Banks on Sentence

Robert Banks

ISBN 0–9550386–0–X

The extracts from the Magistrates' Association Sentencing Guidelines are inuding with the kind permission of the Association.

Copyright Robert Banks

Published by Robert Banks

www.banksr.com   book@banksr.com

Banks on Sentence, PO Box 35, Etchinham, East Sussex TN19 7WS

Typeset by DataConnection, Frome, Somerset

Printed in Great Britain by William Clowes Ltd, Beccles Suffolk

FOREWORD

The process of sentencing becomes more and more complicated as Criminal Justice Acts follow each other. The 2003 Act contributed more than most to this process. The Court of Appeal (Criminal Division) and now the Sentencing Guidelines Council add to the material to which sentencers and others need to refer.

Since the first edition of Robert Banks' book was published in 2002, I know that many have found it a most useful addition to the works of reference on sentencing. Like the first edition it aims to be as comprehensive as possible in guiding the reader towards the proper bracket for sentences for various kinds of offence. The second edition remains reasonably concise and portable. While the summaries of cases or of statutory provisions cannot be a substitute for reference to the relevant text itself, these are a valuable starting point. The author is to be commended for updating and improving his book.

Mr. Justice Crane,
Chairman, Criminal Committee of the Judicial Studies Board

This second edition is different from the first because I am publishing the book myself. This enables me to avoid the expense and bureaucracy of a publisher and retain control of the key decisions. One of these decisions is that the book should retail at about half the price it would have been if it had been published by a traditional publisher with their crippling overheads. Naturally, the operation is an awesome task as I will have to sell the books as well.

There are some key changes from the first edition. Firstly, I have included more of the ancillary orders that are available for specific offences. These are set out more clearly at the beginning of each section. Secondly, there are two years of statistics for the offences which the Home Office keep data. Thirdly, I have expanded the section at the beginning of the book dealing with the traditional way sentences are constructed, (see page vii). Fourthly, I have increased the number of offences included to make the book as comprehensive as possible. Fifthly, I have improved the index as I know how irritating it is when key words are not included in an index. Sixthly, I have endeavoured to incorporate all the key changes made by the Criminal Justice Act 2003 and the Sexual Offences Act 2003 which have so altered sex offences and sentencing. When incorporating those Acts, I have tried to help the reader by incorporating both the old law for the older offences, the old sentencing powers for those offences when they apply, the new offences and the new sentencing law making it clear which is the key date to determine which law applies. Where there are relevant principles for the old offences I have incorporated them in the chapters for the new offences.

All these changes have made the text nearly 50% longer than the first edition. Naturally, I have wanted to ensure that the book is just as portable as the last edition and the print size is as clearly readable as before. To achieve this much thinner paper is used. I regret this but I hope readers will agree that this is better than a bulkier book. The new book is in fact thinner than the last edition.

The book hopes to state the law as at 22 August 2005. It does not include all the latest tariff cases but I hope it includes all the guideline cases and legislation. The Sentencing Advisory Panel recommendations are not listed as the Court of Appeal points out that they do not change the law.

This book could not have been produced without the help and support of the Hon Mr. Justice Crane who gave advice, assistance and wrote the forward. I am also very grateful to HH Judge Barker QC, the new Common Serjeant at the Central Criminal Court for his support and encouragement. David Spens QC, the Criminal Bar Association, the Judicial Studies Board, The Magistrates' Association and the Home Office have been particularly helpful. Others who helped include Helen Leadbeater who wrote some of the summaries and proof read part of the book, Jonathan Page who also wrote some of the summaries, Clara Coxon who proof read the bulk of the book, Mike Lynch from the printers and Ray Smith from the typesetters. I am grateful to them all.

Regrettably the last edition contained a mass of typos. I hope there is not the same problem with this edition. Last time I asked readers to let me know if there were any errors in the book. No one wrote to me! Naturally I ask again for the same help.

The sales will be web and mail order based and not shop based in line with current trends. All personal details sent to me will be retained in a secure system and I will not sell or give any of the information to a third party.

Robert Banks

PO Box 35, Etchingham, East Sussex TN19 7WS   22 August 2005
www.banksr.com   book@banksr.com

ABBREVIATIONS

ABH	Assault occasioning actual bodily harm
AER	The All England Law reports
Att-Gen's	Attorney-General's
CCC	The Central Criminal Court (The Old Bailey)
CCTV	Closed circuit television
Crim L R	The Criminal Law Review
EWCA Crim	The Court of Appeal reference number
CSO	A Community Service Order
ex p	ex parte
GBH	Grievous bodily harm
gram(s)	gramme(s)
ID	Identification
kilo(s)	kilogramme(s)
LCJ	Lord Chief Justice
LSG	Law Society Gazette
News	News report in a newspaper
PDH	Pleas and Direction hearing in the Crown Court
RTR	Road Traffic Reports
QBD	The Queen's Bench Division in the High Court
μg	microgrammes (in drink/drive cases microgrammes in 100 millilitres of breath)
s	section(s)
SJ	Solicitor's Journal
TDA	Taking and driving away (conveyances)
TIC	Offences taken into consideration
WLR	The Weekly Law Reports
YOI	Detention in a Young Offenders' Institute

ABOUT THE BOOK

The chapters are in **BOLD CAPITALS** and the sections within a chapter are in ***bold italics***.

The summaries in the book

The book contains all the cases listed in 1999–2005 (published before May 2005) in the Cr App R (S) law reports other than cases which deal with sentencing orders or procedure. The case summaries are intended to include all the relevant factors. Even cases, which seem out of line or unrepresentative are listed to ensure there is a complete picture.

What is included in the summaries?

The intention is to include all maters that are relevant and exclude all matters that are not relevant. Appellants, applicants, respondents, offenders are all called defendants to make the case simpler. Usually previous cases relied on are excluded because they are either old or already in the book. The decision is the same whether or not no or ten previous cases are used.

The Statistics

The statistics at the beginning of many of the chapters are included with the kind permission of the authorities. The data is compiled by the Home Office and the Editor is very grateful to Graham for extracting the information especially for this book. It was a time consuming task as he was asked for two years' worth of statistics. Strangely the statistics are only for males. The overall statistics are

Crown Court statistics – England and Wales – Males 21+

Year	Plea	Total Numbers sentenced	Type of sentence %					Average length of custody (months)
			Discharge	Fine	Community sentence	Suspended sentence	Custody	
2002	Guilty	31,657	3	3	28	2	62	27.4
	Not guilty	7,376	2	3	15	2	76	44.2
2003	Guilty	33,150	4	3	29	3	59	27.5
	Not guilty	7,010	2	4	16	2	74	46.7

Clearly the accuracy of the statistics depends on those who feed the information into the system. Where a defendant receives the same penalty for different offences there must be problem in deciding which offence to choose as the one to record in the statistics. Committals for sentences are not included. The column for Community sentence includes community rehabilitation orders, community punishment orders, community punishment and rehabilitation orders, curfew orders and DTTO orders. The average length of sentence column excludes life sentences. Where the percentage figures do not add up to 100% this must be because Hospital orders etc. are not included. In the table "–" means nil and 0% means less than 0.5%. Statistics for threats to kill and conspiracy to murder are included together which makes using them very difficult. Similarly production of drugs is listed with supply of drugs.

BASIC SENTENCING PROCEDURES

A The basic route for deciding the sentence

The traditional route for determining a sentence is as follows.

The court assesses:

(1) Whether there is a statutory minimum sentence that must be imposed, like automatic life (for offences committed before 4/4/05), seven years for a third Class A drug trafficking offence or three years for a third domestic burglary offence.

(2) The legal framework namely any guideline from the Sentencing Guidelines Council, any Court of Appeal guideline case, see *B* below, guideline remarks and reported cases, see *C* below. If the case is a serious example of the offence the court will consider the maximum sentence available.

(3) The culpability of the defendant. Criminal Justice Act 2003 s 143(1) provides that the court must consider this.

(4) The impact on the victim or potential victim. Even a tax fraud has a victim.

(5) The aggravating and mitigating features for the offence, see *D* below.

(6) In sexual cases and violent cases in particular the court considers the risk posed by the defendant.

(7) The sentences of defendants connected with the case who have already been dealt with, (if there are any).

Taking into account (1) to (6) the court will decide the appropriate starting point. The court will next consider:

(1) The plea. (See GUILTY PLEA, DISCOUNT FOR)

(2) The character of the defendant both good and bad, see *E, F* and *G* below.

(3) The defendant's personal mitigation, see *H* below.

(4) The pre-sentence and medical reports if there are any.

(5) If it is a sex or violent case the court will consider whether there is a risk to the public. If there is and the statutory criteria are made out the Court will pass one of the new Criminal Justice Act sentences for offences committed on or after 4/4/05 and otherwise consider passing a longer than commensurate sentence (see LONGER THAN COMMENSURATE SENTENCES) or an extended sentence (see EXTENDED SENTENCES).

Taking into account (1) to (5) the court will decide the appropriate sentence. Next it will consider:

(1) Whether costs should be awarded against the defendant.

(2) Whether compensation is appropriate.

(3) Whether there is an ancillary order linked to the offence that should be added to the sentence like disqualification, forfeiture, destruction of drugs, a drug trafficking offences order, a ban on working with children or a football banning order.

However some Judges do not use such a structured approach and just think to themselves, it looks like three years. A similar approach is taken by experienced Magistrates.

B *Guideline/Guideline cases*

There are two types of guidelines. The first are Guidelines from the Sentencing Guidelines Council. The Court must have regard to those that are relevant to the case[1]. The Court of Appeal in R v Millberry *2003 1 Cr App R 142*, said, "We would emphasise that guidelines can produce sentences which are inappropriately high or inappropriately low if sentencers merely adopt a mechanistic approach to the guidelines. It is essential that having taken the guidelines into account, sentencers stand back and look at the circumstances as a whole and impose the sentence which is appropriate having regard to all the circumstances. Double accounting must be avoided and can be a result of guidelines if they are applied indiscriminately".

---

1 Criminal Justice Act 2003 s 172

The Court of Appeal has said that the Reports from the Sentencing Advisory Panel may be useful to sentencers and advocates. However that advice and any draft guidelines from the Sentencing Guidelines Council should not be cited in the Court of Appeal[2].

The second type are guidelines issued by the Court of Appeal. As the name implies these are only a guide. They assist in assessing the starting point. However, the aggravating and mitigating features for the offence may adjust the figure. Guideline cases rarely, if ever, create a maximum for an offence.

C Finding and interpreting comparable cases

Non-guideline reported cases are also only a guide. Some of them are influential, others less so. They only show the operation of the basic principles. More recent cases are more useful than older ones. Some offences like manslaughter are very hard to index because of the infinite variety of ways the offence can be committed. It is important to look at more than one section. However, even if there is a very similar case it does not mean that the same sentence will be passed as in the reported case. Magistrates' Courts normally pass lower sentences than Crown Courts. Many Crown Court judges pass lower sentences than the Court of Appeal judges. Judges differ in their approaches and judges have a discretion when weighing up all the different factors before they pass sentence. The fact the Court of Appeal considers a sentence is not manifestly excessive does not mean that this is the sentence they would have passed. Where the Court of Appeal is considering an appeal by the prosecution (which are cited as *Att-Gen's Reference No 43 of 2001* etc) the sentence that is substituted will be less than the appropriate sentence to take into account the stress etc of the defendant being sentenced twice.

D Aggravating and mitigating features of the offence

The Sentencing Guidelines Council laid down the principles for assessing Culpability, Harm to Victims etc. Aggravating features and Mitigating features for the offences in Sentencing Guidelines Council Guideline Seriousness December 2004 Para 1.6–1.25. www.sentencing-guidelines.gov.uk

E Character General

There are potentially three parts to a defendant's character. First, there is the defendant's criminal record (if there is one). If there is no previous offending the defendant will normally receive a discount for his good character. Where there is only minor offending many years previously, the defendant will also usually receive a discount. The second part is the remarks in the pre-sentence report if one has been ordered. The judge or magistrate does not have to accept the views in the report if he thinks they are wrong but he or she should consider them. Many pre-sentence reports contain a risk assessment analysis which is of increasing importance. The third part is general evidence of good character. It is usually found in witness statements collected by the defence but it can be found in the prosecution case. If the victim of a theft by an employee describes the defendant as hard working and trustworthy over many years up until the theft, that would normally be taken into account.

F Good character – How to apply it

It is not possible to apply mathematical principles about the discount that is applicable. It will all depend on the circumstances. Where there is serious professional criminal behaviour, for example conspiracy to commit armed robbery, good character will be of little significance[3]. At the other end of the scale good character can tip the balance in

---

2 *R v Doidge 2005* The Times 1 March
3 *R v Turner* [1975] 61 Cr App Rep 67. The defendants appealed their sentences for armed robbery. The court in a guideline case said, 'the fact that a man has not much of a criminal record is not a powerful factor in cases of this gravity'.

deciding whether it is necessary to give the defendant a custodial sentence. Good character is more important the older the defendant is. However, it can be very significant for defendants aged under 21. Courts try to avoid sending young people of good character into custody because it can be counter-productive. If the defendant is in employment, custody will normally destroy this and harm his or her chances of finding another position. Further, custody will introduce him or her to a corrupting influence, which will be hard to undo. Courts will prefer a lenient sentence, which may stop them re-offending, rather than a custodial sentence, which may confirm his or her criminal behaviour.

G Bad character – How to apply it

Criminal Justice Act 2003 s 143(2) states that, "in considering the seriousness of an offence committed by an offender who has one or more previous convictions the court must treat each previous conviction as an aggravating factor. It is important that the defendant is not punished twice for the same offence. Therefore the courts will be careful not to add too much to the sentence because of the criminal record. But a criminal record is an important way of considering how the defendant has responded to previous sentences. If non-custodial sentences have not been effective the options of the court will be more limited. Where the criteria for imposing longer than commensurate sentences are satisfied bad character will be of crucial importance.

H Personal mitigation

Criminal Justice Act 2003 166(1) makes provision for a sentencer to take account of any matter that "in the opinion of the court are relevant in mitigating the sentence".

Most sentences are determined primarily by the offence. Occasionally where the defendant has some terrible illness or has taken valiant steps to overcome his/her drug addiction and changed his/her whole lifestyle, courts can exercise mercy and impose a constructive sentence[4].

The majority of personal mitigation has little or no impact on the sentence. If a man with children commits an offence which deserves imprisonment the fact he has children will not normally influence the sentence. Serious offences are in one way aggravated by the fact the defendant committed the offence knowing that if caught the sentence would cause the children to be separated from their father. In principle it would be wrong for those without children to be necessarily sentenced to longer sentences than those with children. Each case will be dealt with on its own facts. However, where a mother appears for sentence the court will consider the impact on the children of the sentence. If she is the sole carer, or particular children will suffer badly, the court will adjust the appropriate sentence not to assist her but to protect the children, (see MOTHERS). If the father is the sole carer, the court will normally consider the impact on the children and then consider an adjustment in the same way.

General

The purposes of sentencing are laid down by Criminal Justice Act 2003 s 142. The section does not apply to offenders under 18, where there is a minimum sentence or where the court is considering a hospital order[5]. The purposes are the punishment of offenders, the reduction of crime, the reform and rehabilitation of offenders and the making of reparations by offenders.

There is a short BASIC PRINCIPLES chapter and one on MERCY. The BASIC PRINCIPLES chapter has sections on *Departing from the sentencing guidance, Prison overcrowding* and *Sentencing is an art etc/Rehabilitation*. The chapter entitled DEFENDANT has sections on *AIDS, defendant has, Disabled defendants, Elderly defendants, Ill health of defendants, Inadequate defendants, Mentally disordered defendants, Personal mitigation, Poor defendants* and *Rich defendants*.

4 *Att-Gen's Reference No 83 of 2001* 2002 1 Cr App R (S) 589
5 Criminal Justice Act 2003 s 142(2)

TABLE OF CASES

The references with a dot refer to paragraph numbers. The roman figures (viii to x) refer to page numbers. Where there is more than one reference the reference in bold is to the fuller entry.

A

Table of Cases

B

C

D

E

H

I

L

M

N

O

Q

R

S

T

X

Y

Z

TABLE OF STATUTES

The references with a dot refer to paragraph numbers. The roman figures (viii to x) refer to page numbers. The more important entries are in **bold**.

TABLE OF STATUTORY INSTRUMENTS

1   ABDUCTION OF A CHILD

1.1   Child Abduction Act 1984 s 1 (by parent) and Child Abduction Act 1984 s 2 (by other person)

Triable either way. On indictment maximum 7 years. Summary maximum 6 months and/or £5,000.

The Criminal Justice Act 2003 creates a summary maximum sentence of 51 weeks, a minimum custodial sentence of 28 weeks and Custody plus. The Home Office says they do not expect to introduce these provisions before September 2006.

CHAPTERS in this book are in bold capitals. The *paragraph titles* are in bold italics. Where a chapter like this one has subsections, the **subsections** are in lower case bold. The four subsections are; A General, B Parent or stepparent, by, C Relative, friend etc. by, D Stranger, by.

Longer than Commensurate sentences and Extended sentences (see 1.3) Abduction is a violent offence for the purposes of passing a longer than commensurate sentence [Powers of Criminal Courts (Sentencing) Act 2000 s 80(2)] and an extended sentence (extending the licence) [Powers of Criminal Courts (Sentencing) Act 2000 s 85(2)(b)] where the offence leads, or is intended or likely to lead, to a person's death or to physical injury to a person[1]. The orders cannot be made for offences committed before 30/9/98 or after 3/4/05. (**See Para 1.3**)

Working with children For section 1 offences where the defendant is aged 18 or over and s/he is sentenced to 12 months or more etc. the court must disqualify him/her from working with children unless satisfied s/he is unlikely to commit any further offences against a child when the court must state its reasons for not doing so[2]. For a defendant aged less than 18 at the time of the offence the court must order disqualification if s/he is sentenced to 12 months or more and the court is satisfied that the defendant will commit a further offence against a child[3]. The court must state its reasons for so doing. There is no power to make this order for section 2 offences. For a Court of Appeal request for this anomaly to be corrected see *R v Prime* 2005 1 Cr App R 203.

Crown Court statistics – England and Wales – Males 21+ – Child Abduction

1.2

Year	Plea	Total Numbers sentenced	Type of sentence %					Average length of custody (months)
			Discharge	Fine	Community sentence	Suspended sentence	Custody	
2002	Guilty	36	8	–	25	6	56	19.8
	Not guilty	9	–	–	22	–	78	21
2003	Guilty	32	3	–	41	–	50	26.9
	Not guilty	3	–	–	100	–	–	–

For details and explanations about the statistics in the book see page vii.

See also FALSE IMPRISONMENT/KIDNAPPING

---

1   As defined by Powers of Criminal Courts (Sentencing) Act 2000 s 161(3). The offences are not sexual offences and may not be treated as violent offences unless the offence led or was likely to lead to physical injury to a person, R v Bailey 2005 2 Cr App R (S) 85.
2   Criminal Justice and Court Services Act 2000 s 28
3   Criminal Justice and Court Services Act 2000 s 29

A General

Longer than commensurate sentences (frequently wrongly called extended sentences) – is it a violent offence?

1.3   Powers of Criminal Courts (Sentencing) Act 2000 s 80(2)(b). the custodial sentence shall be ... where the offence is a violent or sexual offence, for such longer term (not exceeding the maximum) as in the opinion of the court is necessary to protect the public from serious harm from the offender (previously the Criminal Justice Act 1991, s 2(2)(b).)

Powers of Criminal Courts (Sentencing) Act 2000 s 161(3) . . . a violent offence is an "offence which leads, or is intended or likely to lead, to a person's death or physical injury to a person."

R v Newsome 1997 2 Cr App R (S) 69. Look at the facts of the case. Next ask whether the restraining made it a violent offence. The false imprisonment may amount to a violent offence. The court also had to consider whether it was likely to lead to physical injury. Here they were likely to lead to that so it was a violent offence.

R v Nelmes 2001 Times 1 Feb, Judgement 27/11/00. The defendant pleaded guilty to attempted abduction. The defendant who smelt strongly of drink pulled a 3-year-old boy away from his mother who was at a bus station. He said calmly, 'I have come to take your child away.' The mother and boy became very distressed and the mother screamed for help. The mother was able to snatch the child back. The defendant was arrested. The defendant said he was drunk and on medication and could not remember being there or being arrested. He had no relevant previous convictions. Held. The judge purported to extend the sentence. That was not appropriate. The case failed the *R v Newsome* 1997 2 Cr App R (S) 397 test that there should be physical injury or conduct that was likely to lead to physical injury.

Old cases. *R v Wrench* 1996 1 Cr App R (S) 145.

See also **LONGER THAN COMMENSURATE SENTENCES**

B Parent or stepparent, by

Court order, in breach of – Guideline remarks

1.4   *R v A* 2002 1 Cr App R (S) 473. It is the interests of the child which are paramount not the interests or aspirations of the parent. Save in quite exceptional circumstances a person who commits a s 2 offence commits a serious offence, especially if it is done to thwart orders of the court. Orders must be respected by parents who have access to the courts and to legal advice. Real punishment is called for to punish and to deter others.

Court order, in breach of

1.5   *R v Dryden-Hall* 1997 2 Cr App R (S) 235. The defendant the mother of the victim pleaded guilty to two counts of child abduction and a theft. Her husband pleaded guilty to aiding and abetting the abduction. She divorced the father of the children and remarried. In 1993 she applied to her County Court to take her two children to Canada where she had lived and where her family lived. The welfare officer reported to the court and she withdrew her application. The court made an order prohibiting her from taking the children out of the jurisdiction for more than a month without the father consenting. She developed TB and became depressed. She ran up a bill of £1,328 on a store card, (the theft charge). She arranged for Pickfords to quote for a move to Canada. She told a neighbour she was going to Canada. She then flew to Canada with no intention of returning. The father brought proceedings in Canada, which she contested. The children were there for 21 months. The court ordered their return but she stayed behind. When she returned she and her husband were arrested. The welfare officer said the move had had a detrimental effect on the children. She had no previous convictions. Held 9 months was not wrong. However, because of her change in attitude and the interests of the children the sentence was reduced to **4 months** to enable her release very shortly.

R v J A 2002 1 Cr App R (S) 473. The defendant J and D pleaded to aiding and abetting the detention of their daughter, N. T who was J's mother pleaded to conspiracy to abduct a child. The pleas were after a re-arraignment. J and D had two children C and N. C was diagnosed as being a victim of Munchausen Syndrome by Proxy when he was 11. The council made an interim care order and took him from his home. It was said this had led to unnecessary treatment of the child amounting to abuse. J, J's sister and T were also diagnosed with the same syndrome. C remained in care with the consent of J and D. From then J and D raised many complaints about their son's health. They said he was starved, neglected and abused. In contact sessions C had extensive bruising and this was explained by the council in a number of ways. J and D did not accept the explanations and contacted organisations for help including the Child Protection Police. The Council then informed the parents that they were instituting care proceedings for the other child, N although they had no intention of taking her into care. The prosecution said there was a plan hatched by J, T and M, someone styled as a 'child abuse advocate' to remove N from the jurisdiction. T took N to Ireland where they stayed under false names. J reported her daughter missing. M and another arranged for various demands to be made over the Internet and in telephone calls to newspapers and the police. Until they were met T and N would not return. An interim care order and a recovery order were obtained from the High Court. There was also an order that anyone who had knowledge of the whereabouts of N should inform the authorities immediately. J and D knowing the location ignored this and spent a week with their daughter who had been moved to Scotland. D deposited £140 with a charity and an associate of M later withdrew it in Scotland. Police found the house and J, D and N. It was accepted the abduction was prompted in part by others. All defendants were of good character. J was 36. D was 34 and an engineer in the Royal Navy with good naval references. He was not at home for the majority of the relevant time. He had lost his marriage, his children and possibly his career. T was 63. There was a 2 year delay. The judge said the Council was beyond criticism. Held. It is the interests of the child which are paramount not the interests or aspirations of the parent. They had shown a complete contempt for the law. Save in quite exceptional circumstances a person who commits a s 2 offence commits a serious offence, especially if it is done to thwart orders of the court Those who did what the defendants did must expect prison sentences because real punishment is called for and to deter others. The judge took into account the mitigation. Accepting they were under the influences of others the appeals for J and T's **9 months** and D's **6 months** were dismissed.

C Relative, friend etc, by

1.6   *R v Mawdsley* 2001 1 Cr App R (S) 353. The defendant aged 43 pleaded guilty to two counts of abducting a child. He went with his son to the school of one of his son's friends aged 13. The defendant asked for the friend and said he was taking him to the dentist. The boy went with him because he was too scared to say no. His son then asked him to get another boy from another school. He again said he was taking him to the dentist. The boy aged 12 appeared willing to go. He took the boys to his house where they talked and watched TV. The defendant drank cider and on one occasion he took a boy by the ears and spat cider in his face. They stayed for about $2^1/_2$ hours and nothing untoward happened. The defendant had an appalling record for dishonesty but had no convictions for sexual offences. **18 months** was substituted for 2 years.

Police advice, acting against

1.7   *R v Hutchinson* 1999 Unreported 1/10/98. The defendant pleaded guilty to two offences of child abduction. Because of his previous convictions the defendant was known to the police paedophile unit. He was warned by officers to stay away from a 14-year-old boy. The boy asked him to give him a lift home as he was stranded and had no money. He gave him a lift and the police stopped the car and took the boy away. On another occasion he picked him up, and they went to visit a friend. Then they both went to a public lavatory and came out. The boy then went back in. Fifteen minutes later the defendant went to look for him and he wasn't there. The boy was arrested. Held. These were technical offences involving no kind of sexual conduct. **12 months** not 18.

R v A 2000 Unreported 14/9/99. The defendant was convicted of child abduction. He was friendly with a 15-year-old girl. He visited her home and the mother telephoned the police who advised him not to take the girl with him. He met her later and they lived rough together. There was no contact with the mother for 5 days and she was away from home for 9 days. Held. **2 years** was at the top of the bracket but not manifestly excessive.

D Stranger, by

General

1.8   *R v Dean* 2000 2 Cr App R (S) 253. The defendant was convicted of abducting a $4^{1}/_{2}$-year-old boy. He ordered the boy to come to him and not to speak. He threatened to kill him and took hold of his hand. His mother who was watching him shouted to him and the boy broke free and escaped. The defendant drove away. He always denied it. The defendant was then aged 29. When 17 he was put on probation for sending obscene material through the post. It was gay indecent material sent to young boys saying what he would like to do to them. There were 61 TICs. He was sentenced on the basis that it was not a spur of the moment offence because he had travelled away from his home territory. There was no proven sexual motive. The previous offending did give rise for concern. **5 years** was severe but a sentence that the judge was entitled to make to protect the public.

R v Nelmes 2001 Times 1 Feb, 27/11/00. The defendant pleaded guilty to attempted abduction. The defendant who smelt strongly of drink pulled a 3-year-old boy away from his mother who was at a bus station. He said calmly, 'I have come to take your child away.' The mother and boy became very distressed and the mother screamed for help. The mother was able to snatch the child back. The defendant was arrested. The defendant said he was drunk and on medication and could not remember being there or being arrested. He had no relevant previous convictions. Held. The judge purported to extend the sentence and extend the licence. That was not appropriate. The case failed the *R v Newsome* 1997 2 Cr App R (S) 397 test that there should be physical injury or conduct that was likely to lead to physical injury. The case was appalling and caused tremendous distress to the mother, but **2 years** not 3.

R v Prime 2005 1 Cr App R 2003. The defendant pleaded guilty to abducting a child. He had been at a fireworks party where the victim, a 9 year old boy, was also a guest with his mother and siblings. The boy was of low intelligence although he did not have special needs. The defendant asked the boy to go with him to buy some cigarettes and took him to a piece of ground near a supermarket where he asked the boy if he wanted any money, grabbed him by the arm, pulled him to the ground twice, hit him in the face, kicked him in the leg and scratched his face. He then ran off. Some time later two girls found the boy. His left eye was swollen and his eye was slightly closed. The defendant, 36, had one conviction for violent disorder twelve years before. A psychiatric report said he had partial alcohol dependency syndrome. A pre-sentence report referred to the defendant's heavy drinking since his mother's death the previous year, but said that he had demonstrated motivation to change and would accept professional assistance. The report also said that the defendant presented a direct risk of harm to the public especially to children. There were favourable references which said he was hard working. He wrote to the court and expressed regret and remorse. Held. The Crown Court had no power to make an order of disqualification from working with children under the provisions of section 28 of the Criminal Justice and Court Services Act 2000 as an offence under s 2 was, surprisingly, not a qualifying offence. The secretary of state should consider amending the schedule by Order to include it. The court was perturbed by this unexplained conduct which pointed towards an apparent intention to do violence or assault the boy sexually. However the period involved was relatively short, and nothing in the form of sexual touching occurred. What occurred was not substantially premeditated and the boy was not taken away in a vehicle from the area where he lived. The proper sentence was **3 years** not 4.

Sexual motive, for

1.9 *R v Newsome* 1997 2 Cr App R (S) 69. The defendant pleaded guilty to attempted child abduction. He was 43 and approached a girl aged 9 years old as she was gathering conkers in a field. He walked towards her and she backed away. He ran after her and grabbed her by the wrist and an arm. She screamed and kicked him and he let go. The child had feared she could have been pushed into a nearby river. He admitted the offence. He said his was intention was to take her towards the riverbank and indecently assault her. In 1972 he had a conviction for robbery. In 1975 he had a conviction for indecent assault on a girl aged 9. In 1988 he had a conviction for indecently assaulting a girl aged 15 for which he received 4 years. In 1991 he had a conviction for attempted abduction of a 6 year old for which the Court of Appeal gave him probation. The pre-sentence report said that he was a serious risk to young girls. A psychiatrist report said he had long standing paedophile interests. Held. This offence was a 'violent' offence so the judge was right to extend the sentence. However, **5 years** substituted for 6.

R v Adamson 2001 Unreported 19/10/01. 8 year old abducted by a paedophile. 33 months entirely appropriate.

2   ABDUCTION OF A WOMAN

2.1   Sexual Offences Act 1956 s 17

Indictable only. Maximum sentence 14 years.

For offences committed on or after 1/5/04 this offence was repealed[4] and replaced by Sexual Offences Act 2003 S 62(1), (committing an offence with the intention of committing a relevant sexual offence) where the intention is sexual. Otherwise prosecutors can charge kidnapping and false imprisonment.

See also FALSE IMPRISONMENT/KIDNAPPING AND RAPE – *Abduction/false imprisonment etc, and*

---

4   Sexual Offences Act 2003 s 140 & Sch 7

3   ABH – ASSAULT OCCASIONING ACTUAL BODILY HARM

3.1   Offences Against the Person Act 1861 s 47.

Triable either way. On indictment maximum 5 years. Summary maximum 6 months and/or £5,000.

The Criminal Justice Act 2003 creates a summary maximum sentence of 51 weeks, a minimum custodial sentence of 28 weeks and Custody plus. The Home Office says they do not expect to introduce these provisions before September 2006.

There is a new offence of committing an offence with intent to commit a sexual offence, see Sexual Offences Act 2003 s 62. That offence could be ABH.

Anti-Social Behavioural orders Where the defendant has acted in a manner that caused or was likely to cause harassment, alarm or distress to one or more persons not in the same household as the defendant and it is necessary to protect persons from further anti-social acts by him/her the court may make this order[5].

Football Where the offence was committed relevant to a football match and where there are reasonable grounds to believe that making a banning order would help to prevent violence or disorder at or in connection with any regulated football match; the court <u>must</u> make a Football Banning Order, under the Football Spectators Act 1989 s 14A and Sch 1, para 1.

Licensed premises Where the offence is committed on licensed premises the court may prohibit the defendant from entering those premises or any other specified premises without the express consent of the licensee or his agent[6]. The order shall last from 3 months to 2 years[7].

Longer than Commensurate sentences and Extended sentences ABH is a violent offence for the purposes of passing a longer than commensurate sentence [Powers of Criminal Courts (Sentencing) Act 2000 s 80(2)] and an extended sentence (extending the licence) [Powers of Criminal Courts (Sentencing) Act 2000 s 85(2)(b)] where the offence leads, or is intended or likely to lead, to a person's death or to physical injury to a person[8]. The orders cannot be made for offences committed before 30/9/98 or after 3/4/05.

Sexual Offences Prevention Order There is a discretionary power to make this order when it is necessary to protect the public etc[9].

Working with children Where the offence is against a child (aged under 18), the defendant is aged 18 or over and s/he is sentenced to 12 months or more the court must disqualify him/her from working with children unless satisfied s/he is unlikely to commit any further offences against a child when the court must state its reasons for not doing so[10]. For a defendant aged less than 18 at the time of the offence the court must order disqualification if s/he is sentenced to 12 months or more and the court is satisfied that the defendant will commit a further offence against a child[11]. The court must state its reasons for so doing.

[The categories listed are only one factor in the determination of sentence. Usually, the most important matter is the degree of injury inflicted.]

---

5 Crime and Disorder Act 1998 s 1C
6 Licensed Premises (Exclusion of Certain Persons) Act 1980 s 1(1)
7 Licensed Premises (Exclusion of Certain Persons) Act 1980 s 1(3)
8 Powers of Criminal Courts (Sentencing) Act 2000 s 161(3)
9 Sexual Offences Act 2003 s 104 & Sch. 5
10 Criminal Justice and Court Services Act 2000 s 28
11 Criminal Justice and Court Services Act 2000 s 29

Guideline remarks

3.2   *R v Howells Re Robson and Howard* 1999 1 Cr App R (S) 335 at 342. LCJ. Gratuitous violence, directed at members of the public who are going about their business and doing nothing whatsoever to provoke such violence must attract and be understood to attract severe punishment. (For further details see *Stranger in the street, attack on*)

Magistrates' Court Sentencing Guidelines January 2004

3.3   For a first time offender pleading not guilty. Entry point. Is it so serious that only custody is appropriate? Consider the impact on the victim. Examples of aggravating factors for the offence are abuse of trust (domestic setting), deliberate kicking or biting, extensive injuries (may be psychological), head-butting, group action, offender in position of authority, on hospital/medical premises, pre-meditated, victim particularly vulnerable, victim serving the public and weapon. Examples of mitigating factors for the offence are minor injury, provocation and single blow. Examples of mitigation are age, health (physical or mental), co-operation with the police, genuine remorse voluntary and voluntary compensation. Give reasons if not awarding compensation.

For details about the guidelines see MAGISTRATES' COURT SENTENCING GUIDELINES at page 483.

Aircraft, on

See AIRCRAFT OFFENCES – *ABH*

Argument, after

3.4   *R v Jones* 1999 1 Cr App R (S) 427. The defendant pleaded guilty at the Magistrates' Court to ABH. In the street, the defendant after drinking accused the victim of making too much noise. The allegation had been made before. The victim walked on. The defendant grabbed him by the back of the head: 'You better stop making noise at night because I'm fucking sick of it.' The victim walked off again and was struck a heavy blow to the jaw. He fell to the floor. The jaw was broken in two places and required lengthy surgery and a metal plate. The defendant had one conviction, which was for ABH 10 years earlier. The psychiatrist said there might be an element of paranoia. The pre-sentence report said he felt harassed because of an earlier incident on his estate. Held. Because of the serious permanent injuries the sentence of **18 months** was not altered although it was at the top end of the range.

R v Bowers 2005 1 Cr App R (S) 132. The defendant pleaded guilty to ABH. During the early evening of Sunday he was involved in an argument that led to him being banned from a pub. At about 8.15pm he returned and tried to offer an apology to the landlord and the person with whom he was arguing. An argument ensued and again he left. He was later seen in an agitated state with a brick in his hand. The victim, C, saw the defendant threatening someone else, R. C intervened as he thought that the defendant was in trouble and decided to go and speak to him. He said "If you want a fight, put the brick down" and invited him to calm down. The defendant struck C, who fell to the floor and hit his head. The defendant called the police. C suffered a small cut and bruising above his left eye and he suffered a minor fracture around the eye socket. He had extreme and constant headaches and soreness. He was arrested and said that he thought that C was with R; however, he later retracted that account. He pleaded on the basis that the he was under the impression that he was being followed and that harm was about to be done to him. He accepted that C had offered no provocation and that he went beyond self-defence. He was 19 and there were 4 occasions where he had been convicted of assaults. Held. The sentence was out of line with other authorities. Importantly, it was his first custodial sentence and he was in a very highly emotional and distressed state at the time of the incident. **8 months**, not 18.

Children, against See CRUELTY TO CHILDREN *– ABH*

Defendant aged 14–15

3.5 *R v Howells Re Marston* 1999 1 Cr App R (S) 335 at 344. LCJ. The defendant pleaded guilty to ABH. While serving his 9 months detention he pleaded to a Public Order Act 1986, s 4 count for an offence which was committed before the first one and received 3 months consecutive. Both pleas were at the Crown Court. (For details of the first incident see PUBLIC ORDER ACT OFFENCES – s 4). The second incident was about 4 weeks later after the s 4 offence. The victim was in a shop and noticed some youths knocking over a sweet stand. He left and three youths from the shop approached him. One asked him a question and another told him to go. He carried on walking and the first youth punched him in the eye causing him to fall to the ground and repeatedly kicked him. The victim succeeded in tripping him up and stood up. The youth then stood up and seized the victim's jumper. The victim then seized the youth's jacket and the other two shouted 'If you hit him, we hit you.' They then punched and kicked him. The victim again fell where he curled up against the blows. He was pushed on the chest and the three ran off when someone shouted. The victim received bruising, grazing to his eye, cuts and a swollen jaw. The co-defendant was the main aggressor and there was no evidence the defendant kicked the victim. When interviewed he admitted pushing the victim. He was on bail for the first offence. He had a relatively minor dishonesty conviction and two dishonesty cautions. He was said to be remorseful and ashamed. He had been taken away from his family by the local authority. Held. The s 4 offence was an utterly disgraceful and inexcusable episode but abusive language by a 15 year old did not merit custody. For the ABH a very short term of detention would be appropriate. **4 months** YOI for the ABH and no separate penalty for the other not 12 months in all.

Information, to extract

3.6 *R v Reddy and Haslam* 2001 2 Cr App R (S) 216. The defendant R pleaded guilty to a joint count with H and another count of ABH. H was convicted of the joint count of ABH. The victim was the same in both counts. The victim and another man who was having a relationship with R's girlfriend lived in the same block of flats. The victim intervened in a dispute between R and his girlfriend at the block of flats. The following day R was abusive to the victim and others at the same place. At about 3am, the victim tried to make R leave. R punched him in the face a number of times causing him to fall and kneed him in the face. He then grabbed his hair and punched him on the back of the head and kicked him in the face again. R then chased after someone who he feared was going to call the police and returned. He then struck the victim a number of times with his foot. The victim was taken to hospital where a cut to his nose and bumps to his head were seen.

Later the same day at 5pm the two defendants arrived at the block. They pushed their way into the victim's flat. The victim was forced to the floor and R sat on him punching him to the head asking him where his girlfriend and her baby were. H cut the telephone wire. R grabbed the victim by the hair, put him onto a sofa and again demanded to know where the girlfriend was. The victim's head was repeatedly hit against the wall and he was punched in the face by R. H kicked him to the thighs and knees. When the victim again was unable to say where the girlfriend was R once again kicked him in the face. H shouted, 'Old Bill, Old Bill' and R repeatedly karate kicked the victim. R also attempted to gouge out his eyes and head-butted him. The incident lasted about 20 minutes. The judge described it as a premeditated joint attack on a smaller defenceless man and an orgy of violence. He said he gave modest credit for the pleas because of the overwhelming evidence. He said H had participated fully till he shouted 'Old Bill' to stop the violence. Both men were 21 and treated as of good character. The pre-sentence report for R indicated a lack of remorse and lack of insight into his behaviour. Held. The court could not conclude that there was a risk of further offences by these men of good character so as to evoke the powers of longer than normal sentences. R sentence was reduced from 5 years to **3 years** with the earlier ABH sentence of 2 years concurrent remaining. H's sentence was reduced from 5 years to **2¹/₂ years**.

Longer than commensurate sentence (frequently wrongly called an extended sentence)

3.7 Powers of Criminal Courts (Sentencing) Act 2000 s 80(2)(b) ... the custodial sentence shall be ... where the offence is a violent or sexual offence, for such longer term (not exceeding the maximum) as in the opinion of the court is necessary to protect the public from serious harm from the offender. [Previously the Criminal Justice Act 1991 s 2(2)(b).]

R v Reddy and Haslam 2001 2 Cr App R (S) 226. The defendant R pleaded guilty to a joint count with H and another count of ABH. H was convicted of the joint count of ABH. The victim was the same in both counts. The victim and another man who was having a relationship with R's girlfriend lived in the same block of flats. The victim intervened in a dispute between R and his girlfriend at the block of flats. The following day R was abusive to the victim and others at the same place. At about 3am, the victim tried to make R leave. R punched him in the face a number of times causing him to fall and kneed him in the face. He then grabbed his hair and punched him on the back of the head and kicked him in the face again. R then chased after someone who he feared was going to call the police and returned. He then struck the victim a number of times with his foot. The victim was taken to hospital where a cut to his nose and bumps to his head were seen.

Later the same day at 5 pm the two defendants arrived at the block. They pushed their way into the victim's flat. The victim was forced to the floor and R sat on him punching him to the head asking him where his girlfriend and her baby were. H cut the telephone wire. R grabbed the victim by the hair, put him onto a sofa and again demanded to know where the girlfriend was. The victim's head was repeatedly hit against the wall and punched in the face by R. H kicked him to the thighs and knees. When the victim again was unable to say where the girlfriend was R once again kicked him in the face. H shouted, 'Old Bill, Old Bill' and R repeatedly karate kicked the victim. R also attempted to gouge out his eyes and head-butted him. The incident lasted about 20 minutes. The judge described it as a premeditated joint attack on a smaller defenceless man and an orgy of violence. He said he gave modest credit for the pleas because of the overwhelming evidence. He said H had participated fully till he shouted Old Bill to stop the violence. Both men were 21 and treated as of good character. The pre-sentence report for R indicated a lack of remorse and lack of insight into his behaviour. Held. The court could not conclude that there was a risk of further offences by these men of good character so as to evoke the longer than normal sentences powers. R sentence was reduced from 5 years to **3 years** with the earlier ABH sentence of 2 years concurrent remaining. H's sentence was reduced from 5 years to **2¹/₂ years**.

R v Smith 2001 2 Cr App R (S) 160. The defendant pleaded guilty at the Magistrates' Court to ABH. He jumped on a bus ignoring the queue. An 85-year-old woman said something to the effect, 'There's a queue.' After she sat down he got up, approached her and spat in her face. She got up to remonstrate with him and pushed him. Because of their differing sizes it had no effect. He punched her in the face and she fell to the floor. A witness said that you could really hear the crack. She was knocked out for a short time. She was in a lot of pain. There was no medical evidence but the photographs were not a pretty sight. When interviewed he said he wanted her to behave and a man can strike a woman once for being cheeky. He claimed justification. He showed no remorse. The risk of re-offending was assessed as high. A psychiatrist said over the past 20 years there had been a number of incidents of the accused threatening people with a knife, intimidating others and hitting patients or staff. The risk increases when he is intoxicated. Another psychiatrist said the frequency and variety of these incidents indicated they would occur in the future with the same frequency and variety. The judge said the sentence started at 18 months and he extended it to 4 years. Held. It was a quite disgraceful piece of loutish and yobbish behaviour. The base sentence was not too high. It could have been considerably higher. Previously the court had suggested an uplift of 50–100% was appropriate. The extension to **4 years** was abundantly justified. [The police CRO is not referred to].

See also **LONGER THAN COMMENSURATE SENTENCES**

Miscellaneous offences

3.8   *R v Regis and Marius* 1999 2 Cr App R (S) 245. The defendants were convicted of ABH. The defendants were employed as security guards at a 'rave' where some 12,000 people attended. They received no training. The victim became violent and began assaulting someone. Security guards were instructed to remove him. They tried to and he struggled violently. The defendants and two others carried him via a fire exit to where some ambulances were. He continued to struggle. Two paramedics saw the victim being dropped after which he tried to kick the guards. M then kicked him in the head showing anger in his face. He continued to kick him as R joined in kicking him. The paramedics then intervened and stood over him to protect him. The victim later died of drug poisoning unconnected with the defendants. The victim had two or three bruises to the head. R was of good character and M had a number of previous including affray and possession of an offensive weapon. He also had references. Held. Those who kick others especially in the head should expect to go to prison. It was wrong not to differentiate between them. **2 years** for M and **18 months** for R not $3^1/_2$ years for both.

Nurses, doctors etc

R v McNally 2000 1 Cr App R (S) 535. The defendant pleaded guilty to ABH. The defendant who was waiting for his son to be seen by a doctor started shouting at a staff nurse adding, 'You're fucking trying to kill my son.' A doctor tried to intervene and he was very aggressive to him. The doctor began to back away and the defendant hit him in the face causing him to fall backwards. As he fell he hit his head against a table. He suffered a haematoma on the temporomandibular joint, bruising, a cut to his chin and bleeding in the middle chamber of his ear. Hearing loss and tinnitus were present 8 months later. On arrest he apologised. He made a full confession in interview. The defendant was 41 with a good character and at the time was being treated for depression. He was a reliable employee and also had references. Doctors, nurses and their staff are entitled to whatever protection the courts can give. Held. People who use violence against them should expect prison. **6 months** not 12.

3.9   *R v Eastwood* 2002 2 Cr App R (S) 318. The defendant changed his plea on the day of his trial to guilty of ABH. The defendant was drunk, beaten up and found in a ditch. He was taken to hospital and an ECG was thought appropriate. A nurse asked him to turn on his back for it to be done. He said, 'Leave me fucking alone,' and grabbed her index finger and squeezed it tightly. She said it was hurting and asked him to let go. He swore at her and sharply pulled her finger back causing a great deal of pain. He let go, she left and he continued to be abusive and aggressive. The police were called. The finger was swollen and had torn ligaments. Two fingers were splinted and she was on light duties for a week and then had to stop work. Several months later she still hadn't returned to work. Her treatment was continuing and she might require surgery. When interviewed he said he was an alcoholic and didn't remember anything. He did not think the nurse was lying. He had an appalling record including offences of minor violence. Two years before he was convicted of ABH and received 4 months. Held. The assault was unprovoked and caused very considerable suffering and distress. The injury was serious. The need for a severe sentence is obvious. Nurses are particularly vulnerable. The starting point was somewhere between 21 and 24 months. **15 months** substituted for 21 because the late plea may not have been his fault.

Police officer, on

3.10   *R v Casey* 2000 1 Cr App R (S) 221. The defendant pleaded guilty to ABH at the Magistrates' Court and common assault at the Crown Court. The defendant drove the wrong side of a 'keep left' sign, was followed by a police car and was stopped. The police tried to breathalyse him and the defendant tried to move away. A police officer took hold of him and the defendant shouted, 'You fucking bastard,' and he punched the officer. The defendant then pulled him into the road and punched him five or six times to the head. The officer fell to the ground and the defendant sat astride him and punched him repeatedly in the face. A member of the public came to his assistance and pulled the defendant away and the defendant leaned back and twisted the member of the public's knee. This caused ligament damage, which was the common assault matter. The officer returned to work after $3^1/_2$ months. He had suffered bruising and swelling along with short-term memory loss. The defendant said he had taken cocaine and he thought he was being attacked. He had previous convictions including one for ABH when he received 9 months suspended. Held. 3 years reduced to **2 years 3 months** with 9 months concurrent for the common assault unchallenged.

R v Elliott 2000 1 Cr App R (S) 264. The defendant pleaded guilty at a late stage to ABH. Outside a nightclub there were a number of scuffles and fights. Police arrived and tried to arrest the defendant. The defendant struck the officer twice in the back of the head. The officer fell to the ground grabbing the defendant's clothes. As the defendant tried to get away he dragged the officer behind him. The defendant hit him more than once from above. The officer suffered bruising. The defendant was 22 with one previous conviction for an unrelated matter. He was sentenced on the basis that initially he did not know it was a police officer. **8 months** not 12.

R v Broyd 2002 1 Cr App R (S) 197. The defendant pleaded guilty to ABH. Shortly after midnight police attended outside a nightclub and found the defendant being restrained on the ground by 3 door staff. He was struggling but the door staff had the upper hand. The defendant was allowed to get to his feet and was clearly drunk. He refused to co-operate and threatened to hit an officer. After a short struggle he was arrested for threatening behaviour. He was taken to the police vehicle still struggling and he turned to the arresting officer and head-butted him and said, 'Take that.' The blow split the officer's lip and chipped one of his teeth. He was interviewed and admitted the offence. The defendant was 36 with 8 convictions. The last one was in 1991. They were 5 for criminal damage, 2 for threatening behaviour and 1 for obstructing an officer. He had never received a custodial sentence. Held. **9 months** reflected the gravity of the offence. It was wholly appropriate to be of some length to punish and to make clear that custodial sentences will follow assaults on police which cause injury.

R v Cameron 2003 The Times 12 Feb. The defendant pleaded guilty to two counts of ABH at a late stage. At about 6 pm he struck a student who was walking in the street for no apparent reason causing his mouth to bleed. The student called the police and pointed him out to them. The police spoke to the defendant who had a can of beer which was taken off him. He then punched a policeman in the mouth and pushed his thumb into the officer's eye. The officer thought he was trying to pull his eyeball out. He was arrested after a struggle. The officer suffered bruising to the eye with orbital and conjunctival bruising. He also had abrasions to his eyebrow, cheek and lip. The defendant had 20 previous convictions mostly for violence and dishonesty. The vast majority were relatively minor and only one merited a lengthy prison sentence. That was for ABH in 1997, for which he received 30 months. He also had a personality disorder with dis-social and "borderline features." He was prone to antisocial behaviour, substance and alcohol abuse. The risk assessment was assessed as significant. The Judge passed a longer than commensurate sentence. Held. That was wrong because it was not established the public required protection from <u>serious</u> harm. **30 months** not 4 years.

Old cases *R v Fletcher* 1998 1 Cr App R (S) 7. (For a summary of this case see the first edition of this book.)

Prison officer, against

3.11 *R v Mills* 1998 2 Cr App R (S) 198. The defendant made an early plea of guilty to ABH. He had a quarrel with an officer and was placed on report. The next day he threw a jug of boiling water over that officer and swung a sock with batteries at the officer who managed to restrain him. The officer was scalded and in considerable pain but was released from hospital the following day. The defendant was 22 and had a number of previous including affray. He had had four prison sentences. Held. As there was a plea and as it was not the worst case of ABH where the maximum is 5 years, **3 years** substituted for 4.

R v Wilmott 2004 2 Cr App R (S) 19. The defendant pleaded guilty at the Magistrates Court to ABH. He was serving a sentence of 4 years 3 months for two robberies, one of attempted robbery, one of theft and one of battery at Wandsworth prison when he was involved in a disturbance. Prison officers saw red marks on his face and led him to the victim, a prison officer, so he could be escorted to the treatment room to see a nurse. The defendant punched the victim on the face for no apparent reason, breaking his jaw. The victim had an operation for the insertion of two plates. One tooth needed to be removed and two others were loose. Two weeks after the assault he was still only able to eat liquidised food. The defendant aged 25, had 12 previous convictions including two for robbery. A parole assessment said he applied himself after a poor start. He had failed to attend a drugs course and he had a bad adjudication record. Another parole assessment referred to grave concerns about anger management and said he was too volatile to attend an anger management therapy group. A psychiatric report concluded that there was a significant risk of harm to others. Held. This was a serious offence with serious consequences. The Judge failed to give sufficient credit for the plea of guilty and the fact this was single punch without the use of a weapon. **27 months** not 3 years (both were consecutive to existing term.).

For cases about whether the new sentence should be consecutive to the original sentence, see **PRISONERS** – *Total sentence when sentence consecutive to the sentence being served*

Prison officers assaulting prisoners

3.12 *R v Fryer* 2002 2 Cr App R 554. The defendants were convicted after a trial. [The report does not make it clear what the offences were but they were probably ABH.] Three prison officers working at Wormwood Scrubs punched and kicked a prisoner in the segregation unit for $1^1/_2$ to 2 minutes. The officers then made bogus charges which resulted in disciplinary proceedings against the prisoner. Held. Because of the breach of trust **4, 4 and $3^1/_2$ years** upheld.

Racially motivated

See **ABH – RACIALLY AGGRAVATED**

Road rage

See **ROAD RAGE** – *ABH*

School teachers, as victims

3.13   *R v Byrne* 2000 1 Cr App R(S) 282. The defendant pleaded guilty at the Magistrates' Court to ABH. The defendant punched a teacher in the face in a private area at a primary school. The defendant was very angry and was talking about his son. The deputy head had warned the defendant and had tried to stop the defendant reaching the victim. The victim required two stitches for a cut lip and took 2 to 3 weeks to recover. He was teased at school about it and he had difficulty sleeping. He needed stress counselling. The defendant believed a teacher had pinned his son against a wall, which turned out to be entirely false. The victim did not recall his son. The defendant was in work, married with five children and had 10 previous convictions mainly for theft and burglary. None were for assaults. His last offence was in 1990. In 1984 he was convicted of a public order offence when he became angry in a hospital and made a though nuisance of himself. He expressed remorse. Held. Schoolteachers are in a particularly vulnerable position but **9 months** substituted for 15 months.

Stalking   See **STALKING – ABH**

Stranger in the street, attack on

3.14   R v Marples 1998 1 Cr App R (S) 335. The defendant pleaded guilty to ABH. Late at night the victim was in a queue for taxis at a station. Some in the queue had been waiting 45 minutes. The defendant and another went from a seat to the head of the queue. An altercation developed and the defendant struck the man at the head of the queue and tried to push him out of a taxi. The victim then approached and said, 'Now lad.' or something similar. He punched him on the nose fracturing his nose. The defendant said he had been drinking and was feeling sick and had been on the seat for some time. He had marks to his neck from the tussle with the first man. He expressed genuine regret. He was 21 and had 11 previous court appearances but none for violence. He was sentenced to 6 months imprisonment with a concurrent 3 months for a revoked Community Service Order. Held. Because there was a plea of guilty 6 months was reduced to 4 months.

R v Howells Re Robson and Howard 1999 1 Cr App R (S) 335 at 342. The defendants R and H pleaded guilty to ABH. The defendants were in a market square and they saw the victim carrying a case of lager. R aged 18, shouted at him for a beer and the victim smiled and walked on. R ran up to him and punched him saying, 'Don't you grin at me'. The victim fell to the ground and was repeatedly kicked and punched by R and H aged 17. A member of the public shouted out and the two ran off. The victim received a severe black eye but was not detained in hospital. The defendants were arrested several days later and R said he had little recollection of the event and H said he went to help R as the victim was bigger than R. Both defendants were of good character with exemplary work records. They were also genuinely ashamed. Held. Gratuitous violence, directed at members of the public who are going about their business and doing nothing whatsoever to provoke such violence must attract and be understood to attract severe punishment. Conduct of this kind, cannot be tolerated. The custody threshold was passed. Apart from this they appear decent young men. A very short term will suffice. **2 months** detention not 6.

R v Smith 2001 2 Cr App R (S) 160. The defendant pleaded guilty at the Magistrates' Court to ABH. He jumped on a bus ignoring the queue. An 85-year-old woman said something to the effect, 'There's a queue.' After she sat down he got up, approached her and spat in her face. She got up to remonstrate with him and pushed him. Because of their differing sizes it had no effect. He punched her in the face and she fell to the floor. A witness said that you could really hear the crack. She was knocked out for a short time. She was in a lot of pain. There was no medical evidence but the photographs were not a pretty sight. When interviewed he said he wanted her to behave and a man can strike a woman once for being cheeky. He claimed justification. He showed no remorse. The risk of re-offending was assessed as high. A psychiatrist said over the past 20 years there had been a number of incidents of the accused threatening people with a knife, intimidating others and hitting patients or staff. The risk increases when he is intoxicated. Another psychiatrist said the frequency and variety of these incidents indicated they would occur in the future with the same frequency and variety. The judge said the sentence started at 18 months and he extended it to 4 years. Held. It was a quite disgraceful piece of loutish and yobbish behaviour. The base sentence was not too high. It could have been considerably higher. Previously the court had suggested an uplift of 50–100% was appropriate. The extension to **4 years** was abundantly justified. [The police CRO is not referred to].

Victim over 65

3.15   *R v Smith* 2001 2 Cr App R (S) 160. See ABOVE.

4   ABH – RACIALLY OR RELIGIOUSLY AGGRAVATED

4.1   Crime and Disorder Act 1998 s 29[12]

Triable either way. On indictment maximum 7 years. Summary maximum 6 months and/or £5,000.

The Criminal Justice Act 2003 creates a summary maximum sentence of 51 weeks, a minimum custodial sentence of 28 weeks and Custody plus. The Home Office says they do not expect to introduce these provisions before September 2006.

Anti-Social Behavioural orders Where the defendant has acted in a manner that caused or was likely to cause harassment, alarm or distress to one or more persons not in the same household as the defendant and it is necessary to protect persons from further anti-social acts by him/her the court may make this order[13].

Football Where the offence was committed relevant to a football match and where there are reasonable grounds to believe that making a banning order would help to prevent violence or disorder at or in connection with any regulated football match; the court <u>must</u> make a Football Banning Order under the Football Spectators Act 1989, s 14A and Sch 1, para 1.

Licensed premises Where the offence is committed on licensed premises the court may prohibit the defendant from entering those premises or any other specified premises without the express consent of the licensee or his agent[14]. The order shall last from 3 months to 2 years[15].

Sexual Offences Prevention Order There is a discretionary power to make this order when it is necessary to protect the public etc[16].

---

12 As amended by Anti-Terrorism, Crime and Security Act 2001 s39(5) and (6)(a)
13 Crime and Disorder Act 1998 s 1C
14 Licensed Premises (Exclusion of Certain Persons) Act 1980 s 1(1)
15 Licensed Premises (Exclusion of Certain Persons) Act 1980 s 1(3)
16 Sexual Offences Act 2003 s 104 & Sch. 5

Magistrates' Court Sentencing Guidelines January 2004

4.2 For a first time offender pleading not guilty. Entry point. Are Magistrates' sentencing powers sufficient? Consider the level of racial aggravation and the impact on the victim. Examples of aggravating factors for the offence are deliberate kicking or biting, extensive injuries (may be psychological), group action, head-butting, offender in position of authority, on hospital/medical premises, pre-meditated, victim particularly vulnerable, victim serving the public and weapon. Examples of mitigating factors for the offence are minor injury, provocation and single blow. Examples of mitigation are age, health (physical or mental), co-operation with the police, genuine remorse and voluntary compensation. Give reasons if not awarding compensation.

For details about the guidelines see **MAGISTRATES' COURT SENTENCING GUIDELINES** at page 483.

General principles – See RACIALLY AGGRAVATED OFFENCES *General principles*

Defendants aged 17–20

4.3 *R v Kelly and Donnelly* 2001 2 Cr App R (S) 341. The defendants were convicted of a joint count of racially aggravated ABH and D was convicted of a count of racially aggravated ABH on his own. Mr Kapoor the victim of the joint count was driving in his S registered Porsche convertible with Mr Puri the victim of the other count and another. The defendants made racist remarks at them repeatedly using the word, 'Paki'. A witness said the defendants had goaded them and there were many references to the car. Donnelly stabbed Mr Kapoor with a biro and Kelly hit him with a bottle or some heavy object. Mr Kapoor headbutted Kelly. Mr Kapoor had a superficial wound to his chest and bruising. Kelly had a swelling and a small cut to the lip and a tooth was pushed back which he later lost. Kelly was 19 then and had previous convictions but none for violence. He had never lost his liberty. Donnelly was younger than Kelly, had more convictions and had lost his liberty more than once. Held. The judge was correct to give them the same sentence. The ABH was worth 18 months following a trial and the racial element was worth a further 9 months making **27 months** not 3 years' YOI. In the case of Donnelly that was consecutive to a sentence for breach of his release licence.

Att-Gen's Ref No. 92 of 2003 2004 The Times 21 April. The defendant pleaded guilty to racially aggravated ABH two days after his PDH when he pleaded not guilty. In the early hours, a Turkish man left his Kebab shop in Diss with three others. The defendant ran up to them shouting, "Turkish bastards." He struck one with a bottle, threatened another Turk and threw the bottle at him. He missed and the bottle broke on the ground. The defendant who was drunk was arrested nearby. He denied the offence but was picked out on an ID parade. The victim had a broken tooth and a cut in his mouth requiring 15 stitches. The defendant was 20 and had convictions for battery in 1999, (attendance centre), threatening behaviour in 1999, (C/D), common assault in 2000, (action plan), criminal damage in 2000, (fine) and possession of Class A and B drugs. Following his arrest he had joined a drug project and then been sentenced to 12 months for witness intimidation. Held. We would have expected 2 years for the violence and **1 year added** for the racial element. As it was a reference **30 months** YOI not 7 months.

General

4.4 *R v Saunders* 2000 2 Cr App R (S) 71. The defendant was convicted of racially aggravated ABH. He had pleaded guilty to having a bladed article in a public place. Mr Ali parked his car outside his home. The defendant, when fuelled with drink, said, 'I don't like Pakis, fucking Pakis.' and 'kick them out.' Mr Ali went indoors and called the police. Believing they had arrived he went outside. Several of Mr Ali's friends attended. The defendant started pushing Mr Ali and throwing punches at him, wildly, causing him to fall to the ground. He got up and was punched in the face with a powerful blow. As he fell again he was continually hit. On the ground he was kicked in the face and head. As the victim left he held a knife and threatened Mr Ali's friends and sister. The victim had a cut lip grazing and bruising. The defendant denied hitting Mr Ali and said he assaulted him. The defendant was 35 with many previous convictions over 20 years including GBH in 1986 and wounding and affray in 1992. The sentence of **6 months** concurrent for the knife was not challenged. Held. The **42 months** sentence was not susceptible to attack.

R v Bridge 2003 2 Cr App R (S) 23. The defendant pleaded guilty to racially aggravated ABH and racially aggravated common assault. There were two parts to the incident. The defendant's sister and another man, in the course of an incident waved a knife at members of staff at an Indian takeaway. Some shop front windows were smashed with a chair. Police arrived and the defendant's sister was arrested. The defendant was not involved in that incident, but about 10 minutes later approached the proprietor and asked him why he had got his sister arrested. He was heard to call the proprietor a "Paki"; there followed an argument and the defendant was seen to have a short metal bar. The defendant approached the proprietor and a colleague and said "I'll show you what white people are made of" and "you don't know who you're messing around with." The colleague came up behind the defendant and held the defendant in a bear hug. The defendant lifted the metal bar and struck the colleague on the back of the head causing a 5 mm jagged superficial laceration that required stitches. The attack continued and there was some punching and kicking of the proprietor. The defendant's record was a very bad one although he had not had a previous sentence of any substance for violence. The pre-sentence report said the risk of re-offending remains high. Held. **3 years** for the aggravated ABH **and 9 months** for the aggravated common assault, **concurrent** not consecutive.

R v Dickson 2003 2 Cr App R (S) 452. The defendant was convicted of racially aggravated ABH. At about 11pm the defendant returned to the block of flats where he was staying with his sister very drunk. He rang the intercom of the black woman who lived opposite his sister. Having entered he went to the victim's flat and when she came to the door he accused her of saying something to his sister. She denied doing this. He began to shout abuse at her and yelled through her letterbox "I'm going to put a fucking bomb through your letter-box, you black bitch". The victim then opened her door and the appellant spat in her face and continued to shout abuse at her. As she turned to close her door the defendant grabbed her by her hair and pulled her head down. He then kicked and punched her several times to the face and body. When she fell to the ground he continued to kick her to the body, back and legs. Her glasses were smashed. He repeatedly shouted "You black bastard." He was pulled-off the victim by his family. The victim sustained a swollen lip and bruising to her legs. She was treated in hospital with painkillers. He was detained and confronted officers in an aggressive way. In interview he denied the offence but said that he did not like black people. Reports (psychiatric and pre-sentence) indicated that he had entrenched racist with anti-social attitudes towards black people and women. He had previous convictions and for one of those he had been returned to prison (however, the report does not give details). Held. The message needed to be sent out clearly that racism must not be allowed to flourish. The maximum additional sentence that could be passed for the racial aggravation was two years. The sentencer should identify the sentence appropriate for the basic offence and then identify the period to be added for the racial aggravation. The aggravating features were the defendant's habitual racist behaviour, his previous offences and his conduct in relation to those previous offences. This was a disgraceful attack on a woman in her own home. However, the sentence was manifestly excessive. **2¹/₂ years** for the assault, not 4¹/₂ and **1¹/₂ years**, not 2 for the racially aggravated element so **4 years** not 6¹/₂.

R v Graham, Marshall and Watson 2005 1 Cr App R (S) 608. The defendants G, M and W pleaded guilty on the day fixed for trial to racially aggravated ABH. The victim, who was a Rastafarian, went with a woman friend to a public house. W passed the victim's friend and for no apparent reason kicked her. She complained to the victim, who spoke to W to ask if he were responsible. W challenged the victim to a fight. The victim went to leave the public house but then G punched his eye making it bleed. The victim again tried to leave. G and W then repeatedly punched him and M joined in the attack. The victim did not at any stage attempt to hit the defendants. M struck him several times with a snooker cue so hard that the cue shattered. M got another cue and hit the victim again. There were further punches and the attack continued for some time. One of the defendants tore one of the victim's dreadlocks out. One of the group said 'Get the fucking nigger' and 'get the wog'. As the victim and his friend left his friend heard one of the defendants say 'Don't fucking come back here you niggers'. After they left the defendants celebrated their attack, dancing round the public house holding up the victim's hat and dreadlock as trophies. What happened in the public house was caught on CCTV cameras. The victim was taken to hospital bleeding profusely, his right eye was stitched and he was treated for swelling, bruising, a laceration to the back of his head, a very painful fractured rib and pain in his left elbow. In a victim impact statement he said that he was very deeply affected by these events, that the physical scars were slowly healing but that the mental scars had not healed nor were likely to. He had felt deeply the insult to his religion caused by the tearing out of one of his dreadlocks and the subsequent use of it as a trophy. The defendants initially indicated that they would put the prosecution to proof of identity and only when the CCTV was enhanced proving their participation did they plead guilty. The only matter the CCTV did not pick up was the racist statements. W, 26, had twenty nine previous convictions for offences mainly of dishonesty but including affray, assault and public order offences. A pre-sentence report assessed him as being dangerous and posing a high risk of re-offending. M, 24, had fifty previous convictions including four for either assault or wounding. He had many road traffic offences and a conviction for robbery and intimidating a witness. A pre-sentence report assessed him at being at a high risk of re-offending. G, 23, had seventeen previous convictions including one for assault, one for wounding and one for racially aggravated criminal damage which resulted in a prison sentence of 18 months. A pre-sentence report said that he had had a hopeless life in terms of education and work and that his past offending had been linked to cocaine, ecstasy and alcohol. The attack was considered to be, in relation to all the defendants, sadistic and for gratification. All of the defendants had young children. Held. The prolonged nature of the attack, the abuse and the forcible ripping of the dreadlock were aggravating features. The attack did not have the additional aggravating features of planning, being part of a pattern of racist offending, the defendants being member of racist group or the victim being set up for the attack. The credit for pleas to the assault element was diminished or extinguished because of the delay in pleading guilty and the fact that they only pleaded guilty when there was incontrovertible evidence against them. The pleas to the racially aggravated part of the offence merited some although not necessarily substantial credit (as it had never been challenged). The additional period for the racially aggravated part of the offence was somewhat excessive. The judge indicated that without the racial element he would have sentenced W to 4 years and M and G to 3 years 8 months. Imposing the maximum additional period available for this part of the offence (2 years), as the Judge indicated he was doing, was wrong in principle. W **5¹/₂ years** not 6, and M and G **5 years 2 months** not 5 years 8 months.

Racially motivated ABH before s 29 in force

4.5   *R v Williams* 1997 2 Cr App R (S) 97. The defendant pleaded guilty at the earliest opportunity to affray. Police attended in the early hours of the morning after youths had been celebrating after a FA cup final. They found a group of youths facing a corner shop and broken glass on the pavement. The police explained there had been complaints about the noise and bottles being thrown. The group then moved about 5–10 yards and increased in size to about 35. The defendant who was in the group shouted, 'It's only a bastard Paki family complaining. We'll soon have those fuckers out of here.' He was warned by a police officer and said, 'They aren't human. They are fucking Paki bastards.' He was arrested and struggled with his escort. He admitted throwing a bottle at a corner shop but said he had drunk about 12 pints and didn't remember the remark. He was treated as of good character and was in work. **12 months** substituted for 21 months.

R v Earley and Bailey 1998 2 Cr App R (S) 158. The defendants E and B both 18, made an early plea of guilty to ABH. At night the two approached a Pakistani in the street and asked for money. They were larger than him and were frightening and threatening. The victim showed them his empty wallet and he was told, 'You're going to be beaten up anyway, Paki.' He was pulled towards a doorway and punched six or seven times. He fell to the ground and was kicked on the upper part of the body about six times. Police arrived and they kept referring to him as a Paki. The victim was dazed and concussed but suffered no fractures. He was released from hospital after about 40 minutes. E said he had been drinking and had run out of money. E had previous for criminal damage, being carried and breach of bail for which he received a C/D. He was also on bail for assaulting a constable (result not known). B was in breach of a C/D for ABH. Bailey had a Newton hearing about whether it was a racially motivated and lost. The judge started at 2 years and doubled it because it was racially motivated. He gave B 4 years with 3 months consecutive for the C/D. He gave E ¹/₃ off for his plea making 2 years 8 months with 1 month consecutive for the C/D. Held The 2 year starting figure was too low and the doubling of the figure was also wrong. B should have had some discount. Looking at it afresh B's sentence should be **3 years 3 months** with 3 months consecutive. E's sentence was unaltered. The sentences remain severe because they were racially motivated.

R v Miller 1998 2 Cr App R (S) 398. The defendant pleaded guilty to affray. The defendant abused a black man aged 46 by shouting, 'Black bastard', 'Fucking nigger,' as he followed the man with other youths who lagged behind. Then the defendant who appeared to be in a rage hit and kicked the victim's back and head while shouting, 'Black bastard.' The victim was knocked to the ground. The defendant continued to kick him. The victim said he was terrified. The defendant was 20 and had convictions for dishonesty and criminal damage, but none for violence. Held. This offence comes towards the top of incidents that are charged as affray. Because of the aggressiveness of the defendant and the racial motivation **21 months** detention not reduced.

5   ABSTRACTING ELECTRICITY

5.1   Theft Act 1968 s 13

Triable either way. On indictment maximum 5 years. Summary maximum 6 months and/or £5,000.

The Criminal Justice Act 2003 creates a summary maximum sentence of 51 weeks, a minimum custodial sentence of 28 weeks and Custody plus. The Home Office says they do not expect to introduce these provisions before September 2006.

Crown Court statistics – England and Wales – Males 21+
5.2

Year	Plea	Total Numbers sentenced	Type of sentence %					Average length of custody (months)
			Discharge	Fine	Community sentence	Suspended sentence	Custody	
2002	Guilty	7	14	29	14	14	29	13
	Not guilty	1	–	–	–	–	100	12
2003	Guilty	5	–	20	40	–	40	5
	Not guilty	–	–	–	–	–	–	–

For details and explanations about the statistics in the book see page vii.

The cases are listed under THEFT ETC – *Electricity or gas* (including abstracting electricity)

ACCOUNTING, FALSE

See FALSE ACCOUNTING

If there were any cases they would be listed under THEFT ETC

6 AFFRAY

6.1 Public Order Act 1986 s 3

Triable either way. On indictment maximum 3 years. Summary maximum 6 months and/or £5,000.

The Criminal Justice Act 2003 creates a summary maximum sentence of 51 weeks, a minimum custodial sentence of 28 weeks and Custody plus. The Home Office says they do not expect to introduce these provisions before September 2006.

Anti-Social Behavioural orders Where the defendant has acted in a manner that caused or was likely to cause harassment, alarm or distress to one or more persons not in the same household as the defendant and it is necessary to protect persons from further anti-social acts by him/her the court may make this order[17].

Disqualification from driving There are occasions when it is right to make this order[18].

Extended sentences under CJA 2003 For offences committed on or after 4/4/05 there is a mandatory duty to pass an extended sentence when there is a significant risk to members of the public of serious harm etc.[19]. See EXTENDED SENTENCES

Football Where the offence was committed relevant to a football match and where there are reasonable grounds to believe that making a banning order would help to prevent violence or disorder at or in connection with any regulated football match; the

17 Crime and Disorder Act 1998 s 1C
18 Powers of Criminal Courts (Sentencing) Act 2000 s 146 and *R v Cliff 2005* 2 Cr App R (S) 113
19 Criminal Justice Act 2003 s 227–228

court <u>must</u> make a Football Banning Order, under the Football Spectators Act 1989 s 14A and Sch 1, para 1.

Licensed premises Where the offence is committed on licensed premises the court may prohibit the defendant from entering those premises or any other specified premises without the express consent of the licensee or his agent[20]. The order shall last from 3 months to 2 years[21].

Sexual Offences Prevention Order There is a discretionary power to make this order when it is necessary to protect the public etc[22].

Magistrates' Court Sentencing Guidelines January 2004

6.2   For a first time offender pleading not guilty. Entry point. Is it so serious that only custody is appropriate? Consider the impact on the victim. Examples of aggravating factors for the offence are busy public place, football related, group action, injuries caused, people put in fear and vulnerable victim(s). Examples of mitigating factors for the offence are provocation, the defendant did not start the trouble and it stopped as soon as the police arrived. Examples of mitigation are age, health (physical or mental), co-operation with the police, voluntary compensation, genuine remorse and voluntary compensation. Consider compensation. Give reasons if not awarding compensation.

For details about the guidelines see MAGISTRATES' COURT SENTENCING GUIDELINES at page 483.

Guideline remarks – Serious affrays

6.3   *R v Keys* 1987 84 Cr App R 204. LCJ. In cases of very serious affray where it is plain that there was some measure of preparation, central organisation and direction, those who are organisers and ringleaders can expect heavy sentences in the range of **7 years and upwards**. At the other end of the scale, acts of individual participants on the edges of the affray cannot be taken in isolation. Even though a particular defendant never hit an opponent, never threw a missile, never physically threatened anyone, nevertheless, even if he participated simply by encouraging others and shouting insults and threats, he thereby helps to promote the totality of the affray. He must accordingly take some share of the blame for the overall picture. The more he is shown to have promoted the affray, the greater must be his punishment. Where there has been not only a concerted major affray, but also a prolonged and vicious attack on the police, any participant, however slight his involvement may have been, can expect a sentence of at least **18 months to 2 years**. The carrying of weapons, the throwing of missiles and so on ought properly to be reflected in an increase in that minimum.

Aircraft, on

See AIRCRAFT OFFENCES – *Affray*

Football etc related

6.4   *R v Pollinger and Pearson* 1999 1 Cr App R (S) 128. The defendants pleaded guilty to affray. Pollinger also pleaded to common assault. After an equalising goal had been scored at a football match there were two pitch invasions. Rival fans fought. At the first invasion, Pollinger was at the forefront, pushing a player (the common assault). He was escorted off the pitch by policemen. At the second invasion one team cut off the other team's players from their exit. Pollinger ran the length of the pitch. Pearson in the first invasion confronted opposition players aggressively and gesticulated at them. He brushed or pushed a steward away. He was one of the first to invade the pitch in the

---

20 Licensed Premises (Exclusion of Certain Persons) Act 1980 s 1(1)
21 Licensed Premises (Exclusion of Certain Persons) Act 1980 s 1(3)
22 Sexual Offences Act 2003 s 104 & Sch. 5

second invasion and also ran the length of the pitch. The players who gave evidence at the trial of those who pleaded not guilty said they were frightened. Pollinger, aged 27 had a good work record and some previous convictions but none for violence and only one for a public order offence some years previously. Held. Pollinger's sentence of **4 months** and 4 months consecutive was not wrong. However, because of very exceptional personal circumstances the sentences were **suspended**. Pearson aged 32, had convictions for public order offences and other matters up until he was 22. He was in work and had a family. His **4 months** sentence was not altered.

Partner/ex-partner, against

6.5   *R v Howells Re Jarvis* 1999 1 Cr App R (S) 335 at 342. LCJ. The defendant pleaded guilty to affray. He and his co-defendant made a large number of telephone calls to his ex-wife. He was amicable but the co-defendant was aggressive. After about eight calls she unplugged the telephone and later her boyfriend arrived and they went to bed. At about 3.40 am they heard loud banging and the boyfriend got up and saw the defendant and the co-defendant coming up the stairs. When the defendant reached the top of the stairs he shouted, "I'm going to get you, you bastard." The boyfriend tried to shut the door but the defendant pushed it open and grabbed the boyfriend's hair. The ex-wife telephoned the police and the intruders left. After the police had arrived there were two further telephone calls from the co-defendant. The police discovered that the lower door lock had been damaged and the door forced. The defendant was arrested and outlined the friction between him and his ex-wife culminating in her refusal that night to let him have his passport which was at her house. He also said he resented the boyfriend living in what was the matrimonial home and said he had not formed an intention about what to do with the boyfriend but did agree he said he was going to 'get' him. He was 30 with a 15-year-old conviction for assaulting the police, an ABH conviction on his wife in 1994 (probation) and an assault on police conviction also in 1994 (fined £500). The pre-sentence report said his conduct was attributed to drink. He expressed regret. Held. The offence called for a custodial sentence. As it was his first custodial, he had learnt his lesson and there was no continuing danger to his ex-wife or her boyfriend **3 months** not 6.

Police officers, involving

6.6   *R v Sabeddu* 2001 1 Cr App R (S) 493. The defendant was committed for sentence for an affray which was throwing an empty drinks bottle at the police at a May Day demonstration. The defence said it was a "one man affray". He was also committed for possessing a medicinal product for sale. Police stopped him before he went into a warehouse rave party. He was found to have 26 wraps of Ketamine in a wallet concealed up his trousers. He was 18 and of good character. Held. 3 months detention not 8 for the Ketamine. The affray merited a consecutive sentence and was committed on bail for the other. He was part of a large crowd. His action could have precipitated further violence. **6 months** detention was at the top of the bracket but not manifestly excessive.

R v Fox 1999 1 Cr App R (S) 332. The defendant, aged 21 pleaded guilty at the first opportunity to affray at the Magistrates' Court and was committed for sentence. Police were called to an incident at a public house where a crowd of 40 had gathered. A friend of the defendant was arrested and the defendant who had been drinking was abusive and threatening. He produced a bottle, which fell to the ground and smashed. He struggled violently and attempted to strike an officer. The police used CS gas to subdue him. Held. He was of good character and full of remorse. **4 months** substituted for 9 months.

Racially motivated

See **RACIALLY-AGGRAVATED OFFENCES**

Public houses and chip shops etc

6.7   *R v Holmes and Holmes* 1999 2 Cr App R (S) 100. The defendants, GH and AH pleaded guilty to affray at the magistrates and were committed for sentence. The defendants were in a chip shop and tension developed between them and other customers. GH swore, and hit someone on the head. AH joined in and both punched the victim. GH then punched someone who tried to intervene and the victim fell to the ground. GH said he had drunk 8–10 pints and didn't remember much. He did remember punching and kicking the victims. AH said he had 7 pints. They were both of good character with references and in work. **9 months** substituted for 15 months for both.

R v Howells 1999 1 Cr App R (S) 335 at 338. The defendant pleaded guilty to affray. The defendant with two others visited a pub in the evening and behaved in a rowdy manner. One of the other two damaged a barmaid's shoes and the landlord asked the group to pay for the damage. An argument developed and they were asked to leave. The defendant left but the others remained and a fight broke out in which the landlord was punched several times. The fight then continued outside and the defendant was hit on the back of the head. The defendant then hit the assailant a number of blows in retaliation. The victim lost consciousness for 4 minutes and suffered pain, swelling and bruises to his cheek and jaw. One eye was closed and he had a 1" laceration to his lip. Another hit the landlord fracturing his jaw in two places. The defendant's plea was on the basis of excessive self defence. He was 26 and had several convictions including a violent disorder when he was 19 for which he was fined. He had not received a custodial sentence before. He had sole parental responsibility for a very young child. Held. This did pass the custody threshold but **4 months** not 9.

Road rage

See **ROAD RAGE** – *Affray*

AGENT PROVOCATEURS

See **ENTRAPMENT/AGENT PROVOCATEURS**

AGGRAVATED BURGLARY

See **BURGLARY** – **AGGRAVATED**

7   AGGRAVATED VEHICLE-TAKING

7.1   Theft Act 1968 s 12A

Triable either way unless the vehicle was only damaged and the value of the damage is less than £5,000 when it is summary only.

The Criminal Justice Act 2003 creates a summary maximum sentence of 51 weeks, a minimum custodial sentence of 28 weeks and Custody plus. The Home Office says they do not expect to introduce these provisions before September 2006.

On indictment maximum 2 years, and where death is caused 14 years[23]. For offences committed before 27/2/04 the maximum for when death results remains 5 years. Summary maximum 6 months and/or £5,000.

23 Criminal Justice Act 2003 s 285(1).

Anti-Social Behavioural orders Where the defendant has acted in a manner that caused or was likely to cause harassment, alarm or distress to one or more persons not in the same household as the defendant and it is necessary to protect persons from further anti-social acts by him/her the court may make this order[24].

Disqualification from driving Mandatory disqualification of 1 year.

Drug Abstinence Order This was repealed on 4 April 2005.

Endorsement 3 to 11 points.

Imprisonment for public protection For offences when 1) committed on or after 4/4/05 2) death results and 3) when there is a significant risk to members of the public of serious harm etc. there is a mandatory duty to pass a sentence of imprisonment for public protection[25]. For offenders under 18 the duty is to pass detention for public protection or an extended sentence[26].

Sexual Offences Prevention Order There is a discretionary power to make this order when it is necessary to protect the public etc[27].

Crown Court statistics – England and Wales – Males 21+

7.2

Year	Plea	Total Numbers sentenced	Type of sentence %					Average length of custody (months)
			Discharge	Fine	Community sentence	Suspended sentence	Custody	
Without death								
2002	Guilty	256	1	–	22	0	76	12.9
	Not guilty	18	–	–	17	–	83	14.4
2003	Guilty	292	1	0	22	1	74	13.2
	Not guilty	20	10	–	30	–	55	11.7
With death								
2002	Guilty	4	–	–	25	–	75	33
	Not guilty	–	–	–	–	–	–	–
2003	Guilty	2	–	–	–	–	100	42
	Not guilty	1	–	–	–	–	100	24

For details and explanations about the statistics in the book see page vii

Magistrates' Court Sentencing Guidelines January 2004

7.3   For a first time offender pleading not guilty. Entry point. Is it so serious that only custody is appropriate? Consider the impact on the victim. Examples of aggravating factors for the offence are competitive driving: racing, showing off, disregard of warnings e.g. from passengers or others in the vicinity, group action, police chase, pre-meditated, serious injury/damage, serious risk, trying to avoid detection or arrest and vehicle destroyed. Examples of mitigating factors for the offence are passenger only, single incident of bad driving, speed not excessive and very minor injury/damage. Examples of mitigation are age, health (physical or mental), co-operation with the police, genuine remorse and voluntary compensation. Give reasons if not awarding compensation.

24 Crime and Disorder Act 1998 s 1C
25 Criminal Justice Act 2003 s 224–226
26 Criminal Justice Act 2003 s 226 and 228
27 Sexual Offences Act 2003 s 104 & Sch. 5

[Note The ability to award compensation is restricted by the Powers of Criminal Courts (Sentencing) Act 2000 s 130(6) which deals with motor vehicle accidents.]

For details about the guidelines see MAGISTRATES' COURT SENTENCING GUIDELINES at page 483.

General considerations

7.4   *R v Bird* 1993 14 Cr App R (S) 343 at 346. In judging the gravity of the case, the most important of the statutory elements, (a) to (d) of the offence of aggravated-vehicle taking is paragraph (a) that the vehicle was driven dangerously on a road or other public place, for that concerns the culpability of the driver, whereas the incidence and severity of any injury or damage under paragraphs (b), (c) and (d) are to some extent a matter of chance. The aggravating features of this offence will be primarily the overall culpability of the driving: how bad it was and for how long and, to a lesser extent, how much injury or damage, or both was caused. Where drink has played a part no doubt this will affect the dangerousness of the driving.

Alcohol

7.5   *R v Gosling* 2003 1 Cr App R (S) 295. The defendant pleaded guilty to perverting the course of Justice, aggravated vehicle taking and driving whilst disqualified. He was also committed for sentence for no insurance and excess alcohol. In December 2001, after drinking to excess he took his brother's car without his consent. On a by-pass he lost control of the car, hit the central crash barrier, rebounded across three carriageways and hit the nearside crash barrier. The car and the crash barriers were extensively damaged. When the police arrived, he gave his brother's name and the address they shared. At the police station he persisted with the false name. Three days later the police discovered his true identity and when questioned again the defendant admitted he had given a false name. He was 28, with a bad record for dishonesty with 14 convictions for various kinds of theft. In February 2001, he was disqualified for 2 years for dangerous driving. After that he had been convicted of driving whilst disqualified and was given a 180 hours community punishment order and further disqualified. The Judge gave him 18 months for perverting the course of justice and no penalty on the other offences. There were concurrent disqualification orders with 2 years or until he had passes the extended test on the excess alcohol charge. Held. The perverting the course of justice was at the very bottom of the range of seriousness for that kind of offence. The aggravated vehicle taking aggravated by the alcohol and the driving whilst disqualified for the third time in a year was significantly the most serious matter. 3 months not 18 for perverting the course of justice. **9 months** for the vehicle taking and 3 months concurrent for the disqualified driving concurrent. So total 12 months not 18. The disqualification will remain.

Disqualification, for how long?

7.6   *R v Nicholls* 2001 Unreported 15/11/01. See *Police car, being pursued by a*

Police car, being pursued by a

7.7   *R v Frostick* 1998 1 Cr App R (S) 257. The defendant pleaded guilty to aggravated vehicle-taking and driving whilst disqualified. Ten minutes after the car was stolen the police saw it and switched on their lights and their stop sign. The car driven by the defendant cut across the central reservation and accelerated away. It entered a 30 mph zone and travelled at speeds of about 85 mph. It crossed several mini roundabouts at speed and went right at a keep left sign. It stopped in a cul-de-sac. In interview he said he was paid to take the car and didn't stop because he was disqualified. The defendant was 23 and between 1992 and 1995 he had 24 previous convictions. Nearly all concerned motor vehicles particularly TDA and driving offences. He had received 21 months for dangerous driving, driving whilst disqualified and driving a conveyance when he knew it had been taken without authority. Held. As the maximum is 2 years, 18 months was a commensurate sentence, and because of the plea **15 months** not 21 months.

R v Nicholls 2001 Unreported 15/11/01. The defendant pleaded guilty to aggravated vehicle taking, drink/drive, driving whilst disqualified and no insurance. He drove in a stolen car and was seen by police who put their light on to indicate him to stop. He did so but as the officers were about to get out of their car he sped away half on half off the pavement for about 100 metres. He drove through residential streets at between 50 and 60 mph and straight through red traffic lights at 60 mph. After travelling at over 80 mph over a brow of a hill he hit two vehicles at red traffic lights. When tested he was 3 times over the drink/drive limit. When interviewed he admitted speeds of between 80 and 100 mph. He was 29 with two findings of guilt and four convictions mostly for road traffic offences. He had three convictions for drink/drive. He was currently disqualified and had been disqualified six times for periods up to 3 years. The judge indicated the discount for pleading guilty was reduced because of the overwhelming evidence, his drinking and because he was a repeat offender. The sentences were ordered to run concurrently. Held. Credit must be limited because he was caught red-handed. **22 months** for the aggravated vehicle taking was in no way wrong. Because of employment prospects and rehabilitation 5 years disqualification not 10.

AIDS

For where the victim fears s/he might have contracted AIDS although there was no evidence s/he had done so, see VICTIMS – *Victim fears she has contracted AIDS from sex attack*

For where defendant has AIDS see DEFENDANT – *AIDS, defendant has*

8   AIRCRAFT OFFENCES

8.1   Various offences and penalties.

General principles

8.2   *R v Oliver* 1999 1 Cr App R (S) 394. Travelling on an aircraft places a special duty on passengers to co-operate and behave. The safety of the aircraft and the passengers may be put in jeopardy. A relatively small incident may have catastrophic consequences, which may not always be foreseen. Even on a guilty plea to affray it is correct to pass imprisonment.

ABH

8.3   Offences against the Person Act 1861 s 47

Triable either way. On indictment maximum 5 years. Summary maximum 6 months and/or £5,000.

Extended sentences under CJA 2003 For offences committed on or after 4/4/05 there is a mandatory duty to pass an extended sentence when there is a significant risk to members of the public of serious harm etc.[28]. See EXTENDED SENTENCES

R v Beer 1998 2 Cr App R (S) 248. The defendant pleaded guilty to being drunk on an

---

28 Criminal Justice Act 2003 s 227–228

aircraft, and common assault. She was convicted of ABH. Before boarding a transatlantic flight the defendant told the staff she had a drink problem. She was monitored. She was abusive to the staff. She threw her part- full wine glass and her tray at staff and pulled a tie clip off a member of staff who tried to calm her down. She went to the lavatory and consumed the best part of a bottle of whisky. She then fell asleep. On arrival police boarded the plane. She started to swear and shout. She kicked out at a constable with both legs hitting him in the groin. This was very painful. She was abusive and struggled. While handcuffs were placed on her she bent the same officer's hand back causing a painful injury. She lashed out as she was led away and landed a painful blow to the same police officer's leg by kicking him as she was put in a van. That officer was not back on duty 8 months later. One of his testicles was persistently swollen and painful. The wrist injury was still requiring treatment 4 months later. It caused him at times to have shooting pains. Except for a drink/drive offence she was of good character. She had a 12-year-old son. She was sentenced to 6 months, 2 months concurrent and 18 months consecutive. Held. The **18 months** sentence and the overall sentence of 2 years were not excessive.

See also **ABH**

Affray

8.4   Public Order Act 1986 s 3

Triable either way. On indictment maximum 3 years. Summary maximum 6 months and/or £5,000.

Extended sentences under CJA 2003 For offences committed on or after 4/4/05 there is a mandatory duty to pass an extended sentence when there is a significant risk to members of the public of serious harm etc.[29]. See **EXTENDED SENTENCES**

R v Oliver 1999 1 Cr App R (S) 394. The defendant pleaded guilty to affray. The defendant travelled from America with his wife, young daughter and baby. The air steward asked the defendant to move the baby from a cot to one of their laps. He lost his temper, became abusive and moved towards the steward with his hands raised. He calmed down and a little later apologised. He again lost his temper this time with his wife. The cabin staff separated them and moved her away from him. He appeared to try to get to the flight deck and the steward blocked his path. The passengers were frightened and the captain considered diverting the plane. Held. Travelling on an aircraft places a special duty on passengers to co-operate and behave. The safety of the aircraft and the passengers may be put in jeopardy. A relatively small incident may have catastrophic consequences, which may not always be foreseen. Even on a guilty plea it is correct to pass imprisonment. If this offence had been committed on the ground a non-custodial might have been appropriate. However, here **12 months** not 18 months imprisonment.

R v Oliver 1999 1 Cr App R (S) 394. The defendant pleaded guilty on re-arraignment to affray. He, his cousin and his father travelled from Newcastle to Spain. The defendant and his cousin were noisy and rude from the time they reached their seats. All three shouted and swore at each other. The cousin asked for and was found a seat and as she was leaving she pulled his head back by the hair. She pulled his head from side to side and threw a drink in his face. He punched her and she slapped him back. The staff had to intervene and moved them to different parts of the aircraft. With 2 hours still to go he ranted incoherently and kicked the seat in front shouting threats at his cousin. He threatened to open the aircraft door and the captain considered diverting the plane. The staff had to watch him in shifts for the rest of the flight. Police took him off the plane. He was receiving psychiatric treatment for a tendency to panic. Alcohol, drug abuse and his unwillingness to co-operate with the treatment worsened the condition. Held. The

29 Criminal Justice Act 2003 s 227–228

incident was over a very considerable time and for some 2 hours after the drink was thrown. There was considerable anxiety to staff and passengers. Conduct of this sort must be met with a significant sentence. **12 months** can't be criticised.

See also **AFFRAY**

Dangerous goods, delivering for loading

8.5   Air Navigation Order 2000, Arts 60 and 122 and various regulations

Triable either way. On indictment maximum 2 years. Summary maximum £5,000 fine only.

R v Tropical Express Ltd 2002 1 Cr App R (S) 115. The defendant company pleaded guilty to delivering for loading onto an aircraft dangerous goods which he knew or ought to have known were capable of posing significant risk to health and safety etc contrary to the Air Navigation (Dangerous Goods) Regulations 1994, Reg. 4(2) and consigning 13 packages for carriage by air contrary to Air Navigation (Dangerous Goods) Regulations 1994, Reg. 6E. The company was a small company with 12 employees and shipped goods by air. It acted as middleman between those sending freight and air-carriers and their agents. Some of its employees were involved in smuggling cigarettes, which involved a loss to the Revenue of $7.5m. The effective sole Director of the company informed Customs about his suspicions and did all he could to help Customs about it. As an act of revenge against the company the employee involved in the smuggling presented a package property described as 'dangerous goods' at Stansted Airport for shipment to Nigeria. Twice it was rejected by the sales agent because of lack of proper paperwork and the boxes were damaged etc. Later the company, which had rejected the package, telephoned the employee and enquired about the packages. The employee said they had been shipped by Swiss Air without difficulty. This was not withstanding Swiss Air do not ship cargo to Nigeria. Next the employee presented the same goods wrapped up without proper labelling about it being dangerous goods to the same sales agent. They were suspicious and discovered they contained barrels and toxic liquid etc and informed the Civil Aviation Authority. The defendant company had conducted its affairs blamelessly for over 10 years. The sole Director gave evidence for the Customs in the trial about the cigarette trial and the employee was sent to prison. The company had lost its principle customer as a result of the prosecution. The defendant company was fined £20,000 with £18,000 costs. That put the company in a perilous position. Held. Normally the fine would be substantial. This is a wholly exceptional case so **£5,000 fine** and the costs to be taxed and include the sentencing hearing and preparation for that only.

Drunk, being

8.6   *R v Abdulkarim* 2000 2 Cr App R (S) 16. The defendant pleaded guilty to being drunk on an aircraft and smoking in a prohibited part of an aircraft at the Magistrates' Court. The defendant who came from the United Arab Emirates was on a flight from Dubai to London. He smoked repeatedly in a non-smoking section of the plane. Passengers complained and he complied with the requests to stop from the staff only to light another one shortly afterwards. He dropped a lighted cigarette down the side of his seat and was unwilling to assist the staff in retrieving it. He had drunk about eight cans of beer and the staff refused to serve him with anymore. He demanded more and when refused showed his discontent in a forceful way. A doctor who examined him $3^1/_2$ hours after the plane landed said he was still drunk. He was of good character. Held. Strong deterrent sentences are needed but **6 months** substituted for 12.

R v Ayodeji 2001 2 Cr App R (S) 370. The defendant pleaded guilty to being drunk on an aircraft. A count of endangering an aircraft was left on the file. The defendant travelled from Lagos to London. It was a no smoking flight. He persisted in smoking even when told not to. He extinguished a cigarette on a bulkhead and a fire extinguisher had to be used. He was abusive calling a stewardess a 'white bitch' several times. He was very drunk. He suffered from schizophrenia. He had served several long prison sentences including 5 years for attempted robbery. Held. We take a very serious view of the case. Notwithstanding the endangering count being left on the file, the judge was entitled to sentence on the basis the passengers were utterly terrified. The defendant had boarded the plane without his medication and deliberately got drunk. **8 months** was appropriate.

R v Cooper 2004 2 Cr App R (S) 82. The defendant pleaded guilty to being drunk on an aircraft. She and her husband were returning from a holiday in Malta and she was drunk before boarding the flight. They were arguing about their unsatisfactory holiday before and during the flight when this argument involved other passengers, principally the two people sitting directly in front of them. When these people reclined their seats the defendant was verbally abusive. After the plane landed and when it was taxiing towards the terminal the defendant got up from her seat although the seat belt sign was still on, opened the overhead locker, removed her jacket, threw it at the male passenger in the seat in front of her and shouted abuse at him. She tried to punch through the gap between the seats. The purser approached her and asked her to sit down and stop swearing, but she continued to shout abuse at the passengers in front of her. She tried to get out of her seat and the purser had to hold her in her seat until the plane stopped. The defendant was age 38 and of previous good character. A pre-sentence report noted that she was very ashamed of her actions and had expressed remorse. There were character references. Held. She behaved badly but the safety of the aircraft was not endangered in any way while the aircraft was in the air. No actual danger followed from what she did. An appropriate sentence would have been a substantial fine or a community punishment order. She should not have been sent to prison. As she had then served the equivalent of a 6 week sentence, **conditional discharge** not 3 months.

See also **DRUNK**

Endangering an aircraft or any person

8.7   Air Navigation Order 1989 and Civil Aviation Act 1982 s 61

Triable either way. On indictment maximum 5 years[30] (for offences committed before 10/9/04 the maximum remains 2 years). Summary maximum £5,000 fine only.

R v Mullaly 1997 2 Cr App R (S) 343. The defendant pleaded guilty to two offences under the Air Navigation Order and the Civil Aviation Act 1982. The first offence was acting in a manner likely to endanger an aircraft and the second offence was being drunk. The defendant, a US citizen, who was on a transatlantic flight to Manchester was suffering from a cocktail of alcohol and medication. He was asked several times to return to his seat because of his behaviour but he ignored the requests. He banged on the toilet door so it buckled. He banged the luggage rack. He went to the front of the aircraft where he clenched and unclenched his fists. He was incoherent. He pushed a steward who was trying to use a restraining kit. He managed to escape from the handcuffs while passengers guarded him. He got up and swore. The captain considered making an emergency landing in Ireland. The aircrew were in fear. A passenger described it as her worst nightmare. He was treated as of good character. Held. To reflect the plea and his good character the 2 year maximum was wrong. **18 months** substituted.

R v Ryan 2001 2 Cr App R (S) 550. The defendant pleaded guilty, although not at the first opportunity, to endangering the safety of an aircraft or persons therein contrary to the Air Navigation (No 2) Order 1995. On a flight from India the smoke alarm went off in the lavatory. Members of the crew armed with fire extinguishers knocked on the door

---

30 Aviation (Offences) Act 2003 s 2

but there was no response. They gained access and found the defendant there with burnt paper in the lavatory bowl. There was a smell of burnt paper. He said he lit paper to light a cigarette. The other passengers were frightened. He returned to his seat and caused no more trouble. He told police he was burning a receipt to avoid Customs duty. The aircraft materials were fire resistant. The defendant was 35 and had 94 previous convictions including robbery for which he received a $4^1/_2$ year sentence. Held. Those who are tempted to endanger the safety of an aircraft or the passengers should expect deterrent sentences. **15 months** was not excessive.

Endangering safety at aerodromes

8.8   Aviation and Maritime Security Act 1990 s 1

Indictable only. Maximum sentence life.

Dangerous Offender provisions For offences committed on or after 4/4/05 where there is a significant risk to members of the public of serious harm etc. there is a mandatory duty to pass a life sentence when it is justified and otherwise a sentence of imprisonment for public protection[31]. For offenders under 18 the duty is to pass detention for life, detention for public protection or an extended sentence[32].

R v Lees 2003 2 Cr App R (S) 306. The defendant pleaded guilty to disrupting services at an aerodrome with intent contrary to s 1(2)(b) of the 1990 Act and criminal damage. He was a helicopter pilot who used Coventry Airport for leisure purposes. A dispute arose between him and the airport director after the director had mistaken the defendant for someone with a criminal record, wanted by the police. The director appreciated that he had made a mistake, but then he found that the defendant's medical certificate had expired. The defendant said that that was an oversight, however the director excluded the defendant from the airport. However, five weeks later the defendant used the airport to refuel. The director walked over and asked him to leave the airport forthwith or be escorted off. The defendant took off in his helicopter, but instead of leaving he went and hovered at the intersection of the two operational runways. He radioed the control tower that he had a problem with the airport director and that the airport was closed. Two jets waiting to take off had to taxi to a position just off the runway. He then positioned his plane to face one in an intimidating fashion. He caused another helicopter which was coming into land to pull up short so as to avoid a collision. Advised that the director was in the control tower, the defendant said, "I am coming to talk to him". He then flew the helicopter at speed towards the control tower only pulling to a hover directly outside the fourth floor window. He then flew in a loop around the control tower, over-flew the fire station and then circled the control tower again before coming back to hover by the fourth floor window. People tried to calm him. However, he finally said "I've had enough", before dipping the nose of the helicopter and powering it up. It came straight for the control tower, only pulling away at the last minute. The control tower was evacuated. This happened only a month after September 11th 2001. He flew off, but as he did so he clipped a glide path monitor which had to be recalibrated at considerable cost. After landing he was arrested. He was 42 and of exemplary character. He lived for flying. He had glowing references. The PSR said that the defendant was struggling to come to terms with his loss of good character and re-offending risk appeared low. A psychiatric report said he suffered with a moderate to severe post traumatic stress disorder and depression. He was extremely remorseful. Held. Custody was justified. The seriousness was reflected in the fact that the maximum sentence for the offence is life. Accepting that any custodial sentence would lead to loss of his livelihood, coupled with remorse and the mitigation, **2 years** not 3.

---

31 Criminal Justice Act 2003 s 225
32 Criminal Justice Act 2003 s 226 and 228

Firearms etc

8.9   Aviation Security Act 1982 s 4(2)(a)

Triable either way. On indictment maximum 5 years[33] Summary maximum 3 months and/or £5,000 fine only.

Extended sentences under CJA 2003 For offences committed on or after 4/4/05 there is a mandatory duty to pass an extended sentence when there is a significant risk to members of the public of serious harm etc.[34]. See EXTENDED SENTENCES

R v Burrows 2004 2 Cr App R (S) 473. The defendant pleaded guilty at the Magistrates' Court to having with him on an aerodrome an article which appeared to be a firearm, contrary to Aviation Security Act 1982 s 4. When his bag was X- rayed at Stansted Airport it was seen to contain a ball-bearing gun. The defendant had the gun to shoot at targets in his garden. He had put the gun in a compartment in his travel bag weeks before to conceal it from his young daughter and had forgotten it was in there. This account was accepted as truthful. It was accepted that the gun was not a real firearm. The defendant, 44, was a respectable business man and was treated as being of good character. The pre-sentence report said that he was deeply remorseful and the risk of re-offending was low. There were three character references. The episode did not lead to any inconvenience or danger to anyone. Held. A custodial sentence was not wrong in principle. The importance of the need to ensure security in the air cannot be exaggerated. As it was accepted this was a genuine oversight the appropriate sentence was **28 days** not 4 months.

Passengers, interfering with

8.10   *R v Gantz* 2005 1 Cr App R (S) 582. The defendant was convicted of causing a noxious thing to be administered with intent. He and a friend flew from Israel to London. The previous night he had been to a party and taken an ecstasy tablet and smoked cannabis as well as drinking. He also had some cocaine although he claimed he did not knowingly take that. Also travelling to London was the victim, who was pregnant, and her grandmother. The victim was previously unknown to the defendant. The defendant got into conversation with her at the airport and on the plane he was sitting quite close to her. He drank from a bottle of Schnapps on the plane and the cabin crew asked him to stop. He refused and they confiscated the bottle. Next he got into conversation with the victim and handed her a cup of coffee that the flight attendant had made for her. She didn't like the taste and only drank a sip. He asked her to go to a party with him in London and she refused. She perceived him as persistent in his advances although she told him she was married. He later offered to get her an orange juice which she drank. After she had drunk the juice she noticed bits at the bottom of the glass. After that she felt a little unwell and had a rapid pulse with affected vision. She was thought to be suffering from a panic attack. When the plane landed she was taken to hospital and her blood and urine were found to contain traces of ecstasy. Near to where the defendant had been sitting there was an empty Diazepam packet and three ecstasy tablets. It was the Crown case that he had been trying to make her susceptible to his advances by means of the drug. The defendant was 31 and of good character. He never showed any remorse. Held. The fact that the noxious substance was a Class A drug was a seriously aggravating factor. Other aggravating factors were that the victim was a wholly innocent woman, she had not encouraged the defendant's attentions and she was pregnant. When she discovered she had had something administered to her she panicked and was very distressed. The incident was on an aeroplane with limited medical facilities, which would have increased her distress and fear. Although **3 years** was at the upper end of the range of sentence it was not manifestly excessive.

---

33 Aviation (Offences) Act 2003 s 2
34 Criminal Justice Act 2003 s 227–228

Pilots

8.11   There are various offences that could be charged.

R v Grzybowski 1998 1 Cr App R (S) 4. The defendant pleaded guilty to making false entries in his personal flying log, contrary to what is now Air Navigation Order 2000, art 83(2) at the Magistrates' Court. He was a pilot instructor teaching people to fly micro-light aircraft. One of his trainees agreed to pay him petrol money and examination fees to learn to fly. The trainee was dissatisfied with the amount of flying he was receiving. However on his second flight in a particular aircraft when he was flying solo it crashed and he was killed. That evening the defendant handed to the Air Accident Investigation inspectors his log book. It included two entries for trips of the trainee, which hadn't taken place. There were five other entries on days which the trainee couldn't have flown because he was elsewhere. The log also contained his comments. The defendant claimed that the five trips were made but on other days. He claimed the entries helped the trainee to obtain a licence and that he was pressed to do it by the trainee. The trainee's father did not accept that. He was 48 and had a conviction for failing to record that he had taken possession of an aircraft, which was not properly licensed. Held. The log was a record of critical importance. It showed whether young pilots have or had not been properly trained. We profoundly disagree that the custody threshold was not crossed. It called for the sentence of **6 months**, which he had received.

R v Evans 2001 1 Cr App R (S) 442. The defendant pleaded guilty to recklessly acting in a manner likely to endanger a helicopter and anyone therein, contrary to the Air Navigation (No 2) Order 1995 and flying otherwise in accordance with the air opera-tor's certificate. Six months after obtaining a helicopter licence he gave some friends rides without charging at a carnival. He was then approached by someone who wanted to raise money for a registered charity in the name of his autistic son. He then gave rides to members of the public and raised £270. Children were allowed to sit on an adult's laps without being strapped in. One boy moved the control column and an adult had his feet on the control pedals while the helicopter was in flight. The defendant says he told the adult to take them off. An expert said that children sitting unrestrained put the hel-icopter and passengers in danger. The defendant was unemployed with two previous convictions for unrelated offences. The defendant's actions could have been cata-strophic. Held. **3 months** for the endangering, £1,000 for the certificate offence and £5,127.29 prosecution costs were not wrong.

9   AMPHETAMINE

General properties

9.1   *R v Wijs* 1999 1 Cr App R (S) 181. LCJ. Amphetamine is a synthetic stimulant which, in powder or tablet form is a Class B drug. There are two very obvious differ-ences between cannabis and amphetamine: (1) while market prices tend to fluctuate depending on the interplay of supply and demand, and there has been a sharp decline in the street value of amphetamine in the last two years or so, amphetamine has always, weight for weight, been vastly more valuable than cannabis; (2) it has always been the practice to retail amphetamine to consumers in a highly adulterated form. Based on seizures in the last year or two, amphetamine now has a higher concentration of the drug than was once generally the case. While goods seized at the points of importation may contain a high percentage of amphetamine, at a retail level the purity may well be no more than (say) 10% to 12% or even less. It follows that a trafficker in possession of amphetamine stands to earn very much larger sums than a trafficker in possession of the same weight of cannabis; that a relatively small weight of amphetamine of maximum purity will, when adulterated, convert into a very large number of individual doses; and that the weight of amphetamine which a user may hold for his own personal consumption is likely, in many cases, to be much smaller than the weight of cannabis held for personal consumption. For reasons clearly given in *R v Aranguren* 1999 Cr App R 347 sentences in relation to amphetamine should depend not on market value but, on the quantity of the amphetamine calculated on the basis of 100% pure amphetamine base (i.e. the maximum theoretical purity of 73% amphetamine base in amphetamine sulphate, the remaining 27% being the sulphate). As was held in relation to Class A drugs in we should not attempt to distinguish between different drugs in Class B on the basis that one such drug is more or less pernicious than another.

See also **DRUG USERS; IMPORTATION OF DRUGS, POSSESSION OF DRUGS; PRODUCTION OF DRUGS** and **SUPPLY OF DRUGS (CLASS A, B AND C)**

10   ANIMAL CRUELTY

10.1   Protection of Animals Act 1911 s 1 etc.

Summary only maximum 6 month and/or £5,000.

The Home Office has published plans to reform this offence.

Destruction orders There is power to destroy the animal and deprive ownership of the animal and power to disqualify persons from having custody of any animal[35].

Disqualification There is power to disqualify persons from having custody of any animal[36].

Magistrates' Court Sentencing Guidelines January 2004

10.2   For a first time offender pleading not guilty. Entry point. Is it serious enough for a community penalty? Examples of aggravating factors for the offence are adult involving children, animal(s) kept for livelihood, committed over a period or involving several animals, deriving pleasure from torturing or frightening, disregarding warnings of others, group action, offender in position of special responsibility towards animal, premeditated/deliberate, prolonged neglect, serious injury or death and use of weapon. Examples of mitigating factors for the offence are ignorance of appropriate care, impulsive, minor injury, offender induced by others and single incident. Examples of mitigation are age, health (physical or mental), co-operation with the police and genuine remorse. Always consider disqualifying the offender from having custody and depriving him or her of owning the animal concerned.

For details about the guidelines see **MAGISTRATES' COURT SENTENCING GUIDELINES** at page 483.

See also **DOGS**

11   ANIMAL RIGHTS ACTIVISTS

11.1   Various offences and penalties.

Guideline remarks

11.2   *R v Martin* 1999 1 Cr App R (S) 477. Generally the sentences imposed for acts

35 Protection of Animals Act 1911 s 2
36 Protection of Animals Act 1911 s 2

of violence relating to animal rights activism is in almost every case lower than for terrorist offences fuelled by political extremism. There are obvious reasons why this should be so. The political threat presented by such offences is much less potent; and the general level of sophistication is a very great deal lower.

Harassment – Section 4

11.3   *R v Schilling* 2003 2 Cr App R (S) 295. The defendant pleaded guilty to three counts of harassment (s 4, putting people in fear of violence). She campaigned against a company, Huntingdon Life Sciences which specialised in the testing of products, involving the use of animals. She obtained shareholders' telephone numbers and other information and made various threats to them. The first victim had shares as a result of a takeover. He lived with his daughter and he started to receive phone calls in the middle of the night where the defendant told him to sell his shares. She went on to make increasingly frightening threats concerning his car and his home. He also received visits from the defendant and others. On one occasion the victim returned to his home to find his house and garden was being covered in posters depicting pictures of animals apparently being experimented on. When his daughter arrived home the group acted aggressively towards her. She moved from her father's home. He sold his shares at a substantial loss. The second victim obtained some shares following a merger. She received threatening phone calls in which it was obvious that she had been under observation by the defendant. One evening she found her car had been vandalised and that someone had thrown a brick through a window. She sold her shares at a loss. The third victim was a company director and indirectly held shares. The defendant phoned the victim's home. His wife answered. It was apparent to her that the defendant knew where they lived. The wife became increasingly scared as threats were made to the family. Months later the defendant was arrested and interviewed. She made no comment. She was 50. Her first conviction was at 48 and all of her 8 convictions on 6 occasions concerned institutions that carried out experiments on animals. She had received suspended sentences and a conditional discharge in the past. She had committed offences on bail. Although assessed as a medium risk of re-offending, she was now able to distinguish between lawful and unlawful protest. She had shown remorse and a willingness to undergo treatment. Held. She had committed very serious offences that went well beyond the parameters of lawful protest. The principals in *R v Liddle and Hayes* 2000 1 Cr App R (S) 131 were applied. First, the section 4 offence, the more serious, was an aggravating circumstance. Second, there was a history of disobedience because she had committed previous offences of this kind. Third, threats, aggressive behaviour and vandalism had been used. Fourth there had been persistent misconduct in the past. Fifthly, the effects upon the victims had been very serious. However, she had shown a willingness to undergo treatment. **14 months consecutive on each count** (42 months) not 18 months on each (54 months).

See also **ANIMAL CRUELTY**

12   ANIMALS

12.1   *Animal rights activists* See **ANIMAL RIGHTS ACTIVISTS**

Endangered species, purchasing selling etc

12.2   Control of Trade in Endangered Species (Enforcement) Regulations 1997, para 8 Triable either way. On indictment maximum 2 years. Summary maximum 3 months and/or Level 5 fine (£5,000).

R v Eley and Bull 1999 1 Cr App R (S) 252. The defendants E and B pleaded guilty to conspiracy to sell restricted animal specimens. B owned 128 rhinoceros' horn weighing 239 kilos which was 40 years old or older. He had acquired all but one of them before the regulations prohibiting the sale etc came into force. They were from between 77 and 128 rhinos. At least seven came from a critically endangered species. Their value was estimated to be £2.4m. In 1986 B was convicted of murder and sentenced to life imprisonment the sentence for which he was still serving. He asked A to help sell them and she approached E. E approached Christies and Sotheby's. A contacted the Stock Exchange who contacted the RSPCA. B had offered E a commission of 10% and 25% on anything above £10,000 per kg. Two RSPCA inspectors posed as buyers and met E and B who was on home leave. Negotiations continued and because of the sellers' suspicions the RSPCA inspectors were replaced by police officers posing as potential purchasers. Sophisticated arrangements were made to receive the money. There was a meeting in a hotel where £30,000 cash was shown by the police and shortly afterwards the defendants were arrested. E said that he thought it was legal to deal with the articles and if the man from the Stock Exchange had said it was illegal he would not have tried to sell the horn. B also said he thought it was legal. He also said the one horn bought in 1994 on his behalf had an exemption certificate. The pleas were tendered on the basis of recklessness as to the knowledge of the illegality of the activity. E was 54 and treated as of good character. He had character references and a letter from a commander of the Metropolitan police saying that he had performed a valuable service with his technical skill and equipment to trace stolen cars. He suffered from depression, renal damage, hypertension and tinnitus. He also said he was entrapped because throughout the meetings with the RSPCA inspectors and the police they continually avoided giving a straight answer to questions about whether the sales were legal. B was 63 and was an antique dealer at the time. Held. The offence is obviously serious. The quantity was very large. For E whilst not saying the original sentence was wrong, justice can now be made by **6 months** not 9 months. **15 months** for B was entirely correct but the forfeiture order could not stand because the horn had been acquired legally and there were no reasons given for rejecting the submissions made about hardship.

Old case *R v Canning* 1996 2 Cr App R (S) 202 (18 months upheld for keeping and selling Peregrine falcons. The nest was approached and two chicks were missing and falcons found at home address.)

Importing/exporting birds etc. – See **97.2**.

See also ANIMAL CRUELTY, DOGS and ENVIRONMENTAL OFFENCES – *Slaughterhouses and animal incinerators*

13   ANTI-SOCIAL BEHAVIOURAL ORDER, BREACH OF

13.1   Crime and Disorder Act 1998 s 1(10)

Triable either way. On indictment maximum 5 years. Summary maximum 6 months and/or £5,000.

13.2   Guideline remarks

R v Braxton 2003 *Unreported 2/4/03*. A sentence close to the maximum must be reserved for cases of persistent and prolonged breaches or where the behaviour was truly intimidating.

R v Braxton 2005 1 Cr App R (S) 167. This order is a serious infringement upon the liberty of the defendant. When breached the maximum offence may be greater than the maximum for the offences before the court when it was made. The order is a response by Parliament to the increasing concern about the impact on the public of anti-social behaviour in its many constituent forms. It follows that this concern must be reflected in the sentences which the court imposes for breach of the order.

13.3 More than one breach

R v Thomas 2005 1 Cr App R 34. The defendant admitted breaching an ASBO. The ASBO prevented the defendant from entering four stores from which he had entered drunk, stolen items, refused to leave, been abusive to staff and loitered outside. He was an alcoholic with an appalling record of petty offending (237 convictions for 451 offences, 263 for shoplifting). 6 weeks after the ASBO was imposed Magistrates imposed a Community Rehabilitation Order for offences of common assault and theft. 4 days later the defendant breached the ASBO and was later sentenced to 5 months. He was released on licence. 8 days later he entered the same banned store where he stole a teddy bear. He also stole a joint of meat worth £8.28 from a banned Tesco store. Held. He showed a flagrant disregard of the order. He showed a complete disregard for the Community Rehabilitation Order. **18 months** consecutive to 1 month for the theft was justified.

R v Braxton 2005 1 Cr App R (S) 167. The defendant was convicted of breach of two anti-social behavioural orders and assaulting a police officer. Birmingham City Council obtained an anti-social behavioural order which prohibited the defendant entering the City Centre and using threatening behaviour etc. Within two months he had breached the order twice. He was sentenced to 4 years with the Judge saying he did not want the defendant to terrorise members of the public. The Court of Appeal said he was menace and a serious danger to members of the public but reduced the sentence to 2 years. Three months after his release he was seen in the City Centre begging aggressively. The next day he was again seen there begging and slapping a woman on the bottom who refused to give him money. He was arrested and at the police station he saw an officer he knew. He said to him, "Fuck you. Stuart" and spat in his face. The spit went into his eye and mouth. The defendant was 38 with 37 previous court appearances. In the 8 years prior to his release from prison in 2003 he had 9 convictions for threatening behaviour etc. He had 9 convictions for violence albeit usually assault or battery. He received 4 months for writing a letter to the husband of a prison officer threatening to kill the officer. The defendant refused to see the probation officer. The officer's report said he had a variety of social difficulties and will continue to pose problems for anyone involved with monitoring his chosen lifestyle. Held. The anti-social behavioural order is designed to protect the public from this type of distressing misbehaviour. The defendant committed a serious criminal offence even entering the City. He does not appear to understand the nature of the order. **3 years 9 months** and 3 months consecutive for the spit upheld.

See also *R v Braxton 2003 Unreported 2/4/03.*

14   ARMED FORCES, MEMBERS OF

(Present and potential members)

Sentence may bar entry to services

14.1   Ministry of Defence Statement 1980 JP 697. Don't take into account the possibility of the defendant joining the forces as the Ministry of Defence judges the offence by the sentence imposed [Since this was issued the policy for recruitment in the armed forces has changed radically. This statement is only of persuasive force but is a policy which would be natural sentencing for Crown Court judges. The three letters from the author to the Ministry of Defence and the Treasury Solicitors to check that this is still the policy have been ignored.]

Defendant facing discharge

14.2   *R v Francis-McGann* 2003 1 Cr App R (S) 57. The defendant was convicted of perverting the course of Justice. He was a serving army Captain with nine years service. A speed camera photographed his car. When he received the notice he contacted the Criminal Justice Unit saying it could not be him as his car had been exported. He was advised to send in evidence of the exportation. He sent in a letter headed with the army insignia giving details of the "exportation" by him, which was not true. The letter said the car had then been re-plated. He was interviewed and said he could not be sure whether it was his vehicle and challenged the telephone conversation. He had a clean licence and an army officer spoke of his abilities. The army said a community penalty or a custodial sentence would lead to a discharge. The Judge said he would be failing in his duty if he passed any other sentence than custody and gave him **three months** and £1,030 prosecution costs order. Held. We agree with the Judge's comments. On a number of occasions the Court has emphasised that where people persist in perverting the course of Justice to avoid prosecution custody is inevitable. The gravamen was the interference with the administration of Justice and the persistence. It was wholly out of character and will have a disastrous impact on him. It is important for the Court to have serious regard to the effects of any sentence on an individual. We hope a future employer or the Army will bear in mind his good service and the Army should consider whether it is really inevitable that he should lose his commission.

15   ARSON

15.1   CHAPTERS in this book are in bold capitals. The *paragraph titles* are in bold italics. Where a chapter like this one has subsections, the **subsections** are in lower case bold. The subsections are: (1) arson (sometimes known as simple arson). The intent can be reckless or an intention to destroy property; (2) arson being reckless whether life was endangered; (3) arson with intent to endanger life and (4) a life sentence was/was not appropriate.

Anti-Social Behavioural orders Where the defendant has acted in a manner that caused or was likely to cause harassment, alarm or distress to one or more persons not in the same household as the defendant and it is necessary to protect persons from further anti-social acts by him/her the court may make this order[37].

Dangerous Offender provisions For offences committed on or after 4/4/05 where there is a significant risk to members of the public of serious harm etc. there is a mandatory duty to pass a life sentence when it is justified and otherwise a sentence of imprisonment for public protection[38]. For offenders under 18 the duty is to pass detention for life, detention for public protection or an extended sentence[39].

Longer than commensurate sentences and extended sentences It is a violent offence for the purposes of passing a longer than commensurate sentence [Powers of Criminal Courts (Sentencing) Act 2000 s 80(2)] and an extended sentence (extending the licence) [Powers of Criminal Courts (Sentencing) Act s 85(2)(b)][40]. See LONGER THAN COMMENSURATE SENTENCES The orders cannot be made for offences committed before 30/9/98 or after 3/4/05.

37 Crime and Disorder Act 1998 s 1C
38 Criminal Justice Act 2003 s 225
39 Criminal Justice Act 2003 s 226 and 228
40 As defined by Powers of Criminal Courts (Sentencing) Act 2000 s 161(3)

Crown Court statistics – England and Wales – Males 21+

15.2

Year	Plea	Total Numbers sentenced	Type of sentence %					Average length of custody (months)
			Discharge	Fine	Community sentence	Suspended sentence	Custody	
2002	Guilty	313	1	0	27	2	61	34.4
	Not guilty	48	–	2	8	–	81	48
2003	Guilty	339	0	1	26	2	65	34.2
	Not guilty	49	–	–	8	4	76	49

For details and explanations about the statistics in the book see page vii.

Longer than commensurate sentences, how much extra?

15.3   *R v Jones* 2002 1 Cr App R (S) 214. The defendant pleaded guilty to two charges of arson and one charge of vehicle interference at the Magistrates' Court. There were three TICs for arson. Each charge was committed late in the evening or in the small hours after the defendant had been drinking. He set fire to a garage which was used to store furniture and ran off. A few days later he broke into a vehicle ripped the seats and set fire to the foam. He ran off. The vehicle charge was when he got in a van and left when he was seen. The suspicion was he might set fire to the van. He made full and frank confessions and said he was involved in an arson offence every weekend since his release from prison. Fire appeared to excite him. He was in breach of his licence by 278 days. The judge started at 3 years each concurrently and gave an uplift of 6 years making 9 years on each. Held. There were no fires at occupied or domestic premises. The uplift should be 3 so **6 years** instead. [Details of his record and the reports are not given.]

See also LONGER THAN COMMENSURATE SENTENCES

Psychiatric report, need for

15.4   *R v Calladine* 1975 Times 3/12/75. It is unwise to pass sentence without a psychiatric report.

1 Arson (simple arson)

15.5   Criminal Damage Act 1971 s 1(1) and (3)

The offence is triable either way. On indictment maximum Life. Summary maximum 6 months and/or £5,000.

The Criminal Justice Act 2003 creates a summary maximum sentence of 51 weeks, a minimum custodial sentence of 28 weeks and Custody plus. The Home Office says they do not expect to introduce these provisions before September 2006.

Defendant under 17

15.6   *R v Taylor* 2000 1 Cr App R (S) 45. The defendant pleaded guilty to arson. With three others he entered a yard on an industrial estate. A stack of paper was set alight which set fire to other stacks. £250,000 worth of damage was done to the paper. Other businesses also lost £50,000. The defendant admitted lighting the paper saying he was egged on. He also said he tried to put it out and failed. He was of good character. He was then 13, now 14. He had shown increasingly oppositional behaviour at home and was lighting fires at home. He was refusing to attend school. However, he had made good progress at the secure unit. **2 years** not 3 detention substituted.

R v Letham 2000 1 Cr App R (S) 185. The defendant pleaded guilty to arson being reckless whether property was to be destroyed. When he was 16 he sat the last of his GCSE exams. The next day he and another returned to the school and threw stones at the windows causing over £800 worth of damage. The next morning a fire was started in the art block, which caused £400,000 worth of damage. The students' course work for the year was destroyed. He admitted both incidents to the police. He suffered from a depressive illness. He had no previous convictions. He received **2 years** YOI. Held. Less than that could not be justified.

R v Smith 2001 2 Cr App R (S) 376. The defendants were convicted of simple arson. Four boys then aged 15 or 16 bought some petrol and set fire to a comprehensive school. The fire took several hours to extinguish. The damage and cost of hiring Portacabins was £721,000. A large amount of exam course work was lost. An expert concluded petrol had been poured through a broken window. The trial did not take place till about 18 months after the offence. The boys were either of good character or treated as such. There was no suggestion of mental or psychological disorder. The trial judge referred to the boy's boasting about it and the need for deterrent sentences because of the prevalence of these fires. Held. Where a crime is prevalent in an area it was right to pass deterrent sentences. He was right not to distinguish between them. An adult might well be facing 8 years after a trial. **6 years** detention was not excessive.

R v Tingle 2001 2 Cr App R (S) 379. The defendant pleaded guilty at the earliest opportunity to simple arson. Another boy was concerned that his fingerprints might be found at a Primary school that he had burgled. The defendant then 15 after sniffing gas and taking cannabis, which made him less inhibited went with the other boy to the school. The defendant threw a petrol bomb, which he had made earlier, through a window. The main part of the school, which had 460 children, was destroyed. The damage and the cost of replacement classrooms were assessed at £1.1m. All the work of the 4 to 7 year olds was destroyed. A video tape was found showing him, while the school burnt giving a commentary saying he was a hero and being absolutely delighted. The children were adversely affected. He had a previous conviction for causing damage. The pre-sentence report concluded that there was a high risk of him re-offending and a high risk of significant harm to the public. There was no mental disorder but he appeared to satisfy the criteria for, 'socialised conduct disorder.' However, he was genuinely remorseful. Held. Because of the authorities, particularly *R v Storey* 1984 6 Cr App R (S) 104, his plea and so he would not be crushed by the sentence **5 years** not 8 detention.

See also *R v Marklew and Lambert* 1999 1 Cr App R (S) 6 (Life imposed but sentences of 10 years considered appropriate if a life sentence had not been imposed.)

Old cases *R v Bool and White* 1998 1 Cr App R (S) 32, *R v Nicholls and Warden* 1998 1 Cr App R (S) 66, (for a summary of these cases see the first edition of this book.)

Defendant aged 17–20

15.7   *Att-Gen's Ref. Nos. 40–43 of 1997* 1998 2 Cr App R (S) 151. Three defendants pleaded guilty to simple arson. Arson with intent to endanger life counts were left on the file. The three defendants were told they could not come to a house where some young people had gathered. The three went to a public house and then made four petrol bombs from milk bottles and rags etc. They returned to the house and a petrol bomb was thrown at the wall of the house causing damage to a window frame and cracking the window. Another bomb was thrown at a car in the driveway causing damage of about £700. A third unlit bomb was left on the pavement. The fourth was found in a garden nearby. The defendants were 16, 17 and 18 at the time of the offence. One defendant was in breach of a supervision order for offences, which included criminal damage. Another was in breach of a conditional discharge for criminal damage, which involved throwing glass bottles at a building. Held. The appropriate sentence would have been **2¹/₂ to 3 years** YOI and not the combination orders imposed. The sentences were unduly lenient but not increased because of what had happened since including the fact that the community service orders had been largely completed and the defendants were in work.

Domestic premises

15.8 *R v Hales* 1999 2 Cr App R (S) 113. The defendant pleaded guilty to simple arson and was committed for sentence. A householder saw a piece of paper on fire sticking through his letterbox. He opened the door and saw the defendant. He put out the flames while the defendant ran away. When the defendant was arrested he admitted the offence but said he did not know why he did it. An expert said because there was no accelerant the fire would not have taken hold. The defendant was a lonely man who had a drink problem but no previous convictions. He lacked self-esteem. He told the psychiatrist that he had committed other anti-social behaviour when drunk. His employer attended court. Held. **15 months** substituted for 2 years.

Insurance money, to obtain

15.9 *R v Ellis* 1999 1 Cr App R (S) 374. The defendant was convicted of conspiracy to commit arson and 9 counts of conspiracy to defraud. There was a very serious fire at the defendant's warehouse involving cloth and garments stored there by traders including some of his co-defendants. There was no evidence of an accelerant. Police found a list of payments to the loss assessor, which had been made by the conspirators. Investigations revealed that the insurance claims were also inflated. The defendant and the loss assessor arranged the fire and were at the centre of the conspiracies involving the others with an arrangement that the proceeds would be shared. The insurers made full or reduced payments. The defendant obtained 35% of the claims. The total claim was about £2m and £1.5m and was paid. The judge determined the defendant had probably received more than £200,000. He was 60 and of good character with depression. He was described as a ruined man. **7 years** was proper.

Petrol bombs/Petrol

15.10 *Att-Gen's Ref. Nos. 40–43 of 1997* 1998 2 Cr App R (S) 151. Three defendants pleaded guilty to simple arson. Arson with intent to endanger life counts were left on the file. The three defendants were told they could not come to a house where some young people had gathered. The three went to a public house and then made four petrol bombs from milk bottles and rags etc. They returned to the house and a petrol bomb was thrown at the wall of the house causing damage to a window frame and cracking the window. Another bomb was thrown at a car in the driveway causing damage of about £700. A third unlit bomb was left on the pavement. The fourth was found in a garden nearby. The defendants were 16, 17 and 18 at the time of the offence. One defendant was in breach of a supervision order for offences, which included criminal damage. Another was in breach of a conditional discharge for criminal damage, which involved throwing glass bottles at a building. Held. The appropriate sentence would have been **2¹/₂ to 3 years** YOI and not the combination orders imposed. The sentences were unduly lenient but not increased because of what had happened since including the fact that the community service orders had been largely completed and the defendants were in work.

R v Joslin 2003 1 Cr App R (S) 345. The defendant pleaded guilty to attempted (simple) arson. He went to Safeways, which was in a residential area, near a railway station, public house and hospital. He was seen drunk sitting in a shopping trolley and asked to leave. He was next seen in the supermarket's petrol station, which held about 150,000 litres of fuel. An attendant saw him pick up a pump nozzle and try to obtain fuel. When this failed he went to another pump removed the nozzle and lit a lighter. He tried again but the attendant would not activate the pump. A security guard took the lighter from the defendant and the police arrived. He told them, "I just wanted to burn. I picked up the nozzle and had my lighter." There were concerns about his mental health. In interview he said he had drunk about 8 litres of cider and some sherry. Further he said he was depressed and intended to burn himself. He was an alcoholic who was living rough with numerous convictions. His first was arson in 1979 when he received 2 years. Following the break up of his marriage he had set fire to his home to harm himself. His later offending was linked to excessive drinking. The pre-sentence report concluded that given his alcohol dependency, his limited motivation, chaotic lifestyle and his lack of control when intoxicated he posed a serious risk to both himself and the public and the risk of re-offending was high. The psychiatrist said there was no medical recommendation and he needed to do something with his drinking before someone was seriously hurt. The Judge said, "What you did was extremely serious. This could have resulted in a major disaster in this city and it was only through the quick actions of the staff that was prevented. Held. There was obvious force in those comments. Despite the obvious seriousness of what he did we must bear in mind it was attempted simple arson. **3 years** not 4.

Revenge

15.11   *R v Akhter* 2001 1 Cr App R (S) 7. The defendant pleaded guilty to simple arson. The defendant began a probationary period at work and was spoken to about his performance. Just over a year from when he started he learnt from his line manager that things were not going well and he might lose his job. He stole a key and on a Saturday with another poured petrol over his line manager's desk and a severe fire started. £450,000 worth of damage was caused. Thirty people from other parts of the building had to be evacuated. The written basis of plea included that the co-accused put the petrol near the desk and lit it while he acted as look out. He had not intended to go that far or cause the damage that was caused. He was of good character and had 16 references referring to his impeccable character. **3 years** was not manifestly excessive.

2 Arson – reckless whether life would be endangered

15.12   Criminal Damage Act 1971 s 1(2) and (3)

Indictable only. Maximum sentence life.

Guideline remark

15.13   *Att-Gen's Ref. No 1 of 1997* 1998 1 Cr App R (S) 54. The defendant pleaded guilty to arson being reckless whether life would be endangered. If you commit this sort of offence, save in the most exceptional circumstances, an immediate prison sentence must be imposed.

Crime of passion

15.14   *Att-Gen's Ref. No 61 of 1996* 1997 2 Cr App R (S) 316. The defendant pleaded guilty to arson being reckless whether life would be endangered. He was also committed for sentence for animal cruelty and criminal damage. The defendant when worse for drink and in a jealous rage set fire to some of his girlfriend's clothes and maimed their dog with a sledgehammer. He then locked the door and left the terrace house burning. The fire brigade found the dog in a pool of blood and there was £2,000+ damage caused. An elderly man lived on one side and a couple lived on the other side. When asked about those people he said he never gave them a thought. He had only one previous conviction, which was for damaging the car of another boyfriend of his girlfriend. Held. Taking into account all the personal mitigation and that it was a reference, **2 years** not probation.

Death is caused

15.15   *R v Whitbrook and Smith* 1998 2 Cr App R (S) 322. The two defendants aged 17 and 18 pleaded guilty at a late stage to arson being reckless whether life was endangered. A count of manslaughter was left on the file. The Smith family lived oppo-site to Mrs Mitchell and her three sons 9, 10 and 16. Accepting the defendant Smith's idea, Whitbrook lit a firework and put it through Mrs Mitchell's letterbox. The two boys then ran away. The house was engulfed in flames. The 10-year-old boy was found by firemen alive but with 53% burns to his body. He died 3 days later of brain damage and multi-organ failure. The defendants expressed remorse. The Smith family had to leave the area. One defendant was of good character and the other had nothing similar on his record. **3 years** YOI was not altered.

Where there is a conviction for manslaughter, see MANSLAUGHTER – *Fire, by*

Defendant under 17

15.16   *R v Spong and Bromham* 1999 1 Cr App R (S) 417. The defendants pleaded guilty to arson being reckless whether life was endangered. The two boys then 15 and 16 were at a special needs school. They went to a storeroom and each lit a cigarette. They heard someone who they feared was a teacher. They both dropped their cigarettes and ran from the room. £400,000 worth of damage was caused. They were sentenced on the basis that they had given no thought either to the possibility of a fire being caused or to the possibility of lives being endangered. Both defendants were unlikely to re-offend and had responded well over 12 months to the bail support scheme. 21 months and 2 years detention reduced to **15 and 12 months** YOI.

R v C 2002 1 Cr App R (S) 463. The defendant appears to have pleaded guilty to two counts of arson being reckless whether life was endangered. [The judgment does not say what his plea was.] He asked for an offence of arson to be taken into consideration. A 73-year-old woman was asleep in bed alone at about 10.30pm. Her dog woke her up and she looked into the road outside and saw two male figures run off. They returned and they went towards her front porch. She opened the window and remonstrated with them and they ran off again. She went back to bed. Shortly afterwards, she smelt burning and went downstairs and found flames coming through her letterbox. She was able to put the fire out. A rolled up newspaper was in the letterbox. Police discovered a newspaper had been set alight under her car. 12 days later at 6.15pm the victim was watching televi-sion. She smelt burning and found smoke coming through her letterbox. She managed to extinguish the flames and noticed a number of small fires on the hall carpet and the door itself was alight. The house was full of smoke. Police discovered lit firelighters had been put through the letterbox. The front door was badly damaged and the telephone lines had been burnt. The carpet was burnt in places and the wall was damaged by smoke. The victim found the experience terrifying. The defendant then 14 was arrested after setting fire to some bushes. This was the TIC. He admitted the house fire was his idea, and he knew someone lived there. He said the victim sometimes 'moaned at us and some years earlier had refused to return my football when it went into her garden.' He had no previous findings of guilt. He was not unduly sorry for the effects of his actions and was not willing to offer an apology. A child psychiatrist said he was suffering from an attention deficit hyperactivity disorder and an oppositional deficiency disorder. He had been given medication but had stopped taking it. Since then his behaviour had deteriorated and he had been excluded from school. Held. These offences were serious. The elderly lady was sleeping and caused terror. The second arson was even graver. The gravity of the offences and the apparent indifference by the defendant to the consequences called for a substantial sentence. **3 years** detention was entirely right.

See also ARSON – **Life sentence was/was not appropriate** – *Defendant under 17* (**see para 15.35**)

Defendant aged 17–20

15.17   *R v Whitbrook and Smith* 1998 2 Cr App R (S) 322. The two defendants aged 17 and 18 pleaded guilty at a late stage to arson being reckless whether life was endangered. A count of manslaughter was left on the file. The Smith family lived opposite to Mrs Mitchell and her three sons 9, 10 and 16. Accepting the defendant Smith's idea, Whitbrook lit a firework and put it through Mrs Mitchell's letterbox. The two boys then ran away. The house was engulfed in flames. The 10-year-old boy was found by firemen alive but with 53% burns to his body. He died 3 days later of brain damage and multi-organ failure. The defendants expressed remorse. The Smith family had to leave the area. One defendant was of good character and the other had nothing similar on his record. **3 years** detention was not altered.

R v J 2001 Unreported 4/10/01. [A gas fire was used in a failed suicide attempt by a 17 year old. **2^1/$_2$ years** YOI not 4.]

R v Holliman 2002 2 Cr App R (S) 142. (See next section.)

Domestic premises etc with other occupants

15.18   *R v Walker* 1999 1 Cr App R (S) 121. The defendant pleaded guilty to attempted arson being reckless whether life was endangered and reckless as to the starting of the fire. The defendant after drinking 6 pints of lager returned to his flat and had a serious row with his partner. He told her to leave and she did. Feeling sorry for himself he lit the wrong end of a cigarette and dropped it. He thought he had extinguished it. He then went to another room and fell asleep. He woke up with that room full of smoke and broke a vertebra when he escaped out of a window. Occupants in other flats were put at great risk. There was severe damage to the building estimated at £150,000. The defendant had no previous. As a result he had lost his home and his family. **2 years** was not excessive.

R v Parkhurst 1999 2 Cr App R (S) 208. The defendant pleaded guilty to arson being reckless whether life would be endangered. He lived with a woman for 2 or 3 months and she decided she wanted to leave. The two had a lot to drink and he told her he was going to set fire to the place. She fell asleep and she was awoken by the smoke alarm. She was able to escape with her children. The expert said the fire had started in the bedroom with cloth and wood being ignited. A psychiatrist said he had a long history of acting impulsively in response to rejection. He was of 'relatively good character'. **5 years** was stern but not excessive.

Att-Gen's Ref. No 84 of 1998 1999 2 Cr App R (S) 380. The defendant pleaded guilty to arson being reckless whether life would be endangered after the judge had indicated the appropriate sentence. The defendant was unable to accept that his relationship with his partner was over. He pursued her unsuccessfully with calls, letters and presents. She contacted the police who warned him but the letters and presents continued. Early one morning he poured petrol into her kitchen through the cat flap and set it alight. She woke up smelled the smoke and escaped. She was very upset and suffering from smoke inhalation. £10,000 worth of damage was caused. He had a recent conviction for criminal damage when he had placed glass under the wheel of the ex-girlfriend's new boyfriend's car He also had a conviction for making threats to kill in a letter sent to the girlfriend's new address. Held. **3 years** was lenient but as it was a reference and the sentence had been served the sentence was not altered.

Att-Gen's Ref. No 66 of 1997 2000 1 Cr App R (S) 149. The defendant was convicted of arson being reckless whether life would be endangered. He had pleaded guilty to simple arson. He entered his mother-in-law's bungalow in the early hours. He squirted petrol onto the hallway carpet. He lit it. He also set fire to the carpet just outside the bedrooms where his wife, his son, his mother-in-law and brother-in-law were sleeping. He had removed a battery from the smoke alarm a week before. The fire was discovered before very much damage could be caused. He stood to gain between £100,000 and £110,000 on his wife's death. He was of good character and was clinically depressed.

He expressed regret. Held. The appropriate sentence after a trial was within the range 8 to 10 years. **7 years** substituted for 3 years taking into account it was a reference.

R v Harding 2000 1 Cr App R (S) 327. The defendant pleaded guilty at the earliest opportunity to arson being reckless whether life was endangered. His relationship with his wife was difficult and stormy with periods of separation. There were three children two of which were his. Shortly after midnight after he had spent the afternoon and evening drinking he had a violent argument with his wife and started to smash up furniture. With the help of her brother everyone left except the defendant. He lit separate fires in the house and then climbed out of a window and was found outside a police station screaming incoherently. He was distressed and admitted guilt immediately. There was very extensive damage to the house. Most if not all of the rooms of the property, which was owned by the local authority, were burnt out or smoke damaged. The adjoining house where an elderly lady lived was also damaged. Over £20,000 worth of damage was done to the two properties. He was 27 with convictions but nothing comparable. Held. The court takes a very serious view of arson where life is endangered albeit not intentionally because of the propensity of fire to spread rapidly. The offence was aggravated by the closeness of the elderly neighbour. **4 years** was not manifestly excessive.

Att-Gen's Ref. No 98 of 2001 2002 2 Cr App R (S) 85. The defendant was convicted of two counts of arson being reckless whether life would be endangered. He was acquitted by the judge of two counts of arson with intent after the jury failed to agree on those counts. He lived with his wife and his daughter aged 16 and his son aged 11. He had married in 1982 and the relationship had become increasingly unstable. There had been recent incidents of violence. On the day of the fire he refused food his wife offered him and was not on speaking terms with his daughter. At night he called his daughter into his room and asked her why she would not speak to him. When she answered he pushed her onto the bed and slapped her twice. The wife intervened and told the daughter to go to her room which she did. The wife ran out and held onto the door handle to prevent the defendant leaving. The handle pulled out and the wife retreated to her daughter's room. The two prevented the defendant getting into the room by leaning against it etc for 30 minutes. The defendant demanded to get in and said, 'Or I'll set myself alight.' Finally he said, 'You can open the door now I have set myself alight.' Flames and smoke were seen below the door. Attempts to extinguish the flames failed and the daughter broke a window and screamed for help. The daughter climbed onto the window sill. A neighbour broke in through a window and found the front door locked and found the defendant outside his bedroom and told him to leave. He refused. The daughter jumped out of the window into a curtain which was held by neighbours. She broke her arm and hurt her back. She suffered cuts to the foot and a radial fracture to the head. The wife jumped onto a mattress. As she jumped flames could be seen flickering behind her. She suffered a 1" deep cut to her hand from the broken window. The neighbour went back into the house where the defendant remained saying he was going to die there. The neighbour saw that the defendant had made no effort to tackle the flames or unlock the front door dragged him downstairs into the front room. It was discovered he had deactivated the smoke alarm and that there were two seats to the fire in the defendant's bedroom. They were consistent with burning items being dragged to the daughter's bedroom door. There was another seat outside that door. Her bedroom door and frame had been totally burnt away. The house was a mid-terrace property. The defendant was interviewed and denied starting the fires deliberately. He was 46 and of good character with references. He suffering from ill health and had served nearly 7 months. Held. The victims were effectively imprisoned by the fire. The judge overestimated the significance of the medical position. **At least 6 years** should have been imposed. Because it was a reference etc. **4 years** not a community rehabilitation order.

R v Holliman 2002 2 Cr App R (S) 142. The defendant pleaded guilty to arson being reckless whether life was endangered. Some travellers had set up an illegal camp in a car park and on tennis courts. There were 13 caravans. The defendant who had spent the evening drinking went to a petrol station at 2am and bought lighter fuel. He went to the camp site and poured the lighter fuel over a propane gas cylinder besides a caravan containing two adults and three children. He was seen holding something alight and placed it next to the cylinder. A fire was lit between the cylinder and the A frame of the caravan. A passer-by very quickly summoned the police. They extinguished the fire. Only slight damage was caused. Had the fire been allowed to burn it was likely the cylinder would have heated up and exploded causing a fireball so the occupants of the caravan would have been unlikely to survive. The defendant was arrested. He was 20 and was serving in the Royal Navy with no convictions. A large number of character witnesses described him as conscientious, totally reliable etc. He regretted his actions and his risk assessment for re-offending was low. The YOI report described him as very polite and well behaved mature man. Held. There could have been appalling and fatal consequences. **4 years** YOI was severe but not manifestly excessive.

Att-Gen's Ref No. 67 of 2002 2003 1 Cr App R (S) 531. The defendant pleaded guilty to two offences of damaging property. He was convicted after a trial of two offences of arson being reckless as to whether life would be endangered. He was acquitted of arson with intent to endanger life. The defendant had been a member of a social club up until about 1999 where, due to his drinking, there had been several incidents for which he had been warned about his language and general behaviour. He absented himself from the club saying that he had had a breakdown from which he was recovering. He stood for election to the club in 2000 and was unsuccessful. A lady, M had spoken against his candidature and having met her, he told her that he was not happy with the decision. A few days later her car was damaged, with numerous large scratches down both sides. Subsequently the defendant made a complaint about children in the club but was told by a Mr C to leave the children alone. The defendant went round to Mr C's house, banged on the door and window, and told Mrs C that he would throw a brick through their window. Later in 2000 he was barred from the club. In April 2001, the defendant's wife, with their children, left him. In June 2001 Mrs B had an argument with the defendant in a public house. Her husband and the defendant had a fight in the street which resulted in the defendant having a bloody nose and swelling to his eyes. The next day the defendant attended at Mrs B's workplace in an attempt to find out her address. He was not given the address there, but discovered it somehow. At about 01:45 on the following morning, Mrs B was woken by police officers that asked her to open her back door because her front door was on fire. Fortunately someone had driven past who had seen flames and smoke coming from the area of a wheelie bin which had been pushed up against the front door of the house. An expert concluded that the fire was started by material being burned in the letterbox itself. The cost of the damage was between £1,500 and £2,000. The next day, in an unrelated incident, Mr C found scratches to his car. A week later a pedestrian saw smoke coming from the front door of Mr and Mrs C's house. Flames were engulfing the lower part of the house and Mrs C and the children were trapped upstairs by smoke. A passer-by, having climbed the sloping roof at the back of the house rescued her 10 year-old child which had been trapped in a rear bedroom. A younger child was later rescued by fireman using breathing apparatus. This child suffered significant smoke inhalation and a collapsed upper lobe of the lung. She was in a critical condition and spent some time in intensive care before being released from hospital six days later. Mrs C also suffered the affects of smoke inhalation. There was very extensive smoke damage throughout the house. Neighbours woke to find their houses full of smoke and escaped with their own baby. An expert concluded that the fire could have been started by the introduction of burning material through the letterbox.

Later that morning the defendant had been seen walking towards the site of the fire. He said that he was about to call the fire brigade on his mobile telephone, but that it was not working properly. A subsequent examination of the phone revealed no fault. Later that day he went to the police station. Later he admitted that he had been responsible for damaging the cars but he denied that he had started either fire. He said that he was taking anti-depressant medication and that his wife had left him. The defendant was 44 and had no relevant previous convictions. Held. It was hard to believe that a fire would have other than terrified Mrs C with her children in the house. Mr C would have been equally alarmed. Fires were started at night. The occupants were sleeping and the defendant did nothing to alert anyone to what was happening. Taking into account that this was a reference, **5^1/$_2$ years** not 4.

Old cases. *Att-Gen's Ref. No 1 of 1997* 1998 1 Cr App R (S) 54 (For a summary of the case see the first edition of this book.)

Insurance money, to obtain

15.19   See also *R v Zedi* 2001 Unreported 23/10/01.

Police officers targeted

15.20   *R v Trowbridge* 2002 2 Cr App R (S) 154. The defendant pleaded guilty to arson being reckless whether life was endangered. His downstairs neighbours noticed water was coming from his maisonette through their ceiling. The defendant refused to let their plumber in or come to the door. A carpenter tried to gain entry and was sworn at and told to go away. The water flow increased and the supply had to be turned off. The defendant was seen pulling frantically at something in the bathroom. Eventually the police were summoned and they were refused entry in an abusive manner. An officer said he would force the door and broke a glass panel. The defendant shouted, 'Fuck off, I've got petrol.' He then threw petrol at the officer and his clothing was splashed. Then he said he was going to burn the whole place down and lit the petrol causing the curtains to catch fire. The officer moved out of the way quickly and so avoided the flames, which spread to the stairs of the maisonette. A fire extinguisher put the flames out. The defendant jumped out of a rear window and was arrested. When interviewed he said he didn't intent to hurt anyone and he wanted to kill himself and be with his deceased mother. He was 50 and of good character and had no history of starting fires. He told the first psychiatrist that he wasn't going to his dump and marched off. The doctor said he had developed a marked antipathy to the people of Devon, which was where he lived. He was released on bail to be assessed and to see whether a probation order with treatment was suitable. He told them he would rather go to prison than there. The doctor said he was a man of limited intelligence who tended to take up fixed stances and was unable to retreat easily. Another said he needed social services assistance and it was surprising he had been neglected so long. The probation proposal was not feasible. The pre-sentence report said he was very vulnerable and unhappy with considerable difficulties coping with day-to-day issues. His risk assessment for re-offending was assessed as high. In 1996 the judge said he posed a significant risk to people and imposed a life sentence. Since then he had been released, recalled (not for offences but because of difficulties with the probation service supervising his release) and released again. The appeal was heard in December 2001. Held. Throwing petrol at a police officer is extremely grave and could have led to a loss of life. However, the criteria for a life sentence were not present. Since his sentence nothing had happened to suggest he constituted a risk to the public. **4 years** substituted which he had served.

Prison/police property

15.21   *R v Wilson* 2000 1 Cr App R (S) 323. The defendant pleaded guilty to arson being reckless whether life was endangered. A prisoner set fire to his cell and caused about £500 worth of damage. A fire extinguisher put the flames out. His actions had 'been essentially a "cry for help" and to get him out of the health care centre, where he was being harassed and threatened.' He was nearing the end of an 8 year sentence for very serious sexual offences and at the time of the offence was exhibiting bizarre behaviour, including smearing and consuming faeces. He said everyone was against him. A psychiatrist said he met the criteria for narcissistic and paranoid personality disorders. He was not currently showing signs of mental illness. The probation officer, relying on psychiatrists said he was a danger to himself and others including his ex-wife and children. Held. The first pre-condition in *R v Chapman* 2000 was not met so life varied to **10 years** consecutive to sentence for which he was serving. The appropriate sentence of 3 years applying *R v Hales* 1999 2 Cr App R (S) 113 at 115. However, the sentence was extended by 7 years for the protection of the public under [what is now the Powers of Criminal Courts (Sentencing) Act 2000 s 80(2)(b)].

Revenge

15.22   *R v Reynolds* 1999 2 Cr App R (S) 5. The defendant pleaded guilty to arson being reckless whether life was endangered. The defendant who was 21 had a grudge against his brother believing he had burgled his room in the past. The defendant went to his brother's bed-sit, kicked the door down and started a fire on the ground floor and another on the first floor. The damage was extensive. There was no-one else in the bedsitting rooms in the house but the defendant had not checked that. There was however a risk to the adjoining terraced houses. After initial denials to the police he pleaded guilty. Held. He had several previous convictions for burglary. Three of them were committed because of a grudge. There was little remorse. **6 years** was severe but not excessive.

Att-Gen's Ref. No 23 of 2001 2001 2 Cr App R (S) 514. The defendant was convicted of arson being reckless whether life was endangered. He had pleaded guilty to criminal damage. After a 4 year on-off relationship with his girlfriend, he told her he would always find her and burn her house down. After they were living apart he entered her house and was drunk and argumentative. He went to a public house and returned. He rammed his car into the back of her car pushing it towards her house. (This was the criminal damage matter.) She was so scared she left. He rang her saying, 'Get home or I'll burn your house down.' Ten minutes later he called again saying the house was burning and it would teach her a lesson. The blaze was extensive. Part of the house collapsed. It was also discovered that the smoke alarm had been removed before the fire started. The occupier of the adjourning house was away but had someone been there, there would have been a significant risk to anyone inside. He denied it but did not give evidence. He had a previous conviction for effectively a duplicate offence to this one when he had thrown petrol bombs through a girlfriend's window for which he received a 42 month imprisonment sentence. It was described as 'arson endangering life.' He had another conviction for smashing car windows when he thought he had been belittled. Held. The sentence to be expected was **between 6 and 7 years**. Therefore **5 years** substituted for 3½ years because it was a reference.

Similar previous convictions

15.23   *R v Firth* 2002 1 Cr App R (S) 309. The defendant pleaded guilty to arson being reckless whether life was endangered. The defendant lived in a hostel and he set fire to a chair and settee in his flat. He said it was to take his own life and voices in his head were telling him to kill himself and to set fire to the flat. After the room filled with smoke he panicked and changed his mind. He reported the fire to the fire brigade and handed himself in to the police. The flat sustained heavy smoke damage. There were convictions going back to 1976 and in 1997 he was sentenced to 3 years' imprisonment for arson and criminal damage committed in virtually identical circumstances. Again it was claimed he intended to take his own life. The pre-sentence report said the risk of harm to the public and the likelihood of re-offending were extremely high. He did not believe he had any control over his behaviour. There was a high risk of self harm and he was totally preoccupied with killing himself. The psychiatric report said the overall impression was of a disorder of adult personality with evidence for dependency, impulsively and antisocial behaviour particularly in a stressful situation. There was emotional instability and solitary traits. A hospital order was not proposed. He was sentenced to 10 years. Held. He poses a considerable risk to the public and there was a powerful need to protect the public from him. 10 years was manifestly too long but this was pre-eminently a case for a longer than commensurate sentence. Sentence varied to **10 years** as a longer than commensurate sentence.

Unknown motive

15.24   *R v O'Brien* 2003 2 Cr App R (S) 599. The defendant was convicted of arson being reckless as to whether life would be endangered. In the early hours of the morning the defendant went to the flat of a former female friend whilst she was on holiday. He squirted white spirit through the letterbox onto the mail that had built up, which he then lit with a match. A witness discreetly followed him until he was able to point out the defendant to a police officer. The defendant denied having been to the area. In the bag he was carrying, a plastic bottle with a hole in the lid was discovered, with a balaclava, a pair of gloves, a box of matches and a key to the front door of the block of flats. A fire engine attended the flat and extinguished the fire in 7 minutes. However, after the fire brigade had left a second fire broke out in the back bedroom and the entire flat was destroyed. Expert evidence could not identify the cause of the second fire. In interview he denied the offence. It was accepted he knew that the occupants of that flat were away. He was 68 and had a large number of previous convictions resulting in 3, 7, 5 8 and 10 years imprisonment, but none for arson. **6 years** not 10.

Witnesses

See **Perverting the Course of Justice/Contempt of Court/Perjury** – *Witness interference – Arson*

3 Arson – Intending life would be endangered

15.25   Criminal Damage Act 1971 s 1(2) and (3)

Indictable only. Maximum sentence life.

Guideline remarks

15.26   *Att-Gen's Ref. No 47 of 2000* 2001 1 Cr App R (S) 471. The bracket for arson with intent is 8–10 years.

Defendant under 17

15.27   *R v Johnson* 2000 2 Cr App R (S) 235. The defendant pleaded guilty to burglary, arson with intent to endanger life, unlawful wounding, escape from custody, affray, aggravated vehicle-taking, TDA and damaging property. He received 9 years detention concurrent for the arson and the escape counts. For the other offences he received no penalty other than disqualification. He and others stole petrol from a garage and one of them lit it near a house. Just over 3 weeks later he and another escorted an alcoholic home and brutally attacked him. They sprayed graffiti and lit a number of fires about the house. Due to the bravery of members of the public he was dragged unconscious from the property. He spent 5 days in intensive care. The defendant was arrested and detained in a secure unit. While a pool competition was in progress he was asked to return to his room because of his disruptive behaviour. Two staff escorted him and his co-accused attacked one of the staff with a pool cue. He and a third youth armed themselves with pool cues and threatened the staff. He and his co-accused threw pool balls towards the staff one of which caused a deep wound. Furniture was smashed and keys taken enabling the three to escape after they had scaled the perimeter fence with a ladder. A car was stolen and abandoned. The co-accused drove the three off in another stolen car, which crashed. The third youth was killed. These events were the subject matter of the other charges. Held. He had been to courts on five separate occasions. A report said all attempts to reintegrate him had failed. Taking into account the defendant's age and his pleas of guilty a **9 years** global sentence was not wrong.

Domestic premises with occupants

15.28   *Att-Gen's Ref. No 57 of 1998* 2000 1 Cr App R (S) 422. The defendant was convicted of arson, threatening to destroy property and arson with intent to endanger life and two associated counts. He was estranged from his wife but continued to be violent to her after they separated. When she rejected his advances he set fire to the duvet on her bed (count one). Shortly after he poured petrol through the letterbox of her flat and threatened to burn her out (count two). Seven days later in the early hours, while his wife was out and her two young children were in the house with a babysitter he poured petrol through the letterbox in the front door and set it alight (count three). He then left the scene. The front door was the means of escape. Damage was caused but the occupants suffered comparatively minor injuries. He showed no remorse. Held. The appropriate sentence was **8 to 10 years** so as it was a reference **7 years** substituted for 5.

R v McGrath 2000 1 Cr App R (S) 479. The defendant pleaded guilty to arson with intent to endanger life. The defendant returned home after drinking although he wasn't drunk. His partner made a remark about his lorry and he erupted in anger. He kicked the furniture and was violent to her. He locked the back door and poured an inflammable wood preserver over the hall and other rooms. He tried to light it but was unsuccessful. Both doors were now locked. His partner told her son to escape but the defendant pulled him back. He poured the same fluid over the cooker and turned on the gas. The liquid ignited. While his partner tried to put the flames out he tried to fuel the fire. She then tried to escape using her key but he pulled the key out of the lock. She realised he wanted to kill them all. Breathing was now difficult. The son again tried to escape through a window but was stopped. He then stopped her leaving. Eventually he allowed them to leave. £5,000–£8,000 damage was caused. He was of good character. The judge concluded he was a very real danger to the public. **6 years** was not excessive.

Att-Gen's Ref. No 4 of 1999 2000 2 Cr App R (S) 5. The defendant was convicted of arson with intent to endanger life. She and her husband argued and her husband said he wanted a receipt to prove she had been paying the mortgage. At 10pm she left the home saying she was going to work. She didn't go and when she was satisfied he was in bed she returned. Beneath the bed was a can of petrol she had put there sometime before. While he slept she sprinkled inflammatory material over the floor and she lit it. She shut the door and ignored her husband's screams. Three children were on the premises. Held. She had no previous convictions. One would expect a sentence of at least 8 years. Because it was a reference **6 years** was not altered.

Att-Gen's Ref. No 47 of 2000 2001 1 Cr App R (S) 471. The defendant was convicted of arson with intent to endanger life. The victim who had a boy and a girl was depressed and left her flat to move in with her sister. He approached her and said he wanted to use her flat for dealing in crack cocaine. He said he wanted to start that night and he would pay to have the electricity connected and £30 a night. She changed her mind about moving out but allowed him to deal from the flat. The defendant and his associate would be there at night and the victim spent her money mostly on drugs. He went on holiday and on his return was told she had agreed to leave the flat for £7,000 from the council. He didn't think it was worth starting up again. Her children returned to live with her and on the night of the fire her stepson was there too. Shortly after midnight he and his associate knocked on her door and when she answered it the two rushed in. They searched the flat and asked, 'Where's the letter?' Five minutes later there was another knock and she could see it was the same two and she wouldn't let them in. The defendant told the other to kick the door in which he did. They ran upstairs and the defendant poured petrol from a can between the two bedrooms and the kitchen, the kitchen and the hall. She asked what was going on and he poured petrol over her T-shirt. She dialled 999 and he smashed the telephone. He was about to douse the bed where the two boys were asleep and she asked why. He struck her three times with a truncheon and poured petrol over the bed. She tried to wake them and his associate said, 'Not the kids.' She continued waking the boys and saw flames coming from the living room. The boys left taking the little girl with them. The rest left also. It took 30 minutes to extinguish the flames. The fire spread to all parts of the flat and caused £7,000 worth of damage. At his trial he relied on an alibi. He was 36 and had a substantial list of convictions mostly for dishonesty. They was also an ABH and procuring an abortion. His risk assessment was considered high. Held. The bracket for arson with intent is **8–10 years**. This case is at the top of the bracket. Because it was a reference **9 years** not 7.

Domestic premises with occupants – Serious injuries/death

15.29   *R v Manual* 2002 1 Cr App R (S) 526. The defendant was convicted of arson with intent to endanger life, arson being reckless whether life was endangered as an alternative to an intent count and criminal damage. She was acquitted of GBH with intent. After drinking she returned home and as she went through the car park of her block and tore off a mirror from a car, (the criminal damage). Next she went to the flat of a woman who worked in a store and who she believed was responsible for reporting her for shoplifting. She put a rag through the letterbox, doused it in an inflammable liquid and set it alight. The occupant was able to extinguish it but was greatly distressed and shocked. The victim felt unable to live there for 2 months and the door and carpet was damaged. This was the reckless count. The defendant then did the same to another flat in the block. The occupant did not awake immediately and he collapsed in the smoke. He was rescued by the fire brigade and had very serious burns. They were 7.5% burns to his body surface and required full thickness skin grafts. There was smoke damage to his lungs and 3 months later he was still unable to walk more than a short distance. The door and hall were badly damaged and there was extensive smoke damage to the flat and the victim lost a large number of possessions, some of sentimental value. This was the intent count. The defendant was arrested and denied being in dispute with anyone in the block. She was 48 and then of good character. Before she was sentenced she pleaded to the shoplifting. She was divorced with children and had been under psychiatric care for 21 years. She was being treated for a depressive disorder and in 2000 she had been exhibiting very bizarre behaviour. The events occurred 2 weeks after she was discharged. The judge considered the motive for the second attack was to disguise she had committed the first arson. Held. Taking into account her good character **10 years and 8 concurrent** not 12 and 10 concurrent.

R v Hussain 2004 2 Cr App R 497. The defendant pleaded guilty to conspiracy to commit arson and was convicted of conspiracy to commit arson with intent to endanger life and eight counts of manslaughter. The defendant had four co-accused. He and others had made petrol bombs, and the defendant had obtained the petrol. One of the co-accused wanted to attack one of the victims who had been telling tales about his relationship with a girlfriend. In the early hours of the morning the defendant and others drove to the house where the victim was and two of the co-accused threw the petrol bombs at the house. In the subsequent fire eight people died; a woman, her daughter, a student and five girls aged between six months and thirteen years. Four other people escaped the fire. The judge said that the offences of manslaughter came very close to murder, and that no one who heard the evidence of family members who saw the fire would ever forget it. Further it was a gross understatement to say that the surviving family members were devastated. Held. The judge was bound to have regard to the number of persons unlawfully killed. This was manslaughter in horrific circumstances involving eight persons. It could not be argued that **18 years** for the manslaughter charges and a concurrent **14 years** for the conspiracy to commit arson were even arguably manifestly excessive.

Domestic premises without occupants

15.30   *R v Stacey* 1999 2 Cr App R (S) 298. The defendant pleaded guilty to arson being reckless whether life was endangered and arson. One hour after the occupant left her home the defendant poured lighter fuel or something similar through the letterbox of the house. He then lit a match and caused a small fire on a nylon mat. He then telephoned the emergency services and alerted neighbours. The householder's daughter arrived, as the fire services were about to break down the door. The fire was extinguished. The replacement door cost £595. He left a note for the occupier and was given a £5 reward. People were suspicious and the police questioned him. He denied starting the fire. About 6 weeks later firemen saw the defendant foraging in a roadside dustbin. A few minutes later the defendant called the fire station about a fire at a beach hut near where he had been seen. He was there when they arrived and helped to direct traffic and place cones in the road. Fireman found rubbish had been placed between two huts and ignited. £2,450 worth of damage was caused. The defendant was arrested and admitted the offence and said he started it because he was low and wanted attention. He was 38 and had been rejected for the fire service when he was 19. His only relevant conviction was in 1994 for setting fire to a car. It was more of an insurance fraud than a straightforward case of arson. Reports said he had been involved in a considerable amount of crime and was of low intelligence and vulnerable. The offences of arson were committed when he was depressed and upset and were linked to his mother's death. Held. His re-offending risk was described as considerable. Held. **4 years** not 5¹/₂ and **2 years** not 3 for the offences. The sentences remained concurrent.

Petrol bombs

15.31   *Att-Gen's Ref. Nos. 78, 79 and 85 of 1998* 2000 1 Cr App R (S) 371. Two defendants R and O'S were convicted of arson with intent to endanger life relating to two different houses. R had pleaded guilty to arson being reckless whether life was endangered which was not accepted. The third defendant, M was acquitted of those counts but convicted of arson being reckless whether life was endangered relating to the same two houses. R's father had separated from R's mother and had nothing to do with him. One day he heard something, which brought to the surface a long-standing resentment against his father. The three defendants met and R bought some petrol. Two petrol bombs were made and R and O'S threw them at two houses near his father's house. They intended to hit the father's house but made a mistake. The occupants at one house escaped without injury and relatively little damage. At the other house the father jumped from an upstairs window and injured himself. His two children suffered horrific injuries. One had 20% burns with extensive burns to the face hands and legs. The other also had 20% burns with severe burns to face, scalp and other parts of the body. R was now 23, O'S was now 20 and M was now 20. R was the instigator with no similar convictions. O'S was of good character. M was R's girlfriend and under his influence. The judge said she had been used unmercifully. Held. The appropriate sentence for R was **8–10 years** so his **8 years** sentence was undisturbed. It was a very severe sentence for a young man. The judge was entitled to make the distinction between that sentence and the other two defendants. O'S sentence was 5 years and M's was a combination order (probation and 100 hours' CSO).

Revenge

15.32 *R v Flanagan* 1999 1 Cr App R (S) 100. The defendant pleaded guilty to attempted arson being reckless whether life was endangered. The defendant called a hospital where she had previously received psychiatric treatment and said she intended to set fire to Orpington police station. She had previously attacked the station by attacking cars, striking a window with a hammer and had attempted to firebomb the station. For that she was convicted of arson. On the same evening as the call she was found in the foyer of the police station attempting to set fire to a pool of paraffin with a burning piece of paper. An officer put it out. She was 49 and had two previous convictions for arson and a previous conviction for child cruelty. In that case the child had died and it had caused her strong feelings against the police. There were several previous convictions for assaulting the police. She had a history of alcohol abuse, self harm, and anger. One psychiatrist said she had a borderline personality disorder and the other one said she had a severe personality disorder. There was a belief she would commit arson again. Held. **Life was appropriate** but with a 3 year and not 5 year specified term.

Att-Gen's Ref. Nos. 78, 79 and 85 of 1998 2000 1 Cr App R (S) 371. Two defendants R and O'S were convicted of arson with intent to endanger life relating to two different houses. R had pleaded guilty to arson being reckless whether life was endangered which was not accepted. The third defendant, M was acquitted of those counts but convicted of arson being reckless whether life was endangered relating to the same two houses. R's father had separated from R's mother and had nothing to do with him. One day he heard something, which brought to the surface a long-standing resentment against his father. The three defendants met and R bought some petrol. Two petrol bombs were made and R and O'S threw them at two houses near his father's house. They intended to hit the father's house but made a mistake. The occupants at one house escaped without injury and relatively little damage. At the other house the father jumped from an upstairs window and injured himself. His two children suffered horrific injuries. One had 20% burns with extensive burns to the face hands and legs. The other also had 20% burns with severe burns to face, scalp and other parts of the body. R was now 23, O'S was now 20 and M was now 20. R was the instigator with no similar convictions. O'S was of good character. M was R's girlfriend and under his influence. The judge said she had been used unmercifully. Held. The appropriate sentence for R was **8–10 years** so his **8 years** sentence was undisturbed. It was a very severe sentence for a young man. The judge was entitled to make the distinction between that sentence and the other two defendants. O'S sentence was 5 years and M's was a combination order (probation and 100 hours' CSO).

Violent attack, part of a

15.33 *R v Griffin* 1999 1 Cr App R (S) 213. The defendant pleaded guilty to arson with intent to endanger life and causing GBH with intent. The defendant was distressed with the break up of his relationship with the victim. He wrote to his family telling them what he was about to do. The victim came to the premises to pick up some clothing and he pointed a knife at her. She was told she would not get out alive and he stabbed her in the chest. He followed her to the bedroom where he locked the door. There was a struggle over the knife in which the defendant received severe injuries to his hands. After this he recovered the knife and stabbed her several times. By now she was having trouble breathing. Further stab wounds were inflicted and she was told to open her legs. The children then knocked on the front door and he told them to go away. He returned to the bedroom and stabbed her once again in the cheek. The victim became unconscious and awoke up to find a burning duvet on the bed. She got up to get away and the defendant pushed her to the floor and threw the burning duvet over her, which she managed to throw off. She lost consciousness but awoke and escaped. She had burns to shoulders, arms, hands and feet. Held. The defendant had a significant mental illness and some minor previous convictions. Because of plea and the authorities **9 years** not 11 concurrent for both offences.

See also OFFENCES AGAINST THE PERSON ACT 1861, s 18 – *Fire, by*

4   Arson – Life sentence was/was not appropriate

General

15.34   *R v Flanagan* 1999 1 Cr App R (S) 100. The defendant pleaded guilty to attempted arson being reckless whether life was endangered. The defendant called a hospital where she had previously received psychiatric treatment and said she intended to set fire to Orpington police station. She had previously attacked the station by attacking cars, striking a window with a hammer and had attempted to firebomb the station. For that she was convicted of arson. On the same evening as the call she was found in the foyer of the police station attempting to set fire to a pool of paraffin with a burning piece of paper. An officer put it out.

She was 49 and had two previous convictions for arson and a previous conviction for child cruelty. In that case the child had died and it had caused her strong feelings against the police. There were several previous convictions for assaulting the police. She had a history of alcohol abuse, self harm, and anger. One psychiatrist said she had a borderline personality disorder and the other one said she had a severe personality disorder. There was a belief she would commit arson again. **Life was appropriate** but with a 3 year and not 5 year specified term.

R v Simmonds 2001 2 Cr App R (S) 328. The defendant pleaded guilty to arson. His plea of not guilty to arson with intent to endanger life and reckless whether life was endangered was accepted. These had been based on the other houses in the terrace. In 1998 he married his wife who he had known since 1993. He had a long history of mood swings and she eventually obtained an injunction to prevent him going to the matrimonial home. When he received a letter saying she was starting divorce proceedings he bought some petrol from a garage and drove to the former matrimonial home. At 2.50pm he gained entry by smashing a pane of glass and poured petrol round the unoccupied house. The fire took hold quickly. The building was saved but the contents were entirely destroyed. The defendant telephoned the police saying he had made sure the wife was not in the house and he had a shotgun and he intended to use it against people who had hurt him in the past. Knowing the police were pursuing him he said he would blow them out of the sky. When confronted by armed officers he indicated he had a weapon, which turned out to be a wooden-handled axe. The judge considered this was an attempt to invite them to shoot him. He immediately said 'I did it.' He was 37 and of good character. Both of his wives complained of violence. He had had 40 mental health interventions including being sectioned. He had a personality disorder associated with loss of temper and control. There were no psychiatric recommendations from one psychiatrist. Others were more positive. He was considered highly manipulative and had a long and repetitive history of violence to his female partners which was escalating. There was an encouraging prison report. Held. It was a serious case of arson. There were several worrying features in his behaviour. We are concerned about the risk to the public. However, that itself does not justify a life sentence. Something more has to be established. There were no 'most exceptional circumstances.' **6 years** not life.

R v Trowbridge 2002 2 Cr App R (S) 154. The defendant pleaded guilty to arson being reckless whether life was endangered. His downstairs neighbours noticed water was coming from his maisonette through their ceiling. The defendant refused to let their plumber in or come to the door. A carpenter tried to gain entry and was sworn at and told to go away. The water flow increased and the supply had to be turned off. The defendant was seen pulling frantically at something in the bathroom. Eventually the police were summoned and they were refused entry in an abusive manner. An officer said he would force the door and broke a glass panel. The defendant shouted, 'Fuck off, I've got petrol.' He then threw petrol at the officer and his clothing was splashed. Then he said he was going to burn the whole place down and lit the petrol causing the curtains to catch fire. The officer moved out of the way quickly and so avoided the flames, which spread to the stairs of the maisonette. A fire extinguisher put the flames out. The defendant jumped out of a rear window and was arrested. When interviewed he said he didn't intent to hurt anyone and he wanted to kill himself and be with his deceased mother. He was 50 and of good character and had no history of starting fires. He told the first psychiatrist that he wasn't going to his dump and marched off. The doctor said he had developed a marked antipathy to the people of Devon, which was where he lived. He was released on bail to be assessed and to see whether a probation order with treatment was suitable. He told them he would rather go to prison than there. The doctor said he was a man of limited intelligence who tended to take up fixed stances and was unable to retreat easily. Another said he needed social services assistance and it was surprising he had been neglected so long. The probation proposal was not feasible. The pre-sentence report said he was very vulnerable and unhappy with considerable difficulties coping with day-to-day issues. His risk assessment for re-offending was assessed as high. In 1996 the judge said he posed a significant risk to people and imposed a life sentence. Since then he had been released, recalled (not for offences but because of difficulties with the probation service supervising his release) and released again. The appeal was heard in December 2001. Held. Throwing petrol at a police officer is extremely grave and could have led to a loss of life. However, the criteria for a life sentence were not present. Since his sentence nothing had happened to suggest he constituted a risk to the public. **4 years** substituted which he had served.

Old cases *R v Irving* 1998 2 Cr App R (S) 162 (For a summary of this case see the first edition of this book.)

Defendant under 17

15.35   *R v Stanley* 1999 2 Cr App R (S) 31. The defendant pleaded guilty to arson being reckless whether life was endangered on the second day of her trial. A not guilty verdict was entered for a count for intending to endanger life. The defendant, a girl then aged 16 believed that her social worker had said something to those who ran her daughter's nursery so the daughter lost her place. She went to see her social worker. She was told she wasn't available. She then went and got some petrol and returned. She used a pushchair to jam open some doors. Her child was not present. She sprayed petrol from a container onto a counter and some doors. She set fire to it and ran out. There were about 40 people in the building. The damage was limited to about £2,300 because the fire brigade attended extremely quickly. She was arrested and was violent and abusive. There was a long-standing friction between the defendant and the social services. A High Court judge in 1990 had said she had not been served well by the authorities. Held. She had a previous conviction for arson for which she was conditional discharged. She had a child at the time of the fire who was 2 and one born while she was in prison. She appeared to be undergoing an abnormal personality development. The sentencing judge held that she would remain a danger for an unpredictable time. While in prison she and others had attacked a social worker. For that she had been convicted and sentenced to 12 months for affray and wounding. Also she had 10 adjudications in prison. **Life** with a fixed period of 18 months was appropriate.

Grave enough, is the offence?

15.36   *R v Chapman* 2000 1 Cr App R (S) 377. LCJ The first pre-condition for imposing a life sentence for the purposes of public protection was that the offender had committed an offence grave enough to merit an extremely long sentence. *R v Hodgson* 1968 52 Cr App R 113 applied.

R v Wilson 2000 1 Cr App R (S) 323. The defendant pleaded guilty to arson being reckless whether life was endangered or property damaged. A prisoner set fire to his cell and caused about £500 worth of damage. A fire extinguisher put the flames out. His actions had 'been essentially a 'cry for help' and to get him out of the health care centre, where he was being harassed and threatened.' The first pre-condition in *R v Chapman* 2000 1 Cr App R (S) 377 was not met so life varied to **10 years** consecutive to sentence for which he was serving. The appropriate sentence of 3 years was extended (i.e. the licence was extended) by 7 years for the protection of the public under [what is now the Powers of Criminal Courts (Sentencing) Act 2000 s 80(2)(b)].

16   Assault on a Police Officer

16.1   Police Act 1996 s 89(1)

Summary only: maximum 6 month and/or £5,000.

Licensed premises Where the offence is committed on licensed premises the court may prohibit the defendant from entering those premises or any other specified premises without the express consent of the licensee or his agent[41]. The order shall last from 3 months to 2 years[42].

Magistrates' Court Sentencing Guidelines January 2004

16.2   For a first time offender pleading not guilty. Entry point. Is it so serious that only custody is appropriate? Consider the impact on the victim. Examples of aggravating factors for the offence are any injuries caused, gross disregard for police authority, group action, premeditated and spitting. Examples of mitigating factors for the offence are impulsive action and unaware that person was a police officer. Examples of mitigation are age, health (physical or mental), co-operation with the police, genuine remorse and voluntary compensation. Give reasons if not awarding compensation.

For details about the guidelines see **Magistrates' Court Sentencing Guidelines** at page 483.

17   Assisting Offenders

17.1   Criminal Law Act 1967 s 4

Indictable only. The maximum sentence depends on what the maximum sentence is for the person assisted. When the sentence for the other person's offence is fixed by law (i.e. mandatory life for murder), the maximum is 10 years; when the other person's maximum sentence is 14 years or more, the maximum is 7 years; when the other person's maximum sentence is 10–13 years, the maximum is 5 years and in all other cases the maximum is 3 years.

Driving someone away from a crime

17.2   *R v Taylor* 2002 2 Cr App R (S) 385. The defendant made an early plea to doing an act with intent to impede the apprehension of another. He gave his friend a lift to a

---

41 Licensed Premises (Exclusion of Certain Persons) Act 1980 s 1(1)
42 Licensed Premises (Exclusion of Certain Persons) Act 1980 s 1(3)

supermarket where they were going to buy heroin. The friend went and robbed a woman of her handbag and ran back to the car whereupon the defendant drove them away. Police stopped the car. The defendant said he drove off because he feared members of the public might attack them. He was sentenced on the basis he had no knowledge that the friend intended to commit a crime when he got out of the car and when he saw him running with the bag he assumed that there had been a theft. The defendant had a number of convictions principally for drugs and theft. He showed remorse. The co-defendant pleaded guilty to robbery and received 30 months. Held. The level of sentencing to some extent is governed by the seriousness of the offence of the principle offender. **9 months** not 18.

See also **PERVERTING THE COURSE OF JUSTICE/CONTEMPT OF COURT/PERJURY ETC**

ATTEMPTS

Attempts are listed with the full offence except for **MURDER, ATTEMPTED**

AVIATION

See **AIRCRAFT OFFENCES**

18 BAIL OFFENCES

18.1 Bail Act 1976 s 6

Absconding when released on bail

The offence is tried at the court where the offence took place. Maximum sentence at Crown Court (including a committal for sentence) 12 months. Summary maximum 3 months and/or £5,000.

It is possible for the offence to be prosecuted as a Contempt of Court.

The Sentencing Guidelines Council has started the procedure so a guideline can be issued about these offences.

Crown Court statistics – England and Wales – Males 21+ – Failing to surrender to bail
18.2

Year	Plea	Total Numbers sentenced	Type of sentence %					Average length of custody (months)
			Discharge	Fine	Community sentence	Suspended sentence	Custody	
2002	Guilty	52	–	31	2	–	52	2.3
	Not guilty	–	–	–	–	–	–	
2003	Guilty	79	1	14	10	–	65	2.1
	Not guilty	15	–	20	–	–	73	2.1

For details and explanations about the statistics in the book see page vii.

Magistrates' Court Sentencing Guidelines January 2004

18.3   For a first time offender pleading not guilty. Entry point. Is it serious enough for a community penalty? A curfew order may be particularly suitable. Examples of aggravating factors for the offence are leaves jurisdiction, long term evasion, results in ineffective trial date and wilful evasion. Examples of mitigating factors for the offence are appears late on day of hearing, genuine misund-erstanding and voluntary surrender. Examples of mitigation are age, health (physical or mental), co-operation with the police and genuine remorse.

For details about the guidelines see MAGISTRATES' COURT SENTENCING GUIDELINES at page 483.

Absconding

18.4   *R v Deeley* 1998 1 Cr App R (S) 112. The defendant was convicted of failing to surrender to his bail. The defendant was committed to the Crown Court on four charges of burglary in custody. He was released on bail because of the expiry of the custody time limits and appeared when first required to. He then failed to attend his pleas and directions hearing. Three weeks later he was arrested. He said he was trying to face up to his drug addiction, his relationship was strained and he overlooked the date. He was not of good character. Held. This breach was not unusually serious. **3 months** not 6.

R v Clarke 2000 1 Cr App R (S) 224. The defendant admitted failing to answer to his bail. He was arrested on an alcohol duty evasion case and bailed. It was suggested he was an important participant in a £1.2m duty fraud. He didn't turn up for his trial in July 1998 and the trial against the others proceeded. He was arrested in January 1999 after the main trial had finished. He was then tried and acquitted. In April 1999 he was dealt with for the bail offence. The judge considered his absence might have helped him and his co-defendants in their trials. The defendant had said he had received threats. Held. The judge might have given too much attention to the possible advantages of his absence. His criminality is unaffected by the verdict in the trial he absconded from. The judge was entitled to be critical of the suggestion of threats. Because the maximum is 12 months the sentence was reduced to $7^1/_2$ months from 9 months. The court then reconvened itself as the Divisional Court and ordered the relevant period to start from January 1999.

R v Keane 2002 1 Cr App R (S) 383. The defendant pleaded guilty to endangering the safety of rail passengers and failing to surrender to his bail. He was bailed to the Crown Court, failed to answer to his bail and was arrested nearly 4 months later. The defendant was 58 and had no convictions but had a long-standing problem with drink. There was a letter saying he was a hard working and conscientious member of the local community. Held. 15 months for the railway offence cannot be faulted. On the day in question it appears he just could not bring himself to face the music and at the last minute decided not to attend. Taking a broad view of all the circumstances, recognising his good character, the alcohol problems 3 months consecutive for the bail offence was more than necessary to mark what must be accepted as the great inconvenience and cost in time and money caused by his failure to attend. **1 month consecutive** is sufficient.

R v White and McKinnon 2003 2 Cr App R (S) 133. The defendant W failed to attend when facing a Class A drugs offence. He received 6 years for the drugs consecutive to 84 days for breach of licence and 6 months for the bail offence. M faced a burglary and TDA before he absconded. The Crown dropped the burglary and he pleaded to the TDA. He received $5^1/_2$ months for the TDA (maximum 6 months) and 3 months consecutive for the failure to attend. Held. The sentence for failing to attend should not be regarded as having to be proportionate to the gravity of the other offences. There was nothing wrong with W's sentence. M sentence upheld.

Sentence should be consecutive to the sentence imposed for the other offence

18.5 *R v Aroride* 1999 2 Cr App R (S) 406. The defendant pleaded guilty to attempting to obtain property by a deception at the Magistrates' Court and absconded. Held. Failure to surrender to bail is a serious and discrete matter and in principle should attract a separate and **consecutive** sentence.

R v O'Hara 2003 2 Cr App R (S) 121. The defendant pleaded guilty to burglary and breach of bail. The defence argued that it was wrong to pass 2 months consecutive for the breach because of *R v Gorman* 1993 14 Cr App R (S) 120. Held. The Gorman situation was very different because the extra sentence for the bail there changed the remission from $^{1}/_{2}$ to 1/3. Where a defendant had repeatedly failed to honour his obligations under the Bail Act as this defendant has it is appropriate to pass consecutive sentences. 2 months **consecutive** upheld.

R v White and McKinnon 2003 2 Cr App R (S) 133. Held. In principle the absconding sentence should be consecutive. The remarks in *R v Gorman* 1993 14 Cr App R (S) 120 should be confined to the peculiar circumstances of that case.

19   Bail, Offences Committed When The Defendant Is On

19.1 Powers of Criminal Courts (Sentencing) Act 2000 s 151(2). In considering the seriousness of any offence committed while the offender was on bail, the court shall treat the fact that it was committed in those circumstances as an aggravating factor.

The Court must treat this fact as an aggravating factor, see Criminal Justice Act 2003 s 143(3).

Magistrates' Court Sentencing Guidelines January 2004

19.2 Throughout the Guidelines each guideline for the offences says 'If the offender is on bail this offence is more serious.'

For details about the guidelines see **Magistrates' Court Sentencing Guidelines** at page 483.

Consecutive sentence, the offence on bail should attract a

19.3 *R v Stevens* 1997 2 Cr App R (S) 180. It may be proper to make a sentence consecutive to one passed on an earlier occasion, particularly where the second offence was committed on bail for the first offence.

R v Thackwray 2003 The Times 25/11/03. The Judge was entitled to take the commission of the offence when on bail as an aggravating factor even when the defendant was later acquitted of the other offence.

Bankrupt

See **Insolvency Offences**

20 BASIC PRINCIPLES

Departing from the sentencing guidance

20.1 *Att-Gen's Ref. No 83 of 2001* 2002 1 Cr App R (S) 589. What the authorities do not show are the cases where the individual circumstances of the defendant and the mitigation available to him have led to a justified departure from the guidance provided by the reported decisions. It is fundamental to the responsibilities of sentencing judges that while they must always pay proper regard to the sentencing guidance given, they are required also to reflect on all the circumstances of the individual case. Where sentencing judges are satisfied that occasion requires it, they have to balance the demands of justice with what is sometimes described as the calls of mercy.

Att-Gen's Ref. No 84 of 2001 2002 2 Cr App R (S) 226. The defendant pleaded guilty to attempted robbery and having a firearm with intent to resist arrest. He tried to rob a Securicor guard delivering cash to a cash dispenser. Held. Personal factors in relation to offences of this gravity can have only a very small effect in determining what the appropriate sentence is.

Prison overcrowding

20.2 *R v Kefford* 2002 2 Cr App R (S) 495. LCJ. The defendant pleaded guilty to 12 thefts and asked for 9 offences of false accounting to be taken into consideration. Held. It would be highly undesirable if the prison population were to continue to rise. The ability of the Prison Service to tackle a prisoner's offending behaviour and so reduce re-offending is adversely affected if a prison is overcrowded. Courts must accept the realities of the situation. In the case of economic crimes, e.g. obtaining undue credit by fraud, prison is not necessarily the only appropriate form of punishment. Particularly in the case of those who have no record of previous offending, the very fact of having to appear before a court can be a significant punishment. Certainly, having to perform a form of community punishment can be a very salutary way of making it clear that crime does not pay, particularly if a community punishment order is combined with a curfew order. The sentence for a theft from employer involving £11,120 reduced from 12 months to 4 months. The message must go out that courts should imprison only when necessary and for no longer than necessary.

R v Baldwin 2002 The Times 22/11/02. LCJ. The defendant pleaded guilty to conspiracy to supply cannabis and being concerned in the supply of amphetamine. He was a courier for a large-scale drugs enterprise. At the beginning of the police investigation he was sent to prison for 2½ years for possession with cannabis with intent to supply. He served his sentence. Later he was charged with couriering a heat sealing device for amphetamine packing. (There are no details about the cannabis matter.) Until 1993 he was regularly appearing before the courts mostly for dishonesty. There was some violence but no drug offences. There was then a gap till 1998 when there was a section 20 wounding matter. There was employment for him. He had served the equivalent of 12 months imprisonment. Held. He does not represent a high risk of direct harm to the public. He has shown he can hold down responsible employment. Bearing in mind the prison overcrowding and the good prospects he is not going to prey on the public again there are advantages to a fine. A further 12 month sentence is not going to protect the public. So **immediate release** and a **£5,000 fine**. (The problem with this report is there are no details of the cannabis matter and no reference to the impact of the fact he had already been sentenced for other offences connected with the drug enterprise.)

R v Cook 2003 2 Cr App R (S) 315 The defendant pleaded guilty to 9 counts of theft. Over a five-year period he stole about £225,000. The judgement in Kefford did not modify sentencing practices when it came to breaches of trust involving substantial sums of money.

Sentencing is an art etc/Rehabilitation

20.3 *Att-Gen's Ref. No 4 of 1998* 1990 11 Cr App R (S) 517. LCJ. It must always be remembered that sentencing is an art rather than a science; that the trial judge is particularly well placed to assess the weight to be given to various competing considerations; that leniency is not in itself a vice. That mercy should season justice is a proposition as soundly based in law as it is in literature. There were occasions where it was right to take a constructive course and seek to achieve the rehabilitation of the offender. The judge was satisfied it provided the best possible long-term solution for the community and the defendant. It was right to take a constructive course. So far he has been proved right. The prospects of re-offending are now lower than if he had had a custodial sentence. The sentence was lenient on paper but sentencing is not and never can be an exercise on paper; each case, ultimately, is individual. It would be wrong to interfere.

See also **DEFENDANT** and **MERCY**

BENEFIT FRAUD

See **SOCIAL SECURITY FRAUD/HOUSING BENEFIT FRAUD**

21 BIGAMY/MARRIAGE OFFENCES

21.1 Offences Against the Person Act 1861 s 57

Triable either way. On indictment maximum 7 years. Summary maximum 6 months and/or £5,000.

The Criminal Justice Act 2003 creates a summary maximum sentence of 51 weeks, a minimum custodial sentence of 28 weeks and Custody plus. The Home Office says they do not expect to introduce these provisions before September 2006.

Perjury Act 1911 s 3

False statements etc with reference to marriage.

Triable either way. On indictment maximum 7 years. Summary maximum 6 months and/or £5,000.

See also **IMMIGRATION OFFENCES** and **PASSPORT OFFENCES**

Crown Court statistics – England and Wales – Males 21+ – Bigamy
21.2

Year	Plea	Total Numbers sentenced	Type of sentence %					Average length of custody (months)
			Discharge	Fine	Community sentence	Suspended sentence	Custody	
2002	Guilty	3	33	–	67	–	–	–
	Not guilty	3	33	–	67	–	–	–
2003	Guilty	5	40	–	60	–	–	–
	Not guilty	5	40	–	60	–	–	–

For details and explanations about the statistics in the book see page vii.

Immigration controls, to evade

21.3   *R v Cairns* 1997 1 Cr App R (S) 118. The defendant pleaded guilty to bigamy. In August he married a Zimbabwean. This was legitimate. Three weeks later he married a Nigerian. Neither woman was traced. Both marriages were contracted for money. He had a previous conviction for dishonesty but none for this kind of offence. Held. A deterrent custodial sentence was inevitable but **9 months** not 15.

R v Zafar 1998 1 Cr App R (S) 416. The defendants Z and B pleaded guilty to making a false oath or declaration to obtain marriage documents (s 3). The defendant G was convicted of the same offence. The conspiracy was to organise marriages of conveniences for Pakistani immigrants who had entered Belgium illegally. The ceremonies took place in the UK because the arrangements for weddings were easier in the UK. The men were unable to travel to the UK because they were illegal immigrants so their passports were forwarded to the organisers in the UK and a stand-in groom would attend the ceremony. Other members of the conspiracy would attend as witnesses and guests. Shortly after the bride would be taken to Belgium where she would be introduced to the passport holder. They would then go to the Town Hall and register the marriage and that would give the husband the right to remain in Belgium. The authorities would then visit the home address and confirm that the marriage was genuine. The bride would return to the UK and would be paid between £700 and £1,000. B and Z were at the heart of the conspiracy in the UK and played a major part in the recruiting of the brides and arranging the ceremonies. They were not at the 'top of the tree.' G was the partner of B and was also involved with the organisation. She drove the girls to the weddings, bought flowers and rings etc. Z pleaded at the last minute B pleaded at the first opportunity, gave help to the Belgium authorities and showed remorse. Held. There were close parallels between this offence and facilitating illegal entry. Z: **4¹/₂ years** not 5¹/₂. B: **3 years** not 4¹/₂. G: **21 months** not 2¹/₂ years.

First marriage over but no divorce

21.4   *R v Mitchell* 2005 1 Cr App R (S) 193. The defendant pleaded guilty on re-arraignment to bigamy and perjury. In 2000 he made a marriage which effectively lasted only a week and in 2002 his wife petitioned for divorce. In the meantime he had met another woman who lived in the Philippines and they agreed to marry in 2003. He told her he was not married. He went to a register office and signed a notice of marriage including a declaration that his last marriage had been dissolved in 1994 and he had not been married since. Later that month there was a ceremony of marriage. He did not sign or acknowledge the petition for divorce until May 2003. His new wife found out he was still married and police were informed. He was finally divorced from the 2000 wife in August 2003. The defendant, 47, had a not insubstantial record for dishonesty and had served two terms of imprisonment for it. The wife from the Philippines came from a highly religious family who had been appalled when they found out what had happened. She had now forgiven him and they had been properly married. Held. Had he been a man of previously good character there would have been force in the submission that custody was not inevitable. However where a person with a prior record of offences of dishonesty commits the serious offence of perjury there are no exceptional circumstances. **9 months** on each concurrent upheld.

22   BLACKMAIL

22.1   Theft Act 1968 s 21

Indictable only. Maximum sentence 14 years.

Crown Court statistics – England and Wales – Males 21+
22.2

Year	Plea	Total Numbers sentenced	Type of sentence %					Average length of custody (months)
			Discharge	Fine	Community sentence	Suspended sentence	Custody	
2002	Guilty	52	2	–	13	12	71	32.8
	Not guilty	30	–	–	17	–	83	37
2003	Guilty	52	–	2	19	2	77	28.7
	Not guilty	23	–	–	–	–	96	43.6

For details and explanations about the statistics in the book see page vii.

Confiscation For all blackmail offences[1] committed on or after 24 March 2003[2] the court <u>must</u> follow the Proceeds of Crime Act 2002 procedure.

Restitution Order There is power to make an order that the stolen goods etc. in the possession of the defendant or a third party be restored to the owner etc.[3]

Guideline remarks

22.3   *R v Hadjou* 1989 11 Cr App R (S) 29. LCJ. Blackmail is one of the ugliest and most vicious crimes in the calendar of criminal offences and it is perhaps due to the fact that the courts always impose severe sentences that one seldom, if ever, finds a person convicted for a second time for blackmail.

R v Christie 1991 12 Cr App R (S) 540. The offence of blackmail is regarded by the public, and rightly regarded, with loathing and contempt. The typical case of blackmail falls somewhere between robbery and simple theft in seriousness. It is clearly more serious than theft because of the mental anguish, which is so often caused.

R v Davies 2004 1 Cr App R (S) 209. Blackmail is a very nasty offence. A serious view will always be taken but its true gravity does of course vary considerably.

Bills, to enforce unreasonable

22.4   *R v Killgallon and Gray* 1998 1 Cr App R (S) 279. The defendants K and G were convicted of seven counts of blackmail. G would approach small businesses and offer to tarmac their yard or car park for £25 saying he had some tarmac which might other- wise set because of a problem with a wagon etc. If an agreement was made, workman would appear and normally tarmac a greater area than had been agreed. Then G would reappear and demand £25 a square yard. When the customer protested, threats of an extremely intimidating nature were made. Another man who was not apprehended would then attack G, which would intimidate the customer. The threats included threats to burn down their premises, follow people home, firebomb their homes, assault their wives and children and inflict personal violence. K would then appear playing the part of a peacemaker. He would ask for the money and endorsed the threats made. The pros- ecution relied on 39 transactions for which £220,000 had been demanded. £98,000 had been obtained. The figures for the counts in the indictment were £46,000 and £17,000 respectively. G was 36 and effectively of good character and K was 41 and of good character. G was involved later than K. Held. Because the judge had based the sentence on the 39 transactions and not on the counts in the indictment and perhaps the judge had taken an exaggerated view of the offences **6 years** was substituted for 10.

1   Proceeds of Crime Act 2002 s 6 and s 75 and Sch 2 para 9
2   Proceeds of Crime Act 2002 (Commencement No 5, Transitional Provisions, Savings and Amendment) Order 2003
3   Powers of Criminal Courts Act (Sentencing) 2000 s 148(2) and Theft Act 1968 s 24(4)

Debt collecting

22.5   *R v Hart and Bullen* 1999 2 Cr App R (S) 233. Just before a trial for conspiracy to cause GBH the prosecution added a count of conspiracy to blackmail to which the defendants pleaded guilty. Other counts were left on the file. The two defendants went to find a man called Thompson who had links with criminals. The purpose was to recover £20,000, which had been lent to him. They drove to the area where he lived and Thompson's girlfriend received a call saying they were coming to kill him. More calls were made. She was followed by a car, which at one point screeched to a halt and she was told, 'Thompson was going to die.' Threatening messages were left on her answering machine. The defendants went to Thompson's sister's home twice and demanded to know where he was. Threats were made to her and her family. She was terrified. They visited her a third time, entered her premises and forced her boyfriend against a wall. An object was thrust against his stomach and he was threatened with a stabbing if he did not help find Thompson. Next they re-visited his girlfriend.

The defendants were arrested in a hotel and a stun gun, a truncheon, a CS gas canister, a sheath knife, two telephone pagers and a length of fishing wire were found. The basis of plea was that there was no intention to harm anyone, the debt was owed for a business and not connected with drugs and the weapons were not brought there at the behest of either defendant. One defendant was of good character and the other had a list of mostly drug convictions. He was on licence for a 3½ year supply of Class A drug sentence. Held. The judge was able to say that the weapons were ways of enforcing the debt. **4 years** was deserved. The 9 month sentence for breach of the prison licence remained consecutive.

R v Kewell 2000 2 Cr App R (S) 38. The defendant pleaded guilty to blackmail. His relationship broke up and the girlfriend left without making any provision for the money owing in their joint account. The defendant was having difficulty covering his other debts and commitments. She ignored his letters and his threats of legal action. He then sent a letter demanding £300 within 7 days or personal photographs would be distributed to her place of 'work or home or family or worse.' Fearing he might use the Internet she contacted the police. They found the photographs in his computer The defendant was 25 with a new partner and her young son and was working as a soft-ware consultant. He had no previous convictions and expressed remorse. **12 months** substituted for 18 months.

R v Barnes 2003 2 Cr App R (S) 346. The defendant changed his blackmail plea to guilty. In 2000, the victim had been shot through the back of the leg whilst outside the front door of his home. The defendant, whilst adopting an Irish accent, telephoned saying "I am ringing about recent problems you've had. I need a more private telephone number that I can contact you on to discuss it". The victim gave the defendant his mobile phone number. The defendant told him not to involve the authorities. The victim contacted the police. A number of calls were made and the defendant referred to a debt owing and demanded £20,000 telling the victim that he could be shot in the back of the head. The victim said he would pay £15,000. The final call was traced to a phone box where the defendant was arrested. He made no comment in interview. He was 43 with some previous convictions on 12 occasions. For the most serious he received 56 days imprisonment, in 1981. His last one was in 1989. The pre-sentence report said that this offence was out of character. Held. Blackmail is always an ugly offence and in this particular case it was aggravated by the chilling nature of the threats in the knowledge that the victim had already been shot. This case had parallels with R v Cioffo 1996 1 Cr App R (S) 427 which involved the firing of shots at the victim's home and a personal campaign of terror. However, in that case there was no credit for a guilty plea. **4 years** not 7.

See also **Kidnapping Individuals for Ransom/Debt Collecting**

Defendant aged 16–18

22.6 *R v Simmons* 2001 2 Cr App R (S) 170. The defendant pleaded guilty to blackmail. A Cézanne painting worth more than £3m went missing from the Ashmolean Museum which attracted extensive publicity. The defendant then 16 was highly skilled in the use of computers and had a sophisticated knowledge of procedures. He telephoned the curator stating it would be returned for £1m. Two further calls followed and a computer-generated letter was sent saying, 'Your family might get upset if you make the wrong decision.' The curator was told not to tell the police. He sent five e-mails from an Internet café, which were disguised using an encryption programme one of which said the curator should 'watch (his) family and friends die around (him).' The answer was expected by Friday or, 'The culling would start.' There were further threats. Substantial police resources were used to investigate the threats and he was after some difficulty traced. He said he only did it for a joke. The curator's family was extremely upset and suffered major disruption. The effect was devastating and they stopped going out. The defendant had cautions for theft a few months before the offence started. One involved an attempt to use his mother's credit card to obtain £10,000 worth of goods over the Internet. His parents had split up and he was recently told his father was not his biological father. He started a vendetta against his mother and had an overdraft of £2,600 and his family had paid off a large debt of his. The psychiatrist said he had a psychiatric disorder of a conduct disorder unsocial type and an unsettled personality. He was intelligent but had difficulty with authority. Held. Although in many ways he was vulnerable he was also very dangerous. The offence was serious and sophisticated pursued with intelligence and vigour. He had a cynical disregard to what he had done to the curator. **12 months** detention and training was exactly right.

R v Malaj 2004 1 Cr App R (S) 414. Both defendants M and L were convicted of kidnapping and ABH. M was convicted of blackmail and false imprisonment, L had already pleaded guilty to those offences. The defendants were seen in a motor car watching premises of a business run by the victim, a man in his 50s. The victim left these premises at 5pm and was threatened with screwdrivers and told to hand over £50,000. He was forced into the boot of a car and driven away where he was kept bound and gagged in the open for about 2 days. He was given drink but no food. During this time telephone demands to his family for £50,000 were made or he would be killed. The victim was told that he would be held for a week before being killed. After two days period he was tied to a tree and repeatedly kicked in the chest. He was taken to a railway station bound and gagged in the boot of a car where the defendants had been told the ransom money would be handed over. The car was identified and followed. M and L were arrested and the victim was taken to hospital. L said that the demands for money were not his idea and denied assault. He asked for forgiveness for his (limited) role. M denied all offences and said that he had been threatened. M and L were 17 and 18 at the time of the offences and both were of good character. L expressed remorse. Held. These offences were aggravated because they were planned and sought a substantial ransom; the victim was appallingly treated with violence; a tape recording was played to his family that indicated that the victim had been seriously mistreated and the victim had been kept for more than 2 days. M's sentence for kidnapping was reduced from 13 to **11 years' detention**; L's from 10 to **8 years' detention**.

Embarrassing material/behaviour

22.7 *R v Kewell* 2000 2 Cr App R (S) 38. The defendant pleaded guilty to blackmail. The defendant's relationship broke up and his girlfriend left without making any provision for the money owing in their joint account. The defendant was having difficulty covering his other debts and commitments. She ignored his letters and his threats of legal action. He then sent a letter demanding £300 within 7 days or personal photographs would be distributed to her place of 'work or home or family or worse.' Fearing he might use the Internet she contacted the police. They found the photographs in his computer. The defendant was 25 with a new partner and her young son and working as software consultant. He had no previous convictions and expressed remorse. **12 months** substituted for 18 months.

R v Q 2002 1 Cr App R (S) 440. The defendant was convicted of blackmail of his ex-wife. He pleaded guilty to indecent assault on a female (not his ex-wife). The defendant and his wife who was 8 years younger than him became involved in group sex with another couple and the sessions were video taped. Professional pornographic photographs were taken and the pictures sold in America with her face shaded out. There was an acrimonious divorce and a wrangle about the sale of the house. At the end the difference was she wanted £16,000 and he was prepared to settle for £7,000. He threatened to show the video tapes to her parents unless she settled for his figure. Both she and her parents sold their stories to newspapers. He was 34 and of good character. The judge described it as, 'an ugly and odious offence.' He said the defendant tried, 'to rake as much muck' as he could and embarrass her during the trial. He described the defendant as 'cocky and arrogant and something of a predator'. Held. The defendant believed in his claim. **15 months** not 2¹/₂ years with the indecent assault sentence reduced to 3 months consecutive.

Att-Gen's Ref. No. 40 of 2002 2003 1 Cr App R (S) 511. The defendant was convicted of six counts of blackmail in relation to the same elderly victim. The victim had lived alone after retiring and the death of his wife. He lived next door to the defendant who knew all about his savings. The defendant got to know a young woman who in turn got to know the victim. She arrived on one occasion at the defendant's house and told him that the victim had touched her in the crotch area over her trousers and on her breasts over her jumper. She told the defendant that she did not want the police involved. The defendant went round to the victim's house with another man, and in return for a handwritten promise that no action would be taken, the victim promised to pay £5000 if she would keep quiet. However, further demands for money were made and over the next 9 days, in a series of 5 payments, the victim handed over a further £69,000. The victim's life savings were £74,000 and after each payment he had been given an assurance that this would be the last time. But the blackmail continued and the victim hanged himself, leaving a note saying that he was being blackmailed. At the time of conviction, nearly £60,000 of the blackmail proceeds were traced and was made subject to a compensation order. The defendant was aged 25 and of good character. The pre-sentence report assessed his risk of re-offending as relatively low. Held. The victim's life had been destroyed. It was a horrible example of the possible consequences of this type of blackmail and why blackmail is regarded as such a wicked offence, once identified by Lord Lane as one of the most vicious crimes in the calendar of criminal offences. Remembering that it was a reference and that before these events the defendant was a decent young man, **8 years** (concurrent on each count).

R v Davies 2004 1 Cr App R (S) 209. The defendant pleaded guilty to three counts of blackmail. He went to a gay meeting place and watched the victim. On the victim's account the victim started rubbing himself "down below". On the defendant's account the victim took out his penis. The defendant did not respond but he followed the victim home. The defendant said to him his behaviour was unacceptable and he intended to report the matter to the police. The victim said he was sorry but the defendant said it could be resolved in another way. A short time later the victim received a note asking for his jewellery and implying he wouldn't be reported,. The victim handed over rings and pendants worth £630. Another note was received asking for £200. Shortly after midnight another note was received saying his neighbours would be told there was a sex offender living locally. The victim then went to the police. The defendant was arrested and initially denied the offence. A month later he admitted it. He was 37 with a number of convictions but the last was a robbery when he was 21. The pre-sentence report said he was an industrious individual who was devoted to his wife and children. He bitterly regretted his actions and his risk assessment was very low. The property was substantially recovered and it was said to have cost more than he had sold it for. There was a very favourable report from the prison. Held. Blackmail is a very nasty offence. A serious view will always be taken but its true gravity does of course vary considerably. The initial allegation had an element of truth about it which made it difficult for the victim to resist. It was an isolated incident and there was strong mitigation. **2¹/₂ years** was not manifestly excessive.

Embarrassing material/allegations which were fabricated or false

22.8   *R v Daniels* 2002 1 Cr App R (S) 443. The defendant pleaded to blackmail. He delivered three letters to the victim demanding at first £2,000 and later £3,000 suggesting he had visited public lavatories several times to have sex with other men and that the writer had had oral sex with him. The notes made it clear that if the money was not paid the writer would inform his employers and his wife about the sex. The note also said the writer had followed the victim and it revealed personal details about the victim. The victim's secretary opened the second letter. The police and his wife were informed and the defendant was arrested when he went to pick up a package. The victim was married and was put under considerable strain. The defendant knew the victim slightly and they were once professional colleagues. The defendant showed animosity to him and over 30 years had gained pleasure from visiting lavatories and picnic sites to watch people having sex together. His motive was purely vindictive and there was no truth in the suggestions made. He was 52 and effectively of good character with a depressive illness for about 13 years. Held. The motives were to some extent strange and irrational. The offence was designed deliberately to cause pain to the victim. Bearing in mind his medical condition **2 years** not 3.

R v Miah 2003 1 Cr App R (S) 379. The defendant pleaded guilty to 11 counts of blackmail and one count of perverting the course of Justice. He and another selected names from the Directory of Directors and in September 2000 he sent to 44 names from the book a pornographic video involving children. Half of the videos were returned to the address given. In November 2000, he sent a letter to the 44 saying their fingerprints were on the videos and they could be linked with the allegations made by the children. The letter asked the receivers to call or face the disruption of their reputation. It gave a mobile phone number. In February 2001, follow up letters were sent purporting to come from a teacher and an audio cassette with an interview of two males describing alleged abuse. A mobile phone number was given and three people rang and £5,000 was demand. One person, a local councillor was particularly distressed and his work was affected. The defendant's home was searched and the Directory with names highlighted and letter drafts were found. Copies of the actual letters were found on his computer. He was arrested and sought to blame others. He was 38 with a driving whilst disqualified conviction and other matters of marginal relevance. The perverting the course of Justice matter was giving his nephew's details when stopped by the police for speeding. He received 4 months consecutive for that. Held. It was a carefully thought out scheme followed up in stages over a period of months. **4 years** was not excessive for the blackmail.

Kidnapping individuals for ransom/debt collecting

22.9   *R v Rashid* 2004 2 Cr App R (S) 16. The defendant then 21 was convicted of kidnapping, false imprisonment and blackmail. The family of the victim owned a corner shop. One evening 3 masked men burst into the shop. The leader fired a handgun and pistol-whipped the victim and one of the other two men bundled him into a waiting car.

He tried to escape but was stabbed in the back by a machete or long bladed knife. His arms were lacerated as he tried to protect himself. He was forced into the car bleeding heavily, handcuffed and put on the floor. After a time he was hooded and transferred to another car. He identified the defendant as one of the men in the car. The defendant looked after him in the bedroom of a house for 30 hours. During that time the defendant threatened him with violence and sexual assault but did not carry out these threats. He bandaged the victim's wounds. Contact was made with the victim's family and a ransom of £75,000 was demanded. Eventually they placed £35,000 in a hut in a park and the defendant took the victim to Bolton hospital and left him there. He had severe and life threatening injuries; a bilateral haemothorax and deep lacerations to his arms and hand. He required surgery and will suffer permanent restriction of movement in both arms. The defendant had no previous convictions for violence and was acquitted of the charge of section 18 wounding. Held. The sentences for false imprisonment and blackmail should have been concurrent to the sentence for kidnapping, as they were part of the same incident. The defendant kept a badly wounding bleeding man in obvious pain for 30 hours while a ransom was arranged. This was a seriously aggravating feature of the kidnapping. **11 years** not **14.**

R v Burgess 2004 2 Cr App R (S) 85. The defendant was convicted of kidnapping. The victim owed him money for drugs. The defendant saw the victim's car parked outside a flat where crack could be bought. When the victim came out he was dragged into a car by D and taken to a flat. The victim was aged 56 and in poor health. He was kept in a damp and unheated room in a flat for about 10 hours. The defendant threatened, punched, and gave him electric shocks with a stun gun. He contacted the victim's daughters and demanded £3,500. She went to the flat and saw her father. She was present when a threat was made to use the stun gun again. When she left, the defendant told her that if she contacted the police he would have no hesitation in 'taking her father out'. She did contact the police and arrangements were made for the victim to be released on payment of the money. The daughter handed over marked money and he was released. The defendant age 35 had been before the courts on 16 previous occasions including aggravated burglary, burglary and section 18 wounding. Held. There was violence of a particularly unpleasant kind although the victim only suffered minor injuries. The victim's family were involved. The sentence was more severe than was appropriate to the circumstances. **7¹/₂ years** not 9. (There was no conviction for blackmail but that is what the motive was.)

R v Chen 2004 2 Cr App R (S) 91. The defendant aged 28 pleaded guilty on re-arraignment to conspiracy to falsely imprison, conspiracy to blackmail and conspiracy to cause GBH. The victim was a fisherman from China whose family had paid a snakehead gang to arrange for him to come to the UK. After he arrived he claimed asylum and worked under a false name in a restaurant in Manchester. On July 5ᵗʰ a phone call was made asking for him in his real name. The caller was told no one of that name worked there. Two men came to the restaurant and again asked for the victim in his real name, but he refused to acknowledge his identity. 5 or 6 other men arrived at the restaurant, beat him and bundled him into a car. He was punched so that his nose bled. Knives were held to his stomach so he couldn't move. He was made to wear a hood and driven to an address in Manchester where he was subject to brutal beatings and kickings and lost control of his bowels. He eventually revealed his real name and his family's phone number in China. He was asked why he had not paid the money he owed the snakeheads and he said no money was outstanding and he would not pay any more. He was beaten again and threatened that the tendons in his arms and legs would be severed so that he would be disabled. Eventually he signed an IOU for £7,000. The next day three men drove him to the address of one of a co-defendant in London. Another co-defendant told him that the beatings would continue. The defendant arrived at this address in London. He told the victim to call his family and tell them to pay the snakeheads. The victim phoned his brother who promised to pay. Over the next 13 days similar calls were made to China, many of them by the defendant. During them the victim was beaten and his family could hear him yelling and screaming over the phone. The victim described the defendant as 'the snakehead' who took the lead role in contacting his family in China and organising everything including the telephone calls. The defendant hit the victim with an iron bar. Another defendant cut his back twice with a knife. On July 19th when it was apparent no money would be forthcoming the victim was released and put on a train to Manchester. The basis of plea was that: he was not a party to the kidnapping; he accepted participating in one of the assaults on the victim; and he was acting on the instructions of others. Held. The defendant was the organiser on the ground. He took the lead in the phone calls. He was frequently present and was well aware of the level of violence being used against the victim. On one occasion he used violence himself. In the face of overwhelming evidence the pleas were only entered on the first day of trial. Most significantly the violence was of a most severe and brutal kind. There were 14 days of sustained torture and the victim was utterly terrified. The bruising to his body was very severe and extensive. His screams were relayed to his family in a sadistic fashion. **13 years** upheld.

R v Malaj 2004 1 Cr App R (S) 414. Both defendants M and L were convicted of kidnapping and ABH. M was convicted of blackmail and false imprisonment, L had already pleaded guilty to those offences. The defendants were seen in a motor car watching premises of a business run by the victim, a man in his 50s. The victim left these premises at 5pm and was threatened with screwdrivers and told to hand over £50,000. He was forced into the boot of a car and driven away where he was kept bound and gagged in the open for about 2 days. He was given drink but no food. During this time telephone demands to his family for £50,000 were made or he would be killed. The victim was told that he would be held for a week before being killed. After two days period he was tied to a tree and repeatedly kicked in the chest. He was taken to a railway station bound and gagged in the boot of a car where the defendants had been told the ransom money would be handed over. The car was identified and followed. M and L were arrested and the victim was taken to hospital. L said that the demands for money were not his idea and denied assault. He asked for forgiveness for his (limited) role. M denied all offences and said that he had been threatened. M and L were 17 and 18 at the time of the offences and both were of good character. L expressed remorse. Held. These offences were aggravated because they were planned and sought a substantial ransom; the victim was appallingly treated with violence; a tape recording was played to his family that indicated that the victim had been seriously mistreated and the victim had been kept for more than 2 days. M's sentence for kidnapping was reduced from 13 to **11 years' detention**; L's from 10 to **8 years' detention**.

Old cases *R v Walters* 1998 2 Cr App R (S) 167 and *R v Mereu* 1998 2 Cr App R (S) 351, (for a summary of this case see the first edition of this book).

Kidnapping individuals for ransom – Children taken

22.10 *R v Hong* 2001 2 Cr App R (S) 509. Three defendants pleaded guilty to blackmail and false imprisonment. A schoolboy aged 14 was kidnapped from Cambridgeshire and taken to London by all three defendants. The parents were asked for £250,000, which was later reduced to £100,000. They were told that otherwise the boy would be killed. The boy was well treated and not threatened with any violence. The men fled after a telephone call doubtless from someone higher up in the plot. The boy was unharmed. The false imprisonment was the more serious crime. Two had their sentences reduced from 12 to **10 years**. The third defendant who had been recruited for his brawn rather than his brains had **9 years** substituted for 11.

Protection rackets – Guideline remarks

22.11   *R v Hoey and Sherwood* 1992 13 Cr App R (S) 177. Blackmail in the form of a protection racket has got to be stamped out at once. This is blatant, arrogant lawlessness and the sooner it is realised that such conduct will always be severely punished by immediate terms of imprisonment the better.

Protection rackets – Cases

22.12   *R v McDonagh* 2003 1 Cr App R (S) 634. The defendant pleaded guilty at a very late stage to two counts of blackmail. The victim was the licensee of a public house. The defendant began to ask for small amounts of money or cigarettes. Then he began to threaten to hurt the victim or his staff. The first count related to the defendant making threats and receiving about £15 in cash. The other count concerned the defendant saying he wanted money and would be back in 15 minutes. Police officers were present and the defendant was arrested when he returned. In interview he said that the licensee whom, he said, felt sorry for him had given him the money. He denied making any threats. At the time of these blackmail offences he had been on licence for two offences of unlawful wounding and one of attempted robbery, for which he had received seven-and-a-half years about five years earlier. There was an unexpired sentence of 17 months and seven days (s. 116 PCC(S) Act 2000). The sentencing judge ordered that he serve 11 months of his previous sentence, reduced as an act of mercy, consecutive to the sentences for the blackmail. A prison report indicated that the defendant had made significant progress in custody. Held. **2 years and 1 year consecutive** (plus recall), not 2 years and 2 years consecutive (plus recall).

Serious violence inflicted

22.13   *R v Chen* 2004 2 Cr App R (S) 91. The defendant aged 28 pleaded guilty on re-arraignment to conspiracy to falsely imprison, conspiracy to blackmail and conspiracy to cause GBH. The victim was a fisherman from China whose family had paid a snakehead gang to arrange for him to come to the UK. After he arrived he claimed asylum and worked under a false name in a restaurant in Manchester. On July 5th a phone call was made asking for him in his real name. The caller was told no one of that name worked there. Two men came to the restaurant and again asked for the victim in his real name, but he refused to acknowledge his identity. 5 or 6 other men arrived at the restaurant, beat him and bundled him into a car. He was punched so that his nose bled. Knives were held to his stomach so he couldn't move. He was made to wear a hood and driven to an address in Manchester where he was subject to brutal beatings and kickings and lost control of his bowels. He eventually revealed his real name and his family's phone number in China. He was asked why he had not paid the money he owed the snakeheads and he said no money was outstanding and he would not pay any more. He was beaten again and threatened that the tendons in his arms and legs would be severed so that he would be disabled. Eventually he signed an IOU for £7,000. The next day three men drove him to the address of one of a co-defendant in London. Another co-defendant told him that the beatings would continue. The defendant arrived at this address in London. He told the victim to call his family and tell them to pay the snakeheads. The victim phoned his brother who promised to pay. Over the next 13 days similar calls were made to China, many of them by the defendant. During them the victim was beaten and his family could hear him yelling and screaming over the phone. The victim described the defendant as 'the snakehead' who took the lead role in contacting his family in China and organising everything including the telephone calls. The defendant hit the victim with an iron bar. Another defendant cut his back twice with a knife. On July 19th when it was apparent no money would be forthcoming the victim was released and put on a train to Manchester. The basis of plea was that: he was not a party to the kidnapping; he accepted participating in one of the assaults on the victim;

and he was acting on the instructions of others; Held. The defendant was the organiser on the ground. He took the lead in the phone calls. He was frequently present and was well aware of the level of violence being used against the victim. On one occasion he used violence himself. In the face of overwhelming evidence the pleas were only entered on the first day of trial. Most significantly the violence was of a most severe and brutal kind. There were 14 days of sustained torture and the victim was utterly terrified. The bruising to his body was very severe and extensive. His screams were relayed to his family in a sadistic fashion. **13 years** upheld.

Supermarkets and retail stores

22.14 *R v Riolfo* 1997 1 Cr App R (S) 57. The defendant pleaded guilty to blackmail. Between January and April 1995, he threatened Tesco's supermarket that the food had been contaminated with the AIDS virus. He also threatened to inform the press. He demanded £250,000. The money was to be transferred by bank cash machines. He received £7,500 by using a card 73 times. He was caught by police surveillance. It was a sophisticated operation. Nothing was actually infected but an inert substance was injected into certain produce. The defendant was of good character and had lived an industrious life. He had also co-operated with the police. He had had a heart attack and was depressed at the time. **6 years** not 8.

R v Banot 1997 2 Cr App R (S) 50. The defendant pleaded to three counts of blackmail. Harrods received a letter threatening to sabotage their merchandise or their building and demanding £5m. It also said a coded message was to be put in the Evening Standard. This was done. The police mounted a covert operation. Another demand was received. This one contained a threat that food would be poisoned and rodents would be put in the store. Telephone calls were made and the defendant said she could go down to £1m. A threat to set fire to the store was also made. Another man was recruited and there were more telephone calls. The two were arrested. The defendant was 42 and was effectively of good character. She had a significant personality disorder. Held. The judge was right to refer to how vulnerable well-known organisations were and how many resources had been deployed to deal with it. **5 years** substituted for 8 partly because of her personal circumstances.

R v Pearce 2000 2 Cr App R (S) 50. See **EXPLOSIVE OFFENCES** – *Blackmail, and*

R v Dyer 2002 2 Cr App R (S) 490. The defendant pleaded guilty at the first opportunity to 9 counts of blackmail and common assault. Not guilty verdicts were accepted for sending an explosive substance and causing an explosive substance. Both were with an intent to cause GBH. The defendant was short of money and repeatedly demanded £200,000 from Tesco. The money was to be withdrawn from automatic telling machines by way of specially prepared loyalty cards. There were also messages posted in a local paper for communication with the store. After the first letter a post box was set alight. Later, two married pensioners in their seventies received a padded envelope in the post. It exploded creating a large flash and bang in the face of the wife. Smoke got in her eyes and she was in some discomfort for a time. Both were shaken. The device was made of shotgun cartridge powder and match heads. That was the common assault. Seven identical letters were delivered to Tesco customers in the area. The letter said anyone seen shopping in Tesco would be a potential target for bombs. The letters referred to bombs that had been sent to four addresses including the pensioners'. At the three other addresses their packages were at the depot because there was insufficient postage on them. Those packages contained a similar device to the one that went off. Next month a letter said the next generation was ready. Map references were given as to where a bomb was. It covered an area of a square kilometre. 100 police officers, army personnel and bomb disposal officers tried to find it. A month later a further letter was received saying there was no bomb but there was no time to waste. The campaign lasted about six months but he never received any money. The Judge concluded that it was an evil campaign of extortion and intimidation. The planning was with devious cunning and meticulous care. Many customers had been put in fear and there had been enormous public anxiety. Tesco's had incurred great expense and there had been a very extensive police operation. He was 51 and of good character. Held. 14 years in total gave insufficient discount for the plea so **12 years**.

See also **BOMB HOAX ETC.** *Sending false messages Demands made* and **FOOD ETC, CONTAMINATION OF**

23 BLADED ARTICLE, POSSESSION OF A

23.1 Criminal Justice Act 1988 s 139

Triable either way. On indictment maximum sentence 2 years. Summary maximum 6 months and/or £5,000.

The Criminal Justice Act 2003 creates a summary maximum sentence of 51 weeks, a minimum custodial sentence of 28 weeks and Custody plus. The Home Office says they do not expect to introduce these provisions before September 2006.

Magistrates' Court Sentencing Guidelines January 2004

23.2 For a first time offender pleading not guilty. Entry point. Is it so serious that only custody is appropriate? Consider the impact on the victim. Examples of aggravating factors for the offence are group action or joint possession, location of offence, offender under influence of drink or drugs, people put in fear/weapon brandished, planned use and very dangerous weapon. Examples of mitigating factors for the offence are acting out of a genuine fear, carried only on a temporary basis, no attempt to use the weapon and offence not premeditated. Examples of mitigation are age, health (physical or mental), co-operation with the police and genuine remorse.

For details about the guidelines see **MAGISTRATES' COURT SENTENCING GUIDELINES** at page 483.

Weapon not produced

23.3 *R v Datson* 1999 1 Cr App R (S) 84. The defendant pleaded guilty to possessing a bladed article. The defendant was in a public house and moved a knife from his belongings to beneath his jacket. Someone saw and informed the police. The defendant initially refused to be searched but then showed the police the knife in a sheath in his waistband. He told police he had come across the knife when moving items from his former matrimonial home at the request of his partner. Held. We see no reason to disbelieve his account. He had convictions for violence but none for 8 years. The appropriate sentence was community service not immediate custody. As he had served 3 weeks in custody a **conditional discharge** not 2 months.

R v Baldwin 2000 1 Cr App R (S) 81. The defendant pleaded guilty to possessing a bladed article. The defendant was stopped in a supermarket with a trolley with £200 worth of goods in it and arrested for stealing them. Police were called and they found a 5" knife in his sock. He said it was for his own protection. He was 33 and a drug addict with a terrible record for dishonesty. There were no convictions for carrying a weapon. No evidence was offered on the shoplifting count. **6 months** not 18.

R v Brooks and Macintosh 2004 2 Cr App R (S) 357. B was convicted of possession of a bladed article and M pleaded guilty to possession of an offensive weapon. M and a doorman at a public house got into an argument and police were called. M was asked to turn out his pockets and B offered to take the items. A police officer looked at them and found a flick knife hidden within a lighter. B and M were arrested. B volunteered she had a knife in her bag. It was a rusty knife with a five-inch blade. The judge sentenced them on the basis that they went out to licensed premises each knowing the other was armed. Both defendants had previous convictions for violence. M was remorseful and because of this matter had been unable to travel to the US where both of his parents had died to attend their funerals. The court heard there was a job waiting for him if he were to be released in the near future. Held. The sentencing basis suggested that B was involved in the possession of an offensive weapon and they should not have been jointly rather than individually dealt with. M's deprivation of being unable to grieve for his parents was an exceptional circumstance. We also have regard to the employment offered M. **3 months** for B, not 6 and as an exceptional course **3 months** for M not 8.

See also OFFENSIVE WEAPON, POSSESSION OF A

24   BOMB HOAX – PLACING OR DISPATCHING ARTICLES OR SENDING FALSE MESSAGES

24.1   Criminal Law Act 1977 s 51(1) and (2)

The two offences are: (1) placing ... or dispatching an article ... with the intention of inducing in some other person a belief ... that it will explode or ignite ... and (2) communicating any information which he knows or believes to be false to another person with the intention of inducing in him ... a false belief that a bomb or other thing ... liable to explode or ignite is present etc.

Triable either way. On indictment maximum 7 years. Summary maximum 6 months and/or £5,000 fine.

The Criminal Justice Act 2003 creates a summary maximum sentence of 51 weeks, a minimum custodial sentence of 28 weeks and Custody plus. The Home Office says they do not expect to introduce these provisions before September 2006.

Hostage, taking hostage as well

24.2   *R v Mason* 2002 1 Cr App R (S) 122. The defendant pleaded guilty to communicating false information with intent. The prosecution dropped a count of endangering an aircraft and common assault. The defendant was politically active in Trinidad and believed his life was in danger. He went to Switzerland to alert the United Nations about his plight and to claim political asylum. His application was refused and he was put on a plane to Gatwick so he could travel back to Trinidad. He wanted to draw attention to his plight and problems. About 10 minutes before the plane was due to land he took hold of a female member of crew and grabbed her by the neck. A blade of a pair of scissors was held to her throat. She was terrified and he said 'This is a fucking hijack.' Another crew member came to help and she was told there was a bomb on the plane and he threatened to kill his hostage unless his demands were met. He indicated that his Dictaphone was a bomb, which he could activate by pressing a button. The captain arrived and he was told there was a bomb on the plane and that he was to radio the defendant's demands for political asylum to the UK authorities. The captain eventually persuaded the defendant to release his hostage who had been held for a few minutes. The defendant was arrested when the plane landed. He admitted the offence and said he wanted the hostage to feel as frightened as he did about returning to his own country. The hostage was severely traumatised. Some of the passengers were upset and frightened. He was 62 and had no convictions in the UK where he lived for 3 years in the 1990s. He said he had committed a robbery in Barbados. The judge referred to the serious situation of co-pilot landing the aircraft on his own and the injuries to the neck despite the charges, which had been dropped by the prosecution. Held. It was an extremely serious offence. The judge was entitled to take into account the danger to the aircraft. Sentences needed to deter others who wanted to secure their political ends. There was nothing wrong about the **4 years** sentence.

Placing an article with intent

24.3   *R v Bosworth* 1998 1 Cr App R (S) 356. The defendant pleaded guilty to placing an article. The defendant forced a DHL driver to stop and gave him a jiffy bag. The defendant said, 'Make sure Melvyn Ball gets this. Melvyn Ball at DHL.' The driver looked inside and saw there was a hand grenade. The defendant walked away saying, 'Make sure he gets it or you'll never fucking walk again.' The grenade was found to be genuine but with no pin or explosive. The defendant was an ex-employee of DHL with a grudge against them. He had been reprimanded for failing to find a suspicious parcel in a test. He was 29 and had no convictions. Held. It was a very serious and planned offence. A man had been caused great fear. **12 months** was the least he could have hoped to receive.

R v Spencer 1999 Unreported 1/10/98. The defendant pleaded guilty at the Magistrates' Court to (it appears) placing an article and communicating a false message. A package looking like a home made bomb was found by police. The area was evacuated and a controlled explosion took place. Two to three weeks later a call to the ambulance service was made saying there had been a traffic accident. Later a call was made to the police saying there had been no response to the first call. The defendant admitted being responsible for the bomb and the calls. The defendant was mentally retarded and required a great deal of care from his family and others. He was of good character. Held. The court passed a lenient sentence taking into account the defendant's difficulties. The bomb constructed by the defendant was realistic. We are influenced that when he is released from his sentence he will be supervised. **12 months** was not manifestly excessive.

Sending false messages – Demands made

24.4   *R v Barker* 1997 Unreported 7/5/97. The defendant pleaded guilty. He was in dispute with a company over an invention of his. He attached a wire round the company premises, which appeared to go to a parked car. He informed the police there was petrol in a bottle at the end of the wire and it would explode but not hurt anyone. It turned out to be harmless. The police negotiated with the defendant who was demanding money from the company. His solicitor had told him his actions were not illegal. Held. The advice was remarkable. The sentencing bracket was 1–2 years. **9 months** was upheld.

See also **BLACKMAIL**

Sending false messages – No financial demands made

24.5   *R v Harrison* 1997 2 Cr App R (S) 174. The defendant pleaded guilty at the Magistrates' Court to four charges of communicating false information. He made four calls to the London Coliseum Theatre between 5.35 and 6.45pm. The first said there was a bag in the vicinity of the theatre that looked suspicious. The second said he was a member of the IRA and he had planted a bomb in a bin and it was due to go off at 6.30pm that evening and asking why the theatre had not been evacuated. The third said he had seen two men and it was a bomb. The fourth said he was going to operate the bomb by remote control at 7pm and it contained 100lbs. of Semtex. It was a rambling conversation lasting 6 or 7 minutes and it was plain he was under the influence of drink.

He was found in a telephone box making the last call. He admitted the offence. The defendant was 34 and had many previous court appearances. First in 1984 for arson; second in 1988 for arson (probation); third and fourth for dishonesty; fifth in 1991, two for this offence – sending a false message (he had called the fire brigade twice saying there was a fire) (probation); sixth, four bomb hoax offences and using a telephone to send false messages to cause annoyance (he had called the emergency services saying there was a bomb) (2 years and 3 months for breach of probation); seventh in 1994 for calling the fire brigade to attend a non existent fire (fined) and eighth minor dishonesty. He had a personality disorder and needed help for his alcohol problem. His likelihood of re-offending was high. Held. The appropriate sentence for the offence before looking at the defendant was probably near 2 years before a discount for the plea. We have to bear in mind the danger to the public. The only answer is longer periods of custody. **4 years** was severe but not manifestly too long.

R v Cann 2005 1 Cr App R (S) 48. The defendant pleaded guilty before Magistrates to 3 offences of communicating a bomb hoax. On the first occasion he made a call stating that there was a pink bag in a bin near a specified church. Resources were gathered and police officers were deployed to the scene. He rang again later the same evening saying that the police were not dealing with the bomb very well and that the bomb was sensitive and if it were not touched it would go off in an hour. He gave a false name. The next day he telephoned the police to say that there was a bomb in a black car parked in a street. He gave the same false name and was ringing from the same mobile phone. Again the police deployed the necessary resources and made enquiries to trace the subscriber of the phone. The following day, he telephoned on the same mobile phone and gave the same name and again said that there was a bomb in the same black car. He said that the vehicle was in an alleyway. He gave the general location and said that the bomb would go off if it was touched. From his phone details the police attended his home and he was arrested. He implied that it was his neighbour (to whom, he said, he had sold the phone). The neighbour was interviewed but said that although she had bought the phone, she was not sold the SIM card. The defendant later pleaded guilty. He was 22 with no previous convictions. Held. These sorts of offences have always in modern times to be regarded of great seriousness and requiring deterrent sentences. However, **21 months** not 30.

BREACH

See **ANTI-SOCIAL BEHAVIOURAL ORDER, BREACH OF; DRUG TREATMENT AND TESTING ORDER, BREACH OF; RESTRAINING ORDER, BREACH OF** and **SEX OFFENDER ORDER, BREACH OF**

BROTHEL

See **PROSTITUTION**

25   BUGGERY/ASSAULT WITH INTENT TO COMMIT BUGGERY

25.1   These offences were abolished on 1/5/04. Offences from that date should be charged under Sexual Offences Act 2003 s 1, 2, 6 and 69 see **RAPE, SEXUAL ASSAULT BY PENETRATION** and **SEXUAL ASSAULTS ETC. CHILDREN**

Sexual Offences Act 1956 s 12 – Buggery.

Indictable only. Maximum sentence if with a person under 16 or with an animal life imprisonment. If the defendant is 21 or over and the other party is under 18 maximum 5 years (This would apply if the offence was between men and not in private). Otherwise 2 years.

Sexual Offences Act 1956 s 16 – Assault with intent to commit buggery.

Indictable only. Maximum sentence 10 years.

Longer than Commensurate sentences and Extended sentences Both offences are sexual offences for the purposes of passing a longer than commensurate sentence [Powers of Criminal Courts (Sentencing) Act 2000 s 80(2)] and an extended sentence (extending the licence) [Powers of Criminal Courts (Sentencing) Act 2000 s 85(2)(b)][4]. The orders cannot be made for offences committed before 30/9/98 or after 3/4/05.

Notification Where the victim is aged less than 18 at the time of the offence and the defendant is 20 or over and is sentenced to imprisonment or detained in a hospital[5]; the defendant must notify the police within 3 days (or 3 days from his release from imprisonment, hospital etc.) with his name, home address, national insurance number etc. and any change and addresses where he resides for 7 days[6] (in one or more periods) or more in any 12 month period[7]. See SEX OFFENDERS' REGISTER

Working with children Where the offence is against a child (under 16 for buggery and under 18 years for assault with intent) the defendant is aged 18 or over and he is sentenced to 12 months or more etc. or hospital order etc. the court must disqualify him from working with children unless satisfied he is unlikely to commit any further offences against a child when the court must state its reasons for not doing so[8]. For a defendant aged less than 18 at the time of the offence the court must order disqualification if he is sentenced to 12 months or more and the court is satisfied that the defendant will commit a further offence against a child[9]. The court must state its reasons for so doing.

Sexual Offences Prevention Order For these three offences when the notification (see above) criteria are present, there is a discretionary power to make this order when it is necessary to protect the public etc[10].

See also RAPE – *Anal* and RAPE – *Male*

Crown Court statistics – England and Wales – Males 21+
25.2

| Year | Plea | Total Numbers sentenced | Type of sentence % | | | | | Average length of custody (months) |
			Discharge	Fine	Community sentence	Suspended sentence	Custody	
2002	Guilty	27	–	–	4	4	93	63.4
	Not guilty	21	–	–	–	10	90	79.4
2003	Guilty	31	–	–	3	–	97	67.7
	Not guilty	32	—	–	–	–	100	92.2

For details and explanations about the statistics in the book see page vii.

4 Powers of Criminal Courts (Sentencing) Act 2000 s 161(3)
5 Sexual Offences Act 2003 s 80(1)(a) & Sch 3 Para 5 & 9
6 Sexual Offences Act 2003 s 84(1)(c) & (6)
7 Sexual Offences Act 2003 s 83
8 Criminal Justice and Court Services Act 2000 s 28
9 Criminal Justice and Court Services Act 2000 s 29
10 Sexual Offences Act 2003 s 104 & Sch. 3

Guideline case

25.3 *Att-Gen's Ref. No 17 of 1990* 1990 92 Cr App R 288. LCJ There are five aspects which the sentencing Judge should take into account for offences against young children. First, the overall gravity of the offence. Secondly, the necessity for punishment. Thirdly, the necessity to protect the public. Fourthly, the public concern for sexual offences on young children. Fifthly, the deterrent effect.

Old case *R v Willis* 1975 60 Cr App R 146 (This case can no longer be properly applied as non consensual buggery has become rape and the Sexual Offences Act 2003 has transformed the law about homosexual offences to reflect an entirely different attitude to them since 1975.)

Guideline remarks

25.4 Att-*Gen's Ref. Nos. 91, 119 and 120 of 2002*, 2003 2 Cr App R (S) 338 In *R v Millberry* 2003 2 Cr App R (S) 142 at para 8, the Lord Chief Justice said 'There are, broadly three dimensions to consider in assessing the gravity of an individual offence of rape. The first is the degree of harm to the victim; the second is the level of culpability of the offender; and the third is the level of risk proposed by the offender to society. The gravity of each case will depend very much upon the circumstances and it will always be necessary to consider an individual case as a whole taking into account the three dimensions.'

It will be necessary to take account of similar considerations in all cases of sexual interference, whether amounting to rape or not. However, that is not all. In all classes of sexual offences, there will also be the need to deter others from acting in a similar fashion.

Buggery charged when anal rape suggested

25.5 *R v Davies* 1998 1 Cr App R (S) 380. The defendant aged now 21 was convicted of buggery and under age sex [Sexual Offences Act 1956, s 6(1)] with his girlfriend then aged 15. The judge sentenced him on the basis there was no consent. If a man is convicted of buggery it is wrong to sentence him for rape. Where non-consensual sexual intercourse is alleged it must be charged as rape.

Historic abuse – Guideline remarks

25.6 Att-*Gen's Ref. Nos. 91, 119 and 120 of 2002*, 2003 2 Cr App R (S) 338. In *R v Millberry* 2003 2 Cr App R (S) 142, the fact that the offences are of some age is not necessarily a sufficient reason for imposing a lesser sentence than might otherwise have been the case. In Millberry the Court said at para 17: 'in relation to "historic" cases where the offence is reported many years after it occurred. In these cases, also, we consider that the same starting point should apply. The fact that the offences are stale can be taken into account but only to a limited extent. It is, after all, always open to an offender to admit the offences and the fact that they are not reported earlier is often explained because of the relationship between the offender and the victim, which is an aggravating factor of the offence. A different factor that could cause the court to take a more lenient view than it would otherwise is the consequences, which result from the age of the offender. In these cases the experience is that the offender may be only a danger to members of the family with whom he has a relationship. So this is a dimension which can be taken into account if there is a reduced risk of re-offending.'

The same approach is equally applicable to all categories of sexual offending. Where the victims have kept secret what had happened, sometimes following threats made or inducements offered and sometimes out of a sense of shame about what has been done to her, this of itself can aggravate the harm caused by the offence. Before passing a lighter sentence because the offences are stale, the court should weigh the impact on the victim of the matter having remained secret for so long.

Historic abuse

25.7 *R v Leckey* 1999 1 Cr App R (S) 57. The defendant was convicted of large number of counts of buggery and indecent assaults on boys (touching penises, masturbation simulated intercourse etc). There was a group of offences from 1972 to the late 1970s involving six boys aged from 8 to 15 and buggery aged from 11 years. Boys were given gifts and taken on trips. The second group was in 1995 and related to a boy aged 16 and involved masturbation and oral sex. The defendant had no previous convictions. 12 years for the 1970 offences upheld but the consecutive sentence for the later offences reduced from 6 to 3 years making **15 years** not 18 years in all. [Since the appeal the age of consent has been reduced so the second set of offences would no longer be criminal.]

R v Bowers 1999 2 Cr App R (S) 97. The defendant pleaded guilty to five counts of buggery on 2 boys. The offences were committed when the defendant was between 15 and 18. He was 42 when convicted and was a member of a Lads' club as a teenager and abused younger members of the group. The two boys were attacked over a period of 3 years when they were between 8 and 11. He co-operated with the police. The judge noted that the defendant, as an older boy, was in a position of responsibility at the club, and by a combination of encouragement, moneys and treats he systematically abused the boys. One boy suffered deep-rooted psychological problems as a result. The defendant had two unrelated previous convictions. He had excellent references. Because he had now married and had four children the risk of re-offending was assessed as low. Held. The sentence that would have been passed at the time of the offences was a starting point and powerful factor in determining the sentence. That would have been Borstal so **2 years** not 7.

R v R 2000 2 Cr App R (S) 314. The defendant was convicted of attempted buggery of his stepson then aged 10 in 1982–3 and indecent assault (touching and ejaculation) on his daughter when aged 4–5 in 1982–3. There were no threats. He tried to bugger the stepson but he stopped when told it hurt and told the boy to do the same to him but the boy couldn't get an erection. The defendant was now 69 and in poor health. He had no previous convictions. **4 years** and 1 year consecutive was not manifestly excessive.

R v Alden and Wright 2001 2 Cr App R (S) 401. The first defendant A was convicted of 10 counts of buggery, five counts of indecent assault and gross indecency. There were four victims of the buggery and six in all. The second defendant W was convicted of six counts of attempted buggery and four counts of indecent assaults. There were four victims. The victims of both defendants were pupils at an approved school aged between 13 and 16. Many of the boys were vulnerable having been neglected, abused or assaulted. A now 66 committed the offences over a 17 year period from 1966 when he was house master to when he was deputy headmaster. Two boys experienced, 'pain nothing like I'd experienced before,' and 'unbearable pain.' Favours were given and threats made. W now 56 was a housemaster and was then 23–26. His offences were from 1966–9. He used home leave to bribe the boys. Both were of good character. **15 years** for A was fully deserved. **8 years** accurately reflects the factors in W's case.

Att-Gen's Ref. Nos. 35 etc. of 2003 Re GS 2004 1 Cr App R (S) 499 at 542. The defendant was convicted of three counts of buggery and two counts of indecency with a child. The defendant was living with the victim 30 years earlier with other members of the victim's family. When the victim was 11 the defendant took him into the bathroom where he was told to kneel down; Brylcreem was smeared on his bottom and his anus was penetrated by the defendant's penis. On another occasion the victim was taken to a derelict house and penetrated similarly without a lubricant. He cried with pain but the defendant did not desist. There was another occasion of buggery. The victim was also forced to perform oral sex upon the defendant as well as masturbate him. When questioned, the defendant denied the offences. He was 61 and of good character. Held.

This was sexual abuse of young and corruptible boys. The buggery was repeated and the offences occurred over four years. This was also a breach of trust and the victim had suffered significantly. These offences were not committed under the current legislation and so the court could not approach this case as one of male rape; if these offences had been, then significantly longer sentences were required. **6 years** for buggery and 12 months concurrent for indecent assault were right at the lower end of the range for that time.

Att-Gen's Ref. No. 71 of 2003 2004 2 Cr App R (S) 229. The defendant was convicted of four counts of indecent assault on a male, one count of indecency with a child and one of buggery. The assaults happened between 1976 and 1980 when he had abused a boy then aged between 10 and 13. When these events began the defendant was 39 or 40. He took the boy to a laboratory with his father's permission at weekends and abused him, the nature of the abuse escalating over time. The counts related to fondling the victim's private parts over his clothing; touching the victim's penis; performing oral sex on him; smearing Vaseline on the victim's penis and persuading him to bugger the defendant, and buggering the victim and ejaculating inside him. The defendant also made sexual advances to the boy's brother when he was 15 or 16. The victim's interest in his studies declined, he became depressed and was referred to an educational psychologist and he felt dirty and as though he couldn't tell anyone what happened. The aggravating features were that the defendant groomed his victim, he was in gross breach of trust, the boy was very young and there was a considerable gap between his and the defendant's age, the offences were repeated over a long time and they were grave including penetration and oral sex. The defendant, aged 66, suffered from migraines and was caring for his wife who had slowly progressing leukaemia. He had impressive character references. He had one conviction in 1970 for gross indecency with a male. Held. We would have expected a sentence of **6 years**. As it is a reference **4** years not 2 years suspended.

Life sentence – Automatic life for second serious offence
25.8   Powers of Criminal Courts (Sentencing) Act 2000 s 109

R v Wood 2001 1 Cr App R 20. An old offence of non-consensual buggery, (which would now be rape) is not a serious offence for the purposes of the Act.

Life sentence, is it appropriate?
25.9   *R v Bellamy* 2001 1 Cr App R 116. The defendant pleaded guilty to 23 sex abuse counts on five boys aged 12–14 including four counts of buggery and 1 attempted buggery. The abuse lasted 5 years and included inserting objects into the boys' anuses and video recording the activity with the defendant directing every movement. The defendant was aged 50 with two appearances for indecent assaults on boys. The boy in the first case was 14 and the boys in the second case were 13, 14 and 15. The psychiatrist said he had a continuing history of sustained paedophile interest over many years and he falls into a high-risk group in relation to re-offending. He was not in a position of trust to the boys. **Life** was appropriate.

Life sentence – Fixing specified term
25.10   *R v Archer* 1999 2 Cr App R 92. The defendant, a life long paedophile, was sentenced to life for five buggery counts and 10 years in all for 10 indecent assaults counts. He had been sentenced for a string of sex offences since 1955. Held. The appropriate determinate sentence would have been 12 years. Dividing that amount by two and reducing that figure for the time he had spent in custody meant the period should be 5 years 8 months not 9 years. The 10 year sentence was reduced to **8 years** to ensure that he did not remain in prison for the less serious offences after he might have been released for the more serious matters.

Longer than commensurate sentences

25.11   Powers of Criminal Courts (Sentencing) Act 2000 s 80(2)(b) ... the custodial sentence shall be ... where the offence is a violent or sexual offence, for such longer term (not exceeding the maximum) as in the opinion of the court is necessary to protect the public from serious harm from the offender. [previously the Criminal Justice Act 1991 s 2(2)(b).]

Att-Gen's Ref. No 7 of 1997 1998 1 Cr App R (S) 268. The defendant was convicted of seven counts of buggery with boys between 12 and 14 years, four counts of indecent assaults and one offence of possessing indecent photographs. The offences all related to boys between 11 and 15 over a 6 or 7 year period. Held. Because of his good character the judge was not wrong to fail to use the [now s 80(2)(b)] provisions. However, the court said they were not saying the judge would have been wrong if he had used them.

See also LONGER THAN COMMENSURATE SENTENCES

Private, not in

25.12   *R v Bavishi* 2003 1 Cr App R (S) 541. The defendant pleaded guilty to consensual buggery of a male (then 16) in a public place in October 2001. The other male had admitted that he was homosexual and had had sex on a couple of occasions before this incident. The two had met via an internet chat room and had arranged to meet in a secluded wooded area, a place where homosexual encounters were known to have taken place. A complaint of rape was originally made and the defendant had spent nine days in custody. Held. This was a case only just over the borderline of criminal activity. There was next to no chance that being confronted with this sexual activity would embarrass anyone. The offending was minimal. A **conditional discharge** not a fine. (As the defendant had spent the 9 days in custody he had served a greater punishment than the offence deserved. Therefore it would seem wrong to enable a court to re-sentence him if there was a breach. It is suggested the appropriate penalty was £50 or 1 day.)

Stepfathers

25.13   *R v D* 2000 1 Cr App R (S) 120. The defendant was convicted of attempted buggery and two counts of indecent assaults on his stepdaughter when aged 14–15. All the counts were specimen counts. The attempted offence took place in a garden shed. The indecent assaults related to regular consensual sexual intercourse. He was treated as of good character. Sentenced by the Court of Appeal on the basis she might have consented to the attempt. **3 years** and not 7 years with 18 months concurrent for the assaults.

R v R 2000 2 Cr App R (S) 314. The defendant was convicted of attempted buggery of his stepson then aged 10 in 1982–3 and indecent assault (touching and ejaculation) on his daughter when aged 4–5 in 1982–3. There were no threats. He tried to bugger the stepson but he stopped when told it hurt and told the boy to do the same to him but the boy couldn't get an erection. The defendant was now 69 and in poor health. He had no previous convictions. **4 years** and 1 year consecutive was not manifestly excessive.

Taking advantage when victim drunk etc

25.14   *R v Dalton* 2000 2 Cr App R 87. The defendant aged 19 pleaded guilty to buggery of a drunken woman aged 16. She approached him first and after having sex he entered her anally possibly by accident. She appeared to be consenting. Further vaginal intercourse took place. The defendant gave evidence during a Newton enquiry that he didn't know she was drunk. He was disbelieved. The defendant had an impressive reference from his employer. Because the defendant had been in custody after his arrest and after the sentence before being admitted to bail **3 months** not 6 months detention. [The public may question the necessity to use up valuable detention space for an offence most police forces would not consider processing]

Trust, gross breach of (teacher, foster parent etc)

25.15   *R v Paget* 1998 1 Cr App R 80. The defendant was convicted of eight counts of buggery and eight counts of indecent assaults on boys (masturbation and oral sex). It was persistently over 4$^{1}/_{2}$ years on five boys when aged 11–16. He was a foster parent to one and one was allowed to live with him. There were incidents of violence and intimidation. Rewards were given. The defendant had no previous convictions. Held. Buggery sentences of 4 and 5 years with indecent assault counts of 3 years and the five groups of counts being made consecutive totalling **20 years** was not manifestly excessive.

Att-Gen's Ref. No 7 of 1997 1998 1 Cr App R (S) 268. The defendant was convicted of seven counts of buggery with boys between 12 and 14 years, four counts of indecent assaults and one offence of possessing indecent photographs. He entered a late plea to showing indecent photographs. The offences all related to boys between 11 and 15 over a 6 or 7 year period. The defendant now aged 29 showed the boys pornographic films and gave them alcohol and cannabis. Threats were made if the boys told anyone. He made a film about inserting a bottle into a boy's anus. The victims were vulnerable because of their home circumstances. One boy was given permission by the local authority to live with him. At least one had permanent psychological damage as a result of the offences. The defendant had no previous convictions. Held. The judge was not wrong to fail to use the longer than normal sentencing provisions. The appropriate sentence would have been **at least 10 years**. Taking into account it was a reference **9 years** not 7.

R v Alden and Wright 2001 2 Cr App R (S) 401. The first defendant A was convicted of ten counts of buggery, five counts of indecent assault and gross indecency. There were four victims of the buggery and six in all. The second defendant W was convicted of six counts of attempted buggery and four indecent assaults. There were 4 victims. The victims were pupils at an approved school aged between 13 and 16. Many of the boys were vulnerable having been neglected, abused or assaulted. A now 66 committed the offences over a 17 year period from 1966 when he was house master to when he was deputy headmaster. Two boys experienced, 'pain nothing like I'd experienced before,' and 'unbearable pain.' Favours were given and threats made. W now 56 was a housemaster and was then 23–26. His offences were from 1966–9. He used home leave to bribe them. Both were of good character. **15 years** for A was fully deserved. **8 years** accurately reflects the factors in W's case.

Victim aged under 10

25.16   *R v Bowers* 1999 2 Cr App R (S) 97 (See **Para 25.7**)

Victim aged 10–12

25.17   *R v Sullivan* 1999 1 Cr App R (S) 89. The defendant pleaded guilty to three counts of buggery which took place between 1969 and 1972. He and his wife lived near the victim's family and invited the boy then aged 10 to help with some gardening. He took him to a box room ostensibly to show him some guns and records. After messing him around he pushed the victim face down on the floor, removed his jeans and under-pants, forced his legs apart and buggered him. It was very painful. Over the next 2 to 3 years he buggered him on many weekends. He stayed over and was buggered on Friday night and Saturday afternoon. The boy stopped going when he was 12 and had heard it was wrong. The victim suffered trauma and hated the company of men. He found relationships with women difficult. He got married and had three children who he could not pick up. He told his wife about the offences and they split up. The victim reported the offences to the police when he saw the defendant with children. Earlier he had threatened the defendant that he would report him. The defendant was arrested and admitted the offences. He was 73 and of good character and spent his time caring for his wife who he had been married to for 48 years. After his arrest he attempted suicide and had been impotent for 14 years. The minister of the local Church said the defendant had confessed to him and the defendant was a well respected member of the church who helped the disadvantaged. His behaviour in prison was very much to his credit. Held. The sentence was not manifestly excessive. However, it was possible to show mercy particularly because of the defendant's age so **4 years** not 6.

R v Iverson 2000 2 Cr App R 167. The defendant aged 36 pleaded guilty to buggery of a 12 year old girl, two specimen counts of under-aged sex, from when she was 13, and two specimen counts of indecent assault. The offences involved the same girl when she was 12–14. He was in a relationship with her. The buggery caused her pain and thereafter she always refused his requests to repeat it. Gross abnormalities were caused to her vagina and her anus because of her age. She had been seriously disturbed by what had happened. He admitted she expressed love for him but he used her for sex. He had no previous convictions and was married. **5 years** was severe but not manifestly excessive.

R v Clark 2001 1 Cr App R 197. The defendant aged 36 pleaded guilty to three counts of attempted buggery of a boy when 11–13, and 4 counts of indecent assault on the same boy. There was also a TIC for an unspecified offence on a boy when he acted as a scoutmaster. The defendant was a friend of the family of the boy, took him on trips and gave him gifts. Each time the defendant tried to bugger the boy the boy flinched or otherwise indicated he wasn't enjoying it and he desisted. The activity was over a 2 year period. He made full admissions and showed deep remorse. **5¹/₂ years** not 7 with an extended supervision order.

R v Bellamy 2001 1 Cr App R 116. The defendant pleaded guilty to 23 sex abuse cases on five boys aged 12–14 including four counts of buggery and 1 attempted buggery. The abuse lasted 5 years and included inserting objects into the boys' anuses and video recording the activity with the defendant directing every movement. The defendant was aged 50. He was not in a position of trust to the boys. Held. **Life** was appropriate (taking into account the protection of the public and his previous convictions.) The appropriate determinate sentence would have been 16 years.

R v Barker 2001 1 Cr App R 514. The defendant pleaded guilty to two counts of buggery, gross indecency with a child and three counts of indecent assault on a male. They related to two boys then aged 12 and 16. He was also committed for sentence for gross indecency with a child. There were three offences taken into consideration, which were masturbation and oral sex on a boy aged 10–11. After the 16 year old had been drinking, he and another had consensual sex with him. Later consensual sex took place between the defendant and the boy about 20 times. He met the 12 year old by being friendly with children who lived next door to his mother. The boy went to the defendant's flat and another flat. They had masturbation and oral sex. The gross indecency was touching and kissing the 12 year old. The defendant was arrested and admitted the offences. He was 34 and had two convictions for gross indecency with a child and an indecent assault on a male for which he received 6 years in 1993. The pre-sentence report said he posed a serious threat to young boys. The psychiatric report said he had a damaged personality and was emotionally unstable. He assisted the police by giving evidence in the murder trial for the other man who killed a schoolboy. Held. We accept the law reducing the age of consent will be enacted. The 2 year concurrent sentences for the buggery and gross indecency (all against the 16 year old) were not manifestly excessive. However, **8 years** not 10 is the suitable total. The 2 year sentences reduced to 1 year. One indecent assaults on the younger victim reduced from 4 to **3 years**. The other 2 remaining at 4 years extended so total is 1+3+4=8, not 2+4+4=10. The 2 years concurrent for the committal for sentence and the **5 years** extended licence remained.

Att-Gen's Ref. No 60 of 2001 2002 1 Cr App R (S) 396. The defendant pleaded guilty to 11 counts of buggery, one of aiding and abetting buggery and 15 indecent assaults on five boys between 11 and 15. Between 1976 and 1991 he was Chairman of a naturist club. Between 1976 and 1991 he conducted systematic and persistent abuse on five boys. He gained the trust of the parents of the victims and then the victims were groomed, given treats and photographed naked. With each he masturbated, then had mutual masturbation and then buggered four of them. The treats were sweets, drinks, smoking and trips to London. The offences took place when he was 34–45 and he was now 62. Some were abused by his friends. The judge said 'it was a terrible trail of corruption with a lasting and dreadful effect. Some were depressed, unable to take part in sport, form normal relations, lacked a social life, tried to commit suicide and attend psychiatric centres. You pose a real danger to the public.' He reduced the 15 year sentence to 9 because of the delay. Held. The 15 year starting point was right. It is right to make a discount for the delay but it cannot be very great because these offences tend not to come to light very quickly. Taking into account the delay and that it was a reference **12 years** substituted.

Victim aged 13–15

25.18   *Att-Gen's Ref. No 9 of 1996* 1997 1 Cr App R (S) 113. The defendant pleaded guilty at a late stage to buggery of a 14-year-old boy, G and three counts of indecent assault one on a boy of 10 (masturbation), one on a girl aged 12 (hand on her vagina) and one on a boy aged 9 (oral sex). In 1993, the defendant was released from prison after serving 4 years for attempted buggery and indecent assault on an 11-year-old boy. The defendant made friends with G and brought him presents. Sexually explicit material was sent to the boy's address and he threatened him on a number of occasions. The boy's mother sent him a solicitor's letter warning him. When questioned by the police the boy revealed buggery on one occasion. When the defendant's flat was searched sexually explicit material was found including scenes of buggery. Correspondence was found indicating he was seeking strangulation videos from Amsterdam. Held. The offences were carefully planned and two of the victims were threatened with violence. 8 years for the buggery and 4 years concurrent for the indecent assaults was not unduly lenient by reference to the tariff alone. However, taking into account the previous conviction for very similar offences and the fact that he was still on licence when he committed the first offence it was unduly lenient. The lower court should have exercised its powers to pass longer than normal sentences. Taking into account it was a reference **11 years** substituted for 8 on the buggery count with 4 years concurrent for the indecent assaults.

Att-Gen's Ref. No 4 of 1997 1998 1 Cr App R (S) 96. The defendant was convicted of two counts of buggery with one boy when 15 and another boy whose age is unclear, three counts of indecent assaults and indecency with a child (all on boys between about 13 to 15, with masturbation and oral sex). The defendant, aged 54 set up two organisations and asked schoolboys if they would like to join. The intention was to obtain boys. Victims were tied up and blindfolded. One boy was confused about his sexuality and took an overdose of pills, which was not fatal. The defendant had no previous convictions. Held. It was in breach of trust. The correct sentence would have been 5 years and 5 consecutive for the buggery counts. Because it was a reference **4 years** and 4 consecutive with the rest concurrent not 5 years in all.

R v Brierley 2000 2 Cr App R 278. The defendant aged 36–7 at the time of the offences was convicted of buggery of a 14-year-old girl and four counts of indecent assault. The offences involved the same girl over a 5 month period. He was in a relationship with her mother; he turned her attentions to the daughter while the mother was out. The buggery was one incident. He had no previous convictions. Held. He had gravely abused the trust that was placed in him, but **3 years** not 4 for the buggery with the other sentences remaining consecutive.

R v Matthews 2001 2 Cr App R (S) 112. The defendant made a plea not at the first opportunity to buggery. Allegations of rape and indecent assault were left on the file. The defendant aged 31 met the girl aged 15 at a public house. After both had been drinking sexual activity took place and he buggered her. It caused her some pain. The defendant had no previous convictions and an excellent work record. **18 months** substituted for 2$^1/_2$ years.

Victim under 16 – With violence

25.19 *Att-Gen's Ref. No 89 of 1998* 2000 1 Cr App R (S) 49. The defendant was convicted for attempted buggery, six counts of child abduction, six counts of indecent assault, and six counts of indecency with a child. Over a period of 4 years the defendant carried out five sexual attacks on six boys, aged between 11 and 14, as they were walking to or from school on the same common. The last attack was on two boys at the same time. The defendant travelled from Forest Hill to a common in Surrey to carry out these attacks. He seized the boys and forcibly took off their clothing. There was a variety of threats and force used. One was threatened he'd be killed. He inserted a glove in one of the boy's anus to extract faeces. In another he inserted a finger or a stick into the boy's anus. In three of the attacks he forced them to put their penises in his mouth and told them to urinate while he sucked the penis. One boy he tried to bugger but the boy was able to prevent it by tensing his buttocks. One attack was disturbed early on by a police helicopter. One boy was in such a state he was physically sick. The defendant assisted his escape by threats or by taking the boys footwear away or keeping their trousers down. Two were told to swallow his semen. All the victims suffered emotional and psychological harm. The defendant, who was 45, had no previous convictions. The maximum for attempted buggery was increased from 10 years to life after the offence. Held. As this was a campaign of premeditated abduction and grave sexual abuse the appropriate sentence was **18 years without passing a longer than commensurate sentence**. Consecutive sentences were appropriate. Taking into account it was a reference **15 years** in total not 10 years.

26 BURGLARY

26.1 Theft Act 1968 s 9

Triable either way unless (a) the defendant could be sentenced to a minimum of 3 years[11] or (b) where the burglary comprises the commission of, or an intention to commit, an offence which is triable only on indictment (GBH, rape etc)[12] or (c) where the burglary is a dwelling and a person was subjected to violence or the threat of violence[13]. In those cases the offence is triable only on indictment

On indictment maximum 14 years when the building is a dwelling, 10 years otherwise. Summary maximum 6 months and/or £5,000.

11 Powers of Criminal Courts (Sentencing) Act 2000 s 111(2).
12 Magistrates' Courts Act 1980 s 17(1) and Sch 1, para. 28b.
13 Magistrates' Courts Act 1980 s 17(1) and Sch 1, para. 28c. In *R v McGrath* 2004 1 Cr App R (S) 173, violence was inflicted in response to the occupant's force when restraining the burglar. Held. Para 28(c) was not to be taken to mean that the violence must have been part of the effecting of the burglary. It was sufficiently wide to cover cases such as this.

The Criminal Justice Act 2003 creates a summary maximum sentence of 51 weeks, a minimum custodial sentence of 28 weeks and Custody plus. The Home Office says they do not expect to introduce these provisions before September 2006.

Drug Abstinence Order This was repealed on 4 April 2005.

Drug Treatment and Testing Order This is the classic offence for this order. The power is contained in Powers of Criminal Courts (Sentencing) Act 2000 s 52. For how the discretionary power should be exercised see *Att-Gen's Ref No. 64 of 2003* 2004 2 Cr App R (S) 106.

Imprisonment for public protection For offences when 1) the intent is to inflict GBH or do unlawful damage and 2) committed on or after 4/4/05 and 3) when there is a significant risk to members of the public of serious harm etc. there is a mandatory duty to pass a sentence of imprisonment for public protection[14]. For offenders under 18 the duty is to pass detention for public protection or an extended sentence[15].

Minimum sentences Domestic burglary is a specified offence for a 3 year minimum sentence when the offence is a third domestic burglary[16].

Restitution Order There is power to make an order that the stolen goods etc. in the possession of the defendant or a third party be restored to the owner etc.[17].

Sexual Offences Prevention Order Where the intent is to inflict GBH or do unlawful damage there is a discretionary power to make this order when it is necessary to protect the public etc[18].

Working with children For offences committed before 1/5/04, where the intent is to rape a child the defendant is aged 18 or over and he is sentenced to 12 months or more etc. hospital order etc. the court must disqualify him/her from working with children unless satisfied he is unlikely to commit any further offences against a child when the court must state its reasons for not doing so[19]. For a defendant aged less than 18 at the time of the offence the court must order disqualification if he is sentenced to 12 months or more and the court is satisfied that the defendant will commit a further offence against a child[20]. The court must state its reasons for so doing.

Sentencing Trends Notwithstanding the 2003 guideline case the majority of Crown Court Judges give custodial sentences for burglary where they consider the defendant is a professional burglar. This is in tune with public opinion. These sentences are rarely quashed at the Court of Appeal. There is widespread use of the Drug Treatment and Testing orders in the hope that it will be more successful than custody. The response to these orders varies from outstanding success to immediate drug taking and re-offending. As burglary statistics continue to show falls, the fear of burglary remains as high as ever.

14 Criminal Justice Act 2003 s 224–226
15 Criminal Justice Act 2003 s 226 and 228
16 Powers of Criminal Courts (Sentencing) Act 2000 s 111
17 Powers of Criminal Courts (Sentencing) Act 2000 s 148(2)
18 Sexual Offences Act 2003 s 104 & Sch. 5
19 Criminal Justice and Court Services Act 2000 s 28 and Sch 4 Para 3r
20 Criminal Justice and Court Services Act 2000 s 29

Crown Court statistics – England and Wales – Males 21+
26.2

Year	Plea	Total Numbers sentenced	Type of sentence %					Average length of custody (months)
			Discharge	Fine	Community sentence	Suspended sentence	Custody	
Burglary in a dwelling								
2002	Guilty	3,624	1	0	22	1	76	26.2
	Not guilty	396	1	0	13	0	84	29.9
2003	Guilty	3,659	1	0	27	1	70	26.8
	Not guilty	342	1	0	23	1	73	28
Burglary in a building other than a dwelling								
2002	Guilty	671	1	1	25	1	73	21.1
	Not guilty	84	2	–	26	1	69	28.5
2003	Guilty	620	2	0	31	1	66	20.1
	Not guilty	83	2	–	25	–	72	25.9

For details and explanations about the statistics in the book see page vii.

Death is caused

See MANSLAUGHTER – *Burglars/robbers/thieves, by*

Vehicle used to commit the offence

26.3   *R v Stratton* 1988 Times 15/1/88. The defendant burgled an occupied house and an item from the house was found in his car. The defendant had no assets and his car was worth £1,500–£2,000. The court forfeited the car. Held. The forfeiture was extremely appropriate. Perhaps the power should be used more frequently.

Burglary – Domestic

Guideline case

26.4   *R v McInerney* 2003 2 Cr App R 627. LCJ. This guidance is the result of the advice of the Sentencing Advisory Panel dated 9 April 2002. The application of the guidelines must be subject to all the circumstances of the particular case and sentencers in applying the guidelines must tailor their sentence to meet those circumstances. The Court in *R v Brewster* 1998 1 Cr. App R (S) 181 made some comments as to the seriousness of offences of domestic burglary which we regard as still being highly relevant. (These comments are listed below and arranged with the new guidance.)

General

Domestic burglary is, and always has been, regarded as a very serious offence. It may involve considerable loss to the victim. Even when it does not, the victim may lose possessions of particular value to him or her. To those who are insured, the receipt of financial compensation does not replace what is lost. But many victims are uninsured: because they may have fewer possessions, they are the more seriously injured by the loss of those they do have.

The loss of material possessions is, however, only part (and often a minor part) of the reason why domestic burglary is a serious offence. Most people, perfectly legitimately, attach importance to the privacy and security of their own homes. That an intruder should break in or enter, for his own dishonest purposes, leaves the victim with a sense of violation and insecurity. Even where the victim is unaware, at the time, that the burglar is in the house, it can be a frightening experience to learn that a burglary has taken place; and it is all the more frightening if the victim confronts or hears the burglar. Generally speaking, it is more frightening if the victim is in the house when the burglary takes place, and if the intrusion takes place at night; but that does not mean that the offence is not serious if the victim returns to an empty house during the daytime to find that it has been burgled.

The seriousness of the offence can vary almost infinitely from case to case. It may involve an impulsive act involving an object of little value (reaching through a window to take a bottle of milk, or stealing a can of petrol from an outhouse). At the other end of the spectrum it may involve a professional, planned organisation, directed at objects of high value. Or the offence may be deliberately directed at the elderly, the disabled or the sick; and it may involve burglaries of the same premises. It may sometimes be accompanied by acts of wanton vandalism.

Categorising burglary

We divide burglary into low level burglary and a standard burglary which is a burglary which has the following features:

i)   it is committed by a repeat offender;

ii) it involves the theft of electrical goods such as a television or video;

iii) the theft of personal items such as jewellery;

iv) damage is caused by the break-in itself;

v)   some turmoil in the house, such as drawers upturned or damage to some items occurs;

vi) no injury or violence, but some trauma is caused to the victim.

The theft of the electrical goods or the personal items are alternative and the standard burglary does not need to have all of the listed features. Some of the features can be sufficient to bring the offence within the same category.

Aggravating features

The high-level aggravating factors are:

a)   force used or threatened against the victim;

b)   a victim injured (as a result of force used or threatened);

c)   the especially traumatic effect on the victim, in excess of the trauma generally associated with a standard burglary;

d)   professional planning, organisation or execution;

e)   vandalism of the premises, in excess of the damage generally associated with a standard burglary;

f)   the offence was racially aggravated;

g)   a vulnerable victim deliberately targeted (including cases of 'deception' or 'distraction' of the elderly).

(Note The first two factors would make the offence robbery, which has its own guidelines. Factor f) is governed by Powers of the Criminal Courts (Sentencing) Act 2000, s 153. Ed)

The medium-level aggravating factors are:

a)   a vulnerable victim, although not targeted as such;

b)   the victim was at home (whether daytime or night-time burglary;

c)   goods of high value were taken (economic or sentimental);

d)   the burglars worked in a group.

An example of a case that could overlap the two categories would be a case where the victim is especially old, say in his 90s but was not shown to have been targeted because of this. The number of offences may indicate that the offender is a professional burglar which would be a high level aggravating feature but even if they do not fall within this category the number could still be at least a mid level aggravating feature. The fact that the offender is on bail or licence can also be an aggravating feature as can the fact that the offence was committed out of spite.

It is appropriate for the sentencer to reflect the degree of harm done, including the impact of the burglary upon the victim whether or not the offender foresaw that result or the extent of that impact. If, of course, the offender foresees a result of the offending behaviour then that increases the seriousness of the offence.

If the burglary is committed at night, that makes it more likely that the premises are occupied. In addition, we would suggest that an intrusion into an occupied home must be more frightening to the occupants, if they find that they have intruders at a time when they are in the dark, particularly if they are woken from their sleep. A confrontation of the householder, by the burglar, could in our judgment amount to an aggravating feature.

Mitigating features

They are:

a)   It is a first offence;

b)   nothing, or only property of very low value, is stolen;

c)   the offender played only a minor part in the burglary;

d)   there is no damage or disturbance to property;

e)   a timely plea of guilty. Where PCC(S) A 2000, s 111 applies, the reduction is limited to 20% of the determinate sentence of at least three years.

The fact that the crime is committed on impulse may also be a mitigating factor. The offender's age or state of health, both physical and mental, can be a mitigating factor, so can evidence of genuine remorse, response to previous sentences and ready co-operation with the police.

The starting points

For adult offenders, without any aggravating or personal mitigating factors or the discount for a guilty plea, there are three categories for a completed, burglary of domestic premises.

'(1) Low level burglary committed by a first-time domestic burglar (and for some second-time domestic burglars), where there is no damage to property and no property (or only property of very low value) is stolen, the starting point should be a **community sentence**. Other types of cases at this level would include thefts (provided they are of items of low value) from attached garages or from vacant property.

(2) In cases between (1) and (3) the initial approach of the courts should be to impose a **community sentence** subject to conditions that ensure that the sentence is (a) an effective punishment and (b) one which offers action on the part of the Probation Service to tackle the offender's criminal behaviour and (c) when appropriate, will tackle the offender's underlying problems such as drug addiction. If, and only if, the court is satisfied the offender has demonstrated by his or her behaviour that punishment in the community is not practicable, should the court resort to a **custodial sentence**.

(3) In the case of a standard domestic burglary which additionally displays any one of the "high relevance" factors mentioned in, but committed by a first-time domestic burglar, the starting point should be a custodial sentence of **18 months**. The starting point for a second-time domestic burglar committing such an offence should be a custodial sentence of **three years**. When the offence is committed by an offender with two or more previous convictions for domestic burglary the starting point is a custodial sentence of $4^1/_2$ **years**. The presence of more than one "high relevance" factor could bring the sentence for an offence at this level significantly above the suggested starting points.'

(Note. This part and the entire summary are an amalgamation of the parts in the Panel's Report which the court accepted and the court's own views rearranged to make it easier to understand. Ed.)

Other orders

We draw attention to the important powers of court to make restitution and compensation orders. When appropriate, those orders should always be made.

Guideline remarks

26.5   *Att-Gen's Ref. Nos. 19, 20 and 21 of 2001* 2002 1 Cr App R (S) 136. There can be little doubt that the two forms of criminal conduct which causes the public most concern are domestic burglary and street robberies. The effect of such offences goes way beyond the dreadful trauma suffered by the immediate victim and causes large sections of the public to alter their lifestyle to seek to avoid the danger. People are afraid to go out of their homes.

Magistrates' Court Sentencing Guidelines January 2004 – Dwelling

26.6   For a first time offender pleading not guilty. Entry point. Are Magistrates' sentencing powers sufficient? Consider the impact on the victim. Examples of aggravating factors for the offence are force used or threatened (which would make the offence robbery Ed.), group enterprise, high value (in economic or sentimental terms) property stolen, more than minor trauma caused, professional planning/organisation/execution, repeat victimisation, significant damage or vandalism caused, victim injured, victim present at the time and vulnerable victim. Examples of mitigating factors for the offence are first offence of its type AND low value property stolen AND no significant damage or disturbance AND no injury or violence, minor part played, theft from an attached garage and vacant property. Examples of mitigation are age, health (physical or mental), co-operation with the police, genuine remorse and voluntary compensation. Give reasons if not awarding compensation.

For details about the guidelines see MAGISTRATES' COURT SENTENCING GUIDELINES at page 483.

Articles in law journals

26.7   For a detailed analysis of R v McInerney 2003, with statistics and indications that Judges would exceed the Sentencing Advisory Panel's proposals etc. see 2003 Crim L R 243.

Custodial not necessary

26.8   *R v Finney* 1998 2 Cr App R (S) 239. The defendant pleaded guilty to burglary. He lost his job as a chef and with it his accommodation where others lived. The next year at night, he entered an occupied bedsitting room in the building and stole a number of cassettes and a jacket. He tried another room and the occupant recognised him and he left. He admitted the offence in interview. He said he was drunk at the time and he went there because the victim had some of his property, which he hadn't returned.

Despite representations the victim had 'fobbed him off.' The defendant was of good character and genuinely remorseful. Held. Immediate imprisonment was not inevitable. Probation substituted for **9 months**.

R (DPP) v Salisbury JJs 2003 1 Cr App R (S) 560. The defendant pleaded to a domestic burglary. He stole an old lady's handbag. Next day he surrendered to the police before they were aware of the offence. He made admissions and said he had been drunk. The police had not been aware of the offence. He expressed remorse. He was 25 in a settled relationship and in full time employment. There were 15 burglary convictions and other previous. His last sentence was for burglary for which he received 5 years for which he had been released from $2^{1}/_{2}$ years previously. The sentence was a **compensation order of £200 and prosecution costs of £118**. The prosecution appealed. Held. The decision was very surprising and unusual to a significant degree. However because of the very special facts and he because he had shown every indication of having put his past behind him the sentence was within their discretion.

Defendant aged under 18 Guideline case

26.9 *R v McInerney* 2003 2 Cr App R 627. LCJ. The Youth Justice Board is spearheading effective punishment in the community and it is important that, where appropriate, juvenile offenders are dealt with in Youth Court and not the Crown Court. Exceptionally, since domestic burglary is one of the offences which may attract a sentence of long-term detention under the Powers of Criminal Courts (Sentencing) Act 2000, s 91 a young offender may be committed by the Youth Court for trial in the Crown Court with a view to such a sentence being passed. A sentence of long-term detention is available in respect of any offender aged 10 to 17 inclusive who is convicted of domestic burglary.

Where an offender who is now aged 18 or over has two qualifying previous convictions for domestic burglary as a juvenile, a third alleged domestic burglary must be tried in the Crown Court, and the presumptive minimum sentence is a custodial sentence of three years. Although s 111 does not apply until the offender has attained the age of 18, it would seem to follow that for an offender who is under 18 but is charged with a third domestic burglary, a custodial sentence **in excess of 24 months** (the maximum term available for a detention and training order) will be the likely sentence and so the Youth Court should generally commit the case to Crown Court for trial with a view to sentence under s 91.

Defendant aged 12–15

26.10 *R v Brewster* 1998 Re RH 1 Cr App R 220, 1 Cr App R (S) 181 at 187. LCJ The defendant, when 15, pleaded guilty to four burglaries committed in the space of little more than a week. The first involved an unoccupied dwelling where he stole nothing. The next three involved the dwellings of vulnerable people, starting within hours of his release. One involved an epileptic man and his disabled girlfriend, both of whom slept as property worth £225 was stolen. Next he burgled the house of an infirm pensioner in the early hours of the morning. She experienced 'terrible shock'. The next night he broke into the home of a 93-year-old lady and £150 was taken. The defendant had never known his father who was in prison for murder. He had lived with his mother to whom he was close. She suffered from domestic violence. At school he was persistently bullied. The mother disappeared in suspicious circumstances. Until then the defendant was a reasonably stable boy. Unable to come to terms with the situation, he began to use crack cocaine. The offences were committed to fund his addiction. His extended family saw his character change. He became unrecognisable and completely untrustworthy. He was in breach of a supervision order for a residential burglary. He did not receive any treatment at all for his addiction nor adequate counselling. Since his arrest he had absconded twice from local authority care. A psychiatric report said, 'He was clinically depressed and was a very vulnerable, fragile and somewhat immature youth. It was doubted whether he would have resources to survive in a prison environment and he is in urgent need of therapeutic help to address his bereavement, depression and drug addiction. His drug addiction is in fact very much secondary to his bereavement and depression.' He recommended a two-year supervision order including a direction to participate in specified activities for up to 90 days as an alternative to custody and 2 years' aftercare and monitoring. He had served 4 months. Held. The judge accurately described the offences as 'cruel and hateful burglaries' which resulted from 'deliberately targeting the weak and vulnerable'. There was quite exceptional mitigation. If he had been a little older or if the mitigation had not been so exceptional we would not have altered the 4 years detention. **Supervision** substituted.

R v Mills 1998 2 Cr App R (S) 128 at 134. LCJ The defendant pleaded to three burglaries committed in the space a little less than 4 months. He asked for another burglary to be taken into consideration. When 13 he burgled four houses when the occupants were out. On three occasions he broke a window and on two of them he was with other boys. He was arrested for the third burglary and released on bail. He then committed the fourth a month later. A variety of items were stolen. He had findings of guilt for non-domestic burglary and other offences. He was in care and had six placements in 9 months. He had served the equivalent of 11 months after sentence. Held. 18 months was at the top of the range but was not excessive. Taking into account the time served and his need for assistance **supervision** instead.

R v O'Grady 2000 1 Cr App R (S) 112. The defendant pleaded guilty to three distraction burglaries. Two pleas were entered late. The victims were all elderly ladies living alone. The first one involved three boys one of whom asked if she wanted any jobs done and when she said no they waited and entered. 60p was taken. In the second burglary boys entered the home and one asked her if she wanted any shopping done. Another boy went upstairs and stole her purse. The third burglary was very similar with the same two boys. It was clear elderly people had been targeted. The defendant had been sentenced to an attendance centre for common assault. Since his sentence his education had been taken in hand. Held. There had to be a balance between welfare and deterrent and punitive elements. The judge was able to use the then s 53(2) procedure. **6 months** detention was not excessive.

R v D 2001 1 Cr App R (S) 202. The defendant pleaded guilty to burglary and was found guilty of handling stolen goods from another burglary. While the owners were away on holiday, he and the nephew of the victim entered a house by removing a pane of glass and stole a Play Station, games and power tools worth £684. A tap was left running which caused about £60 worth of damage to carpets and one of them urinated over a child's mattress. The nephew was 11. On the same day another house was burgled by a 14 year old and £157 worth of audio equipment and computer accessories were stolen. The defendant tried to sell some of the property on. He said he wanted money to buy his mother a present. He was 14 and had received three formal cautions for criminal damage, theft and common assault. He was sentenced to 12 hours at an attendance centre for theft of a cycle. He also failed to attend and was given no penalty. Held. The judge was entitled to consider the cautions when determining whether he was a persistent offender and to consider he was a persistent offender. Because of his age **8 months** detention not 12.

R v Elliott 2001 2 Cr App R (S) 420. The defendant, aged 14 pleaded to burglary. He and the 13-year-old co-defendant forced the front door and ransacked the home of a friend of the co-defendant. A duvet was sprayed and the co-defendant set it on fire. The defendant put it out. Property worth £1,500 was stolen and £1,000 damage was caused. The victim was very distressed. The defendant had two fairly recent non-domestic burglary convictions and a conviction for handling. The co-defendant's record was worse. The defendant had a disturbed family background and the risk of re-offending was described as high. The judge said it was worth 3 to 4 years for an adult and gave the co-defendant 12 months. Held. There was no reason to distinguish between them so **12 months** not 18.

Old cases *R v Winson and Poole* 1998 1 Cr App R (S) 239. *R v Carr* 1998 2 Cr App R (S) 20. (For a summary of these cases see the first edition of this book.)

Defendant aged 16–17

26.11   *R v Sleeth* 1999 2 Cr App R (S) 211. The defendant, a girl now 17, pleaded guilty to three burglaries. She would get herself invited to the homes of elderly people and then wander round and steal. The victim's ages were 75, 86 and 84. At one she said she was looking for someone, at another she gave the impression she knew the lady and at the last she said she had some rings to sell. She started offending at 11 and her convictions included two burglaries, theft, and GBH with intent. Held. **3 years** detention substituted for 4 because of her age and because she had not served a custodial sentence before.

R v Chapple 2000 1 Cr App R (S) 115. The defendant, when 17, pleaded guilty to a distraction burglary. At about 11.30pm the defendant broke a window and entered using a crowbar. A neighbour called police and they found him inside the flat holding a hammer. He said 'Serves the bitch right, I'll do it again.' He had taken two penknives from the flat. The occupier was at work at the time. He admitted it in interview and when 15 he was convicted of three burglary offences. Each one was a business premise of the householder in the current case. He also had a conviction for theft. Six weeks before the burglary he said to the householder, 'I only got fined £150 at court don't worry I'll break in again at some point, I'll get you back.' **2½ years** detention not 4.

R v Fieldhouse and Watts 2001 1 Cr App R (S) 361. The defendant W pleaded guilty to two counts of burglary, one count of theft and asked for four theft matters to be taken into consideration. F pleaded guilty to one of the burglaries. In the joint burglary the two entered a dwelling house and stole about £2,000 worth of property. F said he knew the occupants and that they would not be in. W's other burglary was at 11.20pm on a house with another while the householder's son was in bed. W's theft matter concerned £2,500 worth of property. W was found at 6am with another and the property that had been stolen from a house nearby. W's TICs were thefts from sheds and vehicles. Some of his offences were committed when he was on bail. They were both now 17. W had three convictions in 1999 for criminal damage, a public order offence and assaulting a police constable. His report said there was a risk of re-offending. F had minor convictions and cautions. F's prison report described him as quiet and well behaved. Held. The judge's approach was impeccable. The gravity of W's offending was such a long-term detention order under (now the Powers of the Criminal Courts (Sentencing) Act 2000, s 91) could well have been made. His 24 months could not be challenged. **8 months** detention for F not 12.

R v Palmer and Others 2004 2 Cr App R 519. The defendant W pleaded guilty to nine counts of burglary with 12 offences of burglary taken into consideration. The defendant P pleaded guilty to one offence of burglary and two of attempted burglary and the defendant O pleaded guilty to one count of attempted burglary two of handling stolen goods and one of driving a conveyance taken without authority. They had four co-accused. The group burgled large houses, normally by forcing entry. They targeted these addresses because there were expensive cars on the driveways. They stole not only the car keys from the houses but other items such as jewellery, watches, laptop computers, cameras and cash. They then drove the cars away with the other property. If the cars were not there they would return on other days with the keys to steal them. W then 17 was involved with nine of these types of burglary in which 8 cars worth in excess of £172,000 were stolen as well as items such as plasma TV sets, jewellery, and cameras. P's offences were burgling the house with W when a plasma TV set worth £9,000 and keys for a Rolls Royce and a Range Rover were taken. Also going to two different houses with expensive cars on the drive, ringing the bells, but the occupants were in and nothing more happened. O was linked to the car worth £10,000 and an Audi car and was seen with others acting suspiciously outside a house where there were expensive cars on the drive. He also handled the plasma TV set. W had 12 previous convictions including ones for aggravated vehicle taking, handling, numerous burglaries of dwelling houses, and offences to do with interfering with motor vehicles. P, 22, was on bail for previous offences of burglary when these offences were committed. He had an extensive record for offences including handling and dwelling house burglaries. A pre-sentence report said that he was doing well in custody and had taken courses including drug programmes. He expressed his shame and said he was determined to avoid re offending. O was 16 and 17 at the time of the offences and 18 when sentenced. His previous convictions were slight with nothing similar. The pre-sentence report set out the extremely difficult crowded and squalid conditions in which he had been brought up. Held. In the case of W if he had been sentenced at age 17 any court would have passed a sentence under Section 91. **5 years** was substantial and severe but justified. In the case of P **3 years** on each count to run concurrently was in no way excessive bearing in mind his record as a whole. In the case of O he was much less involved although he must have realised the seriousness of the overall enterprise. The appropriate total sentence was **18 months** not 2 years.

Old cases *R v Mills* 1998 Re Lamb 2 Cr App R (S) 128 at 137 and *R v Mills* 1998 Re Marsh 2 Cr App R (S) 128 at 140. (For a summary of these cases see the first edition of this book.)

Defendant aged 18–20

26.12 *R v Hanrahan* 1999 1 Cr App R (S) 308. The defendant, now 18 pleaded to a distraction burglary at the home of a 90 year old. He told the lady there was a water explosion and produced something to show he was from the council. He persuaded her to let him in and asked her where the mains tap was. He then persuaded her to go to the cellar while an accomplice stole a watch of great sentimental value worth £100. He had three previous court appearances but none for burglary and had no custodial sentences. He showed remorse and was said to be under the influence of others. Held. A deterrent sentence was called for and 4 years was suitable for someone older or someone who had been in custody before. However, because of the circumstances **3 years** detention not 4.

Where age is not a determining factor, e.g. where the defendant has already served a custodial sentence the case is listed in another category.

Distraction burglaries (entering by a trick and stealing)

26.13 *R v Wright* 1999 2 Cr App R (S) 327. The defendant pleaded guilty to burglary at the Magistrates' Court. The defendant approached the victim and asked to fill a bottle with water for his car. She invited him in. While she went to get a bucket to help him he stole her handbag. He was arrested and identified the bin he had put the bag in and it was recovered. The contents less £35 and her bus pass were found. In 1984 he was convicted of theft when he entered an elderly person's home by asking for a glass of water. He stole two pension books and £94. In 1984 there were two convictions for burglary. In 1992 he was given at least 3 years for obtaining and attempting to obtain property by deception and breach of two suspended sentences. One of them related to a trying to cash someone's pension book. He showed genuine remorse. **3 years** not 4 years.

R v Woodliffe 2000 1 Cr App R (S) 330. The defendant pleaded guilty to two burglaries. He went to an old age pensioner's home saying that he had come about the front light. He then said he needed to check the windows. He asked her to go to her bedroom and listen for banging while he stole her purse containing keys, her bus pass and £14. The same day he visited a 77-year-old man in an old people's complex and said the police and the council sent him. He also said it was cold and asked to be admitted. Once inside he said he was fitting alarms. The victim said he would not pay for any and followed him as he measured up. The defendant was told to leave. He ran out taking £30. The defendant was caught on video and admitted it in interview. He was on licence from a 5 year sentence for five burglaries and an attempted burglary. Those were similar offences to the two new ones. The new sentences were concurrent but consecutive to the order for breaching his licence. Held. *R v Henry* 1998 (above) did not lay down a sentence cannot ever be more than 6 years. **7 years** was severe but not excessive.

R v O'Brien 2002 2 Cr App R (S) 560. The defendant pleaded guilty at the PDH to burglary. He was in breach of his licence and was given 3 months concurrent for that. The victim, an 81 year old lady lived with her son and had the early stages of dementia. She exhibited considerable confusion. She was capable of looking after herself and lived with her son who instructed her not to open the door to anyone without an identity badge. The son returned home and found the tap in the garden running. His mother told him that earlier a man claiming to be from the Water Board visited the house and asked to test the taps. The man went upstairs and stole a mobile phone and £200 from him and a watch from her bedroom. The defendant was traced through fingerprints. When interviewed he denied the offence. He was a drug addict and wrote a letter expressing remorse. (The report does not detail his antecedents or CRO.) The Judge said "Society rightly reserves its deepest censure for those who prey upon vulnerable groups such as the elderly. Throughout your recent criminal career you have mercilessly and relentlessly pursued the old. Time after time you have tricked the elderly into believing you were a public official, tricking your way in and stealing their property. I am determined the elderly have a sustained rest from your activities." Held. He is a professional burglar. His speciality is vulnerable elderly people. He tricks them and steals their property. This type of burglary casts a shadow on the lives of elderly people. They dread the unexpected knock. We entirely agree with the Judge's remarks. The question was had he received sufficient credit for the plea. **8 years** not 9.

R v Dawson 2002 Unreported 26/7/02. The defendant pleaded guilty to burglary at the Magistrates' Court. He and another tricked their way into the home of a 92 year old woman who lived alone, by posing as gas meter readers. To allay her suspicions one of them wrote a fictitious name and address on a piece of paper. While one went with her to the meter the other stole £30 and loose change from her handbag and a £5 note from the mantelpiece. His fingerprints were found by police and he was arrested. In interview he denied the offence. He was 23, a heroin addict and on bail for another offence. His convictions included three for non dwelling house burglaries. He had received probation, community service and 3 months imprisonment. His last conviction was for dangerous driving for which he received a 90 hour community punishment. His sentence was two months for the latest offence. The pre-sentence report indicated there was genuine deep remorse. Held. Because of *R v Wright* 1999 2 Cr App R (S) 327 **3 years** not 4.

R v McInerney 2003 2 Cr App R (S) 240 *at p 260*. The defendant pleaded guilty at the Magistrates' Court to burglary. He entered the home of the victim aged 93 by impersonating a police officer. He showed the victim a fake identification badge bearing his photograph and wore clothes like those of a police officer. He said that he was checking the victim's insurance. He went into every room and spoke to someone on a mobile phone. When the victim became suspicious the defendant offered to let him talk to 'his boss' on the mobile phone. The defendant then locked the victim in his kitchen. When the victim said that he was going to call the police the defendant removed the battery from his phone. The defendant left the house with £140 and a telephone battery. He was later identified by fingerprints and when interviewed he fully admitted the offence saying that he had not targeted the victim and that he did not think that he was 93 but nearer 60. The sentencing judge was sceptical about whether the defendant would have withdrawn if he had known the true age of the victim and was in no doubt that the defendant was targeting the elderly. The defendant was 22 with a record of 39 previous offences including 2 offences of burglary (commercial) for which he received a 2 year sentence. Held. This was a very bad burglary and premeditated, it was aggravated by the age of the victim and the unattractive deceit adopted to carry out this offence. However, $7^1/_2$ years was too high a starting point. **$3^1/_2$ years** not 5.

Old cases *R v Henry* 1998 1 Cr App R (S) 289, *R v Carr* 1998 2 Cr App R (S) 20, and *R v McCamon* 1998 2 Cr App R (S) 81. (For a summary of these cases see the first edition of this book.)

Domestic – Cars – Homes entered to steal keys for high value cars

26.14 *R v Palmer and Others* 2004 2 Cr App R 519. The defendant W pleaded guilty to nine counts of burglary with 12 offences of burglary taken into consideration. The defendant P pleaded guilty to one offence of burglary and two of attempted burglary and the defendant O pleaded guilty to one count of attempted burglary two of handling stolen goods and one of driving a conveyance taken without authority. They had four co-accused. The group burgled large houses, normally by forcing entry. They targeted these addresses because there were expensive cars on the driveways. They stole not only the car keys from the houses but other items such as jewellery, watches, laptop computers, cameras and cash. They then drove the cars away with the other property. If the cars were not there they would return on other days with the keys to steal them. W then 17 was involved with nine of these types of burglary in which 8 cars worth in excess of £172,000 were stolen as well as items such as plasma TV sets, jewellery, and cameras. P's offences were burgling the house with W when a plasma TV set worth £9,000 and keys for a Rolls Royce and a Range Rover were taken. Also going to two different houses with expensive cars on the drive, ringing the bells, but the occupants were in and nothing more happened. O was linked to the car worth £10,000 and an Audi car and was seen with others acting suspiciously outside a house where there were expensive cars on the drive. He also handled the plasma TV set. W had 12 previous convictions including ones for aggravated vehicle taking, handling, numerous burglaries of dwelling houses, and offences to do with interfering with motor vehicles. P, 22, was on bail for previous offences of burglary when these offences were committed. He had an extensive record for offences including handling and dwelling house burglaries. A pre-sentence report said that he was doing well in custody and had taken courses including drug programmes. He expressed his shame and said he was determined to avoid re offending. O was 16 and 17 at the time of the offences and 18 when sentenced. His previous convictions were slight with nothing similar. The pre-sentence report set out the extremely difficult crowded and squalid conditions in which he had been brought up. Held. In the case of W if he had been sentenced at age 17 any court would have passed a sentence under Section 91. **5 years** was substantial and severe but justified. In the case of P **3 years** on each count to run concurrently was in no way excessive bearing in mind his record as a whole. In the case of O he was much less involved although he must have realised the seriousness of the overall enterprise. The appropriate total sentence was **18 months** not 2 years.

Domestic, occupied – One offence

26.15 *R v Brewster* 1998 *Re Woodhouse* 1 Cr App R 220, 1 Cr App R (S) 181 at 187.

LCJ. The defendant, aged 49, pleaded guilty to one night time burglary. At about 4.30 am the female occupant of a ground floor flat, who had not locked her front door, woke up to find the defendant in her bedroom. He told her the front door had been open and he had walked in. He then turned and left. Nothing was taken and he was arrested almost immediately. The defendant had 8 previous convictions of a relatively minor nature, and none for burglary. He had never served a custodial sentence before. He was an alcoholic and full of remorse. He acknowledged the traumatic effect on the victim. Held. For a burglar to enter the bedroom of someone who is asleep is a seriously aggravating feature. No doubt the appellant is a pathetic figure, but it must have been an utterly terrifying experience for the victim. **2 years** was right.

R v McHoul 2003 1 Cr App R (S) 382. The defendant pleaded guilty to theft and failing to surrender to bail at the Magistrates' Court. He was convicted of burglary and committed for sentence. At 6 pm. he entered a flat by forcing two windows and woke the occupier who was in bed. The occupier found the defendant in his lounge attempting to take two bottles of loose change. When challenged the defendant left. Nothing was taken. The occupier recognised him and the defendant was arrested. He released on bail. Nine days later he stole a tool kit worth £15. He then failed to attend court. He was 34 with a drug problem and 13 previous convictions including 15 for theft and three for failing to attend. There were no convictions for burglary. The pre-sentence report asked for an adjournment to consider a DTTO. He was sentenced to **2½ years** with 1 month consecutive for each of the two other offences. Held. The sentence was not manifestly excessive. (This case was heard before R v McInerney 2003.)

See also *Att-Gen's Ref No. 64 of 2003 Re H* 2004 2 Cr App R (S) 106 at 116 (The defendant pleaded guilty to burglary and ABH. The offences had the ingredients of robbery but the court substituted a community rehabilitation order for 4 years.)

Domestic, occupied – More than one offence

26.16   *R v Middlemiss* 1999 1 Cr App R (S) 62. The defendant pleaded to one burglary. He asked for three offences to be taken into consideration. At night he entered a house occupied by a married couple and their two children. At 4.30am the couple were awakened by sounds. While they were investigating them the burglar ran off. Money jewellery, cards, and other property were stolen. The defendant was arrested and he helped locate some but not all of the property. He said he was in the getaway car. The family was distressed particularly the daughter who was referred to a doctor and counsellor. The TICs were two attempted burglaries on the same night and one burglary earlier. He said he was driver and lookout. He was 30 and treated as being of good character. He was genuinely remorseful and the risk of re-offending was assessed as being low. **3 years** was entirely justified.

Domestic, unoccupied – More than one offence

26.17   *R v McInerney* 2003 2 Cr App R (S) 240 *Re. Keating* at 262. The defendant pleaded guilty to two burglaries in the Magistrates' Court. Between 6.30pm and 8.30pm the defendant entered a house whilst the occupiers were away for the weekend. Having made sure that the premises were unoccupied he removed a panel from the back door to gain entry, causing some damage. He stole electrical items, jewellery and a painting to the value of £4,600. £1,700 was later recovered. The second offence was committed 10 days later at 2.30 am when the defendant noticed that the door to another house was open. He took the opportunity to enter. He did not go beyond the kitchen where he saw a wallet and a mobile phone in a handbag and realised that the property might well be occupied. He took those items, valued at £155. He was arrested the next day and made full admissions in interview to both burglaries. Another burglary was admitted in interview and that was taken into consideration at sentence. He was 33 with a record containing 31 offences including 7 burglaries, for which he received 4 months for the most recent. In 1991 he had received 3 years for 2 burglaries. Held. **3 years** not 4.

Drug addicts – Guideline case

26.18   *R v McInerney* 2003 2 Cr App R 627. It is common knowledge that many domestic burglars are drug addicts who burgle and steal in order to raise money to satisfy their craving for drugs. This is often an expensive craving, and it is not uncommon to learn that addicts commit a burglary, or even several burglaries, each day, often preying on houses in less affluent areas of the country. But to the victim of burglary the motivation of the burglar may well be of secondary interest. Self-induced addiction cannot be relied on as mitigation. The courts will not be easily persuaded that an addicted offender is genuinely determined and able to conquer his addiction.

In the case of offences committed because the offender is an alcoholic or a drug addict, while the taking of drink or drugs is no mitigation, the sentencing process must recognise the fact of the addiction and the importance of breaking the drug or drink problem. This is not only in the interests of the offender but also in the public interest since so commonly the addiction results in a vicious circle of imprisonment followed by re-offending. When an offender is making or prepared to make a real effort to break his addiction, it is important for the sentencing court to make allowances if the process of rehabilitation proves to be irregular. What may be important is the overall progress that the offender is making. This is part of the thinking behind drug and treatment orders.

R v Belli 2004 1 Cr App R (S) 490. The defendant pleaded to burglary. Held. The Judge faced a difficult balancing exercise. DTTO is an important part of the court's armoury in dealing with crime. It is far from a soft option. It is incumbent upon a sentencer to give proper consideration to the making a DTTO and not reject it because custody would be appropriate. Nor should it be thought that the option will cease to be available simply because of the scale of offending. At the same time the actual criminality of the offender is by no means an irrelevant consideration.

Drug addicts – Cases

26.19   *R v McInerney* 2003 2 Cr App R 627. LCJ. The record of the offender is of more significance in the case of domestic burglary than in the case of some other crimes. There are some professional burglars whose records show that from an early age they have behaved as predators preying on their fellow citizens, returning to their trade almost as soon as each prison sentence has been served. Such defendants must continue to receive substantial terms of imprisonment. There are, however, other domestic burglars whose activities are of a different character, and whose careers may lack any element of persistence or deliberation. They are entitled to more lenient treatment.

In judging the record it is of course necessary to take into account the type of offence for which the offender has previously been convicted and the number of offences which were considered on any particular occasion. It is of importance that the efforts which an offender has or has not made to rehabilitate himself are taken into account.

R v Belli 2004 1 Cr App R (S) 490. The defendant pleaded to burglary, two thefts and a failing to attend. He broke into a car and stole a C/D player. About 5 weeks later he broke into a cottage while the owner was away on holiday. The premises were ransacked. The phone and TV wire were cut. Goods worth £250 were taken. He was arrested and released on bail. He stole goods at the chemist when he went to pick up his methadone. Since a teenager he had committed numerous offences including robbery and possessing an imitation firearm. Reports indicated he was a candidate for DTTO. The defendant wanted to give up drugs and had shown high motivation. The Judge said drugs were at the root of the offending but said the offences were too serious. Held. The

Judge faced a difficult balancing exercise. But the burglary was not the worst of its kind. **DTTO** not 2 years 9 months.

R v Page Re S 2004 Unreported 8/12/04. S pleaded to burglary, failing to surrender and 3 thefts. He was also dealt with for a breach of a C/D and 2 theft TICs. A 9 year old boy was leaving his flat and he had difficulty securing it. S and another purported to help him. Two days later the boy's mother returned to the flat and found £400 worth of C/Ds and computer games were stolen. There was no forced entry. The thefts were shopliftings. S was a heroin addict and had been to the courts many times with every conceivable disposal tried. He received 3 years for the burglary and 3 months consecutive for the bail offence. Held. The **3 year** sentence was high but bearing in mind the total offences and the number committed on bail the sentence was not excessive.

Drug Treatment and Testing Orders

See **DRUG TREATMENT AND TESTING ORDERS, BREACH OF**

Expensive properties with antiques etc

26.20 *R v Gibbs* 2000 1 Cr App R (S) 261. The defendant pleaded guilty to seven counts of burglary and on three burglary counts pleaded to handling as an alternative. The seven properties were comparatively isolated country houses. Only high value items were taken. £46,000 worth of furniture was taken and £7,000 worth was recovered. Two of the victims were aged 88 and 75. The handling charges related to antique English furniture found in his property in Portugal. The furniture was worth £20,000 and had been burgled from English country houses. His houses were worth £110,000 and £115,000. He was 51 and since 12 had made 18 appearances at court mostly for dishonesty and half of them burglaries. He was sentenced to 10 years for the burglaries, 8 years concurrent for the handling offences, and ordered to pay over £70,000 confiscation, £45,000 compensation and £7,000 prosecution costs. **10 years** was justified.

GBH, with intent to inflict

26.21 *Att-Gen's Ref. No 94 of 2001 Unreported 21/1/02.* [Court would expect 5 years in this attack on the home of the defendant's ex-partner and her parents, with harassment before.]

Hotel rooms

26.22 *R v Massey* 2001 2 Cr App R (S) 371. The defendant, aged 34 pleaded guilty to two burglaries at the Magistrates' Court. He broke into a guest's room at a hotel through a window. From the room and the guest's car he stole property worth £1,500. He also stole the car. The second burglary was also a guest's room at another hotel with access also gained through a window. The property stolen was worth £3,078. He admitted the offences in interview. He had many previous convictions including 36 for burglary and three for attempted burglary. The risk of re-offending was assessed as high. Held. The burglary of a guest's bedroom was much more akin to burglary of domestic premises rather than of a small business. It is close to the burglary of a bedroom. Two and 2 years consecutive not 2 and 3 years so **4 years** not 5 in all.

Persistent burglar – Drug addict

26.23 *R v Kelly* 2003 1 Cr App R (S) 472. The defendant pleaded guilty in the Magistrates' Court to burglary and attempted burglary and to two thefts. One burglary and one attempted burglary were taken into consideration. The burglary was of an unoccupied house; there was considerable damage to gain access and £702.50 cash and goods were taken. The attempted burglary was of an unoccupied house; the appellant went inside storm doors and smashed a window. An inner door was damaged, but nothing was taken. He was under the influence of valium. The thefts were of money taken from an amusement machine at an arcade whilst under the influence of heroin, and of goods worth £150 from a retail shop. The offences taken into consideration were an attempted domestic burglary and a non-domestic burglary. All offences were committed within a six-week period. The defendant was 28 and had 87 previous convictions, 59 of which were for dishonesty. He had spent a total of six years in custody. Prior to arrest he was using half a gram of heroin a day at a cost of £35. A pre-sentence report proposed that he be assessed for a drug treatment and testing order (DTTO). He was assessed as requiring an intensive and structured programme of work. He was given 3 years 8 months in total including 2 months consecutive for a breach of licence. At the time of his appeal he had spent more than seven months in custody. A further assessment was before Court that described the defendant as highly motivated to co-operate with a DTTO. Held. The sentence was not manifestly excessive. The sentencing judge gave too little consideration to the appropriateness of a DTTO disposal. DTTOs provide a chance for a defendant to break his addiction and therefore cease offending. The judge gave disproportionate weight to the scale of offending and thereby diminished the usefulness both to the offender and to the community of a DTTO. A **12-month DTTO** substituted.

Persistent burglar – Minimum 3 years' custody

26.24 Powers of Criminal Courts (Sentencing) Act 2000 s 111. Where a person is convicted of a domestic burglary committed after 30 November 1999 and was 18 or over and he has been convicted of two other domestic burglaries one of which was committed after he had been convicted of the other and both of them were committed after 30 November 1999, the court shall impose a sentence of imprisonment of at least 3 years unless it is of the opinion that there are particular circumstances which relate to any of the offences or to the offender which would make it unjust. [This section is summarised and is slightly amended by the Criminal Justice and Court Services Act 2000.]

Persistent burglar – Minimum 3 years' custody – Guideline case

26.25 *R v McInerney* 2003 2 Cr App R 627. LCJ. The purpose of the section is, in the absence of specific or particular circumstances which would render it unjust to do so, to oblige the court to impose the prescribed custodial sentence. This means that Parliament has chosen a term as the standard penalty. The object of the section quite plainly is to require the courts to impose at least (the minimum sentence). However, that does not preclude situations arising where it would be unjust to impose a sentence of three years, even where the offender qualifies. It may be helpful to give examples of the type of situation where a three-year sentence may be unjust. The sentence could be unjust; if two of the offences were committed many years earlier than the third offence, or if the offender has made real efforts to reform or conquer his drug or alcohol addiction, but some personal tragedy triggers the third offence or if the first two offences were committed when the offender was not yet 16. Section 111 gives the sentencer a fairly substantial degree of discretion as to the categories of situations where the presumption can be rebutted. This approach is supported by the decision of this court in the case of *R v Offen* 2001 1 WLR 253. Understood in this way section 111 can be regarded as reflecting the current sentencing practice of the courts in relation to those who are convicted of burglary on three separate occasions even where the statutory requirements do not apply.

There are some first-time burglaries which on their facts are so serious that a sentence of three years or more might be appropriate but, conversely, some third, fourth or fifth time burglaries where a sentence lower than three years could properly be justified. (The lower sentence being achieved by the reliance on the exception to section 111.) An offender convicted of a single domestic burglary will accrue a qualifying conviction. Equally an offender convicted on one occasion of three burglaries who asked for another three burglaries to be taken into consideration will also only accrue one qualifying offence. The totality of the actual criminal behaviour is important.

Persistent burglar Minimum three years' custody

26.26   *R v Gibson* 2004 2 Cr App R (S) 451. The Judge indicated at one of the case adjournments that if residential accommodation could be found for the defendant she would make a Drug Treatment and Testing Order. It was found and she sent him to prison. Held. Because of the rules when Judges send defendants to prison after the Judge indicates a non custodial it was wrong. His expectation was a "particular circumstance" which made the minimum sentence unjust. DTTO substituted.

Persistent burglar Minimum three years' custody – Attempted burglary

26.27   *R v Maguire* 2003 1 Cr App R (S) 40. Attempted burglary is not a qualifying offence for the purposes of the Act. Sentence quashed.

Persistent burglar – Minimum 3 years' custody – Juvenile convictions Guideline case

26.28   *R v McInerney* 2003 2 Cr App R 627. LCJ. Where an offender who is now aged 18 or over has two qualifying previous convictions for domestic burglary as a juvenile, a third alleged domestic burglary must be tried in the Crown Court, and the presumptive minimum sentence is a custodial sentence of three years. Although s 111 does not apply until the offender has attained the age of 18, would seem to follow that for an offender who is under 18 but is charged with a third domestic burglary, a custodial sentence **in excess of 24 months** (the maximum term available for a detention and training order) will be the likely sentence and so the Youth Court should generally commit the case to Crown Court for trial with a view to sentence under s 91.

Persistent burglar – Minimum 3 years' custody – Plea of guilty

26.29   Powers of Criminal Courts (Sentencing) Act 2000, s 152(3). Where a sentence is to be imposed under the Powers of the Criminal Courts (Sentencing) Act 2000, s 111 nothing in that section shall prevent the court from imposing a sentence of 80% or more of the minimum period. (Section summarised. The section means if he pleads guilty the court can impose a sentence, which is 80% or more of the minimum term.)

R v Smith 2003 1 Cr App R (S) 630. The defendant pleaded guilty to two counts of burglary and asked for one offence of theft to be taken into consideration. The victim of all of the offences was the defendant's mother, who owned a public house. The defendant broke into the bar area at night and smashed open a pay telephone, two gaming machines and stock cupboards and stole cash and food to the value of £850. He caused £600 of damage. At the time of that offence he was on bail pending sentence for a dwelling house burglary for which he received a nine-month sentence. Following his release the defendant's mother found him in his bedroom with some drugs and told him he had to leave. She had left her handbag on the landing from which she discovered £40 was missing after he had gone. That was the theft. At about 9pm that evening, the defendant broke into the residential part of the premises, kicked in the bedroom door and stole £750. He was arrested within a few days and made full admissions in interview. The defendant was 20 with a substantial record of previous convictions including a number of non-dwelling house burglaries. He also had two convictions for dwelling-house burglaries and triggered section 111 of the Powers of Criminal Courts (Sentencing) Act 2000 requiring the judge to impose an appropriate custodial sentence for at least three years, unless it would be unjust so to do. A psychiatric report concluded that the defendant had a history of depressive disorder, had dyslexia and some symptoms of post traumatic stress disorder following abuse as a child. The defendant was severely addicted to heroin. A letter from the defendant's mother was also considered. Held. It was not unjust to impose the statutory minimum. However, the sentencing judge made no mention of the fact that the defendant had pleaded guilty giving the clear impression that he had overlooked section 152 PCC(S) Act 2000 which provides that where a court imposes a sentence under s. 111 it is entitled to reduce the statutory minimum to a sentence not less than 80 per cent of the maximum sentence where an offender has pleaded guilty. **2¹/₂ years** (about 82% of the statutory minimum term) not three years.

Persistent burglar with many previous convictions – One offence

26.30   *R v Banks* 1999 2 Cr App R (S) 231. The defendant pleaded guilty at the Magistrates' Court to burglary. The victims returned to their flat at about 4am and heard a burglar. They went into the street, saw the defendant and gave chase. The defendant was caught nearby. Jewellery and ornaments from the flat worth £20,000 were recovered from a bag he dropped and his person. A report said it appeared he suffered from a personality disorder. In 1989 he was sentenced to 4 years for 29 burglaries and thefts. In 1993 he was sentenced to 3 years for burglary. It was said there was a serious danger he would re-offend. Therefore **4 years** not 5.

R v Jenkins 2002 1 Cr App R (S) 12. The defendant was convicted of burglary. During the day, the defendant broke into an unoccupied dwelling by forcing some French windows. Jewellery worth over £50,000 and a clock worth over £20,000 were stolen. His fingerprints were found near the scene and the clock was found in his garden shed. The jewellery was not found but he had £5,401 in cash was found. He relied on an alibi. He was 56 and on licence from a 2¹/₂ year sentence for burglary. There were twenty burglaries, seven handling offences, three attempted burglaries and four for either house-breaking or attempted house-breaking on his record. He had been a persistent offender for 38 years. The longest sentence was 5 years. His partner suffered from cancer. Held. He is a persistent, professional burglar. This case is similar to *R v Brewster* 1998 1 Cr App R (S) 181 at 187. **8 years** was very severe but not manifestly excessive.

R v Humphreys 2001 Unreported 12/10/01. 6 years not 9 for man with an appalling record for burglary convicted of a single offence

R v Comer 2002 1 Cr App R (S) 147. The defendant was convicted of burglary. The victim saw the defendant walk up the drive and walk into her hall. He said he hadn't done anything wrong and was with the postman delivering a parcel. He left and nothing was taken. He was identified sitting on a park bench nearby. When interviewed he said that he went to the house to look for milk and the door popped open. In November 1999 he received a combination order for a commercial burglary. In total he had four convictions for burglary and had convictions for possession of drugs and theft. He had served three prison sentences. Held. He was a somewhat low level professional burglar. **3 years** not 4

R v O'Brien 2002 2 Cr App R (S) 560. The defendant pleaded guilty at the PDH to burglary. He was in breach of his licence and was given 3 months concurrent for that. The victim, an 81 year old lady lived with her son and had the early stages of dementia. She exhibited considerable confusion. She was capable of looking after herself and lived with her son who instructed her not to open the door to anyone without an identity badge. The son returned home and found the tap in the garden running. His mother told him that earlier a man claiming to be from the Water Board visited the house and asked to test the taps. The man went upstairs and stole a mobile phone and £200 from him and a watch from her bedroom. The defendant was traced through fingerprints. When interviewed he denied the offence. He was drug addict and wrote a letter expressing remorse. (The report does not detail his antecedents or CRO.) The Judge said, "Society rightly reserves its deepest censure for those who prey upon vulnerable groups such as the elderly. Throughout your recent criminal career you have mercilessly and relentlessly pursued the old. Time after time you have tricked the elderly into believing you were a public official, tricking your way in and stealing their property. I am determined the elderly have a sustained rest from your activities." Held. He is a professional burglar. His speciality is vulnerable elderly people. He tricks them and steals their property. This type of burglary casts a shadow on the lives of elderly people. They dread the unexpected knock. We entirely agree with the Judge's remarks. The question was had he received sufficient credit for the plea. **8 years** not 9.

R v Maguire 2003 2 Cr App R (S) 40. The defendant attempted to burgle his girlfriend's ground floor flat. He tried to enter through a window which was already broken. He caused a little more damage. He ran from police, but was caught. In interview he said "I'm guilty. I'm sorry," and that he had no money and he was hungry. He had "a great number of convictions for theft and burglary." Held. Attempted burglary was not a qualifying offence for the automatic 3 years. **18 months** substituted.

R v McInerney 2003 2 Cr App R (S) 240 at p 260. The defendant pleaded guilty at the Magistrates' Court to burglary. He entered the home of the victim aged 93 by impersonating a police officer. He showed the victim a fake identification badge bearing his photograph and wore clothes like those of a police officer. He said that he was checking the victim's insurance. He went into every room and spoke to someone on a mobile phone. When the victim became suspicious the defendant offered to let him talk to 'his boss' on the mobile phone. The defendant then locked the victim in his kitchen. When the victim said that he was going to call the police the defendant removed the battery from his phone. The defendant left the house with £140 and a telephone battery. He was later identified by fingerprints and when interviewed he fully admitted the offence saying that he had not targeted the victim and that he did not think that he was 93 but nearer 60. The sentencing judge was sceptical about whether the defendant would have withdrawn if he had known the true age of the victim and was in no doubt that the defendant was targeting the elderly. The defendant was 22 with a record of 39 previous offences including 2 offences of burglary (commercial) for which he received a 2 year sentence. Held. This was a very bad burglary and premeditated, it was aggravated by the age of the victim and the unattractive deceit adopted to carry out this offence. However, $7^{1}/_{2}$ years was too high a starting point. $3^{1}/_{2}$ **years** not 5.

R v Page 2004 Times 23/12/04. The defendant pleaded to burglary, obtaining services by deception and theft at the Magistrates' Court. He forced a ground floor window of domestic premises and stole £4,800 worth of jewellery. Considerable damage was done and his blood was found on the window. He was arrested and denied the offence. Eighteen days later he and five others went to a restaurant and eat a meal costing £127. The five left and he explained he had no money to pay. He was arrested and he had £4 on him. Twelve days later he was stopped leaving a shop with an oven worth almost £50. He stole an iron from the same shop which was a TIC. The defendant was aged 56 with 49 previous convictions. 40 were shoplifting and 33 burglaries for which he received 7 years in 1977, 5 years in 1981 and 7 years in 1987. Since then he had been convicted at least once a year for shoplifting, drunk and disorderly, criminal damage and minor violence. Since 1987 he had received 4 months, 1 month, 3 months, 3 weeks, 2 months (with a driving whilst disqualified) 14 days twice for shoplifting. $2^{1}/_{2}$ **years** not $3^{1}/_{2}$ for the burglary with 3 and 1 month consecutive making **2 years 10 months** not 3 years 10 months.

Old cases *R v Brewster* 1998 Re Thorpe 1 Cr App R (S) 181 at 188, *R v Brewster* 1998 Re Ishmael 1 Cr App R (S) 181 at 188, *R v Brewster* 1998 Re Blanchard 1 Cr App R (S) 181 at 189, *R v Woods* 1998 2 Cr App R (S) 237 and *R v Hollis* 1998 2 Cr App R (S) 359. (For a summary of these cases see the first edition of this book.)

Persistent burglar with many previous convictions – More than one offence

26.31   *R v Brewster* 1998 1 Cr App R (S) 181 at 187. LCJ The defendant, aged 51, a professional burglar pleaded guilty to three offences of burglary. They were all daytime burglaries of unoccupied flats. A wristwatch valued at £10,000 was stolen. There was no ransacking of the premises. The offences were committed within 3 months, the first one taking place just six months after his release from prison. He made admissions in interview. He had a formidable criminal record, including no fewer than 33 previous convictions for domestic burglary. His criminal career began at the age of 8. Included in it was *R v Brewster* 1980 2 Cr App R (S) 191, when a 10 years sentence was upheld on pleas of guilty to two burglaries in which some £70,000 worth of jewellery was stolen. Lawton LJ said: 'There is no hope of rehabilitating this man. There is no hope that he will be deterred by prison sentences. All that the courts can do with him and his like is to ensure that they do not carry out raids on other people's houses for very substantial periods.' Held. The judge was fully entitled to take into account his appalling record as aggravating the seriousness of the offences. **9 years** was a very severe sentence and was justified. It matters not whether it is structured as 9 years' concurrent or 3 years for each offence consecutive.

R v X 1999 2 Cr App R (S) 294. The defendant pleaded guilty to 'a number of offences of burglary.' He was 30 years of age and had a 'substantial record'. He was a drug addict and his many offences were substantially committed to gain money to fund his habit. In September 1997, he was sentenced for three burglaries of homes, from which he had stolen electrical equipment. There were other less significant offences as well. He was put on probation for two years, with a condition that he reside for 12 months at an identified drug rehabilitation unit. Four days later, he left the unit without permission. A counsellor arranged for him to attend another rehabilitation centre and he went there and remained for about a month but left that centre unilaterally as well. Shortly afterwards, he committed a separate offence of a motoring kind, and served a short sentence for that. In March, he appeared before the justices and admitted the breach of probation. He was committed to the Crown Court for sentence, on bail. Accordingly, he was thereafter on bail as well as still on probation. In April, he broke into a house, divided into bed sitting rooms, during the day time, and stole electrical equipment from several of the rooms. Considerable damage was done to the property. Untidy searches were made and the possessions of the occupants were strewn about. Property worth just over £3,000 was stolen. He pleaded guilty and was sentenced to 4 years concurrently upon each offence. Held. Consecutive sentences would have been fully justified for the original offences and the recent ones. 4 years was appropriate. Because of information provided the offence was reduced to **3$^{1}/_{2}$ years**.

R v Burns 2000 2 Cr App R (S) 198. The defendant, aged 19 pleaded guilty to three burglaries at the Magistrates' Court. He asked for five burglaries to be taken into consideration. The first victim who found the defendant in her kitchen was 66 years old. He asked for some directions and fled with £170, which was taken from the bedroom. Four rooms had been ransacked. Four days later the next victim also found the defendant in her kitchen. An hour later a couple aged 84 and 94 heard banging coming from a bedroom. They found jewellery of sentimental value worth £17,000 had been taken. He had an appalling record, which included 37 offences for burglary. The offences were to finance his heroin addiction. **5 years** was well merited.

R v Palmer and Others 2004 2 Cr App R 519. The defendant W pleaded guilty to nine counts of burglary with 12 offences of burglary taken into consideration. The defendant P pleaded guilty to one offence of burglary and two of attempted burglary and the defendant O pleaded guilty to one count of attempted burglary two of handling stolen goods and one of driving a conveyance taken without authority. They had four co-accused. The group burgled large houses, normally by forcing entry. They targeted these addresses because there were expensive cars on the driveways. They stole not only the car keys from the houses but other items such as jewellery, watches, laptop computers, cameras and cash. They then drove the cars away with the other property. If

the cars were not there they would return on other days with the keys to steal them. W then 17 was involved with nine of these types of burglary in which 8 cars worth in excess of £172,000 were stolen as well as items such as plasma TV sets, jewellery, and cameras. P's offences were burgling the house with W when a plasma TV set worth £9,000 and keys for a Rolls Royce and a Range Rover were taken. Also going to two different houses with expensive cars on the drive, ringing the bells, but the occupants were in and nothing more happened. O was linked to the car worth £10,000 and an Audi car and was seen with others acting suspiciously outside a house where there were expensive cars on the drive. He also handled the plasma TV set. W had 12 previous convictions including ones for aggravated vehicle taking, handling, numerous burglaries of dwelling houses, and offences to do with interfering with motor vehicles. P, 22, was on bail for previous offences of burglary when these offences were committed. He had an extensive record for offences including handling and dwelling house burglaries. A presentence report said that he was doing well in custody and had taken courses including drug programmes. He expressed his shame and said he was determined to avoid re offending. O was 16 and 17 at the time of the offences and 18 when sentenced. His previous convictions were slight with nothing similar. The pre-sentence report set out the extremely difficult crowded and squalid conditions in which he had been brought up. Held. In the case of W if he had been sentenced at age 17 any court would have passed a sentence under Section 91. **5 years** was substantial and severe but justified. In the case of P **3 years** on each count to run concurrently was in no way excessive bearing in mind his record as a whole. In the case of O he was much less involved although he must have realised the seriousness of the overall enterprise. The appropriate total sentence was **18 months** not 2 years.

Victim over 65

26.32   *R v Whittaker* 1998 1 Cr App R (S) 172. The defendant was convicted of four burglaries. The first victim was aged 83 and lost £200 and personal property. He was wearing a balaclava. She was unable to stop him. The second time he wore a mask. The victim was very frightened as he stole £100 and personal property. He was arrested and granted bail. The third victims were a 77-year-old woman and her disabled husband aged 81. He was wearing a hood and the woman tried to stop him but was unable to. He stole her handbag. The fourth involved another old woman who found him in her house. She screamed hysterically. He had a balaclava on. Her husband was knocked over as he took hold of him. He was later taken to hospital. She ran into the street and spoke to the police. The defendant was feeding a drug habit and in 1988 was sentenced to 5 years for burglary. Held. Burglaries against elderly people are regarded as extremely serious. 5 concurrent for each pair consecutive making **10 years** upheld.

R v Guigno 1998 2 Cr App R (S) 217. The defendant was convicted of burgling a bungalow occupied by a married couple aged 87 and 91. At 2.15am he entered her bedroom and when she woke up he carried on searching. She put her hand out and she felt his head. He was challenged twice. Her panic alarm enabled the police to be called and the police outside found him. The contents of her bedroom cabinet had been spread on the floor. At the trial he accepted he was the burglar but said he was too drunk to form the necessary intent. The victims were not called to give evidence. The defendant had no previous convictions for burglary. **3 years** was right.

See also *R v O'Brien* 2002 2 Cr App R (S) 560 and **DISTRACTION BURGLARIES** (where the victim is invariably elderly)

Burglary – Non domestic

Magistrates' Court Sentencing Guidelines January 2004 – Non Dwelling

26.33   Entry point. Is it serious enough for a community penalty? Consider the impact on the victim. Examples of aggravating factors for the offence are forcible entry, group offence, harm to business, occupants frightened, professional operation, repeat victimisation, school or medical premises, soiling, ransacking damage. Examples of mitigating factors for the offence are low value, nobody frightened, no damage or disturbance. Examples of mitigation are age, health (physical or mental), co-operation with the police, genuine remorse and voluntary compensation. Give reasons if not awarding compensation.

For details about the guidelines see MAGISTRATES' COURT SENTENCING GUIDELINES at page 483.

Banks, places for money etc

26.34   *R v Richardson and Brown* 1998 2 Cr App R (S) 87. The defendants pleaded guilty to burglary. An eight-man team used a JCB digger, lorry and car to ram raid a suburban branch of a bank. All the vehicles were stolen. Telephone wires were cut. The police arrived and the group scattered. The lorry was driven at and partly over a police car. The two defendants escaped in the car, which collided with numerous parked cars. The cash machine contained £75,000. R had more previous convictions than B. The judge thought not less than 7 years was appropriate and reduced it to 5 because of the plea. Held. The 2 year only discount was justified and **5 years** was no way too long.

Jewellers

26.35   *R v O'Hara* 2003 2 Cr App R (S) 121. The defendant pleaded guilty to burglary and breach of bail. At about 5 pm he and others forced the back door of a jewellers and ransacked the shop. Display cabinets were broken open and tills forced. There was £1,000 damage and property worth over £3,000 was stolen. The police were notified by the alarm and he and another were caught fleeing. Only some of the property was recovered. He was released on bail and failed to attend. The defendant was 51 with convictions going back to 1962 for theft burglary, TDA and attempted burglary. Since 1990 he had concentrated on stealing from shops to funds his addiction to drink and drugs. The pre-sentence report said he was likely to re-offend. Held. What makes the offence more serious is the shop was a jewellers where it is expected high value easily disposed of property can be found. The public needed to be protected. **3¹/₂ years** was not manifestly excessive.

Shops etc

26.36   *R v Anson* 1999 1 Cr App R (S) 331. The defendant pleaded guilty very late to burglary. At night he burgled Woolworths of property worth £11,913 and caused £2,500 worth of damage. Half the property was recovered from his friends and relatives. He was 28 with a significant criminal record going back many years including burglary both domestic and commercial. **2¹/₂ years** was not wrong.

Sneak thieves

26.37   *R v Creed* 2005 Unreported 2/2/05. The defendant was convicted of burglary at the Magistrates' Court. He was in breach of a DTTO for theft and burglary. The defendant stole a drill from the workshop area not open to the public at the back of a locksmith's showroom while the shop assistant had left to get the post. The assistant found the defendant in the showroom and the drill which was worth £300 was recovered. He was 28 with a deplorable record. In 10 years there were 22 appearances. Held. In reality it was closer to shoplifting than what is commonly regarded as burglary. We apply the R v Page 2004 guidelines. He was fortunate the Judge did not impose prison for the breach of the DTTO. **18 months** not 2 years.

27 BURGLARY – AGGRAVATED

27.1 Theft Act 1968 s 10

Indictable only. Maximum sentence life.

Drug Abstinence Order This was repealed on 4 April 2005.

Dangerous Offender provisions For offences committed on or after 4/4/05 where there is a significant risk to members of the public of serious harm etc. there is a mandatory duty to pass a life sentence when it is justified and otherwise a sentence of imprisonment for public protection[21]. For offenders under 18 the duty is to pass detention for life, detention for public protection or an extended sentence[22].

Minimum sentences Domestic burglary is a specified offence for a 3 year minimum sentence when the offence is a third domestic burglary[23].

Restitution Order There is power to make an order that the stolen goods etc. in the possession of the defendant or a third party be restored to the owner etc.[24].

Sexual Offences Prevention Order There is a discretionary power to make this order when it is necessary to protect the public etc[25].

See also **ROBBERY**

Crown Court statistics – England and Wales – Males 21+

27.2

Year	Plea	Total Numbers sentenced	Type of sentence %					Average length of custody (months)
			Discharge	Fine	Community sentence	Suspended sentence	Custody	
In a Dwelling								
2002	Guilty	119	–	–	10	1	88	52.6
	Not guilty	62	–	–	2	–	92	60
2003	Guilty	125	1	–	8	2	89	52.1
	Not guilty	36	–	–	3	–	97	71.3
Not a dwelling								
2002	Guilty	11	–	–	9	–	82	51
	Not guilty	5	–	–	–	–	100	79.2
2003	Guilty	14	–	–	7	–	86	29.6
	Not guilty	2	–	–	6	–	88	84

For details and explanations about the statistics in the book see page vii.

Guideline case

27.3 For some guidance see **BURGLARY – DOMESTIC** – *Guideline case* R v McInerney 2003 2 Cr App R 627. LCJ Guidelines. However, these guidelines do not deal with the very important element of aggravation.

---

21 Criminal Justice Act 2003 s 225
22 Criminal Justice Act 2003 s 226 and 228
23 Powers of Criminal Courts (Sentencing) Act 2000 s 111
24 Powers of Criminal Courts (Sentencing) Act 2000 s 148(2)
25 Sexual Offences Act 2003 s 104 & Sch. 5

Defendant aged 14–16

27.4   *R v Simpson* 1998 1 Cr App R (S) 145. The defendant aged 16 made an early plea to aggravated burglary and ABH. The victim aged 83 found the defendant in her home in the early hours of the morning. She asked him what he was doing and didn't believe his answer. He tried to go upstairs and the victim called out to her neighbours. He left. A neighbour tried to take hold of him in the garden and the defendant pulled out two knives. A struggle ensued and the defendant bit the neighbour. The wound bled. The defendant also threatened the neighbour with a knife. The defendant had numerous previous convictions mainly for theft etc. He also had 18 burglary convictions many of them of dwelling houses. He had a sad and troubled background. Held. Even taking into account his age, the plea and the circumstances the $3^1/_2$ year sentence was not manifestly excessive

Att-Gen's Ref. No 24 of 1997 1998 1 Cr App R (S) 319. The defendant pleaded guilty to aggravated burglary. In the early hours of the morning he entered the home of a 78-year-old woman who lived alone. She woke up and checked downstairs and returned to bed. She then saw him standing next to her bed with a knife in his hand. His face was covered and he was carrying some tape. She screamed and he fled empty handed. She tried to call the police but the telephone was unplugged. She had seen him twice before when he asked to use her lavatory so he knew her age. He told his foster mother about it and he went with her to the police. He had many previous convictions including numerous for burglary. He had committed burglary the day before the offence. The right sentence would have been 4 years. Taking into account it was a reference $3^1/_2$ **years** detention not 2.

R v Vardy 1999 1 Cr App R (S) 220. The defendant pleaded guilty to aggravated burglary. He asked for two burglaries and two attempted burglaries to be taken into consideration. Shortly after midnight when aged 16 he broke into the home of a 74 year old by smashing a window with a table leg he had brought with him. The householder came down the stairs and the defendant pushed past him and ran out of the house. After the householder had gone upstairs the defendant re-entered the house. The householder again came down the stairs and the defendant rushed at him and struck him over the head with the table leg and the householder fell to the ground. The defendant then struck him on the head at least six times and ran off. The victim had swelling over his head and some cuts. However, he suffered from severe trauma and the attack had severely affected him. The defendant was arrested and denied the offence. However, the police then found his name under some tape on the table leg he had left behind. Of the offences taken into consideration three of them involved dwelling houses. In one he stole £150 worth of Christmas presents and caused £1,700 worth of damage. When he was 14 he was given a conditional discharge for attempted theft. When 15 he was sentenced to 24 hours at an attendance centre for ABH. He had knocked a school friend to the ground and repeatedly kicked him. At the same time he was sentenced for two shopliftings. Later he received 3 months' detention for two ABH offences. He had repeatedly kicked and punched the victim. There was a Newton hearing and the judge found he had lied. The judge said he was a danger to the community. Held. There was gratuitous and severe violence. It was very serious. Had he been older 12 years could not be criticised. However as he is now only 17, **10 years** instead.

R v Bruce 2000 2 Cr App R (S) 376. The defendant pleaded guilty to two burglaries and one aggravated burglary. When 16 he entered the flat of a woman in a housing complex for the elderly. He did not disturb her but took her purse. From then on she was afraid to stay in her flat alone and within a few weeks she died. On the same night in the same complex he entered another flat and stole a purse without waking the occupant. Less than 4 months later a resident aged 72 in the same complex found the defendant in her bedroom. He pulled her out of bed and as she lay on the floor he repeatedly stabbed her with a knife. He left taking no property. She was taken to hospital and found to have four wounds. They were each about $2^1/_2$ " long and 2 cm wide. All had been directed at a life threatening area of the body. The victim was in a lot of pain. He was under the effects of drink and sleeping pills, which would have had a disinhibiting effect. He had a number of previous convictions including five for burglary one of which was residential. **10 years** and 2 years concurrent was entirely right.

Domestic violence
See **DOMESTIC VIOLENCE – General**

Firearm, with
27.5 *R v Matthews and Jacobs* 2002 2 Cr App R (S) 481   The defendants M and J were convicted of aggravated burglary. M also pleaded to prison escape. At 10 p.m. the defendants and another forced their way into a couple's home. They were armed with an imitation firearm and two knives. They threatened the couple and beat the man about the head and body with the gun. She was beaten about the head with a knife handle. They ripped two necklaces from the necks of their victims and also took a small sum of money. They tried to swim across a river but failed and were arrested. M was 24 and had convictions including 6 months YOI for ABH in 1997 and 4 years for wounding and GBH in 1999. J was 35 and had convictions including in 1997 3 years for robbery and having a bladed article in a public place. Held. We have to quash the year extra for breach of M's licence because when he escaped he wasn't on licence. **7 years** for M and 9 years for J whilst severe were not manifestly excessive but to maintain the differential J's sentence was reduced from 9 to **8 years.**

(Note. It would have been preferable if the defendants had been indicted for possession of a firearm with intent to rob.)

Att-Gen's Ref. No. 34 of 2003 2004 1 Cr App R (S) 422. The defendant pleaded guilty to aggravated burglary. The victim, aged 40 was watching television when the doorbell rang and he opened his door to the defendant and another. The other male squirted liquid in the victim's face. The defendant barged the victim backwards and punched him several times to the face. He pointed a pistol-type gun at him. The victim appreciated that it was not a real gun. The defendant demanded that the victim should tell him where the safe was and he would avoid getting hurt. He was pushed into the kitchen and his arms were tied with zip ties; he was then dragged into a bedroom and forced face down on to a bed. £2,000 was taken from bedroom drawers. The victim was tied up with a belt and ties and his vest was put over his face. The defendant was heard to say "Go and get a knife, we'll have to cut him". He was also punched several times in the head. His wallet and camcorder were taken. Other rooms were ransacked. The victim's face was swollen and bleeding. Three days later the defendant was stopped in a car that contained the victim's driving licence and bank cards. The defendant was picked out on an identification parade and footprints linked him to the scene. He made no comment in interview. He was 34 with 21 convictions for 74 offences including offences of violence including GBH. This offence was committed 15 days after the defendant had been sentenced to a community rehabilitation order. Held. This was a very serious offence of its kind. There was a deliberate plan, with two men armed with a firearm, attacking a single man in his own home. They squirted something in his face and there was gratuitous punching. He was tied up and punched again. **9 years** would have been appropriate after a trial; **7 years** with credit for a guilty plea. **5$^1/_2$ years** not 3, as this was a reference.

See also **FIREARMS**

More than one attack
27.6 *R v Daniel* 2000 2 Cr App R (S) 184. The defendant was convicted of aggravated

burglary and attempted aggravated burglary. Both the intents were to inflict GBH. The defendant lived in one of six flats in a house. On his way home early in the morning, the defendant was attacked by an unknown man in the street. The defendant arrived home and kicked the door to the flats open. He was bleeding and brandishing a rather blunt kitchen knife. He pushed past the occupant of the ground floor flat shouting 'Where are they?' The occupier told him to call the police and he said 'Well, you're dead then.' He left and started knocking loudly on another door. He threatened to kill the occupants. Things went quiet. Then he started hitting the door with a hammer saying he would kill them. The door was extensively damaged. The occupants of both flats were terrified. The police arrived. He was arrested in his flat and the hammer and knife were found. He was 27 with numerous previous convictions mostly for dishonesty and violence. There were numerous convictions for burglary. He had been to prison three times. $2^1/_2$ years substituted for 4.

Att-Gen's Ref No. 64 of 2003 Re B 2004 2 Cr App R (S) 106 at 113. The defendant made an early plea to aggravated burglary, two burglaries and an attempted burglary. He asked for 36 offences of burglary and three attempted burglaries to be taken into consideration. In the early hours he broke into a home and stole a handbag. An hour or two later he broke in again. He woke a mother who was with her 10 day old baby. Using a knife he threatened the mother and baby and pulled the mother downstairs to look for her handbag. It wasn't found and she was taken back upstairs where her mother was woken up. He demanded money and took cash and a watch. Later that day after 10 p.m. a householder found the defendant in his home with a stick saying, "I've got a knife." The stick was seized, the alarm pressed and the defendant fled. £4,000 worth of property was stacked by the front door. Half an hour later while a dinner party was in progress he put his arm holding a cane through the letter box. The hostess shouted and the defendant ran off. He was stopped by police and he gave a false address. Fingerprints were taken from the cane and he was arrested. In interview he made admissions saying the offences were to feed his crack habit. He expressed remorse. The total value of property taken in the offences and the TICs was £120,000 of which over £70,000 was recovered. He was 24 with 22 convictions including 2 robberies and 13 burglaries 12 of which were domestic. He was in breach of a licence following a 4 year detention sentence for robbery, false imprisonment and burglary. In that case a knife was used and the victim forced to go to a cash point. The pre-sentence report said there was a high risk of re-offending and said he was suitable for a DTTO order. He was given a DTTO and had absconded from his accommodation. A warrant was issued for his arrest. *Held.* The Court gave guidance for making DTTO orders. Taking into account an offence was at night at a dwelling house with a knife, with the TICs and the fact he was on licence we would expect **6 years**. Because it was a reference, part of the DTTO had been completed and his mitigation **4 years** substituted.

Occupiers suffering injuries

27.7   *Att-Gen's Ref. No 1 of 2000* 2000 2 Cr App R (S) 340. The defendant pleaded to aggravated burglary. He entered a room at a home for nurses and awoke a nurse with a kiss. She moved away and he said 'What is your problem?' She pulled the bedclothes over her head and the defendant tried to pull them off. He started stabbing her with a pair of scissors, which he had found in the room. He ran off. The victim had relatively minor injuries to her arms, neck and chest. He was of good character. *Held.* 5 years would be expected, but as it was a reference **4 years** not 18 months.

R v Barczi and Williams 2001 2 Cr App R (S) 410. The defendants B and W pleaded guilty to aggravated burglary. The victim and his girlfriend broke up acrimoniously. The girlfriend then gave birth. She was the longstanding girlfriend of the brother of W. B lived with W and his family. The defendants travelled from Plymouth to Nottingham and went to the home of the victim wearing balaclavas and surgical gloves. One of them had a piece of wood. They knocked on the door and the victim opened it. Neighbours saw this and called the police. The victim was struck, pushed back in his house and hit repeatedly. He was wrestled to the floor and hit again. His feet and hands were bound with tape. A policeman arrived quickly and arrested the defendants. They didn't resist. The victim suffered from two fractured ribs, bruising, blood in his nose and a cut. Both defendants were of 'exemplary character.' B had served 6 years with the army and his conduct was described as 'exemplary'. W had been in the Royal Navy. Their current work records were good. They said the victim was over pursuing his rights with the children so unsettling the mother. It was feared he would abduct the children or harm the mother. **Held.** After a trial **7 or 8 years** would not have been out of place. **5 years** was not manifestly excessive.

Att-Gen's Ref. Nos. 144, 145 and 146 of 2001 2002 2 Cr App R (S) 503. On 29 January 2001, the defendants P and T pleaded guilty to aggravated burglary. Their basis of plea was not accepted and the case was listed for a Newton hearing. On 26 March 2001 J pleaded not guilty to the same offence. They all absconded. On 15 November 2001 J changed his plea and his basis was also not accepted. At the Newton hearing 2 weeks later they accepted the Crown's case. S, the brother of J and P had an argument with the victim's daughter L. Her boyfriend, C heard about it and went to the brothers' home looking for S who wasn't there. S then went to look C and found him at the victim's home. A fight developed between S and C and the victim intervened, telling them to stop it. S left. Just after midnight, the defendants and between 1 and 4 others ran into the victim's home armed with knives and an axe. They demanded to know where C was. Three or four of them attacked the victim. He was struck and cut with the axe and the knives and punched and kicked. P struck the first blow. T was less involved with the violence than the others. Some ran upstairs and found L who was holding her 10 day old baby. She was hysterical and in fear of her and her baby's life. P pointed a knife at L's sister who was crying. Her sister and mother were also present. When the group realised C was not there they left. The victim was taken to hospital and treated for a 8 cm. superficial laceration across the top of his head which needed 15 stitches, a 1.5 cm. laceration along his eyebrow, a small laceration to the edge of the same eyebrow, a 5 cm. deep laceration to the front of his chest requiring 4 stitches, a 2–3 cm. laceration/abrasion to his forearm and a deep laceration on his thigh requiring 8 stitches. He was in hospital for 3 days and 18 months later he still had numbness in his leg and needed sleeping pills. The defendants were in their early 20s and all had previous convictions but none had had custody. The Judge did not give them full credit for their plea and gave each 30 months. After sentence they had a positive attitude to imprisonment. **Held.** It was an outrageous attack. There was a mob of young men, armed with very dangerous weapons, no doubt gaining courage by being armed and their number, invading a home at night, intent on violence and causing serious violence as well as absolute terror to the victim's family. In an attack like this there is rarely any distinction to be drawn between the defendants. Taking into account their age, their attitude to prison and it was a reference **4 years** is the least we can impose. This will remain consecutive to the 2 months for breach of bail.

Att-Gen's Ref. No. 34 of 2003 2004 1 Cr App R (S) 422. The defendant pleaded guilty to aggravated burglary. The victim, aged 40 was watching television when the doorbell rang and he opened his door to the defendant and another. The other male squirted liquid in the victim's face. The defendant barged the victim backwards and punched him several times to the face. He pointed a pistol-type gun at him. The victim appreciated that it was not a real gun. The defendant demanded that the victim should tell him where the safe was and he would avoid getting hurt. He was pushed into the kitchen and his arms were tied with zip ties; he was then dragged into a bedroom and forced face down on to a bed. £2,000 was taken from bedroom drawers. The victim was tied up with a belt and ties and his vest was put over his face. The defendant was heard to say "Go and get a knife, we'll have to cut him". He was also punched several times in the head. His wallet and camcorder were taken. Other rooms were ransacked. The victim's face was swollen and bleeding. Three days later the defendant was stopped in a car that contained the victim's driving licence and bank cards. The defendant was picked-out on an identification parade and footprints linked him to the scene. He made no comment in interview. He was 34 with 21 convictions for 74 offences including offences of violence including GBH. This offence was committed 15 days after the defendant had been sentenced to a community rehabilitation order. Held. This was a very serious offence of its kind. There was a deliberate plan, with two men armed with a firearm, attacking a single man in his own home. They squirted something in his face and there was gratuitous punching. He was tied up and punched again. **9 years** would have been appropriate after a trial; **7 years** with credit for a guilty plea. **5¹/₂ years** not 3, as this was a reference.

Att-Gen's Ref. No. 104 of 2002 2003 2 Cr App R (S) 682. The defendant was convicted of aggravated burglary and ABH. The defendant broke into the home of a 76-year old widower when he was asleep in his living room one afternoon. He awoke to see a figure at a frosted glass-fronted internal door. When the victim confronted him he hit him on the head with the victim's coal shovel knocking him to the ground. He struck him 3 more times and shouted for him to stay down. The householder got up and backed away but was attacked again: beaten about the face and upper body with the shovel. He fell to the floor and the defendant fled taking the victim's coat, keys and some money. The victim had lacerations to the face and hands, his ribs were either fractured or badly bruised. Seven weeks later a rib was still fractured. He was at the time of the attack recovering from an operation to remove a tumour from beneath his eye. He also had psychological injuries. He had lived in the house for 20 years and nursed his wife there until her death 4 years earlier from terminal cancer. He no longer felt safe or able to return to his home. DNA linked the defendant to the offence. He said in interview that he had seen an open window and climbed in with another man who had carried out the attack. The victim gave evidence at trial. The defendant was 18 at conviction had 12 previous convictions for 26 offences including a conviction for a possessing an offensive weapon 8 days before this offence. He was therefore in breach of the community punishment order that had been imposed. He had not previously received a custodial sentence. Held. This was a burglary bristling with aggravating features. There was a repeated and sustained attack on a victim in his own home who was vulnerable both by age and illness. It caused ugly physical injuries and gravely damaged the victim's sense of security and well-being. **9 years detention** would have been appropriate even for someone so young but as this was a reference **7 years detention** not 4 years.

Att-Gen's Ref. No 4 of 2004 2005 1 Cr App R (S) 108. The defendant was convicted of aggravated burglary. Together with 2 others, he went to a block of flats and rang a doorbell. When someone opened the door he was confronted by the 3 men, armed with 2 knives. They demanded money and the person who opened the door was pushed against the wall as the 3 men entered. The defendant then confronted the other occupant of the flat, grabbed him by the throat, pushed him down onto the bed, threatened him with a knife and ordered him to remove his watch. He demanded money and when the man denied that he had any, the defendant threatened to slash his face and stab his eye out. One of the intruders ripped a gold chain from his neck. One of the intruders stole some cannabis. The defendant then pushed a knife to the side of the face of the other occupant. They left with various electronic items and got into a car. Police traced the car to the defendant. He was identified on a parade. He was 32 with 13 previous convictions, but had never received a custodial sentence. He was a risk to known adults but not to the public at large. His and wife and children had left him as a result of the offence. Held. This was clearly a planned offence by 3 men who went armed to the premises in question. The used the knife did cause injury although it was a relatively superficial injury. The offence took place during the hours of darkness. The offence, without credit, would normally attract **8 years**. Hence **6 years**, not 4.

Old cases *Att-Gen's Ref. No 54 of 1996* 1997 1 Cr App R (S) 245, *Att-Gen's Ref. No 36 of 1997* 1998 1 Cr App R (S) 365, *Att-Gen's Ref. Nos. 37 and 38 of 1997* 1998 2 Cr App R (S) 48 and *Att-Gen's Ref. No 47 of 1997* 1998 2 Cr App R (S) 68. (For a summary of these cases see the first edition of this book.)

See also OFFENCES AGAINST THE PERSON ACT **1861** SECTION **18** *Robbery/Burglary/ Aggravated burglary, and*

Partner, spouse, ex-partner, ex-spouse, against

27.8 *R v Gordon* 2002 1 Cr App R (S) 523. The defendant pleaded guilty to aggravated burglary at an early stage. The defendant who had had two failed marriages and for nearly 2 months lived with the victim a single mother with her children. He didn't tell the truth about his background and he became aggressive and argumentative. When he moved out in August 2000 they remained in contact but she made it clear that she wanted the relationship to be mere friendship. At 3am in the beginning of October he rang her number and she by dialling 1471 discovered he was the caller. About an hour later he gained entry to her home by throwing a gas bottle through a glazed door. He was in combat clothing and was carrying five knives and a piece of rope. He told her to call the police saying he would be 'going down for what I'm going to do.' She did that. She was in the bedroom with 10-year-old daughter and he said he wanted revenge against two of her friends who he blamed for the break up of the relationship. He looked to see if there were signs of another man having been in her bed and threw a knife between her and her daughter. She pushed the daughter down and it missed the daughter by inches. The 3-year-old son came in and the defendant calmed down. The police arrived and found the victim and her daughter cowering against a wall. The defendant had two knives in one hand and three in the other and there was a stand off between him and the officers. He refused to do as he was told and only put the knives down when he was threatened with CS gas. In interview he said he had not intended to harm anyone and had had a moderate amount of alcohol. He was 36 and had convictions for drink/drive and driving whilst disqualified. His job, which had long hours, gave him a high degree of stress. The psychiatrist said it was totally out of character and he was remorseful. Held. This was a very serious offence causing very real terror. Because of the mitigation **5 years** not 7. [Whether the burglary had an intent to steal or cause GBH is not clear.]

Revenge attack on a burglar

27.9 *Att-Gen's Ref. No 10 of 1996* 1997 1 Cr App R (S) 76. The defendant pleaded guilty to aggravated burglary. The defendant had spent much time and effort in building up his business. He was the victim of a burglary in which he lost £25,000 and his guard dog was attacked and seriously injured. He went to the home of the victim, the man he believed was responsible. He pretended he wanted to purchase the tools but was able to look at the inside of the house. Inside the house were the victim's wife, her two children and a neighbour. A few minutes later two cars pulled up and three men got out armed with pieces of wood and ran to the house. The defendant ran to the back door smashed the glass with a baseball bat and broke in. He then broke the lounge door with the bat and met the victim who was armed with a poker. The defendant struck him with the bat repeatedly leaving him lying in a pool of blood. The others in the house had fled upstairs. One of them had to free the victim's tongue, which had caught in his throat. The victim had a depressed occipital fracture of the skull. He was an in patient at hospital three times in the next $7^1/_2$ weeks. The defendant was of good character and co-operated fully with the police. Held. Taking into account it was a reference **4 years** not 15 months.

See also **FALSE IMPRISONMENT/KIDNAPPING** – *Taking the Law into Your Own Hands*

Victim over 65 – Guideline

27.10 *Att-Gen's Ref. Nos. 32 and 33 of 1995* 1996 1 Cr App R (S) 376. LCJ. Both defendants pleaded guilty to aggravated burglary. One also pleaded guilty to attempted robbery. The general effect of the (reported) cases is that where an elderly victim, living alone, is attacked by intruders and is injured the likely sentence will be in double figures. We wish to stress that attacks on elderly people in their homes are particularly despicable and will be regarded by the court as deserving severe punishment. Elderly victims living alone are vulnerable, not only because of their lack of assistance but also because of their own weakness and isolation. Any attack on such a person is cowardly and can only be expected to be visited with a very severe punishment indeed.

Victim over 65 – Cases

27.11 *R v Brady* 2000 1 Cr App R (S) 410. The defendant was convicted of aggravated burglary. The victim was 70 and lived alone. Late in the evening she saw the defendant running up her stairs holding a chisel pointing towards her. He told her to go back to her bedroom and threatened to kill her. He repeatedly asked where the money was. When told there was none he became more aggressive. Eventually she told him it was under the bed. He took it, and a radio and £50. He pulled the telephone from the wall. The defendant had three convictions for robbery and had a sociopathic personality disorder. **7 years** was not manifestly excessive.

Att-Gen's Ref. No 19 of 2000 2001 1 Cr App R (S) 35. The defendant pleaded guilty to aggravated burglary, two counts of false imprisonment and obtaining by deception. He gained entry to the premises of a married couple by pretending to be a police officer. He said he was enquiring about a car and when the husband, aged 82, was in the garage he punched him in the face, gagged him and put material in his mouth and tape over it. The punch broke a tooth and his top denture. He fell unconscious and his hands were bound. When unconscious the husband had been dragged along the garage floor. He was left in the garage. The defendant went into the house and attacked the victim's wife aged 76 by striking her in the face and knocking her down. Pressure was applied to her neck. He taped her mouth for a short time. He bound her hands with tape. She suffered from arthritis and this caused her considerable pain. He said he wanted money but she said she hadn't any. He stole camera equipment and a car. The couple remained bound for 7 hours. They were taken to hospital and suffered psychological problems. The defendant was 22 and had no convictions till about 21. They were for offences of dishonesty including theft from a dwelling. Held. We would have expected following a trial a sentence of **at least 10 years**. On a plea we would have expected 8 years (because of the strong evidence). As it was a reference **7 years** not 5.

Att-Gen's Ref. No 35 of 2001 2002 1 Cr App R (S) 187. The defendant pleaded to aggravated burglary. The victim aged 72 was in bed at 6am and woke up to find the defendant shining a torch in his face and pointing a carving knife at him. The victim was very frightened. The victim was told to sit on the bed and that it was a 'hold up.' The defendant demanded money and the victim said he had no money. The defendant began to search the bedroom and the victim offered £10 from his wallet downstairs. The victim was taken downstairs at knife point and the £10 was handed over. The defendant then ransacked the place. The victim asked him why he didn't get a job and the defendant told him to shut up or he'd use the knife. After 20 minutes the defendant left in the victim's VW Polo car. Property worth £2,000 was stolen including his pension book, alcohol, share certificates and personal documents. The victim was so distressed he could no longer live in his own home. The defendant was 21 or 22 at the time with a conviction for burglary and addicted to heroin. He was in breach of a probation order. When arrested he denied it. Held. It was a terrifying offence. The proper sentence with substantial credit for a plea was **6 years**. As it was a reference **4^1/$_2$ years** not 3^1/$_2$.

R v Harrison 2002 1 Cr App R (S) 470. The defendant pleaded guilty at the first opportunity to aggravated burglary. He asked for 2 shoplifting offences to be taken into consideration. The 61-year-old victim lived with and cared for his 91-year-old bedridden mother. The defendant rang the victim's doorbell at 9.45pm. When the door was opened the defendant said something about being a Catholic and held a crucifix in his hand. He barged in and threatened the victim with a knife and demanded money. The defendant forced him into a corner of the hallway and the victim agreed to give him money if his mother came to no harm, but the victim pushed him back causing a window to smash. The defendant continued to demand money and was given £140 in cash. Suddenly the defendant's behaviour changed and he began to apologise. A neighbour came to help and the defendant was detained. The mother was unaware of the intruder till he was detained. When interviewed the defendant said the knife was for opening sash windows and he thought the address was empty. He showed remorse. Held. This was a grave case with a knife, a vulnerable victim, late in the evening but because of the early plea **5 years** not 7.

Att-Gen's Ref. No. 104 of 2002 2003 2 Cr App R (S) 682. The defendant was convicted of aggravated burglary and ABH. The defendant broke into the home of a 76-year old widower when he was asleep in his living room one afternoon. He awoke to see a figure at a frosted glass-fronted internal door. When the victim confronted him he hit him on the head with the victim's coal shovel knocking him to the ground. He struck him 3 more times and shouted for him to stay down. The householder got up and backed away but was attacked again: beaten about the face and upper body with the shovel. He fell to the floor and the defendant fled taking the victim's coat, keys and some money. The victim had lacerations to the face and hands, his ribs were either fractured or badly bruised. Seven weeks later a rib was still fractured. He was at the time of the attack recovering from an operation to remove a tumour from beneath his eye. He also had psychological injuries. He had lived in the house for 20 years and nursed his wife there until her death 4 years earlier from terminal cancer. He no longer felt safe or able to return to his home. DNA linked the defendant to the offence. He said in interview that he had seen an open window and climbed in with another man who had carried out the attack. The victim gave evidence at trial. The defendant was 18 at conviction had 12 previous convictions for 26 offences including a conviction for a possessing an offensive weapon 8 days before this offence. He was therefore in breach of the community punishment order that had been imposed. He had not previously received a custodial sentence. Held. This was a burglary bristling with aggravating features. There was a repeated and sustained attack on a victim in his own home who was vulnerable both by age and illness. It caused ugly physical injuries and gravely damaged the victim's sense of security and well-being. **9 years detention** would have been appropriate even for someone so young but as this was a reference **7 years detention** not 4 years.

Old cases *R v Eastap, Curt and Thompson* 1997 2 Cr App R (S) 55. (For a summary of this case see the first edition of this book.)

28   BURGLARY – RACIALLY AGGRAVATED

28.1   Theft Act 1968 s 9 and the Powers of Criminal Courts (Sentencing) Act 2000 s 153

Triable either way unless (a) the defendant could be sentenced to a minimum of 3 years[26] or (b) where the burglary comprises the commission of, or an intention to commit, an offence which is triable only on indictment (GBH, rape etc)[27] or (c) where the burglary is a dwelling and a person was subjected to violence or the threat of violence[28]. In those cases the offence is triable only on indictment.

The Criminal Justice Act 2003 creates a summary maximum sentence of 51 weeks, a minimum custodial sentence of 28 weeks and Custody plus. The Home Office say they do not expect to introduce these provisions before September 2006.

On indictment maximum 14 years when the building is a dwelling, 10 years otherwise. Summary maximum 6 months and/or £5,000.

Minimum sentences Domestic burglary is a specified offence for a 3 year minimum sentence when the offence is a third domestic burglary[29].

Restitution Order There is power to make an order that the stolen goods etc. in the possession of the defendant or a third party be restored to the owner etc.[30]

Sexual Offences Prevention Order There is a discretionary power to make this order when it is necessary to protect the public etc[31].

For *General principles* – See RACIALLY AGGRAVATED OFFENCES – *General principles*

Case

28.2 *R v Morrison* 2001 1 Cr App R (S) 12. The defendant was convicted of burglary, which was racially aggravated and racially aggravated criminal damage. He pleaded to affray. The defendant with friends was waiting for their food in a kebab shop. Also waiting was Mr Bashir. The defendant was heard to use the word 'Paki'. He also said 'I can't believe I've got to wait behind a Paki.' One of his friends apologised but the abuse continued. Mr Bashir said 'Tell your mate he is a fucking prick.' At this the defendant lunged forward but was restrained. Mr Bashir was followed and there was a scuffle outside. Mr Bashir reached his home and closed the door behind him. The defendant broke a pane of glass in the door and opened the door. The defendant ran up the stairs brandishing a knife. Mr Bashir believed the defendant intended to kill him and ran into a bedroom and closed the door. As Mr Bashir leant on the door the defendant thrust the knife into the door several times, shouting Fucking Paki, I'm going to get you' etc. This was the basis for the criminal damage count. The defendant then left before the police arrived. Mr Bashir and his friends moved from the area because of their fear. The defendant was 22 with no previous convictions. The judge said the defendant had caused terror to the victim and others in the flat and that normally a $4\frac{1}{2}$ years sentence would be imposed for the burglary and added 2 years for the racial element. Held. *R v Saunders* 2000 1 Cr App R (S) 71 does not mean that the maximum that can be added is 2 years. The extra 2 years was not excessive. **$6\frac{1}{2}$ years** for this serious and horrifying case was justified.

BURIAL, PREVENTING

See OBSTRUCTING THE CORONER/BURIAL, PREVENTING

26 Powers of Criminal Courts (Sentencing) Act 2000 s 111(2).
27 Magistrates' Courts Act 1980 s 17(1) and Sch 1, para. 28b.
28 Magistrates' Courts Act 1980 s 17(1) and Sch 1, para. 28c.
29 Powers of Criminal Courts (Sentencing) Act 2000 s 111
30 Powers of Criminal Courts (Sentencing) Act 2000 s 148(2)
31 Sexual Offences Act 2003 s 104 & Sch. 5

29 CANNABIS

General

Does reclassification affect the guidelines for cannabis supply?

29.1 *R v Mitchell 2004* Unreported 9/11/04. The defendant pleaded guilty to importing cannabis. Held. R v Donovan *2005 1 Cr App R (S) 65* makes clear that in light of the raised maximum penalty for cannabis the reclassification of cannabis should not result in any reduction in sentence.

R v Herridge 2005 Unreported 26/5/05. For supply Parliament clearly intended no change. Where the cannabis is for own use a reduction should be made.

How to assess the different types

29.2 *R v Ronchetti* 1998 2 Cr App R (S) 100. Lord Lane's distinction in *R v Aramah* between cannabis, cannabis resin and cannabis oil should be read as cannabis and cannabis resin being equivalent and cannabis oil being ten times that, as 10 kilos of cannabis or cannabis resin are required to produce 1 kg of cannabis oil.

Cultivation of/production of/management of premises etc. of cannabis

29.2a   Cultivation   Misuse of Drugs Act 1971 s 6

              Production   Misuse of Drugs Act 1971 s 4(2)(a) and (b)

Being concerned in the management of premises and knowingly permitting the production of cannabis Misuse of Drugs Act 1971 s 8(a).

All offences are triable either way. All have on indictment a maximum of 14 years and a summary maximum of 6 months and/or £5,000.

The Criminal Justice Act 2003 creates a summary maximum sentence of 51 weeks, a minimum custodial sentence of 28 weeks and Custody plus. The Home Office says they do not expect to introduce these provisions before September 2006.

Confiscation For production offences and section 8[1] offences the court must follow the Proceeds of Crime Act 2002 procedure for offences committed on or after 24 March 2003[2]. For production offences[3] committed before that date the court must follow the Drug Trafficking Act 1994. There are competing arguments whether the other offence qualifies for the confiscation procedure.

Magistrates' Court Sentencing Guidelines January 2004 – Cultivation

29.3 For a first time offender pleading not guilty. Entry point. Is it serious enough for a community penalty? Consider the impact on the victim. Examples of aggravating factors for the offence are commercial cultivation, large quantity and use of sophisticated system. Examples of mitigating factors for the offence are for personal use, not responsible for planting and small scale cultivation. Examples of mitigation are age, health (physical or mental), co-operation with the police, and genuine remorse.

For details about the guidelines see MAGISTRATES' COURT SENTENCING GUIDELINES at page 483.

Guideline remarks

29.4 *R v Dibden* 2000 1 Cr App R (S) 64. There are four different categories. First, those who grow it for their own use. Secondly, those who grow it for their own use and

---

1   Proceeds of Crime Act 2002 s 75 and Sch 2 para 1(1)(a) and (c)
2   Proceeds of Crime Act 2002 (Commencement No 5, Transitional Provisions, Savings and Amendment) Order 2003
3   Drug Trafficking Act 1994 s 1(1)(a)

also for friends who are supplied free of charge. Thirdly, those who supply friends for money, a commercial operation. Fourthly, those who grow no doubt massive quantities and supply all and sundry.

R v Tuckman 2005 Unreported 11/2/05. The effect of re-classification was limited.

Book – producing a book giving advice on producing cannabis

29.5 *R v Marlow* 1998 1 Cr App R (S) 272. The defendant was convicted of incitement to cultivate cannabis. He pleaded guilty to producing and possessing cannabis. He wrote a book about the cultivating and production of cannabis. It was advertised for sale in Private Eye, Viz and Hemp Nation. Some 500 copies were sold. Police visited his house and found evidence of cannabis production. The defendant was unemployed because of a heart condition, a blood problem and because he suffered from depression. His wife was diabetic and needed his care. He had convictions for possession of drugs, attempted arson, stealing and abstraction of electricity, but they were all before 1977. He was sentenced on the basis the book was not written to earn money and he received 12 months on each count concurrent. Held. The book was an active and widespread encouragement to produce cannabis. A custodial sentence was essential. **12 months** upheld for the book count with 6 months for the other counts substituted.

Own use

29.6 *R v Peters* 1999 2 Cr App R (S) 334. The defendant pleaded guilty to cultivating cannabis and possession of cannabis at the Magistrates' Court. He was committed for sentence. Police searched the bedroom of his flat and found it had been converted for the hydroponic irrigation of cannabis plants. A wooden frame was covered with heavy-duty polythene. The walls were covered with silver reflective material. Water troughs contained 37 mature cannabis plants and 28 cannabis seedlings. 13.7 grams. of cannabis was found in other rooms. If the seedlings were allowed to grow to the height of the others the total yield would be 520 grams with a street value of £1,760. The basis of plea was that it was for his own use to alleviate a medical condition. He suffered from depression, migraines and a skin complaint. He was 34 and had convictions for possession of cannabis and production of cannabis for which he received a probation order. Held. Because of the medical condition **6 months** not 9.

R v Evans 2000 1 Cr App R (S) 107. The defendant pleaded guilty to cultivating cannabis. Police searched his flat and discovered a bedroom had been converted into a hydroponics garden for the growing of cannabis. 21 plants were found in various stages of growth. There were heat lamps and an electric irrigation system. Walls were lined with insulation and plant food and gauges were found. Harvested leaves and flower buds were recovered from other parts of the house. He made full admissions to the police. The plea was on the grounds that 70.6 grams of flowering head material had been produced and the cannabis was for his own consumption. It was worth between £930 and £1,150 on the street. He was 47 and had numerous convictions including several for unlawful possession of drugs and one for supply for which he received 15 months. He had made a complaint about drug dealers and had had a petrol bomb through his letter box. His knee was injured and he received further threats. He said this caused depression and anxiety which was helped by cannabis. **9 months** not 12.

R v Herridge 2005 Unreported 26/5/05. The defendant pleaded guilty at the earliest opportunity to cultivating cannabis. His landlord went to collect the rent and thought he saw a body through the window. The police attended and found no body but did find 52 cannabis plants under cultivation. There was ventilation, heating and extractor fans. In interview he said this was his second crop as the first totally failed. It was readily accepted the amount was consistent with own use. The defendant was 33 and was a habitual and heavy user of cannabis. He had quite a bad criminal record. However his last sentence was in 1995 for a cannabis offence for which he received 2 months. Since arrest he was voluntarily attending a local drug service. Held. Given that a significant element of calculated defiance of the law is required to commit this offence even on a small scale we would expect the offence to ordinarily attract a custodial sentence. But **6 months** not 12.

Old cases. *R v Marsland* 1994 15 Cr App R (S) 665.

Own use and social supply free of charge

29.7   *R v Bennett* 1998 1 Cr App R (S) 429. The defendant pleaded guilty to producing cannabis, possession of cannabis with intent to supply and possessing cannabis. The second plea was entered five weeks after the other two. Police searched his house, garden and garden shed and found 87 cannabis plants, 2 of which had been cut down and some dried and drying cannabis leaf weighing 2.4 kilos. The cannabis' was said to be worth £7,000. There were no sophisticated systems like hydroponic growth or high intensity lighting. There was no evidence of commercial supply. He accepted his involvement in interview and said it was for his own use. The basis of plea was that the potential yield was between $2^1/_2$–3 kilos which would last him 2 years if he had 1–2 oz a week. Some of the cannabis would be supplied to friends without payment. He was 55 and had one conviction for cannabis and that was when he was 20 years old. He was a decent honest man who had always worked until prevented from doing so by an accident. He did charity work and had references. Held. **6 months** not 12.

R v Rafferty 1998 2 Cr App R (S) 449. LCJ. The defendant pleaded guilty at plea before venue to producing cannabis and possessing cannabis. Police executed a search warrant at his home and in his loft they found 10 cannabis plants most of which were 2″ high and covered in sticky buds. Two were a foot high. The loft was well equipped for the hydroponic cultivation of cannabis, which was described as a moderately sophisticated means of continuous plant production. There was a motorised heating and lighting unit and an oscillating fan etc. The yield was estimated to be two crops a year producing 428 grams of cannabis. The THC level for the tops of the plants was estimated to be 11% (the level of THC for imported cannabis was between 3 and 5%). The street value was between £2,500 and £3,750 with £900 for the remaining foliage. He was going to give the person who gave him the plants some of the cannabis. The rest he used and shared with friends. None was to be sold. He was 26 with three children and no assets. He had convictions for burglary, ABH and driving offences. He received $4^1/_2$ years for robbery and carrying a firearm with intent. Since his release in 1995 he had turned his life around and obtained a job as a telephone engineer. He had settled down with a partner and was buying a house on mortgage. He was granted bail after sentence. Held. **4 months** was not excessive.

Old case *R v Blackham* 1997 2 Cr App R (S) 275. Unfortunately this case does not make it clear whether the cannabis was to be sold or not.

Social supply for money

29.8   *R v Dibden* 2000 1 Cr App R (S) 64. The defendant indicated a plea of guilty at the Magistrates' Court to possession of cannabis with intent to supply and producing cannabis. Police searched his premises and found cannabis growing in a bedroom and in a large garage. There were some skunk plants. Considerable effort had been devoted to ensure that the plants had optimum growing conditions. The plants were not ready for harvesting but were 'well on their way.' It was calculated there would be enough for 400 grams making 2,000 cannabis cigarettes. The defendant admitted the offence in interview and said he had fallen into debt. He was 39 with some old irrelevant convictions. Reverences said he was hard-working and honest. Held. This offence comes into the category of commercial supply to friends. **21 months** was not manifestly excessive.

Cannabis intended for commercial supply to the open market

29.9   *R v Knight and Dooley* 1998 2 Cr App R (S) 23. The defendants K and D pleaded guilty to producing cannabis and possessing cannabis with intent to supply. D also pleaded to two counts of possessing a prohibited weapon and possessing cannabis. Police watched D buying gardening equipment for hydroponic propagation. Documents showed £2,400 was spent on PH metres, lights, pumps, hydroponics and growing tanks. Police searched K's home and garage and found the windows and doors sealed with sheeting and tapes. Plants were growing in pumped water. Lamps, fans, seed trays, propagators, plant foods and instruction manuals were found. 11 large plants from which cuttings had been taken were found. 47 plants were in grow-beds. The likely yield was about 555 grams worth between £10,500 and £15,000. In a bedroom plants were being dried. Police found in D's home two locked metal gun cabinets containing an electric stun gun which did not work because it did not have a battery and a pepper spray. £1,800 was found under a floorboard. He claimed the gun and pepper spray were for his own protection. He said he didn't know they were illegal. He bought them in South Africa where they were common defences. *Held*. The cannabis operation was clearly at the beginning of a sophisticated operation intended to be a serious financial enterprise. **3 years** for the production and supply counts concurrent upheld. The firearm sentences reduced from 18 months to 9 months. They remained concurrent to each other and consecutive to the cannabis offences.

R v Jubb 2002 2 Cr App R (S) 24. The defendant pleaded guilty to producing cannabis and possessing cannabis with intent to supply. He rented an industrial unit and 3 months later the police searched it. There were five rooms in it. One was a nursery for plants and the other four contained cannabis plants with climate control, air conditioning etc. There was a large drying area and freezer facilities. There were 705 cannabis plants and 3.78 kilos of prepared flowering tops worth about £37,850. It was estimated there would be four or five harvests a year making £151,000 income for four and £190,000 for five harvests. When interviewed he admitted he was the sole lessee, constructed the entire hydroponic system and cultivated the plants. The written basis of plea said his involvement was to be for a year, he was not the principle and he received no direct share of the sale income. Others financed the project. He was 37 and had been self employed but was not making any 'meaningful money.' *Held*. He was a very important player in charge of the premises and crop production. The operation was on a very large scale and of the most sophisticated kind. His role was central. Deterrent sentences are needed. **5 years** was not in any way manifestly excessive.

R v Liljeros and Alderson 2004 1 Cr App R (S) 486. Both defendants L and A pleaded guilty to different counts of being concerned in the production of cannabis (then class B) with intent to supply and possession of cannabis with intent to supply. L owned factory premises where he constructed a concealed basement to house a cannabis factory with a separate electricity supply. He purchased hydroponics equipment for £24,000. Officers found a trap door to the basement where they found 500 cannabis plants (7.51kg of useful material) at various stages of growth with a wholesale value of between £55,000 and £400,000. In interview he said that he had rented out the premises to another and knew nothing of the operation. A was operating a basement on another industrial estate where police found a hydroponics system containing 114 plants (3.91kg of useful material) valued at £49,000. The basement had cost £16000 to construct. A was interviewed and made no comment. The prosecution abandoned their contentions that the two were linked. Both men were of good character, L was nearly 70. A was 38. *Held*. A 6 year starting point was justified for both (taking account of L's age and A's smaller operation). **4¹/₂ years** each upheld.

Old case. *R v Booth* 1997 1 Cr App R (S) 67, *R v Chamberlain* 1998 1 Cr App R (S) 49 and *R v Green and Withers* 1998 1 Cr App R (S) 437, (for a summary of the last two cases see the first edition of this book).

See also **Drug Users; Importation of Drugs; Possession of Drugs; Production of Drugs** and **Supply of Drugs (Class A, B and C)**

30 Careless Driving/Driving without Due Care and Attention

30.1 Road Traffic Act 1988 s 3

Summary only. Maximum fine Level 4 (£2,500.)

3–9 points. Obligatory endorsement and discretionary disqualification

Magistrates' Court Sentencing Guidelines January 2004

30.2 For a first time offender pleading not guilty. Entry point. Is a discharge or a fine appropriate? Examples of aggravating factors for the offence are excessive speed, high degree of carelessness, serious risk and using a hand-held mobile telephone. Examples of mitigating factors for the offence are minor risk, momentary lapse, negligible/parking damage and sudden change in weather conditions. Examples of mitigation are co-operation with the police, voluntary genuine remorse and compensation. Consider disqualification until test is passed for e.g. defendant's age, infirmity or medical condition. **Starting point fine B.** (100% of weekly take home pay/weekly benefit payment.)

For details about the guidelines see **Magistrates' Court Sentencing Guidelines** at page 483.

Guideline remarks

30.3 *R v Krawec* 1984 6 Cr App R (S) 367. LCJ. The primary considerations are the quality of the driving, the extent the defendant fell below the standard of the reasonably competent driver; in other words the degree of carelessness and culpability. The unforeseen consequences may sometimes be relevant to those considerations. Here the fact the defendant failed to see the pedestrian until it was too late and therefore collided with him was plainly a relevant factor.

Death results – General principles

30.4 R v Krawec 1984 6 Cr App R (S) 367. LCJ. The defendant was convicted of careless driving and acquitted of causing death by reckless driving. We do not think the fact the unfortunate man died was relevant to the charge of careless driving.

R v Morling 1998 1 Cr App R (S) 420. The defendant was acquitted of causing death by dangerous driving and convicted of driving without due care and attention. Held. The principles in *R v Krawec* 1984 6 Cr App R (S) 367 have been applied since then. The court must take care not to let the fact that a death occurred become an aggravating feature. But when examining the degree of culpability, the court is allowed to have regard to the consequences of such carelessness. Thus in this case, even if no death had occurred, it would be perfectly open to the court to say it was a serious act not to have lights because of the consequences which might follow.

R v Simmonds 1999 2 Cr App R (S) 18. The defendant was indicted with causing death by dangerous driving. His plea to careless driving was accepted and no evidence was offered for the causing death count. Held. Considering the statutory changes that have taken place since *R v Krawec* 1984 6 Cr App R (S) 367 we find the concept of a road traffic offence in which the sentencing court is obliged to disregard the fact that a death has been caused as wholly anomalous. The current approach is reflected in *Att-Gen's Ref. No 66 of 1996* 1998 1 Cr App R (S) 16 (a case of causing death by careless driving having consumed alcohol) 'It is nonetheless the duty of the judge, to judge cases dispassionately and to do its best to reach the appropriate penalty, taking account of all the relevant circumstances.' Whether sentencing courts should take into account criminality alone or both the criminality and the consequences of an offence – and in the latter event in what proportions, is ultimately a question of choice and policy. *Krawec* was clearly valid in its context and at its time, but we do not see it as of assistance to sentencing courts in the different context of today. The judge was entitled to bear in mind the death.

R v King 2001 2 Cr App R (S) 503. The decision in *R v Simmonds* 1999 2 Cr App R (S) 18 has marked something of a reconsideration of the approach in this difficult area. The sentencer must still make it his primary task to assess culpability, but should not close his eyes to the fact that death has resulted, especially multiple death where as here, that was all too readily foreseeable.

Death results – Cases

30.5   *R v Simmons* 1999 2 Cr App R (S) 18. The defendant was indicted with causing death by dangerous driving. His plea to careless driving was accepted and no evidence was offered for the causing death count. Driving on a road that was unfamiliar to him the defendant missed his turning. Road conditions were good, but it was dark. He pulled into a wide entrance on his left and without pausing embarked on a sweeping right-hand turn to drive back. The victim, a motorcyclist travelling at 40 mph and in the same direction as the defendant had been travelling swerved and hit the defendant's Range Rover. The victim was catapulted through the air and died. The car behind was unable to stop and also hit the Range Rover. The defendant used his mobile phone to call for an ambulance and the police. At the scene he told police, 'I looked, it was all clear then suddenly this bike came from nowhere.' When interviewed he said, 'I cannot give an explanation as to why I didn't actually see him and I can only assume that he was invisible against the general illumination of other vehicles.' He was in his 60s of good character with an excellent driving record. The judge said it was a tragic error as a result of failing to keep a proper look out. Held. Neither the **£1,000 fine** nor the 12 months disqualification were excessive.

R v King 2001 2 Cr App R (S) 503. The defendant was acquitted of three counts of causing death by dangerous driving and convicted of three charges of driving without due care and attention. [It would appear that two of them were entered in error, as they were all the same offence.] He had accepted the due care matters from the outset. There was a contraflow system in one lane of a dual carriageway with temporary traffic lights in place. The road was straight and visibility was good and warning signs were in place. The defendant drove his HGV vehicle into the back of a queue of traffic and killed three priests in the last car. The sole occupant in the next car was very badly injured. The vehicle before was a lorry. The impact speed was 43 mph in a 40 mph limit. $1^{1}/_{4}$ miles into the contraflow system and 350 metres before impact he was travelling at 50 mph. His defence was he looked down at his tachograph shortly before to calculate when he had to stop driving. He had a good driving record and his only trade was as a HGV driver. The judge described it as 'a quite appalling piece of careless driving.' Held. **£1,500 fine** not £2,250. 2 years not 3 disqualification.

See also **DEATH BY CARELESS DRIVING, CAUSING**

Disqualification, for how long?

30.6   *R v Morling* 1998 1 Cr App R (S) 420. The defendant was acquitted of causing death by dangerous driving and convicted of driving without due care and attention. He drove his tractor on a dual carriageway at $14^{1}/_{2}$ mph without amber flashing lights, rear lights or reflectors as required. The tractor had lights but they could have misled drivers about the position of the trailer. A car hit the trailer and the trailer was lifted into the air and it fell into the offside lane. Another car hit the trailer and the driver sustained head and arm injuries. His wife was killed and one of his children received serious head injuries and the other two received facial and stomach injuries. The defendant was of exemplary character with no convictions. He appealed the disqualification order only. Held. The fact the defendant is an HGV driver is two-edged. The disqualification will hit him hard, but being an HGV driver heightens the culpability of taking the risks he did. It was well within the judge's discretion to impose **12 months disqualification**.

R v Johnson 1998 2 Cr App R (S) 455. The defendant was acquitted of two counts of causing death by dangerous driving and convicted of two counts of careless driving. He tried to negotiate a bend when driving at 40–45 mph. He went on the wrong side of the road and hit a taxi head on and killed the driver and one of the passengers. The road was wet. The defendant was injured. One of his tyres was under inflated. He said the headlights of the taxi dazzled him. The judge said it was a momentary lack of concentration. The defendant was 23 and a student working hard and doing well. He had a lot of travelling to courses to do and was having difficulty with the trains and buses. He was sentenced to a **£500 fine** and appealed a 12 month disqualification order. Held. Applying *R v Krawec* 1984 6 Cr App R (S) 367 the disqualification was too long so **5 months** not 12.

R v Simmons 1999 2 Cr App R (S) 18. See **30.5**

R v King 2001 2 Cr App R (S) 503. See **30.5**

HGV drivers

30.7   *R v Morling* 1998 1 Cr App R (S) 420. The fact the defendant is an HGV driver is two-edged. The disqualification will hit the defendant hard, but being an HGV driver heightens the culpability of taking the risks he did.

CAR RINGING

See THEFT – *Vehicles, car ringing*

CHANGE IN TARIFF YEARS AFTER SENTENCE

See TARIFF, CHANGE IN TARIFF YEARS LATER

CHEATING THE PUBLIC REVENUE

See TAX FRAUD

31   CHILDREN AND YOUNG DEFENDANTS

(Defendants aged under 18)

General principles

31.1   Crime and Disorder Act 1998 s 37. It shall be the principle aim of the youth justice system to prevent offending by children and young persons.

See also CRUELTY TO CHILDREN, MOTHERS and PROSTITUTION, CHILD PROSTITUTES.

Child defendants (aged 10–13)

31.2   Children and Young Persons Act 1933 s 107(1) "Child" means a person under the age of 14.

R v W. 2003 1 Cr App R (S) 502. The defendant, now 12 was convicted when he was 10 of causing GBH with intent. Held. This was a most serious offence. When dealing with a very young person, the court has to have regard to the length of sentence and the perception of the young of that length. By that we mean that a sentence which may be appropriate for someone older may be crushing for someone who is very young. (For more details see **31.12**)

R v T 2004 Unreported 9/11/04. The defendant aged 10 pleaded guilty to three false imprisonment counts, GBH, two ABHs and two robberies. Held. A custodial sentence will ordinarily be available in the form of a Detention and Training Order. If the court is prohibited from making such an order, by reason of age, in general detention under s 91 would not be appropriate. There will however be rare or exceptional cases, very rare if the offender is under 12, when the court can make order s 91 detention for the protection of the public or in the long term interests of the offender. Here a s 91 detention order was essential for the boy and the public. (For more details see p **73.6**)

Education and training

31.3   Children and Young Persons Act 1933 s 44(1). Every court in dealing with a child or young person who is brought before it, either as an offender or otherwise, shall in a proper case take steps for securing that proper provision is made for his education and training.

Welfare

31.3   Children and Young Persons Act 1933 s 44(1). Every court in dealing with a child or young person who is brought before it, either as an offender or otherwise, shall have regard to the welfare of the child or young person and shall in the a proper case take steps for removing him from undesirable surroundings and for securing that proper provision is made for his education and training.

Welfare, The clash between marking the seriousness of the offence and the welfare of the child

31.4   *R v W* 1999 1 Cr App R (S) 488. The defendant was convicted of indecent assault on a 12-year-old girl. He was acquitted of attempted rape. The victim was walking home in the early evening when the defendant caught up with her and started to kiss her. The defendant, who was aged 13, then put his hand down the victim's clothes and touched her vaginal area. The victim pulled his hand away and attempted to escape whereupon the defendant tripped her over, pulled her jogging bottoms down and simulated sexual intercourse on her. The defendant had no previous convictions. Held. These cases are extremely difficult to deal with. It is extremely important that if any woman, whatever age, and in particularly if a child, is sexually assaulted then that is an extremely serious matter and must be dealt with by appropriate punishment. On the other hand when the attacker is no more than a child, the overriding consideration is to do the best to see what can be done to assist him, but at the same time to mark the seriousness of the offence. Here the two principles clash. It was a gratuitous assault but a supervision order rather than **8 months** was appropriate.

R v L and L 2004 1 Cr App R (S) 34. The defendants pleaded guilty in the Magistrates' Court to 5 offences of neglecting their son in a manner likely to cause him unnecessary suffering. They were married to each other and the boy was born in December 2000.

Between 1 October and 23 September 2001 and between mid March and 8 May 2002 the boy was left at home alone on occasions for between 3 and 6 hours. There was no evidence of physical harm. The judge referred to shocking neglect with the boy without food or water and on at least on occasion heaters positioned close to the boy. He was placed with foster carers. A psychologist said the mother had had harsh childhood experiences. She had a learning disability and considerable deficits in understanding basic parenting issues. The pre-sentence report said "the mother was likely to continue to pose a risk of neglecting a child due to her cognitive functioning. The risk may be reduced if she recognises her difficulties and engaged professionals. However she is unwilling or unable to do this. She is not suitable for probation as she was likely to become resentful at what she perceives as intrusion". His report said only a custodial sentence would reflect the gravity of the offences. There were 120 contact sessions with the boy. The new guardian said "custody was not in the interest of the boy as it would delay residential assessment. The boy demonstrates a strong attachment to both parents. He, after the parents' imprisonment, was distressed on the days he would have had contact". Held. It is quite disgraceful that a child so young should be left alone as often as happened here. We do not say the parents did not deserve prison. This is a case where retribution and deterrence should give way to the interests of the child. Here the criminal process should not place obstacles in the way of a viable family life. **6 months suspended** not 2 years.

32   CO-DEFENDANT'S PERSONAL MITIGATION

32.1   *Att-Gen's Ref. No 73 of 1999* 2000 2 Cr App R (S) 209. LCJ. The defendant's sentence was reduced because of the reduction made for the co-defendant because of his personal mitigation. The judge said it was to prevent him having a burning sense of injustice. Held. It is not a reason to reduce the sentence. **18 months** substituted for CSO.

33   COMMON ASSAULT

33.1   Criminal Justice Act 1988 s 39

Summary only. Maximum 6 months and/or £5,000.

However, through the Criminal Justice Act 1988 s 40 the offence is triable on indictment. According to the Divisional Court[4] it is then contrary to s 39 although certain academics and another set of judges at the Divisional Court[5] consider the offence is then contrary to common law. Maximum sentence 6 months (although this could be open to argument).

Anti-Social Behavioural orders Where the defendant has acted in a manner that caused or was likely to cause harassment, alarm or distress to one or more persons not in the same household as the defendant and it is necessary to protect persons from further anti-social acts by him/her the court may make this order[6].

Licensed premises Where the offence is committed on licensed premises and the defendant resorted to violence or offered or threatened to resort to violence, the court may prohibit the defendant from entering those premises or any other specified

4   *DPP v Little* 1992 95 Cr App R (S) 28.
5   *Haystead v DPP* 2000 The Times 2/6/00 164 JP 396.
6   Crime and Disorder Act 1998 s 1C

premises without the express consent of the licensee or his agent[7]. The order shall last from 3 months to 2 years[8].

Magistrates' Court Sentencing Guidelines January 2004

33.2 For a first time offender pleading not guilty. Entry point. Is it serious enough for a community penalty? Consider the impact on the victim. Examples of aggravating factors for the offence are abuse of trust (domestic setting), group action, injury, offender in position of authority, on hospital/medical or school premises, premeditated, spitting, victim particularly vulnerable, victim serving the public and weapon. Examples of mitigating factors for the offence are impulsive, minor injury, provocation and single blow. Examples of mitigation are age, health (physical or mental), co-operation with police, genuine remorse and voluntary compensation. Give reasons for not awarding compensation.

For details about the guidelines see MAGISTRATES' COURT SENTENCING GUIDELINES at page 483.

34   COMMON ASSAULT – RACIALLY OR RELIGIOUSLY AGGRAVATED,

34.1   Crime and Disorder Act 1998 s 29

Triable either way. On indictment maximum 2 years. Summary maximum 6 months and/or £5,000.

The Criminal Justice Act 2003 creates a summary maximum sentence of 51 weeks, a minimum custodial sentence of 28 weeks and Custody plus. The Home Office says they do not expect to introduce these provisions before September 2006.

Anti-Social Behavioural orders Where the defendant has acted in a manner that caused or was likely to cause harassment, alarm or distress to one or more persons not in the same household as the defendant and it is necessary to protect persons from further anti-social acts by him/her the court may make this order[9].

Licensed premises Where the offence is committed on licensed premises the court may prohibit the defendant from entering those premises or any other specified premises without the express consent of the licensee or his agent[10]. The order shall last from 3 months to 2 years[11].

Sexual Offences Prevention Order There is a discretionary power to make this order when it is necessary to protect the public etc[12].

Magistrates' Court Sentencing Guidelines January 2004

34.2   For a first time offender pleading not guilty. Entry point. Is it so serious that only custody is appropriate? Consider the impact on the victim. Examples of aggravating factors for the offence: group action, injury, motivation for the offence was racial or religious, offender in position of authority, on hospital/medical premises, premeditated, setting out to humiliate the victim, victim particularly vulnerable, victim serving the public and a weapon involved. Examples of mitigating factors for the offence: impulsive, minor injury, provocation and single blow. Examples of mitigation: age, health

7   Licensed Premises (Exclusion of Certain Persons) Act 1980 s 1(1)
8   Licensed Premises (Exclusion of Certain Persons) Act 1980 s 1(3)
9   Crime and Disorder Act 1998 s 1C
10 Licensed Premises (Exclusion of Certain Persons) Act 1980 s 1(1)
11 Licensed Premises (Exclusion of Certain Persons) Act 1980 s 1(3)
12 Sexual Offences Act 2003 s 104 & Sch. 5

(physical or mental), co-operation with the police, voluntary compensation and genuine remorse. Consider compensation. Give reasons if not awarding compensation.

For details about the guidelines see MAGISTRATES' COURT SENTENCING GUIDELINES at page 483.

Basic principles see RACIALLY-AGGRAVATED OFFENCES – *General principles*

Cases

Less than 9 months imprisonment

34.3 *R v Beglin* 2003 1 Cr App R (S) 88. The defendant pleaded guilty to racially aggravated common assault at the first opportunity. The victim was in Sainsbury's with his wife, sister and baby daughter. The defendant who was drunk approached him and said "What did you say?" There was no response and he head-butted the victim in the face causing bruising and swelling. Next he tried to punch the victim several times so the victim pushed him and the defendant fell over. He got up and continued to abuse the victim who was eventually compelled to punch him. Shop staff restrained the defendant and as he was led away he shouted "It won't be hard to get you, you Paki bastard. I am from Birmingham." He was 28 with convictions for an affray in 1997, a common assault in 1999 and an ABH 8 days before the offence. He was given a community rehabilitation order. He had written a letter of contrition to the victim. The Judge gave him 12 months without saying how it was made up. Held. That was in error as the Court in *R v Kelly and Donnelly* 2001 2 Cr App R (S) 341 said the proper approach was to firstly consider the proper sentence for the offence and then what should be added. 4 months was appropriate for the offence unaggravated. Any offence that is racially aggravated is serious because of its impact not only on the victim but on the public who should rightly be outraged at such behaviour. 4 months extra was appropriate so **8 months** instead.

R v Foster 2001 1 Cr App R (S) 383. The defendant was convicted of racially aggravated common assault. The defendant in a library approached a mother and child because the child was crying. The mother alleged the defendant touched the child inappropriately and she pushed or punched the defendant's hand away and shouted to the librarian. She also shouted at him 'Fuck off' and he shouted back 'Go away you fucking bitch. Fuck off.' More than once he referred to her as a 'fucking black bitch.' He hit her either on the jaw or on the shoulder. The defendant was treated as of good character. Held. There was nothing wrong with **2 months** imprisonment.

R v Joyce 2002 1 Cr App R (S) 582. The defendant was convicted of racially aggravated common assault, racially-aggravated harassment under s 4 and common assault. Because of her behaviour security guards spoke to her. She was abusive to a black one and emptied her bag on the floor. When she was told to pick the items up she said 'Fuck off you black bastard,' and 'Fucking nigger, the BNP is going to get you.' As she was walking by the victim she struck him a backwards punch with a clenched fist. He punched her in the face. She struck out again and had to be restrained. She continued to swear, strike out and utter racist abuse at the victim. Police arrested her and she abused them and struggled, saying as an example 'All black people are bastards, and they should not be in the country.' They told her they weren't interested in her views. She replied 'You police are scared of niggers, you should try living in South London.' She kicked out at one of the officers and threatened to kill him and his family. She was given warnings and continued the abuse. She spat at another when being taken to the police van. She was now 39 and had 14 court appearances for theft, shoplifting, ABH, criminal damage, assault on police, threatening words, common assault, being drunk and disorderly and possession of a Class A drug. She hadn't received a custodial sentence. The pre-sentence report said there was a high risk of further offences and violence against the public, which would be reduced if she addressed her substance abuse and engaged in strategies to address issues of anger management. She had a glowing prison report and wanted to give birth to her child outside prison. Held. The assault without the racial element was worth 4 months. The racial element was worth 3 months extra so **7 months** not 15.

9 months imprisonment or more

34.4 *R v Webb* 2001 1 Cr App R (S) 112. The defendant was convicted of racially-aggravated common assault and racially-aggravated criminal damage. The defendant and another woman hired a minicab, which was driven by Mr Miah, the victim. There was a dispute over the fare and the two women passengers, who were drunk, screamed racial insults including 'Paki bastard,' and 'Black Bastard.' The defendant who was sitting behind the victim grabbed his hair and pulled his head backwards. They were told to leave and the victim picked up his mobile phone to call the police. The other passenger threw it to the floor and the defendant left the car and kicked the car causing damage to the side panels, the doors, and the front and rear of the car. She also tore off the wing mirror and continued making racial insults. The other woman left the car. The defendant seized the victim by the shirt and punched and slapped him about the face. The other woman joined in the attack. The defendant was arrested and continued to be racially abusive to the victim and to Asians at the police station. The victim suffered multiple bruising, grazing and tenderness. There was £1,600 worth of damage to the car and it was a write-off. The defendant had no relevant previous convictions and had references. Held. **9 months** for the assault and 6 months for the damage were not excessive. Nor was the total excessive when they were made consecutive. However, as she was the sole carer for her just widowed grandfather the **sentences were suspended**.

R v Bell 2001 1 Cr App R (S) 376. The defendant was convicted of racially-aggravated common assault. The defendant after drinking blocked the path of a 65 year old and said 'You black bastards. Why do you fuckers come to this country? You should be in a concentration camp and shot.' The victim ignored him. The defendant then hit him on the back of the head and he fell to the ground where the defendant hit and kicked him, saying 'You black fuckers should be in a fucking camp and shot.' The victim had a cut and graze to his face and head and a cut to his knee. He was in pain and felt dizzy. The defendant had two previous convictions. One was for criminal damage in 1987 and the other one was in 1998 for assaulting a constable. Held. If 6 months was suitable for the common assault the 12 months extra was too great, so **12 months** not 18.

COMPANIES

The principles to follow are listed in the HEALTH AND SAFETY OFFENCES section

For fraud see COMPANY FRAUDS AND FINANCIAL SERVICES OFFENCES

See also MANAGING ETC A COMPANY WHEN BANKRUPT

35   COMPANY FRAUDS AND FINANCIAL SERVICES OFFENCES

35.1   Various statutes and penalties including the Companies Act 1985 and the Financial Services and Markets Act 2000.

Companies Act 1985 s 458 – Fraudulent trading

Triable either way. On indictment maximum 7 years. Summary maximum 6 months and/or £5,000.

The Criminal Justice Act 2003 creates a summary maximum sentence of 51 weeks, a minimum custodial sentence of 28 weeks and Custody plus. The Home Office says they do not expect to introduce these provisions before September 2006.

Disqualification A court may make a disqualification order against a defendant who is convicted of an indictable offence in connection with the management etc. of a company[13].

Crown Court statistics – England and Wales – Males 21+ – Fraud by company director etc.

35.2

Year	Plea	Total Numbers sentenced	Type of sentence %					Average length of custody (months)
			Discharge	Fine	Community sentence	Suspended sentence	Custody	
2002	Guilty	19	–	5	–	11	84	20
	Not guilty	10	–	–	20	10	70	28.6
2003	Guilty	22	–	5	9	–	86	19.3
	Not guilty	8	–	–	25	13	63	33.6

For details and explanations about the statistics in the book see page vii.

Guideline remarks for fraud – City frauds

35.3 *R v Feld* 1999 1 Cr App R (S) 1. LCJ. As well as the guidelines in *R v Barrick* 1985 7 Cr App R (S) 142 the following are relevant considerations:

1 The amount involved and the manner in which the fraud is carried out.

2 The period over which the fraud is carried out and the degree of persistence with which it is carried out.

3 The position of the accused within the company and the measure of control over it.

4 Any abuse of trust which is revealed.

5 The consequences of the fraud.

6 The effect on public confidence in the City and the integrity of commercial life.

7 The loss to the small investors, which will aggravate the fraud.

8 The personal benefit derived by the defendant.

9 The plea.

10 The age and character of the defendant.

It is vitally important if confidence in the City is to be maintained documents sent out in support of rights issues should be honest and complete.

Copyright

35.4 See COPYRIGHT/TRADE MARK OFFENCES/TRADE DESCRIPTION OFFENCES

Fraudulent trading – Companies Act 1985 s 458 – Guideline remarks

35.5 *R v Smith and Palk* 1997 2 Cr App R (S) 167. In broad terms, a charge of fraudulent trading resulting in a deficiency of a given amount was less serious than a specific charge of theft or fraud to an equivalent amount.

Fraudulent trading – Trading with intent to defraud creditors/Long firm fraud

35.6 *Att-Gen's Ref. Nos. 80–1 of 1999 Unreported 13/12/99.* The Crown accepted the motive was to keep company trading rather than benefit personally. The defendants should have received 12 months.

---

13 Company Directors Disqualification Act 1986 s 2.

R v Ward 2001 2 Cr App R (S) 146. The defendant was convicted of two counts of fraudulent trading. He was in sole control of two companies. He failed to pay creditors properly or at all, continued trading and buying goods on credit knowing the companies were insolvent and misappropriated company assets. One company was a sham, which bought furniture on credit and sold it to the other company. The first company had shops and he borrowed £¹/₂m from a bank using his house as security, which was owned by his estranged wife. He was paying a separation agreement with his wife, which would eventually result in the house being transferred to him. His spending on the house contributed to the collapse of the first company. He set up a third company and sold the assets to that company at about ¹/₂ their value. The company debts to creditors for the two companies were £684,000. He was 57 with convictions (not stated). He showed no remorse and lied continually. **3 years** not 4.

R v McHugh 2002 1 Cr App R (S) 330. The defendant pleaded guilty to three counts of fraudulent trading, two counts of acting as an insolvency practitioner without qualification and breach of bail. He and his then future wife were directors of an accountancy company. The company was wound up owing £374,000. The company described itself as chartered accountants which was untrue. The company also claimed that the debts it recovered would be paid into an 'insured and indemnity professional client account.' This was also untrue. There were a "very large number of wrongful and fraudulent activities committed by the defendant". He told one prospective client that his wife was a Detective Sergeant and had access to a variety of information. This was also untrue as she was a traffic warden. The client asked the defendant to collect a debt of £62,000 and the defendant advised him to settle for £34,000 with VAT. There was a long wait for the cheque and when it eventually came the cheque was signed by the defendant and his wife and it bounced. When the Trading Standards Department and the DTI intervened he started running the same business under a different name. He held himself out to be a liquidator twice and gave people a false certificate saying he was. He was arrested and bailed to attend the Crown Court. He failed to attend and was found in the Orkneys. The basis of plea was that the company was not fraudulent at its inception. He was 44 and in 1977 he was convicted of making a false statement to obtain social security. In 1979 he was charged (and presumably had convictions for) with false accounting, obtaining by deception and theft. Held. **3 years** was well deserved. The 6 months for breach of bail remained consecutive.

Old cases. *R v Cook* 1995 16 Cr App R (S) 917, *R v Thobani* 1998 1 Cr App R (S) 227 and *R v Elcock and Manton* 1998 2 Cr App R (S) 126. (For a summary of the last two cases see the first edition of this book.)

Investors, cheating etc

35.7 *R v Gibson* 1999 2 Cr App R (S) 52. The defendant pleaded guilty to three counts of fraudulent trading. His pleas of not guilty to conspiracy to steal, falsifying documents, 13 counts of procuring valuable securities by deception and six counts of theft were accepted. The defendant was an independent financial adviser dealing with investments and pensions. One of the defendant's companies became insolvent and he accepted in a 19 month period over £1m in investments from mainly the elderly or redundant employees. He undertook to invest the money in safe funds but in fact only placed a minute proportion in them and paid out the investors with the new money coming in. Some of the money he spent on himself and his friends. FIMBRA investigators discovered the irregularities and a restraining order was made. There was a £780,000 loss. Nearly all the investors were compensated through the Investors Scheme but they had suffered a great deal of distress. He was 62 and had no convictions. There was a delay of 6¹/₂ years between the offence and the sentence. Held. The public must be protected and others tempted warned that a custodial sentence is inevitable. We accept the denials to theft. There was a real impression that the judge in relying on *R v Clark* 1998 2 Cr App R (S) 95 was treating the case as theft or fraud. That was in error. Because of the judge's lack of credit for the mitigation **3¹/₂ years** not 5. The 10 years disqualification was fully justified.

R v Chauhan and Holroyd 2000 2 Cr App R (S) 230. The defendants C and H pleaded to two counts of engaging in a course of conduct which created a false impression as to the market in investments etc contrary to the Financial Services Act 1986, s 47(2), [now a slightly different Financial Services and Markets Act 2000, s 397(3)]. C also pleaded to making a false entry affecting the property or affairs of the company contrary to the Companies Act 1985, s 450(1). H pleaded just over 6 months after C. H was the principle shareholder and Managing Director of a food manufacturing company, which was floated on the Stock Market in 1992. C was a chartered accountant and finance director appointed in 1990 primarily to assist in the floatation. The two created false company accounts and a false value to the shares in the company by backdating sales contracts, substituting forged documents, inflating the stock values, removing parts of machines to disguise their age and make them appear more valuable and intercepting circulars. In 1990 the auditors were misled about £170,000 worth of debts. In 1992 the auditors were misled about £0.54m of debts. In 1992 for the floatation audit £0.97m worth of false debt were confirmed. In 1992 a sales director discovered what was going on and reported his findings to the auditors. The defendants and H's father tried to discredit the sales director by false versions and printing duplicate invoices. After the floatation they tried to fool the auditor by claiming false amounts of money owing to the company and intercepting circulars sent out to their debtors. False debts to the company of £1.1m were created by forgeries. In 1993 Barclays Bank increased their overdraft to £2.2m. In 1994 receivers were appointed and the total deficit was £4.32m. The members' deficiency who were institutional investors was £1.78m and H and his father's deficiency was £0.45 m. H was 43 and of good character and clinically depressed. His gain was salaries and dividends which was £0.9m of which £0.38m had been paid back. He was made bankrupt and his marriage broke down as a result of the collapse of his company. He was a model prisoner and truly remorseful. C said he was manipulated by H and tried to restrain Directors from the plan and was worried he would be dismissed. Except for his salary of £35,000 a year he received no benefit. From 1997 he gave detailed assistance to the SFO. The judge described this assistance as 'massive'. Held. Having regard to *R v Buffrey* 1993 14 Cr App R (S) 511 at 515 there was insufficient discount for the H's plea. **4 years** not 5 for him. C did not resign and gave respectability to the protracted and serious fraud. There were no exceptional circumstances to suspend his sentence. **18 months** was not manifestly excessive.

Att-Gen's Ref Nos. 48–51 of 2002 2003 2 Cr App R (S) 192. The defendant N pleaded guilty late to conspiracy to defraud. P, L and G were convicted. In 1994, N was released from a 21 month sentence for dishonesty. She set up an investment firm, FR with her son G. At that time L was a solicitor raiding his client account. The Law Society intervened and he moved to another firm. He became the solicitor for FR and pre-pared a contract to be used for the investment programme. It involved funds said to be invested with a "prime bank" offering 100% in a year and a day. L was struck off by the Law Society and he began working for FR from the solicitors' office. L drafted the letter-head undertakings which indicated the funds were protected by his solicitor's indemnity insurance. This was false. P was living in Zurich and promised to provide investors with an exceptionally high rate of return. A significant amount came from small investors. The monies were not invested. P got $2.25m directly. A further $2m was paid to a third party on his instructions. He also disbursed £259,000. N got £449,000 and disbursed a further $550,000. £35,000 went to charity. L got £465,000 and used £160,000 to stave off bankruptcy. G got £170,000. He was the office dogsbody. After her arrest N persuaded an Australian to invest $100,000 promising a very high rate of return. She gave it to her son etc. instead. She diverted two other investments of $30,000 and $50,000 into her US account. She also misused £30,000 from someone trying to raise funds. She pleaded to all those matters. L pleaded to the client account thefts and received 4 years. The Law Society had paid out £679,000. P received 2 years for a fraud committed after this one. P threatened N and eventually arranged for her to be killed. He pleaded guilty to soliciting to murder. He awaits sentence. P was 62, was of good character and had a good work record. N was 60. L was 51 and on his release for fist sentence worked as a kitchen porter. G was 52. The trial judge decided the scheme was dishonest from the start. Held. Taking into account the 10 year maximum, the monies could have been higher, there was no deliberate targeting of small investors and the delay the starting point should have been **7 years**. The appropriate sentence for P was **6 years**, N **5 years** with the 15 months for the other matters consecutive and G **3¹/₂ years**. L had served 4 years and **3 years** making 7 which was enough. Taking into account it was a reference P **5 years** not 4 and N **4 years** not 3. There was no need to return G to prison although his **2 years** consecutive to 15 months for a later offence for which the conviction was quashed was unduly lenient.

Raising money by deception

35.8   *R v Feld* 1999 1 Cr App R (S) 1. LCJ. The defendant was convicted of nine counts of using a false instrument and three counts of making misleading statements contrary to Financial Services Act 1986, s 47, [now a slightly different Financial Services and Markets Act 2000, s 397(3)]. The defendant was Managing Director of a company which owned and managed hotels. The company sought to raise money and a Rights Issue Circular was published which contained serious misinformation. The profit forecast was overstated by £1.6m, the liabilities were understated by £9.5m and the cash balance was stated to be £4.14m when it was only £127,000. The issue was supported by forged documents. The company was under pressure from its banks and was arguably insolvent. The rights issue raised £20.6m and the profits were announced to be £6.1m which was false. Forged documents were sent to the accountants to support that figure. The documents contained fictional income and bogus contracts. The following year the company went into liquidation. The individual shareholders received a voucher from the new owners for £250 and nothing else. The defence said that his family were the greatest losers when the company went into liquidation and the money had been applied to the company. However, it had allowed him to borrow £1.375m from banks, draw his salary for the extra time and continue to maintain his expensive lifestyle. He was of good character with references. Held. The defendant was the dominant figure in the company. His whole lifestyle depended on the continuation of the company. The sentences for the false statements should have been consecutive to the false instruments sentences so **6 years** not 8.

See also INVESTORS, CHEATING ETC

Take over bids, seeking to influence

35.9   *Att-Gen's Ref. Nos. 14–6 of 1995 Unreported 21/3/97.* The three defendants were sentenced for (probably) conspiracy to defraud. They tied to create a false market in shares during a City takeover. No false market was created but that was not for want of trying. The exercise was carefully planned with painstaking organisation and with substantial dishonesty. The defendants were sentenced to CSO. Held. Influencing the fate of a takeover is a very serious matter. Not only may it lead to a fraud on shareholders, but it causes considerable damage to the reputation of the City of London, which is very important to the whole country; and damage to the confidence of the public in its institutions. Rigging a market is quite easy to do with expertise without it being realised. For the instigator and leader the right sentence was 3 years. As it was a reference 2 years. For the active and powerful second in command the right sentence was 30 months. As it was a reference 20 months. For someone who was not a main organiser and who pleaded guilty the right sentence would 15 months. As it was a reference and his failing health **12 months suspended**.

See also EMPLOYMENT, OTHERS WILL LOSE THEIR; INSOLVENCY OFFENCES; PENSION OFFENCES and THEFT ETC

36 COMPUTERS

36.1 Computer Misuse Act 1990 s 1–3

Unauthorised access to computer material (s 1), unauthorised access with intent to commit or facilitate the commission of further offences (s 2) and unauthorised modification of computer material respectively (s 3).

Section 1 is summary only. Maximum 6 months or a Level 5 fine (£5,000). Sections 2–3 are triable either way. On indictment maximum 5 years. Summary maximum 6 months and/or Level 5 fine (£5,000).

The Criminal Justice Act 2003 creates a summary maximum sentence of 51 weeks, a minimum custodial sentence of 28 weeks and Custody plus. The Home Office says they do not expect to introduce these provisions before September 2006.

Interference with company data for revenge

36.2 *R v Lindesay* 2002 1 Cr App R (S) 370. The defendant pleaded guilty at the Magistrates' Court to three charges of causing unauthorised modifications to the contents of a computer contrary to s 3(1) and (7) of the 1990 Act. The defendant was a freelance computer consultant of very considerable experience and repute. He was working on a short-term contract with a computer firm which provided services for a number of clients including maintaining their websites. The company was not satisfied with his work and dismissed him. There was a dispute about the money owed which left him with a sense of grievance. A month later after he had been drinking and acting on impulse he gained unauthorised access to the websites of three companies who were clients of his former employer. They were a supermarket, a communications company and a tour operator. He made use of passports he had been given. He deleted some of the contents to cause inconvenience to his former employer. On two of the sites he moved images around. On the other site, the supermarket one he sent a number of emails informing their customers that prices would go up and they could go elsewhere if they did not like that fact. He changed some of the information on the site about recipes. The computer firm had to do considerable work to restore the sites. The supermarket had to send out E-mails apologising to their customers. Extra security had to be put in place. The site was closed for about 10 weeks. The other companies restored their sites in 3 and $3\frac{1}{2}$ hours. The costs to date were approximately £9,000. There was no damage to the software and no direct revenue loss. When arrested the defendant deeply regretted his actions and wanted to apologise to the three client companies. The defendant was 47 and of good character. He was held in high esteem at Reading University where he was a part time teacher. The police said he was extremely candid. The judge said it was an act of pure unmitigated revenge after a slight. A community penalty was available. Held. The defendant had used the skill and knowledge acquired when working for the company to cause a great deal of work, inconvenience and worry to entirely innocent organisations. It was a breach of trust. **9 months** was not excessive let alone manifestly excessive.

Viruses, – Sending computer viruses

36.3 *R v Vallor* 2004 1 Cr App R (S) 319. The defendant pleaded guilty to three offences of releasing computer viruses onto the Internet, contrary to the Computer Misuse Act 1990, s.3. Over 6 weeks the defendant wrote 3 viruses. The first had been detected in 42 countries and computer systems had been stopped 27,000 different times. This virus was disruptive but not destructive. The second and third viruses had enormously destructive qualities and were programmed to bring the operation of computers to a stop and remove all unsaved data. These viruses only infected 200–300 computers as the police were able to trace him through his internet access quickly. He made full admissions and cooperated with the police. He was "young" and of previous good character. His mother had died in tragic circumstances and the family had suffered a very difficult time. Held. This was a persistent, calculated, disruptive and actually destructive course of conduct involving three offences over a period of time. **2 years** concurrent on each count upheld.

Where the offence is to enable others to watch television without paying, see **Copyright/Trade Mark Offences/Trade Description Offences** – *Television, Enabling access to cable or satellite television for free*

37 Conspiracy

37.1 There are 2 different types of conspiracy. There are statutory conspiracies under the Criminal Law Act 1977 s 1 which form the bulk of conspiracies charged. There are also common law conspiracies of which there are only 2 namely, conspiracy to defraud and conspiracy to corrupt public morals or outrage public decency. For those see **Fraud** and **Public Decency, Outraging**

The Criminal Law Act 1977 s 3 provides for the following maximum penalties for statutory conspiracies:

(a) life, where the offence in question is murder, or is an offence which carries a maximum of life and where the offence has no maximum sentence provided,

(b) the same maximum term of imprisonment to be available as for the offence in question carries and

(c) in all other cases a maximum of a fine.

Conspiracy cases are listed under the offence which was agreed to.

Conspiracy not carried out

37.2 *R v Davies* 1990 The Times 3/10/90. The defendant was convicted of conspiracy to rob. Held. The fact that conspirators had desisted from the planned crime before carrying it out must be reflected in the sentence. If the conspirators desisted because they were overcome with better feelings then great credit must be given. If they desisted because they lost their nerve, none the less they should be not be sentenced as if they had gone ahead with their design.

R v Hardy 2004 Unreported 4/11/04. The defendants H and S were convicted of a conspiracy to import up to 100 kilos of cocaine. The evidence was almost entirely from undercover officers. H was the introducer and attended three meetings after that. Nothing was imported. After his son died, S said he didn't want anything more to do with any plan. H had previously dealt in Class A drugs. S was 60 with a conviction in 1991 for dealing in Class B drugs for which he received 6 years. S had, just before the Court of Appeal hearing, had a successful liver transplant. Held. The reason why a conspiracy to import drugs comes to an end is material to sentence. If the conspiracy is frustrated because the authorities seize the drugs the mitigation is slight. If the conspirators decide of their own free will that they will not continue with the importation the mitigation may be substantial. For this amount where the conspiracy did not come to fruition the starting point is in the order of **14 years.** H **7 years** not 14. Because of S's age and health and his ceasing to be involved **10 years** not 20.

See also WITHDRAWING FROM PLAN – *It should be encouraged*

Penalty for the offence alters during the conspiracy

37.3   *R v Hobbs* 2002 2 Cr App R (S) 425. The defendants were convicted of conspiracy to facilitate the illegal entry into the U. K. of illegal immigrants. During the dates particularised the maximum sentence was raised from 7 to 10 years. The Judge sentenced two of them to 9 and 7 $^1/_2$ years. Held. The better course is to prefe distinct counts for the period before and after the date the maximum changed. Defendants should not be affected adversely, with respect to powers of sentence, by changes in the law occurring during the currency of a conspiracy entered into before the changes. A strict, narrow and certain view as to when the offence is complete should be applied and not a more extensive and flexible construction. Conspiracy is complete when the agreement is made. The Judge was restricted to the old maximums.

CONTAMINATING FOOD

See BLACKMAIL – *Supermarkets and retail stores* and FOOD ETC, CONTAMINATING OF

CONTEMPT OF COURT

See PERVERTING THE COURSE OF JUSTICE/CONTEMPT OF COURT/PERJURY ETC

38   COPYRIGHT/TRADE MARK OFFENCES/TRADE DESCRIPTION OFFENCES

38.1   Copyright, Designs and Patents Act 1988 s 107

Triable either way. On indictment maximum 2 years. Summary maximum 6 months and/or £5,000.

The Criminal Justice Act 2003 creates a summary maximum sentence of 51 weeks, a minimum custodial sentence of 28 weeks and Custody plus. The Home Office says they do not expect to introduce these provisions before September 2006.

Confiscation For all Copyright, Designs and Patents Act 1988 s 107 offences[14] committed on or after 24 March 2003[15] the court <u>must</u> follow the Proceeds of Crime Act 2002 procedure.

Trade Marks Act 1994 s 92

Unauthorised use of a Trade Mark etc.

Triable either way. On indictment maximum 10 years. Summary maximum 6 months and/or £5,000.

14 Proceeds of Crime Act 2002 s 6 and s 75 and Sch 2 para 7
15 Proceeds of Crime Act 2002 (Commencement No 5, Transitional Provisions, Savings and Amendment) Order 2003

Trade Descriptions Act 1968 s 1, 12, 13 and 14

Unauthorised use of a Trade Mark etc.

Triable either way. On indictment maximum 2 years. Summary maximum £5,000.

Crown Court statistics – England and Wales – Males 21+ – Trades Descriptions Act and similar offences

38.2

Year	Plea	Total Numbers sentenced	Type of sentence %					Average length of custody (months)
			Discharge	Fine	Community sentence	Suspended sentence	Custody	
2002	Guilty	56	4	38	27	4	29	10
	Not guilty	10	–	60	10	–	30	6
2003	Guilty	50	12	24	26	6	30	8.6
	Not guilty	11	18	45	9	–	27	18

For details and explanations about the statistics in the book see page vii.

Guideline remarks

38.3   *R v Kemp* 1995 16 Cr App R (S) 941. Offences of counterfeiting normally attract at least a short sentence of imprisonment. They are difficult, time consuming and expensive to detect. The owners of copyright are entitled to be protected.

R v Ansari 2000 1 Cr App R (S) 94. Trade Mark offences undermine reputable companies. The sentencer should consider how professional the enterprise was and the likely or actual profits made.

Car dealers

38.4   *R v Fellows* 2001 1 Cr App R (S) 398. The defendant pleaded guilty to offences under the Trade Descriptions Act 1968, Fair Trading Act 1973, Consumer Transactions (Restrictions on Statements) Order 1976 and the Business Advertisements (Disclosure) Order 1977. There was an offence of supplying goods with a false description and obtaining property arising out of a false odometer reading. The defendant operated a second-hand car business from his home address for just over 18 months. He had dealt with 43 cars. He advertised in local papers giving the impression he was a private seller of a single car. He commonly said it was his daughter's car. The prosecution case was that he was targeting vulnerable people choosing low value cars typically aimed at first time buyers. He sold cars as seen. He accepted he misled buyers but he claimed he was under financial pressure and was ignorant of the law. Held. This was a particularly mean offence causing great anxiety and inconvenience to people whose cars developed faults. **18 months** was severe but not manifestly excessive.

R v Richards and Evans 2004 2 Cr App R (S) 264. R pleaded guilty on re-arraignment to seven counts of supplying goods with a false trade description and one count of offering to supply goods with a false trade description. E pleaded guilty on re-arraignment to five counts of supplying goods with a false trade description, three counts of applying a false trade description to goods and one count of offering to supply goods with a false trade description. The defendants rented units on a trading estate, R's as a valeting service and E selling used cars. Trading standards officers received complaints that a clocked car had been offered for sale from R's premises and that he had been involved in supplying or offering to supply other clocked cars. He continued to offer clocked cars after he knew there was an investigation. He had supplied one to E, who sold four clocked cars after the officers visited him, and the officers found three others on his forecourt during a second visit. They each put in a basis of plea and the court operated on these. The basis of plea for both defendants was essentially that they had no knowledge of the clocking but they accepted that they had failed in their obligation to make sufficient checks on the odometers of the cars before they were involved in the sale of the cars. R, 33, had a considerable record including offences of dishonesty concerned with motor vehicles. A pre-sentence report said he had shown no signs of remorse and there was a risk of re-offending. Evans, 52, had no previous convictions and a pre-sentence report said there was minimal risk of re-offending. He was living on sickness benefit and was not suitable for a community sentence. Held. For E the appropriate sentence was **2 years C/D** on each count, not 6 months imprisonment on each count. For R, who had money available to him and was able to work, it was of primary importance that the innocent purchasers should be compensated for loss, and there should be a degree of parity between the defendants. The appropriate sentence was **2 years C/D** not 6 months imprisonment coupled with compensation orders.

Distributing articles in breach of copyright or with false Trade Marks or descriptions

38.5 *R v Ansari* 2000 1 Cr App R (S) 94. The defendants M, H, L and S pleaded guilty to various unstated offences under the Trade Marks Act 1994 s 92(1)(c). Police raided H's house on an unconnected matter and found garments with well known fashion house labels on them. They started a surveillance operation. This revealed a large scale and sophisticated business in goods with false fashion labels like Versace and Calvin Klein. £74,000 worth of garments were found at one address. M sewed the false labels into every garment. H was in charge of storage of all the goods. He was a major player and the goods he pleaded guilty to were worth between £800,000 and £900,000. L was also a major player who had prior experience in the fashion trade and dealt with the buyers and sellers and the financing of the operation. S was a packer and machinist. £47,900 worth of goods was found in his premises. M was 46, married with three children and with no convictions. He had a legitimate job as a machinist and had lost a baby. H was 41 and effectively without any convictions. He was a trainee pub manager. L was 34 and was in breach of the suspended sentence. He worked in transport. S was 40, married with three children and had no convictions. He was a fork-lift driver. Held. Reputable companies were clearly undermined by this professional enterprise where the likely profits were high. There were no exceptional reasons to suspend M's sentence. **2 years** for M and S and **3 years** for H and L were correct.

Old cases. *R v Yanko* 1996 1 Cr App R (S) 217.

Estate agents

38.6 *R v Docklands Estates Ltd* 2001 1 Cr App R (S) 270. LCJ. The defendant company was convicted of 3 offences of giving a false indication that services had been provided contrary to Trades Descriptions Act 1968, s 13. The company was a family firm of estate agents and had been established for about 6 years. They erected 'Sold' signs on properties in Docklands where they had received no instructions and no permission to erect the signs. Their defence was someone else had done it. The company had unencumbered assets of £77,000 and profits in the last 2 years of £16,000 and £33,000. The family salaries had been deducted. The company had no convictions. The court was shown material which showed fines of £100 being imposed at the Magistrates' Court for these offences. They were ordered to pay £5,203 costs. Held. The improper erection of signs is a nuisance of significant dimensions. It creates a false impression giving the public confidence in the company, which is not justified. Other honest companies are put at a disadvantage. The levels of fines we have been told about are not realistic. We hope the message will go out to Magistrates' Courts that the fines they are imposing are too low. **£2,000 for each** not £7,500 on each.

Making copies in breach of copyright or with false Trade Marks or descriptions

38.7 *R v Bhad* 1999 2 Cr App R (S) 140. LCJ. The defendant was convicted of two counts of applying a Trade Mark without consent (four polo shirts and a sweatshirt), possessing an article used to produce goods with a Trade Mark without consent (a multi-head embroidery machine) and four counts of unauthorised use of Trade Marks (19 polo shirt and a sweatshirt) in total. He ran an embroidery business whose premises were searched by Trading Standards officers. They had three large industrial embroidery machines one of which was connected to a computer. On the computer screen was a 'Reebok' logo. There were the 'Reebok' polo shirts and a sweatshirt which were not genuine. He had no convictions of a similar kind. He was sentenced for just that day's occurrence only with a **£1,250 fine** for the three Trade Mark offences and 4 months on the four Trade Descriptions offences and £6,000 costs. The grounds of appeal argued that it was a single set of facts which gave rise to the seven counts. The Trade Mark offences were alternative counts it was wrong to impose custody on the less serious counts. Held. We recognise the damage done to the legitimate trade by fake products. However, we see force in the defence submissions. The defendant had built up an honest business. It was highly questionable whether the custody threshold was passed. It was anomalous to impose a custodial sentence on the less serious Trade Description offences and a financial penalty on the more serious Trade Mark offences. We quash the prison sentence and impose no penalty on those counts.

R v Gleeson 2002 1 Cr App R (S) 485. The defendant changed his plea at the latest possible stage to guilty of 19 counts of possessing goods bearing a Trade Mark contrary to section 92(1) of the Trade Marks Act 1994 and possessing goods for the labelling and packaging goods contrary to s 92(2)(c). He manufactured copies of music CDs from his home and acquired large quantities of labels, blank CDs and sophisticated printing and shrink wrap equipment. The CDs were indistinguishable from the genuine article. 14 Trade Marks were infringed. He had produced 4,000 CDs and hoped to produce 2,000 a week. The potential loss to the music industry was about £1.5m. The CDs were sold to a distributor for between £1.50 and £2 and he made 50p per CD. That gave him £20,000 and a loss to the owners of £20,000. He was 43 with a conviction for perverting the course of justice in 1988 and conspiracy to supply Class B drugs in 1997. He received 12 months for both. He lived with his elderly mother who was in poor health and had a legitimate job. Held. It is necessary to deter others. We do not tinker with sentences. **30 months** was not manifestly excessive.

R v Passley 2004 1 Cr App R (S) 419. The defendant pleaded guilty at the first opportunity to six counts of possessing goods with a view to sale or distribution which bore a sign identical to or likely to be mistaken for a registered trade mark, contrary to s. 92(1)(c), two counts of possessing an article designed or adapted for making copies of a sign, and two counts of possessing a video recording of a classified work for the purpose of supply, contrary to the Video Recording Act 1984, s.10(1). The defendant was stopped by police officers. He agreed to a search of his home address. Police officers found a large amount of equipment suitable for illegal copying and distributing CDs and DVDs. The equipment was antiquated and unsophisticated. A considerable number of counterfeit computer games, DVDs, CD films and videos were seized. The estimated turnover was £27,000 over two years. He was 34 and of positive good character. The pre-sentence report described him as a responsible hard-working man. As a consequence of custody he had lost his home, his family and the custody of his children. Held. This operation was by no means at the upper end of the scale. A hobby had become a modest, albeit profitable, criminal venture. **12 months** not 21.

Old cases. *R v Gross* 1996 2 Cr App R (S) 189, *R v Lloyd* 1997 2 Cr App R (S) 151 and *R v Dukett* 1998 2 Cr App R (S) 59. (For a summary of the last two cases see the first edition of this book.)

Market traders

38.8   *R v Adam* 1998 2 Cr App R (S) 403. The defendant pleaded guilty to four offences of using an unauthorised Trade Mark, applying a false description and obstructing an authorised officer under the Trades Descriptions Act. In another indictment he pleaded guilty to three offences of using an unauthorised Trade Mark, and obtaining property by deception. Trading standards officers saw the defendant in a market selling illegitimate goods with names on them like 'Calvin Klein, Ralph Lauren and Levi Strauss'. He lied to the officers about his name and address. A week later he was seen selling the same counterfeit goods. Seven months later in another market he was seen doing the same again. On the day of the trial of the first group of offences he pleaded guilty. He then changed his plea to the second group at a different court. It was his case that he was working for another and received £25 a day and the profits went to the stall holder. He was treated as having no convictions. He was 35 and married with four children. He was unemployed, in receipt of benefits and with no savings. Held. The judge was entitled to express scepticism that he was working for someone else. The offence calls for a deterrent sentence. 3 months and 4 months for each group were appropriate. The judge was fully entitled to make them consecutive. **7 months** was severe but he was entitled to pass a severe sentence.

Shops

38.9   *R v Burns* 2001 1 Cr App R (S) 220. The defendant pleaded guilty at the Magistrates' Court to 22 offences of having counterfeit articles for sale in a shop and 31 offences of having counterfeit goods in another shop and storage unit. They were specimen offences. Trading Standard Officers attended his shop and found the clothing featuring counterfeit brand names like Adidas, Ralph Lauren Calvin Klein and Timberland. Five hundred items were seized. They took other clothing from another shop, a van and a storage unit. The value of all the goods was £15,000 and the value of the goods in the charges was £1,300. He was 34 with two recent convictions for Trade Mark infringement for which he was fined. He had financial difficulties. Held. The offences are prevalent. He had ignored the warning he received when last prosecuted. **12 months** was inevitable.

Television, enabling access to cable or satellite television for free

38.10   *R v Carey* 1999 1 Cr App R (S) 322. The defendant pleaded guilty to conspiracy to defraud. Up until March 1994, he ran a company which made electronic devices. In July 1993, BSkyB a satellite television company, had obtained a perpetual injunction against the company prohibiting it from making or trading the devices. In May 1995 the defendant set up another company in Ireland and successfully 'hacked' BskyB's smartcards so enabling viewers to watch programmes without paying BSkyB. BSkyB produced another smartcard and the company successfully hacked that card too. There were about 850,000 sales of the cards. The cost of introducing another smartcard by BSkyB was £30m, although such a figure could not be attributed to the defendant as others were also 'hacking' the cards. The defendant's profit was £20,000. He was 48 and of good character with family responsibilities. Held. The commercial damage was great. The judge was right to concentrate on the company's loss as well as the defendant's gain. **4 years** was not manifestly excessive.

R v Maxwell-King 2001 2 Cr App R (S) 136. The defendant pleaded guilty to three counts of inciting computer misuse by supplying to third parties a device causing unauthorised modifications to a computer. He and his wife were also directors and sole shareholders in a company which pleaded to the same counts, which was not fined but ordered to pay £10,000 prosecution costs. He and his company manufactured and supplied a device, which allowed the upgrading of analogue cable TV so the viewer could access all channels regardless of how many s/he had paid for. Twenty were sold at £30 plus VAT. A number of customers returned the chips because the TV company had been able to disable them electronically. As a result he gave up the scheme. His advertisement had been withdrawn before he was arrested. The chips were advertised on his extensive website. When his premises were raided the FACT officers were able to virtually close him down as they seized all his technical equipment. The loss to the TV company was £14 a device per month. He was 36 and of exemplary character with excellent references. His risk for re-offending was assessed as very low. Held. It was effectively a form of theft. The custody threshold had not been crossed. The appropriate sentence would be a substantial fine or a community sentence. **150 hours' CSO** not 4 months.

R v Parr-Moore and Crumblehulme 2003 1 Cr App R (S) 425 The defendants P and C pleaded guilty to incitement to make and distribute 'cable cubes' contrary to section 3 of the Computer Misuse Act 1990. The defendants formed a company known as CD multimedia that performed many perfectly legitimate commercial activities. However, 'cable cubes' allowed cable television subscribers to view other channels for which they had not paid the subscription. The defendants' own estimate was an average profit of £20 per cube; a total profit of about £6000. Their internet site received about 1000 hits per week of which about 5 per cent turned into actual sales. There was a written basis of plea, accepting that between April and November 1999 they supplied about 300 cubes and that there were a further ten cubes ready for supply in due course. They were both of effectively good character and C was not in the best of health. Held. It was effectively theft and this type of offence was a serious matter, compromising the integrity of the cable network system. Because of the obvious danger of rapid expansion of the popularity of this type of offence, it needed stamping on at the outset. With proper credit for the early guilty pleas, **4 months** not 7 months for each defendant.

R v Iqbal 2004 1 Cr App R (S) 275 The defendant pleaded guilty to conspiracy to defraud. He programmed computer chips to make a cube activator which he sold on the internet. He also sold some cubes by phone registering his BT number in a false name. The cubes were sold for £70 with a discount for bulk purchases and enabled Pay to View to be watched without payment. The profit was in the region of £100,000 with a turnover of £435,000. The loss to the TV company was "on the way to £15m". He was 29, of good character and with a degree in Economics. Held. It was an extremely sophisticated and dedicated crime. The Judge was entitled to add a deterrent element. **5 years** was not wrong.

See also COMPANY FRAUDS AND FINANCIAL SERVICES OFFENCES

CORONER, OBSTRUCTING THE

See OBSTRUCTING THE CORONER/BURIAL, PREVENTING

39 CORRUPTION

39.1 Public Bodies Corrupt Practices Act 1889 s 1 and Prevention of Corruption Act 1906 s 1

Both offences are triable either way. On indictment maximum 7 years. Summary maximum 6 months and/or £5,000.

Commercial

39.2 *R v Anderson* 2003 2 Cr App R (S) 131 The defendant pleaded guilty late to corruption. He was employed as a strategic rail manager by Railfreight. He was in charge of 6 inland terminals that hired additional road haulage from private contractors. The co-accused, C was the manager of a firm of hauliers. C agreed to bribe him with £25,000 from his company's money and the defendant agreed to supply him with £1m worth of business. Payments were made on a small but regular basis, making it easier for C to hide those payments. False invoices that bore no relation to any work actually carried out were set up. The defendant and W were each paid a total of £8,500 from an account that had received £23,651. Subsequent complaints about the service that C's company provided led to an investigation which resulted in the arrest of those involved. The defendant was interviewed and tried to explain it away. He was 56 and a man of good character with a favourable PSR. C received a 240-hour community punishment order and a costs order. **6 months** not 12.

Local government

39.3 *R v Dearnley and Threapleton* 2001 2 Cr App R (S) 201. The defendants were convicted of corruption after a retrial. The defendant D aged 56 was a principle valuer for a Metropolitan Council. He was responsible for its property management including a business centre. Tenders for the centre's security services were invited. A company called ESC was not approached. The defendant T aged 52, was a director of that company's parent company. ESC approached the defendant D and their quote was accepted although it was not the lowest. No formal documentation was presented just invoices. The council also gave the company other work. Two companies connected with T were paid £1m for services provided. Another company connected with T paid off a loan of £5,445 D had obtained to buy a car. The judge described T as greedy. Both had no convictions. The offence was 7 years old. T had spent £75,000 on his legal expenses and was ruined. Held. Custody is inevitable. There was no suggestion of lack of value for money. **12 months** not 18 for both.

R v Bush 2003 2 Cr App R (S) 686. The defendant was convicted of corruption. He was working for a London Borough as the Council's heating manager when he was approached by R who ran a company which repaired and installed hearing systems. The defendant said that he could make things better for R. He could put his company on the contracts list which would allow R's company to tender for the larger contracts. The defendant asked for weekly payments of £100 which R paid continually for 6 years. The defendant made two other demands for £1,000 in cash which R paid. R's company also carried out work at the defendant's home free of charge. R stopped making payments in 1998 and his company was removed from the Approved Contractors List and went into liquidation. The total benefit to the defendant was about £40,000. R pleaded guilty to corruption and received a community punishment order of 150 hours. He also gave evidence for the prosecution at the defendant's trial. The defendant was 49 was of good character. Held. The defendant had solicited the bribes. His corrupt conduct persisted over a period of six years. It was a gross abuse of trust motivated by greed. However, the sentence of **2 ½ years** not 4.

Police officers as defendants

39.4 *R v Donald* 1997 2 Cr App R (S) 272. The defendant pleaded guilty to four counts of corruption after 12½ weeks trial. The first matter was accepting £500 for police information, the second was agreeing to accept £10,000 for police information, the third was agreeing to accept £40,000 for destroying a surveillance log, and the fourth was accepting £18,000 for the removal of the log in the third matter. The defendant was a detective constable serving in No 9 Regional Crime Squad. He was at the heart of a sensitive and vitally important police operation. The money in each matter was negotiated by a criminal, who had gone to the BBC who then filmed and recorded the conversations between the two. The 1st matter was unsolicited and involved Michael Lawson. The second involved Michael Lawson and Kenneth Noye who were both two international criminals being investigated for major drug trafficking. The fourth was a down payment for the third. The defendant had 'glowing recommendations from his superiors.' He received 5 years for the first, 6 years for the second matter consecutive and 5 years concurrent for the other 2 (**11 years** in all). Held. The sentence was severe but not manifestly excessive.

R v Smith 2002 1 Cr App R (S) 386. See *Police officers, trying to corrupt*

See also **POLICE OFFICERS**

Police officers, trying to corrupt

39.5   *R v Brown, Mahoney and King* 2000 2 Cr App R (S) 284. The defendant K pleaded guilty to various conspiracies to pervert the course of justice, conspiracies to corrupt a police officer and corruption. The defendant B was convicted of one conspiracy involving K. The defendant M was convicted of two conspiracies involving K, forming one part of the case. The case fell into three parts. In the first part B was arrested for car fraud. four cars and £17,500 was seized. B's father approached K, a former policeman who approached another former police officer H who approached a Detective Chief Inspector. The Inspector was suspicious and arranged for all further conversations to be recorded. H introduced K to the Inspector and H gave the Inspector £1,000. The Inspector then met B. The cars and the money were returned and K gave the Inspector £5,000. The officer then gave K a letter saying the enquiries into the fraud were at an end.

The second part of the case was when M was charged with two offences of GBH with intent. M's father knew K and he approached the same Detective Chief Inspector. They both agreed that if the papers went missing the case would be tainted. K asked the officer if in exchange for payment he could make some enquiries. Later the Inspector told K he would need to tear up the officers' pocket books and the Identification book at the ID parade for that case. The Inspector asked what sort of money his client was prepared to pay and was told between £5,000 and £10,000. Eventually it was agreed two payments of £2,500 could be made. The first instalment was paid and the papers were produced and destroyed. A further meeting was arranged and K and M were arrested. They were in possession of £2,550.

The third part of the case involved a Henry Moore statue worth about £100,000, which had been stolen from a gallery. K asked the same Detective Chief Inspector whether the £10,000 reward money could be obtained without anyone being arrested. It was agreed K could be registered as an informant in a false name. Later K handed the statue over and was paid the £10,000 reward from the insurance company and £3,000 out of the Informant's fund. He gave £2,000 to the Inspector.

K was 51 with no convictions. His business had gone wrong and he was in financial difficulties. M was 32 and was a builder. He had eight convictions including burglary, handling, theft and possession of cannabis. B was 25 and largely unemployed. He dealt with second-hand cars. He had no convictions. He was described as unsophisticated and somewhat gullible. K was said to have, 'called the shots.' K was given less than the normal credit for his plea because of the strength of the evidence in the tape recordings. Held. An important part of the sentencing process is deterrent. The starting point for K should have been 9 years. Taking into account the mitigation the appropriate sentence was 6 years for the first part of the case and the other sentences concurrent not the 9 he received. B's sentence was reduced from 3 years to **21 months**. M's sentence was reduced from 5 to **3¹/₂ years**.

R v Smith 2002 1 Cr App R (S) 386. The defendants D and H pleaded guilty shortly after a jury was empanelled to a police corruption conspiracy which was over a 4 year period. D was a Sergeant in the CID and H was a drug dealer who was sentenced to 8 years for drug trafficking offences. £130,000 was found at H's home. H supplied D with money and information about other drug criminals and D provided H with information about police and customs operations against other drug dealers. H made tape recordings of the conversations which were found by the police. The corruption started at the beginning of the police officer's career. H suggested planting drugs on other criminals. D adopted H as an informant but did not tell his superior officers. D also dealt with his father's hotel business and it was in 1995 in a poor financial state. H put £10,000 into the hotel business. H then took over the running of the hotel and used it for the storing and distribution of drugs. D then lied about his involvement with H. Five offenders were able to escape when information about the raids on their addresses were leaked to H. The police started investigating and D ignored police instructions. He was told to stop seeing H and he met him the next day and again later. H and D were both arrested and D lied when interviewed. The prosecution could not be precise about the damage caused to the police and the profits made. However the integrity of the police force and its anti-drugs activities were very seriously compromised. H and his associates were major players in the drugs world. D received 7 years, the maximum, and H received 5 years consecutive to the 8 years he had received in his drug case. The judge refused to give D a discount for the plea because the appropriate sentence was 10 years before a small discount for the plea which should have made it $8^1/_2$ years. He said the situation was similar to a specimen charge where one count does not reflect the whole course of conduct. Held. Some discount for the plea should have been made so 6 years for D substituted. H's sentence reduced from 5 to **$4^1/_2$years**.

See also **MISCONDUCT IN PUBLIC OFFICE**

40 COUNTERFEITING CURRENCY

40.1 Forgery and Counterfeiting Act 1981 s 14(1), 15(1), 16(1) and 17(1)

Making [s 14(1)]; passing etc [s 15(1)]; having custody or control of counterfeit notes or coin intending the notes or coins to be passed [s 16(1)]; and making etc counterfeiting materials etc intending the notes or coins to be passed respectively [s17(1)].

All the offences are triable either way. On indictment maximum 10 years. Summary maximum 6 months and/or £5,000.

The Criminal Justice Act 2003 creates a summary maximum sentence of 51 weeks, a minimum custodial sentence of 28 weeks and Custody plus. The Home Office says they do not expect to introduce these provisions before September 2006.

Forgery and Counterfeiting Act 1981 s 14(2), 15(2), 16(2) and 17(2)

Making; delivering; having custody and control of counterfeit notes or coin without lawful excuse; and making etc counterfeiting materials etc without lawful excuse respectively.

Triable either way. On indictment maximum 2 years. Summary maximum 6 months and/or £5,000.

Confiscation For all s 14, 15, 16 and 17 offences[16] committed on or after 24 March 2003[17] the court <u>must</u> follow the Proceeds of Crime Act 2002 procedure.

16 Proceeds of Crime Act 2002 s 6 and s 75 and Sch 2 para 6
17 Proceeds of Crime Act 2002 (Commencement No 5, Transitional Provisions, Savings and Amendment) Order 2003

Guideline remarks

40.2   *R v Crick* 1998 3 Cr App R (S) 275. The defendant pleaded guilty to possessing a press and he made about 150 fake 50p pieces. The coins could not have been put into general circulation and were to be used in vending machines. Held. Coining is a serious offence and calls for immediate imprisonment. However it must be recognised that not all such offences are of the same gravity. At one extreme is the professional forger, with carefully prepared plates, and elaborate machinery, who manufactures large quantities of bank notes and puts them into circulation. A long sentence of imprisonment is appropriate in such a case. At the other end is this case.

Large scale production

40.3   *R v Dossetter* 1999 2 Cr App R (S) 248. The defendants D and J pleaded guilty to two counts of conspiracy to produce counterfeit currency. The defendants C, and M pleaded guilty to one of those counts. D's plea was very late and M's plea was extremely late. J was employed by D in the printing business. After J had left D who was the prime mover approached J to counterfeit US dollars. They needed help and J approached someone who had their own photographic business and who was able to make the necessary transparencies. D and J were able to produce some $200,000 worth of relatively unsophisticated notes. Some went to America where the authorities intervened. About 6 months later they started to produce with a different press and with improved technology $6m worth of notes. They were stored at C's premises and C was paid just over £3,000 for his help. D tried to sell the notes and M used his contacts and an undercover officer agreed to buy $2m. As the deal was about to be finalised officers arrested the courier and the minder at a hotel. J was arrested elsewhere in the hotel. J was interviewed and made admissions. He also showed the police where the other $3.5m worth of notes were and told the officers who else was involved. M was the organiser of the dissemination of the notes. No notes were ever circulated. J and C pleaded at the first opportunity and were prepared to give evidence for the prosecution. D was 46 and of good character. M was 52 with no convictions since 1986. C was 51 and of good character. Held. D's sentence of **7 years** was not manifestly excessive. M's sentence was reduced from 4 to **3 years**. C and J's sentences were reduced from 5 to **3 years** to reflect C's lesser role and J's assistance.

41   CRIMINAL DAMAGE

41.1   There are three criminal damage offences, a) destroying property [s 1(1)], b) making a threat to destroy property [s 2] and c) destroying property reckless whether life would be endangered [s 1(2)]. ARSON is listed separately.

Criminal Damage Act 1971 s 1(1)

The offence is triable either way, where the value of damage is £5,000 or more. Otherwise summary only. On indictment maximum 10 years[18]. Summary maximum, when value is £5,000 or more 6 months and/or £5,000 fine; and 3 months and/or £2,500 otherwise.

The Criminal Justice Act 2003 creates a summary maximum sentence of 51 weeks, a minimum custodial sentence of 28 weeks and Custody plus. The Home Office says they do not expect to introduce these provisions before September 2006.

Anti-Social Behavioural orders Where the defendant has acted in a manner that caused or was likely to cause harassment, alarm or distress to one or more persons

---

18 This is irrespective of what the value is. So if a count is added to the indictment and the value is less than £5,000 the maximum is 10 years, *R v Alden* 2002 2 Cr App R (S) 326.

not in the same household as the defendant and it is necessary to protect persons from further anti-social acts by him/her the court may make this order[19].

Fixed penalties The Anti-Social Behaviour Act 2003 s 43 gives power to an authorised officer of a local authority to issue a £50 fixed penalty for criminal damage, except where the offence was motivated by racial or religious hostility. £80 (£40 if under 16)[20]

Sexual Offences Prevention Order There is a discretionary power to make this order when it is necessary to protect the public etc.[21]

Crown Court statistics – England and Wales – Males 21+

41.2

Year	Plea	Total Numbers sentenced	Type of sentence %					Average length of custody (months)
			Discharge	Fine	Community sentence	Suspended sentence	Custody	
Criminal Damage endangering life								
2002	Guilty	40	–	–	23	–	75	68.5
	Not guilty	5	–	–	20	–	80	87.8
2003	Guilty	44	–	–	11	9	77	37
	Not guilty	7	–	–	–	14	86	143.7
Threats etc. to commit Criminal Damage								
2002	Guilty	50	8	–	26	4	60	24
	Not guilty	5	20	–	20	–	60	27
2003	Guilty	46	7	4	57	–	30	25.4
	Not guilty	5	20	20	–	–	40	39
Other Criminal Damage								
2002	Guilty	372	21	8	48	1	17	9.5
	Not guilty	62	15	10	40	2	19	8.3
2003	Guilty	437	19	8	54	2	11	5.3
	Not guilty	40	15	13	18	5	28	12.5

For details and explanations about the statistics in the book see page vii.

Magistrates' Court Sentencing Guidelines January 2004

41.3 For a first time offender pleading not guilty. Entry point. Is a discharge or a fine appropriate? Consider the impact on the victim. Examples of aggravating factors for the offence are deliberate, group action, serious damage, targeting and vulnerable victim. Examples of mitigating factors for the offence are impulsive action, minor damage, and provocation. Examples of mitigation are age, health (physical or mental), co-operation with the police, genuine remorse and voluntary compensation. Give reasons if not awarding compensation. **Starting point fine C.** (150% of weekly take home pay/weekly benefit payment.)

For details about the guidelines see MAGISTRATES' COURT SENTENCING GUIDELINES at page 483.

Fire, involving See ARSON

---

19 Crime and Disorder Act 1998 s 1C
20 The Penalties for Disorderly Behaviour (Amount of Penalty) Order 2002 Para 2 and Sch. Part II as amended.
21 Sexual Offences Act 2003 s 104 & Sch. 5

Graffiti

41.4   *R v Verdi* 2005 1 Cr App R (S) 197. The defendant pleaded guilty in the Magistrates Court to nine offences of criminal damage and was committed to the Crown Court for sentence. All were spraying graffiti known as 'tagging' on London Underground trains over an 8-month period. He wrote his tag sometimes inside but mostly outside the carriages in black, sometimes covering the whole side of the carriage. He also wrote phrases like 'I drop bombs like Bin' and 'Kill that officer'. The evidence from London Underground was that when a train had graffiti on it was withdrawn from service at a cost of £23,000 a day. If it was repeatedly subject to graffiti that could reduce its service life by five years at a cost of £4 million. It currently cost £10 million to remove graffiti. Once the defendant was almost caught but ran off with others down a tunnel. When officers searched his home they found wire cutters, pens, a dye and spray cans. The defendant, 18, admitted the offences in interview. There was a good pre-sentence report and there was a subsequent prison report which said his conduct was excellent in custody and he was an enhanced prisoner. Held. It should be borne in mind that people who have to chase those running through tunnels run a serious risk of injury from electrified lines. Those who carry out these activities do so for their own gratification and self-advertisement. A deterrent sentence was necessary, but **18 months** not 2 years.

Reckless whether life would be endangered

41.5   Criminal Damage Act 1971 s 1(2)

Indictable only. Maximum sentence life imprisonment.

Dangerous Offender provisions For offences committed on or after 4/4/05 where there is a significant risk to members of the public of serious harm etc. there is a mandatory duty to pass a life sentence when it is justified and otherwise a sentence of imprisonment for public protection[22]. For offenders under 18 the duty is to pass detention for life, detention for public protection or an extended sentence[23].

R v Bonehill 1998 2 Cr App R (S) 90. The defendant made a late plea of guilty to two counts of damaging property in a way likely to endanger life. The victim had had to give evidence at the committal proceedings. The defendant had a relationship with the defendant in which they lived together. After it broke up the house where she lived with her children aged 10 and 12 caught fire in the middle of the night. All three had to jump out of a window to escape. She suspected the defendant was responsible. He then began a campaign of intimidation and she had to move. A brick was thrown through her window and she had to move again. She then discovered that he knew her latest address. When at home with a friend and the children in bed she heard the door banging. She pressed her panic button and found on the floor by the front door a cassette tape in an envelope. A note said that she should play the B side which she did. That side had his voice on it saying how much he loved her. On the A side was him saying, 'I'm going to cut you up like a blood cock pussy whore, (sic) I'm going to torch the house when you're all in it.' The next day a friend told the victim that he was at the door again. Once again a cassette tape was delivered. On it he said he was going to cut her up and she should not go out of the house because he was watching her all the time. It concluded with him saying he would do what he did last time 'when you were all in bed at our last house.' Three days later the victim's brother saw him and held him till the police arrived. After sentence a psychiatric report was written which gave the defendant no assistance. An adverse prison report was also written. Held. **4 years** was severe but it matched the offences which were very serious. Threats of arson are inevitably serious. They would have had an appalling effect on the victim's mind.

22 Criminal Justice Act 2003 s 225
23 Criminal Justice Act 2003 s 226 and 228

R v Mynors 1998 2 Cr App R (S) 279. The defendant pleaded guilty to criminal damage being reckless whether life was endangered. The defendant had arguments with his girlfriend and according to her hit her. She left the house. The police were called and found the girlfriend injured and distressed outside. They smelt gas and broke in. The defendant was found unconscious in a cupboard. A gas pipe had been severed. He told police it was an attempt to commit suicide. He was 43 and had five convictions for violence including rape and wounding and a conviction for arson. He was on probation. A report said he needed psychiatric assistance. **2 years** was not manifestly excessive.

R v Messenger 2001 2 Cr App R (S) 117. The defendant pleaded to guilty to criminal damage being reckless whether life was endangered. The defendant admitted cutting the brake hoses on a car. The driver discovered it, as he was about to take his son to school. The victim was the stepfather of the defendant's ex-girlfriend and there was bad feeling between them. It involved access to his child. The defendant was suffering from severe mental problems connected with the child and an abortion on an unborn child. His only convictions were drug related. **3 years** was not manifestly excessive.

Old case. *R v Dodd* 1997 1 Cr App R (S) 127, (for a summary of this case see the first edition of this book).

See also ARSON – *Arson – Reckless whether life would be endangered*

Threatening to destroy or damage property

41.6   Criminal Damage Act 1971 s 2

Triable either way. On indictment maximum 10 years. Summary maximum 6 months and/or £5,000.

R v Kavanagh 1998 1 Cr App R (S) 241. The defendant pleaded guilty to threatening to destroy or damage property in a way likely to endanger life. In March/April 1996 the defendant was a victim of an assault for which he required 48 stitches in his head. In August he quarrelled with his partner who told him to leave the house. The defendant responded with violence and the partner left the house. Police arrived and found him locked in the flat with the windows closed and a strong smell of gas. The defendant was armed with a large knife and a lighter. He threatened to blow the place up and to stab anyone who came near him. A police officer broke all the windows he could and switched off the gas at the meter. Police tried to calm him down but he brandished seven knives. He was eventually persuaded to leave the flat. A fire officer said the gas from the fire and the oven could easily have ignited and if someone in a neighbouring flat had even turned on a television there might have been an explosion. The defendant said he was on temazepan and painkillers and had drunk 4 pints and 2 large Bacardi rums. He said he did not know why he did it. He was 30 with many previous convictions mainly for dishonesty. A psychiatrist said he was not mentally ill but had symptoms which could be associated with post-traumatic stress disorder. The defendant told him he was very angry and wanted revenge. Held. People in the block were all put in danger. Action of this sort will be met with serious and heavy punishment. With mercy **3 years** not 4.

R v McCann 2000 1 Cr App R (S) 495. The defendant pleaded guilty to threatening to destroy property. The defendant ordered a burger from a kebab shop over the telephone. After it arrived he complained over the telephone that there was sauce in the burger which he had not requested. He was offered a replacement which he declined. He then went to the shop and asked for a refund which was refused. He was abusive to the owner and falsely claimed he had served a long sentence for murder. He said he would return and burn down the shop with the proprietor inside. At 1.30am next morning he returned to the shop which was still open with customers and splashed diesel fuel on the floor and some on the customers. The proprietor's three young children were asleep upstairs. He had a cigarette in his mouth and a lighter in his hand and shouted he was going to burn the place down. The customers ran out in panic while the proprietor leapt on the defendant, took the petrol can and lighter off him and pushed him out of the shop. He restrained him till the police arrived. In interview he said he did not intent to ignite the diesel but wanted to scare them with the fear of being killed. He had four convictions for criminal damage, one for a s 47 assault, one for threatening behaviour and one for possession of explosives. He was 35 and had received no adult custodial sentences. He was sentenced on the basis he had not intended to set the diesel alight. Held. The threat was an ugly and no doubt very frightening episode. In the diesel incident there was great fear but there was importantly no racial or terrorist element. Diesel is not as dangerous as petrol. **3 years** not 6.

42 CRIMINAL DAMAGE – RACIALLY OR RELIGIOUSLY AGGRAVATED

42.1 Crime and Disorder Act 1998 s 30

Triable either way. On indictment maximum sentence 14 years. Summary maximum 6 months and/or £5,000.

The Criminal Justice Act 2003 creates a summary maximum sentence of 51 weeks, a minimum custodial sentence of 28 weeks and Custody plus. The Home Office says they do not expect to introduce these provisions before September 2006.

Anti-Social Behavioural orders Where the defendant has acted in a manner that caused or was likely to cause harassment, alarm or distress to one or more persons not in the same household as the defendant and it is necessary to protect persons from further anti-social acts by him/her the court may make this order.[24]

Sexual Offences Prevention Order There is a discretionary power to make this order when it is necessary to protect the public etc.[25]

Magistrates' Court Sentencing Guidelines January 2004

42.2 For a first time offender pleading not guilty. Entry point. Is it serious enough for a community penalty? Consider the level of racial aggravation and the impact on the victim. Examples of aggravating factors for the offence are deliberate, group action, motivation for the offence was racial or religious, serious damage, setting out to humiliate the victim or vulnerable victim. Examples of mitigating factors for the offence are impulsive action, minor damage, and provocation. Examples of mitigation are age, health (physical or mental), co-operation with the police, genuine remorse and voluntary compensation. Give reasons if not awarding compensation.

For details about the guidelines see **MAGISTRATES' COURT SENTENCING GUIDELINES** at page 483.

General approach See **RACIALLY AGGRAVATED OFFENCES** – *General approach*

Cases

42.3 *R v O'Brien* 2003 2 Cr App R (S) 390. The defendant pleaded to racially aggravated criminal damage. His neighbours were a group of Iraqi asylum seekers. He caused them trouble saying "This is my country. Why have you come to my country?" One evening he threw bricks through their windows and attacked a car he thought belonged to them with an iron bar. While doing this he shouted "Why don't you go back

---

24 Crime and Disorder Act 1998 s 1C
25 Sexual Offences Act 2003 s 104 & Sch. 5

to your country? Come out and fight you son of a bitch. This is my country." The police arrived and he proclaimed "I don't want fucking foreigners in my home. Send them back." He was 35 with previous for damaging property. None had racial overtones. He had a history of depression requiring treatment. He was given 2 months with an uplift of 12 months making a 14 month sentence. The defence said the uplift was too great. Held. We note the Sentencing Advisory Panel recommended the two stage approach and an enhancement within the range of 40–70%, but the sentencer should not be constrained by those figure. There may be cases where the two stage approach is not appropriate. Take the case of a burning book, with slight monetary value but important racial or religious associations. There could be circumstances in which a mechanical or even the flexible application of the 40–70% will not be appropriate. It may fail to regard the overall view. There may be cases where the entire nature of the offence is changed by reason of the racial or religious aggravation. We consider the mere application of a percentage to the 2 month sentence does not fairly reflect the seriousness of this offence. However **6 months** in all not 14.

CRUELTY TO ANIMALS

See **ANIMAL CRUELTY**

43   CRUELTY TO CHILDREN

43.1   This chapter is divided into four sections A Children and Young Persons Act 1933, s 1, B ABH, C Offences against the Person Act 1861, s 18 and D Offences against the Person Act 1861, s 20.

Dividing each section into the different categories etc is somewhat artificial as the important matters for sentence appear to be the defendant's intent, the injuries if any, the length of time over which the offences took place and most crucially of all the trauma of the victim(s). The Courts stress their duty to protect the vulnerable and those who cannot protect themselves.

See also **MANSLAUGHTER** – *Children*

A   Children and Young Persons Act 1933 s 1

43.2   Triable either way. On indictment maximum 10 years. Summary maximum 6 months and/or £5,000.

The Criminal Justice Act 2003 creates a summary maximum sentence of 51 weeks, a minimum custodial sentence of 28 weeks and Custody plus. The Home Office says they do not expect to introduce these provisions before September 2006.

Imprisonment for public protection For offences committed on or after 4/4/05 when there is a significant risk to members of the public of serious harm etc. there is a mandatory duty to pass a sentence of imprisonment for public protection[26]. For offenders under 18 the duty is to pass detention for public protection or an extended sentence.[27]

Licensed premises Where the offence is committed on licensed premises the court may prohibit the defendant from entering those premises or any other specified premises

26 Criminal Justice Act 2003 s 224–226
27 Criminal Justice Act 2003 s 226 and 228

without the express consent of the licensee or his agent.[28] The order shall last from 3 months to 2 years.[29]

Sexual Offences Prevention Order There is a discretionary power to make this order when it is necessary to protect the public etc[30].

Working with children Where the defendant is aged 18 or over and s/he is sentenced to 12 months or more the court must disqualify him/her from working with children unless satisfied s/he is unlikely to commit any further offences against a child when the court must state its reasons for not doing so[31]. For a defendant aged less than 18 at the time of the offence the court must order disqualification if s/he is sentenced to 12 months or more and the court is satisfied that the defendant will commit a further offence against a child[32]. The court must state its reasons for so doing.

Crown Court statistics – England and Wales – Males 21+
43.3

Year	Plea	Total Numbers sentenced	Type of sentence %					Average length of custody (months)
			Discharge	Fine	Community sentence	Suspended sentence	Custody	
2002	Guilty	106	6	1	43	3	47	16.8
	Not guilty	22	5	–	23	–	73	28.7
2003	Guilty	100	5	–	42	5	47	22
	Not guilty	23	–	–	17	13	70	33.8

For details and explanations about the statistics in the book see page vii

Guideline remarks

43.4 *R v Durkin* 1989 11 Cr App R (S) 313. LCJ. The defendant pleaded guilty to a s 20 offence on a boy aged 19¹/₂ months. Held. These cases are among the most difficult a judge has to deal with. First, it is necessary to punish. Secondly, it is necessary to provide some form of expiation[33] of the offence for the defendant. Thirdly, it is necessary to satisfy the public conscience. Fourthly it is necessary to deter others by making it clear this behaviour will result in condign punishment.

R v Ahmed 2003 1 Cr App R (S) 187. The defendant pleaded guilty to ABH. Held. Infants are entitled to care at the hands of those who, despite stresses and strains, nevertheless can contain their temper and control unwelcome impulses. For an attack upon a child, **custody** will almost always be inevitable. But here a community penalty would have been suitable.

Danger, exposing child to

43.5 *R v Laut* 2002 2 Cr App R (S) 21. The defendant pleaded guilty to cruelty. She lived with her husband and her four children, three of whom were from a previous relationship. The husband was violent towards her and several times she made contact with the domestic violence unit. The lock on the washing machine was broken and the defendant asked her son aged 7 to hold it shut. He slipped on some water and his arm went into the exposed drum of the machine while it was on spin. It became entangled in a duvet and he suffered multiple fractures to his arm, which required internal and

28 Licensed Premises (Exclusion of Certain Persons) Act 1980 s 1(1)
29 Licensed Premises (Exclusion of Certain Persons) Act 1980 s 1(3)
30 Sexual Offences Act 2003 s 104 & Sch. 5
31 Criminal Justice and Court Services Act 2000 s 28
32 Criminal Justice and Court Services Act 2000 s 29
33 This means atonement.

external fixation. He made a slow but successful recovery. Both his parents had been in the living room and his father knew what he was doing. About 6 weeks earlier a health visitor had seen the boy holding the door shut and had told the mother it was not appropriate. She said the boy liked doing it. There were insufficient funds to repair the machine. They were both arrested and she admitted the facts and the conversation with the health visitor. She showed remorse. The basis of the plea was it was wilful neglect likely to cause unnecessary suffering or injury to the boy. She was 30 and had no convictions. At the time she was pregnant and since then a baby was born. All her children including the baby were taken into care. She had started divorce proceedings. Her risk of re-offending was assessed as exceptionally low. The parents were treated the same and received 4 months. Held. Without the warning immediate custody would not necessarily be appropriate. The warning made the offence serious wilful neglect requiring imprisonment but because of her character and remorse **12 weeks** instead.

Medical help, delay in seeking

43.6 *R v S* 1999 1 Cr App R (S) 67. The defendant pleaded guilty to cruelty. His girlfriend had his baby and although they were not living together he saw them 2–3 times a week. When his girlfriend returned home he drew her attention to the baby's breathing and telephoned for medical help. He took the baby to hospital and it was found to have bilateral subdural bleeding of two densities and massive retinal bleeding. The defendant confessed to shaking the baby after he was unable to stop him crying. The defence expert said that the injuries were very serious and had the potential to cause permanent blindness. The baby was taken into care and he was denied access. He had expressed shame and guilt. The basis for plea was he had shaken the baby without criminal intent or recklessness. He then realised the baby's health might suffer unless examined by a doctor and fearing what he might have done he delayed for an hour or so seeking medical assistance. He was 24 with no convictions. Held. Because of the basis of the plea, he fell to be sentenced for the delay and not the shaking. **3 months** not 6.

R v Edwards 1999 1 Cr App R (S) 301. The defendant pleaded guilty to cruelty. It was based on a failure to seek medical help. His pleas of not guilty to assault and ill treatment were accepted. An 11-day-old baby suffered cruel injuries, which caused her terrible pain, but the prosecution could not prove which of the two parents had caused them. At 1pm a health visitor called and saw marks and red spots on the baby. The parents were advised to take the baby to a doctor. The doctor saw three marks probably caused by a burning cigarette. Other marks were seen on the soles of her feet, which could have been caused by a pin. The plea was based on a realisation during the evening before the injuries were seen that medical attention should have been sought. The mother had mental problems and was given probation. The defendant was 33 and had one conviction for a wholly dissimilar offence for which he was given a short prison sentence. **12 months** was entirely appropriate.

R v Taggart 1999 2 Cr App R (S) 68. The defendant pleaded guilty to cruelty. It was based on a failure to seek medical help. His pleas of not guilty to assault and ill treatment were accepted. The defendant lived together with his co-defendant, the mother of the victim. He ran the bath taps with the baby in the bath and the plug out. He left the room and heard screams. He returned to find the victim had received severe scalding. Neither defendant sought medical help. The next day the health visitor was refused entry. Not until 5pm that day was a doctor contacted. He arrived and immediately called an ambulance. The bath water was estimated to be approaching 70 C. The hot water system was examined and found to produce hot water far hotter than normal. The baby recovered and was fostered. However, she still experienced flashbacks. The pictures of the baby were horrific. Held. **2¹/₂ years** not 4 ¹/₂

R v Bereton 2002 1 Cr App R (S) 270. The defendant pleaded guilty to cruelty on the first day of his trial. His partner was acquitted of the charge. They lived together and sometime between midnight and 4am their 12-day-old baby received serious injuries. The three were in the same bedroom. There was no call to the emergency services and he and his partner took the baby to the GP's surgery at about 11.15am. The baby was taken to hospital and found to have no external injuries but a drooping eyelid and possibly a bulging eye. A scan found serious injuries to the brain with internal bleeding and swelling. There was an emergency brain operation but the baby died from head injuries. They were caused by impact or shaking. The likelihood was she suffered a severe impact injury to the head, which may have been associated with some shaking. When interviewed he denied causing the injuries and said sometime around 3 or 4am he noticed the baby's eye was swollen. The child was upset, not taking food and vomiting. At 6am his partner had gone to a telephone box to try to obtain advice without success. The prosecution were unable to say which person caused the injuries. An expert said the baby from the moment of injury would not have been remotely normal. She would not have cried and any noises would have been from abnormal breathing. It would have been obvious that she was extremely ill and urgent medical attention was required. He was sentenced on the basis he knew something terrible had happened and he did not obtain medical help, which the baby plainly required. He was 28 and had a conviction for common assault in 1992. There was a delay of 17 months between the incident and the sentence and he showed remorse. Held. We bear in mind the need to protect children from unnecessary suffering and death. **3 years** not 4.

Neglect

43.7   *R v Jackson* 2001 2 Cr App R (S) 259. The defendant on the day his trial was to start, pleaded guilty to three counts of cruelty against his partner's three children. The mother, O pleaded to the same counts and another neglect count to another child. Each count was dated from the victim's birth to when the child was taken into care in 1997. The periods were nearly 4 years, 2 years 8 months and 14 months. In 1991 he invited O to live with his wife and their five children. When he was arrested he and his wife had nine children. These were properly cared for. O gave birth to the three victims. The defendant was domineering and O went to work delivering coal while he stayed at home doing very little. Support from health workers failed. He and O lived at various addresses and in each address the conditions deteriorated. Clothes were unwashed, the children were dirty, nappies were not changed, medical advice not sought, dogs caused unsanitary conditions and there were concerns about the food. There were contrasts between the victims and his children by his wife. The victims aged 4 years, 2 years 8 months and 14 months were not toilet trained, were dressed in urine soaked clothes and the eldest was taking food from the dog's bowl. The house was squalid. The defendant was 50 and had no similar previous convictions. The mother received 1 year in total. Held. **3 years** was not manifestly excessive and the difference in the sentences was understandable.

R v L and L 2004 1 Cr App R (S) 34. The defendants pleaded guilty in the Magistrates' Court to 5 offences of neglecting their son in a manner likely to cause him unnecessary suffering. They were married to each other and the boy was born in December 2000. Between 1 October and 23 September 2001 and between mid March and 8 May 2002 the boy was left at home alone on occasions for between 3 and 6 hours. There was no evidence of physical harm. The judge referred to shocking neglect with the boy without food or water and on at least on occasion heaters positioned close to the boy. He was placed with foster carers. A psychologist said the mother had had harsh childhood experiences. She had a learning disability and considerable deficits in understanding basic parenting issues. The pre-sentence report said "the mother was likely to continue to pose a risk of neglecting a child due to her cognitive functioning.

The risk may be reduced if she recognises her difficulties and engaged professionals. However she is unwilling or unable to do this. She is not suitable for probation as she was likely to become resentful at what she perceives as intrusion". His report said only a custodial sentence would reflect the gravity of the offences. There were 120 contact sessions with the boy. The new guardian said "custody was not in the interest of the boy as it would delay residential assessment. The boy demonstrates a strong attachment to both parents. He, after the parents' imprisonment was distressed on the days he would have had contact". Held. It is quite disgraceful that a child so young should be left alone as often as happened here. We do not say the parents did not deserve prison. This is a case where retribution and deterrence should give way to the interests of the child. Here the criminal process should not place obstacles in the way of a viable family life. **6 months suspended** not 2 years.

R v Bracken 2003 2 Cr App R (S) 324. The defendant pleaded guilty to 2 counts of cruelty to a child. The defendant's partner committed suicide leaving him with their two children, S and C aged less than 2. Thereafter the children's care deteriorated. They appeared generally dirty, under weight and improperly fed. They were exhibiting bruises. The defendant gave lame excuses as to how they were caused. Four months after his partner's death the defendant set up home with a new partner. She contributed very little to the children's upkeep. Upon moving he registered the family with a new medical practice and appeared to have no hesitation in allowing the children to be examined. They were found to have a number of bruises and be underweight. S had multiple bruises of various ages over his face, trunk and groin. There was a recent fracture to his leg that would have required considerable force. He would have been in considerable pain and distress. There were also vertebral fractures likely to have been caused by his being dropped from a height onto the base of his spine or violently shaken. C was found to have significant bruises of various ages over his head and trunk but, unlike S, there was no evidence of rapid weight loss. Both children had been placed into foster care without complication. The PSR said he had problems with anger management and was unable to deal with deep depression. His counsel said after his partner's death the defendant had been inadequate to deal with the situation. Held. Serious though these offences were, and very young though these children were, the total sentence passed was too long. Count 1 (S), **2¹/₂ years** not 4; count 2 (C), **9 months** not 18 months (concurrent). Disqualified from working with children for 7 years remaining

Old case *R v Weaver and Burton* 1998 2 Cr App R (S) 56 (For a summary of this case see the first edition of this book)

Prevent ill treatment, neglect etc. failure to

43.8 *R v Adams and Sherrington* 1999 1 Cr App R (S) 240. The defendants A and S pleaded guilty after their trial had begun to three counts of cruelty to A's baby girl. S was a new partner to A and S admitted squeezing the victim between his legs when she was 15–18 months old (count two). A admitted biting the baby when she was 18 months old (count five). They both admitted failing to prevent her ill-treatment (count six) and failing to seek treatment for her injuries (count seven). A was infatuated with S. The victim was subjected to a course of cruel and violent treatment leading up to her death. The prosecution was unable to say which had caused the particular acts save for the admitted counts. The incident when she was squeezed in a lock was recorded on a Dictaphone. The child screamed in extreme pain. In the 4 weeks before her death bruises were seen by two doctors and a health visitor. Three days before her death S showed the baby to a neighbour, a nurse who saw her limp with bruises all over her face. They were both told to take her straight to hospital. They didn't. In the afternoon of the next day A called an ambulance. The various accounts for the injuries were in conflict. At hospital the baby was found to have several fractures to the skull and irreversible brain damage. There were also bruises of different ages and bite marks. Two days later the ventilator was turned off. A was 32 and treated as of good character and was of limited intelligence. She suffered from post-natal depression. S was 33 and of good character and was the dominant partner. Held. For A 2 years concurrent not 5 for counts six and seven. 2 years not 3 for count five but consecutive rather than concurrent so making **4 years** not 5 in all. S's total sentence of **7 years** was appropriate.

Att-Gen's Ref. No 4 of 2001 2 Cr App R (S) 535. The defendant pleaded guilty to 14 counts of cruelty to children and ABH on the third day of her trial.. Her co-habitee subjected her three children to physical and sexual assaults. Eleven of the counts related to not protecting her children then aged 10, 8 and 6 years old. The children were kicked and punched, their heads were put down the toilet, an attempt to choke one was made, on three occasions paper was put up their anuses and there was digital penetration on another. When seen one was covered in injuries showing the assaults were very persistent and severe. The children gave details of assaults by the defendant and one seemed more afraid of the defendant than her partner. That one's hair was full of lice and she was very badly affected. The partner received 7 years and was described as having a sadistic personality. The defendant had no convictions. She had suffered from violence from her partner who dominated her. She had spent 8 months 1 week in custody before sentence. Held. **2¹/₂ years** would have been appropriate. However, now it would be wrong to interfere with the probation order.

R v Creed 2000 1 Cr App R (S) 304. The defendant pleaded guilty not at the first opportunity to two counts of cruelty to her child (whose age is not in the judgment). Her co-accused and partner was convicted of the murder of the child. The first count was that her partner assaulted the child from time to time between March and October 1997 and the defendant knew this and she had allowed the child to remain at risk. During this time a number of people had noticed bruises, swelling and marks on her. Medical staff also saw a bite mark. At about 8am on 21 October 1997 neighbours of hers heard banging noises. The child had not been to school for 2¹/₂ weeks. Shortly after 9am the defendant received a telephone call at work. She was distraught and was allowed to go home. She arrived no later than 9.30am. After about an hour she made a 999 call saying the baby had fallen down the stairs. The ambulance took the child to hospital and there were no signs of life during the journey. The child was pronounced dead at 12.20pm. 167 bruises were found almost all less than a day old. Some were consistent with her being forcibly poked. Other larger ones were consistent with being hit with a fist or being kicked. She also had a haemorrhage to the intestines and a rib was fractured. Her liver had split which would have caused death within 15 to 20 minutes. The other count was based on causing unnecessary suffering by delaying making the 999 call. She was a senior aircraft woman in the RAF. She was given **3 years** (probably for the first count) and **2 years consecutive** for the other count. Held. The sentences were entirely appropriate.

R v O 2005 1 Cr App R (S) 211. The defendant pleaded guilty at the Magistrates' Court to cruelty to a child. After a tip off police and social services attended her house and they found her six year old daughter and the defendant's boyfriend hiding in a cupboard. The child had extensive bruises over every part of her body. They did not involve broken bones or internal injuries. The child said her mother's boyfriend hit her with a stick which he kept on the top of the cupboard, and that her mother knew what was happening but did nothing effective to stop it. The boyfriend disappeared. The defendant, 26, had had very little support in her life. She tended to drift from one abusive relationship to another. She was of good character. A psychologist said she suffered from dependant personality disorder. She was a victim of violence herself, in particular at the hands of this boyfriend. After the police visit she sought refuge in a hostel from him. She had not seen her daughter for a year. She wrote a letter to the appeal court setting out the extent of suffering the sentence was causing her. Held. A significant feature was the period between her early plea and later sentence, which was seven or eight months, caused by the vain hope that the boyfriend could be brought to trial. She was entitled to a somewhat greater discount and the appropriate sentence was **18 months** not 2 years.

Punishments etc to the children, unlawful

43.9   *R v M* 1998 2 Cr App R (S) 208. The defendant pleaded guilty to three counts of cruelty. The counts were based on bizarre punishments and humiliations. When one girl was about 13 she jokingly told her friend that her father had put her jewellery in the dustbin. The friend asked the father if it was true and his girl was hit in the face and stomach. She was then made to throw the jewellery in the bin and to hit her friend. He sent someone to check that it had been done. Once he required the girls to go to school in their oldest clothes and made the boys lead them with ropes shouting, 'dogs for sale.' His children were made to cut the lawn with nail scissors and to go to bed without food at 4pm. There were other bizarre punishments. The punishments on two children lasted from when they were 5 to 16, and on another between 5 and 14. The defendant aged 41 was of good character. He was frank with the police and he said he was exercising control and sometimes overreacted. He had a personality disorder. The risk of re-offending was minimal. **3 years** in total not 4.

R v P 2004 2 Cr App R (S) 177. The defendant pleaded guilty to cruelty to a child at the Magistrate's Court. She was from the Czech Republic and had been living in this country for three years. She had four children aged two, three, four and six. A social worker visiting her noticed that her four year old son had a blistered injury 8 cm by 6 cm on the outside of his shin showing the imprint of an iron. It was a serious and significant injury. The defendant admitted to the social worker she had caused the injury to teach her son a lesson because he had been naughty. Two days she admitted to a police officer, interpreter and social worker that she had caused the injury because she was cross that her son had tried to burn the carpet with the iron and had also caused cigarette burns to the carpet. She burnt his leg to teach him a lesson. When further interviewed she said she was generally unable to cope with the children. She said she had tested the iron to see how hot it was before she put it against his leg. She expressed sorrow and said she had a great deal of difficulty looking after her children. The defendant, aged 24, had no previous convictions although she had once been cautioned for shoplifting. The pre-sentence report said that she was a lonely, isolated and immature young woman. She did not appreciate the seriousness of the offence and she had had little adult role modelling and minimal support. It assessed the risk of re-offending as low. A report from the Child and Family social worker referred to a number of other injuries suffered by the children, at best caused by neglect and a worst caused deliberately. A psychiatric report said the defendant suffered from an adjustment disorder caused by emigrating to the UK and a further adjustment disorder and bereavement when her children were taken into care. The offence had taken place in an outburst of violence contributed to by the adjustment disorder. She was not a danger to herself, her children or the community at large. Held. The defendant is a very inadequate young woman who has suffered a great deal of stress as a result of her isolation in this country and the demands placed on her by bringing up four small children in such isolated and deprived circumstances. The case involved the deliberate infliction of a very significant and serious injury on a small child. The only sentence that could properly be passed was one of immediate imprisonment. Had the Judge passed a longer sentence we doubt if it would have been susceptible to challenge. **8 months** was entirely right.

Unsupervised, leaving a child or children

43.10 *R v Cameron and Senior* 2000 2 Cr App R (S) 329. The defendants C and S pleaded guilty to three counts of cruelty and no evidence was offered on a count of manslaughter. S the mother of three children also pleaded to ABH. The children were 7, 9 and 13 years old and were left unsupervised while S and her partner C went to a couple of public houses. They were out from a little before 3.30pm and to 9.30pm. Witnesses saw the 13 year old behaving strangely as if drunk. He had tablets with him. The defendants returned home and at 5am an ambulance was called as the boy was having breathing difficulties. He died soon afterwards of methadone poisoning. Other drugs were also detected in his blood. C a drug addict had been prescribed methadone and hid it in the house. S had discovered it and it was kept in their wardrobe where the children were not allowed access. S's ABH was on a social worker, who arrived with police unexpectedly to take two of the children into police protection. She was struck in the face causing a bloody nose. C was 30 and had convictions for dishonesty, criminal damage and possession of cannabis. S was 32 and had one spent conviction. The judge referred to S's history of fecklessness in relation to the care of the children. Held. That remark was in error as she was to be sentenced for leaving the children unsupervised. **12 months** for that was not manifestly excessive nor was the 3 months consecutive for the ABH.

Violence to babies and toddlers (up to 2 years old)

43.11 *R v Isaac* 1998 1 Cr App R (S) 266. The defendant pleaded guilty when first arraigned to cruelty to a child. The defendant had a difficult and unplanned pregnancy. The birth was extremely difficult and prolonged. A forceps delivery failed, as did a Ventouse extraction and she suffered a traumatic birth. An emergency Caesarean section had eventually to be performed. Her son was large, restless, hungry and colicky. He had to be treated for a urinary infection in hospital. When he was discharged the defendant found it very difficult to cope. Her family were supportive but were unable to help her to any great extent. The defendant's mother noticed that the baby had a swollen thigh and was bruised from the groin to the knee. The baby was taken to hospital and was found to have a displaced spiral fracture of the femur probably less than 10 days old and two fractures on both tibias and a fracture on the other femur 2–3 weeks old. The defendant who had learning difficulties denied causing any injury to the baby but could offer no explanation. Later she admitted to a probation officer that she had twisted the baby's legs on 2 occasions. She said he was crying continually and she felt isolated and physically exhausted. Later she was found to be suffering from depression with feelings of helplessness and an inability to cope. A Professor said her post-natal depression predated the injuries. The child was first fostered and then taken into care. Support from the Social Services was now available. Held. 3 years was quite inappropriate. It was totally different from the situation where a baby is injured by a father or other relative. Where injuries are inflicted by a mother suffering from post-natal depression with a difficult pregnancy and an even more difficult birth more than a short custodial is wholly inappropriate. A short custodial was appropriate but as she needs help and encouragement and she has served the equivalent of $8\frac{1}{2}$ months **12 months' probation** instead.

R v Scammell and Mills 1998 1 Cr App R (S) 321. LCJ The defendant M pleaded guilty to unlawful wounding (s 20) and two counts of cruelty to a child. S was convicted of two counts of cruelty to a child. S was the father of the victim and he had lived with M. They parted and S paid M to look after the child while he was at work. The child aged 21 months died of natural causes. However, the post-mortem revealed a skull fracture of 'some little age'; fractures to the fibulae consistent with twisting and pulling of the legs; skin loss to the back of the head underneath of which there was deep bruising; a burn on the back of the hand which extended to the lateral aspect of the elbow; and multiple abrasions and bruises to the head, neck, penis, buttocks and other parts of the body. At the flat the baby's blood was splattered against a wall. M admitted causing the burn. It was not suggested that S was responsible for the blood on the wall and M could not explain it. M gave evidence against S. S was of good character and had a record as a caring mother to her own children. Held. The burn was perhaps the most disturbing injury. The starting point for M was 9 years. The reduction to **6 years** was proper. As S had not committed the most serious assaults the starting point for him was **7 years** and not the 10 year maximum. There was nothing to mitigate that sentence.

R v Kelly 1998 2 Cr App R (S) 368. The defendant pleaded guilty to ill-treating a 5-month-old child of his girlfriend. He and the mother abused drugs. Residents heard the baby screaming and several slaps. A doctor found severe facial bruising which was not part of the basis of his plea. His plea was based on him being responsible for bruising on the head and legs caused by slapping. The doctor concluded considerable force must have been used for those slaps. The defendant was now 23 and had extensive convictions for motor vehicles and one for ABH. The risk of re-offending was said to be high. The mother was given probation. Held. Because it was a plea **2 years** not 3.

R v Adams and Sherrington 1999 1 Cr App R (S) 240. The defendants A and S pleaded guilty after their trial had begun to three counts of cruelty to A's baby girl. The defendant S who was a new partner to A and admitted squeezing the girl between his legs when she was 15–18 months old, (count two). A admitted biting the baby when she was 18 months old, (count five). They both admitted failing to prevent her ill-treatment, (count six) and failing to seek treatment for her injuries, (count seven). A was infatuated with S. The girl was subjected to a course of cruel and violent treatment leading up to her death. The prosecution was unable to say which had caused the particular acts save for the admitted counts. The incident when she was squeezed in a lock was recorded on a Dictaphone. The child screamed in extreme pain. In the 4 weeks before her death bruises were seen by two doctors and a health visitor. Three days before her death S showed the baby to a neighbour, a nurse who saw her limp with bruises all over her face. They were both told to take her straight to hospital. They didn't. In the afternoon of the next day A called an ambulance. The various accounts for the injuries were in conflict. At hospital the baby was found to have several fractures to the skull and irreversible brain damage. There were also bruises of different ages and bite marks. Two days later the ventilator was turned off. A was 32 and was treated as of good character and was of limited intelligence. She suffered from post-natal depression. S was 33 and of good character and was the dominant partner. Held. For A 2 years concurrent not 5 for counts six and seven. 2 years not 3 for count five but consecutive rather than concurrent so making **4 years** not 5 in all. S's total sentence of **7 years** was appropriate.

Violence to children aged 2–4 years

43.12 *R v McWilliam and McWilliam* 2003 2 Cr App R (S) 1. The defendants were convicted of cruelty to a child. In June 1999, they fostered a boy aged 4 and his sister aged 2. Between then and December a number of witnesses such as social workers and staff at his school noticed bruises, cuts and abrasions to the boy's face and body. The defendants told those concerned that the injuries were caused accidentally or by deliberate self-harm. During the last 10 days of his life the number and seriousness of the injuries he received increased significantly. On 20th December two social workers visited and noted that there was massive bruising on the boy's face. The boy gave different explanations to each social worker. On 23rd December between 7 and 8 a.m., neighbours heard a rhythmic banging for half-an hour from the area of the defendants' bedroom. At 08:48 one defendant phoned the emergency services. An ambulance arrived and the boy was unconscious. His body was found to have 55 separate injuries including bruises of various ages and not less than three bite marks and a split cranium. A CT scan revealed a subdural haemorrhage. He never recovered consciousness and died two days later. The pathologist was of the view that there had been several impacts to the head; there were also signs of bleeding in the retina of each eye, indicative of an impact or shaking. After arrest the defendants maintained that the boy had inflicted the injuries himself, or alternatively they were accidental. The defendants were both treated as having good character. Held. This case had distinct aggravating features: that this little boy had been coached by these defendants to maintain to social workers and others that he had injured himself; and, that both of the defendants had lied and lied consistently to members of the public and to two social workers and to others to explain away the injuries to which this boy was subjected. **8 years** upheld.

Violence to children aged 5–10

43.13   *R v O'Gorman* 1999 2 Cr App R (S) 280. The defendant pleaded guilty to cruelty and ABH at the Magistrates" Court. The victim on each count was the same. He was also sentenced for common assault on his co-habitee. The defendant returned home in a foul mood and drank a substantial amount of alcohol. He found his co-habitee's 8-year-old child's room untidy and on and off for 2 hours assaulted the two and broke furniture. The child was grabbed by the neck, thrown around the room, punched on the chin, struck on the eye, and had his head put down the lavatory and the chain pulled. The doctor found multiple areas of bruising and swelling on the boy. His lips were very swollen and there were multiple black bruises indicating where his teeth had knocked the lips. He said the injuries were consistent with repeated forceful blows. The defendant admitted the offences and he had one previous conviction for ABH on a woman in 1987 for which he was fined. He had been a postman for 14 years. Held. Anyone who inflicts violence on a child like this will lose their liberty. Where it was prolonged like here substantial imprisonment will follow. Insufficient credit was given for the early plea so **21 months** concurrent for the attack on the boy not $2\frac{1}{2}$ years with 6 months for the common assault concurrent.

B   Cruelty to children – ABH

43.14   Triable either way. On indictment maximum sentence 5 years. Summary maximum 6 months or £5,000

For ancillary powers see **ABH**.

R v Smith 1999 2 Cr App R (S) 126. The defendant who had two children pleaded guilty to ABH on a 4-year-old child of his partner with whom he lived. He and his partner went out leaving the children, three of her sister's children and another child with a babysitter. The children were staying the night. After arriving home from a party and talking to her sister, the babysitter, they decided to wake up the boy who was asleep to tell him he had been naughty while they were out. He started crying. The other children woke up and the partner and the babysitter left leaving him to look after a 'crisis'. The victim was told by the defendant who was intoxicated to come downstairs and he struck him in the face more than once causing extensive bruising and a cut lip. The defendant was of good character. **4 months** not 6.

R v Rayson 2000 2 Cr App R (S) 317. The defendant made a late guilty plea to ABH. He lived with his girlfriend and her 18-month-old son. She went to visit a friend leaving the son in his care. He rang her to say he had accidentally dropped the son. She came home and saw the son's eye was swollen and bruised. The son was taken to hospital and the defendant repeatedly apologised for dropping him. The hospital found extensive bruising to the left side of the face from the ear to below the jawbone. On the right side there was bruising to the cheek and jawbone. On his forearm there were a collection of tiny petechial (red spots) on the forearm. The injuries to the left side indicated the son had been struck at least twice with considerable force by an adult with an open hand. A similar blow was struck to the right side. The forearm bruising could have arisen from handling or gripping during the assault. The defendant was 34 and of good character and said it was a single loss of temper. Held. Because of the authorities **6 months** not 18.

R v O'Gorman 1999 2 Cr App R (S) 280. The defendant pleaded guilty at the Magistrates' Court to ABH and cruelty to a child. After drinking, the defendant committed a prolonged and fierce attack on his co-habitee's 8-year-old son lasting on and off for about 2 hours only stopping when his co-habitee returned home. He punched him, threw him across the room and put his head inside the toilet basin and flushed the toilet. The doctor found multiple areas of swelling, recent bruises on the head, face, jaw, lips, chin, and upper limbs. They were consistent with repeated forceful blows. The defendant admitted the offences in interview and expressed regret. He had one conviction in 1987 for ABH on a woman for which he was fined. Held. Anyone who uses violence of this nature over a prolonged period must expect a substantial period of imprisonment. Because of the very early pleas **21 months** not $2^{1}/_{2}$ years concurrent on each, concurrent to 6 months for common assault on his co-habitee.

R v Dodgson 2001 1 Cr App R (S) 291. The defendant pleaded guilty to ABH on the son of his co-habitee. When the mother returned she found extensive bruising to the boy's face measuring 10 cms by 7 cms and bruising to an ear. A doctor said the bruising was caused by several blows using a considerable degree of force. The defendant pleaded guilty on the basis of striking the boy twice. He said he was angry the boy had wet himself. Earlier he had said the injuries were an accident. He had been drinking and was remorseful. He was of good character with an employer's reference. The boy recovered quite quickly. The judge said there was substantial force used and it was an extremely dangerous thing to do. Held. It was an isolated incident. **3 months** not 6.

R v Ali 2002 2 Cr App R (S) 542. The defendant pleaded guilty at the Magistrates' Court to ABH and failing to surrender, for which he received a concurrent sentence. He went to the home of his partner to carry out some DIY. He was left in charge of his two children aged 3 years and 9 months. While feeling frustrated about the DIY he prepared some food, which the 3 year old would not eat. He lost his temper, picked up a cane which supported a houseplant and repeatedly hit her with it. When the mother returned she found the victim naked in a shaken and distressed case. The defendant did not try to hide the fact he had hit her. The victim was taken to hospital. There was bruising and linear marks on both cheeks. Three 5 cm. thin red marks with swelling and bruising were found on the left arm. Three 2 cm. red marks and two other marks were found on her right arm. There was bruising between the knuckles and on her stomach there were two 9 cm. red lines. There were further 7 cm. lines on her back. There was redness on her shoulder blade and red lines across her thigh. The injuries were superficial and she was not detained in hospital. He was 22 and treated as of good character. The pre-sentence report said he believed he continued to hit her because she was trying to hide under the sheets and his impression she was not listening to him. The Judge accepted his remorse and found the attack was out of character. His partner and the two children had visited him in prison. Held. It was not possible to establish how many blows were inflicted but in clearly repeated blows in a sustained attack. **12 months** not 18.

R v Ahmed 2003 1 Cr App R (S) 187. The defendant pleaded guilty to ABH at the earliest opportunity. In 1999 he fell in love with K, the mother of the victim, who was from a different ethnic background from him. In March 2000 she was pregnant and his father died and he was sent to Bangladesh to attend to family matters. Whilst there against his wishes he was forced into an arranged marriage. In September the victim was born. By summer 2001 he was living with the victim and K despite the disapproval of his family. He found being estranged difficult and became depressed. He suffered anxiety and panic attacks. While K was at work and the victim was 11 months he took the victim to K's mother saying she kept crying. The mother saw a mark on her cheek and saw the victim was moaning. The defendant said he had no idea how it happened. A paediatrician found an extensive area of bruising on her cheek, compatible with a slap. The defendant was arrested and denied having slapped her. However when interviewed by the writer of the pre-sentence report he said he had tried to put the child to bed and she had cried despite everything he did. He lost his temper and slapped her. He was 21 and when sentenced he was of good character. Since then he had been conditionally discharged for attempted deception. He had a full time job. He was said to be under enormous emotional pressure and his loss of self control was momentary. He was deeply remorseful and K and her family had rejected him. He had no contact with the victim. The pre-sentence report advocated a community penalty. Held. Infants are entitled to care at the hands of those who, despite stresses and strains, nevertheless can contain their temper and control unwelcome impulses. For an attack upon a child, custody will almost always be inevitable. We have paid careful attention to the pre-sentence report. A moment's inability to withstand the erosion of the defendant's general good nature resulted in a transient, albeit visible lesion. When sentenced we would have considered the **community penalty** advocated so strongly in the report. That would be unjust, as he has served 7 weeks in custody so a **conditional discharge** instead.

Old Cases *R v Burrows* 1998 2 Cr App R (S) 407 (For a summary of this case see the first edition of this book.)

See also **ABH**

C Cruelty to children – Offences Against the Person Act 1861 s 18

43.15   Indictable only. Maximum sentence life imprisonment.

For ancillary powers see **OFFENCES AGAINST THE PERSON ACT 1861 s 18**

Att-Gen's Ref. No 34 of 2000 2001 1 Cr App R (S) 359. The defendant was convicted of GBH with intent. He pleaded guilty to s 20 GBH which was not accepted. The defendant was left in charge of his 5-month-old child while the mother went to do evening work. She returned home about $1\frac{1}{2}$ hours later and noticed the baby's condition was not normal. A doctor was called and the baby was taken to hospital. She was found to have bruising to the head with subdural haemorrhage, extensive retinal haemorrhages to both eyes, cerebral contusion and soft tissue injury of the cervical spine. There was also severe brain injury (which was irreparable) and whiplash injury to the neck. The defendant had no convictions. He was not frank about how the injuries were caused. However, it was said to be an isolated incident by a decent and hard working man. Held. The sentencing bracket for an isolated incident by a man of good character following a trial was **4 to 5 years**. Taking it was a reference **$3\frac{1}{2}$ years** not $2\frac{1}{2}$.

R v Murray 2002 1 Cr App R (S) 168. The defendant was convicted of GBH with intent. He had lived with the victim aged 2 years and 3 months and her mother for about $3\frac{1}{2}$ months. One evening the mother went to buy a takeaway meal leaving the child asleep in her bedroom. Neighbours heard cries from the child for much if not most of the 15 to 20 minutes the mother was away suggesting the attack was sustained over most of the period. When the mother returned he put on a convincing performance that he had heard a scream and found the baby had fallen out of her cot. She had several discrete bruises to her face indicating a number of blows. The inside of her mouth and her frenulum was cut. Two different objects had also struck her. One might have been a belt and the other a shoe. When the mother returned the defendant was wearing only one shoe. There were injuries to her head, which indicated she had been struck by a hard surface, which was textured like the wallpaper in the bedroom. There was a long fracture to her occipital bone at the back of the head. For that an extremely severe blow would be required. There was retinal haemorrhage in one eye. The injuries could have led to the most serious consequences but she made a complete recovery although she remained withdrawn and timid which she wasn't before. He and the mother were arrested and he maintained his story. He was 25 and had been discharged from the army for a number of disciplinary incidents. There was a conviction for ABH and the psychiatrist said he was egocentric. Held. He had trouble controlling his temper. **8 years** not 10.

See also OFFENCES AGAINST THE PERSON ACT 1861 s 18

D Cruelty to children – Offences Against the Person Act 1861 s 20

43.16   Triable either way. On indictment maximum sentence 5 years. Summary maximum 6 months or £5,000

For ancillary powers see OFFENCES AGAINST THE PERSON ACT 1861 s 20

Guideline remarks

43.17   *R v Durkin* 1989 11 Cr App R (S) 313. LCJ. The defendant pleaded guilty to a s 20 offence on a boy aged $19^1/_2$ months. Held. These cases are among the most difficult a judge has to deal with. First, it is necessary to punish. Secondly, it is necessary to provide some form of expiation[34] of the offence for the defendant. Thirdly, it is necessary to satisfy the public conscience. Fourthly it is necessary to deter others by making it clear this behaviour will result in condign punishment.

Cases

43.18   *R v H* 2000 1 Cr App R (S) 551. The defendant pleaded guilty at the Magistrates' Court to s 20. The defendant and his wife took their nearly 3-month-old baby to hospital because he was vomiting. The defendant said he had tripped and knocked the baby's head against a door frame and that had occurred before some weeks earlier. Two days later the baby was re-admitted with an unusually large head. A 1 cm bruise was found above the eyebrow with a 5 mms bruise nearby. There was a fracture of the crown bones of the skull resulting in a subdural bleed. A brain scan showed a degree of brain atrophy (wasting of part of it). This might result in learning difficulties in the long term. The mother asked the police and social services to be informed as the defendant had admitted to her he had shaken the baby. When arrested he said he was sorry for what he had done and said his wife had no part in it. In interview he said the baby cried for prolonged periods and he was in pain after an in-growing toenail had been removed. He was agitated and distressed and had shaken the baby and lost his grip. The child had fallen and hit his head on the floor. The child screamed and vomited. His earlier account was false because he was scared. He was 24. His pre-sentence report noted remorse but poor co-operation with the professionals. Another report said he needed therapeutic intervention to address his depressive tendencies. The psychiatric report said he was of low intellectual ability with poor anger control. All the factors and poor verbal skills compromised his parenting ability. He was a risk to his son unless supervised. Treatment and probation was suggested. **2 years** not 4.

R v Busby 2001 1 Cr App R (S) 454. The defendant pleaded guilty to s 20. A s 18 charge was left on the file. In November, his wife had his very premature triplets. They remained in hospital for some time. In February he was in charge of one of them while his wife was asleep. She rang the emergency services to say the child had stopped

34 This means atonement.

breathing. When asked he said he had fallen asleep and she was not breathing. The child was taken to hospital and found to have a large skull fracture and shearing to the brain at the site of the fracture and deep in the brain. The child suffered severe and irreversible brain damage. When interviewed the defendant said the child had lurched backwards and fell hitting her head on the coffee table. He then settled her and he fell asleep. The plea was on the basis of reckless or grossly negligent conduct. He had one previous conviction for assaulting a child which involved hitting the son of a former partner with a slipper. He had separated from his wife and expressed extreme remorse. **2¹/₂ years** not 4 because of the plea and the basis of plea.

R v Brown 2001 2 Cr App R (S) 83. The defendant was convicted of s 20 GBH and cruelty to a child and acquitted of s 18. The defendant and his wife had two children. One was then aged 16 months and the other, the victim was 6 weeks old. The defendant was left alone with them and when the wife called him at about 1pm he said the baby was unwell and he was about to call an ambulance. It was agreed he would take the baby to her and then they both took the baby to hospital. The hospital discovered subdural blood over both cerebral hemispheres and a fracture of the femur. The fracture was the result of tractional forces such as pulling or twisting when the torso was violently shaken. The brain injury was consistent with this. The prosecution case for the cruelty count was that the baby was distressed and he did not assist him. When sentence was passed there was still general retardation of development of the baby. The defendant was 28 and of good character with letters in support. Held. **3 years** was at the upper end of the bracket for se 20 and reflected the mitigation. (The cruelty count was 1 year concurrent.)

See also OFFENCES AGAINST THE PERSON ACT 1861, s 20

CULTIVATION OF CANNABIS

See CANNABIS – **Cannabis, cultivation of/production of/management of premises etc.**

CURFEW SCHEME

See HOME DETENTION CURFEW SCHEME

CURRENCY

See COUNTERFEITING CURRENCY

44   CUSTODY, DISCOUNT FOR TIME SPENT IN

44.1   Criminal Justice Act 2003 s 240, (in force 4/4/05), previously Criminal Justice Act 1967 s 67.

General Principles

44.2   *R v Armstrong* 2002 2 Cr App R (S) 396. The defendant was sentenced for burglaries to a probation order and a DTTO. He breached it and committed another burglary. He was re-sentenced to a probation order and a DTTO with a condition of residence at a treatment centre. He failed to comply with the rules at the treatment centre. He was then dealt with for that breach. The sentencing Judge considered that a four-year sentence was appropriate but reduced it because of the plea and the other mitigation to two and a half years. A little later the Court reconvened and was told that the defendant had spent two periods in custody before each of the probation orders was made. The period was four and a half months the equivalent of a nine-month sentence. The periods would not be automatically deducted from the sentence. The Judge reduced the sentence by 5 months saying the defendant had been treated as favourably as the history of the case merited. Held. The extent to which a period spent in custody should be credited was a matter for the Judge's discretion, *R v McKenzie* 1988 10 Cr App R (S) 299, *R v Wiltshire* 1995 13 Cr App R (S) 642 and *R v Henderson* 1997 2 Cr App R (S) 266. In the ordinary way, if there are not features like the ones in this case, the Judge ought to take into account periods in custody which do not count. Here the defendant had received more than a third discount, the Judge was entitled to take the view he had and sentence imposed could not possibly be described as manifestly excessive. Therefore the appeal is dismissed.

Bail hostels

44.3   *R v Watson* 2000 2 Cr App R (S) 301. The defendant was released on bail with a condition he reside at a bail hostel. He was not permitted to go into the garden or leave except when supervised. He only left to collect his benefit. He was there 11 months before sentence. For 5 months he had been tagged. Held. A Bail Hostel was not to be equated with imprisonment. However, the loss of liberty should be taken into account. More credit for that should have been given.

Community rehabilitation order/Community punishment order etc.

44.4   *R v Broomfield* 2004 2 Cr App R (S) 381.The clear effect of the Criminal Justice Act 1967 s 67(1) is that where a community rehabilitation order is made and a defendant is in breach no period served on remand counts, if the defendant is sentenced to custody. The same approach applies to a community punishment order and a combined community punishment and rehabilitation order.

See also *R v Dale* 2004 2 Cr App R (S) 308.

Defendant earlier in custody for charge not proceeded with/charge defendant acquitted of etc.

44.5   *R v Jarvis* 2002 2 Cr App R (S) 558. The defendant pleaded guilty to escaping. The defendant was charged with aggravated burglary and remanded in custody. The defendant appeared in the Crown Court and he leapt over the dock and was caught. Later the prosecution dropped the burglary charge because a witness had died. The Judge refused to give him credit for the time he was in custody for the other matter. Held. The Judge was right not to give him credit. (For further details see ESCAPE FROM CUSTODY – *Opportunist.*)

Defendant earlier in custody for a conviction which was later quashed

44.6   *R v Roberts* 2000 1 Cr App R (S) 569. The defendant was remanded in custody for drugs offences. Eighteen days later he was sentenced at the Magistrates' Court to 5 months' imprisonment. After he had served his sentence the Crown Court sentenced him to 42 months for the drugs offences. Later a different Crown Court quashed the sentence of 5 months and substituted a conditional discharge. Held. The **42 months** was a perfectly proper sentence. Considering *R v Governor of Wandsworth Prison, ex p Sorhaindo 1999 96(4) LSG 38* it would be appropriate to reduce the sentence by 5 months.

Detention and Training orders

44.7   Powers of Criminal Courts (Sentencing) Act 2000 s 101(8). In determining the term of a detention order for an offence, the court shall take into account any period for which the offender has been remanded in custody in connection with the offence, or any other offence the charge for which was founded on the same facts or evidence.

R v Ganley 2000 Unreported 19/4/00. Time spent in custody on remand will not be deducted from a period to be served under a detention and training order. It has to be taken into account.

R v Inner London Crown Court, ex p I 2000 The Times 12/5/00. The defendant had spent less than 24 hours in custody. Held. The duty under [what is now s 101(8)] is to take account of the time spent. It is not to reflect inevitable time spent in some specific way in the sentence passed.

R v B 2001 1 Cr App R (S) 303. The defendant had spent $3^1/_2$ months in custody. The defence asked for twice the time spent in custody to be deducted from the sentence. The judge refused to do so. He passed a sentence which took into account of all the factors. Held. Taking into account the period in custody or secure accommodation for the purposes of [what is now s 101(8)] does not involve a 1 to 1, day for day or month for month, reduction in sentence let alone a 2 to 1 reduction. The reason for that is that the periods to which the court is entitled to sentence a young defendant to detention and training orders are specified in blocks and deducting precise amounts of time is inconsistent with that provision. Doubling up is not available.

R v Inner London Crown Court, ex p P, N and S 2001 1 Cr App R (S) 343. The defendants had spent 3 days in custody. Held. I would not regard it as appropriate or desirable that any precise reflection should be sought to be given, in making a detention and training order, of a day or two. It is impossible to fine tune by reference to a day or two the sentence which is appropriate.

R v Fieldhouse and Watts 2001 1 Cr App R (S) 361. No rule of general application can be devised to cover the infinitely various situations which may arise. However, the proper approach can perhaps best be illustrated by taking by way of example, a defendant who has spent 4 weeks on remand, which is the equivalent of a 2 month term. The court is likely to take such a period into account in different ways according to the length of the detention and training order which initially seems appropriate. If that period is 4 months, the court may conclude a non-custodial sentence is appropriate. If that period is 6, 8, 10 or 12 months, the court is likely to impose 4, 6, 8 or 10 months respectively. If that period is 18 or 24 months, the court may well conclude that no reduction can properly be made, although the court will of course bear in mind for juveniles the continuing importance of limiting the period in custody to the minimum necessary. The observations to this effect in *R v Mills* 1998 2 Cr App R (S) 128 at 131 still hold good. For those offenders for whom long-term detention under [what is now the Powers of Criminal Courts (Sentencing) Act 2000 s 91] might otherwise be appropriate, a detention and training order of 24 months may be a proper sentence even on a plea of guilty and even when a significant period has been spent in custody. The weekend spent in custody in this case could not sensibly be reflected in the sentence.

R v Elsmore 2001 2 Cr App R (S) 461. The sentence further reduced. (Little or no new matters of principle stated.)

R v Pitt 2002 1 Cr App R (S) 195. The defendant then aged 17 pleaded guilty to unlawful wounding and received 18 months. He had spent 4 months awaiting trial. The maximum was 24 months. Held. Taking the plea and the 4 months into account 15 months was appropriate. That wasn't available, as it was either 18 or 12 months. This Act puts the courts in a straitjacket. Therefore **12 months** substituted.

See also *R v March* 2002 2 Cr App R (S) 448

Article about see Archbold News 17 March 2000.

Drug treatment centre

44.7a   See *R v Armstrong* 2002 2 Cr App (S) 396.

Extradition, time in custody awaiting

44.8   Criminal Justice Act 1991 s 47(2). If, in the case of an extradited prisoner, the court by which he was sentenced so ordered, s 67 of the 1967 Act (computations of sentences of imprisonment) shall have effect in relation to him as if a period specified in the order were a relevant period for the purposes of that section. (Repealed and awaiting commencement order.)

R v Simone 2000 2 Cr App R (S) 332. The defendant absconded during his trial. He was convicted and sentenced in his absence to 6 years. He was arrested in Switzerland and spent 10 months in custody awaiting extradition. Held. The Act presupposes the extradition took place before sentence. Here it did not. Sentence reduced accordingly.

Criminal Justice Act 1991 s 47(2). New sub-section inserted by the Crime and Disorder Act 1998, s119 and Sch 8, para 90 itself amended by the Powers of Criminal Courts (Sentencing) Act 2000 s 165(1) and Sch 9, para 202(3) to make all days served automatically count. (Awaiting commencement order.)

R v Andre and Burton 2002 1 Cr App R (S) 98. The defendants were extradited from New Zealand. The judge did not order all days to be deducted. Held. (Old law) He was entitled to do that on the facts of the case.

Local authority accommodation, remand to

44.9   Criminal Justice Act 1967 s 67(1A)(c). The relevant period means any period…he was remanded or committed to local authority accommodation … under section 23 of the Children and Young Persons Act 1969 or section 37 of the Magistrates' Court Act 1980 and in accommodation provided for the purposes of restricting liberty.

R v Secretary of State for the Home Office, ex p A 2000 2 Cr App R (S) 263. House of Lords. Held. *R v Collins* 1995 16 Cr App R (S) 157 was wrongly decided. The time is not deducted automatically. A's position was closer to a person on bail than in custody. If an allowance was to be made it should be made by the sentencing court and not by an administrative officer of an institution.

Powers of Criminal Courts (Sentencing) Act 2000 s 88(1)(c) Remanded in custody means, remanded or committed to local authority accommodation under section 23 of the Children and Young Persons Act 1969 and placed in secure accommodation [or detained in a secure training centre pursuant to arrangements under subsection (7A) of that section]. The words in brackets are added by the Criminal Justice and Police Act 2001 s 88 adds 'kept in secure accommodation' so affirming the decision in *ex parte A* in the House of Lords. (in force 1/4/02)

See also **Guilty Plea, Discount for**

Custody

For the need to consider prison overcrowding see **Basic Principles** – *Prison overcrowding*

See also **Escape From Custody** and **Prisoners**

45 DANGEROUS OFFENDERS

45.1 The Criminal Justice Act 2003 s 234–236 replace LONGER THAN COMMENSURATE OFFENCES [Powers of Criminal Courts (Sentencing) Act 2000 s 80(2)(b)] and EXTENDED SENTENCES [Powers of Criminal Courts (Sentencing) Act 2000 s 85(2)(b)]. The new provisions apply to offences committed on or after 4/4/05[1]. The new provisions are entitled, "Dangerous offenders".

Offences with a maximum of life

45.2 Dangerous Offender provisions For offences committed on or after 4/4/05 where there is a significant risk to members of the public of serious harm etc. there is a mandatory duty to pass a life sentence when it is justified and otherwise a sentence of imprisonment for public protection[2]. For offenders under 18 the duty is to pass detention for life, detention for public protection or an extended sentence[3].

Offences with a maximum of 10 years up to life

45.3 Imprisonment for public protection For offences committed on or after 4/4/05 when there is a significant risk to members of the public of serious harm etc. there is a mandatory duty to pass a sentence of imprisonment for public protection[4]. For offenders under 18 the duty is to pass detention for public protection or an extended sentence[5].

Offences with a maximum of less than 10 years

45.4 Extended sentences under CJA 2003 For offences committed on or after 4/4/05 there is a mandatory duty to pass an extended sentence when there is a significant risk to members of the public of serious harm etc.[6].

See EXTENDED SENTENCES

DANGEROUS DOGS

See DOGS, DANGEROUS

46 DANGEROUS DRIVING

46.1 Road Traffic Act 1988 s 2

Triable either way. On indictment maximum sentence 2 years. Summary maximum 6 months or £5,000.

The Criminal Justice Act 2003 creates a summary maximum sentence of 51 weeks, a minimum sentence of 28 weeks and Custody plus. The Home Office says they do not expect to introduce these provisions before September 2006.

Depriving defendant of vehicle used There is power to deprive the defendant of the vehicle used[7] for the purposes of committing the offence.

1   Criminal Justice Act 2003 Sections 225(1)(a), 226(1)(a), 227(1)(a) and Criminal Justice Act 2003 (Commencement No 8) Order 2004
2   Criminal Justice Act 2003 s 225
3   Criminal Justice Act 2003 s 226 and 228
4   Criminal Justice Act 2003 s 224–226
5   Criminal Justice Act 2003 s 226 and 228
6   Criminal Justice Act 2003 s 227–228
7   Powers of Criminal Courts (Sentencing) Act 2000 s 143(6) & (7)

Disqualification Minimum disqualification 1 year. The defendant must be disqualified until he/she passes an extended driving test.

Points 3–11 penalty points.

Sentencing notes. Parliament has ignored the problem of the too short maximum sentence. Judges will continue to have to deal with cases of very bad driving which cause very serious injuries by people with bad similar previous convictions. They either have to pass low sentences or water down the principle of a discount for a plea of guilty or both. Eventually Parliament will increase the maximum to 5 or better still 10 years. The defendant's criminality should be the issue and whether the defendant causes death (a Road Traffic Act 1988 s 1 offence maximum 14 years) or puts someone into a coma for life (maximum 2 years) should not create such a huge difference in the maximum sentence available.

Crown Court statistics – England and Wales – Males 21+

46.2

Year	Plea	Total Numbers sentenced	Type of sentence %					Average length of custody (months)
			Discharge	Fine	Community sentence	Suspended sentence	Custody	
2002	Guilty	919	1	6	31	3	59	10.4
	Not guilty	178	2	19	30	2	47	11
2003	Guilty	1,037	1	4	35	2	57	10.5
	Not guilty	173	1	19	30	1	47	10.9

For details and explanations about the statistics in the book see page vii.

Guideline cases

46.3 Some assistance can be found in DEATH BY DANGEROUS DRIVING, CAUSING – *Guidelines*

Magistrates' Court Sentencing Guidelines January 2004

46.4 For a first time offender pleading not guilty. Entry point. Is it so serious that only custody is appropriate? Consider the impact on the victim. Examples of aggravating factors for the offence are avoiding detection or apprehension, competitive driving, racing or showing off, disregard of warnings e.g. from passengers or others in the vicinity, evidence of alcohol or drugs, excessive speed, prolonged, persistent, deliberate bad driving, serious risk and using a mobile telephone. Examples of mitigating factors for the offence are emergency and speed not excessive. Examples of mitigation are co-operation with the police, genuine remorse and voluntary compensation. Give reasons if not awarding compensation.

For details about the guidelines see MAGISTRATES' COURT SENTENCING GUIDELINES at page 483.

Alcohol, driving under the influence – 71 to 100 µg in breath or equivalent

46.5 *R v Friend* 1998 1 Cr App R (S) 163. The defendant pleaded guilty to dangerous driving and no insurance at the Magistrates' Court. The defendant ate and drank with friends and drove home in his van. His insurance had lapsed in the previous month. He was considerably affected by drink and drugs and was $2^{1}/_{2}$ times over the limit and had taken diazepam. He failed to negotiate a left hand bend, crossed the central road markings and collided with an oncoming car. Both cars were very extensively damaged. The other driver received a 5″ cut to his forehead, whiplash injuries and bruising. The defendant told the police he was not the driver. He was 49 and from 1990 onwards had convictions for speeding, failing to provide a specimen, failing to report and failing to stop. He was on bail for and later fined and disqualified for 4 years for excess alcohol. Held. He is a menace to other road users. The photographs are chilling. Balancing the factors **15 months** was entirely appropriate. The £400 fine for the no insurance will be quashed because he has no money.

R v Nichols 1998 2 Cr App R (S) 296. The defendant was convicted of dangerous driving. The defendant drifted from lane to lane on a three lane dual carriageway causing one driver to break heavily. Eventually he drifted into a barrier on the near side of the road of a two lane stretch and stopped. With smoke coming from the tyre and a tyre burst, he reversed at speed into the nearside lane and partly into the offside lane. He drove down the road and into a lay-by where he got out and looked at his vehicle. Then he suddenly drove off again causing other drivers to avoid him. He drove with sparks coming from his nearside wheels at about 50 mph. Eventually he stopped. Police found that the car had extensive damage to the front. The wheel of the tyre that burst had been moved backwards. The steering and suspension was also damaged. Another tyre was deflated. His breath alcohol reading was 78ug. The expert couldn't dispute that the tyre might have burst before the impact. The defendant was now aged 40 and treated as of good character. He was hard working and his two youngest children were in poor health. The youngest was about to have an operation. There was a risk that his company which employed 26 people could collapse. Solicitors acting for Customs confirmed the company was in serious financial difficulties. He received 9 months and since then seven engineers and two apprentices had lost their jobs. Held. He had showed a singular lack of control which arose from excessive consumption of alcohol. With a great deal of hesitation the company mitigation means the sentence should be **6 months** not 9.

Alcohol or drugs charge, sentences should be concurrent with dangerous driving

46.6   *R v King* 2000 1 Cr App R (S) 105. As the dangerous driving arose out of the fact drugs were taken the sentences should be concurrent. See **46.12**

Asleep or being drowsy, driver is

46.7   *R v King* 2000 1 Cr App R (S) 105. See **46.12**

Death results

46.8   As the court is able to consider the victim's injuries it would be odd if the court could not take into account the ultimate injury, death. However, if there is no conviction for causing death by dangerous driving the defendant should not be sentenced for a more serious offence for which he has not been convicted.

R v Simmons 1999 2 Cr App R (S) 18. The defendant was indicted with causing death by dangerous driving. His plea to *careless driving* was accepted and no evidence was offered for the causing death count. The defence argued it was wrong to take into account the death caused. Held. Considering the statutory changes that have taken place since *R v Krawec* 1984 6 Cr App R (S) 367 we find the concept of a road traffic offence in which the sentencing court is obliged to disregard the fact that a death has been caused as wholly anomalous. The current approach is reflected in *Att-Gen's Ref. No 66 of 1996* 1998 1 Cr App R (S) 16 (a case of causing death by careless driving having consumed alcohol) 'It is nonetheless the duty of the judge, to judge cases dispassionately and to do its best to reach the appropriate penalty, taking account of all the relevant circumstances.' Whether sentencing courts should take into account criminality alone or both the criminality and the consequences of an offence – and in the latter event in what proportions, is ultimately a question of choice and policy. *Krawec* was clearly valid in its context and at its time, but we do not see it as of assistance to sentencing courts in the different context of today. The judge was entitled to bear in mind the death.

See also CARELESS DRIVING – *Death results*

Disqualification, for how long? – 3 years or less appropriate

46.9   *R v Hicks* 1999 1 Cr App R (S) 228. The defendant pleaded guilty at the first opportunity to dangerous driving. When 19, he drove with friends at considerable speed in a 30 mph area and where there were traffic calming measures. He said he was trying to keep up with the car he was following. At a bend, which was marked with a slow sign, he did not slow down and lost control of the car. The car skidded across the carriageway, uprooted a tree and struck two teenage girls who were walking on the pavement. After the car had crashed through a wooden fence he did not try to leave the scene. It was estimated that the car was travelling at 71 mph. One girl was thrown into the air but fortunately only received cuts and bruises and a broken thumb. The other girl was trapped under the car, which went over her. She had a fractured femur and severe bruising. She was on crutches for 8 months. Her work and social life had been adversely affected. A witness thought he was going to overtake the car he was following. The defendant worked in the information technology industry and had started a BSc course in computer science. He was due to take his exams shortly. His employers spoke highly of him. He had had his licence for just over a year and had a conviction for doing 50 mph in a 30 mph area. He expressed remorse. The judge said the lowest sentence was 12 months which he reduced to 8 months detention for the plea. Held. The judge was right to describe it as a dreadful piece of driving. The sentence was entirely appropriate. Because of his age and his employment needs **3 years'** not 5 years' disqualification.

R v Burman 2000 2 Cr App R (S) 3. The defendant pleaded guilty at the first opportunity to dangerous driving. The victim was driving his car on a road with a 30 mph limit with his wife the other victim. He saw two cars driving at speed. The defendant's speed was estimated at 59 mph. The defendant clipped the kerb and lost control of his car, which collided with the victim's car. The victims had to be cut from their car and both had fractured sternums and bruising to the chest. The wife also had a broken clavicle. Both suffered from shock. The defendant had three fractured ribs. The court did not sentence him on the basis he was racing. He was 27 and his driving record was, 'not bad.' He had lost his business and his job as a result. His marriage was now over. He expressed remorse at the time and the likelihood of re-offending was assessed as low. He was sentenced to 18 months. Held. It was a bad case. Taking into account the 2 year maximum sentence the starting point was 18 months which we reduce to 12 months for the plea. We reduce the disqualification from 4 to **3 years** because a young man needs a licence to obtain suitable employment.

R v Howells 2003 1 Cr App R (S) 292.The defendant was convicted of dangerous driving. Driving a passenger, he failed to see a motorbike at a roundabout. The driver of the motorbike had to brake heavily to avoid the defendant's car. After the roundabout, the defendant deliberately rammed the bike twice and drew up alongside, causing the driver to swerve and brake. The defendant then swerved and hit the bike's foot peg. The victim gesticulated at the car and kicked the defendant's door panel. The two vehicles moved over and there was a struggle. He was 55 with an exemplary character with a number of impressive testimonials. He had served in the army and then had 17 years of exemplary employment. Following the offence, he was badly affected by anxiety and depression. The Judge sentenced the defendant on the basis he had deliberately used the car as a weapon. Held. In dangerous driving road rage cases, where no accident or injury results and there is no consumption of alcohol but there is ample evidence to suggest furious driving in temper with an intent of causing fear and possibly injury, the appropriate sentencing bracket is between 6 and 12 months. 6 months not 12. **3 years** disqualification was fully merited.

Disqualification, for how long? – More than 3 years or appropriate

46.10   *R v Barker* 1999 1 Cr App R (S) 71. The defendant pleaded guilty to dangerous driving. He drove a van on a country road in the dark. He knew the road well and was in an aggressive hurry. He drove too close to the car in front and the driver of the car gave two warnings by braking which he ignored. When the car and a lorry which was in front stopped to let an oncoming lorry pass at a narrow bridge he pulled out to overtake. He had to brake and his brakes screeched. He then had to reverse his van. He later overtook the car and the lorry and was behind a Range Rover and another lorry. He tried to overtake them both without being able see over a rise in the road. He said he was relying on not being able to see any vehicle headlights in front. However, a driver behind him did see oncoming vehicle lights. The van hit an oncoming motorcycle. The car driver described the defendant's driving as, 'outrageous and dangerous'. The motorcyclist who was driving at a moderate speed was very seriously injured. He was permanently disabled and is now paraplegic. The defendant was 30 with a drink/drive conviction 12 years before, a speeding conviction in 1993, which caused totting up disqualification and a no insurance conviction in 1995. Held. It was a sustained piece of bad driving and it caused very serious injury. He had ignored the brake light warnings and the warning of the incident at the bridge. The bridge incident and the accident were very similar. The maximum is 2 years and the judge must have started at about 20 months before the deduction for the plea. 16 months was severe but not manifestly excessive. **4 years'** not 6 years' disqualification.

R v King 2000 1 Cr App R (S) 105. **5 years** appropriate here. See **46.12**

R v Brindle 2003 1 Cr App R (S) 9. The defendant pleaded guilty to dangerous driving and Section 20. He had pleaded at the Magistrates' Court to failing to report or stop and no insurance. After borrowing a friend's Escort car, he drove three friends at excessive speed in a 30 mph area without insurance. When driving on the wrong side of the road the car struck a pedestrian who was stepping off a traffic island. The victim, aged 16 was thrown into the air and landed on the car and then the road. The car's estimated speed was 50 mph and it was abandoned round the corner where the occupants ran off. Eleven days later he surrendered to the police. The victim spent three weeks in intensive care and eight weeks in hospital. As well as fractures and multiple abrasions he suffered extensive head injuries causing brain injury, which it was hoped, would improve over two years. The defendant was 20 with convictions but none involving vehicles. The Judge said short of killing the victim he could not have caused more harm. Held. This was an exceptional piece of bad driving. He did not deliberately drive the vehicle as a weapon. 21 months detention on both concurrent not 4^1/$_2$ years for the Section 20. **6 years** not 15 years disqualification.

Drugs, when under the influence of

46.11   *R v King* 2000 1 Cr App R (S) 105. See below.

HGV drivers

46.12   *R v King* 2000 1 Cr App R (S) 105. The defendant pleaded guilty to dangerous driving and driving whilst unfit through drink or drugs at the Magistrates' Court. At 6.30am, the defendant was seen to drive his 7.5 tonne lorry in an erratic manner for some time. He drove into a lay-by and hit a parked car. The driver had just gone back into his car and was thrown into the air. The defendant stopped and went to the car. The defendant was certified unfit at the police station. He was unsteady on his feet and drowsy. He had traces of diazepam and barbiturates in his blood. Both could cause drowsiness. A combination would increase that effect. The defendant said he had taken five or six doses of diazepam in the previous 24 hours and he had been out the previous night and had not slept since 10am the previous day. The victim suffered extensive injuries to his shoulder and upper arm. He had a fracture at the base of his spine. He also suffered head injuries, which caused memory loss and other disabilities. He made a good recovery from his physical injuries but it was uncertain whether he had recovered from the head injuries. The defendant's last conviction was for disqualified driving and he was sent to prison for 3 months. The judge passed the maximum sentence of 2 years because he said the defendant had 'been caught red-handed' and the 6 month maximum for drink/drive and made the sentences consecutive. He was disqualified for 5 years. Held. This was a very serious case of dangerous driving made more serious by the drug taking. The drugs could have had a very grave impact on other road users. However, the consecutive sentences were wrong in principle because the dangerous driving arose out of the fact that drugs had been taken. **18 months** and 4 months concurrent substituted. The 5 years' disqualification was correct.

Overtaking

46.13   *R v Barker* 1999 1 Cr App R (S) 71. The defendant pleaded guilty to dangerous driving. He drove a van on a country road in the dark. He knew the road well and was in an aggressive hurry. He drove too close to the car in front and the driver of the car gave two warnings by braking which he ignored. When the car and a lorry which was in front stopped to let an oncoming lorry pass at a narrow bridge he pulled out to overtake. He had to brake and his brakes screeched. He then had to reverse his van. He later overtook the car and the lorry and was behind a Range Rover and another lorry. He tried to overtake them both without being able see over a rise in the road. He said he was relying on not being able see to any vehicle headlights in front. However, a driver behind him did see oncoming vehicle lights. The van hit an oncoming motorcycle. The car driver described the defendant's driving as, 'outrageous and dangerous'. The motorcyclist who was driving at a moderate speed was very seriously injured. He was permanently disabled and is now paraplegic. The defendant was 30 with a drink/drive conviction 12 years before, a speeding conviction in 1993, which caused totting up disqualification and a no insurance conviction in 1995. Held. It was a sustained piece of bad driving and it caused very serious injury. He had ignored the brake light warnings and the warning of the incident at the bridge. The bridge incident and the accident were very similar. The maximum is 2 years and the judge must have started at about 20 months before the deduction for the plea. **16 months** was severe but not manifestly excessive. 4 years not 6 years disqualification.

R v Smith 2002 2 Cr App R (S) 71. The defendant was convicted of dangerous driving. He drove his lorry laden with scrap iron and cars on a wet road in a 60 mph area. He approached a JCB digger at about 30 mph and overtook it on a blind bend without slowing down. The digger was travelling at about 15 mph. He collided head on with the victim who was driving her car at 40–45 mph in the opposite direction. With her was her 3yearold daughter strapped in the back. She tried to break and steer left but skidded on the damp road. Her face was covered in blood and the child was screaming. The front of her car was extensively damaged. The defendant kept approaching her and saying sorry. She had a broken leg, ankle, wrist, and lacerations to her face, scalp and leg. She suffered a whiplash injury and extensive bruising and swelling to her shoulder chest and stomach. She was in plaster for 10 weeks and the child suffered grazes and bruises. The sole cause of the accident was that he overtook on a blind bend. The defendant claimed the digger was indicating left at the time. He was 40 and of good character. The defendant suffered nightmares and had not driven for 6 months. Held. It was over a significant period he was on the wrong side of the road and he could have braked and returned to his side of the road. It was a bad case resulting in the most serious injuries. **4 months** was not manifestly excessive.

Police chases

46.14   *R v Scarley* 2001 1 Cr App R (S) 86. The defendant pleaded guilty to dangerous driving and driving whilst disqualified. The defendant was on bail and disqualified from driving. Police were trying to arrest him for an assault. Police saw him in a car with his brothers. They followed him and lost him and then saw him driving towards them at speed. They had to take evasive action to avoid being hit. Two police cars blocked his path and he braked sharply but hit one of the cars. An officer suffered a whiplash injury, soreness and a headache. The defendant mounted the grass verge narrowly missing another officer. He drove on and abandoned the car and was arrested on foot. He was 36 with an appalling record. He had 157 offences on 40 occasions including violence and road traffic offences. The pre-sentence report said there was a high risk of re-offending. He was given the maximum sentence with no penalty for the other offence and the defence appealed because there was no discount for the plea of guilty. Held. There are exceptions to the rule that a guilty sentence results in a lesser sentence. First, being caught red-handed and having no practical defence to the charge *R v Rogers* 1992 13 Cr App R (S) 80, *R v Landy* 1995 16 Cr App R (S) 908, *R v Reay* 1993 RTR 189. Secondly, where there is a last minute tactical plea; also where there is a need to protect the public or where the charge was representative of a large number of offences, *R v Costen* 1989 11 Cr App R 182. The first example applies here. [The problem in these cases was the maximum sentence was clearly inadequate. It would be much better to have proper maximum sentences and a right to a discount, as having no defence does not always stop the defendant pleading not guilty. Alternatively there could have been a slightly lesser sentence and a consecutive sentence for the other offences.]

R v Jones 2002 2 Cr App R (S) 412. The defendant pleaded guilty to dangerous driving and driving whilst disqualified. At 4.20 p.m. police were alerted to the defendant driving when disqualified and used lights and sirens to indicate he should stop. Instead the defendant drove on the wrong side of the road into oncoming traffic and a chase began. In residential areas he drove at up to 50 mph. Where the speed limit was 20 mph he drove at 50 mph. He swerved in and out of traffic and narrowly missed a van. A sharp handbrake turn was executed causing smoke to come from his tyres. He caused a young girl to cycle into a hedge. When he stopped in a playing field, police had to chase him and he struggled violently. He was abusive and swore at them. He was 32 and had 14 convictions for driving whilst disqualified, 6 for TDA, one recent one for dangerous driving and one for failing to stop after an accident. The probation officer said he did not demonstrate any real insight into the gravity of his behaviour, all sentencing options had been tried and none had had any effect, his behaviour was persistent and entrenched, and there was an extremely high risk of further illegal driving. The Judge said he blamed everyone else for his predicament and this was one of the worst cases of dangerous driving. He received **21 months** for the dangerous driving (2 years being the maximum) and a concurrent sentence for the disqualification count. Held. It is almost always possible to say a particular offence was not the worst of its kind. That does not necessarily mean a sentence approaching the maximum is not justified. Nonetheless care must be taken to consider all the factors carefully before passing a sentence near the maximum. The Judge was able to conclude there was an element of road rage. This was an extremely serious case of dangerous driving, he had an appalling record and he had no apparent awareness of the dangers he posed. The sentence was not manifestly excessive.

R v Phillips 2005 1 Cr App R (S) 627. The defendant pleaded guilty to dangerous driving and driving while disqualified. He was driving a car when police spotted him and pursued him. He drove through a built up area in the wrong direction sometimes at 60mph twice the legal limit. He had to brake hard more than once to avoid collisions. He skidded to a halt and ran off on foot before being caught by the police. The total distance of his pursuit was just over a mile. He was a disqualified driver and therefore had no insurance. The defendant had extensive previous convictions including offences of dishonesty, drug related offending, other motoring matters, seventeen convictions for driving while disqualified and twenty eight for driving with no insurance. He was not long out of prison for offences of driving while disqualified when he committed these offences. A pre-sentence report showed that he did not consider that he drove dangerously. He was described as a long-standing drug addict using heroin and amphetamine. He was in regular employment as a motor mechanic. His risk of re offending was high. Held. There were the following aggravating features: the defendant's previous record for the same offences; the culpability of the offences themselves; the relatively prolonged course of dangerous driving; perhaps most significantly the reason for it – to attempt to outrun justice and avoid another conviction. It is right that this offence was not at the very top of the scale as there was no suggestion of drink or drugs having been taken. The judge was right to sentence him to the maximum sentence for driving while disqualified and to make it consecutive to the sentence for dangerous driving, as the disqualified driving offence was committed in full before the dangerous driving was embarked upon, and the reason for the dangerous driving was that he had committed the offence of driving while disqualified and been detected for it. **18 months** imprisonment for dangerous driving and **6 months consecutive** for driving while disqualified were not manifestly excessive.

See also DEATH BY DANGEROUS DRIVING, CAUSING – *Police chases*

Police officers, traffic wardens, driving at

46.15   *R v Joseph* 2002 1 Cr App R (S) 74. The defendant was convicted of dangerous driving. He parked his jeep outside a bingo hall. When a parking attendant went across to issue a ticket he crossed the road and began a heated argument with him. Next he got in the vehicle turned the wheel towards the attendant and drove it at him. The attendant slid onto the bonnet and was carried for 150 yards. When the attendant got off the defendant drove away. The attendant received a cut finger and some pain to the back and ribs. He didn't require hospital treatment. The defendant surrendered but denied the offence. He was a man of good character who had built up a business. The judge said that those attendants, however unpopular motorists might find them to be, are carrying out an important public duty. They deserve the protection of the courts. Those that drive at them will receive substantial periods of custody as a deterrent to others. Held. We endorse the judge's comments. As the maximum is 2 years and that as a result of this his business had gone into bankruptcy **10 months** not 15. The 2 years' disqualification to remain.

Old case. *R v Charlton* 1995 16 Cr App R (S) 703.

Racing, competitive driving etc

46.16   *R v Arthur* 2001 2 Cr App R (S) 316. The defendant was tried for causing death by dangerous driving. At the close of the prosecution case the judge said there was no case to answer. The defendant then pleaded guilty to dangerous driving. The defendant and the victim raced their cars and the victim died when her car left the road at a bend. The count of causing death failed because the judge ruled that the prosecution could only rely on the final piece of driving. The defendant had driven at dangerous speeds on minor roads and raced through a town at 50–60 mph in a 30 mph area. The two cars were on the wrong side of the road and almost bumper to bumper. The defendant was 25 with convictions for dangerous driving, threatening behaviour, theft and criminal damage. The judge said it was very dangerous driving. He identified racing, excessive speed, prolonged course of driving, a very real danger to others and the death as aggravating factors. Held. The judge was entitled to make the findings he did. **20 months** was a severe sentence but not manifestly excessive.

Road rage

46.17   *R v Howells* 2003 1 Cr App R (S) 292. The defendant was convicted of dangerous driving. Driving a passenger, he failed to see a motorbike at a roundabout. The driver of the motorbike had to brake heavily to avoid the defendant's car. After the roundabout, the defendant deliberately rammed the bike twice and drew up alongside, causing the driver to swerve and brake. The defendant then swerved and hit the bike's foot peg. The victim gesticulated at the car and kicked the defendant's door panel. The two vehicles moved over and there was a struggle. He was 55 with an exemplary character with a number of impressive testimonials. He had served in the army and then had 17 years of exemplary employment. Following the offence, he was badly affected by anxiety and depression. The Judge sentenced the defendant on the basis he had deliberately used the car as a weapon. Held. In dangerous driving road rage cases, where no accident or injury results and there is no consumption of alcohol but there is ample evidence to suggest furious driving in temper with an intent of causing fear and possibly injury, the appropriate sentencing bracket is between **6 and 12 months.** **6 months** not 12. 3 years disqualification was fully merited.

Speeding

46.18   *R v Hicks* 1999 1 Cr App R (S) 228. The defendant pleaded guilty at the first opportunity to dangerous driving. When 19, he drove with friends at considerable speed in a 30 mph area and where there were traffic calming measures. He said he was trying to keep up with the car he was following. At a bend, which was marked with a slow sign, he did not slow down and lost control of the car. The car skidded across the carriageway, uprooted a tree and struck two teenage girls who were walking on the pavement. After the car had crashed through a wooden fence he did not try to leave the scene. It was estimated that the car was travelling at 71 mph. One girl was thrown into the air but fortunately only received cuts and bruises and a broken thumb. The other girl was trapped under the car, which went over her. She had a fractured femur and severe bruising. She was on crutches for 8 months. Her work and social life had been adversely affected. A witness thought he was going to overtake the car he was following. The defendant worked in the information technology industry and had started a BSc course in computer science. He was due to take his exams shortly. His employers spoke highly of him. He had had his licence for just over a year and had a conviction for doing 50 mph in a 30 mph area. He expressed remorse. The judge said the lowest sentence was 12 months which he reduced to **8 months** detention for the plea. Held. The judge was right to describe it as a dreadful piece of driving. The sentence was entirely appropriate. Because of his age and his employment needs 3 years' not 5 years' disqualification.

R v Howells Re Ashby 1999 1 Cr App R (S) 335 at 339. LCJ. The defendant pleaded guilty to dangerous driving and driving with no insurance. The defendant produced some documents to the police about a car. He said he had just bought it. He said he had not driven it because he had had far too much to drink. The officers remained in the vicinity and saw him drive off in it. They followed the car and to start with it was driven slowly. When the police put on their blue light it accelerated to speeds of 60 mph. It drove across two 'Give way' signs and was chased for about a mile when the police lost it. The car was found abandoned nearby. The defendant was arrested and was not breath tested. However, he denied driving the car but admitted drinking a bottle of wine. He was 30 with a substantial record including motoring offences. He had been sent to prison before but had no dangerous driving convictions. Held. The judge was right to recognise the danger he had presented to other road users and that the offence was aggravated by drink. **4 months** was entirely appropriate.

R v Burman 2000 2 Cr App R (S) 3. The defendant pleaded guilty at the first opportunity to dangerous driving. The victim was driving his car on a road with a 30 mph limit with his wife the other victim. He saw two cars driving at speed. The defendant's speed was estimated at 59 mph. The defendant clipped the kerb and lost control of his car, which collided with the victim's car. The victims had to be cut from their car and both had fractured sternums and bruising to the chest. The wife also had a broken clavicle. Both suffered from shock. The defendant had three fractured ribs. The court did not sentence him on the basis he was racing. He was 27 and his driving record was, 'not bad.' He had lost his business and his job as a result. His marriage was now over. He expressed remorse at the time and the likelihood of re-offending was assessed as low. He was sentenced to 18 months. Held. It was a bad case. Taking into account the 2 year maximum sentence the starting point was 18 months which we reduce to **12 months** for the plea. We reduce the disqualification from 4 to 3 years.

Victim(s) seriously injured

46.19   *R v Barker* 1999 1 Cr App R (S) 71. The defendant pleaded guilty to dangerous driving. He drove a van on a country road in the dark. He knew the road well and was in an aggressive hurry. He drove too close to the car in front and the driver of the car gave two warnings by braking which he ignored. When the car and a lorry which was in front stopped to let an oncoming lorry pass at a narrow bridge he pulled out to overtake. He had to brake and his brakes screeched. He then had to reverse his van. He later overtook the car and the lorry and was behind a Range Rover and another lorry. He tried to overtake them both without being able see over a rise in the road. He said he was relying on not being able see to any vehicle headlights in front. However, a driver behind him did see oncoming vehicle lights. The van hit an oncoming motorcycle. The car driver described the defendant's driving as, 'outrageous and dangerous'. The motorcyclist who was driving at a moderate speed was very seriously injured. He was permanently disabled and is now paraplegic. The defendant was 30 with a drink/drive conviction 12 years before, a speeding conviction in 1993, which caused totting up disqualification and a no insurance conviction in 1995. Held. It was a sustained piece of bad driving and it caused very serious injury. He had ignored the brake light warnings and the warning of the incident at the bridge. The bridge incident and the accident were very similar. The maximum is 2 years and the judge must have started at about 20 months before the deduction for the plea. **16 months** was severe but not manifestly excessive. 4 years' not 6 years' disqualification.

R v Hicks 1999 1 Cr App R (S) 228. The defendant pleaded guilty at the first opportunity to dangerous driving. When 19, drove with friends at considerable speed in a 30 mph area and where there were traffic calming measures. He said he was trying to keep up with the car he was following. At a bend, which was marked with a slow sign, he did not slow down and lost control of the car. The car skidded across the carriageway, uprooted a tree and struck two teenage girls who were walking on the pavement. After the car had crashed through a wooden fence he did not try to leave the scene. It was estimated that the car was travelling at 71 mph. One girl was thrown into the air but fortunately only received cuts and bruises and a broken thumb. The other girl was trapped under the car, which went over her. She had a fractured femur and severe bruising. She was on crutches for 8 months. Her work and social life had been adversely affected. A witness thought he was going to overtake the car he was following. The defendant worked in the information technology industry and had started a BSc course in computer science. He was due to take his exams shortly. His employers spoke highly of him. He had had his licence for just over a year and had a conviction for doing 50 mph in a 30 mph area. He expressed remorse. The judge said the lowest sentence was 12 months which he reduced to **8 months** detention for the plea. Held. The judge was right to describe it as a dreadful piece of driving. The sentence was entirely appropriate. Because of his age and his employment needs 3 years' not 5 years' disqualification.

R v King 2000 1 Cr App R (S) 105. See **46.12**

R v Brindle 2003 1 Cr App R (S) 9. The defendant pleaded guilty to dangerous driving and Section 20. He had pleaded at the Magistrates' Court to failing to report or stop and no insurance. After borrowing a friend's Escort car, he drove three friends at excessive speed in a 30 mph area without insurance. When driving on the wrong side of the road the car struck a pedestrian who was stepping off a traffic island. The victim, aged 16 was thrown into the air and landed on the car and then the road. The car's estimated speed was 50 mph and it was abandoned round the corner where the occupants ran off. Eleven days later he surrendered to the police. The victim spent three weeks in intensive care and eight weeks in hospital. As well as fractures and multiple abrasions he suffered extensive head injuries causing brain injury, which it was hoped, would improve over two years. The defendant was 20 with convictions but none involving vehicles. The Judge said short of killing the victim he could not have caused more harm. Held. This was an exceptional piece of bad driving. He did not deliberately drive the vehicle as a weapon. **21 months** detention on both concurrent not 4$^{1}/_{2}$ years for the Section 20. 6 years not 15 years disqualification.

Old cases *R v Stokes* 1998 1 Cr App R (S) 282 (For a summary of this case see the first edition of this book.)

47   DEATH BY CARELESS DRIVING, CAUSING

(Causing death when driving without due care and under the influence of drink or drugs or after failing to provide a specimen)

47.1   Road Traffic Act 1988 s 3A

Indictable only. Maximum sentence 14[8] years. For offences committed before 27/2/04 the maximum is 10 years. Minimum disqualification 2 years[9].

Depriving defendant of vehicle used There is power to deprive the defendant of the vehicle used[10] for the purposes of committing the offence.

Detention It is a specified offence enabling defendant aged 14–17 to be detained[11].

Disqualification The defendant must be disqualified till he/she passes an extended driving test.

Points 3–11 penalty points when the court finds special reasons.

Where a defendant has a conviction for driving while unfit, causing death under the influence of drink, driving with excess alcohol and failing to provide a specimen in previous 10 years' the minimum disqualification is 3 years[12]. There is power to order reduced disqualification for attendance on courses[13].

Funeral expenses The Court may make this compensation order see MANSLAUGHTER – *Funeral expenses of the deceased*

Imprisonment for public protection For offences committed on or after 4/4/05 when there is a significant risk to members of the public of serious harm etc. there is a mandatory duty to pass a sentence of imprisonment for public protection[14]. For offenders under 18 the duty is to pass detention for public protection or an extended sentence[15].

8   Criminal Justice Act 2003 s 285(4)
9   Road Traffic Offenders Act 1988 s 34(1) & (4) & Sch. 2
10 Powers of Criminal Courts (Sentencing) Act 2000 s 143(6) & (7)
11 Powers of Criminal Courts (Sentencing) Act 2000 s 91(2)(a)
12 Road Traffic Offenders Act 1988 s 34(3)
13 Road Traffic Offenders Act 1988 s 34A
14 Criminal Justice Act 2003 s 224–226
15 Criminal Justice Act 2003 s 226 and 228

Sexual Offences Prevention Order There is a discretionary power to make this order when it is necessary to protect the public etc[16].

Crown Court statistics – England and Wales – Males 21+

47.2

Year	Plea	Total Numbers sentenced	Type of sentence %					Average length of custody (months)
			Discharge	Fine	Community sentence	Suspended sentence	Custody	
2002	Guilty	46	–	–	2	–	98	42.2
	Not guilty	5	–	–	–	20	60	48
2003	Guilty	46	–	–	–	–	98	45.4
	Not guilty	5	–	–	–	–	100	40.8

For details and explanations about the statistics in the book see page vii

Guideline cases and remarks

47.3   *R v Cooksley* 2004 1 Cr App R (S) 1. LCJ The level of sentencing in cases of causing death by careless driving when under the influence of drink should not form a separate category from those we have listed for death by dangerous driving. The driving may not exhibit the aggravating factors set out in list for causing death by dangerous driving. In some cases, the only aggravating factor will be the amount of alcohol consumed. In other cases, there may be the aggravating factor of disregarding a warning from a fellow passenger or knowingly driving a poorly-maintained vehicle. There may be previous motoring convictions. There will also be cases where the driving is itself of significance in determining the appropriate sentence. As was made clear in *R v Locke* 1995 16 Cr App R (S) 795, it is not necessary to have an additional count of death by dangerous driving before the full culpability of the offender's driving is taken into account in determining the right sentence. It will be perfectly possible for sentencing judges to fit cases of causing death by careless driving when under the influence of drink into one of the four guideline categories which we propose for causing death by dangerous driving. (See **DEATH BY DANGEROUS DRIVING, CAUSING** – *Guideline remarks*)

Att-Gen's Ref. Nos. 24 and 45 of 1994 1995 16 Cr App R (S) 583 at 586. LCJ. This Court is concerned primarily with the criminality of the person who has caused the death. The fact is that the death is, of itself, a factor in contributing to the length of sentence which should be passed. But essentially we have to look at the cases in the light of the offender's criminality. The length of sentence will very much depend upon the aggravating and mitigating circumstances in the particular case, the extent of the carelessness or dangerousness, and the amount that the offender is over the limit in a case involving excess alcohol. Where an offender is not just over the limit, not even substantially over the limit, but $2^1/_2$ to 3 times over the limit, the sentence which the court must pass is clearly a substantial one. It is insufficient excuse for failing to impose a sufficiently long sentence to look predominantly at the mitigating features and the remorse of the offender.

R v Cororan 1996 1 Cr App R (S) 416 at 419. LCJ. The defendant was convicted of causing death by careless driving after having consumed alcohol. Anyone who is driving with $2^1/_2$ times the permitted alcohol limit must expect a substantial sentence.

R v Chippendale 1998 1 Cr App R (S) 192. There is understandably grave concern about young men who have too much to drink and drive in the face of warnings and

16 Sexual Offences Act 2003 s 104 & Sch. 5

then kill. The court will have regard to the extent of the carelessness and the amount the defendant was over the limit. Personal elements of mitigation such as acute guilt feelings are not matters that should sound greatly in determining the proper sentence.

Alcohol – Guideline remarks

47.4 *Att-Gen's Ref. Nos. 14 and 24 of 1993* 1994 15 Cr App R (S) 640. LCJ. Where a driver is over the limit and kills someone as a result of his careless driving a prison sentence will ordinarily be appropriate. In an exceptional case where the alcohol level is just over the border line and the carelessness is momentary, and there is strong mitigation, a non-custodial may be possible. But in other cases a prison sentence is required to punish the offender, to deter others from drinking and driving, and to reflect the public's abhorrence of deaths being caused by drivers with excess alcohol.

Att-Gen's Ref. Nos. 24 and 45 of 1994 1995 16 Cr App R (S) 583 at 586. LCJ. The length of sentence will very much depend upon the aggravating and mitigating circumstances in the particular case, the extent of the carelessness or dangerousness, and the amount that the offender is over the limit in a case involving excess alcohol. Where an offender is not just over the limit, not even substantially over the limit, but $2^1/_2$ to 3 times over the limit, the sentence which the court must pass is clearly a substantial one. It is insufficient excuse for failing to impose a sufficiently long sentence to look predominantly at the mitigating features and the remorse of the offender.

Alcohol level unknown but driver unfit

47.5 *Att-Gen's Ref. No 10 of 1997* 1998 1 Cr App R (S) 147. LCJ. The defendant pleaded guilty to causing death by careless driving when unfit through drink and aggravated vehicle-taking. A mother left her car on her driveway with a 'crook lock' attached and two boxes of beer in the boot. She went to Scotland with her husband and youngest son leaving her other son and a cousin at the house. Next day there were numerous visitors to the house and there was talk of taking the car. The defendant then 17 expressed reluctance to be involved. The radio and the beer were taken and the defendant and two others went to nearby woods and drank the beer. They came back and appeared drunk. The defendant drove the car with the other two at a speed judged to be between 60 and 70 mph. The defendant lost control at a moderate left hand bend and the car left the road with no noise of skidding or brakes screeching. The car hit a tree and one passenger was killed. The car's speed near the accident was estimated to be between 70 and 90 mph. The speed limit was 60 mph but the greatest speed the bend could be negotiated was 50 mph. The road was dry. The defendant was unconscious for six days. The injury to his frontal lobe of the brain affected his personality. The defendant had a 'dis-social personality disorder.' One doctor said it was exacerbated by the accident and another said it was caused by it. He needed 12 weeks' observation and treatment in a specialist hospital. The judge sentenced him to probation and he was admitted to the hospital. It was not a success. The defendant was of good character. Held. The judge was correct to say 3 years was appropriate. We think 3–4 years if contested and 2–3 years if not. The 2 years since the offence, the injury, his plea and character are significant factors. **12 months** YOI substituted.

R v Roche 1999 2 Cr App R (S) 105. LCJ. The defendant pleaded guilty to causing death by careless driving when under the influence of drink. After 11pm he was driving his cousin after both had been in pubs. The weather was dry and the speed limit was 30 mph. He was driving in the region of 60 to 70 mph. He hit the kerb shortly after negotiating a bend and the car struck a telegraph pole and then a cast-iron post box. The car travelled through the air and partially demolished a bus shelter. His cousin died. The defendant was treated for a minor head injury and was arrested at the hospital. He declined to provide samples of blood or breath. He was subject to very severe stress at the time. The car was found to be defective but that had not contributed to the accident. He said he had had 7 or 8 pints of lager. The victim was not wearing a seat belt although he was. He was 27 and of good character. His re-offending risk was assessed as low and the accident had had a very severe effect on him. He was suffering from profound remorse. The defendant's parents were brother and sister of the victim's parents. The victim's mother treated the defendant almost as a son and had played a large part in bringing him up. The sentence of 4 years was delaying her grieving. Held. There is no room for the degree of indulgence which was shown in the past. Four years can be regarded as merciful. The injured party cannot dictate the sentence for vengeance or compassion. However, this is different and the court can be an instrument of compassion. **3 years** not 4.

Alcohol 36 to 70 µg in breath or equivalent

47.6 *R v Stewart* 1999 2 Cr App R (S) 213. The defendant made a late plea to careless driving after having consumed alcohol. The defendant and a colleague who both worked at Heathrow airport took an unauthorised break and drove to a nearby football club. For $2^1/_2$ hours they drank beer and then the defendant set off at about 6.30 pm to drive the two of them back to work. He drove at speeds between 60–80 mph where there were limits of 40 or 50 mph. He also overtook and undertook other cars. When almost at the airport he was driving at nearly 50 in a 40 mph area on a slip road. A group of young people were crossing the road and he lost control of the car and hit a 13-year-old girl and her friend. He didn't stop and he abandoned the car when it broke down due to damage to it which was very substantial. The girl died and her friend suffered injuries of the utmost gravity. He suffered from multiple fractures and psychological trauma. He was in hospital for about 6 weeks and will suffer permanent and significant disability. The defendant was $1^1/_2$ times over the limit when tested at 8pm. He accepted he required glasses to drive and was not wearing them. He was 35 and of good character. At work he was a team leader preparing aircraft. He had suffered threats and had had to sell his house and move his family. Held. The judge took into account the plea and the threats are not matters which can affect the sentence. The aggravating features were very serious and **5 years** was correct.

R v Thompson 2000 1 Cr App R (S) 84. The defendant was convicted of causing death by careless driving after having consumed alcohol. The victim had spent the evening drinking with friends. They were looking for a minicab. One friend was on one side of the road negotiating with the driver of a cab, which had stopped at a red light. The lights changed and the victim who was wearing dark clothing and the other friend started to cross the road to join the one talking to cab driver. The victim was struck by the defendant's car and thrown into the air. He had major head injuries and died. The friend was also hit. The car on analysis seemed to have been travelling at 23 mph. The defendant remained at the scene and his blood alcohol level was 52mg. The limit is 35. An expert said the victim would have had about 3 seconds to react to the pedestrian and with dark clothing 1.4 seconds. The defendant said in interview he had overtaken a stationary bus and slowed down for the lights. As he approached them they changed and he saw two or three people in front. A witness who was a very experience car driver said the two leapt across very quickly. He said the pedestrians were the cause and the driver could not have done much about it. Others had differing accounts. An expert said alcohol and tiredness played a part for the main parties. The defendant was 44 and of good character and showed remorse. Since starting to drive at 16 he had one speeding conviction. He had references and a very impressive work record. Held. There was only one aggravating feature; he was $1^1/_2$ times over the limit. **2 years** not 3.

R v McNiff 2001 2 Cr App R (S) 275. The defendant then 18 pleaded guilty to causing death by careless driving when over the limit. The defendant spent the day drinking with friends. In the early morning he and a friend drove about 2 miles to a garage to buy cigarettes. On his way back he missed his turning and took the next one. He lost control of the car on a bend. The car hit a tree and the friend was killed. He did his best to help him. His blood reading was 51mg. When interviewed he admitted full responsibility and said he was driving too fast. He was of exemplary character with numerous testimonials. He was deputy head of his school and head boy at his college. The risk of re-offending was described as negligible. He showed deep regret. Held. If a person of older years had pleaded guilty 5 years would have been appropriate. Taking into account his age **3 years 9 months** was not manifestly excessive.

R v Thirumaran 2004 2 Cr App R (S) 179. The defendant pleaded guilty at a relatively early stage to one count of causing death by careless driving when over the prescribed limit for alcohol. He was driving his friend's car with his friend as front seat passenger. There were three other passengers in the back. The car veered to one side, the defendant over-corrected and the car left the road, struck a tree and went down an embankment. The front seat passenger died. The defendant had 61mg of alcohol in 100ml of breath. The defendant admitted to the police that he had been the driver. In mitigation it was said that he had pleaded guilty, was remorseful, and that the victim was his life long best friend. The victim had drunk a substantial amount and realised he was not fit to drive, so he had asked the defendant to drive. The defendant had no previous convictions and had a good work record. The aggravating factor was that he was affected by alcohol. Held. Following *Cooksley*, the case was clearly within the second category although not at the top of it. The starting point is therefore 2 to 3 years imprisonment. **3 years** imprisonment, 5 years disqualification and an order for an extended re-test were not manifestly excessive or even arguably so.

R v Brown 2004 2 Cr App R (S) 224. The defendant was convicted of causing death by careless driving when under the influence of drink. He was driving a car with four passengers in the Old Kent Road at 5.00 am. A witness said the car, going at a little more than average speed, came towards him at a twisted angle while he was on the pavement and then swung round and collided with a tree at the side of the road. One passenger died shortly afterwards. Another suffered a broken neck, a fractured jaw and cracked ribs and was unconscious in intensive care for five weeks, although she made a full recovery. Some four hours later the defendant had 83 mg of alcohol per 100 ml of blood and also traces of cannabis in his blood. The alcohol level represented one and a half times over the legal limit at the time of the accident. The defendant had been out of trouble for twelve years. He stayed at the scene, admitted he had been driving, and showed remorse. Held. The aggravating features were the consumption of alcohol and cannabis, the poor condition of the car tyres and the fact that other passengers were injured. The correct starting point for this offence is 4 to 5 years. We have had regard in particular to the fact that the jury acquitted him of causing death by dangerous driving. The proper sentence is **4 years** not 6 with 5 years disqualification not 8.

Old cases *R v Ocego* 1998 1 Cr App R (S) 408 (For a summary of this case see the first edition of this book.)

Alcohol 71 to 100 μg in breath or equivalent

47.7 *Att-Gen's Ref. No 11 of 1998* 1999 1 Cr App R (S) 145. The defendant pleaded guilty to two counts of causing death by careless driving when over the limit at the first opportunity. The defendant then 21 attended a 21st birthday party where alcohol was freely available. He left in the early hours of the morning and drove in his mother's car on an unfamiliar unlit road. Five other young people were in the car which was designed to carry five people. He drove over a slight brow of a hill and after about 100 metres into a bend for which there was no warning. The car left the road and hit a tree. The defendant was probably the only person wearing a seat belt. Two passengers were thrown from the car and died instantly. One was the defendant's best friend. Another passenger was in hospital for 7 months with a fractured pelvis and severe head injuries. Two other passengers suffered fractured arms. He unsuccessfully tried to help one of those who had died. Two hours after the accident his alcohol reading was 93 μg. He speed as he entered the bend was estimated to be between 40 and 50 mph. He told police he had intended to stay the night at the party. He was a university student of good character. He had many very impressive references. He showed deep, long-lasting remorse. The fathers of one of those killed and one of those injured said the tragedy would only be exacerbated if imprisonment were imposed. Held. We'd expect **4 years**. Taking into account it was a reference, his chance of resuming university in the autumn of next year and he had been at liberty **30 months** not 18 months suspended. 5 years' disqualification not 2.

Att-Gen's Ref. No 91 of 2001 2002 1 Cr App R (S) 466 The defendant pleaded guilty to causing death by careless driving when over the limit at the earliest opportunity. He drove in a built up area with his close friend as his passenger. He was revving very hard and travelling very fast. He was seen to cross the centre markings and to be too close to the kerb. He may have hit the kerb but in any event he lost control of the car and collided with a stationary taxi. He and the passenger were rendered unconscious but he was later able to leave the car. She died of a traumatic rupture of the thoracic aorta and he received minor facial injuries. An expert estimated he was driving at between 30 and 50 mph. When seen by police he said he did not know who was driving. His blood reading was 108 mg (the equivalent of 98 μg in the breath). The test revealed cocaine in the blood. He was 24 and of good character. He called evidence of his good character, the effects both on him and his family and his remorse. He was sentenced to 18 months and had served it. Held. Driving with excess alcohol in any form is conduct which is to be deplored. When the levels reach the level in this case it is of the utmost seriousness. The particular nature of the driving was a straightforward manifestation of a drunken driver quite incapable of controlling his car. This was a bad case. He should have expected **4 or 5 years' imprisonment**. As it was a reference **3 years** instead.

Old cases *R v Chippendale* 1998 1 Cr App R (S) 192 (For a summary of this case see the first edition of this book.)

Alcohol 101 to 130 μg in breath or equivalent

47.8   *R v Ridley* 1999 2 Cr App R (S) 170. The defendant pleaded guilty to three counts of causing death by driving without due care after having consumed alcohol. The defendant and friends visited various public houses and each drank about 12 pints of beer. At about midnight they left a pub in Wigtown and he and four others got into a Fiesta to drive to Carlisle. The owner of the car who survived said 'Someone else had agreed to drive but that didn't happen. The defendant was the last to leave the pub and he got into the driver's seat as it was the only seat left. We all decided to get in the car. No one was dragged in against their will.' It was raining very heavily. The defendant accelerated over the crest of a hill and the car clipped a verge, skidded, turned over and span. The car was extremely badly damaged. Three were killed, the owner of the car spent 2 weeks in hospital and 6 months off work. He spent a lot of time in pain. The defendant's breath reading was 108mg. He suffered from shock and minor cuts and bruises. He came from a good and stable background and was unlikely to re-offend. He received 4 years detention and that had a very severe effect on him and his family. A psychologist said he was finding it extremely difficult to cope with it. Held. Three deaths are much worse than one. He is a vulnerable young man. **2¹/₂ years** substituted.

R v Ndlovu 2001 1 Cr App R (S) 163.The defendant pleaded guilty to causing death by driving without due care after having consumed alcohol. The defendant and two others spent the evening drinking in three pubs with the victim who was due to be married the next day. They travelled back to where the car was parked in another town in a taxi. The defendant offered to drive the others home. There was no criticism of his driving until at a bend he braked heavily and sought to correct the steering. He was driving at about 50 mph in a 30 mph area. A cat came into the road and he lost control. The car hit a garage and the victim who was in the back and not wearing a seatbelt sustained head injuries from which he died. The other passengers sustained injuries of varying degrees. He remained at the scene and sought help. His breath reading was 84 μg and by back-tracking was estimated to be between 106 and 136 μg at the time of the accident. He was 26 and of impeccable character. He was completely devastated. **3¹/₂ years** not 5 and 6 years' disqualification not 10.

R v Porter 2001 2 Cr App R (S) 366. The defendant pleaded guilty to causing death by careless driving when over the limit. The defendant's son was born with breathing difficulties and was rushed to hospital in a critical condition. His wife went to hospital and he stayed at home with their three other young children. He drank 20 bottles of 5% proof lager during the early morning. That evening his wife rang him in a distressed state and asked him to come to the hospital. Although he had family who could have driven him to hospital he drove himself in his van. He claimed he hadn't drunk during the day. He drove in a 40 mph area where there was a line of traffic doing 30–40 mph. He overtook a car causing the driver overtaken to brake heavily to prevent him hitting an oncoming car. He then overtook the next car making an oncoming car brake heavily which caused smoke to come from his wheels. The oncoming car had to go into the kerb. A witness said the van, which was being driven erratically, could not overtake any cars safely, there were no gaps for the van and there was no reason the driver could not have seen the oncoming cars. Other witnesses described the driving as 'stupid', 'erratic' and 'suicidal'. His blood reading 3 hours after the accident was 270mg (the equivalent of 117 μg in the breath). The van hit another car and the driver died 9 days later. The victim was a family man with young children. The defendant also suffered injuries and suffered a severe emotional reaction to the death. He was referred to the community health team. He was 28 and of good character. He was described as a good father and expressed remorse. Held. He was befuddled with alcohol. There are no grounds for interfering with the **4¹/₂ years** sentence.

Old cases *Att-Gen's Ref. No 66 of 1996* 1998 1 Cr App R (S) 16 (For a summary of this case see the first edition of this book.)

Asleep, falling

47.9 *Att-Gen's Ref. No 21 of 2000* 2001 1 Cr App R (S) 173. The defendant pleaded guilty to causing death by careless driving and failing to provide a specimen. Shortly before 1am the defendant drove into the back of a heavy goods vehicle. His passenger died. The defendant was unable to provide a specimen when he was in the ambulance. At the hospital he initially consented to giving a blood test and then later refused. He told the doctor he had drunk 2¹/₂ pints. The HGV's speed was estimated at 43 mph and the defendant's speed was estimated at not less than 73 mph. When interviewed he said he had drunk three glasses of wine. He said he had fallen asleep. The speed limit was 70 mph. The victim was a very close friend of the defendant. They were almost inseparable. The defendant suffered very serious injuries in the accident. He was 40 and had an excess alcohol conviction in 1990. In 1997 he had a conviction for due care for which he was fined £60. He expressed remorse and became extremely morose. He was sentenced to 12 months and had already been approved for the tagging regime. Held. The proper inference to be drawn is that the accident and the death resulted in a substantial part from the alcohol consumed. Taking into account the mitigation, the plea and it was a reference **30 months** substituted.

Att-Gen's Ref. (No 56 of 2002) 2003 1 Cr App R (S) 476. The defendant pleaded guilty to two counts of causing death by careless driving when over the prescribed limit. At about 2.30am just before junction 6 of the M1 the defendant drove into the rear of a Mercedes estate. The Mercedes spun off into fencing causing the deaths of the front seat and rear offside passengers. The rear nearside passenger was severely injured and will never walk again; she had been studying to become a personal fitness trainer. The defendant was unable able to explain what had happened but when he was arrested responded: "I don't know. I may have fallen asleep". When interviewed he admitted he had drunk three bottles of strong stout, although analysis revealed more. His blood alcohol level was at least 69mg per 100mls of blood. (= 44 μg in breath) A back calcu-lation put this within the range 89 to 119mg (=39–52 μg in breath) at the time of the accident. A reconstruction concluded that the Mercedes was travelling at about 65 mph and the defendant's car at about 80 mph at the time of collision. The defendant was 37 and not just a man with no previous convictions but of positive good character. He was in responsible employment and had shown genuine remorse. Immediately after the accident he remained at the scene and did what he could to contact the emergency services. He had been married for just two weeks. Held. The likely explanation was that the defendant had fallen asleep, the likelihood of which was increased by driving late at night with excess alcohol. Those who fall asleep represent an enormous danger to others. Falling asleep is normally the end product of a process of feeling tired and people do have the opportunity to stop and avoid an accident. Where more than one death is caused and where permanent serious injury is added to the factor of two deaths, those are matters that must be give some weight in the sentencing process. The proper sentence would be **4–5 years,** but as it was a reference, **3¹/₂ years** not 2.

See also **DEATH BY DANGEROUS DRIVING** *– Asleep, falling*

Defendant aged 16–17

47.10   Att-Gen's Ref. No 10 of 1997 1998 1 Cr App R (S) 147. LCJ. See **47.13**

R v Brown 2001 1 Cr App R (S) 195. The defendant pleaded guilty to causing death by driving without due care after having consumed alcohol. The defendant who was then 17 drove his mother's car ten days after he had passed his test. He went to a party and drank 2¹/₂ pints of lager. Under some pressure he agreed to drive three of his friend's home. He lost control of the car at a bend and it hit a tree. One passenger died. He ran to a house for help and called the emergency services. His breath reading was 88 μg. He said he had never received any skid training. He was in his sixth form and doing extremely well. He was expecting to go to university. He was of positive good charac-ter and had excellent references. The death had a devastating effect on him. The risk of re-offending was assessed as small. Held. The accident was the result of inexperience rather than alcohol. The judge had a difficult task. **1 year** YOI not 2.

Defendant aged 18–20

47.11   *R v Chippendale* 1998 1 Cr App R (S) 192. The defendant changed his plea to guilty to causing death by driving without due care when unfit through drink. The defendant went to a party intending to leave his car at a friend's house overnight. He then visited a pub, drank more alcohol and went back to the party. Just before 2am he offered to drive two men home. A third declined and advised the other two to get out of the car, as the defendant was not fit to drive. The car hit a brick wall and a passenger died and the defendant and the other man were slightly injured. The defendant said he swerved to avoid an animal but the other survivor didn't see anything. The speed limit was 30 mph and an expert estimated that the car was travelling at least 50 mph and the brakes had been applied very severely causing the wheels to lock. The blood alcohol reading was 68 μg in breath. Backtracking made the reading at the time of the accident 80 *μ*g. The defendant was then 18 and of good character. He showed remorse, admitted the offence to the police and suffered grave emotional trauma from losing a personal friend. Held. There is understandably grave concern about young men who have too much to drink and drive in the face of warnings and then kill. Personal elements of mitigation such as acute guilt feelings are not matters that should sound greatly in determining the proper sentence. The offence was aggravated by the extent he was over the limit, the excessive speed and failure to heed the warning given. **4 years** YOI was not excessive.

R v McNiff 2001 2 Cr App R (S) 275. The defendant then 18 pleaded guilty to causing death by careless driving when over the limit. The defendant spent the day drinking with friends. In the early morning he and a friend drove about 2 miles to a garage to buy cigarettes. On his way back he missed his turning and took the next one. He lost control of the car on a bend. The car hit a tree and the friend was killed. He did his best to help him. His blood reading was 51. When interviewed he admitted full responsibility and said he was driving too fast. He was of exemplary character with numerous testimonials. He was deputy head of his school and head boy at his college. The risk of re-offending was described as negligible. He showed deep regret. Held. If a person of older years had pleaded guilty 5 years would have been appropriate. Taking into account his age **3 years 9 months** was not manifestly excessive.

Defendant distraught etc/What purpose does a prison sentence serve?

47.12   *Att-Gen's Ref. No 36 of 1994* 1995 16 Cr App R (S) 723 at 726. LCJ. The sentencing judge said that human life could not be brought back and he did not think any useful purpose would be served by sending the defendant to prison. Held. We cannot agree with that. There are many cases, unhappily, where offences of this kind are committed by persons of otherwise good character, who will be distraught by what has happened and who will have the fact that they have killed someone with them for the rest of their lives. But to say that no useful purpose is served by sending offenders to prison is to ignore the deterrent factor and the need to establish, to the knowledge of the public (and the driving public in particular), that where one drives with a substantial amount of drink, and one drives in such a way as to kill someone, then a sentence of imprisonment will almost always be required.

Defendant seriously injured

47.13   *Att-Gen's Ref. No 10 of 1997* 1998 1 Cr App R (S) 147. LCJ. The defendant pleaded guilty to causing death by careless driving when unfit through drink and aggravated vehicle-taking. A mother left her car on her driveway with a 'crook lock' attached and two boxes of beer in the boot. She went to Scotland with her husband and youngest son leaving her other son and a cousin at the house. Next day there were numerous visitors to the house and there was talk of taking the car. The defendant then 17 expressed reluctance to be involved. The radio and the beer were taken and the defendant and two others went to nearby woods and drank the beer. They came back and appeared drunk. The defendant drove the car with the other two at a speed judged to be between 60 and 70 mph. The defendant lost control at a moderate left hand bend and the car left the road with no noise of skidding or brakes screeching. The car hit a tree and one passenger was killed. The car's speed near the accident was estimated to be between 70 and 90 mph. The speed limit was 60 mph but the greatest speed the bend could be negotiated was 50 mph. The road was dry. The defendant was unconscious for six days. The injury to his frontal lobe of the brain affected his personality. The defendant had a 'dis-social personality disorder.' One doctor said it was exacerbated by the accident and another said it was caused by it. He needed 12 weeks' observation and treatment in a specialist hospital. The judge sentenced him to probation and he was admitted to the hospital. It was not a success. The defendant was of good character. Held. The judge was correct to say 3 years was appropriate. We think **3–4 years** if contested and **2–3 years** if not. The 2 years since the offence, the injury, his plea and character are significant factors. **12 months** YOI substituted.

Disqualification, for how long?

47.14   *Att-Gen's Ref. No 11 of 1998* 1999 1 Cr App R (S) 145. The defendant pleaded guilty at the first opportunity to two counts of causing death by careless driving when over the limit. The defendant then 21 attended a 21st birthday party where alcohol was freely available. He left in the early hours of the morning and drove in his mother's car on an unfamiliar unlit road. Five other young people were in the car, which was designed to carry five people. He drove over a slight brow of a hill and after about 100 metres into a bend for which there was no warning. The car left the road and hit a tree. The defendant was probably the only person wearing a seat belt. Two passengers were thrown from the car and died instantly. One was the defendant's best friend. Another passenger was in hospital for 7 months with a fractured pelvis and severe head injuries. Two other passengers suffered fractured arms. He unsuccessfully tried to help one of those who had died. Two hours after the accident his alcohol reading was 93 μg. He speed as he entered the bend was estimated to be between 40 and 50 mph. He told police he had intended to stay the night at the party. He was a university student of good character. He had many very impressive references. He showed deep, long-lasting remorse. The fathers of one of those killed and one of those injured said the tragedy would only be exacerbated if imprisonment were imposed. Held. We'd expect 4 years. Taking into account it was a reference, his chance of resuming university in the autumn of next year and he had been at liberty 30 months not 18 months suspended. **5 years'** disqualification not 2.

R v Brown 2004 2 Cr App R (S) 224. The defendant was convicted of causing death by careless driving when under the influence of drink. He was driving a car with four passengers in the Old Kent Road at 5.00 am. A witness said the car, going at a little more than average speed, came towards him at a twisted angle while he was on the pavement and then swung round and collided with a tree at the side of the road. One passenger died shortly afterwards. Another suffered a broken neck, a fractured jaw and cracked ribs and was unconscious in intensive care for five weeks, although she made a full recovery. Some four hours later the defendant had 83 mg of alcohol per 100 ml of blood and also traces of cannabis in his blood. The alcohol level represented one and a half times over the legal limit at the time of the accident. The defendant had been out of trouble for twelve years. He stayed at the scene, admitted he had been driving, and showed remorse. Held. The aggravating features were the consumption of alcohol and cannabis, the poor condition of the car tyres and the fact that other passengers were injured. The correct starting point for this offence is 4 to 5 years. We have had regard in particular to the fact that the jury acquitted him of causing death by dangerous driving. The proper sentence is 4 years not 6 with **5 years** disqualification not 8.

Failing to provide a specimen, after – General principles

47.15   *Att-Gen's Ref. No 21 of 2000* 2001 1 Cr App R (S) 173. The defendant pleaded guilty to causing death by careless driving and failing to provide a specimen. Held. Where the defendant has refused to provide a specimen the gravity lies in part in the fact the defendant has avoided the appropriate sentence for driving with excess alcohol. If the defendant asks to be sentenced on the basis he has drunk only limited alcohol the court should treat that with caution and circumspection. The onus of establishing that lies on the defendant. The court is likely to require him to give evidence. In the absence of evidence a court is able to draw adverse inferences about the amount of alcohol consumed. The ordinary inference will be he has refused because he knows he has consumed alcohol well in excess of the limit. Normally a substantial custodial sentence will be required.

R v Pinchess 2001 2 Cr App R (S) 391. Held. Courts should not examine whether the defendant was below the limit or unaffected by the drinking. They should approach the case as if there had been proven excess alcohol. (The court does not appear to have been referred *to Att-Gen's Ref. No 21 of 2000* 2001 1 Cr App R (S) 173.)

Failing to provide a specimen, after – Cases

47.16   *Att-Gen's Ref. No 21 of 2000* 2001 1 Cr App R (S) 173. The defendant pleaded guilty to causing death by careless driving and failing to provide a specimen. Shortly before 1am the defendant drove into the back of a heavy goods vehicle. His passenger died. The defendant was unable to provide a specimen when he was in the ambulance. At the hospital he initially consented to giving a blood test and then later refused. He told the doctor he had drunk $2^1/_2$ pints. The HGV's speed was estimated at 43 mph and the defendant's speed was estimated at not less than 73 mph. When interviewed he said he had drunk three glasses of wine. He said he had fallen asleep. The speed limit was 70 mph. The victim was a very close friend of the defendant. They were almost insep-arable. The defendant suffered very serious injuries in the accident. He was 40 and had an excess alcohol conviction in 1990. In 1997 he had a conviction for due care for which he was fined £60. He expressed remorse and became extremely morose. He was sentenced to 12 months and had already been approved for the tagging regime. Held. The proper inference to be drawn is that the accident and the death resulted in a substantial part from the alcohol consumed. Taking into account the mitigation, the plea and it was a reference **30 months** substituted.

R v Pinchess 2001 2 Cr App R (S) 391. The defendant was convicted of causing death by careless driving and refusing to provide a specimen. The defendant drove his girl-friend on an unlit road when there was patchy fog. She was 16 and 7 months pregnant with his child. Because of his speed he failed to negotiate a 90° bend with no chevron markings. The car left the road and hit a grass bank. He helped his girlfriend and they walked over a mile to a telephone box to call an ambulance. Both went to hospital by ambulance and the girlfriend started to suffer epileptic fits. On arrival she had a Caesarean operation and her son was born suffering from severe injuries from oxygen starvation brought about by her fits. She had a fracture to her face, fractured ribs, inter-nal bleeding, a blood clot in her arm and ten stitches in her knee. The defendant gave a false name and said they had been abducted by two men who had crashed the car. He said he was not driving the car. He refused to give a blood test and offered urine, which was not accepted by police. He said he had bought four cans of beer and had drunk only one. However, there were no empty cans in the car. He was abusive and unco-operative with the police. Eleven days later the boy died. When interviewed he said he was driv-ing at 50 mph and shortly before the accident the girlfriend had kissed him. He turned to look and when he looked at the road again he was in a fog bank. Next he saw the bend. He admitted the car had failed its MOT. There were defective tyres and brakes but they were not the cause of the accident. He had convictions for assault, dishonesty and driving offences including drink/drive and driving whilst disqualified. He showed distress for the loss of his child and the mother's injuries. He suffered from Reiters syndrome which was very akin to arthritis. In a few years time he would be in a wheel chair. The accident caused the break up with the girlfriend. He had since married another girl and they have now a 2-year-old daughter. Held. We approach this case on the basis alcohol played a part. The aggravating factors were his behaviour at hospital, his denial of being the driver, the girlfriend's injuries and trauma, his record and the condition of the car. His disability was an important factor with the unlikelihood of his being able to drive on his release. There was also the case delay and his change of attitude. Seven years was not outside the appropriate bracket after a trial. However, **5 years** was appropriate taking into account the particular features.

R v Fleming 2005 1 Cr App R (S) 580. The defendant pleaded guilty to causing death by careless driving. He was driving along a main road at four o'clock in the morning and went to turn right. He turned across the path of a motorcycle and when his passenger shouted 'Stop' he stopped in the path of the motorcycle. The driver was killed. The defendant stayed briefly at the scene and then walked home. An ambulance had by then arrived. He was traced to his home and arrested. He obstructed the drink/drive enquiry at every stage. The aggravating features were described as being that he had no driving licence or insurance policy; his behaviour in leaving the scene and being obstructive; a previous conviction for dangerous driving and a blood alcohol offence and repeated convictions for being drunk and disorderly. There was a powerful impact statement from the victim's wife. Held. The sentence was longer than it needed to have been, particularly having regard to the actual driving. **4 years** not 5.

Victim dies after defendant dealt with for careless driving

See **DEATH BY DANGEROUS DRIVING, CAUSING** – *Victim dies after defendant dealt with for dangerous driving*

Victims, the views of the relatives of the

See **DEATH BY DANGEROUS DRIVING, CAUSING** – *Victims, the views of the relatives of the*

48   DEATH BY DANGEROUS DRIVING, CAUSING

48.1   Road Traffic Act 1988 s 1

Indictable only. Maximum sentence 14[17] years. For offences committed before 27/2/04 the maximum remains 10 years.

The Court of Appeal considered that Parliament increased the penalty to deal with the worst type of cases[18]. Therefore cases with the most serious culpability when the sentencing powers were restricted to 10 years can no longer be a guide to the appropriate penalty. However there is no uplift on the

Depriving defendant of vehicle used There is power to deprive the defendant of the vehicle used[19] for the purposes of committing the offence.

Disqualification Minimum disqualification 2 years[20]. The defendant must be disqualified till he/she passes an extended driving test[21]. Specified offence enabling defendant aged 14–17 to be detained[22].

Funeral expenses The Court may make this compensation order see **MANSLAUGHTER –** *Funeral expenses of the deceased*

Imprisonment for public protection For offences committed on or after 4/4/05 when there is a significant risk to members of the public of serious harm etc. there is a mandatory duty to pass a sentence of imprisonment for public protection[23]. For offenders under 18 the duty is to pass detention for public protection or an extended sentence[24].

Points 3–11 penalty points.

17 Criminal Justice Act 2003 S 285(3)
18 R v Gray 2005 Unreported 29/4/05
19 Powers of Criminal Courts (Sentencing) Act 2000 s 143(6) & (7)
20 Road Traffic Offenders Act 1988 S 34(1) & (4) & Sch. 2
21 Road Traffic Offenders Act 1988 s 36(2)(b)
22 Powers of Criminal Courts (Sentencing) Act 2000 s 91(2)(a)
23 Criminal Justice Act 2003 s 224–226
24 Criminal Justice Act 2003 s 226 and 228

Sexual Offences Prevention Order There is a discretionary power to make this order when it is necessary to protect the public etc[25].

See also MANSLAUGHTER – *Vehicle, by*

Crown Court statistics – England and Wales – Males 21+
48.2

Year	Plea	Total Numbers sentenced	Type of sentence %					Average length of custody (months)
			Discharge	Fine	Community sentence	Suspended sentence	Custody	
2002	Guilty	120	–	2	4	8	87	42.1
	Not guilty	41	–	5	2	5	88	33.1
2003	Guilty	126	1	1	–	7	91	46.6
	Not guilty	41	–	–	–	2	98	33.8

For details and explanations about the statistics in the book see page vii.

Guideline case and Guideline remarks

48.3   *R v Cooksley* 2004 1 Cr App R (S) 1. LCJ The Court was told that every year, around 3,500 people are killed on Britain's roads and 40,000 are seriously injured. In total, there are over 300,000 road casualties, in nearly 240,000 accidents, and about 15 times that number of non-injury incidents. The direct cost of road accidents involving deaths or injuries is thought to be in the region of £3 billion a year.

The Approach needed

It is important for the courts to drive home the message as to the dangers that can result from dangerous driving on the road. It has to be appreciated by drivers the gravity of the consequences which can flow from their not maintaining proper standards of driving. Motor vehicles can be lethal if they are not driven properly and this being so, drivers must know that if as a result of their driving dangerously a person is killed, no matter what the mitigating circumstances, normally only a **custodial sentence** will be imposed. This is because of the need to deter other drivers from driving in a dangerous manner and because of the gravity of the offence.

R v Boswell 1984 6 Cr. App R 257 is out of date. Causing death is invariably a very serious crime. Culpability must be the dominant factor when assessing as precisely as possible just where in the level of serious crimes the particular offence comes.

The Aggravating and Mitigating factors

Our list should not be regarded as an exhaustive statement of the factors. In addition it is important to appreciate that the significance of the factors can differ. There can be cases with three or more aggravating factors, which are not as serious as a case providing a bad example of one factor.

Aggravating factors

Highly culpable standard of driving at time of offence

(a)   The consumption of drugs (including legal medication known to cause drowsiness) or of alcohol, ranging from a couple of drinks to a "motorised pub crawl"

(b)   Greatly excessive speed; racing; competitive driving against another vehicle; "showing off"

(c)   Disregard of warnings from fellow passengers

25 Sexual Offences Act 2003 s 104 & Sch. 5

(d) A prolonged, persistent and deliberate course of very bad driving

(e) Aggressive driving (such as driving much too close to the vehicle in front, persistent inappropriate attempts to overtake, or cutting in after overtaking)

(f) Driving while the driver's attention is avoidably distracted, e.g. by reading or by use of a mobile phone (especially if hand-held)

(g) Driving when knowingly suffering from a medical condition which significantly impairs the offender's driving skills

(h) Driving when knowingly deprived of adequate sleep or rest. In *Att-Gen's Ref. No 26 of 1999* 2001 Cr App R (S) 394, it was said that falling asleep at the wheel usually involves a period during which a driver is conscious of drowsiness and difficulty in keeping his or her eyes open and the proper course for a driver in such a position to adopt is to stop driving and rest

(i) Driving a poorly maintained or dangerously loaded vehicle, especially where this has been motivated by commercial concerns.

Driving habitually below acceptable standard

(j) Other offences committed at the same time, such as driving without ever having held a licence; driving while disqualified; driving without insurance; driving while a learner without supervision; taking a vehicle without consent; driving a stolen vehicle

(k) Previous convictions for motoring offences, particularly offences which involve bad driving or the consumption of excessive alcohol before driving.

Outcome of offence

(l) More than one person killed as a result of the offence (especially if the offender knowingly put more than one person at risk or the occurrence of multiple deaths was foreseeable)

(m) Serious injury to one or more victims, in addition to the death(s).

Irresponsible behaviour at time of offence

(n) Behaviour at the time of the offence, such as failing to stop, falsely claiming that one of the victims was responsible for the crash, or trying to throw the victim off the bonnet of the car by swerving in order to escape

(o) Causing death in the course of dangerous driving in an attempt to avoid detection or apprehension

(p) Offence committed while the offender was on bail.

The Mitigating factors

These are:

(a) a good driving record;

(b) the absence of previous convictions;

(c) a timely plea of guilty;

(d) genuine shock or remorse (which may be greater if the victim is either a close relation or a friend);

(e) the offender's age (but only in cases where lack of driving experience has contributed to the commission of the offence), and

the fact that the offender has also been seriously injured as a result of the accident caused by the dangerous driving.'

The Length of sentence

We have set out four *starting points*; no aggravating circumstances 12 to 18 months;

intermediate culpability two to three years; higher culpability five or five years and most serious culpability six years or over. We make clear that *starting points* only indicate where a person sentencing should start from when seeking to determine what should be the appropriate sentence. There is, however, a danger in relation to the higher *starting points* of the sentencer, if he is not careful, of double accounting. The sentencer must be careful not to use the same aggravating factors to place the sentence in a higher category and then add to it because of the very same aggravating features.

No aggravating circumstances

As in the case of sentencing for any offence a sentence of imprisonment should only be imposed if necessary and then for no longer than necessary. In these cases an immediate custodial sentence will generally be necessary. The *starting point* for causing death by dangerous driving should be a short custodial sentence of perhaps **12 to 18 months**. That is the approach that should be adopted even when there is a plea of guilty, though the plea of guilty will justify the appropriate reduction in the length of sentence. This is in relation to an adult offender. We regard as an example of this approach the case of *R v Brown* 2002 1 Cr App R (S) 504. In Brown the defendant momentarily fell asleep while driving his van in daylight, drifted across the road and collided head on with a car travelling in the opposite direction, killing a passenger in it. The mitigating factors were guilty plea, previous good character with an impeccable driving record and the fact that the offender displayed genuine shock and remorse. In addition, the effect on the appellant's life and family was devastating. This Court reduced the sentence to **9 months' imprisonment**.

Brown makes it clear that in order to avoid a custodial sentence there have to be exceptional mitigating features. As exceptional features, we refer to the case of *R v Jenkins* 2001 2 Cr App R (S) 265. In that case the defendant, was 16 years old and with learning difficulties. He lost control of a motorcycle because of its dangerous condition and his pillion passenger, who was his best friend, was killed. He pleaded guilty because it would have been obvious to a competent and careful driver that the condition of his vehicle was dangerous. He was sentenced to detention and a training order for 12 months but the Court of Appeal, while agreeing that the custodial sentence was warranted, 'as a justifiable statement of society's abhorrence of dangerous driving and the use of dangerous vehicles on a public road', took into account that the defendant was not competent to maintain the bike and the fact that his mental condition prevented him from fully appreciating its dangerous condition. In the circumstances there having been delay in the case coming to trial, a **2-year supervision order** was substituted. There obviously can be other exceptional situations and we consider it preferable not to try and anticipate what those situations will be. It is sufficient to emphasize that they have to be exceptional.

Intermediate culpability

An offence involving a momentary dangerous error of judgment or a short period of bad driving may be aggravated by a habitually unacceptable standard of driving on the part of the offender (factors (j) or (k) by the death of more than one victim or serious injury to other victims (factors (l) and (m) or by the offender's irresponsible behaviour at the time of the offence (factors (n) to (p). The presence of one or more of these features could indicate a sentence within the higher range, **2 to 3 years**.

We foresee circumstances, particularly where there is more than one of the factors present referred to above, where **5 years** could be appropriate: if, for example, there is more than one victim. Unfortunately, because of the range of the variety of facts it is not possible to provide more precise guidelines.

In *R v Braid* 2002 2 Cr. App R (S) 509, the offender during daylight and in good conditions overtook a lorry while approaching a blind bend and collided head on with an approaching car. A passenger in the car was killed and, in addition, the driver of the other vehicle suffered injuries which would permanently affect his mobility. This is therefore a case where factor (m) applied and culpability was aggravated by serious injury to another victim in addition to the death of the deceased. The offender pleaded guilty. He was 20 years of age and of good character. The sentencing judge noted he had driven very badly over a short distance. This Court endorsed the view of the sentencing judge that personal circumstances did not weigh heavily in the balance in these cases. The public were entitled to require the courts to reflect the loss of life and to demonstrate that dangerous driving was a serious social evil which, if death results, would lead to a substantial custodial sentence. The appellant should have appreciated that he was approaching a blind corner and that he could not see far enough to ensure that he could pass the articulated lorry safely. In reducing the sentence to 18 months' detention in a young offender's institution, the court was, as it said, reflecting the many mitigating features. However, it also said that the case did not display any of the aggravating features. This would not be true in relation to the present guidelines and if the guidelines had been in force, we would not have expected the Court to interfere with the period of **two years' detention** imposed by the trial judge.

Higher culpability

In relation to contested offences of higher culpability (for example, by the presence of one or two of the factors (a) to (i)) the appropriate starting point would **four to five years**. The exact level of sentence would be determined by the dangerousness of the driving and by the presence or absence of other aggravating or mitigating factors. There will be cases which will involve sentences **higher than five years** because they are bad examples and cases, particularly where there is a plea, where the sentence will be less than four years where there are significant mitigating factors.

The approach that we have just indicated is consistent with the approach of this Court in *Att-Gen's Ref. No 58 of 2000* 2001 2 Cr App R (S) 102; where there was a sustained course of dangerous driving at excessive speeds, 50 mph in a 30 mph area. The offender had also consumed alcohol, although it was unclear whether this contributed to the offence. While driving on the wrong side of the road the offender collided head on with a motorcyclist who was killed. In addition a seven-year-old pillion passenger suffered leg injuries. The offender was an unqualified driver and he had left the scene of the crash immediately although he gave himself up to the police on the following day. On a guilty plea, this Court increased the sentence to $3^{1}/_{2}$ years. That sentence included an allowance for double jeopardy; but for that allowance the sentence would have been **not less than four years**.

The most serious culpability

Custodial sentences of **six years** should be reserved for cases involving an extremely high level of culpability on the offender's part. This might be indicated by the presence of three or more of aggravating factors (a) to (i), although an exceptionally bad example of a single aggravating feature could be sufficient to place an offence in this category. A sentence close to the maximum would be appropriate in a case displaying a large number of these features, or where there were other aggravating factors.

An example is the case of *R v Corkhill* 2002 2 Cr App R (S) 60, where an offender was sentenced to seven years' detention. The Court of Appeal agreed this was a bad case but described it as 'not among the very worse' and reduced the sentence to five years. Bearing in mind that Corkhill was 19 years old and pleaded guilty, we see it as consistent with our starting point.

As an example of the most serious case justifying a total custodial sentence of the maximum of 10 years, we refer to *R v Noble* 2003 1 Cr App R (S) 312. The Court of Appeal made it clear that the maximum sentence was justified not simply by the number of deaths but by the range of other aggravating factors, including driving at an excessive speed while about 2¹/₂ times over the alcohol limit and then seeking to avoid responsibility by claiming one of the victims had been driving.

Att-Gen's Ref. Nos. 24 and 45 of 1994 1995 16 Cr App R (S) 583 at 586. LCJ. This court is concerned primarily with the criminality of the person who has caused the death. The fact that the death is, of itself, a factor in contributing to the length of sentence which should be passed. But essentially we have to look at the cases in the light of the offender's criminality. The length of sentence will very much depend upon the aggravating and mitigating circumstances in the particular case, the extent of the carelessness or dangerousness, and the amount that the offender is over the limit in a case involving excess alcohol. Where an offender is not just over the limit, not even substantially over the limit, but 2¹/₂ to 3 times over the limit, the sentence which the court must pass is clearly a substantial one. It is an insufficient excuse for failing to impose a sufficiently long sentence to look predominantly at the mitigating features and the remorse of the offender.

Att-Gen's Ref. No 76 of 2002 2003 1 Cr App R (S) 519. The public demand that the seriousness of causing death by dangerous driving should be acknowledged. But, dangerous driving varies in its seriousness. We do not accept that in virtually every case of dangerous driving where death results a prison sentence must follow. Often it will follow. In every case there are competing considerations.

R v Gray 2005 Unreported 29/4/05. The Criminal Justice Act 2003 increase in penalty was to deal with the few cases where the 10 year maximum was thought inadequate. It cannot be right that the stating point for all offences should go up proportionately with the increase in new penalty.

Alcohol, driving under the influence – Guideline case

48.4 *R v Cooksley* 2004 1 Cr App R (S) 1. In relation to contested offences of higher culpability (for example, by the presence of one or two of the factors (a) to (i)) the appropriate starting point would **four to five years**. The exact level of sentence would be determined by the dangerousness of the driving and by the presence or absence of other aggravating or mitigating factors. There will be cases which will involve sentences **higher than 5 years** because they are bad examples and cases, particularly where there is a plea, where the sentence will be less than four years where there are significant mitigating factors.

(a) The consumption of drugs (including legal medication known to cause drowsiness) or of alcohol, ranging from a couple of drinks to a "motorised pub crawl"; is the first of the higher culpability list of factors.

The list should not be regarded as an exhaustive statement of the factors. In addition it is important to appreciate that the significance of the factors can differ. There can be cases with three or more aggravating factors, which are not as serious as a case providing a bad example of one factor. For more details see *Guideline case and Guideline remarks.*

Alcohol, driving under the influence – 36 to 70 µg in breath or equivalent

48.5 *Att-Gen's Ref. No 16 of 1998* 1999 1 Cr App R (S) 149. The defendant was convicted of two counts of causing death by dangerous driving. When 22 he went to a pub with two close friends and he drove away with them. None of them were wearing a seat belt. He overtook vehicles on a dual carriageway well in excess of 70 mph. He overtook another vehicle when the road narrowed to a single carriageway, which was potentially dangerous. He entered a roundabout at very close to 70 mph and lost control of the car, which hit a kerb and a crash barrier. Both his passengers were thrown from the car and died shortly after they had arrived in hospital. He left the scene in a state of shock. He gave a false name in hospital where he was treated for a broken shoulder, arm injuries and a head injury. The defendant pretended to the police that he was a passenger. At first he refused to supply a blood specimen but eventually did. By backtracking his reading was between 90 and 120mg at the time of the accident (equivalent to 39–52 μg). In interview he accepted he was driving at about 70 mph and said the brakes had failed. He had two convictions of no relevance and a clean licence. He had an overwhelming sense of grief and was having difficulty in coming to terms with his responsibility. He had become a virtual recluse and had sought counselling. The mother of one of his victims had written a moving letter saying she had forgiven him. The other mother had taken a very different position. He was sentenced to 240 hours' community service. The local press had described him as a murderer who had gone free. The offence was 18 months before and he had completed $^{1}/_{4}$ of his community service. Held. We would have expected **4$^{1}/_{2}$ years**. Taking into account it was a reference and the CSO he had completed **3$^{1}/_{2}$ years** instead.

R v James 2001 2 Cr App R (S) 153. The defendant was convicted of causing death by dangerous driving and driving whilst disqualified. After drinking in a pub with his two nephews he drove them away from the pub in his van. One of the nephews, the victim, sat on the lap of the other in the front passenger seat. None of the three was wearing a seat belt and the defendant was disqualified from driving. The van was seen by police being driven at speed and they gave chase. The van went through a red light and the police put their lights on. Shortly after the van still driving at speed veered across the road and hit an oncoming coach. The victim was thrown from the van and killed instantly. The other nephew was severely injured with head injuries. He was in intensive care for several days. The defendant was also injured. He had 123mg reading of alcohol in his blood, (equivalent to 54 g in his breath). He showed shock and remorse. He was 28 and had an appalling driving record. He had 10 convictions for disqualified driving and two for dangerous driving. One of them was on a motorway when he was trying to escape the police. He also had a conviction for reckless driving and drink/drive. Held. The **8 years** sentence was entirely proper. However, as the judge had considered the fact he was disqualified in considering the aggravating factors it was wrong to make the disqualified driving sentence consecutive. The sentences were made concurrent.

Att-Gen's Ref. No 3 of 2001 2002 2 Cr App R (S) 528. LCJ. The defendant pleaded guilty to two counts of causing death by dangerous driving. The defendant collected her son and then went to a pub and drank on her account three bottles of Special Brew. At 3.30pm when conditions were fine and the road was dry the defendant overtook a two lorries just before the road went from a dual carriageway to a single one. Although there was a gap between the two lorries she overtook both. She cut in quickly after the second to avoid an oncoming lorry. She was travelling at about 80 mph when the limit was 60 mph and hit the grass verge and the car went out of control. She hit two cyclists who were thrown into the air and died. Her car went down an embankment. Both families of the victims were devastated. Her blood reading was 109mg (equivalent to 47 μg of breath) She lacked remorse but depression might have masked that. After her sentence she did show remorse after receiving counselling. She had two speeding convictions. One of them was committed 5 weeks before the accident. Otherwise she was of good character with references. She was a single parent of her son now aged 8. Held. The appropriate sentence was **4–5 years**. Courts are very conscious of the impact of these offences on the relatives and friends of the victims. Courts should consider how bad the driving was and the quantity of alcohol consumed. The allowance made for a reference is about a year. Because of the son and the remorse 3 years not increased.

R v O'Rourke 2005 1 Cr App R (S) 242. The defendant pleaded guilty to causing death by dangerous driving. The defendant, having drunk at least three and a half pints of lager, was driving his 600cc motorcycle with his girlfriend as pillion passenger. The motorbike had worn front and rear brake pads and he knew this. The road had a speed limit of 60 mph. He overtook other vehicles at speeds between 80–100 mph, weaving and out of the traffic. Trying to overtake a car he clipped it with such force that the car spun round and went across the carriageway. In the impact the defendant and his girlfriend were thrown from the motorbike. She died almost straight away from head injuries. He suffered injuries which resulted in the loss of his right testicle and a serious compound facture to his arm. He would have long term problems with stiffness in his right wrist. He had a blood alcohol level of 116 mg in 100ml, (the legal limit being 80). The defendant, 25, had one relevant previous conviction for driving with excess alcohol. He was on licence at the time of this offence for an offence of armed robbery. He did not have a licence or insurance. He had smoked cannabis the previous evening. He was very upset about his girlfriend. A pre-sentence report said that he did not believe he was culpable for his actions. A prison report said he had caused no problems and had no health problems. Held. The judge said that the offence was made worse because the defendant was on licence. He should not have increased the sentence for dangerous driving because the defendant was on licence for another offence while also ordering that the whole of the licence period should be served before this new sentence started. That would be double accounting. This offence fell within the highly culpable bracket. There were aggravating features of consumption of alcohol; excessive speed; aggressive driving and driving a vehicle he knew was poorly maintained. He had never had a licence and had no insurance. The proper sentence for the dangerous driving was **5¹/₂ years** not 6¹/₂. The judge was not wrong to order that the outstanding licence period should be served before this sentence started.

Old cases. *R v Wood* 1998 2 Cr App R (S) 234. (For a summary of this case see the first edition of this book.)

Alcohol, driving under the influence – 71 to 100 μg in breath or equivalent

48.6 *R v Noble* 2003 1 Cr App R (S) 313. The defendant was convicted of causing the death of 6 people with most of the aggravating features in *R v Boswell* 1984 79 Cr App R 277 (the then guideline case) present and he was 2¹/₂ times over the limit. **10 years** not 10 and 5 consecutive making 15. (From the tenor of the Judgement it can be inferred that had the new penalty of 14 years been available the court would have imposed it.) For case details see **48.34**

Alcohol, driving under the influence – Defendant avoids test

48.7 *Att-Gen's Ref. No 58 of 2000* 2001 2 Cr App R (S) 102. The defendant pleaded guilty to causing death by dangerous driving after having pleaded not guilty. The defendant left a pub and drove to his girlfriend's house where they had an argument. He left and was seen by two pedestrians to be driving at about 50 mph in a 30 mph area. The car moved from the kerb to the centre of the road so that oncoming vehicles had to move towards their kerb. The engine was heard revving and after going over a bridge it collided head on with a motorcyclist. The accident was only a short distance from the house. The rider died. The defendant left the scene but surrendered to the police 18 hours later. Held. The defendant had prevented the police from determining his alcohol level. Applying *Att-Gen's Ref. No 21 of 2000* 2001 1 Cr App R (S) 173 the court is able to draw an adverse inference about the amount of alcohol consumed. [For additional details see **48.41**]

Asleep, falling

48.8 *Att-Gen's Ref. No 26 of 1999* 2000 1 Cr App R (S) 394. The defendant pleaded guilty to causing death by dangerous driving. The victim's car broke down on the motorway. The victim lay underneath it and tried to repair it. It was on the hard shoulder. The police coned off the car. The defendant was in a van and was seen to weave about six times from the fast lane to the slow lane in such a way motorists were wary to overtake him. His van suddenly entered the hard shoulder and hit the victim's car. Witnesses did not see his brake lights illuminated. The van rolled over the victim and he was killed instantly. One of his passengers who was waiting outside the car was thrown into the road and suffered major fractures. The other two passengers who were also waiting outside the car also received fractures. One will not regain full use of his arm. The defendant climbed out of his overturned vehicle and scaled a high steel fence to escape. He received major injuries to his hand either in the accident or when climbing the fence. He went to a pub and asked his brother to collect him. When he went to hospital he was arrested and in interview he said he had had 4 hours sleep the previous night. Police found a broken whisky bottle in his van and he said he might have had a small amount. The minimum speed for the van was 45 mph and there was no evidence of braking. The basis of plea was that he must have fallen asleep and the dangerous driving was for no more than a mile. Further when he left the scene he was unaware there were serious injuries caused. The defendant was a professional driver with a very good driving record. He was sentenced to 100 hours' CSO and probation. He had completed the CSO. Held. It was not a momentary falling asleep. There would have been a period of drowsiness etc. 30 months would have been appropriate after a trial. Taking into account the late plea, his personal circumstances and his remorse **21 months** would have been appropriate. As it was a reference and the fact he had completed the CSO **9 months** instead.

R v Price 2001 2 Cr App R (S) 114. The defendant pleaded guilty to two counts of causing death by dangerous driving. The defendant an HGV driver was told by his GP not to drive and see a consultant urgently. He saw the consultant next day who said he had sleep apnoea syndrome. He discovered the defendant had fallen asleep at the wheel of his lorry a month previously and the lorry went into a field. He was again told not to drive. Four days later his lorry was seen on the M1 weaving from the inside lane to the hard shoulder without any indications being given. Forty miles further on and just before a service station he ran into stationary traffic in the slow lane. Two cars were crushed between his lorry and another lorry. The cars and his lorry caught fire and both the car drivers died. The defendant stayed at the scene. He said he planned to pull into the service station. He was of good character and full of remorse. The judge held a Newton hearing about whether he had ignored medical advice and said he could no longer give a full discount for the plea. Held. **4 years** not 5.

R v Brown 2002 1 Cr App R (S) 504. The defendant pleaded guilty to causing death by dangerous driving. The defendant installed satellite dishes throughout Wales and the West Country. One Sunday after working 2 weeks without a break he spent the day installing dishes. He had a short break for lunch. At 4.30pm he drove normally with his employer who fell asleep. He then fell asleep and as the road turned to the left his van went head on into an oncoming car. The passenger of the car was killed. The defendant had 3 broken ribs and other injuries. He was married with two young children and of good character. He was visibly distressed and had character witnesses. The judge said 'he was a sensible man and a sensible competent driver. He had dozed off monetarily.' Held. This was not a case where sleep was fought off over a protracted period. There were no *R v Boswell* (the then guideline case) aggravating features. **9 months** not 18.

R v Hart 2002 Times and Daily Telegraph news 12/1/02. High Court Judge at Crown Court. The defendant was convicted of 10 counts of causing death by dangerous driving. The defendant chatted on the telephone to a person he had contacted through the Internet for 6 (or 5 in the other report) hours until 3am. He set off on a 147 (or 154 in the other report) mile journey and fell asleep. His Land Rover, which was towing a 2 tonne load drifted off the M62. It ran alongside it until it fell into a railway cutting containing the East Coast Main line. An express train ran into it and drove on for another 400 yards before crashing into an oncoming coal freight train. Ten men were killed and 94 casualties. The defendant was 37. Judge's remarks. Every driver and I think I should include myself, has been in or very nearly in that position. Most acknowledge it by taking a break, taking a sleep or handing over to someone else if they can. A driver who presses on takes a grave risk. You chose not to have any sleep in the previous 24 hours. Choosing to drive after plenty of warnings was an aggravating feature. An accident was almost inevitable. There is very little to choose between you and a drink driver. Because of your arrogance in setting off on a long journey without sleep, you caused the worst driving-related accident in the UK in recent history. I accept you are a hard working and decent family man. **5 years** and 5 years' disqualification. [Treat news reports with care. Details of some of the facts can be found in the transcript of defendant's appeal against conviction, *R v Hart* 2003 EWCA Crim 1268].

R v France 2003.1 Cr App R (S) 108. Held. The authorities show in a case where a driver of good character falls asleep due to conventional tiredness and causes one death a sentence of around **21 months to 2 years** is likely on a plea. After a trial that sentence is likely to be in the bracket of **2¹/₂ to 3 years**. Where more than one death is caused, that fact must be reflected and sentences in such cases inevitably increase to a bracket of **2–4 years** on a plea. This period may go higher in cases where the conduct of the driver is particularly bad or the circumstances particularly horrific. Where more than one death is caused and other features are present, such as relevant previous convictions, a known medical condition, deliberate risk taking, or related tachograph offences a sentence of **4–5 years** is likely on a plea.

R v Coulridge 2003 2 Cr App R (S) 43. The defendant was convicted of two counts of causing death by dangerous driving. He had fallen asleep at the wheel of a lorry tractor unit on the M20. His vehicle drifted on to the hard shoulder where it collided with a van which had broken down. The tractor unit had then rebounded out of control and crossed all three lanes of the carriageway and broke through the central reservation. It collided head-on with a BMW containing S and his fiancé who died instantly. The BMW was carried under the front of the tractor unit and there was a further collision before the tractor unit burst into flames. The defendant was dragged to safety. He fell asleep either from a medical condition or from tiredness. Two doctors testified that they had told him that he should not drive as he had already caused a considerable number of minor road traffic accidents. He was 44 and was of effectively good character. Held. It was difficult to imagine a more serious case of its type; however the driving was not dangerous over a prolonged period of time or distance. There was only one aggravating factor. Because of the (then) maximum sentence **6 years** not 8 and disqualification for 8 years not life.

R v Emery 2004 2 Cr App R (S) 141. The defendant pleaded guilty on the first day of trial to causing death by dangerous driving. He was driving a flat bed articulated lorry during the morning rush hour on the M 6, where the traffic ahead near a junction had formed into a queue of slow moving or stationary vehicles. The defendant drove into the back of a van at the rear of the queue at approximately 55 mph with no attempt to slow down or to avoid the collision. The victim, the driver of a car struck by the van, died of multiple injuries. A number of other drivers were injured. The weather was clear and sunny and the road dry. The queue of vehicles was visible for not less than three quarters of a mile. The defendant pleaded guilty on the basis that he had fallen asleep at the wheel and that he ought to have recognised he was feeling tired before he fell asleep. He suffered from obstructive sleep apnoea (OSA) which meant that he had a tendency to fall asleep suddenly. Although he had been diagnosed with this some years before the accident incidental to other medical matters, it was his case that he did not know he had this condition until after the accident. He frequently complained to doctors of sleepiness up to 1996 when he had nasal surgery. He had nodded off at the wheel twice in 1995, although no accidents resulted. A medical report said that he had been treated for OSA and this had led to significant improvements in his alertness, and that it was highly likely he fell asleep at the wheel immediately before this accident. The report concluded that it was probably reasonable for the defendant to conclude that that he was fit to drive after the nasal surgery in 1996. A further medical report said it was possible that he was a poor perceiver of sleepiness. A psychiatric report said that the defendant believed following his surgery that he did not need any further medical assistance. A medical report requested by the Crown said that it was not unreasonable for the defendant to conclude after the 1996 surgery that he did not have a problem with his sleep that might have affected his driving. The defendant, aged 33, said he had been co operative with the police and he was remorseful. The court case had placed him and his family under an enormous strain. He had lost feelings of physical and mental well being as a result of which his marriage had broken up. He did not ever intend to drive a heavy goods vehicle again, so that his career had ended. He was of previous good character with a clean driving licence. A number of character references spoke of him in glowing terms. He had only been driving that day for a short time before the accident and there was no suggestion he had been driving badly or erratically. He was shocked and distraught at the scene but had helped others involved in the accident. He was in poor health suffering from diabetes, obesity and hypertension. As a result of the accident he suffered from severe depression and post-traumatic stress disorder. Held. It was important to note that the defendant pleaded guilty on the basis that he was aware he was feeling tired just before the accident occurred. The Judge made it clear that he sentenced on the basis that the defendant might not have been told he suffered from OSA. The Judge had been entitled to conclude that that the defendant was aware that his sleep pattern had worsened. He was aware of feeling sleepy although it was early in the day and he had only been driving for a short time. **2 years** imprisonment and 5 years disqualification was plainly the right sentence.

See also DEATH BY CARELESS DRIVING – *Asleep, falling* and DANGEROUS DRIVING – *Asleep, falling*

Consecutive or concurrent, should the other sentences be?

48.9   *R v James* 2001 2 Cr App R (S) 153. The defendant was convicted of causing death by dangerous driving and driving whilst disqualified. The defendant was disqualified from driving. Held. As the judge had considered the fact he was disqualified in considering the aggravating factors it was wrong to make the disqualified driving sentence consecutive. The sentences were made concurrent. (For further details see **48.5**)

R v Noble 2003 1 Cr App R (S) 313. It would be wrong in principle to impose consecutive sentences in respect of each death arising from a single piece of dangerous driving. For case details see **48.34**

See also *Multiple deaths*

Defendant aged 15–16

48.10   *R v Jenkins* 2001 2 Cr App R (S) 265. The defendant pleaded guilty to causing death by dangerous driving. The defendant then aged 16 drove his motorbike on a mountain road in Wales with his best friend on the back. He had been given the bike a month earlier and it was in very bad condition. He was wearing a helmet but the passenger was not. The throttle jammed open and was unable to take a bend. The bike hit a wall and the friend was thrown forward and hit his head on the wall. He died. The defendant said the throttle stuck and he was unable to brake. The collision was described as 'low impact'. The bike was found to be totally unroadworthy. The throttle cable was not rooted properly, and the brakes and wheels were also defective. The defendant was of good character. He had mild learning difficulties and showed the deepest remorse. He had become traumatised, very withdrawn, isolated and vulnerable. Held. The judge was faced with a very difficult sentencing problem. A custodial sentence was justified. His mental condition prevented him from fully appreciating the bike's dangerous condition. Taking into account the factors including the long delay before sentence, the fact he needs help and that he had served nearly 3 months **2 years' supervision** not 12 months detention. 3 years' disqualification not 4.

R v Foster 2003 1 Cr App R (S) 547. The defendant pleaded guilty to causing death by dangerous driving. He and his friends bought a car for £25, and when driving at about 11:20pm was involved in a minor collision with a lamppost. Thereafter the defendant drove onto an A road where he was followed by a marked police car. The defendant initially drove off on the wrong side of the road before driving through a red traffic light. The police car, in pursuit, switched on its sirens. The defendant made off to the best of his ability, increasing his speed to about 70 miles an hour in a 40 limit before turning into an estate where the limit was 30 miles an hour. The passengers in the car told the defendant to stop. However, the defendant mounted the pavement, collided with a garden wall and drove off at speed before crossing a junction with another main road which had four lanes. He entered another street at about twice the 30 miles an hour speed limit. He then failed to give way at another junction and he collided with another vehicle with considerable force. The appellant ran off but was quickly arrested. The front seat passenger in the other vehicle died. The driver sustained a broken arm. The rear passenger's leg was broken which required prolonged treatment. The front passenger in the defendant's vehicle sustained serious lacerations to his face and the other passengers sustained minor injuries. The chase had lasted for 1 minute and 24 seconds and the minimum impact speed was estimated to have been 52 miles an hour. The defendant claimed that he had panicked, since he had no driving experience, no licence and no insurance. The defendant was 16 at the time of the offence and there was substantial evidence of remorse. Held. Aggravating features included the grossly excessive and inappropriate speed, over a period of time, a moderately persistent course of bad driving, driving on the wrong side of the road for periods, jumping a series of junctions against the right of way, no insurance and insufficient age to even possess a provisional licence. The victim died because the defendant was trying to avoid being caught by the police. He had been told to stop by his own friends, albeit it at a late stage. This was a truly shocking act of driving, it was prolonged, and sooner or later a terrible accident was inevitable. The judge passed a sentence that fully expressed the aggravating and mitigating factors in this tragic case. **5 years** upheld.

R v Akhtar 2004 1 Cr App R (S) 463. The defendant pleaded guilty to causing death by dangerous driving. The defendant with friends took it in turns to drive a car around a park. The defendant had no driving experience. He drove onto the peripheral road around the park but lost control before colliding with and killing a 71-year-old man walking his dog. He lost control at 47 mph in a 30 mph restriction. The defendant and the others ran off. When interviewed he made no comment at first but later said that he had wanted to brake but by accident hit the accelerator instead of the brake. He said that he ran off without knowing what he had hit. He felt remorse and there was a very low risk of re-offending. He was 16 and of impeccable character. Held. He was driving at greatly excessive speed and showing off, without ever having held a licence, without insurance, whilst a learner without supervision and he failed to stop. **3 years' detention** upheld.

Old case. *R v Carroll* 1998 2 Cr App R (S) 349, (for summary see the first edition of this book).

Defendant aged 17–18

48.11   *R v Nijjer* 1999 2 Cr App R (S) 385. The defendant was convicted of two counts of causing death by dangerous driving. When 18 he left school in his Porsche at lunchtime with two friends. The car had been an 18th birthday present. It was drizzling, the road was damp and it was overcast. In a 30 mph area he overtook a car at 60 mph. He lost control of the car and it mounted the pavement and killed two elderly pedestrians. The defendant and his friends were uninjured and they remained at the scene. He was of good character and he and his family were devastated. The defendant said he never wanted to drive again. He was racked by guilt and self blame and suffered from depression. Held. This was a bad case. Bearing in mind his age, character and remorse **3 years** YOI not 4.

R v Adams 2002 1 Cr App R (S) 373. The defendant pleaded guilty to causing death by dangerous driving. When 17 and holding a provisional licence he took his mother's Ford Escort XR3i without permission. He was not insured. He picked up three friends of similar ages and started driving at a normal speed. The road was dry and the visibility good. He had had about 15 hours' driving experience. In a 40 mph area he accelerated to about 63 mph. A car in front was breaking to turn left into a petrol station. The defendant failed to pay sufficient attention and then swerved to the right to avoid the car, lost control of his car, went across the lane for on-coming traffic and crashed into a concrete bus shelter. The bus shelter collapsed on top of the car and killed the defendant's best friend who died of severe head injuries. Another friend suffered multiple injuries. His femur, left arm and pelvis were each broken in three places. One of his vertebrae was also fractured. His treatment will last 5 years. The car was in good mechanical order. At the time he had no convictions but since the offence he was made the subject of a combination order for assault and racially aggravated assault. He had completed the community service element faultlessly. The risk of re-offending was assessed as low. The judge said he was showing off and sentenced him to 4 years detention. Held. As it was a guilty plea the judge must have started too high. **3 years** YOI substituted.

R v Morton 2003 1 Cr App R (S) 196. The defendant was convicted of causing death by dangerous driving. At 9.30 pm, he then 18, drove his motorbike with his girlfriend on the back and approached a bend at about 60 mph in a 30 mph area. The weather was dry and the road conditions good. He lost control and hit a car. His girlfriend hit the windscreen of the car and died of multiple injuries. His breath test was negative. The motorcycle was examined and was found to be in good working order with no defects. Because of his age the defendant was restricted to bikes with 25kW output. He had removed the devices to restrict the output, which was now 56.2kW. This did not however contribute to the accident. He said he had taken the bend before at 60 mph with his passenger, but this time when he leant the bike would not move with him. He was now 20 with no convictions for motoring offences. He was grief stricken about the loss of his girlfriend with whom marriage was contemplated. His mother said for days after the accident he wouldn't talk or leave his room. He had changed from being outgoing and cheerful to withdrawn, unpredictable and clinically depressed of moderate severity. He made two serious suicide attempts. There was 16 months between interview and trial. Held. This was a tragic case. However we cannot say **2¹/₂ years** YOI was manifestly excessive. Because of his youth and his good motoring record prior to the accident 4 years disqualification not 7.

R v Rooney 2004 2Cr App (S) 135. The defendant aged 17 pleaded guilty to causing death by dangerous driving and driving while disqualified. Driving a car with four passengers in he had driven at excessive speed, navigated a roundabout in an anti-clockwise direction and lost control of the car as he attempted to take a corner. His passengers had screamed at him to slow down but he had ignored them. The car crashed into a tree. One of his passengers was killed. One had a leg amputated. Two were in a deep coma afterwards and were severely disabled as a consequence. The defendant also suffered injuries. He had previous convictions for violence and dishonesty and he had been disqualified from driving for a year which was still in force at the time of this offence. A pre-sentence report said he was deeply remorseful. A psychiatric report said he was over-sensitive with a fragile sense of self-esteem and that he had been greatly affected by his actions. This report also spoke of his remorse. Held. There were 3 highly culpable features of his driving serving to aggravate the offence: excessive speed; disregard of warnings and a deliberate course of very bad driving. The offence was also aggravated because the defendant was driving while disqualified and had not only caused the death of one person but had also effectively destroyed the lives of two or three others. In mitigation there was a timely plea of guilty and a full expression of remorse. The defendant was seriously injured in the accident. It is particularly important that he is only 17. It is vital to focus on the extent of culpability of the offender and bear in mind the mitigating features particularly his age. Alcohol or drugs would have rendered this driving even more culpable. 5 years detention not 7. **7 years** disqualification upheld.

R v Kelly 2005 1 Cr App R 183. The defendant pleaded guilty to two counts of causing death by dangerous driving. He was 17 and had just failed his driving test. He bought a car which did not have an MOT and although he was not insured he drove it unsupervised near his home. When his mother found out she put a lock on the gate so he could not take it on the road. Shortly afterwards the defendant and his friend S sawed through the lock and the defendant drove the car onto the road. S was his front seat passenger. They picked up another boy, 14-year-old B. The defendant drove past a stretch limo which contained off duty police officers, then drove alongside it for a time hooting his horn, then accelerated away down a hill. The speed limit was 60 mph. A witness said his speed was at least 100 mph. He drove into the bend at the bottom of the hill, and lost control of his car which collided with a tree. B died at the scene and S died of his injuries three days later. The defendant was only slightly injured. He was sentenced in the category of higher culpability because of the aggravating features of driving at excessive speed and showing off; driving badly deliberately behind and alongside the stretch limo, accelerating down the hill; not having a licence; driving without insurance; putting his passengers' lives at risk; the fact it was the first time he had driven any distance unsupervised and with passengers and he should not have allowed the two boys particularly B to enter the car. He had no previous convictions and there was positive evidence about his contribution to society. He had achieved six grade A passes at GCSE and was studying part time while working at a useful job in the post office, he felt genuine remorse, both of the boys who died had been his friends. Held. The aggravating features in this case were very serious and a period of **4 years** detention should stand. The period of disqualification was too long. Although there was a high level of culpability account had to be taken of the defendant's age and the likelihood that he had learnt his lesson and that after a few years he would not pose a risk to the public. So 5 years not 10.

Old cases *R v Hajicosti* 1998 2 Cr App R (S) 396 (For a summary of this case see the first edition of this book.)

Defendant not the driver of the car that killed the victim

48.12 *R v Padley* 2000 2 Cr App R (S) 201. The defendant was convicted of causing death by dangerous driving. The defendant then aged 20 drove into a petrol station and challenged another driver to take part in a race. The man ignored him. Later that evening he challenged another man Cragg the co-defendant to race. Cragg agreed. They raced on a single carriageway road, which was a 30ft wide with houses on each side. The road was damp. Cragg whilst being pursued by the defendant lost control of his car and it veered across the carriageway and demolished a brick wall. The car somersaulted back across the road and came to rest on its roof. A girl aged 19 or 20 who was sitting in the back seat of the car was thrown from the vehicle and killed. Another passenger suffered very severe head injuries. The defendant stopped his car and ran back to help. The defendant had three driving convictions. One was for speeding at 40 mph in a 30 mph area when he was on bail for the present offence. It was on the same road as where the accident occurred. The judge said that the defendant was responsible for initiating the whole tragic sequence of events. Held. Cragg received an appropriate sentence of 4 years taking into account his guilty plea. The starting point for the defendant must be 6 years. Despite the fact that the defendant was not the driver of the car which killed the victim, 5¹/₂ years YOI was appropriate.

Defendant's personal mitigation – Guideline remarks

48.13   *R v Braid* 2002 2 Cr App R (S) 509. The Judge said personal circumstances do not weigh heavily in the balance in cases of causing death by dangerous driving. Held. We agree with the Judge about the weight of personal circumstances. Those falling to be sentenced not infrequently have the highest personal credentials and so generate very real sympathy. The courts have to reflect the loss of a precious life and to demonstrate to all that dangerous driving is a very serious social evil, which if it causes death will almost inevitably lead to a substantial custodial sentence.

Disqualification, for how long? – Guideline case and guideline remarks

48.14   *R v Cooksley* 2004 1 Cr App R (S) 1. LCJ The offender being disqualified is a real punishment. The risk represented by the offender is reflected in the level of culpability which attaches to his driving so that matters relevant to fixing the length of the driving disqualification for the offence of causing death by dangerous driving will be much the same as those factors we have listed already. We have adopted four categories.

While those convicted of causing death by dangerous driving are likely to regard disqualification as an onerous part of the punishment for the offence, the main purpose of disqualification is forward-looking and preventative, rather than backward-looking and punitive. A driving ban is designed to protect road users in the future from an offender who, through his conduct on this occasion, and perhaps other occasions, has shown himself to be a real risk on the roads. In general, the risk represented by the offender is reflected in the level of culpability which attaches to his driving, so that matters relevant to fixing the length of the driving disqualification for the offence of causing death by dangerous driving will be much the same as those appearing in the list of aggravating factors for the offence itself. Shorter bans of **two years** or so will be appropriate where the offender had a good driving record before the offence and where the offence resulted from a momentary error of judgment. Longer bans, between **3 and 5 years**, will be appropriate where, having regard to the circumstances of the offence and the offender's record, it is clear that the offender tends to disregard the rules of the road, or to drive carelessly or inappropriately. Bans between **5 and 10 years** may be used where the offence itself, and the offender's record, show that he represents a real and continuing danger to other road users. Disqualification for **life** is a highly exceptional course, but may be appropriate in a case where the danger represented by the offender is an extreme and indefinite one. *R v Noble* 2003 1 Cr App R (S) 31 was described by the Court of Appeal as 'one of those rare cases' where disqualification for life was necessary in order to protect the public.'

We do not agree that the length of the ban should be tailored to take into account the anticipated date of early release of the offender. On the other hand we accept that to extend the ban for a substantial period after release can be counter-productive particularly if it is imposed on an offender who is obsessed with cars or who requires a driving licence to earn his or her living because it may tempt the offender to drive while disqualified.

The balancing of these conflicting considerations is very much the responsibility of the sentencer. In doing so the balancing exercise will require the sentencer to take into account the requirement which now exists that an order must be made that the offender is required to pass an extended driving test.

R v France 2003 1 Cr App R (S) 108. Periods of disqualification vary substantially. The bracket appears to that of **3–6 years**, but likely to be near the top of that bracket where more than one death has been caused but a bad previous driving record is absent.

Disqualification, for how long? – Defendant 16–17

48.15 *R v Kelly* 2005 1 Cr App R 183. The defendant pleaded guilty to two counts of causing death by dangerous driving. He was 17 and had just failed his driving test. He bought a car which did not have an MOT and although he was not insured he drove it unsupervised near his home. When his mother found out she put a lock on the gate so he could not take it on the road. Shortly afterwards the defendant and his friend S sawed through the lock and the defendant drove the car onto the road. S was his front seat passenger. They picked up another boy, 14-year-old B. The defendant drove past a stretch limo which contained off duty police officers, then drove alongside it for a time hooting his horn, then accelerated away down a hill. The speed limit was 60 mph. A witness said his speed was at least 100 mph. He drove into the bend at the bottom of the hill, and lost control of his car which collided with a tree. B died at the scene and S died of his injuries three days later. The defendant was only slightly injured. He was sentenced in the category of higher culpability because of the aggravating features of driving at excessive speed and showing off; driving badly deliberately behind and alongside the stretch limo, accelerating down the hill; not having a licence; driving without insurance; putting his passengers' lives at risk; the fact it was the first time he had driven any distance unsupervised and with passengers and he should not have allowed the two boys particularly B to enter the car. He had no previous convictions and there was positive evidence about his contribution to society. He had achieved six grade A passes at GCSE and was studying part time while working at a useful job in the post office, he felt genuine remorse, both of the boys who died had been his friends. Held. The aggravating features in this case were very serious and a period of 4 years detention should stand. The period of disqualification was too long. Although there was a high level of culpability account had to be taken of the defendant's age and the likelihood that he had learnt his lesson and that after a few years he would not pose a risk to the public. So **5 years not 10.**

Disqualification, for how long? – Less than 5 years

48.16 *R v Garrod* 1999 1 Cr App R (S) 172. 2 years. See **48.29**

R v Everett 2002 1 Cr App R (S) 550. **4 years**. See **48.35**

R v Braid 2002 2 Cr App R (S) 509. The defendant pleaded guilty to causing death by dangerous driving on rearraignment. At 11 am on a clear sunny day he overtook a lorry as he approached a blind corner. He hit an oncoming car head on killing the front seat passenger. Her husband, who was driving, was treated in hospital for six days and released from hospital after four weeks in a wheel chair. He required further treatment and may never fully recover. His left hip was fractured and it required pinning. His daughter aged 17 became the "woman of the house" and found it difficult. His son aged 15 who had learning difficulties requires one to one attention. The defendant was 20 with no convictions. He was suffering from depression relating to his father's disease, Huntington's Chorea and his health concerns about whether he would suffer from the same disease. He was prescribed antidepressants. A psychiatric report said this had impaired his mental state leading to a lack of concentration and maybe a state of disassociation. There were letters from his fiancée, employers and others speaking of his maturity, good sense, his safety as a driver and the burden of his father's illness. Held. The fact he couldn't see far enough should have been apparent. Nevertheless the case does not have any of the aggravating features identified in the authorities and does exhibit many of the features which mitigate the sentence. 18 months YOI not 2 years. **3 years** disqualification not 6.

R v Morton 2003 1 Cr App R (S) 196.The defendant was convicted of causing death by dangerous driving. At 9.30 pm, he then 18, drove his motorbike with his girlfriend on the back and approached a bend at about 60 mph in a 30 mph area. The weather was dry and the road conditions good. He lost control and hit a car. His girlfriend hit the windscreen of the car and died of multiple injuries. His breath test was negative. The motorcycle was examined and was found to be in good working order with no defects. Because of his age the defendant was restricted to bikes with 25kW output. He had removed the devices to restrict the output, which was now 56.2kW. This did not how-ever contribute to the accident. He said he had taken the bend before at 60 mph with his passenger, but this time when he leant the bike would not move with him. He was now 20 with no convictions for motoring offences. He was grief stricken about the loss of his girlfriend with whom marriage was contemplated. His mother said for days after the accident he wouldn't talk or leave his room. He had changed from being outgoing and cheerful to withdrawn, unpredictable and clinically depressed of moderate severity. He made two serious suicide attempts. There was 16 months between interview and trial. Held. This was a tragic case. However we cannot say $2^{1}/_{2}$ years YOI was manifestly excessive. Because of his youth and his good motoring record prior to the accident **4 years** disqualification not 7.

R v Austin 2004 2 Cr.App.R. (S) 88. The defendant, pleaded guilty at the earliest oppor-tunity to causing death by dangerous driving. At 11.20 pm in October he was driving his articulated lorry through the Dartford tunnel. Visibility was good and streetlights were on. The weather was clear and dry. Traffic had to slow down because of well signposted road works, and was reduced to one lane. The traffic in front slowed down and stopped but the defendant did not see this and collided with the back of the Renault Clio in front. The woman passenger died 3 days later from head injuries. The tacho-graph showed he had been driving at 56 mph and that the impact had occurred at a minimum of 50 mph. The impact pushed the Renault to one side and the lorry carried on and collided with four other vehicles, one of them a Vauxhall Corsa. The lorry con-tinued on up an embankment with the Vauxhall trapped underneath it. The driver of the Vauxhall had to be cut out by rescue services and sustained multiple serious injuries including eight broken ribs and a collapsed lung. He was off work for a "significant period of time". A victim impact statement said that his injuries were still affecting the way he performed everyday activities. Four vehicles were written off in the incident. The defendant, aged 38 had no previous convictions. A pre-sentence report stressed his profound remorse. He was considered to have a low risk of re-offending. Held. The aggravating feature was the serious injury to one or more victims. An important factor was that he was driving a long and very heavy vehicle. He must have appreciated the danger to others if it came into contact with their vehicles. This was particularly impor-tant as he was approaching an area where there was congestion ahead. This was not a momentary error of judgement but continued over a distance of 800–1,000 metres when he had been warned of the road works and ought to have been aware of vehicles slow-ing down. There were four mitigating features: the defendant's good driving record stressing that he was a professional lorry driver who drove more than 50,000 miles a year; that he had no previous convictions apart from carrying an excess load, which was not significant; that he entered a timely plea of guilty; and that he had suffered great remorse and genuine shock. Also he was highly unlikely to re-offend. 3 years not 5 years imprisonment, **3 years** not 5 years disqualification.

Disqualification, for how long? – 5 to 6 years

48.17 *R v Blackman* 2001 2 Cr App R (S) 268. **5 years**. See **48.38**

R v Corkhill 2002 2 Cr App R (S) 60. **5 years**. See **48.43**

Att-Gen's Ref. Nos. 32 of 2001 2002 1 Cr App R (S) 517. The defendant pleaded guilty to causing death by dangerous driving. He was committed for sentence for failing to stop, failing to report, driving without a licence and driving without insurance. He was also sentenced for perverting the course of justice, possession of heroin and two counts of possession of cannabis. He was released from YOI in January 2000 and obtained a provisional licence. He had some 4 hours of driving tuition. On 7 May 2000 he drove a stolen car at speed and mounted a pavement. He was arrested and cannabis and heroin were thrown from the car. He was released on bail. His girlfriend's mother left her powerful Ford Galaxy car outside her house and instructed one was to drive it. On 26 May 2000 the defendant used it for a number of journeys and on 27 May 2000 he drank rum in a pub and a club and then drove it at about 40 mph in a 30 mph area with his girlfriend who only had a provisional licence. He failed to see a Give Way sign in time and hit a taxi. His speed then was 20–25 mph. The taxi swung through 180 degrees and the passenger of the taxi died. He got out, looked at the taxi and left the scene. The prosecution said this was to avoid a breath sample being taken. Two days later he surrendered to the police. The defendant was either 18 or 19 (now 20) years old and in 1997 received 15 months YOI. In 1998 for burglary and robbery he received 3 years' detention. There were 439 days unexpired on his licence. He as sentenced to $2^{1}/_{2}$ years for the driving and concurrent sentences on the other offences. No order was made for the breach of the licence. Held. We would expect 5 years detention for the driving in addition to the breach sentence. As it was a reference 4 years detention with 12 months for the breach of licence consecutive and **5 years** not 2 years disqualification.

R v France 2003 1 Cr App R (S) 108. The defendant made an early guilty plea to six counts of causing death by dangerous driving. He was sentenced on the basis he was reading and had no effective control of his lorry on the A1(M). The lorry which was travelling at 55 mph drifted onto the hard shoulder and killed six people who were on the hard shoulder because they had been involved in an accident about 2 minutes earlier. The defendant was 55 and of good character with only one speeding offence which was 15 months before. **6 years** not 8.

Disqualification, for how long? More than 6 years

48.18 *R v McGowan* 1998 2 Cr App R (S) 220. See **48.21**

R v Gilmartin 2001 2 Cr App R (S) 212. **8 years**. See **48.21**

Att-Gen's Ref. Nos. 68 of 2001 2002 1 Cr App R (S) 406. The defendant was convicted of causing death by dangerous driving. The defendant was driving in a 60 mph area without a seat belt talking to his girlfriend on his mobile for 8 minutes. During this time he overtook three vehicles in a way described as 'erratic'. He then overtook another car at the top of a hill which was considered by another motorist as dangerous. He was then behind a Mazda doing 55–60 mph with a Mitsubishi behind him. The Mazda was over-taken near a blind corner on the brow of a hill at a speed 20–30 mph faster than the Mazda. He lost control of his car and hit an oncoming Renault with three adults and a 5-year-old child. One adult was killed and the other two received serious injuries. The child was kept overnight in hospital. The defendant received a broken neck fortunately without spinal damage. When interviewed he said someone was tailgating him and he overtook to get away. He was 26 and was of good character. He had one speeding con-viction in 1992 and was held in high regard by his family and friends. He expressed remorse and was sentenced to a community penalty with 180 hours community service. He had performed 66 hours. Held. We would have expected at least 3 years. Because it was a reference, the hours performed and it was his first custodial **18 months** substituted. The disqualification was increased from 3 to 7 years.

R v Noble 2003 1 Cr App R (S) 313. The defendant was convicted of causing the death of six people with most of the aggravating features in *R v Boswell* 1984 79 Cr App R 277 (the then guideline case) present and $2^{1}/_{2}$ times over the limit. Held. In general very lengthy periods of disqualification should be avoided, but that is subject to the need to protect the public against someone who is a danger on the road. The defendant had already on three occasions either driven with excess alcohol or failed to provide a specimen of breath. He was drunk, but refused to recognise how that impaired his driving ability, with the result that six people died. The lack of recognition on his part is an extremely disturbing. The Judge found that this man would be a danger to other road users indefinitely. In those circumstances, this is one of those rare cases where there was nothing wrong with imposing disqualification for life. For case details see page **48.34**

Old case *R v Lucas* 1998 1 Cr App R (S) 195, (for a summary of this case see the first edition of this book).

Disqualification, for how long? – Defendant under 18

48.19   *R v Jenkins* 2001 2 Cr App R (S) 265. The defendant pleaded guilty to causing death by dangerous driving. The defendant then aged 16 drove his motorbike on a mountain road in Wales with his best friend on the back. He had been given the bike a month earlier and it was in very bad condition. He was wearing a helmet but the passenger was not. The throttle jammed open and was unable to take a bend. The bike hit a wall and the friend was thrown forward and hit his head on the wall. He died. The defendant said the throttle stuck and he was unable to brake. The collision was described as 'low impact'. The bike was found to be totally unroadworthy. The throttle cable was not rooted properly, and the brakes and wheels were also defective. The defendant was of good character. He had mild learning difficulties and showed the deepest remorse. He had become traumatised, very withdrawn, isolated and vulnerable. Held. The judge was faced with a very difficult sentencing problem. A custodial sentence was justified. His mental condition prevented him from fully appreciating the bike's dangerous condition. Taking into account the factors including the long delay before sentence, the fact he needs help and that he had served nearly 3 months 2 years' supervision not 12 months detention. **3 years'** disqualification not 4.

R v Rooney 2004 2Cr App R (S) 135. The defendant aged 17 pleaded guilty to causing death by dangerous driving and driving while disqualified. Driving a car with four passengers in he had driven at excessive speed, navigated a roundabout in an anti- clockwise direction and lost control of the car as he attempted to take a corner. His passengers had screamed at him to slow down but he had ignored them. The car crashed into a tree. One of his passengers was killed. One had a leg amputated. Two were in a deep coma afterwards and were severely disabled as a consequence. The defendant also suffered injuries. He had previous convictions for violence and dishonesty and he had been disqualified from driving for a year which was still in force at the time of this offence. A pre-sentence report said he was deeply remorseful. A psychiatric report said he was over-sensitive with a fragile sense of self-esteem and that he had been greatly affected by his actions. This report also spoke of his remorse. Held. There were 3 highly culpable features of his driving serving to aggravate the offence: excessive speed; disregard of warnings and a deliberate course of very bad driving. The offence was also aggravated because the defendant was driving while disqualified and had not only caused the death of one person but had also effectively destroyed the lives of two or three others. In mitigation there was a timely plea of guilty and a full expression of remorse. The defendant was seriously injured in the accident. It is particularly important that he is only 17. It is vital to focus on the extent of culpability of the offender and bear in mind the mitigating features particularly his age. Alcohol or drugs would have rendered this driving even more culpable. 5 years detention not 7. **7 years** disqualification upheld.

Disqualification, for how long? – HGV/tractor drivers

48.20   *R v Kallaway* 1998 2 Cr App R (S) 220. The defendant pleaded guilty to three counts of causing death by dangerous driving. He disconnected the tachograph on his lorry and worked for 2 days well in excess of the permitted hours. He said it was to earn sufficient money. At 10.20pm the time of the accident he had been driving over the previous period some $39^1/_2$ hours with less than 9 hours' rest. He had his last break 16 hours beforehand. The road went from two lanes to one and there were warning signs about this. There were also cones with amber lights closing off a lane and a set of traffic lights. His lorry ploughed into a line a stationary traffic at about 50 mph. A driver in the last car heard no sign of braking and managed to escape. One car burst into flames. Three people died. Two drivers were significantly injured. Police found the defendant wandering round in a confused state. He was arrested and admitted his involvement. He denied he was asleep. He was 52 and had been a professional driver all his life. He had an unblemished record both as a driver and in work. He showed remorse. Held. The judge had perhaps been overly affected by the fact there were three deaths. That was clearly relevant but the number of deaths is sometimes a matter of chance and does not necessarily reflect the seriousness of the driving which caused the deaths. $3^1/_2$ years not 6 and **5 years'** disqualification not 10.

R v Lunt 1998 2 Cr App R (S) 348. The defendant was convicted of causing death by dangerous driving. The defendant then 23, owned and maintained a tractor and trailer. He was an engineer at Rolls Royce whose work involved test driving vehicles. As a spare time occupation he collected straw bales from farmers' fields. When he started to drive the 21 miles home with a load of straw the trailer lights were working properly. Halfway through the journey they became completely inoperative. On an ill-lit single carriageway in the dark a car drove into the back and the driver was killed. The defendant showed deep remorse and was wholly respectable with references. He was a member of the Institute of Advanced Drivers. The judge said he must have realised the lights were not working and he took a gamble. Held. 8 months upheld but **2 years** not 5 years' disqualification.

R v Wilsdon 1998 2 Cr App R (S) 361. The defendant was convicted of causing death by dangerous driving. At dusk the defendant a farmer drove an unlit slow moving farm vehicle with trailer on an unlit single carriageway country road. It was equipped for crop spraying. A car travelling at about 50 mph drove up behind took avoiding action and swerved to avoid the tractor. It hit an oncoming car head on. The defendant located someone with a mobile to call an ambulance but the first car's passenger was already dead. The headlights of the tractor were obscured by a plastic tank and the rear mudguard, which carried the lights and the reflectors had been removed to allow larger wheels to be fitted. The hazard lights were not visible as they were very dirty. The tractor would only have been visible at about 20 metres. The defendant said he had intended to drive the $^1/_2$ mile home in his pick-up truck taking the chemicals with him but the pick-up got stuck in mud. Although he could have walked and collected another vehicle he took the tractor and took a chance. Held. The gravamen lies in causing the vehicle to go out at dusk with no visible lights. 12 months was in no way excessive. **5 years'** disqualification was not excessive either.

R v Neaven 2000 1 Cr App R (S) 391. The defendant was convicted of causing death by dangerous driving. When it was dark he was driving a low loader which was carrying a dumper truck. He decided to do a U turn through a gap in the central reservation on a dual carriageway. While waiting for a gap in the traffic on the other carriageway the rear part of his lorry was protruding into the fast line of the road. The lights on his vehicle were not visible to those travelling in that lane. A car ran into the lorry and another car ran into that car. The driver of the first car was killed. He was a father of young children. The defendant remained at the scene and rang the police. The defendant was of impeccable character and had an impeccable driving history. He'd had an HGV licence for 25 years. Held. All motorists must realise that if they drive dangerously and thereby kill someone there must be a danger of imprisonment. It was a very dangerous piece of driving. 12 months was not manifestly excessive. However, he had always been a good driver so **2 years'** disqualification not 4.

R v Coulridge 2003 2 Cr App R (S) 43. The defendant was convicted of two counts of causing death by dangerous driving. He had fallen asleep at the wheel of a lorry tractor unit on the M20. His vehicle drifted on to the hard shoulder where it collided with a van which had broken down. The tractor unit had then rebounded out of control and crossed all three lanes of the carriageway and broke through the central reservation. It collided head-on with a BMW containing S and his fiancé who died instantly. The BMW was carried under the front of the tractor unit and there was a further collision before the tractor unit burst into flames. The defendant was dragged to safety. He fell asleep either from a medical condition or from tiredness. Two doctors testified that they had told him that he should not drive as he had already caused a considerable number of minor road traffic accidents. He was 44 and was of effectively good character. Held. It was difficult to imagine a more serious case of its type; however the driving was not dangerous over a prolonged period of time or distance. There was only one aggravating factor. Because of the (then) maximum sentence 6 years not 8 and disqualification for **8 years** not life.

Drugs, driving under the influence of

48.21 *R v McGowan* 1998 2 Cr App R (S) 220. The defendant pleaded guilty at the first opportunity to causing death by dangerous driving and driving whilst disqualified. The defendant left a public house where he had had a pint and a half or two in his girlfriend's car. When travelling at about 60 mph he overtook on a bend 'taking a chance.' He was only able to overtake slowly because his acceleration was poor. A car came into sight and he continued to try to overtake then braked. It caused a skid and he hit the other car head on. The defendant got out and tried to help his passenger who had suffered a ruptured bowel. The defendant left the scene without leaving details and telephoned his girlfriend and told her to report the car as stolen. She reluctantly did so but shortly after told the truth. The driver of the other car was trapped and died 2 weeks later in hospital. The defendant was arrested and denied being the driver. Later he admitted being the driver and expressed remorse. He had been disqualified from driving twice for drink/drive. The judge said he gave the minimum amount for the plea. Held. This case was not near the top of the scale although it was rank bad driving with a bad record. **5 years** not 7 and 8 years' disqualification not 15.

R v Gilmartin 2001 2 Cr App R (S) 212. The defendant pleaded guilty to causing death by dangerous driving. The defendant and two friends spent several hours drinking. He took some ecstasy and later drove off with the two friends. He drove well above the 30 and 40 mph speed limits on residential roads. He lost control of the car, hit a tree and the two friends were thrown from the car. Just before the accident one of the friends shouted a warning. Initially he rang for a taxi to leave the scene but subsequently he stayed at the scene and gave considerable assistance to the police. One passenger died and the other was injured. His blood/alcohol reading was 74mg and by backtracking was 97mg, (the equivalent of 42 μg in the breath). He also had 1,060 μg of ecstasy in his blood which was so high it was mostly seen in fatal overdoses. The defendant had convictions in 1989 and 1990 for reckless driving and drink/drive. He was full of regret and remorse. There was a Newton hearing about whether the ecstasy was taken before or after the accident and the judge found it was taken before the accident although he said the defendant was not deliberately lying. The judge found the manner of driving was due to the effects of ecstasy making him drive faster and faster. Held. The defendant should have the full discount because of the judge's finding he wasn't lying and some of his evidence was accepted. The overarching consideration was the high level of ecstasy. Because of the plea and the other mitigation **6 years** not 7 and 8 years not 10 years disqualification.

R v Austin 2004 2 Cr.App.R. (S.) 88. The defendant, pleaded guilty at the earliest opportunity to causing death by dangerous driving. At 11.20 pm in October he was driving his articulated lorry through the Dartford tunnel. Visibility was good and streetlights were on. The weather was clear and dry. Traffic had to slow down because of well signposted road works, and was reduced to one lane. The traffic in front slowed down and stopped but the defendant did not see this and collided with the back of the Renault Clio in front. The woman passenger died 3 days later from head injuries. The tachograph showed he had been driving at 56 mph and that the impact had occurred at a minimum of 50 mph. The impact pushed the Renault to one side and the lorry carried on and collided with four other vehicles, one of them a Vauxhall Corsa. The lorry continued on up an embankment with the Vauxhall trapped underneath it. The driver of the Vauxhall had to be cut out by rescue services and sustained multiple serious injuries including eight broken ribs and a collapsed lung. He was off work for a "significant period of time". A victim impact statement said that his injuries were still affecting the way he performed everyday activities. Four vehicles were written off in the incident. The defendant, aged 38 had no previous convictions. A pre-sentence report stressed his profound remorse. He was considered to have a low risk of re-offending. Held. The aggravating feature was the serious injury to one or more victims. An important factor was that he was driving a long and very heavy vehicle. He must have appreciated the danger to others if it came into contact with their vehicles. This was particularly important as he was approaching an area where there was congestion ahead. This was not a momentary error of judgement but continued over a distance of 800–1,000 metres when he had been warned of the road works and ought to have been aware of vehicles slowing down. There were four mitigating features: the defendant's good driving record stressing that he was a professional lorry driver who drove more than 50,000 miles a year; that he had no previous convictions apart from carrying an excess load, which was not significant; that he entered a timely plea of guilty; and that he had suffered great remorse and genuine shock. Also he was highly unlikely to re-offend. **3 years** not 5 years imprisonment, 3 years not 5 years disqualification.

Eyesight, poor – accident caused by poor eyesight

48.22   *Att-Gen's Ref. No 88 of 2003* 2004 2 Cr App R (S) 526. The defendant pleaded guilty on the morning of trial to causing death by dangerous driving. He was driving a coach on a maintenance run in the early hours of the morning when he ran down a cyclist on the slip way to a dual carriageway road. It was dark and he simply did not see him. The victim was a 54-year-old man who was a careful cyclist wearing reflective clothing and his bike was fitted with appropriate lights. He sustained multiple injuries and died the next day. The only possible explanation for the accident was that the defendant had defective vision. He suffered from long standing problems with his vision due to diabetes. He had a licence to carry passengers but never contacted the DVLA to tell them he had a problem with his eyes. He had laser surgery on two occasions but although he was given a leaflet saying there is an obligation to tell the DVLA about laser eye surgery he did not tell them. His eyesight fluctuated throughout 2002.

By the time of the accident he seems to have had little or no vision in his right eye and constricted vision in his left eye. He initially told police after the accident he had no problems with his eyesight. His basis of plea was that he genuinely believed his eyesight was sufficiently safe to drive, although he accepted that this could not have been a correct belief. The judge said in sentencing that the defendant knew perfectly well that his eyesight was compromised and at least he should have enquired whether or not he was safe to drive. The defendant, 45, was of positive good character, a family man who did charitable work. The pre-sentence report said he was devastated at having killed someone and tearful and emotional. By the time the report was written he had no sight in one eye and limited sight in the other and used a white stick. He was accompanied wherever he went. His marriage was in difficulty. **Held.** It cannot be accepted that the defendant positively believed his eyesight was adequate for him to be driving. The most difficult feature was that by the time he came to be sentenced he was and always will be effectively blind. This was a dramatic deterioration and the judge was right to give full weight to it, but he possibly gave more weight to it than he should have. The defendant and his wife have now separated and he has had at least two further operations on his eyes since sentencing. The sentence of **2 years suspended for 2 years** was possibly unduly lenient but because it was a reference and the developments in his life since sentencing and condition it was not altered.

Failing to see other vehicles, obstacles etc within time

48.23   *R v Lightfoot* 1999 2 Cr App R (S) 55. The defendant pleaded guilty to two counts of causing death by dangerous driving. In daylight on a dry road where there was good visibility the defendant drove his tractor unit at excessive speeds. Shortly before the accident he was travelling at 67 mph. Ahead was a stationary car waiting to turn right into a lay-by. The speed limit was 60 mph and his permitted limit was 40 mph. Just before the accident his speed was 54 mph. He should have seen the white car 350 yards before but his concentration was such he only saw it when he braked. The brakes were defective and they locked. The tractor unit veered to the right and hit an oncoming a car head on. The driver and his 18-year-old daughter were killed and his wife and younger daughter were injured. The defendant was 33 and of good character with testimonials. He had been a lorry driver since he was 21 and had only one speeding ticket. He expressed genuine shock and remorse. There was a Newton hearing when the judge found the defendant was not aware of the defective brakes. **2 years** not 3.

R v Caucheteux 2002 2 Cr App R (S) 169. The defendant pleaded guilty to three counts of causing death by dangerous driving. In daylight on a dry road where there was good visibility the defendant drove his large lorry and a long trailer on the M6 at a consistent speed of 53 mph. As he approached a queue of traffic he didn't brake or slow down. The last car in the queue took evasive action but was still shunted into the hard shoulder barrier. The next car was propelled into the trailer of the van in front and all three young RAF technicians were killed. Their car was partly under the lorry, which veered into the barrier. The car was pushed under the barrier. Four other cars were pushed forward. Ten other people were injured some seriously. The defendant's lorry had no defects and the alcohol test was negative. There were no skid marks for the lorry. It was estimated he had 32 seconds to slow down for the queue. He could give no explanation for the accident. He was 29 and a French national who drove regularly in the UK. He had no convictions and was deeply affected by the accident and had very positive references. Genuine remorse was shown. In court he asked to speak and made an emotional apology to the relatives and asked for forgiveness. The judge said it was not a momentary loss of concentration, he could not have been looking properly. **Held.** We take into account the number of fatalities but **2 years** not 3.

R v Austin 2004 2 Cr.App.R. (S.) 88. The defendant, pleaded guilty at the earliest opportunity to causing death by dangerous driving. At 11.20 pm in October he was driving his articulated lorry through the Dartford tunnel. Visibility was good and streetlights were on. The weather was clear and dry. Traffic had to slow down because of well signposted road works, and was reduced to one lane. The traffic in front slowed down and stopped but the defendant did not see this and collided with the back of the Renault Clio in front. The woman passenger died 3 days later from head injuries. The tachograph showed he had been driving at 56 mph and that the impact had occurred at a minimum of 50 mph. The impact pushed the Renault to one side and the lorry carried on and collided with four other vehicles, one of them a Vauxhall Corsa. The lorry continued on up an embankment with the Vauxhall trapped underneath it. The driver of the Vauxhall had to be cut out by rescue services and sustained multiple serious injuries including eight broken ribs and a collapsed lung. He was off work for a "significant period of time". A victim impact statement said that his injuries were still affecting the way he performed everyday activities. Four vehicles were written off in the incident. The defendant, aged 38 had no previous convictions. A pre-sentence report stressed his profound remorse. He was considered to have a low risk of re-offending. Held. The aggravating feature was the serious injury to one or more victims. An important factor was that he was driving a long and very heavy vehicle. He must have appreciated the danger to others if it came into contact with their vehicles. This was particularly important as he was approaching an area where there was congestion ahead. This was not a momentary error of judgement but continued over a distance of 800–1,000 metres when he had been warned of the road works and ought to have been aware of vehicles slowing down. There were four mitigating features: the defendant's good driving record stressing that he was a professional lorry driver who drove more than 50,000 miles a year; that he had no previous convictions apart from carrying an excess load, which was not significant; that he entered a timely plea of guilty; and that he had suffered great remorse and genuine shock. Also he was highly unlikely to re-offend. **3 years** not 5 years imprisonment, 3 years not 5 years disqualification.

Att-Gen's Ref. No 85 of 2003 2004 2 Cr App R (S) 371. The defendant pleaded guilty to causing death by dangerous driving. He was driving along a normal A road behind a Mercedes car. The driver of the Mercedes slowed to turn right, which he could not immediately do because of oncoming traffic. He realised the defendant behind him was not slowing down, so he tried to accelerate away. At the last minute the defendant swerved into the oncoming traffic and collided with the victim's car. She was a woman of 73 who had been driving at 40 mph; the impact speed was between 80–100 mph. Her car was struck by the car behind and then again by the defendant's car. She was not wearing a seat belt and died of crush injuries to her chest. The victim's daughter was severely affected by her mother's death. The defendant, 61, suffered rib fractures, head injuries and knee pains. He later had reactive depression and was troubled with flashbacks and anxiety. His short-term memory was impaired. The basis of plea was that the defendant had failed to pay proper attention to the fact that the Mercedes had slowed down to turn right, and had swerved into the incoming traffic only to avoid the Mercedes, and denied any other dangerous driving. He was not adversely affected by alcohol. He was of good character and was remorseful. He remained unable to work and his business failed. It was argued that had the victim been wearing a seat belt she would not have died. Held. The defendant was inattentive over a significant distance. The fact that the victim was not wearing a seat belt could not be regarded as an exceptional circumstance. The appropriate starting point for this offence was **12–18 months**. 12 months imprisonment suspended for two years was too lenient so **8 months**.

See also *Speed, approaching a hazard at excessive*

Health problems, accident caused by

48.24 *R v Davies* 2002 1 Cr App R (S) 579. The defendant was convicted of causing death by dangerous driving. The defendant had been a lorry driver for over 40 years and a history of diabetes. In good conditions on a straight road his lorry veered over to the opposite carriageway and hit a Land Rover a glancing blow. It then hit a Skoda with four occupants and front part of the car virtually ceased to exist. The driver, his girl-friend and their 5-month-old daughter were killed. The other occupant the driver's mother suffered severe lacerations to her forehead and scalp which required about 90 stitches. She had multiple fractures to her cheekbone and eye socket and a fractured collarbone, two fractures to her arm and extensive lacerations to her chest and her underarm area. There were also lacerations to her elbow and arms and a complete loss of movement and feeling in that arm. The defendant was not injured but was in severe shock. He lost control of the lorry after a hypoglycaemic attack and the judge found, 'he didn't have his rations with him. When he felt the attack coming on he didn't stop but carried on.' In 1995 his lorry had also veered across a busy road after a similar attack. No one was hurt but he had received advice and he was authorised to continue driving on the basis he took proper precautions. He was about 65 and of exemplary character with references. He was deeply remorseful and had the strongest feelings of compassion. This judge disqualified him for life. *Held.* Three lives had been lost. A most serious aspect was the previous attack. Some judges might have imposed a lesser sentence because of the strong mitigation but **3 years** was not manifestly excessive. Disqualification for life remained.

Att-Gen's Ref. No 10 of 2004 2005 1 Cr App R (S) 91. The defendant pleaded guilty to causing death by dangerous driving. The defendant had been an insulin dependant diabetic since he was 8. He was 22 when he suffered an infection to his arm that required surgery and was treated with antibiotics. That was having an effect on his insulin requirement at the time of the incident. The defendant had also been addicted to heroin. He purchased a 4 × 4 a few days before the incident. He did not have a driving licence or insurance. He left home with his 10-week-old daughter in the front seat. His movements between 09:30 and 12:15 are not known. At about 12:35 he was driving along a dual carriageway and stopped at some traffic lights before a roundabout. When the lights went green he did not move at first, then rolled a few feet forward. The lights went red and he was blocking the junction. When the lights went green he shot forward, almost hitting the back of the vehicle in front. He then swerved across the 2 lanes of dual carriageway, bounced off the kerb and the central reservation, then swerved into a road on his left with a 30 mph limit. The deceased was walking along the pavement on the defendant's nearside. The defendant's car swerved into the middle of the road and over-corrected, and went onto the pavement striking the deceased. There was no sign of the application of his brakes. The deceased suffered severe head injuries and died 6 days later. The defendant's car continued in a similar manner hitting roadside furni-ture until mechanical failure brought it to a stop. Despite his attempts he was unable to undo the baby seat buckle to release the baby and he then just slumped against the car. When police arrived he was collapsed and there was frothy saliva on his lips. His blood sugar level was low. He said that he had not taken heroin for 2 days; although his blood sample revealed amphetamine and valium. He told police that he had been to his Dr's that morning to seek help with his diabetic control as he knew he was not well. He said that he had had intended to get insurance for the car that morning. He was genuinely remorseful and without previous convictions for driving offences. He had always controlled his diabetes in the past. *Held.* With reference to Cooksley and others 2003 1 Cr App R (S) 1, this was a difficult sentencing exercise. The factor of diabetes explained why the driving of this dreadful standard took place and to that extent it mit-igates the serious nature of the way in which the driving occurred. However, the failure to manage his condition was a seriously aggravating feature and brings it into the top category (**4–5 years** after a trial). The other drugs were not in such quantities to cause a risk of greater harm but were to be seen in the context of his management of his condition. The proper sentence on a plea was **2¹/₂ to 3 years**, but as this was a reference, **2 years**.

See also *Eyesight, poor – accident caused by poor eyesight*

HGV drivers – Guideline remarks

48.25   *R v Caucheteux* 2002 2 Cr App R (S) 169. Those who drove HGV vehicles owed a particular responsibility because of the nature of the vehicles they drove and because the results of the errors could be as in this case catastrophic.

HGV drivers

48.26   R v Neaven 2000 1 Cr App R (S) 391. The defendant was convicted of causing death by dangerous driving. When it was dark he was driving a low loader which was carrying a dumper truck. He decided to do a U turn through a gap in the central reservation on a dual carriageway. While waiting for a gap in the traffic on the other carriageway the rear part of his lorry was protruding into the fast line of the road. The lights on his vehicle were not visible to those travelling in that lane. A car ran into the lorry and another car ran into that car. The driver of the first car was killed. He was a father of young children. The defendant remained at the scene and rang the police. The defendant was of impeccable character and had an impeccable driving history. He'd had an HGV licence for 25 years. Held. All motorists must realise that if they drive dangerously and thereby kill someone there must be a danger of imprisonment. It was a very dangerous piece of driving. **12 months** was not manifestly excessive. However, as he had always been a good driver 2 years' disqualification not 4.

R v Buckingham 2001 1 Cr App R (S) 218. The defendant changed his plea to guilty to causing death by dangerous driving. The defendant was driving an articulated lorry on the motorway. He ran into stationary traffic which was queuing to leave the motorway. Eight cars were damaged and a fire started. One woman was unable to leave her car and died. The defendant was 62 and had one conviction for driving without due care in 1996. He was very remorseful and had suffered from post-traumatic stress disorder. Held. It is important to bear in mind the nature of the vehicle he was driving and the anger and grief of the family and friends of the deceased. In light of his age, trauma, character and remorse **18 months** not 3 years.

R v Price 2001 2 Cr App R (S) 114. The defendant pleaded guilty to two counts of causing death by dangerous driving. The defendant an HGV driver was told by his GP not to drive and see a consultant urgently. He saw the consultant next day who said he had sleep apnoea syndrome. He discovered the defendant had fallen asleep at the wheel of his lorry a month previously and the lorry went into a field. He was again told not to drive. Four days later his lorry was seen on the M1 weaving from the inside lane to the hard shoulder without any indications being given. 40 miles further on and just before a service station he ran into stationary traffic in the slow lane. Two cars were crushed between his lorry and another lorry. The cars and his lorry caught fire and both the car drivers died. The defendant stayed at the scene. He said he planned to pull into the service station. He was of good character and full of remorse. The judge held a Newton hearing about whether he had ignored medical advice and said he could no longer give a full discount for the plea. Held. **4 years** not 5.

R v Taylor 2002 1 Cr App R (S) 76. The defendant was convicted of causing death by dangerous driving. He was driving his lorry and trailer which was 15.5 metres long and approached a junction with a dual carriageway from a side road. Wanting to turn right he crossed one carriageway and stopped in the central reservation with the front of the lorry protruding in the one carriageway and the trailer protruding in the other. It would have been possible to remain in the central reservation without protruding if the angle was right. The trailer had obstructed half of the outside lane of one of the dual carriageways. The deceased was driving her car at about 70 mph in the fast lane and hit the trailer. She didn't see the trailer in time. The dual carriageway was a busy truck road carrying fast moving traffic. It was dark and the speed limit was 70 mph. The road was wet but it wasn't raining. The rear lights of the trailer were not visible because of the angle of the vehicle and because of the colour of the vehicle it merged into the background. The judge said it was an error of judgment. The defendant was a businessman of good character with a good driving record. He had testimonials which spoke extremely highly of him. Held. Following *R v Ollerenshaw* 1999 1 Cr App R (S) 65 [Courts should ask themselves for those who had not previously served custody whether an even shorter period might be equally effective] **4 months** not 8.

R v Vera 2003 2 Cr App R (S) 27. The defendant was convicted of causing death by dangerous driving. He was driving a 7.5-ton lorry on a single-carriageway road. The speed limit was 60 mph. The driving conditions were dry and clear. The road was described as long, straight and boring and was one with which the defendant was familiar. He was driving at about 56 mph when he came over the brow of a hill. Ahead of him and some 16 seconds away was a car being driven by the 72-year-old victim. The car was stationary and indicating to turn right. The defendant simply did not see the car and collided with it pushing it onto the opposite carriageway where it was struck by an oncoming lorry. The victim died later of his injuries. The defendant suffered a broken wrist and concussion. The lorry was subject to a 50 mph speed limit and was slightly over laden. In interview he fully admitted responsibility and showed clear remorse. The question at trial was whether his driving was careless or dangerous. He was 26 and had no relevant previous convictions and was regarded as a good hard-working man. Held. This was more than momentary inattention. However, there had been no bad driving, no deliberate attempt to overtake, no excessive speed, i.e. none of the aggravating features identified in Boswell. **2 years** not 3.

R v Austin 2004 2 Cr.App.R. (S.) 88. The defendant, pleaded guilty at the earliest opportunity to causing death by dangerous driving. At 11.20 pm in October he was driving his articulated lorry through the Dartford tunnel. Visibility was good and streetlights were on. The weather was clear and dry. Traffic had to slow down because of well signposted road works, and was reduced to one lane. The traffic in front slowed down and stopped but the defendant did not see this and collided with the back of the Renault Clio in front. The woman passenger died 3 days later from head injuries. The tachograph showed he had been driving at 56 mph and that the impact had occurred at a minimum of 50 mph. The impact pushed the Renault to one side and the lorry carried on and collided with four other vehicles, one of them a Vauxhall Corsa. The lorry continued on up an embankment with the Vauxhall trapped underneath it. The driver of the Vauxhall had to be cut out by rescue services and sustained multiple serious injuries including eight broken ribs and a collapsed lung. He was off work for a "significant period of time". A victim impact statement said that his injuries were still affecting the way he performed everyday activities. Four vehicles were written off in the incident. The defendant, aged 38 had no previous convictions. A pre-sentence report stressed his profound remorse. He was considered to have a low risk of re-offending. Held. The aggravating feature was the serious injury to one or more victims. An important factor was that he was driving a long and very heavy vehicle. He must have appreciated the danger to others if it came into contact with their vehicles. This was particularly important as he was approaching an area where there was congestion ahead. This was not a momentary error of judgement but continued over a distance of 800–1,000 metres when he had been warned of the road works and ought to have been aware of vehicles slowing down.

There were four mitigating features: the defendant's good driving record stressing that he was a professional lorry driver who drove more than 50,000 miles a year; that he had no previous convictions apart from carrying an excess load, which was not significant; that he entered a timely plea of guilty; and that he had suffered great remorse and genuine shock. Also he was highly unlikely to re-offend. **3 years** not 5 years imprisonment, 3 years not 5 years disqualification.

Old cases. *R v Toombs* 1997 2 Cr App R (S) 228.

HGV drivers – Exceeding permitted hours/fatigue

48.27   *R v Kallaway* 1998 2 Cr App R (S) 220. The defendant pleaded guilty to three counts of causing death by dangerous driving. He disconnected the tachograph on his lorry and worked for 2 days well in excess of the permitted hours. He said it was to earn sufficient money. At 10.20pm the time of the accident he had been driving over the previous period some $39^1/_2$ hours with less than 9 hours' rest. He had his last break 16 hours beforehand. The road went from two lanes to one and there were warning signs about this. There were also cones with amber lights closing off a lane and a set of traffic lights. His lorry ploughed into a line a stationary traffic at about 50 mph. A driver in the last car heard no sign of braking and managed to escape. One car burst into flames. Three people died. Two drivers were significantly injured. Police found the defendant wandering round in a confused state. He was arrested and admitted his involvement. He denied he was asleep. He was 52 and had been a professional driver all his life. He had an unblemished record both as a driver and in work. He showed remorse. Held. The judge had perhaps been overly affected by the fact there were three deaths. That was clearly relevant but the number of deaths is sometimes a matter of chance and does not necessarily reflect the seriousness of the driving which caused the deaths. $3^1/_2$ **years** not 6 and 5 years' disqualification not 10.

R v Porter (No 2) 2002 2 Cr App R (S) 222. The defendant pleaded guilty to three counts of causing death by dangerous driving. A count relating to a false entry on his driver's hour's sheet was left on the file. At 6.55pm in February, the defendant was driving his articulated goods vehicle from Italy to Cheshire on a motorway and he drove into the back of a mobile crane. His vehicle crashed through the barrier, fell 30' and overturned. The driver of the crane lost control of his vehicle and went through the central reservation and overturned and collided with a car and another articulated vehicle. The drivers of all three vehicles died. There was no evidence of pre-impact breaking by the defendant. The estimated speed of the crane was the designated speed of 30 mph and the defendant at something less than 60 mph. One rear indicator light and one tail-light on the crane were not lit. The written basis of plea was that he was under such pressure to meet delivery deadlines that he pushed the limits of his driving hours and rest periods. He did not accept he had tampered with the tachograph. He failed to appreciate the speed of the crane and he must have lost his concentration for a few seconds when approaching the crane. He denied falling asleep. He had a conviction for perverting the course of justice involving a tachograph and driving convictions including speeding and showed remorse. There was a letter from one of the widows describing the devastation on her and her three children. Held. Any motor vehicle is potentially a lethal weapon and if it is driven by someone suffering from fatigue the chances of an accident are greatly increased **4 years** not 5. (The case was reheard in the defendant's presence after his earlier appeal had been dismissed when the defendant wasn't there. see *R v Porter (No 1)* 2002 2 Cr App R (S) 67.)

HGV drivers/tractor drivers – Vehicle lit inadequately

48.28   *R v Lunt* 1998 2 Cr App R (S) 348. The defendant was convicted of causing death by dangerous driving. The defendant then 23, owned and maintained a tractor and trailer. He was an engineer at Rolls Royce whose work involved test driving vehicles. As a spare time occupation he collected straw bales from farmers' fields. When he started to drive the 21 miles home with a load of straw the trailer lights were working properly. Halfway through the journey they became completely inoperative. On an ill-lit single carriageway in the dark a car drove into the back and the driver was killed. The defendant showed deep remorse and was wholly respectable with references. He was a member of the Institute of Advanced Drivers. The judge said he must have realised the lights were not working and he took a gamble. Held. **8 months** upheld but 2 years not 5 years' disqualification.

R v Wilsdon 1998 2 Cr App R (S) 361. The defendant was convicted of causing death by dangerous driving. At dusk the defendant a farmer drove an unlit slow moving farm vehicle with trailer on an unlit single carriageway country road. It was equipped for crop spraying. A car travelling at about 50 mph drove up behind took avoiding action and swerved to avoid the tractor. It hit an oncoming car head on. The defendant located someone with a mobile to call an ambulance but the first car's passenger was already dead. The headlights of the tractor were obscured by a plastic tank and the rear mudguard, which carried the lights and the reflectors had been removed to allow larger wheels to be fitted. The hazard lights were not visible as they were very dirty. The tractor would only have been visible at about 20 metres. The defendant said he had intended to drive the $\frac{1}{2}$ mile home in his pick-up truck taking the chemicals with him but the pick-up got stuck in mud. Although he could have walked and collected another vehicle he took the tractor and took a chance. Held. The gravamen lies in causing the vehicle to go out at dusk with no visible lights. **12 months** was in no way excessive. 5 years' disqualification was not excessive either.

R v Neaven 2000 1 Cr App R (S) 391. The defendant was convicted of causing death by dangerous driving. When it was dark he was driving a low loader which was carrying a dumper truck. He decided to do a U turn through a gap in the central reservation on a dual carriageway. While waiting for a gap in the traffic on the other carriageway the rear part of his lorry was protruding into the fast line of the road. The lights on his vehicle were not visible to those travelling in that lane. A car ran into the lorry and another car ran into that car. The driver of the first car was killed. He was a father of young children. The defendant remained at the scene and rang the police. The defendant was of impeccable character and had an impeccable driving history. He'd had an HGV licence for 25 years. Held. All motorists must realise that if they drive dangerously and thereby kill someone there must be a danger of imprisonment. It was a very dangerous piece of driving. **12 months** was not manifestly excessive. However, as he had always been a good driver 2 years' disqualification not 4.

HGV vehicles – Defective brakes
48.28a   See *Att-Gen's Ref. Nos. 134 of 2004* Unreported 16/12/04. (12 months appropriate for driver knowing the brakes were defective who had substantial mitigation.)

Ice, vision obscured by
48.29   *R v Garrod* 1999 1 Cr App R (S) 172. The defendant was convicted of causing death by dangerous driving. The defendant drove in freezing conditions on a well-lit road one evening. The car mounted a pavement hitting a pedestrian who was thrown into the air and landed on the car's bonnet. The defendant left the vehicle and told witnesses he hadn't seen the man. The man died. The car was examined and there was no evidence that the side window had been de-iced. Ice had formed on the inside and outside of the windscreen. It appeared an attempt had been made to clear a circular part of the windscreen in front of the driving position but ice had reformed. There were a few scratch marks on the nearside of the windscreen. There was no de-icer or scraper

in the vehicle. He told police he left his home a few hundred yards away and had cleaned part of the windscreen. He hadn't cleaned the side windows and he had skidded on the corner. He was of good character. The prosecution put the case as comparable to driving a defective vehicle. Held. That would put it at the lower end of the criminality. **18 months** not 3 years' detention. As his employers would continue his employment if he had a licence 2 years not 3 years' disqualification.

Inattention See *Single misjudgement/inattention*

Injuries, the defendant's own – Guideline case

48.30   *R v Cooksley* 2004 1 Cr App R (S) 1. LCJ The offender's own injuries are a relevant consideration. The injuries can make the sentence of imprisonment a greater punishment than usual. His injuries are also in themselves a punishment and should bring home to the offender, in the most direct possible way, what can be the consequences of dangerous driving. The fact that the offender has been injured should not automatically be treated as a mitigating factor and that only 'very serious, or life changing, injury' should have a *significant* effect on the sentence. Some indication of the scale of the effect is provided by the facts of *R v Maloney* 1996 1 Cr App R (S) 221. The offender had a very severe head injury, severe facial injuries, he lost the sight of his right eye and he lost his right little finger, and there was continuing loss of use of his right arm and leg. This Court reduced the sentence from **5 to 4 years** but in doing so were taking into account, not only the injuries, but the fact that the trial judge had erroneously sentenced the appellant on the basis he had consumed an excessive amount of alcohol.

Mobile phones, defendant using – Guideline case

48.31   *R v Cooksley* 2004 1 Cr App R (S) 1. LCJ In *R v Browning* 2002 1 Cr App R (S) 377 the defendant was a lorry driver who, while sending a text message, veered off the road and killed a man in a lay-by. The court said, and we endorse, 'The use of a mobile phone to read and compose text messages while driving is a highly perilous activity. Even the use of a hand-held mobile phone by a driver whilst moving, a much too common feature of driving today, is self-evidently risky. But the risks of reading and composing, text messages appears to us of a wholly different order and to be to use the judges words, of the most 'blatant nature'. He had pleaded guilty but there had to be a Newton hearing. His evidence was not accepted so he was not entitled to full credit for his plea. The sentence of **5 years** for an offender of good character and who was remorseful was upheld. Browning provides a useful example of what we would regard as being the current appropriate level of sentencing.

Mobile phone, defendant using

48.32   *R v Browning* 2002 1 Cr App R (S) 377. The defendant pleaded guilty to causing death by dangerous driving. The defendant was driving a lorry on a dual carriageway with a dangerous load, helium. 60 metres before a lay-by the lorry began to veer to the left. At the lay-by it scrapped the whole side of a BMW and hit the car in front. A man standing in the lay-by was killed instantly. The defendant stopped and later started crying. The weather was fine. He later claimed he was distracted by papers in his cab. After a Newton hearing the judge found he was composing a text message on his hand held mobile which was transmitted immediately after the accident. The judge concluded that the message had been composed over a distance of about 400 metres, which took the 27 seconds to travel. At the start of that distance he was travelling at 57 mph which he reduced to 49 mph. Also he had received an incoming text message while driving his lorry an hour earlier. Twenty minutes later while still on the move he composed and sent a reply. He had no convictions and a good work record. The judge said he was a decent family man and showed remorse. Since the accident he worked in a yard and he says he never intends to drive a lorry again. Held. The use of a mobile phone to read and to compose text messages while driving is a highly perilous activity. Even the use of a handheld mobile phone by a driver whilst moving, a much more common feature of driving today, is self-evidently risky. But the risks of reading and composing text messages appear to us of a wholly different order and to be of the most blatant nature. It was legitimate for the judge not to give full credit for the plea. An element of deterrence was appropriate for composing a message. **5 years** was not inappropriate.

Att-Gen's Ref. Nos. 68 of 2001 2002 1 Cr App R (S) 406. The defendant was convicted of causing death by dangerous driving. The defendant was driving in a 60 mph area without a seat belt talking to his girlfriend on his mobile for 8 minutes. During this time he overtook three vehicles in a way described as 'erratic'. He then overtook another car at the top of a hill which was considered by another motorist as dangerous. He was then behind a Mazda doing 55–60 mph with a Mitsubishi behind him. The Mazda was overtaken near a blind corner on the brow of a hill at a speed 20–30 mph faster than the Mazda. He lost control of his car and hit an oncoming Renault with three adults and a 5-year-old child. One adult was killed and the other two received serious injuries. The child was kept overnight in hospital. The defendant received a broken neck fortunately without spinal damage. When interviewed he said someone was tailgating him and he overtook to get away. He was 26 and was of good character. He had one speeding conviction in 1992 and was held in high regard by his family and friends. He expressed remorse and was sentenced to a community penalty with 180 hours community service. He had performed 66 hours. Held. We would have expected **at least 3 years**. Because it was a reference, the hours performed and it was his first custodial **18 months** substituted. The disqualification was increased from 3 to 7 years.

Multiple deaths, – Guideline case

48.33   *R v Cooksley* 2004 1 Cr App R (S) 1. LCJ The number of deaths resulting from dangerous driving is relevant to the length of sentence. There are cases in which the defendant is, for example, a coach driver, who drives after being deprived of sleep or under the influence of alcohol, where he must be taken to appreciate that the consequence could be that there will be more than one death if he is involved in an accident. Certainly in that situation, multiple deaths will be a more seriously aggravating feature.

Even where there is no reason to suggest that the defendant is knowingly putting more than one person at risk, the fact that the consequences of dangerous driving are particularly serious, for example involving multiple deaths, is a relevant factor as to the length of sentence. That is the view that will be taken by the public. However, we are certainly not suggesting that the sentence should be multiplied according to the number of persons who sadly lose their life. It is still necessary to regard the offender's culpability in relation to the driving as the dominant component in the sentencing exercise. While the sentence is increased to reflect more than one death the sentence must remain proportionate to the nature of an offence which does not involve any intent to injure.

Multiple deaths – Cases

48.34   *R v Kallaway* 1998 2 Cr App R (S) 220. The defendant pleaded guilty to three counts of causing death by dangerous driving. Three people died. Held. The judge had perhaps been overly affected by the fact there were three deaths. That was clearly relevant but the number of deaths is sometimes a matter of chance and does not necessarily reflect the seriousness of the driving which caused the deaths. (For further details see page **48.20**)

R v Hart 2002 Times and Daily Telegraph news 12/1/02. High Court Judge at Crown Court. The defendant was convicted of 10 counts of causing death by dangerous driving. The defendant chatted on the telephone to a person he had contacted through the Internet for 6 (or 5 in the other report) hours until 3am. He set off on a 147 (or 154 in the other report) mile journey and fell asleep. His Land Rover, which was towing a 2 tonne load drifted off the M62. It ran alongside it until it fell into a railway cutting containing the East Coast Main line. An express train ran into it and drove on for another 400 yards before crashing into an oncoming coal freight train. Ten men were killed and 94 casualties. The defendant was 37. Judge's remarks. Every driver and I think I should include myself, has been in or very nearly in that position. Most acknowledge it by taking a break, taking a sleep or handing over to someone else if they can. A driver who presses on takes a grave risk. You chose not to have any sleep in the previous 24 hours. Choosing to drive after plenty of warnings was an aggravating feature. An accident was almost inevitable. There is very little to choose between you and a drink driver. Because of your arrogance in setting off on a long journey without sleep, you caused the worst driving-related accident in the UK in recent history. I accept you are a hard working and decent family man. 5 years and **5 years'** disqualification. [Treat news reports with care. Details of some of the facts can be found in the transcript of defendant's appeal against conviction, *R v Hart* 2003 EWCA Crim 1268].

R v France 2003 1 Cr App R (S) 108. The defendant made an early guilty plea to six counts of causing death by dangerous driving. He was sentenced on the basis he was reading and had no effective control of his lorry on A1(M). The lorry which was travelling at 55 mph drifted onto the hard shoulder and killed six people who were on the hard shoulder because they had been involved in an accident about 2 minutes earlier. He was 55 and of good character with only one speeding offence which was 15 months before. Held. Cases of causing death by dangerous driving pose a peculiar problem, particularly in multiple deaths cases because in the case of a serious accident, resulting from one particular piece of bad driving, it is very often a matter of chance how many people are killed. For example, if one car is knocked off the road and/or badly damaged, it is quite fortuitous whether there is a lone driver within it or an entire family. Equally, if a person drives recklessly fast round a corner it will be a matter of chance whether an ongoing vehicle is a motor cycle or a charabanc full of passengers. In either case, however many lives are lost, the level of dangerousness, lack of care, or recklessness of the driver will be exactly the same. For these reasons, the classic (then) guideline case of *R v Boswell* 1984 79 Cr App R 277, principally concentrated on features going to the degree and level of blameworthiness involved in the actions of the driver as dictating the proper level of sentence, rather than the number of people killed. Nonetheless, that feature was included as an element which the court must take into account. **5 years** not 6.

R v Noble 2003 1 Cr App R (S) 313. The defendant was convicted of six counts of causing death by dangerous driving. He pleaded to driving whilst disqualified. He and friends spent the day drinking on a 'motorised pub crawl.' He said he had drunk about 12 pints of lager, 1 pint of mixed lager and cider and two Bacardi Breezers. He then drove with others on a wet busy A road at excessive speed. After the dual carriageway narrowed to a single carriageway there was a double bend. Because of his speed he lost control of his car and hit a wall and then two other cars. Three died in both other vehicles and others were injured. The defendant received relatively minor injuries and ran off. On his arrest he said someone else was driving. On his estimate of his drinking his blood/alcohol reading would have been 150 mg in his blood. (The court said he was $2^{1}/_{2}$ times over the limit which gives a different figure.) He was 41 with the following convictions. 1990 failure to provide a specimen. 1991 drink/drive and driving whilst disqualified when he was disqualified for 3 years. In 1997 drink/drive when he received 100 hours' CSO and 4 years' disqualification. He was a family man with a good work record. The judge said he showed breathtaking arrogance in the witness box. Held. This was a horrendous case involving tragedy for many families. There were obvious aggravating features. The motorised pub crawl, the very bad driving record, being disqualified, running off, driving dangerously for a little while before the accident and blaming someone else. The element of chance in the number of people killed by a single piece of dangerous driving underlines the appropriateness of the general principle which applies throughout sentencing for criminal offences, namely that consecutive sentences should not normally be imposed for offences arising out of the same single incident. That is not an absolute principle. It may admit of exceptions in exceptional circumstances. But where such exceptional cases occur, they tend to be ones where different offences are committed. It seems to this court to be wrong in principle to impose consecutive sentences in respect of each death arising from a single piece of dangerous driving. We emphasise in saying that that it is right that the total sentence imposed in such cases should take account of the number of deaths involved. We have read the letters from relatives of several of those who died in the present case. They bring home to any reader the depth of the tragedy which has resulted from the behaviour of this appellant. At the same time, one has to recognise that no prison sentence of whatever length on the offender can make up for the anguish caused or bring back to life those who have been killed. While, therefore, the total sentence should take account of the number of deaths, it cannot be determined by it, if only because of the chance nature of the number of the deaths. The fact that multiple deaths have been caused is not of itself a reason for imposing consecutive sentences. The main focus of the sentencing judge in such cases has to be on the dangerousness of the driving, taking into account all the circumstances of that driving, including the results. It is difficult to imagine a worse case so **10 years** (the maximum) but the sentences should be concurrent so 10 years not 15 (based on consecutive sentences). (From the tenor of the Judgement it can be inferred that had the new penalty of 14 years been available the court would have imposed it.)

See also *Consecutive or concurrent, should the other sentences be?*

Overtaking or starting to overtake, driver

48.35   *R v Nijjer* 1999 2 Cr App R (S) 385. The defendant was convicted of two counts of causing death by dangerous driving. When 18 he left school in his Porsche at lunchtime with two friends. The car had been an 18th birthday present. It was drizzling, the road was damp and it was overcast. In a 30 mph area he overtook a car at 60 mph. He lost control of the car and it mounted the pavement and killed two elderly pedestrians. The defendant and his friends were uninjured and they remained at the scene. He was of good character and he and his family were devastated. The defendant said he never wanted to drive again. He was racked by guilt and self blame and suffered from depression. Held. This was a bad case. Bearing in mind his age, character and remorse **3 years** YOI not 4.

R v Kosola 2000 1 Cr App R (S) 205. The defendant pleaded guilty to causing death by dangerous driving. He was driving with his wife and two children on a single carriageway and overtook some vehicles. He was driving at about 55 mph and collided head on with another car, which was also travelling at about 55 mph. The other car contained three people. One died. One was very badly injured and requires eight pain killing tablets a day. He will never work again. The third suffered fractures, bruising and dislocation. He was unable to work for 14 weeks and needed counselling. The defendant suffered two fractures to his leg, multiple fractures to his ankle and foot. He was in hospital for 9 weeks. He still requires further surgery and uses a crutch to walk. His wife and child suffered minor injuries. He immediately admitted responsibility. He said he still believed he was on a dual carriageway and that he had driven 10,000 miles on English roads in the previous year. He was 32 and was a Captain in the Finnish army who was studying at a military college in England. He had an impeccable character and showed remorse. He army career was very likely to be over and he suffered post-traumatic stress disorder. He claimed he had been confused by the road markings. There was a Newton hearing. He was disbelieved. The judge found he had overtaken a slow moving tanker dangerously. Held. Everybody's injuries and employment changes explain why this case is very serious. His sentence of **12 months** would normally be regarded at the bottom of the sentencing bracket. Exercising mercy because of his character, his probable loss of career, his serious injuries, that the sentence would be served in a foreign country and the effect on his family **8 months** instead.

R v Cusick 2000 1 Cr App R (S) 444. The defendant was convicted of causing death by dangerous driving. He was driving on an A road in the dark between 55 and 60 mph. He didn't overtake the car in front although he could have done. Instead he tailgated it. As he approached a wide left hand bend he overtook the vehicle and within seconds hit an oncoming car. The driver was killed. The driver of the car that was overtaken did not see the accident but it was clear that the defendant's car was for unexplained reasons substantially over the centre line. The defendant's speed at the impact was estimated to be 65–70 mph in a 60 mph limit. He was 49 with an excess alcohol conviction in 1982. Otherwise his licence was for all practical purposes clear. Held. This was a bad case. There was excessive speed and aggression. **2 years** was severe but not excessive.

R v O'Brien 2001 1 Cr App R (S) 79. The defendant pleaded guilty to causing death by dangerous driving on the day his case was listed for trial. In daylight the defendant was in a transit van. At a junction he overtook a car which was travelling at 30 mph. He hit a cyclist who had just emerged from the junction. A week later the cyclist died. The defendant showed remorse from the very beginning. He was 50 and was effectively of good character. The victim's relatives said no useful purpose could be served by a custodial sentence. The judge said it was an impatient and aggressive piece of overtaking at an excessive speed. Held. It was more than a momentary lapse of attention. The judge was right to consider a stern sentence was unavoidable. **12 months** reflected all the factors.

Att-Gen's Ref. Nos. 68 of 2001 2002 1 Cr App R (S) 406. The defendant was convicted of causing death by dangerous driving. The defendant was driving in a 60 mph area without a seat belt talking to his girlfriend on his mobile for 8 minutes. During this time he overtook three vehicles in a way described as 'erratic'. He then overtook another car at the top of a hill which was considered by another motorist as dangerous. He was then behind a Mazda doing 55–60 mph with a Mitsubishi behind him. The Mazda was overtaken near a blind corner on the brow of a hill at a speed 20–30 mph faster than the Mazda. He lost control of his car and hit an oncoming Renault with three adults and a 5-year-old child. One adult was killed and the other two received serious injuries. The child was kept overnight in hospital. The defendant received a broken neck fortunately without spinal damage. When interviewed he said someone was tailgating him and he overtook to get away. He was 26 and was of good character. He had one speeding conviction in 1992 and was held in high regard by his family and friends. He expressed remorse and was sentenced to a community penalty with 180 hours community service. He had performed 66 hours. Held. We would have expected at least 3 years. Because it was a reference, the hours performed and it was his first custodial **18 months** substituted. The disqualification was increased from 3 to 7 years.

R v Everett 2002 1 Cr App R (S) 550. The defendant pleaded guilty to causing death by dangerous driving on the day his case was listed for trial. At 8.15 p.m. the defendant overtook a car which was behind a bus on a narrow winding road with a 60 mph speed limit. He drove right behind the bus. Then on a blind left hand bend he overtook the bus and collided head on with an on coming car. The victim aged 18 with a bright future was burnt to death. His parents were shattered and overwhelmed. The defendant was 35. Held. This was a bad case of an impatient driver who overtook on a blind bend without making any attempt to ascertain whether it was safe to do so. It was a course of the utmost danger. **2 years** and 4 years' disqualification were not excessive.

R v Braid 2002 2 Cr App R (S) 509. The defendant pleaded guilty to causing death by dangerous driving on rearraignment. At 11 am on a clear sunny day he overtook a lorry as he approached a blind corner. He hit an oncoming car head on killing the front seat passenger. Her husband, who was driving was treated in hospital for six days and released from hospital after four weeks in a wheel chair. He required further treatment and may never fully recover. His left hip was fractured and it required pinning. His daughter aged 17 became the "woman of the house" and found it difficult. His son aged 15 who had learning difficulties requires one to one attention. The defendant was 20 with no convictions. He was suffering depression relating to his father's disease, Huntington's Chorea and his health concerns about whether he would suffer from the same disease. He was prescribed antidepressants. A psychiatric report said this had impaired his mental state leading to a lack of concentration and may be a state of disassociation. There were letters from his fiancée, employers and others speaking of his maturity, good sense, his safety as a driver and the burden of his father's illness. The Judge said personal circumstances do not weigh heavily in the balance in cases of causing death by dangerous driving. Held. We agree with the Judge about the weight of personal circumstances. Those falling to be sentenced not infrequently have the highest personal credentials and so generate very real sympathy. The courts have to reflect the loss of a precious life and to demonstrate to all that dangerous driving is a very serious social evil, which if it causes death will almost inevitably lead to a substantial custodial sentence. The fact he couldn't see far enough should have been apparent. Nevertheless the case does not have any of the aggravating features identified in the authorities and does exhibit many of the features, which mitigate the sentence. **18 months** YOI not 2 years. 3 years disqualification not 6.

R v Hoque 2003 1 Cr App R (S) 537. The defendant pleaded guilty to an offence of causing death by dangerous driving. Just after 10:30 pm the defendant was driving a courtesy car, accompanied by a friend. The defendant was not entirely accustomed to the car. He was travelling at 80 miles per hour in a 60 limit and overtook a car thought to be travelling at about 55 to 60 mph. The car swerved violently back to the nearside of the road, rocked from side to side violently, went out of control and collided with an on-coming motor vehicle. The driver of that vehicle sustained grave injuries from which she died. The accident investigator found that the cause of the accident was more to do with the braking and/or steering than speed. The defendant was 24 and of good character with a good job. His employers gave him an excellent reference. He had a single speeding conviction some two years earlier. He was genuinely remorseful, unable to return to work and receiving medication for depression. Held. The feature of this case giving rise to criminality was the overtaking at excessive speed in an unfamiliar car in such a manner that the defendant lost control. This was more than momentary inattention. **2 years** not 3.

R v Roberts 2005 1 Cr App R (S) 187. The defendant changed his plea to guilty on two counts of causing death by dangerous driving. He was driving with his fiancée and with another young woman, C, in the back of his mother's BMW coupe. His mother had asked him to drive the car round the block in a shopping area as it was not easy to park, but he had decided to go for a drive along the by pass. This road had one lane in each direction and a 60mph limit. C saw the car reach a speed of 140 mph. He was overtaking other vehicles by driving in the middle of the road forcing oncoming cars to pull over. One witness estimated he was driving at 100 mph when he saw him. He then entered a bend in the road. A driver who was coming towards him thought he was going to hit her head on; she braked, swerved and saw the defendant braking sharply and swerving. The driver of the car behind her also saw the defendant coming straight at her with his wheels screeching and smoking. She saw him overtake 3 cars and she turned away from him. They missed by two feet. She believed if she had not had both police and army driving training there would have been a collision. The car behind her was driven by E. Her car was marginally on the wrong side of the road in that her rear off-side wheel was over the white line. She collided with the defendant and was killed. The defendant's fiancée was also killed. The defendant was seriously injured, and was left with a limp and a deformity to his arm. C had lacerations to her head. He pleaded guilty on the written basis that he was driving at approximately 100 mph; he was not under the influence of any substance that would have impaired his ability to drive; speed was the only basis for his acceptance that he was driving dangerously; the car driven by E was overtaking and on impact his car was on the right side of the carriage way, although the defendant accepted that because of the speed he was travelling although E braked she did not have time to correct her position; that his dangerous driving was a cause and not the only cause of the deaths, and that another factor was that his fiancée was not wearing a seatbelt. The defendant, 23, had once been a successful auto cross driver and clearly prided himself on being able to drive at speed. He had been disqualified for accumulated speeding offences. He also had five other convictions including failure to provide a specimen of breath and taking a vehicle without consent. A pre-sentence report said he did not take full responsibility for the offences and was bitter about the case. He expressed regret but said he would act in the same way again. His risk of harm to the public was assessed as being high. He was also assessed at being at some risk of self-harm due to depression. There were also medical and psychological reports. He was deeply affected by his injuries and by the death of his fiancée and was suffering from post- traumatic stress, and grief. The aggravating features which put him into the higher *Cooksley* category were: greatly excessive speed; showing off; disregard of warning from fellow passengers; a prolonged persistent and deliberate course of very bad driving; aggressive driving; previous convictions for motoring offences; more than one person killed. Held. This did fall into the most serious category. Balancing the mitigating factors- timely plea of guilty, genuine shock or remorse, serious injury to the offender and the fact that E was slightly on the wrong side of the road- with the aggravating factors **5 years** upheld.

See also *Att-Gen's Ref. No 70 of 2001* Unreported 31/10/01, R v Gray 2005 Unreported 29/4/05 and *R v Penjwnini* 2001 Unreported 15/10/01. 3 years not 4 for overtaking on a bend and *R v Braid* 2002 2 Cr App R (S) 509.

Old cases *R v McGowan* 1998 2 Cr App R (S) 220 and *R v Richards* 1998 2 Cr App R (S) 346 (For summaries of these cases see the 1st edition of this book.)

Police chases

48.36 *R v McGilvery* 2002 2 Cr App R (S) 432. The defendant pleaded guilty to causing death by dangerous driving, driving whilst disqualified and threatening behaviour. In the early hours there was a disturbance involving a group of youths. The police were summonsed and the defendant made off in a car, which he had bought a few weeks earlier, despite the police shouting for him to stop. His car was chased and he travelled at 60–70 mph in a 30 mph area. He weaved from lane to lane and hit a flooded area and drove round a corner. On the wrong side of the road the car flipped into the air. He collided with an oncoming taxi and killed the driver. The defendant was found nearby and made full admissions in interview. He was just short of his 21st birthday and had two convictions for driving with excess alcohol. For the last one he was disqualified for two years 3 months before the offence. Held. This was a truly dreadful offence of its kind, but it cannot be said to be absolutely the worst offence of its kind. Because of the plea **5 years** YOI not 6.

R v Foster 2003 1 Cr App R (S) 547. The defendant pleaded guilty to causing death by dangerous driving. He and his friends bought a car for £25, and when driving at about 11:20pm was involved in a minor collision with a lamp post. Thereafter the defendant drove onto an A road where he was followed by a marked police car. The defendant initially drove off on the wrong side of the road before driving through a red traffic light. The police car, in pursuit, switched on its sirens. The defendant made off to the best of his ability, increasing his speed to about 70 miles an hour in a 40 limit before turning into an estate where the limit was 30 miles an hour. The passengers in the car told the defendant to stop. However, the defendant mounted the pavement, collided with a garden wall and drove off at speed before crossing a junction with another main road which had four lanes. He entered another street at about twice the 30 miles an hour speed limit. He then failed to give way at another junction and he collided with another vehicle with considerable force. The appellant ran off but was quickly arrested. The front seat passenger in the other vehicle died. The driver sustained a broken arm. The rear passenger's leg was broken which required prolonged treatment. The front passenger in the defendant's vehicle sustained serious lacerations to his face and the other passengers sustained minor injuries. The chase had lasted for 1 minute and 24 seconds and the minimum impact speed was estimated to have been 52 miles an hour. The defendant claimed that he had panicked, since he had no driving experience, no licence and no insurance. The defendant was 16 at the time of the offence and there was substantial evidence of remorse. Held. Aggravating features included the grossly excessive and inappropriate speed, over a period of time, a moderately persistent course of bad driving, driving on the wrong side of the road for periods, jumping a series of junctions against the right of way, no insurance and insufficient age to even possess a provisional licence. The victim died because the defendant was trying to avoid being caught by the police. He had been told to stop by his own friends, albeit it at a late stage. This was a truly shocking act of driving, it was prolonged, and sooner or later a terrible accident was inevitable. The judge passed a sentence that fully expressed the aggravating and mitigating factors in this tragic case. **5 years** upheld.

See also **DANGEROUS DRIVING** – *Police chases*

Projecting into the road, vehicle

48.37   *R v Neaven* 2000 1 Cr App R (S) 391. The defendant was convicted of causing death by dangerous driving. When it was dark he was driving a low loader which was carrying a dumper truck. He decided to do a U turn through a gap in the central reservation on a dual carriageway. While waiting for a gap in the traffic on the other carriageway the rear part of his lorry was protruding into the fast line of the road. The lights on his vehicle were not visible to those travelling in that lane. A car ran into the lorry and another car ran into that car. The driver of the first car was killed. He was a father of young children. The defendant remained at the scene and rang the police. The defendant was of impeccable character and had an impeccable driving history. He'd had an HGV licence for 25 years. Held. All motorists must realise that if they drive dangerously and thereby kill someone there must be a danger of imprisonment. It was a very dangerous piece of driving. **12 months** was not manifestly excessive. However, as he had always been a good driver 2 years' disqualification not 4.

R v Taylor 2002 1 Cr App R (S) 76. The defendant was convicted of causing death by dangerous driving. He was driving his lorry and trailer which was 15.5 metres long and approached a junction with a dual carriageway from a side road. Wanting to turn right he crossed one carriageway and stopped in the central reservation with the front of the lorry protruding in the one carriageway and the trailer protruding in the other. It would have been possible to remain in the central reservation without protruding if the angle was right. The trailer had obstructed half of the outside lane of one of the dual carriageways. The deceased was driving her car at about 70 mph in the fast lane and hit the trailer. She didn't see the trailer in time. The dual carriageway was a busy truck road carrying fast moving traffic. It was dark and the speed limit was 70 mph. The road was wet but it wasn't raining. The rear lights of the trailer were not visible because of the angle of the vehicle and because of the colour of the vehicle it merged into the background. The judge said it was an error of judgment. The defendant was a businessman of good character with a good driving record. He had testimonials which spoke extremely highly of him. Held. Following *R v Ollerenshaw* 1999 1 Cr App R (S) 65 [Courts should ask themselves for those who had not previously served custody whether an even shorter period might be equally effective] **4 months** not 8.

Racing, competitive driving etc

48.38   *R v Cooksley* 2004 1 Cr App R (S) 1. In relation to contested offences of higher culpability (for example, by the presence of one or two of the factors (a) to (i)) the appropriate starting point would be **four to five years**. The exact level of sentence would be determined by the dangerousness of the driving and by the presence or absence of other aggravating or mitigating factors. There will be cases which will involve sentences **higher than 5 years** because they are bad examples and cases, particularly where there is a plea, where the sentence will be less than four years where there are significant mitigating factors.

(b) Greatly excessive speed; racing; competitive driving against another vehicle; "showing off"; is the second of the higher culpability list of factors.

The list should not be regarded as an exhaustive statement of the factors. In addition it is important to appreciate that the significance of the factors can differ. There can be cases with three or more aggravating factors, which are not as serious as a case providing a bad example of one factor. For more details see ***Guideline case and Guideline remarks.***

R v Howell 1999 1 Cr App R (S) 449. The defendant pleaded guilty to two counts of causing death by dangerous driving. The defendant with two friends went to Southend where young men raced high performance cars. On his way home at 1.30am he was driving his mother's Ford RS Turbo which had certain modifications made to it on a dual carriageway. The speed limit was 70 mph and he saw a Fiesta car with a similar performance to his mother's car. The driver of the Fiesta had also been racing that day and had taken drink and drugs. He had two passengers. The two drivers decided to race each other. Side by side they travelled for over a mile at speeds of about 100 mph. The defendant was in the nearside lane and the Fiesta in the outer lane. A driver ahead also in the outer lane noticed the two cars driving at speed and stayed where he was. The Fiesta was forced to move into the nearside lane and it clipped the defendant's car causing the cars to crash. The driver and the passenger of the Fiesta were killed. The other passenger was injured. The defendant was quite seriously injured and one of his passengers was very seriously injured. The defendant was 24 and of good character and was a 'thoroughly decent' man with a good work record. $3^{1}/_{2}$ **years** not 4 which would reduce the sentence below the 4 year sentence barrier.

R v Padley 2000 2 Cr App R (S) 201. The defendant was convicted of causing death by dangerous driving. The defendant then aged 20 drove into a petrol station and challenged another driver to take part in a race. The man ignored him. Later that evening he challenged another man Cragg the co-defendant to race. Cragg agreed. They raced on a single carriageway road, which was a 30ft wide with houses on each side. The road was damp. Cragg whilst being pursued by the defendant lost control of his car and it veered across the carriageway and demolished a brick wall. The car somersaulted back across the road and came to rest on its roof. A girl aged 19 or 20 who was sitting in the back seat of the car was thrown from the vehicle and killed. Another passenger suffered very severe head injuries. The defendant stopped his car and ran back to help. The defendant had three driving convictions. One was for speeding at 40 mph in a 30 mph area when he was on bail for the present offence. It was on the same road as where the accident occurred. The judge said that the defendant was responsible for initiating the whole tragic sequence of events. Held. Cragg received an appropriate sentence of 4 years taking into account his guilty plea. The starting point for the defendant must be 6 years. Despite the fact that the defendant was not the driver of the car which killed the victim, **5¹/₂ years** was appropriate.

R v Blackman 2001 2 Cr App R (S) 268. The defendant pleaded guilty to causing death by dangerous driving. The defendant stopped his TVR Sports car at traffic lights on a bypass. A motorbike pulled up beside him. When the lights changed the bike accelerated away and the defendant did the same. He kept close to the bike and crossed a humped railway bridge. Just the other side and 475 metres from the lights a pedestrian was crossing the road. The defendant then travelling at 63 mph braked. The wheels locked and he skidded into the pedestrian. The defendant stopped. He denied he was racing. He said he was squinting because of the sun. The impact on the widow was devastating. He was of good character with references and had a clean licence. He was in full time employment and terrified of going to prison. There was a Newton hearing and the judge found he was driving competitively. He had a good prison report. Held. There was very strong evidence to support the judge's finding. The balancing exercise is very difficult. **3 years** not 4¹/₂ and 5 years' disqualification not 7.

See also *R v Watson* 2001 Unreported 10/8/01.

Att-Gen's Ref. Nos. 68 of 2001 2002 1 Cr App R (S) 406. The defendant was convicted of causing death by dangerous driving. The defendant was driving in a 60 mph area without a seat belt talking to his girlfriend on his mobile for 8 minutes. During this time he overtook three vehicles in a way described as 'erratic'. He then overtook another car at the top of a hill which was considered by another motorist as dangerous. He was then behind a Mazda doing 55–60 mph with a Mitsubishi behind him. The Mazda was overtaken near a blind corner on the brow of a hill at a speed 20–30 mph faster than the Mazda. He lost control of his car and hit an oncoming Renault with three adults and a 5-year-old child. One adult was killed and the other two received serious injuries. The child was kept overnight in hospital. The defendant received a broken neck fortunately without spinal damage. When interviewed he said someone was tailgating him and he overtook to get away. He was 26 and was of good character. He had one speeding conviction in 1992 and was held in high regard by his family and friends. He expressed remorse and was sentenced to a community penalty with 180 hours community service. He had performed 66 hours. Held. We would have expected at least 3 years. Because it was a reference, the hours performed and it was his first custodial **18 months** substituted. The disqualification was increased from 3 to 7 years.

Single misjudgement/Inattention

48.39   *Att-Gen's Ref. No 76 of 2002* 2003 1 Cr App R (S) 519. The defendant pleaded guilty, when the case was listed for trial, to causing death by dangerous driving. At about 9 pm, he was travelling with one passenger when he approached the junction that was marked with a Give Way sign and a warning triangle on the road surface. Road conditions were dry and fine and the defendant's view of the main road was unobstructed.The defendant believed that the main road was clear and at the moment of impact the defendant's car was travelling at about 25 miles per hour. The defendant drove his car across the junction and collided with another vehicle which had right of way. The passenger in the other vehicle died at the scene and the driver suffered extensive bruising and injuries. There was no question of any fault being attributed to the victim's car. The defendant was seen by police and said that he thought that the road was clear and later that the other car had "appeared out of nowhere". The defendant, now 19, was of exemplary character and was a senior aircraftsman employed as avionics technician for the Royal Air Force. He had shown genuine remorse and a number of references had been provided to the Judge. Held. It was not an error brought about by the consumption of drink or drugs nor was the defendant racing. We do not accept that in virtually every case of dangerous driving where death results a prison sentence must follow. Often it will follow. In every case there are competing considerations. The appalling loneliness to which [the victim] will be condemned will blight the rest of his life. So the consequences are catastrophic. However, this was a single misjudgement. He thought that he had checked sufficiently when he had not. Probably he checked too early and probably he should have checked again before deciding to accelerate. He was unlikely to appear in Court again. The sentence was a merciful sentence and a sentence of this kind fell within the proper exercise of the judge's sentencing responsibilities. A **community punishment order and a fine** were not unduly lenient.

Att-Gen's Ref No 80 of 2002 2003 1 Cr App R (S) 599. The defendant pleaded guilty to causing death by dangerous diving. At about 7:30pm he was driving his car with a work colleague. They had been in a public house together earlier. It was dark, road conditions were dry and the weather was good. The road was an unclassified narrow country road with the national speed limit applying. There was an unlit Give Way sign and a 64-metre length of hazard warning line (single white lines) leading up to a crossroads. The defendant accepted that he knew the crossroads and that he did not have priority. Mr S was driving along the main road with his wife in the front passenger seat and his two children in the rear seat. His car collided with the nearside wing of the defendant's car as it was driven deliberately across the junction at a speed of between 50 and 60 miles per hour. There was extensive damage to both vehicles; Mr S's car then struck an electricity pole, snapping it in two. The defendant's passenger was pronounced dead on arrival at hospital. Mrs S suffered very serious injuries, namely a ruptured liver and spleen. She was in intensive care for nearly a month. She was discharged from hospital 5 weeks after the accident. Mr S suffered psychologically but like the defendant and one of his two daughters, suffered only relatively minor physical injuries. The defendant was 23, with no previous convictions of relevance and was deeply affected, suffering with flashbacks and nightmares. Held. This was not a case of momentary inattention. The driving was more serious than that. There were a variety of warnings in relation to this junction by way of a sign and markings on the road. An aggravating feature is the serious injuries suffered by Mrs S. The sentence was unduly lenient. A **short period of custody was called for**. However, as it was a reference and the 100 hours community punishment had been served, no order was made.

R v Vera 2003 2 Cr App R (S) 27. The defendant was convicted of causing death by dangerous driving. He was driving a 7.5-ton lorry on a single-carriageway road. The speed limit was 60 mph. The driving conditions were dry and clear. The road was described as long, straight and boring and was one with which the defendant was familiar. He was driving at about 56 mph when he came over the brow of a hill. Ahead of him and some 16 seconds away was a car being driven by the 72-year-old victim. The car was stationary and indicating to turn right. The defendant simply did not see the car and collided with it pushing it onto the opposite carriageway where it was struck by an oncoming lorry. The victim died later of his injuries. The defendant suffered a broken wrist and concussion. The lorry was subject to a 50 mph speed limit and was slightly over laden. In interview he fully admitted responsibility and showed clear remorse. The question at trial was whether his driving was careless or dangerous. He was 26 and had no relevant previous convictions and was regarded as a good hard-working man. Held. This was more than momentary inattention. However, there had been no bad driving, no deliberate attempt to overtake, no excessive speed, i.e. none of the aggravating features identified in Boswell. **2 years** not 3.

Speed, approaching a hazard at excessive

48.40   *R v Wagstaff* 2000 2 Cr App R (S) 205. The defendant changed his plea to guilty to three counts of causing death by dangerous driving. An accident had caused a build up of traffic on a dual carriageway. A 'slow' sign had been placed well in advance of the hold up. It had a warning strobe light. It was placed to provide maximum impact. In the early afternoon, the defendant drove a horsebox past the sign and his passenger referred to it but the defendant did not take much notice of the remark. She shouted 'Look, there is a police car' and he slowed down a bit. The horsebox hit the stationary traffic and a VW Polo car was almost completely crushed. A husband, wife and child all died. Earlier the passenger had observed the defendant was driving too fast and he was agitated. She had suggested he took a rest and he ignored the advice. The tacho-graph showed he was driving at 51 mph at the moment of impact. The horsebox speed limit was 50 mph. It also showed he had driven for $4^{1}/_{2}$ hours with one break of 19 minutes. That $4^{1}/_{2}$ hours was the maximum amount that was allowed. The defendant claimed he had no memory of the accident. He tried to substitute an earlier tachograph. He was of good character with references. A doctor provided a medical explanation for a loss of concentration. He had not been warned of this. He showed great remorse. Held. The doctor's opinion had to be considered with the warnings from the passenger. The judge had carried out the difficult balancing exercise and had taken into account all the factors. **3 years** was not manifestly excessive.

Speeding – less than 4 years' imprisonment

48.41   *R v Lightfoot* 1999 2 Cr App R (S) 55. The defendant pleaded guilty to two counts of causing death by dangerous driving. In daylight on a dry road where there was good visibility the defendant drove his tractor unit at excessive speeds. Shortly before the accident he was travelling at 67 mph. Ahead was a stationary car waiting to turn right into a lay-by. The speed limit was 60 mph and his permitted limit was 40 mph. Just before the accident his speed was 54 mph. He should have seen the white car 350 yards before but his concentration was such he only saw it when he braked. The brakes were defective and they locked. The tractor unit veered to the right and hit an oncoming a car head on. The driver and his 18-year-old daughter were killed and his wife and younger daughter were injured. The defendant was 33 and of good character with testimonials. He had been a lorry driver since he was 21 and had only one speed-ing ticket. He expressed genuine shock and remorse. There was a Newton hearing when the judge found the defendant was not aware of the defective brakes. **2 years** not 3.

Att-Gen's Ref. Nos. 58 of 2000 2001 2 Cr App R (S) 102. The defendant pleaded guilty at the earliest opportunity to causing death by dangerous driving. The defendant had a provisional licence, left a pub and drove to his girlfriend's house where they had an argu-ment. He left and was seen by two pedestrians to be driving at about 50 mph in a 30 mph area. The car moved from the kerb to the centre of the road so that oncoming vehicles had to move towards their kerb. The engine was heard revving and after going over a bridge it collided head on with a motorcyclist. The accident was only a short distance from the house. The rider died and the passenger aged 7 suffered leg injuries. The defen-dant left the scene but surrendered to the police 18 hours later. An expert concluded the car was on the wrong side of the road and was travelling at about 52 mph. The defendant was 32 and showed every sign of genuine remorse. A basis of plea was accepted which said the speed of the car was about 40 mph and alcohol did not play any part in his man-ner of driving. Held. The defendant had prevented the police from determining his alcohol level. Applying *Att-Gen's Ref. Nos. 21 of 2000* 2001 1 Cr App R (S) 173 the court is able to draw an adverse inference about the amount of alcohol consumed. The judge should not have accepted the basis of plea, but the court was bound by it. Taking into account it was a reference and there were aggravating features **3½ years** not 30 months.

R v Ward 2002 1 Cr App R (S) 221. The defendant pleaded guilty to causing death by dangerous driving based on speed, being too close to the vehicle in front and inattention. The defendant drove four friends behind another a car driven by another friend. In a residential road with a 30 mph speed limit and a slight downhill gradient he was talking and didn't pay sufficient attention to the road. He was too close to the car in front. The car in front braked and he pulled out to avoid hitting it. He panicked, accelerated, overtook the friend's car and drove into a corner at over 50 mph. He hit it, skidded and lost control of the vehicle. It crossed the centre of the road, hit a lamp post and crashed into some parked cars. There was no oncoming traffic. During the manoeuvre hispassengers shouted for him to stop but he did not. A passenger died and he and others were injured. He was then 20 of good character with character references. He showed remorse and the risk of re-offending was assessed as low. There was considerable delay, which was not the defendant's fault. Since the accident he had married and had a daughter. Held. This was not just a momentary lapse. **2 years** not 3.

Att-Gen's Ref. No 50 of 2001 2002 1 Cr App R (S) 245. The defendant was convicted of causing death by dangerous driving. After working at a public house she agreed to drive others in someone else's car to first a pub and then a party. The others were either too drunk or unable to drive. In a 30 mph area there was a lot of laughing in the car and she was driving at 45–50 mph. She approached a sudden blind corner and lost control of the car and went over to the wrong side of the road. One car just managed to get out of the way but she hit a scooter driven by a student. He was thrown onto her windscreen and onto the roof of a parked car and died. Her car hit three parked cars and hit a wall. It was severely damaged and found to have over-inflated tyres and an under-inflated tyre, which could well have affected the stability of the car. All the occupants of her car left the scene and she hid first of all in a garden. All had mobile phones and no one called for assistance. She then went to two pubs. When first interviewed she declined to answer questions and then said that others were joking and bouncing around in the back. One of them tugged her shoulder and she turned round to tell her to leave her alone and the crash happened. She was uninsured at the time. She was 20 with no convictions. Held. The most serious aspect was her simply leaving the scene. 18 months might just have been defensible on a plea of guilty. If contested the appropriate sentence was **3 years**. Because of her youth, her remorse and that it was a reference **2 years** not 18 months YOI.

R v Morton 2003 1 Cr App R (S) 196. The defendant was convicted of causing death by dangerous driving. At 9.30 pm, he then 18, drove his motorbike with his girlfriend on the back and approached a bend at about 60 mph in a 30 mph area. The weather was dry and the road conditions good. He lost control and hit a car. His girlfriend hit the windscreen of the car and died of multiple injuries. His breath test was negative. The motorcycle was examined and was found to be in good working order with no defects. Because of his age the defendant was restricted to bikes with 25kW output. He had removed the devices to restrict the output, which was now 56.2kW. This did not however contribute to the accident. He said he had taken the bend before at 60 mph with his passenger, but this time when he leant the bike would not move with him. He was now 20 with no convictions for motoring offences. He was grief stricken about the loss of his girlfriend with whom marriage was contemplated. His mother said for days after the accident he wouldn't talk or leave his room. He had changed from being outgoing and cheerful to withdrawn, unpredictable and clinically depressed of moderate severity. He made two serious suicide attempts. There was 16 months between interview and trial. Held. This was a tragic case. However we cannot say **2$^1/_2$ years** YOI was manifestly excessive. Because of his youth and his good motoring record prior to the accident 4 years disqualification not 7.

See also R v Hunter 2001 Unreported 1/11/01.

Old cases *R v Chahal* 1998 2 Cr App R (S) 93, *R v Hird* 1998 2 Cr App R (S) 241 and *R v Richards* 1998 2 Cr App R (S) 346. (For a summary of these cases see the first edition of this book.)

Speeding – 4 years or more imprisonment

48.42   *R v Ratcliffe* 2003 2 Cr App R (S) 367. The defendant pleaded guilty to two counts of causing death by dangerous driving. He and a friend had spent the afternoon drinking before going back to the defendant's house where they were joined by others (who included the victims). From his home, the defendant took his parents' BMW into which others (including the victims) climbed. He reversed out of the drive at speed and collided with another car before driving from the village at 70–80 mph. One passenger stated "I looked up to tell [the defendant] to slow down, I could clearly see the speedometer which was showing 100 miles an hour". The defendant entered a right hand bend. A car came from the opposite direction. He lost control and the BMW left the road. The two victims died from head injuries after the car hit a tree. The other passenger suffered bone injuries; the defendant was thrown clear. A back calculation indicated that the defendant would have been over the drink drive limit. He was a provisional licence holder and uninsured. He admitted that he did not have permission to drive the car but had no recollection of the accident. He was now 21 and of good character. There were impressive references. One victim had been his best friend. The other was a friend of over 5 years. It was accepted that he was very remorseful. Held. The aggravating features were (1) he had been drinking; (2) he was showing off to his friends and driving plainly at a greatly excessive speed; (3) he disregarded repeated warnings from the passenger to slow down; (4) this was not a momentary speeding, or error of judgment, but a sustained piece of driving; (5) that he held a provisional licence only and was driving without permission; (6) there had been two deaths and not just one. This had the stamp of the folly and inexperience of young men in proximity to fast cars. However, the sentence fell outside the band of responses. **4 years detention** not 5. Disqualified for 7 years and an extended test.

R v Johnson 2004 2 Cr App R (S) 145. The defendant pleaded guilty on re-arraignment to two offences of causing death by dangerous driving. He was driving a Rover car on a modern single carriageway road with one front seat passenger. Weather conditions were favourable. He pulled sharply away from temporary traffic lights and accelerated down a slight hill leading into a gentle bend. He was travelling at a grossly excessive speed estimated at in excess of 90 mph, and lost control of the car on the bend and skidded into an oncoming car. Going into the skid he was travelling at about 70 mph. and at impact at about 30mph. Even at 70 mph a competent driver should have been able to negotiate the bend. His passenger and a young girl in the rear of the other car died; he and the other driver and another child received serious injuries. He had no memory of the accident. He had no driving licence of any kind and his car was not insured. Aggravating circumstances were that he was driving at greatly excessive speed, that he was committing other offences at the time of this offence, more than one person was killed and there was serious injury to two others. The defendant 'a young man at the time' had no previous convictions, and said that the passenger who died was a friend, and that he suffered serious injuries including a brain injury which was unresolved and which might have persistent consequences. Held. The absence of previous convictions was flimsy mitigation as he had daily driven this vehicle while uninsured and unlicensed. The plea of guilty stood him in good stead as he had no recollection of the events and many defendants in his position would have taken their chances with the jury. The right category for this offence was in the third of the four categories in *Cooksley* 'offences of higher culpability' due to the presence of one or two factors of aggravation in the most serious category. If the Judge had placed him in the highest category he had misjudged the case. **4 years** not 5 years imprisonment and 6 years disqualification upheld.

R v Roberts 2005 1 Cr App R (S) 187. The defendant changed his plea to guilty on two counts of causing death by dangerous driving. He was driving with his fiancée and with another young woman, C, in the back of his mother's BMW coupe. His mother had asked him to drive the car round the block in a shopping area as it was not easy to park, but he had decided to go for a drive along the by pass. This road had one lane in each direction and a 60 mph limit. C saw the car reach a speed of 140 mph. He was over-taking other vehicles by driving in the middle of the road forcing oncoming cars to pull over. One witness estimated he was driving at 100 mph when he saw him. He then entered a bend in the road. A driver who was coming towards him thought he was going to hit her head on; she braked, swerved and saw the defendant braking sharply and swerving. The driver of the car behind her also saw the defendant coming straight at her with his wheels screeching and smoking. She saw him overtake 3 cars and she turned away from him. They missed by two feet. She believed if she had not had both police and army driving training there would have been a collision. The car behind her was driven by E. Her car was marginally on the wrong side of the road in that her rear offside wheel was over the white line. She collided with the defendant and was killed. The defendant's fiancée was also killed. The defendant was seriously injured, and was left with a limp and a deformity to his arm. C had lacerations to her head. He pleaded guilty on the written basis that he was driving at approximately 100 mph; he was not under the influence of any substance that would have impaired his ability to drive; speed was the only basis for his acceptance that he was driving dangerously; the car driven by E was overtaking and on impact his car was on the right side of the carriage way, although the defendant accepted that because of the speed he was travelling although E braked she did not have time to correct her position; that his dangerous driving was a cause and not the only cause of the deaths, and that another factor was that his fiancée was not wearing a seatbelt. The defendant, 23, had once been a successful auto cross driver and clearly prided himself on being able to drive at speed. He had been disqualified for accumulated speeding offences. He also had five other convictions including failure to provide a specimen of breath and taking a vehicle without consent. A pre-sentence report said he did not take full responsibility for the offences and was bitter about the case. He expressed regret but said he would act in the same way again. His risk of harm to the public was assessed as being high. He was also assessed at being at some risk of self-harm due to depression. There were also medical and psycho-logical reports. He was deeply affected by his injuries and by the death of his fiancée and was suffering from post- traumatic stress, and grief. The aggravating features which put him into the higher *Cooksley* category were: greatly excessive speed; showing off; disregard of warning from fellow passengers; a prolonged persistent and deliberate course of very bad driving; aggressive driving; previous convictions for motoring offences; more than one person killed. Held. This did fall into the most serious category. Balancing the mitigating factors- timely plea of guilty, genuine shock or remorse, serious injury to the offender and the fact that E was slightly on the wrong side of the road- with the aggravating factors **5 years** upheld.

Old case. *R v Lucas* 1998 1 Cr App R (S) 195. (For a summary of this case see the first edition of this book.)

See also *Police chases*

Speeding with excess alcohol or drug taking

48.43 *Att-Gen's Ref. Nos. 16 of 1998* 1999 1 Cr App R (S) 149. The defendant was convicted of two counts of causing death by dangerous driving. When 22 he went to a pub with two close friends and he drove away with them. None of them were wearing a seat belt. He overtook vehicles on a dual carriageway well in excess of 70 mph. He overtook another vehicle when the road narrowed to a single carriageway which was potentially dangerous. He entered a roundabout at very close to 70 mph and lost con-trol of the car which hit a kerb and a crash barrier. Both his passengers were thrown from the car and died shortly after they had arrived in hospital. He left the scene in a state of shock. He gave a false name in hospital where he was treated for a broken shoulder, arm injuries and a head injury. The defendant pretended to the police he was a passenger. At first he refused to supply a blood specimen but eventually did. By back-tracking his reading was between 90 and 120mg at the time of the accident (equivalent to 39 and 52 μg). In interview he accepted he was driving at about 70 mph and said the brakes had failed. He had two convictions of no relevance and a clean licence. He had an overwhelming sense of grief and was having difficulty in coming to terms with his responsibility. He had become a virtual recluse and had sought counselling. The mother of one of the victims had written a moving letter saying she had forgiven him. The other mother had taken a very different position. He was sentenced to 240 hours' community service. The local press had described him as a murderer who had gone free. The offence was 18 months before and he had completed $^1/_4$ of his community service. Held. We would have expected **4$^1/_2$ years**. Taking into account it was a reference and the CSO he had completed **3$^1/_2$ years** instead.

R v James 2001 2 Cr App R (S) 153. The defendant was convicted of causing death by dangerous driving and driving whilst disqualified. After drinking in a pub with his two nephews he drove them away from the pub in his van. One of the nephews, the victim, sat on the lap of the other in the front passenger seat. None of the three was wearing a seat belt and the defendant was disqualified from driving. The van was seen by police being driven at speed and they gave chase. The van went through a red light and the police put their lights on. Shortly after the van still driving at speed veered across the road and hit an oncoming coach. The victim was thrown from the van and killed instantly. The other nephew was severely injured with head injuries. He was in intensive care for several days. The defendant was also injured. He had 123mg reading of alcohol in his blood, (equivalent to 54 μg in his breath). He showed shock and remorse. He was 28 and had an appalling driving record. He had 10 convictions for disqualified driving and two fordangerous driving. One of them was on a motorway when he was trying to escape the police. He also had a conviction for reckless driving and drink/drive. Held. The **8 years** sentence was entirely proper. However, as the judge had considered the fact he was disqualified in considering the aggravating factors it was wrong to make the disqualified driving sentence consecutive. The sentences were made concurrent.

Att-Gen's Ref. Nos. 32 of 2001 2002 1 Cr App R (S) 517. The defendant pleaded guilty to causing death by dangerous driving. He was committed for sentence for failing to stop, failing to report, driving without a licence and driving without insurance. He was also sentenced for perverting the course of justice, possession of heroin and two counts of possession of cannabis. He was released from YOI in January 2000 and obtained a provisional licence. He had some 4 hours of driving tuition. On 7 May 2000 he drove a stolen car at speed and mounted a pavement. He was arrested and cannabis and heroin were thrown from the car. He was released on bail. His girlfriend's mother left her powerful Ford Galaxy car outside her house and instructed one was to drive it. On 26 May 2000 the defendant used it for a number of journeys and on 27 May 2000 he drank rum in a pub and a club and then drove it at about 40 mph in a 30 mph area with his girlfriend who only had a provisional licence. He failed to see a Give Way sign in time and hit a taxi. His speed then was 20–25 mph. The taxi swung through 180 degrees and the passenger of the taxi died. He got out, looked at the taxi and left the scene. The prosecution said this was to avoid a breath sample being taken. Two days later he surrendered to the police. The defendant was either 18 or 19 (now 20) years old and in 1997 received 15 months YOI. In 1998 for burglary and robbery he received 3 years' detention. There were 439 days unexpired on his licence. He as sentenced to 2$^1/_2$ years for the driving and concurrent sentences on the other offences. No order was made for the breach of the licence. Held. We would expect **5 years** detention for the driving in addition to the breach sentence. As it was a reference **4 years** detention with 12 months for the breach of licence consecutive and 5 years not 2 years disqualification.

R v Corkhill 2002 2 Cr App R (S) 60. The defendant pleaded at the earliest opportunity to causing death by dangerous driving and driving whilst disqualified. The defendant was an unqualified driver who had been disqualified from driving for 6 months for speeding and driving without insurance or a licence. This was the second time he had been convicted for those offences. Two months later when 18 in the early hours he offered five people a lift in his friend's car. He drove through the centre of Liverpool at high speed. His passengers were terrified and repeatedly shouted for him to slow down but he took no notice. Three girls in the back started crying and asked him to let them out. He drove in excess of 50 mph despite the roads being busy with people and went through a number of red lights. Shortly before the accident he drove at about 50 mph and apparently aimed at a group of people standing in the roadway. Shortly after the victim was crossing the road and had almost reached the other side when the defendant came round a corner extremely fast on the wrong side of the road with the engine revving. The victim stood no chance and was run over. The defendant made no effort to brake or avoid the victim. He drove off at speed and continued to drive dangerously until he abandoned the car at Bootle. He surrendered to the police and accepted he was the driver although he disputed the speeds put to him. The victim's family was devastated by the loss. The defendant showed remorse. He had had a troubled background and had been severely injured by a car when he was 10. He had a clear learning disability, poor social skills and low self-esteem. In 1999 he was treated for depression and was in receipt of incapacity benefit. Held. This was a bad case but could not be described as among "the very worst cases." Because of his plea **5 years** not 7. The disqualification period reduced from 7 to 5 years too.

R v Noble 2003 1 Cr App R (S) 313. The defendant was convicted of six counts of causing death by dangerous driving. He pleaded to driving whilst disqualified. He and friends spent the day drinking on motorised 'pub crawl.' He said he had drunk about 12 pints of lager, 1 pint of mixed lager and cider and two Bacardi Breezers. He then drove with others on a busy A road at excessive speed although the road was wet. After the dual carriageway narrowed to a single carriageway there was a double bend. Because of his speed he lost control of his car and hit a wall and then two other cars. Three from each vehicle died and others were injured. The defendant received relatively minor injuries and ran off. On his arrest he said someone else was driving. On his estimate of his drinking his blood/alcohol reading would have been 150 mg in his blood. (The court said he was $2\frac{1}{2}$ times over the limit which gives a different figure.) He was 41 with the following convictions. 1990 failure to provide a specimen. 1991 drink/drive and driving whilst disqualified when he was disqualified for 3 years. In 1997 drink/drive when he received 100 hours' CSO and 4 years' disqualification. He was a family man with a good work record. The judge said he showed breathtaking arrogance in the witness box. Held. This was a horrendous case involving tragedy for many families. There were obvious aggravating features. The motorised pub crawl, the very bad driving record, being disqualified, running off, driving dangerously for a little while before the accident and blaming someone else. While, therefore, the total sentence should take account of the number of deaths, it cannot be determined by it, if only because of the chance nature of the number of the deaths. The fact that multiple deaths have been caused is not of itself a reason for imposing consecutive sentences. The main focus of the sentencing judge in such cases has to be on the dangerousness of the driving, taking into account all the circumstances of that driving, including the results. It is difficult to imagine a worse case so 10 years but the sentences should be concurrent so **10 years** not 15. (From the tenor of the Judgement it can be inferred that had the new penalty of 14 years been available the court would have imposed it.)

Old case *R v Wood* 1998 2 Cr App R (S) 234 (For a summary of this case see the first edition of this book.)

See also *Failing to see other vehicles, obstacles etc within time*

Temper, driver in a/Aggressive driving

48.44   *R v McGilvery* 2002 2 Cr App R (S) 432. The defendant was convicted of causing death by dangerous driving. He worked as a van driver and he parked in an ambulance bay to make a collection from a Health Centre. The van obstructed the entrance to an underground car park. A chiropodist witness had to drive his car round the van and then went over to the defendant to tell him about the obstruction. The defendant's manner was unpleasant and unconcerned and the chiropodist was told among other things to "piss off". The defendant was seen to be in a temper. He reversed and then drove forward to 11 mph intending to make a three-point turn. The van mounted the pavement and crushed a child who was nearly three and her pushchair. Her mother was standing next to her. The child received dreadful injuries. The defendant apologized to the mother for brake failure on his van. The child died within less than an hour. Vehicle examiners found nothing wrong with the van. The mother had to give evidence and was rendered distraught. The pre-sentence report said he had been devastated by the accident but it hadn't stopped him working as a taxi driver while awaiting trial. (There is no reference to the defendant's age or character.) Held. The defendant's speed was such he could not stop the van from mounting the pavement. This was not a case of inattention or momentary risk taking. It was aggressive driving in a temper over a short distance towards stationary pedestrians plain for all to see. That was an aggravating feature similar to having taken drink. The mother's horror, long term distress and grief can only be imagined. He bears a heavy responsibility for his selfish and self-indulgent conduct. **5 years** not 6.

Unqualified driver

48.45   *Att-Gen's Ref. Nos. 32 of 2001* 2002 1 Cr App R (S) 517. The defendant pleaded guilty to causing death by dangerous driving. He was committed for sentence for failing to stop, failing to report, driving without a licence and driving without insurance. He was also sentenced for perverting the course of justice, possession of heroin and two counts of possession of cannabis. He was released from YOI in January 2000 and obtained a provisional licence. He had some 4 hours of driving tuition. On 7 May 2000 he drove a stolen car at speed and mounted a pavement. He was arrested and cannabis and heroin were thrown from the car. He was released on bail. His girlfriend's mother left her powerful Ford Galaxy car outside her house and instructed one was to drive it. On 26 May 2000 the defendant used it for a number of journeys and on 27 May 2000 he drank rum in a pub and a club and then drove it at about 40 mph in a 30 mph area with his girlfriend who only had a provisional licence. He failed to see a Give Way sign in time and hit a taxi. His speed then was 20–25 mph. The taxi swung through 180 degrees and the passenger of the taxi died. He got out, looked at the taxi and left the scene. The prosecution said this was to avoid a breath sample being taken. Two days later he surrendered to the police. The defendant was either 18 or 19 (now 20) years old and in 1997 received 15 months YOI. In 1998 for burglary and robbery he received 3 years' detention. There were 439 days unexpired on his licence. He as sentenced to 2½ years for the driving and concurrent sentences on the other offences. No order was made for the breach of the licence. Held. We would expect **5 years** detention for the driving in addition to the breach sentence. As it was a reference **4 years** detention with 12 months for the breach of licence consecutive and 5 years not 2 years disqualification.

Victim dies after defendant dealt with for dangerous driving

48.46   *R v Munro* 2001 1 Cr App R (S) 205. The defendant pleaded guilty to dangerous driving and was sentenced to 15 months imprisonment. A week later the case was relisted and the judge suspended the sentence because of the defendant's family circumstances. At that stage which was 7 months after the accident the victim was still in hospital and was a quadriplegic. Thirteen months after the accident the victim left hospital but still required 24 hour care. A month later she died. The defendant was then charged with causing death by dangerous driving. She pleaded guilty and nearly 2 years after her first sentence was given **12 months** imprisonment. The defendant had driven in a highly dangerous way to and from her children's school. She drove at high speed on a road with bends. She lost control of the car both before and after collecting her children. She finally mounted the pavement and knocked over an elderly lady. Since her first sentence she had been stricken with guilt and had difficulty living with what she had done. The sentence of imprisonment had had a very considerable effect on her children which was likely to increase. A recent report showed she had suffered from post-traumatic stress disorder and had attempted to take her life. Held. The judge was faced with a most difficult sentencing problem. The intrinsic culpability of the defendant's conduct had not significantly changed. The victim's quality of life had been destroyed when she had been knocked down. If the defendant had been dealt with for causing death by dangerous driving to start with the judge would have been obliged to pass a sentence of **at least 3 years** which he could not have suspended. Sentences should reflect the gravity of the offences. The judge had balanced all the competing interests and it was hard to criticise his decision. Notwithstanding the new information the appeal was dismissed.

Victims – Guideline case/guideline remarks

48.47   *R v Cooksley* 2004 1 Cr App R (S) 1. LCJ Where death does result often the effects of the offence will cause grave distress to the family of the deceased. The impact on the family is a matter that the courts can and should take into account. However, as was pointed out by Lord Taylor CJ in *Att-Gen's Ref. Nos. 14 and 24 of 1993* 1994 15 Cr. App R (S) 640 at 644: 'We wish to stress that human life cannot be restored, nor can its loss be measured by the length of a prison sentence. We recognise that no term of months or years imposed on the offender can reconcile the family of a deceased victim to their loss, nor will it cure their anguish.'

We refer to the *Practice Direction (Victim Personal Statements) 2002 1 Cr. App R 69* and to *R v Roach* 1999 2 Cr. App R (S) 105 where the Court accepted that they could as an act of mercy reduce a sentence if relatives of a victim indicated that the punishment imposed on the offender was aggravating their distress. The Lord Bingham CJ said, 'the court is not swayed by demands for vengeance and has to be very cautious in paying attention to pleas for mercy'.

Att-Gen's Ref. Nos. 24 and 45 of 1994 1995 16 Cr App R (S) 583 at 586. LCJ. No court can bring back to life those who have been killed. We understand the feelings of those relatives and friends of the deceased who believe that there ought to be a correlation between the loss of life and the length of sentence. We also understand that no length of sentence will ever satisfy those who lose loved ones that a proper correlation has been made. We must emphasise that this court cannot be persuaded by campaigns or by clamour to pass extremely long sentences where the criminality of the offender does not justify it. This court is concerned primarily with the criminality of the person who has caused the death. The fact of the death is, of itself, a factor in contributing to the length of sentence which should be passed. But essentially we have to look at the cases in the light of the offender's criminality.

R v Nunn 1996 2 Cr App R (S) 136. The opinions of the victim or the surviving members of the family about the sentence do not provide any sound basis for reassessing a sentence. If the victim feels utterly remorseful towards the criminal, and some do, the crime has still been committed and must be punished as it deserves. If the victim is obsessed with vengeance, which can in reality only be assuaged by a very long prison sentence, as also happens, the punishment cannot be made longer by the court than would otherwise be appropriate. Otherwise cases with identical features would be dealt with in widely different ways leading to improper and unfair disparity.

Att-Gen's Ref. No 66 of 1996 1998 1 Cr App R (S) 16. LCJ. The families of the victims feel bitter and vindictive towards the defendant whom they see as the author of their irreparable loss. This case contains such a feature. The family members of one of the victims have succeeded in reconciling themselves towards the consequences of this tragedy. The family of the other victim has not. Their feelings are understandable. No one who has not suffered such a loss is in a position to understand how they feel and it would be entirely inappropriate to disparage or belittle the emotions of those who suffer in this way. It is nonetheless the duty of the trial judge and of this court to judge cases dispassionately. The court must of course take account of the understandable outrage felt against any defendant who has caused consequences such as these. That is a sense of outrage shared by the wider public, which feels acute anxiety about the cruel, avoidable loss of life which is a feature of cases such as this. On the other hand, the court must take account of the interests of the defendant who has often, as here, not intended these consequences and is often, as here, devastated by them. The court cannot overlook the fact that no punishment it can impose will begin to match the deep sense of responsibility which defendants often feel. It is important that courts should do their best to approach their task objectively and dispassionately. They should not be overborne or intimidated into imposing sentences which they consider are unjust.

R v O'Brien 2001 1 Cr App R (S) 79. The defendant pleaded guilty to causing death by dangerous driving. The defendant showed remorse from the very beginning. The relatives said no useful purpose could be served by a custodial sentence. Held. The views of the family are to be greatly respected. Applying *R v Nunn* 1996 2 Cr App R (S) 136 and *R v Roche* 1999 2 Cr App R (S) 105 the views of the victims are not a relevant consideration whether they seek leniency or severity save in exceptional circumstances.

R v Porter (No 2) 2002 2 Cr App R (S) 222. All judges are careful not to be over influenced by the devastation that is caused.

Practice Direction (Victim Personal Statements) 2002 1 Cr App R (S) 482. The opinions of the victim or the victim's close relatives as to what the sentence should be are not relevant. Victims should be advised of this.

Att-Gen's Ref No 77 of 2002 2003 1 Cr App R (S) 564. The defendant pleaded guilty to causing death by driving without due care having consumed alcohol above the prescribed limit. The defendant and his passenger were said to be like brothers. They were in fact cousins. The cousin was killed. The defendant was 20, of previous good character and genuinely remorseful. He was deeply depressed, had expressed suicidal thoughts and was spending a great deal of time at his cousin's grave. He had the support of all of his family (including the support of the sisters of the deceased). Since his sentence, a further report said that his attendance and standard of work had been very good. A sister of the deceased wrote movingly: "should [the defendant] be taken away from us now [it] would be devastating". Held. Both the impact of the crime on the victims and impact of the crime on the defendant have to be approached with great care. Just as the impact of the death affects the level of sentence, the impact of death on the defendant may do so too. A husband who is responsible for the death of a beloved wife, or a mother who kills her own child will be carrying his or her own punishment to the grave and that is the sort of feature which may be relevant and weighed in the sentencing decision. It has always been recognised that in an exceptional case a non-custodial sentence is sometimes possible. The ability to exercise mercy and to identify the appropriate case in which mercy should be exercised has long been acknowledged as a judicial attribute. (For further details see next section.)

R v Barker 2003 2 Cr App R (S) 110. The defendant killed the three children of his partner. Held. The attitude of the mother is something the court should take into account. (For more details see MANSLAUGHTER – *Gross negligence*)

See also VICTIMS

Victims, the views of the relatives of the – Defendant related/was friendly with deceased Cases

48.48   *R v Richards* 1998 2 Cr App R (S) 346. The defendant pleaded guilty to causing death by dangerous driving. The defendant then 22, killed his girlfriend by overtaking at excessive speed. He had earlier overtaken another car at speed. He was of good character with seven references and a clean driving record. He was greatly affected by the death and had not driven since. He had no intention of driving in the future. The girl's father said no member of his family wanted the defendant to go to prison and he could not have wished for a better future son in law. Held. Two years was on the high side but not necessarily manifestly excessive. However, he has the burden of killing his own girlfriend and apparently his future wife. This was a grave sentence on its own. The court has a public duty to perform and must be careful not to be swayed by clamour or favour. However, the court cannot ignore that he has retained the confidence and affection of the family who wanted him to marry the victim. Taking those matters into account **12 months** instead. [For further details see 1st edition of this book]

R v Roche 1999 2 Cr App R (S) 105. LCJ. The defendant pleaded guilty to causing death by careless driving when under the influence of drink. He killed his cousin when drunk and speeding. The defendant's parents were brother and sister of the victim's parents. The victim's mother treated the defendant almost as a son and had played a large part in bringing him up. It was very closely-knit family and the victim's mother had written a moving letter. The sentence imposed was delaying the time at which she can grieve. Other members of the family make the same point. A letter from the defendant's mother pointed out the very serious effect which the sentence was having on her and his father. Held. It is not for the injured party to dictate the sentence based on vengeance or compassion. Nonetheless the court can in appropriate circumstances become an instrument of compassion. That is an appropriate response to this case. Although there is no criticism of the 4 year sentence in light of the new material **3 years**.

R v Matthews 2003 1 Cr App R (S) 120. The defendant pleaded guilty to the manslaughter of his brother. The family wrote letters about their support for the defendant and their double loss. Held. Applying *R v Nunn* 1996 2 Cr App R (S) 136, we balance the public duty to indicate the gravity of the offence and on the other hand not adding to the punishment and anguish of the family by a sentence which causes them distress.

Att-Gen's Ref. No 77 of 2002 2003 1 Cr App R (S) 564. On the day of his trial, the defendant pleaded guilty to causing death by driving without due care having consumed alcohol above the prescribed limit, having no insurance and no driving licence. Although the defendant had had a number of driving lessons and a provisional licence he had never taken a test. The defendant and his passenger were said to be like brothers. They were in fact cousins. The defendant had been driven to a public house by his father, having had one or two drinks at home. He did not intend to drive that evening and so had had a further four or five pints of lager. At the end of the evening the defendant's cousin, a long-distance lorry driver, asked the defendant to drive him home in his (the cousin's) car. The defendant, although feeling the worse for drink, agreed. The defendant's girlfriend was also given in a lift. At about 12:40 am the defendant was driving along a single carriageway road, subject to a 60 miles per hour speed limit. There were no road markings or street lighting. The car suddenly veered to the right. This may have been due to the actions of his girlfriend who admitted that she might have grabbed the wheel because she was "messing about, having a laugh". A car travelling in the opposite directions collided with nearside of the car driven by the defendant. The cousin was pronounced dead at the scene; the girlfriend suffered cuts to her forehead and the driver of the other car was unhurt physically, but deeply shocked. A back calculation provided a likely figure of 120 milligrams of alcohol in 100 millilitres of blood at the time of the accident (= 52 µg in breath) (i.e. one and a half times the legal limit). No defects were found to have contributed to the accident and there was no evidence that excessive speed had been a contributory factor. The defendant was 20, of previous good character and genuinely remorseful. He was deeply depressed, had expressed suicidal thoughts and was spending a great deal of time at his cousin's grave. He had the support of all of his family (including the support of the sisters of the deceased). Since his sentence, a further report said that his attendance and standard of work had been very good. A sister of the deceased wrote movingly: "should [the defendant] be taken away from us now [it] would be devastating". Held. Both the impact of the crime on the victims and impact of the crime on the defendant have to be approached with great care. Just as the impact of the death affects the level of sentence, the impact of death on the defendant may do so too. A husband who is responsible for the death of a beloved wife, or a mother who kills her own child will be carrying his or her own punishment to the grave and that is the sort of feature which may be relevant and weighed in the sentencing decision. It has always been recognised that in an exceptional case a non-custodial sentence is sometimes possible. The ability to exercise mercy and to identify the appropriate case in which mercy should be exercised has long been acknowledged as a judicial attribute. This was a lenient sentence and a merciful sentence. **6 month curfew order and a community punishment order** of 180 hours upheld.

DECENCY, OUTRAGING PUBLIC

See **PUBLIC DECENCY, OUTRAGING**

49   DECEPTION, OBTAINING PROPERTY ETC BY

49.1   Theft Act 1968 s 15, 15A and 16. Theft Act 1978 s 1 and 2.

Triable either way. Maximum on indictment, 10 years for s 15 and 15A, 5 years for s 16, 1 and 2. Summary maximum 6 months and/or £5,000.

The Criminal Justice Act 2003 creates a summary maximum sentence of 51 weeks, a minimum sentence of 28 weeks and Custody plus. The Home Office says they do not expect to introduce these provisions before September 2006.

Restitution Order There is power to make an order that the stolen goods etc. in the possession of the defendant or a third party be restored to the owner etc.[26]

Where the offence is in essence obtaining money dishonestly the case is listed under **THEFT ETC**

Magistrates' Court Sentencing Guidelines January 2004
49.2   For a first time offender pleading not guilty. Entry point. Is it serious enough for

26 Powers of Criminal Courts Act (Sentencing) 2000 s 148(2) and Theft Act 1968 s 24(1)

a community penalty? Consider the impact on the victim. Examples of aggravating factors for the offence are committed over lengthy period, large sums or valuable goods, two or more involved, use of stolen credit/debit card, cheque books or giros, and victim particularly vulnerable. Examples of mitigating factors for the offence are for impulsive action, short period and small sum. Examples of mitigation are age, health (physical or mental), co-operation with police, genuine remorse and voluntary compensation. Give reasons for not awarding compensation.

For details about the guidelines see MAGISTRATES' COURT SENTENCING GUIDELINES at page 483.

Driving tests, trying to obtain a pass

49.3   *R v Adebayo* 1998 1 Cr App R (S) 15. The defendant was convicted of conspiracy to obtain property by a deception. He arranged for an impostor to take his driving test. He was 36 and was treated as of good character. He had claimed political asylum and was working as a cleaner. The impostor pleaded guilty and received 3 months varied on appeal to community service. The judge said the difference was the defendant was the beneficiary and hadn't pleaded guilty. He had a good prison report. Held. This offence cannot be tolerated. **6 months** was right.

50   DEFENDANT

AIDS, defendant has

50.1   *R v Stark* 1992 Crim LR 384. The defendant was sentenced to 4 years for drug trafficking. Because of AIDS his life expectancy was estimated by one doctor as not more than a year and another 12–18 months. The offences had originally been allowed to lie on the file because of his condition but 5 weeks later he was arrested for a similar offence. Held. It was not for the Court of Appeal to manipulate a sentence to achieve a social end. That matter was for the Royal Prerogative of mercy. Adjustments could be made as an act of mercy but it would not be right to change radically a perfectly proper sentence. His arrest showed there was a grave risk he would continue to traffic in drugs as long as he was able to do so. The medical reports should be forwarded to the prison authorities.

See also RAPE – *Sexually transmitted disease – Defendant has*

Alcohol, defendant under the influence of/Binge drinking

50.1a   *R v Rees* and Others 2005 Unreported 1/7/05. LCJ The Court dealt with a football related violent disorder case. Held. When it is the habit of young men (and young women) to drink excessively and then behave out of character, it is important that the courts send a message that there are very real dangers in embarking in that sort of binge driking.

Child defendant see CHILDREN AND YOUNG DEFENDANTS

Disabled defendants

50.2   *Att-Gen's Ref. No 2 of 2001* 2001 2 Cr App R (S) 524. The defendant pleaded guilty to seven counts of indecent assault against his stepdaughter when she was between the ages of 8 and 15. The defendant, who was 100% disabled and wheelchair-bound, forced the victim to masturbate him and take his penis in her mouth. The defendant was 49 years of age. Held. The appropriate sentence was **5 years**. Having regard to the fact that this was a reference and the serious disability faced by the defendant which would render imprisonment more difficult to bear **2 years** was appropriate not a probation order.

R v Griffiths 2005 1 Cr App R (S) 600. The defendant was convicted of having an explosive substance with intent, (count 1) and doing an act with intent to cause an explosion (count 2). He had previously pleaded guilty to one count of having an explosive substance (count 3). The defendant went to a co-accused's house and there set about making letter bombs using PE4 -British military high explosive- and detonators. The explosives detonated and caused him serious injuries. £7,000 worth of damage was done to the house. When his own house was searched police found 349g of PE4 (count 3). His motives remained obscure. In the course of the trial he 'belatedly' said he was going to deliver the devices to two people who owed him £5,000 to frighten them into paying the debt, after initially claiming at trial that the explosives had been forced on him by people he had picked up in his minicab earlier in the year. The defendant was 42 with some old previous conviction but nothing approaching this one in seriousness. The longest sentence he had received was 6 months in a detention centre for possession of an offensive weapon. Both his hands had been amputated and he suffered injuries to his thighs, genitalia, anterior trunk, neck and face as well as perforated eardrums. A psychiatric report said there were no suicidal or psychotic issues and he was coming to terms with his injuries. A medical report expressed concern that while in custody he was not receiving the medical care he required. Held. The only substantial point was whether the disability suffered merited further discount beyond making the sentence for count 3 (3 years) concurrent to counts 1 and 2 (**15 years**). It did not.

Elderly defendants

50.3 *R v Suckley* 2001 2 Cr App R (S) 313. The defendant now aged 75 was convicted of attempted murder. Held. It is plain from *R v C* 1992 14 Cr App R (S) 562; *R v S* 1998 1 Cr App R (S) 261 and *R v Anderson* 1999 1 Cr App R (S) 273 regard must be had to age and that a discount is appropriate. Any attempt at an actuarial basis for a discount is inappropriate. It may well be that there is greater scope for exercising mercy in cases where elderly men have committed sexual offences many years earlier. The present sentence has been significantly discounted from almost certainly 15 years which would have been appropriate for a younger man to **11 years**. Such a discount was proper and fair. Appeal dismissed.

Ill health of defendant – Circumstances change after sentence

50.4 *R v Nall-Cain* 1998 2 Cr App R (S) 145. Obiter. Where, for example, there is a deterioration in the defendant's health, or it is impossible, by reason of a prisoner's physical disabilities for the prison to cope with him, the Court of Appeal may exercise mercy.

Ill health enabling the sentence to be suspended

50.5 *R v Stevens* 2003 1 Cr App R (S) 32. The defendant pleaded guilty to offences of false accounting in relation to false claims for income support, housing benefit and council tax. The total amount obtained was £48,066. She co-operated in interview. She was 52 and of good character with a 10 year old daughter. She suffered from ischaemic heart disease, asthma, diabetes, oesophagitis and bilateral hearing loss. There had been many surgical interventions and extensive drug treatments. The pre-sentence report said she was unlikely to re-offend. She received 18 months imprisonment. The prison report said she suffered more frequent angina attacks in prison than at home and that the prison environment will be detrimental to her health. Held. The only question was whether there were exceptional circumstances enabling the sentence to be suspended. There were.

Old cases. *R v Khan* 1994 15 Cr App R (S) 320, *R v Weston* 1996 1 Cr App R (S) 297, *R v Morrish* 1996 1 Cr. App. (S) 215 and *R v Oliver* 1997 1 Cr App R (S) 125; where in each case the sentence was suspended.

Inadequate defendants

50.6 *R v Turner* 2002 1 Cr App R (S) 207. The defendant pleaded guilty to manslaughter on the basis of lack of intent and acting in panic when flustered and under stress. Also diminished responsibility would have been open to him because of his intellectual limitations. He lived with a girl who he had met at a special school. On 12 December 1999 they had a baby. They were both 17 and neither could look after themselves let alone a baby. The relationship was stormy and the arrival of the baby put the relationship under additional and severe strain. Occasionally he would look after the baby with her mother but he seemed not to understand the importance of careful handling. On 15 January 2000 he was left in charge of the baby for the first time. He called his aunt to say the baby was not breathing properly and had gone floppy. When the ambulance came he refused to let them take her because he was worried about his partner. Later the baby was taken to hospital and doctors found haemorrhaging behind both eyes. There was widespread bleeding in the brain. The next day the life support system was switched off. The injuries were consistent with shaken baby syndrome but experts could not say for how long or with what vigour the shaking had been. In interview the defendant admitted shaking his daughter. He said it was a particular difficult day with problems with the local authority etc. The baby started crying and he could not stop it. He shook her twice and supported her head. That he said usually quietened her. When she cried again he shook her without holding her head and he noticed she went floppy. He was of good character. The reports agreed he was a man with very real handicaps with profound social incapacity. He had a borderline learning disability with significant impairment of intellectual and social functioning amounting to an abnormality of the mind. He was vulnerable and dependent on others. If he remained in custody his partner would not be able to cope and would be taken into care. The overwhelming view of the doctors was that custody was entirely inappropriate for him. He had spent 5 months in custody, which he had been unable to cope with. He had to remain in the protection unit. Held. Parents could not escape all the responsibilities for their actions by relying on their own problems. That does not mean in every tragic case where a child is killed custody is inevitable. Exceptional cases merit exceptional sentences. He lacked the mental capacity to appreciate the consequences of his actions and intended no harm to the baby. He was vulnerable and needed protection. He was totally ill equipped to deal with the situation and should never have been put in that position. The sooner he receives support, guidance and medical treatment the better. A **3 year community rehabilitation order** with a condition of treatment and duty to live where approved not $2^{1}/_{2}$ years YOI.

Att-Gen's Ref. No. 69 of 2001 2002 2 Cr App R (S) 593. The defendant was convicted of rape and indecent assault, for which he received no penalty. The victim was 58 and suffered from Huntington's chorea, an appalling progressive disease of the brain. This caused her to suffer from dementia and impairment of the intellectual function, memory and understanding, together with associated psychotic symptoms. She had an IQ of 52 and was a "defective within the meaning of the Sexual Offences Act 1956 s 45". Her condition meant she lost her inhibitions and had a tendency to invent or fill gaps in her memory. She was discharged from the psychiatric department of a hospital and went to a residential care home. Shortly after that the defendant and his brother, M went to visit another resident, P at the home. The defendant was 29 with an IQ of 52. He had a reading and perceptual age of a 9 years old. In some respects he performed like a 6 year old. All four of them were in P's room and there was some horseplay and P encouraged the defendant to ask the victim for sex, which took place. The prosecution case was she repeatedly said words like, "No" and "Stop it". M participated and attempted oral sex and touched her breasts. A care worker heard shouting and discovered the victim with her pants down. The defence was consent. He received 3 years with a 3 years extension. Both sides appealed. Held. It was a very difficult sentencing decision. The defence suggestion that there should have been a guardianship order was wrong because the case was not wholly exceptional such as to warrant a non-custodial. The victim was very vulnerable with child-like tendencies. The aggravating features were that vulnerability, her age and that it took place in a nursing home. The vulnerability was seriously aggravating. Without his impairment the correct sentence would have been 8 years. The correct sentence here would have been **5 years**. Because of the need for a substantial discount as it was a reference and the extended period the sentence was not increased.

See **RAPE** – *Defendant inadequate*

Mentally disordered defendants

50.7   Criminal Justice Act 2003 s 157(1) & (2) Where a defendant is or appears to be mentally disordered, the court must obtain and consider a medical report before passing sentence other than one fixed by law, unless the court considers it is unnecessary to obtain one.

Criminal Justice Act 2003 s 166. This section enables the Court to mitigate the penalties on mentally disordered defendants without many of the restrictions imposed by statute on other defendants.

Att-Gen's Ref. No 83 of 2001 2002 1 Cr App R (S) 589. The defendant pleaded guilty at the first opportunity to robbery. He robbed a small off licence wearing a balaclava mask holding a 12″ chrome object in his hand. He took money, cigarettes and a bottle of brandy. A few days later he went to hospital and admitted himself as a voluntary patient. He told the staff he heard voices and told them about the robbery and permitted them to tell the police. He admitted the offence to the police and said he had a metal bar. Without his help there would have been no evidence. He had minor convictions and was a crack addict. The report said he suffered from a serious mental illness namely schizophrenia. He needed long and consistent management, which would last for a number of years. He came to be sentenced from hospital where he had co-operated with the staff and his condition was stable. It was thought he would be ill equipped to deal with prison and that he would possibly commit suicide if he was sent there. He was sentenced to a community rehabilitation order for 2 years with a requirement that he should reside as directed including hospital and he should take such medication as prescribed. The judge said he considered the normal tariff but considered the circumstances particularly the medical evidence. After sentence a report indicated he had taken advantage of his opportunity and was drug free. Held. What the authorities do not show are the cases where the individual circumstances of the defendant and the mitigation available to him have led to a justified departure from the guidance provided by the reported decisions. It is fundamental to the responsibilities of sentencing judges that while they must always pay proper regard to the sentencing guidance given, they are required also to reflect on all the circumstances of the individual case. Where sentencing judges are satisfied that occasion requires it, they have to balance the demands of justice with what is sometimes described as the calls of mercy. There were occasions where it was right to take a constructive course and seek to achieve the rehabilitation of the offender. The judge was satisfied it provided the best possible long-term solution for the community and the defendant. It was right to take a constructive course. So far he has been proved right. The prospects of re-offending are now lower than if he had had a custodial sentence. The sentence was lenient on paper but sentencing is not and never can be an exercise on paper; each case, ultimately, is individual. It would be wrong to interfere.

R v Walton 2004 1 Cr App R (S) 234. The defendant pleaded guilty to manslaughter. Held. Relying on *R v Mbatha* 1985 7 Cr App R (S) 373, *R v Moses* 1996 2 Cr App R (S) 407, *R v Mitchell* 1997 1 Cr App R (S) 90 and *R v Hutchinson* 1997 2 Cr App R (S) 60 where an offender is suffering from a mental disorder which is susceptible to treatment and a place is available in a special hospital the court should not impose life with the intention of preventing the release of the offender by the Mental Health Tribunal. All the conditions required for a s 37 order are present here so **hospital order with restrictions** substituted for life.

Articles. Sentencing psychopaths: Is the 'Hospital and Limitation Direction' an ill-considered hybrid? 1998 Crim LR 93. Diversion of Mentally Disordered Offenders: Victim and Offender perspectives 1999 Crim LR 805.

Meritorious conduct, defendant's (unrelated to the offence)

50.8   *R v Wenman 2005* 2 Cr App R (S) 13. The defendant pleaded guilty to causing death by careless driving. Shortly before the defendant was sentenced, a motorist swerved to avoid a deer and skidded on ice. His car slid down a bank and into a stream. The motorist lost consciousness and was choking on his blood and saliva. The defendant, who was driving by, saw the red tail lights of the car. He stopped his car and gave assistance. The motorist's car was in a perilous position and was at risk of toppling further into the stream. The defendant telephoned for help, opened the car door and held the victim's head for 30 minutes until assistance arrived. To do so he had to stand in knee deep water. The fire brigade arrived and were not prepared to do anything until they had secured the car. They cut the car around the defendant to free the motorist. Two policemen and the Chief Fire Officer wrote in praise of the defendant. The motorist believed the defendant had saved his life. Held. The behaviour was highly commendable. The defendant was entitled to substantial credit for his selfless and courageous conduct. **3 years** not 4.

Personal mitigation

50.9   *Att-Gen's Ref. No 84 of 2001* 2002 2 Cr App R (S) 226. The defendant pleaded guilty to attempted robbery and having a firearm with intent to resist arrest. He tried to rob a Securicor guard delivering cash to a cash dispenser. Held. Personal factors in relation to offences of this gravity can have only a very small effect in determining what the appropriate sentence is.

Poor defendants

50.10   Criminal Justice Act 2003 s 164(3) (in force 4/4/05) In fixing the amount of any fine to be imposed … a court shall take into account … the financial circumstances of the defendant so far as they are known, or appear, to the court. [previously Powers of Criminal Courts (Sentencing) Act 2000 s 128(3)].

Criminal Justice Act 2003 s 164(4) (in force 4/4/05) Sub-section (3) applies whether taking into account the financial circumstances has the effect of increasing or reducing the amount of the fine. [previously Powers of Criminal Courts (Sentencing) Act 2000 s 128(4)].

Re-sentenced, discount for being

50.11   *R v Broomfield* 2004 2 Cr App R (S) 381. The defendant was in breach of a community punishment and rehabilitation order. When given the order he was in breach of his prison licence. He was sentenced to 9 months with the judge taking into account the 6 months he had served on remand which he considered didn't count towards his sentence. The prison released the defendant after one day because they thought it did. The Judge relisted the case and sentenced him again to 9 months saying the period on remand didn't count. The prison adhered to its view and the court relisted it. The Court was told if it wanted the defendant to serve 9 months it must sentence the defendant to 18 months. The Judge did so. Held. The prison was wrong. 9 months should be reinstated with **one month** discount to reflect the history of the case.

(This discount seems much less generous than the discount given when the defendant is re-sentenced after the prosecution appeal a sentence to the Court of Appeal.)

Rich defendants

50.12   Criminal Justice Act 2003 s 164(3) (in force 4/4/05) In fixing the amount of any fine to be imposed ... a court shall take into account ... the financial circumstances of the defendant so far as they are known, or appear, to the court. [previously Powers of Criminal Courts (Sentencing) Act 2000 s 128(3)].

Criminal Justice Act 2003 s 164(4) (when in force) Sub-section (3) applies whether taking into account the financial circumstances has the effect of increasing or reducing the amount of the fine. [Previously Powers of Criminal Courts (Sentencing) Act 2000 s 128(4)].

R v Jerome 2001 1 Cr App R (S) 316. The defendant was convicted of handling. Computer and other equipment worth in all about £2,739 were stolen in a burglary. The computer was traced to the defendant when a message was sent from the computer to the Internet. His flat was searched and the equipment was found. He was an antiques dealer and his turnover was about £100,000. The judge said he was minded to imprison the defendant but was concerned his business might be permanently wrecked. He was fined £10,000. Held. It is permissible to increase a fine for a wealthy or relatively wealthy offender. However, there must be some proportionality between the scale of the offence and the fine imposed. In handling the value of the goods must be taken into consideration. **£6,000 fine** not £10,000. [Many will consider the sentencing judge's proportionality of just under four times the value is more realistic than the Court of Appeal's proportionality of just over twice the value.]

See also ARMED FORCES, MEMBERS OF; BASIC PRINCIPLES; CUSTODY, DISCOUNT FOR TIME IN; CO-DEFENDANT'S PERSONAL MITIGATION; DRUG USERS; FATHERS; GUILTY PLEA, DISCOUNT FOR; MERCY; MOTHERS AND SOLICITORS

DEFRAUD

See FRAUD

DELAY

For general principles in sexual offences see RAPE – *Historic abuse*

See also INDECENT ASSAULT ON A MAN – *Historic abuse*; INDECENT ASSAULT ON A WOMAN – *Historic abuse* and RAPE – *Historic abuse*

DEPENDANTS

See CRUELTY TO CHILDREN and MOTHERS

DISABILITIES, DEFENDANT'S

See DEFENDANT – *Ill Health* and DEFENDANT – *Disabled defendants*

51   DISABLED, HOSTILITY TOWARDS A DISABLED VICTIM

51.1   Criminal Justice Act 2003 S 146(2)–(3)

Where "the offender demonstrated towards the victim … hostility based on a disability (or presumed disability) of the victim or the offence is motivated … by hostility towards persons who have a disability or a particular disability, the court must treat (that) … as an aggravating factor and must state in open court that the offence was committed in such circumstances."

DISCOUNT

For discount for a guilty plea see GUILTY PLEA, DISCOUNT FOR

For discount for time in custody see CUSTODY, DISCOUNT FOR TIME SPENT IN

For the principle that there is no discount for time served for a conviction which is later quashed see SENTENCES SERVED FOR WHICH THE CONVICTION WAS LATER QUASHED

52   DISQUALIFIED DRIVING

52.1   Road Traffic Act 1988 s 103

Summary only. Under the Criminal Justice Act 1988 s 40(3)(c) it may be included in an indictment.

Maximum sentence 6 months or £5,000. 6 penalty points. Discretionary disqualification.

Depriving defendant of vehicle used There is power to deprive the defendant of the vehicle used[27] for the purposes of committing the offence.

Crown Court statistics – England and Wales – Males 21+
52.2

Year	Plea	Total Numbers sentenced	Type of sentence %					Average length of custody (months)
			Discharge	Fine	Community sentence	Suspended sentence	Custody	
2002	Guilty	171	1	1	46	–	48	3.8
	Not guilty	4	–	–	25	–	75	4.7
2003	Guilty	143	2	2	50	1	43	4.1
	Not guilty	6	–	–	–	–	100	4.8

For details and explanations about the statistics in the book see page vii.

Magistrates' Court Sentencing Guidelines January 2004

52.3   For a first time offender pleading not guilty. Entry point. Is it serious enough for a community penalty? Examples of aggravating factors for the offence are driver has never passed a test, driving for remuneration, efforts to avoid detection, long distance driving, planned long term evasion planned, long term evasion and recent disqualification. Examples of mitigating factors for the offence are emergency established, full period expired but test not re-taken and short distance travelled. Examples of mitigation are co-operation with the police, and genuine remorse.

27 Powers of Criminal Courts (Sentencing) Act 2000 s 143(6) & (7)

For details about the guidelines see MAGISTRATES' COURT SENTENCING GUIDELINES at page 483.

Is the defendant entitled to a discount for pleading guilty?

52.4   *R v Williams* 2001 Unreported 13/7/01. The defendant pleaded guilty to dangerous driving and driving whilst disqualified. The judge considered 5 years was the appropriate penalty. He passed 2 years (the maximum) for the driving and 6 months consecutive (the maximum) for the disqualified driving. The defence appealed the disqualified driving sentence on the basis he was given the maximum because the judge thought the driving penalty was inadequate. Further the defendant had pleaded and the disqualified offence was not of the most serious. Held. We agree with the judge's description that one cannot conceive a more serious case of driving than this. The defendant was entitled to a reduction so **3 months** not 6.

R v Phillips 2005 1 Cr App R (S) 627. The defendant pleaded guilty to dangerous driving and driving while disqualified. He was driving a car when police spotted him and pursued him. He drove through a built up area in the wrong direction sometimes at 60mph twice the legal limit. He had to brake hard more than once to avoid collisions. He skidded to a halt and ran off on foot before being caught by the police. The total distance of his pursuit was just over a mile. He was a disqualified driver and therefore had no insurance. The defendant had extensive previous convictions including offences of dishonesty, drug related offending, other motoring matters, seventeen convictions for driving while disqualified and twenty eight for driving with no insurance. He was not long out of prison for offences of driving while disqualified when he committed these offences. A pre-sentence report showed that he did not consider that he drove dangerously. He was described as a long-standing drug addict using heroin and amphetamine. He was in regular employment as a motor mechanic. His risk of re offending was high. Held. There were the following aggravating features: the defendant's previous record for the same offences; the culpability of the offences themselves; the relatively prolonged course of dangerous driving; perhaps most significantly the reason for it – to attempt to outrun justice and avoid another conviction. It is right that this offence was not at the very top of the scale as there was no suggestion of drink or drugs having been taken. The judge was right to sentence him to the maximum sentence for driving while disqualified and to make it consecutive to the sentence for dangerous driving, as the disqualified driving offence was committed in full before the dangerous driving was embarked upon, and the reason for the dangerous driving was that he had committed the offence of driving while disqualified and been detected for it. **18 months** imprisonment for dangerous driving and **6 months consecutive** for driving while disqualified were not manifestly excessive.

See also GUILTY PLEA – *Discount Is a discount appropriate*

53   DOGS, DANGEROUS

53.1   Dogs dangerously out of control in a public place

Dangerous Dogs Act 1991 Section 3(1)

Summary only. Maximum sentence 6 months and/or £5,000 fine.

Disqualification from having dogs For this offence there is a discretionary power to order the destruction of the dog and the disqualification of the defendant from having custody of dogs[28].

---

28 Dangerous Dogs Act 1991 Section 4(1)

Dogs injuring a person in a public place or where a dog is not permitted

Dangerous Dogs Act 1991 Section 3(1) and (3)

Triable either way. Maximum sentence 2 years. Summary maximum sentence 6 months and/or £5,000 fine.

The Criminal Justice Act 2003 creates a summary maximum sentence of 51 weeks, a minimum sentence of 28 weeks and Custody plus. The Home Office says they do not expect to introduce these provisions before September 2006.

Anti-social behavioural orders For both offences, where the defendant has acted in a manner that caused or was likely to cause harassment, alarm or distress to one or more persons not in the same household as the defendant and it is necessary to protect persons from further anti-social acts by him/her the court may make this order[29].

Destruction There is a requirement to order destruction of the dog, unless the court is satisfied that the dog would not constitute a danger to public safety and a discretionary power to order the defendant to be disqualified from having custody of dogs[30].

Disqualification from having dogs There is a discretionary power to order the defendant to be disqualified from having custody of dogs[31].

Aggravated offences – (Persons injured) Guideline remarks

53.2   *R v Cox* 2004 2 Cr App R (S) 287. LCJ. Parliament has demonstrated by the penalties the clearest intention that the courts should in no small measure look at the consequences of the offence when determining the penalty. An analogy can be seen with dangerous driving.

Aggravated offences – (Persons injured) (Dangerous Dogs Act 1991 s 3(1) and (3))

53.3   *R v Cox* 2004 2 Cr App R (S) 287. LCJ. The defendant changed her plea to guilty of the aggravated offence. She lived with her husband, five children, five dogs, a number of puppies and some cats. Seven dogs ran in a pack in a park and attacked a seven year old boy. His clothes were ripped off and people came to help. He was taken to hospital and was there for 5 days. He had multiple puncture wounds, lacerations to his arms, legs, face, chest and stomach. He twice required surgery. She was 38, of good character and genuinely upset. She allowed the dogs to be destroyed immediately and said she never intended to own dogs again. Her report said she did not seem to have a proper understanding of the responsibility of dog ownership. The plea was on the basis that she had failed to ensure the dogs were kept indoors. Held. The extent of the negligence sets the scene for the potential escape of the dogs which creates the risk of injury and the potential extremely serious injury. She intended no injury. It is not difficult to anticipate serious scarring and psychological damage to the victim. Her home circumstances were chaotic. Poor care and control of her dogs was very probably symptomatic of her lifestyle. **3 months** not 9 months with a 10 year disqualification.

Destruction of the dog, On the facts correct

53.4   *R v Holland* 2003 1 Cr App R (S) 288. The defendant pleaded guilty to allowing a dog to enter an adjoining property. The offence was in the aggravated form because the dog caused injury. Her son left his bull terrier with her for six weeks. A neighbour noticed that the dog had a propensity to wander into adjoining property. On a Sunday, the neighbour had her family including her grandchildren to lunch. The grandchildren played with a ball and the dog forced apart the fencing and ran towards them. The father of them managed to seize his son but the dog gripped the ankle, then the leg and then the

29 Crime and Disorder Act 1998 s 1C
30 Dangerous Dogs Act 1991 Section 4(1) and (1A)
31 Dangerous Dogs Act 1991 Section 4(1) and (1A)

chest of his daughter aged 8. The girl's father and uncle hit the dog with punches and a mop handle but they were resisted. The dog stopped only when the defendant called. The girl was hysterical and the dog had bitten a hole 10″ in diameter just above her knee. She has a permanent scar and a phobia for dogs for life. The defendant was fined £250, disqualified from having dogs for 10 years and the dog was ordered to be destroyed. The defence appealed the destruction order and the disqualification. They relied on a petition from people from the area where the defendant's son lived to say the dog was not dangerous and a letter from "Sublyme Bull terriers" saying the writer had seen the dog in the council kennels and assessed its well being. Held. This was the aggravated offence so the Judge had to order destruction unless satisfied it did not constitute a danger to public safety. There was no evidence the dog was other than a danger. The petition provides no evidence of the type which the court would require to avoid destruction. We are unable to attach any weight to the letter. We agree with the order.

Disqualification from having custody, On the facts correct

53.5   *R v Holland* 2003 1 Cr App R (S) 288. (For details see above) The Judge said he was disqualifying the defendant not to punish her but he wanted to ensure that the victim would know there were no dogs next door when she visited her grandparents. The defence also provided a number of testimonials from people who knew the defendant and her dogs. Held. The Judge's approach to disqualifying the victim was for a legitimate purpose. A balance should be struck between the sensitivities of the victim and the restrictions on the freedom of the custodian. The Judge was right to conclude that the risk of emotion, if not physical harm, to the child was a continuing one and the onus of demonstrating that the defendant was a fit and proper person to have custody of a dog remained on her. She can in the future make an application to shorten the period where the court is likely to consider the breed of the dog, the existence of secure fencing and who her neighbours are.

54   DOMESTIC VIOLENCE

54.1   This can be charged under a wide variety of offences.

Sentencing Advisory Panel The Panel have produced a report which can be found at www.sentencing-guidelines.gov.uk

Sentencing predictions As the offences receive more political interest and with the prosecution sentence appeals expect the sentences to rise. The once common lenient sentences when the couple had sorted out their differences or when the end of the relationship had been accepted will become rarer. This is good news for those who have campaigned for change but bad news for those at the Home Office looking for prison space.

Definition

54.2   CPS definition adopted by the Home Secretary. Any criminal offence arising out of physical, sexual, psychological, emotional or financial abuse by one person against a current or former partner in a close relationship, or against a current or former family member[32].

General

54.3   *Att-Gen's Ref. No. 138 of 2002* 2004 1 Cr App R (S) 114. The defendant pleaded guilty at his PDH to aggravated burglary with intent to inflict GBH, ABH, common assault and theft. The defendant married the victim in 1994. There were 3 children

---

32 Sentencing Advisory Panel Consultation paper 12 July 2004.

although the eldest, R was now thought not to be his. He was violent to his wife and on occasions the police were called but there were no court proceedings. In 2001 she moved out of their home to stay with her stepfather. She told the defendant R was not his. Two months after she left, she received a telephone call from him saying he wanted to talk to her. She agreed to meet because she was worried he might tell R he was not her father. They met in a pub car park and he asked to borrow her phone. She refused and he pulled her to the ground and straddled her. He shouted as he snatched the mobile, "I've got evidence to prove you were shagging someone when you were with me." She suffered a cut lip. This was the common assault and the theft. At 2.45 next morning, he broke his way into her stepfather's house. He violently opened the lounge door, turned the lights on and said, "Guess who. You're been shagging my best mate and I am going to kill you." He was holding a knife with a 5"–7" blade. Her stepfather and her brother came downstairs and asked what he was doing. He said, "This is pay back time." He punched the stepfather twice causing a periorbital laceration and a contusion over his ear. The stepfather retreated to call the police and get dressed. The victim was seized by her dressing gown and dragged to the front door. The gown was ripped off and she was dragged out of the house wearing only her knickers. He ordered her against her will into his van which was parked outside. The stepfather drove his new Ford Focus across the drive to block the exit. The defendant deliberately reversed into the driver's door of the Focus while the stepfather was inside. For some time the stepfather was unable to get out. The victim managed to escape and run into the house and he pulled her out again. He slapped her on the top of the head. This was the ABH. The police arrived and had to use CS gas spray to restrain him. In interview he admitted her account was true. He said he was hurt and angry and took the knife because he thought he would be outnumbered. He said he had had 15 pints. The pre-sentence report said he found it hard to deal with the break up of his marriage and he hoped she would return. The children had continued to live with him after the incident. He was now 30 with a conviction for a common assault on his sister in 1991 and attempted theft in 1997. He was fined for both. He received 18 months, was disqualified from driving for 3 years and ordered to pay compensation of £2,130. While in custody everything can be relied on in his favour. He was a trusted model prisoner. Since his release he has been allowed to have contact with his children. Held. So far as the children are concerned he has been a loving father. They are likely to be very seriously affected if he is returned to custody. The Judge should have imposed **5–6 years**. It was not necessary for him to be a long term prisoner so **3$^{1}/_{2}$ years** substituted.

See CRUELTY TO CHILDREN, HARASSMENT S 4, MANSLAUGHTER, *Relationship killings*, OFFENCES AGAINST THE PERSON ACT 1861 S 18 *Relationship attacks*, THREATS TO KILL, *Relationship attacks*

55 DRINK DRIVING

55.1 The chapter is divided into four subsections, (A) Excess alcohol, (B) Drugs driving under the influence of, (C) In charge and (D) failure to provide a roadside breath test. FAILING TO PROVIDE A SPECIMEN is listed separately.

Depriving defendant of vehicle used There is power to deprive the defendant of the vehicle used[33] for the purposes of committing the offence.

Football The Road Traffic Act 1988 s 4 and 5 are relevant offences under the Football Spectators Act 1989 s 14A and Sch 1, para 1. Where (a) the offence was committed during a journey and the court makes a declaration that the offence related to football matches and (c) there are reasonable grounds to believe that making a banning order

---

33 Powers of Criminal Courts (Sentencing) Act 2000 s 143(6) & (7)

would help to prevent violence or disorder at or in connection with any regulated football match; the court must make a Football Banning Order, (except where the defendant is given an absolute discharge).

High Risk Offenders Where a defendant has been disqualified for being $2^1/_2$ or more times over the limit, or has two or more disqualifications for drink driving within 10 years or has a disqualification for failure to provide a specimen[34] s/he will be classified by the DVLA as a High Risk Offender. They will be treated as persons potentially suffering from a disability requiring medical investigation[35].

A Excess alcohol/Driving etc when unfit

55.2 Road Traffic Act 1988 s 4(1) and 5(1)(a)

Summary only. Maximum 6 months or a Level 5 fine (£5,000).

Disqualification Minimum disqualification 1 year. 3–11 penalty points if special reasons not to disqualify are found. Where a defendant has a conviction for driving while unfit, causing death under the influence of drink, driving with excess alcohol and failing to provide a specimen in previous 10 years, minimum disqualification is 3 years[36]. There is power to order reduced disqualification for attendance on courses[37].

Magistrates' Court Sentencing Guidelines January 2004

55.3 For a first time offender pleading not guilty. Entry point. Depends on reading. Examples of aggravating factors for the offence are ability to drive seriously impaired, causing injury/fear/damage, police pursuit, evidence of nature of the driving, type of vehicle, e.g. carrying passengers for reward/large goods vehicle and high reading (and in combination with above). Examples of mitigating factors for the offence are emergency, moving a vehicle a very short distance and spiked drinks. An example of mitigation is co-operation with the police. Offer a rehabilitation course.

Breath	Blood	Urine	Disqualify not less than	Guideline
36–55	80–125	107–170	12 months	B[38] fine
56–70	126–160	171–214	16 months	C fine
71–85	161–195	215–260	20 months	
86–100	196–229	261–308	24 months	Consider community penalty
101–115	230–264	309–354	38 months	
116–130	265–300	355–400	32 months	Consider custody
131+	301+	401+	36 months	

R v St Albans Crown Court, ex p O'Donovan 2000 1 Cr App R (S) 344. The defendant was convicted of driving with excess alcohol. The guidelines only apply where there are no special reasons. For more details see below.

For details about the guidelines see **MAGISTRATES' COURT SENTENCING GUIDELINES** at page 483.

Disqualification, for how long?

55.4 *R v St Albans Crown Court, ex p O'Donovan* 2000 1 Cr App R (S) 344. The defendant was convicted of driving with excess alcohol. The defendant was moving his

34 Motor Vehicles (Driving Licence) Regs. 1999 Para 74 (1)
35 Motor Vehicles (Driving Licence) Regs. 1999 Para 74 (1)
36 Road Traffic Offenders Act 1988 s 34(3)
37 Road Traffic Offenders Act 1988 s 34A
38 1 B =100% and C =150% of weekly take home pay/weekly benefit payment.

car in a pub car park. He bumped another car and had 103mg of alcohol in his blood. The prosecution accepted that he lived 5 minutes' walk away and he was not going to drive out of the car park, but was simply moving his car to attempt to clear the access to the rear of the pub. The car was partially blocking a service gate. He was 39 with no relevant convictions. He was a forklift driver on building sites and his loss of job would affect his ex-wife and two daughters who he supported. He was sentenced to **£750 fine** and 20 months' disqualification with a 5 month reduction for going on a course. He appealed to the Crown Court who dismissed his appeal. Each court found special reasons to exist. The Crown Court relied on the Magistrates' Guidelines. Held. It would be hard to justify disqualification of more than 12 months. The guidelines only apply where there are no special reasons. The disqualification was reduced to **12 months** with 3 month reduction for going on a course.

B Drugs, under the influence of

55.5   *R v O'Prey* 1999 2 Cr App R (S) 83. The defendant pleaded guilty to perverting the course of Justice, driving whilst disqualified and possession of cannabis. He was committed for sentence for driving whilst unfit through drugs. Police stopped his car because it was being driven "terribly" on the M3. He gave a false name (presumably the perverting matter). He admitted he had smoked cannabis and spat some out. He was then 24 with dishonesty convictions and had received custody for robbery. He was disqualified for 2 years for drink/drive. Held. The judge was in a difficult position because he had not been charged with dangerous driving. He could not be sentenced for it by using the cannabis count. The proper sentence for the driving whilst disqualified was **3 months**, for the perverting count 3 months, for the unfit charge 6 months and 1 month (not 3 years) concurrent for the cannabis. The rest were consecutive making 12 months not $3^1/_2$ years.

C In charge

55.6   (Whilst unfit through drink or drugs, when refusing to provide a specimen and when over the alcohol limit.)

Road Traffic Act 1988 s 4(2), 5(1)(b) and 7(6)

Summary only. Maximum 3 months or Level 4 (£2,500).

When the Criminal Justice Act 2003 280(2) Sch 26 Para 38 is in force the maximum sentence will become 51 weeks[39]. The Home Office does not expect to increase this before September 2006.

Discretionary disqualification. Mandatory endorsement (subject to special reasons). 10 penalty points. There is power to order reduced disqualification for attendance on courses[40].

Magistrates' Court Sentencing Guidelines January 2004

55.7   For a first time offender pleading not guilty. Consider disqualification **Starting point fine C.** (150% of weekly take home pay/weekly benefit payment.)

For details about the guidelines see **MAGISTRATES' COURT SENTENCING GUIDELINES** at page 483.

D Failure to provide roadside breath test

55.8   Road Traffic Act 1988 s 6(4)

Summary only. Maximum fine Level 3 (£1,000). Discretionary disqualification. 4 penalty points. Mandatory endorsement (subject to special reasons).

39 Criminal Justice Act 2003 s 280(2) Sch 26 Para 38
40 Road Traffic Offenders Act 1988 s 34A

Magistrates' Court Sentencing Guidelines January 2004

55.9 For a first time offender pleading not guilty. **Starting point fine A.** (50% of weekly take home pay/weekly benefit payment.)

For details about the guidelines see MAGISTRATES' COURT SENTENCING GUIDELINES at page 483.

DRIVERS' HOURS

See TACHOGRAPH AND OTHER DRIVERS' HOURS OFFENCES

DRIVING TEST

See DECEPTION, OBTAINING PROPERTY ETC BY – *Driving tests, trying to obtain a pass*

56   DRUG TREATMENT AND TESTING ORDER, BREACH OF

56.1 On 4/4/05, the Drug Treatment and Testing Order (DTTO) was replaced by the Drug Rehabilitation Order[1]. The DTTO breach provisions are contained in Powers of Criminal Courts (Sentencing) Act 2000 s 56 Sch 3 Paras 1-9. Breach provisions for the new order are found in Criminal Justice Act 2003 Sch 8.

General principles

56.2 *R v Robinson* 2002 2 Cr App R (S) 434. On 14 February 2001 the defendant was given a DTTO for 12 months and a 2-year probation order, (now called a community rehabilitation order). He later pleaded guilty to two domestic burglaries committed on 1st and 23rd February 2001. He was 43 with about 40 convictions mostly for dishonesty, and in particular burglary, attempted burglary and theft. He had a few convictions for violence and drug offences. The majority of the offences were drug related. He was using heroin and his first DTTO appointment was 22 February 2001. He had been prescribed methadone. He responded to the DTTO in an extremely positive fashion and had attended all appointments and group sessions punctually. The Judge sentenced him to 15 months for each burglary consecutive, making 2½ years and referred the breach to the original Judge. Held. It is not wrong in principle to impose custody after a DTTO has recently been imposed. Whether a custodial sentence should be passed must be a matter for the exercise of judicial discretion. If a sentencing Judge decides not to impose custody and to permit the drug treatment and testing procedures to continue there are five possible options. He can (1) make no order; (2) defer sentence; (3) grant a conditional discharge; (4) make a community rehabilitation order and (5) make a new and further DTTO. No order might well have been appropriate here but generally it is unlikely to be desirable to make no order. In most cases it will be desirable to a make a further DTTO or a community rehabilitation order, or both. If a community rehabilitation order is imposed, additional requirements over and above those in relation to the DTTO can be imposed. A breach of the second DTTO would also amount to a breach of the original order.

If the court considers that there is no alternative to a custodial sentence there are three options. The first and usual one will be to revoke the DTTO and pass custodial

1   Criminal Justice Act 2003 s 332 and Sch 37 Part 7 and Criminal Justice Act 2003 (Commencement No 8 and Transitional and Saving Provisions) Order 2005 Sch 1

sentences for the original offence and the new offence. That option is only available at the Crown Court under Schedule 3, para 11(2) of the 2000 Act. On release the Secretary of State can include in his licence a drug testing requirement under the Criminal Justice and Court Services Act 2000 Section 64, if the offender was sentenced to a trigger offence as defined in Schedule 6 to the Act. The second option would be to leave the DTTO in force. Generally this Court has disapproved of community sentences running at the same time as custodial sentences, see *R v Fontano* 2001 1 Cr App R (S) 48. It might be appropriate to leave the DTTO in force where the custody is short in comparison to the DTTO. It would be desirable for the Court to ascertain the extent the provisions of the DTTO that could be complied with in custody. The third possibility would be to revoke the DTTO and replace it with a drug abstinence order (Note This was repealed on 4 April 2005).. The statutory requirements must be satisfied and it is to be noted that there is no treatment element in the order and it is only available in notified courts. However this power is a theoretical possibility and unlikely to be practical option. We doubt whether the original Judge had any power to deal with the breach of the DTTO after it had been referred to him. His only power would be to revoke it. The second Judge should have dealt with it.

It is now possible to see that revoking the order and imposing a custodial sentence was not the most appropriate course, because the DTTO had not in the few days since it was made had any time to have any material effect. The risk of re-offending was substantial but he was showing every sign of determination to make the dramatic changes necessary to come off heroin and stop committing offences. It is well known that a high proportion of criminal offences are committed to fund drug habits. Judges should be alert to pass sentences which have a realistic prospect of reducing drug addiction whenever it is possibly sensible to do so. This case provides such an example. The first shoots of his determination were becoming visible before the second Judge and are now more obvious. For ten months he has remained drug free. It is in the interests of the public and the defendant for a DTTO to be made. It shall be for 12 months will the same conditions as before. The community rehabilitation order will remain for a further 12 months.

Examples

56.3 *Att-Gen's Ref No 89 of 2003* 2004 2 Cr App R (S) 502. The defendant pleaded guilty on the first day of trial to aggravated burglary and affray. He entered a flat with a large kitchen knife and pushed his way in past the 73-year-old woman occupant. She tried to take refuge on the balcony but he smashed the glass in and put the knife to her chest saying he was not going to hurt her. Her screams alerted neighbours, who couldn't get in but told the woman that the police were on their way. The defendant left the flat, taking a small knife from the kitchen with him. That was the aggravated burglary offence. He then went to the next-door flat where the eighty-year-old occupier and his daughter were able to disarm him. He was described as jumping around like a lunatic. His flatmate arrived and tried to get him to leave but the defendant picked up an axe and started waving it about. Eventually he was disarmed and police arrived. That was the affray charge. The defendant had ten previous convictions including robbery and common assault. At the time of these offences he was the subject of a 12 months community rehabilitation order and a 100-hour community punishment order. His basis of plea was that he had been acting in a state of paranoia and fear brought on by consumption of crack cocaine. A pre-sentence report said he was remorseful and that he had committed the offence under the influence of drugs. His previous response to community sentences had been poor. He was assessed as medium to high risk of causing harm to others and his risk of re-offending was high. He had completed a Restorative Justice Programme whilst on remand and he had met the 73 year old woman victim. She had expressed the view he needed treatment rather than custody. The judge had made a DTTO order. Reports showed that he was highly motivated although there had been some lapses of attendance and some relapses into taking crack cocaine. It was said this was much less than many others in the first stages of a DTTO. The author of a report from the Probation Drugs Team expressed the hope that he would be allowed to continue with the DTTO. A further report from the Probation Drugs Team said that the defendant had finished a structured day care programme but that he had had difficulties because of emotional upsets and that although his attendance as generally good he was due to receive a final warning for recent absences. He was about to start an eight-week programme aimed at crack cocaine users. He had been co-operative and well mannered. His recent test result showed only one use of crack cocaine out of seven tests. He had spent seven months eight days in custody awaiting sentence. **Held.** His motivation was not gain but his delusions. It must have been a terrifying ordeal for the victim of the burglary. The community penalty at the time of sentence was unduly lenient because he had failed to comply with the conditions of the orders then in force: he had had the opportunity of addressing his addiction problem and had failed to do so. However, exceptionally the public was now more likely to be protected by allowing the **15 month DTTO** to remain. If it were breached the defendant would receive **a lengthy custodial sentence.**

DRUGS MONEY

For acquiring, possessing or using the proceeds of drug trafficking see **MONEY LAUNDERING ETC**

57   DRUG USERS

Guideline case

57.1   *R v McInerney* 2003 2 Cr. App. R. 627. It is common knowledge that many domestic burglars are drug addicts who burgle and steal in order to raise money to satisfy their craving for drugs. This is often an expensive craving, and it is not uncommon to learn that addicts commit a burglary, or even several burglaries, each day, often preying on houses in less affluent areas of the country. But to the victim of burglary the motivation of the burglar may well be of secondary interest. Self-induced addiction cannot be relied on as mitigation. The courts will not be easily persuaded that an addicted offender is genuinely determined and able to conquer his addiction.

In the case of offences committed because the offender is an alcoholic or a drug addict, while the taking of drink or drugs is no mitigation, the sentencing process must recognise the fact of the addiction and the importance of breaking the drug or drink problem. This is not only in the interests of the offender but also in the public interest since so commonly the addiction results in a vicious circle of imprisonment followed by re-offending. When an offender is making or prepared to make a real effort to break his addiction, it is important for the sentencing court to make allowances if the process of rehabilitation proves to be irregular. What may be important is the overall progress that the offender is making. This is part of the thinking behind drug and treatment orders.

Guideline remarks

57.2   *Att-Gen's Ref. No 105 of 2002* 2003 2 Cr App R (S) 319. Of course it is in the interests of the public that those who commit criminal offences in order to feed their drug habit should, if possible, be weaned from that habit; because, if they are, the public may, in the future, suffer less from the depredations than they have in the past.

On the other hand, the imposition of a community penalty for offences of robbery, taking into account many other offences including 6 other offences of robbery, even if the offence at the time of sentence was a promising candidate for a DTTO, would usually be wholly inappropriate, having regard to the public interest and the interests of the victims.

Determined efforts to break addiction

57.3 *Att-Gen's Ref. No 34 of 1999* 2000 1 Cr App R (S) 322. LJC. The defendant pleaded guilty to robbery 4 months after the PDH hearing. The defendant who had partly covered his face with a shirt came up to the victim in a park and grabbed him by his jacket. He also grabbed hold of a valuable gold chain, which was round his neck. The defendant produced a hypodermic syringe, which appeared to contain a brown liquid and accused the boy of selling drugs to his brother. He held the syringe about a foot away from his neck and threatened to give him AIDS if he didn't get the chain off. The boy was terrified and the syringe was moved close to the boy's legs in a stabbing motion. Eventually the chain was undone. The defendant ran off with it. The next day he went to the shop where the boy worked and asked if he was accusing him of being the robber. He warned the boy not to make trouble for himself. He was arrested and gave an alibi. He was 25 and had convictions for burglary, common assault, drink/drive and failing to provide a specimen. They were all drug related. He didn't co-operate with a probation order and was given CSO, which he breached and he then served a short period of custody. There were reports from drug rehabilitation units, which said he was committed to overcoming his addiction and was doing his utmost to sort out his life. He arranged his own interviews and all tests were negative. To interfere with the programme would jeopardise the recovery. He was now in a residential unit. The progress was very good. The stay would be for up to 9 months funded by the council. The risk to the public was now described as being very low. He was given 18 months suspended and suspended sentence supervision order. Held. What distinguishes this from the normal case of a defendant saying they will cure themselves is that here he has taken vigorous, persistent, constructive and determined action. That made it exceptional so the sentence could be suspended. The sentence did not fall outside the options open to the judge.

Att-Gen's Ref. No 48 of 1999 2000 1 Cr App R (S) 472. LCJ. The defendant pleaded guilty to conspiracy to steal. During a 9 month period he stole tools from vans during the night. Each loss was between £100 to £3,000 and he was arrested and bailed twice. He co-operated with the police and admitted involvement in 25 thefts. In all the property stolen was worth £25,000. He was 28 and had a long list of convictions including burglary and some which were similar to this offence. He looked after his disabled father who was 'highly dependant' on him. The defendant had been addicted to amphetamines but had voluntarily sought help at a clinic. The judge recognised he had made a determined effort to conquer his drug problem and the public interest was best served by a course of treatment. He was placed on **probation** for 2 years with a condition of attendance at a centre for 30 days. Although there had been one lapse back into drug taking the latest reports were positive. One said he had attended the regularly at the centre and the writer considered a custodial sentence would be counterproductive. Held. If he had been convicted the ordinary sentence would have been 18 months to 2 years. With a plea and his mitigation a sentence in the order of **12 months** would have been in no way excessive. Sentencing courts must retain an element of discretion. The sentence was merciful and one open for the judge to pass so not unduly lenient.

Exceptional cases

57.4 *R v Brewster* 1998 Re RH 1 Cr App R 220, 1 Cr App R (S) 181 at 187. LCJ. The defendant, when 15 pleaded guilty to four burglaries committed in the space of little more than a week. The offences were committed to finance his addiction to crack cocaine. Because of wholly exceptional personal circumstances the court substituted a **supervision order** for an otherwise perfectly appropriate 4 years' detention. The court said, 'No one should interpret this judgment as detracting in any way from the general rule that there is no mitigation in drug addiction.'

DRUGS

See **DRUG USERS; EXPORTATION OF DRUGS; IMPORTATION OF DRUGS (A, B AND C); POSSESSION OF DRUGS; PRODUCTION OF DRUGS; SUPPLY OF DRUGS (A, B AND C); AMPHETAMINE; CANNABIS; ECSTASY; LSD AND OPIUM**

For driving under the influence of drugs see **DRINK DRIVING**

58 DRUNK

58.1 Drunk   Licensing Act 1872 s 12

Summary only. Maximum fine Level 1 (£200).

Drunk and disorderly   Criminal Justice Act 1967 s 91

Summary only. Maximum fine[41] Level 3 (£1,000).

1.

Football related   Sporting Events (Control of Alcohol etc.) Act 1985 s 2

Summary only. Maximum fine Level 2 (£500).

Fixed penalty (for first two offences only) £50 for s 12 offences (£30 if under 16) and £80 for s 91 offence (£40 if under 16) [42]

Football For (1) a Sporting Events offence and (2) a drunk offence which was committed relevant to a football match the court <u>must</u> make a Football Banning Order where there are reasonable grounds to believe that making a banning order would help to prevent violence or disorder at or in connection with any regulated football match, under the Football Spectators Act 1989 s 14A and Sch 1, para 1.

Magistrates' Court Sentencing Guidelines January 2004 – Drunk and disorderly

58.2 First time offenders who plead not guilty. Entry point. Is a discharge or a fine appropriate? Examples of aggravating factors for the offence are offensive language or behaviour, on hospital/medical premises or school premises and with a group. Examples of mitigating factors for the offence are induced by others, no significant disturbance and not threatening. Examples of mitigation are health (physical or mental), co-operation with the police, and genuine remorse. **Starting point fine A.** (50% of weekly take home pay/weekly benefit payment)

Magistrates' Court Sentencing Guidelines January 2004 – Football related

58.3 First time offenders who plead not guilty. Entry point. Is a discharge or a fine appropriate? Examples of aggravating factors for the offence are group action and offensive language/behaviour. Examples of mitigating factors for the offence are induced by others, no significant disturbance and not threatening. Examples of

41 *R v Broughtwood* 2002 Unreported 26/06/02. A sentence of one day's imprisonment is unlawful
42 The Penalties for Disorderly Behaviour (Amount of Penalty) Order 2002 Para 2 and Sch. Part II as amended.

mitigation are age, health (physical or mental), co-operation with the police, and genuine remorse. **Starting point fine A.** (50% of weekly take home pay/weekly benefit payment). Must impose a banning order or give reasons why no order.

For details about the guidelines see MAGISTRATES' COURT SENTENCING GUIDELINES at page 483.

See also DRINK DRIVING

Aircraft, on

See AIRCRAFT OFFENCES – *Drunk, being*

DUE CARE

See CARELESS DRIVING

59   DUTY EVASION

59.1   Customs and Excise Management Act 1979 s 170(2)

Triable either way. On indictment maximum sentence 7 years. Summary maximum 6 months and/or £5,000 or three times the value of the goods which ever is greater.

The Criminal Justice Act 2003 creates a summary maximum sentence of 51 weeks, a minimum sentence of 28 weeks and Custody plus. The Home Office says they do not expect to introduce these provisions before September 2006.

Forfeiture There are powers to forfeit the goods and cars, ships etc used in duty evasion.

See also TAX FRAUD

Guideline case

59.2   *R v Czyzewski* 2004 1 Cr App R (S) 289. We adapt the Sentencing Advisory Panel's advice. The principal factors are the level of duty evaded; the complexity and sophistication of the organisation involved; the function of the defendant within the organisation and the amount of personal profit to the particular defendant. An offence will be aggravated if a defendant:

(1) played an organisational role;

(2) made repeated importations, particularly in the face of a warning from the authorities;

(3) was a professional smuggler, to which we shall return.

(4) used a legitimate business as a front;

(5) abused a position of privilege as a customs or police officer, or as an employee, for example, of a security firm, ferry company or port authority;

(6) used children or vulnerable adults;

(7) threatened violence to those seeking to enforce the law;

(8) dealt in goods with an additional health risk because of possible contamination; or

(9) disposed of goods to under-aged purchasers.

In addition to these factors there are statutory aggravating features of offending while on bail or having previous convictions.

7. Evidence of professional smuggling will include:

(1) a complex operation with many people involved;

(2) financial accounting or budgets;

(3) obtaining goods from several different sources;

(4) integration of freight movements with commercial organisations;

(5) sophisticated concealment methods such as forged documents or specially adapted vehicles;

(6) varying of methods and routes;

(7) links with illicit oversees organisations; and

(8) The value of goods involved is a potential indicator of professional smuggling,

Mitigating factors will include, a prompt plea of guilty, co-operation with the authorities, particularly in providing information about the organisation and, to a limited extent, previous good character. Pressure from others to commit the offence may, depending on the circumstances, afford mitigation.

Following trial, for a defendant with no relevant previous convictions and disregarding any personal mitigation, the following starting points are appropriate:

(i)   where the duty evaded is less than £1,000, and the level of personal profit is small, a moderate fine, If there is particularly strong mitigation, and provided that there had been no earlier warning, a conditional discharge may be appropriate;

(ii) where the duty evaded by a first time offender is not more than £ 10,000, which approximately equates to 65,000 cigarettes, or the defendant's offending is at a low level, either within an organisation or persistently as an individual, a community sentence or curfew order enforced by tagging, or a higher level of fine. The custody threshold is likely to be passed if any of the aggravating features which we have identified above is present.

(iii) where the duty evaded is between £10,000 and £100,000, whether the defendant is operating individually or at a low level within an organisation, up to 9 months

(iv) when the duty evaded is in excess of £100,000, the length of the custodial sentence will be determined, principally, by the degree of professionalism of the defendant and the presence or absence of other aggravating factors; subject to this, the duty evaded will indicate starting points as follows: £100,000 to £500,000, **9 months to 3 years**; £ 500,000 to £1 million, **3 to 5 years**; in excess of £1 million, **5 to 7 years**. Where very many millions of pounds in duty have been evaded, it may be appropriate to impose consecutive sentences or, alternatively, to charge an offence of cheating the public revenue, for which the maximum sentence is life.

These guidelines are not a straightjacket. Finally, where licensed premises have been used for the sale of smuggled goods, the court should notify the licensing authority.

Old case. *R v Dosanjh* 1999 1 Cr App R (S) 107.

Magistrates' Court Sentencing Guidelines January 2004 – low level offender £1,000–£10,000

59.3   For a first time offender pleading not guilty. Entry point. Is it serious enough for a community penalty? Examples of aggravating factors for the offence are abuse of power (e.g. use of children/vulnerable adults), offender is Customs/Police officer, playing an organisational role, professional operation, repeated imports over a period of time, substantial amount of duty evaded, threats of violence, importing two or more types of goods and warning previously given. Examples of mitigating factors for the offence are co-operation with authorities, no evidence of pre-planning, small amount of duty evaded and under pressure from others to commit offence. Examples of mitigation are age, health (physical or mental), co-operation with the authorities, genuine remorse and voluntary restitution. Restitution should be made. Above £10,000 seek advice.

For details about the guidelines see **MAGISTRATES' COURT SENTENCING GUIDELINES** at page 483.

Confiscation/Deprivation orders/Disqualification

59.4 *R v Czyzewski* 2004 1 Cr App R (S) 289. Sentencers should also bear in mind their powers to order: confiscation of assets under the Proceeds of Crime Act 2002 (Crown Court only); compensation in a clear case under Powers of Criminal Courts (Sentencing) Act 2000 s 130 (Crown Court and, subject to a limit of £5,000, Magistrates' Court also); deprivation, particularly of vehicles, under the Powers of Criminal Courts (Sentencing) Act 2000 s 143 (both Crown Court and Magistrates' Court); and disqualification from driving, where a motor vehicle has been used (Crown Court only). The court should warn the defence before making the order.

R v Doick 2004 2 Cr App R (S) 203. The defendant pleaded guilty to attempting to evade £164,000 worth of duty on cigarettes he had carried on his lorry to Dover docks. He said he was offered £500 to import them. He was 34, had no previous convictions and throughout his working life had been an HGV driver. He lost his job. Held. He yielded to temptation on one occasion. 6 months was the very minimum sentence he could have received. The court emphasised in *R v Wright* 1979 1 Cr App R (S) 82 that once a man had served his sentence he should be given help to re-establish himself in an honest life and disqualification may hinder that rehabilitation. Disqualification is a useful tool in many cases. Those who aid criminal gangs to import dutiable goods should not have disqualification end on their release. However here it was not in the public interest to deprive him of his employment. Taking into account his character and his need for a licence **6 months** not 12.

Value less than £10,000

59.5 *R v Czyzewski* 2004 1 Cr App R (S) 289. Where the duty evaded is less than £1,000, and the level of personal profit is small, a **moderate fine**. If there is particularly strong mitigation, and provided that there had been no earlier warning, a **conditional discharge** may be appropriate. Where the duty evaded by a first time offender is not more than £ 10,000, which approximately equates to 65,000 cigarettes, or the defendant's offending is at a low level, either within an organisation or persistently as an individual, a **community sentence or curfew order enforced by tagging**, or a higher level of **fine**. The custody threshold is likely to be passed if any of the aggravating features which we have identified above is present.

R v Latif 1999 1 Cr App R (S) 191. The two defendants, M and N were brothers and they made an early guilty plea to evading duty on 154 cartons of cigarettes. They were committed for sentence. The defendants flew to Stockholm and back to London. Each journey was via Prague. They obtained green-edged EC baggage tags in Stockholm and 154 cartons of cigarettes in Prague. At Heathrow their luggage was searched and the cigarettes found. In interview they admitted the offence and told the probation officer that the bulk would be sold on. Both were of good character. M was 40 with a wife and three children. N was 32 and had a wife and two children. They had been in regular work and expressed remorse. They were considered unlikely to re-offend and were suitable for community service. Held. The principle factor in any case will be the duty lost. Custody was right to deter others. **6 months** not 9. [Unfortunately the report does not refer to the value of the duty lost.]

R v Czyzewski 2004 Re D 1 Cr App R (S) 289 at 297. D pleaded guilty to four offences of duty evasion. On five occasions, he was stopped by Customs at Heathrow Airport.

Each time he was in possession of cigarettes. In May 2001 he had 10,800 cigarettes. In July 2002 he had 15,200 cigarettes. In January 2003 he had 3,000 cigarettes. In February 2003 he had 3,200 cigarettes. The total duty evaded was £5,729. On each of the first four occasions the cigarettes were seized and the defendant was issued with a notice of seizure and he was warned that a record would be kept of the seizure. He was arrested on the fifth occasion. He was and of good character. The author of the pre-sentence report concluded that there was a significant risk of re-offending. Held. The repeated conduct was an aggravating factor. **9 months** upheld.

Value £10,000–£100,000

59.6 *R v Czyzewski* 2004 1 Cr App R (S) 289. Where the duty evaded is between £10,000 and £100,000, whether the defendant is operating individually or at a low level within an organisation, **Up to 9 months.**

R v Ollerenshaw 1999 1 Cr App R (S) 65. The defendant pleaded guilty to three counts of evasion of excise duty. Police officers stopped a van because they thought it was overweight and found it was laden with cigarettes and alcohol. There were 500 cigars, almost 20,000 cigarettes, 10 kilos of rolling tobacco, 49 litres of spirits, 165 litres of beer and 1.5 litres of wine. He said he had bought it duty free across the Channel and intended selling them to his family and friends. He said he had made about ten trips between Dover and Calais in all and five trips from Sheffield to Dover. He said on two of the trips he had been warned by Customs. He also said the profit was about £1,000. The evaded duty amounted to some £10,000. He was 46, unemployed and effectively of good character. Held. When a court is considering imposing a comparatively short period of custody that is 12 months or less it should ask itself particularly when the defendant has not previously served a sentence of custody whether a shorter period might be equally effective. Applying that **9 months** not 12.

R v Czyzewski 2004 Re W 1 Cr App R (S) 289 at 297. W pleaded guilty to duty evasion. He collected tobacco from a tobacco packing unit on three separate occasions. Illegally imported tobacco was used. On the first two occasions he picked up 20 bags and on the third 60 bags. His job was to transport them to a lay-by on a motorway where he would hand over the goods. He was paid £200 a trip. It was estimated that about £60,000 worth in duty had been handled by the applicant. Held. The role of W was a very subsidiary role indeed. We have no doubt that custody was necessary but **6 months** not 9.

Value £100,000–£500,000

59.7 *R v Czyzewski* 2004 1 Cr App R (S) 289. When the duty evaded is in excess of £100,000, the length of the custodial sentence will be determined, principally, by the degree of professionalism of the defendant and the presence or absence of other aggravating factors; subject to this, the duty evaded will indicate starting points as follows: £100,000 to £500,000, **9 months to 3 years**.

R v Dosanjh 1999 1 Cr App R (S) 107. The defendant pleaded guilty to evasion of duty. Police stopped a van because it seemed to be overweight. The defendant was a passenger. A large number of cans of beer were found. His home was searched and a total of about 86 litres of spirits, 68 litres of wine, 4,500 cigarettes and 8 litres of beer were found. The defendant said they were from duty free shops. At his house were names and telephone numbers of off-licences. There were also receipts of goods for off-licences. Inquiries revealed that the defendant had made a total of 82 trips across the channel between November 1995 and September 1996 in a variety of vans or mini buses that had been hired in his name. On two occasions, customs officials in Dover had stopped the defendant, and alcohol and cigarettes had been confiscated. The total duty evaded was £164,000. The defendant was now 26 years of age with a conviction for driving while disqualified and a forgery offence but no convictions for an offence of this kind. Held. For amounts between £100,000 and £500,000, **2 to 3 years** on a guilty plea, and **up to 4 years**, following a trial, will generally be appropriate. It was repeated wholesale importation in a van hired in his name, despite two previous warnings. **3 years** was at the top of the bracket which we have indicated, following a guilty plea. It was not so manifestly excessive that this court should interfere.

R v Czyzewski Re B 2004 1 Cr App R (S) 289 at 295. B pleaded guilty at an early stage to duty evasion. M was convicted of the same count. Bryan was a lorry driver and he imported about 1.25 million cigarettes for a promised payment of £3,000. M was the organiser. The duty evaded was £164,000. Both were 34. B was of good character. M had convictions for theft and handling a good many years ago but no custodial sentences. B **9 months** not 2¹/₂ years. M **2¹/₂ years** not 4.

Old case. *R v Mann* 1998 2 Cr App R (S) 275, for a summary of the case see the first edition of this book.

Value £500,000–£1m

59.8 *R v Czyzewski* 2004 1 Cr App R (S) 289. When the duty evaded is £500,000 to £1 million, **3 to 5 years**.

R v Lee 2002 2 Cr App R (S) 41. The defendant changed his plea to guilty for seven counts of duty evasion which were specimen counts. The EU had introduced an anti dumping duty to protect the EU market from cheap imports from countries with state subsidies or cheap labour. Between August 1994 and September 1997 a company of which the defendant was the beneficial owner arranged with a Hong Kong supplier to purchase Chinese silicon which was subject to the duty. The defendant's company was registered in Liberia and administered in Jersey. The silicon was sold to a company who had contracted to buy silicon of either Western or Australian origin. The defendant stipulated that the silicon should be packaged in plain bags and that Hong Kong should appear as the port of loading. He forged certificates showing the silicon was Australian. 1,960 metric tonnes of silicon was imported in at least 33 importations. The defendant was not responsible for the payment of the duty but the duty evaded was £600,000. He was sentenced on the basis that at the beginning but for a very short time he thought he was buying Australian silicon. His profit was $200,000. He was 51 and of good character. The case meant he could no longer trade in metal and he had lost his livelihood. Held. The appropriate starting point was **4 years**. **30 months** was not manifestly excessive.

R v Czyzewski 2004 1 Cr App R (S) 289. He convicted of two counts of duty evasion on cigarettes. The goods included about 2.5 million illicit cigarettes. One consignment was seized. One arrived two days earlier and was delivered to an industrial estate. The duty evaded in these two counts was approximately £ 670,000 and VAT in excess of £150,000. He was an organiser. In 1995 he received 3 years for supplying a Class A drug. He has other convictions. **4 years** upheld.

Value £1m–£5m

59.9 *R v Czyzewski* 2004 1 Cr App R (S) 289. When the duty evaded is very many millions of pounds, it may be appropriate to impose consecutive sentences or, alternatively, to charge an offence of cheating the public revenue, for which the maximum sentence is life.

R v Flaherty and McManus 2000 1 Cr App R (S) 250. The defendants F and M pleaded guilty to evasion of duty. From November 1996 to February 1997 F was involved in removing spirits intended for exports from bonded warehouses. M was involved from the very end of November to February. Fraudulent paperwork was used and the goods were sold at less than half price. F organised the storage space and some of the documentation. M organised the distribution, signed dockets, hired vehicles etc. The Customs mounted a surveillance operation and the duty evaded was estimated to be £1.2m. F was 41, of good character and a model prisoner. M was 45 with convictions including 1 for deception for which he received 18 months. He also was a model prisoner. The defence contended that there were others more involved and the Judge had been wrong to start at 7 years. Held. The judge started at 7 years and then reduced it because of their relatively subordinate roles. There was no fault in **4 years** for F and **5 years** for M.

Value over £5m

59.10   *R v Dosanjh* 1999 1 Cr App R (S) 107. For amounts in excess of £500,000, sentences in the region of **4 years, increasing to the maximum of 7 years**, when £1m pounds or more in duty is evaded, will be appropriate, following a trial, with a suitable discount for a plea of guilty. In exceptional cases, where very many millions of pounds in duty are evaded, consecutive sentences may be appropriate; alternatively, it may be appropriate to charge conspiracy to cheat, which is capable of attracting higher sentences than those already indicated.

R v Towers 1999 2 Cr App R (S) 110. The defendant pleaded guilty to six counts of being concerned in dealing with goods for which duty had not been paid. He asked for 59 (or 62) similar offences to be taken into account. Over a year he diverted high value goods such as alcohol from bonded warehouses to the black market. He used forged documents, aliases and set up 13 companies to facilitate the fraud. The loss was over £6m. He wasn't the only principal and was involved in the paperwork. He was 53 and had a number of convictions including nine for deception in 1986 for which he received 5 years. Held. This crime is prevalent. The judge could not be faulted for the course he took in imposing 5 years on one count and 2 years consecutive for the other counts making 7 years which was the maximum sentence. However, it could be reduced to **6 years** because of matters raised when we cleared the court.

Att-Gen's Ref. No 90 of 1999 2001 2 Cr App R (S) 349. The defendant pleaded guilty at an early stage to conspiracy to cheat the Inland Revenue and assisting another to obtain the benefit of criminal conduct by money laundering. There was a massive conspiracy to cheat the Inland Revenue of £18m of alcohol and tobacco duty over 3 years. 800 containers of dutiable goods were bought, transported, stored and sold. The second conspiracy was the laundering of the proceeds. He was a director of two French companies and deceived the French tax authorities. He also produced false accounts to support the fraud. The organising brains of the conspiracy pleaded guilty and was sentenced to 9 years. Afterwards the defendant continued the conspiracies and set up other companies to assist. He visited the organiser in prison. He was also involved in printing the false documents. To launder the proceeds he invested in French properties through off-shore companies. His payment was £1,700 a month. At the start he was 23 or 24 years old and was of good character with excellent references. He had a degree in accountancy and was married and his wife suffered from ill health. His benefit was assessed at £100,000 and a confiscation order of just over £1,000 was made. Others received 5, 4 and 3 years for conspiracy to cheat. Four years had elapsed since his arrest. Held. 2 years suspended for 2 years was unduly lenient. We would have expected $3^{1}/_{2}$ **to 4 years**. Because of the delay, that it was a reference and he had received a non-custodial sentence **18 months** instead.

EARNINGS, MEN LIVING ON IMMORAL

The offence was abolished on 1/5/04. For the old and the new law see **PROSTITUTION**.

60   ECSTASY

Constituency

60.1   *R v Warren and Beeley* 1996 1 Cr App R (S) 233 at 236. LCJ. Most ecstasy tablets contain 100 mgs of active constituents. Accordingly 5,000 tablets could contain 500 grams. That should equate with 500 grams of heroin or cocaine.

Dangers of

60.2   *R v Broom* 1993 14 Cr App R (S) 677. Ecstasy in the odd unusual case can kill and does kill.

R v Wright 1998 2 Cr App R (S) 333 at 335. Ecstasy is a drug whose dangerousness is not to be underestimated and which is unfortunately often retailed in premises where young people may be found gathered together who simply do not understand or appreciate the possible dangers.

See also DRUG USERS; IMPORTATION OF DRUGS; POSSESSION OF DRUGS; PRODUCTION OF DRUGS and SUPPLY OF DRUGS (CLASS A, B AND C)

EDUCATION

See SCHOOL, FAILURE TO SECURE REGULAR ATTENDANCE

ELDERLY DEFENDANT

See DEFENDANT – *Elderly*

61   ELECTION OFFENCES

61.1   Representation of the People Act 1983 Various sections and penalties.

Forging proxy vote details

61.2   *R v Lewis* 1998 1 Cr App R (S) 12. The defendant pleaded guilty to eight counts of making a false instrument and eight counts of using those instruments. The defendant was a candidate in local elections. When voters said they would be unable to attend the polling booth she persuaded them to sign proxy voting forms. She pleaded guilty on the basis that she forged the details but she had the specific authority of the voter. She denied any of the information was false and denied she had forged any of the signatures. She said all had expressed a willingness to vote for her and she was simply taking a short cut. Held. Prison was not wrong in principle. She was interfering with the electoral process and undermining confidence in it. **1 month** not 2 giving her immediate release.

ELECTRICITY

The penalties and statistics are listed under chapter ABSTRACTING ELECTRICITY

The cases are listed under THEFT ETC – *Electricity or gas (including abstracting electricity)*

62   EMPLOYMENT, OTHERS WILL LOSE THEIR

62.1   *R v Nichols* 1998 2 Cr App R (S) 296. The defendant was convicted of dangerous driving. The defendant drifted from lane to lane on a three lane dual carriageway causing one driver to brake heavily. Eventually he drifted into a barrier on the near side of the road of a two lane stretch and stopped. With smoke coming from the tyre and a tyre burst he reversed at speed into the nearside lane and partly into the offside lane. He drove down the road and into a lay-by where he got out and looked at his vehicle. Then he suddenly drove off again causing other drivers to avoid him. He drove with sparks coming from his nearside wheels at about 50mph. Eventually he stopped. Police found that the car had extensive damage to the front. The wheel of the tyre that burst had been moved backwards. The steering and suspension was also damaged. Another tyre was deflated. His breath alcohol reading was 78µg. The expert couldn't dispute that the tyre might have burst before the impact. The defendant was now aged 40 and treated as of good character. He was hard working and his two youngest children were in poor health. The youngest was about to have an operation. There was a risk that his company which employed 26 people could collapse. Solicitors acting for Customs confirmed the company was in serious financial difficulties. He received 9 months and since then seven engineers and two apprentices had lost their jobs. Held. He had showed a singular lack of control which arose from excessive consumption of alcohol. With a great deal of hesitation the company mitigation means the sentence should be **6 months** not 9.

See also *Company frauds and financial services offences*

ENDANGERED SPECIES

See ANIMALS – *Endangered species* and IMPORTATION/EXPORTATION OF PROHIBITED/ RESTRICTED GOODS *Birds etc.*

63   ENTRAPMENT/AGENT PROVOCATEURS, SIMILAR SITUATIONS

63.1   Where police conduct amounts to state generated crime the court may stay the count in the indictment[1]. However the police are permitted to make test purchases (either where a statute authorises it or when it has been authorised by senior officers) and take part in similar activity.

Police etc collect evidence of continuing activity, e.g. drug dealing

63.2   *R v Springer* 1997 1 Cr App R (S) 217. The defendant pleaded guilty at the Magistrates' Court to three charges of supplying heroin and was committed to the Crown Court. The defendant was a suspected drug dealer. The police tested their suspicions by making three telephone calls. He was asked, 'Have you got anything.' He replied, 'Yeah,' and arrangements were made to meet him. In response to each call a meeting was arranged and about 1.5grams of heroin was supplied. The calls were recorded and the meetings were videoed. The defence argued that he was entitled to a discount because of entrapment. Held. There was a need for the police to adopt this method of detection. There was need for there to be more than one supply to provide evidence he was a dealer. This was not a case of entrapping a suspect into supplying

1   *R v Looseley* 2000 Unreported 13/4/00

drugs who would otherwise never have engaged in that activity. *R v Underhill* 1979 1 Cr App R (S) 270 at 272 applied. Here there was legitimate police activity and not activity that could provide mitigation or any reduction at all.

R v Mayeri 1999 1 Cr App R (S) 304. The defendant pleaded guilty at the earliest opportunity to four counts of supplying ecstasy. One tablet was involved in each case. Four undercover police officers approached him in a nightclub and he agreed to sell them a tablet for £10. He claimed there was an element of entrapment. The defendant relied on *R v Tonnessen* 1998 2 Cr App R (S) 328 Held. The entrapment argument is not a good one. Where undercover officers discover a man is prepared to sell drugs by approaching him it is not a matter the courts need normally take into account as amounting to entrapment. It might be said 'Seller beware.' These premises are frequently used to sell drugs.

Journalists, by

63.3   *R v Tonnessen* 1998 2 Cr App R (S) 328. The defendant pleaded guilty to supplying heroin. The defendant was approached by a man who claimed to know her. He was accompanied by two others who turned out to be from the *News of the World*. They said they worked for a Sheikh and they were instructed to buy drugs. She was a heroin addict and a cannabis user and said these drugs were widely available. They said they wanted to buy heroin and asked her whether she was prepared to get it for them. They gave her £50 and she bought four wraps of heroin. She and a friend spent the rest of the evening with them. Immediately after her name and photograph appeared in the paper. The police felt obliged to arrest her and she admitted the offence. After the publicity she was assaulted and received a threat to her life. She was 31 and had already served a prison sentence for an unrelated offence. She had no supply convictions. She suffered from a serious pre-cancerous condition. The judge did not refer to the involvement of agent provocateurs and appeared not to have taken it into account. The defence said there can be considerable mitigation where it can be shown that the offence would not otherwise have been committed. The defence submitted that it was legitimate for policemen to entrap criminals. When the entrapment is by journalist even more consideration and more weight should be given. Held. We consider there is substance in those submissions. However, it merited immediate custody. We cannot ignore the fact that she was set up. If these men had been police officers that would provide mitigation. Different considerations must apply to investigatory journalists. Their purpose was perfectly honourable. But we feel the public would be left with a sense of unease by the identification in the paper. The consequences were most unfortunate. It is appropriate to reflect the entrapment in the sentence. It should have been expressly mentioned in the remarks. In the exceptional circumstances we reduce the sentence from 12 months to **6 months**.

Refer to it in the sentencing remarks, must

63.4   *R v Tonnessen* 1998 2 Cr App R (S) 328. The judge did not refer to the involvement of agent provocateurs and appeared not to have taken it into account. Held. Applying *R v Mackey* 1993 14 Cr App R (S) 53, it should have been expressly mentioned in the remarks.

64   ENVIRONMENTAL OFFENCES

64.1   Various offences and penalties.

The principles to follow when dealing with companies as defendants are listed in the **HEALTH AND SAFETY OFFENCES** section.

Sentencing Advisory Panel The Panel has produced a report about environment offences which can be found at www.sentencing-guidelines.gov.uk

Crown Court statistics – England and Wales – Males 21+ – Public Health
64.2

For details and explanations about the statistics in the book see page vii.

Year	Plea	Total Numbers sentenced	Type of sentence %					Average length of custody (months)
			Discharge	Fine	Community sentence	Suspended sentence	Custody	
2002	Guilty	7	14	29	43	–	14	2
	Not guilty	7	14	57	14	–	14	6
2003	Guilty	18	17	50	17	–	17	12.3
	Not guilty	5	20	40	40	–	–	–

Magistrates' Court Sentencing Guidelines, January 2004

64.3   A deliberate breach of the legislation by a company or an individual with a view to profit seriously aggravates the offence

For details about the guidelines see MAGISTRATES' COURT SENTENCING GUIDELINES at page 483.

Guideline remarks

64.4   *R v Anglian Water Services Ltd* 2004 1 Cr App R (S) 374. The environment in which we live is a precious heritage and it is incumbent on the present generation to preserve it for the future. Rivers and watercourses are an important part of that environment and there is an increasing awareness of the necessity to preserve them from pollution. There is a heavy burden on (water companies) to do everything possible to ensure that they do not cause pollution.

Slaughterhouses and animal incinerators

64.5   *R v Clutton Agricultural Ltd* 2001 Unreported 27/11/01. The defendant company and two of its directors were convicted in total of thirty six counts. The company was a family company operating incinerators and two directors who were brothers ran it. Local authorities attach conditions for incinerators to combat BSE and records had to be kept. For each count against the company there was one for a director. One pair of counts was carrying out the operation in breach of conditions laid down. This was contrary to Environmental Protection Act 1990 s 23(1)(a). The company used three incinerators at a time although they were permitted to use only two in the conditions. The company had in fact applied to use three but their application was refused. Three years later on appeal permission was granted. The offences were committed when the appeal was pending. Two pairs of counts were for carrying out the operation otherwise than in accordance with the conditions. This was incinerating far in excess of the permitted 250 kilos of carcasses an hour. Twelve pairs of counts were either providing false figures or failing to provide accurate figures to the local authority. Accurate records were sent to the Intervention Board but false and lower figures were sent to the local authority to hide the amount of incineration and therefore the breach of conditions. Three pairs of counts were for failure to burn or deliver carcasses. The company had to incinerate carcasses within six days. When this couldn't be done in time the company was obliged to return them. Instead the carcasses were frozen until they could be burnt. One director was a solicitor and none of the defendants had any convictions. The company and the directors had access to considerable funds. The judge held that there was no environmental damage or any danger to human health from the offences. He said the offences were committed for profit and it was wholly dishonest. He fined the company **£25,000** and the directors **£15,500** and **£9,000**. A costs order of £80,000 out of £100,000 was made to take into account the defendants were not convicted on all the charges. Held. Courts need to show by the fines that this game is not worth the candle. There was no error in this sentence.

Waste, unauthorised keeping, treating or depositing

64.6   Environmental Protection Act 1990 s 33

Triable either way. On indictment maximum 5 years for special waste and 2 years otherwise. Summary maximum 6 months and/or £20,000.

R v Moynihan 1999 1 Cr App R (S) 294. The defendant pleaded guilty to two counts of unauthorised keeping and depositing of controlled waste without a licence, obtaining services by deception, two counts of forgery and an attempted obtaining by deception. The defendant's family had a number of businesses including a company, which manufactured industrial incinerators and one which incinerated clinical waste. In the early 1990s the companies ran into financial difficulties and the defendant systematically cheated the Inland Revenue over VAT. In 1995 he started to accept large volumes of clinical waste before he had obtained the necessary licences. He tried to have the waste disposed of by another operator but that proved to be inadequate and he hired a number of containers to store the waste. An environmental protection officer ordered him to remove it and instead of deposing it lawfully he moved it to a disused factory. The Waste authority intervened and disposed of it at a cost to the Authority of £200,000. The nature of the waste created a potential risk to the public. It included incontinence pads, human tissue and syringes. The deception counts concerned the forging of an authorisation that he was able to use the incinerator, obtaining financial services by claiming he was able to use the incinerator, forging a performance bond to obtain a contract and stating a fictitious income in connection with a mortgage. He was 33 with a young family. In 1997 he had been convicted of cheating the Inland Revenue over the VAT. He received a 3 year sentence. He had no other convictions and was now a 'ruined man.' He received **18 months** in all for the environmental offences, consecutive to 9 months in all for the dishonesty offences consecutive to the VAT sentence he was still serving making 5¼ years in all. Held. There was nothing wrong with the sentences and we would expect the sentences for the dishonesty to be consecutive to the environmental offences. However the total was too long. The sentence was rearranged to make the total **4½ years**.

R v Ferguson 2001 1 Cr App R (S) 312. The defendant pleaded guilty at the 11th hour to causing the disposal without a licence of controlled special waste in or on land. CSS an English company accepted for payment over 2,000 45 gallon drums labelled Nitrochlorobenzene (NCB) from an Italian company. Plans to recycle them were abandoned, as it wasn't economic. 1,120 drums were lawfully disposed of at a cost of £110 a drum. The defendant who worked for Blue Circle had an interest in blending chemicals. He set up a company with someone connected with a Belgium cement producer and the company was paid over £40,000 to take 738 drums of NCB. The contents were not suitable for the Belgium company and the venture was abandoned and he split from his partner. When the defendant was ordered to remove 184 drums from transport yard he took them to a warehouse in Greenwich and contacted the London Waste Regulation Authority. They found the drums and disposed of them. The defendant disclaimed responsibility for them. The basis of plea included that he was told by CSS that it was a product and not waste and the drummed material was properly stored, did not suffer from significant leakage or deterioration and was not highly toxic. He was 56 and treated as of good character. The defendant was to receive a salary of £60,000 from the new company and was to receive payment of £200,000 (defendant said £100,000) over a 5 month period. He had considerable other assets. Compensation was being claimed through the civil courts. He was **fined £30,000** (£25,000 within 2 months and then £2,000 a month) and **£50,000 prosecution costs**. Held. The defendant had avoided the cost of storage on specially licensed land for profit. Sometime before they were stored at the transport yard he knew it was waste. There was nothing wrong with the judge's approach.

R v O'Brien and Enkel 2000 2 Cr App R (S) 358. The defendants O and E changed their plea to guilty to two counts of causing controlled waste to be deposited without a licence [s 33 (1)(a], no written description of controlled waste [s 33(1)(c)(ii)] and no signed transfer note [s 33(5)]. E was offered £4 a tyre to dispose of 2,000 tyres. He agreed. O and E were running a company and they said they could store the tyres or dispose of them as mats in playgrounds or to farmers. O and E hired a van and rented a compound for £80 for 3 weeks. The tyres were dumped there and a neighbour complained. The total gain was £8,304 for 2 days' work. O was arrested and admitted he did not have a licence. The tyres were not removed. The cost of removal was £12,000–£12,500. O was 36 with no convictions for waste offences. E was 34 with a conviction in 1995 for counterfeiting but no waste convictions. Held. The lack of danger can be seen in the fact that no licence is needed to store the tyres. The case does not pass the custody threshold. A **fine or CSO** is appropriate. As they had served their 8 month sentence no order made.

Old cases. *R v Garrett* 1997 1 Cr App R (S) 109.

Water Resources Act 1991 s 85

64.7   Polluting controlled waters.

Triable either way. On indictment maximum 2 years and unlimited fine. Summary maximum 3 months or a fine of £20,000.

R v Milford Haven Port Authority 2000 2 Cr App R (S) 423. The company pleaded guilty to causing oil to enter controlled waters under s 85. A pilot of the company was guiding a tanker carrying about 130,000 tonnes of crude oil into Milford Haven dock. He committed a serious navigational error and the tanker grounded on rocks. Initially the tanker lost 2,500 tonnes of oil. Within 6 days the tanker lost a further 69,300 tonnes of crude oil and some bunker oil. There was widespread pollution to the coastal waters which were beautiful and environmentally sensitive. There were many sites of special scientific interest and conservation. Various forms of marine life were killed and birds suffered as a result. Those who were dependent on visitors also suffered. The spill was among the largest ever recorded. The clean up costs were estimated to be £60m. The basis of plea was that the offence was one of strict liability and the authority was not at fault nor guilty of any breach of duty, whether negligent, reckless or deliberate or of any misconduct. There was no record of offending or history of non-compliance or warnings unheeded. The judge gave modest credit for the plea because there was no defence and the plea was late. The company was ordered to pay £825,000 prosecution costs. Held. Had it not been an offence of strict liability the culpability would have been much greater. However, Parliament creates an offence of strict liability when it considers the doing or not doing of a particular thing is so. Here the danger of oil pollution is so potentially devastating, so far reaching and so costly to rectify Parliament attaches a criminal penalty where no lack of care or due diligence need be shown. The company cannot escape a very substantial penalty. Public bodies are not immune from appropriate penalties because they have no shareholders and the directors are not in receipt of handsome annual bonuses. However, it is proper for the judge to take that factor into account. If a substantial financial penalty will inhibit the proper performance by a statutory body of the public function it has been set up to perform that factor should not be disregarded. It was understandable that the company delayed the plea until agreement had been reached about the basis even though a plea was inevitable. There is material to show the fine imposed could not be recouped from the customers. The judge did not have information we have which shows the authority's inability to borrow etc and pay the fine imposed without cutting back on expenditure or losing business. **£750,000 fine** not £4m.

R v Anglian Water Services Ltd 2004 1 Cr App R (S) 374. The defendant company pleaded guilty to causing sewage effluent to be discharged into a river, contrary to the Water Resources Act 1991, s.85(3). For between three and five hours the defendant company released about 200 tonnes of untreated sewage into a local river. A combination of mechanical failure (a retaining gate had not prevented sewage passing into the river) and faulty monitoring equipment (a contamination monitor which would have diverted the flow and raised the alarm) caused the release. The monitor had been broken for three weeks. The release had been catastrophic for fish and wildlife over about 2 km of river. The defendant took what steps it could by re-oxygenating the river as soon as it could and the river had recovered by the next day. In mitigation, there was a plea of guilty, co-operation with the Environment Agency, restoring the river and achieving improvement to prevent a recurrence. The defendant had 64 convictions for sewage discharge although this was seen in context of the size of the operation and effectively disregarded. The water company covered 20% of England and Wales serving $5^1/_2$ m people and had a comparatively good record. Held. With reference to *R v F Howe and Son (Engineers) Ltd* 1999 2 Cr App R (S) 37 there were certain material factors to be considered: the extent to which the defendant fell short in his duty, the risk of death or serious injury, the skimping of proper precautions to make or save money to gain a competitive advantage, the deliberate breaching of a duty in order to maximise profit, the degree of risk and danger created by the offence, the extent of the breach or breaches, evidence of repetition or failure to heed warnings, the financial profit (if any) occurring to the defendant as a result of the offence, admission of guilt and a plea of guilty at an early opportunity, the taking of prompt and effective measures to rectify any failures and a good record of compliance with the law. Further, the fine should reflect the means of the defendant. In *R v Yorkshire Water Services Ltd* 2002 2 Cr App R (S) 13 there were four failures leading to seventeen offences of supplying water unfit for human consumption. Fines were reduced from £199,000 to £80,000. Here the company had done what it could to rectify the situation and there was no question of the defendant having deliberately cut corners to save cost. Fine reduced from £200,000 to **£60,000**.

See also COMPANIES and WATER

65 ESCAPE FROM CUSTODY

65.1 Escape from and breach of prison are both common law offences. Both offences are indictable only. Both offences have no maximum sentence provided so the maximum is life.

Prison Act 1952 s 39

Aiding prisoner to escape etc.

Indictable only. Maximum 10 years.

Crown Court statistics – England and Wales – Males 21+
65.2

Year	Plea	Total Numbers sentenced	Type of sentence %					Average length of custody (months)
			Discharge	Fine	Community sentence	Suspended sentence	Custody	
2002	Guilty	230	3	2	17	0	78	7.2
	Not guilty	5	–	–	–	–	80	9.2
2003	Guilty	302	2	2	18	0	78	5.3
	Not guilty	5	–	–	–	–	100	4.4

For details and explanations about the statistics in the book see page vii.

Guideline remark

65.3   *R v Sutcliffe* 1992 13 Cr App R (S) 538. It is quite essential for the courts to mark out the seriousness of escapes from custody, whether in the Magistrates' Court or the Crown Court, by immediate sentences of imprisonment. It is not only intended as a punishment but also as a clear deterrent to others.

R v Jarvis 2002 2 Cr App R (S) 558. The defendant pleaded guilty to escaping and appealed. The defence posed a series of questions. (1) Was it pre-planned? (2) What level of violence was used and what level of injury, if any, was suffered? (3) Was the attempt successful and if so how long was the defendant at large? Held. We bear in mind the criteria which have been helpfully summarised. Those who seek to escape violently must expect a custodial sentence.

Carefully planned

65.4   Old cases. *R v Wilson* 1993 14 Cr App R (S) 314.

Running from the dock – Opportunist

65.5   *R v Wilson* 1998 2 Cr App R (S) 267. LCJ. The defendant pleaded guilty to escape. The defendant was arrested for driving matters and appeared at the Magistrates' Court where his bail application was refused. As the dock officer moved towards him the defendant ran to the side of the dock, with the officer after him. The defendant vaulted over the door and ran into the court foyer. As the officer pushed the door open it swung sharply against an usher and injured her arm causing two cuts. The officer fell over the usher and they both fell to the ground. The defendant escaped. He visited his daughter in hospital and went home where he was arrested two days later. He said sorry in interview and when taken back to court he apologised personally to the officer. The driving offences were discontinued. He was 23 with one hundred and fifty offences on thirty occasions. He had 18 custodial sentences including one for robbery for which he received 12 months. They included violence and drugs. He had an unfortunate family background and had a history of drug abuse. **9 months** not 18.

R v Roberts 1998 2 Cr App R (S) 455. The defendant pleaded guilty to escape. The defendant appeared at a Magistrates' Court and without warning jumped over the dock. He was followed by officers but got away and he was at large for six weeks. He was 29. His sentence was consecutive to 18 months for other offences for which no appeal was made. Held. Escape is always a serious offence. An important factor is whether the escape was opportunist or carefully planned. **9 months** not 18.

R v Jarvis 2002 2 Cr App R (S) 558. The defendant pleaded guilty to escaping. The defendant was charged with aggravated burglary and remanded in custody. The defendant appeared in the Crown Court and the case was adjourned. He leapt over

266

the dock and was tackled by two security officers and an off duty police officer before he could get through the court doors. There was a struggle lasting four to five minutes. The police officer sustained a slight cut to his knuckle. Later the prosecution dropped the burglary charge because a witness had died. The Judge refused to give him credit for the time he was in custody for the other matter. Held. The Judge was right not to give him credit. Bearing in mind the criteria (see *Guideline remarks*) **6 months** not 12.

EVIDENCE

For giving evidence for the co-defendant, see GUILTY PLEA, DISCOUNT FOR – *Co-defendant, giving evidence for*

For giving evidence in a Newton hearing, see GUILTY PLEA, DISCOUNT FOR – *Newton hearing, defendant takes part in*

For giving evidence for the prosecution, SEE INFORMANTS/GIVING EVIDENCE FOR THE PROSECUTION

EXCESS ALCOHOL

See DRINK DRIVING – *Excess alcohol*

EXCISE DUTY EVASION

See TAX FRAUD AND DUTY EVASION

66   EXCISE LICENCE, FRAUDULENT USE ETC

66.1   Vehicle Excise and Registration Act 1994 s 44

Triable either way. On indictment maximum 2 years. Summary maximum £5,000.

Magistrates' Court Sentencing Guidelines January 2004

66.2   First time offenders who plead not guilty. Entry point. Is a discharge or a fine appropriate? Examples of aggravating factors for the offence are bought fraudulently, deliberately planned, disc forged or altered, long term defrauding and LGV, HGV, PCV, PSV, taxi or private hire vehicle. Examples of mitigation are co-operation with the police and genuine remorse. **Starting point fine B.** (100% of weekly take home pay/weekly benefit payment)

For details about the guidelines see MAGISTRATES' COURT SENTENCING GUIDELINES at page 483.

67   EXPLOSIVE OFFENCES

67.1   Explosive Substances Act 1883 s 2, 3 and 4

Indictable only. Maximum for s 2 and 3 is life and for s 4, 14 years.

The chapter is divided into two sections, (A) Causes an explosion and (B) Making or possessing explosives.

Dangerous Offender provisions For both s 2 and s 3 offences when committed on or after 4/4/05 where there is a significant risk to members of the public of serious harm etc. there is a mandatory duty to pass a life sentence when it is justified and otherwise a sentence of imprisonment for public protection[2]. For offenders under 18 the duty is to pass detention for life, detention for public protection or an extended sentence[3].

Sexual Offences Prevention Order For offences under section 2 and 3 there is a discretionary power to make this order when it is necessary to protect the public etc[4].

A   Causes an explosion with intent to endanger life etc.

67.2   Explosive Substances Act 1883 s 2 and 3

General

67.3   *Att-Gen's Ref. No. 13 of 2002* 2003 1 Cr App R (S) 48. The defendant was convicted of possession of an explosive substance with intent (Section 3) and simple possession (Section 4). After a period in the army, he became a computer software engineer and lived with his partner. She went abroad for work and he started a relationship with a colleague at work, C. After a year she ended it and started a relationship with D. The defendant bombarded her with telephone calls and text messages. He approached an army friend and asked him to find someone to get rid of D. The friend did not help and the defendant attempted to revive the relationship with C. About seven months later a gamekeeper found an explosive device on a dry stone wall. This was the Section 4 offence. It was a test device that had malfunctioned. Three days later a walker found in a field eight devices with warheads in two halves which could when required be joined together. They were fragmentation bombs with three kilos of metal nuts packed around a pipe bomb. Inside was nitro-cellulose and nitro-glycerine. If detonated the force would have been great. The nuts and shrapnel would travel at high speed causing very serious if not fatal injuries if they struck anyone. Three of the devices were particularly sophisticated and able to be detonated by remote signal. They contained mercury tilt switches, which would operate as an anti handling mechanism. If disturbed they would detonate. The firing devices were of particular sophistication not previously seen. Five devices had labels, which could be set for a delay of between one and seven hours. It was believed D was the target. There was a long, detailed and expensive police investigation, which the Judge described as huge. It emerged the defendant had bought a mobile in the name of an old school friend to buy the parts and had hired a car for seven days. There were false plates at his home matching a car used by someone who lived three miles away. When interviewed he claimed to be the victim of a blackmail plot forcing him to buy the parts. His defence at trial was that he intended to conduct a hoax bombing campaign ending with the taking of his own life. He was 41, of good character and a JP undergoing training. The Judge sentenced him to 5 years and 18 months concurrent. *Held.* Bearing in mind the offence was with an intent to endanger life, the sophistication, there were so many devices, the anti-handling mechanisms and the planning we would have expected at least **12 years**. As it was a reference **9 years** substituted.

R v Wildy 2004 1 Cr App R (S) 99. The defendant was convicted of having an explosive substance with intent to endanger life or cause serious injury to property and doing an

---

2   Criminal Justice Act 2003 s 225
3   Criminal Justice Act 2003 s 226 and 228
4   Sexual Offences Act 2003 s 104 & Sch. 5

act with intent to cause an explosion. He rented a house and he and his co-defendant G were there when there was an explosion in the kitchen which blew out most of the windows in the house and broke the kitchen windows and doors. G was very badly injured and was not available for questioning for some time. When he was questioned he refused to answer. The defendant suffered only minor injuries and when questioned lied. Investigations revealed letter bombs were being manufactured with PE4, a powerful, British military explosive. A list of items required for the construction of the devices was found. Twenty grams of PE4 were recovered with two detonators, complete home made pressure switches and two envelopes addressed to businessmen known to have connections with organised crime. He was 59 with no convictions. **Held.** The scheme was to endanger the lives of two people who could well have been killed. **15 years** was not manifestly excessive.

R v Griffiths 2005 1 Cr App R (S) 600. The defendant was convicted of having an explosive substance with intent, (count 1) and doing an act with intent to cause an explosion (count 2). He had previously pleaded guilty to one count of having an explosive substance (count 3). The defendant went to a co-accused's house and there set about making letter bombs using PE4 -British military high explosive- and detonators. The explosives detonated and caused him serious injuries. £7,000 worth of damage was done to the house. When his own house was searched police found 349g of PE4 (count 3). His motives remained obscure. In the course of the trial he 'belatedly' said he was going to deliver the devices to two people who owed him £5,000 to frighten them into paying the debt, after initially claiming at trial that the explosives had been forced on him by people he had picked up in his minicab earlier in the year. The defendant was 42 with some old previous conviction but nothing approaching this one in seriousness. The longest sentence he had received was 6 months in a detention centre for possession of an offensive weapon. Both his hands had been amputated and he suffered injuries to his thighs, genitalia, anterior trunk, neck and face as well as perforated eardrums. A psychiatric report said there were no suicidal or psychotic issues and he was coming to terms with his injuries. A medical report expressed concern that while in custody he was not receiving the medical care he required. **Held.** The only substantial point was whether the disability suffered merited further discount beyond making the sentence for count 3 (3 years) concurrent to counts 1 and 2 (**15 years**). It did not.

Blackmail, and

67.4 *R v Pearce* 2000 2 Cr App R (S) 50. The defendant pleaded to nine counts of blackmail, three ABHs, causing an explosion likely to endanger life, doing an act with intent to cause an explosion likely to endanger life, unlawful wounding, two counts of possessing firearms with intent to commit an indictable offence, possessing explosives and possessing a prohibited weapon. He was the 'Mardi Gras bomber' who over 3½ years waged a campaign against Barclays Bank and Sainsbury's. In the Barclays Bank campaign he deployed 25 devices of six different types intending to produce explosions. Some were boxes designed to fire shotgun cartridges, others were modified gas cylinders filled with diesel fuel and a detonating charge and some were designed to fire pellets from a two barrel shotgun. One victim received minor injuries, one narrowly avoided injury to the eye, and a passing car was engulfed with flames with the driver managing to escape. The devices could cause serious injury and death. In the campaign against Sainsbury's he used a similar extremely ingenious mechanism involving shotgun cartridges. A man was injured. Another device went off in someone's car and one struck a man causing multiple puncture wounds. That victim had to end his athletic career. Others exploded in the street without causing injuries. He wanted very substantial sums of money from the bank and £½m from Sainsbury's. For each there was an ingenious method of payment to avoid the risk of being caught. He was 62 and needed psychiatric treatment. His life expectancy was 4–5 years. Held. A hospital order was not appropriate. **21 years** in all was entirely appropriate.

See also BLACKMAIL

Kill the victim, intending to

67.5 *R v McDonald* 2002 2 Cr App R (S) 113. The defendant pleaded guilty to causing an explosion likely to endanger life. The defendant, the intended victim W and the victim's wife worked for a firm of electrical engineers. The defendant was a technological systems manager. W's wife left him and went to live with the defendant. When she returned to W the defendant was openly talking about killing W and making it look like an animal rights act as the company was working on a large contract for a company which used animals for research. He wrote letters threatening to hurt employees of various companies if the company given the contract continued animal testing. A sophisticated bomb was prepared packed with screws, which could be set off by remote control. He put the bomb beneath the driver's seat of W's van which was parked outside his home and waited. W went to the van and the defendant changed his mind. W saw the bag and went back home. The defendant detonated the bomb in part to cover his tracks. The screws were scattered over 200' and embedded themselves in window frames of houses. A gas meter nearby narrowly avoided being seriously damaged. The defendant left and wrote a letter to the companies saying 'It could be you next.' When arrested he made a full confession. No report suggested there was anything aggressive about him. He was of good character and had been in the army but it was not sug-gested he had gained any bomb making skills there. His commanding officer wrote a testimonial for him. Held. It was jealous anger. **10 years** was severe but appropriate.

See also MURDER, ATTEMPTED – *Murder, conspiracy to*

B Making or possessing explosives

67.6 Explosive Substances Act 1883 s 4

Defendant aged 14–15

67.7 *R v Milsom* 1998 1 Cr App R (S) 306. The defendant pleaded guilty to making an explosive substance, having an explosive substance and possession of a prohibited weapon. He asked for offences of making an explosive device and stealing chemicals to be taken into consideration. In 1995 the defendant started experimenting with explosives. By the summer of 1996 he had an obsession with making explosives from common and domestic chemicals. In July 1996 he received a conditional discharge for setting off an explosion. Four days later he set off another explosion using icing sugar and weed killer in a biscuit tin with a fuse. It caused a ball of flame and a woman in a house nearby was terrified. He attended the police station and admitted making four explosions. In October 1996, the day before he was due to be interviewed about an offence of criminal damage for which he was later conditionally discharged, he was stopped by police who found on him another explosive device, two homemade pipe guns containing 10 grams of screwpin heads, tacks and ball-bearings. He said he was going to sell the device. A search of his room revealed further ingredients for explosive devices. The defendant admitted the equipment was for flares for Bonfire Night and said the pipegun was for self defence. He said he would never do any damage with his bombs. The pre-sentence report described him as arrogant, anti-authoritarian and reckless. The time on remand had shifted his views but he remained naïve and emotionally frozen. The risk of re-offending was estimated to be medium to high. A psychiatrist said he seemed to have an emotional disorder called 'conduct disorder' involving manic depressive mood swings. He recommended 18 months in a secure unit. Since his sentence he had made progress. Held. The defendant was presenting great risks to the public although he didn't intend the risks to be created. It was unfortunate he had been cautioned three times leading up to these offences. Custody was right but it ought to be kept to the minimum. **3 years** detention in total not 4.

R v O 2001 Unreported 17/7/01. 6 months detention upheld for a 15 year old.

Home-made devices as a hobby

67.8   *R v Lloyd* 2001 2 Cr App R (S) 493. The defendant pleaded guilty to making explosives. More serious charges were left on the file. He made four devices each about 8cm long in the form of empty gas canisters containing a mixture of weedkiller and sugar. He handed them to a co-defendant who later told a prison officer about them after reading about a bomb in a newspaper. Police searched the defendant's home and found a closed copper pipe, a printed circuit board, 2″ silver CO_2 canisters and three full pots of weedkiller. He was sentenced on the basis the devices were to make a loud bang and enable him to show off. There was no intent to injure. He had a long-standing hobby of making fireworks and explosives and had 14 convictions including firearms and offensive weapon offences. There were none for explosives. He had a chronic personality disorder with depression. He made a witness statement against a co-defendant and was prepared to give evidence against him. Held. Explosive devices in the wrong hands are capable of causing untold injury and misery to innocent people. $3^1/_2$ **years** could not be criticised.

See also **TERRORISM**

68   EXPORTING DRUGS

68.1   For statute and penalties see **IMPORTATION OF DRUGS (CLASS A, B AND C)**

Basic principles

68.2   *R v Powell* 2000 Times 5/10/00. LCJ. There was no difference in criminality between the importation and exportation of controlled drugs.

69   EXTENDED SENTENCES

69.1   Sexual and Violent offences are dealt with under four different systems. For offences committed (a) before 1 October 1992 there is no statutory powers to increase the sentences; (b) from 1 October 1992 to 29 September 1998 there was power to pass a sentence to protect the public from serious harm from him; (c) from 30 September 1998 to 3 April 2005 there are the Longer than Commensurate and the first Extended Sentence powers and (d) from 4 April 2005 there are the Dangerous Offender provisions created by the Criminal Justice Act 2003.

The new extended sentence replaces both the **LONGER THAN COMMENSURATE SENTENCE** and the old Extended Sentence. The old extended sentence colloquially meant the extended licence part of a sentence. (Strictly speaking the extended sentence was considered to refer to the whole term.)

Extended Sentences (New)

69.2   Criminal Justice Act 2003 s 227–8

The new extended sentence applies to offences where the maximum sentence is less than 10 years. The offence must be committed on or after 4/4/05[5], or end on or after 4/4/05[6].

Courts can only pass an extended sentence for a specified offence. Each offence that is specified has this power to pass an extended sentence listed at the beginning of its chapter.

Criteria required

69.3   Criminal Justice Act 2003 Section 227(1)–(2). Where a person aged 18 or over is convicted of a specified offence and the court considers that there is a significant risk to members of the public of serious harm occasioned by the commission by him of further specified offences the court must impose an extended sentence of imprisonment for life which is … equal to the aggregate of (a) the appropriate custodial term and (b) a further period (the extension period) for which is of such length as the court considers necessary for the purpose of protecting members of the public from serious harm occasioned by the commission by him of further specified offences.

Criteria required – Assessing whether there is a significant risk

69.4   Criminal Justice Act 2003 Section 229(2). If the offender has not been convicted in the UK of any relevant offence or was aged under 18, the court in making the assessment (whether there is a significant risk to members of the public of serious harm) (a) must take into account all such information as is available to it about the nature and circumstances of the offence and (b) may take into account any information which is before it about any pattern of behaviour of which the offence forms part, and (c) may take into account any information about the offender which is before it.

Criminal Justice Act 2003 Section 229(3). If at the time the offence was committed the offender was aged 18 or over and had been convicted in any part of the UK of one or more relevant offences, the court must assume that there is such a risk (whether there is a significant risk etc.) unless … the court concludes that it would be unreasonable to conclude that there is such a risk.

Extended sentence not adequate / mandatory duty to impose

69.5   Criminal Justice Act 2003 Section 225. Where a person aged 18 or over is convicted of a serious offence and the court is of the opinion that there is a significant risk to members of the public of serious harm occasioned by the commission by him of further specified offences the court must impose a sentence of imprisonment for life if (i) (the maximum for the offence is life), and the court considers that the seriousness of the offence, or of the offence and one or more offences associated with it, is such as to justify the imposition of a sentence of imprisonment for life.

Criminal Justice Act 2003 Section 226. This section contains a similar provision for persons under 18 and imposes a duty to the court to impose a sentence of detention for life.

Maximum/minimum periods

69.6   Criminal Justice Act 2003 Section 227(4). The extension period must not exceed (a) 5 years in the case of a specified violent offence, and (b) 8 years in the case of a specified sexual offence. The court must impose at least 12 months.

Criminal Justice Act 2003 Section 228. This section contains similar provisions for those over 18. The appropriate custodial term has to be at least 12 months.

5   Criminal Justice Act 2003 s 225(1)(a), 226(1)(a), 227(1)(a) and Criminal Justice Act 2003 (Commencement No 8) Order 2005
6   Criminal Justice Act 2003 s 234

Extended Sentences (Old)

69.7   An old extended sentence is a sentence which has an extended licence period, Powers of Criminal Courts (Sentencing) Act 2000 s 85(2)(b).

The court can also pass a sentence which is longer than commensurate, Powers of Criminal Courts (Sentencing) Act 2000 s 80(2). This is frequently (wrongly) called an extended sentence but that is not what the section calls it. See LONGER THAN COMMENSURATE SENTENCES.

Guideline case/Guideline remarks

69.8   *R v Nelson* 2002 1 Cr App R (S) 565. The first stage is to decide on the sentence which would be commensurate. The second stage is to consider whether a longer period in custody is needed to protect the public from serious harm from the offender. If so, a longer than commensurate custodial sentence will be called for. The third stage, in relation to a sexual offence or a violent offence for which the appropriate custodial sentence is 4 years or longer, is to consider whether that sentence, whether commensurate or longer than commensurate, is adequate to prevent the commission by the offender of further offences and secure his rehabilitation. If not, an extended sentence is called for. Also, there may be cases in which, because of the power to impose an extended licence period, a longer than commensurate sentence may not be necessary. Judges should always take care to use the correct terminology when passing sentence. In particular, a longer than commensurate sentence should be so described: it is not an extended sentence.

R v Pepper 2005 Unreported 28/4/05. Protection may be a reason for passing a longer than commensurate sentence, but it is not of itself a reason for passing an extended sentence, the purpose of which is to prevent the commission of further offences and to secure the offender's rehabilitation.

Commensurate term, and a

69.9   *R v Nelson* 2002 1 Cr App R (S) 565. One purpose of an extended sentence is to reduce the likelihood of re-offending, and it is therefore particularly suitable where a commensurate custodial term is too short for this to be done in prison and where the normal licence period, if any, will not be long enough to permit attendance at a treatment programme in the community. This will arise particularly in relation to less serious sexual offences, where the likelihood of re-offending appears high, but where a longer than commensurate sentence cannot be justified because the offender does not present a risk of serious harm to the public.

R v Creasey 1994 15 Cr App Rep. (S) 671. The appellant there had a record of convictions for relatively minor indecent assaults, and he pleaded guilty to other comparatively minor offences. The trial judge imposed a longer than commensurate sentence of 5 years. The Court of Appeal substituted a sentence of 21 months as being commensurate because, although the offences were unpleasant and distressing, they did not require protection of the public from serious harm. The trial judge had fallen into the trap of assessing the seriousness of the risk of re-offending rather than the seriousness of the anticipated harm. Such a case might now be regarded as one where an extended sentence could and should be imposed with a commensurate custodial term. Similarly, in *R v JT* 2001 1 Cr App Rep. (S) 205, a 78 year old offender pleaded guilty to comparatively minor acts of indecency. He had 10 previous convictions for sexual offences. He was sentenced to an extended sentence of 10 years, with a custodial term of 4 years expressed as a longer than commensurate sentence, together with an extension period of 6 years. Held. There was a clear risk of further offending but we are not satisfied that a longer than commensurate sentence was necessary to protect the public from serious harm. So that sentence is quashed and a commensurate sentence of 3 years is substituted. The extension period of 6 years, however, is upheld. These are the sort of cases where an extended sentence incorporating a commensurate sentence is appropriate. We add that the use of an extended sentence, with a relatively short custodial term, less than 12 months, was endorsed in *R v Ajaib* 2001 1 Cr App R (S) 105.

Consecutive to other sentences

69.10   *R v Cridge* 2000 2 Cr App R (S) 477. It should not be consecutive to other sentences.

R v Nelson 2002 1 Cr App R (S) 565. There have been conflicting views expressed in this Court as to whether the legislation permits the imposition of consecutive extended sentences. Whatever the position as a matter of statutory interpretation, we are in no doubt that sensible practice requires that extended sentences should not, generally, be imposed consecutively.

R v G 2004 Unreported 21/10/04. Good sentencing practice requires the avoiding of consecutive extended sentences and also the avoiding of any consecutive sentence where an extended sentence is passed, save where the court is exercising its power to require the balance of an unexpired term to be served, which must come first.

R v B 2004 The Times 10/12/04. An extended sentence should not be made consecutive to another extended sentence. There was no objection to passing an extended sentence consecutive to a determinate one. The occasion for it may well arise in sexual offences where some of the offences were committed before September 1998 and some after that.

Counsel, should warn

69.11   *R v Nelson* 2002 1 Cr App R (S) 567. Where a sentencer is considering imposing an extended sentence, counsel should be warned of this.

R v Evans 2004 The Times 22/3/05 (the judgement date in the report is wrong). LCJ. The Judge drew attention to the courts power to extend the sentence in the context of the reports before the court. She gave no indication to counsel that she required submissions about extended sentences. Held. The three year extended sentence was entirely sensible. If counsel are not invited to make submissions we will consider whether any valid point arises and consider whether to reduce or set the order aside. But the order will not be quashed simply because counsel was not invited to make submissions.

Extended, the sentence should be

69.12   *R v Green* 2002 Unreported 31/7/02. The defendant pleaded guilty to rape and was assessed as high risk. Held. There was nothing wrong with 6 years custody and 4 years extended licence.

Att-Gen's Ref. No. 192 of 2003 2004 2 Cr App R (S) 395. The defendant changed his plea to guilty to manslaughter on the grounds of provocation. He and the victim were friends and drinking partners, and had known each other for about six years. The victim was addicted to heroin, had undergone periods of hospitalisation for drug-induced schizophrenia and was a heavy drinker. He was undergoing a methadone programme. Shortly before his death he had broken his leg and had been discharged from hospital with his leg in a cast. The defendant was a binge drinker. On the 29th of April the defendant and the victim were seen by a community nurse in the victim's flat. She did not think either was drunk. Another nurse visited the following day and the defendant answered the door, drunk and said he had killed the victim. He was tearful. The victim had 19 stab wounds. At least three had penetrated the heart. The defendant said that on the 29th they had been drinking heavily at a public house; that they had had an argument following the defendant dropping a video recorder belonging to the victim. The victim said the defendant now owed him £240 for the recorder. He also hit the defendant on the head with his crutches. Later the argument erupted again and the victim hit the defendant with his crutch, burnt his shoulder with a cigarette, and struck him again in an escalation of violence. The defendant went to the kitchen, fetched a knife and stabbed the victim repeatedly. He told police he had been pushing the victim around on his bicycle for the previous two weeks taking him to his drug dealer. The victim had hit him with the crutches on previous occasions. There was well-supported evidence that the defendant in the past had shown kindness to the victim and that this kindness had been met with abuse and violence. A taxi driver had seen the victim hitting the defendant with his crutches and trying to punch him because of an argument over the fare on the 29th, and the landlord of a public house saw the victim verbally abusing the defendant on the 28th. The defendant, 37, had 24 convictions for being drunk and disorderly, a conviction for unlawful wounding by means of a knife and five convictions for possession of an offensive weapon – in each case a knife. He demonstrated genuine regret. A psychiatric report said that the defendant did not suffer from any abnormality of mind, that he was a serious alcoholic, and that perhaps he had stored up anger against the victim and then disinhibited by the alcohol there was a sudden and temporary loss of control. Held. **7 years** was an entirely appropriate sentence. The reference only related to the period of licence as the sentence was not extended for licence purposes under section 84. In that respect the sentence was unduly lenient and the offender should be subject to licence throughout the 7 year period of his sentence as that would help him in the rehabilitation process.

How long should the sentence be? – Guideline case

69.13   *R v Nelson* 2002 1 Cr App R (S) 567. The court must decide what period will be adequate to secure the offender's rehabilitation and to prevent re-offending. This will often be difficult. But, in some cases, involving less serious sexual offences where the custodial term is relatively short, the court may be able to take advice on the availability and length of treatment programmes and tailor the extension period accordingly. In all cases the court should consider whether a particular extension period can be justified on the evidence available. A long extension period should usually be based on a clear implication from the offender's criminal record or on what is said in a pre-sentence report or a psychiatric report. The objective, where possible, should be to fix the length of the extension period by reference to what can realistically be achieved within it. When the defendant is clearly dangerous the custodial term will usually be longer than commensurate and a long period of extended licence will often be called for. The length of an extension period is subject to a statutory maximum of 5 years in relation to a violent offence and 10 years in relation to a sexual offence and the combined total of the custodial term and the extension period is limited to the maximum for the offence. It is clear from *R v Gould* 2000 2 Cr App R (S) 173 that a court imposing an extended sentence should bear in mind that the offender may ultimately serve the whole or part of the extension period in custody. But, as the legislature's intention in introducing extended sentences is clearly to place an offender at risk of recall for some considerable time, it would be illogical to require strict proportionality between the duration of the extension period and the seriousness of the offence. Proportionality with the seriousness of the offence is, of course, of central importance to a custodial term. But it should not be a primary factor in determining the length of an extension period. It does, however have some relevance and the implications of the overall sentence should be borne in mind.

How long should the sentence be? – Cases

69.14   *R v Gould* 2000 2 Cr App R (S) 173. The defendant was sentenced to a 5 year custodial term. Here **2 years** extension not 5 appropriate.

R v Nelson 2002 1 Cr App R (S) 567. The defendant was sentenced for indecent assault. The 15 year old school girl victim was walking home and she noticed a man, in a parked car, apparently watching her. She arrived home and was alone. The defendant rang the doorbell. The girl saw him and, after a time, went downstairs, where she was confronted by the defendant, standing in the kitchen, by the back door. He asked if a man called Tony lived there and, when told he did not, he asked a further series of questions, including whether she would give her father his telephone number. When she bent over a table to write it down, the appellant seized her arm and put his other hand over her mouth. He threatened to kill her unless she was quiet. She was terrified. She found difficulty in breathing and started crying. The appellant dragged her upstairs, keeping her mouth covered, and saying 'Shut up or I'll kill you'. He dragged her into the bedroom and threw her on the bed. He lay on top of her, starting to kiss her and simulating intercourse. He seemed angry. He squeezed her right breast, painfully. She begged him to get off. He asked her if he could feel her 'pussy'. She was very frightened and shaking and said no. The defendant said: 'It's all right I'm not going to rape you.' He reached inside her tracksuit bottoms and touched her vagina, without digital penetration. She was crying even more violently and feared she would be raped. The appellant stopped and got off the bed. He threatened he would return and kill her if she told anybody and left. The attack lasted about 5 minutes. When her father returned home the victim was distressed and hysterical and later had to take time off school. She had difficulty sleeping. The defendant was now 32 years and had convictions for blackmail and impersonating a police officer 1991. He received 2 years suspended. The pre-sentence report said there was a significant risk of the appellant re-offending. The psychiatrist's report said he had a 20% risk of re-offending. The judge passed a 5 year sentence with a 5 year extension. Held. This was a very serious offence committed by a stranger, in the victim's home. The judge was entitled to pass an extended period of licence. **2** not 5 years for the extension.

R v Figg 2004 1 Cr App R (S) 409. The defendant was convicted of indecent assault. He was acquitted of rape. He had sexual intercourse with a girl aged just 13. He was 48 and was treated as of good character. The psychiatric report said he had little if any notion as to why sexual activity may lead to harm and damage. The Judge felt obliged not to exceed the maximum for the (old) Sexual Offences Act 1956 s 6. Held. The judge was wrong to consider he was bound by the maximum for the other offence. The maximum for section 6 of 2 years was manifestly inadequate. But **3 years** extension not 8.

R v Christian 2003 1 Cr App R (S) 1. The defendant was convicted of attempted robbery and indecent assault. The victim was walking through an isolated small garage area. The defendant who was drunk grabbed her from behind and tried to pull her over and tried to put his hands over her mouth. Next he put his mouth on her breast and squeezed it. He tried to take her rings off and lunged at her shoulder bag but was unable to dislodge it. Then he moved his hands down to the woman's crotch and tried to lift up her skirt. She managed to elbow him in the stomach and punch him in the groin. He eventually released his grip and she escaped. Nothing was stolen and she suffered no physical injuries. Three days later she saw him again and he said, "I ain't fucking finished with you yet, bitch". She ran away. Two days later he was arrested and denied the offences. Less than a month earlier, he had assaulted a 13 year old and had grabbed her jacket. She managed to get free. When on bail for this he committed the attempted robbery. He was convicted by the Magistrates for an assault and for an unknown offence and received a community rehabilitation order. There were no other convictions. He told the psychiatrists he had been an alcoholic for 20 years and usually drank himself into oblivion. The psychiatrist's report for the Magistrates' Court considered he was a chronic alcoholic and had a disorganised personality who posed a risk, as he did not appear to appreciate personal boundaries. The psychiatrist for the Crown Court said he posed a risk when under the influence of alcohol. Further his alcohol abuse had lead to personality changes in terms of poor social behaviour and loss of impulse control. He said he was likely to re-offend when he resumes his heavy alcohol intake. The pre-sentence report said he poses a high risk to the public and indications suggest that violence would be characteristic of the high likelihood of sexual offending. The Judge made the sentences concurrent and made an extended sentence with the licence part **5 years**. Held. The two offences showed a pattern. $4^1/_2$ years in total was lenient. He was unlikely to co-operate with rehabilitation. For a chronic alcoholic with anti-social and anti-women tendencies a long period of supervision is necessary for the protection of the public. The extension was not wrong.

Longer than commensurate sentence, and an extended sentence

69.15 *R v Thornton* 2000 2 Cr App R (S) 47. 5 years longer than commensurate changed to a 2 years custodial term with a 3 years extension period.

R v Nelson 2002 1 Cr App R (S) 567. The two sentences will be appropriate, where a violent or sexual offence is committed by a seriously dangerous offender, in relation to whom a life sentence, if available, might well be passed, thereby permitting the offender to be released only when the executive believes that the risk posed by him has been greatly reduced. In such a case, the offender would of course be subject to recall for the rest of his life. It is appropriate to combine an extended period of licence with a longer than commensurate custodial term for an offender who presents a serious danger to the public but where a life sentence is not available because the maximum penalty is, for example, a lesser determinate sentence. There may also be cases in which a discretionary life sentence is available for the offence but the criteria which have to be established before such a sentence can be passed may not all be present (e.g. *R v Chapman* 2000 1 Cr App R (S) 377). Where a longer than commensurate sentence is called for, it should usually be accompanied by an extension period because a seriously dangerous offender, attracting a longer than commensurate sentence, may well commit further offences.

Low risk, – only a low risk

69.16 R v M 2004 The Times 18/8/04. LCJ The Judge accepted he only presented a low risk of offending. Held. He could be sentenced to an extended sentence. It was for the Judge to decide. He had been satisfied the statutory criteria had been made out.

Magistrates' Courts

69.17 *R v Nelson* 2002 1 Cr App R (S) 567. Where magistrates think the normal period of licence is inadequate they should commit to the Crown Court for sentence. A Youth Court may have the power to pass an extended sentence but the legislation is obscure and the point may merit scrutiny on some future occasion.

Maximum, – the sentence should not exceed the maximum

69.18 Powers of Criminal Courts (Sentencing) Act 2000 s 85(5). The term of an extended sentence passed in respect of an offence shall not exceed the maximum term permitted for that offence.

R v L 2000 2 Cr App R (S) 506. The defendant pleaded guilty to three counts of indecent assault on girls aged around 13 or 14. The defence argued relying on *R v Hinton* 1995 16 Cr App R (S) 523 that although the maximum is 10 years the maximum for unlawful sexual intercourse with a girl aged 13–15 is only 2 years so where there are sexual acts falling short of sexual intercourse there should be a judicially imposed maximum of 2 years. The Judge sentenced him to 12 months with 3 years extension. Held. The Judge was right to accept that argument. However the term should not exceed the maximum, Powers of Criminal Courts (Sentencing) Act 2000 s 85(5). As the defendant should have received a discount and should not have received the maximum the extended period should be reduced to 6 months. (Powers of Criminal Courts (Sentencing) Act 2000 s 85(2) appears to define the term of an extended sentence as the custodial part and the licence period.)

Old offences

69.19   Criminal Justice Act 1991 Section 44. The original power before the 2000 Act. This Act came into force on 1 October 1992.

European Convention of Human Rights Article 7. Nor shall a heavier penalty be imposed than the one that was applicable at the time the offence was committed.

Powers of Criminal Courts (Sentencing) Act 2000 Section 85(1)(a). This section (giving power to order extended sentences) applies to sentences committed on or after 30 September 1998. (Summarised) This Act re-enacted the powers in the Crime and Disorder Act 1998 s 58.

Powers of Criminal Courts (Sentencing) Act 2000 Section 86(1). Where a prisoner is serving a sentence for sexual offences committed before 30 September 1998 the court may extend the licence period from $^3/_4$ of the term to the whole term. (Summarised)

R v Massie 2003 1 Cr App R (S) 414. For offences committed prior to 1992, the court has no power to pass any extended sentence of the kind permitted by Section 85 of the 2000 Act.

Proportionate, should it be

69.20   *R v B* 2005 Unreported 17/1/05. While proportionality with the seriousness of the offence has some relevance and the implications of the overall sentence should be borne in mind, strict proportionality between the duration of the extension period and the seriousness of the offence should not be a primary factor in determining the length of an extension period. While it is established in the decisions of *R v Nelson* 2002 1 Cr App R (S) 565 and *R v Cornelius* 2002 Unreported 23/1/02 that strict proportionality between length of an extension and the seriousness of an offence is not the primary consideration in determining the length of the extension, because the measure is designed to provide greater protection for the public, those decisions state that proportionality has some relevance and the implications to the overall sentence has to be borne in mind.

Reduce the custodial term because the sentence is extended, don't

69.21   *R v Nelson* 2002 1 Cr App R (S) 565. It is not appropriate to reduce the custodial term because an extended licence period is being imposed [see *Att-Gen's Ref. No 40 of 2001* Unreported 9/5/01].

Short sentences, and – Sexual offences

69.22   *R v Ajaib* 2001 1 Cr App R (S) 105. There is power to order an extended sentence when the sentence is 9 months imprisonment. However here, the extension period should be reduced from 2 years to **15 months**.

Short sentences, and – Violent offences

69.23   *Powers of Criminal Courts (Sentencing) Act 2000 s 85(3) Where the offence is a violent offence the court shall not pass an extended sentence where the custodial term is less than 4 years.*

R v Pepper 2005 Unreported 28/4/05. It is not appropriate to impose shorter consecutive sentences totalling 4 years in order to be able to invoke s 85.

Treatment programmes

69.24   *R v Nelson* 2002 1 Cr App R (S) 565. One purpose of an extended sentence is to reduce the likelihood of re-offending, and it is therefore particularly suitable where a commensurate custodial term is too short for this to be done in prison and where the normal licence period, if any, will not be long enough to permit attendance at a treatment programme in the community. This will arise particularly in relation to less serious sexual offences, where the likelihood of re-offending appears high, but where a longer than commensurate sentence cannot be justified because the offender does not present a risk of serious harm to the public.

For definition of sexual and violent offence see Longer than Commensurate Sentences – *Sexual offence, what is?* and *Violent offence, is it?*

See also Incest – *Extended sentences* and Offences Against the Person Act 1981 s 18 – *Extended sentences*

Extradition, Time Spent in Custody Awaiting

See Custody, Discount for Time Spent in – *Extradition, time in custody awaiting*

70   Failing to Provide a Specimen

70.1   Road Traffic Act 1988 s 7(6)

Summary only. Maximum 6 months or £5,000.

Depriving defendant of vehicle used There is power to deprive the defendant of the vehicle used[1] for the purposes of committing the offence.

Disqualification Minimum disqualification 1 year, unless defendant in charge. Where a defendant has a conviction for driving while unfit, causing death under the influence of drink, driving with excess alcohol and failing to provide a specimen in previous 10 years, minimum disqualification is 3 years[2]. There is power to order reduced disqualification for attendance on courses[3].

Points 3–11 penalty points if special reasons not to disqualify are found.

Magistrates' Court Sentencing Guidelines January 2004

70.2   For a first time offender pleading not guilty. Entry point. Is it serious enough for a community penalty? Examples of aggravating factors for the offence are ability to drive seriously impaired, caused injury/fear/damage, evidence of nature of the driving, police pursuit, type of vehicle, e.g. carrying passengers for reward/ large goods vehicle,. Examples of mitigation for the offence: not the driver. Examples of mitigation are genuine remorse and voluntary completion of alcohol impaired driver course (if available). Offer a rehabilitation course. Minimum 24 months disqualification.

For details about the guidelines see Magistrates' Court Sentencing Guidelines at page 483.

---

1   Powers of Criminal Courts (Sentencing) Act 2000 s 143(6) & (7)
2   Road Traffic Offenders Act 1988 s 34(3).
3   Road Traffic Offenders Act 1988 s 34A

71   FAILING TO STOP/FAILING TO REPORT

71.1   Road Traffic Act 1988 s 170

Summary only. Maximum 6 month and/or Level 5 £5,000. 5–10 points.

Depriving defendant of vehicle used There is power to deprive the defendant of the vehicle used[4] for the purposes of committing the offence.

Magistrates' Court Sentencing Guidelines January 2004

71.2   First time offenders who plead not guilty. Entry point. Is a discharge or a fine appropriate? Examples of aggravating factors for the offence are evidence of drinking or drugs, serious injury and serious damage. Examples of mitigating factors for the offence are believed identity to be known, failed to stop but reported, genuine fear of retaliation, negligible damage, no-one at scene but failed to report and stayed at scene but failed to give/left before giving full particulars. Examples of mitigation are co-operation with the police, genuine remorse and voluntary compensation. **Starting point fine C.** (£150 when defendant has £100 net weekly income.)

For details about the guidelines see **MAGISTRATES' COURT SENTENCING GUIDELINES** at page 483.

72   FALSE ACCOUNTING

72.1   Theft Act 1968 s 17

Triable either way. On indictment maximum 7 years. Summary maximum 6 months and/or £5,000.

Crown Court statistics – England and Wales – Males 21+
72.2

Year	Plea	Total Numbers sentenced	Type of sentence %					Average length of custody (months)
			Discharge	Fine	Community sentence	Suspended sentence	Custody	
2002	Guilty	165	4	5	38	13	40	11.7
	Not guilty	22	–	5	36	5	55	12.4
2003	Guilty	130	5	8	42	8	38	14
	Not guilty	22	5	32	27	–	36	11.9

For details and explanations about the statistics in the book see page vii.

There are no cases, but similar cases are listed under **THEFT ETC**

73   FALSE IMPRISONMENT/KIDNAPPING

73.1   Both offences are common law offences.

Both offences are indictable only with a maximum sentence of life[5].

---

4   Powers of Criminal Courts (Sentencing) Act 2000 s 143(6) & (7)
5   *R v Szczerba* 2002 2 Cr App R (S) 385 at 392

Dangerous Offender provisions For offences of false imprisonment and kidnapping committed on or after 4/4/05 where there is a significant risk to members of the public of serious harm etc. there is a mandatory duty to pass a life sentence when it is justified and otherwise a sentence of imprisonment for public protection[6]. For offenders under 18 the duty is to pass detention for life, detention for public protection or an extended sentence[7].

Longer than Commensurate sentences and Extended sentences Both offences are violent offences for the purposes of passing a longer than commensurate sentence [Powers of Criminal Courts (Sentencing) Act 2000 s 80(2)] and an extended sentence (extending the licence) [Powers of Criminal Courts (Sentencing) Act 2000 s 85(2)(b)] where the offence leads, or is intended or likely to lead, to a person's death or to physical injury to a person[8]. The orders cannot be made for offences committed before 30/9/98 or after 3/4/05. See LONGER THAN COMMENSURATE SENTENCES

Sexual Offences Prevention Order For both offences, there is a discretionary power to make this order when it is necessary to protect the public etc[9].

Working with children For both offences, where the offence is against a child (aged under 18), the defendant is aged 18 or over and s/he is sentenced to 12 months or more or a hospital order etc. the court must disqualify him/her from working with children unless satisfied s/he is unlikely to commit any further offences against a child when the court must state its reasons for not doing so[10]. For a defendant aged less than 18 at the time of the offence the court must order disqualification if s/he is sentenced to 12 months or more and the court is satisfied that the defendant will commit a further offence against a child[11]. The court must state its reasons for so doing.

Crown Court statistics – England and Wales – Males 21+ – Kidnapping etc.
73.2

Year	Plea	Total Numbers sentenced	Type of sentence %					Average length of custody (months)
			Discharge	Fine	Community sentence	Suspended sentence	Custody	
2002	Guilty	173	2	–	17	2	75	36.8
	Not guilty	30	–	–	17	–	83	37
2003	Guilty	192	4	2	13	2	78	41.8
	Not guilty	93	–	1	6	–	86	65.3

For details and explanations about the statistics in the book see page vii.

Guideline case

73.3   *R v Spence and Thomas* 1983 5 Cr App R (S) 413. LCJ. The defendant pleaded to kidnapping. Held. There is a wide possible variation between one instance of the crime and another. At the top end of the scale comes the carefully planned abductions where the victim is used as a hostage or where ransom money is demanded. Such offences will seldom be met with less than 8 years or thereabouts. Where violence or firearms are used or there are other exacerbating features such as detention of the

6   Criminal Justice Act 2003 s 225
7   Criminal Justice Act 2003 s 226 and 228
8   Powers of Criminal Courts (Sentencing) Act 2000 s 161(3)
9   Sexual Offences Act 2003 s 104 & Sch. 5
10 Criminal Justice and Court Services Act 2000 s 28
11 Criminal Justice and Court Services Act 2000 s 29

victim over a period of time, then the proper sentence will be very much longer than that. At the other end of the scale are those offences which can perhaps scarcely be classed as kidnapping at all. They very often arise as a sequel to family tiffs or lover's disputes, and they seldom require anything more than 18 months and sometimes a great deal less.

General

73.4 *R v Richardson* 2000 2 Cr App R (S) 373. The defendant pleaded guilty to theft and false imprisonment. The defendant at night visited the victim, a lady of 89 who he knew. He asked to use the lavatory. She followed him. She said he should leave. He refused and appeared to be on drugs. He was aggressive and threatened to hurt her. He pushed her into her sitting room and forced her into an armchair. He tied a jumper over her face. He asked for £20. On a number of occasions she attempted to get out of the chair but he pushed her back. She was repeatedly threatened that she would be hurt if she told anyone about him. She allowed him to make a call for a taxi. When the taxi arrived he snatched her bag and stole £20. He tore the telephone wire from the wall. Because the telephone did not work and she could not manage the steps in the dark she had to stay in all night unable to contact anyone. Before the police started to look for him he went to a police station and confessed to a robbery. His account was very similar to the victim's although he claimed to have told her he wasn't going to hurt her. The defendant was very anxious she should not have to go to court and therefore did not contest her account. He had a bad record with 12 appearances in the last 10 years 7 of which were for robbery. He had three convictions for burglary, three convictions for theft in a dwelling house and three convictions for theft from a person. He expressed remorse. The reason for his offending was crack cocaine. Held. It was so serious a DTTO was inappropriate. In light of the mitigation **4 years** substituted for 5.

Arranged marriages, to force an

73.5 *R v Khan and Bashir* 1999 1 Cr App R (S) 329. The defendants pleaded guilty to kidnapping and administering a noxious thing. The defendants were a husband and wife with three children. The eldest child was a girl aged 20. The parents tried to persuade her to go to Pakistan for an arranged marriage. She did not want to go and she left home and started a course at a local university. On 21 December 1997 she returned home when she discovered that her grandfather had died and agreed to stay there over the New Year period. On 27 December she was asked to wear some Asian clothes and she refused. Next day she was given some drinks which had sleeping pills in it. She was taken to Manchester airport and told she was in hospital. There were three plane tickets bought. One was for her, one for her mother and the other for her brother. She was very weak and drowsy. Her strange behaviour in not wanting to board the flight was spotted by security staff and the police were informed. She received medical treatment and recovered. The wife received 6 months 'out of mercy for her children' and the husband 2 years. Held. The wife's sentence even taking into account the children was an extremely merciful one. Her appeal has no merit. There was nothing which could justify suspending her sentence. The husband's sentence was reduced to **12 months** because of disparity.

Att-Gen's Ref. Nos. 8, 9 and 10 of 2002 2003 1 Cr App R (S) 272. The defendants K, H and N pleaded guilty to kidnapping. They were the father and uncles respectively of the 19 year old student victim. She had been brought up in the traditional Muslim way and it was envisaged she would have an arranged marriage. However, she developed a relationship with a non-Muslim boyfriend. She went to live with him and the parents reported her missing. The police found them and reported that she was safe and happy. Her address was not revealed. About two months, later the three defendants called at the address. N had a metal bar, K seized her and passed her to the others and H carried her to a car. As K left he threatened the boyfriend. She was taken to H's address and guarded for a day. Her mother tried to persuade her to tell the police she had voluntarily left her boyfriend. She feared she would be taken against her will to Pakistan and forced into an arranged marriage. The next day, following some arrests K drove the victim to the police station. K was 47, N was 26 with a good job and supported his family and H was 30. They were of good character. The Judge asked to see counsel and told them that the victim acknowledged that this was to be expected, prison was counterproductive and it would do harm to community relations. The defendants then changed their pleas and no evidence was offered against three others. They were given 3 year conditional discharges with £250 costs. Held. The defendants were motivated by strong and genuinely held religious beliefs and they thought it was in her best interests. The appropriate sentences for the father was **18 months** and **12 months** for the others. The court felt constrained because prosecuting counsel had not indicated any dissent. Because of the Judges remarks and other factors the sentences were not varied.

Blackmail, and   See **BLACKMAIL**   (Where the motive is blackmail the case is listed under **BLACKMAIL** whether or not there was a conviction for blackmail.)

Defendant aged 10–14

73.6   *R v T* 2004 Unreported 9/11/04. The defendant aged 10 pleaded guilty to three false imprisonment counts, GBH, two ABHs and two robberies. He and two others dragged a 12 year old boy to a shed outside a derelict bungalow. The boy was put in a dustbin and punched and kicked to the head and body. He was taken into the bungalow where two more boys joined the assailants. The boy was struck with chair legs about the head and body. He was next taken to the bathroom where he was taunted and told to wash or else he would be killed. Then the boy was taken to the living room where he was tied to a bench with electrical flex. When the boy managed to stand up he was kicked in the stomach which caused him to fall after which one of them stamped on his face. In hospital he was treated for extensive bruising. Shortly after on the same day, the defendant and two others approached J and K aged 12 and 11. They asked for money and dragged them to the bungalow. They were put in the same shed and their bags were taken. The defendant picked up a metal bar. J was taken to the bungalow, searched and some biscuits taken from him. The defendant hit him with the bar. L was taken from the shed, searched and also had biscuits taken from him. Both boys were pushed into chairs. The defendant jumped on K and another jumped on and kicked J. The boys were told to suck one of the boy's "dick", to kiss each other, spit in each others mouths and put their tongues in each others mouths. The boys refused. J's trousers and boxer shorts were taken off. K started screaming and he was told if he didn't stop he would be killed. A passer-by heard what was going on and the assailants ran away. All the victims were seriously traumatised. The defendant had a chaotic and traumatic childhood. His father was killed. He was permanently excluded from school at 8. He was disruptive and aggressive at placements. He was heavily involved in anti-social behaviour. An anti-social behaviour order was made a few weeks before the offences. The pre-sentence report recommended s 91 detention. Held. It is very rare for someone of the defendant's age to be detained. But a s 91 detention order was essential for the boy and the public. **3 years** did take into account the guilty plea.

Defendant aged 15–17

73.7   *Att-Gen's Ref. Nos. 36 and 37 of 1998* 1999 2 Cr App R (S) 7. The defendants L and J pleaded guilty to false imprisonment and L pleaded to wounding (the October incident). J also pleaded to wounding with intent and unlawful wounding and L also pleaded to affray (the September incident). In September at about 9.25 pm the defendant J then 17 picked a fight with one of a group of students and punched one of them in the mouth and face several times. He then took a bottle of beer off the victim and smashed it over his head. The students made off. L then 15 and J pursued them throwing rubbish from a skip at them. A passer-by was walking her dog and J attacked her with a broken bottle. She had a 3" wound to her cheek and 1" wounds to her nose and chin. For a number of weeks she could not talk properly or eat solid foods and she was off work for 9 weeks. The defendants were released on bail and about 4 weeks later at about 9 pm J and L approached a group of teenagers. J jumped on one of them aged 16, and started to struggle with him. L threatened the group, and was restrained by a member of his group. J then said to L 'Come on, let's go and get the filthy Paki'. J and L then followed three of them to a path running along a lake. J and L forced the three to climb over the gate into the park and threatened to 'batter' or kill them. Once in the park the three were forced to sit upon a bench. J punched one of them in the face and pushed a lighted cigarette into his face causing burn marks. L forced him against a tree, and J said he was going to kill him. The three were terrified and ran away, with L in pursuit. One climbed over some spiked railings, and suffered a 5 cm and 2 cm cut to his thigh. Both were deep. This was L's wounding charge. One of the three managed to run away and the third was forced by J and L to walk across the park until he too escaped. The three teenagers were so terrified that they were unable to estimate the period of time during which they had been detained. Both J and L were arrested and when interviewed disputed the victims' account of events. L was of good character. J had an ABH conviction involving an attack with two others on a man in the early hours. The man was knocked to the ground, kicked and punched. J had also been cautioned for affray and assaulting a police officer. A report indicated that L's use of drugs was the most significant factor in his aggressive behaviour. J also had a serious history of drug and alcohol abuse. The judge gave L a deferred sentence J received $3^1/_2$ years for the wounding with intent and 6 months for the false imprisonment. Held. The intimidation of the teenagers was deliberate and sustained and the offence had a very unpleasant racist overtone which demanded an immediate custody. The deferred sentence was unduly lenient. Had L contested his guilt **15 months** detention would have been appropriate for the false imprisonment. With his plea **10–12 months** detention would have been merited. As it was a reference **8 months** detention with no separate penalty for affray. Had J pleaded not guilty a total of **7 years** detention would have been appropriate for the section 18 and false imprisonment offences. On a plea of guilty **5 years** would have been merited. Taking into account it was a reference and the false imprisonment **4 years** for the s 18 offence.

Drug offences, linked to See Supply of Drugs – ***Drug gang using violence Firearms, with (real or imitation)***

73.8   *Att-Gen's Ref. No 17 of 1999* 2000 1 Cr App R (S) 215. The defendant pleaded to false imprisonment, having a firearm in a public place and taking a vehicle without consent. The defendant arranged for a hire car to be delivered to his home. When it arrived the defendant threatened the driver with what the driver believed to be a shotgun. The defendant said he would 'take your head clean off.' The victim heard two clicks. The defendant also said he had served 15 years already for shooting someone. He handcuffed the victim's hands behind him and ordered him upstairs at gunpoint. His legs and mouth were taped and he was asked for money. The defendant left the house taking the car keys with him. The victim escaped and called the police. Police found him at his sister's address. He had a loaded revolver in his waistband (the subject matter of the firearm count) and a large knife in his back pocket. He admitted the offences in interview. The defendant had been released from prison 11 months before for two robberies and firearm offences. He had received 12 years. He was sentenced on the basis the driver had believed he had been threatened by a gun but it was a hollow tube. Held. We would expect a total sentence of **at least 10 years**. Because it was a reference **4 years** for the false imprisonment, and for the firearm matter consecutive making **8 years** in all consecutive with the taking a vehicle 4 months concurrent not $5^1/_2$ in all.

R v Wheeler 2002 2 Cr App R (S) 263. The defendant pleaded guilty to possessing a firearm with the intent to cause a belief that violence would be used, having a firearm with intent to commit an indictable offence, possession of a prohibited weapon and false imprisonment. He had a relationship and moved in with the victim. He said he had served in the French Foreign Legion and was highly experienced in explosives, firearms and weapons. About a year later after arguments she told him to leave. He did so and found it hard to accept and made repeated efforts to see her. She felt pestered. Five months later he waited outside the garden centre where she worked and $^3/_4$ hour later he entered the centre and told her to go into an office. He had a pistol loaded with two live rounds and told her and her colleague, A, to telephone the police. He pointed the gun at her and said he wasn't messing about, he was serious. He talked about his relationship with her and she became extremely frightened. The gun appeared cocked and it appeared to remain so. He talked about Hungerford and Dunblane and said her son was going to be an orphan. She was detained for 12 hours and he wouldn't let her go to the lavatory. The defendant threatened to kill himself. A chose to remain although the defendant said he could go. Eventually the defendant surrendered to the police. A said he was not seriously worried about his or her safety. When interviewed the defendant said he waited till the school emptied. The victim had persuaded him not to let the police shoot him. He was at his lowest ebb ever and the gun was to stop her leaving. The defendant was 44 and had no previous record for this kind of offence. He had had periods of depression. Held. The incident was terrifying. It was planned and the pistol was loaded with 2 bullets. These were very grave offences of the utmost seriousness. **7 years** was not manifestly excessive.

See also **FIREARMS**

Hostage, more than one

73.9   *R v Cockeram* 1999 2 Cr App R (S) 120. The defendant pleaded guilty to five counts of false imprisonment. At about 10pm, under the influence of alcohol the defendant entered a newsagent and purchased a packet of cigarettes. There were three members of staff present. As he received his change he produced a 12" carving knife and shouted 'Shut the fucking doors.' The knife was put to an assistant's throat. The doors were shut but not locked and a customer entered the shop. One assistant was ordered to bring the customer over to the counter. When another customer entered the first managed to escape and contacted the police. When another customer entered there were five hostages who were made to sit on the floor. The defendant pointed the knife at them and said he had nothing to lose. Armed police arrived and surrounded the shop. He became irrational. He smashed a display of Easter Eggs and threatened to cut the throat of an assistant. He also apologised and offered them cushions, cigarettes and drink. After time the hostages felt more comfortable with him and when he was arrested they shouted at the police not to hurt him because he hadn't hurt them. He released the hostages at 2.15am. One had in fact suffered a small bruise. All suffered some psychological harm. The defendant said he had not intended to rob the shop and expressed regret and remorse. He had a number of previous convictions and an impressive recent employment history. Held. This was not a case of solitary hostage taking which can be even more frightening. There was no material violence or pre-planning. These features put it at the lower end of the scale, so **5 years** not 6.

***Longer than commensurate sentences (frequently wrongly called extended sentences) –
Is it a violent offence?***

73.10   Powers of Criminal Courts (Sentencing) Act 2000 s 80(2)(b). … the custodial
sentence shall be … where the offence is a violent or sexual offence, for such longer
term (not exceeding the maximum) as in the opinion of the court is necessary to protect
the public from serious harm from the offender. (Previously the Criminal Justice Act
1991, s 2(2)(b).)

Powers of Criminal Courts (Sentencing) Act 2000 s 161(3). … a violent offence is an
'offence which leads, or is intended or likely to lead, to a person's death or physical
injury to a person.'

R v Cochrane 1994 15 Cr App R (S) 708. The defendant pleaded guilty to robbery. Held.
The definition of a violent offence does not require that the physical injury be serious.
It does not include psychological harm. Here no injury was actually done. Sometimes
shock may amount to ABH. This was not that case. The defendant denied he intended
to cause physical injury. The judge accepted that. It was not necessary to show that
injury was a necessary or probable consequence. The only issue was whether the acts
were likely to lead to physical injury. Here it could have done if the shopkeeper had
resisted or the defendant had lost control. 6 years was arguably too high if the sentence
was commensurate with the facts of the offence. However, it was a perfectly proper
sentence for a man foreseeably likely to cause serious harm to the public.

R v Williams 1999 1 Cr App R (S) 105. The defendant pleaded guilty to kidnapping,
ABH, indecent assault and driving whilst disqualified. He stopped an 8 year old girl and
put his hand over her mouth. Next he dragged her to his car. When she screamed he told
her not to look at him and he drove off with her crying. He drove for some miles and
stopped in a country lane. He touched her on her stomach and on her right thigh. She
kicked out at him. When she tried to attract attention he drove off and when he stopped
again he asked her to open her legs. Then he told her to get out and asked for a kiss
which she refused. He opened the zip of his trousers and she eventually managed to
get out and she ran to a nearby house. She had bruises to her arms, legs and back and
several scratch marks to her chest. Her top was ripped and she had a lump on her throat.
When arrested he said he needed help, he was sorry and gave full admissions. He was
26 with no previous sexual convictions. He told the doctor that he fanaticized about
offences with young girls. The doctor said he suffered from a psychopathic personality
disorder and the risk of re-offending was exceptionally high. Held. The Judge was right
to make the offence longer than commensurate, but **9 years** not 14.

Att-Gen's Ref. No 113 of 2001 2002 2 Cr App R (S) 269. The defendant pleaded guilty
to five counts of robbery. The victims were all elderly and attacked in their own homes
after dark. He was masked and they were terrified. He demanded money and he put his
hand over two of their mouths. He brushed past one and caused her to fall. Another
victim was tied up. The judge was not satisfied the offences were violent. Held. Bearing
in mind the ages of the victims and what was done to each of them, the real possibility
of fractures, asphyxia and cardiac arrest, each was a violent offence. The defendant was
lucky not to have caused physical injury and this demonstrates its likelihood.

R v Szczerba 2002 2 Cr App R (S) 385. The defendant pleaded guilty to false imprisonment. He broke into the home of a 71-year-old widow who lived alone. The window
was smashed and the telephone wires cut. The widow was terrified and he demanded
money. He picked up her walking stick and threatened to kill her and threatened to
punch and stab her. He sprayed her face with hair spray. That caused discomfort
for some weeks. He put his hands round her throat for some 2 minutes and applied
pressure. She thought she was going to die. He was there for $1^3/_4$ hours. The judge
found her physical and mental health had suffered. Held. The offence led to physical

injury and the defendant's conduct was 'likely to lead to physical injury.' Although mere risk is insufficient to give rise to a violent offence, it does not have to be shown that injury was 'a necessary or probable consequence.' Conduct which could very well lead to injury is properly characterised as likely so to lead. It was a violent offence.

See also LONGER THAN COMMENSURATE SENTENCES

Public servants (Doctors etc)

73.11 *Att-Gen's Ref. No 45 of 2000* 2001 1 Cr App R (S) 413. The defendant pleaded guilty to false imprisonment and robbery. A doctor visited a female patient who was a heroin addict. She was also the defendant's girlfriend. The doctor explained to both of them that he was not going to prescribe any medication. They explained their displeasure and then the doctor tried to leave. The defendant's activity caused the doctor to ask 'Are you barring my exit?' The defendant replied 'I've done 7 years and I'll do it again.' He then armed himself with a large knife and held the knife at the doctor's chest. He demanded the doctor's bag. The doctor who was frightened gave the defendant two tablets. The defendant demanded a sleeping pill, which he was given. The doctor was allowed to leave but was in a highly distressed condition. Fortunately the doctor had a driver who became suspicious and called the police who arrived.

The defendant appeared to be under the influence of drink or drugs or both and the police found him incoherent. The defendant had an appalling record including offences of violence and dishonesty. He was on licence at the time. Held. A sentence of **4 or 5 years** would be appropriate. However, as it was a reference the **30 month**s sentence was not altered.

Relationships, failed

73.12 *R v Lucas* 2000 1 Cr App R (S) 5. The defendant was convicted of false imprisonment. He had had a relationship with a woman for 18 years. They had three children but they had separated. 6 months later he went to her home. He struck her on the head, which knocked her unconscious. He took her and his one-year-old daughter to his car. She was made to drive him and the baby to a park where he claimed to have dug a grave for her. The woman managed to escape. He followed and prized her from the hold of someone she had approached and took her back to his car. He drove off. When he heard his car being circulated as wanted by the police he drove her home. She was too frightened to make a complaint for 10 months. She had injuries of a cut above the right eye, a bite mark and bruising in various different places. He had no previous for violence. Held. Whether it is a domestic dispute or by a stranger is neither here nor there. It was a quite terrifying experience. **2 years** could not be faulted.

Att-Gen's Ref. No 42 of 2000 2001 1 Cr App R (S) 393. The defendant pleaded guilty during his trial to four counts of false imprisonment, making threats to kill, ABH and inflicting GBH. The defendant had a troubled relationship with a 23 year old who from time to time returned to her mother. In June 1997, he slapped her and pulled her by the hair into the cellar. He pushed her into the coal cellar and shut her inside. He released her after two hours. He became angry again and told her to go back in. She did so because she feared an assault. This continued over 4 days although from time to time she was let out. This activity was the first count. In July 1997, she gave birth. A week later he punched her and pushed her down the cellar steps and locked her in the coalhouse. He let her out to feed the baby and picked up a crossbow and loaded it with a bolt. He told her he could kill her and get away with it. She believed she was going to be killed. This lasted for about a minute. He punched and kicked her and put a belt round her neck, which he pulled tight. This activity was the second false imprisonment count and the threats to kill. In November 1997 they moved to a flat. In December he punched and kicked her. He grabbed her between the legs and tore her right labia majora, causing her bleeding and immense pain. She said she wanted to end her life and he said, 'go on then' and gave her some Tamazepam tablets, which she took. The offender became extremely violent and pushed her head through a plasterboard wall. He forced her to swallow shampoo to bring up the tablets, which she did. At 9–10 pm he tied her to a stool with flex and put a sock in her mouth. He slapped and punched her till the early hours. This activity was the third false imprisonment. He was then sentenced to 30 months imprisonment for wounding etc which involved fighting men unrelated to the victim. The last false imprisonment was when he punched her, made her undress and tied her to the bedposts. He whipped her back and legs. She had black eyes, cut lips, a swollen face, bruising to her body and wheel marks. The ABH related to when he punched her and pushed a burning cigarette against her chest. This was followed by more punching. The GBH involved an incident when they out with friends and he slapped her. She refused to go home. He said he would break her jaw. He grabbed her hair and dragged her to the front door. The friends told him to stop. He kicked and punched her in the face. She was taken to the kitchen where it was repeated. She was pregnant again. He banged her head on the floor. She had to be taken to hospital. He was taking crack or heroin during all the false imprisonments and the occasion of the ABH. He was arrested and she gave evidence at the trial. Just before she was to be cross-examined he pleaded guilty. The defendant had helped police in an unrelated matter. He had two ABH findings of guilt as a juvenile as well as the 30 month sentence. *Held.* **6 or 7 years** was appropriate. Because it was a reference **5 years** not 30 months, consecutive to 11 remaining of a 30 month sentence.

R v Hibbert 2002 2 Cr App R (S) 106. The defendant pleaded guilty to false imprisonment and was acquitted of two rapes. He had known the victim since they were teenagers at school. They had a short relationship then and remained friends. In 2000 they met in a pub and they started going out together. Four months later they moved into a flat together. Two months later she discovered he had run up a bill of £500 for sexual chat lines. She spoke to him about it but as he was so drunk she decided to go out. At 11.30pm she returned with a take away meal for them both but as he was drunk and arguing she went to bed and locked her door. He kicked open the door, pushed her backwards and placed his hand over her mouth to prevent her screaming. The argument continued in the bathroom where he grabbed her. They returned to the bedroom where he found her diary and read entries about her former boyfriend. He became very angry and tore up the diary. There a short struggle and he said he was going to commit suicide by jumping off the Humber Bridge. He told her to go to sleep and he lay in front of the door preventing her leaving. When she awoke he was asleep and she pushed a note though the bedroom window asking for help. When he awoke he left the room and locked the door behind him. She went back to sleep and 3 hours later they both woke up and started talking in a more reasonable manner. They had sex and then he fetched a Stanley knife and he was going to tie her up and jump off the Bridge. He slashed his wrists with the knife and told her she could leave when he was dead. Then he rang his former partner and told her he had slashed his wrists. She rang back and persuaded him to let the victim go. The victim left about 13 hours after it all started. She was at times during the incident very frightened and made repeated requests to leave. The police arrived and arrested him, he said he was sorry. 5 years before he had been convicted of wounding his previous partner when drunk. He stabbed her with a pair of scissors and received probation. **3¹/₂ years** was not manifestly excessive.

R v Ashbridge 2002 2 Cr App R (S) 408. The defendant was convicted of kidnapping and a Section 20 wounding. He was acquitted of Section 18 count. After a nine-year stable relationship with Tracey he told her in a letter it was all over. In the next month, she met the victim. The defendant then sought a reconciliation, which she declined. The defendant became distressed and believed the victim was involved with drugs. He later became obsessive about the new relationship. She agreed to go to Spain with him for a week but at the end of the week she said she would not resume their relationship. The defendant put a bug on the victim's phone. Shortly before the kidnap the defendant waited outside the victim's home and sought a confrontation. The victim was able to avoid it. In a period of days the victim received six threatening telephone calls. At 11.30 p.m. the victim received a silent call followed by a knock on his door. A man told him his car was damaged and he was lured outside. Two more men arrived and tried to bundle the victim into a car. The victim resisted and someone said, "Stab him." He was stabbed three times to the thigh penetrating the muscle layers. The wounds were 3 cms and less in length. He was forced into the footwell of the car and a blanket was placed over his head. While held down, he heard the defendant giving directions to the men on a two-way radio. After ten minutes, the car stopped and the defendant spoke to the victim and said, "You know what this is about. If you go to the police we will come and get you again. Leave Tracey alone but let her down gently". He was taken out of the vehicle with his head still covered. As he removed the blanket he saw the car drive away. He walked to a house where he received help. He was shocked and frightened. The ambulanceman found he was bleeding badly with his blood pressure well down indicating hypovolaemic shock. His hospital treatment was successful and was discharged in the afternoon. He was able to return to work a week later. He was 34 with no convictions. There was evidence of positive good character. The Judge sentenced him on the basis he had used three heavily built men and the victim had nearly lost his life. Held. There was no direct evidence there was a danger the victim nearly lost his life. The aggravating features were (1) the planning and some of the sophistication in the arrangements; (2) the use of a knife; (3) the serious injury; and (4) the abandonment of the victim. The mitigation was the limited duration of the detention, the good character and the defendant's loss of equilibrium in the face of a disintegrating relationship. **5 years** not 7.

Att-Gen's Ref. No. 2 of 2004 2005 1 Cr App R (S) 55. The defendant was convicted of false imprisonment. The defendant formed a relationship with the victim who was the same age as him for about 3 weeks. He was possessive and the victim broke off the relationship (on his birthday). She removed her belongings from his flat. Two days later they agreed to meet in a public house, where they argued. However, she agreed to go back to his flat. He jealously accused her of having a relationship with someone else and they argued. The victim tried to leave but the defendant prevented her from doing so by sitting astride her. He pressed her windpipe, slapped her, punched her on the face, legs and stomach; and this assault lasted, according to her, approximately 45 minutes. He then pulled her into his bedroom and stripped her naked, he handcuffed her, first to himself and then to the bed, She was terrified that he was going to rape her. She was grabbed by the throat and he put his hand over her mouth. She remained like that between 1am and 7am. She was released from the cuffs and managed to escape. He was 22 without previous convictions. Held. The appropriate bracket was **2 to 3 years**. He had completed 100 hours of CPO and as this was a reference, **18 months** not a combination order (100 hours and 2 years' supervision).

Revenge

73.13 *Att-Gen's Ref. Nos. 73–4 of 2001* 2002 1 Cr App R (S) 451. The defendants W and S pleaded guilty to false imprisonment. W also pleaded to unlawful wounding. The pleas were entered on the day fixed for their trial. Over 6 months the victim and W had a casual sexual relationship. W called the victim and said she was coming to collect a TV set. W went to the victim's home and watched television with him for about an hour. About midnight she took a small fruit knife and accused him of raping her while she was asleep some days before because she had a love bite on her back and her knickers were wet. He denied it. She was very angry and waved the knife and stabbed him in the leg and smashed a mug over his head. She then took a pill probably ecstasy. She rang S to take her away from his flat. When S got there she repeated the rape allegation, shouted and stabbed the victim in his other leg. She said his life was in her hands. S spat at the victim's face and the victim became progressively more frightened. W said they would take the victim out of the flat and told S to tie him up. S tied him with electrical wire and slapped him across the face. The victim was put in a car next to S with W driving. W instructed S to cover the victim's eyes and S did so with sellotape. The victim's head was covered with a cloth. When the victim moved his head S punched him about the eye. The victim was also stabbed in the arm and a cigarette lighter was applied to his forehead. He heard W on her mobile saying the victim was dying and she was going to kill him. When the car came to a halt S told the victim to be quiet or he would be killed. The victim was headbutted and thereafter blacked out. He was released after an 8–10 hour ordeal and was terrified and distressed with three stab wounds requiring two, two and three stitches, two small burns and bruising. Items of the victim's jewellery were found on W. The defendants accepted violence took place but denied they did it. W was 42 and had previous convictions for violence. S was 21 and had no convictions for violence. S was sentenced **to 9 months** and had been released on a tag. The sentence was due to end in just over 2 weeks. Held. Those that perceive themselves to be victims of crime should not take matters into their own hands. The victim's detention was long and frightening with him not being able to see. There was considerable violence used. We would have expected **4 years** for W and **2 years** for S. As it was a reference **3 years** not 18 months for W. S's sentence not altered because of the progress he had made since it was passed.

R v Stacey 2004 2 Cr App R (S) 463. The defendant was convicted at a retrial of false imprisonment and common assault. He had been in the process of buying a house he had long been interested in when the vendor, the victim of these offences, withdrew the house from sale. He phoned the defendant to tell him and later the same day the defendant barged his way into the victim's house and began to abuse him in words such as 'You're a fucking spineless git', 'You're not a fucking man of your word … you've let my kids down'. The victim had had two triple coronary by-pass graft operations and the defendant knew this. The victim started to panic and tried to leave the house but was prevented by the defendant. The defendant continued to shout and swear at him using racist language: the victim belonged to one of the ethnic groups the defendant was being abusive about. The victim told the defendant that he would call the police if he didn't leave, at which the defendant ripped the phone from the wall throwing it on the floor where it broke. He punched the victim in the face and said 'That's not all I'm going to do. You see that heart of yours, I am going to fucking cut it out'. The victim was extremely frightened and had to take some medication; he asked the defendant to call an ambulance but he refused, and he retreated to a couch and pulled a quilt over his head while the defendant knelt down and continued to shout and swear at him. Eventually the defendant left. The victim estimated the events had lasted some two hours. His face was swollen and his jaw was stiff. He was very depressed at what had happened. The defendant, 39, had some previous convictions, including assaulting his partner four years earlier by slapping her round the head. He had never served a custodial sentence. He was a successful businessman enjoying a lavish lifestyle. He had suffered from bi-polar disorder but by the time of this offence there was little evidence that it was affecting his judgement. He produced an impressive number of character references. A pre-sentence report said he showed no empathy for his victim and sought to minimise and justify his conduct and he seemed controlling manipulative and intimidating. Held. The defendant could well have been intending to bully the victim into reinstating the deal. This was a terrifying ordeal which lasted for some time and left its mark. This was a tough sentence, but **3** years was not manifestly excessive.

Robbery, and See **ROBBERY**

Sexual

73.14 *R v Williams* 1999 1 Cr App R (S) 105. The defendant pleaded guilty to kidnapping, ABH, indecent assault and driving whilst disqualified. He stopped an 8 year old girl and put his hand over her mouth. Next he dragged her to his car. When she screamed he told her not to look at him and he drove off with her crying. He drove for some miles and stopped in a country lane. He touched her on her stomach and on her right thigh. She kicked out at him. When she tried to attract attention he drove off and when he stopped again he asked her to open her legs. Then he told her to get out and asked for a kiss which she refused. He opened the zip of his trousers and she eventually managed to get out and she ran to a nearby house. She had bruises to her arms, legs and back and several scratch marks to her chest. Her top was ripped and she had a lump on her throat. When arrested he said he needed help, he was sorry and gave full admissions. He was 26 with no previous sexual convictions. He told the doctor that he fanaticized about offences with young girls. The doctor said he suffered from a psychopathic personality disorder and the risk of re-offending was exceptionally high. Held. The Judge was right to make the offence longer than commensurate, but **9 years** not 14.

R v Ellis 1999 1 Cr App R (S) 245. The defendant pleaded guilty to kidnapping and indecent assault against a 23-year-old woman. The defendant followed the victim after she had been shopping and caused her to go into a graveyard where he indecently attacked her for a period of 45 minutes. The doctor found 10 areas of recent bruising around her neck, her ear, her arm, wrists, finger, both knees and damage to her private parts. The defendant was 37 and had a previous conviction of abduction and indecent assault against an 18-year-old girl. After that offence he did not accept offers of treatment. His risk of re-offending was assessed by a psychiatrist as serious. This was based on the similarity of the offences, his denial of important aspects of the offence, his unstable personality and his social isolation. The judge was of the opinion that the defendant was likely to commit similar offences in the future. Held. **Life** sentence for the kidnap was appropriate. 6 years concurrent for the indecent assault not 9 years.

Att-Gen's Ref. No 77 of 1998 1999 2 Cr App R (S) 336. (The title in the law report is wrong.) **7 years** was lenient but not varied.

R v Willoughby 1999 2 Cr App R (S) 18. The defendant was convicted of false imprisonment, indecent assault and ABH. In the early hours, the defendant entered a student's accommodation block. He found an 18-year-old student in the bathroom. As she left a cubicle he came up behind her and put his hand over her mouth. She was pushed into a cubicle so she faced the wall. He slapped her three or four times and locked the door. He put what he claimed to be a knife against her neck and forced her to perform oral sex on him. After he had ejaculated he forced her to swallow, said he was sorry and left. At the time of the offence he was 43. He had 6 previous court appearances for assault and dishonesty, gross indecency with a child, kidnapping, indecent assault, attempted kidnapping, and false imprisonment. The psychiatric evidence indicated that he was 'a high risk' because of his repetitive sexual offending. Held. It was appropriate to look at the purpose of the imprisonment. **Life** was appropriate here.

Att-Gen's Ref. No 22 of 1999 2000 1 Cr App R (S) 253. The defendant was convicted of false imprisonment, indecent assault and putting a person in fear of violence under the Protection from Harassment Act 1997. The victim after a long and violent relationship with another moved next door to where the defendant lived. They began a sexual relationship and he moved in with her. That relationship deteriorated and he was asked to move out and he went back next door. She found another man. The defendant saw them together and resented it. She gave up her job and stayed with a girlfriend so the defendant could not find her. Because she had two dogs to look after she returned home. That same evening, at about midnight as she went to let the dogs out, the defendant jumped over a shared gate. He pushed her back in the house. He demanded to know who she had been talking to on the telephone. He dragged her into the living room. He took her car keys and threatened to set her car on fire. He pulled out the stereo plug and the telephone plug. At about 3am he said he wasn't leaving until they had sex. He put his arms around her and pressed his erection against her. She protested. He tried to kiss her. There was a struggle and he knelt astride her and unbuttoned his trousers. He then masturbated himself ejaculating over her breasts. At about 4.30am he left making her promise she would not get him into trouble. At 9am he returned and asked for the same assurance. The victim was so distraught she was admitted into a psychiatric hospital for 4 weeks where she had been treated before. On her release he harassed her persistently saying she was dead and he would get her together with her old partner. She had to be re-admitted to hospital for 6 weeks. At the trial she had to give evidence. The defendant had previous for rape, receiving 4 years. He also had convictions for burglary and theft. Held. The appropriate sentence would have been **6 years** but as it was a reference **4¹/₂** years not 3.

When linked to prostitution see PROSTITUTES, CONTROLING ETC. – *Trafficking*

Taking the law into your own hands

73.15 *Att-Gen's Ref. No 15 of 1999* 2000 1 Cr App R (S) 128. The defendant was convicted of kidnapping, false imprisonment and having a firearm with intent to kidnap. The defendant was burgled and lost some jewellery. When seen by police he was very volatile, aggressive and threatened to kill whoever was responsible. Later he suspected the victim was responsible and one evening he with three others all wearing balaclavas kidnapped him using a handgun. He pushed into a car and taken to an isolated lane. The handgun was put to his ear and he was told to retrieve the stolen property. The gun which was capable of firing blanks was discharged. The attackers made off and the victim was found 'absolutely terrified' with blood on his face and crying. His hearing was affected for 1¹/₂ days. He had been detained for ¹/₄ hour. The defendant showed no remorse. He was 28 with some dissimilar convictions, which were not as serious. He was in good employment and had testimonials for charitable work. In 1992 he was given an award for saving a drowning man. The victim had a bad record. Police had to install a panic button in the defendant's home to protect him and his girlfriend from attacks. Held. There were serious aggravating features here. Three or 4 years was called for. As it was a reference **2¹/₂ years** not 18 months.

R v AS 2000 1 Cr App R (S) 491. The defendant pleaded guilty to false imprisonment. The defendant's daughter complained of indecent assault. A man was interviewed by the police and denied it. The CPS decided there was insufficient evidence. The suspect was assaulted and the defendant was arrested and charged. He was obsessive in his views as to what should happen. He was kept in custody for 6 months and acquitted. He remained obsessed, which caused his marriage to break up and his business to collapse. He suffered from a form of depression and took to drink and drugs. Inflamed by a cocktail of cocaine, vodka, rage and obsession he went to the suspect's house. The suspect was in bed and the defendant smashed a Calor gas bottle through the lounge window. He went in with a 5 litre oil can. He entered the bedroom and told the defendant to lie down. He showed him the oil can and threatened to set him alight. In fact the can contained water not oil. The police arrived. He said he had sufficient petrol to burn the suspect alive. Over 150 police became involved over 7 hours. He forced the man to write a confession, which he did. He considered it was not sufficient so he forced him to write another. He let the man go when the police promised to arrest him. He then barricaded himself in a room for a further $1^1/_2$ hours. In interview he said he never had any intention of harming the man. At the Appeal Court he said he now accepted the CPS decision. He had previous convictions for drugs and violence but nothing of this kind. Held. 4 years not improper, but as an act of mercy to a broken man **3 years**.

R v Meek and Meek 2001 2 Cr App R (S) 12. The two defendants father and son pleaded guilty to six counts of false imprisonment. The father ran a company, which had factory area and a yard, which had skips and was also used as a car park. His son worked there. Intruders entered their premises and smashed windows, damaged vehicles and the like. The police were unable to track down the culprits. Later six boys aged 12 or 13 entered the yard. Men with airguns, sticks, bars and a hockey stick came on the scene. The boys tried to run away. Someone said 'Don't run or we'll shoot you.' Three boys were shot with an airgun. The younger defendant struck one with the hockey stick. The boys were herded into the factory. The older defendant was waiting for them in there. The boys were made to stand in six inches of dye and questioned about the damage. They denied it, which was not accepted. They then had to sit in the dye. One was punched and they were all threatened. The older defendant was sentenced on the basis he did not have a weapon. The younger defendant was sentenced on the basis that he had struck only two boys and only once and that he left the area after the boys were herded in. The father was 52 and the son 20. Both were treated as of good character and were hard working men. Nothing but good had been said about them. They were sentenced on the basis that they believed the boys had been involved in the earlier incidents. Their home was also attacked. **1 year** substituted for 2 years imprisonment and YOI.

R v McHale 2001 2 Cr App R (S) 417. The defendant was convicted of kidnapping and two ABHs. He was the area manager of a construction company and with another interviewed a supervisor who they believed was responsible for stealing some company machinery. The supervisor denied it and the defendant lost his temper, became abusive and punched him. While the victim tried to defend himself he butted him in the face and pushed his head so it broke one of the windows. The attack continued and he was finally hit with a paving brick. The victim suffered pain, bruises to his head and back and a cut. Two days later the defendant and two others went to see the next victim, another company employee suspected of theft and told the other two to put the victim in the back of the van. The victim failed to escape and was questioned about the missing items in the back of the van. The defendant drove the van off and the victim was threatened which included using a knuckleduster which one of them had. When the van stopped the defendant went to the back of the van and asked where the stolen items were. He got in and said, 'Right lads, get him and break his legs.' The victim was punched repeatedly to the head and body and grabbed around the throat. The victim was exceedingly frightened. Eventually he was released and he had seven cuts to his head, numerous cuts to his hands and tenderness to his chest. The defence was he acted in self defence in the first matter and had nothing to do with the second matter. He was of good character with testimonials. The pre-sentence report said his risk of re-offending was low. He was sentenced on the basis he had acted out of character. Held. These were serious assaults. People cannot be permitted to take the law into their own hands. Severe prison sentences are virtually inevitable for this sort of conduct by people of good character. **3 years** not $3^1/_2$.

Old case *R v Chapman* 1994 15 Cr App R (S) 196.

Unexplained attack

73.16 *Att-Gen's Ref. No. 25 of 2004* 2005 1 Cr App R (S) 58. The defendant pleaded guilty to false imprisonment and asked for a common assault to be TIC'd. He moved into the victim's house as one of two lodgers. About 6 weeks later the victim returned to her home with a male friend having been out to celebrate her birthday. They put music on and danced. The defendant was jealous and started mumbling and behaving oddly. The victim asked him what was wrong and he told her to go away. He then suddenly slapped her with his open hand and she slapped him back. He slapped her again, harder, causing her to reel back. Her male friend stood up to stop any further violence. The defendant said that, "if he was to start he would kill him". The defendant went into the kitchen and was heard opening drawers and removing knives. The police were called and the defendant was found lying down on the kitchen floor, bare-chested. He was lying on top of the wooden curtain pole which he had torn from the kitchen window. There were two knives near his head and others nearby. He was arrested after a struggle and taken away. The victim packed up the defendant's belongings for collection and did not want him to contact her in any way. He was bailed on condition that he lived a considerable distance away. 3 days later at about 3.30 pm he telephoned and spoke to her twice before she went out. About an hour later she was sitting in her living room with the other lodger when the defendant burst in, by the back door, which he locked behind him. Pushed the other lodger out and locked the front door. The victim was crying and shaking; she tried to call the police but the defendant ripped the phone wires from the wall. The victim's 9-year old son and daughter returned home and were both ejected from the house by the defendant. He then told the victim to sit down and he removed his upper clothing. He picked up some knives and tied them around himself before tying himself to the banisters. He threw the house keys behind him onto the stairs out of the victim's reach. Police arrived at about 5pm. The defendant was shouting and irate. He told the victim to speak to the police from the window and tell them to return to the station or he would kill them both. He put the blade of the knife to her throat and another knife to his own in full view of the police for about 2 minutes. He ordered her upstairs and when he returned downstairs. She jumped from the first floor window and onto an adjacent roof and then escaped. He continued to shout at the police occasionally throwing objects at them. He was eventually rendered unconscious by police using a Taser gun. The next day he said that he had consumed a large amount of alcohol but never intended to harm her and only made 'empty' threats. He said he had mental problems which caused him to be violent and he was sorry for his actions. There were no physical injuries to the victim. He was 46 and had previous convictions for dishonesty and some 17 years earlier, one ABH. A psychiatric report said "His judgment was likely to have been impaired by mental illness precipitated by unaccustomed consumption of alcohol … He did not represent a serious risk of re-offending." A PSR said that he may remain at medium to high risk of offending and harm unless he was able to learn new strategies. He spent 10 weeks on remand. Held. This was an extremely difficult sentencing exercise. It would properly have been **3 years** on a guilty plea as there was very great anxiety caused to the victim. Weighing the public interest as well as the defendant's interest, it would not progress the defendant and he had completed the majority of his CPO. Coupled with the fact it was a reference and the fact that the offence was out of character, although unduly lenient, the sentence remained.

FALSE INSTRUMENT, USING A

Where the false instrument is used to steal see THEFT ETC

See also COUNTERFEITING CURRENCY, ELECTION OFFENCES and PASSPORT OFFENCES

FAMILY

See **CRUELTY TO CHILDREN, FATHERS** and **MOTHERS**

FATHERS

See **CRUELTY TO CHILDREN** and **MOTHERS**

74   FIREARMS

74.1   Various different penalties under the Firearms Act 1968 and the Firearms (Amendment) Act 1997 s 2 to 8 and other legislation.

CHAPTERS in this book are in bold capitals. The ***paragraph titles*** are in bold italics. Where a chapter (e.g. arson) has subsections, the **subsections** are in lower case bold.

Automatic life Offences under Firearms Act 1968 s 16, 17(1) and (2)[12] and 18 are specified offences for automatic life[13] if committed before 4/4/05.

Confiscation For all Firearms Act 1968 s 3(1) offences[14] committed on or after 24 March 2003[15] the court must follow the Proceeds of Crime Act 2002 procedure. For all Customs and Excise Management Act 1979 s 68(2) and 170 offences[16] committed on or after 24 March 2003[17] which concern firearms or ammunition the court must follow the Proceeds of Crime Act 2002 procedure.

Dangerous Offender provisions For offences under s 16, 17(1), 17(2) and 18 when committed on or after 4/4/05 where there is a significant risk to members of the public of serious harm etc. there is a mandatory duty to pass a life sentence when it is justified and otherwise a sentence of imprisonment for public protection[18]. For offenders under 18 the duty is to pass detention for life, detention for public protection or an extended sentence[19].

Imprisonment for public protection For s 16A offences committed on or after 4/4/05 when there is a significant risk to members of the public of serious harm etc. there is a mandatory duty to pass a sentence of imprisonment for public protection[20]. For offenders under 18 the duty is to pass detention for public protection or an extended sentence[21].

Minimum sentences Offences under Firearms Act 1968 s 5(1)(a), (ab), (aba), (ac), (ad), (ae), (af), (c), and (1A)(a) committed on or after 22/1/04 carry a minimum sentence of 5 years for defendants aged 18 years or over unless there are exceptional circumstances[22]. The minimum sentence does not apply where the defendant is

12 *R v Buckland 2000 2 Cr App R (S) 217*
13 Powers of Criminal Courts (Sentencing) Act 2000 s 109(5)
14 Proceeds of Crime Act 2002 s 6 and s 75 and Sch 2 para 5(2)
15 Proceeds of Crime Act 2002 (Commencement No 5, Transitional Provisions, Savings and Amendment) Order 2003
16 Proceeds of Crime Act 2002 s 6 and s 75 and Sch 2 para 5
17 Proceeds of Crime Act 2002 (Commencement No 5, Transitional Provisions, Savings and Amendment) Order 2003
18 Criminal Justice Act 2003 s 225
19 Criminal Justice Act 2003 s 226 and 228
20 Criminal Justice Act 2003 s 224–226
21 Criminal Justice Act 2003 s 226 and 228
22 Firearms Act 1968 S 51A inserted by Criminal Justice Act 2003 S 287

indicted with another offence involving a prohibited weapon[23]. There is no power to reduce the 5 years because the defendant pleaded guilty[24].

Sexual Offences Prevention Order For offences under the Firearms Act 1968 s 16, 16A, 17(1), 17(2) and 18 there is a discretionary power to make this order when it is necessary to protect the public etc[25].

Crown Court statistics – England and Wales – Males 21+

74.2

Year	Plea	Total Numbers sentenced	Type of sentence %					Average length of custody (months)
			Discharge	Fine	Community sentence	Suspended sentence	Custody	
2002	Guilty	228	9	6	20	6	58	25.8
	Not guilty	22	–	5	–	5	91	59.1
2003	Guilty	277	5	4	22	7	61	31.7
	Not guilty	57	–	4	7	2	81	54.5

For details and explanations about the statistics in the book see page vii.

Guideline case

74.3   *R v Avis* 1998 1 Cr App R 420. LCJ. The numbers convicted of some firearms offences has very sharply increased. The unlawful possession and use of firearms is generally recognised as a grave source of danger to society. The reasons are obvious. Firearms may be used to take life or cause serious injury. They are used to further the commission of other serious crimes. Often the victims will be those charged with the enforcement of the law or the protection of persons or property. In the conflicts, which occur between competing criminal gangs, often related to the supply of drugs, the use and possession of firearms provoke an escalating spiral of violence. The appropriate level of sentence for a firearms offence, as for any other offence, will depend on all the facts and circumstances relevant to the offence and the offender, and it would be wrong for this court to seek to prescribe unduly restrictive sentencing guidelines. It will, however, usually be appropriate for the sentencing court to ask itself a series of questions:

(1)   What sort of weapon is involved? Genuine firearms are more dangerous than imitation firearms. Loaded firearms are more dangerous than unloaded firearms. Unloaded firearms for which ammunition is available are more dangerous than firearms for which no ammunition is available. Possession of a firearm which has no lawful use (such as a sawn-off shotgun) will be viewed even more seriously than possession of a firearm which is capable of lawful use.

(2)   What (if any) use has been made of the firearm? It is necessary for the court, as with any other offence, to take account of all circumstances surrounding any use made of the firearm: the more prolonged and premeditated and violent the use, the more serious the offence is likely to be.

(3)   With what intention (if any) did the defendant possess or use the firearm? Generally speaking, the most serious offences under the Act are those which require proof of a specific criminal intent (to endanger life, to cause fear of violence, to resist arrest, to commit an indictable offence). The more serious the act intended, the more serious the offence.

23 *Att-Gen's Ref. No 114 of 2004 2005 Crim L R 142*
24 *R v Jordan 2004 Unreported 14/12/04*
25 Sexual Offences Act 2003 s 104 & Sch. 5

(4) What is the defendant's record? The seriousness of any firearm offence is inevitably increased if the offender has an established record of committing firearms offences or crimes of violence.

Where there are breaches of s 4, 5, 16, 16A, 17(1) and (2), 18(1), 19 or 21 of the Firearms Act, 1968 the custodial term is likely to be of considerable length, and where the four questions suggested above yield answers adverse to the offender, terms at or approaching the maximum may in a contested case be appropriate. An indeterminate sentence should however be imposed only where the established criteria for imposing such a sentence are met.

Some of the sentences imposed for these offences in the past, sometimes by this court, have failed to reflect the seriousness of such offences and the justifiable public concern which they arouse. Save for minor infringements which may be and are properly dealt with summarily, offences against these provisions will almost invariably merit terms of custody, even on a plea of guilty and in the case of an offender with no previous record.

[No cases heard before *R v Avis* 1998 are listed as that case indicates that past sentences were on occasions too low.]

Airports   See **AIRCRAFT OFFENCES** – *Firearms*

Consecutive or concurrent sentences

74.4   *Att-Gen's Ref. No 77 of 2003* Unreported 21/12/04. The defendant pleaded guilty to supplying cannabis, offering to supply cocaine, producing cannabis, three counts of possession of a prohibited weapon and three other firearm counts. Held. The firearms offences should have been consecutive not concurrent.

See also **ROBBERY** – *Firearms, with* – *Consecutive or concurrent sentences*

Death results

See **MANSLAUGHTER** – *Firearms, with*

Debt collecting

74.5   *R v Lavin* 2000 1 Cr App R (S) 226. The defendants KL, TL and SW pleaded guilty to possessing a firearm with intent to commit an indictable offence. TL also pleaded guilty to possessing prohibited ammunition. The pleas were entered late after a plea basis was agreed and the prosecution agreed to drop a more serious count. Police on surveillance duties saw a car containing the three defendants acting suspiciously near some shops and post offices. They stopped the car. SW was wearing a hood and gloves. A lump hammer, a holdall, two hats, a small handgun, an earpiece and four further pairs of gloves were found. The safety catch on the firearm was down and the gun was cocked with live ammunition in the magazine and a live round in the chamber. A large amount of ammunition was found at TL's home. The basis of plea was that indictable offence in the count was a debt owed to TL, which was not enforceable through the courts. The gun was only to be showed to the debtor and not to be used. The firearm had come into their possession because someone wanted it looked after rather than sought for the task. KL was 40 and had a number of convictions mostly for dishonesty but there was one firearm conviction. TL was 48 and had numerous convictions for motoring offences and dishonesty but none for firearm. SW was 40 with dishonesty convictions and no firearm offences. The judge said there was a local problem with the use of guns in Merseyside and SW was the least involved. He also said that gave a substantial discount for the pleas entered. Held. The judge was in the best position to judge local problems. KL, **6 years** not $7^1/_2$. TL, **6 and 1 years consecutive** not $7^1/_2$ and $1^1/_2$ consecutive. SW, **5 years** not 6.

Defendant aged under 18 years

74.6   *R v Thomas* 2000 2 Cr App R (S) 155. The defendant pleaded guilty to possessing a firearm when committing a Sch 1 offence and theft. The defendant went to a 'peep' show and asked for change. He left and returned and seized a cash bag containing £122 from the cashier. He was chased through the streets. A police officer caught him and an imitation handgun was found on him. It wasn't used but was of convincing appearance. He said he just liked carrying it. The defendant was 17 and had findings of guilt for failure to surrender to bail, criminal damage and possession of a bladed article. Held. The law on imitation firearms exists to prevent anyone minded to commit a criminal offence from carrying firearms or imitation firearm. If someone carries an imitation firearm when committing an offence but does not produce it and has some entirely credible or innocent reason for its possession the court might be persuaded to unusual leniency. Otherwise it calls for a substantial custodial sentence. Taking into account the defendant's youth and his plea 15 months cannot be described as excessive. **15 months and 3 months consecutive** YOI was not wrong.

R v Burnip 2002 Unreported 12/8/02. The defendant pleaded guilty to having an imitation firearm with intent to resist arrest, threats to kill, having an offensive weapon and affray. He attacked police when they had been called by his mother because of his behaviour. We would have expected at least 18 months but because of his progress with his drug problem the community rehabilitation order was undisturbed.

Disposing of the firearm

74.7   *R v Morgan* 2004 1 Cr App R (S) 134. The defendant pleaded guilty to possessing a prohibited weapon and possessing a firearm. He asked for three other firearm matters to be taken into account. He was seen disposing a quantity of firearm parts in a municipal skip. There were two Stirling submachine guns in various states of dismantlement, 19 ammunition magazines, two dummy rocket propelled grenades, a blank firing pistol, a rifle, tools and various firearm components. The police were told and he was arrested. He said he worked for the Ministry of Defence between 1989 and 1999 and it was all scrap which he used for repairs on real or display weapons for various army units. The basis of plea was none could be fired, their barrels were plugged and bolted and the Army categorised them as scrap. An experienced armourer would need to do a considerable amount of work to make them fire. The defendant had stored them in his mother's shed. He was 35 and of good character. The Judge was concerned that the machine guns would make very convincing imitation firearms. Held. His initial possession of the items was lawful. This was a highly irresponsible offence. There remained the risk of these items falling into the wrong hands. **9 months** upheld.

Exporting firearms see *Importing/exporting firearms*

False imprisonment, and

See FALSE IMPRISONMENT – *Firearms, with (real or imitation)*

Firearms Act 1968 s 1

74.8   Possession of a firearm

Triable either way. Maximum sentence 5 years. Summary maximum 6 months or £5,000

R v Baer 1999 1 Cr App R (S) 441. The defendant pleaded guilty to possessing a firearm, possessing ammunition and handling stolen goods at the Magistrates' Court. He was committed for sentence. The police searched the defendant's home in connection with a motoring matter. The defendant told them he had a small handgun in the attic. It was duly found with 50 rounds of ammunition. The defendant said he had lawfully bought them in the US at the suggestion of his friend who he was living with.

On his return to this country he had brought them back and they had remained in the house unused and untouched. The defendant was 38 with one minor conviction. Held. The gravity of the offence is the risk of them falling into the wrong hands. These facts are very unusual. **12 months** not 18 with the other sentences remaining concurrent.

R v Wharton 2000 2 Cr App R (S) 339. The defendant made an early plea to possession of a firearm. The police executed a search warrant at the defendant's home and found a revolver hanging on the living room wall. It was of modern Italian reproduction with a cylinder with blocked chambers. However, in a cupboard was a cylinder which when fitted made a working firearm. The defendant said it was an ornament which he had had a number of years and had cost him £25. He was 44 with dissimilar convictions between 1974 and 1985, none of which were for violence. He was divorced who looked after his children 3 days a week. **2 months** not 6 months.

R v Lamb 2002 Unreported 24/9/02. The defendant pleaded guilty on the first day of his trial to possessing a firearm without a certificate and possession of ammunition. For many years he had had a turbulent relationship with his former wife. Police were called to her home and found on the kitchen table parts of a firearm which when assembled was a self loading pistol. There was also ammunition which fitted the pistol. He was sentenced on the basis he owed money to another and when he defaulted that person asked him to take possession of it for a day or two. It was received in a disassembled state and the defendant never contemplated using it. He was 46 with many convictions, the last was in 1997 for a wholly different offence. The judge said he passed a deterrent sentence. Held. We are sceptical of the basis of plea, but we accept it. We support the judge in his views that severe sentences are appropriate, but because of the plea and the basis of plea **3 years** not 4.

R v Beaumont 2004 1 Cr App R (S) 393. The defendant pleaded guilty at the Magistrates' Court to possessing a firearm without a certificate, possessing ammunition without a certificate and to possessing cannabis. Police officers executed a bench warrant at the defendant's home. He was seen attempting to conceal a package that contained a single barrel 12 bore shotgun in poor condition and the barrel had been cut down. Officers also found 23 cartridges and some cannabis. When interviewed he said that he bought the shotgun and cartridges for £100 and said that he simply attended to mount the gun. He was 27 with just two convictions, both for having a bladed article (2 years C/D). He expressed remorse. He had four young children. He was of low risk of re-offending. Held. There is nothing to show that he had any intention to use the items in a violent way. **2 years** not 3.

Firearms Act 1968 s 1 and 4(4)

74.9   Possession of a shortened shotgun or firearm which has been converted.

Triable either way. Maximum sentence 7 years. Summary maximum 6 months or £5,000

R v Gourley 1999 2 Cr App R (S) 148. The defendant pleaded guilty to possessing a firearm. The police searched the defendant's home and found a single barrelled sawn-off shotgun and 17 shotgun cartridges in two plastic bags under a child's bed in one of the bedrooms. The gun was capable of being fired and the cartridges could be used in the gun. He said he had bought the gun from some gypsies for his own protection. The defendant had a conviction for violence and had a good work record. The judge said that on a not guilty plea 6 years would be the sentence. Held 6 years was too close to the statutory maximum. **3 years** substituted for 4.

R v Holmes 1999 2 Cr App R (S) 383. The defendant pleaded guilty to possession of a firearm whilst a prohibited person, possession of a shortened shotgun, and possession of a loaded shotgun in a public place. A householder went to look at a car and saw a sawn off shotgun in the passenger footwell through a partially open window. The police were called and found the shotgun, which was loaded with two cartridges. The police traced the defendant, aged 42, as the hirer of the vehicle and arrested him. He admitted the gun belonged to him and said he had bought it with the intention of committing suicide. He said he took some pills and ended up in hospital. In 1990 he was sentenced to 4 years for possession of drugs with intent to supply. He had heart and artery problems, which he tended to exaggerate. The psychiatrist said the possession of the shotgun for a possible suicide fitted in with his presentation and his behaviour at the time. The prison report says he always uses his medical and psychological problems to get what he wants. Held. Leaving the firearm there was extreme irresponsibility and recklessness. We are quite unmoved by the submission that his intention to commit suicide means he is less culpable. There was nothing wrong with **2¹/₂ years** on each concurrent.

R v Campbell 2000 1 Cr App R (S) 291. The defendant appears to have pleaded guilty to possession of a shortened shotgun, and a prohibited firearm. Police officers searched his flat after a disturbance in which he threatened someone and kicked a car. For the disturbance he received 6 months in all for possession of an offensive weapon and criminal damage. In a cupboard they found a sawn off shotgun in pieces in a black bin liner. In another cupboard they found an automatic machine pistol, which was a prohibited weapon and over 900 rounds of ammunition in a suitcase. Neither was loaded but both were in working order. He was sentenced on the basis he thought the items were stolen goods and he didn't look at them. (This was no defence because of *R v Steele* 1993 Crim LR 298) He had had them for 10 days and was to receive no payment. [The judgment does not refer to his character.] Held. 3¹/₂ years would have been appropriate if he had known but as he didn't **2 years** substituted.

R v Herbert 2001 1 Cr App R (S) 77. The defendant pleaded guilty to possession of a shortened shotgun and possession of a firearm when prohibited. Police officers executed a search warrant at the defendant's home address and found a sawn-off shotgun with two live cartridges concealed in a bed. The firearm was in working order and the cartridges fitted the shotgun. At a Newton hearing he claimed he was looking after it for a short while for £50 for a man he was terrified of. This was not accepted and he was sentenced on the basis it was for his own purposes. The defendant was 29 with eleven previous convictions including three for ABH for one of which he was sentenced to 12 months. There were no convictions for firearms. Held. The weapon had no lawful use and was a criminal's weapon for use in violent and serious crime. Although there was no evidence of any contemplated offence the court was entitled to assume that it was for unlawful use should the occasion arise. His prohibition aggravated the offence. **4 years** on each concurrent was not manifestly excessive.

Firearms Act 1968 s 2

74.10 Possession of a shotgun

Triable either way. Maximum sentence 5 years. Summary maximum 6 months and/or £5,000.

Firearms Act 1968 s 3(1)(a)

74.11 Manufacturing a firearm

Triable either way. On indictment maximum sentence 5 years.

Summary maximum 6 months and/or £5,000.

Confiscation For all s 3(1) offences[26] committed on or after 24 March 2003[27] the court must follow the Proceeds of Crime Act 2002 procedure.

26 Proceeds of Crime Act 2002 s 6 and s 75 and Sch 2 para 5(2)
27 Proceeds of Crime Act 2002 (Commencement No 5, Transitional Provisions, Savings and Amendment) Order 2003

Firearms Act 1968 s 4

74.12   Converting weapons and shortening the barrel of a shotgun.

Triable either way. Maximum sentence 10 years. Summary maximum 6 months and/or £5,000.

R v Avis 1998 2 Cr App R (S) 178 – LCJ. Where there are breaches of s 4 of the Firearms Act 1968 the custodial term is likely to be of considerable length, and where the four questions suggested above (see *Guideline case*) yield answers adverse to the offender, terms at or approaching the maximum may in a contested case be appropriate.

R v Hampson 2005 1 Cr App R (S) 227. The defendants A and D, who were brothers, changed their pleas to guilty to conspiracy to convert an imitation firearm into a firearm. When police officers searched D's home they found £12,000 in cash, prohibited firearms which had been converted from blank firing parts, parts of prohibited firearms, improvised ammunition, a modified blank firing gun, parts removed from a blank firing gun and debris from dismantled ammunition. Experts established that imitation firearms had been converted by sawing off the barrels and inserting tubing to create new barrels. They were then able to fire live ammunition. Blank cartridges had been converted by drilling out the cartridge and inserting a missile. Police then searched A's home and found a rifle and self loading pistol, eight prohibited firearms converted from blank firing guns, prohibited ammunition, improvised bulleted ammunition, debris and dismantled ammunition. A was 48 years old and had a bad record of over 77 offences including two previous firearms offences. D also had a bad record of 23 offences including numerous offences of dishonesty. He did not have any previous convictions for firearms. Held. These guns were crude but nonetheless lethal. It was a well-organised and continuing conspiracy. Those who involve themselves in converting firearms for use on the street deserve little or no sympathy and cannot complain when they receive sentences of this length. **6 years** for A and **5¹/₂** years for D were upheld.

Firearms Act 1968 s 5

74.13   Possession etc. of a prohibited weapon or ammunition.

Offences under sub-sections 5(1)(a), (ab), (aba), (ac), (ad), (ae), (af), (c), and (1A)(a) committed on or after 22/1/04 are indictable only[28], and become specified offences enabling defendants aged 16–17 to be detained[29]. All other offences are triable either way.

Maximum sentence 10 years. Summary maximum 6 months and/or £5,000.

Minimum sentences For offences under those sub-sections above committed on or after 22/1/04 there is a minimum sentence of 5 years for defendants aged 18 years or over unless there are exceptional circumstances[30]. The minimum sentence does not apply where the defendant is indicted with another offence involving a prohibited weapon[31]. There is no power to reduce the 5 years because the defendant pleaded guilty[32].

Firearms Act 1968 s 5 – Guideline case

74.14   *R v Avis* 1998 2 Cr App R (S) 178. LCJ. Where there are breaches of s 5 of the Firearms Act 1968 the custodial term is likely to be of considerable length, and where the four questions suggested above (see *Guideline case*) yield answers adverse to the offender, terms at or approaching the maximum may in a contested case be appropriate.

28 Criminal Justice Act 2003 Section 288
29 Powers of Criminal Courts (Sentencing) Act 2000 s 91(1A) and (3)–(4) substituted by Criminal Justice Act 2003 s 289(2)
30 Firearms Act 1968 S 51A inserted by Criminal Justice Act 2003 s 287
31 *Att-Gen's Ref. No 114 of 2004 2005 Crime LR 142*
32 *R v Jordan 2004 Unreported 14/12/04*

Firearms Act 1968 s 5 – Possession of a prohibited weapon

74.15   *R v Wright* 2000 1 Cr App R (S) 109. The defendant pleaded guilty to possession of a prohibited weapon, possession of ammunition and possessing a firearm when prohibited. Police officers searched his flat and he managed to remove a revolver from his sofa without the officers noticing. He passed it to his partner but she was searched. It was a Smith and Wesson and fully loaded with six bullets. Because of its length it was prohibited. It was functioning normally. He said it was for his own protection and he was concerned because he had helped the police about the death of a close friend. The defendant had a conviction for conspiracy to rob where no robbery took place and no weapon was involved for which he received 4 years. Held. There was no actual use made of it, it was possessed for a short time and it was for self-defence. After considering the questions in *R v Avis* 1998, **2 years** not 4.

R v Campbell 2000 1 Cr App R (S) 291. The defendant appears to have pleaded guilty to possession of a shortened shotgun, and a prohibited firearm. Police officers searched his flat after a disturbance in which he threatened someone and kicked a car. For the disturbance he received 6 months in all for possession of an offensive weapon and criminal damage. In a cupboard they found a sawn off shotgun in pieces in a black bin liner. In another cupboard they found an automatic machine pistol, which was a prohibited weapon and over 900 rounds of ammunition in a suitcase. Neither was loaded but both were in working order. He was sentenced on the basis he thought the items were stolen goods and he didn't look at them. (This was no defence because of *R v Steele* 1993 Crim LR 298) He had had them for 10 days and was to receive no payment. [The judgment does not refer to his character.] Held. 3 ½ years would have been appropriate if he had known but as he didn't **2 years** substituted.

R v Aplin 2000 2 Cr App R (S) 89. The defendant pleaded guilty at the Magistrates' Court to possession of ten prohibited weapons and five charges of possessing prohibited ammunition. The defendant, aged 58 was a registered firearm dealer held in high regard by members of a Rifle and Pistol Club, which he ran, and by members of the police force who used the club. A fire broke out in a bedroom above the garage of the house where the defendant was staying. The firemen discovered 46 prohibited firearms and ammunition in the garage and called the police. In the house the police discovered cabinets containing firearms. The firearms only became prohibited by the 1997 legislation. The firearms were stored without the knowledge of the family that lived there and before the change in the law were worth about £30,000. The defendant said that the firearms belonged in part to the club and the rest belonged to his business. When the changes to the law were taking place he stored the firearms in Germany at a gun club and club members used them there. However, because there were so many firearms he was asked to end the arrangement. He failed to sell them in Germany and then could not benefit from the UK surrender and compensation policy. He brought them back to the UK illegally. He claimed he held them in the hope of obtaining compensation. The family whose home the firearms were stored had problems with their insurance claim because of the illegal storage of firearms and the defendant had to compensate them £16,000 from his pension fund. Held. The prevailing purpose of the legislation was safety. Keeping lethal weapons in insecure conditions was serious. He treated himself above the law. The sentence had to have a deterrent element. He exposed his friends and others to a very significant level of risk. Applying *R v Avis* 1998 2 Cr App R (S) 178 **18 months** not 3 years because of his age, character and the financial loss.

R v Morgan 2004 1 Cr App R (S) 134. The defendant pleaded guilty to possessing a prohibited weapon and possessing a firearm. He asked for three other firearm matters to be taken into account. He was seen disposing a quantity of firearm parts in a municipal skip. There were two Stirling submachine guns in various states of dismantlement, 19 ammunition magazines, two dummy rocket propelled grenades, a blank firing pistol, a rifle, tools and various firearm components. The police were told and he was arrested. He said he worked for the Ministry of Defence between 1989 and 1999 and it was all scrap which he used for repairs on real or display weapons for various army units. The basis of plea was none could be fired, their barrels were plugged and bolted and the Army categorised them as scrap. An experienced armourer would need to do a considerable amount of work to make them fire. The defendant had stored them in his mother's shed. He was 35 and of good character. The Judge was concerned that he machine guns would make very convincing imitation firearms. Held. His initial possession of the items was lawful. This was a highly irresponsible offence. There remained the risk of these items falling into the wrong hands. **9 months** upheld.

Firearms Act 1968 s 5 – Manufacture of a prohibited weapon

74.16   *R v Luty* 1999 2 Cr App R (S) 81. The defendant pleaded guilty to manufacturing a prohibited weapon and possession of ammunition. He asked for two offences of possession of a firearm to be taken into consideration. The defendant visited a photographer and said he had designed a weapon and he wanted the 80 parts photographed for a service and assembly manual. The photographer told the police who searched the defendant's home. They found a workshop with a very large number of assorted pieces of metal, weapon parts, gun magazines and diagrams. They also found a home-made sub-machine gun and six Luger cartridges. Residue showed the gun had been fired. It could only fire single shots but with adjustment it could probably fire bursts of ammunition. In interview he said he had been engaged in the project for 2 years for a book to be published in the US. The book was now published and it explained how to construct a sub-machine gun. Other prototypes were the subject matter for the TICs. The defendant had a conviction for possession of a loaded firearm in a public place for which he was fined. He was considered a loner with anger towards society. It was accepted the gun was not to be used for crime or to injure anyone. Held. The offence was aggravated by the deliberate breaking of the law, which he disapproved of, and his previous conviction. A heavy sentence was inevitable. **4 years** was severe but the sentence properly reflects society's revulsion for guns and was not manifestly excessive.

Att-Gen's Ref No 120–1 of 2004 2005 Unreported 22/4/05. The defendants, H and B, pleaded guilty on the first day of trial to three counts on which they were jointly charged: (1) conspiracy to manufacture prohibited weapons; (2) conspiracy to sell or transfer prohibited weapons; and (3) conspiracy to possess firearms with intent to enable others to cause fear of violence. Over a ten-month period they obtained from two suppliers in London a large quantity of blank firing handguns and corresponding blank ammunition. They then converted the weapons into lethal prohibited weapons capable of firing the ammunition, and sold the weapons and ammunition directly to interested criminal parties or through one of their supplying shops. On a conservative basis they made and sold more than 150 weapons. The weapons were destined for the criminal fraternity. Their pleas followed unsuccessful submission by their counsel to exclude evidence. After this H's counsel received a message from the judge that if the defendants pleaded guilty they would receive full credit. Written bases of plea were submitted for both men. H's said that he was not responsible for the manufacture of all guns (over 300 were referred to in the evidence). B's said that although he had been a party to the conspiracy in count one he had played a minimal role in the manufacture; that the conduct charged in the other two counts was incidental to that charged in the count one, and that he had a lesser role than H. The judge indicated to counsel in chambers that both men would receive full credit for their pleas and that his provisional view was that he would sentence concurrently on all counts as they were part and parcel of the same enterprise. The prosecutor indicated to the judge he could not agree the proposed bases of plea although there were some assertions of fact he could not gainsay; in particular it was the Crown's case that the defendants were involved over the course of the conspiracy with hundreds of guns. The aggravating features were identified as being the vast quantity of weapons involved; the 10 month length of the conspiracy and the defendants' intention to equip criminals with fully functioning firearms to put fear into others. H was 47, B 45. Held. This was a case where the prosecution evidence was strong and it was not a case for a full discount for pleas of guilty. Where the seriousness and range of the separate counts calls for a higher sentence than any of them on its own there should be consecutive sentences. Despite the judge's early indication that he had concurrent sentences in mind he gave no commitment to that course and the defendants cannot have had a legitimate expectation that he would impose concurrent sentences. These conspiracies required sentences of a very high order not 6 years. The appropriate starting point for these offences was about **15 years** reduced to **9 years** after allowing for the full discount promised to the defendants by the judge and taking into account it was a reference.

Firearms Act 1968 s 16

74.17   Possession with intent to endanger life

Indictable only. Maximum sentence life.

Automatic life Section 16 is a specified offence for automatic life[33] for offences committed before 4/4/05.

Firearms Act 1968, s 16 – Guideline case, guideline remarks

74.18   *R v Avis* 1998 2 Cr App R (S) 178. LCJ. Where there are breaches of section 16 of the Firearms Act, 1968 the custodial term is likely to be of considerable length, and where the four questions suggested above (see *Guideline case*) yield answers adverse to the offender, terms at or approaching the maximum may in a contested case be appropriate.

Dangerous Offender provisions For offences committed on or after 4/4/05 where there is a significant risk to members of the public of serious harm etc. there is a mandatory duty to pass a life sentence when it is justified and otherwise a sentence of imprisonment for public protection[34]. For offenders under 18 the duty is to pass detention for life, detention for public protection or an extended sentence[35].

Att-Gen's Ref. Nos. 58–61, 63–66 of 2002 147 SJ 296. In a contested case simple possession of a firearm together with ammunition with intent to endanger life merits a sentence of between **7–8 years**.

Firearms Act 1968, s 16 – Cases

74.19   *R v Avis* 1998 Re Thomas 2 Cr App R (S) 178 at 189. LCJ. Thomas pleaded guilty to two counts of possessing a firearm with intent to endanger life, six counts of selling or transferring firearms unlawfully; and two counts of selling or transferring ammunition unlawfully. The pleas were entered at the beginning of his trial after the judge had made a ruling on the evidence. Thomas was a firearms dealer who sold three revolvers and ammunition for them to an undercover police officer for £1,160 in a car park. Thomas told the officer that he could supply firearms regularly and easily. At a further meeting at a railway station Thomas sold the officer two pump action shotguns which had been shortened. He also sold three pistols and ammunition for all five weapons. The total price was £1,220. Thomas was arrested. He was 66 and had no convictions. He had a very large number of testimonials. He had for many years been involved with charity work and was held in high esteem. He was sentenced to 9 years on each endanger count; 4 years for the selling firearms counts and 2 years for

33 Powers of Criminal Courts (Sentencing) Act 2000 s 109(5)
34 Criminal Justice Act 2003 s 225
35 Criminal Justice Act 2003 s 226 and 228

ammunition counts. They were all concurrent making a total of **9 years**. Held. The judge's starting point would have been 12 years. The use of firearms by armed robbers and drug dealers is prevalent and on the increase. A person who provides firearms in the certain knowledge that they are going to be used by criminals commits a grave offence. The judge took the mitigation fully into account and he could not sensibly have reduced the sentence further.

Att-Gen's Ref. No 49 of 1998 1999 1 Cr App R (S) 396. The defendant pleaded guilty two days before his trial to possession of a firearm with intent to endanger life, and other lesser and connected firearm offences. The defendant's flat was searched. The defendant struggled and kicked out at the officers. In the airing cupboard they found a plastic bin bag containing a self-loading pistol and a clip for the pistol containing six rounds of ammunition and thirty one other rounds. The firearm was a prohibited weapon and in working order. In interview he said there had been a lot of gang related trouble and it was for his own protection. He accepted he was a member of one of the gangs. He was 23 and had convictions for drugs and wounding. Held. If the matter had been contested **8 years** would have been appropriate. For a late plea **7 years** was appropriate. As it was a reference **6 years** not 30 months.

Att-Gen's Ref. No 2 of 2000 2001 1 Cr App R (S) 27. The defendant was convicted of possession of a firearm with intent to endanger life and possessing ammunition. Police made an arrest and went to the man's home address. Inside was the defendant and the police saw him through a window throw an object into a cupboard. It was found to be a sock with a Smith and Wesson self-loading pistol with one round in the breech and 13 in the magazine. The safety catch was off. It was in good condition and was a prohibited weapon. The defendant was 33 and had no convictions. Held. We would have expected a sentence of at least **7 years**. Because it was a reference **6 years** not 4.

R v Marney 2002 1 Cr App R (S) 506. See page **74.37**.

Firearms Act 1968 s 16A

74.20 To have in his possession any firearm or imitation firearm with intent (a) by means thereof to cause, or (b) to enable another person by means thereof to cause, any person to believe that unlawful violence will be used against him or another person.

Indictable only. Maximum sentence 10 years.

Imprisonment for public protection For offences committed on or after 4/4/05 when there is a significant risk to members of the public of serious harm etc. there is a mandatory duty to pass a sentence of imprisonment for public protection[36]. For offenders under 18 the duty is to pass detention for public protection or an extended sentence[37].

R v Avis 1998 2 Cr App R (S) 178. *LCJ*. Where there are breaches of section 16A of the Firearms Act, 1968 the custodial term is likely to be of considerable length, and where the four questions suggested above (see **GUIDELINE CASE**) yield answers adverse to the offender, terms at or approaching the maximum may in a contested case be appropriate.

Firearms Act 1968, s16A – Airguns, air rifles, air pistols

74.21 *R v Avis* 1998 Re Torrington 2 Cr App R (S) 178 at 189. LCJ. The defendant pleaded guilty to possessing a firearm with intent to cause fear of unlawful violence. In the early hours, the defendant's stepson, Roberts walked home from a local public house was confronted by about seven men. Abuse was exchanged and one of the men kicked him. The defendant, who had been drinking, was told about it and he fetched two air rifles, handing one to Roberts. Each was loaded and primed. The two men went to the scene of the earlier incident and Roberts identified a man called Sanjit Singh as

36 Criminal Justice Act 2003 s 224–226
37 Criminal Justice Act 2003 s 226 and 228

the person who had kicked him. The defendant kicked Mr Singh and he pointed the gun at his face. Mr Singh pushed the gun away, but this caused the weapon to be accidentally discharged. The defendant then primed the weapon and reloaded. Mr Singh ran off in fear. The police then arrived. The defendant told the police where he had hid the guns. The defendant was of good character. He had been off work since January 1996 through ill health. He was also suffering from depression. Held. This case had the aggravating feature that loaded weapons were taken to a public place, where one was discharged, albeit accidentally. The **18 months** he received was the correct sentence.

R v Thompson 1999 2 Cr App R (S) 292. The defendant pleaded guilty to possession of a firearm with intent to cause another to believe unlawful violence would be used. The defendant aged 58, went to a public house with an air pistol. He had no ammunition with him. He was very drunk and he took exception to a remark about his age and produced the pistol, and said 'No-one fucks with me.' The man who made the remark pulled up his shirt and pointed at his heart although he did not regard it as a joke. The incident subsided. Later he was arrested. He had suffered from depression although the psychiatrist said the incident should be treated as an isolated offence and he was not psychiatrically disturbed. Between 1990 and 1993 he was convicted of ABH four times and affray. There were no convictions since. **4 months** not 2 years.

R v Carey 2000 1 Cr App R (S) 179. The defendant was convicted of possession of a firearm with intent to cause fear or violence. Following reports of a male firing an airgun into the street, police went to the defendant's home. They saw him at an open window pointing a firearm in their general direction, shouting 'Fuck off you lot. I'll let you have it if you come at me with a shotgun.' He was told not to be silly but he put the butt of the rifle to his shoulder and his eye to the sight pointing the gun at the police. He said, 'I'll do it. I'll fucking have you.' A crack was heard followed by a bang. A police cordon was mounted, and pupils were kept in at school. He was arrested and two air rifles and air pellets were found. He was 43 with a number of convictions but none between 1989 and 1997. The judge believed all the time in custody would count towards his sentence, but it didn't because of another conviction and sentence. Held. **2 years** cannot possibly be said to be manifestly excessive.

R v Doyle 2001 2 Cr App R (S) 8. The defendant pleaded guilty to possession of a firearm with intent to cause a person to fear unlawful violence would be used. After 1am the defendant and two others went to a take away restaurant and she tried to buy a bottle of whisky. When the member of staff refused to sell the drink she became angry and shouted at him that she would kill him. She produced a handgun and said 'Give me the drink or I'll blow your fucking head off.' The member of staff who was used to firearms from his previous career did not think the gun was real and was not frightened. The customers of the restaurant gasped in disbelief. One of her friends pulled her away and they left. Just after that or before she entered the restaurant she discharged the gun through a window of an off-licence. The ball hit a bottle behind where the proprietor was standing. She was filmed on CCTV outside brandishing a gun and on one occasion waving it in the direction of another man. She was arrested at her home and the gun was found in some undergrowth. It was an air pistol, which resembled a Browning 9 mm handgun. On the night she had drunk a large amount of alcohol and had consumed anti-depressant drugs. She was 26 and had no convictions. She had suffered abuse as a child and had a history of alcohol abuse and suicide attempts. Held. **3 years** was not excessive.

Firearms Act 1968, s 16A – Handguns

74.22   *R v Avis* 1998 1 Cr App R 420. LCJ. The defendant was convicted of possessing a firearm with intent to cause fear of violence. Avis was involved in a serious dispute with his sister. A neighbour saw her face had blood on it and she was heading for her car, parked nearby and noticed Avis pursuing her shouting 'You fucking want it'. Avis was holding a handgun, which he appeared to be trying to load with a magazine. He pointed the gun at her and made the gun click three times. He put the handgun to her head. She and her children reached the car and whilst she was trying to put the children in the car Avis was still trying to make the gun work. He approached her again and put the handgun to the back of her head. This time when he clicked the gun there was a loud bang and a wall was struck by a bullet and crumbled. A witness said she didn't know whether the sister moved her head or Avis purposely missed. The sister drove off in the car shouting to Avis 'I'll get you for this.' Shortly after this she drove back and it appeared she was going to confront Avis who appeared on the scene. Almost immediately the police arrived and Avis left. The gun was found nearby. It was a Colt. 45 semi-automatic pistol with one live round in the magazine and in poor condition. Avis was arrested and was 35. He had convictions for violence. In 1995 he was placed on probation for affray. The sister, unlike many victims, did not appear to have suffered psychological distress. Held. The sentence of 8 years was above the prevailing level of sentence being imposed at the time. We reduce it to **6 years**. However, in future offences such as this could well attract sentences of the length first imposed.

R v Thynne 2001 Unreported 23/7/01. **2½ years** upheld on a plea. Attack on lover with violence.

Att-Gen's Ref. No 7 of 2001 Unreported 29/11/01. **1 year** substituted for CSO.

R v Wheeler 2002 2 Cr App R (S) 263. The defendant pleaded guilty to possessing a firearm with the intent to cause a belief that violence would be used, having a firearm with intent to commit an indictable offence, possession of a prohibited weapon and false imprisonment. He had a relationship and moved in with the victim. He said he had served in the French Foreign Legion and was highly experienced in explosives, firearms and weapons. About a year later after arguments she told him to leave. He did so and found it hard to accept and made repeated efforts to see her. She felt pestered. 5 months later he waited outside the garden centre where she worked and ³/₄ hour later he entered the centre and told her to go into an office. He had a pistol loaded with two live rounds and told her and her colleague, A, to phone the police. He pointed the gun at her and said he wasn't messing about, he was serious. He talked about his relationship with her and she became extremely frightened. The gun appeared cocked and it appeared to remain so. He talked about Hungerford and Dunblane and said her son was going to be an orphan. She was detained for 12 hours and he wouldn't let her go to the lavatory. The defendant threatened to kill himself. A chose to remain although the defendant said he could go. Eventually the defendant surrendered to the police. A said he was not seriously worried about his or her safety. When interviewed the defendant said, he waited till the school emptied. The victim had persuaded him not to let the police shoot him. He was at his lowest ebb ever and the gun was to 'stop her leaving.' The defendant was 44 and had no previous record for this kind of offence. He had had periods of depression. Held. The incident was terrifying. It was planned and the pistol was loaded with two bullets. These were very grave offences of the utmost seriousness. **7 years** was not manifestly excessive.

Att-Gen's Ref. No. 114 of 2004 Crim L R 142. The defendant pleaded guilty to possession of a firearm with intent to cause fear of violence and two counts of possession of a bladed article at the first opportunity. Police were called to a night club after a shot was fired. The defendant was pointed out to them and they followed him to an alleyway. He tried to get rid of the gun, a Bruni 1911. He also had two folding lock-knives and was wearing a bullet proof vest. In interview he said he was threatened by another group in the club and thought his brother was likely to be shot. The gun had been converted to fire steel balls however it was unable to produce sufficient energy to activate the recoil process. It was a prohibited weapon. The defendant had no previous convictions and was assessed as having a low risk of re-offending. However because of the feud the risk of causing serious harm was assessed as high. The Judge said he could not be sure that the bullet would have the capacity to kill someone. Held. **3 years consecutive to 6 months** for the knives was within the ambit of the Judge's sentencing powers.

Old case *R v Roker* 1998 2 Cr App R (S) 254 (For a summary of this case see the first edition of this book.)

Firearms Act 1968, s 16A – Imitation weapons, ball bearing guns starting pistols etc

74.23   *R v Avis* 1998 Re Barton 2 Cr App R (S) 178 at 187. The defendant, aged 20, pleaded guilty to two dwelling house burglaries, possessing an imitation firearm contrary to s 16A of the Firearms Act 1968 and a count of commercial burglary. The last two were committed on bail. He also asked for three offences of domestic burglary and four of commercial burglary to be taken into account. In the early hours of a morning Barton, who had been drinking, approached a car containing three young men, produced a replica handgun and pointed it at them. He demanded a lift. He held the gun within inches of the face of one of them and immediately pulled the trigger and the gun clicked. It made a noise like an imitation pistol. The man was not sure whether it was imitation and was in shock. He aimed a blow at Barton who was leaning into the car and got out of the car and punched at Barton who fell but then got up again. The man chased him and Barton turned and fired the gun again. Although he did not think anything was fired from it, the man was still fearful. Barton was arrested. Between 1994 and 1996 he had been convicted on numerous occasions, including twenty one offences of theft and taking vehicles and two public order offences, including his most recent conviction for affray for which he received 8 months' detention. The judge regarded the occupants of the car as absolutely terrified thinking their lives were in danger. He was sentenced to a total of **5 years** detention (3 years in all for the other offences and two years for the firearm offence consecutive). Held. The judge rightly said this was a terrifying offence. The total was not excessive.

R v Steele 1999 1 Cr App R (S) 369. The defendant pleaded guilty to possessing an imitation firearm with intent to cause another to believe violence would be used. The defendant's relationship with his girlfriend F, aged 17 broke up and each accused the other of harassment. He said associates of hers had used violence against him. He went to the police about it four days before the offence and was carrying a metal pole about 3' in length. He said it was for his self defence and it was taken off him. The police advised him against carrying weapons. He left blaming the police for taking her side. He then borrowed a starting pistol from a friend, which was capable of firing blanks. He had no cartridges for it. He went to the F's flat and was told F was not at home. F and two young women were abusive to one another and the defendant managed to get into the hall. He pointed the pistol at F and the two others and told the two to go away. F believed it was a real gun and was very fearful. All the women ran away and F went to the police station. The defendant admitted the offence. He was 22 and had been in minor trouble as a juvenile and had been cautioned for criminal damage. He had no convictions for violence. He was sentenced on the basis there had been provocation and he had ignored the advice given earlier. **9 months** not 18.

Att-Gen's Ref. No 49 of 1999 2000 1 Cr App R (S) 436. The defendant pleaded guilty to possession of a firearm with intent to cause fear of violence. The defendant after drinking hired a taxi at about 1.30am to take him home. He was asked for £5 and he said his money was in the house. The defendant went in and after he didn't return the taxi driver knocked on his front door and then returned to his taxi. The defendant approached the taxi and demonstrated that he appeared to be holding a gun and magazine clip. He made a movement to suggest he was cocking a gun. He asked what the fare was and was told it was now £5.80. The defendant told the taxi driver to think again. There was a conversation during which he continued to make it appear he was prepared to use the gun. He said he was on crack cocaine and eventually the taxi driver left and contacted the police. Armed police attended and after $^1/_2$ hour he was arrested. In the attic the police found a replica Beretta handgun and four rounds of replica ammunition. It was made of metal and plastic. He was 33 and his criminal record contained nothing of significant gravity. He was sentenced to 100 hours' community service, costs and compensation. Held. Anything less than **2 years** was inappropriate. **12 months** substituted because it was a reference and because he had performed 68 hours of the community service and had paid the £250 costs.

R v Crawford 2001 1 Cr App R (S) 119. The defendant pleaded guilty to four counts of possession of a firearm with intent to cause a person to fear unlawful violence, possession of a bladed weapon and common assault. The defendant was refused a drink at a public house because he was drunk. He swore and abused another customer. The relief manager of the public house told him to leave and the defendant headbutted him. He was ejected and the defendant was abusive and said he was going to shoot him. He pulled an imitation handgun from his pocket and the manager trapped the firearm in the doors of the public house. A customer said it was a toy and the defendant said 'I'm having you,' and ran off. About $2^1/_2$ hours later he went into a club and was refused a drink. He started to leave and was followed out. The defendant pulled out an imitation handgun and pointed it at the member of staff. He was told to behave himself. The defendant went home and got a kitchen knife and returned. The same member of staff saw him outside and saw him throw a glass into a builder's yard. He called the defendant a twat. The defendant took out the knife and there was a struggle. The defendant was headbutted and forced to drop the knife. A handgun fell to the ground and the defendant staggered off. He was arrested and released on bail. He failed to surrender to it.

About 6 months later he was drinking at a public house with two women and a man and telephoned his wife when he was emotional. Afterwards he became angry and pulled out a pistol and said he was going to kill someone and himself. The man said 'Don't be stupid, you couldn't hurt a fly with that.' The defendant fired the gun at the wall and the woman he was with was terrified. He said he was going to shoot himself and put the barrel into his mouth. It was then realised the gun was for firing blanks. The defendant then fell asleep. The two men went to another public house and were so drunk that they practically fell over. The defendant asked a customer to change a £1 coin and he refused. The defendant removed an imitation gun and made a cocking motion. The customer was in fear of his life. They were ejected from the public house. The defendant was 43 with 16 mainly motoring convictions. **3 years** in total not 5.

R v Mernin 2001 2 Cr App R (S) 24. The defendant made an early plea to possession of a firearm with intent to cause fear of violence. Shortly after midnight the defendant entered a shop of a petrol station with camouflage netting over his head. He asked to go to the kitchen area for water and this request was refused. He appeared unsteady on his feet and his speech was slurred. He was given a drink of water. He then asked the assistant what he would do if he pointed a gun at him and asked for the money in the till. The assistant was shocked but told the defendant he would not get any money and he would call the police. The defendant asked another customer for a cigarette and the panic button was pressed. The defendant made to leave and asked the assistant about another member of staff and told him to mention Mr Mernin, which was the defendant's name. He also said he had been released from prison that day. About 30–40 feet away he took a gun from his waistband and pointed it at the assistant and put his finger on the trigger. Three or four seconds later he put it back in his waistband, laughed and left the shop. The assistant was terrified and believed the firearm to be real and that the defendant was about to shoot him. Police arrested him nearby and he said 'I've got HIV and Hepatitis C. I hope you lot get it.' Police found a blank cartridge firing imitation firearm resembling a Colt Magnum which was very realistic. The defendant was 29 and was a heroin addict. He had convictions but none that had attracted custody. He expressed remorse and had Hepatitis C and had been thought to be HIV positive. Held. **3 years** was a severe sentence for a man in the defendant's condition but it was not excessive.

R v Poggiani 2001 2 Cr App R (S) 305. The defendant was convicted of possession of a firearm with intent to cause fear of violence. (If this is the toy pistol isn't it an imitation firearm?) He had pleaded guilty to possession of ammunition at the Magistrates' Court. About 10 months before the offence the victim, a neighbour of the defendant, had run out of his own house carrying a cap gun and had shouted at children who were playing with a ball near his car. He fired the gun twice. As a result the defendant's nephew had nightmares. This caused a dispute between the two. Six days before the neighbour was due to be sentenced, the defendant shouted abuse at him to provoke him into violence and it was not successful. The defendant left and returned with a toy pistol, which he pointed at the neighbour. He twice pretended to fire it and the neighbour's wife heard it click twice. He put the gun against the head of the neighbour's 6-year-old son and said 'Bang, bang, you're dead.' The child ran into his house crying. The defendant surrendered to the police and they found three large bullets, twenty one smaller bullets and ten bullet heads in a hole in his kitchen wall. They had been both charged with similar offences and the neighbour was ordered to perform 150 hours' community service. The defendant was 30 and had convictions including two for threatening behaviour etc with intent to cause fear. **6 months** not 12.

Att-Gen's Ref. No 71 of 2001 2002 2 Cr App R (S) 79. The defendant pleaded guilty at the first opportunity to possession of an imitation firearm with intent to cause fear of violence. The defendant was driven to a job interview by a friend and produced a starting pistol. He fired two shots out of the window saying he was having fun and reloaded it. The friend protested but the defendant shouted at someone in the street and fired the pistol at him. The friend dropped him off and contacted the police. After the interview the defendant called his partner on his mobile and his behaviour was sufficiently odd for a man in a group of three to say something to the defendant. The defendant said he had nothing to do with the three and they should get on with their work. One said it was just funny to watch him. The defendant said, 'Just wait a minute, I'll fucking show you' and he produced, loaded and cocked the pistol. One tried to take cover and another was too frightened to move. The defendant discharged the pistol towards the ground. One of the three thought the pistol was aimed at one of his friends. The defendant went to a café apparently unconcerned and was arrested. The pistol was found to be loaded with three blanks. He said the pistol just happened to be in his pocket and he used it to scare pigeons. Once he had an established relationship and a steady job. He started drinking which led to a drink/drive conviction and that led to the loss of his job and then the break up of his relationship. He was 36 with no convictions of 'particular relevance'. He had a serious altercation with his partner and when the police attended he threatened them with a pickaxe handle. He received 4 months. He was sentenced to 100 hours' CSO and had performed the 'greater part of it'. He refused to see a psychiatrist. Held. The gravity for this offence can vary enormously and in certain extreme circumstances a non-custodial might be appropriate. Less than **2 years** here was not appropriate. More than 2 would not necessarily be inappropriate. Taking into account it was a reference and the hours performed **1 year** instead.

Att-Gen's Ref. No 36 of 2001 2002 1 Cr App R (S) 241. The defendant pleaded guilty to possessing an imitation firearm with intent to cause fear of violence. He was a licensee and he and his friend were drinking heavily at another pub. An argument broke out with another group that had also been drinking heavily. The quarrel spilled out into the car park and his friend was knocked out. They defendant ran back to his pub which was in the same road and retrieved an 8mm replica self-loading pistol capable of firing blanks. He ran back with it and chased two from the other group waving his gun. One tried to get in a taxi and the defendant got in still brandishing the gun and demanded to know who had hit his friend. The name was revealed and the defendant threw the man out of the cab and he ended up sleeping on the ground. Four weeks later he was still off work on antidepressants. The defendant was arrested and the pistol was found under his bed. He claimed it was for his own protection. He was 40 and had three irrelevant dishonesty convictions when young. He had disposed of his share of the pub in which he had sunk his savings because of this case and had started a small grocery shop with his wife. They had both since become depressed. The pre-sentence report said he was industrious and law abiding. Held. An appropriate sentence would be **2 years**. Because of the sale of the pub and his character etc **18 months** would be justified. As it was a reference **9 months** not a £500 fine.

Att-Gen's Ref. No 75 of 2001 2002 2 Cr App R (S) 455. The defendant pleaded guilty at the first opportunity to possession of an imitation firearm with intent to cause fear of violence. The defendant, a French lorry driver, drove his lorry and trailer on the M25 at about 60 mph in the centre lane very close to a car. The two drivers both pulled into the fast lane and the defendant had to swerve back into the centre lane. The driver of the car made an offensive gesture with his finger at the defendant. The defendant responded by putting his arm out of the cab pointing a large pistol at the driver of the car for a few seconds. Other motorists were terrified and the police were contacted. An armed response was called and the defendant was questioned. A Desert Eagle pistol with an empty magazine was found, but no ammunition. It was designed to fire ball bearing but classified as an imitation firearm. In interview the defendant claimed the other driver had flashed his lights to allow him to go on. He said he carried the pistol to cause fear but for his own defence. He was 23 and only had a driving conviction. Held. The wielding of a firearm, by a driver of an HGV vehicle, travelling at considerable speed on a motorway and deliberately threatening a driver is a serious example of the use of a firearm albeit an imitation for the purposes of causing fear. The consequences of such activity are not difficult to imagine in terms of evasive driving by others immediately or indirectly threatened. For a foreign national for whom prison would be more difficult to bear we would expect **12–15 months**. Taking into account it was a reference and he had paid the fine of £250, **8 months** instead.

Att-Gen's Ref. (No 42 of 2002) 2003 1 Cr App R (S) 93. The defendant pleaded guilty at the earliest opportunity to possessing an imitation firearm with intent to cause fear of violence. The defendant had gone to a public house where he slapped a young woman in the face. A doorman intervened and saw the defendant pull what appeared to be a handgun from the waistband of his trousers, which he cocked and fired into the air. The defendant then left the public house and was followed by the doorman. He turned and pointed the gun at the doorman and discharged it from a distance of about 12 feet. Unbeknown to the doorman, the gun was in fact a starting pistol. In interview he admitted the offence, explaining that he had been drinking and had taken cocaine. To use his own words he was, "just in a state". He had previous convictions for wounding with intent and for violent disorder. He expressed remorse and regret to the probation officer. The defendant's father was seriously, if not terminally, ill. He had completed 85 hours of the imposed community punishment order and all but £100 of the compensation and costs orders (totalling £650) had been paid. Held. The least sentence would have been **2 years**, but as it was a reference and the number of hours already completed, **12 months** not 200 hours Community Punishment Order.

R v Khan 2003 1 Cr App R (S) 554. The defendant pleaded guilty to possessing an imitation firearm with intent to cause fear of violence. At 11:30pm the defendant confronted the head doorman of a nightclub with a firearm. He challenged him as to why he had refused another man entry to the club. The doorman explained that the other man was a drug dealer and that he was not going to be permitted to enter the nightclub. The defendant made his way to his car and from somewhere between the front seats picked up a handgun in a holster, making sure that the doorman could see it. He reversed his car, opened the driver's door and stood up holding the weapon in his right hand across his body. At no stage did the weapon leave the holster. The defendant said to the doorman "Do you want to reconsider?" The doorman replied "No." The defendant drove off. In interview the defendant said that it was in fact a mobile phone and not a gun. However, five months later he pleaded guilty. The defendant was 30 with one previous court appearance for offences of assault and criminal damage. Held. The use of firearms, both real and imitation, is a growing menace in the area of Leeds and Bradford. Because the weapon was never removed from the holster and the event lasted for seconds only, **2 years** not 3. If it had been removed **3 years** would have been proper.

R v Brown 2004 1 Cr App R 192. The defendant was convicted of a section 16A offence. At about 9.50pm, he approached two 16 year old boys, B and C who were sitting on some grass drinking. He had a slight acquaintance with them and asked for a drink. B refused and was sarcastic. The defendant produced a ball-bearing gun capable, if it was in working order, of firing plastic pellets. It wasn't in working order. He pointed the gun at B's face and threatened to blow his jaw off. B wasn't scared as he recognised it as a ball-bearing gun. After 5 seconds he pointed the gun at C's chest. At first C had thought it was a real gun but he soon realised what the gun was. A police car drove by and the defendant made off. Two days later police found the gun at his home. The defendant was 18 and had 9 court appearances for common assault, criminal damage, TDA, battery, ABH, driving offences and for breaches of court orders. He had received sentences of 4 months (twice) and 6 months detention and training. He was now in breach of a supervision order. Reports said he had a pattern relating to assaults on former girlfriends, he had difficulty in controlling his temper, there was alcohol abuse and that he lacked maturity. The defendant had suffered from violence from an early age. Held. It is far too common for youths to walk around with guns as accessories or because it make them feel better. **3 years detention** was severe and at the top end but not manifestly excessive.

R v Owen 2004 2 Cr App R (S) 514. The defendant pleaded guilty to possessing an imitation firearm with intent to cause fear of violence. He was with a group of youths in Liverpool and when a police car passed by he made a pistol gesture at it. The police got out and approached the group. The defendant ran off and was chased by a police officer into an alleyway. There he turned and pointed a gun at the officer. The defendant then ran off, throwing the gun over a wall. It was a ball bearing gun, and therefore an imitation firearm. The officer thought it was a real gun and that he was about to be shot. The defendant, 28, had a large number of previous convictions including two for ABH on a police officer. He had convictions for dishonesty, but nothing for firearm offences. A pre-sentence report said that he perceived himself as a victim of discrimination and undue attention from the police. Held. This involved a direct threat with an apparently real weapon to police officers doing their duty at night chasing an offender. In Liverpool guns are a serious problem. A message must be sent. Although **5 years** was severe it was not manifestly excessive.

Firearms Act 1968, s 16A – Shotguns

74.24 *R v Hewitt* 1999 1 Cr App R (S) 256. The defendant was convicted of possessing a firearm with the intent to cause fear, possession of a firearm when prohibited and possession of ammunition when prohibited. He visited his estranged wife's house and produced a sawn off shotgun which had been strapped to his leg and two cartridges. His wife asked him what the gun was for and he replied, 'Where's Sean?' No threats were uttered. She asked again and he ran away. The police searched his home and found six cartridges but no firearm. He was sentenced on the basis he did not intend his wife any harm but that he wanted her to believe that serious harm was intended to Sean his cousin. He was then 34 and had convictions but none since 1990. Held. The total should have been **3 years** not 4.

R v Corry 2000 1 Cr App R (S) 47. The defendant pleaded guilty on the day his case was listed for trial to possession of a firearm with intent to cause fear of violence. The victim who knew the defendant heard someone outside his home and opened his front door. He saw the defendant about 2 feet from the door and being fearful he started to close the door. The victim was able to see the defendant produce a shotgun, which appeared shortened from behind his back. It was pointed at his head. He shut the door and heard someone say to the defendant, 'Why don't you do something about it?' The victim ran upstairs and the shotgun was discharged at the door. The pellets made a hole in the bottom of the door and hit the hall floor where the victim had been standing. The victim called the police. The defendant was arrested and denied the offence. He was then 23 and had five court appearances including two separate non dwelling house burglaries. There were no offences of violence. His basis of plea was that he had not fired the weapon and his intention was limited to threatening the victim with it. Held. This was gangsterism. The starting point is 6 years and he was entitled to only half of the usual discount. Therefore **5 years** not 7.

R v Wright 2000 1 Cr App R (S) 109. The defendant pleaded guilty to shortening the barrels of a shotgun, possessing a shortened shotgun with intent to cause a person to fear violence and possession of 138 grams of amphetamine. Police executed a search warrant at the defendant's farm and found a van which contained six shotgun cartridges, amphetamine worth at street value nearly £2,000, scales and a 12 bore shortened shotgun loaded with two live 12 bore cartridges. The stock of the gun had been broken off and the trigger guard was missing. The fore-end was held on by tape. The defendant claimed that his daughter had been attacked and he and his family had been threatened. He said intruders had put a gun to his throat and two weeks before he had been assaulted by a group of people who had broken his leg. He was treated at hospital where he gave a false name. He said he had stolen the firearm from a house and shortened it. He had used it in self-defence when he had discharged the gun over the heads of people who had arrived with lumps of wood and a hockey stick. He had not reported the attacks to the police. He was sentenced to 30 months for each of the firearm matters and 6 months for the drugs all concurrent. Held. It was important to remember the triggers were not protected, the condition of the gun was very poor, it was a classic weapon for serious crime, because of its aim and accuracy no one would use it for self-defence and it was loaded. The court needs to turn to only one authority, *R v Avis* 1998 2 Cr App R (S) 178. People cannot take the law into their own hands. It cannot possibly be said that **30 months** was manifestly excessive.

R v Porter 2001 1 Cr App R (S) 241. The defendant pleaded guilty to possessing a shotgun with intent to cause a person to fear violence and making threats to kill. A 21-month old girl was woken up in the evening by a car alarm on a housing estate. The car belonged to the defendant and the girl's father shouted out of his window for the alarm to be turned off. The woman next to the car said it wasn't her car and the father spoke to her again and she became abusive. About 10 minutes later the defendant knocked on the father's door and said he heard he wanted a word with him. The father who was carrying his daughter opened the door and explained it was about the car alarm. The defendant said he was talking to the wrong person and he was out of his league. He then pointed a sawn off shotgun at him and told him he wanted a word and he should leave the flat. He placed both his hands on the gun and the father heard two clicks. The gun was still aimed at the father and he was told he would be shot. There was a further verbal altercation and the father managed to close his door. The defendant was arrested and his father was later pursued by police in his car and the shotgun was thrown out of the car window. It hit the road and went off. A cartridge was in one barrel and there were seventeen cartridges, which fitted the shotgun in a plastic bag. The defendant had a bad record, which included violence. The defendant said in a note for the judge that at the time the shotgun was unloaded. There was no Newton hearing and he was sentenced on the basis the gun was loaded. Held. **4 years** not 5 because of earlier decisions of the court and the defendant might have had a legitimate grievance about the sentencing comments.

Firearms Act 1968 s 17(1)

74.25   Making use of a firearm with intent to resist arrest.

Indictable only. Maximum sentence Life imprisonment.

Automatic life Section 17(1) is a specified offence for automatic life[38] for offences committed before 4/4/05.

Dangerous Offender provisions For offences committed on or after 4/4/05 where there is a significant risk to members of the public of serious harm etc. there is a mandatory duty to pass a life sentence when it is justified and otherwise a sentence of imprisonment for public protection[39]. For offenders under 18 the duty is to pass detention for life, detention for public protection or an extended sentence[40].

R v Avis 1998 2 Cr App R (S) 178. LCJ. Where there are breaches of s 17(1) of the Firearms Act 1968 the custodial term is likely to be of considerable length, and where the four questions suggested above (see *Guideline case*) yield answers adverse to the offender, terms at or approaching the maximum may in a contested case be appropriate.

Att-Gen's Ref. No 120 of 2001 Unreported 23/1/02. If there had been a trial **8 years' detention** would have been appropriate. With the plea and other mitigation 5 years would be appropriate. As it was a reference **4 years**.

R v Duffy 2005 1 Cr App R (S) 373. The defendant pleaded guilty to having a firearm or imitation firearm with intent to resist arrest, possessing an imitation firearm with intent to cause fear of violence, and making a threat to kill. The defendant was causing a disturbance and when police were called they discovered that he was wanted on a warrant. The defendant called to police out of an upstairs window, produced a black handgun, pointed it a police officer and said 'I am going to shoot you'. The officer feared for his safety and told the defendant to put the gun down. He didn't. He pointed the gun at three other officers and threatened to shoot them. The officers took the defendant's girlfriend away and the defendant shouted and pointed a gun at the arresting officer: 'Let her go or I will shoot her'. Armed officers were called. They believed the gun was a replica. The defendant put his gun down when officers released his girlfriend. He then produced a petrol can and threatened to burn the house down and showed another weapon which the police believed correctly to be a plastic toy. The other weapon was an ornamental flintlock musket. There was a siege which resulted in the area being cordoned off which lasted from 3.00am to 11.30am. The judge said the offence was very frightening for the officers and it was aggravated by the defendant being wanted on warrant at the time. The defendant, 21, had a bad record for violent behaviour including affray, assault and ABH. Held. The judge was right to pass a severe sentence in this case. **5 years** for the possession with intent to resist arrest, 3 years for

38 Powers of Criminal Courts (Sentencing) Act 2000 s 109(5)
39 Criminal Justice Act 2003 s 225
40 Criminal Justice Act 2003 s 226 and 228

the possession with intent to cause fear of violence, and 3 years for making a threat to kill, all concurrent to each other, were entirely appropriate.

Firearms Act 1968 s 17(2)

74.26   Being arrested for a Schedule 1 offence and being in possession of a firearm. Indictable only. Maximum sentence Life.

Automatic life Both sub-sections 17(1) and 17(2) are specified offences for automatic life[41] where the offence was committed before 4/4/05.

Dangerous Offender provisions For offences committed on or after 4/4/05 where there is a significant risk to members of the public of serious harm etc. there is a mandatory duty to pass a life sentence when it is justified and otherwise a sentence of imprisonment for public protection[42]. For offenders under 18 the duty is to pass detention for life, detention for public protection or an extended sentence[43].

Firearms Act 1968, s 17(2) – Cases

74.27   *R v Avis* 1998 2 Cr App R (S) 178. LCJ. Where there are breaches of s 17(2) of the Firearms Act 1968 the custodial term is likely to be of considerable length, and where the four questions suggested above (see **Guideline case**) yield answers adverse to the offender, terms at or approaching the maximum may in a contested case be appropriate

R v Tudor 1999 1 Cr App R (S) 397. Tudor pleaded guilty to wounding and possession of a firearm whilst committing a Sch 1 offence. Three poachers armed with air rifles entered his land to shoot rabbits. Because of the problems he had had in the past with poachers and threats the defendant and his son were carrying guns. They saw the men and told them to give up their guns. The men appeared to comply with the request and then ran off. The defendant shouted at them to stop but they continued to run so he fired his gun aiming about 10 feet away from them when 30–40 feet away from them. One of the men was hit in the arm, nose and head. He fired again without incident. The plea was on the basis of recklessness. The defendant was 51 and of good character. The neighbourhood held him in high regard. Held. The wound to the nose was very close to the eyes. It must be made clear that people, even if they have a licence, who in anger use a shotgun recklessly are almost invariably going to receive a custodial sentence. 18 months was too long so **3 months** substituted. (The court did not refer to *R v Avis* 1998.)

R v Thomas 2000 2 Cr App R (S) 155. The defendant pleaded guilty to possessing a firearm when committing a Sch 1 offence and theft. The defendant went to a 'peep' show and asked for change. He left and returned and seized a cash bag containing £122 from the cashier. He was chased through the streets. A police officer caught him and an imitation handgun was found on him. It wasn't used but was of convincing appearance. He said he just liked carrying it. The defendant was 17 and had findings of guilt for failure to surrender to bail, criminal damage and possession of a bladed article. Held. The law on imitation firearms exists to prevent anyone minded to commit a criminal offence from carrying firearms or imitation firearm. If someone carries an imitation firearm when committing an offence, does not produce it and has some entirely credible or innocent reason for its possession the court might be persuaded to unusual leniency. Otherwise it calls for a substantial custodial sentence. Taking into account the defendant's youth and his plea 15 months cannot be described as excessive. **15 months and 3 months consecutive** YOI was not wrong.

---

41 Powers of Criminal Courts (Sentencing) Act 2000 s 109(5) and *R v Buckland 2000 2 Cr App R (S) 217*
42 Criminal Justice Act 2003 s 225
43 Criminal Justice Act 2003 s 226 and 228

Firearms Act 1968 s 18(1)

74.28   Having a firearm or imitation firearm with intent to commit an indictable offence.

Indictable only. Maximum sentence Life.

Automatic life Section 18(1) is a specified offence for automatic life[44] where the offence was committed before 4/4/05.

Dangerous Offender provisions For offences committed on or after 4/4/05 where there is a significant risk to members of the public of serious harm etc. there is a mandatory duty to pass a life sentence when it is justified and otherwise a sentence of imprisonment for public protection[45]. For offenders under 18 the duty is to pass detention for life, detention for public protection or an extended sentence[46].

R v Avis 1998 2 Cr App R (S) 178. LCJ. Where there are breaches of s 18(1) of the Firearms Act 1968 the custodial term is likely to be of considerable length, and where the four questions suggested above (see *Guideline case*) yield answers adverse to the offender, terms at or approaching the maximum may in a contested case be appropriate

R v Avis 1998 Re Marquez 2 Cr App R (S) 178 at 190. LCJ. The defendant was convicted of having a firearm with intent to commit an affray, having an imitation firearm with intent to commit an affray and possession of a firearm. Police tried and failed to stop a car in which he was travelling with two other youths. There was a car chase. The defendant was seen to tumble from the passenger side and a police officer saw him throw an object from his jacket before running off. He was arrested and was returned to the point where he had emerged from the car. A self-loading automatic Colt pistol was recovered. A police car had followed the car until it collided with a wall. A search of the car revealed a black woollen hat with eye holes cut in it and an imitation gun. The Colt pistol was in full working order although no ammunition was found. The imitation firearm was a good copy of a Baretta self-loading pistol. The Crown were unable to say for what purpose the gun and the imitation gun were being carried but contended that they must have been intended for an unlawful display of force that would inevitably cause considerable fear. The defendant was 19 and of good character. His girlfriend had given birth to a child and following her admission to hospital after a nervous breakdown the defendant had had to shoulder a major part of the responsibility for care of the child. He was sentenced to **42 months** for having the firearm with intent and other concurrent sentences. Held. The aggravating features present in this case were that a real firearm was involved and that all the circumstances, including the adapted hat with the eye holes cut in it, suggest that whatever the precise objective was, it was something that involved a degree of preparation. Even allowing for the good character and age the sentence passed was not in any way manifestly excessive.

Att-Gen's Ref. No 26 of 2001 2002 1 Cr App R (S) 3. LCJ. The defendant was convicted of possession a firearm with intent to commit an indictable offence, two counts of threats to kill and an ABH. He pleaded guilty to possessing a firearm without a certificate, possessing a prohibited weapon and selling a prohibited weapon. The defendant married and early on the marriage deteriorated. After 'unhappy incidents' his wife obtained a non-molestation order. He went abroad but kept in touch. He returned without warning and at 3am he broke into the former family home where his wife, her sister and her mother were sleeping. He went into the sister's room and she woke up and began screaming. He grabbed hold of her and put a stun gun to her neck. Initially she thought it was an ordinary gun. Then he dragged her into his wife's bedroom. He had a leather holster, cable ties and handcuffs and said, "I have come back to end it all

---

44 Powers of Criminal Courts (Sentencing) Act 2000 s 109(5)
45 Criminal Justice Act 2003 s 225
46 Criminal Justice Act 2003 s 226 and 228

and I'm taking you and your mother with me. I'm going to kill you and your mother." He said he had no reason to live and asked to hold his baby and he treated her affectionately. The sister began to hyperventilate and a doctor was called. The ambulance arrived and he took the gun from the holster saying it was real. He removed and replaced the magazine so everyone knew it was loaded. At some stage he tried to handcuff the sister and the mother but he was easily dissuaded. The police arrived and he allowed the older three to go to hospital leaving the baby with the defendant. An eighteen hour siege followed and there was no harm to the baby. A large number of officers were involved. He threatened to kill himself. Eventually the defendant was distracted and he was seized. A self-loading pistol and stun gun designed to discharge electricity were recovered. The sister had bruising to the neck. The effect on the 3 victims was very substantial. He was 57, had no convictions and was depressed about the marriage. Held. The breach of the court order was very important indeed. The attack was premeditated and carefully planned. Women are very vulnerable to men who decide to behave in this way. 5 years would have been the very lowest sentence appropriate. As it was a reference **4 years** not $2^1/_2$.

Firearms Act 1968 s 19 — *See Violent Crime Reduction Act 2006 s 41.* 7 yrs or 12 mth.

74.29   Having in a public place a loaded shotgun, an air weapon or a firearm whether loaded or not or an imitation firearm[47].

Triable either way unless an air weapon when it is a summary only offence.

On indictment maximum 7 years. Summary maximum 6 months and/or £5,000.

R v Avis 1998 2 Cr App R (S) 178. LCJ. Where there are breaches of s 19 of the Firearms Act 1968 the custodial term is likely to be of considerable length, and where the four questions suggested above (see ***Guideline case***) yield answers adverse to the offender, terms at or approaching the maximum may in a contested case be appropriate

R v Fatinikun 1999 1 Cr App R (S) 412. The defendant pleaded to two counts of having a loaded firearm in a public place, possessing ammunition and possessing a firearm when prohibited at the Magistrates' Court. He was committed for sentence. The defendant tried to get into a nightclub and the doorman felt what he thought was a gun and refused him access unless he could be more fully searched. The police were called about an unconnected incident and approached the defendant who ran off. They chased and caught him. He was searched and the police found cannabis and two bullets. His car was searched and a Derringer pistol with a sawn-off barrel loaded with two bullets of the same type as on the defendant was found. Also found was a revolver type pistol loaded with two bullets. The defendant was then almost 18 and had convictions for carrying a firearm with intent to commit an indictable offence and burglary. The risk of re-offending was assessed as high. The sentencing judge sentenced him on the basis the doorman had felt his telephone. The defendant was in breach of his licence for the burglary conviction and was ordered to serve an extra 4 months. Held. Because the maximum was 7 years the discount for the plea was inadequate. **4 years** substituted for 6 years with the 4 months remaining consecutive.

R v Morris 1999 2 Cr App R (S) 146. The defendant pleaded guilty to possession of a firearm and ammunition in a public place, possession of a converted firearm and handling stolen goods. The defendant and the co-accused went to a wood to bury a shotgun and ammunition. The police intervened and the items were found. At the defendant's home was found a de-activated assault rifle and an AK Rifle under the floorboards. Both weapons had been stolen from a friend of his in a burglary a month before. After that the shotgun had been shortened and was for the co-defendant's use

---

47 This wider offence was inserted by Anti-Social Behaviour Act 2003 s 37. In force for offences from 20/1/04, Anti-Social Behaviour Act 2003 (Commencement No 1 and Transitional provisions) Order 2003.

who said he had a buyer for it. He was of good character and had known the co-accused who received 10 years since school. Held. He was weak person who was manoeuvred by a professional criminal to get himself out of his dilemma. Without those features 3$^1/_2$ years could not be criticised. With them **18 months** instead.

R v Holmes 1999 2 Cr App R (S) 383. The defendant pleaded guilty to possession of a firearm whilst a prohibited person, possession of a shortened shotgun, and possession of a loaded shotgun in a public place. A householder went to look at a car and saw a sawn off shotgun in the passenger footwell through a partially open window. The police were called and found the shotgun, which was loaded with two cartridges. The police traced the defendant, aged 42 as the hirer of the vehicle and arrested him. He admitted the gun belonged to him and said he had bought it with the intention of committing suicide. He said he took some pills and ended up in hospital. In 1990 he was sentenced to 4 years for the possession of drugs with intent to supply. He had heart and artery problems, which he tended to exaggerate. The psychiatrist said the possession of the shotgun for a possible suicide fitted in with his presentation and his behaviour at the time. The prison report says he always uses his medical and psychological problems to get what he wants. Held. Leaving the firearm there was extreme irresponsibility and recklessness. We are quite unmoved by the submission that his intention to commit suicide means he is less culpable. There was nothing wrong with **2$^1/_2$ years** on each concurrent.

Firearms Act 1968 s 21(4)

74.30   Possession of a firearm when prohibited (when convicted of an offence and sentenced to certain terms of imprisonment).

Triable either way. Maximum sentence 5 years. Summary maximum 6 months and/or £5,000.

R v Avis 1998 2 Cr App R (S) 178. LCJ Where there are breaches of s 21 of the Firearms Act 1968 the custodial term is likely to be of considerable length, and where the four questions suggested above (see *Guideline case*) yield answers adverse to the offender, terms at or approaching the maximum may in a contested case be appropriate

R v Hill 1999 2 Cr App R (S) 388. The defendant was convicted of possessing a firearm when prohibited, possession of a firearm, possession of a shotgun and possession of ammunition. Police officers conducted a search of the defendant's home and found a double-barrelled 12 bore shotgun, a .22 rifle without a bolt, forty four .22 cartridges and thirty two .22 rifle cartridges. The defendant said the shotgun and rifle had been left at his home for safe keeping by a third party when he was in prison. The defendant had a long list of convictions all of them for dishonesty, except one in 1975 which was causing injury with an air pistol. Held. Although the maximum is the same for s 21(4) and possession of a firearm, *R v Avis* 1998 2 Cr App R (S) 178 makes it clear it is more serious. There was nothing to suggest that he intended to use either of the firearms. **18 months** not 2$^1/_2$ years for the prohibited count with the other sentences remaining concurrent.

R v Holmes 1999 2 Cr App R (S) 383. The defendant pleaded guilty to possession of a firearm whilst a prohibited person, possession of a shortened shotgun, and possession of a loaded shotgun in a public place. A householder went to look at a car and saw a sawn off shotgun in the passenger footwell through a partially open window. The police were called and found the shotgun, which was loaded with two cartridges. The police traced the defendant, aged 42 as the hirer of the vehicle and arrested him. He admitted the gun belonged to him and said he had bought it with the intention of committing suicide. He said he took some pills and ended up in hospital. In 1990 he was sentenced to 4 years for the possession of drugs with intent to supply. He had heart and artery problems, which he tended to exaggerate. The psychiatrist said the possession of the shotgun for a possible suicide fitted in with his presentation and his behaviour at the time. The prison report says he always uses his medical and psychological problems to get what he wants. Held. Leaving the firearm there was extreme irresponsibility and recklessness. We are quite unmoved by the submission that his intention to commit suicide means he is less culpable. There was nothing wrong with **2¹/₂ years** on each concurrent.

R v Brizzi 2000 1 Cr App R (S) 126. The defendant was convicted of possessing a firearm when prohibited. Police officers observed the defendant riding a mountain bike next to another man who was walking beside him. As the officers approached he accelerated away and rode up a curb. He dropped the bike went up a small alleyway and put his hand in a privet hedge. He then walked towards the police who found a. 25 Beretta semi automatic pistol at the spot in the hedge where he had put his hand. The gun was found to misfire repeatedly. After cleaning it was found to function normally. It was a prohibited weapon but was not linked to any recorded offending. The defendant was 30 and had a conviction for supplying drugs for which he received 5¹/₂ years. He had 22 court appearances but no firearm convictions. Held. As maximum sentence is 5 years, the gun could not be fired properly, there was no evidence it had been used, it was not loaded, the magazine had been removed and there was no ammunition **2¹/₂ years** not 4.

R v Hair 2000 1 Cr App R (S) 118. The defendant pleaded guilty to two counts of possession of a firearm and possession of ammunition. The defendant's house was searched and police found a Smith and Wesson revolver with a shortened barrel and 104 rounds of live ammunition. She said her stepson asked her to store them for him, when they lived in Sunderland and she took them with her when she moved to Blackburn. There was no lawful purpose for the revolver. The ammunition fitted the weapon. The defendant was 38 with no convictions. Held. The weapon was intended for using in crime. Just like drug offences persons of good character who do not appear to be criminally minded are used by others to lodge weapons. This offence is extremely serious. **2 years** was not manifestly excessive.

R v Corrish 2001 1 Cr App R (S) 436. The defendant pleaded guilty to possessing a firearm when a prohibited person. A woman saw the defendant and another out of her window approach her door. One of them was carrying what appeared to be a shotgun. It was in fact a. 22 air rifle. The barrel was wrapped in a bin bag. They knocked on her door and she asked what they wanted. They asked her to open the door and she was terrified. She didn't open the door and they shouted and swore at her. They then hammered on the door. She and her aunt who was with her ran and hid in a coal shed. The defendant was arrested. He was 30 and had a large number of convictions including several for violence and public order offences. In the last four years he had received custodial sentences for threats to kill, affray, possession of an offensive weapon, criminal damage, GBH, and robbery. There were no convictions for firearms. He was also sentenced to 254 days consecutive to the firearm sentence because he was in breach of his licence after his release from a robbery sentence. Held. Because the maximum is 5 years **18 months** was substituted for 2¹/₂ years. There was no reason to alter the consecutive sentence for the breach.

R v Allen 2001 2 Cr App R (S) 359. The defendant made a plea not at the first opportunity to possession of a prohibited firearm. He had earlier pleaded guilty to possession of ammunition. Police visited the defendant's home to arrest him for an unrelated matter. They said they were going to search his home address and he told them he had a small. 25 automatic pistol. He showed them where it was. It was a 6.35 mm Titan self-loading pistol with a missing pin. A cartridge which fitted the pistol was also found. He said he had acquired it in America and had not fired it since 1974. At that time he was a serving member of the USAF in Germany. It was his property but he was then permitted to possess it. He brought the gun to England in 1979 and intended to move to Jamaica. When his partner died he changed his mind. He kept it as a souvenir. He told the immigration service about it who told him to register it or remove the pin. He was 51 and had no relevant convictions. He had references and it was estimated there was a very low risk of him re-offending. Held. **6 months** not 12 months with the 3 months for the ammunition remaining concurrent.

See also *R v M* 2001 Unreported 11/10/01. **2$^{1}/_{2}$ years** not 3$^{1}/_{2}$.

Imitation firearms – Guideline remarks

74.31 *R v Avis* 1998 1 Cr App R 420. LCJ. Where imitation firearms are involved, the risk to life and limb is absent, but such weapons can be and often are used to frighten and intimidate victims in order to reinforce unlawful demands. Such imitation weapons are often very hard to distinguish from the real thing – for practical purposes, impossible in the circumstances in which they are used – and the victim is usually as much frightened and intimidated as if a genuine firearm had been used. Such victims are often isolated and vulnerable.

Imitation firearms – Automatic life

74.32 *R v Buckland* 2000 2 Cr App R (S) 217. LCJ. Possession of an imitation firearm under Firearms Act 1968, s 16, 17 and 18 is a "serious offence" for the purposes of the Crime (Sentences) Act 1997, s 2 (now the Powers of Criminal Courts (Sentencing) Act 2000 s 109) (automatic life).

Imitation firearms – Cases

74.33 *R v Thomas* 2000 2 Cr App R (S) 155. The defendant pleaded guilty to possessing a firearm when committing a Sch 1 offence and theft. The defendant went to a "peep" show and asked for change. He left and returned and seized a cash bag containing £122 from the cashier. He was chased through the streets. A police officer caught him and an imitation handgun was found on him. It wasn't used but was of convincing appearance. He said he just liked carrying it. The defendant was 17 and had findings of guilt for failure to surrender to bail, criminal damage and possession of a bladed article. Held. The law on imitation firearms exists to prevent anyone minded to commit a criminal offence from carrying firearms or imitation firearm. If someone carries an imitation firearm when committing an offence does not produce it and has some entirely credible or innocent reason for its possession the court might be persuaded to unusual leniency. Otherwise it calls for a substantial custodial sentence. Taking into account the defendant's youth and his plea 15 months cannot be described as excessive. **15 months and 3 months consecutive** YOI was not wrong.

Importation/exportation of firearms

74.34 Customs and Excise Management Act 1979 s 50, 68, 170(1) and (2)

Triable either way. On indictment maximum sentence 7 years. For offences committed in Great Britain for a prohibited weapon or ammunition restricted Firearms Act 1968 S 5(1)(a), (ab), (aba), (ac), (ad), (ae), (af), (c), and (1A)(a) committed on or after 22/1/04 offences the maximum sentence is 10 years[48]. Summary maximum 6 months and/or £5,000 or three times the value of the goods which ever is greater.

Confiscation For all s 68(2) and 170 offences[49] committed on or after 24 March 2003[50] which concern firearms or ammunition the court must follow the Proceeds of Crime Act 2002 procedure.

---

48 Customs and Excise Management Act s 50(5A) 68(4A) and 170(4A) inserted by Criminal Justice Act 2003 s 293
49 Proceeds of Crime Act 2002 s 6 and s 75 and Sch 2 para 5
50 Proceeds of Crime Act 2002 (Commencement No 5, Transitional Provisions, Savings and Amendment) Order 2003

R v Gal 2001 1 Cr App R (S) 221. The defendant pleaded guilty to importing two handguns and ammunition. The defendant's car was searched at Dover docks. Customs found inside his luggage in the boot two semi-automatic pistols and 225 rounds of ammunition. About 200 of the rounds fitted one or other of the handguns. He was a foreign national and had no convictions. He was sentenced on the basis he was not a tourist but was here to deliver the guns and ammunition to someone involved in a criminal enterprise. His account was rejected. Held. The judge was right to say importing firearms was *every* bit as serious as importing drugs. It increases the arsenal of weapons in the country. **5 years** was severe but not manifestly excessive.

See also IMPORTATION/EXPORTATION OF PROHIBITED/RESTRICTED GOODS – *CS* – *Gas sprays*

Knowledge that he possessed firearms, no

74.35 *R v Campbell* 2000 1 Cr App R (S) 291. The defendant appears to have pleaded guilty to possession of a shortened shotgun and a prohibited firearm. Police officers searched his flat after a disturbance in which he threatened someone and kicked a car. For the disturbance he received 6 months in all for possession of an offensive weapon and criminal damage. In a cupboard they found a sawn off shotgun in pieces in a black bin liner. In another cupboard they found an automatic machine pistol, which was a prohibited weapon and over 900 rounds of ammunition in a suitcase. Neither was loaded but both were in working order. He was sentenced on the basis he thought the items were stolen goods and he didn't look at them. (This was no defence because of *R v Steele* 1993 Crim L R 298.) He had had them for 10 days and was to receive no payment. [The judgment does not refer to his character.] Held. 3½ years would have been appropriate if he had known but as he didn't **2 years** substituted.

Protecting your property

74.36 *R v Tudor* 1999 1 Cr App R (S) 397. Tudor pleaded to wounding and possession of a firearm whilst committing a Sch 1 offence (s 17(2)). Three poachers armed with air rifles entered his land to shoot rabbits. Because of the problems he had had in the past with poachers and threats the defendant and his son were carrying guns. They saw the men and told them to give up their guns. The men appeared to comply with the request and then ran off. The defendant shouted at them to stop but they continued to run so he fired his gun aiming about 10 feet away from them when 30–40 feet away from them. One of the men was hit in the arm, nose and head. He fired again without incident. The plea was on the basis of recklessness. The defendant was 51 and of good character. The neighbourhood held him in high regard. Held. The wound to the nose was very close to the eyes. It must be made clear that people even if they have a licence who in anger use a shotgun recklessly are almost invariably going to receive a custodial sentence. 18 months was too long so **3 months** substituted. (The court did not refer to *R v Avis* 1998.)

Robbery and

See ROBBERY – *Firearm, with* and *Defendant aged 16–17 – Firearm, with*

Self defence, firearms for

74.37 *R v Marney* 2002 1 Cr App R (S) 506. The defendant pleaded guilty to two offences of possessing a firearm with intent to endanger life, four counts of possessing ammunition, possessing a prohibited weapon and possessing a firearm. Police officers mounted a surveillance operation and watched him store items in three of his vehicles. He was arrested in one of his Landcruisers and they found a loaded Beretta pistol with a round in the breach. In his Skoda they found forty five rounds of ammunition which fitted the Beretta and a loaded .22 Ruger rifle with a round in the breach and nine rounds of ammunition in the magazine. There were 336 rounds of ammunition for the rifle and a silencer for it. In his other Landcruiser they found a silencer suitable for the Beretta. The defendant was 34 and a traveller. He had an extensive record for dishonesty and violence. In 1996 he sustained gunshot wounds to the elbow and buttocks. In 1997 he sustained gunshot wounds to the face, chest and buttocks. He nearly died. The reason for holding these guns was for self-defence after the attempt to murder him. Those incidents arose out of a feud, which had very serious criminal overtones. He broke from the normal code of those from his background and co-operated with the police and one of those he named was sent to prison. Others were arrested but proceedings against them were discontinued. The police advised him to leave the area but he refused. He installed video cameras, bullet proof windows, wore body armour and acquired the firearms. The basis of plea was that the firearms were intended to protect him and were not to be used against the public. Held. Firearm offences are always very serious; more so when committed with men with substantial criminal records. The courts recognise the need for deterrent sentences and the acute public concern at the ever-rising tide of possession of deadly weapons. The firearms were immediately available to use with deadly effect. This was a wholly exceptional case and the judge failed to reflect those exceptional circumstances. Nothing justified him in arming himself but **8 years** not 10.

Sieges, police

74.38 *R v Duffy* 2005 1 Cr App R (S) 373. The defendant pleaded guilty to having a firearm or imitation firearm with intent to resist arrest, possessing an imitation forearm with intent to cause fear of violence, and making a threat to kill. The defendant was causing a disturbance and when police were called they discovered that he was sought on a warrant. The defendant called to police out of an upstairs window, produced a black handgun, pointed it a police officer and said 'I am going to shoot you'. The officer feared for his safety and told the defendant to put the gun down. He didn't. He pointed the gun at three other officers and threatened to shoot them. The officers took the defendant's girlfriend away and the defendant shouted and pointed a gun at the arresting officer: 'Let her go or I will shoot her'. Armed officers were called. They believed the gun was a replica. The defendant put his gun down when officers released his girlfriend. He then produced a petrol can and threatened to burn the house down and showed another weapon which the police believed correctly to be a plastic toy. The other weapon was an ornamental flintlock musket. There was a siege which resulted in the area being cordoned off which lasted from 3.00am to 11.30 am. The judge said the offence was very frightening for the officers and it was aggravated by the defendant being wanted on warrant at the time. The defendant, 21, had a bad record for violent behaviour including affray, assault and ABH. Held. The judge was right to pass a severe sentence in this case. **5 years** for the possession with intent to resist arrest, 3 years for the possession with intent to cause fear of violence, and 3 years for making a threat to kill, all concurrent to each other, were entirely appropriate.

Supplying firearms to criminals

74.39 *R v Avis* 1998 Re Thomas 2 Cr App R (S) 178 at 189. LCJ. Thomas pleaded guilty to two counts of possessing a firearm with intent to endanger life, six counts of selling or transferring firearms unlawfully; and two counts of selling or transferring ammunition unlawfully. The pleas were entered at the beginning of his trial after the judge had made a ruling on the evidence. Thomas was a firearms dealer who sold three revolvers and ammunition for them to an undercover police officer for £1,160 in a car park. Thomas told the officer that he could supply firearms regularly and easily. At a further meeting at a railway station Thomas sold the officer two pump action shotguns which had been shortened. He also sold three pistols and ammunition for all five weapons. The total price was £1,220. Thomas was arrested. He was 66 and had no convictions. He had a very large number of testimonials. He had for many years been involved with charity work and was held in high esteem. He was sentenced to 9 years on each endanger count; 4 years for the selling firearms counts and 2 years for ammunition counts. They were all concurrent making a total of **9 years**. Held. The judge's starting point would have been 12 years. The use of firearms by armed robbers and drug dealers is prevalent and on the increase. A person who provides firearms in the certain knowledge that they are going to be used by criminals commits a grave offence. The judge took the mitigation fully into account and he could not sensibly have reduced the sentence further.

75 FISHING OFFENCES

75.1 Over-fishing etc

Fisheries Act 1981 s 5, 12, 17 and 30(2)

There are many different orders made under this Act which create offences including some triable either way. There are various penalties.

Cases

75.2 *R v Anglo-Spanish Fisheries Ltd* 2001 1 Cr App R (S) 252. The defendant company pleaded guilty at the Magistrates' Court to an offence under the Fisheries Act 1981 s 30(2) and the relevant EEC regulations. There were three charges of failing to record accurately the quantity of fish, one of landing a quantity of undersized fish and one of failing to keep a drawing of a fish storage room. The Spanish company owned a British registered boat, which was boarded by officers from the Sea Fisheries Inspectorate. They weighed the fish on board and compared it to the entries in the logbook. There was significant under-recording of three fish. There was no recording of Megrim a fish much sought after in Spain in the book. 1,154 kilos of the fish was found on board. To conceal the Megrim an elaborate scheme of deception had been devised. The top layer of the boxes of fish was covered by Witch, a fish for which there was no quota, and the boxes were labelled Witch. The Witch fish was over-recorded. Of the other two fish in the charges of failing to record, the fish was hidden under nets and empty boxes. The total value of the under declared fish was £12,400. In 1998 the company had four convictions dealt with at the same courts as this offence for similar charges for over-quota fishing. The company was fined £80,000 with £6,371 prosecution costs. The company was fined in total **£115,000** and ordered to **pay £3,869 prosecution costs**. It appealed the fine in this case for failing to record the amount of Megrim fish for which it was fined £80,000. Held. Policing and enforcement of the quota system is exceptionally difficult for ships nominally registered in the UK but who operate out of ports of other countries. There was a paramount need to protect the fishing stocks. The offences were extremely serious and were motivated by greed. Penalties must strip the offenders of the profits and act as a very real deterrent. The penalties imposed were no more than adequate. The judge would have been justified in imposing substantially larger fines on the other charges. We are surprised the judge did not suspend the fishing licence.

R v Ramosa 2005 1 Cr App R (S) 396. The defendant company pleaded guilty to eleven counts of failing to comply with EU provisions relating to fisheries. The offences were strict liability and concerned failing to record quantities of fish and the alteration of log books, pursued with a commercial motive. The eleven counts spanned sixteen months for approaching £1/2m worth of undeclared fish. The defendant company had no previous convictions. Held. The defendant company had pleaded guilty to strict liability offences but that did not inhibit the judge from sentencing on the basis that there were aggravating features of knowledge and a commercial motive. The company could have purchased additional quota entitlements for £50,000. **£250,000 fines** not £500,000.

76 FOOD ETC, CONTAMINATING OF

76.1 Various offences including, Public Order Act 1986 s 38(1)

Contaminating goods with intent to cause the alarm, anxiety, injury or economic loss.

Triable either way. On indictment maximum 10 years. Summary maximum 6 months and/or £5,000.

Putting items in food in supermarket

76.2 *R v McNiff* 2001 2 Cr App R (S) 275. The defendant pleaded guilty to two offences under s 38. He asked for seven offences to be taken into consideration. Customers of Tesco found pins, needles and nails in food and the police were told. He pleaded in count one to putting needles in some Turkish Delight and in a chicken and pins in other items. Police watched him push something into a packet of scones. A pin was found and this was count two. He was arrested and had a piece of paper with three pins attached. Videos of the store showed him handling items, which were later found to be contaminated. Some of the pins were not discovered till the customers were eating. Injuries were limited to a pierced tongue, some pin-pricks and soreness. The conduct was over a period of months. On three occasions the entire stock of pick and mix sweets were destroyed. The investigation involved considerable amount of police and store staff work. He was 56 with no convictions and references. Between 1995 and 1999 he became profoundly deaf. His motive was not clear but it wasn't financial. The cause might have been his difficulty in expressing his distress and difficulties. He cared for his mother who was in her 90s and expressed remorse. Held. The seriousness of the offence is shown by the 10 year maximum sentence. The potential for serious injury is obvious. Notwithstanding the personal mitigation the seriousness must be marked. **3 years** was not excessive.

See also **BLACKMAIL –** *Supermarkets and retail stores*

77 FOOD SAFETY OFFENCES

77.1 Food Safety Act 1990 s 7, 8, 14, and 15

Rendering food injurious to health, selling food not complying with food safety requirements, selling food not of a nature or quality demanded, and falsely describing or presenting food etc.

Triable either way. On indictment maximum 2 years. Summary maximum 6 months and/or £20,000, (£5,000 for s 15).

The Criminal Justice Act 2003 creates a summary maximum sentence of 51 weeks, a minimum sentence of 28 weeks and Custody plus. The Home Office says they do not expect to introduce these provisions before September 2006.

Licences If the defendant is licensed under Slaughterhouses Act 1974 s 1 or 6 there is power to cancel the licence[51].

---

51 Food Safety Act 1990 s 35 (4)

Crown Court statistics – England and Wales – Males 21+ – Adulteration of food
77.2

Year	Plea	Total Numbers sentenced	Type of sentence %					Average length of custody (months)
			Discharge	Fine	Community sentence	Suspended sentence	Custody	
2002	Guilty	10	20	–	70	–	10	6
	Not guilty	–	–	–	–	–	–	–
2003	Guilty	1	–	100	–	–	–	–
	Not guilty	2	–	100	–	–	–	–

For details and explanations about the statistics in the book see page vii.

Preparing food without a licence

77.3   *R v Altaf* 1999 1 Cr App R (S) 429. The defendant elected trial for using premises for cutting of chickens without a licence, an offence under regulations made under the Food Safety Act 1990, s 16 and 17. He then pleaded guilty at the Crown Court. He had been involved in the distribution and selling of chickens for some time. He cut them up after they had been slaughtered elsewhere. His application for a licence was turned down. He was in the process of moving his business to premises where he had successfully obtained a licence. He continued using the other premises. Ministry inspectors visited the premises and found multiple breaches of the regulations. Flies were found in the work area, there was inadequate rodent protection, meat was stored in filthy cardboard boxes, meat was in contact with the cardboard and had spilt onto the floor, the reception, handling and dispatch of the exposed meat was unhygienic, chilling facilities were inadequate and there were dirty knives and other equipment. He had co-operated with the Ministry and was of good character. The offence was only punished by a fine at the Magistrates' Court. Held. It was quite impossible to say custody was wrong in principle for serious and multiple breaches of the regulations. Injury to health could have occurred. Because of the plea and other mitigation **3 months** not 6.

78   FOOTBALL OFFENCES

78.1   Various offences including the Football (Offences) Act 1991 s 4

Going onto a playing area or an adjacent area to which the spectators are not permitted

Summary only. Maximum fine Level 3 (£1,000).

Football For (1) all Football (Offences) Act 1991 offences, (2) Football Spectators Act 1989 s 2(1), 5(7), 14J(1) and 21C(2) offences, (3) Sporting Events (Control of Alcohol etc.) Act s 2 and 2(A) offences and (4) offences committed relevant to a football match the court must make a Football Banning Order where there are reasonable grounds to believe that making a banning order would help to prevent violence or disorder at or in connection with any regulated football match, under the Football Spectators Act 1989, s 14A and Sch 1, para 1.

Magistrates' Court Sentencing Guidelines January 2004 – Football (Offences) Act 1991 s4

78.2   First time offenders who plead not guilty. Entry point. Is a discharge or a fine appropriate? Examples of aggravating factors for the offence are being drunk, deliberate provocative act and inciting others. Examples of mitigation are age, health (physical or mental), co-operation with the police, and genuine remorse. **Starting point fine A.** (50% of weekly take home pay/weekly benefit payment). Must impose a banning order or give reasons why no order made. NB Community rehabilitation and curfew orders are the only available penalties for this offence.

For details about the guidelines see MAGISTRATES' COURT SENTENCING GUIDELINES at page 483.

See also AFFRAY – *Football etc related*, and OFFENCES AGAINST THE PERSON ACT **1861, s 20** – *Sporting*. For drunken football related offences see also DRUNK

For a Violent Disorder case see R v Rees and Others 2005 Unreported 1/7/05.

79 FORGERY

Where the forgery is used to steal see THEFT ETC

Crown Court statistics – England and Wales – Males 21+
79.4

Year	Plea	Total Numbers sentenced	Type of sentence %					Average length of custody (months)
			Discharge	Fine	Community sentence	Suspended sentence	Custody	
2002	Guilty	10	30	–	30	–	40	14.3
2003	Guilty	8	25	13	50	–	13	30
	Not guilty	3	–	–	–	–	100	12
Other forgery								
2002	Guilty	203	5	6	35	1	53	15.4
	Not guilty	44	2	5	14	5	73	15.7
2003	Guilty	238	5	5	29	8	52	14.7
	Not guilty	52	4	8	25	4	60	11.7

For details and explanations about the statistics in the book see page vii.

See also COUNTERFEITING CURRENCY, ELECTION OFFENCES and PASSPORT OFFENCES

80 FRAUD

80.1 Various offences with differing penalties.

Crown Court statistics – England and Wales – Males 21+ – Fraud other than by a company director
80.2

Year	Plea	Total Numbers sentenced	Type of sentence %					Average length of custody (months)
			Discharge	Fine	Community sentence	Suspended sentence	Custody	
2002	Guilty	1,098	4	3	37	6	50	17.1
	Not guilty	220	3	5	25	3	65	26.8
2003	Guilty	1,078	4	4	36	5	50	18.7
	Not guilty	236	6	5	25	4	60	30.5

For details and explanations about the statistics in the book see page vii.

Advance fee frauds

80.3   *R v Boothe* 1999 1 Cr App R (S) 98. The defendant pleaded guilty to attempting to obtain property by deception and having a false instrument. The victim a US businessman received an unsolicited letter purporting to be from the Government of Nigeria inviting his company to receive $17.5m in excess fees in return for which he would receive 30% commission. He received faxes apparently from the Nigerian Government and the Central Bank of Nigeria. As a result he paid £17,000 legal fees, cable charges of $14,000, $26,150 for an Insurance Release Bond, $25,000 signing fees, $25,500 handling charges, a further sum for VAT, $3,124 for postage $28,000 insurance fees, a $13,500 security charge and stamp duty fees as well as two fountain pens and two fax machines. He contacted the US Secret Service and they asked him to continue to go along with the arrangements. He did so and was told by the fraudsters to go to London and pay $200,000 VAT to Gary Boothe. As arranged he met the defendant who produced further documents from the Central Bank of Nigeria. It was arranged the money would be exchanged the following day. They met again the next day and $200,000 was exchanged for some documents and a forged cheque for $17.5 m. Police then arrested Boothe and he had an ID card for the Central Bank of Nigeria on him. In interview he said he was a lawyer for the Bank and he believed the cheque was genuine. He was 31. Held. This advance fee fraud was at that time prevalent. This was not a breach of trust case but guidance can be obtained from those cases. The victim was a greedy and willing participant in this scam, but that does not destroy the defendant's criminality. The defendant came late into the scheme. **2½ years** in all not 3½.

R v Iwuji 2001 1 Cr App R (S) 456. The defendant pleaded guilty to conspiracy to defraud. The victim who was employed in Saudi Arabia received a fax regarding blocked funds in Nigeria. He contacted the sender of the fax who claimed to be a highly placed official in the Nigerian National Petrol Corporation. The sender said there was $30.5m from an over invoiced contract which was available to be transferred to an account abroad. The victim received false documents purportedly from the Petrol Corporation, the Ministry of Finance at the Funds Disbursement Unit in Lagos and the Central Bank of Nigeria. There were a number of telephone calls and faxes. The victim was asked to pay an administration fee of £5,500, and asked to travel to London. He did so and was met by a chauffeur and was driven to the defendant who was posing as Dr Moore. Eventually he paid the fee and was told the cheque had been stopped because of the lack of a VAT receipt. He was shown a number of forged documents including a cheque for $30.5m. He was told to pay $305,000 and he contacted the police who conducted an undercover operation and the defendant was arrested. The defendant was involved in planning the fraud by using false cheques, false documents and creating a false organisation in London. Accommodation and cars were hired. He was 28. In 1996 he received 30 months for possessing false instruments with intent to use. It involved cloned credit cards. Held. He is a determined fraudster who failed to heed the warning of his last sentence. Because of that and that he was attempting to obtain a larger figure than *R v Boothe* 1999 1 Cr App R (S) 98 there can be no criticism of **3¹/₂ years**.

R v Dekson 2005 1 Cr App R (S) 630. The defendant was convicted of six offences of conspiracy to defraud, four counts of obtaining services by deception and having a false instrument (a passport). His wife was convicted with money laundering. The conspiracy was an advance fee fraud. The defendant conspired with others to carry out a number of such frauds. Two victims, P from the US and C from Hong Kong gave evidence. They were both contacted by letter purporting to come from an official in a Nigerian Petroleum company seeking to remove over-invoiced money from Nigeria. They were invited to make a bank account available for this purpose and promised a significant fee. Following a flurry of bogus documents they were invited to London where a conspirator played the role of a friend. They were taken to a bank and seated out of sight of the cashier while the conspirator pretended to receive a draft and handed it to another conspirator playing the role of a delighted recipient. The victim in each case was shown the draft briefly to convince him it was genuine but he was informed that although this was his draft it could not be released until a fee was paid. The conspirator 'friend' offered to shoulder some of the fee himself. After this there was another percentage handling charge, then a bribe to a Nigerian official and then an increase in the bribe fee. C was told the bank draft was for $55 million. P was told he would receive 25 per cent of $71 million. The frauds in relation to these two extracted a total of £1.7 million. £950,000 of that had been frozen and was likely to be recovered. The defendant was the guiding spirit and a large proportion of the £1.7 million went to him. He opened bank accounts fraudulently or used them fraudulently. He had many documents in a self-storage box showing links to names used in respect of the deception counts. There were forged drafts for millions of pounds and dollars. There was a passport, which was the false instrument count. The defendant had a conviction for obtaining and going equipped, which had been committed after the conspiracy to defraud started and was part of the evidence in the trial. The judge said his plea indicated that he lacked remorse and that he had involved his wife in his activities and had done nothing to soften the blow when it fell on her. 18 months consecutive for the obtaining of services was unchallenged. Held. On the advance fee fraud the fact that the victims were not themselves innocent can be overstated. They drew in others who were entirely innocent and it is a likely consequence of this kind of offending that the victims will in desperation lay hands on or borrow money from others who as a result may suffer indirectly. This category of case is special by its prevalence, and the high degree of skill, psychological insight and organisation used in it. There is a role for a deterrent element in sentencing. The amounts involved were substantial. **6 years** for the conspiracy to defraud was not manifestly excessive. The passport offence was reduced from 18 months to 12 making 8¹/₂ years not 9.

Charity fraud

80.4 *R v Day and O'Leary* 2002 2 Cr App R (S) 421. The defendants changed their plea on the morning their case was listed for trial to guilty to three counts of conspiracy to defraud. The two set up a company and gave the impression that it was registered as a charity. Staff were sought, badges obtained and collecting boxes ordered. Count 1 related to collecting money over 14 months pretending it was for a young boy with a congenital heart condition. His story had been reported in the local paper. Count 3 was similar and was over 3¹/₂ months. Count 4 was collecting for a genuine charity over two weeks. The total sum obtained was probably between £10,000 and £30,000. Only £50 was ever given to charity. They were 39 and 43 and were either of good character or were treated as such. Held. They exploited public goodwill and in some cases private grief. There was a dual deceit to the public detriment and an undermining of public confidence. We have obtained guidance from the authorities concerning cowboy builders and con-men preying on the elderly. The Barrick and Clark line of cases were very different. **4 years** was severe but intentionally so.

See also THEFT ETC – *Charity offences*

Confidence tricks   See THEFT – *Confidence tricks*

Documents, Selling bogus

80.5   *Att-Gen's Ref. Nos. 57–8 of 2003* 2004 2 Cr App R (S) 182. Aresh and Ali Daryadel were convicted of conspiracy to defraud and fraudulent trading. They used a business to defraud customers, principally asylum seekers, by selling them documents which purported to be licences which allowed the holder to drive in the UK for up to 5 years. Each customer was charged £450.00. The system used to provide the licences was quite complex and after the victims had paid they received documents with a similar appearance to a genuine DVLA driving licence and an international driver's permit. The fraud operated for some 20 months. The lowest estimate of defrauded customers was 488. The income generated was of the order of £250,000.The licences were advertised in Turkish, Russian and Farsi language newspapers sold in the UK, and they deceived some police officers, court officials and insurance companies. After the police in London began to make enquiries there was a break in the defendants' activities at the end of which a solicitor acting on their behalf wrote to the police in dicating that they intended to resume their activities on the basis of legal advice they had obtained indicating they were not breaking the law. However the jury found that the defendants knew that what they were doing was dishonest. The aggravating features were that the victims had trusted in the defendants, they were foreign nation- als of limited means, and particularly vulnerable. The victims drove vehicles when they were not insured. Police and court officials could be deceived when attempting to administer justice. The fraud was committed over a significant period of time. After they had been arrested and released the defendants continued to defraud customers. Arash was the principal, and at the time he was subject to a supervision order for 10 offences of obtaining a pecuniary advantage by deception. Arash, 32, suffered from a depressive disorder requiring treatment and medical supervision. He was not suffering from that at the time the offences were committed, but he had been before and afterwards. There was a risk of self-harm and suicide if he were to be sent to prison. Ari, 26, had received treatment for high blood pressure and acute anxiety. He was said to harbour ideas of self-harm. He was a lesser figure in the fraud than Arash. Held. We take into account that the investigation has had a devastating effect on the families of the defendants, and that confiscation orders were made of £60,000 and £55,000 with periods of imprisonment in default. (Note this is not permissible because Criminal Justice Act 1988 s 72(5) forbids confiscation being taken into account when determin- ing the appropriate sentence) We also take into account their current state of health and the fact that it will be a shattering blow to go into custody now. The appropriate sentence for Arash was **4 years** imprisonment and for Ali **2¹/₂ years**. As it was a reference **3** years for Arash not 18 months suspended and **21 months** for Ali not 12 months suspended.

Elderly victims

80.6   *R v Duggan* 1999 2 Cr App R (S) 65. The defendant was convicted of six counts of procuring the execution of a valuable security. Theft and other counts were left on the file. He was an unqualified accountant who ran a perfectly legitimate business until he got heavily in debt over a speculative land development. He took £400,000 from the funds of a widow aged 85 by persuading her to invest in a particular account. By deception and forgery he kept his creditors at bay. He misled her to sign documents. When she asked for an explanation he lied. It carried on for about 3 years by which time £688,000 had been obtained. Held. The vulnerable victim was carefully targeted. It was a grave case of prolonged financial defalcation. There was no repayment. 4 years consecutive to 5 making **9 years** was entirely right.

See also *Wills*

Employers, frauds against the defendant's

80.7 *R v Oprey and Pinchbeck* 2002 1 Cr App R (S) 317. The defendants O and P pleaded to conspiracy to defraud and other dishonesty etc counts. A large hotel group employed them at one of their hotels in Harrogate. P was general manager between 1989 and 1997. O started working there before P arrived and was financial controller. P and O were paid at the end £47,000 and £21,000 in salaries. Between 1992 and 1997 P organised events at a nearby conference centre on his own behalf and for his own profit and used the hotel's facilities. Over the years the hotel paid for £140,000 of the costs. The company paid for the band at his wedding reception and £3,000 worth of hotel champagne was taken there and most was drunk. Other wine was taken for his own use. O was sentenced on the basis she failed to prevent the payment of the invoices by the hotel. She was also obstructive to the suppliers when their invoices were not paid. She didn't put the details on the computer so Head Office couldn't see them. There were unpaid invoices worth £130,000 found at her home. P was 52 and O was 61 with no convictions and had made no personal gain. She suffered from poor health. Both were made bankrupt. The defence said P was an extremely successful manager with a very respected reputation. O agreed to give evidence against P and then P made a late plea. The judge said the fraud was ingenious, sustained and profitable and P was dishonest, greedy and devious. Held. P had committed quite separate acts of dishonesty, which could have been made the subject of consecutive sentences. It was in P's favour the judge did not do that. P's plea although late was a very strong piece of mitigation so **3 years** not 4. Without O, P could not have continued the fraud and she had obstructed the investigation. Because of her health and mercy **9 months** not 12. It would be wrong to suspend her sentence.

Guilty plea, late

80.8 *R v Buffrey* 1993 14 Cr App R (S) 511 at 514. LCJ. The defendant made a late plea to conspiracy to trade fraudulently and other connected counts. The Court of Appeal considered to what extent – when someone pleads guilty at a late stage and so saves the holding of a very lengthy trial – ought the sentence which would otherwise have been imposed be discounted? Held. It must not be thought by those who are minded to commit fraud that after indulging in devious deception – which necessitates a long trial to unravel it – they can by pleading guilty at a late stage, earn such praise from the court for their public-spirited acceptance of what they have done that they can have a great reduction of their sentence. But some reduction must be made and because frauds of this kind are complex and do take a long time to unravel, they have become a burden on the criminal justice system. They are very costly, both in time and money. They cause stress to jurors, judges, those who conduct them and not least the witnesses and the defendants. These matters justify the court in applying a considerable discount where someone late in the day pleads guilty. There is no absolute rule as to what the discount should be. There will be considerable variance between one case and another. As a general guidance something of the order of one third would very often be appropriate.

R v Oprey and Pinchbeck 2002 1 Cr App R (S) 317. The defendants O and P pleaded guilty to conspiracy to defraud and other dishonesty etc counts. O agreed to give evidence against P and then P made a late plea. Held. P's plea although late was a very strong piece of mitigation.

Identity frauds – Guideline remarks

80.9   *R v Odewale and Others* 2004 2 Cr App R (S) 240. Identity fraud is a particularly serious form of conspiracy to defraud. The Judge was fully entitled to take into account the prevalence of this kind of fraud.

Identity frauds – Cases

80.10   *R v Odewale and Others* 2004 2 Cr App R (S) 240. The 3 defendants, O, Os and A were convicted with others of a conspiracy to defraud financial institutions by means of identity theft. They took over the identity of former residents of various properties, obtained false documents such as driving licences or utility bills and opened accounts at banks or building societies in these names. They then obtained loan facilities and credit and debit cards. They made 140 applications to financial institutions using 63 names and 100 of these were successful. The fraud lasted from January 2000 to March 2002. O was involved throughout; his fingerprints were on many of the forms used in the conspiracy and he was present at a number of transactions at the institutions. Os had been involved since November 2000 and was in possession of a fraudster's kit of false documents, disposable gloves and property newspapers. He had profited significantly. A was involved from early 2001. He had been the gatherer of the potential addresses and identities. The financial loss to the institutions was at least £500,000. O, 26, had a previous conviction for conspiracy to defraud for which he had been sentenced to 12 months imprisonment, and a number of other convictions for minor dishonesty. Os, 25, had a conviction for attempting to obtain property by deception, and for using a false instrument. He had offered to plead guilty to substantive charges but this had been refused by the Prosecution. A had a conviction for using a false instrument. The judge said, 'a disproportionate number of participants in these sorts of crimes, are either Nigerians or people who have connections to other Nigerians, the court has a responsibility … to seek to deter others'. Held. The judge should not have made those remarks and it is regrettable that he did so. The language used may well have given the impression that their Nigerian background added to the defendants' sentences. An element of deterrence was appropriate in the sentences but not on the basis described by the judge. O **6 years** not 8, Os **4 years** not 5, and A **3 years** 4.

Att Gen's Ref. 73 of 2003. 2004 2 Cr App R (S) 337. The defendant pleaded guilty on 'virtually the day of trial' to conspiring with others to defraud UK banks and institutions over a period of 10 months. The fraud involved the use of computers and other equipment to transfer details from genuine credit cards to blank petrol station cards and these cards were then used by employees of petrol stations to take cash from the tills. Numerous items were found in the defendant's house and car including encoded loyalty cards, two computers, card readers and writers. An examination of the use of the cards found at his and other addresses indicated that 150 cards were involved and the total loss was in the region of £1.5 million. The defendant pleaded guilty on the basis that his benefit was £125,000; that he was a distributor of the cards; and that he himself was not a manufacturer, although he was physically close to the manufacturer. The defendant had no previous convictions. 'Various matters of co operation' were taken into account. He was only involved for part of the run of the conspiracy and although he was charged in 2001 he was not dealt with until 2003. Held. The appropriate sentence would have been **4 years**. As it was a reference **3 years** not 16 months.

Att-Gen's Ref. No. 86 of 2003 2004 2 Cr App R (S) 421. The defendant pleased guilty to conspiring to defraud the Co-Op Bank between November 2001 and August 2002. He had worked at the bank since 2000 as a customer advisor and he passed on details of customers' accounts and security details obtained through his employment to two co-accused, M and Mc. They then transferred money fraudulently to accounts they controlled. The total amount transferred was £46,725 and this was the global loss sustained. The defendant shared a house with M and another. Items containing bank security information and £1,400 in cash were found at the address. Aggravating features were the breach of trust, the sustained nature of the fraud, and the pivotal role of the defendant. In a basis of plea he said he was the facilitator of the fraud, which had been M's idea. He said his benefit was only £1,900. The defendant, 22, accepted in a pre-sentence report that without him the fraud could not have taken place and expressed regret. Since his arrest he had found new employment. He said that he had found himself in financial difficulties. There were character references. It was a long time from discovery of the fraud to sentence and it was relatively unsophisticated. The defendant had completed the curfew order imposed on him because of further delays in the Court of Appeal. He had served over one third of the community punishment order imposed on him. He was living at home with supportive parents, was in a steady job and taken City and Guild exams. Held. So far as the amount is concerned, the relevant factor was the loss to the victims rather then the personal benefit. The imposition of a prison sentence now would be wholly counter productive. We also take into account that both co-offenders, who had considerable criminal records, avoided custodial sentences. The appropriate sentence was **2 years** reduced to **16 months** because of the plea, not community punishment of 240 hours together with a 4-month home curfew order. But because of the exceptional circumstances the sentence will stand.

R v Chirila 2005 1 Cr App R (S) 523. The three defendants pleaded guilty to conspiracy to defraud. Banking staff were monitoring cash withdrawals. Unusual activity was repeatedly noted at one Automatic Teller Machine at about 3.15am and the police attended where they found the defendants. They were searched and fifty-four mobile phone top-up cards were found together with £9,600 cash and a list of PIN numbers. They gave false names but further enquiries revealed a hotel room where a large quantity of sophisticated high-tech equipment was found along with £18,200 in cash. A magnetic strip reader was installed at the entrance to the lobby containing the ATMs and an incredibly small, wireless camera was installed to record PIN numbers as customers typed in their details. Fifty-five customers had been defrauded. Another bank had also been targeted to the tune of £3,340. The defendants had transferred £130,000 to Romania over the previous eight months but for the period relevant to their pleas only £22,500 had been transferred. Each had false documents and was an illegal immigrant. All were of previous good character and aged 28, 25 and 24. Held. These offences are now prevalent. A strong deterrent element must be incorporated into these sentences in the same way that a strong deterrent element is employed against those who bring drugs into this country. The sophistication of the fraud and the limited credit for the guilty pleas (the evidence was overwhelming) meant that **6 years** was upheld.

See also *R v McKechnie* 2002 EWCA Crim 3161 and *R v Taj* 2003 EWCA Crim 2633.

Insurance frauds

80.11 *R v Mehboob* 2000 2 Cr App R (S) 343. The defendant was convicted of four offences of conspiracy to defraud. Earlier he had pleaded guilty to three similar counts. There were 23 co-defendants. He was at the centre of seven separate conspiracies to defraud insurance companies by fabricating road traffic claims between September 1992 and April 1994. He was the central figure and the instigator of the fraud where the accidents were either fictitious or the accidents had not happened in the way the claimants stated. The fraud required a great deal of ingenuity and planning. He thought up the fictitious accidents, communicated with the insurance companies, filled in the documentation etc and corrupted others. The total claimed was £34,162. The total loss to the insurance companies was £13,358 and the total gain to the defendant was £6,147. He was of good character. Held. The mischief of this offence is that it is easy to commit and difficult to detect. **4 years** not 5.

R v Hurst 2004 1 Cr App R (S) 482. The defendant pleaded guilty to conspiracy to defraud. The defendant was charged with P who was the defendant's son in law. The defendant had built up a business over a number of years repairing and re-spraying used plant. He and P were partners. One night an extremely serious fire broke out resulting in almost £3 m loss and damage. P later confessed that he had employed a third person to set the fire; he was under the impression that the business was failing. P told the defendant soon after the fire. The defendant made a false statement to the police stating that he was with P at the time of the fire. The defendant also proceeded to lodge a claim with his insurers and made a false statement to the assessor 10 days after the fire. In interview P later fully confessed; the defendant made no comment. The basis of plea was the defendant had discovered that the fire had been set after the fire had taken place but before he made his statement to the loss adjuster. He had co-operated in attempts to mitigate the loss caused to other traders by the fire. He was 65 and of positive good character. His wife had been receiving psychiatric help for many years and he was now in substantial debt. Held. A custodial sentence of some substance was called for. The defendant chose to fall prey to the temptation to make a false claim. The help he gave to other traders and the fact that he did not start the fire were important features. **18 months** not 3 years.

Old cases. *R v Guppy* 1995 16 Cr App R (S) 25 and *R v Nall-Cain* 1998 2 Cr App R (S) 145. (For a summary of the last case see the first edition of this book.)

Investments, false promises/bogus investment schemes etc

80.12   *R v Andre and Burton* 2002 1 Cr App R (S) 98. The defendant B pleaded guilty to conspiracy to defraud eight people of £185,659.54. The defendant A pleaded guilty to dishonestly retaining a wrongful credit of £93,770 and two counts of issuing a cheque (one for £500 and the other for £325) knowing or being reckless whether they would be honoured. The two defendants had lived together as a couple for many years. They went from Australia to America where they set up a company, which was later used in the frauds and came to the UK. They stayed in expensive hotels, employed a chauffeur and butler. They hired a Bentley and later a Rolls Royce and left the hotel bills unpaid. They created the impression they had access to enormous sums of money. B agreed to sponsor the Royal Windsor Horse Show for $250,000. Through that B promised someone involved that an investment of £75,000 could give a return of £6.8 m. He paid the money and the money went to America where the FBI retrieved it. A US businessman and a retired accountant were told that B was a very successful international bond dealer. They paid $300,000, which was spent within a month on staff, a horse and a car etc. B claimed to three other people she had just bought a German bank and profits were there for the taking. They were told an investment of $150,000 would offer a return of $13.5 m in 10 months. They paid the money with a promised return of $1.5 m after 35 days. That money was spent within a month. B agreed to buy a farm from a Norfolk farmer. At the same time she persuaded the farmer to invest $300,000 which would raise $1.5 m in 35 days. The cheque was payable to A. A kept half of it which was the wrongful credit offence she pleaded to. Two Swiss men were told a similar story and lost $300,000. £50,000 of that went into A's account. They left the country and went to New Zealand from where they were extradited. The total losses on B's defraud count were £557,000. A's 2 cheque offences related to her

sponsoring the Arab Horse Show and the cheques were to the winners. She appreciated the cheques were unlikely to clear. A was 51 and had two unrelated convictions in
Australia. B was 58 and had a substantial record for dishonesty in Australia and New
Zealand between 1961 and 1999. While in New Zealand awaiting extradition she
served 6 months for false pretences. Held. The judge was entitled to reduce the credit
for the guilty plea because the pleas were late. A had benefited from all the high living
in the defraud count and lent herself to the enterprise. Because A was effectively of
good character and had a lesser role the 8 months consecutive for the two cheque
offences would run concurrently so 3 years in all. B's fraud was serious, sophisticated
and large scale. It was on individual investors. **5 years** was entirely appropriate.

R v Hooper 2003 2 Cr App R (S) 569. The defendant pleaded guilty to 10 counts of
obtaining a money transfer by deception and 3 counts of forgery. The defendant worked
as a financial adviser for $2^{1}/_{2}$ years but ran-up substantial debts with his employers. He
left and was no longer registered with the Personal Investment Authority. However, he
proceeded to set up his own company. Victim 1 (B) was 81, he lived alone and had no
close family. Victim 2 (D) was 84 and also lived alone. Both were persuaded by
him to invest money when he was legitimately employed, however they subsequently
paid over cheques (B, £10,000 and D, £52,000) to him after he had formed his own
company (the obtaining a transfer by deception counts). The deception of D took place
over about a year. In a basis of plea he admitted that he had dishonestly obtained monies
from D and B by giving them the false impression that monies were to be used to
purchase investments for them. B was repaid, D was not. The forgery counts related to
forged signatures of a business colleague on three cheques totalling £28,584 (the
cheques were subsequently not honoured). The total un-recovered loss was £52,538. He
was 29 and of previous good character. He expressed remorse. He was sentenced to
12 months in respect of the deception against B, 2 years in respect of the deceptions
against D (consecutive) and 12 months (concurrent) for the forgery counts. Held. There
was a breach of trust which was particularly large as D and B had entered into an important fiduciary relationship with the defendant. The victims were elderly and socially
isolated. He knew that those who acted on his advice did so without protection. **3 years**
was not manifestly excessive.

When by arson see **ARSON** – *Insurance money, to obtain* and **ARSON** – *Arson –
Reckless whether Life would be Endangered – Insurance money, to obtain*

Property frauds

80.13   *R v Palmer (No. 2)* 2003 2 Cr App R (S) 5. The defendant was convicted of two
counts of conspiracy to defraud. In 1985 the defendant began a development of the first
of a number of holiday resorts in Tenerife in which he sold timeshare interests in
apartments. From about 1990 timeshare interests were sold by systematic fraud on
a very large scale, based on false and dishonest promises as to the resale value of
customers' existing timeshare interests using a technique known as Buy/Sell. Timeshare
owners were told that their existing interests would be sold promptly and at highly
attractive prices provided that they bought fresh interests in the defendant's resorts, to
be financed by such sales. A variation known as buy/rent was practised on a similar
scale. Purchasers were induced to buy on the spot without any pause for reflection.
It was represented to them that the resale or rental of their timeshares would be undertaken by a named independent company with a good reselling record. They paid for
registration with such a company regardless of resale. The reality was that the market
for resold timeshares was at best slack. Prices in rental forecasts were known by the
defendant to be unreal. Customers risked being left with two or more timeshares rather
than one. The operation of the defendant's companies was part of the overall fraud
under his control and influence. At trial the prosecution called forty eight customers,

however the evidence identified 16,600 customers. Orders were made in favour of approximately four hundred named losers. The confiscation ordered was £33 m. Held. Some assistance on the losses suffered by customers could be gleaned from the compensation orders that totalled in excess of £2 m. The defendant's criminality was to be measured primarily by the widespread use of the fraudulent techniques. There was no doubt that the fraud was very widespread indeed and properly measured as one causing significant, though not as yet fully quantified losses. **8 years** upheld.

Wills

80.14 *R v Spillman and Spillman* 2001 1 Cr App R (S) 496. The defendant A made a late guilty plea to conspiracy to defraud, two thefts of cheques from the testator and forgery of a will. The defendant D was convicted of the same conspiracy. They were husband and wife involved in a sophisticated scheme to swindle an elderly lady's beneficiaries out of £1.8 m by creating and forging a will, which made them beneficiaries. A fake letter was sent to the elderly lady's long-standing solicitor withdrawing her instructions from the firm. A's mother posed as the testator and made a will with a firm of solicitors the testator had never used. A and D witnessed it. After the testator died A and D continued to represent the fake will was valid. A's mother gave evidence for the prosecution and explained how D had recruited her and drove her to the testator's house where all the photographs of the testator had been removed. She then posed as the testator. Shortly after the testator died a vigilant solicitor intervened. The plot was very nearly successful. A had a conviction (not specified). A's report detailed the abuse she had suffered from her mother, her stepfather and her husband. She suffered from battered woman syndrome. She was said to passively accept events. The judge said he rejected that and the views of the pre-sentence report after listening to the trial. Held. This was an extremely serious fraud involving an enormous sum and the grossest breach of trust. The judge's approach was entirely proper. **5 years 3 months** for A was severe and justified. D's sentence of **7 years** was not manifestly excessive.

For fraudulent trading and generally see COMPANY FRAUDS AND FINANCIAL SERVICES OFFENCES and THEFT ETC

FRAUDULENT TRADING

See COMPANY FRAUDS AND FINANCIAL OFFENCES – *Fraudulent trading*

81 GAY

Buggery, gross indecency and soliciting were abolished on 1/5/04.

Hostility towards a gay victim

81.1 (as an aggravating factor)

Criminal Justice Act 2003 s 146(2)–(3)[1] Where "the offender demonstrated towards the victim … hostility based on a the sexual orientation (or presumed sexual orientation) of the victim or the offence is motivated … by hostility towards persons who are of a particular sexual orientation, the court must treat (that) … as an aggravating factor and must state in open court that the offence was committed in such circumstances."

See BUGGERY; RAPE – *Anal rape, Homophobic rape* and *Male rape*

1 This section came into force on 4 April 2005.

GBH – GRIEVOUS BODILY HARM

See BURGLARY – *GBH, with intent to inflict, Offences Against the Person Act 1861 s 18* and *Offences Against the Person Act 1861 s 20*

82   GOING EQUIPPED TO STEAL

82.1   Theft Act 1968 s 25

Triable either way.

On indictment maximum 3 years. Summary maximum 6 months and/or £5,000.

Disqualification from driving If the offence concerns the theft or taking of a motor vehicle the offence carries discretionary disqualification[2]

Drug Abstinence Order This was repealed on 4 April 2005.

Crown Court statistics – England and Wales – Males 21+
82.2

Year	Plea	Total Numbers sentenced	Type of sentence %					Average length of custody (months)
			Discharge	Fine	Community sentence	Suspended sentence	Custody	
2002	Guilty	88	6	3	36	1	53	11.1
	Not guilty	23	4	9	39	–	48	15.1
2003	Guilty	103	10	2	38	1	50	10.9
	Not guilty	28	–	–	32	–	64	12.6

For details and explanations about the statistics in the book see page vii.

Magistrates' Court Sentencing Guidelines January 2004

82.3   First time offenders who plead not guilty Entry point. Is it serious enough for a community penalty? Examples of aggravating factors are group action, sophisticated, number of items, people put in fear, sophistication and specialised equipment. Examples of mitigation are age, health (physical or mental), co-operation with police, and genuine remorse. Consider forfeiture and destruction.

For details about the guidelines see MAGISTRATES' COURT SENTENCING GUIDELINES at page 483.

See also THEFT ETC – *Telephone boxes*

GRIEVOUS BODILY HARM

See BURGLARY – *GBH, with intent to inflict, Offences Against the Person Act 1861, s 18* and *Offences Against the Person Act 1861, s 20*

2   Road Traffic Offenders Act 1988 s 9, 34, 97 and Sch. 2 Part II

GROOMING

See **SEXUAL ASSAULT ETC. CHILDREN**

83 GROSS INDECENCY

83.1 Sexual Offences Act 1956 s 13

This offence was abolished on 1/5/04. Where the other party is a child or where there is no consent offences from that date would be charged under Sexual Offences Act 2003 s 7 and 3 respectively. See **SEXUAL ASSAULT ETC. CHILDREN** and **SEXUAL ASSAULT TOUCHING**

84 GUILTY PLEA, DISCOUNT FOR

84.1 Criminal Justice Act 2003 s 144[3] formerly Powers of Criminal Courts (Sentencing) Act 2000 s 152(1). In determining what sentence to pass on an offender who has pleaded guilty, a court shall take into account (a) the stage the offender indicated his plea of guilty and (b) the circumstances in which the indication was given. [Section summarised.]

Before the Sentencing Guideline Council issued their Guideline experience shows the full discount is a third so a 3 year starting point becomes 2 years on a plea. As the sentence lengthens most judges reduce the fraction. So for a 15 years starting point the defendant would receive 11–12[4] and not 10 years. There remains a significant discretion with some judges generous and others not so generous. The same principles apply to fines, community service hours etc. However, a guilty plea doesn't prevent a life sentence being passed. The new guidelines are likely to be ignored (and rightly so) by judges who want to encourage a defendant to plead guilty just before the trial starts. If the stated discount is 10% (see **84.15**) few defendants will see the discount as significant. It will be the victims in those cases who will suffer from any rigid application of the guidelines.

Sentencing Guidelines Council Guideline Guilty Plea December 2004

84.2 This is distributed among the sub headings, see also www.sentencing-guidelines.gov.uk

Magistrates' Court Sentencing Guidelines January 2004 (issued before the SGC Guideline)

84.3 The law requires the court to reduce the sentence for a timely guilty plea but this provision should be used with judicial flexibility. A timely guilty plea may attract a sentencing discount of up to one third but the precise amount of discount will depend on the facts of each case and a last minute plea of guilty may attract only a minimal reduction. Credit may be given in respect of the amount of a fine or periods of community service or custody. Periods of mandatory disqualification or mandatory penalty points cannot be reduced for a guilty plea.

In deciding what sentence to pass on a person who has pleaded guilty the court has to take into account the stage in the proceedings at which that plea was indicated and the

---

3 The section came into force on 4 April 2005
4 For that calculation see *Att-Gen's Ref. Nos. 19, 20 and 21 of 2001* 2002 1 Cr App R (S) 136

circumstances in which the indication was given. If the court imposes a less severe penalty than it would have given, it must state this in open court. It would be a matter of good practice for the court to say how much credit has been given, with a brief reason for the decision.

The principles of 'discount' apply as much to Magistrates' Courts as they do to Crown Courts. A timely guilty plea may attract a sentencing discount of up to a third but the precise amount of discount will depend on the facts of each case. A change of plea on the day set down for trial may attract only a minimal reduction in sentence; the court must still consider whether credit should be given.

Reductions apply to fines, periods of community sentences and custody. An early plea of guilty may also affect the length of a disqualification or the number of penalty points. However, minimum periods of disqualification and mandatory penalty points cannot be reduced for a guilty plea. Reasons should be given for decisions.

Ancillary orders

84.4   Sentencing Guidelines Council Guideline Guilty Plea December 2004 Para B 2.5. The guilty plea reduction has <u>no</u> impact on sentencing decisions in relation to ancillary orders. www.sentencing-guidelines.gov.uk

See also *Disqualification and penalty points*

Approach, Recommended

84.5   Sentencing Guidelines Council Guideline Guilty Plea December 2004 Para C 3.1. 1) The Court decides sentence for the offences taking into account TICs; 2) The court selects the amount of reduction by reference to the sliding scale; 3) the court applies a reduction to the sentence decided on; and 4) the court should usually state what the sentence would have been if there had been no reduction. www.sentencing-guidelines.gov.uk

Articles about

84.6   Article about the discount see Archbold News 2003 2 December p 3.

Co-defendant, giving evidence for

84.7   *R v Lawless* 1998 2 Cr App R (S) 176. The defendant pleaded guilty to affray and his co-defendant was convicted of the same offence. The defendant gave evidence for him. The judge sentenced them both to 21 months saying the defendant had thrown his credit away because the jury must have found his evidence to be lies and it was wholly discredited. Held. It is important that a co-defendant should not be inhibited from giving evidence. He was entitled to a discount so **15 months** instead.

R v Hickman 2000 2 Cr App R (S) 176. The defendant made a late plea of guilty to robbery and his co-defendant pleaded not guilty and was convicted of the same offence. The defendant gave evidence for him. The Judge took the lying into account and sentenced them both to the same sentence. Held. The principle in *R v Lawless* 1998 2 Cr App R (S) 176 has to be applied. **3$^{1}/_{2}$ years** not 4.

Conspiracy conviction which relates to many different offences

84.8   *R v Smith* 2002 1 Cr App R (S) 386. The defendants D and H pleaded guilty shortly after a jury was empanelled to conspiracy which was over a four year period and involved police corruption. C and S pleaded guilty to kidnapping. D was a sergeant in the CID and H was a drug dealer who was sentenced to 7 years for drug trafficking offences. £130,000 was found at his home. H supplied D with money and information about other drug criminals and D provided H with police and customs operations against other drug dealers. H made tape recordings of the conversations which were found by the police. The corruption started at the beginning of the police officer's career. H suggested planting drugs on other criminals. D adopted H as an informant but did not tell any superior. D also dealt with his father's hotel business and it was in 1995 in a poor state. H put £10,000 into the business. H then took over the running of the hotel and used it for the storing and distribution of drugs. D then lied about his involvement with H. Five offenders were able to escape when information about the raids on their addresses were leaked to H. The police started investigating and D ignored instructions. He was told to stop seeing H and he met him the next day. They were both arrested and lied when interviewed. The prosecution could not be precise about the damage caused to the police and the profits made. However, the integrity of the police force and its anti-drugs activities were very seriously compromised. H and his associates were major players in the drugs world. D received 7 years, the maximum and H received 5 years consecutive to the 8 years he had received in his drug case. The judge refused to give D a discount for the plea because the appropriate sentence was 10 years before a small discount for the plea to 8¹/₂ years. He said the situation was similar to a specimen charge where one count does not reflect the whole course of conduct. Held. Some discount for the plea should have been made so **6 years** substituted. H's sentence reduced from 5 to **4¹/₂ years**.

Detention and training orders where the adult maximum is less than 14 years

84.9 Sentencing Guidelines Council Guideline Guilty Plea December 2004 Para E 5.6. A detention and training order of 24 months may be imposed on an offender aged under 18 if the offence is one which would but for the plea have attracted a sentence of long-term detention in excess of 24 months under the Powers of Criminal Courts (Sentencing) Act 2000 s 91. www.sentencing-guidelines.gov.uk

R v Kelly 2002 1 Cr App R (S) 40. The defendant pleaded guilty to causing GBH. He was aged 15. Held. As the maximum for the offence was 2 years' detention and training it was wrong to give him the maximum. **18 months** substituted.

R v Marley 2002 2 Cr App R (S) 73. The defendant pleaded guilty to violent disorder. He was aged 16 when the offence was committed. As the maximum for the offence was less than 14 years 2 years was the absolute maximum in this case. Held. Had not 2 years been the maximum this appeal would not have succeeded. As he pleaded guilty he was entitled to a discount so **18 months** not 2 years.

R v March 2002 2 Cr App R (S) 448. The defendant had to be given a discount when he had pleaded and had spent 8 months on remand. 6 months reduction given.

Disqualification and penalty points

84.10 Magistrates' Court Sentencing Guidelines 2004 An early plea of guilty may also affect the length of a disqualification or the number of penalty points. However, minimum periods of disqualification and mandatory penalty points cannot be reduced for a guilty plea.

Extended sentences

See *Longer than commensurate/extended sentences/indeterminate sentences*

How great should the discount be? – Basis principles

84.11 Criminal Justice Act 2003 s 444[5] formerly Powers of Criminal Courts (Sentencing) Act 2000 s 152(1). In determining what sentence to pass on an offender who has pleaded guilty, a court shall take into account (a) the stage the offender indicated his plea of guilty and (b) the circumstances in which the indication was given. [Section summarised.]

---

5   The section came into force on 4 April 2005

Sentencing Guidelines Council Guideline Guilty Plea December 2004 Para D 4.1 The level of reduction should be a proportion of the total sentence imposed, with the proportion based upon the stage in the proceedings at which the guilty plea was entered. Save where minimum sentences apply the level of reduction will be gauged on a sliding scale ranging from a maximum of 1/3, where the plea was entered at the first reasonable opportunity, reducing to 1/4 where a date of trial has been set and to a maximum of 1/10 where the plea is entered at the door of the court or after the trial has begun. Where the plea comes very late it is still appropriate to give some reduction. www.sentencing-guidelines.gov.uk

How great should the discount be? – Defendant caught red handed

84.12   Sentencing Guidelines Council Guideline Guilty Plea December 2004 Para E 5.2. Since the purpose of giving credit is to encourage those who are guilty to plead at the earliest opportunity, there is no reason why credit should be withheld or reduced on these grounds alone. The normal sliding scale should apply. www.sentencing-guidelines.gov.uk

How great should the discount be? – Early plea

84.13   *R v McDonald* 2002 1 Cr App R (S) 585. The defendant pleaded guilty to robbery at the first opportunity. His co-defendant pleaded 6 weeks later. They each received 4 years. Held. There was no ground for distinguishing between their culpability or their criminality. It is important those who plead at the earliest opportunity should know that they will receive, and be seen to receive, the greatest possible credit for the early stage at which the plea is tendered. Although the offending might well have deserved a term of 4 years the sentence will be reduced to 3^1/$_2$ **years** to mark positively the earliest stage at which the he gave his plea.

How great should the discount be? – Early plea – Magistrates' Court, plea before venue

84.14   *R v Rafferty* 1998 2 Cr App R (S) 449. LCJ. The defendant pleaded guilty before venue. Held. It is no longer appropriate for counsel to say the defendant pleaded at the first opportunity if the plea was not entered before venue. If the plea is first entered at the Crown Court and there is no satisfactory explanation was it was not tendered earlier will receive less discount than if they pleaded at the Magistrates' Court and less discount than they received hitherto. (The part about receiving less discount than hitherto is not being followed by most Crown Courts judges because they are aware of the terrible pressures on their lists. Therefore they wish to encourage as many defendants as possible to plead guilty by giving those that plead when the indictment is first put the full discount.) In the usual case where a defendant enters a plea at plea before venue s/he should be entitled to a greater discount than a person who delays making that plea until the Crown Court.

R v Barber 2002 1 Cr App R (S) 548. In many cases, the appropriate discount for a prompt plea of guilty, at the Crown Court to an offence triable only on indictment is of the order of one third. In relation to either way offences, where such a plea is entered before venue, a greater than 1/3 will often be appropriate.

How great should the discount be? – Late plea

84.15   Sentencing Guidelines Council Guideline Guilty Plea December 2004 Para D 4.1 Save where minimum sentences apply there is a maximum of 1/10 where the plea is entered at the door of the court or after the trial has begun. Where the plea comes very late it is still appropriate to give some reduction. www.sentencing-guidelines.gov.uk

R v Delaney 1998 1 Cr App R (S) 325. The defendant made a late plea to robbery and making use of a firearm with intent. The judge gave him **11^1/$_2$ years** saying there was a 2¹/₂ years' discount for the late plea. Held. The discount for the late plea was within the judge's discretion.

R v Okee and West 1998 2 Cr App R (S) 199. The defendants pleaded guilty at the last minute. The judge passed a **4¹/₂ years** sentence saying with no plea it would have been 5 years. The defence said there was insufficient credit given. Held. Those who run their not guilty pleas to the wire should know that the discount will be substantially and visibly reduced. The 10% discount here was ample.

See also FRAUD – *Guilty plea, late*

How great should the discount be? – Maximum considered too low

84.16 Sentencing Guidelines Council Guideline Guilty Plea December 2004 Para E 5.3. The sentencer cannot remedy perceived defects (for example an inadequate charge or maximum penalty) by refusal of the appropriate discount. www.sentencing-guidelines.gov.uk

Cases before the guideline. *R v Scarley* 2001 1 Cr App R (S) 86 and *R v Williams* 2001 Unreported 13/7/01, (for a summary of these cases see the first edition of this book).

How great should the discount be? – Plea indicated shortly after PDH

84.17 *R v Djahit* 1999 2 Cr App R (S) 142. The defendant pleaded not guilty at his PDH hearing. His counsel then asked for an adjournment so a conference could take place. A few days later the conference took place and a letter was sent to the court saying he would plead guilty. At the sentencing hearing the judge said he would only give partial credit for the guilty plea, as it hadn't been entered at the earliest opportunity. Held. The fact he did not plead earlier appears to have been the responsibility of the solicitors who had failed to organise a conference before the PDH. The defendant was entitled to a full discount.

How great should the discount be? – Tactical not guilty plea to retain privileges

84.18 Sentencing Guidelines Council Guideline Guilty Plea December 2004 Para D 4.3 v. If a not guilty plea was entered and maintained for tactical reasons (such as to retain privileges whilst on remand), a late plea should attract very little, if any discount. www.sentencing-guidelines.gov.uk

Fraud   See FRAUD – *Guilty plea, late*

Health and Safety offences

See HEALTH AND SAFETY OFFENCES – *Guilty plea, Discount for*

Longer than commensurate/extended sentences/indeterminate sentences

84.19 Sentencing Guidelines Council Guideline Guilty Plea December 2004 Para E 5.1. Where the court has determined that a longer than commensurate, extended sentence, or indeterminate sentence is required for the protection of the public, the minimum custodial term but not the protection of the public element of the sentence should be reduced to reflect the plea. www.sentencing-guidelines.gov.uk

Magistrates' Court

84.20 Sentencing Guidelines Council Guideline Guilty Plea December 2004 para E 5.4. Where two or more summary only offences are to be sentenced and where the maximum is 6 months the sentence for each should is reduced to reflect the guilty plea, it may be appropriate to make them consecutive. This will not undermine the general principle. However the total should make some allowance for the plea. Where there is a guilty plea the 6 month maximum may be imposed where otherwise it would have attracted a sentence of 9 months after a committal. www.sentencing-guidelines.gov.uk

Article. Sentence discounts in Magistrates' Courts 2000 Crim LR 436.

Minimum sentences for third Class A drug trafficking offence or third domestic burglary

84.21   Powers of Criminal Courts (Sentencing) Act 2000 s 110 and 111.

Powers of Criminal Courts (Sentencing) Act 2000 s 152(3). Where a sentence is to be imposed under the Powers of the Criminal Courts (Sentencing) Act 2000, s 110 and 111 nothing in that section shall prevent the court from imposing a sentence of 80% or more of the minimum period. [Section summarised. The section means if the defendant pleads guilty the court can impose a sentence, which is 80% or more of the minimum term.]

See also BURGLARY – *Persistent burglar – Minimum 3 years' custody – Plea of guilty, –* SUPPLY OF DRUGS **(Class A, B and C)** – *Persistent Class A supplier etc. – Minimum – 7 – years' custody Plea of guilty* and IMPORTATION OF DRUGS **(Class A, B and C)** – *Persistent Class A offender. – Minimum 7 years' custody – Plea of guilty*

Newton hearing, defendant takes part in

84.22   Sentencing Guidelines Council Guideline Guilty Plea December 2004. Para D 4.3 iv. If there is a Newton hearing and the offender's version is rejected, this should be taken into account in determining the level of reduction. www.sentencing-guidelines.gov.uk

R v Hassall 2000 1 Cr App R (S) 67. The judge was entitled to reduce the discount that would otherwise be given where there was a Newton hearing and his account was disbelieved. The judge was wrong to give the defendant no credit for his plea. The sentence was reduced.

Non Custodial sentences

84.23   Sentencing Guidelines Council Guideline Guilty Plea December 2004. Where an offence crosses the threshold for imposition of a community or custodial sentence, application of the reduction principle may properly form the basis for imposing a fine or discharge rather than a community sentence, or an alternative to an immediate custodial sentence. Where the reduction is applied in this way, the actual sentence imposed incorporates the reduction. www.sentencing-guidelines.gov.uk

Purpose

84.24   Sentencing Guidelines Council Guideline Guilty Plea December 2004. A reduction in sentence is appropriate because a guilty plea avoids the need for a trial, shortens the gap between charge and sentence, saves considerable cost and in the case of an early plea, saves victims and witnesses from concerns about having to give evidence. www.sentencing-guidelines.gov.uk

Rape   see RAPE – *Guilty plea*

State that the sentence has been discounted, judge must

84.25   Powers of Criminal Courts (Sentencing) Act 2000 s 152(2). If the court imposes a lesser sentence because of the guilty plea it shall state in open court it has done so. [Section summarised.]

See also *R v Bishop* 2000 1 Cr App R (S) 432.

85   Handling Stolen Goods

85.1   Theft Act 1968 s 22

Triable either way. On indictment maximum 14 years. Summary maximum 6 months and/or £5,000.

The Criminal Justice Act 2003 creates a summary maximum sentence of 51 weeks, a minimum sentence of 28 weeks and Custody plus. The Home Office says they do not expect to introduce these provisions before September 2006.

Restitution Order There is power to make an order that the stolen goods etc. in the possession of the defendant or a third party be restored to the owner etc.[1].

Crown Court statistics – England and Wales – Males 21+
85.2

Year	Plea	Total Numbers sentenced	Type of sentence %					Average length of custody (months)
			Discharge	Fine	Community sentence	Suspended sentence	Custody	
2002	Guilty	1,199	4	3	42	2	48	12.1
	Not guilty	184	4	9	39	2	45	18.7
2003	Guilty	1,203	5	4	43	2	45	13.9
	Not guilty	202	4	10	36	3	46	19.8

For details and explanations about the statistics in the book see page vii.

Guideline case

85.3   *R v Webbe* 2002 1 Cr App R (S) 82. LCJ. The difficulty of issuing guidelines in relation to handling arises from the enormous variety of possible sentences (which may be suitable) according to the circumstances. The offence can attract a penalty from a conditional discharge or modest fine at one end, up to 14 years (imprisonment) at the other. The relative seriousness of a case depends upon the interplay of different factors. One important issue is whether the handler has had advance knowledge of the original offence; or has directly or indirectly made known his willingness to receive the proceeds of the original offence, as compared with a handler who has had no connection with the original offence but who has dishonestly accepted the stolen goods at an undervalued (price). Where the handler has had knowledge of the original offence, the seriousness of the handling is inevitably linked to the seriousness of that original offence. The link to the original offence explains the need for the high maximum penalty of 14 years' imprisonment, which might otherwise look anomalous. Sentences approaching the maximum should clearly be reserved for the most serious and unusual cases where the handler had previous knowledge of a very serious offence such as an armed robbery, which itself carries life imprisonment as its maximum.

The replacement value of the goods involved is often a helpful indication of the seriousness of the offence. Monetary value in itself should not be regarded as the determining factor. There is an obvious difference, for example, between the gravity of receiving in a public house £100 worth of stolen television sets, and the gravity of receiving £100 in cash from the proceeds of a robbery which has taken place in the receiver's presence. Furthermore, accurate values in relation to the property received may very often be extremely difficult to ascertain. Other factors significantly affecting the relative seriousness of the handling offence, are the level of sophistication of the

1   Powers of Criminal Courts Act (Sentencing) 2000 s 148(2)

handler, the ultimate designation of the goods, the criminal origin of the goods, the impact on the victim, the level of profit made or expected by the handler, and, especially in cases of actual or intended disposal of goods, the precise role played by the handler. Handling cases at or towards the lower end of the scale are characterised by the handler having no connection with the original offence, an absence of sophistication on the part of the handler, the less serious nature of the original offence, the relatively low value of the goods and the absence of any significant profit.

The following nine factors aggravate the offence: (1) The closeness of the handler to the primary offence. [We add that closeness may be geographical, arising from presence at or near the primary offence when it was committed, or temporal, where the handler instigated or encouraged the primary offence beforehand, or, soon after, provided a safe haven or route for disposal]; (2) Particular seriousness in the primary offence; (3) High value of the goods to the loser, including sentimental value; (4) The fact that the goods were the proceeds of a domestic burglary; (5) Sophistication in relation to the handling; (6) A high level of profit made or expected by the handler; (7) The provision by the handler of a regular outlet for stolen goods; (8) Threats of violence or abuse of power by the handler over others, for example, an adult commissioning criminal activity by children, or a drug dealer pressurising addicts to steal in order to pay for their habit; (9) As is statutorily provided by s 151(2) of the Powers of Criminal Courts (Sentencing) Act 2000, the commission of an offence while on bail.

The mitigating factors are low monetary value of the goods, the offence was a one-off offence, committed by an otherwise honest defendant, there is little or no benefit to the defendant, and voluntary restitution to the victim.

Magistrates' Court Sentencing Guidelines January 2004

85.4   First time offenders who plead not guilty Entry point. Is it serious enough for a community penalty? Consider the impact on the victim. Examples of aggravating factors for the offence are high level of profit accruing to handler, high value (including sentimental) of the goods, provision by handler of regular outlet for stolen goods, proximity of handler to primary source, seriousness of the primary offence, sophistication, the particular facts e.g. the goods handled were the proceeds of a domestic burglary, and threats of violence or abuse of power by handler in order to obtain goods. Examples of mitigating factors for the offence are isolated offence, little or no benefit accruing to handler and low monetary value of goods. Examples of mitigation are age, health (physical or mental), co-operation with police, genuine remorse and voluntary compensation. Give reasons for not awarding compensation.

For details about the guidelines see **MAGISTRATES' COURT SENTENCING GUIDELINES** at page 483.

Antiques, valuable jewellery etc

85.5   *R v Dixon* 2002 2 Cr App R (S) 18. The defendant pleaded guilty to assisting in the retention etc. of stolen goods. While the victims were away attending a funeral, their house was burgled and antiques worth £255,000 were stolen including two clocks by Thomas Tompion worth together £230,000. Police searched the defendant's home and he showed them the stolen antiques. He said he was looking after them for someone else who he declined to name. He was 40 and was treated as of good character. His wife had a depressive illness and his daughter special needs. He was sentenced on the basis he was not a professional handler and had been prevailed upon against his better judgment to store the items. Nor could he be expected to know the clocks were so valuable. **18 months** not 3 years.

R v Chalcraft and Campbell 2002 2 Cr App R (S) 172. The defendant J pleaded guilty to four counts of attempting to handle stolen property. The defendant N pleaded to three such counts. They both had changed their plea. J had two jewellery shops. Following information jewellery was being received there an undercover officer started to sell them jewellery. J bought small items from him and then introduced him to N and he bought some items from him in pubs. As the contact developed the officer made it clear he was a burglar and the items were stolen. In fact the items were goods recovered which the owners had not claimed. N said the officer should take a gold watch and he would pay £1,000 for a 1930s Rolex. Next day he sold jewellery to J for £90. Six days later he told J a box saying he had stolen it from a house in Brighton. J said he would make enquires. Later he sold jewellery to J for £380. J warned him to be careful. There were further sales and J paid £40 and £50 and N paid £30. They were told where items were stolen from. Again J told him to be careful. The officer then used four antique candlesticks, which had been provided by another dealer. They were worth £10,500 retail. On J's direction N was shown a single candlestick and he showed it to J. They agreed to pay £320 for them. Both were arrested and denied they knew the goods were stolen. J returned some items, which he had on display. J was 40 and of good character and spoken of highly. N was 39 and had a number of offences including in 1997 convictions for burglary, theft and 3 deceptions for which he received a deferred sentence followed by CSO. N's role was less than J. Held. Monetary value should not be the determining factor. The case was aggravated by the closeness to the primary offence, the items were thought to be from domestic burglary, the high level of profit and they were both a regular outlet. The fact they had been targeted by police and there were no victims was mitigation. **10 months** for J not 15. **8 months** for N not 12.

R v Gwyer 2002 2 Cr App R (S) 246. LCJ. The defendant was convicted of nine counts of handling stolen property. For almost 4 months he received property stolen from residential burglaries. It was mostly antiques – porcelain, silver, clocks, furniture and the like. He and his associate sold the items through auctioneers where £16,160 was obtained. The Judge considered the replacement value was substantially more. The property was handled shortly after the burglaries. The judge considered they were professional fences for antiques. He was 43 and a roofer. There were convictions for dishonesty, poaching, firearm offences but none for handling. He hadn't served a custodial sentence. There was a delay of $2^1/_2$ years and he was under considerable stress. Held. Because of the delay and the stress **4 years** not 5.

Art, works of

85.6 *R v Love* 1999 1 Cr App R (S) 75. The defendants L and S were convicted of two counts of handling. Defendant T changed his plea at the beginning of the trial. They were all involved in the disposal of art. T was the principle, acting as broker to the thieves. He recruited L and S to assist. S made his flat available. L was responsible for transport. In 1995 a painting worth £10,000 was stolen from a country house. Also in 1995 a 42-item pottery collection was stolen from a museum valued at £100,000. It was regarded as part of the National Heritage. The following month T met an undercover police officer posing as an agent for a purchaser. T asked for £60,000 for the pottery. Next T and S met the officer and £52,000 was agreed for 37 items of pottery. T was followed to S's flat. £10,000 was handed over for the first tranche of property. S took the money to L who was in a car outside. The car dove off to collect the pottery and returned with the first tranche and the painting. S and L were arrested at the scene and T surrendered later. L was 50 with dishonesty convictions up to 1982. In 1981 he received $2^1/_2$ years for handling stolen antiques. S was 44 and had 10 convictions including 6 for burglary. T was 34 and was effectively of good character. He was the sole carer for his ill wife. Held. **3 years 9 months** not 7 years for S and L. Because of his character, plea and mitigation **3 years 3 months** for T not 6.

Old case. *R v Davies* 1998 2 Cr App R (S) 193 (for summary see first edition of this book).

Businessman defendant

85.7   *Att-Gen's Ref. No 70 of 1999* 2000 2 Cr App R (S) 28. The defendant was convicted of conspiracy to steal computer equipment and conspiracy to handle stolen computer equipment. He pleaded guilty to conspiracy to handling stolen goods and taking part in a company when an undischarged bankrupt. The defendant ran a computer supply and repair business. He suffered 3 burglaries and he wasn't insured. The losses were substantial. He then started to sell substantial quantities of stolen computer equipment. He involved members of staff to act as drivers and payers of cash. He had discussions about stealing a lorry load of computers worth £250,000. He agreed to pay £50,000 for the computers. This was the conspiracy to steal count. The judge treated the defendant as a man of good character and the offences as rather stale. Held. The offences were worth at least 4 years following a trial. Because it was a reference and because the defendant had already been released from prison **30 months** not 12 months in all. [Unfortunately there is no reference to the estimated value of goods involved in the handling counts.]

Car ringing

See THEFT – *Vehicles – Car ringing*

Compensation, confiscation and restitution

85.8   *R v Webbe* 2002 1 Cr App R (S) 82. LCJ.A court should always have in mind the power to make restitution orders under s 148 and 149 of the Powers of Criminal Courts (Sentencing) Act 2000, to make compensation orders under s 130 of the Powers of Criminal Court (Sentencing) Act 2000, and to make confiscation orders in relation to profits, under the Criminal Justice Act 1988 and the Proceeds of Crime Act 1995. A Magistrates' Court cannot, of course, make a confiscation order in a case of handling. But it is open to magistrates, in such a case, to commit to the Crown Court for sentence.

Custody threshold

85.9   *R v Webbe* 2002 1 Cr App R (S) 82. LCJ. So far as the custody threshold is concerned, the defendant either with a record of offences of dishonesty, or who engages in sophisticated law breaking, will attract a custodial sentence. It is in relation to the length of that sentence that the aggravating and mitigating features will come into play, as will the personal mitigation of the offender, who may appropriately, in accordance with *R v Ollerenshaw* 1999 1 Cr App R (S) 65, be dealt with by a somewhat shorter sentence than might, at first blush, otherwise have seemed appropriate. Note *R v Ollerenshaw* 1999 laid down, 'that where a court was considering imposing a comparatively short period of custody, of about 12 months or less, it should ask itself whether an even shorter period might be equally effective in protecting the interests of the public and punishing and deterring the criminal. There might be cases where 6 months might be just as effective as 9, or 2 months as effective as 4.'

R v Burke 2002 Unreported 30/8/02. The defendant appears to have pleaded guilty to handling and three counts of theft. In December 01 he stole an electric toothbrush from Boots worth £40. He was released on bail and failed to attend. In March 02 he stole some clothing worth £90 from Marks and Spencer. He was released on bail and in April 02 he stole some razor blades from Woolworths. After a scuffle with the police he was searched and 10 credit cards and a cheque book were found. The items had been stolen from a robbery two days before. He was 35, from America and of good character. The pre-sentence report said there was a real risk of further offending. He was addicted to crack and a DTTO was suggested. He refused the offer as he felt he couldn't keep to the requirements. Held. The offences were aggravated by the possession of the cards etc. a short time after the robbery and the breaches of bail. He had prevented a non-custodial option. **9 months** was not manifestly excessive. (The pleas and the offences are not directly referred to.)

Defendant aged 10–13

85.10   *R v T and F* 2001 1 Cr App R (S) 294. The defendant F pleaded to robbery. The defendant T pleaded guilty to handling. The victim was walking home when F grabbed her from behind and pressed a closed penknife into her neck. F demanded her handbag and dragged and pushed her over a small fence. The victim fell and F grabbed her bag off her shoulder and ran off. The defendants both then 13 were arrested and T pointed out a bin where the bag was found. £15 and cash was missing. T admitted being given £5. A month later the victim still had a fear of being out alone. Without her admissions there was no evidence against T. T had been dealt with for 11 offences in less than a year. She had six robberies, two thefts and a common assault against her. Her mother had severe mental problems. She had tried to commit suicide and involve T in it. As a result she was taken into care. Her placement with foster parents broke down and she went to a community home. She made substantial progress but was volatile. She was said to be extremely emotionally and psychologically damaged. It was said there was no risk of re-offending. Held. Taking into account her age and that it was only £5 **12 months** not 18 months' detention and training.

Defendant aged 14–17

85.11   *R v Webbe* 2002 Re Mitchell and Davis 1 Cr App R (S) 82. LCJ. The defendants M and D pleaded guilty to handling. M's brother seized a lady's handbag as she was out walking. There was a short struggle and she screamed. She was punched once in the face. The defendants and others were standing nearby. The brother ran off with the handbag, which contained credit and bankcards, keys and £6. The others ran off with him. The woman was bruised and grazed. D received £5 and M nothing. The two Mitchell brothers contacted the police and were arrested. M admitted holding some of the items as the young men went through the victim's handbag. But he said he handed them back. He left the scene with the others. He told the police the names of the robbers. D was arrested and said they had searched the bag and shared the contents. He had had £5 from the robbery. He accepted that there had been a conversation before-hand about committing a robbery. M was then 17 He had a conviction for a serious sexual offence, for which he was sentenced to 3 years' detention but no convictions for dishonesty. D was then 16. He had a number of convictions for stealing. 1 month before the offence a supervision order was imposed on him. **12 months** detention not 18 for both.

Fines and compensation more appropriate than custody

85.12   *R v Webbe* 2002 1 Cr App R (S) 82. LCJ *R v Khemlani* 1981 3 Cr App R (S) 208, shows the sentence that was appropriate for a man of good character, who pleaded guilty to handling 350 stolen watches (wholesale value £7,350). He was sentenced to 3 months' imprisonment. But the Court of Appeal took the view that the matter could be far better met by imposing a fine and making a compensation order in favour of the owners of the goods.

Monetary value – Value less than £1,000 – Guideline

85.13   *R v Webbe* 2002 1 Cr App R (S) 82. LCJ Where the property handled is of low monetary value and was acquired for the receiver's own use, the starting point should generally be a moderate fine or, in some cases (particularly, of course, if a fine cannot be paid by a particular defendant) a discharge. Such an outcome would, in our judgment be appropriate in relation to someone of previous good character handling low value domestic goods for his own use. By low value we mean less than four figures. A community sentence may be appropriate where property worth less than four figures is acquired for resale, or where more valuable goods are acquired for the handler's own use. Such a sentence may well be appropriate in relation to a young offender with little criminal experience, playing a peripheral role. But adult defendants with a record of dishonesty are likely to attract a custodial sentence.

Monetary value – Value less than £1,000 – Cases

85.14   *R v Osinowo* 2001 Unreported 23/10/01. The defendant pleaded guilty on re-arraignment to handling. He also pleaded guilty to a bail offence for which he was fined. He allowed another, Q to use his bank account to pay in cheques. The victim discovered her chequebook had been taken and a cheque for £4,700 was paid into his bank account. He was charged and a verdict of not guilty was entered for that. Police searched his home and discovered a blank cheque. He said Q gave it to him. No attempt had been made to use the cheque. The defendant was a 23-year-old student of good character when the offence was committed. Since then he had been given a community service order and had not performed any work. His pre-sentence report said that another order would not be appropriate. *Held.* The offence of handling is always serious and that certainly applies to cheques. A short custodial sentence was right and the judge was justified in suspending it. However, **4 months suspended** not 12.

Monetary value – £1,000 – £100,000 – Guideline

85.15   *R v Webbe* 2002 1 Cr App R (S) 82. LCJ In the more serious cases there will be some for which the range of 12 months to 4 years are likely to be appropriate if the value of the goods involved is up to around £100,000. [Note this guideline only relates to offences in the 4th and most serious level of seriousness. The 3rd category is offences which cross the custody threshold and the fourth is 'more serious offences'.]

Monetary value – £1,000 – £100,000 – Cases

85.16   *R v Jerome* 2001 1 Cr App R (S) 316. The defendant was convicted of handling. Computer and other equipment worth in all about £2,739 were stolen in a burglary. The computer was traced to the defendant when a message was sent from the computer to the Internet. His flat was searched and the equipment was found. He was an antiques dealer and his turnover was about £100,000. The judge said he was minded to imprisonment the defendant but was concerned his business might be permanently wrecked. He was fined £10,000. *Held.* It is permissible to increase a fine for a wealthy or relatively wealthy offender. However, there must be some proportionality between the scale of the offence and the fine imposed. In handling, the value of the goods must be taken into consideration. **£6,000 fine** not £10,000. [Many will consider the sentencing judges' proportionality of just under four times the value is more realistic than the Court of Appeal's proportionality of just over twice the value.]

R v Webbe 2002 1 Cr App R (S) 82. LCJ. Webbe pleaded guilty to attempting to handle and handling stolen watches. Police officers found three watches and £250 in cash in the boot of his car. One was an 18-carat gold watch with a retail value of £7,700. That was the handling offence. The attempt count related to two other linked chronographs, each with a retail value of £1,150. In interview the appellant made no comment. But later, he said that he had paid £200 for the watches, to a man he had met in the street. He was of good character. A pre-sentence report indicated the defendant's regret and that he was not a man who had criminal attitudes or a general disrespect for the law. The risk of re-offending was minimal. The total retail value of the goods was slightly over £10,000. *Held.* The defendant was not forthcoming in interview and could have provided the police with more help about the source and circumstances of his acquisitions. Taking into account the good character, the goods were apparently for his own use, the plea and the observations made in *R v Ollerenshaw* 1999 1 Cr App R (S) 65 (at custody threshold) **4 months** not 15 months.

Monetary value – Over £100,000 – Guideline case

85.17 *R v Webbe* 2002 1 Cr App R (S) 82. LCJ In the more serious cases where the value of the goods is in excess of £100,000, or where the offence is highly organised and bears the hallmarks of a professional commercial operation, a sentence of 4 years and upwards is likely to be appropriate, and it will be the higher where the source of the handled property is known by the handler to be a serious violent offence such as armed robbery. [Note. This guideline relates to offences in the fourth and most serious level of seriousness, although most offences of this value would fall into that category. The third category is offences, which cross the custody threshold and the fourth is 'more serious offences.']

Monetary value – Over £100,000 – Cases

85.18 *R v Webbe* 2002 Re White 1 Cr App R (S) 82. LCJ White pleaded guilty late to three counts of handling and a late count. The value involved was some £210,000. He leased a warehouse, which was searched by the police. There were found cigarettes, and alcohol, which had been stolen from two parked trailers two days before. The goods worth £72,000 were recovered. Also found were two trailers which, with their loads, had been stolen that day. Other stolen goods and trailers were found. At the time, he had been on bail for a remarkably similar offence. The judge concluded that the applicant had run a dishonest business yard, making it available to others for the disposal of dishonest goods. He was 36 and had convictions predominantly involving motor vehicles. He was sentenced to **2¹/₂ years** consecutive to 3 years he was currently serving. Held This was large scale professional receiving by a man with a criminal record. Goods reached him remarkably quickly after they had been stolen. The offences were committed while he was on bail for other serious offences. The sentence was a modest sentence.

Persistent offenders – Guideline case

85.19 *R v Webbe* 2002 1 Cr App R (S) 82. LCJ. *R v Battams* 1979 1 Cr App R (S) 15, shows the sentence of imprisonment which was appropriate for a receiver of stolen goods, obviously known in the locality as a person willing to assist in the disposal of such goods, however modest the sums of money involved. In that case, a sentence of 18 months was reduced to **12 months**, to take account of the appellant's physical disability. In *R v Bloomfield* 1995 16 Cr App R (S) 221, the Court of Appeal noted that the appropriate sentencing bracket for a receiver, who dealt regularly with thieves and burglars providing a regular outlet, was between 2 and 4 years' imprisonment, although, in that particular case, which was a one-off offence, a significantly lower sentence was imposed, namely 15 months for receiving three stolen caravans, for which he, a caravan dealer, had paid £9,000. As we have earlier indicated, sentences significantly higher than 4 years also may be appropriate where a professional handler, over a substantial period of time, demonstrated by his record or otherwise, has promoted and encouraged, albeit indirectly, criminal activity by others.'

Persistent offenders – Cases

85.20 *R v Webbe* 2002 Re Moore 1 Cr App R (S) 82. LCJ. Moore pleaded guilty to two offences of handling. He asked for 47 other offences, including 17 burglaries and 27 thefts, to be taken into consideration. The total value of the goods in the indictment was somewhat less than £2,000. The value of the TIC property was some £20,000. Two houses were burgled on the same day. A day or two later the defendant converted some of the property into cash at a pawnbrokers. He tried to sell the stolen property again and was arrested by police. His home was searched and stolen items were seized. He was 26 and had 60 convictions including burglary, theft and handling. Held. It is not generally desirable that a very large number of offences should be taken into consideration when there are comparatively few offences in the indictment and when the offences taken into consideration are of a different kind from those in the indictment. It is far preferable for the indictment to reflect the general level of criminality of a particular defendant. **4 years** was not manifestly excessive.

Professional handlers

85.21   *R v Webbe* 2002 1 Cr App R (S) 82. LCJ. In the more serious cases where the value of the goods is in excess of £100,000, or where the offence is highly organised and bears the hallmarks of a professional commercial operation, a sentence of 4 years and upwards is likely to be appropriate, and it will be the higher where the source of the handled property is known by the handler to be a serious violent offence such as armed robbery.

R v Gwyer 2002 2 Cr App R (S) 246. See ANTIQUES, VALUABLE JEWELLERY ETC

Robbery, proceeds of

85.22   *R v Webbe* 2002 1 Cr App R (S) 82. LCJ. The sentence will be higher where the source of the handled property is known by the handler to be a serious violent offence such as armed robbery.

R v Triumph and Ramadan 1999 Unreported 2/2/99. T pleaded guilty to handling and R was convicted of it. Both were acquitted of robbery. There was a robbery of a Securicor van and CS gas was spayed in the driver's face. The stolen property was found in the possession of the defendants 8 hours later. Both had convictions for dishonesty. Held. **4 years and 6 years** were severe but due to the short time after the offence and that it was a violent offence the sentence was not manifestly excessive.

R v Burke 2002 Unreported 30/8/02. The defendant appears to have pleaded guilty to handling and three counts of theft. In December 01 he stole an electric toothbrush from Boots worth £40. He was released on bail and failed to attend. In March 02 he stole some clothing worth £90 from Marks and Spencer. He was released on bail and in April 02 he stole some razor blades from Woolworths. After a scuffle with the police he was searched and 10 credit cards and a cheque book were found. The items had been stolen from a robbery two days before. He was 35, from America and of good character. The pre-sentence report said there was a real risk of further offending. He was addicted to crack and a DTTO was suggested. He refused the offer as he felt he couldn't keep to the requirements. Held. The offences were aggravated by the possession of the cards etc. a short time after the robbery and the breaches of bail. He had prevented a non-custodial option. **9 months** was not manifestly excessive. (The pleas and the offences are not directly referred to.)

Vehicles, stolen

85.23   *R v Okoro* 1997 Unreported 7/10/97. The defendant was convicted of 6 counts of handling stolen cars valued at £200,000. They were stolen in London and destined for Ghana. The defendant was a shipping agent who helped make arrangements for the containers and falsified details of payments. Held. It was a prevalent crime. **4 years** was not manifestly excessive.

HARBOURING DRUGS

See IMPORTATION OF DRUGS (CLASS A, B AND C) – *Harbouring*

86   HARASSMENT S 2

86.1   Pursuing a course of harassment.

Protection from Harassment Act 1997 s 2

Summary only. Maximum sentence 6 months and/or Level 5 fine (£5,000).

Anti-Social Behavioural orders Where the defendant has acted in a manner that caused or was likely to cause harassment, alarm or distress to one or more persons not in the same household as the defendant and it is necessary to protect persons from further anti-social acts by him/her the court may make this order[2].

Restraining order There is power to make a restraining order to protect the victim etc from further conduct[3]. These powers are amended by Domestic Violence, Crime and Victims Act 2004 s 12 etc. and there is power from 31/3/05 to impose an order after an acquittal.

Guideline case

86.2   *R v Liddle and Hayes* 2000 1 Cr App R (S) 131. The court should consider: (1) Is the offence a s 2 or a s 4 offence? (2) Is there a history of disobedience to court orders in the past? (3) The seriousness of the defendant's conduct, which can of course range from actual violence through to threats, down to letters, which of course may even express affection rather than any wish to harm the victim. (4) Is there persistent misconduct by the defendant or a solitary instance of misbehaviour? (5) The effect upon the victim, whether physical or psychological. Does the victim require protection? What is the level of risk posed by the defendant? (6) The mental health of the offender. Is the defendant willing to undergo treatment or have the necessary help from the probation service, which is readily available under special schemes? (7) What is the defendant's reaction to the court proceedings? Is there a plea of guilty? Is there remorse? Is there recognition of the need for help? For a first offence a short sharp sentence may be appropriate, though much will depend on the factors of repetition and breach of court orders and the nature of the misconduct. Obviously, the facts of each case vary and the facts of any particular case may require a longer sentence. For a second offence longer sentences of about **15 months** on a plea of guilty would be an appropriate starting point, and from then on it is possible to see from the maximum of 5 years where each case fits into the statutory framework working from the figure of 15 months, which may be appropriate. [Unfortunately the court does not say whether the sentences are for s 2 or 4 or both.]

Magistrates' Court Sentencing Guidelines January 2004

86.3   First time offenders who plead not guilty. Entry point. Is it serious enough for a community penalty? Consider the impact on the victim. Examples of aggravating factors for the offence are disregard of warning, excessive persistence, interference with employment/business, invasion of victim's home, involvement of others, use of violence or grossly offensive material and where photographs or images of a personal nature are involved. Examples of mitigating factors for the offence are initial provocation and short duration. Examples of mitigation are age, health (physical or mental), co-operation with the police, genuine remorse and voluntary compensation. Consider making a restraining order. Give reasons if not awarding compensation.

For details about the guidelines see **MAGISTRATES' COURT SENTENCING GUIDELINES** at page 483.

---

2   Crime and Disorder Act 1998 s 1C
3   Protection from Harassment Act 1997 s 5

Ex-partners

86.4   *R v Liddle and Hayes* 2000 1 Cr App R (S) 131. The defendant L pleaded guilty to two breaches of a restraining order. A Crown Court injunction was made restraining him from harassing his ex-wife. In breach of that he was convicted at the Magistrates' Court of harassment, (s 2), and of harassment, causing fear of violence (s 4). He was sentenced to a combination order including community service. A new restraining order was made for his ex-wife, his child and her parents. Four months later he was again convicted at the same court of three breaches of the new restraining order. He was conditionally discharged. Five months later he pleaded guilty at the Crown Court to two breaches of the order and was sentenced to 9 months imprisonment. He was released on 12th October 1998 and on 25 February 1999 he pleaded guilty to two more offences. They were sending two letters to his ex-wife, an exchange of words with her and sending three letters to her from prison. One of the offences was 2–3 weeks after his release from prison. His ex-wife was distressed and clearly annoyed. He was 32 and his pre-sentence report said he did not present a risk of serious harm to the public, but could pose such a risk to his wife and daughter should he persevere with his obsessional views about returning to his wife. A psychiatric report said he was not mentally ill and had no history of violent behaviour. Held. In the main he had only written letters. It is little mitigation that the letters were not threatening or objectionable. There was only one incident in the street. The effect on the victim and the need for protection are well in our minds. **8 months** and 4 months consecutive consecutive to the 3 months recall not 21 months.

Stranger

86.5   *R v Liddle and Hayes* 2000 1 Cr App R (S) 131. The defendant H was convicted of two offences of harassment. He began to harass a young woman who he saw by chance. She rebuffed his advance but he persisted in harassing her. He was charged with harassment and sentenced to two months consecutive on each. The court made a lifetime restraining order. Eight months after the conviction he rang her door bell. He then ran away but was caught by a friend of the victim's. Six weeks later she received a letter written by him revealing his knowledge of her daily life and inferentially suggesting that he had been observing her in order to make those revelations. He was 39. A pre-sentence report said he was obsessional about this young lady. He has lived with his mother for a long period and has never been in full-time employment. Held. It was mainly letters. There was one incident at her home, which was at the bottom of the range. The effect on the victim was distress and annoyance rather than any more. **8 months** and 3 months consecutive not 2 years.

Telephone calls

86.6   *R v Sutton* 2001 2 Cr App R (S) 414. The defendant pleaded guilty to harassment. The defendant and an elderly man were good friends and the defendant helped him out for 15 years. When items went missing the elderly man asked a relation to tell the defendant not to visit again and to give him £500 as a thank you. The elderly man died. The relative, one of the victims gave the defendant the money and told him he didn't think the defendant was responsible for taking items. The defendant strongly denied the thefts and what the relative said. The defendant then made five threatening telephone calls and sent him a funeral brochure and two brochures of memorial headstones. Two further calls were made which were taken by the relative's wife demanding £10,000 or the relative would be killed. He eventually admitted making the calls and said he wanted to get his own back and he was very hurt by what the victims had said. He was 31 with no convictions. The pre-sentence report said it was very unlikely he would re-offend. He had depressive symptoms which had improved. They were linked to the death of the elderly man. The victims asked that the sentence should not be too harsh. Two prison reports commented favourably on his work and raised questions about his safety. **1 year** not 3 with a 5 year restraining order remaining.

See also **PUBLIC ORDER ACT 1986** and **STALKING**

87   HARASSMENT S 2 – RACIALLY OR RELIGIOUSLY AGGRAVATED

87.1   Pursuing a course of harassment, which is racially aggravated.

Protection from Harassment Act 1997 s 2 and the Crime and Disorder Act 1998 s 32(1)(a)

Triable either way. On indictment maximum sentence 2 years. Summary maximum 6 months and/or £5,000.

Anti-Social Behavioural orders Where the defendant has acted in a manner that caused or was likely to cause harassment, alarm or distress to one or more persons not in the same household as the defendant and it is necessary to protect persons from further anti-social acts by him/her the court may make this order[4].

Restraining orders There is power to make a restraining order to protect the victim etc from further conduct[5]. These powers are amended by Domestic Violence, Crime and Victims Act 2004 s 12 etc. and there is power from 31/3/05 to impose an order after an acquittal.

Sexual Offences Prevention Order There is a discretionary power to make this order when it is necessary to protect the public etc[6].

Magistrates' Court Sentencing Guidelines January 2004

88.2   First time offenders who plead not guilty Entry point. Is it so serious that only custody is appropriate? Consider the impact on the victim. Examples of aggravating factors for the offence are disregard of warning, excessive persistence, interference with employment/business, invasion of victim's home, involvement of others, motivation for the offence was racial or religious, setting out to humiliate the victim, use of violence or grossly offensive material and where photographs or images of a personal nature are involved. Examples of mitigating factors for the offence initial provocation and short duration. Examples of mitigation are age, health (physical or mental), co-operation with the police, and genuine remorse and voluntary compensation. Consider making a restraining order. Give reasons if not awarding compensation.

For details about the guidelines see **MAGISTRATES' COURT SENTENCING GUIDELINES** at page 483.

General approach   See **RACIALLY AGGRAVATED OFFENCES** – *General approach*

Employers

87.3   *R v Gaunt* 2004 2 Cr App R (S) 194. The defendant pleaded guilty on rearraignment to racially aggravated harassment. He was the general manager and later the managing director of a Transport Services firm. Between 1997 and 2001 the victim, a black man with moderate learning difficulties, worked there and was subjected by three other employees to verbal and physical abuse with racist overtones. The defendant pleaded guilty on the basis that he was aware of at least two incidents, these being that

---

4   Crime and Disorder Act 1998 s 1C
5   Protection from Harassment Act 1997 s 5 and the Crime and Disorder Act 1998 s 32(7).
6   Sexual Offences Act 2003 s 104 & Sch. 5

firstly the victim was forced into a grab device and secondly that he had objects thrown at him; that by reason of his inaction those responsible for these incidents may have taken his inaction as an encouragement of their conduct; and that he did not see any of the acts of cruelty to which the victim was subjected. It was said that the degree of cruelty and abuse to which the victim was subjected was much greater and more serious than the two incidents the defendant knew about. The defendant was a man of exemplary character who had built up the business so that it had become extremely successful. He had extremely impressive references. In his personal life he had no racist tendencies and had friends across the communities. Held. This type of case must be considered on its own facts, and pre-eminent will be the extent of knowledge of the aider and abettor. The judge lost sight of the point that the defendant stood in a totally different position from his co-accused, not in the sense that he did not perform any acts himself, but that he knew a very small part of what was happening. That made a substantial difference in the case. **6 months** not 18.

Neighbours

87.4   *R v Shand* 2002 1 Cr App R (S) 291. The defendant pleaded guilty to racially aggravated harassment. The defendant and the victim were neighbours. They were both white. The victim's partner was Afro-Caribbean and her three children were of mixed race. One afternoon he started shouting, 'England, fucking blacks, nigger lovers,' outside his gate. He was looking towards the victim's flat and appeared drunk. She found it intimidating and called the police who spoke to him about it. A week later, the defendant saw the victim's partner and shouted, 'Nigger lover,' and continued shouting, 'England. If you're happy and white clap you're hands. Fucking black bastards.' He called the victim a 'whore,' 'drug dealer' and 'prostitute.' The police arrived about an hour later and talked to the defendant. He went back inside. At 11.30pm that night when she and the children were in bed he started shouting saying he was going to kill her and her days were numbered. The abuse continued till the police arrived and took him away. The next day at 8.30am he was back shouting loudly, 'Nigger lover, jungle bunnies, cock sucker, England.' 'Combat 18 was going to bomb you niggers out.' Eight days later there was further similar abuse and the next day he threatened to kill the victim and her children and set fire to her house. A month later there was more abuse. The victim was absolutely distraught. The defendant was 39 and had convictions for threatening behaviour, affray and in 1997 for racially threatening behaviour on the same victim for which he received 28 days imprisonment. His problem was drink. He showed remorse and had lost his home of 16 years. Held. This was the most disgraceful conduct. There was nothing wrong with **15 months**.

Police officers etc, directed at

87.5   *R v Jacobs* 2001 2 Cr App R (S) 174. The defendant was sentenced for harassment (presumably s 2) which was racially aggravated and common assault. (The plea is not given in the report.) The defendant then 20 was arrested and taken to a police station. A police officer asked the defendant to remove two rings she was wearing. She said, 'I don't want you Paki filthy hands on me. I don't want that Paki touching me.' She also told the custody officer she didn't want a foreigner touching her. She was restrained and the rings were removed. She struggled and continued shouting racial abuse. In the cell she shouted abuse. Later she abused the same officer again. She admitted the offence in interview. She had a public order conviction in 1997 for which she received an attendance centre order. Her psychiatric report said she would respond to probation perhaps with psychiatric treatment. Held. Police officers are entitled to be protected from racial abuse but **3 months** not 9.

See also **PUBLIC ORDER ACT 1986** and **STALKING**

88 HARASSMENT S 4 / PUBLIC NUISANCE

88.1 Putting people in fear of violence.

Protection from Harassment Act 1997 s 4

Triable either way. On indictment maximum sentence 5 years. Summary maximum 6 months and/or £5,000.

The Criminal Justice Act 2003 creates a summary maximum sentence of 51 weeks, a minimum sentence of 28 weeks and Custody plus. The Home Office says they do not expect to introduce these provisions before September 2006.

Public Nuisance

Common law so indictable only. There is no maximum provided so the maximum is life imprisonment.

Anti-Social Behavioural orders Where the defendant has acted in a manner that caused or was likely to cause harassment, alarm or distress to one or more persons not in the same household as the defendant and it is necessary to protect persons from further anti-social acts by him/her the court may make this order[7].

Extended sentences under CJA 2003 For offences committed on or after 4/4/05 there is a mandatory duty to pass an extended sentence when there is a significant risk to members of the public of serious harm etc.[8]. See EXTENDED SENTENCES

Restraining orders There is power for section 4 offences to make this order to protect the victim etc from further conduct[9]. These powers are amended by Domestic Violence, Crime and Victims Act 2004 s 12 etc. and there is power from 31/3/05 to impose an order after an acquittal.

Sexual Offences Prevention Order For offences under section 4, there is a discretionary power to make this order when it is necessary to protect the public etc[10].

Guideline case

88.2 *R v Liddle and Hayes* 2000 1 Cr App R (S) 131. The court should consider: (1) Is the offence a s 2 or a s 4 offence? (2) Is there a history of disobedience to court orders in the past? (3) The seriousness of the defendant's conduct, which can of course range from actual violence through to threats, down to letters, which of course may even express affection rather than any wish to harm the victim. (4) Is there persistent misconduct by the defendant or a solitary instance of misbehaviour? (5) The effect upon the victim, whether physical or psychological. Does the victim require protection? What is the level of risk posed by the defendant? (6) The mental health of the offender. Is the defendant willing to undergo treatment or have the necessary help from the probation service, which is readily available under special schemes? (7) What is the defendant's reaction to the court proceedings? Is there a plea of guilty? Is there remorse? Is there recognition of the need for help? For a first offence a **short sharp sentence** may be appropriate, though much will depend on the factors of repetition and breach of court orders and the nature of the misconduct. Obviously, the facts of each case vary and the facts of any particular case may require a longer sentence. For a second offence longer sentences of about **15 months** on a plea of guilty would be an appropriate starting point, and from then on it is possible to see from the maximum of 5 years where each case fits into the statutory framework working from the figure of 15 months, which may be appropriate. [Unfortunately the court does not say whether the sentences are for s 2 or 4 or both.]

7 Crime and Disorder Act 1998 s 1C
8 Criminal Justice Act 2003 s 227–228
9 Protection from Harassment Act 1997 s 5
10 Sexual Offences Act 2003 s 104 & Sch. 5

Magistrates' Court Sentencing Guidelines January 2004

88.3   First time offenders who plead not guilty Entry point. Is it so serious that only custody is appropriate? Consider the impact on the victim. Examples of aggravating factors for the offence are disregard of warning, excessive persistence, interference with employment/business, invasion of victim's home, involvement of others, threat to use weapon or substance (including realistic imitations), use of violence or grossly offensive material and where photographs or images of a personal nature are involved. Examples of mitigating factors for the offence are initial provocation and short duration. Examples of mitigation are age, health (physical or mental), co-operation with the police, and genuine remorse and voluntary compensation. Consider making a restraining order. Give reasons if not awarding compensation.

For details about the guidelines see MAGISTRATES' COURT SENTENCING GUIDELINES at page 483.

Animal rights activists

see ANIMAL RIGHTS ACTIVISTS – *Section 4*

Obsessive behaviour to opposite/ex-partners

88.4   *R v Miah* 2000 2 Cr App R (S) 439. The defendant was convicted of harassment and intimidating a witness. The defendant then 22 years old wanted to start a relationship with the victim who was a 15 or 16-year-old schoolgirl. He used to wait for her outside school and hug her and hold her hands. She didn't want a relationship with him at all. He threatened to cut her hands off with a knife. A man saw them and came and rescued her. Two weeks later she ran away from him and he caught up and shouted abuse at her and punched her in the face and kicked her on the ground. Onlookers called the police. She suffered bruises. Over 6 weeks later he came in to a fast food restaurant where she worked and she ran into the back office. He called out, 'Fucking bitch,' and said he had a gun and was going to get her. He was arrested and released on bail. $3^{1}/_{2}$ months later the victim was walking home from work with a friend and he ran up to them with his fists clenched and said, 'Fucking bitch.' Her friend told him to leave her alone and there was a short argument. He then threw some papers down and said, 'Fucking bitch, read that. That is what you wrote,' referring to her witness statement. He took hold of her wrists and frog marched her to the station (police presumably) swearing at her. He dragged her to some gardens and his mood changed with him asking her not to leave him. His mood changed back and he said, 'Leave me, fucking bitch. You are going to pay in the end.' She walked away and he shouted after her. He was arrested and was remanded in custody. He was of good character. Those that wrote reports found he lied and continued to deny the offences. One report said he was irrational and might be obsessed with the victim. No treatment was suggested. There was no contrition and the risk of re-offending was described as high. Held. Here the persistent and impact on the victim must be regarded. The judge should assess the form of sentence and length of sentence most likely to lead to the defendant behaving and not breaching the restraint order. **18 months** not $2^{1}/_{2}$ years with the intimidation sentence of 6 months concurrent and a restraining order remaining.

R v Onabanjo 2001 2 Cr App R (S) 27. The defendant pleaded guilty at the Magistrates' Court to putting another in fear contrary to s 4 and common assault. He had a $2^{1}/_{2}$ year relationship with the victim and they had an 18 month old son. She told him the relationship was over and she moved back to her old flat. He went to her flat argued with her and pulled her across the floor by her feet causing friction burns which were not serious. He was charge and released on bail. The there were a number of other incidents of which three were over 6 days and were; threatening to kill her twice on the telephone and once in the street after he had blocked her way. Within the 6 days he entered her flat through a window at 12.45 am. She awoke to find him at the foot of her bed repeatedly asking for them to get back together. He stayed for $^1/_2$ hour and she said she wasn't frightened then. He also sent letters of affection. He said the conduct was connected with his concern for his son. He was then 21 and had 4 years before been bound over for threatening words and behaviour. Three years later he received 2 years detention for 3 robberies and 1 attempt. He had a problem with alcohol and expressed genuine remorse. Held. The repeated threats by a man who is capable of unpredictable behaviour made the offence particularly serious. The **12 months** and 3 months for the assault were not excessive. Neither was it wrong to make the sentences consecutive. Nor was the 15 months excessive.

R v Tully 2003 1 Cr App R (S) 268. The defendant pleaded guilty to putting a person in fear contrary to section 4. He and his wife met in 1980 and married in 1983. Both had four children and they had one together. She said the marriage was violent. He denied that. They separated seven times. In 2001, She moved into the home of J keeping the address secret. Two weeks later the defendant visited the address and told J, "When I find them I'll kill them." She and J left the area and went to Devon. She instructed solicitors for a divorce. He wrote a threatening letter to her solicitor saying he was prepared for prison to get revenge. She and J were out walking and the defendant appeared in front of them. He raised his fist at J and threatened them, saying "I'll be back to get you." About two months later she received another threatening letter from the defendant. Next day she saw him and contacted the police. They issued him a protection from harassment warning. About a week later, another letter said he had befriended some gypsies and they could get anything including guns. Further he did not care about prison as his life was not worth living and next time he visited he had a present for them. She and J then went to Sunderland. Fifteen days after the gypsy incident, he found them and pushed a letter into her hand and said to J, "You better have a serious talk with her, to get her to come back to me and the family, or I'll knife you in the neck with a big knife." She and J then entered a club. As she phoned the police, she saw the defendant running across the road towards her waving a large butcher's type knife. The doormen shut the door and he shouted, "This is what you are going to get. You're fucking dead." The letter was the same as the others veering from love to hate, jealousy and resentment and to the pain of being deserted. He was arrested and said his sole intention was to get her back. He was 56 and effectively of good charac-ter. Since his arrest there had been no contact with the wife, they had been divorced and he had found a new relationship. The judge found he had deliberately caused terror and threatened extreme violence. He gave him 8 months and a two year restraining order. The defence asked for a short sharp sentence to be substituted. Held. This was persistent harassment. **8 months** was in no way excessive.

R v Kennedy 2004 Cr.App.R. (S.) 97. The defendant pleaded guilty to harassment on his ex partner. In early 1996 he had been placed on probation for destroying property and ABH on the victim. Later in 1996 he was placed on probation for common assault on her. On one occasion she had sought an injunction and by 2002 the relationship was over as far as she was concerned; she required him to leave the family home and told him that she had started a relationship with another man, H. Shortly afterward the defendant broke into the house, armed himself with 2 knives and a lump hammer and attacked H with a hammer, causing minor injuries. He also caused damage in the house. For this aggravated burglary he received 15 months imprisonment. The day after he was released from prison he went in a drunken state to the house and banged repeatedly on the door causing the glass to crack. The victim's son persuaded him to leave before the police arrived. The police said they would give him a harassment warning but apparently did not. The defendant wrote a letter to his sons, which contained threats of future action: 'one day there will be an almighty eruption and the fall out will be catastrophic'; 'I will decide when the game is over and it ain't over till I say ... war of attrition'; 'You can't run and you can't hide'. The defendant went to a police station expressing fears for his mental health and for a short time he was a voluntary in-patient at a hospital where he was treated for depression. After that he went to collect his son from the house and the victim told the defendant he was not supposed to be there. The next day he returned to the house. The victim told him to leave. He said 'You deny me my kids'. In fact she had encouraged contact between the defendant and their children. He said 'You have ripped my heart out. I am going to kill you.' He then spoke to his mother on the phone and was heard to say: 'Either I am going to die or they are'. After the phone conversation he said he was going to petrol bomb the house. He was then arrested. The victim said she was now frightened that he would return and that she was always looking round to see if he was in the house. There was no psychiatric report available to the sentencing judge. The pre- sentence report said the defendant seemed determined to make changes in the future, but that he had not shown any sustained motivation to change his drinking behaviour which played a critical part in his offences or to move on from his immature, self indulgent and damaging behaviour towards the victim and their children. He had breached his bail terms. A post-sentence report said that progress had been made and that he had undergone an enhanced thinking skills programme in prison. He was taking anti-depressant medication and was less aggressive. He had a good report from his landing officer. **Held.** The harassment began the day after the defendant was released from prison. There were explicit threats designed to cause fear. Threats were made both face to face and in a letter. The behaviour was persistent and it produced a significant effect on the victim. The defendant's offending was not at the lower end of the scale. **18 months** imprisonment for the harassment was not manifestly excessive. The portion of unexpired sentence to be served consecutive recalculated to 210 days.

Sexual

88.5 *R v Underwood Re A* 2005 1 Cr App R (S) 478 at 490. The defendant pleaded guilty to fifteen counts of harassment contrary to s. 4 and one count of intimidating a witness. The offences took place over about $3\frac{1}{2}$ years and were similar. The victims were aged between 14 and 17. The defendant would begin by approaching and sometimes appearing to befriend the victims. He made them flex their biceps and felt their arms, chests and legs. He would ask them to lean over and perform squatting exercises while he rested his weight against their backs or buttocks. He often required them to perform these exercises in his car or in some lonely area. In some cases they were harassed in this way for periods exceeding three years. Some saw him daily, others less frequently. He undoubtedly intimidated the victims. The separate witness intimidation concerned a victim of harassment who came across the defendant by accident. The defendant said to him "I want you out of this ... better for you if you were not involved". They talked for about 20 minutes. He was 43 with a very long record including 30 months for threats to kill that occurred after these offences. Most of his previous convictions were for violence on police officers and offences of dishonesty. **Held.** He represented a danger to young men. An overall sentence of **5 years** for harassment was not arguably manifestly excessive nor was a consecutive **12-months** for witness intimidation.

Telephone calls

88.6 *R v Hill* 2000 1 Cr App R (S) 8. The defendant made an early plea to harassment by putting someone in fear contrary to s 4. A 13-year-old girl left her bus pass on a bus. It had her personal details including her telephone number on it. She was unknown to the defendant but he repeatedly telephoned her at her home in Rotterdam. Generally the calls were made at night between 7.15 pm and 9 am. Sometimes he would hang up, sometimes he started heavy breathing and sometimes he asked her questions about what she was doing. There were also questions about what she was wearing and threats to see her at school. He also claimed to know personal details about her. The girl became very frightened and was frightened to leave her home. On one day he told her he wanted to shag her and talked about coming to her house and ripping her clothes off. Eventually the telephone number was changed and this caused considerable inconvenience to her father over his business calls. The defendant was 24 when he appeared at court he had no convictions. Later he pleaded guilty to a similar offence for which he received 2 months concurrent. He had a history of depressive symptoms and an inadequate and immature personality. Held. The victim was at a vulnerable stage. However, **12 months** not 18.

R v Eskdale 2002 1 Cr App R (S) 118. The defendant pleaded guilty to causing a nuisance to the public by making threatening, obscene and malicious telephone calls. Over 2 weeks he made about 1,000 telephone calls. There were 15 complainants. Four were telephoned in the middle of the night, three very late in the evening and the rest very late in the morning. In some he said he had followed them or was outside their homes. They were made for his sexual gratification. As an example he telephoned a pregnant 28-year-old wife whose telephone was ex-directory and spoke to her by name and asked if her husband was in. He then said he was outside and said, 'I'm going to come inside and fuck you. Don't put the telephone down or you'll regret it.' She did put the telephone down and tried to ring her husband but the defendant was blocking the line. Eventually she went to a neighbour who assisted her. In another he threatened to stab the female victim if she put the telephone down. The worst case was when he rang a young woman whose flat overlooked a darkened car park. At 1am it woke her up and he said she had better do as he said or he would come and rape her. She was alone and very frightened. He made her stand in front of the window and take her clothes off and threatened to enter the flat if she refused. It was clear he was watching her. He told her to touch her breasts and vagina and told her to put her bottom against the window and part her cheeks. He also told her to stop crying or he'd come and fuck her. She was also made to simulate sex with a banana and her mouth. She was told not to tell anyone or he'd come and get her. She felt disgusted and violated. She had to leave her flat and live with her father. The defendant was arrested. He had in 1990 a conviction for using the telephone system to send offensive matter and several burglaries and threats to kill. The burglaries were to steal underwear. Later in 1990 a conviction for using the telephone system to send indecent matter. In 1993 he received $5^1/_2$ years for indecent assault. In 1996 a conviction for using the telephone system to send offensive matter and to cause annoyance for which he received imprisonment. When serving the $5^1/_2$ year sentence he received treatment but after his release he committed further offences and was recalled to prison. The probation officer considered his offending was escalating in a dangerous way. There was considered a serious risk of harm to the public. The psychiatrist described his abnormally high sex drive with anger, social isolation and little self-control and the likelihood he gains gratification from humiliating women. Adding despite extensive treatment he was a danger to women. Held. The judge was confronted with an exceptionally difficult sentencing exercise. **9 years** was a very severe sentence but it was justified.

R v Preston 2002 1 Cr App R (S) 419. The defendant pleaded guilty to harassment causing fear at the Magistrates' Court. Within 6 of her release from prison she made 46 menacing calls to a 63 year old lady who was a complete stranger. The victim lived with her sister and suffered from high blood pressure. The calls were abusive and threatening. One day there were 19 calls containing threats to stab her, burn her house down and kill her. Sometimes the calls would be silent. She was arrested and told the police, 'I am going not guilty because I want to know what the bitch looks like.' She was 27 with a substantial history of offending. She had convictions for repeated offences of theft, assault, Public Order offences, intimidating a witness, harassment and racially aggravating threatening behaviour. In 2000 she received 19 months for threats to kill, threatening behaviour, affray and common assault. The psychiatrist's report said she suffered from an emotionally unstable personality disorder. The judge sentenced her to the 10 months for the breach of her licence and **2¹/₂ years consecutive**. Held. There was a history of disobedience to the court orders in the past. The sentence was inevitable.

R v Harley 2003 2 Cr App R (S) 16. The defendant pleaded guilty to causing a public nuisance. Police enquiries centred around two mobile telephones, both of which were traced to the defendant. Over a three-month period he made 4845 calls to in excess of 1000 people. There was a pattern in relation to the calls: some were silent; some were explicitly and unpleasantly sexual. One woman received 18 calls, another 53 calls and another 40 calls of an unpleasant and explicitly sexual kind. The defendant was arrested 2 months after the calls had finished. In interview he admitted to owning the phones and admitted to calling one of the women before making no further comment. He was interviewed 6 weeks later and he admitted telephoning the 45 women named on the indictment. He agreed that he made sounds as if to indicate he was masturbating on occasions. He said that he gained no sexual gratification but that he was trying to see what the reaction would be. He stopped making the calls when he learned, by chance, of the effect that such calls could have. He was 32 and of good character. Held. Such activity required a significant sentence. This case had unusual features: (1) the defendant was of previous good character; (2) he committed these offences at a time when was suffering from clinical depression; (3) the offences were committed over a comparatively short period of time; and (5) the psychiatric report concluded that the risk of repetition was minimal. **9 months** not 21.

R v Newton 2003 2 Cr App R (S) 437. The defendant pleaded guilty to 4 counts of harassment (section 4), 1 count of harassment (section 2) and a breach of bail. There were 10 further harassment (section 4) offences to be taken into consideration. Over a 15 month period the victims had all come into contact with the defendant through his work as a landscape gardener. The first victim received about three calls a day, every other day for two weeks, the last of which contained threats of violence towards her daughter. The second victim received 25 calls of a sexual nature on one day. The third victim received about 10 calls on two separate weeks a month apart. The fourth victim received numerous calls over about 1 year. The offences to be taken into consideration were calls to other women over the same period. He was arrested and initially denied the offences. He later made full admissions, saying that he had been on drugs at the time and did not know what had made him do it. He said that he was trying to seek help. He was 37 and had various convictions for violence and dishonesty. There was one conviction (10 years earlier) for using telecommunications systems to send offensive matter. He had one conviction for "a sex-related" ABH that was 5 years old. The defendant had some insight into his behaviour and had expressed remorse. A psychiatric report concluded that he had a disorder or personality of the dissocial type with co-existing harmful use of drugs. Held. These offences involved obscene, sexually explicit and offensive material. They were graphic, disgusting with an explicit violent content. This was a campaign of repeated obscene and threatening phone calls. These were serious offences causing considerable anxiety and fear. **3¹/₂ years** (plus 3 months consecutive for the breach of bail) upheld.

R v Lowrie 2005 1 Cr App R (S) 530. The defendant pleaded guilty to twelve offences of public nuisance. Over a month he telephoned the emergency services on twelve occasions. These included the fire service to say that his house was burning down and two engines were dispatched, Two days later he called the ambulance service twice saying that he had been assaulted, the police to say he was about to commit suicide and the coastguard claiming that he was suicidal. Six days later he called an ambulance giving false details and saying that his friend had taken an overdose. He also called the fire service days later saying that a pub was on fire. Fire engines were dispatched. There was also a call to the coastguard that resulted in a search and rescue operation. He was 24 was an appalling record for exactly this type of offending. He had since 16 been sentenced for repeated calls to the emergency services and received every type of disposal including, most recently, 5 years' imprisonment. The current offending occurred within 3 months of his release from that sentence. Psychiatrists thought that he had a psychopathic disorder and specifically either an antisocial or emotionally unstable personality disorder. The risk of reoffending was assessed as high. Held. Despite the psychiatric mitigation, society is entitled to expect the courts to provide protection against hoax callers. **8 years** upheld.

See also **PUBLIC ORDER ACT 1986** and **STALKING**

89   HARASSMENT S 4 – RACIALLY OR RELIGIOUSLY AGGRAVATED

89.1   Putting people in fear of violence, which is racially aggravated.

Protection from Harassment Act 1997 s 4 and the Crime and Disorder Act 1998 s 31(1)(a)

Triable either way. On indictment maximum sentence 7 years[11]. Summary maximum 6 months and/or £5,000.

Anti-Social Behavioural orders Where the defendant has acted in a manner that caused or was likely to cause harassment, alarm or distress to one or more persons not in the same household as the defendant and it is necessary to protect persons from further anti-social acts by him/her the court may make this order[12].

Extended sentences under CJA 2003 For offences committed on or after 4/4/05 there is a mandatory duty to pass an extended sentence when there is a significant risk to members of the public of serious harm etc.[13]. See **EXTENDED SENTENCES**

Restraining Order There is power to make a restraining order to protect the victim etc from further conduct[14]. These powers are amended by Domestic Violence, Crime and Victims Act 2004 s 12 etc. and there is power from 31/3/05 to impose an order after an acquittal.

Sexual Offences Prevention Order There is a discretionary power to make this order when it is necessary to protect the public etc[15].

General approach   See **RACIALLY AGGRAVATED OFFENCES** – *General approach*

Magistrates' Court Sentencing Guidelines January 2004

89.2   First time offenders who plead not guilty Entry point. Are magistrates' sentencing powers sufficient? Consider the impact on the victim. Examples of aggravating factors for the offence are disregard of warning, excessive persistence, interference with employment/business, invasion of victim's home, involvement of others, motivation for the offence was racial or religious, setting out to humiliate the victim, to use weapon or substance (including realistic imitations), use of violence or grossly offensive material

---

11 Where the jury convict of s 4 as an alternative to the racially-aggravated offence the maximum sentence at the Crown Court is the Magistrates' Courts' maximum, *R v Alden* 2002 2 Cr App R (S) 326.
12 Crime and Disorder Act 1998 s 1C
13 Criminal Justice Act 2003 s 227–228
14 Protection from Harassment Act 1997 s 5 and the Crime and Disorder Act 1998 s 32(7).
15 Sexual Offences Act 2003 s 104 & Sch. 5

and where photographs or images of a personal nature are involved threat, use of violence or grossly offensive material and where photographs or images of a personal nature are involved. Examples of mitigating factors for the offence initial provocation and short duration. Examples of mitigation are age, health (physical or mental), co-operation with the police, genuine remorse and voluntary compensation. Consider a committal for sentence. Consider making a restraining order. Give reasons if not awarding compensation.

For details about the guidelines see **MAGISTRATES' COURT SENTENCING GUIDELINES** at page 483.

Cases

89.3 *R v Joyce* 2002 1 Cr App R (S) 582. The defendant was convicted of racially-aggravated common assault, racially aggravated harassment under s 4 and common assault. Because of her behaviour in a department store security guards spoke to her. She was abusive to a black one and emptied her bag on the floor. When she was told to pick the items up she said, 'Fuck off you black bastard,' ' and 'Fucking nigger, the BNP is going to get you.' As she was walked by the victim she struck him a backwards punch with a clenched fist. He punched her in the face. She struck out again and had to be restrained. She continued to swear, strike out and utter racist abuse at the victim. Police arrested her and she abused them and struggled, saying as an example, 'All black people are bastards, and they should not be in the country.' They told her they weren't interested in her views. She replied, 'You police are scarred of niggers, you should try living in South London.' She kicked out at one of the officers and threatened to kill him and his family. She was given warnings and continued the abuse. She spat at another when being taken to the police van. She was now 39 and had 14 court appearances for theft, shoplifting, ABH, criminal damage, assault on police, threatening words, common assault, being drunk and disorderly and possession of a Class A drug. She hadn't received a custodial sentence. The pre-sentence report said there was a high risk of further offences and violence against the public, which would be reduced if she addressed her substance abuse and engaged in strategies to address issues of anger management. She had a glowing prison report and wanted to give birth to her child outside prison. Held. The assault without the racial element was worth 4 months. The racial element was worth 3 months extra so **7 months** not 15.

R v Clark 2004 2 Cr.App.R. (S.) 1. The defendant pleaded guilty on re-arraignment to racially aggravated harassment (s 4). He got on a underground train in the evening rush hour when the carriage was crowded and people were standing. He was blocking the space between the seats. The victim said 'Excuse me may I come through?' He put his fist in front of her face and said 'You fucking bitch, you cunt, I will fuck you. I will not let you through. Get out and go back to your own fucking country.' She was upset and feared he would assault her. She said 'Don't you ever talk to me like that.' He continued to be abusive saying things like: 'You fucking come here, claim asylum and social security and you fucking Indians.' An off duty policewoman on the train told him to stop making racist comments. He was abusive to her and said 'You're just a fucking kid. What can you do?' The officer told him to let the victim through and he said to the victim 'Go on you fucking bitch, I'll get you.' He moved slightly and let her through. The police officer gave the victim her seat and the defendant said 'You're fucking mad to give up your seat to this woman. You shouldn't stand up for them. Are you fucking mad?' The victim got off the train and the police officer remained after her own stop because the defendant was clearly drunk, swearing, making racist and anti-police comments. When the train reached the end of the line he had calmed down and gave his details to the officer. He was arrested later. The victim was upset for some days after the incident and was nervous of travelling on the underground. The pre-sentence report indicated a lack of remorse and said that the defendant's main problem was alcohol. He was initially evasive, abrupt and abusive to the person making the report. He presented as angry and agitated. After the interview for the report he lay on the floor and went to sleep. When asked to leave by security he became very abusive and aggressive and was forcibly removed from the building. The report said that there was a high likelihood of him committing offences of a similar nature given that he appeared drunk most of the time. He aged about 42, had 29 previous convictions and numerous prison sentences over 20 years. These were mainly for fraud; there were also 5 offences against the person. This was the first racially aggravated offence. Since being in custody a prison report indicated that he was settling down and was causing no great problems in prison. Held. We take into account that he was attacked by a group of youths 6 years before and his leg was broken with a metal pole; and that since the offence he had been attending weekly counselling session for his alcohol addiction. The sentence was too high taking into account his mitigation and his plea of guilty. Serious though it was, this offence was not at the very top end of the bracket. **12 months**, not **21 months**.

R v Underwood Re A 2005 1 Cr App R (S) 478 at 490. The defendant pleaded guilty to fifteen counts of harassment contrary to s. 4 and one count of intimidating a witness. The offences took place over about $3^{1}/_{2}$ years and were similar. The victims were aged between 14 and 17. The defendant would begin by approaching and sometimes appearing to befriend the victims. He made them flex their biceps and felt their arms, chests and legs. He would ask them to lean over and perform squatting exercises while he rested his weight against their backs or buttocks. He often required them to perform these exercises in his car or in some lonely area. In some cases they were harassed in this way for periods exceeding three years. Some saw him daily, others less frequently. He undoubtedly intimidated the victims. The separate witness intimidation concerned a victim of harassment who came across the defendant by accident. The defendant said to him "I want you out of this … better for you if you were not involved". They talked for about 20 minutes. He was 43 with a very long record including 30 months for threats to kill that occurred after these offences. Most of his previous convictions were for violence on police officers and offences of dishonesty. Held. He represented a danger to young men. An overall sentence of **5 years** for harassment was not arguably manifestly excessive nor was a consecutive **12-months** for witness intimidation.

See also **PUBLIC ORDER ACT 1986** and **STALKING**

HARASSMENT S 5

See **BREACH OF A RESTRAINING ORDER**

90   HARASSMENT AND UNLAWFUL EVICTION OF TENANTS

90.1   Protection from Eviction Act 1977 s 1

Triable either way. On indictment maximum 2 years. Summary maximum 6 months and/or £5,000.

Anti-Social Behavioural orders Where the defendant has acted in a manner that caused or was likely to cause harassment, alarm or distress to one or more persons not in the same household as the defendant and it is necessary to protect persons from further anti-social acts by him/her the court may make this order[16].

---

16 Crime and Disorder Act 1998 s 1C

Restraining order There is power to make a restraining order to protect the victim by prohibiting the defendant from doing anything described in the order[17]. The order may be for a specified period or till further order[18].

Crown Court statistics – England and Wales – Males 21+
90.2

Year	Plea	Total Numbers sentenced	Type of sentence %					Average length of custody (months)
			Discharge	Fine	Community sentence	Suspended sentence	Custody	
2002	Guilty	1	–	–	–	–	100	3
	Not guilty	2	50	–	–	–	50	3
2003	Guilty	1	–	–	100	–	–	–
	Not guilty	2	–	50	50	–	–	–

For details and explanations about the statistics in the book see page vii.

Threats and aggression

90.3   *R v Khan* 2001 2 Cr App R (S) 553. The defendant was convicted of interfering with the peace or comfort of an occupier, unlawful eviction, theft and doing an act intending to pervert the course of justice. The victim a single mother aged 33, her boyfriend and her three children including her baby rented a flat owned by the defendant. There was some delay in the rent being paid because of benefit problems and that situation was explained to the defendant. She was told her 6 month agreement would not be renewed His agent started legal proceedings but said this was just a formality because he was expecting the rent money. However the defendant started calling round and saying he needed the flat for his wife. While the victim was out he and four associates went to the flat and kicked in the door breaking the frame. They disturbed and broke much of its contents. The stereo and speakers were smashed, the TV was broken, the beds were turned upside down, and one of them was broken in two. The baby's cot and toys were also broken. After discovering this, the family went to the victim's mother. A number of items were taken from the flat including an electric fan. After a couple of hours, the boyfriend went to the flat to pick up some of the baby's clothes. He was met by the defendant and four others and he said they had no right to be there. One of them replied it was 'fuck all to do with him' and the defendant wanted his house back. That man was aggressive and threatening and the boyfriend found him intimidating. The boyfriend was told to leave immediately and if the victim returned to the flat her face would be rearranged. The lock on the flat door was changed. Police attended and found the defendant and four other men inside and the defendant said he was repossessing the flat for non-payment of rent. The defendant was released on bail with a condition not to contact directly or indirectly any prosecution witness. Two months later, a car in which the defendant was a passenger approached the boyfriend. The man who had intimidated him got out of the car and asked to see the victim. They both went to where the victim was living and the man asked her how much she wanted to drop the case. When she told him to deal with the solicitors the man became aggressive and told her if the defendant went to prison she would get nothing. He also said the most she would get would be £1,500, with half paid now and the rest when the case was dropped. The defendant was 26 and of good character. His wife was ill and spoke no English. Held. There was no basis for interfering with the **16 months** for the three flat offences. Perverting offences are treated seriously because they

---

17 Protection from Harassment Act 1997 s 5(1)
18 Protection from Harassment Act 1997 s 5(3)

undermine justice. 8 months for it was not excessive. Neither was **2 years** in total in any way excessive.

Old case. *R v Madarbakus* 1992 13 Cr App R (S) 542.

Hare Coursing

See **Hunting/Hare Coursing**

91   Health and Safety Offences

This chapter also deals with the principles for sentencing a company defendant

91.1   Various statutes, regulations and penalties. The main one is Health and Safety at Work etc Act 1974 s 2(1) and 33(1) and (1A) (Failing to discharge the duty to ensure the health, safety and welfare of employees.)

Triable either way. On indictment maximum an unlimited fine. Summary maximum £20,000. For offences against s 33(1)(g) or (o) the maximum on indictment includes 2 years and the summary maximum includes 6 months imprisonment.

Sentencing trends. The prosecution tends to under indict perhaps because of lack of confidence or because they want to avoid trials where they may not obtain their costs. Defence counsel's current tactic is to provide a list of very selective cases at the Crown Court and the Court of Appeal to try to minimise the fine. Those lists often ignore the fact that the low fines are because of lack of means rather than lack of culpability. The Lord Chancellor and the Court of Appeal have made it clear that the current level of fines are too low. Poor health and safety standard continue to maim and kill at work particularly where Health and Safety standards are poor. Judges are likely to reflect these factors in higher fines particularly for large companies. Unless the fines are large it will not cause shareholders or directors to notice the orders of the court. Where there is doubt that the company will institute adequate changes to their Health and Safety procedures deferring sentences will become routine. This power is not restricted to occasions where the court is considering a custodial sentence.

Crown Court statistics – England and Wales – Males 21+
91.2

Year	Plea	Total Numbers sentenced	Type of sentence %					Average length of custody (months)
			Discharge	Fine	Community sentence	Suspended sentence	Custody	
2002	Guilty	18	11	83	–	6	–	–
	Not guilty	6	–	100	–	–	–	–
2003	Guilty	23	13	87	–	–	–	–
	Not guilty	7	–	100	–	–	–	–

For details and explanations about the statistics in the book see page vii.

Guideline case
91.3   *R v Howe and Son Ltd* 1999 2 Cr App R (S) 37. There had been increasing recognition in recent years of the seriousness of health and safety offences. In assessing the

gravity of the breach look at how far short of the appropriate standard the defendant fell. It is often a matter of chance whether death or serious injury results from even a serious breach. Generally where death is the consequence of a criminal act it is regarded as an aggravating feature of the offence. The penalty should reflect public disquiet at the unnecessary loss of life. Financial profit can often be made at the expense of proper action to protect employees and the public. Cost cutting is a crucial tool in achieving a competitive edge. A deliberate breach of the health and safety legislation with a view to profit seriously aggravates the offence. There is some evidence that proportionately more accidents occur in companies with less than fifty employees than those with a large staff. The standard of care imposed by the legislation is the same regardless of the size of the company. Other matters that may be relevant to sentence are the degree of risk and extent of the danger created by the offence; the extent of the breach or breaches, for example whether it was an isolated incident or continued over a period and, importantly, the defendant's resources and the effect of the fine on its business. Particular aggravating features will include (1) a failure to heed warnings and (2) where the defendant has deliberately profited financially from a failure to take necessary health and safety steps or specifically run a risk to save money. Particular mitigating features will include (1) prompt admission of responsibility and a timely plea of guilty, (2) steps to remedy deficiencies after they are drawn to the defendant's attention and (3) a good safety record.

The objective of prosecutions is to achieve a safe environment for those who work there and for others who may be affected. A fine needs to be large enough to bring that message home where the defendant is a company not only to those who manage it but also to its shareholders. The level of fines imposed generally for offences of this nature are too low.

R v Colthrop Board Mills Ltd 2002 2 Cr App R (S) 359. The company pleaded guilty to an offence under the Health and Safety at Work etc Act 1974 s 2(1) and the Provision and Use of Work Equipment Regulations 1974 Reg. 11. An experienced charge-hand either slipped or became entangled in a machine. His arm was passed or pulled through a join and he received a serious crush injury to his hand and arm. He was in hospital for 4 weeks. The company discontinued trading and realised assets of about £17m. Held. Companies like this can expect to receive penalties up to at least £$^{1}/_{2}$ m for serious defaults and proportionately lesser sums if the limitation upon means or some lesser blame justifies it. The £$^{1}/_{2}$m figure should not be seen a maximum. As time goes on and awareness of the importance of safety increases, the courts will uphold sums of that amount and even in excess of them in serious cases, whether or not they involve what could be described as major public disasters.

Guideline remarks

91.4   *R v P & O European Ferries (Irish Sea Ltd)* 2005 2 Cr App R (S) 113. For companies of this substance the fine has to be of sufficient significance not only to reflect the seriousness of the offence and the defendant's culpability but also to include an appropriate sting, in financial terms, so as to send a message both to managers and shareholders and indeed other employers in this field.

Magistrates' Court Sentencing Guidelines, January 2004

91.5   The main Health and Safety offences are:

Health and Safety at Work Act 1974 33(1)(g) and (o) failing to comply with an improvement or prohibition notice, or a court remedy order.

Section 33(1)(a) – breaching general duties in sections 2 to 6 Health and Safety at Work Act.

Section 33(1)(c) – breach of health and safety regulations or licensing conditions.

It is important to seek guidance from the legal adviser in all these serious cases. The Court of Appeal, in *R v Howe* 1999 2 Cr App R (S) 37 gave guidance on health and safety sentencing.

Seriousness

Offences under these Acts are serious, especially where the maximum penalty in the Magistrates' Court is £20,000. Imprisonment is available for some offences. It is important to be careful when accepting jurisdiction as to whether the cases ought properly to be heard in the Crown Court. This is especially so when dealing with large companies. In *R v Howe*, the Court of Appeal said that a fine needs to be large enough to bring home to those who manage a company, and their shareholders, the need to protect the health and safety of workers and the public. A company is presumed to be able to pay any fine the court is minded to impose unless financial information to the contrary is available to the court before the hearing. A deliberate breach of the legislation by a company or an individual with a view to profit seriously aggravates the offence. If a guilty plea is made for an either way offence, again a committal for sentence under section 4 Powers of Criminal Courts (Sentencing) Act 2000 might be more appropriate. Simple cases can, of course, be dealt with by the Magistrates' Court. In the case of *R v Friskies Petcare (UK) Ltd* 2000 2 Cr App R (S) 401 it was recommended that the Health and Safety Executive should list in writing the aggravating features of the case, and the defence should do likewise with the mitigating features, so as to assist the court in coming to the proper basis for sentence after a guilty plea. Matters to consider when assessing seriousness include:

1   offence deliberate or reckless breach of the law rather than carelessness;
2   action or lack of action prompted by financial motives – profit or cost-saving or neglecting to put in place
3   preventative measures or avoiding payment for relevant licence;
4   considerable potential for harm to workers or public;
5   regular or continuing breach, not isolated lapse;
6   failure to respond to advice, cautions or warning from regulatory authority;
7   death or serious injury or ill-health has been a consequence of the offence;
8   ignoring concerns raised by employees or others;
9   an awareness of the specific risks likely to arise from action taken but ignoring them;
10   previous offences of a similar nature;
11   extent of damage and cost of rectifying it (expensive clean up operation required);
12   attitude to the enforcing authorities;
13   offending pattern;
14   serious extent of damage resulting from offence (but lack of actual damage does not render the offence merely technical; it is still serious if there is risk);
15   animal health or flora affected;
16   defendant carrying out operations without an appropriate licence;
17   other lawful activities interfered with.

Other factors may provide some mitigation:

1   the offender's minor role with little personal responsibility;
2   genuine lack of awareness or understanding of specific regulations;
3   an isolated lapse.

There may be some offender mitigation:

1   prompt reporting;

2   ready co-operation with regulatory authority;

3   good previous record;

4   timely plea of guilt.

Sometimes in a case much more damage has occurred than could have been reasonably anticipated. Any sentence should give weight to the environmental impact but should primarily reflect the culpability of the offender.

The level of fines – general approach

A fine is considered by the Sentencing Advisory Panel to be the appropriate form of penalty for both companies and individuals for these offences. The normal principles of the Criminal Justice Act 1991 should apply and the seriousness of the offence and the financial circumstances of the defendant should be taken into account. The level of fine should reflect the extent to which the defendant's behaviour has fallen below the required standard. High culpability should be matched by a high fine even though actual damage turned out to be less than might reasonably have been anticipated. In line with *R v Howe*, the level of the fine should reflect any economic gain from the offence by failure to take precautions. It has been said that a deliberate failure to take the necessary precautions can be a form of stealing commercial advantage from law-abiding competitors. In all cases with corporate offenders the company's financial circumstances must be carefully considered. No single measure of ability to pay can apply in all cases. Turnover, profitability and liquidity should all be considered. It is not usual for an expert accountant to be available in summary cases. If a company does not produce its accounts the court can assume that the company can pay whatever fine the court imposes. In most cases it is hard to imagine a company failing to provide such information, although with large known companies of national or international standing this may not be a necessary requirement. Where necessary the payment of fines can be spread over a longer period than the usual 12 months, if payment in full would be unduly burdensome on say, a smaller company.

Fining too little?

A fine suited to the circumstances of a small local company would make no impact at all on a multi-national corporation with a huge turnover. The fine to any company should be substantial enough to have a real economic impact, which together with attendant bad publicity would pressure both management and shareholders to tighten their regulatory compliance. Such fines on large companies might often be beyond the summary fines limit and in such circumstances the case should be transferred to the Crown Court for trial or sentence. Where the court does not transfer the case of a larger company to the higher court magistrates should look to a starting point near the maximum fine level then consider aggravating and mitigating factors.

Fining too much?

Care should be taken to ensure that fines imposed on smaller companies are not beyond their capability to pay. The court might not wish the payment of the fine to result in the company not being able to pay for improved procedures or cause the company to go into liquidation or make its employees redundant.

Other sentencing options

Whilst fines will be the usual outcome in proceedings of this sort, other sentencing options are available. A discharge will rarely be appropriate. Compensation should be considered if there is a specific victim who has suffered injury, loss or damage. You should give reasons if you decide not to make a compensation order. The current limit

is £5,000 per offence, although substantial civil claims are often pending in such cases.
• The legislation provides for the possibility of directors and senior managers appearing before the courts, and custodial sentences are available in specific instances. The courts have power to disqualify directors under the Company Directors Disqualification Act 1986. This is important particularly in Health and Safety enforcement and breach of an order is itself a criminal offence carrying a term of imprisonment for up to two years.

For more information, access the environmental offences training materials on the Magistrates'

Association website. www.magistrates-association.org.uk

A deliberate breach of the legislation by a company or an individual with a view to profit seriously aggravates the offence

For details about the guidelines see MAGISTRATES' COURT SENTENCING GUIDELINES at page 483.

Basis for sentence, there must be a proper

91.6 *R v Friskies Petcare Ltd* 2000 2 Cr App R (S) 401. Problems can arise when there is a dispute about whether the court sentenced the defendant on the basis on which the case was presented. This case illustrates the problem. The Health and Safety Executive should list in writing not merely the facts of the case but the aggravating features as set out in *R v Howe and Son Ltd* 1999 2 Cr App R (S) 37. It should be served and the defence should set out in writing the mitigating features. If there is an agreed basis it should be in writing.

Costs

91.7 *R v Howe and Son Ltd* 1999 2 Cr App R (S) 37. The power to award costs is contained in s 18(1) of the Prosecution of Offences Act 1985 and permits an order that the defendant pay to the prosecutor such costs as are just and reasonable. This includes the cost of the prosecuting authority carrying out investigations with a view to prosecution, see *R v Associated Octel Ltd* 1997 1 Cr App R (S) 435. Sometimes costs awarded have been scaled down so as not to exceed the fine. Neither the fines nor the costs are deductible against tax and therefore the full burden falls upon the company.

Magistrates' Court Sentencing Guidelines, January 2004 The prosecution will normally claim the costs of investigation and presentation. These may be substantial, and can incorporate time and activity expended on containing and making the area safe. Remediation costs for pollution offences may also be significant. For water pollution offences enforcing authorities are able to recover them through the criminal courts (Water Resources Act 1991, as amended). In other cases there are powers for the courts to order offenders to remedy the cause of the offence, or for the Environment Agency to require them to undertake clean-up at their own expense, or for the agency to carry out remedial costs and seek to recover them through the civil courts.

The enforcing authorities' costs should be fully recouped from the offender. The order for costs should not be disproportionate to the level of the fine imposed.

The court should fix the level of the fine first, then consider awarding compensation, and then determine the costs. If the total sum exceeds the defendant's means, the order for costs should be reduced rather than the fine. Compensation should take priority over both the fine and costs. As always, magistrates should seek the advice of the legal adviser on sentencing options and guidelines in all cases.

Costs, apportioning them

91.8 *R v Harrison* 1993 14 Cr App R (S) 419. The defendant pleaded to trade description offences. The Judge considered the first defendant was the principle defendant and stood to gain financially from the offence and had the means to pay whereas the second defendant who was his son had little to do with running the business. He therefore made the principle defendant pay all the costs. Held. Where there are several defendants it will usually be appropriate when making a costs order to look to see what would be a reasonable estimate of the costs if each defendant was tried alone. However the Judge's approach was proper.

R v Fresha Bakeries Ltd 2003 1 Cr App R (S) 202. The defendant company, H Ltd., its sister company, B, the Chief Executive of the group, M, the chief engineer at the plant and J the production director pleaded guilty to offences under the Health and Safety at Work Act 1974 Sections 2 and 3. The companies and M pleaded guilty at the first appearance. B and J pleaded guilty the day before the trial was fixed. Two workmen were burnt to death trying to repair a bread oven when major breaches of Health and Safety procedures took place. (See **DEATH IS CAUSED**.) It was agreed by the prosecution, defence and the Judge that he should fix the overall financial penalty as if it was a single company and apportion the fine and costs elements between the companies. The defendants were able to pay a significant fine. The pre-tax profits of Freshas were £250,000 and H Ltd. profits were £400,000. The Judge distinguished *R v Ronson and Parnes* 1992 13 Cr App R (S) 153 (where costs were adjusted so they were what they would have been if the defendant was tried alone) and calculated the costs to included the work up and until sentence not withstanding their early plea. Freshas was fined £250,000 with costs of £175,00, H Ltd was fined £100,000 with £75,000 costs, B was fined £10,000 with £5,000 costs, J was fined £1,000 and M was fined £2,000. The revised figure for the costs when the companies pleaded guilty was £108, 451. The revised figure when the other defendants pleaded was £283, 307. Held. It was a very bad case. There was no basis for holding the **fines totalling £350,000** were manifestly excessive. It may be appropriate to order the defendant who is more responsible to pay a greater share of the costs than he would pay if he was tried alone. The Judge was entitled to conclude the corporate defendants bore a greater responsibility than the individual defendants. However the Judge took too little account of the fact that the companies had no control over the proceedings against B and J. If they had pleaded when the companies did the costs would have been significantly less. Taking into account the costs incurred for the proposed trial after the corporate defendants had pleaded guilty and the reduced costs figure now available Fresha's costs should be £105,000 and H Ltd's costs should be £45,000.

Death is caused

91.9   *R v Hall and Co Ltd* 1999 1 Cr App R (S) 306. The company pleaded guilty to an offence under the Health and Safety at Work etc Act 1974 s 2(2) at the Magistrates' Court. At the company's builder's' yard an employee was helping to load a lorry. The lorry reversed, ran over him and killed him. The injuries were very serious. The following failures were identified: (1) the vehicle could not be reversed without danger to pedestrians; (2) there were no fixed mirrors to assist drivers to see round blind corners; (3) the vehicle had no reversing alarm; (4) the procedure for lookouts was regularly flouted. On the day there were none; (5) there was no proper risk assessment as required by Reg. 3 of the Management of Health and Safety at Work Regulations 1992. Six months before the incident the company was fined £750 for another s 2 breach but the circumstances were far removed from this case. The company was part of the Ready Mix Group of companies. The defendant's turnover was £180m and the parent company's turnover was £4 billion. The judge said the failures created an obvious risk to the safety of employees. Held. That risk necessarily encompassed the risk of a fatal accident. A severe penalty was required. **£150,000** was a proper fine.

R v Howe and Son Ltd 1999 2 Cr App R (S) 37. It is often a matter of chance whether death or serious injury results from even a serious breach. Generally where death is the consequence of a criminal act it is regarded as an aggravating feature of the offence. The penalty should reflect public disquiet at the unnecessary loss of life.

R v RIMAC Ltd 2000 1 Cr App R (S) 468. The company pleaded guilty to an offence under the Health and Safety at Work etc Act 1974 s 2 at the Magistrates' Court. The victim a 19-year-old trainee who was asked to move some plastic piping in an area which was used for storage. He fell through a suspended ceiling onto the floor 9 feet below. He died 2 days later of head injuries. The area was not load bearing. The only safe way to cross the ceiling was to use crawling boards. No verbal instructions of any kind were given on how he should do the task. There was no real recognition of this being a hazardous area despite access to it being easy. No warnings were displayed. The use of the area as a storage area may well have misled someone into believing that it was in fact load bearing. There was no supervision of the deceased. The company was **fined £60,000** (payable in four quarterly instalments) and ordered to pay £9,723 costs. Held. The risk was obvious, foreseeable and continuing. The penalty should reflect the public disquiet at the unnecessary loss of life. The mitigating factors were: (1) prompt admission of responsibility; (2) the good safety record of the company: and (3) steps had been promptly taken to remedy the deficiency. The accounts show the company can well afford both the fine and the costs. A fine needs to be large enough to bring the message home not only to those that manage it but also to its shareholders. The fine and costs were right.

R v Friskies Petcare Ltd 2000 2 Cr App R (S) 401. The company pleaded guilty to an offence under the Health and Safety at Work etc Act 1974 s 2(1) at the Magistrates' Court. The company was a large manufacturing concern producing cat food. A company welder and process technician went into a silo in which the meat was mixed by metal stirrers to repair a stirrer. The welder was wearing steel toe capped boots and was connected to an electric arc welding unit. The welder remained still and the technician realised he was undergoing an electric shock. The technician had to go 30 metres up a ladder, along a gantry and through a locked gate to turn the power off. The welder died of electrocution in a damp environment. The inspector concluded that the victim came into contact with the exposed and live parts of the welding electrode holder and/or the welding electrode itself while in contact with the metal silo creating a complete electrical circuit. The clothing did not provide sufficient resistance. The power point was too far away. The breaches had been going on for some time and no-one's attention was drawn to the Health and Safety pamphlets about welding. There was no system in place, which alerted the technicians to the risks. No steps were taken to avoid the risks. The inspector said it was well known in the trade that those circumstances were potentially dangerous. The company disputed this. There was a prompt admission of responsibility, steps were taken to remedy the deficiencies and the company had a good safety record. The company's pre-tax profits were some £40m. The judge said the company had put profit before safety. The defence said in mitigation that this wasn't the case and no one questioned that assertion at the time. After the sentence the prosecution wrote saying that was not their case. Held. Reported cases show that fines in excess of £$^1/_2$ m tend to be reserved for cases where a major public disaster occurs e.g. the collapse of the Heathrow railway tunnel – that is to say where the breaches put large numbers of people at risk of serious injury or more. A fine of £425,000 was imposed on a major retail company when the trial judge said that the working practices dated back to the dark ages and safety was sacrificed for profit. This case was in neither of those categories. We agree with the 'judges' description that the defendants fell a long way short of doing what was reasonable and practical. Applying *R v Howe and Son Ltd* 1999 2 Cr App R (S) 37 **£250,000 fine** not £600,000.

R v Keltbray Ltd 2001 1 Cr App R (S) 132. The company pleaded guilty to Health and Safety at Work etc Act 1974 s 2(1). It was based on breaches of Construction (Health, Safety and Welfare) Regulations 1996. The company was demolishing a building. Two workmen were cutting a well hole and a floor slab on the eighth floor collapsed. They fell and died. Before the work started there had been written risk assessments. A dangerous method was used to do the cut on the eighth floor. The workman chose a quicker method than the one planned. They were being paid on the basis of a full day's work even if they managed to finish early. This was approved by the ganger even though the company did not approve it. There was no harness or other protection provided. No foreman was supervising contrary to the risk assessment. After the accident procedures were altered. The company had an excellent work record for demolition. They had no convictions and were not the subject of any complaints from the Health and Safety Executive. It had won awards. The company made profits of £191,000 in 1997 and £211,000 in 1998. The company was ordered to pay £8,037.87 costs. Held. This potentially dangerous operation requires firm supervision. A highly dangerous operation was permitted. Harnesses which were the fall back means of safety were not present. The **£200,000 fine** was appropriate.

R v Aceblade Ltd 2001 1 Cr App R (S) 366. The company pleaded guilty to failing to ensure the health and safety of an employee. The victim was lifting a piece of stone on his crane and the crane fell over. The driver's cab was crushed and he was killed. A warning device had been bypassed a few weeks before the accident. The directors did not know this. The tyres were under-inflated which contributed to the instability. The crane had been inspected a month before when it was working properly. There was no proactive system for the inspection of the crane. There was a prompt admission of responsibility and a timely plea. Steps were made to remedy the deficiencies and the company had a good safety record. In 1999 the company profit was £113,608 and in 2000 there was a £7,901 loss. Legal expenses in this case, health and safety spending and investment had contributed to the fall. The directors' remuneration remained the same. The accountants said the cost of the accident was about £134,000 including loss of production. They were **fined £20,000** with £6,648.98 legal costs and £15,000 health and safety costs. The fine was payable over 42 months. Held. The payment period was not too long. The penalties were entirely justified.

R v Fresha Bakeries Ltd 2003 1 Cr App R (S) 202. The defendant company, H Ltd., its sister company, B, the Chief Executive of the group, M, the chief engineer at the plant and J the production director pleaded guilty to offences under the Health and Safety at Work Act 1974 Sections 2 and 3. The companies and M pleaded guilty at the first appearance. B and J pleaded guilty the day before the trial was fixed. The companies made bread on a large scale. At the Fresha's site there were three ovens consisting of long metal encased tunnels, which operated at 260°C. The dough travelled through the oven on a conveyor belt taking 17 minutes to pass through. One of the metal grids, which made up the conveyor belt came off in one of the ovens and landed on the bottom of the oven. D, the chief engineer and the man responsible for Health and Safety decided to do the repair in house. It was decided to shut the oven down for eight hours. Ten or eleven grills were removed from the conveyor belt to create a gap for two men to occupy. They would enter the oven and walk or crawl at the speed of the belt so that they wouldn't be trapped or crushed. In fact the oven was turned off for only two hours and it was suggested that the men wanted to get on with the job so that they could watch the Cup Final. No one looked at the temperature gauge and the oven was at 100°C. The men took walkie-talkies and after 10 minutes the messages became garbled and they passed out. The belt kept going and they were at the bottom of the oven. When one somehow got to the exit below the belt he could not get through the gap. The hole was enlarged with a crowbar and he was pulled out. He had been in the oven for 20 minutes and suffered extensive skin loss over his body. He died of heat exposure. The other was trapped in the machinery, badly burnt and died of multiple injuries. The safety memorandum applicable was not referred to or applied. A permit should have been drafted and signed only when the temperature reached a safe level. The oven should have been off for 12 hours. When Fresha's was bought in 1996, it was in a run down state and B set about improving the Health and Safety matters. An improvement notice was served in 1997 and a few months later there was an accident in the flour silo, which could have been fatal. There hadn't been a meeting of the Safety Council for 7 months. The Crown relied on amongst other matters the fact the system devised fell far short a reasonable safe system, there was no risk assessment and there was a lack of appropriate training, planning, monitoring and supervision at all levels. The defence relied on amongst other matters, the major efforts made after the events to deal with the Health and Safety issues, the breach wasn't deliberate, the money spent before and after the accident on Health and Safety and the absence of convictions for the companies. The defendants were able to pay a significant fine. The pre-tax profits of Freshas were £250,000 and H Ltd. profits were £400,000. Freshas was fined **£250,000** with costs of £175,00, H Ltd was fined **£100,000** with £75,000 costs, B was fined **£10,000** with £5,000 costs, J was fined **£1,000** and M was fined **£2,000**. Held. It was a very bad case. There was no basis for holding the fines totalling **£350,000** were manifestly excessive. The cost orders were revised. (For details see COSTS, APPORTIONING THEM.)

R v P & O European Ferries (Irish Sea Ltd) 2005 2 Cr App R (S) 113. The defendant pleaded guilty at the Magistrates Court at the first opportunity to a Section 2(1) offence and a lighting offence under the Docks Regulations 1988. The company operated ferry services with a yard where containers were loaded and unloaded. An HGV driver reversed into another lorry. Later the lorry hit and killed another worker. The Health and Safety Executive considered pedestrian employees were exposed to safety risks. Visibility was partially obscured. The audio system fitted to the machine that lifted containers was ineffective and a mirror was missing. There was a lack of training of staff. There was no demarcation of pedestrian areas. The company had held some risk assessments but there was no specific risk assessment about loading and pedestrians. The lighting was in places under 5–6 lux when the minimum was 10 lux. It was accepted the breaches were careless rather than deliberate to save costs. Since the accident there had been full compliance with the requirements. Held. Save for the death there were no significant aggravating features and numerous mitigating ones. There was no avoidance of previous warnings. The sentence had to reflect the disquiet at the death. **£200,000** not **£250,000** and **£25,000** not £50,000 with £18,400 costs.

R v Yorkshire Sheeting 2003 2 Cr App R (S) 548. The defendant company pleaded guilty at the Magistrates' Court to a section 3(1) offence of not ensuring the health of a non-employee. A self employed roofer was working on the roof of a warehouse and inadvertently stepped back onto a roof light. The worker fell though and hit a concrete floor six metres below and died. The company was the sub-contractor who issued a method statement saying they would erect safety nets for the entire warehouse. A risk assessment said the risk of a fall was low. There was no provision for the covering of the roof lights. The weekend before the work was to commence vandals put the scissor lifts out of action so not all the nets could not be put in place. The company decided to cone off the area without nets. By the next Wednesday a battery charger was removed so a lift could not be used to continue with the netting. By Thursday half the bays were netted. The contractor's safety officer was concerned about the absence of netting and the holes where the roof lights had been removed. The roof lights in the working area were covered. The site manager was to ensure that no-one worked in the areas without nets. There was to be a spare bay on either side of the working area. However no cones or demarcation was deployed. There was some evidence to suggest the workers were told not to work outside the permitted area. The victim fell through an un-netted roof light. 50% of fatalities in the industry were through falls and most were through fragile roofs. The prosecution case was the low assessment was wrong, no access should have been permitted without full netting, the rest of the roof should have been marked out and strict instructions about the banned area should have been issued. However it was not suggested the motivation was cost cutting. The defendant's turnover in 1999 was £6m with £105,000 profits. In 2000 the turnover was over £8.7 m with £388,000 profits. The co-defendant company was the contractor who was fined £10,000 with a proportion of the costs. Both companies were well respected. The defendant had no convictions and an excellent safety record. It had cooperated with the authorities in every way. The Judge assessed the blame as 10%/90% between the contractor and subcontractor. Held. Save for the death there were no aggravating factors. All the mitigating factors identified in R v Howe 1999 2 Cr App R (S) 37 were present. Although a serious default **£60,000** was appropriate not £100,000. Because of the way the costs had been apportioned the fine was reduced to **£55,000**.

Death is caused – not directly attributable to the breach

91.10   *R v Cardiff City Transport* 2001 1 Cr App R (S) 141. The company pleaded guilty to an offence under the Health and Safety at Work Act etc 1974 s 2 at the Magistrates' Court. On a Sunday, at the company's bus depot an employee moved a bus into an allocated space. He ran off the bus and was knocked to the ground by another bus, which was travelling at the regulation 10 mph. The other driver had no opportunity to avoid him. The victim struck his head on the ground and died shortly after. The Health and Safety inspectors concluded that there was no risk assessment for pedestrians and vehicle movements. There were three specific failings: (1) the bus was travelling the wrong way in the one way system. The one way system was not enforced at all times, as Sunday was seen as an exception; (2) high visibility clothing was needed for those engaged in moving vehicles round the depot; (3) the speed limit should not have been increased from 5 to 10 mph. The prosecution accepted that there was no causal link between the death and the breaches. The death did however highlight the unsafe system and increase the risk of the type of collision, which in fact occurred. The basis of the plea was that the company had failed make the risk assessment about pedestrians and vehicles, failed to identify the need for high visibility clothing and failed to enforce the one way system. The company had a good safety record and had no convictions. It had always co-operated with the Health and Safety Inspectorate. The company profits were between £300,000 and £$^1/_2$m in the previous 3 years. The failings were not connected with increasing profit. Held. It is essential that employers are made acutely aware of the need to ensure the highest possible standards. However, the company had behaved very responsibly since the accident. No one had suggested high visibility clothing before the accident. The change of speed limit was after they had consulted an expert. Had the death been caused by the breaches a fine of considerably more than £75,000 would have been appropriate. **£40,000 fine** not £75,000.

Directors etc

91.11   Health and Safety at Work Act 1974 s 37. Power to convict directors etc who consent, connive etc to an offence committed by a body corporate.

R v Davies 1999 2 Cr App R (S) 356. he defendant was a director and pleaded guilty to neglecting his duty under the Health and Safety at Work etc Act 1974 s 2(1). His company and two other companies also pleaded guilty to breaching their duties. His company made plastic cases. The process created heat, which was dispelled in a cooling tower. That created the risk of legionnaires' disease. In an earlier incident at another plant the production manager caught the disease and died. As a result that company went into liquidation. It was not suggested that was the fault of the defendant.

The defendant then became the director of the new company. Neither he nor the person responsible for the cleaning of the towers had any knowledge of the regulations or the guidelines for cleaning the towers. The system was shut down over Christmas for 11 days when it remained stagnant. One of the defendants, a cleaning company wrote in a survey 8 years before of the problem of bacteria which was present and chlorination but pointing out the cost of having the towers shut down for a full clean. They were regular inspections and chlorination but no actual cleaning. The defendant said he was relying on the cleaning company, as neither he nor anyone from his company were experts. The basis of the plea was that the defendant believed he had taken all the necessary steps and the system was being properly supervised by the cleaning company. The only neglect was his failure to ensure that their company's employer who was responsible for the cleaning went on a course. His ability to pay was not in question. The defendant was bought into the proceedings at a late stage and argued that he should not be responsible for the costs before he was a defendant. The cleaning company was fined £15,000 and he and his company was fined £25,000. Held. The primary responsibility must remain with the employers. It is not adequate to simply transfer it to an expert third party. At all stages the employer must supervise the independent contractor rather than the independent contractor supervise the employer. They must carry the greater responsibility. Because of the basis of plea **£15,000 fine** not £25,000. At whatever stage the defendant was brought in costs would have been incurred and the defendant must pick up his share of the responsibility for those costs. £10,000 costs order for him upheld.

Directors and small companies both prosecuted. Avoid double punishment

91.12 *R v Rollco Screw and Rivet Co Ltd* 1999 2 Cr App R (S) 436. LCJ. The defendant company and two of its directors who were father and son pleaded guilty to failing to ensure the health and safety of employees and persons other than their employees. The defendants were prosecuted for stripping out asbestos in breach of the regulations and exposing employees and others to risks. The father was in charge of the contractual arrangements. The son was considered the father's lieutenant and did not fully appreciate the risks. The total fines and costs for the company was £40,000 fine and £30,000 costs. The father was fined £6,000 and £2,000 costs. The son was fined £4,000 and £2,000 costs. Held. In a small company the directors are likely to be the shareholders and therefore the main losers if a severe sanction is imposed on the company. One must avoid a risk of overlap and must not impose double punishment. On the other hand it is important that fines should be imposed which make it clear that there is a personal responsibility on directors and they cannot simply palm off their responsibilities to the corporation of which they are directors. The proper approach is to answer two questions. First, what financial penalty does the offence merit? Secondly, what financial penalty can a defendant, whether corporate or personal reasonably be ordered to meet? Addressing the first question the total fine for the company and the directors was £50,000. In considering that question we have to bear in mind the glaring public need for effective sanctions where the health and safety of the public are so obviously at risk. The situation is the more important when, as here, the ill-effects of exposure to brown asbestos may take many years to appear. In the interim of course no individual can know whether he will ultimately suffer or not. The division of **£40,000** and **£10,000** was an appropriate split. The total sum divided between the two was an appropriate recognition of the gravity of this offending. The directors' appeal was dismissed. The fine on the company was reduced on other grounds.

Employees etc partly/fully to blame

91.13 *R v Patchett Engineering Ltd* 2001 1 Cr App R (S) 138. The company pleaded guilty to Health and Safety at Work etc Act 1974 s 2(1). The company supplied an egg collecting machine to a farm. A young worker who was collecting eggs caught his jacket in the machine and was found suspended from a drive shaft. The clothing had tightened round his neck and he was strangled. The worker must have climbed up the frame of the cage to reach the position where his clothing was caught. The likely explanation was that he noticed the top tier tray was not in place and he climbed up to let it down without turning the machine off. The defence argued that there was no need for the worker to act in the unorthodox way he did and it was not foreseeable. The judge rejected this. Held. The judge was right. Workers will take short cuts and not follow proper practices. The need to guard the shaft should have been apparent. When it was designed someone should have considered operatives do on occasions take short cuts. The statutory duty has as one of its objects, the protection of workers who may be neglectful of their own safety in a way, which should be anticipated.

Guilty plea, discount for

91.14 *R v Thames Trains* 2004 Court transcript at p 11 5/4/04. High Court Judge at CCC. The defendant company pleaded to two Health and Safety charges. Held. The conventional discount for early acceptance of guilt and for cooperation with a prosecuting authority is one third which I apply here.

Health and Safety at Work etc Act 1974 s 2(1), 33(1) and (1A)

91.15 Failing to discharge the duty to ensure the health, safety and welfare of the employees

Triable either way. On indictment maximum sentence unlimited fine. Summary maximum £20,000. For offences against s 33(1)(g) or (o) the maximum on indictment includes 2 years and the summary maximum includes 6 months imprisonment.

(The cases are broken up into financial groups to assist but many state principles, which apply to all the groups)

Less than £50,000 fine

91.16 *R v Howe and Son Ltd* 1999 2 Cr App R (S) 37. The company pleaded guilty to (1) Health and Safety at Work etc Act 1974 s 2(1) (2) failing to maintain an electric cable to a machine under Reg. 4(2) of the Electricity at Work Regulations 1989, (3) failing to make a suitable and sufficient assessment of the risks of the electric cable to the machine, contrary to Reg. 3 of the Management of Health and Safety at Work Regulations 1992, and (4) failing under Reg. 11 of the Electricity at Work Regulations 1989 to ensure that means were provided to protect the electrical system supplying the machine from excess current. A 20-year-old employee of the company was electrocuted when he was cleaning the factory when it was shut down for that purpose. A cable to a machine called Freddy was damaged and the machine became 'live' and the boy was unable to let go. The damage to the cable was consistent with the cable having been crushed by a heavy load. The socket into which the 15 amp cable had been plugged was fitted with 32 amp fuses, which had been subsequently bridged by fuse wire. There was a circuit breaker called an RCD that had been deliberately interfered with so it was inoperable. A Health and Safety Inspector found in a number of instances that someone had tried to install contactors but the piece of equipment was not working and he had to rectify it. A fitter had advised the company both orally and in writing that they were overloading the electrical supply. The fitter was never asked to look at Freddy. The judge sentenced on the basis that the company's employees did not themselves interfere with the RCD. There was 13 months between the installation of the RCD and the accident. During this time the company made no effort to check the RCD or indeed even to check whether the test button was operating. The test button could have been pressed at any time and would have revealed that the device was not working. Good practice dictated that it should have been checked every 3 months. The company was a small precision engineering company then with 12 employees. It is now 10. The company accounts reveal that for 1996–7 the annual turnover was £355,000 and the net profit after tax was £26,969 and the net book value of the company was £129,288 but this included £68,227 in respect of assets held under finance leases and hire purchase contracts. The company did not pay any dividends and retained its annual profit in order to finance improvements and acquire further machinery. Neither of the working directors received an income in excess of £20,000 per annum. There was no pension scheme and no company car. Following the accident the company spent £15,000 on a complete overhaul of its electrical system. The company had no previous convictions nor has it received warnings from the Health and Safety Executive. Held. The company had no system at all for checking its electrical equipment. The fatality was an accident waiting to happen. This was a bad case and the electrical state of the equipment was appalling. There appears to have been a flagrant disregard for the safety of the company's employees. Corners were cut and no real attention was paid to electrical safety. The judge gave inadequate weight to the financial position of the company maybe because such financial information as he had was not supplied until the very last moment. This is a small company with limited resources. The appropriate fine was one totalling **£15,000** on count one of the indictment with no separate penalty in respect of the other offences not £48,000 in all. There was no reason to scale down the £7,500 costs when the prosecutor's total costs exceeded £12,000.

R v Cappagh Ltd 1999 2 Cr App R (S) 301. The company pleaded guilty to failing to discharge its duty under Health and Safety at Work etc Act 1974 s 2(1). An employee was cleaning a concrete crushing machine. Safety guards to prevent access to the crushing part had not been fitted and were lying derelict some 50 yards away. The supervisor told him to turn the machine on. The employee was drawn into the machine some way and was crushed to death. The judge took into account the good safety record of the company but said the facts were extremely disturbing. The company's profits for 1996–7 were £150,000. Held. The 'judge's approach was proper and there was no basis to say the **£40,000** fine was excessive.

R v Rollco Screw and Rivet Co Ltd 1999 2 Cr App R (S) 436. LCJ. The defendant company and two of its directors who were father and son pleaded guilty to failing to ensure the health and safety of employees and persons other than their employees, [Section 2(1) and 3(1)]. The company employed 12 or more employees in the manufacture of screws and rivets. Both directors were keen the roof, which was in poor condition, should be repaired and knew it contained asbestos. The company contracted two co-defendants from another company to remove the brown asbestos from the roof. Brown asbestos is the most dangerous of all kinds of asbestos and requires the greatest care in handling. An asbestos worker, Mr Evans contracted with the two co-defendants to remove the asbestos. None of them possessed an asbestos licence. A vehicle hired by Mr Evans was seen unloading bags of asbestos at a number of unauthorised sites. An investigation took place. That discovered that the asbestos was removed with inadequate equipment, with an absence of air locks, effective masks and protective clothing. Asbestos was disseminated over the factory premises. 200–300 bags had been fly-tipped. Children had taken an interest in some of them. During the work father and son visited the premises regularly. When the work was finished employees were directed to clear up the mess. The son organised this. The father was in charge of the contractual arrangements. The son was considered the father's lieutenant and did not fully appreciate the risks. The company's profits were £51,000 in 1994–5, £24,000 in 1995–6 and £33,000 in 1996–7. There was a loss of £122,000 in 1997–8 which attributable in part to roof costs, fines, court costs and legal fees. A modest profit was expected in 1998–9. The total fines and costs for the company was **£40,000 fine** and £30,000 costs. The father was fined **£6,000** and £2,000 costs. The son was fined **£4,000** and £2,000 costs.

Held. We give the guidelines in *R v Howe and Son Ltd* 1999 2 Cr App R (S) 37 our unqualified support. The proper approach is to answer 2 questions. Firstly what financial penalty does the offence merit? Secondly what financial penalty can a defendant, whether corporate or personal reasonably be ordered to meet? Addressing the first question the total fine for the company and the directors was £50,000. In considering that question we have to bear in mind the glaring public need for effective sanctions where the health and safety of the public are so obviously at risk. The situation is the more important when, as here, the ill-effects of exposure to brown asbestos may take many years to appear. In the interim of course no individual can know whether he will ultimately suffer or not. The division of **£40,000** and **£10,000** was an appropriate split. The total sum divided between the two was an appropriate recognition of the gravity of this offending. We are not persuaded there was disparity between the father and son and the contractors on the other hand because the Judge made it plain that the business of the contractors had plummeted and that the fines on the 2 contractors would have been very much greater had that not been so. We are not satisfied that the fine for the son who is relatively young with commitments and a young child is one he can't pay. The directors' appeal was dismissed. The company's costs were reduced to £20,000 because the period of payment over 6 years 5 months was too long a period.

R v Cardiff City Transport 2001 1 Cr App R (S) 141. The company pleaded guilty to an offence under the Health and Safety at Work etc Act 1974 s 2 at the Magistrates' Court. On a Sunday, at the company's bus depot an employee moved a bus into an allocated space. He ran off the bus and was knocked to the ground by another bus, which was travelling at the regulation 10 mph. The other driver had no opportunity to avoid him. The victim struck his head on the ground and died shortly after. The Health and Safety inspectors concluded that there was no risk assessment for pedestrians and vehicle movements. There were three specific failings (1) The bus was travelling the wrong way in the one way system. The one-way system was not enforced at all times, as Sunday was seen as an exception. (2) High visibility clothing was needed for those engaged in moving vehicles round the depot. (3) The speed limit should not have been increased from 5 to 10 mph. The prosecution accepted that there was no causal link between the death and the breaches. The death did, however, highlight the unsafe system and increase the risk of the type of collision, which in fact occurred. The basis of the plea was that the company had failed make the risk assessment about pedestrians and vehicles, failed to identify the need for high visibility clothing and failed to enforce the one way system. The company had a good safety record and had no convictions. It had always co-operated with the Health and Safety Inspectorate. The company profits were between £300,000 and £½m in the previous 3 years. The failings were not connected with increasing profit. Held. It is essential that employers are made acutely aware of the need to ensure the highest possible standards. However, the company had behaved very responsibly since the accident. No one had suggested high visibility clothing before the accident. The change of speed limit was after they had consulted an expert. Had the death been caused by the breaches a fine of considerably more than £75,000 would have been appropriate. **£40,000 fine** not £75,000.

£50,000 to £100,000 fine

91.17   *R v Firth Vickers Ltd* 1998 1 Cr App R (S) 293. The defendant company pleaded guilty to failing to ensure the health and safety of employees from 1 to 3 November 1995. Failure to maintain plant and provide safe systems of work were particularised. The firm had a foundry employing about 300 people. On 2 November 1995 the foundry was making a ring which was heavier than anything cast before Two tons of molten metal at 1,500°C was poured into a mould and some escaped. It sprayed out in a jet and four men were caught. Three received substantial injuries. One received 40% burns and was in hospital for 10 weeks. He will probably not return to work. Another was in hospital for

6 nights. The machine was designed to hold 5 tons. The Health and Safety report said parts had become worn and the accident was caused by the top plate, which was inadequately retained by enough and strong enough pins. The top plate and the side wall were found to be distorted. There was no effective seal. The company overhauled their whole safety procedures with a new officer audits and training etc. That cost £60,000. A new managing director was appointed. An employee had been burnt in a fault on a different machine in 1993. For that the company was fined £10,000. It also involved the spray of molten metal. There was another incident in April 1994 when no one was injured. Two employees were splashed in September 1994. That incident was not reported to the Health and Safety Executive. In 1994–5 employees expressed their concerns about the ejection of molten metal. Throughout 1995 the employee that was most seriously injured who was also splashed in 1994 complained about the unrepaired top plate. On the day of the offence that employee had made requests about the steel plate. Those requests were ignored. The company was fined **£100,000** and ordered to pay £6,600 costs. It was suggested the judge gave undue weight to the earlier incidents and requests. Held. The previous incidents are very relevant for they showed that no proper re-assessment of the risks was made in due time. Potentially this machinery could cause very serious injuries and yet its guarding was known to be defective. The relatively modest cost of the guard eventually fitted underlined the company's failure to take any proper care in this hazardous employment. The judge had properly considered the history to see if it was an isolated oversight or indicative of something greater. The history was relevant in considering their inactivity. It was a serious case. The criminality was not wrongly inflated. The fine was upheld.

£100,001 to £¹/₂m fine

91.18   *R v Hall and Co Ltd* 1999 1 Cr App R (S) 306. The company pleaded guilty to an offence under the Health and Safety at Work etc Act 1974 s 2(2) at the Magistrates' Court. At the company's builder's yard an employee was helping to load a lorry. The lorry reversed, ran over him and killed him. The injuries were very serious. The following failures were identified: (1) the vehicle could not be reversed without danger to pedestrians; (2) there were no fixed mirrors to assist drivers to see round blind corners; (3) the vehicle had no reversing alarm; (4) the procedure for lookouts was regularly flouted. On the day there were none; (5) there was no proper risk assessment as required by Reg. 3 of the Management of Health and Safety at Work Regulations 1992. Six months before the incident the company was fined £750 to another s 2 breach but the circumstances were far removed from this case. The company was part of the Ready Mix Group of companies. The defendant's turnover was £180m and the parent company's turnover was £4 billion. The judge said the failures created an obvious risk to the safety of employees. Held. That risk necessarily encompassed the risk of a fatal accident. A severe penalty was required. **£150,000** was a proper fine.

R v Friskies Petcare Ltd 2000 2 Cr App R (S) 401. The company pleaded guilty to an offence under the Health and Safety at Work etc Act 1974 s 2(1) at the Magistrates' Court. The company was a large manufacturing concern producing cat food. A company welder and process technician went into a silo in which the meat was mixed by metal stirrers to repair a stirrer. The welder was wearing steel-toe capped boots and was connected to an electric arc welding unit. The welder remained still and the technician realised he was undergoing an electric shock. The technician had to go 30 metres up a ladder, along a gantry and through a locked gate to turn the power off. The welder died of electrocution in a damp environment. The inspector concluded that the victim came into contact with the exposed and live parts of the welding electrode holder and/or the welding electrode itself while in contact with the metal silo creating a complete electrical circuit. The clothing did not provide sufficient resistance. The power point was too far away. The breaches had been going on for some time and no-one's attention was drawn to the Health and Safety pamphlets about welding. There was no system in place, which alerted the technicians to the risks. No steps were taken to avoid the risks. The inspector said it was well known in the trade that those circumstances were potentially dangerous. The company disputed this. There was a prompt admission of responsibility, steps were taken to remedy the deficiencies and the company had a good safety record. The company's pre-tax profits were some £40m. The judge said the company had put profit before safety. The defence said in mitigation that this wasn't the case and no one questioned that assertion at the time. After the sentence the prosecution wrote saying that was not their case. Held. Reported cases show that fines in excess of £$^1/_2$ m tend to be reserved for cases where a major public disaster occurs e.g. the collapse of the Heathrow railway tunnel – that is to say where the breaches put large numbers of people at risk of serious injury or more. A fine of £425,000 was imposed on a major retail company when the trial judge said that the working practices dated back to the dark ages and safety was sacrificed for profit. This case was in neither of those categories. We agree with the judge's description that the defendants fell a long way short of doing what was reasonable and practical. Applying *R v Howe and Son Ltd* 1999 2 Cr App R (S) 37 **£250,000 fine** not £600,000.

R v Colthrop Board Mills Ltd 2002 2 Cr App R (S) 359. The company pleaded guilty to an offence under the Health and Safety at Work etc Act 1974 s 2(1) and the Provision and Use of Work Equipment Regulations 1974 Reg. 11. The company produced carton board on a very large machine. In 1999 a Health and Safety inspector visited the factory and issued an improvement notice requiring the company to carry out a risk assessment. The inspector identified employees accessing dangerous areas of machinery to carry out cleaning and maintenance work as particular problems and asked for action without delay. The company's risk assessment which took place after a delay and a successful application for an extension of time found the joins between the rollers in the machine as carrying a substantial risk of death or serious injury to an employee in the event of an accident. The gravity of the injury was assessed as 'at its highest' and the likelihood of an accident as 'moderate'. No remedial steps were taken. An experienced charge-hand leant through the handrails of the machine and he either slipped or became entangled in the machine. His arm was passed or pulled through a join and he received a serious crush injury to his hand and arm. Several bones were broken in the hand, there were friction bones to the shoulder and back and a deep cut to his palm. He was in hospital for 4 weeks. After the accident the danger was removed promptly, simply and inexpensively. The company discontinued trading and realised assets of about £17m. In about 40 years the joins in the machine must have been cleaned about 126,000 times without accident. In 1994 the company had a s 2(1) conviction when a hand had been drawn into another join on another machine. It was fined £6,500. In 1995 there was a conviction under the Factories Act 1961, s 14(1) for an accident when another employee was drawn into another join on another machine. The fine was £3,000 with £1,000 costs. Held. Companies like this can expect to receive penalties up to at least £$^1/_2$m for serious defaults and proportionately lesser sums if the limitation upon means or some lesser blame justifies it. The £$^1/_2$m figure should not be seen a maximum. **£200,000** not £350,000 fine in total with £5,000 costs unaltered.

R v Keltbray Ltd 2001 1 Cr App R (S) 132. The company pleaded guilty to an offence under the Health and Safety at Work etc Act 1974 s 2(1). It was based on breaches of Construction (Health, Safety and Welfare) Regulations 1996. The company was demolishing a building. Two workmen were cutting a well hole and a floor slab on the eighth floor collapsed. They fell and died. Before the work started there had been written risk assessments. A dangerous method was used to do the cut on the eighth floor. The workman chose a quicker method than the one planned. They were being paid on the basis of a full day's work even if they managed to finish early. This was approved by the ganger even though the company did not approve it. There was no harness or other protection provided. No foreman was supervising contrary to the risk assessment. After the accident procedures were altered. The company had an excellent work record for demolition. They had no convictions and were not the subject of any complaints from the Health and Safety Executive. It had won awards. The company made profits of £191,000 in 1997 and £211,000 in 1998. The company was ordered to pay £8,037.87 costs. Held. This potentially dangerous operation requires firm supervision. A highly dangerous operation was permitted. Harnesses which were the fall back means of safety were not present. The **£200,000 fine** was appropriate.

R v Avon Lipiatt 2003 2 Cr App R (S) 427. The defendant company pleaded guilty to two Health and Safety counts under sections 2(1) and 3(1). In December 1999, the company obtained the contract to install gas from Transco. They took on the Transco employees. In May 2000, two employees attended a terrace house, No 186 to install gas. Because the road had recently been resurfaced they decided to run the new pipe from the gas pipe to the next but one house, No 182. They used a cable avoidance tool to check for other pipes. The tool did not work adequately and the test was negative. In fact there was a gas pipe to No 184. The occupier of No 184 knew this but was not asked. An employee used a mole to tunnel which hit the gas pipe to No 184. The pipe was dented and the mole turned off. The employee dug down and found the pipe without realising it was a gas pipe and reversed the mole. Gas from the fractured pipe escaped into No 184. The pipe was connected from 186 to No 182 and it was tested. While the employees were filling in the trench they had dug there was an explosion which knocked an employee onto some nearby railings. His clothes caught fire and he was badly burnt. The other employee was uninjured. No 184 was unoccupied but completely destroyed. There was destruction at the other two houses. The occupier of No 186 pushed back by the blast and suffered injuries to her back and shoulders. The team leader had not attended the company's one day's training check. The prosecution said the company had disregarded the procedures and had failed to heed the warnings about using moles in their booklet. The Health and Safety Inspector said, the site risk assessment was inadequate and failed to identify obvious risks; training and supervision was insufficient; instructions on safety was inadequate as there should have been specific warnings against moling and there was a significant failure on the part of management to convey the dangers of moling to the operatives. The prosecution accepted there was no financial gain because of the breaches, the company took appropriate steps to tighten up the moling procedures and otherwise the company had "in place Health and safety structures" with a good record. The company had 1,000 employees and had made a loss of £2m in 1999–2000 on a £38m plus turnover. New financial material was available to the Court of Appeal, (not in the report.) Held. The dangers of fracturing gas pipes are well known. Before a mole is used precautions should have been taken to detect cables and pipes underground. If proper equipment had been used the pipe would have been found. The company was being punished for their failure to ascertain their new employees' competence and if necessary retrain them. It was that failure which led to the accident. **£150,000** in all not £250,000 with £43,804 costs undisturbed.

Health and Safety at Work etc Act 1974 s 3(1) and 33(1)(a) and (1A)

91.19   Failing to discharge the duty to ensure the health, safety and welfare of persons other than employees.

Triable either way. On indictment maximum sentence unlimited fine. Summary maximum £20,000. For offences against s 2(1)(g) or (o) the maximum on indictment includes 2 years and the summary maximum includes 6 months.

R v Rollco Screw and Rivet Co Ltd 1999 2 Cr App R (S) 436. LCJ. The defendant company and two of its directors who were father and son pleaded guilty to failing to ensure the health and safety of employees and persons other than their employees, [s 2(1) and 3(1)]. The company employed 12 or more employees in the manufacture of screws and rivets. Both directors were keen that the roof, which was in poor condition, should be repaired and knew it contained asbestos. The company contracted two co-defendants from another company to remove the brown asbestos from the roof. Brown asbestos is the most dangerous of all kinds of asbestos and requires the greatest care in handling. An asbestos worker, Mr Evans contracted with the two co-defendants to remove the asbestos. None of them possessed an asbestos licence. A vehicle hired by Mr Evans was seen unloading bags of asbestos at a number of unauthorised sites. An investigation took place. That discovered that the asbestos was removed with inadequate equipment, with an absence of air locks, effective masks and protective clothing. Asbestos was disseminated over the factory premises. 200–300 bags had been fly-tipped. Children had taken an interest in some of them. During the work father and son visited the premises regularly. When the work was finished employees were directed to clear up the mess. The son organised this. The father was in charge of the contractual arrangements. The son was considered the father's lieutenant and did not fully appreciate the risks. The company's profits were £51,000 in 1994–5, £24,000 in 1995–6 and £33,000 in 1996–7. There was a loss of £122,000 in 1997–8 which attributable in part to roof costs, fines, court costs and legal fees. A modest profit was expected in 1998–9. The total fines and costs for the company were **£40,000 fine** and £30,000 costs. The father was fined **£6,000** and £2,000 costs. The son was fined **£4,000** and £2,000 costs. Held. We give the guidelines in *R v Howe and Son Ltd* 1999 2 Cr App R (S) 37 our unqualified support. The proper approach is to answer two questions. First, what financial penalty does the offence merit? Secondly, what financial penalty can a defendant, whether corporate or personal reasonably be ordered to meet? Addressing the first question the total fine for the company and the directors was £50,000. In considering that question we have to bear in mind the glaring public need for effective sanctions where the health and safety of the public are so obviously at risk. The situation is the more important when, as here, the ill-effects of exposure to brown asbestos may take many years to appear. In the interim of course no individual can know whether he will ultimately suffer or not. The division of £40,000 and £10,000 was an appropriate split. The total sum divided between the two was an appropriate recognition of the gravity of this offending. We are not persuaded there was disparity between the father and son and the contractors on the other hand because the judge made it plain that the business of the contractors had plummeted and that the fines on the two contractors would have been very much greater had that not been so. We are not satisfied that the fine for the son who is relatively young with commitments and a young child is one he can't pay. The directors' appeal was dismissed. The company's costs were reduced to £20,000 because the period of payment over 6 years 5 months was too long a period.

Instalments, paying fines etc by

91.20   *R v Olliver and Olliver* 1989 11 Cr App R (S) 10. LCJ. There is nothing wrong in principle for the period of payment (for a fine) being longer than a year providing it is not an undue burden and so too severe a punishment having regard to the offence and the nature of the offender. A 2 year period will seldom be too long and in an appropriate case 3 years will be unassailable. Every effort is required to find alternatives to custodial sentences.

R v Rollco Screw and Rivet Co Ltd 1999 2 Cr App R (S) 436. LCJ. The defendant company and two of its directors who were father and son pleaded guilty to failing to ensure the health and safety of employees and persons other than their employees, [s 2(1) and 3(1)]. The defendants were prosecuted for stripping out asbestos in breach of the regulations and exposing employees and others to risks. The father was in charge of the contractual arrangements. The son was considered the father's lieutenant and did not fully appreciate the risks. The total fines and costs for the company was £40,000 fine and £30,000 costs, (£5,000 within a year and the rest at £1,000 a month). The father was fined £6,000 and £2,000 costs, (£1,000 a month). The son was fined £4,000 and £2,000 costs. Held. Reminding ourselves of *R v Olliver and Olliver* 1989 11 Cr App R (S) 10 the court was at pains to avoid stipulating any period which should not be exceeded. With a personal defendant there are arguments for keeping the period within bounds. Those arguments are much weaker, if indeed they apply at all when one is considering a corporate defendant. There is not the same anxiety as is liable to afflict an individual and it is acceptable for a fine to be payable by a company over a substantially longer period than might be appropriate for an individual. It is not necessarily a more severe course to order a larger sum over a longer period than a smaller sum over a shorter period, since the former course may give the company a greater opportunity to control its cash flow and survive difficult trading conditions. If it wants the company can pay the sums sooner than it need. This period of payment over 6 years 5 months was excessive. Because of that the fine is reduced to £20,000 so the payment period is **5 years and 7 months** which is an appropriate payment period.

R v Aceblade Ltd 2001 1 Cr App R (S) 366. The company pleaded guilty to failing to ensure the health and safety of an employee. They were fined £20,000 with £15,000 costs. The fine was payable over **42 months**. Held. The payment period was not too long

Magistrates' accepting jurisdiction

91.21 *R v Howe and Son Ltd* 1999 2 Cr App R (S) 37. Magistrates should always think carefully before accepting jurisdiction in Health and Safety at work cases, where it is arguable that the fine may exceed the limit of their jurisdiction or where death or serious injury has resulted from the offence. [This guidance is repeated in the Magistrates' Guidelines.]

Means, the defendant/company

91.22 Magistrates' Court Sentencing Guidelines amendment June 2001

Defendants in such cases are frequently companies with huge annual turnovers. Our aim should be for any fine to have an equal impact on rich and poor. Financial penalties must relate to the companies' means and we should accustom ourselves, in appropriate cases, to imposing far greater financial penalties than have been generally imposed in the past. In 1998, the Lord Chancellor spoke to the Magistrates' Association about the disquiet being expressed about the level of sentences for these offences. He particularly suggested the maximum penalties were there to be used in appropriate cases. He said, 'You should not flinch from using them if you believe that they are deserved.' In all cases with corporate offenders the company's financial circumstances must be carefully considered. No single measure of ability to pay can apply in all cases. Turnover, profitability and liquidity should all be considered. It is not unusual for an expert accountant to be available. If a company does not produce its accounts the court can assume that the company can pay whatever fine the court imposes. In most cases it is hard to imagine a company failing to provide such information, although with large (well) known companies of national or international standing this may not be a necessary requirement. Where necessary the payment of fine can be spread over a longer period that the usual 12 months, if payment in full would be unduly burdensome on say, a smaller company. The fine should be substantial enough to have real economic impact. Care should be taken to ensure that fines imposed on smaller companies are not beyond their capacity to pay. The court might not wish the payment of the fine to result in the company not being able to pay for improved procedures or cause the company to go into liquidation or make its employees redundant.

R v Howe and Son Ltd 1999 2 Cr App R (S) 37. Any fine should reflect not only the gravity of the offence but also the means of the offender, and this applies just as much to corporate defendants as to any other, see of the Criminal Justice Act 1991 s 18 (3). Difficulty is sometimes found in obtaining timely and accurate information about a corporate defendant's means. The starting point is its annual accounts. If a defendant company wishes to make any submission to the court about its ability to pay a fine it should supply copies of its accounts and any other financial information on which it intends to rely in good time before the hearing both to the court and to the prosecution. This will give the prosecution the opportunity to assist the court should the court wish it. Usually accounts need to be considered with some care to avoid reaching a superficial and perhaps erroneous conclusion. Where accounts or other financial information are deliberately not supplied the court will be entitled to conclude that the company is in a position to pay any financial penalty it is minded to impose. Where the relevant information is provided late it may be desirable for sentence to be adjourned, if necessary at the defendant's expense, so as to avoid the risk of the court taking what it is told at face value and imposing an inadequate penalty. Where a defendant is in a position to pay the whole of the prosecution costs in addition to the fine there is no reason in principle for the court not to make an order accordingly. The court must look at the whole sum (fine and costs) and consider the impact upon him.

R v Patchett Engineering Ltd 2001 1 Cr App R (S) 138. The company pleaded guilty to an offence under the Health and Safety at Work etc Act 1974 s 2(1). A worker died. The company was fined £75,000 and ordered to pay £5,000 costs. Held. *R v Howe and Son Ltd* 1999 2 Cr App R (S) 37 and *R v Hall and Co Ltd* 1999 1 Cr App R (S) 306 suggest subject to the defendant's ability to pay the fine could have been higher. The judge did take the means into account. We have more information than he did. Six of its 11 staff have been laid off. The £80,000 fine and costs would be likely to mean that the company could not keep its head above water. **£20,000 fine** substituted.

R v Supremeplan Ltd 2001 1 Cr App R (S) 37. The company pleaded to an offence under the Health and Safety at Work etc Act 1974 s 2. It ran a mobile delivery hot food business. A safety device on a warmer was bypassed and there was a build up of gas in a compartment. When an employee lit the burner in a van there was a flash flame and she received burns to her face and hands. The company was owned by two directors who had taken out in the previous year less than £10,000 on a turnover of £140,000. The year's profit was £11,500. The judge described the van as a death trap. He made a compensation order for £3,000. Held. The company fell far short of the appropriate standard of care. Taking into account the means of the company **£7,500 fine** not £25,000.

Previous incidents/convictions

91.23 *R v Firth Vickers Ltd* 1998 1 Cr App R (S) 293. The defendant company pleaded guilty to failing to ensure the health and safety of employees from 1 to 3 November 1995. Failure to maintain plant and provide safe systems of work were particularised. The firm had a foundry employing about 300 people. On 2 November 1995 the foundry was making a ring which was heavier than anything cast before Two tons of molten metal at 1,500° C was poured into a mould and some escaped. It sprayed out in a jet and four men were caught. Three received substantial injuries. One received 40% burns and was in hospital for 10 weeks. He will probably not return to work. Another was in hospital for 6 nights. The machine was designed to hold 5 tons. The Health and Safety report said parts had become worn and the accident was caused by the top plate, which was inadequately retained by enough and strong enough pins. The top plate and the side wall were found to be distorted. There was no effective seal. The company overhauled their whole safety procedures with a new officer audits and training etc. That cost £60,000. A new managing director was appointed. An employee had been burnt in a fault on a different machine in 1993. For that the company was fined £10,000. It also involved the spray of molten metal. There was another incident in April 1994 when no one was injured. Two employees were splashed in September 1994. That incident was not reported to the Health and Safety Executive. In 1994–5 employees expressed their concerns about the ejection of molten metal. Throughout 1995 the employee that was most seriously injured who was also splashed in 1994 complained about the unrepaired top plate. On the day of the offence that employee had made requests about the steel plate. Those requests were ignored. The company was fined **£100,000** and ordered to pay £6,600 costs. It was suggested the judge gave undue weight to the earlier incidents and requests. Held. The previous incidents are very relevant for they showed that no proper re-assessment of the risks was made in due time. Potentially this machinery could cause very serious injuries and yet its guarding was known to be defective. The relatively modest cost of the guard eventually fitted underlined the company's failure to take any proper care in this hazardous employment. The judge had properly considered the history to see if it was an isolated oversight or indicative of something greater. The history was relevant in considering their inactivity. It was a serious case. The criminality was not wrongly inflated. The fine was upheld.

Public Bodies

91.24   *R v British Railways Board* 1991 Unreported extract at 2000 2 Cr App R (S) at 430. High Court Judge at CCC. The company was sentenced for Health and Safety offences following the Clapham rail crash. Held. In the case of a public authority that is funded by the taxpayer or, as here, by a combination of the taxpayer and the fare-paying public, the question of penalty raises an acute problem. A swingeing fine of the magnitude that some might consider appropriate could only be met by the board either by increasing the burden on the fare-paying passengers – which is hardly logical, having regard to the fact that it is for the benefit of the fare-paying passengers that this legislation exists – or by reducing the funds available for improvements in the railway system in general. That can hardly be regarded as a desirable state of affairs. On the other hand, I must bear in mind the necessity of marking the disapproval of society at the failures demonstrated by those charged with British Rail management leading up to and causing this accident. An insignificant fine would rightly bring down on myself and upon the whole system of justice universal condemnation. I therefore have to steer a narrow course between those two alternative hazards. **£250,000 fine** imposed.

R v Milford Haven Port Authority 2000 2 Cr App R (S) 423. The company pleaded guilty to causing oil to enter controlled waters. A pilot committed a serious navigational error and a tanker grounded on rocks causing a crude oil spill which was among the largest ever recorded. The authority was a public trust port. Held. Public bodies are not immune from appropriate penalties because they have no shareholders and the directors are not in receipt of handsome annual bonuses. However, it is proper for the judge to take the factor into account. If a substantial financial penalty will inhibit the proper performance by a statutory body of the public function it has been set up to perform that factor should not be disregarded.

Railway accidents

91.25   *R v Great Western Trains Co Ltd* 1999 Unreported. Extract of judgment see 2000 2 Cr App R (S) at 431. High Court Judge at CCC. The company pleaded guilty to Health and Safety breaches, which contributed to the causes of the Southall train crash. Seven died and there were 150 casualties. The company had a good safety record. Prompt action was taken to prevent further breaches of Health and Safety requirements. Held. The company fell short of the standard required and it was a serious failure. The court needs to bring home to those who run substantial transport undertakings that eternal vigilance is required to ensure accidents do not occur. The company operated a system where there was no alternative in place when the AWS system was isolated. It was a serious fault of senior management. Sentence **£1.5m fine**.

For an extract of the judgment in the Clapham rail crash prosecution see *R v British Railways Board* 1991 Unreported extract at 2000 2 Cr App R (S) at 430.

R v Thames Trains 2004 Times news report 6/4/04. High Court Judge at CCC. The defendant, a train operator, pleaded guilty to two charges at the Magistrates' Court relating to the Paddington rail crash. The charges were that it had failed to ensure the health and safety of its employees and its non-employees. A driver who had only qualified 13 days went through a red signal and his train crashed into an express train travelling in the opposite direction. The trains had a closing speed of 130 mph. 31 people died. 400 others were injured many very seriously. The crash would have been avoided if the driver had been properly trained. Views of the signal were interrupted and problems with the sun may have contributed to the failure to read the signal. The signal had a very poor record of drivers passing it at red. The company also failed to arrange for the driver to attend Signal passed at danger training awareness or made him aware of the problems around Paddington. The Lord Cullen enquiry stopped short of concluding the omissions were causative of the disaster. The company had no convictions for heath and safety breaches. Sentencing remarks. There was considerable mitigation in their attitude to driver information and safety generally. The signal was designed, created and maintained by others who should have taken steps to eliminate the dangers. They cooperated fully with the enquiry and were frank in their failures. The company should have acted to curb a continuing risk. It had made a serious admission in its failure to warn the driver about signal. The serious safety breaches had "immeasurably awful consequences." It was not a case of putting profit before safety but the fine must be big enough to act as a lasting reminder to management and shareholders of the importance of safety. It must mark the seriousness of the risk involved – a seriousness underlined by the extent of the disaster. The early plea is worth a discount of a third. **£2 million fine** with £75,000 prosecution costs. (Although this summary was taken from the transcript treat news reports with care.)

Shipping

91.26 *R v Armana Ltd* 2005 1 Cr App R (S) 7. The defendant company pleaded guilty before Magistrates Court to being the owner of a fishing vessel which entered the safety zone around an offshore installation, contrary to the Petroleum Act 1987, s 23(2). This is a strict liability offence. The defendant company's fishing trawler was in the North Sea, captained by a man with 28 years experience; the second mate had 13 years trawling experience. At a handover the Captain made it clear to the second mate that he must watch out for gas installations and a particular installation was pointed out to him. Visibility at handover was between 1 and 2 miles but soon deteriorated to less than 200 yards. The second mate did not follow instructions to reduce speed, sound the fog signal or call the Captain's assistance. For some unexplained reason, the trawler changed course unnecessarily about 1.2 nautical miles from the installation. This was thought to be through human error. Although the installation had picked up the trawler as she approached, she was not alerted due to a faulty radio on the installation. When the installation was seen, it was too late to prevent a (glancing) collision. The Health and Safety Executive prosecuted. The subsequent cost of putting right the damage to the installation, the evacuation of its 128 personnel, a structural survey and remedial work was put at over £650, 000. The Captain pleaded guilty and was fined £3,000 for a similar charge. The second mate pleaded guilty to failing to prevent a collision, contrary to the Merchant Shipping (Distress Signals & Prevention of Collisions) Regulation 1996 (IS 1996/75) and was fined £1,000. Held. the Company's liability was at the bottom of the scale. The company did not encourage or acquiesce in any breach of safety regulations and had employed an experienced crew and deck officers. It operated to reduce the risk in safety procedures. It had a clean safety record and had cooperated fully with the investigation and pleaded guilty at the first opportunity. It had suffered significant financial losses of about £1m in loss of catch revenues, the insurance excess and an increased insurance premium. The company was in a parlous financial state. In fixing the fine in cases such as this amongst the features that the Court has to have regard to are the level of culpability, the financial circumstances of the defendant and consequences and potential consequences to others of the breach of safety which the Court is examining. **£15, 000 fine** not £40,000.

HEALTH, DEFENDANT'S POOR STATE OF

See **DEFENDANT** – *Ill health*

HEROIN

See **IMPORTATION OF DRUGS (CLASS A, B AND C); OPIUM; POSSESSION OF DRUGS; PRODUCTION OF DRUGS** and **SUPPLY OF DRUGS (CLASS A, B AND C)**

HISTORIC ABUSE

For general principles see **RAPE** – *Historic abuse*

See **INDECENT ASSAULT ON A MAN** – *Historic abuse*; **INDECENT ASSAULT ON A WOMAN** – *Historic abuse* and **RAPE** – *Historic abuse*

92   HOME DETENTION CURFEW SCHEME

Also known as Tagging

Foreign Nationals not eligible
92.1   *R v Al-Buhairi* 2004 1 Cr App R (S) 496. There is no certainty as to the release of any defendant. This is far too a speculative area. We are not persuaded that any allowance should be made.

Should not be considered when fixing the sentence
92.2   *R v Alkazaji* 2004 2 Cr App R (S) 291. LCJ The Judge wanted the defendant released before she had her baby. He thought there was every prospect she would be tagged. However in prison she tested positive for drugs. Held. In general it is inappropriate for a Judge to take into account the possibility, the likelihood or the almost certainty that the defendant will be released under a tagging or residential order. There is always a degree of uncertainty. Pass the appropriate sentence and do not take into account administrative arrangements. (Sentence altered on other grounds see **MOTHERS**.)

See also *R v Dale* 2004 2 Cr App R (S) 308, (same principle stated).

93 HOMOSEXUAL OFFENCES

93.1 Buggery, gross indecency and soliciting were abolished on 1/5/04.

HOMOSEXUAL VICTIMS

For hostility to a gay victim see GAY *Hostility towards a gay victim*

HOSPITALS

See INDECENT ASSAULT ON A WOMAN – *Breach of trust – Nurse* and PATIENTS, ILL TREATING ETC

94 HUNTING/HARE COURSING

94.1 Hunting Act 2004 s 1 and 5

Hunting a wild mammal with a dog and participating in a hare coursing event etc.

Both offences are summary only. Maximum fine Level 5 (£5,000).

The Act came into force on 18 February 2005.

Forfeiture There is power to forfeit dogs, hunting articles and vehicles[19].

ILL TREATING

See ANIMAL CRUELTY; CRUELTY TO CHILDREN and PATIENTS, ILL TREATING ETC

95 IMMIGRATION OFFENCES

95.1 Immigration Act 1971 s 25, 25A and 25B

Assisting unlawful immigration, helping asylum seeker to enter UK and assisting entry to UK in breach of deportation order or exclusion order respectively. These offences came into force on 10/2/03[1]

Triable either way. On indictment maximum 14 years. Summary maximum 6 months and/or £5,000.

Immigration Act 1971 s 25 (This offence was replaced by those above on 10/2/03[2])

Assisting illegal entry and harbouring

---

19 Hunting Act 2004 s 9
1 Nationality, Immigration and Asylum Act 2002 s 143 and Nationality, Immigration and Asylum Act 2002 (Commencement No 2) Order 2003
2 Nationality, Immigration and Asylum Act 2002 s 143 and Nationality, Immigration and Asylum Act 2002 (Commencement No 2) Order 2003

Triable either way. On indictment maximum 10 years. Summary maximum 6 months and/or £5,000. The penalty was increased from 7 to 10 years from 14 February 2000.

Immigration Act 1971 s 24A

Obtaining leave etc by deception

Triable either way. On indictment maximum 2 years. Summary maximum 6 months and/or £5,000.

Confiscation For all s 25, 25A and 25B offences[3] committed on or after 24 March 2003[4] the court <u>must</u> follow the Proceeds of Crime Act 2002 procedure.

Crown Court statistics – England and Wales – Males 21+ – Assisting illegal entry
95.2

Year	Plea	Total Numbers sentenced	Type of sentence %					Average length of custody (months)
			Discharge	Fine	Community sentence	Suspended sentence	Custody	
2002	Guilty	104	4	–	5	7	85	16.5
	Not guilty	36	–	–	–	6	94	32
2003	Guilty	88	2	–	2	5	91	14.9
	Not guilty	29	–	3	10	3	83	34.5

For details and explanations about the statistics in the book see page vii.

Guideline case

95.3 *R v Le and Stark* 1999 1 Cr App R (S) 422. LCJ. The problem of illegal entry is on the increase. The offence calls very often for deterrent sentences. The following are aggravating features: (1) where the offence has been repeated; (2) where there is financial gain; (3) where it involves a stranger rather than a spouse or a close member of the family; (4) in a conspiracy where it has been committed over a period; (5) high degree of planning, organisation and sophistication; (6) there are a large number of illegal immigrants as opposed to one or a very small number. Plainly the more prominent the role of the defendant the greater the aggravation of the offence.

Guideline remarks

95.4 *R v Ali* 2002 2 Cr App R (S) 115. The defendant pleaded guilty to an offence under s 24A. Held. Previous good character and personal circumstances are of very limited value. Cases will be sentenced on a deterrent basis.

Disqualification from driving

95.5 *R v Woop* 2002 2 Cr App R (S) 281. The defendant pleaded guilty on rearraignment to facilitating the illegal entry of thirty five people. He drove his lorry to the freight depot on the French side of the channel tunnel. A Customs officer asked him what he was towing and he said, 'Quartz sand.' A custom officer found movement and thirty five people were found. The defendant denied knowledge of them. He was a 38-year-old German man of good character with two young children. The trip was to fund treatment for his wife's chronic asthma. That treatment was not covered by their health insurance. Held. The gravity and prevalence of this offence requires no special emphasis. Sentences are heavy and intended to deter. Six years was too long so 5 years substituted. The offence had nothing to do with his driving. He earns his living from driving. The disqualification was reduced from 5 to **3 years**.

3   Proceeds of Crime Act 2002 s 6 and s 75 and Sch 2 para 4 as substituted by Nationality, Immigration and Asylum Act 2002 s 114 and Sch. 7 Para 31
4   Proceeds of Crime Act 2002 (Commencement No 5, Transitional Provisions, Savings and Amendment) Order 2003

Driving illegal immigrants through ports etc – Commercial motive

95.6   *R v Winn* 1999 1 Cr App R (S) 154. The defendant pleaded guilty to facilitating an illegal entrant. He drove his lorry off a ferry and was stopped by Customs. He said he was on his own but sixteen illegal immigrants were found in the back of the vehicle. The sentencing judge reluctantly accepted that he only knew there were four of them. He was 40 and of good character with financial difficulties. He received 4 years. Held. Sentences will contain a deterrent element. Suppose the judge had in mind a sentence of 6 years following a trial that would be 1 year less than the maximum of 7 [now 10]. That could not be right for a first offence. **3 years** substituted.

R v Le and Stark 1999 1 Cr App R (S) 422. LCJ. The defendant S, pleaded guilty at the Magistrates' Court to facilitating illegal entry. The defendant and another were questioned when they arrived in England from France in a camper van. They both said there were only two people travelling in the van. They said the large number of bags in the van were being taken to friends. The van was searched and two men were found in the luggage locker and a woman and six children were found under bedding. Two of them said they had paid a large sum of Deutschmarks to be conveyed from Kosovo to England. The defendant said he had only been paid 4,400 DM as expenses and one of his employees had asked him to bring members of his family to the UK. He was of good character with references. **3¹/₂ years** not 5.

R v Liddle 2000 2 Cr App R (S) 282. The defendants L and B were convicted of assisting illegal entry. V pleaded guilty to the same count. Police came across a lorry driven by L with V as the co-driver. Also found was a transit van driven by B with twenty illegal immigrants in the back. L and V had gone abroad to collect goods and the immigrants were picked up and brought over. The van was to collect the immigrants. The motive for all three was money. L was to receive £200 and the other amounts were not known. V's basis of plea was he had not gone abroad to pick the immigrants up. He admitted telephoning numbers on both sides of the Channel. L was 47 and treated as of good character. He had been a hard worker as a driver. B was 43 with no convictions. He was the sole carer of three children. V was 30 with no convictions. He had a good military record but was in financial difficulties He had two children aged 15 and 12 and showed remorse. The judge said he started at 6 years and he would give a discount for the delay and would have given a substantial discount to V for his plea but had to take into account the part he had played. Held. Each had played a vital part in the operation. The smuggling in of strangers was an aggravating factor. The judge was entitled to sentence them to the same sentence. With a maximum of 7 years to start at 6 was wrong. **3 years** not 4 for all.

R v Woop 2002 2 Cr App R (S) 281. The defendant pleaded guilty on rearraignment to facilitating the illegal entry of thirty-five people. He drove his lorry to the freight depot on the French side of the channel tunnel. A Customs officer asked him what he was towing and he said, 'Quartz sand.' A custom officer found movement and thirty-five people were found. The defendant denied knowledge of them. He was a 38 year old German man of good character with two young children. The trip was to fund treatment for his wife's chronic asthma. That treatment was not covered by their health insurance. The Judge sentenced him to 5 years and when told the maximum was increased to 10 years he increased it to 6 years. Held. The gravity and prevalence of this offence requires no special emphasis. Sentences are heavy and intended to deter. It was permissible for the judge to increase the sentence but 6 years was too long so **5 years** substituted. The disqualification was reduced from 5 to 3 years.

R v Wacker 2003 1 Cr App R (S) 92. The defendant was convicted of conspiracy to facilitate illegal entry and 58 counts of manslaughter. Sixty illegal immigrants travelled from China to Holland where they were loaded into an adapted container on the defendant's lorry. The only ventilation was a small vent at the front. 4½ kilometres from Zeebrugge the lorry stopped and the vent was closed. The deaths were caused by lack of air. The basis for the manslaughter was gross negligence. The defendant was a Dutch national. It was not suggested that he intended to harm the victims in any way. He received **8 years** for the conspiracy and 6 years consecutive for the manslaughter counts. The defence argued the total was too much and the Attorney General argued the 6 years for the manslaughter counts was too lenient although the total sentence was not challenged. Held. Professional smuggling of large numbers of illegal immigrants is in itself a serious matter. The causing of so many deaths to avoid detection puts this case in a category of its own. **14 years** was not manifestly excessive. Concurrent sentences were the correct approach so 14 years for the manslaughter, which would not have the appearance of devaluing the loss of life. (Now the maximum sentence for this offence has been increased the 8 year sentence here is unlikely to be a true guide to the likely sentence in similar cases from 10/2/03.).

R v Nikalakos 2002 2 Cr App R (S) 526. The defendant pleaded guilty to facilitating the entry of an illegal immigrant. Held. 18 months would not be excessive for a non-commercial motive so no appeal here where there was a commercial motive.

R v Sackey 2004 2 Cr App R (S) 456. The defendant pleaded guilty to breaching immigration laws (s 25). He was a German national who was stopped at Dover docks with a passenger in his car. The passenger gave the name of Quainoo and produced a German identity document bearing that name, although the photo on it did not resemble him. The defendant said he had known his passenger for about a year as 'Paddy' only. The defendant had on him a driving licence also in the name of Quainoo. The passenger was returned to France. Ferry records showed that the defendant had travelled to the UK five times in the previous six months and on four of these occasions he had a passenger named Quainoo. The defendant said this was a common name in Ghana, and the driving licence belonged to his passenger. The defendant, 39, had no previous convictions. He had a wife and children. Held. The judge was entitled to conclude from the name Quainoo and the driving licence that the defendant was part of a professional enterprise. That was an aggravating feature. **2 years** was not manifestly excessive.

Old cases. *R v Goforth* 1997 1 Cr App R (S) 234; *R v Aziz and Niaz* 1996 2 Cr App R (S) 44; *R v Ungruth* 1996 2 Cr App R (S) 205; *R v Brown* 1997 1 Cr App R (S) 112; *R v Matloob* 1997 1 Cr App R (S) 298; *R v Farah* 1997 2 Cr App R (S) 333.

Driving illegal immigrants through ports etc – Compassionate motive

95.7 *R v Le and Stark* 1999 1 Cr App R (S) 422. LCJ. The defendant L, a Vietnamese refugee was convicted of facilitating illegal entry. He arrived from Ostend with a fellow Vietnamese and showed a Customs officer two Home Office travel documents one in his name and one in another. Looking at his companion the officer considered the age in the document didn't match the companion. When interviewed the defendant said he had met his passenger in Belgium and he had agreed to give him a lift to England. The judge did not decide it was for commercial gain and left the issue open. The defendant was 35 with a conviction for an entirely different matter. He was separated from his wife and had responsibility for his 6-year-old son. Held. While he might have received payment there was no evidence of financial gain nor participation in a commercial operation. **2½ years** not 3½.

R v Ahmetaj 2000 1 Cr App R (S) 66. The defendant a Dutch national pleaded guilty at the Magistrates' Court to assisting illegal entry. He was committed for sentence. The defendant's car was searched and 2 Yugoslav nationals were found hiding in the boot. He was a former Yugoslav national from Kosovo who said an acquaintance had asked him to give the two men a lift from Holland to France and the two men had persuaded him to take them to England for a small sum to contribute to the petrol money. He was

31 and of good character. Held. It is inevitable he would be sympathetic to their plight when Kosovo had suffered ethnic cleansing. It was an isolated offence with no financial gain or commercial organisation. **18 months** not 2 years.

R v Toor and Toor 2003 2 Cr App R (S) 349. The defendants A and MH who were brothers were convicted of being knowingly concerned in facilitating the entry of an illegal immigrant. A fortnight before the offence one of the defendants' brothers (T) reported the loss of his passport. He then booked a return airline ticket from Manchester to Athens. A week later he obtained a replacement passport and flew to Athens to meet another brother (MT). MT's photograph was replaced for T's in the "lost" passport. These two brothers then flew from Athens to Brussels and then travelled overland to Calais. The defendants then sailed from Dover to Calais with family. Another ticket was purchased for travel between Calais to Dover on which MT's name was added. At 4.40am MT attempted to pass through immigration controls at Dover using the altered passport, which was spotted as such by an immigration officer. A (aged 38) and MH (aged 36) were of good character. Held. Referring to R v Le and Stark 1999 a Cr App R (S) 422, since that time the maximum sentence had increased from 7 to 10 years. In the circumstances of this case it was necessary for a deterrent sentence. **2¹/₂ years** upheld.

Old cases. *R v Ozdemir* 1996 2 Cr App R (S) 64 and *R v Angel* 1998 1 Cr App R (S) 347 (for a summary of the last case see the first edition of this book).

Large scale organisation

R v Saini and others 2005 1 Cr App R (S) 278. S and D pleaded guilty to conspiracy to facilitate illegal immigration. K had pleaded guilty to the same count 5 months earlier. Others were also involved. D was the head of a sophisticated operation which provided a complete illegal entry service. The immigrants came from India, the Middle East and Europe. The conspirators forged passports and visas, arranged passage to the UK, provided coaching in personal details to be given in English and arranged free legal representation if any were caught, when they were advised to claim political asylum. The motivation was financial with clients paying a fee of between £3,000 and £8,000. Thirty-four immigrants had been caught and it was not possible to put a figure on the number the group had dealt with, save to say that it was a significant number, and the profits must have been significant. D was the principal and he travelled extensively through Europe, to India and North Africa. S was an Indian living in Leipzig who was arrested at D's address in Birmingham. He had been under surveillance and had been recorded on several occasions discussing forged travel documents and the facilitation of illegal entry into the UK. He was more of a foot soldier than D, not a planner or an organiser, and he said his motivation was to help his sister get back to India or go to the US. He did not receive any money for his help. K was D's lieutenant. He met the immigrants in Europe, handed over the forged documents and escorted them back to the UK. He admitted to 20–25 expeditions. He accepted he had received £2,500–£3,000 for his services. D, 44, a family man, had previous unrelated convictions. He did not have a rich lifestyle. S, 38, was of previous good character and had behaved well in prison. He had to serve his sentence in the UK while his family in Germany could not afford to visit him. K was 50. Held. For D: there need not be any actual danger or exploitation as far as the immigrants are concerned to put a conspiracy like this close to the maximum sentence of 10 years. The sentence of **7¹/₂ years** was not excessive. For S: **5 years** was not excessive. For K: he was given greater credit than S for a prompt admissions and an earlier plea. The sentence of **4 years** was not manifestly excessive.

Obtaining leave etc by deception

95.8   *R v Ali* 2002 2 Cr App R (S) 115. The defendant pleaded guilty at the Magistrates' Court to seeking to obtain leave to enter by a deception (s 24A). Immigration officials were investigating Pakistanis who were claiming asylum pretending to be Afghans. They spoke to the defendant who gave a false name and falsely said he was born in Afghanistan. Checks revealed he was a Pakistani who had entered the country on a different date than he claimed. He was arrested and admitted the deception. He was 24 and had no convictions. He worked in a bakery and had never claimed any benefits. He regularly sent money to his ill parents in Pakistan. He said he wanted to return to Pakistan. He had a good prison report. Held. Offences will be treated very seriously. The offence was prevalent. Previous good character and personal circumstances are of very limited value. Cases will be sentenced on a deterrent basis. As the maximum is 2 years, **12 months** not 18.

Prostitution, for

See **PROSTITUTES, CONTROLING ETC.** – *Trafficking*

See also **BIGAMY** – *Immigration controls, to evade* and **PASSPORT OFFENCES**

IMMORAL EARNINGS, MEN LIVING ON

The offence was abolished on 1/5/04. For cases under the old and the new law see **PROSTITUTION.**

IMPEDING

For impeding the apprehension or prosecution of an another person see **ASSISTING OFFENDERS**

96   IMPORTATION OF DRUGS (CLASS A, B AND C)

96.1   Customs and Excise Management Act 1979 s 170(1)(b) and (2)(b)

Triable either way unless the defendant could receive the minimum sentence of 7 years for a third drug trafficking offence when the offence is triable only on indictment.

The Criminal Justice Act 2003 creates a summary maximum sentence of 51 weeks, a minimum sentence of 28 weeks and Custody plus. The Home Office says they do not expect to introduce these provisions before September 2006.

On indictment maximum Class A – life, Class B and C – 14[5] years. For offences involving Class C drugs committed before 29/1/04 the sentence is 5 years. On summary conviction 6 months (3 months for Class C drugs) and/or £5,000 or three times the value of the goods which ever is greater.

For drugs on the high seas destined for other countries the offences are prosecuted under Criminal Justice (International Co-operation) Act 1990, s 19 which has the same penalties (save the three times the value of the goods is omitted) and has the same 'triable either way' provisions.

Confiscation For all importation offences[6] the court <u>must</u> follow the Proceeds of Crime Act 2002 procedure for offences committed on or after 24 March 2003[7] and Drug Trafficking Act 1994 procedure for offences committed before that date.

5   Criminal Justice Act 2003 s 284 and Sch. 28 Para 2.
6   Proceeds of Crime Act 2002 s 75 and Sch 2 para 1(2)(a) (b) and (c) or Drug Trafficking Act 1994 s 1(1)(a) (depending on the date of the offence).
7   Proceeds of Crime Act 2002 (Commencement No 5, Transitional Provisions, Savings and Amendment) Order 2003

Minimum sentences For offences committed on or after 30 September 1997, supply is a specified offence for minimum 7 years for third Class A drug trafficking offence[8]. See *Persistent class A offenders*.

Travel Restrictions For importation and exporting offences committed on or after 1/4/02 where 4 or more year's imprisonment is appropriate the Court is under a duty to consider whether it is appropriate to make a travel restriction order[9]. Where there is a direction in the order the Secretary of State may retain the defendant's passport[10].

Crown Court statistics – England and Wales – Males 21+

96.2

Year	Plea	Total Numbers sentenced	Type of sentence %					Average length of custody (months)
			Discharge	Fine	Community sentence	Suspended sentence	Custody	
Class A								
2002	Guilty	316	–	–	0	0	99	69.2
	Not guilty	115	–	–	–	1	–	99 137.3
2003	Guilty	224	–	–	0	–	99	82.4
	Not guilty	85	–	1	–	–	99	130.4
Class B								
2002	Guilty	137	–	–	2	1	96	27.4
	Not guilty	64	–	–	–	–	100	43
2003	Guilty	100	–	1	3	3	93	32.9
	Not guilty	36	–	–	–	–	97	54.8
Class C								
2002	Not guilty	1	–	–	–	–	100	10
2003	Guilty	1	–	–	–	–	100	6
	Not guilty	1	–	–	–	–	100	9

In 2002 and 2003 there were 77 and 48 offences respectively where the Class of drug was not recorded. In 2002 and 2003 there were 8 recorded offences of exporting drugs each year. All those defendants received custody. For details and explanations about the statistics in the book see page vii.

The chapter is divided into nine sections, namely (A) General principles, (B) Amphetamine, (C) Cannabis, (D) Cocaine, (E) Ecstasy, (F) Heroin, (G) LSD, (H) Opium and (I) Steroids.

A General Principles

Guideline cases – Class A

96.3 *R v Aramah* 1982 76 Cr App R 190. LCJ. Large scale importations, that is where the weight of Class A drugs at 100% purity is of the order of 500 grams or more, sentences of **10 years** and upwards are appropriate. Where the weight at 100% purity is of the order of 5 kilos or more, sentences of **14 years** and upwards are appropriate. It will seldom be that an importer of any appreciable amount will deserve less than **4 years**, [as adapted by *R v Bilinski* 1987 86 Cr App R 146 LCJ. and *R v Aranguren* 1994 99 Cr App R 347 LCJ.]

8 Powers of Criminal Courts (Sentencing) Act 2000 s 110
9 Criminal Justice and Police Act 2001 s 33
10 Criminal Justice and Police Act 2001 s 33(5)

R v Van der Leest 1997 Unreported 16/6/97. Where a massive quantity of Class A drugs has been imported, a sentence significantly in excess of 20 years, after a trial, should be reserved for exceptional cases e.g. where the amount of drugs is truly enormous, or the defendant is to be sentenced for more than one such importation, or he has a previous record for serious drug dealing or he is at the pinnacle of responsibility for the particular importation. Here 170 kilos of ecstasy worth £10m merited **20** not 25 **years** after a trial and **15** not 18 **years** after a plea for those very close to the centre of the operation.

Guideline remarks – Class A – large scale conspiracies

96.4 *Att-Gen's Ref. Nos. 99–102 of 2004* 2005 Unreported 7/2/05. We do not depart from the principle that the amount of drugs is only one of the factors to which regard must be paid. However generally speaking where a massive quantity of Class A drugs have been imported, a sentence of significantly in excess of **20 years** after a trial should be reserved for exceptional cases where for example the amount of drugs is truly enormous or the defendant is taking part in more than one importation or the defendant is at the pinnacle of responsibility of that particular importation.

Assisting the Crown

96.5 *R v Aramah* 1982 76 Cr App R 190. LCJ. It is particularly important that offenders should be encouraged to give information to the police, and a confession of guilt coupled with considerable assistance to the police can properly be marked by a substantial reduction.

Believing goods to be a different drug

96.6 *R v Bilinski* 1987 9 Cr App R (S) 360. The drugs were heroin although the defendant believed they were cannabis. Held. It was a relevant sentencing consideration.

R v Ngiam 2002 1 Cr App R (S) 150. The defendant pleaded guilty to possessing 50 kilos of heroin (at 47%) with intent to supply. She was sentenced on the basis she thought it was cannabis and she was a courier. Held. The fact she believed it was cannabis was a mitigating factor but it did not mean the Judge was obliged to sentence her as if it was cannabis.

Att-Gen's Ref. No. 14 of 2002 2003 1 Cr App R (S) 70. The defendant was convicted of importing cocaine. The prosecution accepted that she didn't know the drug was cocaine. Held. Applying *R v Ngiam* 2002 1 Cr App R (S) 150 she was entitled to some discount for not knowing the goods were cocaine but she was not entitled to be sentenced on the basis the drug was in a less serious category.

See also SUPPLY OF DRUGS, *Believing the goods to be a different drug*

Cannabis – Guideline cases

96.7 *R v Aramah* 1982 76 Cr App R 190. LCJ. Importation of very small amounts for personal use can be dealt with as if it were simple possession. (See POSSESSION OF DRUGS). Otherwise importation of amounts up to about 20 kilos of herbal cannabis, or the equivalent in cannabis resin or cannabis oil, will, save in the most exceptional cases, attract sentences of between **18 months and 3 years**, with the lowest ranges reserved for pleas of guilty in cases where there has been small profit to the offender. There are few, if any, occasions when anything other than immediate custodial sentence is proper in this type of importation. Medium quantities over 20 kilos will attract sentences of **3 to 6 years** imprisonment, depending on the amount involved, and all the other circumstances of the case. [As adapted by later cases.]

R v Ronchetti 1998 2 Cr App R (S) 100. Following a trial, the importation of 100 kilos of cannabis by persons playing more than a subordinate role, should attract a sentence of **7 to 8 years**. Following a trial, for importations of 500 kilos or more, by such persons, **10 years** is the appropriate starting point. Larger importations will attract a higher starting point. That starting point should rise according to the role played, the weight involved, and all the other circumstances of the case up to the maximum of 14 years. The fact that, in a particular case of massive importation, an even greater quantity of the drug might one day have to be dealt with by the courts, is not in itself, a reason for not imposing the maximum sentence for those at the top of the organisation.

See also **Cannabis – Class C (previously B) – Does reclassification affect the guidelines for cannabis supply?** (at **96.25**)

Conspiracy not carried out

See CONSPIRACY – *Conspiracy not carried out*

Couriers

96.8 *R v Rimmer* 1999 1 Cr App R (S) 234. The defendant pleaded to importing amphetamine. Held. A courier can be involved in a wide variety of ways. The critical fact is the degree and extent of his involvement and the nature of the enterprise.

Defendant does not speak English etc.

96.9 *R v Rainho* 2003 1 Cr App R (S) 389. The defendant was convicted of importing 10 kilos of cocaine She was 53 and with a good character after checks were made in Brazil. She spoke no English and the defence said prison would bear more harshly on her. Held. That is not something which much weight can be given. Otherwise those are simple circumstances which would lead to the selection of particular types of courier by drug dealers, in order to encourage couriers to believe that sentences would be mitigated on account of those personal circumstances. It is to be noted that prisoners can be repatriated to their own country to serve part of their sentences. (For more details see **96.33**)

Defendant under 18 – Class A

96.10 *R v J* 2001 1 Cr App R (S) 280. The defendant pleaded guilty to importing 1.66 kilos of pure cocaine. When aged 15, she went to Jamaica with another aged 22 to buy drugs for resale in UK. They each had a bag with a hidden compartment in which the drugs were hidden. The drugs were found at Gatwick. They expected to be paid between £4,000 and £5,000. She had no previous convictions. She had started working and had become addicted to drugs. She lost her job and was unable to purchase drugs. The pre-sentence report said she had a pattern of frequent wilful behaviour since she was 13 and was vulnerable. Held. Because of her age **$5^1/_2$ years** not $6^1/_2$ detention.

Defendant aged 18–20 – Class A

96.11 *R v Bristol* 1998 1 Cr App R (S) 47. The defendant was convicted of importing cocaine. She arrived from Jamaica with almost 1.5 kilos of cocaine concealed in the soles of three sandals. The drugs were 85% pure with a street value of £96,000. She was 18 with no convictions. She had been in care since the age of 9. She was said to be vulnerable and easily influenced by a man much older than herself. Held. The sentence was perfectly proper save for the age and vulnerability of the defendant. Those who intend to bring drugs into the country will select the vulnerable, the young and those of good character. Those factors which will justify a substantial discount carry less weight in importation cases. However, in all the circumstances **8 years** YOI not 10.

Drugs not destined for UK

96.12 *R v Mouzulukwe* 1996 2 Cr App R (S) 48. The defendant claimed the drugs were destined for the US. Held. That made no difference whatsoever to the sentence.

R v Maguire 1997 1 Cr App R (S) 130. The defendant was convicted of being concerned with cannabis in transit on the high seas, contrary to the Criminal Justice (International

Co-operation) Act 1990 s 19(2)(b). The boat carrying the drugs was on the high seas in international waters and not in UK waters. The boat was going to Holland where the maximum would have been 4 years. The likely sentence would have been 18 months. Held. That was irrelevant. Courts should use English cases.

See also *Foreign penalties are irrelevant, future*

Drugs worth less than defendant thought

96.13   Old cases. *R v Afzal* 1991 13 Cr App R (S) 145.

Exporting drugs

96.14   *R v Powell* 2000 The Times 5/10/00. LCJ. There was no difference in criminality between the importation and exportation of controlled drugs.

Foreign penalties are irrelevant, future

96.15   *R v Ogburu* 1992 The Times 14/10/92. Ignore foreign penalties in the future.

R v Nwoko 1995 16 Cr App R (S) 612. A Nigerian defendant faced a further term imprisonment on his return. Held. It was not a relevant consideration.

R v Ukoh 2004 The Times 28/12/04. The defendant pleaded guilty to importing 3.13 kilos of heroin at 100%. He was a Nigerian who feared further imprisonment on his return home because the government were, it was claimed, reactivating a 1990 decree. Held. We affirm *R v Ogburu* 1992 and *R v Nwoko* 1995. No Judge can anticipate what the law and practice in a foreign state will be or how it will be applied when the defendant is released. The Home Secretary can decide in each case whether it will be unduly harsh to return the defendant.

See also *Drugs not destined for UK*

Good character

96.16   *R v Aramah* 1982 76 Cr App R 190. LCJ. Good character of a courier of drugs was less important than good character in other cases. The large scale operator looks for couriers of good character and for the people of a sort which is likely to exercise the sympathy of the court if they are arrested. Consequently one will frequently find students, sick and elderly people used as couriers for two reasons: first of all they are vulnerable to the offer of quick profit, and secondly, it is felt that the courts will be moved to misplaced sympathy in their case.

R v Rainho 2003 1 Cr App R (S) 389. The good character of a courier in Class A drugs is something which can be of little consequence. Those behind the trade exploit the good character. (For more details see **96.33**)

Harbouring

96.17   (Cases of harbouring etc. drugs with intent to evade the prohibition are normally sentenced as if the defendant was involved in the onward distribution of drugs in an importation case. Importation being a continuing offence[11]. This level of sentence will equate with a supply sentence, where sentences approaching those imposed for importation can be imposed[12]. The nearer the defendant is to the importation the greater will be the sentence.)

R v Unlu 2003 1 Cr App R (S) 524. The defendant was convicted of harbouring heroin with intent to evade the prohibition on importation of it. Customs officers mounted a surveillance operation on the defendant and his co-defendant. The defendant drove to his home address followed by the co-defendant driving a van. Once there, a suitcase and holdall were taken from the defendant's house and placed in the van. The defendants

11 DPP v Doot 1973 57 Cr. App. R. 600
12 R v Aramah 1982 76 Cr. App. R. 190

drove in convoy to a quiet residential area, stopped and waited, before the defendant received two calls on his mobile phone. Following the second call the defendant got back into his car and started to drive off at which point they were arrested. The suitcase and holdall contained 54.8 kilograms of heroin at 40–47% purity, giving 24 kilograms at 100% purity with an estimated street value of more than £2.8 m. At trial each defendant sought to blame the other. The judge said that all the indications were that the defendant was very close to the source of the drugs and that he sought to involve the co-defendant who had not been involved before that day. The defendant was 28, married with a child and of good character. The judge described him as a ruthless operator, clever and wily. A co-defendant received nine years. Held. The duration over which drugs are stored may (depending on the circumstances) be of very little significance. In cases of harbouring of this kind the position almost always is that the harbourer is at the shore end, as it were, of the importation process. There was no basis to conclude that the judge's assessment of respective culpability was wrong. **16 years** was not too long.

Own use

96.18   *R v Aramah* 1982 76 Cr App R 190. LCJ. Importation of very small amounts of cannabis for personal use can be dealt with as if it were simple possession. (See **POSSESSION OF DRUGS**)

R v De Brito 2000 2 Cr App R (S) 255. The defendant is entitled to a discount if the importation is solely for the consumption of the offender, but the larger the amount the smaller the discount. This is because whatever the intention of the offender may be, the larger the amount the greater the danger that the drugs may pass into the hands of others.

Old cases. *R v McLean* 1994 15 Cr App R (S) 706.

Persistent Class A offender – Minimum 7 years

96.19   Powers of Criminal Courts (Sentencing) Act 2000 s 110. Where a person is convicted of a class A drug trafficking offence committed after 30 November 1999 and was 18 or over and he had been convicted of two other class A drug trafficking offences one of which was committed after he had been convicted of the other, the court shall impose a sentence of imprisonment of at least 7 years except where the court is of the opinion that there are particular circumstances which relate to any of the offences or to the offender which would make it unjust. [This section is summarised and is slightly amended by Criminal Justice and Court Services Act 2000.]

Persistent Class A offender – Minimum 7 years' custody – Plea of guilty

96.20   Powers of Criminal Courts (Sentencing) Act 2000 s 152(3) Where a sentence is to be imposed under the Powers of the Criminal Courts (Sentencing) Act 2000, s 110 nothing in that section shall prevent the court from imposing a sentence of 80% or more of the minimum period. [Section summarised. The section means if s/he pleads the court can impose a sentence, which is 80% or more of the minimum term.]

Purity – What is required?

96.21   *R v Morris* 2001 2 Cr App R (S) 297. We have considered a large number of authorities. The relevant principles are the amount of Class A or B drug with which a defendant is involved is a very important but not solely the determinative factor in sentencing. Evidence as to the scale of dealing can come from many sources other than the amount with which a defendant is directly connected. Amounts should generally be based on the weight of drug involved at 100% purity, not its street value; see *R v Aramah* 1982 4 Cr App R (S) 407 at 409 and *R v Ronchetti* 1998 2 Cr App R (S) 100 at 104 as to cannabis; *R v Aranguren* 1994 99 Cr App R 347 at 351 as to cocaine; *R v Warren & Beeley* 1996 1 Cr App R 120 at 123A as to ecstasy and *R v Wijs* 1999 1 Cr App R (S) 181 at 183 as to amphetamine. But, in some circumstances, reference to the street value of the same weight of different drugs may be pertinent, simply by way of cross check, e.g. 1 kilo of LSD is worth very much more than 1 kilo of heroin, and 1 kilo of amphetamine is worth very much more than 1 kilo of cannabis. Weight depends on purity. The purity of drugs such as cocaine, heroin and amphetamine powder, can be appropriately determined only by analysis. The weight of drugs such as ecstasy, in tablet, or LSD, in dosage, form, can generally be assessed by reference to the number of tablets or doses and, currently, an assumed average purity of 100 mgs of ecstasy (*R v Warren & Beeley* 1996 1 Cr App R (S) 233 at 236) and 50 micrograms of LSD (*R v Hurley* 1998 1 Cr App R (S) 299 at 304) unless prosecution or defence, by expert evidence, show the contrary (*R v Warren & Beeley* 1996 1 Cr App R (S) 233 at 236, and *R v McPhail* 1997 1 Cr App R (S) 321 at 322) Purity analysis is essential for sentencing purposes for cases of importation, or in other circumstances, where 500 grams or more of cocaine, heroin or amphetamine are seized. It may be desirable in cases where quantities less than 500 grams of those substances are seized. But, bearing in mind the cost of purity analysis and that analysis may cause delay, purity analysis will not generally be required where a defendant is in possession of only a small amount consistent with either personal use or only limited supply to others. In such a case the court can be expected to sentence only on the basis of a low level of retail dealing, but taking into account all the other circumstances of the particular case. But, as purity can indicate proximity to the primary source of supply, if there is reason for the prosecution to believe that a defendant in possession of a small quantity of drugs is close to the source of supply and is wholesaling rather than retailing, it will be necessary for purity analysis to be undertaken before a court can be invited to sentence on this more serious basis. In the absence of purity analysis or expert evidence, it is not open to a court to find or assume levels of purity, except in the case of ecstasy and LSD in the circumstances to which we have referred.

B Amphetamine – Class B

B Amphetamine – Class B – Guideline case

96.22 *R v Wijs* 1998 2 Cr App R 436. On conviction of importing amphetamine a custodial sentence will almost invariably be called for save in exceptional circumstances or where the quantity of the drug is so small as to be compatible only with personal consumption. The ordinary sentence following a contested trial (subject to all other considerations, and on quantities calculated on the basis of 100% purity) should be (1) Up to 500 grams: **up to 2 years**. (2) More than 500 grams but less than $2^1/_2$ kilos: **2–4 years**. (3) More than $2^1/_2$ kilos but less than 10 kilos: **4–7 years**. (4) More than 10 but less than 15 kilos: **7–10 years**. (5) More than 15 kilos: **upwards of 10 years**, subject to the statutory maximum of 14 years.

Amphetamine – Class B – Less than 5 kilos

96.23 *R v Rouse* 1997 Unreported 22/10/96. The defendant pleaded guilty to importation of 2.25 kilos at 45%. He was a mere courier. **4 years** not 5 years.

R v West 1998 2 Cr App R (S) 310. The defendant was convicted of importing 3.1 kilos of amphetamine at a minimum purity of 95%. A DHL parcel was intercepted in Belgium. It was addressed to the UK. The drugs were removed and the Customs made a controlled delivery. There was no answer so they left a card. The defendant's co-accused picked up the parcel from the depot and took it to a van outside. The defendant who was in the van drove him away at speed. The van was lost but some time later was found and the two were arrested. The defendant was now 27 and had a degree of mental handicap. He had convictions for theft and burglary but nothing for drugs. Held. The defendant was if not at the heart of the enterprise very near it. **6 years** not 8.

Old cases. *R v Purcell* 1996 1 Cr App R (S) 190

Amphetamine – Class B – 5 kilos and more

96.24   *R v Wijs* 1999 Re Donaldson 1 Cr App R (S) 181 at 184. The defendant was convicted of importing 33 kilos of amphetamine (equivalent to 30 kilos at 100% pure amphetamine base) with a street value of about £4.7 m. Two other defendants were convicted of importing cannabis, which were bought in at the same time. The drugs were brought into this country by another by car, in bags. The car was stopped at Harwich and the drugs were removed. The bags were re-filled. The car went to a meeting place at a hotel where Donaldson was seen in a gold Mercedes. The judge described him as a substantial organiser in a vastly profitable enterprise. Held. The judge having heard the evidence was entitled to sentence on that basis. **12 years** was not excessive.

R v Rimmer 1999 1 Cr App R (S) 234. The defendant made a very late plea to importing amphetamine. Four boxes of 74.5 kilos of amphetamine (32 kilos at 100%) arrived at Heathrow Airport from Belgium. Their street value was between £3.75 m and £4 m. Sugar was substituted for the drugs. The man who collected them took them to his home. The defendant arrived there and put the boxes in his car and took them to Liverpool. As he approached Liverpool he conducted some very odd manoeuvres on the road. In interview he claimed it was contraband tobacco. He was a 29-year-old happily married family man with a good character and references. He was unemployed and in financial difficulties. The judge said he was in sole charge of a very valuable cargo over quite a significant time. Held. A courier can be involved in a wide variety of ways. The critical fact is the extent of his involvement and the nature of the enterprise. **6 years** was severe but because of the late plea, the extent of his involvement and that it was a very substantial enterprise it was not manifestly excessive.

See also AMPHETAMINE

C   Cannabis – Class C (previously B)

Cannabis – Class C (previously B) Does reclassification affect the guidelines for cannabis importation?

96.25   On 29/1/04, Cannabis was transferred from a Class B drug to a Class C drug[13], However at the same time the penalty for importing Class C drugs was increased to 14 years[14] so the maximum sentence remained the same. The changes only apply to offences committed on or after 29/1/04.

R v Mitchell 2004 Unreported 9/11/04. The defendant pleaded guilty to importing cannabis. Held. R v Donovan *2005 1* Cr App R (S) *65* makes clear that in light of the raised maximum penalty for cannabis the reclassification of cannabis should not result in any reduction in sentence.

R v Herridge 2005 Unreported 26/5/05. For supply Parliament clearly intended no change. Where the cannabis is for own use a reduction should be made.

Cannabis – Class C – Guideline cases

96.26   *R v Aramah* 1982 76 Cr App R 190. LCJ. Importation of very small amounts for personal use can be dealt with as if it were simple possession (see POSSESSION OF DRUGS). Otherwise importation of amounts up to about 20 kilos of herbal cannabis, or the equivalent in cannabis resin or cannabis oil, will, save in the most exceptional cases, attract sentences of between **18 months and 3 years**, with the lowest ranges reserved

13 Misuse of Drugs Act 1971 (Modification)(No 2) Order 2003.
14 Criminal Justice Act 2003 s 284 and Sch. 28 Para 2.

for pleas of guilty in cases where there has been small profit to the offender. There are few, if any, occasions when anything other than immediate custodial sentence is proper in this type of importation. Medium quantities over 20 kilos will attract sentences of **3 to 6 years** imprisonment, depending on the amount involved, and all the other circumstances of the case. (As adapted by later cases.)

R v Ronchetti 1998 2 Cr App R (S)100. Following a trial, the importation of 100 kilos of cannabis by persons playing more than a subordinate role, should attract a sentence of **7 to 8 years**. Following a trial, for importations of 500 kilos or more, by such persons **10 years** is the appropriate starting point. Larger importations will attract a higher starting point. That starting point should rise according to the role played, the weight involved, and all the other circumstances of the case up to the maximum of 14 years. The fact that, in a particular case of massive importation, an even greater quantity of the drug might one day have to be dealt with by the courts, is not in itself, a reason for not imposing the maximum sentence for those at the top of the organisation.

Cannabis – Class C – Under 1 kilo

96.27   *R v Aramah* 1982 76 Cr App R 190. For very small amounts for personal use deal with as simple possession which is often met with a fine.

R v Browne 1999 Unreported 31/3/99. The defendant made a late guilty plea to importing through the post three packages of herbal cannabis from South Africa. The combined weight of cannabis was about 500 grams worth about £1,750 on the street. He was 33 and of good character. Held. It wasn't a single instance and the benefit of the plea was diluted by the lateness of it but **2 months** not 3.

Cannabis – Class C – 1–19 kilos

96.28   *R v Astbury* 1997 2 Cr App R (S) 93. The defendant pleaded guilty at the Magistrates' Court to importing 1,100 grams of herbal cannabis and a little over 20 grams of cannabis resin. The drugs were found in his car at Dover. The prosecution accepted it was for own use. He was committed for sentence. Held. **3 months** not 9.

Old cases. *R v Blyth* 1996 1 Cr App R (S) 388, *R v Klitkze* 1995 16 Cr App R (S) 445.

Cannabis – Class C – 20–99 kilos

96.29   *R v Frazer* 1998 1 Cr App R (S) 287. The defendant pleaded guilty to importing 36 kilos of herbal cannabis. He took the drugs through the green channel and he was stopped. He was 50 and it was his third conviction for importing cannabis into the country. He had received 6 months and 2 years. Held. **6 years** was a high sentence at the top end of the bracket but because it was a commercial importation by someone convicted for the third time it was not manifestly excessive.

R v Wijs Re Church and Haller 1999 1 Cr App R (S) 181 at 186. The defendants H and C were convicted of importing 39 kilos of cannabis resin with a street value of £132,900. The drugs were brought into this country by car by another. The car was stopped at Harwich and the drugs were removed by Customs. They were re-filled. The car went a hotel where H and C arrived. H was given two bags, which had contained cannabis. H and C were arrested. H had met the driver once in Holland and once at the hotel to arrange the delivery. H was sentenced on the basis that he was substantially involved and C was involved on a lesser basis. For H, **5 years** not 7. For C, **4 years** not 5.

Old case *R v Damen* 1997 Unreported 12/12/97, (for a summary of this case see the first edition of this book.)

Cannabis – Class C – 100 kilos to 1 tonne

96.30   *R v Vickers* 1999 2 Cr App R (S) 216. The defendant was convicted of importing 402 kilos of cannabis and 301 kilos of cannabis resin. The cannabis was found in his lorry when it searched at Dover ferry port. Held. As it was his lorry he could not be described as in a subordinate role. He was not an ordinary courier, he was master of his own lorry. Therefore **10 years** was not excessive.

R v Golder 2000 1 Cr App R (S) 59. LCJ. The defendant, a lorry driver pleaded guilty to importing cannabis resin. In May 1998 he was seen transferring boxes from his lorry to a van. Sixteen days later he entered the country at Dover and drove his lorry to Warwickshire. He transferred boxes containing 141 kilos of cannabis to his car and then drove the car to a meeting place where he transferred the boxes to another car. He and the driver of the other car were arrested. The cannabis was worth about £$^1/_2$m. He agreed he had smuggled six similar boxes in May. He said he was paid £8,200 for the first trip and £200 a box for the second trip. He was now 35 and effectively of good character and had co-operated with the Customs officers. He was sentenced on the basis he knew the second consignment was drugs but not the first. **5$^1/_2$ years** not 7.

Att-Gen's Ref. Nos. 36–8 of 1999 2000 2 Cr App R (S) 303. The defendants D, B and H were convicted of a conspiracy to import and supply cannabis. The defendant N pleaded guilty on a limited basis. D was the prime mover and the others were his lieutenants. Police conducted a surveillance operation. D was seen to pay £10,000 into a bank. The cashier said, "Paying in again." He said, "Yes." D made three visits to Spain one year. N, B and H also visited Spain. 400 kilos of cannabis resin with a street value of about £800,000 was packed in containers in two cars. N drove it and he was stopped. D was the prime mover and appeared to be reasonably affluent. The others were said to be lieutenants. B had no signs of wealth. He worked as a minicab driver. H worked as a valet for cars. N was an unemployed warehouseman. D was 35 and the rest varied from 29–39. They had no convictions. N had served his sentence. Held. D should have received 9 years. As he has absconded it didn't matter it was a reference so 9 not 7. B and H should have received **6 years**. However, it was not now appropriate to increase their 4 year sentences. N should have received **3$^1/_2$ years** not 2$^1/_2$ but as he has been released the sentence will not be increased.

Old cases. *R v Ronchetti* 1998 2 Cr App R (S) 100 (for a summary of this case see the first edition of this book).

Cannabis – Class C – Over 1 tonne

96.31   *R v Bisset and Wray* 2000 2 Cr App R (S) 397. The defendants B and W pleaded guilty to importing 1,151 kilos of cannabis in a very sophisticated false compartment of a lorry. B was acting on behalf of the Spanish principle who had arranged the exportation. B also supervised the unloading of the lorry in London and the transfer of the drugs to the next in the chain. Customs videoed the unloading of the drugs and then arrested both defendants. W was not the principle in the UK but very close to him. The judge said he was an able lieutenant. W had recruited the man who had the premises where the drugs were stored in this country. B was 40 and of good character. W was 36 and had an old conviction for theft. Held. The **11 years** sentences were severe but not excessive because of the amount of drugs, the roles played, and the limit for the credit for the plea of guilty because they were caught red-handed.

Old cases. *R v Fishleigh* 1996 2 Cr App R (S) 283 and *R v Maguire* 1997 1 Cr App R (S) 130 (for a summary of the last case see the first edition of this book).

See also CANNABIS

D   Cocaine – Class A

Cocaine – Class A – Under 1 kilo (at 100% purity)

96.32   *R v Aranguren* 1994 99 Cr App R 347. Where the Class A drugs are 500 grams or more (at 100% purity) the sentences will be **10 years** and upwards.

R v White 1999 1 Cr App R (S) 325. The defendant pleaded guilty to importing 477 grams of cocaine, (386 grams at 100% purity). A man was approached to import drugs and he informed the police who put him in touch with customs. He agreed to take part in the plan and inform customs. He was told two women would visit him. The defendant and another woman visited him and she assessed his suitability and was the go-between. She attended further meetings where instructions were given and spending money handed over. The informer was told that as this was his first trip he would be returning with a Class C drug. He was instructed to go to Jamaica and there was given a pair of training shoes to wear. He returned to the UK and the shoes were found to contain the drug, the street value of which was £59,390. She was sentenced on the basis that she believed the cannabis was to be imported. She was a 38-year-old mother with three children and two foster children and some spent convictions. There was some evidence of her attempting to assist the authorities. Held. **5^1/$_2$ years** not 6^1/$_2$.

R v De Brito 2000 2 Cr App R (S) 255. The defendant pleaded guilty to two counts of importing cocaine. He had received two envelopes and together they contained 21.5 grams of cocaine. One was 5.59 grams and the other 4.94 grams at 100% purity. He was sentenced on the basis it was for his own use. The defendant was 37 and of good character. Held. **2 years** could not be criticised.

Att-Gen's Ref. No. 14 of 2002 2003 1 Cr App R (S) 70. The defendant was convicted of importing just over a kilo of cocaine. At 100% it was 707 grams. She had earlier pleaded guilty and during a Newton hearing to determine whether she thought the drug was cocaine or cannabis she was allowed to change her plea because of the account she gave. The first jury failed to agree. She arrived at Gatwick airport and it became apparent she had something concealed under her skirt. When asked about drugs she pointed to her midriff. She was arrested and the cocaine was found in a girdle round her waist. In interview she said, "she didn't know what the packages contained. She was desperately short of money and needed to buy expensive medication for her sick mother. She earned a small amount as a telephonist. Someone approached her in the street and offered her $3,000 to carry some packages, which contained a herb illegal in Brazil and the US but nowhere else. He gave her a ticket and $1,205 which was found on her. He also claimed he helped charities." She was 32 and a Brazilian national with a good character. The prosecution accepted that she didn't know the drug was cocaine. The Judge was moved by a letter she wrote to the court and gave her 3^1/$_2$ years. Held. The Judge's starting point of **11 years** was entirely appropriate. The vulnerability and personal characteristics can only play a very small part in the sentencing process. It was not appropriate to treat her as having pleaded guilty. Applying *R v Ngiam* 2002 1 Cr App R (S) 150 she was entitled to some discount for not knowing the goods were cocaine but she was not entitled to be sentenced on the basis the drug was in a less serious category. The least sentence he could impose was **6 years**. Because it was a reference **5 years** substituted.

R v Robinson 2004 2 Cr App R (S) 392. The defendants R and W were convicted of importing cocaine. Customs officers searched them after a flight from Jamaica. R's sandals contained 412 grams of cocaine (70 grams at 100%). W's shoes contained 461 and 160 grams of cocaine (288 grams at 100%). The total street value was £17,995. At trial they relied on duress saying they were told they would be shot if they did not agree to carry the drugs. Both were 17. The Judge declined to make a finding whether or not they were coerced to carry the drugs. Held. The fair course would be for us to accept they were coerced. Taking into account their age, immaturity and the coercion **3^1/$_2$ years** detention not 4.

Old cases. *R v Bell* 1995 16 Cr App R (S) 93; *R v Nwoko* 1995 16 Cr App R (S) 612.

Cocaine – Class A – 1–9 kilos (at 100% purity)

96.33   *R v Aranguren* 1994 99 Cr App R 347. LCJ. Where the Class A drugs are 500 grams or more (at 100% purity) the sentences will be **10 years** and upwards. Five kilos or more (at 100% purity) is worth **14 years** and upwards.

R v Guy 1999 2 Cr App R (S) 24. The defendant pleaded guilty to importing cocaine. Customs Officers at Gatwick airport stopped the defendant, his then girlfriend, and her child after they had travelled from Jamaica. They were en route to Manchester. A search of their luggage revealed packages of 3.95 kilos of cocaine, which at 100% purity was 2.29 kilos. The packages were replaced with dummies. Guy and his girlfriend were arrested and he was frank with the customs officers and he co-operated with them. Later that day different Customs Officers met the defendant in Manchester. The co-accused was expected to meet the defendant there and he too was arrested. His co-accused was tried, convicted and received 12 years. The defendant gave evidence against him. He also gave also gave significant information to Customs. The defendant received 8 years. The co-accused's conviction was quashed on appeal and he was acquitted at the retrial. The defendant did not give evidence in that trial. He was 26 and was a person of positive good character. Held. The sentence on the co-accused was entirely appropriate. The defendant was significantly less involved than him. The starting point in the case of Guy ought to have been **10 years**. He was entitled to 50% discount so **5 years** instead.

R v Rainho 2003 1 Cr App R (S) 389. The defendant was convicted of importing 10 kilos of cocaine (7.6 kilos at 100%). The street value was just under £1m. She flew from Rio de Janeiro to Gatwick were the drugs were found in her suitcase. There was $4,500 US on her. She was interviewed and claimed she thought she was carrying money and that she was to be met later that day and was to be paid $10,000 US. She was 53 and with a good character after checks were made in Brazil. She spoke no English and the defence said prison would bear more harshly on her. Held. That is not something which much weight can be given. Otherwise those are simple circumstances which would lead to the selection of particular types of courier by drug dealers, in order to encourage couriers to believe that sentences would be mitigated on account of those personal circumstances. It is to be noted that prisoners can be repatriated to their own country to serve part of their sentences. The good character of a courier in Class A drugs, is something which can be of little consequence. Those behind the trade exploit the good character. The tariff was **14 years and upwards. 15 years** was not manifestly excessive.

R v Cassidy 2005 1 Cr App R (S) 200. The defendant pleaded guilty to the importing of cocaine. He had opened two mailboxes using the name King, giving a false address and showing forged documents. Six deliveries were made to the boxes. The last delivery was intercepted. It was from the West Indies and contained ten packages of cocaine equivalent to 4.27 kg at 100 % purity, concealed in engine parts. He collected a substitute package and was arrested. The defendant said that he was involved through a friend. The friend had told him that he and a man called King ran photo studios and they wanted to expand into West London. The friend asked the defendant to help him by setting up the mailboxes and collecting photographic and framing equipment from them. Presumably the friend provided the documents. When the defendant collected the first consignment he became suspicious and confronted his friend who told him the package contained cannabis. He then tried to back out but was reminded that he owed the friend several thousand pounds. He was told he could work off his debt by £250 every time he made a collection, and he would additionally be paid £150 for every collection. He was threatened with violence to him and his family if he refused. He was shocked when he found out the amount of cocaine seized. He had assumed the amounts were about half a kilogram each. There was nothing to contradict his account of his involvement and that was the basis on which he was sentenced. The defendant, 38, had previous convictions all for dishonesty. He was an habitual gambler. He told the author of the pre-sentence report he was running his own building firm and making £30,000 a year. Held. The weight of cocaine suggested a starting point close to **14 years**, but the fact that there were four previous consignments had to be factored in, together with the mundane level of the defendant's involvement which was akin to a courier. The correct starting point would have been **16 years**. An appropriate sentence bearing in mind his early pleas of guilty and frankness with the police meant that **11 years** not 16.

Old cases. *R v Brougham* 1996 2 Cr App R (S) 88; *R v Bristol* 1998 (See **Para 96.11**), *R v McLeary* 1997 Unreported 10/4/97 and *R v Watson* 1997 Unreported 10/3/97.

Cocaine – Class A – 10–24 kilos (at 100% purity)

96.34   Old cases. *R v Scamaronie* 1992 13 Cr App R 702; *R v Serdeiro* 1996 1 Cr App R (S) 251; *R v De Four* 1996 2 Cr App R (S) 106.

Cocaine – Class A – Over 25 kilos (at 100% purity)

96.35   *R v Akyeah* 2004 1 Cr App R (S) 239. The defendant was convicted of importing 38.9 kilos (at 100%) of cocaine. She was stopped by Customs on arrival from Ghana. A Customs officer examined her suitcase and noticed a chemically smell. She said it was flour. The drugs were found and she answered questions without a solicitor. She said she was to be met outside and agreed to stand there for 45 minutes. No-one approached her. She was now 34, a mother and of good character. There was £10,000 in her bank account. The Judge said, "You are an intelligent woman with a business which was ideal cover. You are not a poor impoverished courier." **20 years** not 23.

Old case. *R v Richardson* 1994 15 Cr App R (S) 876.

E Ecstasy – Class A

Ecstasy – Class A – Guideline case

96.36   *R v Warren and Beeley* 1996 1 Cr App R (S) 233 at 237. LCJ. For the importation of 5,000 tablets or more of ecstasy tablets (assuming that each tablet contained an active constituent close to the average of 100 mgs) the appropriate sentence would be of the order of **10 years** and upwards. For 50,000 tablets or more **14 years** or more.

Ecstasy – Class A – Less than 5,000 tablets or equivalent

96.37   *R v Warren and Beeley* 1996 1 Cr App R (S) 233. LCJ. Both defendants W and B in unconnected cases pleaded guilty to importing ecstasy tablets. W was searched by customs officers at Ramsgate and they found 1011 tablets taped to his chest. He was 43 with three unrelated convictions. Held. **5 years** not 6. Customs Officers at Sheerness searched B after he arrived from the continent. They found 1,585 tablets of ecstasy in his sock. He was expecting £500 and a debt of £800 he owed the person organising it to be written off. He claimed the dealer had made threats. He had no relevant convictions. Held. **6 years** not 7.

R v Wijs 1999 2 Cr App R (S) 181 at 184. The defendant pleaded guilty to importing ecstasy, amphetamine and cannabis, obstructing a customs officer and impeding the detention of drugs. A customs officer searched the defendant, who was with his 17-year-old girlfriend, after he had disembarked from a ferry from Holland. The defendant was searched and he produced 1.34 grams of cannabis from his shoe. His girlfriend was also searched and she produced 15 ecstasy tablets from inside her sock. There was 35.9 grams of cannabis concealed in her vagina. The appellant was taken to hospital and he dropped 58 amphetamine tablets, and 5 tablets of ecstasy which had been concealed in his rectum. While at the hospital he tried to grab the packages and abscond, which gave rise to the last two counts. The street value of the 20 ecstasy tablets (containing somewhat over 1 gram of pure ecstasy) was £240, the value of the 58 amphetamine tablets (containing 2.03 grams of pure amphetamine) was £205 and the value of the 37.24 grams of cannabis was £151.56. The judge regarded it as a commercial importation by the defendant who had used his girlfriend as an assistant. The judge gave only a nominal discount for his plea since the evidence was quite overwhelming. He received 7 years for the ecstasy, 15 months' concurrent for the amphetamine and 6 months consecutive for the obstructing and impeding counts making $7^{1}/_{2}$ years in all. The girlfriend, who pleaded guilty to all the counts except the last two, received a total of 6 months detention. Held. The judge was entitled to say he had involved his young girlfriend. Although the defendant certainly merited a longer sentence than she did the difference was too great. The guideline decisions are not to be applied with mathematical precision. This court in *R v Warren and Beeley* 1996 1 Cr App R (S) 233 at 237, indicate that for the importation of 5,000 tablets or more of ecstasy tablets (assuming that each tablet contained an average of 0.1 grams) the sentence would be of the order of 10 years and upwards. The appellant pleaded guilty and the importation was of 20 tablets only, which contained less of the active ingredient than was assumed in *R v Warren and Beeley* to be the norm, so **2 years** not 5. In view of the very small quantity of amphetamine 15 months for that was excessive. 9 months substituted making $2^{1}/_{2}$ in all.

Ecstasy – Class A – 100,000 tablets or more

96.38   *R v Van der Leest* 1997 Unreported 16/6/97. The defendant V pleaded guilty to importing 170 kilos of ecstasy worth £10m. G was convicted of the same offence. 630,000 tablets of ecstasy was sent by lorry from Holland to Manchester. In a surveillance operation V was seen flying from Holland to Manchester shortly before the importation and he was met by G. V was arrested as the lorry was unloaded. G left the scene in a car at the same time as V's arrest and seven boxes of ecstasy were recovered from that car. G had made many telephone calls to Holland and visited Holland in the months before. The judge said V was equally involved as G. Held. The judge was right to say that G was "very close to the centre of the operation." However, **20 years** not 25 years for G and **15 years** not 18 for V.

R v Main and Johnson 1997 2 Cr App R (S) 63. The defendants M and J were convicted of attempting to import 1.2 million tablets of ecstasy worth £23.5m in a van, and conspiracy to supply ecstasy. Officers searched premises and found the two defendants, 25 kilos and 111,275 tablets of ecstasy. The house received deliveries of imported ecstasy. Both were considered 'main persons' in the organisation in this country. J was 54 and had heart disease. Held. **24 years** concurrent on each defendant upheld.

R v Ellis and Avis 2000 1 Cr App R (S) 38. Both defendants E and A were convicted of a conspiracy to import 115,000 ecstasy tablets from Belgium. Another person was arrested in Belgium with the tablets before they could be imported. The defendants were under surveillance and seen making preparation for the importation and flying around in a small aircraft. The drugs were about 75% purity representing 88,000 at 100%. Their street value was about £1m. The trial judge sentenced A as the principle. The prosecution said they were equally involved. Held. The appropriate bracket for this amount is more than 14 years and less than 20. Because the conspiracy was not successful **16 years** for both not 18 and 22 years.

Old cases. *R v Tattenhove* 1996 2 Cr App R 91.

See also ECSTASY

F   Heroin – Class A

Heroin – Class A – Guideline case

96.39   *R v Aramah* 1982 76 Cr App R 190. LCJ. Large-scale importations of Class A drugs, that is where the weight of the drugs at 100% purity is of the order of 500 grams or more, sentences of **10 years** and upwards are appropriate. Where the weight at 100% purity is of the order of 5 kilos or more, sentences of **14 years** and upwards are appropriate. It will seldom be that an importer of any appreciable amount will deserve less than **4 years**, [as adapted by *R v Bilinski* 1987 86 Cr App R 146. LCJ and *R v Aranguren* 1994 99 Cr App R 347. LCJ.]

Heroin – Class A – Under 1 kilo (at 100% purity)

96.40   *R v Aranguren* 1994 99 Cr App R 347. Where the Class A drugs are 500 grams or more (at 100% purity) the sentences will be **10 years** and upwards.

R v Siebers 2002 2 Cr App R (S) 28. The defendant pleaded guilty to the importation of 0.496 kilos of heroin (at 100%). She was stopped at Waterloo Station after travelling from Brussels on the Eurostar. Her ticket showed she was due to return in about an hour. She said she had come to see her boyfriend. Underneath her clothing were found four packages held by elasticised back support. They contained 1.986 kilos of heroin at 25%. The street value was £70,000. She was a foreign national, 18 and of good character. She had an unhappy background and had been pressurised to do it by an older man who offered marriage and money. Held. Couriers very often have a sad background, immaturity, youth and vulnerability. The judge made proper allowance for these factors. The appeal over **5 years** detention dismissed.

Old cases. *R v Daniel* 1995 16 Cr App R 892; *R v Mouzulukwe* 1996 2 Cr App R (S) 48.

Heroin – Class A – 1–10 kilos (at 100% purity)

96.41   *R v Ukoh* 2004 The Times 28/12/04 The defendant pleaded guilty on re-arraignment to importing 3.97 kilos of heroin (3.13 kilos at 100%). He flew from Lagos to City airport and he was searched. Custom officers found the drugs. He had no convictions. The Judge treated him as a courier and said he gave little credit for the plea because it was after Customs officers had flown to Nigeria to investigate his then defence of duress. His wife in Nigeria had admitted her affidavit and photograph supporting the defence were false. Held. He was a trusted courier not a mere foot soldier. **12 years** was within the appropriate bracket.

Heroin – Class A – 10–50 kilos (at 100% purity)

96.42   *R v Aranguren* 1994 99 Cr App R 347. LCJ. Five kilos or more (at 100% purity) is worth **14 years or more**.

R v Kayar 1998 2 Cr App R (S) 355. The defendant was convicted of importing 10.3 kilos (purity unknown). The heroin was concealed in the sides of 20 boxes of clothing which arrived at Stansted airport from Turkey. The defendant was in charge of the UK end of this operation. He planned and tested the system and arranged with others the actual importation. He was considered to be 'a ruthless character' but he had no previous convictions. He was 35 and Turkish and had been in the UK for 18 years. He spoke little English and had a disabled son of 17. Held. **16 years** not 20. The deportation order was confirmed.

R v Billson 2002 2 Cr App R (S) 521. The defendant pleaded guilty to importing 82.6 kilos of heroin, (49 kilos at 100%). He drove his car from Belgium and through the Channel Tunnel where he was stopped by Customs. Officers found the drugs in the boot and he said, "I know it is drugs." The basis of plea was that he was acting as a courier at all times and was paid £2,000 cash for expenses and was to be paid £50,000 once the drugs were delivered. He said the money was needed to bail out his business and there was information to support the business difficulties. He was 44 and of good character. His wife had health problems and the Judge took into account his remorse and his positive attitude he had written in a letter. He received 17 years. Held. The Judge was right to have deterrence at the forefront of her mind. However her notional sentence before deductions was too high. It must have been 22 years or more. Sentences in excess of 20 years should be reserved for those higher up the chain of command, or those involved in a series of importations or for larger quantities than this. After a trial the proper sentence would have been **20 years**. After deductions the sentence will be **14 years**.

Old cases. *R v Latif and Shahzad* 1994 15 Cr App R (S) 864; *R v Patel* 1995 16 Cr App R (S) 267; and *R v Serdeiro* 1996 1 Cr App R (S) 251.

Heroin – Class A – Over 50 kilos (at 100% purity)

96.43   *R v Kaynak* 1998 2 Cr App R (S) 283. The defendant A pleaded guilty and K, H and S were convicted of conspiracy to import 200 kilos of heroin (100 kilos at 100% purity). None of the defendants were at the top of the chain. H was a Czech coach driver who was seen to hand packages from his coach to S and A. K and A were stopped in a car and 66 kilos of heroin were found. S was found to have large sums of cash and a bag identical to one in which heroin had been packed. A's car was parked in the car park of S's apartment block and 73 kilos of heroin were found in the car. 9 kilos were found in K's flat. H's coach was again seen at the place where packages were seen being transferred but no-one turned up. He drove back to Ramsgate Dock to leave the country and 50 kilos of heroin were found in the coach. K was a courier-cum-errand boy who was not a middle ranker more a cog. At the trial he claimed duress. H was a high ranking courier. He also claimed duress. S was a mid ranker who claimed not to be involved. A was also a mid ranker but slightly below S. He provided some assistance to the authorities. Held. K **18 years** not 24. H was assigned too high a role by the judge so **18 years** not 26 years. S, **24 years** not 30. A, **15 years** not 20.

R v Dimitrov and Nedelkov 1999 Unreported 14/6/99. The defendants D and N were convicted of importing 65.1 kilos of heroin worth in excess of £10m. N drove the lorry with the drugs from Bulgaria to Hull. Customs discovered it and took N to hospital. They then created the fiction he was still in hospital when he was taken into police custody. D came over from Bulgaria and collected the lorry believing the drugs were still on board. For 5 days he drove round England until he was arrested. N was 52 and D 43. They were of good character. The judge described it as a very sophisticated and professional operation based on a legitimate consignment of furniture. He did not regard N as one of the top men but someone who took the load through seven countries. He thought D had been sent over to retrieve the situation. N knew no English. Held. N **18 years** not 24 and D **12 years** not 16.

R v Kulunk 2002 Unreported 12/04/02. The defendant pleaded guilty on the eighth day of his trial to conspiracy to supply heroin. Well in excess of 44 kilos of heroin were found. The deliveries were 80 kilos of heroin a week. The amount involved was well in excess of £100m. The judge considered the defendant to be the prime mover and started at **30 years**. He took into account his plea and his good character and sentenced him to **26 years** which was upheld.

R v Izzigil 2002 Unreported 25/04/02. The defendants were co-conspirators with Kulunk (above) and they were convicted of importation. Held. The scale of the importation required exceptional and severe sentences. **18 years** and **20 years** upheld.

Old cases. *R v Richardson* 1994 15 Cr App R (S) 876; *R v Middelkoop and Telli* 1997 1 Cr App R (S) 423; *R v Kaya* 1996 Unreported 12/6/96 and *R v Mulkerrins* 1997 Unreported 20/6/97.

See also OPIUM

G LSD – Class A

96.44   Old cases. *Att-Gen's Ref. Nos. 3, 4, and 5 of 1992* 14 Cr App R (S) 191.
See also **LSD**

H Opium – Class A

Opium – Class A – Guidelines

96.45 *R v Mashaollahi* 2001 1 Cr App R (S) 96. The court should proceed on the assumption that any given consignment of opium is unadulterated and of 100% purity. Should the defence wish to persuade a judge that the active ingredient was of a lesser percentage it is open to them to call the evidence. Heroin is eight times more valuable than opium, so 40 kilos of opium at 100% would be equivalent to 5 kilos of heroin at 100%. There is at least the remote possibility that opium might be imported to convert it into morphine or heroin. Then base the sentence on the amount of heroin or morphine that could be produced from the opium seized. The ratio to apply would be 10:1 i.e. 10 kilos of opium would be needed to produce 1 kilo of morphine or heroin assuming average levels of purity. The guideline for the importation of opium should be based on weight, crosschecked with street value to ensure that at least an approximate equivalence with heroin and cocaine is maintained. For importation of opium, the appropriate guidelines would be, **14 years** and upwards for 40 kilos or more of opium, **10 years** and upwards for 4 kilos or more of opium. To this rule of thumb we would make one exception and that is in cases where it is established that the importation of opium was carried out for the purpose of conversion into morphine or heroin we consider that the appropriate sentence should be based on the equivalent value of those drugs.

See also OPIUM

I Steroids – Class C

96.46 *R v Abdul* 2001 1 Cr App R (S) 8. The defendant was convicted of conspiracy to import steroids, conspiracy to supply steroids, and theft of cash and drugs from his employers. The defendant was a qualified pharmacist who used his position at work as a locum pharmacist to import "massive quantities" of steroids and supply them. He was a bankrupt who was in severe financial difficulties. Held. The steroid offences were very serious indeed. **3 years** concurrent for the steroids, 1 year for the thefts consecutive upheld.

See also DRUG USERS

97 IMPORTATION/EXPORTATION OF PROHIBITED/RESTRICTED GOODS

97.1 Customs and Excise Management Act 1979 s 50(2) s 68(2) and s 170(2)

Triable either way. On indictment maximum 7 years. On summary conviction 6 months and/or £5,000 or three times the value of the goods which ever is greater.

Confiscation For all s 68(2) and 170 offences[15] committed on or after 24 March 2003[16] which concern firearms or ammunition the court must follow the Proceeds of Crime Act 2002 procedure.

Notification For offences under Customs and Excise Management Act 1979 s 170 where the good were prohibited by Customs Consolidation Act 1876 s 42 (indecent or obscene articles) and (a) the photograph showed a person under 16 and (b)(i) the defendant is 18 or over or (ii) the defendant is sentenced to at least 12 months imprisonment; the defendant must notify the police within 3 days (or 3 days from his/her release from imprisonment, hospital etc.) with his/her name, home address, national insurance number etc. and any change and addresses where s/he resides for 7 days[17] (in one or more

15 Proceeds of Crime Act 2002 s 6 and s 75 and Sch 2 para 5
16 Proceeds of Crime Act 2002 (Commencement No 5, Transitional Provisions, Savings and Amendment) Order 2003
17 Sexual Offences Act 2003 s 84(1)(c) & (6)

periods) or more in any 12 month period[18]. See **Sex Offenders' Register** (It seems illogical sections 50(2) and 68(2) do not also trigger notification.)

Sexual Offences Prevention Order There is a discretionary power, when the notification (q.v.) criteria are present and when it is necessary to protect the public etc[19].

Birds etc.

97.2 *R v Sissen* 2001 1 W L R 902. The defendant was convicted of four counts of importing endangered species. Three related to Lear's Macaws and one to six Headed Macaws birds. He travelled by car to Yugoslavia and Slovakia and bought three Lear's Macaws from a dealer and the other six birds from someone else. He smuggled the birds back possibly in a concealed compartment in his petrol tank. He paid £50,000 for the nine birds. He didn't have enough money for the ninth bird so he made a later journey to buy it. There were only twenty pairs of breeding Lear Macaws left in the wild. At his home there were five hundred parrots. He was 61 and had previous convictions for dealing (or importing?) endangered species 20 years earlier. The Judge said it was an elaborate scheme. The defendant lost the £50,000. Held. Whether the reason for the breach of the restriction is profit, obsession or conservation as this defendant contends, all contribute to the illegal market which underlies the capture of these birds from the wild. These are serious offences. **30 months** was not wrong in principle. However **18 months** substituted because of his age, it was his first custodial sentence and the loss of money.

R v Jungthirapanich 2003 1 Cr App R (S) 551. The defendant pleaded guilty on the day fixed for his trial to fraudulently evading a restriction on the importation of twenty three wild birds of prey (a protected species). The defendant, a Thai national who was educated in Britain, became involved in the co-defendant's business which involved the sale of wild birds and other animals. In 1999, the two of them travelled to Thailand and made enquiries about smuggling birds of prey to Britain. The appellant sent a fax to the co-defendant, who had returned to Britain, setting out how the operation would work. The birds would be secured in plastic tubes and then placed in suitcases. The appellant bribed officials at Bangkok airport to get the suitcases through the security processes. The co-defendant then went to Thailand and returned with Brahminy Kites. Days later the defendant returned with two further suitcases. He met up with the co-defendant. Customs officers who had been observing them arrested them. The birds were found. All had been alive at the start of the journey. Six had died in transit. Three had not been fit to travel. The rest had sustained pressure injuries due to the plastic tubes, asphyxia and hypothermia consistent with the time spent in the unpressurised and unheated hold of the aircraft. A vet's opinion was that the birds had suffered gross cruelty and suffering. The value of the birds was about £25,000. It was accepted that he had acted throughout under the influence of the aggressive and bullying character of the co-defendant and that he may not have been acting for personal profit. He was 23 and of entirely good character. A co-defendant who was convicted after a trial on this count and 21 other counts concerning birds and wild animals and related offences received a total sentence of six and a half years. On this count alone he received three years. Held. The degree of influence that the co-defendant had over the defendant and the nature of the defendant's motivation, together with personal mitigation were taken into consideration. **15 months** not 22.

R v Humphrey 2004 1 Cr App R (S) 252. The defendant was convicted of 22 counts of importing endangered birds and other associated counts. The rare birds included Eagle owls and Brahminy Kites. 3 counts related to mammals like Golden Cheeked Gibbon. He met his two co-defendants off a flight from Thailand. They had twenty three birds

---

18 Sexual Offences Act 2003 s 83 & Sch 3 Para 14
19 Sexual Offences Act 2003 s 104 & Sch. 3

of prey in plastic tubes. Some had died in transit. They searched his home and found other birds. There were forged documents suggesting the birds had been acquired lawfully. He had a bad record but nothing similar. The Judge referred to his appalling cruelty, his lies and the birds' rarity. Held. The Judge was right to pass an exemplary sentence. There was extreme and sickening cruelty. **5¹/₂ years** in total not 6¹/₂. (The total number of birds is not revealed.)

CS Gas sprays/weapons

97.3 *R v Sidhu* 2004 1 Cr App R (S) 199. The defendant pleaded guilty to four counts of illegal importation and two counts of possession of prohibited articles. Customs intercepted a package addressed to the defendant containing a large CS Gas spray, four extendible batons, two combined CS Gas sprays and stun guns and 13 smaller CS Gas or gel sprays. Two further CS Gas sprays were found at his home address. He explained he bought the goods on the Internet. Initially he sought to pretend he was importing the articles to show how easy it was. Later he accepted his motive was commercial. The defendant was of good character with positive references. His prison report was good. He had been a doorman and the case had destroyed his hope of becoming a prison officer. His report said he posed no risk. **2 years** not 3.

See also R v Price 2005 The Times 25/7/05

Firearms See FIREARMS – *Importation/Exportation of Firearms*

Pornography

97.4 Extended sentences under CJA 2003 For offences 1) involving indecent and obscene articles and 2) committed on or after 4/4/05 there is a mandatory duty to pass an extended sentence when there is a significant risk to members of the public of serious harm etc.[20]. See EXTENDED SENTENCES

R v Dunn 1999 Unreported 28/10/99. The defendant pleaded guilty at the Magistrates' Court to importing two obscene video-tapes and possession of indecent photographs. A package from Russia addressed to him was intercepted. It contained the tapes which had boys aged 6–13 taking part in buggery etc. As a result, Customs went to his flat. He had seven computer disks containing 6,428 indecent images of children engaged in various sexual acts with adults and each other. He was of impeccable character and was sentenced to 8 months' imprisonment. It was accepted that the material was for his own use, and he was in a poor state of health. For that reason in particular, his sentence was halved to **4 months**. (This case appears now out of line with current sentencing.)

R v Hirst 2001 1 Cr App R (S) 152. The defendant pleaded guilty to conspiracy to import indecent or obscene material. He was involved in a sophisticated and cleverly set up operation to import hard core pornography. The main man absconded and the defendant was described as his right-hand man. The defendant's prime role was the use of his home to receive pornographic video spools and to copy them onto blank video cassettes. He also arranged forward transmission of the videos to customers and addressed jiffy bags with addresses in England knowing they would be sent to Belgium for the pornographic material to be dispatched. He was involved for about five weeks and was paid £500 a week. 236 videos were found at his home some of which were blank. Also found were materials for copying videos, mailing lists, customer orders and a large quantity of jiffy bags. The material was revolting and sickeningly vile. It included coprophilia, defecation, scatophagy, urolagnia, enema, domination, bestiality, sadomasochism and simulated rape. He was 51, of good character and under extreme financial pressure. He showed remorse and the risk of re-offending was assessed as very low. Held. He played an important role. **12 months** might be regarded as severe but it was not manifestly excessive.

20 Criminal Justice Act 2003 s 227–228

R v O'Carroll 2003 2 Cr App R (S) 104. The defendant was convicted on three counts of importing indecent material. A number of boxes arrived at Heathrow from Qatar addressed to him. Inside them Customs officers found photograph albums containing photographs of young children. When interviewed he said that he had taken the photographs and sent them, but in his view they were not indecent. None of the photographs showed children engaging in any kind of sexual activity or being degraded in any way. Essentially they were photographs taken of children playing or being with adults. Two were of the same child who was being dressed, or undressed, apparently by his mother. The other photograph was of a very young child who was sitting naked astride a man, presumably his father. They were presumably taken using a relatively long-distance lens and the defendant was in no way personally involved with any of the children concerned. He claimed that the photographs had an artistic quality, but admitted that he had a paedophilic interest in the photographs. A probation officer reported that the defendant found them to be erotic and that the photographs did provide him with sexual stimulation. There was a high risk of re-offending. He was 57 with one previous conviction for conspiracy to corrupt public morals for which he was imprisoned for two years in 1981. *Held.* The offences were no less, but no more, than bringing to this country the three photographs. The seriousness of importing indecent material into this country was not to be minimised and nothing in this case had any bearing on cases involving the internet. The offences did not pass the custody threshold so **no sentence** and not 9 months' imprisonment quashed, because he had served $3^{1}/_{2}$ months.

INADEQUATE DEFENDANT

See **DEFENDANT** – *Inadequate*

98   INCEST

98.1   Sexual Offences Act 2003 s 64–65

Sex with an adult relative. Section 64 the defendant penetrates and section 65 the defendant is penetrated. The offences came into force on 1/5/04

Both offences are triable either way. On indictment maximum 2 years. Summary maximum 6 months and/or £5,000.

The Criminal Justice Act 2003 creates a summary maximum sentence of 51 weeks, a minimum sentence of 28 weeks and Custody plus. The Home Office says they do not expect to introduce these provisions before September 2006.

Offences committed before 1/5/04 are charged under Sexual Offences Act 1956 s 10 and 11. These sections were repealed on 1/5/04 and replaced by new offences under the Sexual Offences Act 2003 including the ones above. For offences committed against a child under the new law see **SEXUAL ACTIVITY WITH A CHILD FAMILY MEMBER** (q.v.)

Old offences – Sexual Offences Act 1956 s 10 Incest by a man

Indictable only. Maximum sentence if girl under 13 Life imprisonment. Otherwise 7 years. Maximum for an attempt if girl under 13, 7 years otherwise 2 years.

Sexual Offences Act 1956 s 11 Incest by a woman

Indictable only. Maximum sentence 7 years. For attempted offences 2 years.

Extended sentences under CJA 2003 For offences committed on or after 4/4/05 there is a mandatory duty to pass an extended sentence when there is a significant risk to members of the public of serious harm etc.[21]. See **EXTENDED SENTENCES**

Longer than Commensurate sentences and Extended sentences Sexual Offences Act 1956 s 10 and 11 are both sexual offences[22] for the purposes of passing a longer than commensurate sentence [Powers of Criminal Courts (Sentencing) Act 2000 s 80(2)] and an extended sentence (extending the licence) [Powers of Criminal Courts (Sentencing) Act 2000 s 85(2)(b)]. The orders cannot be made for offences committed before 30/9/98 or after 3/4/05. See **EXTENDED SENTENCE** and **EXTENDED SENTENCES** and **LONGER THAN COMMENSURATE SENTENCES**

Notification For offences under (1) Sexual Offences Act 1956 s 10 (where the other party was under 18) and (2) Sexual Offences Act 2003 s 64–65 where (a) the defendant is aged less than 18 and is sentenced to imprisonment for 12 months or more or (b) the defendant is 18 or over and is sentenced to imprisonment or detained in a hospital; the defendant must notify[23] the police within 3 days (or 3 days from his/her release from imprisonment, hospital etc.) with his/her name, home address, national insurance number etc. and any change and addresses where s/he resides for 7 days[24] (in one or more periods) or more in any 12 month period[25]. See **SEX OFFENDERS' REGISTER**

Sexual Offences Prevention Order There is a discretionary power, when the notification (q.v.) criteria are present and when it is necessary to protect the public etc[26].

Working with children Where the offence is under Sexual Offences Act 1956 s 10 and 11 and is (a) having sexual intercourse with a child (b) the defendant is aged 18 or over and (c) s/he is sentenced to 12 months or more etc. or a hospital order etc. the court must disqualify him/her from working with children unless satisfied s/he is unlikely to commit any further offences against a child when the court must state its reasons for not doing so[27]. For a defendant aged less than 18 at the time of the offence the court must order disqualification if s/he is sentenced to 12 months or more and the court is satisfied that the defendant will commit a further offence against a child[28]. The court must state its reasons for so doing.

Crown Court statistics – England and Wales – Males 21+

98.2

Year	Plea	Total Numbers sentenced	Type of sentence %					Average length of custody (months)
			Discharge	Fine	Community sentence	Suspended sentence	Custody	
2002	Guilty	30–	–	–	17	10	73	42.8
	Not guilty	9–	–	–	–	–	100	77.7
2003	Guilty	22	5	–	18	5	73	49.7
	Not guilty	5	–	–	–	–	100	57

For details and explanations about the statistics in the book see page vii.

Guideline case

98.3   *Att-Gen's Ref. No 1 of 1989* 1989 90 Cr App R 141. LCJ The view taken by the

21 Criminal Justice Act 2003 s 227–228
22 Powers of Criminal Courts (Sentencing) Act 2000 s 161(2)(a)
23 Sexual Offences Act 2003 s 80(1)(a) & Sch 3 Para 4, 11 and 32
24 Sexual Offences Act 2003 s 84(1)(c) & (6)
25 Sexual Offences Act 2003 s 83
26 Sexual Offences Act 2003 s 104 & Sch. 3
27 Criminal Justice and Court Services Act 2000 s 28
28 Criminal Justice and Court Services Act 2000 s 29

legislature of the gravity of this offence has to be judged by the maximum penalties which can be imposed. Incest by a man with a girl under 13 has a maximum penalty of life. Incest by a man with a female over 13 carries a maximum sentence of 7 years. The gravity of the offence of incest varies greatly according, primarily, to the age of the victim and the related matter, namely the degree of coercion or corruption. Aggravating factors, whatever the age of the girl may be, are:

(1) If there is evidence that the girl has suffered physically or psychologically from the incest;

(2) If the incest has continued at frequent intervals over a long period of time;

(3) If the girl has been threatened or treated violently by or was terrified of the father;

(4) If the incest has been accompanied by perversions abhorrent to the girl, e.g. buggery or fellatio;

(5) If the girl has become pregnant by reason of the father failing to take contraceptive measures;

(6) If the defendant has committed similar offences against more than one girl.

Possible mitigating features are:

(1) A plea of guilty. It should be met by an appropriate discount, depending on the usual considerations, that is to say how promptly the defendant confessed and his degree of contrition and so on;

(2) If it seems that there was a genuine affection on the part of the defendant rather than the intention to use the girl simply as an outlet for his sexual inclinations;

(3) Where the girl has had previous sexual experience;

(4) Where the girl has made deliberate attempts at seduction;

(5) Where, as very occasionally is the case, a shorter term of imprisonment for the father may be of benefit to the victim and the family.

(The rest of the guidelines are split up into the various sections for the different ages for the victim.)

Guideline remarks

98.4   *Att-Gen's Ref. Nos. 91, 119 and 120 of 2002 2003* 2 Cr App R (S) 338. In *R v Millberry* 2003 2 Cr App R (S) 142 at para 8, the Lord Chief Justice said, 'There are, broadly three dimensions to consider in assessing the gravity of an individual offence of rape. The first is the degree of harm to the victim; the second is the level of culpability of the offender; and the third is the level of risk proposed by the offender to society. The gravity of each case will depend very much upon the circumstances and it will always be necessary to consider an individual case as a whole taking into account the three dimensions.' It will be necessary to take account of similar considerations in all cases of sexual interference, whether amounting to rape or not. However, that is not all. In all classes of sexual offences, there will also be the need to deter others from acting in a similar fashion.

Extended sentences (i.e. extending the licence period)

98.5   *R v M* 2003 1 Cr App R (S) 283. The defendant pleaded guilty to eight counts of incest. He lost contact with his daughter very early in her life. They met again when she was 23 and shortly after he moved in with her and her four children. They were both alcoholics. About two to three weeks later, when she was 24 and they were both drunk, sex took place. Sexual intercourse continued with consent and without force from November 1997 to December 2000 when she went to the police. In 1999 she gave birth to his child. There was no genuine affection between the two and he just used her as a sexual outlet. He accepted that what he had done had had a serious impact on his daughter. He was 45 with no convictions of any real significance and had a depressive disorder. The pre-sentence report said the risk of committing a similar offence was slim and there was no longer any contact between them. The psychiatrist said he showed genuine remorse and he had become suicidal. Held. The duration of the relationship, the birth of the child, the serious impact on the daughter and his age and maturity were serious aggravating features. $2^1/_2$ years might be regarded as high but it was not manifestly excessive. In order for an extended licence period to be imposed, the Court must conclude that the licence period would be inadequate for the purpose of preventing the commission of further offences and for securing his rehabilitation. Those circumstances were not present so the **extension was quashed**.

See also EXTENDED SENTENCES

Girl under 13 years – Guideline case – (old law)

98.6 *Att-Gen's Ref. No 1 of 1989* 1989 90 Cr App R 141. LCJ. The most difficult area is that involving girls under the age of 13. As in the case of those between 13 and 16, sexual intercourse is an offence, quite apart from the parental relationship. For victims under 13, however, a further factor comes into play. Although the girl may 'consent' to the act of intercourse in such a way as to render a charge of rape inappropriate, the girl is, from the very relationship, in a particularly vulnerable position, which the father is in a position to exploit due to her dependence and inexperience and, possibly, fear of disrupting relations between mother and father if she lets it be known what is happening, or fear of her father if she refuses to comply with his demands. In those circumstances the crime, although falling far short of rape, has some of the unpleasant aspects of that particular crime.

A broad guide to the level of sentence where the girl is under 13 and where there has been no plea of guilty follows. It is here that the widest range of sentence is likely to be found. If one can properly describe any case of incest as the 'ordinary' type of case, it will be one where the sexual relationship between husband and wife has broken down the father has probably resorted to excessive drinking and the eldest daughter is gradually, by way of familiarities, indecent acts and suggestions, made the object of the father's frustrated sexual inclinations. If the girl is not far short of her 13th birthday and there are no particularly adverse or favourable features on a not guilty plea, a term of about **6 years** on the authorities would seem to be appropriate. The younger the girl when the sexual approach is started, the more likely it will be that the girl's will was overborne and accordingly the more serious would be the crime. [Note. The imprisonment figures in this guideline case were issued before the changes to the release dates brought about by the Criminal Justice Act 1991 s 32–40. The figures should be considered in line with the Practice Statement (Crime Sentencing) 1992 95 Cr App R 948. However, since then the actual release dates are not greatly different and in recent years the courts have been slow to make reductions because of the 1991 changes.]

Girl under 13 years – Cases – (old law)

98.7 *R v O* 2004 1 Cr App R (S) 130. The defendant pleaded guilty on re-arraignment to three counts of incest and two counts of indecent assault. The offences were specimen offences between 26 and 34 years ago. He assaulted his daughter from when she was aged 5 to 13 so much so that she could not remember a time when the father wasn't having sex with her. The indecent assaults were very frequent. Once she was told to perform oral sex on him and she refused so he hit and shouted at her until she did. The incest was from 1970–76 when she was aged between 7 and 12. Once when she was 7 or 8 he pulled her into her sleeping bag on a camping holiday, had sex with her causing her pain and making her have trouble urinating afterwards. The offences caused her great distress and she had suicidal thoughts with a number of drug overdoses taken. She left home as soon as she could at 16 and severed her connections with her family for a long time. She became socially isolated and developed psychological problems. When the defendant heard that there were police enquires he rang the investigation officer and was told the officer could not speak to him. He stated he was pleading guilty to all the charges. When interviewed he admitted the indecent assaults. He was 64 and of good character. He was a hard working man and except for the offences he was a good father in every respect. Now he had an irregular heart beat, high blood pressure and an underactive thyroid and obesity. Held. These were very serious offences which took place over a sustained period when the victim was very young. It was a grave breach of trust. But insufficient account was taken of his age and early and frank openness so **8 years** in total not 12.

Girl under 13 years – Brother, by – Aged 13–15 – (old law)

98.8 *R v C and C* 2002 1 Cr App R (S) 14. The defendants pleaded guilty to acts of incest with their sisters when they were younger. The offences were committed 14 years before conviction when the defendants were between 14 and 16 and the sisters between 9 and 13. Held. **8 months** not 3 years.

Girl aged 13–15 years – Guideline case – (old law)

98.9 *Att-Gen's Ref. No 1 of 1989* 1989 90 Cr App R 141. LCJ. Where the girl has achieved the age of 13 it will in most cases mean she has reached puberty. This of course is the demarcation line chosen in the 1956 Act. Sentences in this area seem to vary between about **2 years to 4 or 5 years** on a plea of guilty, depending on the mitigating or aggravating factors. A broad guide to the level of sentence where the girl is 13 to 16 and where there has been no plea of guilty is: Here a sentence between about **5 years and 3 years** seems on the authorities to be appropriate. Much the same principles will apply as in the case of a girl over 16, though the likelihood of corruption increases in inverse proportion to the age of the girl. [Note. The imprisonment figures in this guideline case were issued before the changes to the release dates brought about by the Criminal Justice Act 1991 s 32–40. The figures should be considered in line with the Practice Statement (Crime Sentencing) 1992 95 Cr App R 948. However since then the actual release dates are not greatly different and in recent years the courts have been slow to make reductions because of the 1991 changes.]

Girl 13–15 years – Fathers – (old law)

98.10 *R v MH* 2001 2 Cr App R (S) 454 The defendant pleaded guilty to seven counts of incest with his daughter over a period of 6 years when the girl was 15 to 21. When the girl started a sexual relationship with a boyfriend he resented it and after an incident between him and the boyfriend that relationship broke up. He decided he was going to teach her about sex. He engaged in sexual activity with her when she was aged 14 without active protest on her part. She simply suffered what was going on. On her 15th birthday he first had sexual intercourse her. He would sleep in her bedroom and have intercourse with her 2–3 times a week often with his wife's (the girl's mother) knowledge. He moved out of the family home with his daughter and the two effectively lived as husband and wife. She permitted that to keep the peace and because she was financially dependant on him. He was 47 and had no relevant convictions. The judge said that the defendant had destroyed her womanhood and destroyed the trust that should exist between a father and daughter. Held. The judge was correct in his remarks, therefore **4¹/₂ years** was high but we will not disturb it.

Girl/Woman aged 16 or more – Guideline case

98.11 *Att-Gen's Ref. No 1 of 1989* 1989 90 Cr App R 141. LCJ. At one end of the scale is incest committed by a father with a daughter in her late teens or older who is a willing participant and indeed may be the instigator of the offences. In such a case the court usually need do little more than mark the fact that there has been a breach of the law and little, if anything, is required in the way of punishment. A broad guide to the level of sentence where there has been no plea of guilty is: where the girl is over 16, generally speaking a range from **3 years down to a nominal penalty** will be appropriate depending, in particular, on whether force was used, on the degree of harm, if any, to the girl, and the desirability, where it exists, of keeping family disruption to a minimum. The older the girl the greater the possibility that she may have been willing or even the instigating party to the liaison, a factor which will be reflected in the sentence. In other words, the lower the degree of corruption, the lower the penalty.

Girl/woman aged 16 or more – Fathers

98.12   *R v B* 1999 1 Cr App R (S) 174. The defendant pleaded guilty to incest with his daughter and supplying cannabis to her. The defendant, who was 42 years of age, had spent the evening with his daughter, who was aged 20. Both of them had been drinking heavily and shared a cannabis cigarette. He and his daughter were sleeping in the same room, though in separate beds. During the night the defendant asked his daughter to join him in his bed and engaged in sexual intercourse with her. The woman did not move nor communicate with her father during the act. She pretended to be asleep. When he pleaded guilty she said she wanted to withdraw the complaint and that she loved him. The defendant had no relevant convictions. The judge noted that the defendant had abused his position of trust and had taken advantage of his daughter's vulnerability as she was under the influence of alcohol and cannabis. Held. The hitherto good relationship between the father and daughter should not be disrupted longer than was necessary therefore **6 months** not 18 months.

Girl/Woman aged 16 or more – With pregnancy/baby born

98.13   *R v M* 2003 1 Cr App R (S) 283. The defendant pleaded guilty to eight counts of incest. He lost contact with his daughter very early in her life. They met again when she was 23 and shortly after he moved in with her and her four children. They were both alcoholics. About two to three weeks later, when she was 24 and they were both drunk, sex took place. Sexual intercourse continued with consent and without force from November 1997 to December 2000 when she went to the police. In 1999 she gave birth to his child, which was proved by scientific evidence. There was no genuine affection between the two and he just used her as a sexual outlet. He accepted that what he had done had had a serious impact on his daughter. He was 45 with no convictions of any real significance and a depressive disorder. The pre-sentence report said the risk of committing a similar offence was slim and there was no longer any contact between them. The psychiatrist said he showed genuine remorse and he had become suicidal. Held. The duration of the relationship, the birth of the child, the serious impact on the daughter and his age and maturity were serious aggravating features. **2$^{1}/_{2}$ years** might be regarded as high but it was not manifestly excessive. However the circumstances were not present to warrant an extended licence period so that was quashed.

R v GM 2002 1 Cr App R (S) 112. The defendant was convicted of three counts of incest. They were representative counts for a 21 month period of regular incest with his daughter. He was acquitted of rape and other counts of incest for a different period. A fortnight after his 15th birthday his then girlfriend of a similar age gave birth to a daughter, the victim. That relationship continued on a tenuous basis for two years or so. They then lost touch. Twelve years later he met her again. There was perfectly proper contact for two years or more. The defendant's marriage then broke up. He continued to see his daughter and just short of her 17th birthday the relationship became sexual. She had had no other sexual experience before. When she became pregnant, he encouraged her to have a late termination for his own protection. In the state of some depression she made a suicide attempt. He was 38 with no other convictions. The trial judge came to the clear conclusion that his relationship always had selfish and manipulative elements. He also considered the relationship contributed to her depression. Held. The fact that the two had not grown up in the same household was a relevant consideration and provides some differentiation from a case when a man exploits a girl who has been dependant upon him as a parent. Neither the termination nor her mother's suspicions made to him deterred him from continuing. There was a proper basis for saying some emotional damage had been done to her. **3½ years** not 5.

R v B 2003 1 Cr App R (S) 484. The defendant pleaded guilty to five counts of incest. At the time the defendant was on licence for murdering his wife in 1973. Having been released in 1990 he re-established contact with his daughter. She had left her husband and had with her three children. In 1996 he began a sexual relationship with her (then aged 24), with intercourse taking place on 10 occasions. No contraception was used and the daughter became pregnant. The child died when she was a few months old. By 1997 the relationship was over, although it was not reported until 2000. On arrest the defendant made a full confession. The daughter had consented fully and letters written by her reflected the love that she felt for him. He was 63. There was no element of corruption or seduction and the defendant had provided her with emotional and financial support during the relationship. **9 months** not 18.

Historic abuse – Guideline remarks

98.14 *Att-Gen's Ref. Nos. 91, 119 and 120 of 2002* 2003 2 Cr App R (S) 338 In *R v Millberry* 2003 2 Cr App R (S) 142. The fact that the offences are of some age is not necessarily a sufficient reason for imposing a lesser sentence than might otherwise have been the case. In Millberry the Court said at para 17: 'in relation to "historic" cases where the offence is reported many years after it occurred. In these cases, also, we consider that the same starting point should apply. The fact that the offences are stale can be taken into account but only to a limited extent. It is, after all, always open to an offender to admit the offences and the fact that they are not reported earlier is often explained because of the relationship between the offender and the victim, which is an aggravating factor of the offence. A different factor that could cause the court to take a more lenient view than it would otherwise is the consequences, which result from the age of the offender. In these cases the experience is that the offender may be only a danger to members of the family with whom he has a relationship. So this is a dimension which can be taken into account if there is a reduced risk of re-offending.'

The same approach is equally applicable to all categories of sexual offending. Where the victims have kept secret what has happened, sometimes following threats made or inducements offered and sometimes out of a sense of shame about what has been done to her, this of itself can aggravate the harm caused by the offence. Before passing a lighter sentence because the offences are stale, the court should weigh the impact on the victim of the matter having remained secret for so long.

Historic abuse cases

98.15 *R v O* 2004 1 Cr App R (S) 130. The defendant pleaded guilty on re-arraignment to three counts of incest and two counts of indecent assault. The offences were specimen offences between 26 and 34 years ago. He assaulted his daughter from when she was aged 5 to 13 such she could not remember a time when the father wasn't having sex with her. The indecent assaults were very frequent. Once she was told to perform oral sex on him and she refused so he hit and shouted at her until she did. The incest was from 1970–76 when she was aged between 7 and 12. Once when she was 7 or 8 he pulled her into her sleeping bag on a camping holiday, had sex with her causing her pain and making her have trouble urinating afterwards. The offences caused her great distress and she had suicidal thoughts with a number of drug overdoses taken. She left home as soon as she could at 16 and severed her connections with her family for a long time. She became socially isolated and developed psychological problems. When the defendant heard that there were police enquires he rang the investigation officer and was told the officer could not speak to him. He stated he was pleading guilty to all the charges. When interviewed he admitted the indecent assaults. He was 64 and of good character. He was a hard working man and except for the offences he was a good father in every respect. Now he had an irregular heart beat, high blood pressure and an underactive thyroid and obesity. Held. These were very serious offences which took place over a sustained period when the victim was very young. It was a grave breach of trust. But insufficient account was taken of his age and early and frank openness so **8 years** in total not 12.

See also RAPE and SEXUAL ACTIVITY WITH A CHILD FAMILY MEMBER

INDECENCY, GROSS

This offence was abolished on 1/5/04. Where the other party is a child or where there is no consent the offence from that date would be charged under Sexual Offences Act 2003 s 7 and 3 respectively. See SEXUAL ASSAULT ETC. CHILDREN and SEXUAL ASSAULT TOUUCHING

99   INDECENCY WITH CHILDREN

99.1   This offence created by Indecency with Children Act 1960 s 1(1) (gross indecency with a child) was abolished on 1/5/04. Offences committed after that date would be charged under Sexual Offences Act 2003 s 7, 9, 16, 25 see SEXUAL ACTITITY BREACH OF TRUST, SEXUAL ACTIVITY CHILD FAMILY MEMBER, SEXUAL ASSAULT ETC. CHILDREN.

For offences before 1/5/04 see INDECENT ASSAULT ON A WOMAN and INDECENT ASSAULT ON A MAN.

100   INDECENT ASSAULT ON A MAN

100.1   Sexual Offences Act 1956 s 15

Indecency with Children Act 1960 s 1(1) (gross indecency with a child under 14).

Both offences are triable either way. On indictment maximum 10 years. Summary maximum 6 months and/or £5,000.

The Criminal Justice Act 2003 creates a summary maximum sentence of 51 weeks, a minimum sentence of 28 weeks and Custody plus. The Home Office says they do not expect to introduce these provisions before September 2006.

Both offences were abolished on 1/5/04. Offences committed after that date would be charged under Sexual Offences Act 2003 s 3, 7, 9, 16, 25 *Sexual activity breach of trust, Sexual activity child family member, Sexual assault etc. children* and *sexual assault touching*.

There is a new offence of committing an offence with intent to commit a sexual offence, see Sexual Offences Act 2003 s 62.

Longer than Commensurate sentences and Extended sentences Indecent assault is a sexual offence[29] for the purposes of passing a longer than commensurate sentence

29 Powers of Criminal Courts (Sentencing) Act 2000 s 161(2)(a)

[Powers of Criminal Courts (Sentencing) Act 2000 s 80(2)] and an extended sentence (extending the licence) [Powers of Criminal Courts (Sentencing) Act 2000 s 85(2)(b)]. The orders cannot be made for offences committed before 30/9/98 or after 3/4/05. See *Longer than Commensurate Sentences,* EXTENDED SENTENCES and LONGER THAN COMMENSURATE SENTENCES

Notification Where the other party is under 18 or the defendant is sentenced to at least 30 months imprisonment or a hospital order with a restriction, the defendant must notify the police within 3 days (or 3 days from his release from imprisonment, hospital etc.) with his name, home address, national insurance number etc. and any change and addresses where he resides for 7 days[30] (in one or more periods) or more in any 12 month period[31]. See SEX OFFENDERS' REGISTER

Sexual Offences Prevention Order There is a discretionary power to make this order, when the notification (q.v.) criteria are present and when it is necessary to protect the public etc[32].

Working with children Where the offence is against a child (aged less than 18), the defendant is aged 18 or over and s/he is sentenced to 12 months or more etc. the court must disqualify him/her from working with children unless satisfied s/he is unlikely to commit any further offences against a child when the court must state its reasons for not doing so[33]. For a defendant aged less than 18 at the time of the offence the court must order disqualification if s/he is sentenced to 12 months or more and the court is satisfied that the defendant will commit a further offence against a child[34]. The court must state its reasons for so doing.

Crown Court statistics – England and Wales – Males 21+
100.2

Year	Plea	Total Numbers sentenced	Type of sentence %					Average length of custody (months)
			Discharge	Fine	Community sentence	Suspended sentence	Custody	
2002	Guilty	142	2	1	23	4	71	32.9
	Not guilty	83	1	–	8	5	84	32.1
2003	Guilty	140	4	1	17	4	72	34.7
	Not guilty	74	3	4	16	1	76	36.3

For details and explanations about the statistics in the book see page vii.

Magistrates' Court Sentencing Guidelines January 2004

100.3   First time offenders who plead not guilty Entry point. Is it so serious that only custody is appropriate? Consider committal for sentence. Consider the impact on the victim. Examples of aggravating factors for the offence are age differential, breach of trust, injury (may be psychiatric), prolonged assault, very young victim, victim deliberately targeted, victim serving the public and vulnerable victim. An example of mitigating factors for the offence is slight contact. Examples of mitigation are age, health (physical or mental), co-operation with the police, genuine remorse and voluntary compensation.

For details about the guidelines see MAGISTRATES' COURT SENTENCING GUIDELINES at page 483

30 Sexual Offences Act 2003 s 84(1)(c) & (6)
31 Sexual Offences Act 2003 s 83 & Sch. 3 Para 8
32 Sexual Offences Act 2003 s 104 & Sch. 3
33 Criminal Justice and Court Services Act 2000 s 28
34 Criminal Justice and Court Services Act 2000 s 29

Guideline remarks

100.4   *Att-Gen's Ref. Nos. 91, 119 and 120 of 2002*, 2003 2 Cr App R (S) 338 In *R v Millberry* 2003 2 Cr App R (S) 142 at para 8, the Lord Chief Justice said, 'There are, broadly three dimensions to consider in assessing the gravity of an individual offence of rape. The first is the degree of harm to the victim; the second is the level of culpability of the offender; and the third is the level of risk proposed by the offender to society. The gravity of each case will depend very much upon the circumstances and it will always be necessary to consider an individual case as a whole taking into account the three dimensions.'

It will be necessary to take account of similar considerations in all cases of sexual interference, whether amounting to rape or not. However, that is not all. In all classes of sexual offences, there will also be the need to deter others from acting in a similar fashion.

Guideline remarks – Child victims

100.5   *R v Lennon* 1999 1 Cr App R (S) 19. The defendant, was convicted of indecent assault on the 9-year-old daughter of his co-habitee. The court reviewed 43 authorities on indecent assault on a child. Held. It is never easy to sentence in these cases. The circumstances of each case will vary greatly. The judge must tailor the sentence to the particular facts. In most cases the personal circumstances of the defendant will have to take second place behind the plain duty of the court to protect victims and to reflect the clear intention of Parliament that offences of this kind are to be met with greater severity than in former years when the position of the victim may not have been so clearly focused in the public eye. (It is assumed that the same policy for female victims would be extended to male victims.)

Breach of trust – Educational

100.6   *R v Bromiley* 2001 1 Cr App R (S) 255. The defendant pleaded guilty to ten counts of indecent assault on five boys aged 12 and 14 in her residential school for those with learning difficulties. She was a care assistant at a residential school for boys with learning difficulties. She was later promoted to senior care assistant. The offences took place in 1984, 1986/7 and between 1995 and 1999. On two occasions she approached one boy in a dormitory and had sexual intercourse with him. On another occasion she invited another victim to her flat, initiated sexual activity and engaged in sexual intercourse with him. She had sexual intercourse with another boy who sent her a love letter. She said she loved him. She had sexual intercourse with two further boys both at her flat and on the school premises. The boys were all willing parties. She was 37 and of previous good character. She had a history of failed relationships with men. Her risk of re-offending was assessed as high. The judge noted the frequency and severity of the abuse on vulnerable boys. He also noted she had a 9-year-old son who would suffer should his mother face a custodial sentence. He said that her punishment would be nothing like as severe as it would have been had she been a man. Held. Sexual abuse of the young in residential homes is currently a matter of serious and acute public concern. Those of either sex, who are in positions of trust in such homes, must expect to go to prison for a substantial time if they prey sexually on those in their care. The offences were a grave breach of trust and had a man had sexual intercourse with girls of such an age he would have faced a very long sentence. Therefore **5 years** was not manifestly excessive.

R v S 2004 1 Cr App R (S) 303. The defendant pleaded guilty to indecently assaulting a male. The victim was a 13 year-old pupil at a special school which catered for children with emotional and behavioural difficulties. He was on medication for Attention Deficit Hyperactive Disorder. The defendant was a classroom assistant. The victim sent her a note saying that he loved her and she started sending him text messages and letters. He reciprocated. The defendant was suspended but within 2 days had made an arrangement for the two of them to meet. She gave him alcohol and intercourse then took place. In interview she declined to comment. She was 33, of good character and married with 3 children for whom she was the main carer. The middle child suffered with autism, epilepsy and related behavioural problems. She was remorseful about the offence. Held. She abused a position of trust, had groomed him and custody was warranted. Her imprisonment will cause severe difficulties within her household. However, taking account of the mitigation, **5 months** not 9.

Breach of trust – Friend etc. of the victim's family

100.7   *Att-Gen's Ref. Nos. 35 etc. of 2003 Re RD 2004* 1 Cr App R (S) 499 at 519. The defendant pleaded guilty to eight counts of indecent assault. The first victim, aged about 7, stayed the night with the defendant's daughter. He slept the night in a bed with the defendant who touched and played with his penis. The second victim (his brother) was 9 and also slept in the same bed as the defendant and awoke to find he was being masturbated. The boy then masturbated the defendant to ejaculation. The defendant also performed oral sex on the boy. This was repeated on another occasion when another boy was present and each masturbated the other. The abuse continued at the defendant's home in Spain. The third brother (who was about 11) also went on nine holidays with the defendant. He spent the night before each holiday with the defendant who masturbated him and performed oral sex on him. The boy would also masturbate the defendant. The family of the fifth victim (aged about 10) met the defendant through the Spanish holidays. The defendant provided the boy with many gifts. There was mutual masturbation, oral sex performed by both and simulated intercourse by the defendant on the boy; the abuse lasted for 4 years. During an investigation in this country, the defendant went to live in Spain where he served a sentence of 9 years for the abuse of two boys who were on holiday there. On his return to the UK he was arrested and made full admissions. The counts were considered specimen counts. The offences had a marked impact on the lives of the victims and their families. He was 63. Held. Although the Court was entitled to take into account the fact that had he faced a sentence that included both the Spanish and UK offences it would not have been much longer than the 9 years he received in Spain. There was no element of retribution for the UK offences in the Spanish sentence and the suffering of these victims demanded a longer sentence. **Seven years** would have been appropriate if the Spanish sentence was disregarded. Five years was appropriate taking into account the Spanish sentence. As this was a reference **4 years** and not $2^1/_2$.

Att-Gen's Ref. No 34 of 2004 2005 1 Cr App R (S) 172. The defendant pleaded guilty to indecent assault on a male. The defendant, 47, befriended his victim, aged 14, after they met at a football referees' course. They continued to meet sometimes at similar places and the defendant would often telephone him at home. The defendant suggested that the victim spend two nights at his home so that they could go to a football match. The victim's parents had spoken to the defendant but had never met him and believed he was a lone parent looking after two sons. They agreed to the plan. When the victim arrived at the defendant's home the defendant said he would put up a Z bed for the victim in his own room. The defendant's two sons aged 16 and 19 each had their own bedroom and were present in the house throughout. That evening the defendant asked the victim about his relationship with his parents. This upset the victim and the defendant put his arms round him. They went to the bedroom and undressed to their underpants. The defendant again asked the victim about his family life and again the victim became upset. The defendant asked the victim to lie down on his bed and put his arm round him. The victim went to sleep on the defendant's bed. Later the defendant took the victim's hand and placed it over his crotch area. He placed his hand under the victim's shorts and touched his penis. The victim removed the hand and turned over but the defendant put his hand on the victim's penis and pulled his shorts down and began to rub the victim's bottom, opening and closing his buttocks. The victim then felt something inserted in his bottom which went in quite far. He did not know what it was. The defendant then touched the victim's penis again making it erect and pressed his own penis against the victim's buttocks for some time. Eventually at 4.00 am the victim left the house wearing only a fleece and boxer shorts and phoned 999. Reports showed he had developed difficulties sleeping and some behavioural problems that affected his family life and school work. He had post-traumatic stress disorder and had had a long period of counselling. The defendant had no previous convictions. At the Crown Court it was said in mitigation that if he was sent to prison for more than 6 months he would lose his home and his sixteen year old son would have nowhere to live because he could not live with his mother. A letter from the boy's mother at the Court of Appeal made it clear this was not true and that the boy had been living mainly with her at the time of the offence. The pre-sentence report assessed the risk of non sexual re-offending as low but said sexual offending might be a higher risk as the defendant struggled with understanding why he offended and had a limited acceptance of the victim's perspective. The aggravating features included abuse of trust used to exploit a vulnerable victim away from home by taking advantage of his home problems to commit the offence. It was accepted that the grooming was limited to the evening of the offence. Held. Harm of a psychological nature is not less important than physical harm. This was a serious assault involving masturbation and penetration. The appropriate sentence was **2¹/₂–3 years**. As it was a reference **2 years** not 6 months with 2 years not 2¹/₂ years extended licence period.

Old case. *R v Nicholson* 1998 1 Cr App R (S) 370, (for a summary of this case see the first edition of this book).

Att-Gen's Ref No 53 of 2004 2005 1 Cr App R (S) 272. The defendant pleaded guilty to forty five counts of indecent assault on a male person. The offences took place in the 1970s and early 80s over a period of seven years and involved three boys, each being abused over a five-year period. In each case the boys, who were related to each other, were aged between 8 and 13. The abuse occurred when the defendant was aged between 36 and 43. In each case the abuse involved numerous incidents of masturbation of the boy by the defendant and of oral sex both on the boy and on the defendant. In the case of one of the boys there were incidents of masturbation where the defendant inserted his penis between the boy's legs with the boy lying face downwards. There were no offences of buggery or any kind of anal penetration. The offences arose out of a relationship between the defendant and the families of the boys. There were regular family holidays together and in time the boys were allowed to travel with the defendant alone on holiday. The defendant bought presents for the boys and gave them treats as inducements. He promised one boy he would leave him £500 in his will. He also used threats and punishments. He locked a boy out of his hotel room for refusing to perform oral sex on him, and he threatened to take back presents already given if the boy did not do what he was asked. The first victim estimated he had been subject to at least three hundred instances of abuse over 5 years. The second and third victims said the abuse had happened on almost every occasion when they were alone with the defendant. In each case the abuse began when the victim was about 8 and had a profound effect. One victim in his impact statement said he thought of the abuse every day and the fear he had of anyone finding out. He was unable to allow anyone to get close to him. The second victim had suffered from severe depression and suicidal feelings. The third said memories of the abuse had seriously affected his relationship with his wife and children and he could not stand physical contact with his children. The defendant, now 65, had no previous convictions. A pre-sentence report said that he did not want to consider the harm he has caused and that he continued to see the boys as complicit in the offences. He was in relatively poor health. Held. The relevant factors here were the ages of the victims, their number, the nature of the sexual misconduct, the frequency, the breach of trust, the impact and the systematic grooming. His plea of guilty was important, and the court had regard to a limited degree that the offences took place 22 and 30 years ago. It also noted his failure to appreciate the harm he did and his lack of remorse. The appropriate sentence was **7 years** not 5; taking into account it was a reference, **6 years** substituted.

Breach of trust – Religious, Youth clubs etc

100.8 *R v Staples* 2001 2 Cr App R (S) 517. The defendant was convicted of seventeen counts of indecent assault on boys who were between the ages of 8 and 11. The defendant was a leader of a Cub group and over a period of 3 years abused the boys in his care. The offences happened after the defendant had managed to separate the victims from the rest of the boys. The abuse included touching the victims' penises both over and underneath their clothing and removing both his and one of the victims' trousers and lying on top of him. There was no evidence any of the boys had been harmed by the experience. The defendant was 33 and of good character. Held. On all the offences except one there was minimal touching usually over rather than under their clothing. The offences were pre-meditated and involved a gross breach of trust, therefore **4 years** was not a manifestly excessive sentence.

Att-Gen's Ref. Nos. 35 etc. of 2003 Re JC 2004 1 Cr App R (S) 499 at 538. The defendant pleaded guilty early to three charges of indecent assault. The offences started about 27 years earlier, when the defendant was a teacher of a Church of England School. At the age of 8 the first victim became an altar boy under the defendant's care. The defendant was trusted by the boy's family and became the boy's mentor. The defendant touched him and masturbated him frequently when he stayed with the boy's family and when on holiday with the boy. The abuse occurred when the boy was between 12 and 16. About 20 years later the defendant met the second victim when he was on holiday. He touched the boy on occasions and put his hand into the boy's trousers and stroked his groin area. When interviewed he made full admissions and expressed remorse. Aged 66, he was of exemplary character with impressive references and presented a low risk. Held. The offences involved 2 boys, a gross breach of trust and there was an element of grooming. The sexual assaults against the first victim were serious and had a significant effect upon him. The correct sentence would have been **2½ years** as far as the first victim was concerned (reduced to **15 months** as this was a reference) and six months in respect of the second victim; not a community rehabilitation order.

Defendant abused as a child

100.9 *Att-Gen's Ref. Nos. 35 etc. of 2003 Re TC 2004* 1 Cr App R (S) 499 at 544. The defendant pleaded guilty to three counts of indecent assault on a male person, two counts of indecency with a child and once count of gross indecency. Held. He had abused three different boys in a serious way over a substantial period of time. However, where the abuse of the defendant by others when he was young is clearly established and where there is an obvious link with his own offending, some allowance should be given for that fact. The older the offender gets and the more remote his offending becomes to the harm that he has suffered the smaller the allowance given.

Defendant under 16

100.10 *Att-Gen's Ref. Nos. 35 etc. of 2003 Re H 2004* 1 Cr App R (S) 499 at 522. The defendant was convicted of three indecent assaults on a male under 10, three of indecency with a child and three of rape of a boy under 16. All offences were committed on the same boy nearly six years younger than he was. The allegations were that he had regularly abused this boy, the sexual assault included acts of oral sex and buggery. They had started when the boy was 5 and the defendant was 11. The boys became close friends when their families moved close. They frequently played together and were often in each others bedrooms. The abuse all occurred within a 2 year period until the boy moved away. There was no compulsion involved. Held. Offences of this kind on such a young child even committed by a young defendant should have been marked by a custodial sentence of some sort. However, as this was a reference and the defendant had made progress since the original sentencing, he had an apprenticeship, an **Intensive Supervision and Surveillance Programme** will be imposed instead of a community rehabilitation order.

Defendant 17–21

100.11 *Att-Gen's Ref. Nos. 35 etc. of 2003 Re TC 2004* 1 Cr App R (S) 499 at 544. The defendant pleaded guilty to three counts of indecent assault on a male person, two counts of indecency with a child and one count of gross indecency. He also pleaded guilty to nine counts of making an indecent photograph of a child. He was the cousin of one of the victims and babysat often. When the victim was 8 the defendant had touched his penis over his clothing. About a week later the boy slept at the defendant's home and the defendant had touched his penis and put his finger into his bottom. He also made the boy touch his erect penis. A few weeks later the defendant pulled the victim's underpants down and started touching his penis before putting his own penis into the boy's mouth and ejaculating over his face. About a year later the defendant put his penis into the boy's anus (although a plea was accepted that fell short of the full offence of buggery). The second victim was pushed into a lavatory where the defendant showed him his penis before masturbating and ejaculating over the boy's arm. Both victims were also taken into some woods where the defendant took down his own trousers and then touched their penises and ejaculated. The defendant also took Polaroids of the first victim naked. On another occasion the defendant had ejaculated in the presence of one of the first victim's 9-year-old friends. The defendant was interviewed but denied the allegations. His computer was seized and contained 9 discs containing 200 images of children involved in various sexual activities. There were also pictures and a CD with images of adults anally penetrating children. There were also 2,000 deleted pictures. The pictures ranged from level 1 to 4 and were reflected across the 9-count indictment. He admitted that he had looked at these pictures and that it had reminded him of what his grandfather had done to him. The defendant's mother gave evidence supporting that contention, which the Court accepted. He was now 21 and of good character. Held. He had abused three different boys in a serious way over a substantial period of time. He had been in a position of responsibility. He was 17 when the offending commenced. However, where the abuse of the defendant is clearly established and where there is an obvious link with his own offending, some allowance should be given for that fact. The older the offender gets and the more remote his offending becomes to the harm that he has suffered the smaller the allowance given. **12 months** for the indecent assaults, 6 months for the indecency with a child and gross indecency offences and 9 months for each offence of making an indecent image of a child were unduly lenient but unaltered in the circumstances of this case. All sentences were concurrent. Extended sentences of 4 years imposed. (The age of the defendant at the time of the offending appears to be 17–19.)

Defendant 65 or over

100.12 *Att-Gen's Ref. Nos. 35 etc. of 2003 Re EE 2004* 1 Cr App R (S) 499 at 526. The defendant pleaded guilty on the day of trial to five counts of indecent assault. The first four counts represented individual offences committed against the first victim. The fifth count was a sample count covering the offences committed against the second victim. More than 25 years ago the defendant was a church minister who took advantage of his privileged position to seek opportunities to abuse two of his boy parishioners. The first victim became involved in church readings and this required him to practise either in the church or at the manse where the defendant lived. During such practice sessions the defendant would place his hand on the victim's genital area on top of his clothing during classes lasting up to 90 minutes. Such instances occurred whilst the victim was between 9 and 14. The second victim was abused when he was about 12. The defendant visited the victim's bedroom when he was in bed and put his hand under the blanket and touched the boy's penis. He then began to masturbate him; this incident was repeated on one occasion. He was abused twice at the manse when the victim went to prepare an essay. His shorts were pulled down and he was masturbated to ejaculation. Following his arrest 22 years later he initially denied the allegations and then answered no comment. He was 82 and of good character. He suffered with multiple sclerosis most of his adult life. A psychiatric report described him as "very vulnerable" but there were no other health difficulties. Held. There were no exceptional circumstances that permitted the suspension of the sentence. **12 months**, not 2 years suspended for 2

Female defendant

100.13   *R v Bromiley* 2001 1 Cr App R (S) 255. See **100.6**.

R v F 2000 2 Cr App R (S) 292. See **100.19**.

Historic abuse – Guideline remarks

100.14   *Att-Gen's Ref. Nos. 91, 119 and 120 of 2002*, 2003 2 Cr App R (S) 338 In *R v Millberry* 2003 2 Cr App R (S) 142. The fact that the offences are of some age is not necessarily a sufficient reason for imposing a lesser sentence than might otherwise have been the case. In Millberry the Court said at para 17: 'in relation to "historic" cases where the offence is reported many years after it occurred. In these cases, also, we consider that the same starting point should apply. The fact that the offences are stale can be taken into account but only to a limited extent. It is, after all, always open to an offender to admit the offences and the fact that they are not reported earlier is often explained because of the relationship between the offender and the victim, which is an aggravating factor of the offence. A different factor that could cause the court to take a more lenient view than it would otherwise is the consequences, which result from the age of the offender. In these cases the experience is that the offender may be only a danger to members of the family with whom he has a relationship. So this is a dimension which can be taken into account if there is a reduced risk of re-offending.' The same approach is equally applicable to all categories of sexual offending. Where the victims have kept secret of what had happened, sometimes following threats made or inducements offered and sometimes out of a sense of shame about what has been done to her, this of itself can aggravate the harm caused by the offence. Before passing a lighter sentence because the offences are stale, the court should weigh the impact on the victim of the matter having remained secret for so long.

Historic abuse

100.15   *Att-Gen's Ref. No 5 of 2001* 2001 2 Cr App R (S) 473. LCJ. The defendant was convicted of three offences of indecent assault against an 8-year-old boy. In 1986, two older friends of the victim who were 13 or 14 took the boy to the defendant's flat and the defendant then 31 asked him to perform oral sex on him. The abuse was secured in the first instance by preventing the victim from escaping and pushing on his chest. The acts had a marked effect on the boy who in his middle teens became reclusive, anxious and confused. The defendant was now 45. In 1987, he was convicted of indecent assault against the other two boys. He was put on probation and since then he had behaved responsibly. Held. To corrupt a child of the victim's age was a serious matter. If the offences had been committed recently the appropriate sentence would be **4 years**. Having regard to the age of the offences, the successful probation order and that it was a reference **2 years** was appropriate not 6 months.

Att-Gen's Ref. Nos. 35 etc. of 2003 Re EE 2004 1 Cr App R (S) 499 at 526. The defendant pleaded guilty on the day of trial to five counts of indecent assault. The first four counts represented individual offences committed against the first victim. The fifth count was a sample count covering the offences committed against the second victim. More than 25 years ago the defendant was a church minister who took advantage of his privileged position to seek opportunities to abuse two of his boy parishioners. The first victim became involved in church readings and this required him to practise either in the church or at the manse where the defendant lived. During such practice sessions the defendant would place his hand on the victim's genital area on top of his clothing during classes lasting up to 90 minutes. Such instances occurred whilst the victim was between 9 and 14. The second victim was abused when he was about 12. The defendant visited the victim's bedroom when he was in bed and put his hand under the blanket and touched the boy's penis. He then began to masturbate him; this incident was repeated on one occasion. He was abused twice at the manse when the victim went to prepare an essay. His shorts were pulled down and he was masturbated to ejaculation. Following his arrest 22 years later he initially denied the allegations and then answered no comment. He was 82 and of good character. He suffered with multiple sclerosis most of his adult life. A psychiatric report described him as "very vulnerable" but there were no other health difficulties. **Held.** There were no exceptional circumstances that permitted the suspension of the sentence. **12 months**, not 2 years suspended for 2

Longer than commensurate sentences

100.16   *R v Nicholson* 1998 1 Cr App R (S) 370. The defendant was convicted of nine counts of indecent assault on two brothers who were aged 12 and 10. The defendant, who was 56 years, befriended the victims and persuaded their mother that he was a suitable person to take them out for the day. The abuse included touching the victims' private parts both over and underneath their trousers. The defendant had two previous convictions of indecent assault and one conviction of indecency with children. **Held.** Although the assaults were serious they could not be said to be the kind of assaults which would expose the public to serious harm.

See also LONGER THAN COMMENSURATE SENTENCES

Victim under 10

100.17   *Att-Gen's Ref. No. 141 of 2001* 2003 1 Cr App R (S) 28. The defendant pleaded guilty at the Magistrates' Court to five offences of indecent assault and four of gross indecency. His step grandson, K aged 5 complained the defendant had touched his penis. He immediately admitted it and said he had abused three of the other step grandchildren. Two were girls, D and K (same letter unfortunately) both born in 1992. One was a boy, S born in 1990. He said he would go to the police but he went abroad. Eleven days later he returned and went to the police. He told them it was opportunistic and he needed help. Further he was abused as a boy and never hurt them. When interviewed he said he had abused S when he was 5 on four or five occasions. Both would be naked and the boy would be asked to lie down and the defendant would lie on top of him with his penis between the boy's legs. The boy would be asked to close his legs and the defendant would simulate intercourse until he ejaculated. The boy's penis would also be touched. On other occasions he would put his hand down S's trousers. D was abused from 5 onwards on a fortnightly or monthly basis in much the same way as S. He also touched and kissed her vagina and on one occasion put his penis in her mouth. Over 4 years there were over a hundred assaults on her. The girl K was only abused twice. That was similar including kissing and touching her vagina. The boy K was also abused twice in the same way. The defendant said if the boy told anyone he would never see his grandfather again. There was a gross indecency and indecent assault for each child and an extra indecent assault for D. He was now 49 and on life licence for murder and attempted murder with firearms imposed in 1975. In 1989 he was convicted of indecently assaulting a boy aged 8 or 9. He received a conditional discharge. The Judge sentenced him to 3$^1/_2$ years on each and extended his licence to 18 months. Held. We would have expected a total sentence of **5–6 years. 4$^1/_2$ years** substituted with the extension remaining.

Att-Gen's Ref No 53 of 2004 2005 1 Cr App R (S) 272. The defendant pleaded guilty to forty five counts of indecent assault on a male person. The offences took place in the 1970s and early 80s over a period of seven years and involved three boys, each being abused over a five-year period. In each case the boys, who were related to each other, were aged between 8 and 13. The abuse occurred when the defendant was aged between 36 and 43. In each case the abuse involved numerous incidents of masturbation of the boy by the defendant and of oral sex both on the boy and on the defendant. In the case of one of the boys there were incidents of masturbation where the defendant inserted his penis between the boy's legs with the boy lying face downwards. There were no offences of buggery or any kind of anal penetration. The offences arose out of a relationship between the defendant and the families of the boys. There were regular family holidays together and in time the boys were allowed to travel with the defendant alone on holiday. The defendant bought presents for the boys and gave them treats as inducements. He promised one boy he would leave him £500 in his will. He also used threats and punishments. He locked a boy out of his hotel room for refusing to perform oral sex on him, and he threatened to take back presents already given if the boy did not do what he was asked. The first victim estimated he had been subject to at least 300 instances of abuse over 5 years. The second and third victims said the abuse had happened on almost every occasion when they were alone with the defendant. In each case the abuse began when the victim was about 8 and had a profound effect. One victim in his impact statement said he thought of the abuse every day and the fear he had of anyone finding out. He was unable to allow anyone to get close to him. The second victim had suffered from severe depression and suicidal feelings. The third said memories of the abuse had seriously affected his relationship with his wife and children and he could not stand physical contact with his children. The defendant, now 65, had no previous convictions. A pre-sentence report said that he did not want to consider the harm he has caused and that he continued to see the boys as complicit in the offences. He was in relatively poor health. Held. The relevant factors here were the ages of the victims, their number, the nature of the sexual misconduct, the frequency, the breach of trust, the impact and the systematic grooming. His plea of guilty was important, and the court had regard to a limited degree that the offences took place 22 and 30 years ago. It also noted his failure to appreciate the harm he did and his lack of remorse. The appropriate sentence was **7 years** not 5; taking into account it was a reference, **6 years** substituted.

Att-Gen's Ref. No 5 of 2001 2001 2 Cr App R (S) 473. See **100.15**.

R v Staples 2001 2 Cr App R (S) 517. See **100.8**.

Victim aged 10–12

100.18   *R v Bromiley* 2001 1 Cr App R (S) 74. See **100.6**.

Att-Gen's Ref. Nos. 35 etc. of 2003 Re RD 2004 1 Cr App R (S) 499 at 519. The defendant pleaded guilty to eight counts of indecent assault. The first victim, aged about 7, stayed the night with the defendant's daughter. He slept the night in a bed with the defendant who touched and played with his penis. The second victim (his brother) was 9 and also slept in the same bed as the defendant and awoke to find he was being masturbated. The boy then masturbated the defendant to ejaculation. The defendant also performed oral sex on the boy. This was repeated on another occasion when another boy was present and each masturbated the other. The abuse continued at the defendant's home in Spain. The third brother (who was about 11) also went on 9 holidays with the defendant. He spent the night before each holiday with the defendant who masturbated him and performed oral sex on him. The boy would also masturbate the defendant. The family of the fifth victim (about 10) met the defendant through the Spanish holidays. The defendant provided the boy with many gifts. There was mutual masturbation, oral sex performed by both and simulated intercourse by the defendant on the boy; the abuse lasted for 4 years. During an investigation in this country, the defendant went to live in Spain where he served a sentence of 9 years for the abuse of 2 boys who were on holiday there. On his return to the UK he was arrested and made full admissions. The counts were considered specimen counts. The offences had a marked impact on the lives of the victims and their families. He was 63. Held. Although the Court was enti-tled to take into account the fact that had he faced a sentence that included both the Spanish and UK offences it would not have been much longer than the 9 years he received in Spain. There was no element of retribution for the UK offences in the Spanish sentence and the suffering of these victims demanded a longer sentence. **Seven years** would have been appropriate if the Spanish sentence was disregarded, five years would have been appropriate. As this was a reference 4 years and not $2^1/_2$. (Although one boy was just under 10 the rest were over so is listed in the 10–12 section).

Old cases. *R v Nicholson* 1998 1 Cr App R (S) 370. For a summary see the first edition of this book or **100.16**.

Victim aged 13–15

100.19   *R v F* 2000 2 Cr App R (S) 292. The defendant, a woman pleaded guilty to five counts of indecent assault on two 15-year-old boys and two counts of permitting premises to be used for the smoking of cannabis. She had three children and children used to visit her. On three occasions one of the victims visited the defendant where con-sensual sexual intercourse and oral sex took place. On two other occasions the second victim participated in consensual sexual foreplay with the defendant. The victims drank freely and used cannabis with her and her children. Her 5-year-old boy was curious about cannabis and sniffed some from a bucket and was sick. The defendant had not interfered. The pre-sentence report said she was a vulnerable and dependant person-ality with a degree of learning difficulty. She 'presented as extremely immature.' Held. The defendant was neither a predatory sex offender nor a risk to the public therefore **6 months** not 12.

R v Lee 1998 2 Cr App R (S) 272. The defendant, who was aged 45, pleaded guilty to indecent assault on a consenting 14-year-old boy. The counts were specimen counts. The defendant met the victim near public lavatories where they engaged in mutual mas-turbation. For a period of 5 months thereafter the victim visited the defendant in his flat and consented to mutual masturbation and fellatio. The victim asked for money and was given it on every visit. He showed the boy some pornographic films. The defen-dant had previous convictions for gross indecency in 1987 with a consenting male and was fined £150. In 1991 he had a conviction for indecent assault on a 15-year-old girl. He received 28 days suspended. In 1993 he was convicted of two indecent assault offences on a physically and mentally disabled man. The offences were committed in the lavatory of a public house. He was given probation for that. The pre-sentence report recommended a 3 year probation order involving a Sex Offender Treatment programme. The judge said that the defendant presented a potential risk to young boys or children, certainly to vulnerable members of the public. Held. Young boys must be protected against themselves. **$2^1/_2$ years** not $3^1/_2$ years.

Att-Gen's Ref. No 41 of 2000 2001 1 Cr App R (S) 372. The defendant pleaded guilty to two counts of indecent assault on a 13-year-old boy and three counts of taking inde-cent photographs of a child. The victim attended a school for children with special needs and on his way to school bumped into the defendant, whom he did not know. The defendant began to talk to the boy and took him for something to eat at McDonalds. The defendant took the boy swimming and then drove him home. The defendant arranged to meet the victim later the same evening and took him to his flat. They watched an '18' film and the victim was given a mobile phone. They met again and the defendant asked the boy to pose for him for £20. The photographs included one with the victim naked with his legs apart and the defendant on top of him simulating intercourse. Another photograph showed the roles reversed. These were the basis for the indecent assault. There were other photographs of the boy masturbating and others that showed him with an erection. In addition photographs of other children were found. The defendant was 39 and had two convictions for gross indecency. They involved masturbation of a mentally defective teenage boy. For this offence he was sentenced to probation with a Sex Offender Treatment programme. He had left his accommodation without notifying anyone and had ignored the treatment programme. Held. The gravity of the appropriate sentence lay in the grooming of the handicapped victim and the giving of money and gifts. **2¹/₂ years** substituted.

Att-Gen's Ref. No 54 of 2003. 2004 2 Cr App R (S) 196. The defendant was convicted of one count of indecent assault on a male and two counts of taking indecent photographs of a child. The defendant, then 50, made contact through an internet chat room with the victim, then aged 15. The defendant said he was 19. They exchanged phone numbers and the defendant frequently phoned and sent text messages to the victim. The victim said he wanted to buy a scooter and the defendant offered to send him money to buy a scooter. He sent the victim small presents with a note signed 'Jenny' – the victim told his mother 'Jenny' was a new friend. The defendant introduced him to another male on the internet, and the victim and this other person masturbated in front of each other by means of a web camera. The defendant started to contact the victim through personal e-mail and asked the victim to be his boyfriend. The victim refused saying he was not homosexual. The defendant asked again two days later and the victim agreed, he said in order to stop the defendant asking. The defendant offered to buy a scooter for the victim and spoke to the victim's mother on the phone confirming that the victim had won a scooter in a competition. The victim said he could not have a scooter till he was 16. The defendant told him he wanted oral sex with him. He told the victim he had paid £1,000 deposit to a firm in Darlington, near the victim, for the scooter. He drove hundreds of miles from Sussex to see the victim and they met briefly in the evening. The following day they met again and drove to a hotel in Darlington where the defendant hired a family room. At this time the victim was four weeks from his sixteenth birthday. The defendant took Polaroid photographs of the naked victim. The victim gave the defendant the phone number of a friend who was also a 15 year old boy. Eighteen months before the friend and the victim had taken part in sexual activity together. The next day the victim met the defendant in his car. Also in the car were the victim's friend and another 17 year old boy. All four of them went to the hotel room, where the defendant masturbated himself and the victim and performed oral sex on him. The other two boys watched. There was further contact after this. On the day of his 16th birthday the victim collected the scooter and the day after that he again met the defendant in a hotel and sexual activity took place between them. This led to a count of rape against the defendant but he was acquitted of that on the basis that the activity was consensual. Three days later the victim's mother confronted him and he told her the truth. The defendant was arrested in the hotel room and he gave police the two photographs of the victim. In his room were four pairs of handcuffs, two tubes of lubricating jelly and the Polaroid camera. The day after this the victim's mother told the police that he was threatening suicide because he was so ashamed of what had happened. The prosecution said the aggravating features were use of the internet, lying about his name and age initially, using expensive presents to corrupt his victim, deceiving the victim's mother and sister by use of the name 'Jenny', carefully planning the indecent assault, committing the assault in the presence of two others, and the severe affect on the victim. In mitigation he had no previous convictions for sexual activities. The indecent assault on the Jury's finding was a consensual act when the victim was nearly 16. After he was 16 the victim voluntarily continued his activity with the defendant and another man. The victim was medically examined and had suffered no (presumably physical) harm. The deception about the defendant's age only lasted until they met when the victim was well aware of the defendant's age. Held. The appropriate sentence for the offending as a whole was **3^1/$_2$ years**, with an extended licence period of **3** years. As it was a reference, **2^1/$_2$** years imprisonment on all counts to run concurrently, not **21** months, with an extended licence period of **3** years. There must also be an order disqualifying him from working with children.

Att-Gen's Ref. No 34 of 2004 2005 1 Cr App R (S) 172. The defendant pleaded guilty to indecent assault on a male. The defendant, 47, befriended his victim, aged 14, after they met at a football referees' course. They continued to meet sometimes at similar places and the defendant would often telephone him at home. The defendant suggested that the victim spend two nights at his home so that they could go to a football match. The victim's parents had spoken to the defendant but had never met him and believed he was a lone parent looking after two sons. They agreed to the plan. When the victim arrived at the defendant's home the defendant said he would put up a Z bed for the victim in his own room. The defendant's two sons aged 16 and 19 each had their own bedroom and were present in the house throughout. That evening the defendant asked the victim about his relationship with his parents. This upset the victim and the defendant put his arms round him. They went to the bedroom and undressed to their underpants. The defendant again asked the victim about his family life and again the victim became upset. The defendant asked the victim to lie down on his bed and put his arm round him. The victim went to sleep on the defendant's bed. Later the defendant took the victim's hand and placed it over his crotch area. He placed his hand under the victim's shorts and touched his penis. The victim removed the hand and turned over but the defendant put his hand on the victim's penis and pulled his shorts down and began to rub the victim's bottom, opening and closing his buttocks. The victim then felt something inserted in his bottom, which went in quite far. He did not know what it was. The defendant then touched the victim's penis again making it erect and pressed his own penis against the victim's buttocks for some time. Eventually at 4.00 am the victim left the house wearing only a fleece and boxer shorts and phoned 999. Reports showed he had developed difficulties sleeping and some behavioural problems that affected his family life and school work. He had post-traumatic stress disorder and had had a long period of counselling. The defendant had no previous convictions. At the Crown Court it was said in mitigation that if he was sent to prison for more than 6 months he would lose his home and his sixteen year old son would have nowhere to live because he could not live with his mother. A letter from the boy's mother at the Court of Appeal made it clear this was not true and that the boy had been living mainly with her at the time of the offence. The pre-sentence report assessed the risk of non sexual re-offending as low but said sexual offending might be a higher risk as the defendant struggled with understanding why he offended and had a limited acceptance of the victim's perspective. The aggravating features included abuse of trust used to exploit a vulnerable victim away from home by taking advantage of his home problems to commit the offence. It was accepted that the grooming was limited to the evening of the offence. Held. Harm of a psychological nature is not less important than physical harm. This was a serious assault involving masturbation and penetration. The appropriate sentence was **2^1/$_2$–3 years**. As it was a reference **2 years** not 6 months with 2 years not 2^1/$_2$ years extended licence period.

R v S 2004 1 Cr App R (S) 303. The defendant pleaded guilty to indecently assaulting a male. The victim was a 13 year-old pupil at a special school which catered for children with emotional and behavioural difficulties. He was on medication for Attention Deficit Hyperactive Disorder. The defendant was a classroom assistant. The victim sent her a note saying that he loved her and she started sending him text messages and letters. He reciprocated. The defendant was suspended but within two days had made an arrangement for the two of them to meet. She gave him alcohol and intercourse then took place. In interview she declined to comment. She was 33, of good character and married with three children for whom she was the main carer. The middle child suffered with autism, epilepsy and related behavioural problems. She was remorseful about the offence. Held. She abused a position of trust, had groomed him and custody was warranted. Her imprisonment will cause severe difficulties within her household. However, taking account of the mitigation, **5 months** not 9.

101   INDECENT ASSAULT ON A WOMAN/GROSS INDECENCY WITH A CHILD

101.1   Sexual Offences Act 1956 s 14

Indecency with Children Act 1960 s 1(1) (gross indecency with a child under 14).

Both offences are triable either way. On indictment maximum 10 years. Summary maximum 6 months and/or £5,000.

The Criminal Justice Act 2003 creates a summary maximum sentence of 51 weeks, a minimum sentence of 28 weeks and Custody plus. The Home Office says they do not expect to introduce these provisions before September 2006.

Both offences were abolished on 1/5/04. Offences committed after that date would be charged under Sexual Offences Act 2003 s 3, 7, 9, 16, 25 see SEXUAL ACTIVITY BREACH OF TRUST, SEXUAL ACTIVITY CHILD FAMILY MEMBER, and SEXUAL ASSAULT ETC. CHILDREN, SEXUAL ASSAULT TOUCHING.

There is a new offence of committing an offence with intent to commit a sexual offence, see Sexual Offences Act 2003 s 62.

Longer than Commensurate sentences and Extended sentences Indecent assault and gross indecency with a child are both sexual offences[35] for the purposes of passing a longer than commensurate sentence [Powers of Criminal Courts (Sentencing) Act 2000 s 80(2)] and an extended sentence (extending the licence) [Powers of Criminal Courts (Sentencing) Act 2000 s 85(2)(b)]. The orders cannot be made for offences committed before 30/9/98 or after 3/4/05. See EXTENDED SENTENCE, LONGER THAN COMMENSURATE SENTENCES, EXTENDED SENTENCES and LONGER THAN COMMENSURATE SENTENCES

Notification For both offences, where the other party is under 18 or the defendant is sentences to at least 30 months imprisonment or a hospital order with a restriction, the defendant must notify the police within 3 days (or 3 days from his release from imprisonment, hospital etc.) his name, home address, national insurance number etc. and any change and addresses where he resides for 7 days[36] (in one or more periods) or more in any 12 month period[37]. See SEX OFFENDERS' REGISTER

Sexual Offences Prevention Order For both offences, there is a discretionary power to make this order, when the notification criteria (see above) are present and when it is necessary to protect the public etc[38].

35 Powers of Criminal Courts (Sentencing) Act 2000 s 161(2)(a)
36 Sexual Offences Act 2003 s 84(1)(c) & (6)
37 Sexual Offences Act 2003 s 83 & Sch. 3 Para 7
38 Sexual Offences Act 2003 s 104 & Sch. 3

Working with children For both offences where the defendant is aged 18 or over and s/he is sentenced to 12 months or more etc. the court must disqualify him/her from working with children unless satisfied s/he is unlikely to commit any further offences against a child. In this the court must state its reasons for not doing so[39]. For a defendant aged less than 18 at the time of the offence the court must order disqualification if s/he is sentenced to 12 months or more and the court is satisfied that the defendant will commit a further offence against a child[40]. The court must state its reasons for so doing.

Crown Court statistics – England and Wales – Males 21+
101.2

Year	Plea	Total Numbers sentenced	Type of sentence %					Average length of custody (months)
			Discharge	Fine	Community sentence	Suspended sentence	Custody	
2002	Guilty	713	3	1	29	2	64	28.7
	Not guilty	527	0	2	11	2	83	28.5
2003	Guilty	720	3	1	24	3	66	27.3
	Not guilty	441	2	1	12	4	79	29.8

For details and explanations about the statistics in the book see page vii.

Magistrates' Court Sentencing Guidelines January 2004

101.3 First time offenders who plead not guilty Entry point. Is it so serious that only custody is appropriate? Consider committal for sentence. Consider the impact on the victim. Examples of aggravating factors for the offence are age differential, breach of trust, injury (may be psychiatric), prolonged assault, very young victim, victim deliberately targeted, victim serving the public and vulnerable victim. An example of mitigating factors for the offence is slight contact. Examples of mitigation are age, health (physical or mental), co-operation with the police, genuine remorse and voluntary compensation.

For details about the guidelines see MAGISTRATES' COURT SENTENCING GUIDELINES at page 483.

See also RAPE

Guideline remarks

101.4 *Att-Gen's Ref. Nos. 91, 119 and 120 of 2002* 2003 2 Cr App R (S) 338 In *R v Millberry* 2003 2 Cr App R (S) 142 at para 8, the Lord Chief Justice said, 'There are, broadly three dimensions to consider in assessing the gravity of an individual offence of rape. The first is the degree of harm to the victim; the second is the level of culpability of the offender; and the third is the level of risk proposed by the offender to society. The gravity of each case will depend very much upon the circumstances and it will always be necessary to consider an individual case as a whole taking into account the three dimensions.'

It will be necessary to take account of similar considerations in all cases of sexual interference, whether amounting to rape or not. However, that is not all. In all classes of sexual offences, there will also be the need to deter others from acting in a similar fashion.

Guideline remarks – Child victims

101.5 *R v Lennon* 1999 1 Cr App R (S) 19. The court reviewed forty three authorities on indecent assault on a child. Held. It is never easy to sentence in these cases. The

39 Criminal Justice and Court Services Act 2000 s 28
40 Criminal Justice and Court Services Act 2000 s 29

circumstances of each case will vary greatly. The judge must tailor the sentence to the particular facts. In most cases the personal circumstances of the defendant will have to take second place behind the plain duty of the court to protect victims and to reflect the clear intention of Parliament that offences of this kind are to be met with greater severity than in former years when the position of the victim may not have been so clearly focused in the public eye.

R v Stapley 2001 1 Cr App R (S) 302. LCJ. The defendant, aged 67 and of good character, fondled the breasts of a 13 year old. He showed her indecent photographs. Held. The courts have to have regard to the public perception of the way offences of this sort are treated and have to make it plain, in order to discourage and to deter others that custodial sentences will invariably be passed.

Guideline remarks – The victim

101.6   *Att-Gen's Ref. No 31 of 2000* 2001 1 Cr App R (S) 386. The effect on the victim is a very important consideration. Women are entitled to walk home without fear of being attacked by men.

Breach of trust – Doctor

101.7   *R v Ghosh* 1999 1 Cr App R (S) 225. The defendant was convicted of two counts of indecent assault on a patient aged 20. The victim had been receiving treatment for breast pain when the defendant handled her breasts in an examination, which did not conform to the usual clinical guidelines. The victim also complained of back pain and the defendant suggested that a massage would reduce the discomfort. The following day whilst performing the massage the defendant squeezed the victim's bottom and breasts and inserted a finger several times into her anus and vagina. As a consequence the victim found it difficult to go to the doctor. The defendant who was aged 57 had one unrelated conviction. As a consequence of the conviction the defendant has lost his income, his wife and his profession. He suffered from ill health. Held. As these offences were committed in breach of trust, 3 years cannot be criticised. As an act of mercy **2 years** not 3 was appropriate.

Att-Gen's Ref. No 6 of 1999 2000 2 Cr App R (S) 67. The defendant, an osteopath was convicted of four counts of indecent assault on patients. We would expect at least **30 months**.

Att-Gen's Ref No 79 of 2004 2005 1 Cr App R (S) 619. The defendant pleaded guilty on re-arraignment to twenty three counts comprising five counts of indecent assaults on a female, ten counts of making an indecent photograph of a child and eight counts of possession of an indecent photograph of a child. The defendant was a GP. Over a period of seven months he indecently assaulted five of his female patients by conducting unnecessary or inappropriate vaginal examinations. Sometimes he recorded these examinations using a hidden digital camera. Count one of indecent assault related to a woman who complained of feeling sick after eating. On her third visit he conducted a vaginal examination without wearing gloves, inserting a speculum inside her, then with gloves he rubbed her clitoris and conducted a high internal examination, which lasted for five minutes. She noticed that a tissue box close to her had a hole cut out through which she could see a lens. She later complained to her mother and a nurse in the surgery. The tissue box with the circular hole was found. Eventually police examined the GP's home computer and found recordings of the defendant examining undressed female patients. They also discovered child pornography downloaded from the Internet. This victim then lost confidence in the medical profession and her relationship with her partner broke down. Count two of indecent assault related to a 74 year old woman who was extremely vulnerable with cognitive impairment as well as physical disabilities. One of the sequences in the home computer showed the defendant examining her at home. He did not wear gloves; he fondled her breasts; he helped her remove her pants to expose her private parts; he rubbed her clitoris and digitally penetrated her; he massaged her buttocks and placed his penis against them; and he made her kneel down on the bed and having exposed her vaginal area filmed her from behind. She was not told of the offences committed against her. Count 4 was the making of an indecent image of a nine year old girl. A sequence in the home computer showed her removing her tights and then a view of her perineum. She had been taken to see the defendant by her father and the defendant had said that he needed to take a vaginal swab. Counts five and six related to the indecent assault and the taking of an indecent photograph of a seven year old girl. Again there was a sequence in the computer showing the defendant's ungloved hand repeatedly massaging her clitoris and parting her labia. The girl's mother had taken her to the surgery because the girl suffered from stomach cramps and wet herself. The defendant said he would have to take a vaginal swab and conduct an internal examination. The girl's mother had been present during the examination but had not been aware of what he was doing. In view of her age the girl was not told of the sexual nature of the conduct against her but she was told the defendant did something wrong and that he took photographs of her. She no longer trusted doctors and became distressed and worried when she had to see one. She had been a confident child but needed, after this, to be chaperoned and did not like being away from her family. Her mother was also distressed by what happened in her presence. Count seven of indecent assault related to an unknown female seen in a sequence on the computer; the defendant was stimulating her clitoris with no medical justification. The last count of indecent assault, count nine, related to a fifteen year old girl who was taken to the defendant with a vaginal discharge. Her mother was present at the examination. She saw him persisting in a rubbing motion. He spent two minutes with his hand under the sheet rubbing the girl's vagina. This victim showed a significant change in her personality and attitude to men, becoming withdrawn and unable to forget the incident. She lost interest in her proposed career as a beauty therapist. Counts 11–26 were sample counts relating to indecent images found on his computer downloaded from the Internet, none of them depicting his patients. In all 1600 indecent images were retrieved. The vast majority were at level 1, but there were twenty three at level 2, thirty five at level 3, eighteen at level 4 and one at level 5. The aggravating features were said to be that these offences were committed against patients in a gross breach of trust; they were repeated and six patients were the victims of the misbehaviour; at least four of the patients had their examinations recorded; some of the indecent assaults involved penetration; some of the victims were particularly vulnerable by reason of age and, in the case of the elderly patient, mental impairment; that patient also suffered indignities and was treated in a particularly humiliating and degrading fashion; the offences had a considerable impact on the lives of some of the victims and there was a very large number of indecent images of children found. The defendant, 30, was of previous good character and demonstrated genuine remorse. He was shy and introverted with a skin disorder. Reports showed him to have a medium risk of re-offending which would arise if he had access to children or vulnerable adults in the future. Held. It was pertinent that there were serious consequences to at least three victims. There was high degree of culpability because of the breach of trust of the doctor-patient relationship. This was a case where a deterrent element in relation to doctors or those acting as doctors should be incorporated into the sentencing process. The appropriate sentence would have been at least an **extended sentence of 8 years** with a custodial element of **5¹/₂ years,** not an extended sentence of 5¹/₂ years with a custodial element of 5¹/₂ years. As this was a reference **4¹/₂ years** custody extended to **8 years**.

Breach of trust – Friend of victim's family – Victim aged less than 10 – Under 4 years appropriate

101.8   *Att-Gen's Ref. No 54 of 1997* 1998 2 Cr App R (S) 324. The defendant pleaded guilty to three counts of indecent assault on three girls, one count of indecent assault on a boy and four counts of indecency with children. The four victims, who were aged between 9 and 13 and were children of friends of the defendant, were allowed to stay overnight on the defendant's boat. The defendant touched and digitally penetrated the girls' vaginas, touched the boy's penis, drew over the victim's naked bodies with washable pens and procured them to draw over his penis whilst he was naked. The offences were over 'a long time'. The defendant, who was 53, was of previous good character. The sentencing judge rejected the defendant's denials of sexual motivation and that the children were lying. Held. Having regard to the position of trust the defendant was in, the age of the victims and the degree of indecent assault a total sentence in the region of **3 years** would have been appropriate. As it was a reference, **27 months**, not 12 months.

R v W 1999 2 Cr App R (S) 150. The defendant, who was 34 years of age, pleaded guilty to two counts of indecent assault on his niece, who was aged 6 years. The victim had to stay with the defendant and his wife because her mother was in hospital. The defendant entered the victim's bedroom, removed her underwear and touched her vagina; on one occasion he digitally penetrated her. The conduct caused the victim pain and as a result she became tearful and clingy and often reluctant to go upstairs or sleep on her own. The defendant was of previous good character. Held. It was inappropriate for the sentencing judge to note that these offences were 'not much short of rape'. The risk of the defendant molesting children in the future was medium to low and he accepted the impact that his conduct had had on the victim. **2¹/₂ years** not 5 years was appropriate.

Att-Gen's Ref. No 46 of 1999 2000 1 Cr App R (S) 310. The defendant pleaded guilty to nine counts of indecent assault and eight counts of indecency with a child. Some were sample counts. The defendant assaulted three children aged between 7 and 8, one child aged between 5 and 6 and one girl of 15 years of age. The defendant was a friend of the victims' families and would occasionally visit their houses. The younger victims suffered digital penetration and were forced to touch the defendant's penis and take it in their mouths. In addition the defendant touched the 15-year-old victim's breasts over her clothing. The defendant, who was 55 years of age, had no relevant similar convictions. The risk of re-offending was assessed as significant. He was sentenced to 3 years probation with the condition of attendance at sex offenders' programmes. In breach of the conditions he had gone abroad. After sentence although prohibited from seeing his grandchildren by his daughter he said, 'She'll come round in time.' His attitude to the offences had not changed. Held. The appropriate sentence if he had contested the case was **6 years** and **4 years** as he pleaded. As it was a reference **3 years** substituted. His licence should be extended so it was 3 years from his release.

R v Massie 2003 1 Cr App R (S) 414. The defendant changed his plea to guilty to four counts of indecent assault. The defendant met two families through the Church and he and his wife babysat the victims. Count 1 was between 1975 and 1982 and involved a girl aged between 5 and 10 years old. He went to the victim's bedroom and pulled back the bedclothes. Next he touched the girl's vaginal area over her pants. To escape the girl used the excuse that she needed to go to the lavatory where she locked herself in. The incident was not repeated. The other counts related to three consecutive nights in 1981 or early 1982 while he babysat for another family. He committed almost exactly similar offences. That victim told her family and it was discussed privately within the church authorities and no action was taken. The counts were not specimen counts. He was now 49 with a number of convictions for dishonesty and minor violence, which save for one, were more than 20 years old. The Judge ignored them. In August 2001 the girls now in their 30s contacted the police. The defendant was interviewed and made frank admissions about the offences. The pre-sentence report referred to his remorse and the risk of re-offending was medium but reasonably well contained. It recommended a community rehabilitation order. The total sentence was 15 months with an extended sentence of 3 years. The Judge said he wanted to ensure the defendant was under supervision and subject to treatment. He had served 22 weeks in custody. Held. For offences prior to 1992, the court has no power to pass any extended sentence of the kind permitted by Section 85 of the 2000 Act. Sexual abuse of children, other than of the most minor nature, which this was not, is not normally to be described as falling short of the custody threshold. The priority here is for the rehabilitation of the defendant and the protection of the public as the Judge wanted. We intend to achieve that by substituting a **community rehabilitation order** coupled with a **condition to undertake a Sex Offender Treatment Programme**.

Breach of trust – Friend of victim's family – Victim aged less than 10 – Less than 4 years appropriate

101.9 *R v D* 2001 2 Cr App R (S) 281. The defendant pleaded guilty to two counts of indecent assault on a girl who was aged 5. The defendant was married to the victim's grandmother and had offered to look after the victim and her brother. The defendant began to tickle the victim's stomach and then removed her trousers and digitally penetrated her. The defendant then took the girl upstairs and made her lie on top of him so that her vagina touched his penis; he then digitally penetrated her again. The defendant, who was 29, had four convictions for indecent assault against his stepdaughter aged 11, who was the victim's aunt. That abuse involved digital penetration. The sentencing judge said that this was a very revealing previous conviction. Where children are concerned 'once is too often, twice is completely and utterly unacceptable. You are an ongoing danger to children'. Held. **4 years** longer than commensurate and an extension period of 3 years was not a manifestly excessive.

R v Sweeney 1998 2 Cr App R (S) 43. The defendant, who now was 65, pleaded guilty to seventeen counts of indecent assault on seven girls aged between, 6 and 14 for offences committed between 1962 and 1993. The six victims were either related to the defendant or he was a friend of their families. The abuse for the most part consisted of frequent digital penetration of their vaginas but also included attempts to make the victims masturbate him. The abuse had caused one of the girls to bleed and another was in such pain that she would lie awake all night crying. One of the victims took an overdose as a result of the abuse. The defendant had no previous convictions and was a pillar of the community. The pre-sentence report said he was a continuing risk to children. The sentencing judge noted that the offending did not involve violence. Held. Because of the relatively moderate nature of the sexual activity **7 years** not 9.

R v Burton-Barri 1999 2 Cr App R (S) 252. The defendant, who was 63 when convicted, pleaded guilty to forty four counts of indecent assault, taking indecent photographs of a child and gross indecency with a child. Twenty three counts were for indecent assault, sixteen on females and seven on males. The ages were from 8 upwards. The abuse took place over a period of 25 years with children of friends of the defendant and his own stepchildren. He inveigled his way into the confidence of the parents by acts of kindness and generosity. The offences took place when the defendant offered to baby-sit the victims and included videoing the defendant performing oral sex on the victims and having the act reciprocated. Vaginal and anal penetration took place and he inserted objects into one of the victims' anus. Presents were given. The defendant was 63 with convictions in 1992 for gross indecency with a child and taking indecent photographs. Held. The sentence had to reflect the fact that although the abuse was appalling it was not as appalling as it could have been. It had to be borne in mind that the defendant should not have been sentenced as he might have been for committing rape or buggery. **10 years** not 14$^1/_2$ years was appropriate.

Breach of trust – Friend of victim's family – Victim aged 10–12

101.10 *Att-Gen's Ref. No 77 of 1999* 2000 2 Cr App R (S) 250. The defendant was

convicted of three counts of indecent assault. The defendant indecently assaulted his niece for about a year when she was between the ages of 10 and 11, when she was staying at his house. The defendant put his hand inside the girl's knickers and touched the victim's vagina and would occasionally expose his penis to her. The defendant, who was 46 years of age, had no relevant previous convictions and after conviction he admitted the offences and expressed deep remorse. The defendant was given probation with conditions. Since his sentence a report told of his high level motivation and that his relationship with his partner was in tact and that his own children were not at risk. His risk of re-offending was described as being relatively low. Held. Having regard to the progress the defendant has made a **3 years** probation order was not unduly lenient, it was within the residual discretion of the judge to take an exceptional course.

Att-Gen's Ref. No 1 of 2001 2001 2 Cr App R (S) 469. LCJ. The defendant was convicted of indecent assault on a 10-year-old girl. The defendant was a good friend of the victim's stepfather and would visit their home with his wife once a fortnight. The defendant sat the victim on his lap and digitally penetrated her. The defendant, who was 55 years of age, had one previous conviction for indecent assault against his daughter when she was 6 years old. When bathing the child the defendant inserted a finger into her vagina. The defendant was in ill health. The sentencing judge noted that the defendant had breached the trust not only of the victim but also of her parents and that his plea of not guilty had meant that the victim had had to give evidence. Held. The appropriate sentence was 3 years. As it was a reference **21 months** was appropriate not a probation order.

See also *Att-Gen's Ref. No 27 of 2001* 2002 1 Cr App R (S) 42. 27 months on a man who indecently assaulted friends of his daughter.

Breach of trust – Nurse

101.11 *Att-Gen's Ref. No. 115 of 2001* 2003 1 Cr App R (S) 42. The defendant pleaded guilty to indecent assault on the second day of his trial after his admissibility argument had failed. The victim had already been brought to Court. Counts of rape, sexual intercourse with a mental patient and with a mental defective were not proceeded with. The defendant was a full time night staff nurse at a nursing home for 50 severely mentally ill or elderly residents. He was the team leader in charge of five staff. The victim was 47 and suffered from paranoid schizophrenia, which gave her delusions and auditory hallucinations. She required 24 hour supervision and had borderline intelligence and was incapable of giving lawful consent to sexual intercourse. He was sentenced on the basis of his account in interview, which was as follows. She visited his room and asked for help in sleeping etc. three times. He went to her room and she said she wanted him inside her because he was her husband. She took his hand and began to rub it against her vagina. She unzipped his trousers and took his penis out and rubbed it against her vagina. She then threatened to scream. She next lay on her back with her legs apart. Then she rubbed his penis up and down her vagina. It carried on till he ejaculated over the bed and the floor. He claimed he not she was the victim. There was no evidence of any serious or lasting emotional or other consequence to the victim. He was now 58 with a positive good character and his employment lost. The pre-sentence report indicated a degree of failure to acknowledge his guilt and consequently there was some risk of reoffending. He was given a 12 month sentence suspended for 2 years with a suspended supervision order. Seven and a half months had elapsed since then. Held. It was a gross breach of trust. There was no basis for suspending the sentence. Giving every allowance to his plea, character and taking into account it was a reference **6 months** substituted.

Breach of trust – Police officer – Victim aged 13–15

101.12 *R v Cairns* 1998 1 Cr App R (S) 434. The defendant pleaded guilty to three counts of indecent assault on girls who were between the ages of 13 and 14. They were specimen counts. The defendant, who was 23 at the time of the first assault, was a serving police officer who assisted in the running of a youth club. The defendant persuaded the first victim, who was aged 14 to enter into a sexual relationship with him. The indecency progressed from the defendant kissing the victim and fondling her breasts over her clothing to engaging in mutual oral sex and digital penetration of her vagina. This conduct took place both in the defendant's flat and in the countryside. The second victim was abused just before she was 13. The defendant touched the victim's breasts and vagina over her clothing when they were in a stockroom together and on occasions forced her to masturbate him and perform oral sex upon him. The second victim also engaged in sexual activity when the first victim was also present. The defendant kissed the third victim, who was 13, when he was driving her home. Intimacy progressed as with the other two victims. The defendant was 36 and of previous good character. Held. The defendant was not only in a position of trust but as a serving police officer a position of authority. The offences were not the worst kind of indecent assault, therefore **5 years** not 7 years was appropriate.

Breach of trust – Taxi driver – Victim aged 16+

101.13   *R v Saboor* 2000 1 Cr App R (S) 40. The defendant was convicted of indecent assault against a passenger in his minicab. The victim and her male friend travelled in the defendant's minicab after an evening out. The companion was dropped off whilst the victim was asleep. The defendant moved into the backseat and digitally penetrated the woman. The defendant, who was 28, had no previous convictions. The sentencing judge noted that this assault was made worse as it was committed by a person in a position of trust. Held. This was a very serious assault. Society rightly looks to the courts to offer what protection it can to those who use taxicabs and expose themselves to the possibility of attack by the drivers. **3 years** was an appropriate sentence. Having regard to the personal circumstances of the defendant including his wife was unable to speak English and the death of three of their children from an inherited lung disorder and as an act of mercy **2 years**.

R v Sailani 2001 Unreported 13/7/01. The defendant was convicted of indecent assault. He was a taxi driver who kissed one of his passengers at night on the cheek and tried to kiss her on the lips. She refused to allow him and he brushed his hand across her breasts. Held. The trust between the taxi driver and the passenger must be maintained. People who travel at night need protection. The breach of trust was serious but **9 months** not 2 years. The deportation order quashed.

Breach of trust – Teachers etc – Victim aged 10–12

101.14   *Att-Gen's Ref. No 44 of 2000* 2001 1 Cr App R (S) 460. The defendant pleaded guilty to eight counts of indecent assault on a girl, five of which related to girls under 13 and one count of indecent assault on a male. They spanned from 1969–1977. The victims were pupils aged 11–13 at a private preparatory school where he was deputy headmaster and then headmaster. He would administer punishment for poor spelling etc. He required them to lie across his lap and sometimes he would remove their knickers to expose their buttocks. He would then perform circular hand movement on the girls. The offences came to light in 1977 and nobody told the police or thought it appropriate to inform the police. He was 67. He pleaded guilty after the judge had indicated that he would not go to prison. The judge gave him **18 months suspended**. Held. We doubt there were exceptional circumstances to suspend the sentence, but no order made because the prosecution had been involved in the plea bargain.

See also SEXUAL INTERCOURSE, BREACH OF TRUST – *Teachers*

Breach of trust – Workplace – Victim aged 13–15

101.15   *Att-Gen's Ref. No 25 of 1997* 1998 1 Cr App R (S) 310. The defendant was

convicted of two counts of indecent assault on a girl aged 15 years. The defendant, who was 64 years of age owned a pet shop and the victim was placed with him on work placement. Over the course of the first week he made lewd comments towards her, cuddled her, squeezed her bottom on several occasions, ran his hand over her bare back, kissed and bit her neck, stroked her upper thigh, felt her right breast underneath her clothing and squeezed her vagina over the top of her jeans. The acts were done despite the protestations of the victim. He gave her £5 and told her not to tell anyone. She was worried about being given a bad report. The victim was very distressed and became withdrawn. There was no remorse. The defendant had a previous conviction for indecent assault 11 years earlier. Held. He was in a position of trust. The conduct was a campaign of sexual harassment towards a girl, though it was not the worst indecent assaults. The only mitigation was his age. **12 months** was the appropriate sentence. As it was a reference **8 months** not a £500 fine.

See also **Workplace**

Deception, by – Pretending to be a Doctor – Victim aged 13–15

101.16   *Att-Gen's Ref. No 62 of 1998* 2000 2 Cr App R (S) 286. The defendant, who was now 59 years of age, was convicted of four offences of indecent assault on women, six of obtaining property by deception, three of unlawful wounding, two of supplying prescription-only medicines, and nine of perverting the course of justice. For 8 years the defendant passed himself off as a doctor, establishing a laboratory and styling himself as Dr, BSc, MSc, PhD, and DSc. The defendant was not medically qualified and an expert said that he had very little knowledge and experience. He carried out vaginal examinations on female patients. A 15-year-old girl had something inserted between her legs, and she screamed. The defendant inserted his finger into the vagina of a 25-year-old woman and on the next day he pretended to take a sample from her by inserting a stick into her vagina. He then inserted his finger and touched her clitoris. The victim was very upset. The defendant told her that she was suffering from a sexually transmitted disease. Other women were told that they had sexually transmitted diseases and one had a wooden spatula inserted into her vagina and the other was examined with a speculum. The 3 older victims' relationships with their partners broke up. The defendant had convictions for ABH for which he received 3 months and obtaining property by deception for which he received 6 months. Held. The appropriate sentence for the indecent assault and related offences was **5–6 years** with 2 years consecutive on the second indictment for perverting the course of justice. The sentence of 5 years was unduly lenient. Having regard to the age of the defendant, his state of health and that this was a reference it was not necessary to increase the **5 years** sentence.

Defendant aged 10–13

101.17   *R v W* 1999 1 Cr App R (S) 488. The defendant was convicted of indecent assault on a 12–year-old girl. He was acquitted of attempted rape. The victim was walking home in the early evening when the defendant caught up with her and started to kiss her. The defendant, who was aged 13, then put his hand down the victim's clothes and touched her vaginal area. The victim pulled his hand away and attempted to escape whereupon the defendant tripped her over, pulled her jogging bottoms down and simulated sexual intercourse on her. The defendant had no previous convictions. Held. These cases are extremely difficult to deal with. It is extremely important that if any woman, whatever age, and in particular if a child, is sexually assaulted then that is an extremely serious matter and must be dealt with by appropriate punishment. On the other hand when the attacker is no more than a child, the overriding consideration is to do the best to see what can be done to assist him, but at the same time to mark the seriousness of the offence. Here the two principles clash. It was a gratuitous assault but a **supervision order** rather than 8 months was appropriate.

Defendant aged 14–15

101.18 *R v D* 1998 2 Cr App R (S) 292. The defendant, then aged 15, pleaded guilty to three counts of indecent assault on a 4–year-old girl. The defendant was the son of a friend of the victim's mother and was a babysitter for the victim and her brothers. On two occasions he placed his finger in the victim's anus and vagina and on one occasion placed his penis into her mouth. He also masturbated himself. The abuse became apparent when the victim claimed that the defendant had 'shagged' her. He tried to bribe her into silence. The defendant had no convictions but had two cautions for offences of buggery against his sister and brother. He had buggered his sister once when she was aged five and he was 12 years old, and buggered his brother who was aged ten on a number of occasions. He had then failed to respond to the help that was available. The pre-sentence report said unless he received help the risk of re-offending was high. A supervision order was recommended. The sentencing judge held that the defendant constituted a significant risk to children and that a custodial sentence was essential. Held. The defendant is plainly a dangerous man in relation to sex offences and children. The offences were extremely serious. There was no doubt he needed therapy and deserved punishment. There were no Sexual Offenders programmes in YOI. Until he had the therapy he constituted a significant risk to young children. A substantial custodial sentence was required to punish him and protect young children. If it was [the then s 53] detention he would receive therapy in a secure environment. **4 years' detention** was severe but not manifestly excessive.

R v B 2000 1 Cr App R (S) 177. The defendant pleaded guilty to three counts of indecent assault on a female child, one count of indecent assault on a boy aged 3 years, and one count of committing gross indecency with a child. One of the counts was a specimen count. The defendant when aged 14 and 15 baby-sat the victims, two of whom were his half-sisters, who were aged 4 and 6. The male victim was the son of a friend of the defendant's stepmother. The defendant touched and sucked the boy's penis, touched the female victims vaginal area, encouraged one of the victims to perform oral sex on him and simulated sexual intercourse upon her. The defendant was of previous good character. He showed signs of being unable to control his behaviour without therapeutic help. The pre-sentence report said a high level of therapeutic input was required. Held. This type of offence will always pose problems for a court. Balanced against the interests of the offender in seeking a way to prevent further offending are, of course, the damage to his victims and the public abhorrence for this type of crime. We are not saying custody was wrong in principle, but now he has served a short period of custody it is possible to take a different course. **Supervision order** not 2 years' detention.

Att-Gen's Ref. No 61 of 1999 2000 1 Cr App R (S) 516. LCJ. The defendant pleaded guilty to indecent assault on a girl aged 12. His not guilty plea to attempted rape was accepted. The victim was walking home from school when the defendant, who was 14, approached her. She agreed to go into some bushes with him where he asked her to have sexual intercourse with him. When she refused he pushed her to the ground and forced his penis into her mouth. On withdrawing his penis he ejaculated over her leg. Held. Such behaviour was not less unacceptable because it was committed by one of such youthful age. A supervision order was an unduly lenient sentence; the appropriate sentence was **12 months detention**. As this was a reference the court could not impose more than 6 months and it would not be in the public interest that he should serve such a short period of detention; therefore a **supervision order** was undisturbed.

R v TW 2001 1 Cr App R (S) 128. The defendant pleaded guilty to three counts of indecent assault on a girl of 5 or 6 years of age. A not guilty verdict was entered on two rape counts. The defendant knew the victim through her brother, as they were school friends. Over the period of a year, the defendant, put his penis into the victim's mouth, lay on top of her with his penis between her thighs and touched the outside of her vagina. The defendant, who was 14 years of age, had no previous convictions. The risk of the defendant re-offending was low, particularly if the defendant became involved in a relationship with a child of his own age, but that only a custodial sentence would do. After sentence the education he received was undemanding and obstructed by others. Held. Looking at it from the defendant's point of view it would be better if he was seeing a psychiatrist and being educated outside. The sentencing judge imposed the correct sentence of **15 months**. Sentence reduced to **12 months** so as not to interfere with the next academic year.

Defendant aged 16–17

101.19 *R v Oldfield* 2000 1 Cr App R (S) 73. The defendant pleaded guilty to indecent assault on a 20 year old woman as she was walking home in the early hours of the morning. The defendant, who was 16 years of age, grabbed the victim from behind and pushed her to the ground and pinned her down. He put one hand over her mouth and the other seized her wrists. He forced his hand down her trousers and inside her underwear where he touched her vagina. The force broke the top button and the zipper. A man who was nearby frightened the defendant and the defendant escaped, stealing the victim's purse. The victim was hysterical and had scratches to her neck and breastbone. The defendant had two previous convictions for ABH, which had no sexual element. The risk of offending and the risk to the public was assessed as high. There was no sign of any mental illness. The sentencing judge noted that the defendant was lucky that the man intervened as he may have been facing a charge of attempted rape. An indefinite supervision order was made. Held. Having regard for the age of the defendant **3 years** not 4 years.

R v Gallagher 2002 2 Cr App R (S) 523. The defendant pleaded guilty to indecent assault. When just 16 he drove his mother's car with permission. In broad daylight the victim aged 29 was walking home from shopping. He drove the car and blocked her path more than once. He got out took hold of her and asked for a kiss. He felt her breasts particularly the nipples and touched and pressed her vagina. He unzipped his fly and took out his penis. He pressed himself against her and thrust it until he ejaculated, although she was not immediately aware of that. She was in great distress and thought he was in his early 20s. He was arrested 8 months later after a DNA match. In interview he denied the offence. There was one previous conviction for interfering with a motor vehicle. He was from a travelling family and had limited educational attainments. He had casual employment as a labourer and had had a number of girlfriends. Both the psychiatric report and the pre-sentence report said the offence was impulsive and unpremeditated. Further he had a high sex drive and presented a high risk of reoffending and would benefit from focused treatment. Held. Looking at him today we understand why she thought he was in his early 20s. This case is very much at the serious end of the range. The victim was a stranger who was in real fear of being raped. However she was not undressed. His extreme youth weighs with us. **3 years** detention not 4.

Extended sentences (i.e. licence extended)

101.20 Powers of Criminal Courts (Sentencing) Act 2000 s 85 (previously the Crime and Disorder Act 1988 s 58).

R v Barros 2000 2 Cr App R (S) 327. The defendant pleaded guilty to indecent assault of a female. The defendant left a pub and about 1am he met the victim outside a supermarket. She was under 16 and they began kissing. The defendant touched the victim over her clothes and pulled her skirt up and digitally penetrated her vagina. The girl said that she wanted to go. The defendant took the victim's hand and put it on his penis over his trousers. After pulling the victim to the ground and holding her, she struggled free and ran away. At that stage the defendant said he was not trying to have sex with the victim. When interviewed the defendant admitted the offence. The defendant, now aged 36, had no previous convictions. He was sentenced on the basis that he thought the victim to be 17 years old the sentence was 4 years with an extended period of licence of 3 years under what is now s 85. Held. 4 years cannot be justified after a guilty plea and this was not an appropriate case for an extended licence.

R v Thornton 2000 2 Cr App R (S) 47. **5 years** extended sentence for a man who put his hand up the victim's skirt and pulled down her tights.

R v Pullen 2002 1 Cr App R (S) 17. **3¹/₂ years** with an extension period of **2 years** for a man who dragged a woman off her bicycle and squeezed her breast.

R v L 2000 2 Cr App R (S) 506. The defendant pleaded guilty to three counts of indecent assault on girls aged around 13 or 14. The defence argued relying on *R v Hinton* 1995 16 Cr App R (S) 523 that although the maximum is 10 years the maximum for unlawful sexual intercourse with a girl aged 13–15 is only 2 years so where there are sexual acts falling short of sexual intercourse there should be a judicially imposed maximum of 2 years. The Judge sentenced him to 12 months with 3 years extension. Held. The Judge was right to accept that argument. However the term should not exceed the maximum, Powers of Criminal Courts (Sentencing) Act 2000 s 85(5). As the defendant should have received a discount and should not have received the maximum the extended period should be reduced to 6 months. (Powers of Criminal Courts (Sentencing) Act 2000 s 85(2) appears to define the term of an extended sentence as the custodial part and the licence period.)

See also *R v Horrobin* 2002 2 Cr App R (S) 566 and EXTENDED SENTENCES

Factual basis for sentence after an acquittal for rape

101.21   *R v Gillespie* 1998 2 Cr App R (S) 61. The defendant was acquitted of attempted rape, but pleaded guilty to indecent assault on a 14–year-old girl. The defendant was a door-to-door salesman and gained access to the victim's house when she was alone by asking to use the lavatory. The victim alleged that the defendant forcibly undressed her and attempted to rape her though only succeeded in touching the outside of her vagina with his penis. The jury rejected this account. Held. The judge when sentencing the defendant on the count of indecent assault either based his judgment on the evidence of the victim, which is wrong as this was rejected by the jury, or failed to make clear which part of the victim's evidence he was accepting. The court did not know on what factual basis the judge sentenced and was left with a feeling that it was inconsistent with the jury's acquittal of attempted rape. The indecency was not of the worst kind, therefore **6 months**, not 4 years.

R v Iles 1998 2 Cr App R (S) 63. The defendant was acquitted of rape but convicted of indecent assault on a 15-year-old girl, arising out of the same facts. The defendant had admitted the act of intercourse to the police. The victim was very drunk and had been raped earlier by a third party; the defendant was aware of this. The defendant then had consensual sexual intercourse with the victim, which amounted to indecent assault as the victim was under 16 and in law could not consent. The defendant has previous convictions but not for sexual offences. Held. The maximum sentence for unlawful sexual intercourse is 2 years. The defendant should be treated as though he pleaded guilty therefore **15 months** not 2 years.

See also: *R v Gore* 1998 1 Cr App R (S) 413. The sentencing basis of the judge could not stand. It will have to be based on a consenting victim here.

Father/stepfather, by – Victim under 10 – Less than 3 years appropriate

101.22   *R v Lennon* 1999 1 Cr App R (S) 19. The defendant, who was 52, was convicted of indecent assault on the 9–year-old daughter of his co-habitee. The defendant had masturbated and subsequently jumped onto the victim, pulled off her trousers and underwear and attempted to penetrate her with his penis. It was treated as a single act. Held. Each sentence must be tailored to the particular facts. **2 years** was not manifestly excessive. [Facts are in short supply in this case.]

Att-Gen's Ref. No 35 of 1998 1999 1 Cr App R (S) 400. The defendant, who was 61, pleaded guilty to four counts of indecent assault on two girls aged between 7 and 11. The victims were the daughters of the defendant's girlfriend with whom he was staying. The defendant invited the victims into his bed when he was naked and subsequently placed his penis between their legs. The defendant was arrested but without any evidence except for the girls there was no prosecution for a year. This conduct occurred on a second occasion after the defendant had shown the victims a pornographic video. The defendant was treated as being of good character. The judge noted the defendant remained a high risk unless his behaviour was fully addressed. Held. The appropriate sentence was **12–18 months** considering his age and the plea. As it was a reference **9 months** was appropriate not a probation order.

Att-Gen's Ref. No 20 of 1998 1999 1 Cr App R (S) 280. The defendant pleaded guilty to four counts of gross indecency and three counts of indecent assault on the daughter of his co-habitee, who was between 8 and 11. The counts were specimen counts. The defendant had touched the victim's vagina with his penis, his finger and a vibrator, masturbated in front of her and ejaculated onto her naked leg. It was accepted that he had not digitally penetrated her. The defendant, who was 37, had a record but no previous convictions of this kind. The Judge gave him a $3^1/_2$ year probation order. The girl was dismayed the defendant might lose his liberty. Held. This was very grave conduct, considering the defendant was in a position of responsibility and that the offences were repeated on several occasions over a number of years. We would have expected **4 years**. As it was a reference and going to prison for him will be particularly harsh **2 years**.

Att-Gen's Ref. Nos. 35 etc. of 2003 Re EM 2004 1 Cr App R (S) 499 at 530. The defendant pleaded guilty to six counts of indecent assault on a female under 13 that occurred about 24 years earlier. The offences were against his daughter when she was between 7 and 8. He told her to go to her bedroom and sit with her legs open. He then exposed his penis and took hold of her hand and placed it on his penis. She pulled her hand away and said that she did not want to do it but the defendant took her hand again and placed it on his penis and made her masturbate him holding his hand over hers. He made her masturbate him to ejaculation. He then digitally penetrated her vagina and caused her pain. This conduct was repeated every Saturday whilst her mother was out of the house. When interviewed he denied the allegation but admitted touching her vagina on two occasions. He later pleaded on a full facts basis. He was 57 and of good character. Held. This was a gross breach of trust with a young victim and repeated over an appreciable amount of time. It had a significant impact on the defendant. **3 years** would have been appropriate, but **18 months** as this was a reference and taking account of the progress he had made whilst subject to the community rehabilitation order.

Att-Gen's Ref. No 72 of 1999 2000 2 Cr App R (S) 79. The defendant was convicted of six counts of indecent assault, and one of indecency and taking an indecent picture. The first girl, H, his stepdaughter, was abused when she was 4 or 5, 5 or 6 and 7 twice. The second girl, G had been fostered and then adopted when she was 12. She was abused when she was 13 or in one count possibly younger. His early abuse was touching the girl's vagina in the bath. When H was 7 she made her touch his penis. G was asked to play strip poker and when she lost they both had all their clothes off and the defendant became all excited and asked her to touch him. She refused. Later he made G unroll a condom on his erect penis. G was also asked twice to lie on a scanner once with her bra and once without. He also made her masturbate him to ejaculation. Both girls had to give evidence. The defendant was of good character and had given up his job to be a Minister and was highly regarded by the church. He lost his home, his job and his vocation. He showed no remorse. **2¹/₂ years** in total not 12 months.

Att-Gen's Ref. No 15 of 2001 2001 2 Cr App R (S) 532. LCJ. The defendant was convicted of gross indecency on his 4-year-old stepdaughter and perverting the course of justice. The defendant had consumed a considerable amount of alcohol when his wife found him astride the girl. The defendant had pulled down the child's underwear and was masturbating over her. His wife came in and found him astride the girl and there was semen on the crotch of her knickers and her T-shirt. The defendant tried to destroy the evidence by putting the sheet in the washing machine while she attempted to prevent it. She also tried to call the police and he ripped the phone out of the socket. When she tried to use her mobile to call the police he snatched it. He was arrested and denied the incident. The defendant, who was 23 years of age, had no relevant convictions. He was in the Navy with promotion prospects. He was dismissed from the services, lost £8,000 in pension rights and lost Navy quarters. He also lost being with his two daughters and his stepdaughter. He received 6 months for the indecency and 2 months consecutive for the perverting the course of justice. Held. The 2 months was adequate and rightly consecutive. A sentence must be imposed as a deterrent. The appropriate sentence was **2¹/₂ years**. As it was a reference **18 months** not 6 months.

Att-Gen's Ref. Nos. 35 etc. of 2003 Re EM 2004 1 Cr App R (S) 499 at 530. The defendant pleaded guilty to six counts of indecent assault on a female under 13 that occurred about 24 years earlier. The offences were against his daughter when she was between 7 and 8. He told her to go to her bedroom and sit with her legs open. He then exposed his penis and took hold of her hand and placed it on his penis. She pulled her hand away and said that she did not want to do it but the defendant took her hand again and placed it on his penis and made her masturbate him holding his hand over hers. He made her masturbate him to ejaculation. He then digitally penetrated her vagina and caused her pain. This conduct was repeated every Saturday whilst her mother was out of the house. When interviewed he denied the allegation but admitted touching her vagina on two occasions. He later pleaded on a full facts basis. He was 57 and of good character. Held. This was a gross breach of trust with a young victim and repeated over an appreciable amount of time. It had a significant impact on the defendant. **3 years** would have been appropriate, but **18 months** as this was a reference and taking account of the progress he had made whilst subject to the community rehabilitation order.

Att-Gen's Ref. Nos. 35 etc. of 2003 Re AC 2004 1 Cr App R (S) 499 at 538. The defendant pleaded guilty at the Magistrates' Court to seven charges of indecent assault; five on his older daughter between 18 and 14 years earlier, two on his younger daughter two years earlier. The offences against the older daughter were committed when she was between 6 and 11. The charges were specimens and took place when the defendant and the girl were alone in his bed during the day and at night regardless of whether others were at home or not. The defendant encouraged the girl to remove her knickers and then would touch her vagina. He placed his erect penis between her thighs from behind and then thrust until he ejaculated. He did the same with her on top of him. On one occasion he grabbed her hand and placed it on his penis even though she said she did not want to touch it. The abuse continued until she refused to allow it to continue. The abuse against the younger girl started when she was aged 6. It was similar although she had masturbated him to ejaculation. He stopped seeing the younger daughter and said to police that he felt sick at what he had done. He was 47 and without previous convictions. Held. This was the abuse of two daughters involving a gross breach of trust. The assaults involved simulated intercourse and ejaculation and there were repeated indecent assaults. The period of abuse was conducted over 17 years and both victims had suffered trauma. The appropriate sentence would have been **3 years**. As it was a reference, **2 years** concurrent for each offence with a three year extended sentence for the offences against the younger victim instead of 12 months with an extended sentence of 12 months.

Father/stepfather, by – Victim under 10 – 3 to 4 years appropriate

101.23   *Att-Gen's Ref. No 32 of 1998* 1999 1 Cr App R (S) 316. The defendant pleaded guilty to five offences of indecent assault and one of indecency, with the daughter of his co-habitee, who was between the ages of 6 and 8. The defendant, who was aged 44, admitted to behaving indecently with the child on between 15 and 20 occasions, which included simulating sexual intercourse, digital penetration of the victim's vagina and anus, and mutual oral sex. The child was extremely traumatised and had to receive treatment for her mental condition. The defendant had no previous convictions and had demonstrated genuine remorse. The psychiatrist's report stated that the defendant had distorted the boundaries between affection and sexuality with his stepdaughter. The judge noted that the defendant was not a 'true paedophile' and presented a low risk of re-offending. Held. **3 years** was lenient but not an unduly lenient.

Att-Gen's Ref. No 61 of 1998 1999 2 Cr App R (S) 226. LCJ. The defendant pleaded guilty to eight counts indecent assault on the handicapped daughter of the woman with whom he cohabited. The victim suffered from quadriplegia, cerebral palsy and dystonia, which affected her limb movements and voice. The defendant was the father figure of the house. Over a 2 year period when the victim was between the ages of 9 and 11 the defendant forced the victim to masturbate him, digitally penetrated her, performed oral sex on her and forced her to reciprocate. The acts were not reported and it wasn't until 3 years later her school nurse was told about it. The defendant, who was 40, had no previous convictions for similar behaviour. The judge noted that the child's trust had been abused and the child's innocence betrayed. Held. The appropriate sentence on a trial was 4 years or more. On a plea it should have been **3 years**. As it was a reference **2 years** not a probation order.

Father/stepfather, by – Victim under 10 – More than 4 years appropriate

101.24   *Att-Gen's Ref. No 66 of 1999* 2000 1 Cr App R (S) 558. The defendant was convicted of seven counts of indecent assault on his three daughters, who were aged between 7 and 13 over a period of 4 or 5 years. The defendant's wife had died and he had been left to look after the victims and a fourth child, a boy aged 10. The conduct included digital penetration, touching the victim's breasts, simulating sexual intercourse and forcing the victims to masturbate him. Two of the victims left home at the age of 13 because of the defendant's conduct. The defendant, who was 51, had previous convictions though none had a sexual element and these were not taken into account by the sentencing judge, though the serious breach of trust was noted. Held. **4$^1/_2$–5 years**. As this was a reference, **3$^1/_2$ years** not 2$^1/_2$ years.

Att-Gen's Ref. No 77 of 2000 2001 2 Cr App R (S) 94. The defendant was convicted of six counts of indecent assault against his two daughters who were between the ages of 9 and 14. The defendant was a strong disciplinarian and as such his daughters feared him. The defendant began to abuse his eldest daughter when she was 10. The defendant touched the girl's breasts and vagina, digitally penetrated her and simulated sexual intercourse with her. When the defendant's younger daughter was between the ages of 9 and 13 he subjected her to abuse such as digital penetration, sucking her breasts and simulating sexual intercourse with her. The abuse was over a 4 year period. The defendant, who was 52 years of age at the time of conviction, had no previous convictions. Held. The appropriate sentence was **4 years**. As it was a reference **3 years** not 12 months.

Att-Gen's Ref. No 2 of 2001 2001 2 Cr App R (S) 524. The defendant pleaded guilty to seven counts of indecent assault against his stepdaughter when she was between the ages of 8 and 15. The defendant, who was 100% disabled and wheelchair-bound forced the victim to masturbate him and take his penis in her mouth. The defendant was 49 years of age. Held. The appropriate sentence was **5 years**. Having regard that this was a reference and the serious disability faced by the defendant which would render imprisonment more difficult to bear **2 years** was appropriate not a probation order.

Old case. *R v S* 1998 2 Cr App R (S) 17 (For summary see 1st edition of this book.)

Father/stepfather, by – Victim aged 10–12

101.25   *R v L* 1999 1 Cr App R (S) 347. The defendant pleaded guilty to six counts of indecent assault on his daughter aged 12. The offences took place over a period of 3 months when the victim was in the sole care of her father and consisted of, touching the victim's breasts and vagina, placing her hand on his erect penis when it was exposed and through his clothing and pinning her down whilst kissing her. The defendant, who was 46 years of age, had no previous convictions. The pre-sentence report said unless he addressed his offending there was a high risk of re-offending. The trial judge had regard that there was no force, no threats and no penetration but that children were entitled to protection from the courts. Held. These offences were a gross breach of trust and as the defendant was unwilling to accept the seriousness of what had happened **2 years** was not manifestly excessive.

Att-Gen's Ref. No 43 of 1999 2000 1 Cr App R (S) 398. LCJ. The defendant was convicted of two counts of indecent assault on his daughter, who was aged between 10 and 11, and one count of gross indecency. The offences took place when the victim's mother was either asleep or out of the house. The defendant rubbed his penis on the victim's vaginal area, stroked her breasts and forced the victim to hold his penis. The defendant, who was 45, had no previous convictions. The probation officer said he was unlikely to offend again. The judge noted that these were not the worst assaults imaginable as there had been no violence or threat of violence and no penetration. The defendant was sentenced to 6 months. Held. The sentence was unduly lenient. The appropriate sentence for these offences was **15–18 months**; having regard that this was a reference **9 months**. As the defendant had already served his 6 months it would be destructive and advanced no relevant public interest for him to be returned to prison.

Att-Gen's Ref. Nos. 35 etc. of 2003 Re DS 2004 1 Cr App R (S) 499 at 533. The defendant pleaded guilty to two specimen counts of indecent assault committed about 8 years earlier. About half a dozen incidents were relied on. The defendant had formally adopted the victim and was on occasions left in charge of her. He began to enter her bedroom and, first shutting the door, put his hands on her body, touched her beneath her nightdress and knickers and digitally penetrated her vagina. Despite her complaints and physical resistance, he lifted her legs and licked her vagina and genital area. The last occasion of abuse involved him seizing her by the hair and trying to force his erect penis into her mouth. The attack only ceased when she bit his penis. She had been profoundly affected by the abuse as had her mother and her brother who had witnessed it. He was 38, good character and expressed remorse. Held. The case was aggravated by the victim's young age, the different forms of abuse, the breach of utmost trust, the fact that it was repeated and that it had a significant effect on the victim and her family. A sentence of **4½–5 years** should have been imposed, hence **3½ years** as this was a reference.

Att-Gen's Ref. No 31 etc. of 2004 Re AC 2005 1 Cr App Rep (S) 377 at 389. The defendant AC pleaded guilty to fourteen counts of indecent assault on his step-daughter. His wife (the victim's mother) suffered from physical and mental health problems and was dependant on the defendant's care and support. Four years before the incident the victim (who was then 10) had told her mother that the defendant had been abusing her but no action was taken following his denials. Three years later a social worker interviewed the victim (who was then 14) who said that she had been touched between her legs by the defendant when aged between 5 and 11. The defendant admitted indecently assaulting her about once a week in a bedroom and in a lock-up garage whilst her mother was out. He had touched her genital area both over and under her pants. The defendant said that no further touching had occurred after the initial complaint, four years earlier. The victim did not wish to be interviewed on video or attend court. But for his admissions there would have been no evidence against him. She said she did not want the defendant to go to prison because she and her elder brother would have to live with her mother and care for her. She did not get on with her mother. The defendant was 44 and of good character. He had shown genuine remorse. Held. The victim's wishes were not based on a feeling that he did not deserve to go to prison. Also the judge had placed too much weight on the 3-year gap between the last offence and his sentencing. Bearing in mind the breach of trust and frequency of the offending, **3 years** would have been appropriate. As this was a reference, **2 years** with an **extended licence of 2 years** not 9 months custody with a 2 year extended licence.

Historic abuse – Guideline remarks

101.26   *Att-Gen's Ref. Nos. 91, 119 and 120 of 2002,* 2003 2 Cr App R (S) 338 In *R v Millberry* 2003 2 Cr App R (S) 142. The fact that the offences are of some age is not necessarily a sufficient reason for imposing a lesser sentence than might otherwise have been the case. In Millberry the Court said at para 17: 'in relation to "historic" cases where the offence is reported many years after it occurred. In these cases, also, we consider that the same starting point should apply. The fact that the offences are stale can be taken into account but only to a limited extent. It is, after all, always open to an offender to admit the offences and the fact that they are not reported earlier is often explained because of the relationship between the offender and the victim, which is an aggravating factor of the offence. A different factor that could cause the court to take a more lenient view than it would otherwise is the consequences, which result from the age of the offender. In these cases the experience is that the offender may be only a danger to members of the family with whom he has a relationship. So this is a dimension which can be taken into account if there is a reduced risk of re-offending.'

The same approach is equally applicable to all categories of sexual offending. Where the victims have kept secret what had happened, sometimes following threats made or inducements offered and sometimes out of a sense of shame about what has been done to her, this of itself can aggravate the harm caused by the offence. Before passing a lighter sentence because the offences are stale, the court should weigh the impact on the victim of the matter having remained secret for so long.

Historic abuse – Victim(s) aged under 10

101.27   *R v Burton-Barri* 1999 2 Cr App R (S) 252. The defendant, who was 63 when convicted, pleaded guilty to forty four counts of indecent assault, taking indecent photographs of a child and gross indecency with a child. Twenty three counts were for indecent assault, sixteen on females and seven on males. The ages were from 8 upwards. The abuse took place over a period of 25 years with children of friends of the defendant and his own stepchildren. He inveigled his way into the confidence of the parents by acts of kindness and generosity. The offences took place when the defendant offered to baby-sit the victims and included videoing the defendant performing oral sex on the victims and having the act reciprocated. Vaginal and anal penetration took place and he inserted objects into one of the victims' anus. Presents were given. The defendant was 63 with convictions in 1992 for gross indecency with a child and taking indecent photographs. Held. The sentence had to reflect the fact that although the abuse was appalling it was not as appalling as it could have been. It had to be borne in mind that the defendant should not have been sentenced as he might have been for committing rape or buggery. **10 years** not 14$\frac{1}{2}$ years was appropriate.

R v R 2000 1 Cr App R (S) 244. The defendant pleaded guilty at a late stage in the trial to four counts of indecent assault against his niece and nephew over a period of 4 years. Counts of rape and attempted buggery were not persued. When the assaults began in 1971 the victims were aged 10 and 8 respectively and the defendant was 14 years of age. The defendant digitally penetrated the female victim and performed oral sex on her. The male victim was forced to masturbate the defendant and perform oral sex on him. The defendant was arrested in 1997. He was now 41 with a number of convictions for dishonesty and violence but no sex convictions. There was no sexual misconduct for 25 years. Held. The correct approach is to sentence him with the penalty, which would have then been appropriate. These offences included a significant degree of breach of trust, however consideration must be given to the fact that the defendant was little more than a child when he committed these offences. **2 years** not 4 years was appropriate.

Att-Gen's Ref. No 15 of 2000 2001 1 Cr App R (S) 82. The defendant was convicted of nine counts of indecent assault on a girl, four counts of indecency on a boy and two counts of indecency with children. The defendant sexually abused his 3 children over a period of 11 years from 1966 to 1977. The defendant abused his eldest daughter when she was between the ages of 9 and 15 by touching her vaginal area with his hand and his penis, digitally penetrating her and masturbating in her presence. The defendant abused his adopted son when he was between the ages of 5 and 12 by forcing the boy to masturbate him and reciprocating the act and forcing his penis into the boy's anus. The defendant's adopted daughter was abused over an 18 month period between the ages of 12 and 13. The defendant masturbated in her presence, digitally penetrated the victim, forced his penis into her mouth and achieved slight vaginal penetration with his penis. The defendant who was 71 when convicted was arrested over 20 years after the offences occurred. He had no previous convictions. Due to the date that the offences took place the maximum sentences were 5 years for the counts on a girl under 13, 2 years for the offences with a female over the age of 13 and 10 years for the indecent assault on a male. Held. The appropriate sentence in this instance would have been at least **6 or 7 years**. Taking into account the defendant's age and the fact that he had poor health and his reliance on a wheelchair for movement 6 was appropriate. As it was a reference **4 years** not 2 years suspended.

Att-Gen's Ref. No 28 of 2000 2001 1 Cr App R (S) 307. LCJ. The defendant pleaded guilty to two counts of indecent assault on a girl under the age of 10 and two counts of indecency with a child. The offences began in 1973 when the victim was 4 and continued until 1980. The abuse took place on an almost daily basis, where the defendant would fondle the victim, and coerce her to masturbate him. When the girl asked him to stop he did so. The defendant, who was 51 years of age, also indecently assaulted the son of a woman with whom he lived after the failure of his marriage to the first victim's mother. His new partner found the defendant in the kitchen with the defendant's penis in the boy's mouth. He said to the boy, 'Come on swallow it.' This relationship also ended. He showed remorse and took very seriously the gravity of his offending. The reports indicated that he was not predatory and offences would only occur in the family context. He was sentenced to probation and the order was progressing well and the defendant had obtained employment. Held. The appropriate sentence would have been **3 years** on a plea. As it was a reference 2 years would have to be imposed of which the defendant would only serve 1 year. The probation order imposed by the sentencing judge was for 3 years, therefore the public would be better protected by the continuation of this order. **3 years probation order** was appropriate in these exceptional circumstances.

R v Massie 2003 1 Cr App R (S) 414. The defendant changed his plea to guilty to four counts of indecent assault. The defendant met two families through the Church and he and his wife babysat the victims. Count 1 was between 1975 and 1982 and involved a girl aged between 5 and 10 years old. He went to the victim's bedroom and pulled back the bedclothes. Next he touched the girl's vaginal area over her pants. To escape the girl used the excuse that she needed to go to the lavatory where she locked herself in. The incident was not repeated. The other counts related to three consecutive nights in 1981 or early 1982 while he babysat for another family. He committed almost exactly similar offences. That victim told her family and it was discussed privately within the church authorities and no action was taken. The counts were not specimen counts. He was now 49 with a number of convictions for dishonesty and minor violence, which save for one, were more than 20 years old. The Judge ignored them. In August 2001 the girls now in their 30s contacted the police. The defendant was interviewed and made frank admissions about the offences. The pre-sentence report referred to his remorse and the risk of re-offending was medium but reasonably well contained. It recommended a community rehabilitation order. The total sentence was 15 months with an extended sentence of 3 years. The Judge said he wanted to ensure the defendant was under supervision and subject to treatment. He had served 22 weeks in custody. Held. For offences prior to 1992, the court has no power to pass any extended sentence of the kind permitted by Section 85 of the 2000 Act. Sexual abuse of children, other than of the most minor nature, which this was not, is not normally to be described as falling short of the custody threshold. The priority here is for the rehabilitation of the defendant and the protection of the public as the Judge wanted. We intend to achieve that by substituting a **community rehabilitation order** coupled with a condition to undertake a Sex Offender Treatment Programme.

Att-Gen's Ref. Nos. 91, 119 and 120 of 2002 Re NJK 2003 2 Cr App R (S) 338 at 343. The defendant pleaded guilty to two indecent assaults and four counts of indecency with a child. Between 1993 and 1995 when a friend of the defendant's daughter was only 7 or 8 he created opportunities to be alone with the friend. He put his hand down the girl's top and rubbed her bare chest on two occasions. On two other occasions he made the girl masturbate him. Twice he made the girl take part in oral sex. She was told by him that if she mentioned it his daughter would be taken away making her lose her father. In 2001, the victim told the mother of her boyfriend and the defendant was arrested. At first he denied the offences. The offences had a profound effect on the victim and her family. The victim found it difficult to trust men and became paranoid and depressed. Her relationships suffered particularly with her mother. The mother felt guilty about making the victim stay overnight and needed anti-depressants. He was 44 with no convictions. There was genuine remorse. Held. Not less than **4 years** was appropriate. Because it was a reference **3 years** not a community rehabilitation order.

Att-Gen's Ref. Nos. 91, 119 and 120 of 2002 Re CCE 2003 2 Cr App R (S) 338 at 345. The defendant pleaded guilty at a very early stage to three indecent assaults. In 1991, while fitting windows at a house where he was working he put his hand down a six year old girl's underpants and touched her vagina. It was repeated more or less on a daily basis for three weeks. On one occasion he persuaded her to place her hand on his penis and move it up and down. She said nothing for 10 years. During this time she remained upset and angry and increasingly so. Her education suffered and she was self conscious about her body. She argued with her parents and was suspected of harming herself. The defendant was 55 with a similar conviction in 1995 for which he received 12 months. His health was poor suffering from severe back pain following an accident at work. As a result of the offences he separated from his wife. The PSR said, "He was genuinely aware of the terrible psychological harm he had caused and hates himself for it having suffered abuse as a teenager himself. He presents a continuing risk unless and until he receives treatment." Held. Had he admitted these offences in 1995 he might have received a shorter sentence. That was his fault. The consequence has been that the victim has had to live with her secret for a further six years. The sentence should have been **18 months**. As it was a reference **12 months** not 6.

Att-Gen's Ref. Nos. 35 etc. of 2003 Re EM 2004 1 Cr App R (S) 499 at 530. The defendant pleaded guilty to six counts of indecent assault on a female under 13 that occurred about 24 years earlier. The offences were against his daughter when she was between 7 and 8. He told her to go to her bedroom and sit with her legs open. He then exposed his penis and took hold of her hand and placed it on his penis. She pulled her hand away and said that she did not want to do it but the defendant took her hand again and placed it on his penis and made her masturbate him holding his hand over hers. He made her masturbate him to ejaculation. He then digitally penetrated her vagina and caused her pain. This conduct was repeated every Saturday whilst her mother was out of the house. When interviewed he denied the allegation but admitted touching her vagina on two occasions. He later pleaded on a full facts basis. He was 57 and of good character. Held. This was a gross breach of trust with a young victim and repeated over an appreciable amount of time. It had a significant impact on the victim. **3 years** would have been appropriate, but **18 months** as this was a reference and taking account of the progress he had made whilst subject to the community rehabilitation order.

Att-Gen's Ref. Nos. 35 etc. of 2003 Re AC 2004 1 Cr App R (S) 499 at 538. The defendant pleaded guilty at the Magistrates' Court to seven charges of indecent assault; five on his older daughter between 18 and 14 years earlier, two on his younger daughter two years earlier. The offences against the older daughter were committed when she was between 6 and 11. The charges were specimens and took place when the defendant and the girl were alone in his bed during the day and at night regardless of whether others were at home or not. The defendant encouraged the girl to remove her knickers and then would touch her vagina. He placed his erect penis between her thighs from behind and then thrust until he ejaculated. He did the same with her on top of him. On one occasion he grabbed her hand and placed it on his penis even though she said she did not want to touch it. The abuse continued until she refused to allow it to continue. The abuse against the younger girl started when she was aged 6. It was similar although she had masturbated him to ejaculation. He stopped seeing the younger daughter and said to police that he felt sick at what he had done. He was 47 and without previous convictions. Held. This was the abuse of two daughters involving a gross breach of trust. The assaults involved simulated intercourse and ejaculation and there were repeated indecent assaults. The period of abuse was conducted over 17 years and both victims had suffered trauma. The appropriate sentence would have been **3 years**. As it was a reference, **2 years** concurrent for each offence with a three year extended sentence for the offences against the younger victim instead of 12 months with an extended sentence of 12 months.

Old case *R v Sweeney* 1998 2 Cr App R (S) 43 (For a summary see the 1st Edition of this book.)

Historic abuse – Victim(s) aged 10–12

101.28   *R v JW* 2000 1 Cr App R (S) 234. The defendant, who was now aged 80 years, pleaded guilty to fourteen counts of indecent assault on his daughter over a period of 4 years when the girl was aged between 11 and 15. The counts were specimen counts. The offences were committed 40 years earlier. The assaults included digital penetration of her vagina, forcing the victim to touch his erect penis and to masturbate him and simulating sexual intercourse with her. The victim was threatened with violence if she did not comply. The pre-sentence report referred to his lack of insight into his responsibility. The sentencing judge noted that these offences occurred when the maximum sentence was 2 years, save where the victim was under 13, where the maximum was 5 years. Held. The offences had grave consequences. According to modern sentencing standards the appropriate sentence would perhaps go into **double figures**. For the sentencing standards at the time 8 years would have been likely on a guilty plea. Delay is a factor to be taken into account but the weight to be attached is limited. Great caution is required lest discount is accorded for what is in truth an aspect of the crime itself. Age is another factor but there is no particular ailment or hardship here. The present and future interest of the victim is of high priority. Taking into account the time that has passed and the age of the defendant **3¹/₂ years** was appropriate and will send the right message to him.

R v North 2001 1 Cr App R (S) 109. The defendant pleaded guilty to four counts of indecent assault on a girl who was between the ages of 10 and 13. The offences took place between 1979 and 1982. The defendant befriended the victim's mother and became a frequent visitor to her home. The defendant touched the girl on her vagina and masturbated in front of her. On one occasion the defendant took the victim to his home and showed her a pornographic film and held a vibrator against her, outside her clothing. There was neither penetration nor digital penetration. From 1988 the defendant sent the victim money, first, through her mother and subsequently directly. In 1998 the victim made the allegations. The defendant was now 73 years old and was treated as of good character. He showed remorse and was in failing health. The sentencing judge noted that there was not a high risk of the defendant re-offending but there was some risk to the public. Held. The defendant had groomed and trained a young girl for his own sexual gratification, and there was a grave breach of trust. If recent the sentence would in no way be excessive. The court must take into account the maximum sentence available at the time that the offences were committed, which was 5 years. On this basis alone **2 years** not 3.

R v L 2000 2 Cr App R (S) 506. The defendant pleaded guilty at the Magistrates' Court to three offences of indecent assault and one count of gross indecency. Between January and March 1991, he caused his 11 year old daughter to masturbate him on 6 or 8 occasions. Finally he had mutual oral sex with her and that brought him to his senses. Ten years later, he went to his local police station and confessed to the offences for religious reasons. He said he wanted to close this chapter in his life and handed the police a letter from his daughter saying she supported her father in his actions but did not want him to be prosecuted. She made a statement saying there had been sexual impropriety but did not want her father charged. She also said she was not affected mentally or physically by it and she "wanted to let it lie". He was 50. The Judge said he regretted that he could not find any exceptional circumstances to suspend the sentence and gave him **9 months**. He had served 2 months. Held. The offences were horrible. The fact that he promptly ceased was a very important feature of this case. Custody was not wrong in principle. The circumstances were exceptional so the sentence will be **suspended** for 2 years.

Historic abuse – Victim(s) aged 13–15

101.29 *Att-Gen's Ref. Nos. 91, 119 and 120 of 2002 Re TAG 2003* 2 Cr App R (S) 338 at 341. The defendant was convicted of two rapes, two indecent assaults and two counts of cruelty to children. He used extreme violence on his daughter for her most minor transgressions. He would strike her with a knife and throw her round the room. He abused her verbally and carved "I hate you" on her bed head. He put her in the lavatory and banged her head on the door. When she was 8 or 9 and lying between her parents in bed she woke up to find him pressing her vagina. In late 1980 or early 1981, his daughter told her friend aged 13 to wait in her bedroom. The defendant came in, pinned her against a wall, forced her to the floor and raped her. He threatened to kill her if she told anyone. Previously he had shown her pornographic and violent films. While doing this he had frequently felt her breasts. She was a virgin and since then had suffered repeated nightmares. As an adult she had matrimonial problems which needed counselling that may refer back to the rape. Between August 1980 and August 1982 he took another of her daughter's friends aged 12 or 13 on a motorbike to a field where he forced her to the ground, put his arm round her throat, slapped her and raped her. Her lip bled and he blamed her for struggling. In about 1973, when his son was 7 he severely smacked him. When he was 8 he made the boy stand on a chair in front of his sister before pulling down his trousers and whipping him with the buckle end of a belt. He was 54 and when 20 or 21 he was given a suspended sentence for rape. The PSR said there was a high risk of further offending. Held. Each rape on its own called for 8 years at least because of the age of the victim. If concurrent the total sentence should have been 12 years for each of the rapes and 3 years for each of the cruelty counts consecutive making 15 years. **15 months** was the least sentence for the assaults because of the girls' age, their vulnerability and the breach of trust. Those sentences should be concurrent to the others. Because it was a reference 11 years for the rapes and 2 years consecutive for the cruelty making 13 years not 8 years for the rapes, 3 for the cruelty and **9 months** for the assaults all concurrent.

Internet – Guideline remarks

101.30   *Att-Gen's Ref. No. 39 of 2003* 2004 1 Cr App R (S) 468. Where a man considerably older than a teenager makes contact with young girls using the internet and this leads to sexual offences against the girls, it needs to be clearly understood that sentences will be to the top of the range.

Kidnapping, and

See FALSE IMPRISONMENT/KIDNAPPING – *Sexual*

Kissing – (not breach of trust)

101.31   *R v Tabit* 2000 2 Cr App R (S) 298. The defendant, who was aged 42, was convicted of indecent assault. Both the victim, who was 18 years of age, and the defendant worked in a shop. The defendant had attempted to kiss the victim but she had said 'no'. She was frightened. The next day the victim was in the stock room and she saw him outside and locked the door. For 25 minutes the defendant kept calling the victim's name and trying to open the door. As she left the stockroom when she thought he had gone he grabbed her in a bear hug and pushed her onto some crates. He tried to kiss her twice but she pushed him away, she felt very scared. The defendant was much bigger than the victim. The victim was tearful and shaken. After the incident the victim had to leave her job. The defendant had no previous convictions. At trial the judge commented that the serious aspect was that the defendant was more than twice as old as the victim and that his actions had frightened her. The defendant's risk assessment was described as high because he continued to deny the offence. Held. This was not the most serious offence of indecent assault, therefore **4 months** not 9 months.

R v Aziz 2003 1 Cr App R (S) 40. The defendant was convicted of indecent assault. Towards dusk an 18 year old student was walking across a field at her College. The defendant walked towards her and smiled at her. She carried on and then felt his hand on her shoulder. He complimented her on her hair and she made it absolutely clear she wanted him to go. He pestered her for her name and seized her hand. She tried to pull away and he refused to let go. While he questioned her, she continued to try to pull away and when she did he grabbed her and pulled her towards him. He put his arm around her waist and tried to kiss her on the mouth, but she turned away. There was struggling for several minutes during which he kissed her on the cheek. She pushed him away but he kept hold of her hand and repeatedly questioned her. Finally she ran away. The incident had lasted between 10 and 15 minutes. She was absolutely terrified, distraught and in tears. He was arrested nearby and told police she had kissed him first and she wasn't held against her will. He was 23 and had an impeccable character. There were four references. His mother suffered severe anaemia and abdominal pains. The conviction hit him and his family hard. Because of his denials, the pre-sentence report said there was a risk of re-offending. Held. The serious element was the sheer persistence. Immediate custody was inevitable, but **8 months** not 12.

Att-Gen's Ref. No. 46 of 2001 Unreported 24/7/01. The defendant was convicted of two counts of indecent assault and pleaded guilty to one count of indecent assault. He and his wife were close friends with Mr. and Mrs. A. On occasions he kissed and touched Mrs. A inappropriately. In 1996 at his house when Mr. and Mrs. A had been invited for a meal, he grabbed Mrs. A from behind and touched her bottom. After the meal as Mr. and Mrs. A were leaving he reached between her legs and grabbed her in the area of her vagina. She then had a double mastectomy but this did not stop the defendant from continually grabbing and touching her. A couple of months later at about 10.30pm the defendant appeared uninvited in her bedroom. She went to put the kettle on and he pinned her against the patio doors. He stroked her in her vaginal region. She felt his erect penis against her and feared she might be raped. She pushed him away and ran. He followed and forced her legs apart and a dog came into the room and he left. She was extremely upset but did not tell her husband who was then a police officer. In 1997 the defendant was cautioned for indecently assaulting a female in a pet shop. He had twice kissed her and placed her hand on his erect penis. In 1999, while working as a builder he went with some marble to a customer, Mrs. E. She asked him how much it would cost and he kissed her on the cheek and said that was payment enough. While working in one of the bedrooms, he placed his hands on either side of her face and began kissing her and forcing his tongue into her mouth. She was shocked and repeatedly mentioned her children who were downstairs. She told him to leave and he grabbed her hand and placed it on his erect penis. He was arrested and charged and at the Magistrates' Court he was seen by Mr. A, who was now a security officer. Mr. A told Mr. E about the earlier matters which he had now been told about. The defendant pleaded to this later matter. He was 53 and of good character. Held. The appropriate sentence was **15–18 months**. Because it was a reference **9 months** not £1,500 fine.

Longer than commensurate sentences

101.32 *R v Langton* 1998 1 Cr App R (S) 217. The defendant pleaded guilty to indecent assault on a 10-year-old girl. The defendant was a friend of the family of the victim and had offered to baby-sit her and her two brothers. When the victim was preparing for bed the defendant went into her bedroom and watched her undress. Later in the evening the victim got up and went downstairs wearing only her nightdress and underwear. The defendant cuddled her, invited her to sit on his knee and touched her over her clothing near her vagina. She got off and ran upstairs. In interview the defendant added that he touched the girl on her chest. The defendant had two convictions for buggery of an 8 year old boy when he was 14; a conviction for indecently assaulting a young boy when he was 15 and a conviction for indecently assaulting a 6 year old girl when he was 17. The presentence report said he constituted a danger particularly to young children. The sentencing judge noted that the defendant constituted a danger to young children, and there remained a risk that he would re-offend. He passed a longer than commensurate sentence. Held. No strictly mathematical approach should be adopted in longer than commensurate cases, and it may well be that a much longer sentence than a commensurate sentence is perfectly proper, particularly in an extreme or particularly difficult case. Having regard to the risk the defendant posed **4 years** was proper.

R v Parsons 1999 Crim LR 918 Judgement 31/8/99 (the date in the report is wrong). The defendant was convicted of gross indecency with a child. In an alleyway he came towards three girls aged 13, 14 and 14 with a young boy. His penis was exposed and he was masturbating. The girls were very frightened and embarrassed. They reported it to the police who arrested the defendant who denied the offence. He was 38 and had 28 sexual convictions. Since he was 13 there was a pattern of indecent assaults or indecent exposures with women and in one case a young boy. All the other victims were teenage girls or women who were strangers to him. The last one was an attempted abduction of a girl under 16 for which he received 4 years and 3 months for indecent exposure. He was in breach of his licence for that offence with 11 months outstanding. The psychiatric report made plain that, 'he was a recidivist sex offender. There was little evidence to indicate that any of the treatment he had received had any beneficial effect. There was a high risk of re-offending.' The defendant claimed his victims enjoyed his behaviour and that it had no impact on them. He didn't want treatment because he considered those giving it were unreasonable. The Judge considered he was a grave risk and untreatable. Held. The sentence for the offence had been increased and that reflects Parliament's view that the offence is potentially very serious and damaging and should be dealt with more severely than in the past. Because of his past offending **6 years** as a longer than commensurate sentence was not manifestly excessive. The breach of licence should be consecutive not concurrent.

See also *R v Osman* 2000 2 Cr App R (S) 112. The defendant touched a woman's bottom on a tube train. He had seven convictions for indecent assault on a woman. The judge gave him 30 months. Held. The power to impose a longer than commensurate sentence could not be invoked. The requirement that the public required protection from serious harm was not present. (For further details see Train on a, Stranger)

R v D 2001 2 Cr App R (S) 281. The defendant pleaded guilty to two counts of indecent assault on a girl who was aged 5. The defendant was married to the victim's grandmother and had offered to look after the victim and her brother. The defendant began to tickle the victim's stomach and then removed her trousers and digitally penetrated her. The defendant then took the girl upstairs and made her lie on top of him so that her vagina touched his penis; he then digitally penetrated her again. The defendant, who was 29, had one previous court appearance for four offences of indecent assault against his stepdaughter aged 11, who was the victim's aunt. That abuse involved digital penetration. The sentencing judge said that this was a very revealing previous conviction. Where children are concerned 'once is too often, twice is completely and utterly unacceptable. You are an ongoing danger to children'. Held. **4 years** longer than commensurate and an extension period of 3 years was not a manifestly excessive sentence.

See also Longer than Commensurate Sentences and *Persistent offender*

Partner/acquaintance, on

101.33   *R v Coles* 1999 1 Cr App R (S) 372. The defendant was convicted of indecent assault on a woman who consented to go to his hotel room with him. He was acquitted of attempted rape. The victim had spent the evening drinking at a hen night in a hotel. The defendant met the victim in a hotel bar and they began to drink together. In the early hours of the morning the victim went with the defendant to his hotel room. As the victim tried to leave the defendant pushed her onto the bed and removed her lower clothing and all of his own clothes. When the victim escaped the defendant followed her to the lift doors and prevented her from escaping. He told her, 'You're drunk. No one will believe you.' He returned to his room but the door had closed. The victim tried to wake her room-mate and others for help. Eventually the room-mate opened the door and she ran in distressed and crying. He tried to follow her in. The incident had lasted 5–10 minutes. The defendant, who was 31 years of age, had a number of previous convictions though none involved a sexual element. Held. This was serious offence and outrageous behaviour. **2^1/$_2$ years** not 4 years was appropriate.

R v C 2000 1 Cr App R (S) 533. The defendant pleaded guilty to indecent assault on his partner, with whom he had lived for 10 years. The victim and the defendant who had been drinking had gone to bed, at which point the defendant removed her nightdress and attempted to perform oral sex upon her without her consent. He demanded that she perform oral sex on him and pulled her head to his penis. When she refused to perform oral sex he digitally penetrated her anus and vagina. This caused her pain. He threatened to bugger her unless she performed oral sex on him, which she subsequently did. She was crying and very upset. He then inserted his fingers into her vagina and anus which was painful. She attempted to escape by going to the lavatory but he accompanied her and ordered her back upstairs. She was so frightened she complied. She thought he was a different person and was treating her like an animal. He again forced her to perform oral sex while fingering her anus and vagina. When she said she had had enough he slapped her and pushed her back on the bed. Eventually he released her and she ran to her mother's house which was across the road. The incident had lasted about an hour. When interviewed he said he had been drinking heavily and admitted his behaviour to the victim had changed over recent weeks. The defendant, who was 35 years old, had previous convictions for violence but none for sexual offences. Before the offence there had been no violence in the relationship. The relationship ended but she visited him in prison. The incident happened on Friday and he pleaded guilty at the Magistrates' Court on the following Monday. **Held.** Conduct such as this, when it takes place in a well-established relationship, was just as unacceptable and unlawful as when the parties knew nothing of each other. **2¹/₂ years** not 3¹/₂ years was appropriate.

R v Sully 2000 1 Cr App R (S) 62. The defendant pleaded guilty to two counts of indecent assault on his girlfriend. The victim and the defendant had engaged in a sexual relationship for 6 years, during which time the defendant had used such objects as a vibrator and a carrot on the victim. The victim did not enjoy this form of sexual activity. On the evening of the offence the defendant drove the victim to a car park and he started to masturbate himself. She demanded to be taken home but he drove them to a remote area after stopping off to buy a cucumber. He had already equipped himself with a roll of tape and a knife. She again demanded to be taken home. The defendant told her that he wanted to have sexual intercourse with her, to which she refused. He then threatened her with a knife and said he would tape up her mouth if she refused. She begged him to let her go. He pulled down her trousers and underwear, rubbed Vaseline onto her vagina and inserted a cucumber into her whilst digitally penetrating her anus. She screamed. He forced his fingers into her anus saying he was going to bugger her. He was unable to because of her struggling. He took the cucumber out of her vagina. The victim refused to take the defendant's erect penis in her mouth and he ejaculated over her face. He released her and apologised. Throughout the incident he remained on top of her. When he arrived home he apologised and said he was going to commit suicide. The victim had scratch marks on her breast thigh and arm. The defendant, who was 34, had eight previous convictions, two of which were for violence, but none were for sexual offences. For a number of years he had fantasised about violent sex particularly anal rape. The judge noted that this attack was planned and that the defendant was totally merciless in treating the victim as a sex object. **Held.** This was a dreadful case. The combination of sexual perversions was worse than rape. **7 years** was severe but not manifestly excessive.

Persistent offender

101.34 *Att-Gen's Ref. No 47 of 1998* 1999 1 Cr App R (S) 464. The defendant pleaded guilty to five counts of indecent assault on five different women as they were using a multi-storey car park. They were on 5 different days. The defendant targeted the victims when they were alone and seized their bottoms, twice he exposed himself and on one occasion he placed his hand up the victim's skirt and touched the top of the inside of her leg. The victims were all effected by the incidents and some were psychologically damaged. The defendant was 25 and had 8 convictions for indecent assault including a conviction in 1994 for burglary with intent to commit rape, indecent assault and ABH for which he received 5 years. On his release he started to attend a Sex Offenders programme.

His first group therapy meeting was on the same day as the first offence. The psychiatrist said progress was slow and he had no victim empathy. He concluded the defendan was a grave danger to the public. His later report said, 'he was extremely dangerous partly because the defendant considers treatment a waste of time. He is an untreatable psychopath whose offending behaviour was likely to escalate.' Held. The defendant constituted a serious risk to the public and there was a serious risk that he would re-offend. **6 years** not 2 years was appropriate as a longer than normal sentence being passed under the then Criminal Justice Act 1991, s 2 (2)(b).

R v Osman 2000 2 Cr App R (S) 112. The defendant pleaded guilty at the Magistrates' Court to indecent assault on a woman. The victim was sitting next to her sister in law on a tube train. The defendant sat next to the victim and touched her bottom through his pocket. She felt very uncomfortable and turned her back towards him. He then moved several of his fingers against her bottom with his hand which was again in his pocket. She pushed him in the chest and abused him. An employee of the railway who heard the abuse reported him to the police. He was 41 with seven convictions for indecent assault on a woman. He had had probation and 21 months imprisonment. The pre-sentence report said he was a recidivist whose potential for escalating offending in the future was significant. The report also referred to the defendant's considerable progress. The judge gave him credit for seeking treatment. Held. He was a persistent offender. He was getting more prone to take risks. The Judge's approach was not consistent with the requirement that a sentence must be commensurate with the seriousness of the offence, Criminal Justice Act 1991 s 2(2)(a) (now Powers of Criminal Courts (Sentencing) Act 2000 s 80(2)(a)) The assault was brief and the victim was with a friend. The power to impose a longer than commensurate sentence could not be invoked. The requirement that the public required protection from serious harm was not present. **12 month** not 30.

Att-Gen's Ref. No 46 of 2000 2001 1 Cr App R (S) 407. LCJ. The defendant pleaded guilty to indecent assault on a 35–year-old woman in her car. The victim was visiting shops in the course of her business as a sales consultant. Having returned to her car she wrote up her report. The defendant got into the car and asked the victim for a lift. The victim found the man cheeky but not, at this point, threatening. The defendant tried to steer the car into an alley though it came to rest in a lay-by. She demanded he get out of her car. The defendant then grabbed her thigh and said, 'Come on love.' She tried to hit him and he pushed something into her ribs, saying, 'I've got a knife'. The defendant then put his hands over her breasts. He got out of her car and sped away. The whole incident lasted 10 minutes. The defendant, who was 46 years of age, had previous convictions for offences against the person, four convictions for sexual offences in 1981–8, of which three were for rape (one included an act of buggery), 21 convictions for theft and others for offences involving weapons. The 1981 three rapes were on lone women on footpaths at night. He received 7 years. In 1988 he received 6 years for robbery. The sentencing judge noted that whilst he was able to pass an extended sentence this would still not be long enough for the defendant to benefit from a sexual offender treatment programme whilst in prison. Therefore a treatment programme to last for the duration of his probation order was more appropriate. Held. The judge weighed up the competing considerations in a fair and appropriate manner. **3 years probation order** with a requirement to attend a sexual offender's treatment programme for the duration was not unduly lenient.

R v Briggs 2003 2 Cr App R (S) 615. The defendant was convicted of indecent assault. He was acquitted of kidnapping and false imprisonment based on the same incident. A 15 year old girl was walking in the rain. The defendant, now aged 46 stopped his car and offered her a lift. After about 5 minutes he rubbed her knee and said he wanted to shag her. She asked him to stop the car and she let herself out crying. She sought help at a nearby house. In 1980 he was sentenced to 7 years for rape and two serious indecent assaults. In 1986 he was sentence to 10 years for the attempted rape of an 11 year old. In 2000 he pleaded guilty to three offences involving the propositioning three women. In one he pulled up his car alongside a 16 year old girl and questioned her about sex. He asked a 40 year old woman to come to his car and she ran away. 20 minutes later he did the same to a 23 year old. The psychiatrist said he was a recidivist sexual offender. He assessed the risk of further acts of serious harm as high. The pre-sentence report referred to his emotional loneliness, empathy deficits and deviant fantasies. The risk of re-offending was assessed as very high. The Judge referred to his total lack of remorse. Held. The proved allegation was she entered his car and when she indicated she wanted nothing more he desisted. 2 years was the right commensurate sentence taking the instant offence into account. It would not be right to impose a longer than commensurate sentence of more than 1 year. However we cannot ignore his 10 years of no serious offending. So **2 years** (not longer than commensurate) with an extended sentence of 3 years, instead of 4 years for the offence made up to 8 years as a longer than commensurate sentence with a 2 year extended sentence (making total possible sentence 10 years).

See also *R v De Silva* 2000 2 Cr App R (S) 408. Children aged 6 and 8. Touching their vaginal areas in the bath. Previous for rape, buggery, indecent assault etc. **3 years** not 5 years longer than commensurate.

See also *Longer than commensurate sentences*

Prostitute, on a

101.35   *Att-Gen's Ref. No 65 of 1999* 2000 1 Cr App R (S) 554. The defendant, who was aged 43, pleaded guilty to indecent assault on a prostitute on the day his case was listed for trial. The victim was engaged by an escort agency to provide sexual services for the defendant. She visited the defendant at his flat and during sexual activity the defendant put live maggots into her vagina. She was unable to see this. As he inserted them with his finger he held her head in a tight grip. When she could see she saw a plastic bag on the bed with live maggots in it. She tried to get out but the defendant prevented her from leaving by sitting on her. She panicked and he became aggressive. He then held a knife to her face and thrust it at her four times as she tried to escape. She ran out of the house naked. The victim said the offence had had a devastating effect on her. Her college work and her family life had suffered she said beyond recognition. She didn't want to be cuddled by her husband or her children. The defendant had three previous convictions for sexual offences. The pre-sentence report said he was not motivated to reduce the risk of re-offending. Held. This was an exceptionally unpleasant and serious sexual assault and the victim was threatened with a knife, therefore **3 years** not 12 months was appropriate. [The sentence was made a longer than commensurate sentence.]

Public place, in a – Stranger

101.36   *R v Amin* 1998 1 Cr App R (S) 63. The defendant pleaded guilty to two counts of indecent assault and one count of common assault against three women in public during the early hours of the morning. The defendant approached two of the victims as they walked together and assaulted one and indecently assaulted the other by grabbing her left breast with so much force as to cause her pain. Twenty minutes later the defendant offered the third victim a lift home. When the victim declined the defendant grabbed her right breast. The defendant, who was 25, had no convictions. There was a very low risk of the defendant re-offending and his conduct was considered to be out of character. Held. These offences lay at the lower end of the scale of gravity. **6 months** not 18 months was appropriate.

Att-Gen's Ref. No 29 of 1999 2000 1 Cr App R (S) 209. The defendant, who was 37 years of age, was convicted of indecent assault on a 28-year-old female. He was acquitted of rape. The defendant offered to buy the victim a drink in a public house, which she refused. The victim delayed leaving the pub to avoid him. However, when she left she found the defendant at a bridge waiting for her. He put his hand round her shoulders and attempted to kiss her. When she resisted he placed her hands down her shorts and tried to touch her vagina. He pushed her into the driveway of a bungalow and placed both hands over her bottom and pulled her towards her. He undid his belt and pushed her on her shoulders and caused her to fall to the ground. He took hold of her shorts and underwear and pulled them to her ankles. He tried to persuade her to masturbate him but she refused. He then masturbated himself and ejaculated over her. He then rubbed his semen around her vaginal area. When she got home she was crying and shaking. The defendant had no previous convictions and a good work record. At trial he contended she consented. The sentencing judge noted that the defendant had targeted the victim and then lay in wait for her. Held. Having regard for the seriousness of the offence the proper sentence should have been $3^1/_2$–4 years. Taking into consideration that this was a reference **2 years 9 months**.

Robbery and indecent assault

See **ROBBERY** – *Sexual*

Serious attack causing terror

101.37   *R v Fletcher* 2002 2 Cr App R (S) 568. The defendant pleaded guilty to indecent assault and threats to kill. Counts of rape and false imprisonment were ordered to lie on the file. The defendant contrived a need for a business meeting at the victim's home. Previously there had been some sexual relations between them. The basis of it was fictitious. Having arrived there late in the morning with chains and handcuffs, he produced a knife and said if she wasn't quiet he would slit her throat and leave her children motherless. He indicated he would then kill himself. To survive she had to do exactly as he demanded. She was handcuffed so she could be secured with the padlock and chains. He then released the handcuffs. Then over four hours or so he demanded she underwent the most humiliating of experiences, (which understandably are not detailed). She had to kneel so he could have complete domination over her. He made her lick his feet and other parts of his body. She was completely terrified and shaking with fear. At one point he apologised with tears. Eventually after making her promise not to turn him in she drove him home. When arrested and in his defence case statement he claimed consent. He had committed a similar offence 9 years earlier in 1991. For the threats to kill and false imprisonment he received 8 years. The psychologist reports both said he minimised the seriousness of his conduct, that he had a deep personality defect and when under stress he would remain without much, if not any, hope of cure a grave danger to women. The Judge said he didn't think he had ever come across a case of indecent assault in such frightening, humiliating, long drawn-out and generally sexually disgusting circumstances. He gave him 10 years, longer than commensurate for the indecent assault when the maximum is 10. He said he had to protect women. On the threats to kill he gave him 4 years consecutive. The defence argued that the longer than commensurate sentence should not be consecutive, he should receive a discount for his plea and matters arising out of the same incident should be concurrent. Held. The Judge was right to pass a sentence to reflect the seriousness and to protect the public from a dangerous man. The principle or practice that same incident counts should be concurrent is always subject not only to exceptional circumstances but also more fundamentally to considerations of justice particularly that the total sentence must properly reflect the seriousness of the criminality involved. The Judge was right to find 10 years was too low. Here it was necessary to reflect the gravamen of the two offences and the total seriousness by consecutive sentences. It follows as the sentences are consecutive it will not be appropriate to make the sentence longer than commensurate. So **8 and 4 years consecutive**.

Should the sentence exceed the 2 year maximum sentence under Sexual Offences Act 1956 s 6?

101.38   *R v Figg* 2004 1 Cr App R (S) 409. The defendant was convicted of indecent assault. He was acquitted of rape. He had sexual intercourse with a girl just aged 13. The Judge felt obliged not to exceed the maximum for the (old) Sexual Offences Act 1956 s 6. Held. The judge was wrong to consider he was bound by the maximum for the other offence. The maximum for section 6 of 2 years was manifestly inadequate.

R v Cronshaw 2005 1 Cr App R 469. The defendant was acquitted of rape but convicted of unlawful sexual intercourse with a girl under 16 and two offences of indecent assault on the same girl. The Judge gave him $3^1/_2$ years. The defence argued he should not be sentenced more for the indecent assaults than for sexual intercourse (maximum sentence 2 years). Eight earlier authorities were reviewed. Held. In *R v Jones* 2003 2 Cr App R (S) 134 not cited in *R v Figg* 2004 1 Cr App R (S) 409, there is a settled practice in treating 2 years as the maximum appropriate for indecent assault bought where a charge under Section 6 would have been brought had not the 12 month time limit not expired. Whether that settled practice applies depends on the facts of any case. The principle lying behind the practice is that it would not be fair or appropriate to do so, see *R v Quayle* 1993 14 Cr App R (S) 726 and *R v Hinton* 1995 16 Cr App R (S) 523. Cases where it would apply are where indecent assault is indicted because the time limit has expired and where the indecent assault is the foreplay leading to the sexual intercourse. In other cases such as *R v Figg* 2004 1 Cr App R (S) 409 where Section 6 was unlikely to be charged the practice may not apply. If the acts of indecent assault are separate and distinct as they were in R v Figg 2004 regarded as acts of grooming by a man considerably older it would not apply. We do not see R v Figg 2004 overruling the earlier authority. The sentence was rearranged. 2 years with an 18 month extended period substituted.

Teachers   See **Breach of trust – Teachers**

Touching over the clothes

101.39   *Att-Gen's Ref. 70 Of 2003* 2004 2 Cr App R (S) 254. The defendant pleaded guilty on the first day of trial to indecent assault on a 10 year old girl. He lived near the girl's family and knew them well. With her father's permission she went with the defendant to the end of his garden to look at fox cubs. He touched and rubbed her over her clothes on the chest area. She walked away and told her parents. He pleaded guilty on the basis, which was accepted, that he rubbed her chest; he made a comment about Page 3 and said she would grow; that he intended his behaviour as a joke although he now accepted it was inappropriate. A report from a probation officer said the defendant had only a limited awareness of the consequences of the offence. He assessed the likelihood of re-offending as low. He concluded the only alternatives were treatment at a sex offenders' centre or a CD and/or a curfew order. A further report assessing his suitability for the sex offenders' course expressed the same concerns about the defendant's lack of understanding of his offence and its effects. Because he denied any sexual intent he was not suitable for the treatment course. The defendant, 64, had effectively no previous convictions and nothing of this nature. He declined to move after these events, so the victim's family moved. The victim was somewhat anxious about meeting the defendant in the area. Held. The £500 compensation order made to the victim was inappropriate and should not have been made. The right sentence would have been **a community rehabilitation order.** This would have given a probation officer the opportunity to discuss the offence with him and may have resulted in him having treatment. The **CD** for 3 years was lenient but not unduly lenient.

Train, on a – Stranger

101.40   *R v Tanyildiz* 1998 1 Cr App R (S) 362. The defendant was convicted of indecent assault on a woman who was travelling on a tube train. Two plain clothes police officers noticed the defendant, who was 34, boarding different tube trains and standing close behind female passengers. He was described as being sexually aroused on at least one occasion. The victim described how the defendant had pushed his erect penis against her bottom on three separate occasions during her journey. The defendant was a political asylum seeker and was of good character. Held. Offences of this nature were easy to commit and difficult to detect and were highly unpleasant and could be frightening for the victim. Taking account of his inability to speak English and his problems in Turkey, **3 months** not 6 months was appropriate.

R v Yazbek 1998 1 Cr App R (S) 406. The defendant was convicted of indecent assault on a woman who was travelling on an underground tube train. The defendant stood unnaturally close to the victim and was reluctant to move as other passengers wanted to board the train. The victim felt the defendant rubbing himself against her groin area and was observed rubbing his right upper arm across her right breast. The defendant, who was 62 years of age, had no previous convictions. The sentencing judge noted that the defendant had caused the victim shock, humiliation, and degradation and took advantage of her intentionally. Held. **3 months** was not an excessive sentence.

R v Diallo 2000 1 Cr App R (S) 426. The defendant was convicted of indecent assault on a woman on an underground train. The victim was travelling to work and had to stand as there were no seats on the tube. The victim felt the defendant rubbing himself across her buttocks. The defendant, who was 30, was French and of previous good character. He was assessed as suitable for CSO but in need of supervision. The judge noted that this assault was pre-meditated and was serious because it lasted several minutes, rather than a matter of seconds. Held. **3 months** was not an excessive sentence.

R v Osman 2000 2 Cr App R (S) 112. The defendant pleaded guilty to indecent assault on a woman at the Magistrates' Court. The victim was sitting next to her sister in law on a tube train. The defendant sat next to the victim and touched her bottom through his pocket. She felt very uncomfortable and turned her back towards him. He then moved several of his fingers against her bottom with his hand which was again in his pocket. She pushed him in the chest and abused him. An employee of the railway who heard the abuse reported him to the police. He was 41 with seven convictions for indecent assault on a woman. He had had probation and 21 months imprisonment. The pre-sentence report said he was a recidivist whose potential for escalating offending in the future was significant. The report also referred to the defendant's considerable progress. The judge gave him credit for seeking treatment. Held. He was a persistent offender. He was getting more prone to take risks. The Judge's approach was not consistent with the requirement that a sentence must be commensurate with the seriousness of the offence, Criminal Justice Act 1991 s 2(2)(a) (now Powers of Criminal Courts (Sentencing) Act 2000 s 80(2)(a)) The assault was brief and the victim was with a friend. The power to impose a longer than commensurate sentence could not be invoked. The requirement that the public required protection from serious harm was not present. **12 month** not 30.

Uninvited intruder – Stranger

101.41   *R v Woodcock* 1998 1 Cr App R (S) 383. The defendant was convicted of indecent assault. At 1.55am the defendant, who was 35, was let into the victim's house by someone else and then barged his way into the victim's bed-sitting room. She was 21 and made it plain she did not want him there. He was drunk, she was undressed and ready for bed. He put his hand under her quilt and touched the victim's knee and made lewd comments about her body. The defendant requested that the victim masturbate him, although she refused he exposed his penis to her. She said she was crying with fright. The defendant fell asleep and she was able to escape. Wearing only a nightdress she went to a call box and called the police. Real terror could be heard in her voice. The defendant had several previous convictions for violence, though none for sexual violence. Held. The barging in was a serious aggravating feature. **2 years** not 33 months was appropriate.

Victim under 10

101.42   *Att-Gen's Ref. No. 141 of 2001* 2003 1 Cr App R (S) 28. The defendant pleaded guilty at the Magistrates' Court to five offences of indecent assault and four of gross indecency. His step grandson, K aged 5 complained the defendant had touched his penis. He immediately admitted it and said he had abused three of the other step grandchildren. Two were girls, D and K (same letter unfortunately) both born in 1992. One was a boy, S born in 1990. He said he would go to the police but he went abroad. Eleven days later he returned and went to the police. He told them it was opportunistic and he needed help. Further he was abused as a boy and never hurt them. When interviewed he said he had abused S when he was 5 on 4 or 5 occasions. Both would be naked and the boy would be asked to lie down and the defendant would lie on top of him with his penis between the boy's legs. The boy would be asked to close his legs and the defendant would simulate intercourse until he ejaculated. The boy's penis would also be touched. On other occasions he would put his hand down S's trousers. D was abused from 5 onwards on a fortnightly or monthly basis in much the same way as S. He also touched and kissed her vagina and on one occasion put his penis in her mouth. Over 4 years there were over one hundred assaults on her. The girl K was only abused twice. That was similar including kissing and touching her vagina. The boy K was also abused twice in the same way. The defendant said if the boy told anyone he would never see his grandfather again. There was a gross indecency and indecent assault for each child and an extra indecent assault for D. He was now 49 and on life licence for murder and attempted murder with firearms imposed in 1975. In 1989 he was convicted of indecently assaulting a boy aged 8 or 9. He received a conditional discharge. The Judge sentenced him to $3^{1}/_{2}$ years on each and extended his licence to 18 months. Held. We would have expected a total sentence of **5–6 years. $4^{1}/_{2}$ years** substituted with the extension remaining.

Att-Gen's Ref No 79 of 2004 2005 1 Cr App R (S) 619. The defendant pleaded guilty on re-arraignment to twenty three counts comprising five counts of indecent assaults on a female, ten counts of making an indecent photograph of a child and eight counts of possession of an indecent photograph of a child. The defendant was a GP. Over a period of seven months he indecently assaulted five of his female patients by conducting unnecessary or inappropriate vaginal examinations. Sometimes he recorded these examinations using a hidden digital camera. Count one of indecent assault related to a woman who complained of feeling sick after eating. On her third visit he conducted a vaginal examination without wearing gloves, inserting a speculum inside her, then with gloves he rubbed her clitoris and conducted a high internal examination, which lasted for five minutes. She noticed that a tissue box close to her had a hole cut out through which she could see a lens. She later complained to her mother and a nurse in the surgery. The tissue box with the circular hole was found. Eventually police examined the GP's home computer and found recordings of the defendant examining undressed female patients. They also discovered child pornography downloaded from the Internet. This victim then lost confidence in the medical profession and her relationship with her partner broke down. Count two of indecent assault related to a 74 year old woman who was extremely vulnerable with cognitive impairment as well as physical disabilities. One of the sequences in the home computer showed the defendant examining her at home. He did not wear gloves; he fondled her breasts; he helped her remove her pants to expose her private parts; he rubbed her clitoris and digitally penetrated her; he massaged her buttocks and placed his penis against them; and he made her kneel down on the bed and having exposed her vaginal area filmed her from behind. She was not told of the offences committed against her. Count 4 was the making of an indecent image of a nine year old girl. A sequence in the home computer showed her removing her tights and then a view of her perineum. She had been taken to see the defendant by her father and the defendant had said that he needed to take a vaginal swab. Counts five and six related to the indecent assault and the taking of an indecent photograph of a seven year old girl. Again there was a sequence in the computer showing the defendant's ungloved hand repeatedly massaging her clitoris and parting her labia. The girl's mother had taken her to the surgery because the girl suffered from stomach cramps and wet herself. The defendant said he would have to take a vaginal swab and conduct an internal examination. The girl's mother had been present during the examination but had not been aware of what he was doing. In view of her age the girl was not told of the sexual nature of the conduct against her but she was told the defendant did something wrong and that he took photographs of her. She no longer trusted doctors and became distressed and worried when she had to see one. She had been a confident child but needed, after this, to be chaperoned and did not like being away from her family. Her mother was also distressed by what happened in her presence. Count seven of indecent assault related to an unknown female seen in a sequence on the computer; the defendant was stimulating her clitoris with no medical justification. The last count of indecent assault, count nine, related to a fifteen year old girl who was taken to the defendant with a vaginal discharge. Her mother was present at the examination. She saw him persisting in a rubbing motion. He spent two minutes with his hand under the sheet rubbing the girl's vagina. This victim showed a significant change in her personality and attitude to men, becoming withdrawn and unable to forget the incident. She lost interest in her proposed career as a beauty therapist. Counts 11–26 were sample counts relating to indecent images found on his computer downloaded from the Internet, none of them depicting his patients. In all 1600 indecent images were retrieved. The vast majority were at level 1, but there were twenty three at level 2, thirty five at level 3, eighteen at level 4 and one at level 5. The aggravating features were said to be that these offences were committed against patients in a gross breach of trust; they were repeated and six patients were the victims of the misbehaviour; at least four of the patients had their examinations recorded; some of the indecent assaults involved penetration; some of the victims were particularly vulnerable by reason of age and, in the case of the elderly patient, mental impairment; that patient also suffered indignities and was treated in a particularly humiliating and degradin fashion; the offences had a considerable impact on the lives of some of the victims and there was a very large number of indecent images of children found. The defendant, 30, was of previous good character and demonstrated genuine remorse. He was shy and introverted with a skin disorder. Reports showed him to have a medium risk of re-offending which would arise if he had access to children or vulnerable adults in the future. Held. It was pertinent that there were serious consequences to at least three victims. There was high degree of culpability because of the breach of trust of the doctor-patient relationship. This was a case where a deterrent element in relation to doctors or those acting as doctors should be incorporated into the sentencing process. The appropriate sentence would have been at least an **extended sentence of 8 years** with a custodial element of **5¹/₂ years,** not an extended sentence of 5¹/₂ years with a custodial element of 3¹/₂ years. As this was a reference **4¹/₂ years** custody extended to **8 years**.

See also *Breach of trust – Friend of Victim's Family – Victim Less than 10 Less than 4 Years Appropriate*

Victim aged 10–12

See *Breach of Trust – Friend of Victim's Family – Victim Aged 10–12 Breach of Trust* and *Victim Aged 10–12 –Teacher Victim Aged 10–12*

Victim aged 13–15 – less than 2 years appropriate

101.43   *R v Martley* 2000 1 Cr App R (S) 416. The defendant pleaded guilty to indecent assault on a 15-year-old girl. The victim was walking home at night having spent the evening drinking a considerable amount of alcohol. The defendant met the victim and began to help her home. The two kissed each other and the victim voluntarily pulled down her trousers and underwear. The defendant attempted, unsuccessfully, to have sexual intercourse with the victim and subsequently digitally penetrated her. This caused a small tear. She became nauseous and vomited. All sexual activity stopped. She tried to resume kissing but he wasn't interested. She was sick again and he offered to take her home. She declined the offer and asked him to leave as she would look after herself. An hour later a woman found her and the victim made no complaint. The defendant saw police tape at the scene and thought she had been murdered and went to the police station. The age gap between the two was 'limited.' The defendant was of previous good character and in work. The judge noted that the defendant, knowing the victim was drunk, had taken gross advantage of the situation. Held. As the activity was consensual the offence could have been charged as attempted unlawful sexual intercourse, for which the maximum is 2 years. The judge did take into account the defendant's guilty plea therefore he must have had a starting point which exceeded that for unlawful sexual intercourse therefore **9 months** not 2 years.

R v Stapley 2001 1 Cr App R (S) 302. LCJ. The defendant pleaded guilty at the Magistrates' Court to indecent assault on a 13 year old girl. The defendant met the victim through her 15-year-old friend who delivered newspapers to the defendant's home. The two girls were walking past the defendant's home just after Christmas when he told them that he had a present for them and invited them into his house. The defendant showed the girls two photographs of himself, one showed him with an erect penis and the other with a naked woman. The defendant undid the blouse of the victim and placed his hands on her breasts and fondled them. The girls left and he gave them £10. They went to a shop and he followed them and remained outside for about 20 minutes. The girls left after he had gone. The defendant, who was 67 years of age, had no previous convictions. As a result of his conviction he had lost his home. Held. The defendant did not use violence towards the victim and the girls were not involuntarily detained. **1 year** was appropriate not 2.

See also **Breach of Trust – Workplace – Victim Aged 13–152**

Victim 13–15 – Cases – 2 years or more appropriate

101.44   *R v Blackman* 1998 2 Cr App R (S) 280. The defendant was convicted of indecent assault on a 14 year old girl. He was acquitted of attempted rape. The defendant went driving with the victim whom he knew. The victim accepted that she comforted the defendant whose grandfather had recently died and that she kissed him and lowered her own trousers and underwear. The defendant then attempted to have sexual intercourse with her and masturbated over her pubic area. The victim who was a virgin found it very, very distressing. The defendant, who was 20, had no previous convictions. He was sentenced on the basis that he knew that the victim did not consent. Held. **2$\frac{1}{2}$ years** was severe but not excessive.

R v Wellman 1999 2 Cr App R (S) 162. The defendant was convicted of indecent assault on a 13-year-old girl. The victim was a friend of the defendant's 14-year-old daughter, with whom he lived. The defendant supplied the girls with a considerable amount of alcohol and eventually the victim became sick. The victim and her friend shared the defendant's double bed, whilst he slept on the sofa. The victim woke three times during the night and found the defendant in the bed. On the second occasion he had his hand down the girl's pyjama trousers and on the third occasion his hands were inside her underwear after which her digitally penetrated her vagina. The defendant, who was 58, had previous convictions though none of a sexual nature and none of any kind in recent years. Held. **2 years** was entirely appropriate.

R v Parsons 1999 Crim LR 918 Judgement 31/8/99 (the date in the report is wrong). The defendant was convicted of gross indecency with a child. In an alleyway he came towards three girls aged 13, 14 and 14 with a young boy. His penis was exposed and he was masturbating. The girls were very frightened and embarrassed. They reported it to the police who arrested the defendant who denied the offence. He was 38 and had 28 sexual convictions. Since he was 13 there was a pattern of indecent assaults or indecent exposures with women and in one case a young boy. All the other victims were teenage girls or women who were strangers to him. The last one was an attempted abduction of a girl under 16 for which he received 4 years and 3 months for indecent exposure. He was in breach of his licence for that offence with 11 months outstanding. The psychiatric report made plain that, 'he was a recidivist sex offender. There was little evidence to indicate that any of the treatment he had received had any beneficial effect. There was a high risk of re-offending.' The defendant claimed his victims enjoyed his behaviour and that it had no impact on them. He didn't want treatment because he considered those giving it were unreasonable. The Judge considered he was a grave risk and untreatable. Held. The sentence for the offence had been increased and that reflects Parliament's view that the offence is potentially very serious and damaging and should be dealt with more severely than in the past. Because of his past offending 6 years as a longer than commensurate sentence was not manifestly excessive. The breach of licence should be consecutive not concurrent.

R v Cronshaw 2005 1 Cr App Rep (S) 469. The defendant was convicted of one offence of unlawful sexual intercourse and two offences of indecent assault. He was acquitted of rape. The victim was 14 with a mental age of 12. She ran away from home and met the defendant by chance. He invited her back to his flat where she was given food and a bath. He undressed her before digitally penetrating her, having oral intercourse and then full intercourse (using a condom). The following morning, she said she was 15. She remained at the flat for another two days but there was no further sexual activity. The defendant tried to persuade her to contact her family. Police attended the flat for unrelated reasons and asked how old she was. She initially gave false details, supported by the defendant before he admitted that she was under 16. He maintained that he thought that she was over 16 at the time of the intercourse and that she had at all times consented. He presented a significant risk of harm and expressed no remorse. She had been a virgin and was clearly vulnerable. He was 24 with no previous violent or sexual offences. Held. On the facts, the only proper basis for sentencing the defendant was that whilst he may have believed that she was consenting to all of the activities, he knew that she was under 16. There is a settled practice in treating 2 years' imprisonment as the maximum sentence appropriate to a charge of indecent assault brought in the circumstances where a charge of unlawful sexual intercourse would have been properly brought, but for the expiry of the 12 month time limit relating to that offence. Here, the indecent assaults, albeit separately charged, could properly be regarded as being part of the prelude or foreplay to the act of intercourse and therefore the convention is applicable. For the indecent assaults concurrent extended sentences of **3 years 6 months** were appropriate, with the custodial term at **2 years** (not $3^1/_2$ years custodial).

See also **Breach of Trust – Police Officer– Victim Aged 13–15** and **Deception, by Pretending to be a Doctor – Victim Aged 13–15**

Victims under 16 who consent – Guideline remarks

101.45   *R v L* 2000 2 Cr App R (S) 506. The defendant pleaded guilty to three counts of indecent assault on girls aged around 13 or 14. The defence argued relying on R v Hinton 16 Cr App R (S) 525 that although the maximum is 10 years the maximum for unlawful sexual intercourse with a girl aged 13–15 is only 2 years so where there are sexual acts falling short of sexual intercourse there should be a judicially imposed maximum of 2 years. Held. The Judge was right to accept that argument.

Violence, injuries caused

101.46   *Att-Gen's Ref. No 31 of 2000* 2001 1 Cr App R (S) 386. The defendant pleaded guilty to indecently assaulting an 18-year-old female student and to common assault. After an evening out the victim waited to board a bus and became aware of the defendant and his companion. On the bus she was very worried about the defendant and his companion. He left the bus at the same time as her and ran up behind her without warning. He grabbed her vaginal area from behind. She pushed her hands back and he released his grip. He then attempted to grab her breasts from behind but her heavy jacket prevented him from doing so. She was able to pull free. The defendant then attempted to put his hand up the victim's skirt. He said words to the effect, 'you really want it'. She tried to walk away but he kept grabbing her. When a couple came near he walked away and when they were out of sight he ran after her. He then tried to put his hand up her skirt a third time. She screamed for her mother and he punched her in the face. Her screams were heard and he ran off. She sustained bruising. The incident effected the victim very adversely. She had nightmares and avoided the company of men. Her studies were affected. The defendant was also 18 years old and of good character. Held. The effect of this on the victim is a very important consideration. Women are entitled to walk home without fear of being attacked by men. A probation order was an unduly lenient sentence. **18 months YOI** was an appropriate sentence. It was not necessary to extend the licence.

Att-Gen's Ref. No 83 of 1999 2001 2 Cr App R (S) 511. The defendant was convicted of indecent assault on a woman at a New Year's Eve party. The victim attended the party with her boyfriend. She proposed to him over the loudspeaker and he accepted. She later went outside to get some fresh air. The defendant aged 31, approached her and threatened her with a 9' metal file. He then punched and dragged her away from the club where he inserted the metal file into her vagina several times. The defendant then inserted his fist inside her. The defendant punched the victim whilst the file was inside her. The blows rendered her unconscious. She was taken to hospital in an ambulance in considerable pain. She had bruises to her forehead, grazing on the nose, swollen lips and friction type graze marks in her private parts. She also had an unpleasant vaginal discharge. He had no convictions and was of exemplary character. Held. The appropriate sentence was **6 years**. As it was a reference **5 years** was appropriate not 3 years.

Old case *Att-Gen's Ref. No 39 of 1997* 1998 2 Cr App R (S) 336 (For a summary of this case see the 1st edition of this book.)

Workplace, at

101.47   *R v Wakefield and Lancashire* 2001 Times 12/1/01 Judgment 6/11/00. The defendants W and L were convicted of indecent assault on a work colleague aged 50. They were 41 and 33. L in front of others pushed the victim against a filing cabinet and simulated intercourse with her and grabbed her between the legs. It was repeated and she had to leave work as she was severely depressed. Held. This was prolonged, humiliating and degrading. L was a cowardly bully and W was in a position of authority and did nothing about it. W then assaulted her. Held. Women were entitled to be protected. **12 and 21 months** were unimpeachable.

See also **Breach of Trust – Workplace**

INDECENT PHOTOGRAPHS

See **PORNOGRAPHY**

102 INFANTICIDE

102.1 Infanticide Act 1938 s 1

A woman causing the death of her child when her mind was disturbed

Indictable only Maximum life

Dangerous Offender provisions For offences committed on or after 4/4/05 where there is a significant risk to members of the public of serious harm etc. there is a mandatory duty to pass a life sentence when it is justified and otherwise a sentence of imprisonment for public protection[41]. For offenders under 18 the duty is to pass detention for life, detention for public protection or an extended sentence[42].

Sexual Offences Prevention Order There is a discretionary power to make this order when it is necessary to protect the public etc[43].

Working with children Where the defendant is aged 18 or over and she is sentenced to 12 months or more or a hospital order etc. the court must disqualify him/her from working with children unless satisfied s/he is unlikely to commit any further offences against a child when the court must state its reasons for not doing so[44]. For a defendant aged less than 18 at the time of the offence the court must order disqualification if s/he is sentenced to 12 months or more and the court is satisfied that the defendant will commit a further offence against a child[45]. The court must state its reasons for so doing.

Sentencing notes The Judge will normally be greatly influenced by the psychiatric reports. Usually the Judge will show understanding and give assistance rather than punishment while recognising the importance that a life has been taken.

See also **MOTHERS**

103 INFORMANTS/GIVING EVIDENCE FOR THE PROSECUTION

103.1 The going rate for a plea of guilty at the Crown Court is up to $^1/_3$ off. If the plea is indicated at the Magistrates' Court more than $^1/_3$ can be discounted. If the defendant gives evidence for the prosecution s/he can expect up to another $^1/_3$ off. The Court of Appeal tends to work on a 50% discount for giving evidence and plea, which is not so generous. It is expected the Crown Court will continue with their approach as a person who may risk his/her life and will endure a difficult time in prison should expect at least the same discount for giving evidence, ($^1/_3$), as the man who pleads guilty ($^1/_3$).

Articles

103.2 For an article about the law and some problems that have arisen see Archbold News 2003 2 December p 5.

General principles

103.3 *R v King* 1986 82 Cr App R 120 at 122. LCJ. One then has to turn to the amount by which the starting figure should be reduced. The quality and quantity of the material disclosed by the informer is one of the things to be considered, as well as accuracy and the willingness or otherwise of the informer to confront other criminals and to give evidence against them in due course if required in court. Another aspect to consider is

41 Criminal Justice Act 2003 s 225
42 Criminal Justice Act 2003 s 226 and 228
43 Sexual Offences Act 2003 s 104 & Sch. 5
44 Criminal Justice and Court Services Act 2000 s 28
45 Criminal Justice and Court Services Act 2000 s 29

the degree to which he has put himself and his family at risk by reason of the information he has given; in other words the risk of reprisal. The reasoning behind this practice is expediency. It is to the advantage of law-abiding citizens that criminals should be encouraged to inform upon their criminal colleagues. They know that if they do so they are likely to be the subject of unwelcome attention, to say the least, for the rest of their lives. They know that their days of living by crime are probably at an end. Consequently, an expectation of substantial mitigation of what would otherwise be the proper sentence is required in order to produce the desired result, namely the information. The amount of that mitigation, it seems to us, will vary from about $\frac{1}{2}$ to $\frac{2}{3}$ reduction according to the circumstances.

R v A and B 1999 1 Cr App R (S) 53. LCJ. Where defendants co-operate with the prosecuting authorities, not only by pleading guilty but by testifying or expressing willingness to testify, or making a witness statement which incriminates a co-defendant, they will ordinarily earn an enhanced discount, particularly where such conduct leads to the conviction of a co-defendant or induces a co-defendant to plead guilty. It has been the long standing practice of the courts to recognise by a further discount of sentence the help given, and expected to be given, to the authorities in the investigation, detection, suppression and prosecution of serious crime: see for example *R v Sinfield* 1981 3 Cr App R (S) 258; *R v King* 1985 7 Cr App R (S) 227 and *R v Sivan* 1988 10 Cr App R (S) 282. The extent of the discount will ordinarily depend on the value of the help given and expected to be given. Value is a function of quality and quantity. If the information is accurate, particularised, useful in practice, and hitherto unknown to the authorities, enabling serious criminal activity to be stopped and serious criminals brought to book, the discount may be substantial.

Danger, the defendant exposes him/herself to

103.4   *R v A and B* 1999 1 Cr App R (S) 53. LCJ. Where by supplying valuable information to the authorities, a defendant exposes himself or his family to personal jeopardy, it will be ordinarily recognised in the sentence passed.

Document handed to the judge about an informant – Procedure

103.5   *R v X* 1999 2 Cr App R (S) 294. The defendant pleaded guilty to a number of burglaries. A confidential document prepared by a police officer at a high level was passed to the judge. Prosecution counsel began a Public Interest Immunity application before the judge over the document. The defence asked to see the document and the judge refused the request. Held. The proper principles to be followed are:

1   It is convenient to remember that a document of this kind is supplied at the request of the defendant.

2   Except to the extent that the defendant's contention that he has given assistance is supported by the police, it will not generally be likely that the sentencing judge will be able to make any adjustment in sentence. A defendant's unsupported assertion to that effect is not normally likely to be a reliable basis for mitigation.

3   The courts must rely very heavily upon the greatest possible care being taken, in compiling such a document for the information of the judge. The judge will have to rely upon it, without investigation, if police enquiries are not to be damaged or compromised and other suspects, guilty or innocent, are not to be affected. The document in the present case had not been prepared with sufficient care. Those who prepare such documents, and senior officers who verify them, must realise the importance of ensuring that they are complete and accurate.

4   Except in very unusual circumstances, it will not be necessary, nor will it be desirable for a document of this kind to contain the kind of details which would attract a public interest immunity application.

5   If very exceptionally such a document does contain information attracting a public interest immunity consideration, then the usual rules about the conduct of such an application will apply. In particular, the Crown Court (Criminal Proceedings and Investigation Act) (Disclosure) Rules 1997 will apply. The defence can and should be told of the public interest immunity application.

6   Absent any consideration of public interest immunity, which we take to be the general position, a document of this kind should be shown to counsel for the defence, who will no doubt discuss its contents with the defendant. That is not, we emphasise, because it will be necessary to debate its contents, but it is so that there should be no room for any unfounded suspicion that the judge has been told something potentially adverse to the defendant without his knowing about it. A defendant is entitled to see documents put before the trial judge on which he is to be sentenced. Expeditions to the judge's chambers should not be necessary in these cases. There should never normally be any question of evidence being given, nor of an issue being tried upon the question of the extent of the information provided.

7   If the defendant wishes to disagree with the contents of such a document, it is not appropriate for there to be cross-examination of the policeman, whether in court or in chambers. The policeman is not a Crown witness, he has simply supplied material for the judge, at the request of the defendant. It would no doubt be possible, in an appropriate case, for a defendant to ask for an adjournment to allow any opportunity for further consideration to be given to the preparation of the document. Otherwise, if the defendant does not accept what the document says, his remedy is not to rely upon it. Cross-examination on the usefulness of the information would almost inevitably be contrary to the public interest. It would be likely to damage enquiries still in train, trials yet to come, suspects guilty or innocent and quite possibly the defendant in the instant case.

8   No doubt, the learned judge should ordinarily disregard such a document, if asked by the defendant to do so. In such case, he will no doubt not then be minded to entertain any submission that the defendant has given valuable assistance to the police.

9   If the judge does take the document into consideration he will, no doubt, say no more than is in accordance with the present practice, namely that he has taken into consideration all the information about the defendant, with which he has been provided.

Giving evidence in the first trial but not in the re-trial

103.6   *R v Guy* 1999 2 Cr App R (S) 24. The defendant gave evidence in the first trial and the co-defendant was convicted. The Court of Appeal quashed the conviction and the defendant did not give evidence at the retrial. The co-defendant was acquitted. Held. The appropriate discount here is 50%. His failure to give evidence in the 2nd trial should not be held against him. If he had given evidence, a further slight reduction might have been justified.

Family informing on the defendant

See **SUPPLY OF DRUGS (A, B AND C)** – *Informing on the defendant, family*

Future help

103.7   *R v A and B* 1999 1 Cr App R (S) 53. LCJ. Account will be taken of help given and reasonably expected to be given in the future.

See also *Sentence, information given after*

Giving evidence in major cases

103.8   *R v Sehitoglu and Ozakan* 1998 1 Cr App R (S) 89. The defendants S and O made early guilty pleas to conspiracy to possessing heroin. S gave information and evidence in a linked murder case, which his part had been crucial. He had also given information and assistance in a significant drugs conspiracy. He was due to give evidence in that case and he was described as the lynch pin in both cases. He and his family were very seriously at risk. The police were satisfied his account was true and accurate. The judge started at 25 years for S and reduced it to 15 because of the assistance he had given. Held. The case falls into the highest category of drug trafficking. On a trial the sentence for O and S would be in the region of 24 years. The information, assistance, evidence given and the risks to S and his family mark this as a case where the maximum possible reduction should be made. Applying *R v King* 1985 7 Cr App R (S) 227 the reduction for S should be? off the starting figure before one considers the plea. The sentence should then be reduced to **8 years**.

R v Guy 1999 2 Cr App R (S) 24. The defendant pleaded guilty to importing cocaine. The defendant, his then girlfriend, and her child were stopped by customs officers at Gatwick airport after a flight from Jamaica when they were on route to Manchester. A search of their luggage revealed packages of 3.95 kilos of cocaine, which at 100% purity was 2.29 kilos. The packages were replaced with dummies. Guy and his girlfriend were arrested and he was frank with the customs officers and he co-operated with them. Later that day different customs officers met the defendant in Manchester. The co-accused was expected to meet the defendant there and he too was arrested. His co-accused was tried, convicted and received 12 years. The defendant gave evidence against him. He also gave also gave significant information to Customs. The defendant received 8 years. The co-accused's conviction was quashed on appeal and he was acquitted at the retrial. The defendant did not give evidence in that trial. He was 26 and was a person of positive good character. Held. The sentence on the co-accused was entirely appropriate. The defendant was significantly less involved than him. The starting point in the case of Guy ought to have been 10 years. He was entitled to 50% discount so **5 years** instead.

Poor information

103.9   *R v A and B* 1999 1 Cr App R (S) 53. LCJ. If the information given is unreliable, vague, lacking in practical utility or already known to the authorities, no identifiable discount may be given or, if given, any discount will be minimal.

Sentence, information given after

103.10   *R v A and B* 1999 1 Cr App R (S) 53. LCJ. The defendants A and B pleaded guilty to importing ecstasy. The sentencing judge was told they were already assisting Customs. At the Court of Appeal the police said there was additional information given which related to a major mostly international crime. This information was found to be correct. Also there was further information which was described as high in the scale of valuable intelligence. Held. If a defendant is sentenced following a contested trial without supplying valuable information before sentence or expressing willingness to do so, the Court of Appeal will not ordinarily reduce a sentence to take account of information supplied by the defendant after sentence. So much is made clear by *R v Waddingham* 1983 5 Cr App R (S) 66 at 68–9, with commentary at 1983 Crim LR 492; *R v Debbag and Izzet* 1991 12 Cr App Rep(S) 733 at 736–7 and *R v X* 1994 15 Cr App R (S) 750 with commentary at 1994 Crim LR 469. The reason for this general rule is that the Court of Appeal is a court of review; its function is to review sentences imposed at first instance, not to conduct a sentencing exercise of its own from the beginning. Thus it relies entirely, or almost entirely, on material before the sentencing court. A defendant who has denied guilt and withheld all co-operation before conviction and sentence cannot hope to negotiate a reduced sentence in the Court of Appeal by co-operating with the authorities after conviction. In such a situation a defendant must address appropriate representations to the Parole Board or the Home Office. To this general rule there is one apparent, but only partial exception. It sometimes happens that a defendant pleads guilty and gives help to the authorities, for which help credit is given, explicitly or not, when sentence is passed. In such a case the sentencing court will do its best to assess and give due credit for information already supplied and information which, is reasonably hoped, will thereafter be supplied. But it may be that the value of the help is not at that stage fully appreciated, or that the help greatly exceeds, in quantity or quality or both, what could reasonably be expected when sentence was passed, so that in either event the credit given did not reflect the true measure of the help in fact received by the authorities. In such cases this court should review the sentence passed, adjusting it, if necessary. Applying those principles A and B are entitled to some additional credit. Therefore A's sentence reduced from 13 to **11 years** and B's from 14 to **12 years**.

R v R 2002 The Times 18/2/02. LCJ. The defendant provided significant information in relation to the offence he pleaded guilty to after he has been sentenced. Held. He was entitled to rely on it. However, it would not have the same weight, as it would have carried if it was given before sentence.

R v K 2003 1 Cr App R (S) 12 The defendant was sentenced and after that gave assistance and promised to give more. Held. The Court cannot criticise the sentence imposed on the material the Judge had before him. It would normally follow that the Court cannot interfere with the sentence passed. It may well be appropriate for the prison authorities and the Parole Board to consider what has transpired since the sentence was passed. The sentence was upheld.

See also *Future help*

104   INSOLVENCY OFFENCES

104.1   Insolvency Act 1986 s 206–211, 262A and 353–62 and 389 (and many other sections)

Fraud, misconduct and falsification etc when a company is to be or is wound up.

Non disclosure, concealment of property, falsification, making false statements and fraudulent disposal of property etc. by a bankrupt.

The offences are triable either way[46]. On indictment maximum 7 years (except for s 207, 354(3), 357–8, 360–2 and 389 where it is 2 years). Summary maximum 6 months and/or £5,000.

Where the defendant is convicted in connection with the liquidation or receivership of a company etc there is power to disqualify from being a director, receiver etc[47].

The chapter is divided into two sections (A) General and (B) Managing a company when bankrupt

---

46 Insolvency Act 1986 s 431 and Sch 10.
47 Powers of Criminal Courts (Sentencing) Act 2000 s 146

Crown Court statistics – England and Wales – Males 21+ – Bankruptcy offences
104.2

Year	Plea	Total Numbers sentenced	Type of sentence %					Average length of custody (months)
			Discharge	Fine	Community sentence	Suspended sentence	Custody	
2002	Guilty	40	15	5	50	5	25	7.5
	Not guilty	10	–	–	50	–	50	6.4
2003	Guilty	55	18	7	51	9	15	8.9
	Not guilty	3	33	33	33	–	–	–

For details and explanations about the statistics in the book see page vii.

A General

Guideline remarks

104.3   Some guidance can be found in *R v Theivendran* 1992 13 Cr App R (S) 601. See below.

Failing to disclose property to a liquidator

104.4   *R v Bevis* 2001 Cr App R (S) 257. The defendant changed his plea to guilty for failing to disclose company property and details of its disposal to the liquidator contrary to the Insolvency Act 1986, s 208(1)(a). He was a 'partner or present office holder' in a company which was wound up. (What the property was and how much it was worth is not revealed in the report.) He was 53 and of good character. The defence said there was no self-enrichment. Held. The section implies dishonesty so he has a defence if he wants to prove he had no dishonesty. He did not seek to do so. There is a distinction between this offence and fraudulent trading but it strikes at the root of winding up companies. **9 months** not 18. 2 not 4 years disqualification from being a director.

B Managing a company when bankrupt

104.5   Company Directors Disqualification Act 1986 s 11

Triable either way. On indictment maximum 2 years. Summary maximum 6 months and/or £5,000.

Guideline remarks

104.6   *R v Theivendran* 1992 13 Cr App R (S) 601. LCJ. The underlying purpose of the Acts (Insolvency Act 1986 and Company Directors Disqualification Act 1986) is to rationalise the law of insolvency and in general to enable those who have suffered business failure to get back on their feet as rapidly as may be consistent with fairness to the creditors. If the contravention has been flagrant … a custodial sentence would in principle be appropriate. If, on the other hand, there are no aggravating features, such as previous offences of the same kind or personal profit gained in the fraud of creditors, that may be taken into account as justifying suspension of the sentence. [The need for exceptional circumstances to suspend sentences was in force shortly after the judgment.]

Cases

104.7   *R v Ashby* 1998 2 Cr App R (S) 37. The defendant was convicted of four counts of taking part in the management of a company when an undischarged bankrupt. The offences were over a 2 year period. The companies were Tottenham Hotspur Football Club and its associated companies. The defendant effectively ran the company on behalf of Terry Venables. He signed cheques, chaired meetings and gave executive orders. He was 53 and of good character with references. The defence said he turned the company round from near bankruptcy to prosperity and there was no allegation of fraudulent personal enrichment. They also said the sentence had an utterly devastating effect on him. The sentencing judge described it as wholly flagrant and over a considerable time and said the more blatant and repeated the offences the greater the necessity for a clear deterrent warning to others. Held. Under the current legislation the judge did not have the option of suspending the sentence. Unhesitatingly we conclude **4 months** was not too long.

See also *R v Vanderwell* 1998 1 Cr App R (S) 439.

See also COMPANY FRAUDS AND FINANCIAL SERVICES OFFENCES ETC and THEFT ETC

INSTRUMENT, USING A FALSE

Where the forgery is used to steal see THEFT ETC
See also COUNTERFEITING CURRENCY; ELECTION OFFENCES and PASSPORT OFFENCES

INSURANCE

See FRAUD – *Insurance frauds*

105   INSURANCE, NO

105.1   Road Traffic Act 1988 s 143
Summary only. Maximum Level 5 fine, £5,000.
Discretionary disqualification. Obligatory endorsement. 6–8 points.

Magistrates' Court Sentencing Guidelines January 2004

105.2   First time offenders who plead not guilty Entry point. Is a discharge or a fine appropriate? Examples of aggravating factors for the offence are defective vehicle, deliberately driving without insurance, gave false details, LGV, HGV, PCV, PSV, or minicabs and no reference to insurance ever having been held. Examples of mitigation for the offence are accidental oversight, genuine mistake, responsibility for providing insurance rested with another – parent/owner/lender/hirer and smaller vehicle e.g. moped. Examples of mitigation are difficult domestic circumstances and genuine remorse. Starting point fine B (100% of weekly take home pay/weekly benefit payment)

For details about the guidelines see MAGISTRATES' COURT SENTENCING GUIDELINES at page 483.

Magistrates' Association Guidance May 2001

105.3   Supplementary Guidance May 2001: The offence causes particular concern to magistrates who sometimes say that 'it is cheaper to pay a fine rather than insure one's car'. However, although it is possible to purchase a roadworthy car for £200 or £300, for a young male driver to insure that car third party only, will cost three or four times that and as we know only too well, the temptation is to drive the car without insurance. The chances of being caught are slim and if he is caught he will only face a very small fine since he is on low income. The implied alternative is that he should be fined at least the cost of the insurance, regardless of the fact that the fine will be way beyond his ability to pay and will probably end up being written off. Magistrates should have regard to the advice in the Guidelines which suggests that for driving with no insurance they should carefully consider the option of disqualification, a much greater penalty than any fine. Even if the driver is not disqualified he will have 6–8 points on his licence and face disqualification on a second offence under the totting up procedure. The outcome of this however is that it is unlikely that he will become legally insured in the future and the cycle often ends with a term of imprisonment for disqualified driving.

Certainly the solution to the problem is not in imposing fines which the defendants are unable to pay and which bear no relation to their income. A more efficient system of enforcement of the law, so that the chances of a driver getting away with it are greatly reduced may be a part of the solution.

The prevalence of the offence of driving without insurance must relate in part to the difference between the cost of the car and the cost of insurance. Magistrates must continue to administer the law by following the current edition of the Magistrates' Court Sentencing Guidelines.

JURY OFFENCES

For interfering with jurors etc see PERVERTING THE COURSE OF JUSTICE/CONTEMPT OF COURT/PERJURY ETC – *Jury interference*

JUSTICE, PERVERTING THE COURSE OF

See PERVERTING THE COURSE OF JUSTICE/CONTEMPT OF COURT/PERJURY ETC

KIDNAPPING

See FALSE IMPRISONMENT/KIDNAPPING.
When for ransom see BLACKMAIL – *Kidnapping individuals for ransom*

KILL, THREATS TO

See THREATS TO KILL

LANDLORDS

See HARASSMENT AND UNLAWFUL EVICTION OF TENANTS

LAUNDERING, MONEY

See MONEY LAUNDERING

106   LICENCE, BEING IN BREACH

106.1   Powers of Criminal Courts (Sentencing) Act 2000 s 116(1) and (2)

Courts have power to return to prison those defendants who were sentenced after 30 September 1992 and during their licence period commit an offence punishable with imprisonment. The return may be for the whole or part of the remaining term of imprisonment. Magistrates' Courts have no power to return to prison for more than 6 months but may commit the defendant to the Crown Court for sentence on bail or in custody.

This section of the book does not deal with the details of the provisions but just how long should be imposed.

Basic principles

106.2   *R v Taylor* 1998 1 Cr App R (S) 312 at 318 sub nom *R v Secretary of State for the Home Department, ex p Probyn* (a QBD and Court of Appeal case). First decide the appropriate sentence for the new offence. Then consider whether to order a return to prison. Consider the nature and the extent of any progress made by the defendant since his release and the nature and gravity of the new offence and whether it calls for a custodial sentence. Have regard to the totality both in determining whether to return to prison and whether the period of return should be concurrent or consecutive and how long the return term should be.

R v Blades 2000 1 Cr App R (S) 463. LCJ. The fact there is a discretionary power makes clear that no iron rules can be or should be laid down which would pervert the nature of the discretionary power. The commission of a further offence during the licence period shows that a defendant has not availed himself of the opportunity to live a law abiding existence and has not taken advantage of the probationary opportunity offered. There is a public interest in making quite clear to defendants and to the public in general that if a defendant commits serious further offences or a further serious offence while on licence there is a real and not simply a theoretical price to pay.

Double accounting

106.3   *R v O'Rourke* 2005 1 Cr App R (S) 242. The judge said that the offence was made worse because the defendant was on licence. Held. He should not have increased the sentence because the defendant was on licence for another offence while also ordering that the whole of the licence period should be served before this new sentence started. That would be double accounting.

Examples – Reduced period appropriate

106.4   *R v Cox* 2000 2 Cr App R (S) 57. The defendant was sentenced to 4 months consecutive for two charges of dangerous driving and was ordered to serve the whole of the 2 years and 73 days of his breached licence following an 8 year sentence for robberies and related offences. The pre-sentence report said he had made very determined efforts to rehabilitate himself. Held. The Judge had not applied his mind to whether or the term should be reduced in accordance with *R v Taylor* 1998 1 Cr App R (S) 312. The breach term should be reduced to **1 year 73 days**.

R v Griffiths 2000 2 Cr App R (S) 224. On 27 May 1999 the defendant was sentenced to 15 months for burglary which was committed on 31 March 1998 and 20 months and 21 days for a breach of his licence for a sentence of 6 years for manslaughter. Since the burglary he had given up drugs and settled down with a girlfriend who confirmed he was not taking drugs. He had also found work and kept out of trouble. In prison he had a successful record of negative tests for drugs. Held. Applying *R v Taylor* 1998 1 Cr App R (S) 312, the considerable progress during the relevant period is very much to his credit. A person must generally expect to go back to prison. However, his efforts must be reflected in the total sentence. Accordingly **6 months** substituted consecutive to the new sentence.

Att-Gen's Ref. Nos. 32 of 2001 2002 1 Cr App R (S) 517. The judge should have ordered detention for the breach. 439 days left. 12 months consecutive to the sentence for the new matter added.

R v Martin 2002 2 Cr App R (S) 516. The defendant pleaded guilty at the Magistrates' Court to theft. In 1997 he was convicted of robbery and sentenced to 8 years. On 2 March 2001, he was released on parole and kept his appointments with his probation officer. On 27 June 2001 he was arrested in a shop wearing some stolen trousers under track suit bottoms. They were worth £20. He had a pair of wire-cutters suitable for removing security tags. He was 37 and a heroin addict with a very bad record. He had four robbery convictions on three occasions and twenty nine convictions for theft and kindred offences. There were nine other offences. The report said he appeared to be making real efforts to remain drug free and was enjoying the support of his parents and renewed contact with his children. The Judge referred to two aggravating features. Firstly the offence was committed when he was on licence and secondly the wire cutters. The judge ordered the total remaining period, 2 years and 264 days to be served first and 3 months consecutive for the theft. The defence submitted that the Judge had (1) approached the sentence the wrong way round; (2) been wrong not to consider the theft sentence first; (3) failed to consider whether the defendant constituted a real risk of causing serious harm to the public; (4) failed to regard the significant progress the defendant had made and (5) failed to consider the total sentence. Held. There is much force in these submissions. **6 months** for breach of the licence substituted making 9 months in all.

See also *R v Russell* 1998 2 Cr App R (S) 375 and *R v Martin* 2002 2 Cr App R (S) 516 [second offence minor].

Examples – Full amount ordered to be served

106.5   *R v Walker* 1998 2 Cr App R (S) 245. The defendant pleaded guilty at his first appearance to three counts of supplying crack cocaine. In August 1994 he was sentenced to 3 years for supplying crack cocaine. Two months after his release he was seen by an officer in Brixton conducting an undercover drugs operation. The officer asked if he had any crack. The officer was asked to follow him and he did. A short distance away the defendant broke off a piece of crack from a large piece and sold it to the officer for £50. It weighed 321 mgs. A few days later there was another meeting and two wraps were sold for £40 each. Their total weight was 253 mgs. The next day he sold 197 mgs of crack for £20 to another under-cover officer. That wrap was spat from his mouth. He was arrested three months later and lied in his interview. The risk of re-offending was described as considerable, although there were some indications that he was trying to lead a more settled life. The judge sentenced him to 3 years 11 months consecutive to **16 months** for being in breach of his licence for the previous supply offence. The sentence had been varied because the judge had misstated his parole position. Held. The 3 years 11 months sentence was entirely proper. He could not have complained if it had been longer. These offences were committed in flagrant breach of his licence. Some judges might have given a reduction for the 3 month period after the offences when he was not offending but the judge could not be criticised for not doing so. The total was not excessive.

Att-Gen's Ref. No 89 of 1999 2000 2 Cr App R (S) 382. The full period should have been made to run consecutively. For details see ROBBERY – *Domestic premises – Victim over 65 – Victim injured or attacked*

R v Bolt 1999 2 Cr App R (S) 202. The defendant pleaded guilty to theft. His accomplice stole a handbag from the floor of a pub near a customer and the two drove off together. The police caught them. He was 28 and had an appalling record. There were thirty convictions since he was 11. He had been sentenced to 3 and 5 years. This offence was committed 3 months after his release from the 5 years. The judge ignored the defence version that it was an impulse theft. Held. The judge should have indicated his view to counsel. An impulse theft is worth 12 months not 2 years. The earlier sentence had not deterred him. He had been released very shortly before. There was no reason why he should not serve the remainder of the earlier sentence.

R v Taylor 2002 1 Cr App R (S) 490. The defendant pleaded guilty to robbery in which knives were used. The offence was committed 3 months after his release from a 7 year sentence for an armed robbery on a post office. He had two other convictions for robbery. There were 684 days unexpired on his licence. The defendant who was equally to blame received 6 years. The co-defendant had an appalling record but no convictions for robbery. Held. The defendant's sentence was reduced from 12 years to **10**. We do not ignore that he had difficulties in coming to terms with life in the community but it was wholly outweighed by the offence being committed 3 months from precisely the same offence. There was no element of double punishment. All he had done was deprived himself of the benefit of his licence. The total was not too long. The 684 days were not reduced and were to remain consecutive. That was within the judge's discretion.

Judge does not say whether the days to be served are to be consecutive or not

106.6   *R v Prince* 1999 2 Cr App R (S) 419. The defendant pleaded guilty to offering to supply cocaine. He was in breach of his licence following his release from a $2\frac{1}{2}$ year sentence for robbery. There were 224 days left to serve. Held. The sentence should be reduced to 12 months. Although the judge when he activated the 224 days left to serve didn't say whether they were consecutive or concurrent they should be served consecutively. The amount should be 6 months consecutive not 224 days.

R v Twisse 2001 2 Cr App R (S) 37. The defendant was convicted of possessing heroin with intent to supply, possessing cocaine with intent to supply. He had pleaded guilty to simple possession of ecstasy. Police officers stopped the defendant as he was about to get into a car. They searched him and his flat. They found 23 ecstasy tablets, 23.37 grams of cocaine, the street value was up to £2,200, 42.5 grams of heroin the street value was up to £3,400. The appellant was arrested and interviewed and claimed the drugs were for his own use. He was 35 years of age and had nine previous court appearances mostly for robbery, sometimes including firearms. In 1993, he was sentenced to 11 years for attempted robbery and carrying a firearm with intent to commit an indictable offence. He was released on licence in 1998. He was sentenced to 6 years and ordered to serve the whole 1,670 days of an unexpired term of the 11 year sentence. (That was illegal, as the maximum is the time from the breach to the end of the sentence). Held. The judge did not pay sufficient regard either to the appellant's history following his release on licence or to the principle of totality. $2\frac{1}{2}$ **years** consecutive substituted.

Longer than commensurate sentences, consecutive to See LONGER THAN COMMENSURATE SENTENCES – *Consecutive to other sentences, the longer than commensurate sentence should not be*

Recall by Secretary of State, and

106.7   *R v Stocker* 2003 2 Cr App R (S) 335. The defendant breached his licence and the Secretary of State exercised his power to recall the defendant under Criminal Justice Act 1991 s 39. Later the court ordered him to serve the full period of the breach of the licence. Held. The Judge should deduct the time the defendant had served following his recall.

See also *R v Sharkley* 2000 1 Cr App R (S) 541

LIVING OFF THE EARNINGS OF PROSTITUTION

The offence was abolished on 1/5/04. For the old and the new offences see
PROSTITUTION.

107   LONGER THAN COMMENSURATE SENTENCES

107.1   Powers of Criminal Courts (Sentencing) Act 2000 s 80(2)(b). The custodial
sentence shall be ... where the offence is a violent or sexual offence, for such longer
term (not exceeding the maximum) as in the opinion of the court is necessary to protect
the public from serious harm from the offender, (previously Criminal Justice Act 1991
s 2(2)(b)).

Sexual and Violent offences are dealt with under four different systems. For offences
committed (a) before 1 October 1992 there is no statutory powers to increase the
sentences; (b) from 1 October 1992 to 29 September 1998 there are powers to pass a
sentence to protect the public from serious harm from him; (c) from 30 September 1998
to 3 April 2005 there are the first Longer than commensurate and Extended Sentence
powers and (d) from 4 April 2005 there are the Criminal Justice Act 2003 provisions.
These provisions are for Dangerous Offenders and give powers to pass life sentences
and (new) Extended sentences. See **EXTENDED SENTENCES**.

Commencement There is no power to pass this sentence for offences committed before
30/9/98.

Extended sentences An extended sentence is a sentence which has an extended licence
period, Powers of Criminal Courts (Sentencing) Act s 85(2)(b). Unfortunately many
people including Judges refer to a Longer than commensurate sentence as an extended
sentence but that is not what the section calls it. Where judges refer to a longer than commensurate sentence as an extended sentence, 'longer than commensurate' is substituted
to distinguish the sentence from a real extended sentence. See **EXTENDED SENTENCES**.

There is no power to order this sentence for offences committed on or after 4/4/05.

Consecutive to other sentences, the longer than commensurate sentence should not be
107.2   *R v Johnson* 1998 1 Cr App R (S) 126. The defendant pleaded guilty to
three robberies and a s 20 wounding. The offences were committed 3 months after
he was released from a 5 year sentence for robberies. The judge passed a longer
than commensurate sentence of 10 years and ordered it to be consecutive to the
unexpired portion of his previous sentence. Held. After considering *R v King* 1995
16 Cr App R (S) 987 and the words of the s 2(2)(b) it was illogical to order that the
period assessed for the protection of the public should commence on some date in
the future. It was therefore in principle generally undesirable to order an extended
sentence to run consecutive to any subsisting sentence. They should be ordered to run
concurrent thus ensuring that the extended sentence runs from the date the sentence is
passed.

R v Cuthbertson 2000 Crim LR 61. Same rule applied.

R v Sullivan 2000 2 Cr App R (S) 318. The sentences should not be ordered to run consecutively. Sentence of **4 years** made concurrent to the 167 days for breach of licence.

R v Sowden 2000 2 Cr App R (S) 360. The defendant pleaded guilty to robbery and
theft. He had a bad record. He received 1 year for the theft and 5 years extended for the
robbery consecutive. Held. We are bound to follow *R v Walters* 1997 2 Cr App R (S)
87 and hold the extended sentence should not be consecutive to the other sentence.

R v Ellis 2001 1 Cr App R (S) 148. Rule applied.

R v Everleigh 2002 1 Cr App R (S) 130. Rule applied.

R v Fletcher 2002 2 Cr App R (S) 568. The defendant pleaded guilty to indecent assault and threats to kill. The Judge gave him 10 years, longer than commensurate for the indecent assault when the maximum is 10. On the threats to kill he gave him 4 years consecutive. The defence argued that the longer than commensurate sentence should not be consecutive, he should receive a discount for his plea and matters arising out of the same incident should be concurrent. Held. The principle or practice that same incident counts should be concurrent is always subject not only to exceptional circumstances but also more fundamentally to considerations of justice particularly that the total sentence must properly reflect the seriousness of the criminality involved. The Judge was right to find 10 years was too low. Here it was necessary to reflect the gravamen of the two offences and the total seriousness by consecutive sentences. It follows as the sentences are consecutive it will not be appropriate to make the sentence longer than commensurate. So **8** and **4 years** consecutive.

R v Blackwell 2003 The Times 15/12/03. The sentencer in a grave case is entitled to achieve the protection of the public by imposing a consecutive longer than commensurate which in total exceeds the statutory maximum for the individual offence.

Duty to pass

107.3   *R v Avis* 1998 Re Goldsmith 2 Cr App R (S) 178 at 192. LCJ. The defendant pleaded guilty to attempted robbery and having a firearm with intent to commit an indictable offence. The defendant was 49 and was a persistent armed robber. The judge said that viewed in isolation 10 years' imprisonment was the correct sentence but when he considered the need to protect the public, a longer sentence of **15 years** was appropriate. Held. The long sentences the defendant had served had done nothing to deter him. Even without resorting to s 2(2)(b) of the 1991 Act 10 years was justified for this armed robbery. The judge was right that the s 2(2)(b) power should be exercised. It is clear the defendant is likely to commit further offences of this very serious kind. The sub-section requires that the court 'shall' pass such sentence 'as is in the opinion of the court necessary to protect the public from serious harm from the offender'. Since a previous 15 year sentence did not deter him from re-offending, it is difficult to see how the necessary period of protection required should be any shorter. The sentence was an entirely proper one.

Extended sentence and a longer than commensurate sentence

107.4   *R v Thornton* 2000 2 Cr App (S) 47. 5 years longer than commensurate changed to a **2 years** custodial term with a **3 years** extension period.

R v Nelson 2002 1 Cr App R (S) 567. The two sentences will be appropriate, where a violent or sexual offence is committed by a seriously dangerous offender, in relation to whom a life sentence, if available, might well be passed, thereby permitting the offender to be released only when the executive believes that the risk posed by him has been greatly reduced. In such a case, the offender would of course be subject to recall for the rest of his life. It is appropriate to combine an extended period of licence with a longer than commensurate custodial term for an offender who presents a serious danger to the public but where a life sentence is not available because the maximum penalty is, for example, a lesser determinate sentence. There may also be cases in which a discretionary life sentence is available for the offence but the criteria which have to be established before such a sentence can be passed may not all be present (e.g. *R v Chapman* 2000 1 Cr App R (S) 377). Where a longer than commensurate sentence is called for, it should usually be accompanied by an extension period because a seriously dangerous offender, attracting a longer than commensurate sentence, may well commit further offences.

Guilty plea and imposing the maximum sentence

107.5   *R v Lovett* 2003 1 Cr App R (S) 320. The defendant pleaded guilty to Section 20 on a Section 18 indictment. After drinking cider and vodka and taking cannabis and cocaine, he had an argument with the victim in the victim's girlfriend's kitchen. The defendant then took a knife from the kitchen drawer and slashed the victim's face. The victim slumped to the floor and the defendant said, ``I'm fucking going to kill you.'' The girlfriend interposed her body between them and the defendant left. There was no real motive. The victim had a deep laceration over his eyelid and across the bridge of his nose. There was also a 1cm cut over his upper eye lid and a 2cm superficial laceration to the cheek. The plea of guilty was based on the defendant being too drunk to form a specific intent. The defendant was 28. His violent and alcohol offences were: two ABH offences in 1992, assault on police and drunk and disorderly in 1995, excess alcohol in 1998, drunk and disorderly in 2000 and possession of a bladed instrument in 2001. The pre-sentence report said all his offences were drink related and he presents a high risk of harm to the public. The psychiatrist said his violence appears to have an impulsive element and he is likely to cause injury in the future. Held. This was a very serious offence, committed by a man who presents a continuing danger to the public of serious harm. The description of the injuries does not describe their seriousness, nor how very close the victim came to sustaining very serious damage indeed. He could have lost an eye. His throat could have been cut. The Judge was right to make the offence longer than commensurate. The defendant had little option but to plead guilty. The credit for the plea is minimal. This is one of the exceptional cases where the Judge was right to take the view that the protection of the public must be paramount. **5 years** (the maximum) was the right sentence.

Sentence must not be out of proportion/out of scale

107.6   *R v Mansell* 1994 15 Cr App R (S) 771. LCJ. The judge has to balance the need to protect the public on the one hand with the need to look at the totality of the sentence and see that it is not out of all proportion to the nature of the offending.

R v Crow 1995 16 Cr App R (S) 409. LCJ. Where (the then) s 2(2)(b) is applied, the sentence should, whilst long enough to give necessary protection to the public, still bear a reasonable relationship to the offence for which it is being imposed.

R v Howatt 1997 Unreported 8/7/97. The defendant was convicted of rape. He forced his way into a flat, and threatened the victim with a knife. He then raped her. He had four previous convictions for indecent assault. Held. The use of the section must not result in a sentence out of all proportion to the sentence that would otherwise be imposed. **15 years** not 18.

R v Gabbidon and Bramble 1997 2 Cr App R (S) 19. One defendant was sentenced to 27 years for very grave domestic robberies. The judge had considered 18 years suitable for the overall figure and added 50% under the then s 2(2)(b). Held. That was out of scale. Without extending the sentence 15 years would have been appropriate. To reflect the need to protect the public 5 additional years is right making **20 years** in all.

R v Langton 1998 1 Cr App R (S) 217. The defendant pleaded guilty to indecent assault on a 10-year-old girl. The defendant had two convictions for buggery of an 8 year old boy when he was 14; a conviction for indecently assaulting a young boy when he was 15 and a conviction for indecently assaulting a 6-year-old girl when he was 17. The pre-sentence report said he constituted a danger particularly to young children. The sentencing judge noted that the defendant constituted a danger to young children, and there remained a risk that he would re-offend. He passed a longer than commensurate sentence. Held. No strictly mathematical approach should be adopted in longer than commensurate cases, and it may well be that a much longer sentence than commensurate sentence is perfectly proper, particularly in an extreme or particularly difficult case. Having regard to the risk the defendant posed 4 years was proper. For further details see INDECENT ASSAULT ON A WOMAN – *Longer than commensurate sentences,*

R v Winfield 1999 2 Cr App R (S) 116. The defendant was convicted of robbery. He and two others were in a public house. One followed the victim, who had drunk about five pints, into the lavatory. The victim's gold chain was seized and there was a struggle. The victim received a bite on the finger. The defendant and the other man joined them and all three kicked and punched the victim. The door was closed to stop those who had heard the commotion from entering. The victim became unconscious and lost his gold chain, his bracelet, a gold watch, a ring and £30. Police found him covered in blood with a boot mark on his forehead. At hospital he was found to have a 2″ cut to his head and bruising to his temple, nose, cheek and near his eye. He stayed there for a few days. The defendant had a bad record (details not given). He was given a longer than commensurate sentence of 8 years. Held. Ordinarily the offence would warrant 5 years. The court had to balance the need to protect the public and ensure the sentence is not out of all proportion to the nature of the offending. It must also ensure there is no double counting. Double counting is when a sentence has a deterrent factor built in and is extended without taking into account that existing deterrent factor. That deterrent factor caters for the necessity to protect the public. **6 years** not 8.

R v Smith 2001 2 Cr App R (S) 160. The defendant pleaded guilty to ABH. The judge said the sentence started at 18 months and he extended it to 4 years. Held. It was a quite disgraceful piece of loutish and yobbish behaviour. The base sentence was not too high. It could have been considerably higher. Previously the court had suggested an uplift of 50–100% was appropriate. The extension to **4 years** was abundantly justified.

R v Briggs 2003 2 Cr App R (S) 615. The defendant was convicted of indecent assault. He was acquitted of kidnapping and false imprisonment based on the same incident. A 15 year old girl was walking in the rain. The defendant, now aged 46 stopped his car and offered her a lift. After about 5 minutes he rubbed her knee and said he wanted to shag her. She asked him to stop the car and she let herself out crying. She sought help at a nearby house. In 1980 he was sentenced to 7 years for rape and two serious indecent assaults. In 1986 he was sentenced to 10 years for the attempted rape of an 11 year old. In 2000 he pleaded guilty to three offences involving the propositioning of three women. In one he pulled up his car alongside a 16 year old girl and questioned her about sex. He asked a 40 year old woman to come to his car and she ran away. 20 minutes later he did the same to a 23 year old. The psychiatrist said he was a recidivist sexual offender. He assessed the risk of further acts of serious harm as high. The pre-sentence report referred to his emotional loneliness, empathy deficits and deviant fantasies. The risk of re-offending was assessed as very high. The Judge referred to his total lack of remorse. Held. The proved allegation was she entered his car and when she indicated she wanted nothing more he desisted. 2 years was the right commensurate sentence. It would not be right to impose a longer than commensurate sentence of more than 1 year, bearing in mind the need for proportionality. However we cannot ignore the 10 years of no serious offending. So **2 years** with an extended sentence of 3 years, not longer than commensurate instead of 4 years commensurate and 4 years longer than commensurate with a 2 year extension period making total possible sentence of 10 years.

See also ARSON – *Longer than commensurate sentences, how much extra?* and OFFENCES AGAINST THE PERSON ACT 1861, s 18 – *Longer than commensurate sentences, how much extra?*

Serious harm, Must establish it was necessary to protect the public from

107.7   *R v Cameron* 2003 The Times 12/2/03. The defendant pleaded guilty to two counts of ABH at a late stage. At about 6pm he struck a student who was walking in the street for no apparent reason causing his mouth to bleed. The student called the police and pointed him out to them. The police spoke to the defendant who had a can of beer which was taken off him. He then punched a policeman in the mouth and pushed his thumb into the officer's eye. The officer thought he was trying to pull his eyeball out. He was arrested after a struggle. The officer suffered bruising to the eye with orbital and conjunctival bruising. He also had abrasions to his eyebrow, cheek and lip. The defendant had 20 previous convictions mostly for violence and dishonesty. The vast majority were relatively minor and only one merited a lengthy prison sentence. That was for ABH in 1997, for which he received 30 months. He also had a personality disorder with dis-social and ``borderline features.'' He was prone to antisocial behaviour, substance and alcohol abuse. The risk assessment was assessed as significant. The Judge passed a longer than commensurate sentence. Held. That was wrong because it was not established the public required protection from *serious* harm. **30 months** not 4 years.

Serious offences, should it be used for the most

107.8   *R v Chapman* 1994 15 Cr App R (S) 844. The defendant was a persistent armed robber. Held. He is a dangerous man who is a menace to society. It is clearly necessary to protect the public. We apply (the then) s 2(2)(b) provisions.

R v Christie 1995 16 Cr App R (S) 469. It is incumbent when considering whether to apply (the then) s 2(2)(b) to guard against the danger of effectively imposing an element of the sentence twice. That is because the commensurate sentence is likely to contain an element which is designed to achieve the protection of the public, it is wrong in principle to apply s 2(2)(b) in order to achieve a sentence of greater length.

R v Gabbidon and Bramble 1997 2 Cr App R (S) 19. The defendants were sentenced to **27** and **17 years** concurrent for very grave domestic robberies. Held. *R v Chapman* 1994 15 Cr App R (S) 844 and *R v Christie* 1995 16 Cr App R (S) 469 were clearly in conflict. There was a clear need to protect the public. We prefer the approach in *Chapman*. It is better the courts applies Lord Taylor (LCJ)'s balance, the need to protect the public and the need to look at the totality of the sentence.

Use of powers wrong but sentence correct

107.9   *R v Rai and Robinson* 2000 2 Cr App R (S) 120. The defendants received a longer than commensurate sentence of 15 years. The judge did not state that the reason for that was their propensity to violence. Held. It was unnecessary to extend the sentence, as 15 years was not inappropriate. Where the court passes an extended sentence but the sentence was correct this court will not reduce that sentence even if it considers the use of the statute was wrong. The sentence was upheld without relying on the statute.

R v Sowden 2000 2 Cr App R (S) 360. The defendant pleaded guilty to robbery and theft. He had a bad record. He received 1 year for the theft and 5 years extended for the robbery consecutive and an extended licence. Held. We are bound to follow *R v Walters* 1997 2 Cr App R (S) 87 and hold the extended sentence should not be consecutive to the other sentence. However, 5 years could be imposed without extending the sentence. 1 year consecutive was correct. Appeal dismissed.

The following chapters have *Longer than commensurate sentences* sections: Abduction of a Child, ABH, Buggery, False Imprisonment/Kidnapping, Indecent Assault on a Man, Indecent Assault on a Woman, Offences Against the Person Act 1861, s 18, Offences Against the Person Act 1861, s 20, Public Decency, Outraging, Robbery and Threats to Kill.

108   LSD

Don't treat the drug as less serious than other Class A drugs

108.1   *R v Hurley* 1998 1 Cr App R (S) 299 at 302. LCJ. Principle stated.

How should the amount of drugs be presented to the court?

108.2   *R v Hurley* 1998 1 Cr App R (S) 299 at 303. LCJ. Don't use resale value. Although it may be appropriate for the street value to be given to give an idea of the scale of the operation. The number of impregnated squares usually of approximately ¼ inch in size, provides the best way. There is however evidence that it is now the fashion for dosage units to approximate to 50 microgrammes and since any effect is unlikely to be detectable very much below 25 microgrammes a dose of 50 micro-grammes is accepted as being a realistic dose. The practical evidence suggests that in the market place this is the average level of dose as judged by the seizures which are made. Of course, one would not expect the squares to be impregnated with exactly 50 microgrammes. There must be a plus or minus. If, however, one takes the number of squares as the primary starting point, then allowance must be made appropriately upwards or downwards if there is convincing evidence that the squares are signifi-cantly more or less heavily impregnated. By 'significantly' we have in mind something in excess of 10microgrammes one way or the other. It is therefore possible, where weaker dosage units are intentionally produced, to adjust the scale accordingly, while bearing in mind that in such a situation those who produce these squares may well have done so quite deliberately in order to maximise their profits. Since the object of the legislation is to deter the use of unlawful drugs and strip dealers of their profits, it seems to us appropriate that the penalties should be related to the number of dosage units put, or to be put, on the market, subject to such adjustment as may be appropriate in the light of a significant deviation from the standard dose. The sentence therefore should ordinarily be based on the number of squares to be marketed, assuming an LSD content of about 50 microgrammes of pure LSD per square, plus or minus about 10 microgrammes, but with discretion in the sentencer to vary the sentence upwards or downwards where there is any more significant variation.

Scientific evidence

108.3   *R v Hurley* 1998 1 Cr App R (S) 299 at 302. LCJ. Dr Jansen and Professor Nichols told us that in the 1960s and 1970s LSD was regularly used in much larger quantities than is usual today. They testified that it was at about a dose of 50microgrammes that most people start to begin to experience hallucinatory effects.

See also **DRUG USERS; IMPORTATION OF DRUGS; POSSESSION OF DRUGS; PRODUCTION OF DRUGS** and **SUPPLY OF DRUGS (CLASS A, B AND C)**

109   MAGISTRATES' COURT SENTENCING GUIDELINES

Implementation date: 1 January 2004

Quotes for previous guidelines

109.1   'They are of course only guidelines. They do not curtail your independent discretion to impose the sentences you think are right, case by case. But they exist to help you in that process, to give you a starting point and to give you more information in reaching your decisions. And, importantly, they help to assist the magistracy to maintain an overall consistency of approach.' Lord Irvine (Lord Chancellor)

'I think it most important that, within discretionary limits, Magistrates' Courts up and down the country should endeavour to approach sentencing with a measure of consistency, and I have no doubt that these Guidelines will contribute powerfully to that end.' Lord Bingham of Cornhill (former Lord Chief Justice)

R v Krawec 1984 6 Cr App R (S) 367. LCJ. It cannot be emphasised too strongly the guidelines are not a tariff.

Section 1 – User Guide

109.2   These Sentencing Guidelines cover offences with which magistrates deal regularly and frequently in the adult criminal courts. They provide a sentencing structure, which sets out how to: establish the seriousness of each case and determine the most appropriate way of dealing with it. They provide a method for considering individual cases and a guideline from which discussion should properly flow; but they are not a tariff and should never be used as such. These guidelines are based on a first time offender pleading not guilty.

Using the sentencing structure

109.3   The sentencing structure used for these Guidelines was established by the Criminal Justice Act 1991. This reaffirms the principle of 'just desserts' so that any penalty must reflect the seriousness of the offence for which it is imposed and the personal circumstances of the offender. Magistrates must always start the sentencing process by taking full account of all the circumstances of the offence and making a judicial assessment of the seriousness category into which it falls. It is important that the court makes clear the factual basis on which the sentence is based. In every case, the Criminal Justice Act 1991 requires sentencers to consider: Is discharge or a fine appropriate? Is the offence serious enough for a community penalty? Is it so serious that only custody is appropriate? If the last, in either way cases, justices will also need to consider if Magistrates' Courts' powers are sufficient.

The format of the Sentencing Guidelines

1. Consider the seriousness of the offence

109.4   Magistrates must always make an assessment of seriousness following the structure of the Criminal Justice Act 1991. The guideline sentences are based on a first time offender pleading not guilty. However, the Sentencing Guidelines do give a starting point guideline for each offence. Where the starting point guideline is a community penalty, refer to the guidance under '*Community Penalties*', below. Where the starting point guideline is custody, think in terms of weeks and credit as appropriate for a timely guilty plea. For some either way offences the guideline is 'are your sentencing powers sufficient?' This indicates that magistrates should be considering whether the seriousness of the offence is such that 6 months (or 12 months in the case of two or more offences) is insufficient, so that the case must be committed to the Crown Court. If the case is retained in the Magistrates' Court a substantial custodial sentence is likely to be necessary. It should be noted that if magistrates consider (say) 9 months to be the appropriate sentence, to be reduced for a timely guilty plea to six months, then the case falls within their powers and must be retained. Subject to offender mitigation, six months would appear to be the appropriate sentence. However, if sentence is passed on this basis the court should specifically say so in its reasons.

2. Consider aggravating and mitigating factors

109.5   Make sure that all aggravating and mitigating factors are considered. The lists in the Sentencing Guidelines are neither exhaustive nor a substitute for the personal judgment of magistrates. Factors which do not appear in the Guidelines may be important in individual cases. If the offence was racially aggravated, the court must treat that fact as an aggravating factor under statute (Powers of Criminal Courts (Sentencing) Act 2000 s 153). If the offence was committed while the offender was on bail, the court must treat that as an aggravating factor under statute (s 153 Powers of Criminal Courts (Sentencing) Act 2000). Consider previous convictions, or any failure to respond to previous sentences, in assessing seriousness. Courts should identify any convictions relevant for this purpose and then consider to what extent they affect the seriousness of the present offence.

3. Take a preliminary view of seriousness, and then consider offender mitigation

109.6 When an initial assessment of the seriousness of the offence has been formed, consider the offender. The Guidelines set out some examples of offender mitigation but there are frequently others to be considered in individual cases. Any offender mitigation that the court accepts must lead to some downward revision of the provisional assessment of seriousness, although this revision may be minor. Remember, however, that the guideline sentences are based on a first time pleading not guilty. A previous criminal record may deprive the defendant of being able to say that he is a person of good character.

4. Consider your sentence

109.7 The law requires the court to reduce the sentence for a timely guilty plea but this provision should be used with judicial flexibility. A timely guilty plea may attract a sentencing discount of up to one third but the precise amount of discount will depend on the facts of each case and a last minute plea of guilty may attract only a minimal reduction. Credit may be given in respect of the amount of a fine or periods of community service or custody. Periods of mandatory disqualification or mandatory penalty points cannot be reduced for a guilty plea.

5. Decide your sentence

109.8 Remember that magistrates have a duty to consider the award of compensation in all appropriate cases, and to give reasons if compensation is not awarded. See **Compensation Orders**

Establishing the seriousness of the offence

109.9 In establishing the seriousness of the case before them, courts should: (1) make sure that all factors, which aggravate or mitigate the offence are considered. The lists in the Guidelines are neither exhaustive nor a substitute for the personal judgment of magistrates. Factors which do not appear in the Guidelines may be important in individual cases; (2) consider the various seriousness indicators, remembering that some will carry more weight than others; (3) take into account, as a seriousness factor the impact of the offence upon the victim. (4) note that, by statute, racial and religious aggravation increases the seriousness of any offence-s 153 Powers of Criminal Courts (Sentences) Act 2000, but see the note on specific racially-aggravated offences created under s 29–32 of the same Act; (5) always bear in mind that, by statute, the commission of an offence on bail aggravates its seriousness; (6) consider the effect of using previous convictions, or any failure to respond to previous sentences, in assessing seriousness. Courts should identify any convictions relevant for this purpose and then consider to what extent they affect the seriousness of the present offence; (7) note that, when there are several offences to be sentenced, the court must have regard to the totality principle. This means that the overall effect of the sentence must be commensurate with the total criminality involved.

When the court has formed an initial assessment of the seriousness of the offence(s), consider any offender mitigation.

Victim personal statements

109.10 A victim personal statement gives victims a formal opportunity to say how the crime has affected them. Where the victim has chosen to make such a statement, a court should consider and take it into account prior to passing sentence. (LCJ Practice Direction made 16 October 2001) Evidence of the effects of an offence on the victim must be in the form of a s 9 statement or expert's report and served on the defence prior to sentence. Except where inferences can properly be drawn from the nature or circumstances surrounding the offence, a sentencer must not make assumptions unsupported by evidence about the effects of an offence on the victim. The court must pass what it judges to be the appropriate sentence having regard to the circumstances of the offence and of the offender, taking into account, so far as the court considers it appropriate, the consequences to the victim. The opinions of the victim or the victim's close relatives as to what the sentence should be are not relevant.

Reduction in sentence for guilty pleas

109.11 Powers of Criminal Courts (Sentencing) Act 2000 s 152 In deciding what sentence to pass on a person who has pleaded guilty the court has to take into account the stage in the proceedings at which that plea was indicated and the circumstances in which the indication was given, If the court imposes a less severe penalty than it would have given, it must state this in open court. It would be a matter of good practice for the court to say how much credit has been given, with a brief reason for the decision.

The principles of 'discount' apply as much to magistrates' courts as they do to Crown Courts. A timely guilty plea may attract a sentencing discount of up to a third but the precise amount of discount will depend on the facts of each case. A change of plea on the day set down for trial may attract only a minimal reduction in sentence; the court must still consider whether credit should be given.

Reductions apply to fines, periods of community sentences and custody. An early plea of guilty may also affect the length of a disqualification or the number of penalty points. However, minimum periods of disqualification and mandatory penalty points cannot be reduced for a guilty plea. Reasons should be given for decisions.

Pre-sentence reports and SSRs

109.12 The purpose of all reports is to provide information to help the court decide the most suitable sentence. They are required in most cases where the threshold of "serious enough" (community penalties) or "so serious" (custody) is reached-and should only be sought in such cases. They can be in the form of a PSR (pre-sentence report) or SSR (specific sentence report). PSRs are written reports to assist the courts in determining sentence. In accordance with National Standards they contain: a full risk assessment and a proposal for sentence commensurate with the risk of harm, likelihood of re-offending, the nature of the offence and the suitability of the offender. A PSR must be provided within 15 working days of the court's request or any agreed shorter time period.

A SSR is a PSR for legal purposes as it meets the definition of s 162 of the Powers of Criminal Courts (Sentencing) Act 2000. SSRs are designed to speed up the provision of information to courts to allow sentencing without delay in relatively straightforward cases. They are a specific limited enquiry undertaken at the request of the court into an offender's suitability for a particular community sentence. They are designed to be available on the day requested (or next morning). If there is doubt about a defendant's suitability for a specific sentence report the probation officer may recommend an adjournment for a full PSR.

Giving reasons

109.13   Magistrates should normally give reasons for their findings and decisions; this is obligatory under the Human Rights Act 1998: (1) the offender should be told the reasons for the decision; (2) the victim will want to know the reasons for the decision; (3) the public is entitled to know what is going on in the criminal justice system, and to have confidence in it. (4) If a sentence is unusual the case for reasons is doubly important; (5) ill-informed criticism in the media may be reduced if reasons have been given in public and recorded; (6) in preparing an SSR or a PSR, or in implementing a community sentence, the probation service must know what the magistrates had in mind and what findings of fact were made; (7) if a case has to be adjourned, and a differently constituted bench sits next time, the later bench must know the reasons for the decisions of the earlier bench; and (8) the reasons will be necessary if there is an appeal by way of case stated.

There are now many instances where the giving of reasons is required by law: (1) why bail is refused; (2) why the offence is so serious as to justify prison; (3) why a defaulter is being sent to prison; (4) if a compensation order is not awarded; (5) if a sentence is reduced because of a guilty plea; (6) if the court does not disqualify the driver or endorse his licence for "special reasons" and (7) If the court does not impose a "totting up" disqualification.

Having reached their findings through a structured approach, it is perfectly proper for the magistrates to seek the advice and assistance of the legal adviser in how best to formulate and articulate their reasons for the purposes of the pronouncement. It is the responsibility for the legal adviser to provide justices with any advice they require properly to perform their functions, whether or not the justices requested that advice. The Practice Direction on the functions and responsibilities of Justice's Clerks and authorised legal advisers, made by the Lord Chief Justice on 2 October 2000, makes it clear that this responsibility extends to giving advice on the appropriate decision making structure to be applied in any given case, reminding the bench of the evidence, and assisting the court where appropriate as to the formulation of reasons and recording of those reasons.

Fining

109.14   Fines are suitable as punishment for cases which are not serious enough to merit a community penalty, nor so serious that a custodial sentence must be considered. The aim should be for the fine to have equal impact on rich or poor and before fixing the amount of a fine, the court must inquire into the offender's financial circumstances, preferably using a standard means form. A fine must not exceed the upper statuary limit. Where this is expressed in terms of "level" the maxima are Level 1 £200, level 2 £500, Level 3 £1,000, Level 4 £2,500 and Level 5 £5,000. The fine must reflect the seriousness of the offence and must be proportionate both to the offence and the offender. A reduction must be considered for a guilty plea – up to a third if the plea was timely (see **109.11**), and the appropriate announcement made. Where compensation is awarded this must take priority over fines or costs (see **Compensation orders.**).

Where a defendant is to be fined for several offences and his means are limited it may be better to fix the relevant fine level for the most serious offence and order 'no separate penalty' on the lesser matters. The suggested fines in these *Guidelines* are given as either A, B or C. These represent 50%, 100% and 150% of the defendant's weekly take home pay/benefit. (Weekly take home pay or benefit means weekly income after all deductions made by an employer (take home pay) or the amount of weekly benefit payment.) These levels take into account ordinary living expenses. This guidance should not be used as a tariff and every offender's means must be individually considered. The defendant should be given a document which sets out the total fines, rate of payment, date of first payment and place of payment before leaving the court.

Assessing means

109.15   Before fixing the amount of any fine the Powers of Criminal Courts (Sentencing) Act 2000, section 128 requires the court to enquire into the financial circumstances of the offender so far as they are known. Defendants should be asked to complete a means form to provide this information. The first figure needed is take home pay/benefit which is used to ensure the fairest approach to those in different financial circumstances – the guideline fines (which are only a starting point) are based on this income and reflect ordinary living expenses. The court should be aware of other information including:

- whether the offender has savings or other disposable or realisable capital assets;
- liability to pay outstanding fines;
- level of outgoings.

And should in every case consider individual circumstances, but outgoings will only be relevant if they are out of the ordinary and substantially reduce ability to pay, leading to undue hardship. The financial circumstances of third parties, e.g. other members of the family, are irrelevant, save insofar as the offender derives income or benefit from such persons, or he is thereby relieved of a proportion of household expenses. If for any reason the magistrates are not satisfied with the information they have received, and they feel they cannot sentence until they have such information, they may adjourn the case for further information to be supplied, and they may make a financial circum-stances order requiring a statement of means to be provided, Powers of the Criminal Courts (Sentencing) Act 2000, section 126.

The fine is payable in full on the day and the defendant should always be asked for immediate payment. If periodic payments are allowed, the fine should normally be payable within a maximum of 12 months. It should be remembered however, that for those on very low incomes it is often unrealistic to expect them to maintain weekly payments for as long as a year. The fine should be a hardship, depriving the offender of the capacity to spend the money on 'luxuries', but care should be taken not to force him or her below a reasonable 'subsistence' level.

Fining in the defendant's absence

109.16   If, having been given a reasonable opportunity to inform the court of his means, the offender refuses or fails to do so, the magistrates may draw such inference as to means as they think just in the circumstances, using all available information. It is inappropriate simply to fine the maximum level. See also the guidance on fine enforcement at the end of these guidelines. Our order is as follows.

1.   Decide sentencing band according to seriousness. Consider the aggravating and mitigating features of the offence, plus any personal mitigation relating to the offender – decide that a fine is appropriate.

2.   Decide level of fine according to seriousness taking the above factors into account, decide on the level of fine (A, B or C) that reflects those factors.

3.   Obtain financial information. The court is required by statute to enquire into finan-cial circumstances and to take them into account so far as they are known. Full information (from means form/questioning in court) should cover income, savings (if any) and outgoings including other court fines.

4.   Set fine. A fine is meant to have an equal impact on rich and poor. To ensure a fair approach the starting point in all cases should be weekly take home pay/weekly benefit payment. Select level A (50%), level B (100%) or level C (150%) of this

weekly amount according to decision on seriousness (see 2 above). NB these levels already take into account ordinary living expenses.

5. Consider factors relevant to individual case. Outgoings: these are only relevant if they are out of the ordinary and substantially reduce ability to pay, leading to undue hardship. Timely guilty plea: give credit where appropriate. Compensation/costs if these are applicable then total financial penalty must be considered in relation to known means, including savings. If means insufficient for all three elements, apply usual priority of compensation – fine – costs. Confirm original figure or justify any change.

6. **Announce amount of fine**: seek immediate payment. If payment in full not possible, seek immediate part payment. If time is asked for, consider all information above in setting level of payments/time to clear total sum.

Costs

109.17   The following guidance was given by the Court of Appeal in *R v. Northallerton Magistrates' Court ex parte Dove* 2000 1 Cr App R (S) 136:

1. An order for costs to the prosecutor should never exceed the sum which, having regard to the defendant's means and any other financial order imposed upon him, he is able to pay and which it is reasonable to order him to pay. 2. Such an order should never exceed the sum which the prosecutor had actually and reasonably incurred. 3. The purpose of the order is to compensate the prosecutor and not to punish the defendant. 4. The costs ordered to be paid should not in the ordinary way be grossly disproportionate to the fine imposed for the offence. If the total of the proposed fine and the costs sought by the prosecutor exceeds the sum which the defendant could reasonably be ordered to pay, it was preferable to achieve an acceptable total by reducing the sum of costs ordered, rather than by reducing the fine. 5. It is for the defendant to provide the justices with such data relevant to his financial position as would enable them to assess what he could reasonably afford to pay, and if he fails to do so the justices are entitled to draw reasonable inferences as to his means from all the circumstances of the case. 6. It is incumbent on any court, which propose to make any financial order against a defendant, to give him a fair opportunity to adduce any relevant financial information and to make any appropriate submissions.

Compensation orders

The Legal Framework

109.18   As well as assessing the seriousness of the offence, including the impact on the victim, and any mitigating factors affecting the offender, the court is under a duty to consider compensation in every case where loss, damage or injury has resulted from the offence, whether or not an application has been made (Powers of Criminal Courts (Sentencing) Act 2000, s.130).

Priorities

109.19   If the sentence is to be financial, then the order of priorities is compensation, fine, costs. If the sentence is to be a community penalty, the court should consider carefully the overall burdens placed on the offender if a compensation order is to be made too. If the sentence is to be custody, then a compensation order will be unlikely unless the offender has financial resources available with which to pay immediately or on release.

Giving Reasons

109.20   If, having considered making a compensation order, the court decides that it is not appropriate to make one, it has a statutory duty to give its reasons for not ordering compensation.

Limitations on Powers

109.21   Magistrates have the power to award compensation for personal injury, loss or damage up to a total of £5,000 for each offence. An exception is where the injury, loss or damage arises from a road accident: a compensation order may not be made in such a case unless there is conviction of an offence under the Theft Act or if the offender is uninsured and the Motor Insurers' Bureau will not cover the loss. If in doubt, seek advice from the legal adviser. Compensation should only be awarded in fairly clear, uncomplicated cases: if there are disputes and complications, the matter should be left to the civil courts.

No Double Compensation

109.22   Any victim may bring a civil action for damages against the offender: if that action is successful, the civil court will deduct the amount paid by the offender under a compensation order. In this way, there should be no double compensation. The same applies where the victim receives a payment under the Criminal Injuries Compensation Scheme. The magistrates' court should therefore take no account of these other possibilities.

Criminal Injuries Compensation Scheme

109.23   The Criminal Injuries Compensation Scheme provides state compensation for the victims of crimes of violence, particularly those who are seriously injured. The minimum award is currently £1,000. Courts are encouraged to make compensation orders, whether or not the case falls within the Criminal Injuries Compensation Scheme, in order to bring home to offenders themselves the consequences of their actions.

The Purpose of Compensation Orders

109.24   The purpose of making a compensation order is to compensate the victim for his or her losses. The compensation may relate to offences taken into consideration, subject to a maximum of £5,000 per charge. Compensation for personal injury may include compensation for terror, shock or distress caused by the offence. The court must have regard to the means of the offender when calculating the amount of the order.

The Approach to Compensation

109.25   In calculating the gross amount of compensation, courts should consider compensating the victim for two types of loss. The first, sometimes called 'special damages', includes compensation for financial loss sustained as a result of the offence – e.g. the cost of repairing damage, or in cases of injury, any loss of earnings or dental expenses. If these costs are not agreed, the court should ask for evidence of them. The second type of loss, sometimes called 'general damages', covers compensation for the pain and suffering of the injury itself and for any loss of facility.

Calculating the Compensation

109.26   The amount of compensation should be determined in the light of medical evidence, the victim's sex and age, and any other factors which appear to the court to be relevant in the particular case. If the court does not have sufficient information, then the matter should be adjourned to obtain more facts. The Table below gives some general guidance on appropriate starting points for general damages for personal injuries. Once the court has made a preliminary calculation of the appropriate compensation, it is required to have regard to the means of the offender before making an order. Where the offender has little money, the order may have to be scaled down significantly. However, even a compensation order for a fairly small sum may be important to the victim.

Type of injury	Description	Starting point
Graze	Depending on size	Up to £75
Bruise	Depending on size	Up to £100
Black eye		£125
Cut: no permanent scar	Depending on size and whether stitched	£100–£500
Sprain	Depending on loss of mobility	£100–£1,000
Finger	Fractured little finger, recovery within month	£1,000
Loss of non-front tooth	Depending on cosmetic effect	£500–£1,000
Loss of front tooth	Depending on cosmetic effect	£1,500
Eye	Blurred or double vision	£1,000
Nose	Undisplaced fractured of nasal bone	£1,000
	Displaced fracture of bone requiring manipulation	£1,500
	Not causing fracture but displaced septum requiring sub-mucous resection	£2,000
Facial scar	However small, resulting in permanent disfigurement	£1,500
Wrist	Closed fracture, recovery within month	£3,000
	Displaced fracture, limb in plaster, recovery in 6 months	£3,500
Leg or arm	Closed fracture of tibia, fibula, ulna or radius, recovery within month	£3,500
Laparotomy	Stomach scar 6–8 inches (resulting from operation)	£3,500

Community sentences

109.27   The purpose of a community sentence is to provide a rigorous and effective punishment for an offender whose offence requires more than a financial penalty but is not so serious as to necessitate imprisonment. A community sentence has three principal elements: restriction of liberty, reparation and prevention of re-offending. Community sentences include:

- attendance centre orders;
- community rehabilitation orders with or without special requirements;
- community punishment orders;
- community punishment and rehabilitation orders;
- curfew orders;
- drug treatment and testing orders.

The restrictions on liberty imposed by the sentence must be commensurate with the seriousness of the offence and the order must be the one most suitable for the offender. It is generally good practice to require a pre-sentence or specific sentence report when considering whether to impose a community sentence. Where a report is considered necessary the shorter report should be requested whenever this will be sufficient, to enable the case to be finalised more speedily. In ordering such a report the court should indicate any relevant findings of fact, view of the level of seriousness and the aim of the sentence. In pronouncing sentence the court should stress the need of the offender to co-operate and the consequences of breach. Penalties for breach of a community sentence are:

- a fine of up to £1,000, the order to continue;
- community punishment of up to 60 hours, the order to continue;
- revocation and re-sentencing for the original offence (in which case the probable sentence will be custody);
- attendance centre order.

See the revised National Standards and the new inter-agency publication *Towards Good Practice* – Community Sentences and the Courts.

The court may ask to be kept informed of the offender's progress under the order.

Electronic monitoring of curfew orders

109.28   Curfew orders enforced by electronic monitoring are available for offenders aged ten and over. The curfew order is a community sentence requiring an offender to remain at a specified place from 2 to 12 hours a day on from 1 to 7 days a week, for a maximum period of six months. The court must obtain and consider information about the proposed curfew address including the attitude of others affected by the order. The order must take account of religious beliefs, employment, education and the requirements of other community orders. The offender's consent is not required.

The aims of the order are:

- to restrict liberty in a systematic controlled way;
- to make it harder for the offender to commit further crimes;
- to interrupt the pattern of offending by removing the offender from the circumstances of his/her offending;
- provide clear evidence of curfew compliance.

The order can be used as a stand alone order, in combination with any other community order, or can be added to a pre-existing community order. When considering whether to impose an order the offence must be assessed by the court to be 'serious enough' for a community penalty. When ordering a pre-sentence report the court should specifically ask the probation service to carry out a curfew assessment in all appropriate cases.

Breach of court orders

109.29   The breach of court orders should never be treated lightly. They should be rigorously enforced. In making any pronouncement on sentence the breach should be given special mention. A failure by the court to respond effectively to a breach can:

- erode public confidence in the courts;
- undermine the work of the agency supervising the order;
- allow the offender to feel he has 'got away with it'.

The offender should be clearly told of the seriousness of the offence and, if the court decides to allow an order to continue, be told what is expected of him/her and the likely consequence of any further breach. In the case of community sentences there are National Standards revised in April 2002 which lay down strict enforcement requirements for the probation service.

Racially or religiously aggravated offences

109.30   There are special provisions on racial and religious aggravation, under the Crime and Disorder Act 1998 as amended. There are two forms of aggravation: an offence is racially or religiously aggravated EITHER if it is racially or religiously motivated, OR if in committing the offence the offender demonstrates racial or religious hostility (e.g. by making a racist remark). The guideline case for sentencing for these offences is *Kelly and Donnelly 2001*, and three situations should be treated separately:

i)   there are a few specific racially or religiously aggravated offences in the Crime and Disorder Act, which have higher maximum penalties than the non-aggravated versions of those offences (e.g. common assault, ABH, criminal damage, etc). Where a defendant is convicted of one of these special offences, the court should determine its sentence for the basic offence (such as criminal damage or assault), and then decide how much to add for the racial or religious aggravation. When the sentence is announced, the court should state how much it added to the basic offence in order to reflect the racial or religious aggravation.

ii)   most offences do not have a specific racially or religiously aggravated version, however. Here, the general principle applies, which is that racial or religious aggravation is a factor that should increase the severity of the sentence.

iii)   where an offender is convicted of an offence which has a racially or religiously aggravated version, but is convicted only of the basic offence, it is wrong in principle to pass a higher sentence on racial or religious grounds. If the racially or religiously aggravated version of the offence is not charged or not proved, that is the end of the matter.

Road traffic offences

Disqualification

109.31   Some offences carry mandatory disqualification. This mandatory disqualification period may be automatically lengthened by the existence of certain previous convictions and disqualifications. Sentencers should not disqualify defendants in their absence although there is provision in statute to do so provided that an offender is given adequate notice of the hearing at which the court will consider disqualification. This discretionary power should only be exercised in out of the ordinary circumstances. As with all decisions of this type, account should be taken of human rights legislation. The court must give cogent and explicit reasons for any decision to disqualify in absence.

Penalty points and disqualification

109.32   All endorsable offences carry also as an alternative discretionary power to disqualify instead of imposing penalty points. Dangerous driving carries an obligatory minimum disqualification of one year and a mandatory extended re-test. For any offence which carries penalty points the courts have a discretion to order a re-test provided there is evidence of inexperience, incompetence or infirmity. It would be an ordinary test except where disqualification is obligatory when an extended test would be required. The number of variable penalty points or the period of disqualification is targeted strictly at the seriousness of the offence and in either case must not be reduced below the statutory minimum, where applicable. Offences committed on different occasions may carry points, even where they are dealt with on the same occasion.

Disqualification until a test is passed

109.33   A magistrates' court **must** disqualify an offender until he passes an *extended driving test* where he is convicted of an offence of dangerous driving. The court has a **discretion** to disqualify until a test is passed where the offender has been convicted of an offence involving obligatory disqualification. In this case it is the ordinary driving test that must be undertaken. An offender disqualified as a 'totter' under the penalty points provisions **may** also be ordered to re-take a driving test, in which case it will be the *extended test*. The discretion is likely to be exercised where there is evidence of inexperience, incompetence or infirmity; or the disqualification period imposed is lengthy (i.e. the offender is going to be 'off the road' for a considerable time).

Disqualifications for less than 56 days

109.34   A disqualification for less than 56 days is also more lenient in that it does not revoke the licence and cannot increase subsequent mandatory periods even if it is imposed under the points provisions.

Reduction for guilty plea

109.35   The precise amount of credit for a timely guilty plea will depend on the facts of each case. It should be given in respect of the fine or periods of community sentence or custody. An early guilty plea may also affect the length of a disqualification or the number of penalty points but cannot apply so as to reduce minimum mandatory periods of disqualification.

The multiple offender

109.36   Where an offender is convicted of several offences committed on one occasion, it is suggested that the court should concentrate on the most serious offence, carrying the greatest number of penalty points or period of disqualification. The application of the totality principle may then result in the court deciding to impose no separate penalty for the lesser offences, or to reduce fines for these offences below the level which might normally be imposed.

Totting

109.37   Repeat offenders who reach 12 points or more within a period of three years become liable to a minimum disqualification for 6 months, and in some instances 12 months or 2 years – but must be given an opportunity to address the court and/or bring evidence to show why such disqualification should not be ordered or should be reduced. Totting disqualifications, unlike other disqualifications, erase all penalty points. Totting disqualifications can be reduced or avoided for exceptional hardship or other circumstances. No account is to be taken of non-exceptional hardship or circumstances alleged to make the offence(s) not serious. No such ground can be used again to mitigate totting, if previously taken into account in totting mitigation within the three years preceding the conviction.

New drivers

109.38   Newly qualified drivers who incur 6 points or more during a two-year probationary period from the date of passing the driving test will automatically have their licence revoked by the Secretary of State and will have to apply for a provisional licence until they pass a repeat test. This total must include any points imposed prior to passing the test provided they are within three years.

Fixed penalties

109.39   If a fixed penalty was offered, the court should consider any reasons for not taking it up and, if valid, fine the amount of the appropriate fixed penalty (provided the amount is within the means of the offender), endorse if required, waive costs and allow a maximum of 28 days to pay. If a fixed penalty was refused or not offered, the court should consider whether there are aggravating factors which merit increasing the fine or there should be any credit for a guilty plea.

Fine enforcement

109.40   Unless an offender is appearing at the fine enforcement court because a review date was fixed when the fine was imposed, he will be either answering to a summons or on a warrant following a summons; in both instances he will probably have also had a reminder (court practices differ in this respect). The court should first receive information about the history of the case(s): the offence, the original means form, the date of the sentence, the order of the court regarding payment and the record of payment to date. Then, an up-to-date means form should be considered, followed by questioning by the legal adviser and/or the magistrates to establish any change of circumstances since the fine was imposed and the reason given for the failure to pay as ordered. The court can remit fines after a means enquiry and may order it if the court 'thinks it just to do so having regard to a change of circumstances' which may reasonably be found where:

- the defaulter's means have changed;

- information available to the court on a means enquiry was not before the sentencing court;

- arrears have accumulated by the imposition of additional fines to a level which makes repayment of the total amount within a reasonable time unlikely;

- defaulters are serving a term of imprisonment, remission may be a more practical alternative than the lodging of concurrent warrants of imprisonment;

- compensation and costs cannot be remitted but in circumstances where payment is unlikely or impractical due to the defaulter's means or circumstances the sum may be discharged or reduced. Victims and claimants should be consulted and given an opportunity to attend a hearing. NB: Excise penalties (which include fines and back duty for using an untaxed vehicle) cannot be remitted. The Magistrates' Courts Act 1980 s 82 requires that before a court may issue a warrant of commitment for non-payment of fines it must have: 'considered or tried all other methods of enforcing payment of the sum and it appears to the court that they are inappropriate or unsuccessful'. The court must record the reasons for not trying each of the methods. The options are:

- Detention in the precincts of the court (Magistrates' Courts Act 1980 s 135)

- **Money Payment Supervision Order:** for those under 21 years of age the court must place the defaulter under such an order (before making any decision to submit to detention) unless satisfied it is undesirable or impracticable so to do.

- **Attendance Centre Order:** for under 25 year olds only. It requires a defaulter to attend for two or three hours on a Saturday at a local attendance centre. The total number of hours must not exceed 24 if the defaulter is under 16 or 36 when he/she is 16 or over. NB. Not all sentencers have an Attendance Centre available to them.

- **Deduction from Benefit:** the court may request the Department for Work and Pensions to make payments direct from the offender's benefit, subject to any right of review or appeal he may have.

- **Attachment of Earnings Order:** the order requires an employer to make periodical payments from the defaulter's earnings to the court so this method is only suitable where the defaulter is in settled employment. A protected earnings rate (the rate below which his earnings will not be reduced as a result of the order) needs to be fixed together with a normal deduction rate, after enquiring into the defendant's means and needs and obligations.

- **Distress Warrant:** authorises the bailiffs to seize goods belonging to the defaulter and sell them in order to pay the fine, together with the bailiff's costs. Its issue may be postponed on terms.

- **Warrants of overnight detention:** the defaulter can be held overnight in the police station. He must be released at eight o'clock the following morning or the same morning if arrested after midnight.

- **Imprisonment:** the court must conduct a means enquiry before finding the defaulter guilty of culpable neglect or wilful refusal to pay. An opportunity must be provided for legal representation. The aim in fixing a period of commitment should be to identify the shortest period which is likely to succeed in obtaining payment and the periods prescribed in schedule 4 of the Magistrates' Courts Act 1980 (set out below) should be regarded as maxima rather than the norm. The period of imprisonment may be suspended pending regular payments. Where such payments are not made, the defaulter should be brought back before the court for consideration of whether the period of imprisonment should be implemented.

Maximum periods of imprisonment in default of payment

109.41   An amount not exceeding £200 7 days

An amount exceeding £200 but not exceeding £500 14 days

An amount exceeding £500 but not exceeding £1,000 28 days

An amount exceeding £1,000 but not exceeding £2,500 45 days

An amount exceeding £2,500 but not exceeding £5,000 3 months

An amount exceeding £5,000 but not exceeding £10,000 6 months

An amount exceeding £10,000 12 months

(The Crown Court has additional powers, £10,000 but not exceeding £20,000 12 months; £20,000 but not exceeding £50,000 18 months; £50,000 but not exceeding £100,000 2 years; £100,000 but not exceeding £250,000 3 years; £250,000 but not exceeding £1m 5 years and an amount exceeding £1m 10 years.)

Notes   Search: magistrates can order the defaulter to be searched and any money found on him/her to be used to pay the fine.

110   MAKING OFF WITHOUT PAYMENT

110.1   Theft Act 1978 s 3

Triable either way. On indictment maximum sentence 2 years. On summary maximum 6 months and/or £5,000.

Restitution Order There is power to make a restitution order under Powers of Criminal Courts (Sentencing) Act 2000 s 148.

For the tariff for general dishonesty offences see THEFT ETC

Magistrates' Court Sentencing Guidelines January 2004

110.2   For a first time offender pleading not guilty. Entry point. Is a discharge or a fine appropriate? Consider the impact on the victim. Examples of aggravating factors for the offence are deliberate plan, high value, two or more involved and victim particularly vulnerable. Examples of mitigating factors for the offence are impulsive action and low value. Examples of mitigation are age, health (physical or mental), co-operation with the police, genuine remorse and voluntary compensation. Give reasons if not awarding compensation. Starting point fine B. (100% of weekly take home pay/weekly benefit payment)

For details about the guidelines see MAGISTRATES' COURT SENTENCING GUIDELINES at page 483.

MANAGING A COMPANY WHEN BANKRUPT

See INSOLVENCY OFFENCES

111   MANSLAUGHTER

111.1   Offences Against the Person Act 1861 s 5 and the Homicide Act 1957 s 2(3)
Indictable only. Maximum sentence life imprisonment.

Domestic Violence, Crime and Victims Act 2004 s 5 introduces a new offence of causing or allowing the death of a child or vulnerable adult.

CHAPTERS in this book are in bold capitals. The *paragraph titles* are in bold italics. Where a chapter (e.g. arson) has subsections, the **subsections** are in lower case bold.

Automatic life Manslaughter is a specified offence for automatic life[1] for offences committed before 4/4/05.

Dangerous Offender provisions For offences committed on or after 4/4/05 where there is a significant risk to members of the public of serious harm etc. there is a mandatory duty to pass a life sentence when it is justified and otherwise a sentence of imprisonment for public protection[4]. For offenders under 18 the duty is to pass detention for life, detention for public protection or an extended sentence[5].

Depriving defendant of vehicle used There is power to deprive the defendant of the vehicle used[2] for the purposes of committing the offence.

Disqualification from driving When committed by a driver of a motor vehicle, there is obligatory disqualification for 2 years unless there are special reasons and endorsement with 3–11 points[3]. The court must order him to be disqualified till he has passed the appropriate driving test unless there are special reasons.

Funeral expenses The Court may make this compensation order[6] see *Funeral expenses of the deceased*

Longer than Commensurate sentences and Extended sentences Manslaughter is a violent offence for the purposes of passing a longer than commensurate sentence [Powers of Criminal Courts (Sentencing) Act 2000 s 80(2)] and an extended sentence (extending the licence) [Powers of Criminal Courts (Sentencing) Act 2000 s 85(2)(b)][7]. These provisions will continue to apply to offences committed after 29/9/98 and before 4/4/05.

Sexual Offences Prevention Order There is a discretionary power to make this order when it is necessary to protect the public etc[8].

Working with children Where the offence is against a child (aged under 18), the defendant is aged 18 or over and s/he is sentenced to 12 months or more or a hospital order etc. the court <u>must</u> disqualify him/her from working with children unless satisfied s/he is unlikely to commit any further offences against a child when the court must state its reasons for not doing so[9]. For a defendant aged less than 18 at the time of the offence the court must order disqualification if s/he is sentenced to 12 months or more and the court is satisfied that the defendant will commit a further offence against a child[10]. The court must state its reasons for so doing.

---

1   Powers of Criminal Courts (Sentencing) Act 2000 s 109(5)
2   Powers of Criminal Courts (Sentencing) Act 2000 s 143(6) & (7)
3   Road Traffic Offenders Act 1988 s 34(1), (4) & Sch 2 Part II
4   Criminal Justice Act 2003 s 225
5   Criminal Justice Act 2003 s 226 and 228
6   Powers of Criminal Courts (Sentencing) Act 2000 s 130(1)(b)
7   Powers of Criminal Courts (Sentencing) Act 2000 s 161(3)
8   Sexual Offences Act 2003 s 104 & Sch. 5
9   Criminal Justice and Court Services Act 2000 s 28
10 Criminal Justice and Court Services Act 2000 s 29

The cases are in part divided into sections for the weapon that was used, as that part of the case is usually clear. Much more important factors are the intent and the surrounding circumstances. One of the most critical factors is whether there was an intent to kill or cause GBH, which would be present, when the offence is based on diminished responsibility or provocation. It is not possible to divide the cases by intent because many of the cases provide insufficient information.

Crown Court statistics – England and – Wales Males 21+
111.2

Year	Plea	Total Numbers sentenced	Type of sentence %					Average length of custody (months)
			Discharge	Fine	Community sentence	Suspended sentence	Custody	
			Manslaughter					
2002	Guilty	137	–	–6	4	83	61.8	
	Not guilty	76	–	1	1	3	93	72.9
2003	Guilty	110	–	2	5	2	76	55.5
	Not guilty	70	–	–	–	4	96	80.1
			Manslaughter due to diminished responsibility					
2002	Guilty	14	–	–	–	–	43	51.6
	Not guilty	2	–	–	–	–	50	84
2003	Guilty	17	–	–	–	–	41	57.6
	Not guilty	5	–	–	–	–	100	84

For details and explanations about the statistics in the book see page vii.

Guideline remarks

111.3   *R v Boyer* 1981 Cr App R (S) 35. The offence of manslaughter attracts the widest band of sentences for any offence known to this court. The sentence can vary from life imprisonment to a conditional discharge.

R v Butler 1999 2 Cr App R (S) 339. Little use is gained in sentencing in manslaughter cases from an exhaustive view of the authorities since it is clear that this court has repeatedly said that sentencing in manslaughter cases is (a) very difficult, and (b) turns on the particular facts of the cases under consideration.

R v Barker 2003 2 Cr App R (S) 110. Manslaughter cases of this kind (gross negligence) are very difficult because the court is sentencing for consequences the defendant did not intend. The public interest requires the imposition of a prison sentence where lives are taken in these circumstances. (For more details see **111.34**)

Guideline remarks – Diminished responsibility

111.4   *R v Chambers* 1983 5 Cr App R (S) 190. LCJ. In diminished responsibility cases there are various courses open to a judge. His choice of the right course will depend on the state of the evidence and the material before him. If the psychiatric reports recommend and justify it, and there are no contrary indications, he will make a hospital order. Where a hospital order is not recommended, or is not appropriate, and the defendant constitutes a danger to the public for an unpredictable period of time, the right sentence will, in all probabilities, be one of life imprisonment. In cases where the evidence indicates that the accused's responsibility for his acts was so grossly impaired that his degree of responsibility for them was minimal, then a lenient course will be open to the judge. Provided there is no danger of repetition of violence, it will usually be possible to make such an order as will give the accused his freedom, possibly with some supervision. There will however be cases in which there is no proper basis for a hospital order; but in which the accused's degree of responsibility is not minimal. In such cases the judge should pass a determinate sentence of imprisonment, the length of which will depend on two factors: his assessment of the degree of the accused's responsibility and his view as to the period of time, if any, for which the accused will continue to be a danger to the public.

Babies
See CHILDREN

Body, dismembering and disposing of the

111.5   *R v Frisby* 2002 1 Cr App R (S) 289. The defendant was convicted of manslaughter on the basis of provocation. Held. (Two judge court.)The dismembering and disposal of the body was not a proper matter to take into account. It would have been a proper matter in relation to murder as showing some form of pre-planning but not for manslaughter. Sentence reduced from 8 years to **6 years**.

R v Brooks 2004 1 Cr App R (S) 315. The defendant was convicted of manslaughter on the basis of provocation. Held. (Three judge court including Rose LJ) We disagree with *R v Frisby* 2002 1 Cr App R (S) 289 There may be cases when diminished responsibility is the basis in which dismembering may not have an aggravating effect. Where provocation is concerned dismembering may well have an aggravating effect just as it does in murder in accordance with the Practice Statement last year. Here it was an aggravating factor.

Burglars/Robbers/Thieves, by

111.6   *R v De Jesus Amarel* 1999 Unreported 11/6/99. The defendant pleaded guilty to manslaughter and robbery. The victim, aged 72 had befriended the defendant aged 26. However the defendant and another agreed to steal from him. They gagged him, and the other punched him. They found £180 and tied him up and gagged him. They left him to die while they went to buy drugs. The defendant played the lesser role in the violence but took a full part in the manslaughter. He was due to give evidence against the other. Held. **10 years** and 8 concurrent was not excessive.

Att-Gen's Ref. Nos. 19, 20 and 21 of 2001 2002 1 Cr App R (S) 136. The defendants B, F and C pleaded to attempted robbery. They denied murder. On the third day of their murder trial B and F pleaded to manslaughter and C pleaded to conspiracy to rob. A 59-year-old Norwegian man was walking in Blackpool town centre and the three defendants attacked him from behind. He was pushed to the ground and kicked to the head and body. They didn't find his wallet. People came to his help and the three fled. The victim was very badly beaten and suffered extensive bruising to the face. Ninety minutes later a 60-year-old man was walking home nearby. He was attacked from behind and robbed of £270 and a sovereign ring. He staggered home, collapsed and died. There were nine fractures to seven of his ribs. Four penetrated his chest cavity. The victim had pre-existing emphysema and respiratory problems caused by the fractured ribs which led to his rapid decline. The cause of death was 'blunt force chest and neck injuries'. The manslaughter basis of plea was that the chest injuries were caused by F falling on him and/or sitting on him in order to restrain him while his property was stolen. C's basis of plea to the conspiracy was he withdrew before the violence begun and he wasn't responsible for the death. B was 36 and of effective good character. He was married with two children. He had a good work record as a security guard and had been discharged from the army with exemplary character. He was separated from his wife and at a low ebb in a hostel. F was 26 and the Judge ignored his record. He broke the 'wall of silence' and assisted in the recovery of part of the property. C was 16 at the time and had spent a 'very considerable period' in custody and none of it would count to his sentence. B and F received 7 years for the manslaughter with 5 concurrent for the attempted robbery. C received **2 years detention and training** but the effective sentence would be a little short of **4 years**. Held. The offences were not opportunist. The first offence involved considerable gratuitous violence. Even without a death or unintended serious injury resulting, these two offences following pleas of guilty merited for an adult **at least 6 years**. The risk of serious harm was a high one. Deterrent sentences were demanded. There was no good reason why the sentences for the 2 attacks were concurrent. They were quite distinct matters. We would have imposed a sentence of 12 years for the manslaughter and **3 years consecutive** for the attempted robbery making **15 years**. For a plea that would be **11 to 12 years**. Taking into account it was a reference 10 years for B and F, made up of **9 years** for the manslaughter and 1 year consecutive for the attempt. The 1 year is artificially low to take account it was a reference. C when 16 had faced a murder charge when he bore no responsibility for the death. As the appropriate sentence for an adult was 6 years C's sentence was not unduly lenient.

R v Simpson 2002 2 Cr App R (S) 234. LCJ. The defendant made an early guilty plea to manslaughter and two robberies. The first victim, an 89-year-old lady was returning to her flat after picking up her pension and doing some shopping. As she was walking up the stairs to the flat the defendant pulled her shopping bag firmly backwards. It contained her purse with £6 in it. She tried to resist and he gave it a heavier pull. She fell backwards and slid down the concrete stairs. He ran off with the bag. She was found to have a fracture to her neck and femur. A plate and screws were inserted. The operation appeared straightforward but she suffered two consequential chest infections and died about a month after the robbery. Almost immediately after the first robbery, the defendant 'thumped' a 76-year-old lady in the back and then pulled at her bag. It contained her pension book, documents and purse. The victim had just returned from collecting her pension. He pulled at it until she let go and drove away. The defendant was now 40 with convictions going back to the early 1970s. Over the years he had been in and out of prison for dishonesty and driving offences. In 1995 he received 4 years for two robberies and one of the victims was an 83 year old lady who was followed from picking up her pension and knocked to the ground. The second robbery was similar. After the manslaughter offence he was sentenced to 3 years for burglary and serious driving offences. He needed £200 a day for heroin. Held. These offences are mean beyond words, easy to commit, highly prevalent and dangerous both to life and limb of the elderly victims. When they are committed by dangerous acts and death occurs severe sentences are called for. There can be no fault with the sentence of 7 years for the robberies because of his record and the circumstances. The **10 years** for the manslaughter as an overall sentence could not be faulted. The sentences remained consecutive to the sentence he was serving.

R v Ginley 2002 2 Cr App R (S) 277. The defendant was convicted of manslaughter and attempted robbery. The 57-year-old victim and his disabled wife were helping out at their frozen food warehouse. Because of ill health they were semi-retired and their sons had taken the business over. In 1987 the victim had had a triple bypass and his wife was paralysed down one side and in a wheelchair. In the late morning the defendant and another entered the warehouse. One pulled a balaclava down over his face and demanded to know where the safe was. He put a knife with a 10″ blade to the victim's throat and put him in a headlock. There was a scuffle in which the victim was prodded in the ribs a number of times with the knife. The wife pointed to the safe in the office and picked up a stick to go to her husband's aid. The second man who was masked grabbed her stick and pushed her in her wheelchair to the other side of the office away from the panic button. The victim shouted the police were on their way and the robbers left believing the panic button had been pressed. The victim then pressed the panic button and the police attended quickly. The victim gave the number of the car to an officer, collapsed and died of a heart attack. The pathologist said, 'death could have occurred at any time but trauma and excitement could precipitate a heart attack. More likely than not the victim would have been alive had it not been for the struggle.' The defendant was 21 when sentenced and had convictions but none for violence. Held. The judge quite rightly took the view that this was a robbery of an extreme kind. It was a prepared robbery. There was nothing wrong with 9 years for the robbery without considering the death. The 3 years extra for the death was wholly appropriate. **12 years** upheld. (The poor health of the victim is not listed as a factor in the judgement confirming the principle defendants do not receive a reduction when the defendant is of poor health.)

R v Clark and Lappin 2002 2 Cr App R (S) 353. The defendant L pleaded guilty to manslaughter and robbery at the first opportunity. C pleaded guilty to robbery. At about midnight the 32-year-old alcoholic victim was walking in the street with two bottles of cider. He was beaten and robbed of the two bottles. L punched him and caused quite 'horrific injuries'. They were a closed and swollen eye, which required three stitches, a cut to the lip and a broken nose. The victim was discharged from hospital and asked to return in the morning. Unfortunately he suffered from a liver disease and his blood would not clot. When he returned the next morning his nose would not stop bleeding and he suffered a cardiac arrest. He died 16 days later of multiple organ failure as a result of bleeding caused by his facial injuries. The pathologist said the injuries were consistent with several punches and could be one rather forceful punch and a lesser punch. The basis of plea was, 'C asked the victim for a cigarette and the victim probably thought he was going to be robbed and swung a bottle at L. At that stage they didn't intend to rob him and L punched him and both men fell to the ground. When L was on top of the victim he told C to take the bottles which he did. As L walked away the victim grabbed his jumper and L punched him on the nose causing the fatal injury.' L was then 19 with 12 convictions including attempted robbery, theft, assault on police, criminal damage, threatening behaviour, burglary and possession of an offensive weapon. He had served 4 months YOI. Held. The aggravating feature was that the offence occurred during a robbery. **6 years** YOI was not obviously too long.

Att-Gen's Ref. Nos. 108–9 of 2002 2003 2 Cr App R (S) 608. The defendants were convicted of manslaughter, conspiracy to rob and threatening to kill. The defendant, together with a third man, went to the victim's 12th floor flat to rob him. They recruited another to trick the victim into opening his front door. After the door was opened all three burst in. The victim ran to his bedroom where his 3-year old daughter was asleep. The men demanded the keys to his sports car and the victim refused. One of the men had a folding knife; the other had a claw hammer. One of them threatened to shoot him. One of them grabbed his daughter and threatened to kill her. The victim, in panic, threatened to climb out of the window unless they released the child. Then a man held on to the child and the victim climbed out of the window. The three defendants left. As the victim was clinging to the ledge the police arrived at the foot of the block and as they went in the defendants were leaving. The police were told a different floor from the one on which the events were taking place. Inside the flat, a friend tried to pull the victim back in but the victim lost his friend's grasp and fell to his death. One defendant denied presence, the other admitted presence but denied playing any part in the robbery. Both defendants were 22, one was of good character, the other had one conviction for possessing a bladed article 3 years earlier. Held. There were 3 male invaders who were armed with at least one and probably two weapons. The threats that they made, to the child were despicable and understandably induced intense fear. The defendants left without rendering him any assistance and they sought to mislead the police about where he might be found. The manslaughter would normally attract a sentence of between **10 and 12 years**; the conspiracy to rob, a sentence of at least 7 years. For the manslaughter, 6 years was unduly lenient; **9 years** substituted. For the conspiracy to rob, 4 years was unduly lenient; 6 years substituted. All concurrent.

R v Silkstone 2004 2 Cr App R (S) 416. The defendant pleaded guilty to manslaughter and robbery. She had a co accused, O, who pleaded guilty to murder and robbery. The defendant aged 16 agreed to help O rob someone of a car. The plan was that she would activate a pelican crossing to bring a car to a stop and O would eject the driver and drive off with the defendant. O was dressed in a black Ninja type suit showing only a small area round his eyes. He had a knife with a long blade. When the defendant activated the pelican crossing the 54-year-old victim stopped his car and O got in it and immediately attacked him with the knife. O ejected the victim and the defendant got in the car leaving the victim lying in the road. He died at the scene having sustained four stab wounds to the face and one to the chest. The defendant and O abandoned the car, burnt the property they had taken from it, burnt their own clothes and left the area. The basis of plea was that she knew that O had a knife and was aware that he might use it during the robbery to threaten the driver. She had no previous convictions. A pre-sentence report was highly favourable, saying she had experienced problems which may have led her to become too close to O. She could not have anticipated O's behaviour and that she had allowed herself to be manipulated. She expressed remorse and regret and was very conscious of the trauma caused to the victim's family. The report said she would not offend again and posed no risk of future harm to the public. Held. It was a well-made point that the sentence should not be so heavy as to crush her spirit, but her role was a key one and fell to be dealt with severely. Natural revulsion at the viciousness of the attack by O should not be reflected in the level of sentence appropriate for this defendant, given her lack of intention that it should occur. The appropriate starting point for the manslaughter was **9 years**, reduced to **6 years** for the guilty plea and a further year for her youth, good character and lack of future danger. **5 years detention** for the manslaughter and 4 years for the robbery to run concurrently, not 8 and 7 concurrent.

Old cases. *R v Brophy* 1995 16 Cr App R (S) 652; *Att-Gen's Ref No 68 of 1995* 1996 2 Cr App R (S) 358.

Children – Neglect, starvation etc

111.7 *R v Watts* 2002 1 Cr App R (S) 228. The defendant changed her plea to guilty to manslaughter. She was a single mother and sole carer for her 20-month-old daughter and her 9-month-old son, the victim. During the pregnancy of the son she made it clear she did not want the baby. Afterwards she would deny his existence and told her GP that she hated him. Nannies were employed and found a catalogue of neglect. Some were not paid. While she was at work she provided childcare for the older child but saved money by not providing it for her son. She made a 999 call and emergency services found the boy dead. He was unchanged, unwashed, unfed and had been in a cold room for hours. He was caked with faeces and grossly underweight. He had a bedsore and had been starved over a long period. There was severe skin breakdown on both the buttocks and the penis. The cause of death was severe malnutrition and dehydration. She was of normal intelligence and led an active social and sex life. She had no friends and was estranged from her family. She had a severe untreatable personality disorder of an anti-social and histrionic variety and was an inveterate and skilful liar. One psychiatrist said, 'She will remain concerned with her own hedonistic satisfaction and short term gratification. She will continue to lie, fail to meet her financial obligations, steal and defraud. She will place blame and responsibility on others and take none herself.' Held. The photographs are horrific. The prolonged history of starvation, dehydration and cruel neglect are appalling. It is difficult to think of a more serious case of manslaughter by neglect. There was no sufficient evidence to suggest she posed a grave risk to the public so **10 years** not life.

R v Onley 2005 1 Cr App R (S) 122. The defendant pleaded guilty to the manslaughter of her son, aged 18 months. She was a single mother aged 20 with a nursery nursing qualification and was aware of the needs of a very young child. She lived with her mother and brother when the child was first born but then moved to a rented flat of her own. Her family were very supportive. She worked part time as a clerical assistant 3 days a week. Although she suffered from post-natal depression she appeared to be coping adequately and was not an abusive to the child. However, in the early months of 2003 she appeared able to maintain her lifestyle of socialising with her friends in pubs and clubs. She found herself in debt and so began working as an escort/prostitute. She started a relationship with a driver from the agency and began to spend increasingly less time with her child. 2 weeks before his death she took him to the GP with a cough, nappy rash and a high temperature. She left the child for long periods without a babysitter or anyone to look in on him. Bottles of milk and orange juice were placed in his cot. He was left in a soiled cot with increasingly severe nappy rash which became a significant source of fluid loss. The flat was equally unkempt. On the day of his death in May she left him 7 hrs 45 minutes earlier to discover him dead from dehydration caused by excoriation of the skin from severe nappy rash in a hot environment. In interview she initially (falsely) claimed that she left her son assuming that babysitters were on their way. In fact no babysitters had been arranged. She pleaded guilty to gross negligence manslaughter. Held. There was gross neglect during the last 6 or 7 days of this boy's appalling life. **6 years detention** upheld.

Children – With violence

111.8   *R v Pigott* 1999 1 Cr App R (S) 392. The defendant was convicted of manslaughter when the prosecution had rejected that plea before the trial for murder. The defendant aged then 23, lived with his son aged 9 months and the son's mother. When the mother was out he consumed four cans of lager and 2 litres of cider. The baby cried and he struck him with his hand or fist. The baby died due to head injuries including a fracture to the left parieto-occipital bones. There was no previous history of violence to the baby. **6 years** YOI substituted for 10

R v Yates 2001 1 Cr App R (S) 428. The defendant pleaded guilty to manslaughter. The defendant was caring for his 3-month-old baby girl while the mother was in bed unwell. He was unable to stop the baby crying. He shook her violently causing the baby to be limp and silent. She was taken to hospital where her head was swollen because of bleeding in her brain. Surgery was not successful and her life support systems were turned off. A post-mortem revealed that significant trauma to the baby's brain had been sustained 1 to 2 weeks before her admission to hospital. The left-sided subdural haematoma, which had led to her death, was probably inflicted on the same day as her admission. There was also a fracture of the skull. He was sentenced on the basis, 'that he had lost his temper when he had been unable to calm her. He had shaken her on two occasions. There were no direct blows and he was not responsible for the fracture. As soon as he realised harm had been done he immediately told his wife.' He had six previous spent convictions for violence, but had served no period of custody. The other children of theirs were said to be well parented. Held. The cases reveal the bottom bracket for baby cases is 2 years but in a most exceptional case a non-custodial is appropriate. Here **5 years** not 7 was appropriate.

R v Webb 2001 1 Cr App R (S) 524. The defendant pleaded guilty to manslaughter and cruelty to a child. The defendant lived with his wife and baby daughter. He became agitated with her. He scalded her accidentally but was reluctant to obtain medical advice. Later, his wife noticed that the baby screamed when her left arm was touched. Five days later when in hospital for an infection she was found to have a fractured rib. Eighteen days later the baby was rigid and her vision was unfocused. She was sent to hospital. Bruising on the neck, breastbone and rib cage developed. Three days later she died. At hospital the defendant said he had accidentally dropped her on her head. The baby was found to have a substantial skull fracture, the rib fracture seen earlier and three other fractures. The skull fracture could not have been accidental. Severe squeezing had caused the rib fracture. The injuries had been caused on no less than four separate occasions, and must have resulted in severe pain for something like 7 days. He later made admissions to a doctor saying he had deliberately hit her head on the cot and had pushed her head violently on to the bed dropping her twice. He had no previous convictions. It would be wrong to reduce the **5 years** sentence.

R v Turner 2002 1 Cr App R (S) 207. The defendant pleaded guilty to manslaughter on the basis of lack of intent and he acted in panic when flustered and under stress. Also diminished responsibility would have been open to him because of his intellectual limitations. He lived with a girl who he had met at a special school. On 12 December 1999 they had a baby. They were both 17 and neither could look after themselves let alone a baby. The relationship was stormy and the arrival of the baby put the relationship under additional and severe strain. Occasionally he would look after the baby with her mother but he seemed not to understand the importance of careful handling. On 15 January 2000 he was left in charge of the baby for the first time. He called his aunt to say the baby was not breathing properly and had gone floppy. When the ambulance came he refused to let them take her because he was worried about his partner. Later the baby was taken to hospital and doctors found haemorrhaging behind both eyes. There was widespread bleeding in the brain. The next day the life support system was switched off. The injuries were consistent with shaken baby syndrome but experts could not say for how long or with what vigour the shaking had been. In interview the defendant admitted shaking his daughter. He said it was a particular difficult day with problems with the local authority etc. The baby started crying and he could not stop it. He shook her twice and supported her head. That he said usually quietened her. When she cried again he shook her without holding her head and he noticed she went floppy. He was of good character. The reports agreed he was a man with very real handicaps with profound social incapacity. He had a borderline learning disability with significant impairment of intellectual and social functioning amounting to an abnormality of the mind. He was vulnerable and dependent on others. If he remained in custody his partner would not be able to cope and would be taken into care. The overwhelming view of the doctors was that custody was entirely inappropriate for him. He had spent 5 months in custody, which he had been unable to cope with. He had to remain in the protection unit. Held. Parents could not escape all the responsibilities for their actions by relying on their own problems. That does not mean in every tragic case where a child is killed custody is inevitable. Exceptional cases merit exceptional sentences. He lacked the mental capacity to appreciate the consequences of his actions and intended no harm to the baby. He was vulnerable and needed protection. He was totally ill equipped to deal with the situation and should never have been put in that position. The sooner he receives support, guidance and medical treatment the better. A **3 year community rehabilitation order** with a condition of treatment and duty to live where approved not $2^{1}/_{2}$ years YOI.

R v Wright 2003 1 Cr App R (S) 257. The defendant was convicted of manslaughter and cruelty to a child. In December 1998, she began to cohabit with her co-accused. She had two children of her own. He had a child, L then 5. She was cruel and spiteful to the L. She was heard to swear and shout at L and strike her head with a fist, causing L to fall. She also inflicted punishments on L. A neighbour saw L forced to stand silent facing the wall in front of a heater for an hour while her two children watched television. As a result of this treatment L began to physically decline. In January 2000, she was losing weight and her hair was coming out in handfuls. She also had bruises. In May 2000, paramedics went to the house and found her body. The Crown case was she had killed L with a forceful kick to the abdomen. The blow had been struck some days before she was found. She was 31 and of limited abilities. She received 10 and 5 years consecutive. Held. The sentencing bracket is **12 to 15 years**. The total sentence should be **12 years**. The cruelty sentence should remain, but it should be concurrent.

R v Bennett 2004 1 Cr App R (S) 396. The defendant was convicted of manslaughter and acquitted of murder (on the basis of provocation). The victim was the defendant's son who was $3^1/_2$ months old when he died between 10 pm and 2 am one night. The mother of the child woke up to find the defendant telling her that the child was not breathing. They both tried resuscitation and the emergency services were called. The child had suffered severe brain damage and was pronounced dead. The death was caused by violent shaking and probably a substantial blow. There were substantial head injuries caused by a force equivalent to a fall on the head from a height of 6 feet. The defendant admitted that he had shaken the child that night as he was frustrated at the child's crying. He also admitted shaking him on earlier occasions. At trial he said that he gave those answers to protect the child's mother. The defendant had been under considerable stress. He was 29 and had no experience of parenting. He had no record for violent offending, however the violence inflicted on the child was severe. Held. In the spectrum of provocation that can justify a jury reducing the offence from murder to manslaughter this offence was at the low end of that spectrum. **9 years** upheld.

Old cases. *R v White* 1995 16 Cr App R (S) 705; *R v Brannan* 1995 16 Cr App R (S) 766; *R v Staynor* 1996 1 Cr App R (S) 376; *R v Leggett* 1996 2 Cr App R (S) 77 and *R v Cawthorne* 1996 2 Cr App R (S) 445.

Concurrent, should the sentence be concurrent or consecutive to the sentence for the illegal activity

111.9   *R v Wacker* 2003 1 Cr App R (S) 92. The defendant was convicted of conspiracy to facilitate illegal entry and 58 counts of manslaughter. Sixty illegal immigrants travelled from China to Holland where they were loaded into an adapted container on the defendant's lorry. The deaths were caused by lack of air. The basis for the manslaughter was gross negligence. He received 8 years for the conspiracy and six consecutive for the manslaughter counts. The defence argued the total was too much and the Attorney General argued the 6 years for the manslaughter counts was too lenient although the total sentence was not challenged. Held. The causing of so many deaths to avoid detection puts this case in a category of its own. Concurrent sentences were the correct approach so there is no danger of punishing the underlying criminality twice. Therefore **14 years** for the manslaughter substituted, which would not have the appearance of devaluing the loss of life.

Crime of passion   See *Passion, Crime of*

Defendant aged under 16

111.10   *Att-Gen's Ref Nos. 68 and 69 of 1996* 1997 2 Cr App R (S) 280. Two girls L and H who were aged 13 and 12 at the time of the offence pleaded guilty to manslaughter. At a fairground there were a number of incidents involving girls fighting. Two who had been involved on earlier occasions sought to leave the site but were followed by the two defendants who were part of a much larger group. One girl was encouraged to fight H and she eventually agreed to do so. They fell to the ground and H managed to sit on her punching the girl in the chest and on the head. The victim of the manslaughter said the girl had had enough and intervened. L seized her by the hair and pulled her off balance and kicked her chest and head as she lay on the ground. H also kicked her between the eye and the ear. After a Newton hearing both were sentenced on the basis of one kick as victim lay defenceless on the ground. Both had no previous convictions. Held. It was worth **2 to 3¹/₂ years** detention, so the 2 year sentence remained undisturbed.

R v KC 2005 1 Cr App R (S) 545. The defendant was convicted of manslaughter. The unlawful act relied on was arson being reckless as to whether life was endangered. He was playing with his friends, on their bicycles at the rear of a retail park. One of whom was the deceased, who was 15. The group had removed pallets and pieces of wood from a waste container in order to construct ramps to cycle over. That container was a large metal box that was half full of paper, wood and cardboard. It had large metal doors that could be secured shut. At some point another friend put the deceased's bike inside the container whilst the defendant restrained the deceased. When released the deceased went to retrieve the bike and they closed the door on him and secured it. The defendant and his friend then went on top of the container and dropped pieces of wood though a narrow gap around the doors. Unbeknown to the boys the pieces of wood were causing the doors to become incapable of release. A short while later, the defendant lit a piece of paper and despite attempts to discourage him, posted the lit paper through the narrow gap. A small fire started inside the container and despite frantic efforts they could not release the doors. They stopped a passer-by immediately and the defendant summoned the fire brigade. The deceased made frantic pleas. When the fire brigade arrived they released the doors and retrieved the deceased who had 30% burns and tragically died some hours later. Reports indicated a low risk of re-offending, remorse and regret. He had positive references from school and had made exceptional progress since his detention. He was 15 and without convictions. Held. **3 years** detention not 4.

Old cases. *R v G* 1993 14 Cr App R 349 and *R v Coffey* 1994 15 Cr App R (S) 754.

Defendant aged 16–17

111.11 *R v Hamilton* 1999 1 Cr App R (S) 187. The defendant was convicted of manslaughter. The defendant aged 17 at the time visited his grandmother aged 83 to steal money from her to pay for drugs. She disturbed him and he strangled her. There was no sign of mental illness. Held. In view of the defendant's youth, his minor record and the fact the attack was not persisted or repeated **8 years** detention substituted for 10 years.

R v Jeans 1999 2 Cr App R (S) 257. The defendant pleaded guilty to manslaughter. There were two different parties attended by young people. One was orderly and attended by the victim and the other was disorderly and drunken and attended by the defendant then aged 16¹/₂. Later in the street when people from the two parties met, three youths from the defendant's group heckled the other group. Either the defendant or someone else from his group struck someone from the other group on the head with a piece of wood. The defendant then struck the victim with his piece of wood on the upper lip. The victim's nasal septum was torn away at the base. The victim lost consciousness and fell backwards. Unusually the shock to the brain caused the heart and breathing to stop. The defendant had two previous convictions for ABH and common assault. He had suffered abuse as a child. Remorse was shown from the outset. Held. Because of his youth and the surprising consequences of what he did, **4 years** detention substituted for 6 years.

R v Murray 2001 2 Cr App R (S) 17. The defendant was convicted of manslaughter of his stepfather after years of abuse. The defendant's mother married the victim when the defendant was 14. The relationship between the victim and his wife and his stepson deteriorated. The victim was seriously violent to his wife. He ripped down a curtain rail, smashed a telephone, threatened to break the TV set with a meat cleaver, tore off cupboard doors and threw knives at the defendant's bedroom door. The defendant, who was 17, told his mother that he did not want his stepfather at the flat. The stepfather was told about the remark and said he was not going to be dictated to by a 17 year old. He left a public house and went home. He found the defendant in and seized him by the shirt. He produced an iron bar weighing about 2lbs. The defendant was told to return to his flat. He refused and the victim hit him and threatened to hit and harm him. He prodded the defendant in the stomach with the bar quite firmly. The bar was raised. The defendant punched him to the face and grabbed the bar. The victim fell to his knees and the defendant managed to take the bar. The victim started to rise and the defendant hit him up to eight times with the bar. The victim's skull was hopelessly shattered. The defendant gave himself up to the police. He gave a full and frank account to the police. The defendant had no previous convictions and had many very positive reports. **18 months** detention and training order not 5 years detention.

Att-Gen's Ref No 63 of 2001 2001 1 Cr App R (S) 326. The defendant was convicted of manslaughter by reason of provocation. He had earlier pleaded guilty to manslaughter on the basis of a lack of intent and the prosecution had not accepted the plea. After a trial he was acquitted of murder and convicted of manslaughter. When 17, he was a regular at the pub where the victim was the manager. He was warned about his behaviour on a number of occasions. Shortly before the incident he was barred. He went to a party and then with friends at about 9.30pm he went to the victim's pub. He hid behind the pillar and the victim saw him and went to speak to him. An argument developed and the defendant punched him once, hard on the jaw. The victim was propelled backwards onto a gaming machine and then fell. He never regained consciousness. The defendant was dragged from the pub by a friend kicking as he went to another pub where he boasted he had beaten up the victim. The cause of death was bleeding in the skull because of a rupture to an artery. The blow had rotated the head. The defendant was arrested having tried to run away. In interview he said he had drunk about 12 bottles of beer and the victim had started talking to him as though he was 'a thicky' and showing him up to his friends. He also lied. In 1994 he was cautioned for ABH. In 1998 he pleaded to common assault on a fellow schoolboy. In 2000 there was another common assault when he punched another boy. He received 3 months detention. In December 2000 there was another ABH in which he kicked the victim twice in the head. He received 5 months detention. He was on bail for this when he killed the victim. His parents were heroin addicts and he had been drinking alcohol since 15. Since leaving school he had always been in work. His father and uncle were 'hard men' and he had been taught that men deal with conflict through violence. His risk of re-offending was assessed as high. He showed genuine remorse. Held. The judge appreciated the importance of affording protection to landlords particularly from those they have excluded. There was no weapon. Some judges would have passed more than **3 years**. It was lenient but not unduly lenient.

R v Walters 2005 1 Cr App R (S) 569. The defendant pleaded guilty to manslaughter on the basis of gross negligence and to a separate charge of ABH. The ABH occurred first, when the defendant attacked a man who was already being attacked by another man, P. The defendant kicked him on the nose and joined several others who were demanding his mobile phone. The victim was treated for a bruised, swollen nose as well as cuts to his body. He made a no comment interview and was later identified on a parade. The manslaughter occurred quite separately, three months later. The victim was an alcoholic and known to the defendant's mother. He was a pathetic character and treated as a punch bag by, amongst others, the defendant. At times he would sleep in a disused outbuilding on a mattress on the floor. On the night he died, the victim was so drunk that his partner would not allow him to remain at home so he set off with the defendant to the outbuilding where he lay in a drunken state. During some horseplay some lighted clothing landed on the mattress. The defendant ran off but did not raise the alarm. Sadly the victim died of extensive burns. The defendant was assessed as a high risk of re-offending and had an alcohol problem. A psychological report said that he was a highly marginalized member of society. He was 18 when sentenced with convictions for various relatively minor offences and had had supervision in the past. Held. The defendant by his criminal conduct had taken an innocent life and this had followed an earlier offence of unprovoked violence on another man. There could have been no complaint if the judge had passed consecutive sentences that had given the same total sentence. In any event, the sentence of **6 years** for the manslaughter (with 18 months concurrent for the ABH) was not manifestly excessive.

Old cases *R v Swatson* 1997 2 Cr App R (S) 140 and *Att-Gen's Ref No 51 of 1997* 1998 2 Cr App R (S) 313. (For summaries of these cases see the first edition of this book.)

Defendant aged 16 – 17 – Knives

111.12   *R v Mills* 1998 Re Holder 2 Cr App R (S) 128 at 143. LCJ. The defendant was acquitted of murder and convicted of manslaughter. There was a trivial dispute in a playground not involving the defendant in which a boy was chased. The police were called and it ended. The boy was chased again by a large number of boys and sticks and bottles were thrown at him. The defendant caught up with him and stabbed him with a $2-2^1/_2$" knife which penetrated his heart. He had been to the Youth Court twice for TDA and for handling and assault with intent to resist arrest. There were testimonials. Held. Where a defendant deliberately goes out with a knife which is carried as a weapon, and uses it to cause death, even if there is provocation, he should expect a sentence in a contested case in the region of **10 to 12 years. 9 years** detention was not too long.

R v Saif 2001 2 Cr App R (S) 458. During a murder trial the defendant pleaded guilty to manslaughter on the basis of insufficient intent. The defendant knew the victim but was not a friend of his. When aged 16, at the end of a party the host, the defendant, the victim and a girl remained. There was an exchange of insults and the defendant called the deceased, 'green teeth.' The deceased replied with words like, 'smelly Arab.' The defendant who had been drinking a great deal was challenged to go outside. He declined. There was some evidence that the defendant was egged on to fight and he was frightened of a fight. The deceased then went upstairs to the lavatory and the defendant followed him with a knife. The deceased emerged and the defendant lunged at him saying, 'If you want me to fight him, I will fight him.' They went to the ground. A punch was thrown. The victim was holding his chest and an ambulance was called. He was found to have five stab wounds with one to the heart. The defendant started crying and the victim died. The trial judge described it as close to murder. The defendant had one caution and no previous convictions. **7 years** detention not 9 was appropriate.

See also *R v Turner* 2002 1 Cr App R (S) 207

R v Devlin and Cooper 2004 2 Cr App R (S) 102. D aged 16 at the time of the offence and C aged 17 were convicted of manslaughter. These two and two others kicked and stabbed the victim as he was walking home shortly after midnight. He later died. The participation of these two was accepted by the crown as being secondary in that they had either used violence or encouraged others to do so, and they continued to participate in the attack after they were aware that one of the others had a knife. The jury's verdict implied that they foresaw the real possibility that the knife would be used to cause injury although not serious injury or death. One of the 8 or 9 eyewitnesses gave evidence that he thought the attack was racially motivated and that evidence was relied on by the sentencing judge. The evidence was "I couldn't be clear, but something like 'Shut up you Paki' "and "I think I heard 'Shut up you Paki' cried out. That's what I thought I heard." The sentencing judge said he had no doubt this was a racially motivated attack and he treated that as an aggravating factor. There were post-sentence reports speaking favourably of D, and extremely favourable reports from the YOI on C. Held. There is considerable do1ubt whether it was open to the judge to conclude that there was proof to the necessary criminal standard that these 2 defendants were racially motivated. There was no such specific count in the indictment. Although they had been convicted on the basis of joint enterprise it did not follow that their motivation must have been the same as the others. The judge did not, as he should have done, indicate the sentence he would have thought appropriate without the feature of racial aggravation. Taking into account their age and the seriousness of the offence **7 years** not 9 for both.

R v Silkstone 2004 2 Cr App R (S) 416. The defendant pleaded guilty to manslaughter and robbery. She had a co accused, O, who pleaded guilty to murder and robbery. The defendant aged 16 agreed to help O rob someone of a car. The plan was that she would activate a pelican crossing to bring a car to a stop and O would eject the driver and drive off with the defendant. O was dressed in a black Ninja type suit showing only a small area round his eyes. He had a knife with a long blade. When the defendant activated the pelican crossing the 54-year-old victim stopped his car and O got in it and immediately attacked him with the knife. O ejected the victim and the defendant got in the car leaving the victim lying in the road. He died at the scene having sustained four stab wounds to the face and one to the chest. The defendant and O abandoned the car, burnt the property they had taken from it, burnt their own clothes and left the area. The basis of plea was that she knew that O had a knife and was aware that he might use it during the robbery to threaten the driver. She had no previous convictions. A pre-sentence report was highly favourable, saying she had experienced problems which may have led her to become too close to O. She could not have anticipated O's behaviour and that she had allowed herself to be manipulated. She expressed remorse and regret and was very conscious of the trauma caused to the victim's family. The report said she would not offend again and posed no risk of future harm to the public. Held. It was a well-made point that the sentence should not be so heavy as to crush her spirit, but her role was a key one and fell to be dealt with severely. Natural revulsion at the viciousness of the attack by O should not be reflected in the level of sentence appropriate for this defendant, given her lack of intention that it should occur. The appropriate starting point for the manslaughter was **9 years**, reduced to **6 years** for the guilty plea and a further year for her youth, good character and lack of future danger. **5 years detention** for the manslaughter and 4 years for the robbery to run concurrently, not 8 and 7 concurrent.

Old cases. *Att-Gen's Ref. No 28 of 1994* 1995 16 Cr App R (S) 589.

Defendant aged 18–20

111.13   *R v Anucha* 1999 2 Cr App R (S) 74. The defendant pleaded guilty to manslaughter, two counts of robbery and a count of battery. The defendant and another stole £60 by pulling a shop assistant away from the till. Six days later the defendant returned and was recognised and the assistant refused to open the till. The defendant tried to open it. The assistant went next door to call the police and returned. The defendant accused him of injuring him on the earlier occasion and punched him three times in the face. Thirteen days later the defendant who was then aged 19, used a minicab. The driver was the deceased and he drove it to a petrol station to fill up with petrol. The deceased became worried and tried to ring the police. The defendant left the cab became aggressive and shouted, 'You don't want to take me'. He then punched the victim twice in the face causing him to fall hitting his head hard on the ground. On the same day the defendant returned to the shop and opened the till while another held the assistant as £200 was stolen. Three weeks later the victim died. The defendant had seven previous convictions for robbery, one for attempted robbery, three for theft and two for assault.

A report indicated crack cocaine lay behind the offending. The sentencing judge invoked the 'longer than normal sentence' statutory provisions. **6 years** YOI not 8 for the manslaughter consecutive to 3 years for the two robberies.

R v Bosanko 2000 2 Cr App R (S) 108. The defendant pleaded guilty to manslaughter. On the defendant's 18th birthday, he, the victim and another sat outside a public house drinking strong lager. The defendant became aggressive to the victim and others. The three then visited the home of a women. The three continued drinking and the victim and defendant continued quarrelling. The defendant was unsettled and hyperactive. There was a scuffle between the two inside and a fight outside. The third person described them both as equally to blame and both stupid. The victim was next seen getting up and at the same time made an extremely insulting remark about the defendant's mother. The defendant struck the victim with a single blow, which knocked him over, and his head cracked against the ground. He died in hospital of fractures and swelling of the brain. The defendant had a conviction for unlawful wounding with a knife the previous year and one for ABH when he had knocked down a female who fractured her cheek bone and caused her head to hit the pavement. **4¹/₂ years** YOI substituted for 6.

R v Al-Hameed 2000 2 Cr App R (S) 158. LCJ. The defendant was convicted of manslaughter to which he had been prepared to plead guilty to when he faced a murder count. The age of defendant the is not recorded but would be less than 21. The defendant and the victim had a bad relationship due to a problem between the defendant and the victim's half-sister. On account of this the victim had confronted and assaulted the defendant twice. The defendant was told the victim was looking for him and was going to beat him up. The defendant went from his house to where the victim lived with a knife. The victim arrived there at about 11pm. There was an exchange of words and the victim went to the garden and challenged him to a fight. The defendant did not respond. The victim returned and they met in the kitchen. The defendant produced his knife. He later said he did this because he feared the victim was going to attack him. The victim fell on the knife, which penetrated his chest. There was no evidence of a deliberate stab or a lashing out at the victim. The conviction was based on the defendant producing and holding the knife and that the victim may have fallen or stumbled on the knife. He had no previous convictions. **4 years** YOI upheld.

R v Thompson 2001 1 Cr App R (S) 249. The defendant was convicted of manslaughter on an insufficient intent basis after a murder trial. When aged 18 the defendant was celebrating the New Year when a confrontation developed. He and another were pursued by the deceased and two others who were older and bigger than the defendant was. The defendant picked up a yard brush and a scuffle developed. After the defendant had been injured, he hit the deceased with the brush on the neck, which caused extensive internal bleeding. The defendant had no previous convictions and had impressive references. **3¹/₂ years** YOI substituted for 4¹/₂.

R v Refern 2002 2 Cr App R (S) 155. Three defendants R, B and O pleaded guilty to manslaughter. All three after drinking heavily and taking drugs attacked a 40 year old in a car park. He was punched to the ground and kicked by all three in a deliberate and violent beating. He died of an extensive brain haemorrhage. R was 28 (all ages are taken from the time of the offence), and had been to the courts on 23 occasions for offences of dishonesty, criminal damage, arson and possession of an offensive weapon. One had resulted in custody. He had a good prison report and had an excellent work record in prison. B aged 19, had had 17 court appearances including offences of dishonesty, criminal damage, affray, and three convictions for ABH. Those three did not appear particularly serious. He had had several custodial sentences. He expressed remorse. O who was 21, had 18 court appearances mostly for dishonesty. He had had four custodial sentences. He expressed remorse. The prison report said he was quiet and polite. All were dealt with equally. Two were sentenced to 6¹/₂ years imprisonment, the other to 6¹/₂ years YOI. Held. All reduced to **5¹/₂ years**. An order under the Crime and Disorder Act 1986 extending the supervision to 8 years was undisturbed.

R v Murphy 2001 2 Cr App R (S) 384. The defendant was convicted of manslaughter. The defendant aged 19, left his home to walk to Plaistow to meet his girlfriend. He met some teenagers who told him that, 'A madman was going nuts.' Further that he was sniffing glue and chasing little kids. One of the teenagers was in possession of a knife. The defendant took it, put it in his back pocket and went to confront the glue-sniffer, the victim. The defendant found him and challenged him. He also took the knife out of his pocket. The victim told the defendant he did not want a fight. The defendant said he was going to stab him. The two moved together and started to fight. They fell to the ground and the defendant stabbed the victim. The defendant ran away and fled to Ireland. The wound had penetrated the heart. Later he surrendered. He claimed self-defence. He had three convictions. One was for robbery. One was for being aggressive to two boys in a park, being arrested and becoming violent and assaulting two police officers. The third was a non-domestic burglary. He was using Class A drugs. There was no mental disorder. Held. The sentencing bracket was **8–10 years** detention so **9 years** with an extended period of supervision on licence was undisturbed.

R v Heslop 2004 1 Cr App R (S) 427. The defendant pleaded guilty to manslaughter on an indictment for murder. The defendant noticed that one of his friends, the deceased, (aged 16) was wearing one of his shirts. The victim said that the defendant's brother had sold it to him. The defendant was "mad" and asked his brother, who denied selling the shirt. The defendant went and found the deceased and shouted aggressively at him. The victim stood up and the defendant punched him on the head. The deceased fell back and the defendant punched him. The pathologist suggested there were seven blows. The defendant was dragged away, leaving the deceased unconscious. The victim never recovered consciousness. He pleaded on the basis that he momentarily lost control using no more than moderate force. He was 18 and had one previous conviction (disorderly behaviour and criminal damage). He was full of remorse and unlikely to re-offend. References spoke well of him. Held. There was very strong mitigation. **2¹/₂ years' detention**, not 3¹/₂.

R v Harty 2002 2 Cr App R (S) 253. See **111.19**

R v H 2001 Unreported 22/10/01. Because of his plea, remorse and he was 18, **2** not 4 years YOI.

Old case. *R v McLean* 1998 2 Cr App R (S) 250. (For a summary of this case see the first edition of this book.)

Diminished responsibility – Homicide Act 1957 s 2

111.14   The basis for a conviction for manslaughter is not as important as the individual circumstances. The diminished responsibility cases are listed under the general categories. However if there is a plea based on diminished responsibility it means the defendant accepts that he or she intended to kill or cause GBH to the victim.

Doctors killing patients

111.15   *R v Mulhem* 2003 The Times news report 23/9/03, Internet sites. Nottingham Crown Court. High Court Judge. The defendant, a hospital doctor, changed his plea to guilty of manslaughter on the day his second trial was to start. His first trial had to be abandoned because of the defendant was said to be having a nervous breakdown. The victim aged 18 who suffered from cancer went to hospital for two days of routine chemotherapy. He should have received a spinal injection of cytosine on the first day and vincristine intravenously on the next day. A senior houseman asked the defendant to supervise him. The defendant had only been at the hospital for two days. The first drug was correctly administered. The defendant then handed the junior the vincristine and told him to inject it into his spine. The defendant had failed to note what was written on the victim's haematology chart, failed to see which drug should have been administered and failed to check the syringe which clearly stated the drug must never be injected spinally. The junior checked his instructions twice and was told to go ahead. The drug entered the central canal of the victim's nervous system and led to an agonising, creeping paralysis. He suffered multiple organ failure and a month later died when his life support system was turned off. The defendant was 36 and born in Syria. He received 10 months for unrelated assaults and had spent 11 months on remand. **8 months consecutive** making 18 months and immediate release. (Treat news reports with care.)

R v Sinha 2004 The Times news reports 17/3/04 and 6/4/04. Chester Crown Court. High Court Judge. The defendant was convicted of manslaughter. He worked as a locum GP for five days and four nights in the week he was called to visit the victim who was in excruciating pain from arthritis. Her husband explained her medical condition and offered him her medical charts which he refused to look at. He administered three times the safe dose of morphine sulphate. She suffered from severe kidney problems and died. He was 68. Sentencing remarks. The public must have confidence in their general practitioners. **15 months**. (Treat news reports with care.)

R v Walker 2004 The Times news reports 24/6/04. CCC Former High Court Judge The defendant pleaded guilty to manslaughter. He worked as a surgeon and during a liver operation in 1995 he continued to operate after finding the tumour was twice the size he had expected and was near important blood vessels. He removed the liver and spread it out and turned his back on the patient to have his photograph taken. Other staff were horrified by this. The victim lost pints of blood and died. He was not qualified to perform the operation. He was 47 and was suspended in 1999 by the GMC after ten botched operations which left four dead and others maimed. The panel heard 16 anaesthetists refused to work with him. He was struck off in 2001 for performing surgery beyond the limit of his skill. He appealed and was allowed to continue working so long as he didn't perform operations. Only then was a police investigation launched. When he was charged he was again suspended. Sentencing remarks. There are exceptional circumstances enabling the sentence to be suspended. The hospital had not done enough to stop the defendant operating on patients. There was a lamentable systemic failure. The hospital failed to act with the vigour the public are entitled to expect. The fault was compounded by the coroner's failure to hold an inquest and an in house post-mortem which was misleading. There was an astonishing delay in setting up a determined investigation. It was not the defendant's fault he was allowed to go on operating, subject to restrictions for another two years. **21 months suspended**. (Treat news reports with care.)

Old cases. *R v Saha* 1994 15 Cr App R (S) 342 (Doctor regularly over subscribing a drug to a patient. Convicted. 21 months was not excessive.)

Drug abuse – Guideline remarks

111.16   *R v Braybrooks* 2003 1 Cr App R (S) 603. The defendant was convicted of manslaughter. The defendant injected the victim with heroin. Held. A clear pattern of sentences appears with the Court emphasising the need for stern deterrent sentences where the supply of heroin is concerned, particularly in the circumstances which have led to death. The scope for mitigation may be limited. The authorities demonstrate that, after a trial, a sentence of **5 years** is appropriate in such cases.

Drug abuse

111.17   *R v Atherton* 2002 1 Cr App R (S) 498. The defendant pleaded guilty on re-arraignment to manslaughter. The defendant was a heroin addict and lived in a hostel

for the homeless where he supplied other residents with heroin. The victim a
33-year-old alcoholic and heroin addict knocked on the defendant's door and was told
to go away. Later the defendant said to others he planned to take the victim's medication in return for heroin. Later again the defendant injected himself and the victim with
heroin. The victim fell unconscious and the defendant and another carried him to the
bathroom where they left him. The defendant left the hostel and when he came back in
the evening he pretended to find the body and shouted for help. The victim was
found dead. Next day he told a friend that he had cleaned the syringe and placed it in
the victim's hand. The cause of death was multiple drug toxicity. The defendant was
arrested and denied he knew how the victim had died. He had been present once before
when a resident had died of heroin injection. Another had died in similar circumstances.
Held. The judge was entitled to take into account the prevalence of his offence in South
Wales but **5 years** not 6.

R v Powell 2002 2 Cr App R (S) 532. The defendant pleaded guilty at the PDH hearing
to manslaughter and supplying a drug. The victim was a heavy drinker and a user of
heroin. She previously had been hospitalised for overdoses of drink and drugs. She drank
³/₄ of a bottle of vodka and 3 cans of lager. Her partner put her to bed and left her. She
spent the night at a friend's house and drank more alcohol. The friend refused her request
to buy drugs for her and she visited the defendant's flat. There she took some more
heroin although the defendant and his flat mate tried to dissuade her from having anymore. They warned her of the dangers of overdosing and she replied, "I've done it loads
of fucking times." At her request the defendant injected her with more heroin. She became
incoherent and her faced turned blue. The defendant and his flat mate tried to arouse her
and then called an ambulance. She died. Tests showed 353 mgs of alcohol in her blood,
(4¹/₂ times over the limit). There was also morphine well within a range where death
results. The toxic effect of the opiate would have been significantly increased by the high
level of alcohol consumed. The defendant was arrested and initially denied injecting her
with heroin. Shortly after he admitted it. The defendant named his supplier who was successfully prosecuted. Held. These cases are always very difficult and everything that can
be done to discourage drug abuse should be done. More credit for the plea and other
matters should have been given so **3 years** and 2 concurrent not 5 years and 3 concurrent.

R v Braybrooks 2003 1 Cr App R (S) 603. The defendant was convicted of manslaughter
and doing an act tending and intended to pervert the course of justice. The victim was a
friend of the appellants. They were both habitual users of heroin. One evening the victim
went to the defendant's house where she and her boyfriend had already taken heroin. The
defendant injected the victim with heroin. Evidence revealed that she would not have
been able to inject herself. Another man visited the house and saw the victim slumped on
the bedroom floor. The defendant and her boyfriend were sitting on the bed heavily under
the influence of heroin. The defendant said to this visitor that the deceased had taken a
number of temazepam tablets and had been drinking strong cider. She had been unable to
inject herself and had pestered the defendant to inject her. The defendant reluctantly had
agreed so to do. They all began to panic and summoned an ambulance. They agreed that
they would all say that the victim had injected herself whilst they were in another room.
A post-mortem concluded that the cause of death was opiate, alcohol and temazepam. A
toxicologist concluded that the quantities of alcohol and temazepam could significantly
have increased the effects of the heroin. The defendant continued to lie about what had
happened and it was that persistent lying that was the basis for the pervert count. Held. A
clear pattern of sentences appears with the Court emphasising the need for stern deterrent
sentences where the supply is heroin is concerned, particularly in the circumstances which
have led to death. The scope for mitigation may be limited. As the authorities demonstrate
that, after a trial, a sentence of **5 years** is appropriate in such cases. The sentence of five
years for manslaughter was manifestly the correct one and the learned judge was right

to pass a consecutive sentence for the second count. Bearing in mind the personal mitigation, those sentences to be concurrent and not consecutive. So **5 years** not six.

R v Ruffell 2003 2 Cr App R (S) 330. The defendant was convicted of manslaughter through gross negligence. The defendant, the deceased and H went to the defendant's mother's house after an evening of drinking. They purchased heroin and cocaine on the way. The defendant and H were experienced drug users. The deceased was not. All three took the drugs and H said that the deceased started going "a bit off colour, a bit white." H and the defendant tried to revive him by putting him near an open window and splashing water on his face before putting him in a bath of water. He was then carried downstairs, wrapped in towels and placed near a radiator. H left at about 1 am. At about 6am a neighbour heard groaning and "come on, come on". At 7.05 am the defendant had phoned the deceased's mother and told her that her son had been sick after drinking a bottle of vodka. He further said: "I ain't done nothing". At this stage the deceased was outside and his mother told the defendant to bring him inside and cover him with a blanket. It was a cold morning. Three hours later the deceased was found by workmen and neighbours on the path. He died of hypothermia and opiate intoxication. Held. The defendant was well aware that the deceased was in a very bad shape as a result of injecting heroin. It must have been obvious that it was a very cold morning. He agreed to take the deceased back inside. To deliberately leave someone in a bad condition out in cold weather when he could quite easily have brought him inside, as he said he would, put a serious reflection on the case. However, the sentence was longer than the type of sentence imposed for this type of case. **2 years** not 3.

R v Parfeni 2003 2 Cr App R (S) 362. The defendant was convicted of manslaughter by gross negligence and of supplying heroin and cocaine. She was a crack and heroin addict and had known the 39 year old victim for weeks. Having left a pub, the victim phoned him and they then met. They went to King's Cross where the defendant purchased heroin and crack. At the defendant's flat the victim was introduced to Miss M. They all smoked crack whilst the defendant prepared some heroin and she then helped to inject it into the victim. The victim had no known prior involvement with drugs. He made a noise as if in pain, lay down on the defendant's bed and fell asleep. The defendant searched him and took £80 and his credit cards, which the defendant went out and used. She returned about 3 hours later and said to Miss M that she was going to "put him to sleep". She returned to the living room and said to Miss M "I did it twice. I've put him to sleep". That morning Miss M and the defendant went out shopping. When they returned to the flat they found the victim lying on his stomach and vomit coming from his mouth. He was not breathing. The defendant said to Miss M "We are in big shit. This is between you and me. If you tell anyone, I'm going to kill you or put you in prison for life". She then called an ambulance. When police officers arrived she told them that they had both taken crack and heroin and then gone shopping and that when she had returned she had found him dead. A post mortem concluded that death had been caused by a heroin overdose. She was later arrested and made no comment in interview. She was well aware of the risk of injecting heroin as her brother had been convicted of murder by heroin overdose 7 years earlier. Held. This grossly negligent act was carried out for the purposes of greed. The victim was vulnerable. The defendant was aware of the risks of heroin injection. The offence was aggravated by the behaviour of the defendant after she had found Burgess apparently dead. The facts of this case were sufficiently different from Att-Gen's Refs Nos. 19–21 of 2001 2002 1 Cr App R (S) 33 for the Court not to pass a deterrent sentence. So **10 years** not 12.

See also *R v Davison* 2001 Unreported 22/3/01.

Old cases. *Att-Gen's Ref No 5 of 1995* 1996 1 Cr App R (S) 85, *Att-Gen's Ref No 39 of 1995* 1996 2 Cr App R (S) 125 and *R v Edwards* 1998 Unreported 28/4/98

See also **SUPPLY OF DRUGS (CLASS A, B AND C)** – *Death is caused*

Drunken attack

See *No reason/minor provocation/drunken attack*

Farm accident

111.18   *R v Crow* 2002 2 Cr App R (S) 219. The defendant and his father were convicted of manslaughter on the grounds of gross negligence though their reckless disregard for safety over months. They were co-owners of a farm, which employed a 16-year-old placement from an agricultural college who was enthusiastic and popular. The boy drove a JCB telescopic farm Loadall with a brush attachment to clear mud from an A road next to a field which had been recently harvested. He parked the vehicle off the road but the raised bucket protruded at the height of its boom $1^1/_2$ metres into the road. A passing lorry hit the bucket and the JCB rolled onto the boy and crushed him. He died that night. The defendants had failed to heed warnings from the Health and Safety Executive that the boy should not be permitted to drive the JCB until he had undergone a course. Despite this he had used the vehicle regularly and on the day of the accident the father had instructed him to brush the farmyard and a road. The son was away on his honeymoon. The boy had used the JCB on the A road before. The son had a positive good character and there was an excellent safety record at the farm. The business (income?) was assessed as £300,000. The parents of the victim wrote a moving letter saying nothing would be achieved by sending them to prison. Their defence was to blame their employees. The Judge identified three aggravating features. There was a high degree of recklessness, forseeability of serious injury or death and failure to heed explicit warnings. He determined that the son was marginally more responsible because his role was 'chief executive.' He expressed a wish to ensure someone was looking after the farm when the son was in prison. The father received 12 months suspended based on health and life expectancy. Held. There was no error in the judge's approach. However since sentence the father's health had deteriorated and to fulfil the judge's wish the **15 months** sentence was **suspended**.

Fighting (no knife)

111.19   *R v Elton* 1999 2 Cr App R (S) 58. The defendant was convicted of manslaughter and causing GBH with intent both charges involving the same victim. He had also pleaded guilty to common assault on Adrian Berry. In a public house the defendant struck Adrian Berry forcibly twice for no apparent reason. This was the common assault. The defendant was ejected. Adrian Berry and others returned to their hotel and the defendant arrived there. The defendant and the victim, one of Adrian Berry's group, got into a verbal altercation, which degenerated into a fight. The defendant chased the victim out of the hotel and the victim was next seen lying in the road. The defendant admitted punching the victim several times and kicking him once in the face. Forensic evidence revealed that the victim had been killed by being crushed by a heavy vehicle. It also revealed that the victim had injuries to his face and mouth, which were typical of those produced by a violent assault. The injuries were consistent with the victim receiving a severe kick to the face, but being alive when hit by the vehicle. The basis for the prosecution case was that the victim had been left in a situation where he would be 'subject to some harm'. The defendant when 16 and 18 had been convicted of common assault. Held. 4 not 5 years for the GBH because it should be detached from the death. The manslaughter was completely unintended and it should be dealt with as a bad case of manslaughter by gross neglect. **6 years** substituted for 8. 1 year for the common assault unaffected with all sentences concurrent.

R v Harty 2002 2 Cr App R (S) 253. The defendants pleaded to manslaughter at the first opportunity. He and the victim were brothers and part of a large family of travellers.

After a christening party there was hard core drinking and the two were driven back to their caravan site and they shouted at each other, 'I can beat you.' This was not an uncommon exchange. When the van neared the site the defendant jumped out and the two men started fighting. The victim fell back in the van and his wife drove him to her cousin's caravan leaving the defendant behind. She wanted to stop the fighting. The defendant went to the caravan, stripped to the waist and challenged his brother again. They started fighting and the victim fell to the ground. The defendant kicked him in the mouth and deliberately jumped on his stomach with both feet. His wife took him to hospital and he died of massive internal bleeding. The fights were not uncommon. The defendant was then 19 and had a dissocial personality disorder. He had a great deal of suppressed anger which related to his dislocated and deprived childhood. The anger was brought to the fore when he drank. He showed genuine remorse. Held. There were serious features particularly the stamping and the excessive and unwarranted violence. But because of the plea, his age, it was his own brother and the remorse **4 years YOI** not 5.

See also *R v Powell* 2002 2 Cr App R (S) 532.

Old cases. *R v Crimp* 1995 16 Cr App R (S) 346; *R v Harrison* 1996 2 Cr App R (S) 250, *R v Lloyd-Williams* 1997 1 Cr App R (S) 41 and *R v McMinn* 1997 2 Cr App R (S) 219. (For a summary of the last two cases see the first edition of this book.)

Fighting with the death being caused by the fall not any blow – Guideline remarks

111.20   *R v Coleman* 1992 13 Cr App R (S) 508. LCJ. We are considering a person who receives a blow, probably one blow only, to the head or face, is knocked over by the blow and unfortunately cracks his head on the floor or the pavement, suffers a fractured skull and dies. It is to be distinguished sharply from the sort of case where a victim on the ground is kicked about the head. It is to be distinguished sharply from the sort of case where a weapon is used in order to inflict injury. It is to be further distinguished from where the actual blow itself causes the death. This is the case of a fall almost accidentally resulting in a fractured skull. The starting point for this type of offence is **12 months** on a plea of guilty. Then one looks at the mitigation and aggravating features. No premeditation, a single blow of moderate force, remorse and immediate admissions are all mitigation. Indications that the defendant is susceptible to outbreaks of violence, the assault was gratuitous and unprovoked, more than one blow all tend to aggravate the offence.

Fighting with the death being caused by the fall not any blow – Cases

111.21   *R v Henry* 1999 2 Cr App R (S) 412. The defendant pleaded guilty to manslaughter which he had indicated at the first opportunity. The defendant's wife went out for the evening leaving the defendant to look after the children aged 5 and 1. Leaving one child with his in-laws and taking the other he drove to pick his wife up. However, she had left a public house with another man. He then saw them in the street arms linked. They stopped and kissed each other. The defendant shouted across but the wife refused to get into his car. The defendant ran across the road and punched the other man in the face. The victim fell backwards, and struck his head on a manhole cover. He died of injuries to his skull and brain caused by the fall. The blow was of considerable force. It broke the victim's jaw and had lifted him off the ground. The defendant after initial denials expressed remorse. He was 31 and had no previous convictions. There were excellent character references. He told the probation officer he didn't drink and had never hit anyone before. He was a model prisoner. Held. **18 months** substituted for 4 years. Had the blow been less ferocious it would have been less.

R v Cannon 2001 1 Cr App R (S) 286. The defendant pleaded guilty to manslaughter, which had been tendered at an early stage. The defendant's brother broke the glass door of a restaurant as he was leaving. The proprietor, Mr Lau left the restaurant to talk to him. The defendant then left the restaurant. The defendant mistakenly thought that Mr Lau was striking the brother whereas he was merely grabbing hold of him to detain him. There was an altercation in which Mr Lau struck the defendant causing pain and the defendant struck Mr Lau twice in the face with a clenched fist. Mr Lau fell backwards and struck his head on the pavement receiving his fatal injury or injuries. The defendant had been drinking heavily. He had previous convictions for violence including assaulting a constable. He showed remorse. Held. The court accepted the need to protect shopkeepers at night. **3^1/$_2$ years** substituted for 7.

R v Gratton 2001 2 Cr App R (S) 167. The defendant pleaded guilty to manslaughter. The defendant and the victim were friends. The deceased believed the defendant fancied his girlfriend (wrongly they said). After drinking a lot during the day, they went home when the public house closed. The defendant and the victim were seen arguing. The defendant was put to bed on the sofa by his girlfriend and the victim. The defendant's girlfriend went into the garden and was joined by the victim. They sat opposite each other on chairs. The victim leaned forward put his hands on her knees and gave her a quick kiss on the lips as a thank you gesture. Unfortunately the defendant had come out and had seen it. He walked up to them quickly saying, 'You fucked up with your missus, now you are trying it on with mine.' He threw two or three punches to the victim's face causing the victim and his chair to tip back. His head hit some rocks in a rockery. He appeared to be dead when the ambulance attended. The defendant showed great remorse. He thought he saw a 'snog.' He was 31 and was treated as of good character. He had an excellent work record. There were many references. The defendant received **9 months**. Held. It would not be right to suspend it.

R v Edwards 2001 2 Cr App R (S) 540. The defendant was convicted of manslaughter. At a country club the victim and the defendant who did not know each other had an argument. The defendant was aggressive and offered to see the other outside. One of the defendant's friends tried to pull him away. The victim left the club and was followed by the defendant. The victim suddenly turned and squared up to the defendant. The defendant punched the victim once with his fist to the mouth and chin. The victim fell back and struck the base of his head on the hard surface of the car park. The defendant was aggressive and offensive to someone who sought to explain that the victim had gone over to apologise. The victim died two days later. The fall and not the blow caused the death. The skull had fractured. The defendant, who had been a keen amateur boxer, was 40 with two previous convictions. One was for s 20 wounding in 1979. He had a large number of letters and testimonials. The judge spoke of his positive good character and described the blow as not a blow of great force. **18 months** not 30 months.

R v Matthews and Hewson 2002 1 Cr App R (S) 279. The defendants M and H now 20 and 19 pleaded to manslaughter. M also pleaded to burglary. While staff were busy at 11pm in a pub M went behind the bar and took £133. This was the burglary. Outside he saw G a 17-year-old quiet lad and asked to him to hide the money. The next day he asked G for it back and G said it had gone missing. He gave M £20 but M threatened him saying, 'If I don'n\t get the rest soon I'm gonna smash your face in.' G promised to get the money and invented a story so he got £50 from his grandfather and gave it to M. M still wasn't satisfied. The next day, M boasted to H and a group of youths what he would do if he didn't get the money. He would smash him in the face and knock him out with one blow. H picked up a broom handle and said he would wrap this round his head while you punch him. H continued to encourage M to hit G and asked, 'Are you going to hit him? Bet you don't hit him. Could you one time him.' One timing means knocking someone out with one punch. They came across G with others in the street. M confronted him and G pleaded with him saying he would get the money somehow. H continued to incite M saying, 'You're a shit bag. I thought you were going to knock him out,' and 'Come on hurry, I've got somewhere to go.' This incitement continued. Eventually M punched G who fell backwards and hit is head on a paving slab. G went into a fit or spasm. It was clear he was badly hurt save perhaps to M and H. They appeared to revel in the violence and M said, 'Oh yes, sweet punch,' 'Check that punch out' and 'Knock out.' H said, 'That was a bad punch. Check it out he's having a fit. I'm buzzing off. It was a sweet punch.' While G lay unconscious M took his watch. Because of the fit he was unable to prise open the fingers so he forced his fingers apart with his teeth. M then told the witnesses to lie about the attack. Eventually G was taken to hospital and died of double basal fracture to the skull caused by the head hitting the stone. M changed his account in interview but in the second admitted hitting him. Later he said it was an accident. H denied inciting him but admitted laughing as G lay on the ground. M had convictions for five ABHs, intimidating witnesses, three of threatening behaviour, battery and offences of dishonesty. H had fewer including ABH, arson, threatening behaviour and dishonesty. Held. There is an important distinction between the one punch cases and M's case. The fatal violence had been pre-meditated. It was to obtain the proceeds of the burglary. He announced his intention to do so. He made unwarranted demands above and beyond the return of the ill-gotten gains. H did everything possible to encourage M to attack G. At the scene there was no remorse. This was wholly unprovoked and pre-meditated violence which led to the death of this very young man. M's **4¹/₂ years** detention with 6 months consecutive for the burglary and H's **2 years** detention were sentences of some severity but entirely justified.

Att-Gen's Ref. No 100 of 2001 2002 2 Cr App R (S) 365. The defendant pleaded guilty to manslaughter and two counts of ABH. After drinking heavily the defendant was in a pick up truck with another in a city centre. At around 2.00–2.20am he called three people over to him and punched them in the face. Each bent down to hear what he was saying. The first victim was struck a hard punch and the defendant drove off at speed. The first two victims suffered bruising. The third victim was knocked backwards and his head struck the pavement and he was rendered unconscious. The defendant told his colleague to, 'Quick, drive, drive.' The victim died within 36 hours and the pathologist found injuries to the nose and lips, which were consistent with a single blow of at least moderate force. Death was due to a blunt force injury to the back of the head as a result of the fall. The victim was 34 and about to finish his 4 year degree course and had bright prospects. When interviewed the defendant lied and said the victim had thrown at punch at him. The defendant was 22 and of good character with most favourable references. He showed remorse. Held. This was a premeditated, deliberate and wholly unprovoked blow to an innocent passer-by. The defendant drove off. This was a serious case. 5 years would be appropriate. As it was a reference **4 years** not 3.

See also Att-Gen's Ref. No 124 of 2001 Unreported 22/1/02.

Old case. *R v Williams* 1996 2 Cr App R (S) 72.

Fire, by

111.22   *R v Hills* 1999 2 Cr App R (S) 157. The defendant was convicted of manslaughter. The defendant visited an estate to pick up a car he had just purchased. He had with him some car accessories including an empty petrol can. A group of youths approached him, as he appeared drunk. He went to a garage and filed the can with petrol. He met up with the youths again and after some banter chased two girls in a drunken manner. He said to them, 'Do you want to see something freaky?' As a boy reached him he poured petrol on to him and lit a cigarette lighter over the neck of the can. The boy was thrown to the ground and covered in flames. He had 47% burns to his body and died. The defendant said he had taken methadone that morning. Held. This offence was consistent with the sentences where a knife has been used but its use was entirely unpremeditated. **8 years** substituted for 10 years.

R v Malik 2003 2 Cr App R (S) 669. The defendant was convicted of manslaughter (instead of murder) and of arson with intent to endanger life. In the early hours of the morning the defendant intentionally set fire to a mid-terrace house by pouring petrol through a letterbox. It was a revenge attack against a man who, he believed, had facilitated an adulterous relationship between the defendant's wife and another man. The target escaped but an innocent tenant died from fumes whilst trying to escape from a window. The previous convictions were not relevant to sentence. A plea to manslaughter had been offered on two occasions but had been rejected. Held. The loss of an innocent life in such horrific circumstances make a substantial sentence inevitable. This was completely uncharacteristic behaviour on the defendant's part, carried out when his distressing and deteriorating personal situation had pushed him to the brink and then beyond. **12 years** not 15.

R v Hussain 2004 2 Cr App R 497. The defendant pleaded guilty to conspiracy to commit arson and was convicted of conspiracy to commit arson with intent to endanger life and eight counts of manslaughter. The defendant had four co-accused. He and others had made petrol bombs, and the defendant had obtained the petrol. One of the co-accused wanted to attack one of the victims who had been telling tales about his relationship with a girlfriend. In the early hours of the morning the defendant and others drove to the house where the victim was and two of the co-accused threw the petrol bombs at the house. In the subsequent fire eight people died; a woman, her daughter, a student and five girls aged between six months and thirteen years. Four other people escaped the fire. The judge said that the offences of manslaughter came very close to murder, and that no one who heard the evidence of family members who saw the fire would ever forget it. Further it was a gross understatement to say that the surviving family members were devastated. Held. The judge was bound to have regard to the number of persons unlawfully killed. This was manslaughter in horrific circumstances involving eight persons. It could not be argued that **18 years** for the manslaughter charges and a concurrent 14 years for the conspiracy to commit arson were even arguably manifestly excessive.

R v Walters 2005 1 Cr App R (S) 569. The defendant pleaded guilty to manslaughter on the basis of gross negligence and to a separate charge of ABH. The ABH occurred first, when the defendant attacked a man who was already being attacked by another man, P. The defendant kicked him on the nose and joined several others who were demanding his mobile phone. The victim was treated for a bruised, swollen nose as well as cuts to his body. He made a no comment interview and was later identified on a parade. The manslaughter occurred quite separately, three months later. The victim was an alcoholic and known to the defendant's mother. He was a pathetic character and treated as a punch bag by, amongst others, the defendant. At times he would sleep in a disused outbuilding on a mattress on the floor. On the night he died, the victim was so drunk that his partner would not allow him to remain at home so he set off with the defendant to the outbuilding where he lay in a drunken state. During some horseplay some lighted clothing landed on the mattress. The defendant ran off but did not raise the alarm. Sadly the victim died of extensive burns. The defendant was assessed as a high risk of re-offending and had an alcohol problem. A psychological report said that he was a highly marginalized member of society. He was 18 when sentenced with convictions for various relatively minor offences and had had supervision in the past. Held. The defendant by his criminal conduct had taken an innocent life and this had followed an earlier offence of unprovoked violence on another man. There could have been no complaint if the judge had passed consecutive sentences that had given the same total sentence. In any event, the sentence of **6 years** for the manslaughter (with 18 months concurrent for the ABH) was not manifestly excessive.

Old cases. *R v England* 1995 16 Cr App R (S) 776 and *R v Archer* 1998 2 Cr App R (S) 76. (For a summary of the last case see the first edition of this book.)

See also ARSON – *Death is caused*

Firearms, with

111.23 *R v Jackson* 1999 2 Cr App R (S) 77. The defendant pleaded guilty to manslaughter and to doings acts tending to pervert the course of justice. The victim was living with one woman and also having an affair with the defendant's daughter. The daughter thought she was pregnant by him but in fact wasn't. The defendant received a telephone call saying the victim wanted the daughter to stop pestering him. The defendant's partner on hearing this got into a rage and demanded that the defendant speak to the victim. The defendant went to the victim's house. The victim went into the street with a bullet-proof vest. They both got into the defendant's car. He was sentenced on the basis the victim cocked the gun and held it to the defendant's neck. The gun was knocked out of his grasp and picked up by the defendant. The defendant made threats and a struggle developed in which the gun was discharged twice. The defendant disposed of the gun and initially relied on an alibi. He also had the car cleaned and disposed of which was the background to the perverting charge. The defendant had one deception offence in the last 20 years. Held. **5 years** substituted for 8 with 2 years consecutive for the perverting remaining as before.

R v Kent 2004 2 Cr App R (S) 367. The defendant pleaded guilty to possession of a firearm with intent to cause a person to fear violence and manslaughter. There was a confrontation between amongst others the defendant, the victim of the firearms offence G, then aged 15, and the victim of the manslaughter F, then aged 19. The defendant left that confrontation and armed himself with a handgun with at least three rounds of ammunition and sought a further confrontation with G and F. That took place at 7.00pm in a narrow residential street. A substantial crowd mainly of young people was present. The defendant fired two shots which passed close to G. It was accepted that the purpose of the shots was to frighten rather than to injure G. The defendant fired a third shot which struck F in the lower abdomen causing fatal injuries from which he died a few hours later. It was accepted again that the principal intention was to frighten and that he did not have the intent required for murder. The defendant, 23, had a plentiful record of low to medium tariff offending, but nothing like the gravity of these offences. He was not a gang member. Held. The totality of the sentence was rather too long, and 12 years would have been sufficient. The firearms sentence was reduced from 5 to **2** years but only because of the court's view on totality. The sentence for manslaughter remained **10** years to run consecutively.

Old cases. *R v Klair* 1995 16 Cr App R (S) 660; *R v Pittendrigh* 1996 1 Cr App R (S) 65, *Att-Gen's Ref. No 2 of 1997* 1998 1 Cr App R (S) 27 and *R v Howell* 1998 1 Cr App R (S) 229. For summaries of the last two cases see the first edition of this book.

Frightened to death,

111.24   *R v Scammell* 2002 1 Cr App R (S) 293. See **111.55**.

Funeral expenses of the deceased, power to make an order for compensation for the

111.25   Powers of Criminal Courts (Sentencing) Act 2000 s 130(1). The court may on application or otherwise make an order requiring him to make payments for funeral expenses or bereavement in respect of a death resulting from an offence other than death due to an accident arising out of the presence of a motor vehicle on a road.

Powers of Criminal Courts (Sentencing) Act 2000 s 130(3). A court shall give reasons if it does not make a compensation order in a case where this section empowers it to do so.

R v Williams 1989 Unreported 10/3/89. It is important that sentencers bear in mind the words (which had just been added to the then statute giving the court power to order compensation for funeral expenses). If the court decides not to order compensation it must give its reasons.

Harassed by neighbours, after being

111.26   Old case. *R v Wright* 1995 16 Cr App R (S) 877.

Health

See Victim's health precarious/eggshell skull

Knife, with – Guideline remark cases

111.27   *Att-Gen's Ref. No 33 of 1996* 1997 2 Cr App R (S) 10. Where a defendant deliberately goes out with a knife which is carried as a weapon, and uses it to cause death, even if there is provocation, he should expect a sentence in a contested case in the region of **10 to 12 years**.

R v Mills 1998 Re Holder 2 Cr App R (S) 128 at 143. LCJ. The case of *Att-Gen's Ref. No 33 of 1996 1997* 2 Cr App R (S) 10 does provide a tariff for manslaughter.

Old cases. Ignore all cases before *Att-Gen's Ref. No 33 of 1996*, above.

Knives – 5 years imprisonment or less

111.28   *Att-Gen's Ref. No 3 of 1999* 1999 2 Cr App R (S) 433. The defendant pleaded guilty to manslaughter. Two drunken men walked past the defendant's home and one of them appeared to damage the defendant's wife's car. She protested and they swore at her. The defendant became aware of this and he armed himself with a hunting knife, which he removed from its sheath. The knife had been in a cupboard. He and his wife followed the young men and they turned and confronted them. One picked up some timber and the other was carrying a bottle. A fight ensued initiated by the two young men. The defendant was hit by the timber and the bottle. The defendant then knifed one of them three times and he died. One stab was to the head, one was to upper chest and the third to his right chest. Genuine remorse was expressed. The defendant had an excellent record with character references showing his integrity, his generosity and his lack of aggression. Held. The case would merit a 4 year sentence. It might have merited 3 years because of the exceptional circumstances, but not less than that. Since the conviction his family has had to move and his wife's health had suffered. **2 years** immediate imprisonment substituted for 2 years suspended.

Att-Gen's Ref. No 19 of 1999 2000 1 Cr App R (S) 287. The defendant was convicted of manslaughter on the grounds of provocation. He had agreed to plead to that before the trial but it was not accepted. Some neighbours became annoyed at the defendant's dog. The RSPCA was contacted but the found the dog to be in perfectly good condition. After the dog had barked all one evening, neighbours gathered to complain and the police were called. Eventually when the defendant came home, neighbours expressed their anger and the victim and others surrounded his car. Some witnesses described the deceased trying to pull the car door off and pull the defendant out. The children in the car were terrified. The car drove off and someone shouted that they would kill the dog. The defendant went to the home of a friend and armed himself with a knife. He returned with another and found damage to his windows and the fence of his home. The deceased was standing by a front door four doors away from the defendant's home and directed abuse at the defendant. The defendant walked towards him and a fight ensued. They fell to the ground and the defendant stabbed him in the neck. The stab wound would have required moderate force. He died within a few minutes. The defendant was 22 and was effectively of good character. Held. This case was significantly different from the *Att-Gen's Ref. No 33 of 1996* 1997 2 Cr App R (S) 10 where a 10–12 year starting point was set. The sentence of **5 years** was lenient but within the permissible parameters for this offence. It was not unduly lenient.

R v Jarrett 2003 1 Cr App R (S) 154. The defendant pleaded guilty to manslaughter on a murder indictment. The deceased reported his car stolen and he suspected youths from a particular estate where it was found had taken it. He drove there and a verbal confrontation took place with a group of youths. The deceased swung his arm at the defendant and he lunged back striking him in the chest with a penknife at least twice. Some witnesses said another held the deceased just as he was struck by the defendant. The basis of plea was the defendant acted to defend himself against a perceived, unwarranted attack and the use of the knife was disproportionate to the deceased conduct. The defendant was 19 with convictions on 4 occasions. Since then he'd been before the Court twice for breaches of community service. The pre-sentence report, which was largely favourable said, "He had been brought up in a violent and offending-orientated environment. His explanation for carrying the knife was that there had been two very recent incidents which had put him in great fear. He was not confident that he was physically robust enough to protect himself unarmed. He insists he acted on impulse, thinking that he was about to be seriously attacked. His attitude to the offence was of complete disapproval." Held. We have considered *Attorney-General's Ref. No. 33 of 1996* 1997 2 Cr App R (S) 10 which dealt with a defendant who intended either fatal force, or to cause really serious injury, but where it was not murder because of provocation. It appeared to be directed to the sort of manslaughter which occurs when a public house or dance hall is emptying and some fracas develops and a knife causes a fatal blow. This case is excessive self defence. It does not fit comfortably within the principle in the 1996 reference. There was very strong mitigation. The knife was not carried for aggression or in anticipation of violence. There was strong mitigation in his substantial references and his efforts to put the past behind him and improve his lot. The Judge was right to emphasise the need to deter those who carry knives, but **5 years** YOI not 7.

R v Matthews 2003 1 Cr App R (S) 120. The defendant pleaded guilty to the manslaughter of his brother. The brothers were engaged in a drunken argument at their mother's flat about the defendant's help with the deceased's drug problem. The argument became more and more heated and the defendant stabbed the deceased once with a small kitchen knife which was in the room. The knife penetrated the heart. The defendant tried to resuscitate him in vain. The Crown accepted the defendant deeply regretted what he had done and was immediately distraught. He was 33 with bad previous convictions including a robbery in 1999 for which he received 5 years. On his release he had established a stable family life with his partner and daughter. The family wrote letters about their support for the defendant and their double loss. Held. It is clear that 5 years for manslaughter by use of a knife was within the range of proper sentences. Applying *R v Nunn* 1996 2 Cr App R (S) 136, we balance the public duty to indicate the gravity of the offence and on the other hand not adding to the punishment and anguish of the family by a sentence which causes them distress. This was not a case where there was a deliberate argument with a knife. 5 years reduced to **3¹/₂ years** to reflect the added distress of the family.

R v Law 2003 2 Cr App R 593. The defendant pleaded guilty to the manslaughter of his brother. A family reunion was arranged to celebrate the reconciliation between the defendant's brother and his daughter. The defendant had been instrumental in that reconciliation. Alcohol was consumed. The atmosphere was happy and cordial at the meal. Afterwards there was an argument between the brothers and the defendant was punched in the face. The defendant spat back. The defendant was ejected from the premises as was the brother's daughter. However, she fell and cut her nose. They went home together. When the brother arrived later the door was answered by his daughter and he saw the cut on her nose. He thought that the cut had been caused by the defendant and immediately went "mad". At one point the defendant was pinned on a sofa by his brother where he was punched and held around the neck and told that he was going to be "fucking killed". The defendant managed to get out from under his brother and ran to the kitchen. The fight continued in the kitchen and a kitchen draw came open and fell onto the floor. Both ended up on the sitting room floor with the defendant beneath his brother. The brother stood up, collapsed and died. He had suffered a stab wound to the arm and fatal wound to the abdomen. The defendant had no recollection of the stabbing. The defendant was to be treated upon the basis that it was not he who originally picked up the knife and that the knife only came into his possession during the course of the struggle. He was 41 and had a number of previous convictions including affray and threatening behaviour. He was genuinely remorseful and loved his brother. Held. The authorities indicate how difficult it is to sentence in manslaughter cases and how at the end of the day each case must be decided on its own facts. **4 years** not 5.

Knives – 6 to 7 years imprisonment

111.29   *R v Wade* 2000 2 Cr App R (S) 445. The defendant was convicted of manslaughter after a murder trial. There was a history of violence between the defendant and the victim who had known each other for about 10 years. For 9 months before the killing they had been involved in selling drugs. The victim accused the defendant of stealing from their joint supply of heroin. The victim demanded payment and later stole some of the defendant's property from his address. The defendant threatened the victim with a shotgun and most of the property was returned. However the victim maintained he was owed £2,000 for the heroin. The victim, armed with a knife, visited the defendant's address with another. The victim had given the other visitor £2,000 to look after. They were refused access. Later the victim visited the address alone and was stabbed to death. The defendant who had a cut on his hand was seen with a large wad of notes which it was suggested he had taken from the victim. The victim was found to have 11 stab wounds five of which were to the head, one to his shoulder, one to the neck and three to his chest. Any of the three could have been fatal. The room was in disarray and a knuckle-duster was found. The defendant surrendered himself to the police and said, 'I did it. I fucking killed him' In interview he said the defendant had beaten him in the past. He said the victim had threatened him and a struggle took place and the defendant took the knife from him. The fatal blows were then struck. The jury rejected self-defence but concluded he had been provoked. **7 years** not 9.

R v Dillon 2002 1 Cr App R (S) 172. The defendant was convicted of manslaughter by reason of provocation after a murder trial. The victim believed the defendant had stolen his girlfriend's purse. The defendant was angry because he claimed the victim had threatened the defendant's ex-wife and their daughter in numerous telephone calls. He threatened to kill the victim and his girlfriend. The victim went in search of the defendant to confront him and during the day had a great deal to drink. He told a barmaid the defendant was going to 'get it.' When he found the defendant in a pub he abused him and both squared up to each other. A scuffle broke out with both exchanging punches. The fight was short and the defendant forced the victim to the floor face down. The defendant sat astride his legs and stabbed him twice with a knife in the lower back. The first blow did not penetrate very far but the second blow was with great force and the blade went up to the hilt penetrating 10 cm. The defendant left and the victim was taken to hospital. The victim had very severe internal bleeding and major damage to the arteries and veins. He died the following morning. When arrested the defendant said, 'The bastard got what he deserved. He threatened my daughter and missus.' The defendant had swelling on his temple caused by a blunt instrument. The victim was found to have had a knuckleduster. The defendant was sentenced on the basis it was not known who originally had the knife. The defendant was about 36 and had a conviction for robbery in 1985. Held. **7 years** not 9 and the judge was wrong to consider he was danger to the public so the extension to the licence quashed as the statutory requirement were not present.

Att-Gen's Ref. No. 192 of 2003 2004 2 Cr App R (S) 395. The defendant changed his plea to guilty to manslaughter on the grounds of provocation. He and the victim were friends and drinking partners, and had known each other for about six years. The victim was addicted to heroin, had undergone periods of hospitalisation for drug-induced schizophrenia and was a heavy drinker. He was undergoing a methadone programme. Shortly before his death he had broken his leg and had been discharged from hospital with his leg in a cast. The defendant was a binge drinker. On the 29th of April the defendant and the victim were seen by a community nurse in the victim's flat. She did not think either was drunk. Another nurse visited the following day and the defendant answered the door, drunk and said he had killed the victim. He was tearful. The victim had nineteen stab wounds. At least three had penetrated the heart. The defendant said that on the 29th they had been drinking heavily at a public house; that they had had an argument following the defendant dropping a video recorder belonging to the victim. The victim said the defendant now owed him £240 for the recorder. He also hit the defendant on the head with his crutches. Later the argument erupted again and the victim hit the defendant with his crutch, burnt his shoulder with a cigarette, and struck him again in an escalation of violence. The defendant went to the kitchen, fetched a knife and stabbed the victim repeatedly. He told police he had been pushing the victim around on his bicycle for the previous two weeks taking him to his drug dealer. The victim had hit him with the crutches on previous occasions. There was well-supported evidence that the defendant in the past had shown kindness to the victim and that this kindness had been met with abuse and violence. A taxi driver had seen the victim hitting the defendant with his crutches and trying to punch him because of an argument over the fare on the 29th, and the landlord of a public house saw the victim verbally abusing the defendant on the 28th. The defendant, 37, had 24 convictions for being drunk and disorderly, a conviction for unlawful wounding by means of a knife and five convictions for possession of an offensive weapon – in each case a knife. He demonstrated genuine regret. A psychiatric report said that the defendant did not suffer from any abnormality of mind, that he was a serious alcoholic, and that perhaps he had stored up anger against the victim and then, disinhibited by the alcohol, there was a sudden and temporary loss of control. Held. **7 years** was an entirely appropriate sentence. The reference only related to the period of licence as the sentence was not extended for licence purposes under section 84. In that respect the sentence was unduly lenient and the offender should be **subject to licence throughout the 7 year period of his sentence** as that would help him in the rehabilitation process.

Knives – 8 years imprisonment or more

111.30   *R v Bowen* 2001 1 Cr App R (S) 282. LCJ. The defendant was convicted of manslaughter after a murder trial. The defendant had drank beer and was carrying a knife, which was carried so he could cut cocaine. In a snooker hall the two victims approached him and he stabbed them both in the neck. Then he kicked one of them. The fatal wounds were severe. The defendant claimed self-defence, which was rejected. Held. The basis was manslaughter because of provocation. One witness had heard one of the victims saying, 'Paki bastard.' The two deaths were an important aggravating factor. The defendant had previous convictions for violence but none since 1986. **12 years** concurrent substituted for 14 concurrent.

Att-Gen's Ref. No. 143 of 2002 2004 1 Cr App R (S) 102. The defendant was convicted of manslaughter on the basis of lack of intent and acquitted of murder. He did not offer manslaughter as a plea and ran in the main an accident offence. It was a retrial after the first jury disagreed. He was driving in his van with his 14 year old son. He had some chef knives he had stolen some months earlier from his employer near his feet. A man, J, unknown to him who was much the worse for drink walked into the road unsteadily in front of the van. He may have tried to kick the vehicle. J behaved abusively and the defendant took the largest chef knife got out of the van and stabbed

J once in the liver and the heart. J died and the defendant drove off. Held. The knives were not carried in the van as weapons but he deliberately took a knife from the van. The very least sentence was **8 years**. Because it was a reference **6 years** not 5.

R v Lahbib 2005 1 Cr App R (S) 342. The defendant after facing a count of murder was convicted of manslaughter. He was a Moroccan national who had married an Englishwoman and had been in the country about four years. He was working as a kitchen porter and sometimes visited a particular public house. The previous year he had been attacked on two occasions while travelling home from work late at night and since that time had carried a lock knife to scare people off. On this evening he visited the public house and played snooker. He drank some beer but was not drunk. The victim, entirely unprovoked by the defendant, walked up to him and punched him in the face. While the defendant was on the ground the victim kicked him at least once. The manager was called and although eye-witnesses tried to explain that the defendant had done nothing wrong the manager insisted both men leave the pub. Outside the victim attacked the defendant again, lashing out and shouting. The defendant did not retaliate but put up his hands and ran away. When the defendant got home he realised his watch was missing and went back to the pub to try to find it. People in the pub saw him looking at the floor by the snooker table. The victim had also returned to look for items. At they left the pub the defendant said something to the deceased and outside the victim shouted drunkenly at the defendant and attacked him again. The defendant told the victim he had a knife but this did not stop the attack. The defendant took the knife out, there was a scuffle and the victim received four injuries from the knife of which one stab wound to the heart was the fatal injury. The jury did not say whether the verdict of manslaughter was returned on the basis of provocation or lack of intent to cause serious harm. The defendant, 27, had no convictions and was described by character witnesses as gentle and kind. Held. The final confrontation was not planned. The defendant did not draw his weapon during the initial assault on him in the pub, or when manhandled from the pub by the licensee, or during the second assault on him outside the pub by the victim, which demonstrated that he did not carry the weapon intending to use it as a weapon of offence. **8 years** not 10 years.

Old cases *R v Pitt* 1998 1 Cr App R (S) 58 (For summary see first edition of this book.)

Life sentence/Automatic life sentence – Fixing specified term

111.31   *R v Secretary of State for Home Department, ex p Furber* 1998 1 Cr App R (S) 208. The general rule for young offenders is to fix the period at half the determinate period.

R v Caswell 1999 1 Cr App R (S) 467. Consider first what would be appropriate if a determinate sentence was passed. Divide that term by two although not every prisoner is entitled to have $\frac{1}{2}$ deducted. Then deduct the time the defendant has been on remand. Here it was worth 8 years. Because the defendant had not done well in prison after division $4\frac{1}{2}$ years. Deducting 6 months for the time he had spent in custody **4 years** substituted.

R v McStay 2003 1 Cr App R (S) 176 at 180–1. The Judge passed an automatic life sentence. Held. Judges should deduct the period in custody after they have divided the notional determinate sentence in half. The amount of time in custody should be an exact figure and not rounded up or down. If the figure is not known it is not wrong for the Judge to fix the term and add, "less the number of days spent in custody for this offence, with liberty to apply within 28 days in default of agreement as to that number of days." We recommend that Judges imposing automatic life should, after stating the period, the method of calculation, and the effect of the specified period add words to the effect that the defendant will remain in custody unless and until the Parole Board is satisfied that it is no longer necessary for the protection of the public he should be detained. That will stop any misunderstanding as to the period.

Old cases. *R v Iqbal* 1997 2 Cr App R (S) 226.

Medical

See DOCTORS KILLING PATIENTS

Mentally disturbed defendants

111.32   *R v Walton* 2004 1 Cr App R (S) 234. The defendant pleaded guilty to manslaughter. Held. Relying on *R v Mbatha* 1985 7 Cr App R (S) 373, *R v Moses* 1996 2 Cr App R (S) 407, *R v Mitchell* 1997 1 Cr App R (S) 90 and *R v Hutchinson* 1997 2 Cr App R (S) 60 where an offender is suffering from a mental disorder which is susceptible to treatment and a place is available in a special hospital the court should not impose life with the intention of preventing the release of the offender by the Mental Health Tribunal. All the conditions required by a s 37 order are present here so hospital **order with restrictions** substituted for life.

Neglect, gross

111.33   *R v Sogunro* 1997 2 Cr App R (S) 89. The defendant was convicted of manslaughter and false imprisonment. The defendant shut his fiancé in a room without food or drink because he believed she was possessed by the devil. She died of starvation and neglect but was not found until 10 months after her death. Defendant had no previous convictions. **6 years** and 3 years concurrent upheld.

R v Elton 1999 2 Cr App R (S) 58. The defendant was convicted of manslaughter and causing GBH with intent both involving the same victim. He had pleaded guilty to common assault on Adrian Berry. In a public house the defendant struck Adrian Berry forcibly twice for no apparent reason. This was the common assault. The defendant was ejected. Adrian Berry and others returned to their hotel and the defendant arrived there. The defendant and the victim, one of Adrian Berry's group, got into a verbal altercation, which degenerated into a fight. The defendant chased the victim out of the hotel and the victim was next seen lying in the road. The defendant admitted punching the victim several times and kicking him once in the face. Forensic evidence revealed that the victim had been killed by being crushed by a heavy vehicle. It also revealed that the victim had injuries to his face and mouth, which were typical of those produced by a violent assault. The injuries were consistent with the victim receiving a severe kick to the face, but he was alive when hit by the vehicle. The basis for the prosecution case was that the victim had been left in a situation where he would be 'subject to some harm'. The defendant when 16 and 18 been convicted of common assault. Held. 4 not 5 years for the GBH because it should be detached from the death. The manslaughter was completely unintended and it should be dealt with as a bad case of manslaughter by gross neglect. **6 years** substituted for 8. 1 year for the common assault unaffected with all sentences concurrent.

See also *Children – Neglect, starvation etc*

Negligence, gross

111.34   *R v Devine* 1999 2 Cr App R (S) 409. The defendant was convicted of manslaughter. The defendant had after drinking heavily jumped, ran or walked into the path of a motorcyclist. The bike skidded and the rider hit a lamppost and died. The defendant received minor injuries. He said he had mixed alcohol with his medication for depression. The defendant had previous convictions for domestic burglary (receiving 30 months' youth custody), common assault, possession of an offensive weapon and threatening behaviour. He had been warned on earlier occasions about drinking when on medication. He had also on occasions staggered into the road, no doubt imperilling motorists. Held. Gross negligence manslaughter cases are notoriously difficult. He had pleaded not guilty but he could hardly be criticised for asking for a jury's verdict.

The **3¹/₂ years** sentence, consecutive to 3 months for unrelated offences was reduced to 2¹/₂ years.

R v Barker 2003 2 Cr App R (S) 110. The defendant was convicted of three counts of manslaughter. He drove his partner and their three young children and a friend to a recreation area by an old chalk pit that had been filled with water. There were other friends following them in another car. The defendant stopped the car and talked with his friends in the other car about where they were going to park. The defendant got back into his car with the driver's door open and with one foot out of the car keeping it open. He drove towards a cliff. The car approached the cliff. It seemed to go faster before it slowed down but went over the cliff into the lake. The defendant, his friend and his partner managed to get out but tragically the three children aged two, five and six were drowned. Shortly after the accident he gave a number of different explanations: including the pedal had got stuck under the mat, there was petrol on the carpet and his foot slipped, the mat was underneath the accelerator, the accelerator got stuck in the mat and his foot got stuck as they were coming up the slope. The vehicle was eventually examined but no defects were found. He had no licence or insurance. He was interviewed and said that a few days before the accident he had noticed that the accelerator had got stuck and he accepted that on this occasion the accelerator had got stuck because he had floored it. He was 23 and had some irrelevant previous convictions. There was a low risk of re-offending assessed and extreme remorse. Psychiatric material revealed post-traumatic stress disorder. There was a petition with a large number of signatures and a statement from the mother of the children asking for leniency in very dignified terms. Held. The public interest required the imposition of a prison sentence where lives are taken in these circumstances. However, the attitude of the mother is something that the Court rightly ought to take into account. **3 years** not 5.

R v Ruffell 2003 2 Cr App R (S) 330. The defendant was convicted of manslaughter through gross negligence. The defendant, the deceased and H went to the defendant's mother's house after an evening of drinking. They purchased heroin and cocaine on the way. The defendant and H were experienced drug users. The deceased was not. All three took the drugs and H said that the deceased started going "a bit off colour, a bit white". H and the defendant tried to revive him by putting him near an open window and splashing water on his face before putting him in a bath of water. He was then carried downstairs, wrapped in towels and placed near a radiator. H left at about 1am. At about 6am a neighbour heard groaning and "come on, come on". At 7.05am the defendant had phoned the deceased's mother and told her that her son had been sick after drinking a bottle of vodka. He further said: "I ain't done nothing". At this stage the deceased was outside and his mother told the defendant to bring him inside and cover him with a blanket. It was a cold morning. Three hours later the deceased was found by workmen and neighbours on the path. He died of hypothermia and opiate intoxication. Held. The defendant was well aware that the deceased was in a very bad shape as a result of injecting heroin. It must have been obvious that it was a very cold morning. He agreed to take the deceased back inside. To deliberately leave someone in a bad condition out in cold weather when he could quite easily have brought him inside, as he said he would, put a serious reflection on the case. However, the sentence was longer than the type of sentence imposed for this type of case. **2 years** not 3.

R v Parfeni 2003 2 Cr App R (S) 362. The defendant was convicted of manslaughter by gross negligence and of supplying heroin and cocaine. She was a crack and heroin addict and had known the 39 year old victim for weeks. Having left a pub, the victim phoned him and they then met. They went to King's Cross where the defendant purchased heroin and crack. At the defendant's flat the victim was introduced to Miss M. They all smoked crack whilst the defendant prepared some heroin and she then helped to inject it into the victim. The victim had no known prior involvement with

527

drugs. He made a noise as if in pain, lay down on the defendant's bed and fell asleep. The defendant searched him and took £80 and his credit cards, which the defendant went out and used. She returned about 3 hours later and said to Miss M that she was going to "put him to sleep". She returned to the living room and said to Miss M "I did it twice. I've put him to sleep". That morning Miss M and the defendant went out shopping. When they returned to the flat they found the victim lying on his stomach and vomit coming from his mouth. He was not breathing. The defendant said to Miss M "We are in big shit. This is between you and me. If you tell anyone, I'm going to kill you or put you in prison for life". She then called an ambulance. When police officers arrived she told them that they had both taken crack and heroin and then gone shopping and that when she had returned she had found him dead. A post mortem concluded that death had been caused by a heroin overdose. She was later arrested and made no comment in interview. She was well aware of the risk of injecting heroin as her brother had been convicted of murder by heroin overdose 7 years earlier. Held. This grossly negligent act was carried out for the purposes of greed. The victim was vulnerable. The defendant was aware of the risks of heroin injection. The offence was aggravated by the behaviour of the defendant after she had found Burgess apparently dead. The facts of this case were sufficiently different from *Att-Gen's Refs Nos. 19–21 of 2001 2002* 1 Cr App R (S) 33 for the Court not to pass a deterrent sentence. So **10 years** not 12.

R v Hood 2004 1 Cr App R (S) 431. The defendant was convicted of manslaughter. He was the sole carer of his wife. She was in poor heath with osteoporosis and diabetes. Both she and the defendant were heavy drinkers. She suffered a fall and broke a number of bones. However, the defendant did not call an ambulance for 3 weeks. She was debilitated, very thin and had pressure sores. About 5 weeks later she died. Her poor health and the low standard of care received from the defendant had contributed both directly and indirectly to her debilitated state. Held. On any view this was a case of pure omission. She was reluctant to go to hospital. Ultimately the defendant called for medical assistance. His neglect was not the only cause of her death. **30 months**, not 4 years.

Old cases. *Att-Gen's Ref. Nos. 26 and 27 of 1994* 1995 16 Cr App R (S) 675; *R v Kite* 1996 2 Cr App R (S) 295.

No reason/Minor provocation/Drunken attack

111.35 *Att-Gen's Ref. No. 118 of 2001* 2002 2 Cr App R (S) 537. The defendant pleaded guilty to manslaughter as an alternative to murder based on a lack of intent owing to his drunken state. He and the victim were both unemployed alcoholics living together in a squalid maisonette. They gave each other mutual support and companionship which was regularly marred by both verbal and physical arguments when one of them was drunk. The victim was 67 and a small man of comparatively slight build. The defendant was tall, much fitter and of bigger build. The defendant became very drunk and hit the victim twice with a heavy lump of wood, which had a large protruding nail in it. It was to be used as firewood. The first blow hit the side of the head causing deep internal bruising and a fracture to the scull. It probably rendered the victim unconscious. The second blow hit the arm. The nail pierced an artery. No medical help was sought and the victim bled to death. Eighteen hours later the defendant contacted a friend and he tried to surrender to the police. The police station was closed and the police were then called. Police found the body with the lump of wood still next to it. Test showed the victim was not intoxicated. He was 44 with no convictions. In prison without alcohol he had reverted to his normal character and had behaved sensibly. He was due to be released in a month. Held. The proper sentence was in the range **4 to 5 years**. Because it was a reference and the other factors **3 years** not 27 months.

R v Byrne 2003 1 Cr App R (S) 338. The defendant was acquitted of murder and convicted of manslaughter. He and the victim abused heroin. They met in the street and then both went to the victim's house where they took temazepam and heroin. They then set off for the pub and on the way both consumed some strong cider. At the pub they arranged to buy some crack cocaine. While waiting, the defendant played pool and the victim sold some mobile top up cards. The defendant told police in interview the victim came back to the pool table and abused the defendant in various ways including calling him a wanker, smirking and goading him. The defendant lost his temper, picked up a pool cue and struck the victim with the thick end of the cue. It hit a vulnerable part of the neck and the blow caused the artery to split. The Judge held the jury's basis for their verdict was provocation and not lack of intent and the blows were very severe. He also said, "Your life from start to finish has been one of criminality, sometimes violent, more often dishonesty. I dare say a lot of it is down to your abuse of drugs. That is entirely of your own making." Held. *Attorney General's Ref. No. 33 of 1996* 1997 2 Cr App R (S) 10 makes it clear that sentences in double figures and up to 12 years will be appropriate for provocation cases where a weapon has been deliberately carried other than a brief moment provocation when a weapon has been deliberately carried with the contemplation that it may be used. Here the weapon was carried for a brief moment and the provocation was moderate. **8 years** was at the top end but not outside the range.

R v Wadsworth 2004 1 Cr App R (S) 13. The defendant pleaded guilty to manslaughter. A murder count was dropped. The victim aged 16 went out to celebrate his GCSE results and his obtaining a job in engineering. He spent the evening in public houses. Walking home with his brother the two crossed a road to avoid some rowdy youths which included the defendant. The defendant said, "Let's go and smack those lads". The victim needed to urinate and as he zipped up his trousers the defendant punched him in the face. A second blow had such force the victim was knocked to the ground. His head hit the road surface causing a skull fracture and fatal brain injury. As the victim lay helpless on the ground the defendant kicked him hard in the head. The defendant in interview lied but did describe the kick as like a penalty kick. He was 17 and had no convictions. He expressed remorse and had 15 character witnesses. Held. The decision to offer a manslaughter plea was surprising. The kick was hard and was a serious aggravating feature. **8 years** was at the top end of the scale but not manifestly excessive. As he was young and had no convictions the two year extension to the sentence was quashed.

R v Reece 2005 1 Cr App R (S) 99. The defendant pleaded guilty to manslaughter on an indictment for murder. The deceased, CJ and his partner JL left home with the defendant and his partner, DF and went to the pub where they were joined by others including DR (the defendant's brother). At closing time they left with the defendant and the deceased straggling behind. DF heard them shouting. She told them to be quiet and carried on walking. When she looked back she saw the deceased swaying and then fall to the ground. The defendant arrived back at the deceased's house and was heard to say that the deceased was in the road. The babysitter, KH, went outside and saw the deceased staggering. The defendant went up to the deceased and started a conversation. Both were extremely drunk, but he heard the defendant tell the deceased that he was going to hit him again. KH tried to separate them but got nowhere. He returned and got DR. When KH and DR returned they found the deceased lying on the ground. The defendant had kicked the deceased at least once whilst he was on the ground. The blow was of sufficient strength to leave a bruise and shoe impression his cheek. He died early the following day from a brain-bleed caused by the kick. In interview the defendant could remember nothing of the incident. He had had 13 pints. He was 20 with convictions for harassment and racially aggravated common assault. He presented a high risk of reoffending. He was distressed. Held. Unlike *R v Eaton* 1989 11 Cr App R (S) 475 and *R v Redfern* 2001 2 Cr App R (S) 33, the attack involved only the defendant. There was one kick of moderate severity. A kick with the shod foot is just as serious as the used of a weapon. **5 years detention**, not $6^1/_2$.

Old cases. *R v Bourne* 1995 16 Cr App R (S) 237; *R v Bamborough* 1995 16 Cr App R (S) 602.

One punch manslaughter

111.36   *R v Edwards* 2001 2 Cr App R (S) 540. Where a single blow produced tragic consequences clearly unintended, the gravity of the consequences does have to be marked by a custodial sentence in most cases.

R v Grad 2004 2 Cr App R (S) 218. The defendant was convicted of manslaughter. He was with a group of friends at a nightclub on a balcony overlooking the club's beer garden. One of his group spat some beer over the balcony which landed on the victim in a second group. There was verbal abuse between the two groups and bottles and glasses were thrown by the second group towards the group on the balcony, and some witnesses said glasses were thrown down from the defendant's group. One of the glasses thrown up by the second group hit the defendant and cut his head, which bled profusely. The security staff ushered the defendant's group out of the club. One of the second group followed them because he wanted to continue with the confrontation, and shouted abuse outside but was then restrained by security staff. The victim had followed him out, not because he was looking for trouble but because he wanted to support his friend. The defendant approached the victim and punched him once in the head (according to the witnesses) or the top of the neck (according to the scientific evidence.) The punch was delivered with moderate force. The victim fell to the floor and was motionless. The defendant did not play any part in any fighting save for that single punch. The victim died almost immediately. The medical evidence was that the cause of death was a very unusual combination of circumstances: a haemorrhage in the brain caused by the combination of the twisting of the neck by the blow, the angle of the blow and the dilation of the blood vessels caused by the victim's drinking. The defendant and his friends had left the scene but when he heard of the death he surrendered voluntarily to the police. The prosecution said the offence was as near to accident as a criminal offence could be. He was of previous good character. He had made a financial contribution to the victim's family and there was a wide range of references showing he had good business qualities and a bright future. There were letters showing that the companies he was involved with were suffering serious difficulties because of his imprisonment. He had shown genuine remorse. Held. The combination of factors which led to the death were very unusual. It was understandable that the defendant did not plead guilty having regard to the parties before the court. This was a case where the seriousness of the offending must be marked by a custodial sentence. The appropriate sentence is at the very bottom of the bracket for this type of case. **9 months** substituted for 18 months.

Att-Gen's Ref. No. 133 of 2002 2003 2 Cr App R (S) 645. The defendant was convicted of manslaughter on an indictment alleging murder. He used to drink in a pub where he became friendly with the victim, who was 65. On one occasion the defendant had gone back to the victim's flat where the victim had made a homosexual advance. The defendant threatened to kill the victim if their paths crossed again. By chance, about 4 months later, the defendant met the victim again in the street when both were drunk. The victim was found some minutes later lying on the pavement with blood pouring from his head and vomit by his mouth. He had six fractures to the skull with significant external injuries to the right side of the head. The defendant was arrested shortly afterwards. In interview the defendant produced a prepared statement denying having seen the victim that night. At trial evidence was advanced that one punch could have caused the victim to fall with the fatal injury caused by his head hitting the pavement. He was 39 with previous convictions for common assault. Held. The risk of death was not apparent. Consideration should be given to the plea proffered, the age and criminal record of the defendant, the nature of the violence, the context in which the incident occurred, any premeditation and the defendant's conduct after the event. This offence was the result of single punch which was not premeditated but it was an unprovoked attack after a grudge by a younger man on an older man. There was no contrition. **2¹/₂ years** was unduly lenient. **3 years** would not have been inappropriate and therefore no interference with the sentence as this was a reference.

Att-Gen's Ref. No. 139 of 2002 2003 2 Cr App R (S) 653. The defendant was convicted of manslaughter. At about 03:30 on New Years day the defendant drove his taxi to collect a fare from a party. No-one claimed the taxi and the offender was angry that his time had been wasted. The deceased stepped out from the party for some fresh air and following an exchange the defendant punched the deceased once with a clenched fist to the right-hand side of the deceased's head. The defendant left the scene and continued to work. The deceased was dead by the time the ambulance had arrived. The cause of death was probably the punch. The amount of alcohol the deceased had consumed had caused a relaxation of his neck muscles. The defendant surrendered to a police station two days later and in interview said that he had acted in self-defence. He was 26 and had a previous conviction for two offences of ABH for which he had received a combination order. He showed remorse. The trial judge sentenced him on the basis that the deceased had made a racist remark, there was provocation by the deceased and that the defendant had been confronted by him. Held. A custodial sentence of 2 years would have been appropriate. When considering whether that sentence could be suspended, provocation was incapable by itself of being an exceptional circumstance unless the gravity of the provocation was itself wholly exceptional. Here there was racial abuse, a confrontation and the deceased had consumed a large amount of alcohol and this had led directly to his death. These factors were capable of giving rise to exceptional circumstances so **2 years** could be **suspended**.

R v Cheetham and Baker. 2004 2 Cr App R (S) 278. C pleaded guilty to manslaughter. B was convicted of manslaughter. B pleaded guilty to two robberies and other counts of making a false instrument etc. for which he received concurrent sentences of 2 years etc. C pleaded guilty on the basis that he was at a party where everyone drank a great deal. C believed that a young woman at the party had been assaulted by the victim and he was told at the party that the victim was a woman beater who had assaulted his own girlfriend. C was distraught at what he believed to be the victim's behaviour towards women and he followed the victim from the party and struck him a single blow to the face. The victim fell back and struck his head causing injuries which led to his death. B then began kicking and stamping on the victim. The basis of plea did not include any joint enterprise between B and C. After B's trial the judge sentenced B on the basis that they had engaged in a joint enterprise and that both were equally responsible for the single blow which caused death. He made no finding on what might have happened after the victim was on the ground. C, 45, had previous convictions including one for robbery. He was genuinely remorseful and had an exemplary army record. The pre-sentence report said he was at a relatively low risk of re-offending. A prison report said he had caused no problems. B, 24, also had previous convictions including one for robbery. Pre-sentence reports indicated he was at a high risk of re-offending. A psychiatric report concluded he had learning difficulties and a long-standing personality disorder, although he was not mentally ill. A prison report said he was volatile and had not expressed remorse and that he was a bully. Held. We must sentence C on his basis of plea. B **3 years** not 6 consecutive to 4 years for the robberies. C **2 years** not 4.

Passion, Crime of

111.37   *R v Henry* 1999 2 Cr App R (S) 412. The defendant pleaded guilty to manslaughter. He had indicated his plea at the first opportunity. The defendant's wife went out for the evening leaving the defendant to look after the children aged 5 and 1.

Leaving one child with his in-laws and taking the other with him, he drove to pick up his wife. However, she had left a public house with another man. He then saw them in the street with arms linked and saw them stop and kiss each other. The defendant shouted across but the wife refused to get into the car. The defendant ran across the road and punched the other man in the face who fell backwards, and struck his head on a manhole cover. He died of injuries to his skull and brain caused by the fall. The blow was of considerable force. It broke the victim's jaw and had lifted him off the ground. The defendant after initial denials expressed remorse. He was 31 with no previous convictions and had excellent character references. He told the probation officer he didn't drink and had never hit anyone before. He was a model prisoner. Held. **18 months** substituted for 4 years. Had the blow been less ferocious it would have been less.

R v Gratton 2001 2 Cr App R (S) 167. The defendant pleaded guilty to manslaughter. The defendant and the victim were friends. The deceased believed the defendant fancied his girlfriend (wrongly they said). After drinking a lot during the day, they went home when the public house closed. The defendant and the victim were seen arguing. The defendant was put to bed on the sofa by his girlfriend and the victim. The defendant's girlfriend went into the garden and was joined by the victim. They sat opposite each other on chairs. The victim leaned forward put his hands on her knees and gave her a quick kiss on the lips as a thank you gesture. Unfortunately the defendant had come out and had seen it. He walked up to them quickly saying, 'You fucked up with your missus, now you are trying it on with mine.' He threw two or three punches to the victim's face causing the victim and his chair to tip back. His head hit some rocks in a rockery. He appeared to be dead when the ambulance attended. The defendant showed great remorse. He thought he saw a 'snog.' He was 31 and was treated as of good character. He had an excellent work record. There were many references. The defendant received **9 months**. Held. It would not be right to suspend it.

R v Rumbol 2001 2 Cr App R (S) 299. The defendant was convicted of manslaughter. The defendant, a professional boxer formed a relationship with a 17-year-old girl, called Carlie. It faded and she resumed her relationship with the victim, her former boyfriend. The defendant who was possessive of her when they were together became consumed with jealousy. Shortly before his 21st birthday he lay in wait for the victim as he walked to the bus for work. The victim was struck by one blow, which caused him to fall to the ground. The defendant was heard to say, 'Stay away from Carlie, just stay away from her.' The defendant ran off. The victim died the next morning. The pathologist said the rupture of the vertebral artery was cause by a single hard blow. The defendant had never been in trouble before. Held. Because of his character and because he never intended to cause any serious harm to the victim **6 years** not 7.

Att-Gen's Ref. Nos.74, 95 and 118 of 2002 Re H 2003 2 Cr App R (S) 273 at 285. The defendant pleaded to manslaughter of his wife on the basis of provocation. The couple had married in 1986 and had four children aged 14, 12, 7 and 2$\frac{1}{2}$. In 2001, the marriage ran into difficulties. She considered he was spending too much time at work where he was a successful solicitor. He thought she was spending too much time at her karate classes and was too close to the instructor. In October 2001, she became intimate with the instructor. On 20 December 2001 he confronted her about a possible affair with the instructor. She denied it. By Christmas Day night he was upset and cried. She called him pathetic and told him not to keep her awake. On Boxing Day she asked him to leave and with reluctance he moved to a hotel. On the next three days he talked to his wife about the problems and discussed them with his doctor and partners. The following day he visited his wife to collect his clothes and say goodbye to his children. She said he had something to say to him. He said he wasn't strong enough to hear it and wanted time. She persisted and said, "I don't love you. We're finished". She said her feelings for the instructor were "big style" and he had feelings for her. She added in a week she will have slept with him. Later he claimed she said she had slept with him. He attacked her with a knife and continued as she tried to escape. As the eldest child tried to revive her the child became covered in blood. The defendant stabbed himself with the knife and the second child took it out of his chest. The third child saw some of the incident and heard the defendant say, "Please don't die on me I love you so much. The youngest child was crying next to the mother and the defendant said, "She was going to leave me. I want to die". The knife was probably a bread knife. The wife had 11 stab wounds. Two completely penetrated her body. One penetrated her heart. He needed an operation. In interview he said he had "lost it totally" and "It's like they say you can see a red mist. I was bellowing like a bull." It appeared he hadn't eaten or slept for several days before the incident. He was 39 and of good character. There was no history of aggression or violence inside or outside the marriage. There was medical evidence of a particular severe "acute stress reaction" in addition to physical and psychological exhaustion, making him unusually susceptible to what his wife had said. **$3^1/_2$ years** was not lenient still less unduly lenient.

Att-Gen's Ref. Nos.74, 95 and 118 of 2002 Re W 2003 2 Cr App R (S) 273 at 288. The defendant was acquitted of murder of his partner and convicted of manslaughter on the basis of provocation. He had earlier offered to plead to manslaughter but his offer was rejected. The couple met as teenagers and had two young children. In 2001 they bought a house together but there were difficulties between them. She left with the children two months later. The defendant found it difficult to accept the relationship was over and found out she was seeing another man. He made a threatening call to the new man but later rang back and had a normal conversation with him. Thirteen months after she left she agreed to visit him to talk. Shortly after he told his parents and his brother he had killed her. Police found her with a plastic bag in her mouth. She had died of asphyxia. There was bruising to her jaw line consistent with the defendant covering her mouth and nose with his hands. He told the jury he felt heart broken at losing his wife. He reacted badly to the loss of his children. He was not sleeping. He showed her some photographs of the children and she said, "I've got the kids. You have only the photographs." Later she said she was thinking of setting up with the new man, with him being the surrogate father and moving to Manchester. Further, she didn't care if she had hurt him. At that stage he "just boiled over, red haze, gripped hold of her, adrenaline really going, heart pounding." One psychiatrist said he suffered from an adjustment order and could be clinically depressed. The other disagreed and said he was in a depressed and unhappy mood. The defendant was 26 and of good character. Witnesses said he put everything into the relationship working long and anti-social hours so his wife could have everything she wanted. She took more than she gave, going out frequently and spending more than they could afford causing financial problems. Her sister said she was using him and he was hardworking and decent. He was sentenced on the basis he had not been violent to her before. The trial Judge said he thought it right to be merciful. Held. He was entitled to be merciful. **4 years** upheld.

Old case. *R v Light* 1995 16 Cr App R (S) 824.

See also *Relationship attacks*

Plead, defendant offering to plead and offer rejected

111.38   *R v Bertram* 2004 1 Cr App R (S) 186. The defendant offered to plead guilty to manslaughter and the prosecution rejected the offer. His defence put forward at his trial for murder was inconsistent with a plea to manslaughter. The Judge refused to give the defendant any credit for his plea. Held. He should have some credit for his offer. It was unrealistic for him to plead guilty to manslaughter at the beginning of the trial.

Police officers on duty as victims

111.39   *R v Rule* 2003 1 Cr App R (S) 224. The defendant pleaded guilty to manslaughter. On 18 December 2000, shortly after midnight, he drove in a friend's car at 52 mph in a 30 mph area towards an officer with a speed gun. The road was well lit with clear visibility. The officer, the victim stepped off the pavement and raised his hand to signal to the defendant to stop. There was ample time to stop and his two passengers screamed at him to stop. He seemed to increase his speed and the other officers shouted at the victim to get out of the way. The brakes were not applied. The road was wet and the officer might have slipped. The defendant tried to swerve round the officer but the car hit him. The officer hit the bonnet and then the windscreen and was carried along until he fell onto the road. He died shortly afterwards and the defendant abandoned the car. The defendant surrendered to the police after the police were able to identify him through his mobile phone. In interview he said he didn't stop because he was banned and he wanted to spend Christmas with his family. He was 26 with 58 previous offences on 15 occasions. He had been disqualified twice in 1996 for 18 months and in 1998 for 18 months for drink/drive and disqualified driving. On 3 October 2000, he was banned from driving for excess alcohol for 3 years. Held. Police officers acting in the course of their duty on the roads require and should be given the protection of the courts against this sort of conduct. He thought only of his own position. Although we accept he tried to avoid the officer, he had driven with a total disregard for human safety or human life. The offence was of a very high level of criminality. He showed genuine remorse. A severe deterrent sentence was required and that is what the **9 years** was. However 9 years not 15 years disqualification.

R v Parfitt 2005 1 Cr App R (S) 221. The defendant was convicted of manslaughter when tried for murder and pleaded guilty to theft, driving while disqualified, burglary and taking a conveyance. He stole a car and drove it although he was disqualified. When police officers saw him driving it he left the car and went to a house where he persuaded the occupant to call him a taxi. When the taxi came he left the house but was seen by a police officer. The defendant jumped into the driver's door of the taxi; the taxi driver ran after him and jumped into the passenger seat. The police officer got his arm or arms into window to try to stop the car but the defendant drove off, dragging the victim with the car. He swerved from side to side to try and dislodge him while the taxi driver tried to grab the key to stop the car. The victim shouted 'Stop it, you'll kill me'. After about 100 yards the victim was dislodged. He fell and hit his head on a bollard. He died two days later. The taxi driver grabbed the key and the car stopped. The defendant ran away. He later broke into an outhouse and stole goods and took a van He was arrested the following day after a violent struggle. He had indicated from an early stage that he was guilty of manslaughter, and the jury knew he accepted that. At the time of the offence his licence had been revoked from a sentence of imprisonment for robbery because he had breached his licence by taking drugs and failing to attend probation appointments. Held. It was correct to approach this as though the defendant had pleaded guilty to manslaughter. This was an aggravated form of manslaughter: committed by a man in breach of his licence, in the course of committing offences, and when approached by a police officer doing his duty. Two people were telling him to stop; the taxi driver and the police officer. This case was right up in the top bracket and **12 years** was not manifestly excessive. When a person has committed offences and causes injury to another in an attempt to escape, and particularly when that other is a police officer, those offences should as a matter of principle attract a consecutive sentence. There was nothing wrong with **12 months consecutive** for the other offences.

Provocation

111.40   *R v Byrne* 2003 1 Cr App R (S) 338. The defendant was convicted of manslaughter. Held. *Att-Gen's Ref. No. 33 of 1996* 1997 2 Cr App R (S) 10 makes it clear that sentences in double figures and **up to 12 years** will be appropriate for provocation cases where a weapon has been deliberately carried other than a brief moment provocation when a weapon has been deliberately carried with the contemplation that it may be used. (For further details see No Reason/Minor Provocation/ Drunken Attack)

Att-Gen's Ref. Nos.74, 95 and 118 of 2002 2003 2 Cr App R (S) 273. Limiting our observations to cases of manslaughter committed after provocation arising out of possessiveness, jealousy or unfaithfulness, we would not seriously disagree with the proposition that the ordinary sentencing range lies between **5 and 7 years**, though that is not to overlook what was said in *R v Light* 1995 16 Cr App R (S) 824 about most cases resulting in sentencing "of the order of **7–8 years**".

Sentencing Advisory Panel The panel have produced a report about provocation which can be found at www.sentencing-guidelines.gov.uk

For an article about sentencing in provocation cases see 2004 Crim L R 501.

[For other cases of provocation see the individual sections for the type of death etc.]

Reckless manslaughter

111.41   Cases on this manslaughter are listed under the general headings.

Relationship killings – Men killing wives or partners – Guideline remarks – Provocation

111.42   *Att-Gen's Ref. Nos.74, 95 and 118 of 2002* 2003 2 Cr App R (S) 273. Limiting our observations to cases of manslaughter committed after provocation arising out of possessiveness, jealousy or unfaithfulness, we would not seriously disagree with the proposition that the ordinary sentencing range lies between **5 and 7 years**, though that is not to overlook what was said in *R v Light* 1995 16 Cr App R (S) 824 about most cases resulting in sentencing "of the order of **7–8 years**".

Relationship killings – Men killing wives or partners

111.43   *R v Caswell* 1999 1 Cr App R (S) 467. The defendant pleaded guilty to manslaughter on the grounds of diminished responsibility. A boy now aged 21 killed his older gay lover after the relationship was over following a row about money. He severely beat, kicked and stamped on the deceased causing grievous multiple injuries to the face head and body. The defendant was found to have a severe emotional and personality disorder. He was sentenced to life, which was not challenged. Held. If there had been a determinate sentence passed **8 years** would have been appropriate.

R v Butler 1999 2 Cr App R (S) 339. The defendant pleaded guilty to manslaughter. The defendant, aged 22, was released from custody and spent his time drinking and taking amphetamine and cocaine. He also resumed living with his girlfriend. One week after being released he had an argument with her in the street. She punched him and he punched her. She then got a knife and threatened him. Both went to their house where a violent struggle took place in the hallway. She tried to use the knife again. He then strangled her. The force of that had caused her to have a vasovagal reflex. He pleaded on the basis that he had injured her in the course of disarming her but had gone beyond self-defence. He had a bad record including five appearances for violence including actual bodily harm involving a weapon. **6 years** was entirely correct.

R v Sexton 2000 2 Cr App R (S) 94. The defendant pleaded guilty to manslaughter on the grounds of diminished responsibility based on depression. The defendant's business got into difficulties so he mortgaged his house and eventually went bankrupt. He hid this from his wife to whom he was devoted. The bailiffs possessed the home but to prevent his wife discovering he re-entered the premises. She was very devoted to the house. Five days later they were leaving the house together and she remarked a plant needed to be replanted. At this he seized a spade from the garage and hit his wife hard across the head. He drove around in his car for 28 hours with her body in the boot. Then he surrendered himself to the police. He said he had been trying to tell the wife but never found a suitable opportunity. He showed deep remorse. He had a blameless character, to whom violence of any kind was alien. He was considered sane. Held. Partly because it was a crime based on love not hatred **3 years** not 5.

R v Hampson 2001 1 Cr App R (S) 288. The defendant pleaded guilty to manslaughter on the grounds of diminished responsibility based on depression. The defendant's wife was reported missing. He said she had left home after their marriage had broken down. This he repeated later. When formally arrested for murder he admitted killing her because of years of friction and arguments. He said she went on and on and he had to shut her up. After continual verbal abuse he picked up a hammer and struck her three times. He buried her in the garden where the police found her. He felt he couldn't leave his wife because his daughter was extremely close to him. He was 44 with no previous convictions. He also had had mild to moderate personality problems over the years. He was suffering from moderate to severe depression. **4 years** substituted for 6.

R v Frisby 2002 1 Cr App R (S) 289. The defendant was convicted of manslaughter on the basis of provocation after a murder trial. After his marriage to the victim in 1994 she continued to see her boyfriend and drank. Over Christmas 1999 she disappeared. Fifteen months later a dog found her skull. The defendant wrote a note saying the victim had grabbed their eldest child and kicked her in the buttocks. They had argued and she threw a hammer at him. He picked it up and struck her on the head several times and he then dismembered and disposed of the body. The torso was cut up and put in the sea and river. The head was buried. He was 42 and of good character. Held. The dismembering and disposal of the body was not a proper matter to take into account. It would have been a proper matter in relation to murder as showing some form of pre-planning but not for manslaughter. Sentence reduced from 8 years to **6 years**.

R v Veysi 2003 1 Cr App R (S) 14. The defendant pleaded guilty to manslaughter by reason of diminished responsibility. He walked into a police station and said he had killed his wife with a rolling pin and then strangled her. He also said he had intended to kill his three children and had tried to strangle himself. Police went to his home and found a note on the bedroom door saying, "Please do not open. Call the police." His wife's body was found inside under a duvet next to a rolling pin. They also found some knotted sheets in the attic. The post mortem confirmed the defendant's account. Bruising was found round the defendant's neck. He expressed his sorrow at having killed his wife. He was 37 and said he had debts of between £35,000 and £40,000. There were no convictions of relevance. The Judge had four psychiatrists' reports who agreed the defendant had developed a serious depressive illness. The risk of danger to his children was not quantified. One said in view of recent history there is a risk to future partners. The Judge gave him life with a $3\frac{1}{2}$ year minimum to serve. The Court of Appeal obtained a new and comprehensive psychiatric report, which said he had recovered from his depressive episode and there was no sign of any other psychiatric disorder. There was a full and symptom free recovery. His awareness of his condition and willingness to respond to the problems of a relapse make the chance of a relapse causing a recurrence remote. The risk of future violence, including to his children was assessed as low. Held. The Judge adopted a cautious approach but with the new material the defendant does not present such a danger to justify life. **5 years** substituted with his licence extended by 3 years.

Att-Gen's Ref. Nos.74, 95 and 118 of 2002 Re S 2003 2 Cr App R (S) 273 at 283. The defendant was tried for murder and acquitted by direction of the Judge. He was retried for manslaughter and convicted. The defendant phoned his doctor to report his partner had fallen and was unconscious. She died the next day in hospital of a head injury. The defendant denied hitting her and said she died of a fall. She had four area of bruising to the left cheek. Only two could be attributed safely to the defendant and one of these caused 5 fractured or missing teeth. The victim had 361 mg of alcohol in her blood ($4^1/_2$ times the driving limit). The reason for the attack was unknown but there was no evidence it was premeditated. The judge assumed the defendant was stressed as a result of the victim's problems. The defendant was 33 and had convictions for dishonesty and criminal damage and had served short prison sentences for drink/drive. There were no convictions for violence and no evidence of previous violent conduct towards the victim. He had an excellent prison report. Held. The least unfavourable factual basis would be an attack with a fist. **$3^1/_2$ years** seems lenient but the Judge was in a far better position to assess culpability than we are. We are not interfering.

Att-Gen's Ref No 49 of 2004 2005 1 Cr App R (S) 358. The defendant pleaded guilty to manslaughter at the earliest opportunity. At the time of the offence he was on licence for another violent offence. There was a Newton hearing. The victim was a 22 year old woman who had been in a relationship with the defendant for a little more than seven months. They both attended a barbecue and then went onto a public house where they were both drunk. They quarrelled. The victim was crying and the victim's sister suggested she left the offender but the victim said if she did that he would kill her. She went home and there was a drunken fight in which the defendant lost his temper and punched her in the face and then applied considerable pressure to her chest, from which crushing injury she died. There was medical evidence that an object such as a penis, finger, hand or inanimate object had been introduced into her anus with considerable force. There were tears to the skin around the anus and damage to the underlying muscle. After the Newton hearing the Judge found that the trauma to the chest was the result of compression and the defendant had inflicted the non-consensual injuries to the anus. The defendant, 38, had a total of 27 previous convictions included repeated convictions for violence: four for s 20 wounding, four for ABH, one for common assault, and one for aggravated burglary. In mitigation it was said this was not premeditated violence, it was a short fight apparently initiated by the victim. The defendant showed remorse after the killing and tried to call an ambulance. Held. The defendant tried to contest the manner of his victim's death and lessen his blameworthiness, and of even greater account was the extent of violence used including the forceful penetration of her anus. This was an aggravating feature which had to be reflected in sentence. The commensurate sentence would have been between **7 and 8 years**. This was a man who cannot control his violent instincts especially when he has been drinking. This was a case where a longer than commensurate sentence in the order of **10 years** should have been passed. As it was a reference **9 years** not 6.

See also *Att-Gen's Ref. No 118 of 2001* 2002 2 Cr App R (S) 537 [Drunk, lump of wood – **5 years** proper].

Old cases. *R v Irons* 1995 16 Cr App R (S) 46; *Att-Gen's Ref No 43 of 1995* 1996 2 Cr App R (S) 74 and *R v Tzambazles* 1997 1 Cr App R (S) 87 (for summary of the last case see 1st edition of this book).

See also ***Passion, crime of***

Relationship killings – Women killing husbands or partners

111.44   *R v Fell* 2000 2 Cr App R (S) 464. The defendant pleaded guilty to manslaughter. The defendant started having sex with the victim when she was 14 and he was 19. When she was 16 they started living together. He recruited her to take part in his criminal activities. Once he left her and she took an overdose. She briefly went into care and was expelled from school. She had a miscarriage and took a further overdose. She said he became violent to her two or three times a week. She was dependent on him. As her depression deepened she began to take cannabis. He was sent to prison and on his release continued to beat her up. He frequently locked her up. She handled a cheque-book stolen by him and was given probation. She did not respond well to the order. She was seen by a psychiatrist and because of the injuries twice by the police. She would respond to the violence by attacking him. Those who lived nearby frequently heard shouting, screaming and crying. On the day she decided to leave there was an argument and the defendant punched him. He grabbed her and locked her in the bathroom. A visitor let her out and she picked up a knife and waved it at him. He picked up the knife, put it down and went to attack her. She picked it up, there was a struggle and he grappled with her. The struggle continued and the knife went into his back. She was seen to be immediately distressed. She was arrested and found to have bruising to her upper arms, breasts, neck, back and legs. During the interviews she sobbed uncontrollably. A psychiatrist found a number of features of battered women's syndrome namely: (a) a chronic depressive illness; (b) a feeling of hopelessness and helplessness and despair; (c) inability to act effectively; (d) inability to see any escape from the situation or any future; (e) self blame for the violence inflicted upon her by her male partner; (f) a failure to see that what was happening was abnormal because she was isolated from reality; shame and a poor sense of worth and (g) submission as a form of self protection. The prosecution psychiatrist also found a number of features of battered women's syndrome. The probation officer listed the new improvement to her character and life and said a custodial sentence was likely to destroy the very positive steps which had been achieved. There was a job, a new relationship and reconciliation with her family. She had been in custody about a year. **2 years' probation** not 4 years YOI.

R v Lawrenson 2004 1 Cr App R (S) 44. The defendant pleaded guilty to manslaughter on the grounds of diminished responsibility. The victim was her current boyfriend who stayed at her home regularly. They went to a public house and returned home. Her alcohol level in her blood was 288. They started arguing in front of her sons aged 16 and 13 and she hit him several times. When she wanted to leave the victim tried to stop her. She stabbed him once with a knife above the nipple. Police arrived after and she said, "It's just the drink. He started it." The pre-sentence report said, "The victim had inflicted psychological abuse on her and was very controlling. He isolated her from her friends and had raped her on a number of occasions. She said she was convinced that the victim was going to rape her again". The risk of re-offending was assessed as low. The psychiatric report said, "she was psychologically damaged with a borderline personality disorder. There was a history of abuse from when she was a young child. She had suffered a series of abusive and violent relationships. She also suffered from alcohol dependency and battered woman syndrome". Another report said she had made two serious suicide attempts and suffered from post-traumatic stress disorder, battered woman syndrome and a personality disorder. She was 38 and of good character. An updated pre-sentence report said, "She had made excellent progress in prison and valued the therapy she had received there. The preferred option would be release today to a probation hostel." **3 years** not 5.

Old cases. *R v Higgins* 1996 1 Cr App R (S) 271; *R v Cutlan* 1998 1 Cr App R (S) 1 and *R v Howell* 1998 1 Cr App R (S) 229. (For a summary of the last two cases see the first edition of this book.)

See also *Crime of passion*

Religious beating/imprisonment

111.45   *R v Sogunro* 1997 2 Cr App R (S) 89. The defendant was convicted of manslaughter and false imprisonment. The defendant shut his fiancé in a room without food or drink because he believed she was possessed by the devil. She died of starvation and neglect but was not found until 10 months after her death. The defendant had no previous. **6 years** and 3 years concurrent upheld.

Old case. *R v Patel* 1995 16 Cr App R (S) 827.

Revenge attack

111.46   *Att-Gen's Ref. Nos. 33–4 of 2001* 2002 1 Cr App R (S) 400. The defendants were convicted of manslaughter. [The case is unclear about what the prosecution case was so the case is not summarised.]

R v Malik 2003 2 Cr App R (S) 669. The defendant was convicted of manslaughter (instead of murder) and of arson with intent to endanger life. In the early hours of the morning the defendant intentionally set fire to a mid-terrace house by pouring petrol through a letterbox. It was a revenge attack against a man who, he believed, had facilitated an adulterous relationship between the defendant's wife and another man. The target escaped but an innocent tenant died from fumes whilst trying to escape from a window. The previous convictions were not relevant to sentence. A plea to manslaughter had been offered on two occasions but had been rejected. Held. The loss of an innocent life in such horrific circumstances make a substantial sentence inevitable. This was completely uncharacteristic behaviour on the defendant's part, carried out when his distressing and deteriorating personal situation had pushed him to the brink and then beyond. **12 years** not 15.

Att-Gen's Ref 64 of 2004 2005 1 Cr App R (S) 595. The defendant, who was indicted for murder, indicated a month before trial that she would plead guilty to manslaughter on the ground of lack of intent. The victim was a 68-year-old alcoholic man who was subjected to two separate attacks in his home at night. There was a witness to both the attacks, although the witness was drunk throughout. The defendant was not involved in the first attack, in which two men assaulted the victim and tried to steal money from him. They shook him and slapped him in the face and subsequently pleaded guilty to assault with intent to rob. Police and ambulance men were called after this first incident but the victim refused medical help. He was seen to be semi conscious and very drunk. Within an hour or two the defendant went to his flat looking for her daughter. She was described as being 'steaming drunk' and accused the victim of molesting her children. The victim had old convictions for unlawful sexual intercourse and indecent assault on a 10-year-old girl. The defendant threw a television set at him, which hit him in the lower part of the face and upper chest. He fell. She then picked up a piece of wood used as a door prop and brought it, jagged end down, into his stomach several times with considerable force. She threw a clock and clock radio at him, hitting his head and chest. Next she took a mirror and a clock and walked off, later telling a friend that these items came from a paedophile's house. Police were called the next morning by which time the victim was dead, He had three large lacerations in his small bowel which resulted in three litres of blood entering his abdomen and other injuries. It would have needed a significant degree of force to inflict these injuries. The aggravating features were described as being the sustained and forceful attack; a weapon was used; the victim's age, his vulnerability and defencelessness; the attack was unprovoked and the defendant had left without seeking medical help for the victim. The defendant, 41, was of good character. She was responsible for the care of three children aged 16, 8 and 4. She showed genuine remorse. The possibility of her committing a similar offence was said to be very low. In prison she had achieved the highest possible status and had taken a number of courses including anger management and alcohol control. A psychiatric report said she had an unhappy history and a fragile relationship with a man. Held. We bear in mind above all the family circumstances of the defendant. The judge was unduly influenced by the mitigation and paid too little regard to the gravity of the offence. If she had been a man without this mitigation the least sentence which could have been passed would have been **5 or 6 years**. In her case the appropriate sentence would have been **4$^{1}/_{2}$ years. 3$^{1}/_{2}$ years** not 2$^{1}/_{2}$.

Road Traffic

See *Vehicle, by*

Robbers

See *Burglars/robbers/thieves, by*

Self defence, after/Lawful restraint or eviction etc., after

111.47 *R v Frankcom* 2003 1 Cr App R (S) 91. The defendant pleaded guilty to manslaughter on a murder indictment. He, his girlfriend, the deceased and two others were at his girlfriend's flat in the early hours of New Years Day. The deceased, who was his girlfriend's brother, and the defendant were in high spirits and poured wine down each other's throats. However the deceased became increasingly irritating and his behaviour deteriorated. An argument developed between him and the girlfriend and she asked him to leave. He refused saying he would take anyone on. He took hold of the defendant's face and the defendant tried to pacify him and asked him to leave. The girlfriend and two others went to the kitchen and they were all crying. The deceased followed. He was again asked to leave and responded by putting his face close to her face and she punched or pushed him back. Next he punched the telephone from her hand and she hit him in the face with it. His response was to say, "Hit me again" and the defendant asked him to leave again. The deceased took off his T-shirt and said, "Come on then." The defendant said he didn't want a fight and told the deceased to, "Fuck off" with a slap. The girlfriend fell on the sofa and was hit by the deceased. He and the defendant started to fight and the defendant got the deceased in a headlock, which he held for some time refusing to release it. The deceased made gurgling and spluttering noises and the girlfriend told the defendant to stop. His response was, "He shouldn't be hitting a girl then, should he?" One witness heard the defendant say, "I love you. I didn't want to do this, but this is the last time you'll hit my girlfriend." One witness said the headlock did not look powerful while another said the defendant was very angry, shaking with the force of his grip, his anger and hatred. Further the deceased's hand and lip had turned blue. That witness asked the defendant to release his grip and the defendant refused to do so saying, "I am the people's champion," and "He'll never hit Kelly again." The police were called on the phone twice until the defendant eventually released his grip. There was some 15 minutes between the calls. When the defendant was told the deceased had died he sobbed. The medical evidence was that death was caused by neck compression and that holding a neck in an arm hold was hazardous. In interview the defendant said he didn't know whether to believe the deceased was going blue and didn't know whether the deceased was faking it. The Crown's case was that it was excessive self-defence. The defendant was of good character and it was accepted that the conduct was wholly out of character. In prison he had shown an exemplary character. Held. The more serious elements are the element of persistence and the very long time the deceased was held in a headlock. There was a high degree of careless disregard, which places the case in a more serious category. On conviction the starting point would be in the region of **5 years**. Because of the plea **3^1/$_2$ years** substituted.

Sexual

111.48 *R v Blakemore* 1997 2 Cr App R (S) 255. The defendant was convicted of manslaughter and doing an act to pervert the course of justice. The defendant sold some land and workmen found a young man's body buried. The body was wrapped in plastic and tied with a rope. Marks on the neck indicated that he had been strangled with a rope or ligature. The boy had been dead for some 10 years. Sentenced on the basis he had died posing for bondage photographs taken by the defendant. **5 and 3 years consecutive** not 7 and 5 years consecutive.

Old case. *R v Billia 1996* 1 Cr App R (S) 39.

Self defence, Excessive

111.49   *R v Jarrett* 2003 1 Cr App R (S) 154. The defendant pleaded guilty to manslaughter on a murder indictment. The deceased reported his car stolen and he suspected youths from a particular estate where it was found had taken it. He drove there and a verbal confrontation took place with a group of youths. The deceased swung his arm at the defendant and he lunged back striking him in the chest with a penknife at least twice. Some witnesses said another held the deceased just as he was struck by the defendant. The basis of plea was the defendant acted to defend himself against a perceived, unwarranted attack and the use of the knife was disproportionate to the deceased conduct. The defendant was 19 with convictions on 4 occasions. Since then he'd been before the Court twice for breaches of community service. The pre-sentence report, which was largely favourable said, "He had been brought up in a violent and offending-orientated environment. His explanation for carrying the knife was that there had been two very recent incidents which had put him in great fear. He was not confident that he was physically robust enough to protect himself unarmed. He insists he acted on impulse, thinking that he was about to be seriously attacked. His attitude to the offence was of complete disapproval." Held. We have considered Attorney-General's Ref. No. 33 of 1996 1997 2 Cr App R (S) 10 which dealt with a defendant who intended either fatal force, or to cause really serious injury, but where it was not murder because of provocation. It appeared to be directed to the sort of manslaughter which occurs when a public house or dance hall is emptying and some fracas develops and a knife causes a fatal blow. This case is excessive self defence. It does not fit comfortably within the principle in the 1996 reference. There was very strong mitigation. The knife was not carried for aggression or in anticipation of violence. There was strong mitigation in his substantial references and his efforts to put the past behind him and improve his lot. The Judge was right to emphasise the need to deter those who carry knives, but **5 years** YOI not 7.

Two or more killings

111.50   *R v Bowen* 2001 1 Cr App R (S) 282. The defendant was convicted of manslaughter after a murder trial. In a snooker hall the defendant drank beer. He was carrying a knife, which he had so he could cut cocaine. The two victims approached him and he stabbed them both in the neck. Then he kicked one of them. The fatal wounds were severe. The defendant claimed self-defence, which was rejected. Held. The basis of the conviction was manslaughter because of provocation. One witness had heard one of the victims saying, 'Paki bastard.' The two deaths were an important aggravating factor. He had previous convictions for violence but not since 1986. **12 years** concurrent substituted for 14 years concurrent.

R v Wacker 2003 1 Cr App R (S) 92. The defendant was convicted of conspiracy to facilitate illegal entry and 58 counts of manslaughter. Sixty illegal immigrants travelled from China to Holland where they were loaded into an adapted container on the defendant's lorry. The only ventilation was a small vent at the front. $4^{1}/_{2}$ kms from Zeebrugge the lorry stopped and the vent was closed. This was to avoid discovery and the defendant's fingerprints were found on the outside covering of the vent. The ferry trip took longer than expected and nearly 6 hours later customs officers searched the container and found the victims. The two survivors told how 2 hours after the vent was closed those inside became distressed and found difficulty in breathing. There was also a lot of screaming and no one came to help. The deaths were caused by lack of air. The basis for the manslaughter was gross negligence. The defendant was a Dutch national. It was not suggested that he intended to harm the victims in anyway. He received 8 years for the conspiracy and six consecutive for the manslaughter counts. The defence argued the total was too much and the Attorney General argued the 6 years for the manslaughter counts was too lenient although the total sentence was not challenged. Held. Professional smuggling of large numbers of illegal immigrants is in itself a serious matter. The causing of so many deaths to avoid detection puts this case in a category of its own. **14 years** was not manifestly excessive. Concurrent sentences were the correct approach so 14 years for the manslaughter, which would not have the appearance of devaluing the loss of life.

R v Hussain 2004 2 Cr App R 497. The defendant pleaded guilty to conspiracy to commit arson and was convicted of conspiracy to commit arson with intent to endanger life and eight counts of manslaughter. The defendant had four co-accused. He and others had made petrol bombs, and the defendant had obtained the petrol. One of the co-accused wanted to attack one of the victims who had been telling tales about his relationship with a girlfriend. In the early hours of the morning the defendant and others drove to the house where the victim was and two of the co-accused threw the petrol bombs at the house. In the subsequent fire eight people died; a woman, her daughter, a student and five girls aged between six months and thirteen years. Four other people escaped the fire. The judge said that the offences of manslaughter came very close to murder, and that no one who heard the evidence of family members who saw the fire would ever forget it. Further it was a gross understatement to say that the surviving family members were devastated. Held. The judge was bound to have regard to the number of persons unlawfully killed. This was manslaughter in horrific circumstances involving eight persons. It could not be argued that **18 years** for the manslaughter charges and a concurrent 14 years for the conspiracy to commit arson were even arguably manifestly excessive.

Uncertainty over jury's verdict

111.51 *R v Cawthorne* 1996 2 Cr App R (S) 445. There were three bases for this manslaughter conviction, insufficient intent, provocation or gross negligence. The foreman was asked if he wanted to indicate the basis and he declined. The judge sentenced the defendant on the basis of lack of sufficient intent. Held. It was quite proper for the foreman to decline. Having considered the authorities, we are quite clear that whether the judge asks is entirely a matter for the trial judge's discretion. In many cases the judge will not wish to do so, and doing so will throw an unnecessary additional burden on the jury. In a case like the present, and there are many other cases of this nature, there are grave dangers in asking juries. For example they may not all have reached it by the same route. The judge was entitled to decide the basis of the sentence.

R v Bowen 2001 1 Cr App R (S) 282. The jury was not asked which basis it was. The judge did not indicate whether it was provocation or lack of sufficient intent. Held. It was for the Court of Appeal to decide.

R v Byrne 2003 1 Cr App R (S) 338. The defence case in the defendant's murder trial was there was a lack of intent. The judge left the issue of provocation to the jury. The jury convicted of manslaughter and the judge decided it was not appropriate to ask them for the basis of their verdict. Held. The judge was entitled not to ask and decided that the basis of the verdict was provocation. The judge has a duty to explain his decision and it would have been better if he had gone into greater detail. The sentence was upheld.

R v Bertram 2004 1 Cr App R (S) 186. The judge is not bound to accept the most favourable version to the defence. The Judge should carefully apply the criminal standard of proof and give the defendant the benefit of any doubt.

Unprovoked attach (or minor provocation) with fists and/or feet

111.52 *R v Harrison* 1996 2 Cr App R (S) 250. An unlucky punch in the course of a spontaneous fight is very different from a wholly unprovoked blow to an innocent bystander.

R v Anucha 1999 2 Cr App R (S) 74. The defendant pleaded guilty to manslaughter, two counts of robbery and a count of battery. The defendant and another stole £60 by pulling a shop assistant away from the till. Six days later the defendant returned and was recognised and the assistant refused to open the till. The defendant tried to open it. The assistant went next door to call the police and returned. The defendant accused him of injuring him on the earlier occasion and punched him three times in the face. Thirteen days later the defendant who was then aged 19, used a minicab. The driver was the deceased and he drove it to a petrol station to fill up with petrol. The deceased became worried and tried to ring the police. The defendant left the cab became aggressive and shouted, 'You don't want to take me'. He then punched the victim twice in the face causing him to fall hitting his head hard on the ground. On the same day the defendant returned to the shop and opened the till while another held the assistant as £200 was stolen. Three weeks later the victim died. The defendant had seven previous convictions for robbery, one for attempted robbery, three for theft and two for assault. A report indicated crack cocaine lay behind the offending. The sentencing judge invoked the 'longer than normal sentence' statutory provisions. Held. **6 years** not 8 years detention for the manslaughter consecutive to 3 years for the two robberies.

R v Cheetham and Baker. 2004 2 Cr App R (S) 278. C pleaded guilty to manslaughter. B was convicted of manslaughter. B pleaded guilty to two robberies and other counts of making a false instrument etc. for which he received concurrent sentences of 2 years etc. C pleaded guilty on the basis that he was at a party where everyone drank a great deal. C believed that a young woman at the party had been assaulted by the victim and he was told at the party that the victim was a woman beater who had assaulted his own girlfriend. C was distraught at what he believed to be the victim's behaviour towards women and he followed the victim from the party and struck him a single blow to the face. The victim fell back and struck his head causing injuries which led to his death. B then began kicking and stamping on the victim. The basis of plea did not include any joint enterprise between B and C. After B's trial the judge sentenced B on the basis that they had engaged in a joint enterprise and that both were equally responsible for the single blow which caused death. He made no finding on what might have happened after the victim was on the ground. C, 45, had previous convictions including one for robbery. He was genuinely remorseful and had an exemplary army record. The presentence report said he was at a relatively low risk of re-offending. A prison report said he had caused no problems. B, 24, also had previous convictions including one for robbery. Pre-sentence reports indicated he was at a high risk of re-offending. A psychiatric report concluded he had learning difficulties and a long-standing personality disorder, although he was not mentally ill. A prison report said he was volatile and had not expressed remorse and that he was a bully. Held. We must sentence C on his basis of plea. B **3 years** not 6 consecutive to 4 years for the robberies. C **2 years** not 4.

Att-Gen's Ref. No 44 of 1998 1999 1 Cr App R (S) 458. The defendant was convicted of manslaughter. The defendant after drinking went to his former matrimonial home where he kicked in the door. When his wife and another man returned, the defendant started shouting. He then attacked the other man. He was punched and knocked to the ground and then kicked 7 or 8 times, including on the face. The deceased suffered a myocardial insufficiency by reason of hypertensive heart disease. The attack had significantly contributed to his death. The defendant had no previous convictions. Held. Taking into account it was a reference **3¹/₂ years** not 2¹/₂.

R v Keaney 2001 1 Cr App R (S) 126. The defendant was convicted of manslaughter. After drinking about 14 pints the defendant came across a group of Asian taxi drivers. A dispute developed and a number of punches were thrown. The defendant was knocked to the ground. He got up punched an entirely innocent 62-year-old West Indian bystander. He fell over causing injury to the back of the head and severe brain damage from which he died.

The defendant ran away and was arrested the next day. The pathologist said the blow was heavy and above moderate. He was sentenced on the basis it was not a racially-aggravated attack. There was some remorse and he was treated as of good character. Held. This case is more serious than the cases cited. There was a substantial age gap (62 and 30), the victim was blame-free, the blow was described as severe, guilt was contested and the defendant had had far too much to drink. However, **3 years** substituted for 7.

R v Refern 2002 2 Cr App R (S) 155. Three defendants R, B and O pleaded guilty to manslaughter. All three after drinking heavily and taking drugs attacked a 40 year old in a car park. He was punched to the ground and kicked by all three in a deliberate and violent beating. He died of an extensive brain haemorrhage. R was 28 (all ages are taken from the time of the offence), and had been to the courts on 23 occasions for offences of dishonesty, criminal damage, arson and possession of an offensive weapon. One had resulted in custody. The defendant had a good prison report citing an excellent work record in prison. B aged 19, had had 17 court appearances including dishonesty, criminal damage, affray, and three convictions for ABH. Those three did not appear particularly serious. He had had several custodial sentences. He expressed remorse. O, who was 21, had 18 court appearances mostly for dishonesty. He had had four custodial sentences. He expressed remorse. The prison report said he was quiet and polite. All were dealt with equally. Two were sentenced to $6^{1}/_{2}$ years imprisonment, the other to $6^{1}/_{2}$ years detention. Held. All reduced to **$5^{1}/_{2}$ years**. An order under the Crime and Disorder Act extending the supervision to 8 years was undisturbed.

R v Hamar 2001 2 Cr App R (S) 295. The defendant pleaded guilty to manslaughter. Having drunk about 12 pints, the defendant joined a taxi queue in which the victim was standing. There was a scuffle involving the victim in which the defendant was struck. They both left and a CCTV camera recorded what happened. The defendant gratuitously struck the victim a single bow to the side of his head causing him to fall to the ground banging his head. The defendant walked away. The victim was taken to hospital and died. The post mortem disclosed the cause of death was fractures to the skull with associated bruising and swelling. Further the injuries were consistent with a fall onto the back of the head. Sentenced on the basis of striking the victim a, 'haymaking blow of tremendous force.' The defendant had been released from custody 3 months before. Held. The judge was right to take a serious view and **$4^{1}/_{2}$ years** was severe but not excessive.

R v Heslop 2004 1 Cr App R (S) 427. The defendant pleaded guilty to manslaughter on an indictment for murder. The defendant noticed that one of his friends, the deceased, (aged 16) was wearing one of his shirts. The victim said that the defendant's brother had sold it to him. The defendant was "mad" and asked his brother, who denied selling the shirt. The defendant went and found the deceased and shouted aggressively at him. The victim stood up and the defendant punched him on the head. The deceased fell back and the defendant punched him. The pathologist suggested there were seven blows. The defendant was dragged away, leaving the deceased unconscious. The victim never recovered consciousness. He pleaded on the basis that he momentarily lost control using no more than moderate force. He was 18 and had one previous conviction (disorderly behaviour and criminal damage). He was full of remorse and unlikely to re-offend. References spoke well of him. Held. There was very strong mitigation. **$2^{1}/_{2}$ years' detention**, not $3^{1}/_{2}$.

Att-Gen's Ref. No 100 of 2001 2002 2 Cr App R (S) 365. See **111.21**.

See also *Fighting*

Vehicle, by

111.53 Obligatory disqualification and endorsement and 3–11 penalty points when by the driver of a motor vehicle[11].

---

11 Road Traffic Offenders Act 1988 s 9, 34, 97 & Sch 2, Part II

R v Gault 1995 16 Cr App R (S) 1013. LCJ. The defence sought to equate manslaughter committed by a vehicle with the statutory offences of causing death by dangerous/ careless driving. The statutory offences are capped with a limit to their sentence. The maximum for manslaughter is life. A different approach is required for offences of manslaughter with a vehicle.

Att-Gen's Ref. No 16 of 1999 2000 1 Cr App R (S) 524. LCJ. The defendant was convicted of manslaughter, theft and conspiracy to cause actual bodily harm. There was bad blood between the defendant's co-defendant, Marsh and Danny Marlow, the victim. It was about money and snooker. About a month before the incident, the co-defendant had approached a taxi which Danny Marlow was driving and hit the driver's window with a brick. Marsh became obsessed with him and approached someone requesting that he should put the 'frighteners on him'. He refused and Marsh approached the defendant asking him to frighten Marlow with telephone calls and assault him causing minor injuries. This was the basis of the conspiracy conviction. One evening Marlow left a public house and on his way home was assaulted and knocked to the ground. The defendant hit him with the stolen car he was driving and made no attempt to stop. He suffered a severe injury and died. The medical evidence indicated he had been run over by a car and dragged along the road. It also suggested that the victim was lying in the road when hit. The stolen car was set on fire. **5 years** was not unduly lenient.

Att-Gen's Ref. No 14 of 2001 2002 1 Cr App R (S) 106. The defendant was convicted of manslaughter and pleaded to attempting to pervert the course of justice. The defendant had defective vision which requires spectacles for driving. Without spectacles his vision was blurred from 30 cm and from there on the blurring increased. Shortly after his release from custody he left his spectacles in Salisbury and decided to drive from Bournemouth to Salisbury in a car he had just bought. It had no insurance. He was warned by a colleague before he set off and he said he was prepared to take the risk and would leave early to avoid the dark. In fact he left as it was getting dark and after driving 20 miles at 40 mph he hit an 18-year-old girl who was crossing the road. It was a 40 mph area but he was not speeding. She was in dark clothing and the road was poorly lit. It was accepted even if wearing glasses he probably would not have been unable to avoid her but it would have given him an opportunity to slow down and sound the horn. It was accepted he never really saw her at all. He carried on driving and another car passed over her legs. She died from being hit by the defendant's car. Next he set the vehicle alight and removed the registration plates. His defence to the manslaughter was that he was wearing glasses and in interview he said, 'I won't get in my car without my glasses on. I'm lethal. I wouldn't even make it down the road. I wouldn't be able to see about 3 'in front of me.' The jury were directed that to convict they must be sure he wasn't wearing glasses. He was 22 and was genuinely remorseful from early on. Held. Had he been convicted of death by dangerous driving the proper sentence should not have been less than 5 years. For manslaughter the sentence should have been of the order of **5–6 years** with 9 months for the perverting count consecutive. As it was a reference **4 years 3 months** for the manslaughter not 3 years and 9 months consecutive for the perverting matter not concurrent.

Att-Gen's Ref. Nos. 64 of 2001 2002 1 Cr App R (S) 409. The defendant offered to plead guilty to manslaughter and his offer was rejected. Later it was accepted and the murder charge was dropped. The defendant lived near the victim and was close to her sister and the sister's boyfriend who lived with her. The relationship between the victim and her sister soured, probably because of the victim's resumption of drug taking. The defendant was drawn into the dispute and he discovered that yellow paint had been poured over his van, a window had been smashed and its tyres were slashed. He blamed (no doubt in good faith) the victim and blamed her for causing the general disruption in his life. There was a discussion between the defendant and the sister and their partners and the defendant stormed out very angry stating he was going to get the deceased. He lost his temper and drove off at speed. He chatted to some people and said, 'Watch this.' He revved his engine and drove the van at the victim and another. The van mounted the pavement, went across a grass verge and hit the victim who was walking on the pavement. It had travelled 50 yards. She went onto the bonnet, struck her head, travelled some distance, fell to the ground and later died of head injuries in hospital. The defendant drove off at speed smiling. The sister's boyfriend persuaded him to contact the police and he did so. He claimed he tried to avoid her. The victim was 35 with four children but only one living with her. He was sentenced on the basis it was to frighten her and was a deliberate act and that the van was travelling at 15mph. He was 24, extremely deaf and had no convictions. He was deeply remorseful and not a violent man by nature. Held. The sentence should have been **6 years** not $3^1/_2$. Because it was a reference and because of his difficulties **$4^1/_2$ years** substituted.

R v Rule 2003 1 Cr App R (S) 224. The defendant pleaded guilty to manslaughter. On 18 December 2000, shortly after midnight, he drove in a friend's car at 52mph in a 30 mph area towards an officer with a speed gun. The road was well lit with clear visibility. The officer, the victim, stepped off the pavement and raised his hand to signal to the defendant to stop. There was ample time to stop and his two passengers screamed at him to stop. He seemed to increase his speed and the other officers shouted at the victim to get out of the way. The road was wet and the officer might have slipped. The defendant tried to swerve round the officer but the car hit him. The brakes were not applied. The officer hit the bonnet and then the windscreen and was carried along until he fell onto the road. He died shortly afterwards and the defendant abandoned the car. The defendant surrendered to the police after the police were able to identify him through his mobile phone. In interview he said he didn't stop because he was banned and he wanted to spend Christmas with his family. He was 26 with 58 previous offences on 15 occasions. He had been disqualified twice in 1996 for 18 months and in 1998 for 18 months for drink/drive and disqualified driving. On 3 October 2000, he was banned from driving for excess alcohol for 3 years. Held. Police officers acting in the course of their duty on the roads require and should be given the protection of the courts against this sort of conduct. He thought only of his own position. Although we accept he tried to avoid the officer, he had driven with a total disregard for human safety or human life. The offence was of a very high level of criminality. He showed genuine remorse. A severe deterrent sentence was required and that is what the **9 years** was. However 9 years not 15 years disqualification.

R v Wright 2004 1 Cr App R (S) 40. The defendant was convicted of manslaughter. He was acquitted of murder. Some youths threw some gravel at each other and some hit the defendant's van as he was driving by. He stopped the van causing skid marks. He then confronted the youths. Others congregated and a fairly violent fight developed. He was headbutted, kneed to the groin and punched in the face. There were 8–10 blows and eventually he returned to his van with a cut to his eyebrow which bled into his eye. He drove the van, swerved across the road and mounted the kerb clipping one person and scooping up the victim aged 18 onto the bonnet. The defendant drove at 10–20 mph with the victim on the bonnet 60 metres to a roundabout where the victim slid off. He landed on his head. The defendant did not stop and two days later tried to remove his van's windscreen which had been damaged in the incident. On hearing about the victim's critical condition on the radio he went to the police. In interview he lied. The victim died. The defendant was of good character with two references. **8 years** was severe but not manifestly excessive.

R v Franks 2005 1 Cr App R (S) 51. The defendant was convicted of manslaughter on an indictment charging him with murder. The defendant with a male friend and two girls were driving around in a stolen car having been drinking and taking cocaine. In the evening they stole a mobile telephone from somebody who happened to be sitting at an adjoining table. The loser of the phone and his associates gave chase. This group detained the defendant's friend and the defendant drove off dangerously. The defendant returned to collect his friend moments later. His friend ran down the road and was chased by the deceased. The defendant followed them in the car at considerable speed. He swerved suddenly to the left and struck the deceased, causing him severe injuries. The defendant drove off but lost control a little further on and hit a wall. He then decamped and fled. He returned later and set light to the car in an attempt to destroy the evidence. However, having discovered that the deceased had died, he surrendered himself to the police. He later pleaded guilty to causing death by dangerous driving but disputed ever having swerved to his left prior to hitting the deceased. The conviction was on the basis that he had swerved but had not intended serious harm to the deceased. He was 18 at the time of sentence and had only minor previous convictions. He was sentenced to 12 years in total: for the manslaughter, 10 years; 12 months consecutive for perverting the course of justice (firing the car); 9 months consecutive for dangerous driving (leaving the scene the first time); 3 months consecutive for the theft of the phone. Held. He was young with only minor previous convictions and there was a risk that by imposing consecutive sentences for the theft and the dangerous driving, he was being sentenced twice for those offences. Hence, for manslaughter, **9 years** (not 10); the theft and dangerous driving sentences would be concurrent making a total sentence of **10 years**.

Old cases. *R v Sherwood* 1995 16 Cr App R (S) 513; *Att-Gen's Ref. No 68 of 1995* 1996 2 Cr App R (S) 358 and *R v Ripley* 1997 1 Cr App R (S) 19. (For a summary of the last case see the first edition of this book.)

Victim over 65

111.54   *Att-Gen's Ref. Nos. 57, 58 and 59 of 1997* 1999 1 Cr App R (S) 31. All three female defendants pleaded guilty to manslaughter, two by reason of no intent to cause serious harm and the third on account of diminished responsibility. All three went to the flat of a 74-year-old man who was being cared for by one of them, Beveridge. They wanted revenge because the old man had answered questions from the police about a social security claim made by Beveridge. The claim had involved the old man. He was attacked by being smothered by bedclothes and his belt was used to strangle him. He was also struck. His body was not discovered for 4 or 5 days during which time Beveridge used his pension book to obtain his pension. Beveridge who was the leader and who at the plea showed remorse was given **7¹/₂ years detention** and **3¹/₂ concurrent** for the pension book robbery. The second girl showed early remorse but had stamped on the victim's face and was given **5 years** and **3¹/₂ years** concurrent. The last girl, who was of very limited intelligence and susceptible to pressure, and had relied on diminished responsibility received **3¹/₂ years** for the manslaughter. None of the sentences were held to be unduly lenient.

R v Kime 1999 2 Cr App R (S) 3. The defendant was convicted of manslaughter having earlier offered to plead guilty to it. He was acquitted of murder. At about 10 p.m., the defendant who was then aged 21 was drunk. He was with his girlfriend and he heard the victim aged 80 and others laughing in the street. He went over to them and asked him, 'Are you fucking laughing?' Before there was an opportunity to reply he shouted again and punched the victim in the head with moderate force. There was some evidence of a second blow. He collapsed and during the following evening the victim suffered a cardiac arrest which had been hastened by the shock and the facial injuries. The injuries had caused heavy bleeding. The defendant had a number of previous convictions including common assault, criminal damage and had served a custodial sentence. A psychiatric report said he had a propensity to act very dangerously when under the influence of alcohol. Held. **6 years** was severe but not excessive.

Victim's health precarious/eggshell skull/one would not expect victim to die

111.55   *R v Harrison* 1996 2 Cr App R (S) 250. A blow sufficient to fracture an eggshell skull is very much less culpable than one which fractures a normal skull. [This means that the sentencing factor is the force of the blow and not the victim's individual characteristics.]

R v Scammell 2002 1 Cr App R (S) 293. The defendant pleaded guilty to manslaughter. The defendant lived near the victim and heard the victim had blamed him for breaking his neighbour's window. The next day the defendant got drunk and called the victim 'queer' to his friends. He went to the victim's house and banged on the door. The victim closed it, which the defendant tried to prevent. The defendant then attacked the door and was bitten by the victim's Alsatian dog. He threw red paint on the door, kicked it and began to scream and shout. A friend caught up with him and found him in a temper about the bite. The friend tried to calm him down and another friend arrived and both tried to restrain him. But the defendant threw six or seven stones or rocks through the window and into the room the victim lived. He continued to shout threats including threats to kill him. Later the victim was found dead and the windows smashed. There was glass everywhere including on top of the victim. A wheelbrace and baseball bat was found on the bed which it was suggested the victim had to protect himself. The victim was 68 and suffered from severe coronary heart disease. Any stressful incident could have led to cardiac arrhythmia and death. It was not suggested the defendant knew about the bad heart. The defendant was 21 and in 1998 had a conviction for criminal damage. He had abused a bus driver and was ejected from the bus. He kicked out at the bus door and smashed the glass in the door. When the bus returned he threw a brick though the bus windscreen. The pre-sentence report said he needed to give up intoxicants, mature and get a job. The psychiatric report said he was being treated for depression and threatened self harm. The judge said the victim died of fright. Held. The intention was to damage property rather than commit physical harm. The plea to manslaughter indicates an acknowledgment there was a risk of harm to the deceased from his conduct but not that death was envisaged. It was aggravated by drunkenness and his decision to go there. The misconduct was over a period of time. Taking into account his age 4 years would have been appropriate after a trial so **2 years 9 months** not $3\frac{1}{2}$ years.

R v Grad 2004 2 Cr App R (S) 218. The defendant was convicted of manslaughter. He was with a group of friends at a nightclub on a balcony overlooking the club's beer garden. One of his group spat some beer over the balcony which landed on the victim in a second group,. There was verbal abuse between the two groups and bottles and glasses were thrown by the second group towards the group on the balcony, and some witnesses said glasses were thrown down from the defendant's group. One of the glasses thrown up by the second group hit the defendant and cut his head, which bled profusely. The security staff ushered the defendant's group out of the club. One of the second group followed them because he wanted to continue with the confrontation, and shouted abuse outside but was then restrained by security staff. The victim had followed him out, not because he was looking for trouble but because he wanted to support his friend. The defendant approached the victim and punched him once in the head (according to the witnesses) or the top of the neck (according to the scientific evidence.) The punch was delivered with moderate force. The victim fell to the floor and was motionless. The defendant did not play any part in any fighting save for that single punch. The victim died almost immediately. The medical evidence was that the cause of death was a very unusual combination of circumstances: a haemorrhage in the brain caused by the combination of the twisting of the neck by the blow, the angle of the blow and the dilation of the blood vessels caused by the victim's drinking. The defendant and his friends had left the scene but when he heard of the death he surrendered voluntarily to the police.

The prosecution said the offence was as near to accident as a criminal offence could be. He was of previous good character. He had made a financial contribution to the victim's family and there was a wide range of references showing he had good business qualities and a bright future. There were letters showing that the companies he was involved with were suffering serious difficulties because of his imprisonment. He had shown genuine remorse. Held. The combination of factors which led to the death was very unusual. It was understandable that the defendant did not plead guilty having regard to the parties before the court. This was a case where the seriousness of the offending must be marked by a custodial sentence. The appropriate sentence is at the very bottom of the bracket for this type of case. **9 months** substituted for 18 months.

R v Ginley 2002 2 Cr App R (S) 277. The defendant was convicted of manslaughter and attempted robbery. The 57-year-old victim and his disabled wife were helping out at their frozen food warehouse. Because of ill health they were semi-retired and their sons had taken the business over. In 1987 the victim had had a triple bypass and his wife was paralysed down one side and in a wheelchair. In the late morning the defendant and another entered the warehouse. One pulled a balaclava down over his face and demanded to know where the safe was. He put a knife with a 10″ blade to the victim's throat and put him in a headlock. There was a scuffle in which the victim was prodded in the ribs a number of times with the knife. The wife pointed to the safe in the office and picked up a stick to go to her husband's aid. The second man who was masked grabbed her stick and pushed her in her wheelchair to the other side of the office away from the panic button. The victim shouted the police were on their way and the robbers left believing the panic button had been pressed. The victim then pressed the panic button and the police attended quickly. The victim gave the number of the car to an officer, collapsed and died of a heart attack. The pathologist said, 'death could have occurred at any time but trauma and excitement could precipitate a heart attack. More likely than not the victim would have been alive had it not been for the struggle.' The defendant was 21 when sentenced and had convictions but none for violence. Held. The judge quite rightly took the view that this was a robbery of an extreme kind. It was a prepared robbery. There was nothing wrong with 9 years for the robbery without considering the death. The 3 years extra for the death was wholly appropriate. **12 years** upheld. (The poor health of the victim is not listed as a factor in the judgement confirming the principle defendants do not receive a reduction when the defendant is of poor health.)

R v Clark and Lappin 2002 2 Cr App R (S) 353. The defendant L pleaded guilty to manslaughter and robbery at the first opportunity. C pleaded guilty to robbery. At about midnight the 32-year-old alcoholic victim was walking in the street with two bottles of cider. He was beaten and robbed of the two bottles. L punched him and caused quite 'horrific injuries'. They were a closed and swollen eye, which required three stitches, a cut to the lip and a broken nose. The victim was discharged from hospital and asked to return in the morning. Unfortunately he suffered from a liver disease and his blood would not clot. When he returned the next morning his nose would not stop bleeding and he suffered a cardiac arrest. He died 16 days later of multiple organ failure as a result of bleeding caused by his facial injuries. The pathologist said the injuries were consistent with several punches and could be one rather forceful punch and a lesser punch. The basis of plea was, 'C asked the victim for a cigarette and the victim probably thought he was going to be robbed and swung a bottle at L. At that stage they didn't intend to rob him and L punched him and both men fell to the ground. When L was on top of the victim he told C to take the bottles which he did. As L walked away the victim grabbed his jumper and L punched him on the nose causing the fatal injury.' L was then 19 with 12 convictions including attempted robbery, theft, assault on police, criminal damage, threatening behaviour, burglary and possession of an offensive weapon. He had served 4 months YOI. Held. The aggravating feature was that the offence occurred during a robbery. **6 years** YOI was not obviously too long.

Victims, the views of the relatives of the

111.56 The law is most clearly stated in the cases about causing death by dangerous and careless driving. See **DEATH BY DANGEROUS DRIVING, CAUSING** – *Victims, the views of the relatives of the*

MANUFACTURE OF DRUGS

See **PRODUCTION OF DRUGS**

MARRIAGE OFFENCES

See **BIGAMY/MARRIAGE OFFENCES**

112   MEDICINE OFFENCES

112.1   Medicines Act 1968 s 7, 8, 31, 31, 34 and 67

Sell, supply, export etc medicinal products, substances etc.

Triable either way. On indictment maximum 2 years. Summary maximum £5,000.

Selling – Defendant aged 18–21

112.2   *R v Sabeddu* 2001 1 Cr App R (S) 493. The defendant pleaded guilty at the Magistrates' Court to possessing a medicinal product for selling. Police stopped him before he went into a warehouse rave party. He was found to have 26 wraps of Ketamine in a wallet concealed up his trousers. He was 18 and of good character. He also faced sentence for committal for an affray which was throwing an empty drinks bottle at the police at a May Day demonstration. Held. No guidelines exist for Ketamine. We are not fully informed of its dangers so this should not be seen as a precedent in a case where there is such evidence. **3 months** YOI not 8.

Viagra

112.3   *R v Groombridge* 2004 1 Cr App R (S) 84. The defendant pleaded guilty to 5 counts of selling Viagra outside the prescription system and an advertisement offence for which he receive no penalty. The 5 counts were specimen charges. Over 16 months he sold £630,000 worth of Viagra on the internet and on the telephone. Each pill was sold for £15. Typical sales were 1,000 pills a week. He claimed his net profit was £289,000. He also claimed the offences were committed carelessly or recklessly. A Newton hearing was held to determine this and the defendant was roundly disbelieved. The Crown did not prove any individual had suffered but relied on risk to the public because of the drug's dangerous side effects. He was 41 with convictions for violence, dishonesty, four for drug possession and one for drug supply. He had recently been released from prison. His company was fined £50,000 and a varied confiscation order for £630,000 was made. Held. This was serious, persistent and deliberate offending. **12 months** was not excessive.

See also *R v V* 2002 Unreported EWCA Crim 108.

See also **Drug Users; Importation of Drugs; Possession of Drugs; Production of Drugs** and **Supply of Drugs (Class A, B and C)**

Mentally Disordered Defendants/Persons

See **Defendant** – *Mentally disordered defendants* and **Sexual Activity with Mentally Disordered Persons**

113 Mercy

Mercy should season justice

113.1 *Att-Gen's Ref. No 4 of 1989* 1990 11 Cr App R (S) 517. LCJ. It must always be remembered that sentencing is an art rather than a science; that the trial judge is particularly well placed to assess the weight to be given to various competing considerations; that leniency is not in itself a vice. That mercy should season justice is a proposition as soundly based in law as it is in literature.

Att-Gen's Ref. No 83 of 2001 2002 1 Cr App R (S) 589. What the authorities do not show are the cases where the individual circumstances of the defendant and the mitigation available to him have led to a justified departure from the guidance provided by the reported decisions. It is fundamental to the responsibilities of sentencing judges that while they must always pay proper regard to the sentencing guidance given, they are required also to reflect on all the circumstances of the individual case. Where sentencing judges are satisfied that occasion requires it, they have to balance the demands of justice with what is sometimes described as the calls of mercy. There were occasions where it was right to take a constructive course and seek to achieve the rehabilitation of the offender. The judge was satisfied it provided the best possible long-term solution for the community and the defendant. It was right to take a constructive course. So far he has been proved right. The prospects of re-offending are now lower than if he had had a custodial sentence. The sentence was lenient on paper but sentencing is not and never can be an exercise on paper; each case, ultimately, is individual. It would be wrong to interfere.

See also **Defendant**

Meritorious Conduct

See **Defendant** – *Meritorious conduct*

114 Misconduct in Public Office

Common law offence.

114.1   Indictable only. The maximum sentence is life.

Police officers as defendants

114.2   *R v Keyte* 1998 2 Cr App R (S) 165. The defendant was convicted of conspiracy to commit misconduct in a public office. He was a police officer who made 192 unauthorised enquiries on police national computer. They were mainly about the registered keepers of motor vehicles. He supplied the information to a private investigation company, which was connected with his co-accused who was a friend of the defendant and an ex-police officer. The sums gained were not large. The defendant was 42 and of good character. He was a father of four children and his partner was suffering from ill health. He had lost his job. Held. The integrity of the police national computer is of absolutely vital importance. Police officers are given considerable powers and privileges. If they dishonestly abuse their position and do so for profit, then not only must a prison sentence follow but it must of necessity be a severe one. We take into account the devastating effect of the prison sentence and the mitigation but **2 years** was not manifestly excessive.

R v Nazir 2003 2 Cr App R 671. The defendant pleaded guilty to misconduct in a public office. A younger probationer police officer issued a fixed penalty notice to the driver of a vehicle. The passenger told the police officer that she knew the defendant, a police officer based at the same station. The next day the defendant approached the probationer and invited him to toss a coin to see who should get the notice. The probationer lost and handed the notice to the defendant, but reported the incident. The defendant was questioned by a senior officer and explained frankly that he intended to destroy the ticket. He was 32 and of good character and had now lost his job. Held. His conviction led to the loss of his job (with the consequential financial losses) and the loss of his accommodation. He had expressed remorse. **1 month** not 3

See also CORRUPTION AND POLICE OFFICERS

AG Ref 140 of 2004 - Sawl   RvKASSIM (CA)
                                 14/4/05

MOBILE PHONES

See DANGEROUS DRIVING – *Magistrates' Court Sentencing Guidelines* and DEATH BY DANGEROUS DRIVING, CAUSING – *Mobile phone, defendant using*

MONEY

See COUNTERFEITING CURRENCY and MONEYLAUNDERING

115   MONEY LAUNDERING ETC

115.1   Proceeds of Crime Act 2002 s 327–9   (In force from 24/2/03)

Section 327: concealing etc. criminal property.

Section 328: entering into an arrangement etc about criminal property.

Section 329: acquiring using and possessing criminal property.

For offences committed before 24/2/03 Criminal Justice Act 1988 s 93A, 93B and 93C. (Criminal conduct money) and Drug Trafficking Act 1994 s 49, 50 and 51 (drug trafficking money) remain in force.

Both old and new offences are triable either way. On indictment maximum 14 years. Summary maximum 6 months and/or £5,000.

Confiscation For offences under sections 327 and 328 committed on or after 24 March 2003[12] the court must follow the Proceeds of Crime Act 2002 procedure[13]. For offences under Drug Trafficking Act 1994 s 49, 50 and 51 the court must follow the Drug Trafficking Act procedure[14]. For offences under Criminal Justice Act 1988 93A, 93B and 93C the court must follow the Criminal Justice Act 1988 procedure[15]. See CONFISCATION.

The Court of Appeal has ruled that the prosecution can indict for the Criminal Justice Act 1988 Sections and the Drug Trafficking Act 1994 together[16] so the counts in the indictment do not always distinguish between drug trafficking and other money.

Crown Court statistics – England and Wales – Males 21+
115.2

Year	Plea	Total Numbers sentenced	Type of sentence %					Average length of custody (months)
			Discharge	Fine	Community sentence	Suspended sentence	Custody	
2003	Guilty	3	–	–	–	–	100	35
	Not guilty	2	–	–	–	–	100	78

For details and explanations about the statistics in the book see page vii.

Guideline remarks

115.3 *R v O'Meally and Morgan* 1994 15 Cr App R (S) 831. LCJ. It is impossible to lay down guidelines. Cases are infinitely variable.

R v Greenwood 1995 16 Cr App R (S) 614. The defendant pleaded guilty to assisting another to retain the proceeds of drug trafficking. Launderers are nearly as bad but not quite as bad as those that do the actual dealing.

R v Basra 2002 2 Cr App R (S) 469. Held. Money laundering is a stand alone offence where the constituent elements may be many and varied. There may be circumstances where the launderer has no knowledge of the source of the money laundered and indeed may choose not to know. He may know that it represents the proceeds of criminal activity, but beyond that he is careful not to ask any questions. Many such offenders say they are ignorant of the origin of the proceeds in question and that this should isolate them from the original crime. In this case the maximum sentence for money laundering is 10 years, (Note in fact it is 14 years) whereas the maximum sentence for the evasion of duty was 7 years. The former makes allowance for the many and varied antecedent offences to which it could relate. There is no necessary direct relationship between the sentence for the laundering offence and the original antecedent offence. The criminality in laundering arises from the encouragement and nourishment it gives to crime in general. Without it many crimes would be rendered much less fruitful and perhaps more difficult to perpetrate. Nonetheless the sentence for laundering cannot be wholly disproportionate to the sentence for the original antecedent offence, where the offence is that of being involved in an arrangement whereby the retention or control of the proceeds of criminal conduct.

12 Proceeds of Crime Act 2002 (Commencement No 5, Transitional Provisions, Savings and Amendment) Order 2003
13 Proceeds of Crime Act 2002 s 6 and s 75 and Sch 2 para 2
14 Drug Trafficking Act 1994 s 1 and 2
15 Criminal Justice Act 1988 s 72 and 72AA
16 *R v El-Kurd* [2001] Crim LR 234

R v Monfries 2004 2 Cr App R (S) 9. The defendant was convicted of conspiracy to assist another to retain the proceeds of drug trafficking/criminal conduct money. Held. The relevant considerations that apply in cases of this type include the following: (i) The circumstances of assisting another to retain the benefit of drug trafficking and/or criminal conduct vary so widely that this Court has not to date provided detailed guidelines. (ii) There is not necessarily a direct relationship between the sentence for the laundering offence and the original antecedent offence. Where, however, the particular antecedent offence can be identified, some regard will be had to the appropriate sentence for that offence, when considering the appropriate sentence for the laundering offence. (iii) The criminality in laundering is the assistance, support and encouragement it provides to criminal conduct. (iv) Regard should be had to the extent of the launderer's knowledge of the antecedent offence. (v) The amount of money laundered is a relevant factor.

Confiscation

115.4   *Att-Gen's Ref. No. 4 of 2003* 2005 1 Cr App R (S) 407. [Note the title in the Cr App R (S) is incorrect, it should read No. 4 not No. 3] The defendant was convicted of conspiracy to convert or transfer the proceeds of drug trafficking or of criminal conduct contrary to Criminal Law Act 1977 s 1. Because it could not be said which route the defendant was convicted the Judge held he had no power to conduct a confiscation hearing. Held. Conspiracy under the 1977 Act means an agreement which will necessarily amount to or involve the commission of any offence or offences. It meant that he had been convicted of offences under both the Drug Trafficking Act 1994 and the Criminal Justice Act 1988. Confiscation proceedings shall take place.

Criminal conduct money – up to £1m

115.5   *R v Gonzales and Sarmiento* 2003 2 Cr App R (S) 36. S aged 24 and G aged 48, both pleaded guilty to conspiracy to assist another to retain the benefit of criminal conduct. They travelled from Colombia via Miami and Paris. They booked into a London hotel and over the next three days collected bags from men known to them whilst under covert surveillance. On their third day they were arrested and their room was searched where the money (£693,555), gloves, carbon paper and clingfilm were found. The other items were thought to relate to an attempt to evade metal detectors at an airport. In interview G said that she had travelled to London to buy clothes. S said that she had been invited to London by G to help with the banking of an inheritance. It was accepted at sentence that both defendants suspected that the money was the proceeds of crime as opposed to drug trafficking and that their state of mind was one of suspicion rather than belief. Both were of good character. S's mother had been taken to hospital since her arrest and her father had died whilst she was in custody. G was a mother of two and her sentence had been in excess of that which she had been led to believe she would receive. Held. A relevant factor was the amount of money laundered. However, as the volume of money increases the gravity of the offence necessarily increases, although not in direct proportion with the sum involved. Inherent in the accepted basis of plea was substantial mitigation. This was a single trip, not drugs money and "suspicion" only. Both have had serious family problems (the case report makes no mention of what G's problems were). **3 years** not 5.

R v Monfries 2004 2 Cr App R (S) 9. The defendant was convicted of conspiracy to assist another to retain the proceeds of drug trafficking/criminal conduct money. She had been involved in laundering about £30,000 in several transactions between Jamaica and England. The money was transferred via agencies established in newsagents and travel agents. She had sent the money as a favour and had not questioned its provenance. She was aged 37 and had two previous convictions for possession of a controlled drug in 1991 and 1994. These were called not substantive by the judge. He also was unable to say whether she was involved for profit or through fear and whether the money was drugs related or not. She had two children aged under 17. Held. Because of the mitigation **15 months** not 2 years.

R v Yoonus 2005 1 Cr App R (S) 207. The defendant pleaded guilty on re-arraignment to two offences of conspiracy to convert the proceeds of drug trafficking and/or other criminal conduct. He conspired to convert sterling, which was the proceeds of crime, and 'street money' into large denomination currencies. A co-defendant had a number of businesses which had bureaux de change in them. At one of these, a hotel, the defendant was allowed to use a room and other people would bring bags of money to him. Customs and Excise officers kept watch and saw a co-defendant enter a house and leave with a rucksack. Later the defendant was seen to go into the hotel with the rucksack. Another co-defendant was then arrested coming out of the hotel with US$300,000 on him. On another occasion he was observed in Portsmouth dealing with various co-defendants, including one who was later found to have US$580,000 on him. A further total of US$1,166,000 was found at the home of co-defendants. That was count one. The second count related to the defendant's dealings with co-defendants on two days when he made exchanges at the hotel and in a car. The defendant pleaded guilty on the basis that some of the observations related to him carrying on legitimate business; not all of the money recovered could be attributed to money laundering; and in relation to count two he said there were two transactions with a co-defendant when he knew the money came from crime. The defendant, 31, was of previous good character. He denied that the money was the proceeds of drug trafficking or other serious crime, and that was accepted by the judge. It was not a sophisticated scheme and he was the labourer for others. He received very little financial benefit, probably as little as £5,000. Held. It was not shown the money came from serious crime and the dishonesty was only part of a legitimate commercial operation. The sums involved were significant. He received insufficient credit for his plea: so **4 years** not 6. (Without a monetary figure for criminal part of the cash transferred this case is of only limited assistance.)

Criminal conduct money – £1m and up to £20m

115.6   *R v Everson* 2002 1 Cr App R (S) 553. The defendants S and B pleaded guilty to conspiracy to convert and remove from the jurisdiction criminal conduct money. The judge gave them the full discount for the plea. The defendant E was convicted of the same count. The conspiracy was over nearly 2 years and masterminded by S's brother in Gibraltar. Stirling notes, all the proceeds of crime, were exchanged for foreign currency of higher denomination, bank drafts and electronic transfers. Over £15m was laundered through a Bureau de Change in Victoria in London. There were at least 150 transactions. Some of the amounts were very large. S was the runner making most of the deposits. The money came from B and E. B was stopped as he was about to board a flight to Athens with his cleaner. They had nearly £169,000 worth of Swiss francs and Deutschmarks in their hand luggage. E was arrested and found to have a large amount of cash and a note in his jeep. The note referred to a shipment of training suits. When the consignment was intercepted it was found to contain £8.67m worth of cigarettes. He was deeply involved in the smuggling of cigarettes and the investment of the proceeds. His role was to cloak the operation with respectability. £1 m was transferred by shares. His laundering was close to £2m. None of the defendants were principles. The personal profits were said to be relatively modest. The judge found B was deeply involved in the regular laundering of the proceeds of cigarette smuggling. S was of good character. In 1984 B was convicted of evading duty and received 2 years. In 1991 he was sentenced to 10 years for drug smuggling. E was of good character and his partner had health problems. The defence relied on the fact the maximum for smuggling cigarettes was 7 years. The prosecution could not say what the duty evaded was. Held. As it was a conspiracy count it did not relate to just one evasion of duty so we are not impressed with counsel's argument. The Judge had looked at the totality of the sums. However, **3¹/₂ years** not 4¹/₂ for S, **5 years** not 6 for B and **6 years** not 7 for E.

R v Basra 2002 2 Cr App R (S) 469. The defendant pleaded guilty to assisting another to obtain the benefit of criminal conduct money. He exchanged £1.2m into foreign currency at a bureau at Victoria Station. He was sentenced on the basis it was the proceeds of jewellery smuggled from Uganda. His role was a middleman and the VAT evaded was £215,000. He carried on exchanging after his first arrest. **3¹/₂ years** not 5.

R v Hagan 2004 1 Cr App R (S) 207. The defendant pleaded at the earliest opportunity to concealing the proceeds of criminal conduct money. He was employed as a courier to travel from Liverpool to London to exchange euros at a bureau. He was arrested after he left a bureau with the equivalent of £50,000 in euros. The total value laundered was just over £1m. His gain did not exceed £250 a trip. He was treated as being of good character. The Judge said he started at 9 years and gave him 6 years. **4 years** substituted.

Criminal conduct money – £20m or more

115.7   *R v El-Kurd* 2001 Crim LR 234. The defendant was convicted of two conspiracies to remove criminal conduct money and two conspiracies to convert criminal conduct money. He was the proprietor of a Bureau de Change where over £70m was laundered over a 2 year period. Suitcases and holdalls of low value sterling notes were exchanged for high value foreign notes particularly Dutch guilders, Deutschmarks and Swiss Francs. The laundering activities did not appear in the exchange's books and the defendant had 55 bank accounts in England, Wales and Jersey. Held. As he wasn't convicted of laundering drugs money and the maximum was 14 years. **12 years** not 14.

Drugs money – Up to £50,000

115.8   *R v Gray* 2001 1 Cr App R (S) 99. The defendant pleaded guilty to the acquisition, possession or use of the proceeds of drug trafficking and possession of cannabis. Police searched his home and he produced a small piece of cannabis. Another piece was found in a speaker. They also found a letter from a man in prison asking for help with some "dosh" and in another speaker they found £15,725 which contained traces of cocaine, cannabis, heroin and amphetamine. He told police it was his savings for a business buying and selling houses. His plea was entered on the basis that he had received a call from the man in prison the night before who informed him there was cash in the speakers which he had previously asked him to remove from the premises. He realised the cash stored in the speakers was the proceeds of drugs. He had not responded to the letter and was relieved that his dilemma about what to do with the money ended with the arrival of the police. He was 41 with convictions and a low risk assessment for offending from the probation officer. Held. It was surprising the Crown accepted the basis of plea. As it was he had to be sentenced on that very limited role and that he stood to gain nothing. Therefore **15 months** not 2 years.

Old case. *R v Greenwood* 1995 16 Cr App R (S) 614.

Drugs money – £200,000 up to £1m

115.9   *R v Simpson* 1998 2 Cr App R (S) 111. The defendants S, F and L pleaded to conspiracy to possessing the proceeds of drug trafficking. A and D pleaded to possessing the proceeds of drug trafficking. G pleaded to assisting another to retain the benefit of drug trafficking. They were part of a well-organised drug syndicate, which during 1995 was raising £¹/₂m every 2–3 weeks principally selling Class A drugs. The money was taken to Ireland to be laundered. S made regular trips to Ireland. F and L delivered £540,000 to S in London and S was arrested with the cash at Heathrow airport. From tape recordings F and L were thoroughly familiar with workings of the whole organisation. After S's arrest A visited him in prison on a number of occasions.

It was agreed he would take over S's role in dealing with the Croydon end and receive the cash generated there. A was arrested with £$\frac{1}{2}$m of cash which he had been handed at Victoria Station by D. D had earlier been contacted at home by the dealers and asked to take the money there. He had the money for a maximum of 1$\frac{1}{2}$ hours and was paid £200. The judge said this was not the first time F and L were involved in disposing of the proceeds of drug trafficking. They were very much higher up than the bottom rung of the conspiracy. L was subordinate to F and became involved later than F did. A's criminal responsibility was considered the same as F. G's basis of plea was that he had twice in 1995 facilitated the export of money and on each occasion didn't know the amount involved and his role was as back up. The judge said G knew S, F, L and A well and played quite a prominent role in the business. However, he didn't seem to have made much money out of his involvement. D was sentenced for the one occasion and he knew there was a substantial amount of cash but didn't know how much money there was. F had convictions for a number of offences of dishonesty but none for drugs. L was of good character. A was 42 and had a number of convictions. There were no drug trafficking convictions and he had testimonials. D was 31 and for practical purposes of good character. G was 29 and of good character with testimonials. F and L's benefit was assessed at £20,000 and £10,000 and they were ordered to pay £10,000 and £8,800 respectively. A's benefit was £519,500 and the judge made a confiscation order in that amount. No order was made against G. Held. S's **11 years** was severe but not manifestly excessive. F's **9 years** and L's **7 years** were not manifestly excessive. The judge was wrong to equate A with F so **7 years** not 9 for A. Although D did not plead at the first opportunity, **4 years** not 5. The judge by saying G had played a prominent role was implicitly rejecting the basis of plea so **5 years** not 6. (For details about S see *Drugs money – £1m and up to £20m*)

Drugs money – £1m and up to £20m

115.10 *R v Simpson* 1998 2 Cr App R (S) 111. The defendant S pleaded guilty at an early stage to conspiracy to possessing the proceeds of drug trafficking. He was part of a well-organised drug syndicate, which during 1995 was raising £$\frac{1}{2}$ m every 2–3 weeks principally selling Class A drugs. The money was taken to Ireland to be laundered. S made regular trips to Ireland. F and L delivered £540,000 to S in London and S was arrested with the cash at Heathrow airport. He admitted his involvement in interview. S was sentenced on the basis he had made five earlier trips, the total sum transported by him being approximately £2.5m and he was paid £25,000 to £30,000 per trip. S received 11 years with a £948,700 confiscation order. It was contended that **11 years** on a plea equated with 14 years if contested which was the maximum. Held. S's role was crucial and pivotal. As he was caught red-handed we doubt whether a 3 year discount would have been appropriate. It was a severe sentence but not manifestly excessive. (For details about the co-defendants see *Drugs money – £200,000–£1m*)

Drugs money – £20m or more

115.11 *R v Sabharwal* 2001 2 Cr App R (S) 329. The defendant was convicted of conspiracy to facilitate the proceeds of drug trafficking. He exchanged £52m into guilders and £1,288,000 into other currencies between April 1998 and May 1999 using two London exchange centres who kept no records of the transactions. The £$\frac{1}{2}$m notes were seized and analysed. They were contaminated throughout with heroin, cocaine and two forms of ecstasy. He was living on benefits. Held. **12 years** was entirely appropriate.

Solicitors

115.12 *R v Duff* 2003 1 Cr App R (S) 466. The defendant pleaded guilty to two counts of failing to disclose knowledge or suspicion of money laundering contrary to the Drug Trafficking Act 1994, s 52(1). This involved £60,000 and £10,000. The defendant qualified as a solicitor in 1984. In 1991 he established his own practice, 90% of his work was conveyancing and the rest was personal injury work. In 1993 or 1994 he met G through their mutual interest in motor racing. He started to act for G and his business associate, H. They also became friendly. In April 1997 the defendant was given £60,000 in cash by G of which £10,000 was to pay for litigation. The rest was to be invested in an office run by the defendant and G. In May 1997 G paid the defendant £10,000 as an investment in a company to solicit personal injury work. The venture failed. In 1998 G and H were arrested for possession of cocaine worth £5m. To start with the defendant acted for G and H and then just G. Six months later a charge of conspiracy to import was added. The defendant accepted from then he had doubts about G's innocence. The defendant returned the £50,000 investment money. In October 1998 he obtained literature from the Law Society and concluded he was not under any duty to disclose. In 1999 G and H were tried and convicted and the trial focused on the defendant's dealing with G. After the trial the defendant took advice from another solicitor who advised he had no duty to report the dealings. The defendant was arrested and was not frank about the facts. There was a 15 month delay between his arrest and charge and 18 months before the case came to court. The defendant was of good character with a wife and three children. He suffered from adverse and sometimes inaccurate publicity and his firm collapsed. The judge said the clear message had to go out that offences of this type would not be overlooked. Held. Money laundering is a very serious matter and we agree with the judge. **6 months** was not in any way excessive.

116   MOTHERS

Child, the interests of the child

116.1   *R v Hier* 1998 2 Cr App R (S) 306. The defendant pleaded guilty to GBH with intent. She lived with the victim and their two sons aged 2 and 3 and her three other children. The victim admitted he had been violent to her and had been arrested for it three times. Several times the defendant had moved with her children to a woman's refuge. She instigated a reconciliation and when the relationship broke down moved back to the refuge with the children. She, when slightly intoxicated and some women friends went to a bar where the victim was. He asked about the children and she said they were being looked after. She asked him to dance and they did. He went to another public house. The defendant went in and accused him of chatting up the girls. He calmed her down and then they argued. She suggested they go outside and he walked away to join his girlfriend. She started crying and he and the girlfriend might have goaded her. He went to buy a drink and stood besides her. She hit him with a bottle more than once causing a large laceration to his ear, four cuts to the back of the head, one to his temple and one to his other ear. She told a barman it had given her satisfaction. She was arrested and accepted responsibility and shock at the extent of the injuries. She was 39 and in breach of a CD for ABH. She had struck a female on the head causing bruises. There were four convictions including the ABH and an assault on police in 1981. She expressed affection for the victim and expressed genuine regret. She was on anti-depressants. The refuge expressed concern for the children. Three were with their father all sharing a bedroom in his brother's three bedroom house with three other children. Two ran away to a mountain nearby. The youngest were with the victim who was also staying with his brother and sharing a room with the children. The victim also expressed concern about his children. Held. It was a very serious offence. The living conditions of each of the children are highly unsatisfactory. The circumstances are now so exceptional to enable the sentence to be suspended. **18 months suspended**

for 12 months (reduced because of the time in custody) with a supervision order not 18 months immediate imprisonment.

R v Smith 2002 1 Cr App R (S) 258. The defendant pleaded guilty to evading duty on tobacco etc. 105 trips were made with £365,000 evaded. She made 35 return trips evading some £70,000. Her father, mother and sister were co-defendants. The father was the prime mover. All 4 had been stopped by Customs. She was 28, with three children aged 7 and 2¹/₂ years and 8 months. The middle one was epileptic. Her husband was the breadwinner and was experiencing extreme difficulty in arranging adequate care for the children. She was of good character. She received **12 months** and the defence asked for it to be suspended. Held. This was a sustained participation in a major fraud notwithstanding warnings when they were stopped. The circumstances are of course harrowing from the perspective of the children. No one can fail to be moved by the children's plight but sadly the picture painted is all too familiar in cases where a young mother becomes involved in serious criminal activity. This Court is always most reluctant to see a mother of young children sentenced to imprisonment. Unhappily sometimes it is inevitable. The sentence was merciful. A suspended would not have been justified.

R v L and L 2004 1 Cr App R (S) 34. The defendants pleaded guilty in the Magistrates' Court to five offences of neglecting their son in a manner likely to cause him unnecessary suffering. They were married to each other and the boy was born in December 2000. Between 1 October and 23 September 2001 and between mid March and 8 May 2002 the boy was left at home alone on occasions for between 3 and 6 hours. There was no evidence of physical harm. The judge referred to shocking neglect with the boy without food or water and on at least on occasion heaters positioned close to him. He was placed with foster carers. A psychologist said the mother had had harsh childhood experiences. She had a learning disability and considerable deficits in understanding basic parenting issues. The pre-sentence report said, "the mother was likely to continue to pose a risk of neglecting a child due to her cognitive functioning. The risk may be reduced if she recognises her difficulties and engaged professionals. However she is unwilling or unable to do this. She is not suitable for probation as she was likely to become resentful at what she perceives as intrusion". His report said only a custodial sentence would reflect the gravity of the offences. There were 120 contact sessions with the boy. The new guardian said, "custody was not in the interest of the boy as it would delay residential assessment. The boy demonstrates a strong attachment to both parents. He, after the parents' imprisonment was distressed on the days he would have had contact". Held. It is quite disgraceful that a child so young should be left alone as often as happened here. We do not say the parents did not deserve prison. This is a case where retribution and deterrence should give way to the interests of the child. Here the criminal process should not place obstacles in the way of a viable family life. **6 months suspended** not 2 years.

R v Alkazaji 2004 2 Cr App R (S) 291. The defendant pleaded guilty to theft and other offences. She was a drug addict. The Judge wanted the defendant released before she had her baby. He thought there was every prospect she would be tagged. However in prison she tested positive for drugs. Held. The sentence was a lenient one. It is undesirable that the baby should be born into custody. From all the material before the court, it seems that the birth of the baby may be a positive feature which will change her approach to offending. We don't criticise the sentence. However the protection of the public is more likely to be achieved if we give her one more opportunity to take advantage of a **community rehabilitation order**.

R v Collins 2005 1 Cr App R (S) 103. The defendant pleaded guilty to perverting the course of public justice. During the course of theft of a transit van, the van's owner was run over and killed. The defendant's boyfriend was identified as possibly involved. When the defendant was seen by police she provided a preliminary statement in which she said that she had been aware of the incident, having heard about it on television.

She said that she had not talked to her boyfriend about it. Her boyfriend was arrested but denied any involvement. She made a full statement (s.9 CJA 67) stating that the personality of her boyfriend had changed and he had been observed by her as unable to sleep and having been distressed. She stated that her boyfriend had told her that he had gone out with a friend to "do a little tickle" (steal a car) and that the friend had admitted running over the victim and that her boyfriend had been the person responsible thereafter for telephoning the ambulance in relation to what had occurred. She said that she had been very shocked by what she had been told and she detailed a conversation that she had overheard between her boyfriend and his friend talking about their involvement in the matter. Both the boyfriend and his friend were arrested and changed with murder, then remanded in custody. 2 months later the defendant told the police that the conversation that she had recounted had in fact never happened and that she had lied. The police interviewed her and she admitted her witness statement contained lies. She was 19 and had no previous convictions. She had two small children ($2^{1}/_{2}$ and $5^{1}/_{2}$), had suffered depression and had attempted suicide on two occasions. She was heavily pregnant when she made her witness statement. Held. There was nothing wrong in principle in custody. The making of a witness statement implicating people in an offence of murder, falsely, strikes at the very heart of the administration of justice. A custodial sentence on a young mother kept away from her young children means the impact of such a sentence is worse than it would be for someone else not in that situation committing the same offence. **9 month's detention**, not 18.

See also CHILDREN AND YOUNG DEFENDANTS, CRUELTY TO CHILDREN and INFANTICIDE

Dishonesty, offences of when of good character

116.2   *R v Bowden* 1998 2 Cr App R (S) 6. The defendant pleaded guilty to four counts of theft and asked for 12 similar matters to be taken into consideration. The defendant was elected Treasurer of a Parent Teacher Co-operative. She held the cheque books etc and persuaded her co-signatory to sign blank cheques. She didn't prepare the accounts when they were due. A member of the group attended her house to request the books at the next day's meeting. The next day the books were not available and she submitted a letter of resignation saying she couldn't juggle the roles of mother and treasurer and saying the paperwork had been lost. In fact she had taken £2,983 in 16 withdrawals. She made full admissions in interview. She was 35 and of good character. She said she intended to pay the money back but it had got out of hand. She was a single mother with four children aged 15, 14, 11 and 8. She had spent the money on necessities. She lived on benefit and disability benefit. The pre-sentence report said the behaviour stemmed from difficult home circumstances, stress, debts and poor health. Two of the children suffered from chronic asthma, one from depression, one from attention deficit, hyperactivity disorder and a language disorder and one from brain damage, epilepsy and severe learning difficulties. The pre-sentence report said separation would be very traumatic for the children. She was given 12 months and a special needs worker had moved into her home. Held. 12 months was excessive. The compensation order of £2,983 was too heavy. Custody was not in principle incorrect. The appropriate sentence was **6 months** and 1 day. The exceptional circumstances justified a **suspended sentence** and a suspended supervision order. Both orders made with the compensation order upheld but varied to £100 a month.

R v Mills 2002 2 Cr App R (S) 229. LCJ. The defendant pleaded guilty to two offences of obtaining services by deception. She completed an application for credit at a store and claimed that the Merseyside Fire Service had employed her for 3 years. This was untrue. Credit facilities were granted. For 12 months she had made the minimum payments. She made no more payments. With interest and charges, the account was £5,682.66 in debt. She also purchased goods to the value of £714 from another store. A

10% deposit was paid. She applied for credit to finance the balance. In her application she claimed to have been employed by Allwood Joinery for 6 years. This was quite untrue. Some months after a finance company issued a credit card to the appellant, which she then used. She said she had not knowingly applied for, or expected to receive, the card. By the time that account was closed, it was approximately £5,438 in debit, and only £43.76 had been paid. She was arrested and when interviewed she admitted that she had made the false representations on each application. She had borrowed £4,000 from her mother to pay off part of the debt. She was 33 years of age and the sole carer of two children aged 11 and 4. She had no previous convictions or cautions and had references. They said that she did voluntary work at a local charity shop and gave her time to a voluntary agency assisting parents with young children. A pre-sentence report recommended a community sentence. The judge said, 'Those who commit offences of this kind, knowing perfectly well that there is really no chance of them ever being able to pay for the goods concerned, go to prison.' Held. The appellant was deeply sorry for the way she had behaved and the offences had been committed to provide for her children. The first factor that has to be take into account is that apart from 'the clang of the prison door' type of sentence, which gives a prisoner the opportunity of knowing what is involved in imprisonment, the ability of the prison service to achieve anything positive in a short prison sentence is very limited. Secondly, with a mother who is the sole supporter of two young children, you must consider them if the sole carer is sent to prison. Finally, take into account the current situation with the female prison population. Since 1993 there has been a remarkable increase. Short prison sentences are always difficult for the prison service to accommodate. The ability to imprison mothers close to their homes in the community is difficult. The difficulties in the prison population to which we have referred does not mean that if an offence is such that it is necessary to send an offender to prison, they should not be sent to prison. But in a borderline case, where the offence does not in particular involve violence but is one with financial consequences to a commercial concern, it is very important to take into account the facts to which we have referred. The courts should strive to avoid sending people like her to prison and instead use punishments in the community. It is true that obtaining credit is easy. Commercial concerns are entitled to the protection of the courts. It was wrong in principle to send her to prison. The minimum period should be passed for this category of offending. If it was necessary to send her to prison, all that would be required was the clang of the prison door. One month not 8 months should have been imposed. It would have been right to impose a **community punishment** order in this case then but now we will make a community rehabilitation order for 6 months.

117   MURDER

Common law. Indictable only. Mandatory sentence of life.

Automatic life For offences committed before 4/4/05, murder is a specified offence for automatic life[17] (so if the defendant on release commits another serious offence before 4/4/05 the murder conviction will count as a previous serious offence).

Funeral expenses The Court may make this compensation order see *Funeral expenses of the deceased*

Sexual Offences Prevention Order There is a discretionary power to make this order when it is necessary to protect the public etc[18].

17 Powers of Criminal Courts (Sentencing) Act 2000 s 109(5)
18 Sexual Offences Act 2003 s 104 & Sch. 5

Working with children Where the defendant is aged 18 or over and the offence is against a child the court must disqualify him/her from working with children unless satisfied s/he is unlikely to commit any further offences against a child when the court must state its reasons for not doing so[19]. For a defendant aged less than 18 at the time of the offence the court <u>must</u> order disqualification if the court is satisfied that the defendant will commit a further offence against a child[20]. The court must state its reasons for so doing.

Crown Court statistics – England and Wales – Males 21+
117.1

Year	Plea	Total Numbers sentenced
2002	Guilty	47
	Not guilty	223
2003	Guilty	47
	Not guilty	169

For details and explanations about the statistics in the book see page vii

Defendant under 18 at the time of the offence

117.2   Powers of Criminal Courts (Sentencing) Act 2000 s 90. Where a person convicted of murder appears to the court to have been aged under 18 at the time the offence was committed, the court shall (notwithstanding anything in this or any other Act) sentence him to be detained during Her Majesty's pleasure.

Defendant under 21 on the day of conviction

117.3   Powers of Criminal Courts (Sentencing) Act 2000 s 93. Where a person aged under 21 is convicted of murder the court shall sentence him to custody for life unless he is liable to be detained under s 90 (of this Act).

R v Burgess 2003 1 Cr App R (S) 371. At the time of the murder he was 17. The Court laid down how the term should be set for those under 18.

Defendant 21 or over on the date of conviction

117.4   Murder (Abolition of Death Penalty) Act 1965 s 1. No person shall suffer death for murder and a person convicted of murder shall be sentenced to imprisonment for life.

Funeral expenses of the deceased, power to make an order for compensation for the

117.5   Powers of Criminal Courts (Sentencing) Act 2000 s 130(1). The court may on application or otherwise make an order requiring him to make payments for funeral expenses or bereavement in respect of a death resulting from an offence other than death due to an accident arising out of the presence of a motor vehicle on a road.

Powers of Criminal Courts (Sentencing) Act 2000 s 130(3). A court shall give reasons if it does not make a compensation order in a case where this section empowers it to do so.

R v Williams 1989 Unreported 10/3/89. It is important sentencers bear in mind the words (which had just been added to the then statute giving the court power to order compensation for funeral expenses). If the court decides not to order compensation it must give its reasons.

Guilty plea

117.6   Reduction in Sentence for a Guilty plea guideline 16/12/04. Sentencing Guidelines Council's guideline. See www.sentencing-guidelines.gov.uk

---

19 Criminal Justice and Court Services Act 2000 s 28
20 Criminal Justice and Court Services Act 2000 s 29

R v Last 2005 The Times 31/1/05. The guidelines apply to life sentences passed before the guidelines were issued. The law was examined and explained.

Recommendations to the Secretary of State

117.7 Murder (Abolition of Death Penalty) Act 1965 s 1(2) On sentencing any person convicted of murder to imprisonment for life the Court may at the same time declare the period which it recommends to the Secretary of State as the minimum period which in its view should elapse before the Secretary of State orders the release of that person on licence.

Setting the minimum term

117.8 *Practice Statement Minimum Periods (Life Imprisonment) 2002* 2003 1 Cr App R (S) 218: The word minimum term should replace the word 'tariff'. The normal starting point for an adult is 12 years and the higher starting point is 16 years.

Consolidated Criminal Practice Direction (Amendment No 6) 2004 2 Cr App R 385.

R v Peters 2005 Unreported 10/3/05.

(As this book is about sentences passed not recommendations the texts are not summarised.)

118 MURDER, ATTEMPTED – MURDER, CONSPIRACY TO – MURDER, SOLICITING

118.1 Attempted murder. Criminal Attempts Act 1981 s 1(1). Indictable only. Maximum is life[21].

Conspiracy to murder. Criminal Law Act 1977 s 1(1). Indictable only. Maximum is life[22].

Soliciting to murder Offences against the Person Act 1861 s 4. Indictable only. Maximum is life[23].

Automatic life For offences committed before 4/4/05, attempted murder, conspiracy to murder, incitement to murder and soliciting to murder are specified offences for automatic life[24].

Dangerous Offender provisions For these three offences when committed on or after 4/4/05 where there is a significant risk to members of the public of serious harm etc. there is a mandatory duty to pass a life sentence when it is justified and otherwise a sentence of imprisonment for public protection[25]. For offenders under 18 the duty is to pass detention for life, detention for public protection or an extended sentence[26].

Longer than Commensurate sentences and Extended sentences All three offences are violent offences for the purposes of passing a longer than commensurate sentence [Powers of Criminal Courts (Sentencing) Act 2000 s 80(2)] and an extended sentence (extending the licence) [Powers of Criminal Courts (Sentencing) Act 2000 s 85(2)(b)][27]. The orders cannot be made for offences committed before 30/9/98 or after 3/4/05.

---

21 Criminal Attempts Act 1981 s 4(1)(a).
22 Criminal Law Act 1977 s 3(1)(a) and 3(2)(a).
23 Offences against the Person Act 1861 s 4.
24 Powers of Criminal Courts (Sentencing) Act 2000 s 109(5)
25 Criminal Justice Act 2003 s 225
26 Criminal Justice Act 2003 s 226 and 228
27 Powers of Criminal Courts (Sentencing) Act 2000 s 161(3)

Sexual Offences Prevention Order For all three offences, there is a discretionary power to make this order when it is necessary to protect the public etc[28].

Crown Court statistics – England and Wales – Males 21+
118.2

Year	Plea	Total Numbers sentenced	Type of sentence %					Average length of custody (months)
			Discharge	Fine	Community sentence	Suspended sentence	Custody	
Attempted Murder								
2002F	Guilty	21	–	–	–	5	71	106.5
	Not guilty	34	–	–	–	–	100	129
2003	Guilty	25	–	–	–	–	92	96
	Not guilty	54	–	–	–	–	94	158.8
Threat or conspiracy to murder[29]								
2002	Guilty	124	3	1	31	4	60	29.9
	Not guilty	42	–	–	17	2	71	36.1
2003	Guilty	141	4	2	26	6	57	29.4
	Not guilty	61	2	–	10	3	74	59.9

For details and explanations about the statistics in the book see page vii.

Guideline remarks – Attempted murder

118.3   *R v Powell* 1998 1 Cr App R (S) 84. Attempted murder is often more serious than murder as it involves the intention to kill which is not necessary in murder cases.

R v Smith 1999 2 Cr App R (S) 212. Factors to have particular regard to are: (1) an intent to kill will have been established; (2) the failure to implement the intent will not normally be a cause for indulgence or credit to be accorded to the defendant; (3) the motive and the premeditation; (4) the recognition of some proportional correlation between the sentence and the minimum recommendation the judge would have made had murder been committed; (5) the plea; (6) the defendant's age; (7) where there are other sentences, the totality.

Assisting others who want to kill

118.4   *R v Chapman* 1999 2 Cr App R (S) 374. The defendant was convicted of conspiracy to murder. His co-accused was violent to his girlfriend and they separated. He became obsessed by her, obtained a gun and made a number of threatening calls to her. He was arrested and met the defendant in prison. While there he recruited others to make threatening calls to the girlfriend. He was returned to prison and expressed an intention to kill her. He persuaded the defendant to write a letter at his dictation which included threats to kill. The defendant was charged with that and was acquitted by a jury. The co-accused then persuaded the defendant to assist him to kill the girlfriend. He told others in prison about the plan and an undercover police officer approached the co-accused posing as a contract killer. The co-accused's instructions were taped. The co-accused then exchanged letters with the defendant who was also still in prison about plans to kill her. Both their cells were searched and the correspondence was found. The defendant was arrested. At his trial the defendant said he had no real intention of carrying out the plan. He was 26 with an appalling record for dishonesty but no

28 Sexual Offences Act 2003 s 104 & Sch. 5
29 Presumably this is threats to kill and conspiracy to murder.

convictions for violence. The co-defendant had three convictions for ABH, two for kidnapping, one each for arson, false imprisonment and possession of a firearm. The psychological reports on the defendant differed in their conclusions. They were both sentenced to 8 years. Held. The defendant should have received less than the co-accused. One had convictions for violent acts of retribution against former girlfriends. The other had no convictions for violence. The co-accused was the prime mover and had issued earlier threats. **6 years** substituted.

Conspiracy not carried out   See CONSPIRACY – *Conspiracy not carried out*

Contract killings – Guideline remarks

118.5   *R v Smith* 1999 2 Cr App R (S) 212. The range for (vengeance) cases is **14 to 20 years**. Contract killing or for enforcement of drug (disputes) gives rise to sentences at the upper end.

Contract killings – Cases

118.6   *R v Mason and Sellars* 2002 Unreported 22/3/02. The defendants M and S were convicted of conspiracy to murder. M was also convicted of possessing a firearm with intent to endanger life. There was a history of conflict between them and the victim. They all drank in the same pub. They plotted over months to kill him and paid a hit man £6,000 to kill the victim who died in the street. He was shot in the neck with a shotgun. The victim was a violent and unpleasant man. M had an extensive criminal record principally for dishonesty and a conviction for armed robbery and was sentenced to automatic life. Held. We must take into account the plan succeeded. The appropriate determinate sentence for M was **22 years**. As S did not represent a serious danger to the public **20 years** not life.

R v Khalil 2004 2 Cr App R (S) 121. H pleaded guilty on re-arraignment to conspiracy to murder. Y aged 50 was convicted of the same count. K was acquitted. Y's 20 year old daughter married the victim against Y's wishes. Y had wanted her to marry her cousin in Pakistan. He tried to separate the couple and appeared at court in a charge of harassment of the victim. He decided to have the victim killed. H was involved in the conspiracy from the outset. H made contact with a man who he believed to be a hit man but who was an undercover police officer. Much of the activity was recorded. After discussions between H and the police officer it was agreed the police officer would go to the court dealing with Y's harassment charge so that the victim could be identified to him. Other men handed £30 to the officer for expenses and pointed out the victim to him. H and the officer agreed that the officer would be paid £4,000 for killing the victim. The officer later told H that he had killed the victim and there was a meeting the next day in which H told the officer he would be paid on proof that he had killed the victim. Y was of previous good character. The judge identified six serious aggravating circumstances in relation to both men: the motive was wholly inadequate; it was revenge on the victim for having married his wife secretly and prevented her marriage to her cousin; a contract killer was involved; a large sum of money was put up to ensure the killing was carried out; it was intended that the victim be killed not just harmed; four others were drawn into the conspiracy to do the dirty work. Held. The range of sentence between **14–20 years** considered appropriate for attempted murder was appropriate in this case. H and Y should be treated equally. H benefited from a generous discount for his guilty plea. **16** years for Y upheld. **12 years** not manifestly excessive for H.

Criminal gangs, killings by etc

118.7   *R v Powell* 1998 1 Cr App R (S) 84. The defendant was convicted of attempted murder and possessing a firearm with intent to endanger life. The defendant was acquitted of three other shooting incidents in Birmingham, Stoke Newington and

Peckham in London. The victim was 17 and sold cannabis. Near midnight he was in the Ladbroke Grove area of London with two others involved in selling drugs. They were joined by two women. A car pulled up and the defendant and another two men got out. The defendant pulled out a gun and fired it at the victim who fell to the ground. He was taken to hospital and it was found a bullet had entered his chest and damaged his spine. The victim was left permanently paraplegic. Held. This was either a contract killing or a killing concerned with the enforcement of order amongst drug dealers. It was at the top end of the scale for this kind of offence. However, **20 years** not 25.

R v Docking and others *2005 1 Cr App R (S) 675*. D was convicted of attempted murder, possession of a shotgun with intent to endanger life, dangerous driving and driving while disqualified. In a separate indictment but arising out of related events W, L and C were convicted of conspiracy to commit criminal damage and conspiracy to commit GBH. C was also convicted of unlawful wounding. The unlawful wounding arose when Cook went to the home of man called Fletcher and wounded him with a weapon. Fletcher at that stage declined to report the matter to the police. A few weeks later C, W, L and another man drove to Fletcher's house with three weapons: a cosh, a baseball bat and a loaded gun. They put on balaclavas and kicked in the side door to his home. W stayed in the car. L stayed outside smashing car windows. Two vehicles belonging to Fletcher were damaged. C and the other man went inside the house, where Fletcher was with his son and three other people. Fletcher had a shot aimed at his head but he put his hand up and the shot broke his wrist. The gun jammed and was then used to beat him about the head. The gunman was alleged at trial to be C but he was acquitted of attempted murder. D then tried to avenge what had happened to Fletcher. D and a woman companion were in a car that blocked a car in which L and two other men were travelling. The woman handed a sawn off shotgun to D and he fired the gun through the window of the other car. Pellets hit L and the driver of the car, who then took off, pursued by D, at speeds of up to 100mph. D rammed the other car and shouted 'I'm going to shoot you, you fucking bastards. You're dead, you're dead.' He fired again breaking a window in the car. He got out of the car with a gun and a baseball bat. The three men ran off. When arrested D gave a false alibi involving a girlfriend who was later prosecuted for making a false statement. D, 24, had a substantial criminal record as a car thief and burglar and was described by the judge as a career criminal and very dangerous. He still had some months of a licence period for burglary and other matters to run at the time of these offences. W and C were both 21. L was 22. Each of them had four previous convictions including offences of drug possession. The judge said he was satisfied that C and L were prime movers. Held. In relation to D the judge was entitled to impose a deterrent sentence particularly having regard to the use of firearms in Sheffield. **16 years** not 18 years for attempted murder concurrent not consecutive to the 2 years for dangerous driving. So 16 years not 20 years. W's **8 years** detention for conspiracy to commit GBH was severe but not even arguably manifestly excessive. For L the judge was entitled to conclude that he knew a loaded firearm was being carried and **14 years** detention for conspiracy to commit GBH was not even arguably excessive. C's sentences of **12 years** detention for the conspiracy to cause GBH, **2 years** detention to run **consecutively** for the unlawful wounding were upheld.

Obsessive attacks

118.8 *R v Suckley* 2001 2 Cr App R (S) 313. The defendant who was now 75 was convicted of attempted murder, GBH with intent and ABH. He was a neighbour of the victims, a husband, his wife and their son. He had built his house and their house. In 1990 they exchanged properties. In 1995 when his wife died his personality changed and the relationship with the neighbours deteriorated. By 1999 he had become obsessed with complaining about them. He said they moved his tools and scratched his windows. The complaints appeared to be trivial and ill founded. He left two telephone messages for the police but they were not followed up. The next day the husband, aged 52, started early to cut his hedge. He wanted to avoid the heat of the day. At 9am his wife and son were sweeping up the cuttings. The defendant revved his engine and reversed his transit van at them. He hit all three. The wife was knocked into the hedge unconscious and the husband was knocked away. The son was hit by the central part of the bonnet and hit the windscreen, which broke. He landed on the road. The defendant reversed over the son and knocked the husband who was trying to rescue him. He drove forward and reversed over the son three or four times. Then he parked his van and told a neighbour, "These people have made my life hell for the passed 3 years." The son had a fractured nose and femur with multiple fractures to the rib, pelvis, spine and foot bones. He was in intensive care for 3 weeks and in hospital for 4 weeks. He was in a wheel chair and it was hoped he would be able to walk again. The wife had a fractured pelvis with a head injury. She was in intensive care for 5 days and in hospital for a month. She continued to suffer from memory and concentration problems. The husband suffered bruising and was in hospital for 2 days. The psychiatric report said the defendant had a paranoid psychotic illness of an unknown cause. Another said his persecution delusions were evidence of a mental disorder specifically paraphrenia. Held. It is plain from *R v C* 1992 14 Cr App R (S) 562; *R v S* 1998 1 Cr App R (S) 261 and *R v Anderson* 1999 1 Cr App R (S) 273 that regard must be had to age and that a discount is appropriate. Any attempt at an actuarial basis for a discount is inappropriate. The present sentence has been significantly discounted from almost certainly 15 years, which would have been appropriate for a younger man to **11 years**. Such a discount was proper and fair. Appeal dismissed.

Police officers, on

118.9   *R v Morrison* 2002 2 Cr App R (S) 75. The defendant was convicted of three counts of attempted murder and a count of wounding with intent. He married in 1988 and had two children. In 1995 his wife discovered he was having an affair and in 1997 they were divorced. In June 1999 he accused his ex-wife of turning the children against him. He threatened to kill her and they rarely spoke although contact with his daughters continued. In August 1999, she borrowed his car and collected her daughter from a previous relationship. Forty-five minutes later she returned and he became angry because he did not accept where she had been. That evening he rang her and sounded drunk. He said he loved her, asked her why she had been away so long and called her a bitch because she wouldn't take him back. There were further calls during that evening and he said he was going to kill her. The calls were recorded and in the last one he said 'I'm coming up now. I've decided what to do with you. I'm going to kill you and get you out of the way.' Fifteen minutes later he arrived at her home with a Samurai sword. He used the sword to break down the door. She ran upstairs and shut the door and held onto the handle of the door of the bedroom to stop him coming in. He thrust the sword through the door three times but she wasn't hit. (This was the first attempted murder – **10 years**.) Police arrived and an officer got out of a van. The defendant ran towards him with the sword raised. The officer retreated to the van and sat in the driver's seat. The defendant raised the sword and brought it down on the windscreen twice but it didn't break. He followed the van as it reversed and raised the sword again. That officer decided to wait for an armed response unit to arrive. A dog van attended and the defendant hid behind an electricity junction box. Suddenly he ran at the dog van which reversed. The defendant caught up with it and brought the sword down on the windscreen in a dagger like movement aiming at the driver. It went through the windscreen but missed the officer. The driver drove away. (This was the second attempted murder – **15 years**.) Another officer arrived in a patrol car and saw the attack on the van. He decided to disarm the defendant by knocking him over. His bonnet hit the defendant's knees. The defendant fell down but got up, picked the sword up, walked towards the car and raised the sword which he brought down like an axe smashing the windscreen in front of the PC. The PC panicked and his attempts to drive away failed. The defendant struck the roof of the car with the sword a number of times. He then drove the sword through the open window towards the officer's head. He slashed and stabbed at the PC's head and body. The roof was hit again. The PC managed to run away. The tendons to his wrists had been cut. (This was the third attempted murder – **16 years**.) Another officer arrived, knocked the defendant over and he was arrested. The defendant was 40 with three convictions, two of which were for ABH. He expressed remorse. Held. It was a very serious incident. **16 years** in all was not excessive.

Relationship/emotional – Guideline remarks

118.10   *R v Davis* 2001 1 Cr App R (S) 186. The defendant pleaded guilty to attempted murder. Held. Decisions of this court show offences involving savage attacks by a partner who either does not want himself removed or does not want the partner to go. A sentence of **12 years** on conviction is certainly not unusual, and may well be appropriate and usual.

Relationship/emotional – Cases – 5 years or less

118.11   *Att-Gen's Ref. No 117 of 2001* 2002 2 Cr App R (S) 374. The defendant was convicted of attempted murder. About 5 years before the offence he separated from his wife and started a relationship with the victim. The new partner believed it was a good, open and honest relationship. He was loving and affectionate and never violent. He hid from her his debts but his partner's death would not have helped with that. At 5.45 am he approached her in bed, held her hands and said he loved her. He took up a pillow on which he had wrapped some cling film. He forced it over her face and she struggled. She was able to scream and he abandoned his attempt. She asked him what he had done and he said he didn't know what she was talking about. A pathologist found petechial haemorrhages in her eyes consistent with her nose and mouth being covered for at least a minute. The defendant denied the offence in interview. His former wife said he had never been violent or aggressive and there was no sign of a mental disorder. He was of good character and his manager said he was responsible and trustworthy. No explanation for the offence emerged. Held. The range of sentences for attempted murder is wide. **5 years** was lenient but not unduly lenient.

R v Molyneux 2004 1 Cr App R (S) 138. The defendant pleaded guilty to soliciting murder. She married in 1980 and had four children. There was an acrimonious divorce and she believed her husband was hiding assets abroad. She contacted an inquiry agent who said she said she wanted her husband dead. There was a series of calls. Her husband withdrew his offer to let her stay in the matrimonial home. She said to the agent it would be better if it was done while she was in Canada. The agent contacted the Sunday People and a reporter met her posing as a hitman with an audio and video recorder running. She said, "She wanted him gone for ever. He's an absolute bastard. He has admitted 15 cases of adultery and I will not lose my house". She gave him details of her husband's car and his photograph. She said she was thinking of making it look like a carjacking. He told her it would cost £20,000 and asked her if she was 100% sure as she had to think of the children. She said, "Yeah". The reporter went to the police. While she was in Canada the reporter phoned her and said Clive would be in contact. An undercover officer posing as Clive phoned and asked if she was happy to go ahead and she said, "I haven't any doubts at all". She was sentenced on the basis she had been inveigled by the inquiry agent. The husband and the children asked for leniency. Held. Inveiglement is an important factor. **5 years** upheld.

R v Francis 2003 2 Cr App R (S) 689. The defendant pleaded guilty to attempted murder. His mother was a widow and underwent a series of hip operations which were not a complete success. She could walk with two sticks only. The defendant was extremely supportive of her and moved in with her. She was 85 at the time of the offence. He was made redundant by his employers and had managed to find a new job that he found more stressful. He had recently been involved in a road traffic offence and was on anti-depressant medication. Four days before the offence he did not get out of bed and was visited by his GP who increased his medication. Over the next few days the defendant decided to commit suicide and to kill his mother. He believed that there would be no one to look after his mother after his death and he was concerned about the effect his death would have on her. As his mother came out of her lavatory he hit her over the head with a shillelagh. She fell down and he hit her again. She called to him to stop and tried to get to the telephone, but the defendant pushed her down. He held her by the throat and told that he was having to kill her because there would be no one to look after her after he had committed suicide. He then struck her on the back of her head with one of her sticks. He then stopped what he was doing and called for assistance. He then went outside and asked a neighbour to help his mother. She was taken to hospital where she had injuries to her head and neck. He said in interview that he had intended to kill her as painlessly as possible and then hang himself. The Judge accepted that he did not pose anything more than a remote theoretical risk. It was accepted that at that time he had been completely out of kilter and unbalanced. He had no convictions and there were many character references including a letter from his mother who wrote a moving letter about how good a son he had been to her. Held. The defendant put into affect a premeditated plan to kill his mother, for reasons which were not altogether altruistic. His warped sense of thinking did not absolve him from responsibility. **4 years** unchanged.

Relationship/emotional – Cases – More than 5 years

118.12   *R v Davis* 2001 1 Cr App R (S) 186. The defendant was convicted of attempted murder. His relationship with the victim broke down after a domestic argument and she asked him to leave. He chased her and stabbed her in the back and stomach. He dragged her down the road and slashed her face substantially with a kitchen knife. The victim was expected to have permanent and cosmetically disfiguring scars on her face and to have facial muscle weakness. Her life had been altered and she had problem eating and drinking. She could not sleep and felt the events would haunt her forever. He was 37 and she was 36. Held. The photographs show very frenzied injuries. There was no mitigation. **12 years** upheld.

R v Hough 2001 1 Cr App R (S) 258. The defendant pleaded guilty to attempted murder. After a 20 year relationship the victim, aged 36, left the defendant, aged 66, and took their five children with her. She blamed the deterioration of the relationship on his violence. He blamed it on her affair with another man. He met her and two of the children in the street and tried to persuade her to return home. She refused. They went to a friend's house, as neutral territory and talked. He tried to persuade her to return and she continued to refuse to do so. He went home which was close by and returned shortly afterwards. He asked her to go upstairs so they could speak privately. She feared he would attack her but he assured her he would not. They went upstairs and he asked her to sit down. He asked to see her personal alarm as she had said she had one. In fact she didn't have one. He leant towards her, she thought to cuddle her but he produced a knife. Using both hands he tried to stab her in the stomach. Luckily as she was wear-ing a strong fabric the knife buckled. She kicked him and he pulled out a second knife and stabbed her in the top of the forehead and the knife passed between the skin and the skull. The knife exited 4″ further down her forehead just above the right eye. She screamed and he ran off leaving the knife in place. She went to hospital and he went to the police station and told them he had stabbed her because she was messing with another man and he wished her dead. In interview he said he tried to 'get rid of the bitch.' He said he went home to get the knives and he wanted to make sure he got rid of her. He said he intended to kill her because she deserved it. His last conviction was in 1976 for sex with a girl under 16. His last custodial sentence was in 1961. He was unemployed and had earlier told the third man he had nothing to live for. Held. On a fight the sentence would be **8–9 years**, so with the mitigation **6 years** not 8.

R v Robinson 2003 2 Cr App R (S) 54. The defendant was convicted of incitement to murder. She had formed a relationship with S in 1975 and they lived together. S started an affair and then left her. The defendant then began to take in lodgers, one of whom, G, had criminal connections. The defendant decided to enlist G's help to find a contract killer to kill S's new lover. Police heard about the plan. Consequently she was introduced to an undercover police officer who the defendant told she wanted S's new partner murdered. A figure of £5,000 to £6,000 was agreed and another meeting was arranged. She met another undercover officer who, she was told, would actually carry out the killing. Three meetings with this second officer followed where a photograph of the other woman and a map were handed over together with £100 expenses. A price of £10,000 was agreed and £5,000 was paid. This officer was told that he would be contacted. A date was set and then put off for a few days. At a further meeting the defendant told this officer that the contract could not go ahead because G had been telling people what was planned and it had all become too risky! She was arrested and interviewed. She denied intending the other woman should be killed and maintained that it had all been a fantasy. She suffered from a dependant personality disorder and was suffering from depression. She was 58 and of good character. Held. The gravity of the offence and sentencing policy dictated that a strong deterrent element should be included in the sentence. The judge had been entitled to take the view that the plans made were detailed and calculating; lasting over a significant period of time and the only reason for calling them off was a fear of being discovered. **7 years** upheld.

R v Gouldthorpe 2004 1 Cr App R (S) 248. The defendant was convicted of attempted murder. His partner decided to terminate their relationship and went to live with her parents. He took it badly and pestered her so much so that she sought police advice. Police cautioned him and he was told to leave her alone. He travelled from Torquay to Plymouth with a knife to catch her as she took the bus to work. He approached her from behind. She was seized and he slashed her across the throat three times, saying "I don't take rejection lightly." The wounds were more than 2″ long and within a short distance of vital blood vessels. Next he pushed her to the ground and plunged the knife into her chest nearly inflicting fatal injuries. He left and drove to Dartmoor where he poured petrol over himself and his car. He lit it and then extinguished the flame on himself and was taken to hospital where he was treated for burns. When interviewed he said he wanted to speak to her but had no memory of the incident. His only conviction followed the break up of another relationship. He trashed the woman's flat, hammered the walls, damaged her belongings and put her clothing in the bath with bleach. The defence psychiatrist said he posed a continuing and perhaps escalating risk to other women with whom he might develop a relationship. Held. This was a well planned, pre-meditated, determined and sustained attack. **12 years** was right. With the psychiatric evidence three years on top as a longer than commensurate sentence was justified making **15 years**.

R v Palmer 2005 1 Cr App R (S) 604. The defendant was convicted of attempted murder. The victim was his former partner and mother of his two year old child. They had separated four or five weeks before the attack. There were difficulties over access to the child and the victim was concerned enough about his attitude to her to speak to her parents and work colleagues. The day before the attack she was threatened by a woman who shouted at her that she was 'going to get it'. The next day arrangements were made for her to leave work early and to be escorted to her car by a colleague. Just after the colleague left her by her car she saw the defendant; she managed to get into the car but the defendant prevented her from locking it and attacked her. He hit her head and then got into the car and made a frenzied attack on her with a knife. At one point she managed to get the knife away from him and he slumped in the passenger seat and said he was sorry. She thought the attack was over and released her grip on the knife. He grabbed it from her and continued the attack saying 'Die you bitch'. She managed to sound the car horn so that her colleague was alerted and the defendant ran off. The defendant later returned to the scene and was arrested by the police. He showed them where the knife was. The victim had sixteen lacerations to her head, neck, shoulders, arms, legs and hand. She had a potentially life threatening injury to her neck below her ear which required a number of operations to close the wound and stem the blood loss. She was off work for five months, her daughter reacted against her and had to be cared for by the victim's mother. The victim suffered headaches and nervousness and was left with scars, nightmares and anxiety. She had to change her job. The defendant, 28, was of good character. A number of people spoke well of him and gave evidence on his behalf. It was accepted that he did not present a future risk. Held. The most powerful mitigation was the defendant's good character. Account was also taken of the fact that this incident had to be viewed against the background of a volatile and sometimes violent relationship, that the defendant did not present a future risk and that the injuries were substantially less serious than those in the case of *R v Davies 2001 1 Cr App R (S) 186*. **10 years** not 12.

Old cases. *R v Gibson* 1997 2 Cr App R (S) 292; *R v D* 1998 1 Cr App R (S) 110; *R v Wooton* 1998 1 Cr App R (S) 296 and *R v Rahman* 1998 1 Cr App R (S) 391. (For a summary of the last three cases see the first edition of the book.)

Sadistic offences

118.13   *R v Dalziel* 1999 2 Cr App R (S) 272. The defendant made a late guilty plea to attempted murder. Just under a month after being released from a 2 year sentence for blackmail the defendant then 19 called at the front door of an 82-year-old widower who was blind and lived with his guide dog. The defendant claimed he was from Age Concern and was invited in. They talked and the defendant was given strawberries and cream. After taking the dirty dishes to the kitchen the two returned to the living room and the defendant drew the curtains. He then seized the victim from behind and held a knife to his throat. He was threatened that his throat would be cut if he did not do what he was told. The victim's hands were tied behind his back with flex and over $^1/_2$ hour he removed his trousers and underwear and buggered him. He took him to the bathroom where he made the victim lie on the floor while he had a shower. Next he took him to his bedroom and ransacked it. Then he was taken to the living room where he was tied up with flex round the legs and throat and gagged. The defendant found and sprinkled a can of lighter fuel and whisky over the victim and the room. Finally he set light to a piece of paper and left the house to burn. The victim was terrified for himself and the dog which had been tethered. The flames spread quickly and travelled up between the victim's bare legs which began to burn. He managed to remove the gag and shout for help. Neighbours heard the screams, kicked the door down and dragged him free. The victim had reddening to the scrotum and penis and multiple partial thickness burns to the legs, stomach, hand and soles of the feet. They required skin grafts. The defendant had the blackmail conviction and dishonesty offences but none for violence. Psychiatric reports indicated he was very dangerous. He had fantasies of torturing and killing people and had tortured animals. His psychopathic disorder was untreatable. Held. Examination of comparable horrific cases of attempted murder and similar offences indicate a broad range of **14–18 years** for a contested case. It was not surprising the defendant was given life. **18 years** or close could have been the starting point. Taking into account the plea and his youth **14 years** would not be too high. His dangerousness should not increase the sentence, as that's why it was life. The specified period was therefore $^1/_2$ the 14 years so **7 years** not 12 years.

Att-Gen's Ref. Nos. 15 and 16 of 2002 2003 1 Cr App R (S) 161. The defendants L and M were convicted of attempted murder. The two defendants were in a lesbian relationship and held a party to celebrate their engagement at M's flat. The victim, a 13 year old boy who had not previously met either of the defendants attended the party. He drank far too much alcohol and was sick over one of the guests and on a bed. He might have fallen over L's 4 year old boy. The defendants became angry and slapped and punched the boy. They undressed him and put him under a cold shower. The clothes were rinsed and he was redressed in the wet clothes. After he had been sick again, the defendants carried him out to a grassy area where he was subjected to a prolonged, sadistic and brutal assault over some two hours. They returned to him two or three times continuing the attack on the helpless boy. A passer-by heard one of them say, "If you do it again, I'll kill you." Others living nearby heard sounds of breaking glass on several occasions. On the first return to the flat M was seen to take a Stanley knife and L was seen to put a kitchen knife into the back of her trousers. They also took a bottle and a can of beer and were seen to have blood on their hands. Between 2 and 2.30 am M suggested people should get some sleep and a bit later she woke one of them up to look at the body. When they looked at the body, she asked him if the boy was still alive. He seemed to them to be dead and she said, "I stabbed him in the side and we slit his throat. They returned to the flat and L said he was dead and, "I stabbed him and I couldn't stop stabbing him." Further she said she had slit his throat and stabbed him in the chest and there was nothing that could be done for him. M called an ambulance at 3.03 am. The boy was found in a pool of blood and broken glass. He had lacerations to his throat, head and chest and his pulse was faint. He was close to death. He had 23 stab wounds and areas of bruising and abrasions to the head, torso and limbs. In interview and at trial both sought to blame each other. L was then 21 and had only a caution for common assault. A psychiatrist detected a degree of instability of personality exacerbated by drug and drink abuse. She had incidents of self harm and suicide gestures while awaiting trial. M was then 17 and had a conviction for aggravated vehicle taking and two cautions. A psychiatrist said she had a history of emotional disturbance and she presented a low risk of causing future harm to others. M's relationship with L was assessed as very destructive, volatile and dangerous. M was considered vulnerable and easily influenced. Held. We derive the greatest assistance from *R v Dalziel* 1999 2 Cr App R (S) 272 which gives the **14 to 18 year** bracket for an adult. We would have expected 14 years for L and 11 years detention for M. As it was a reference **11 years** for L and **8$^1/_2$ years** for M.

Stranger(s), attacking

118.14   *R v Comer* 2002 2 Cr App R (S) 476. The defendant was convicted of three counts of attempted murder. He spent most of Saturday with his best friend drinking in public houses and in one joined a private party where he had a fight over a spilt drink. The friend broke the fight up and someone handed the friend a knife, which he recognised as the defendant's knife. The friend noticed the defendant was getting "wound up." As they walked home in the early hours the defendant appeared to black out and collapse. He quickly recovered and threatened to beat his friend up if he did not return the knife. The knife was returned and the friend walked away. Shortly afterwards the defendant stabbed three perfect strangers in separate incidents. The first victim suffered unpleasant but not particularly serious injuries. Fortunately the knife struck the victim's jacket zip. The second victim suffered a collapsed lung. In hospital he was in "extremis", with no blood pressure and on the point of dying. He had a full thickness hole in his heart, with the coronary artery severed. He was loosing blood at the rate of three to four pints a minute. A nurse who was passing by attended to the third victim and kept him alive until an ambulance arrived. He had a large hole in his liver and suffered a cardiac arrest. When arrested the defendant asked, "Have I killed anyone? What have I done?" He was asked how many people he had stabbed and he said three or four. He said he had taken a $^1/_4$ ounce of amphetamine. A blood test revealed 235 mg of alcohol and a low concentration of amphetamine. At the police station he said, "It was like a pressure value going off, not a power thing. It felt good doing it and I felt good. I was just on autopilot. I knew I was putting my hand out and hitting people. I don't know why." In interview he expressed bewilderment and remorse.

He was 29 with no convictions and eight character witnesses. They said temperamental, ill-tempered or aggressive. He was successful in work. He was of high intellect but suffered from depression. There was insufficiency of memory consistent with mild brain damage caused by repeated minor head injuries. The effects could have been accentuated by drugs. When sober and free from intoxicants those abnormalities did not make him a danger to others. There was no mental illness. He was sentenced to 20, 20 and 16 years concurrent. Held. There was no discernible motive. There were difficulties understanding what went on and why. **16 years** substituted.

Vengeance – Guideline remarks

118.15   *R v Smith* 1999 2 Cr App R (S) 212. The range for (vengeance) cases is **14 to 20 years**. Contract killing or for enforcement of drugs (disputes) gives rise to sentences at the upper end.

Vengeance – Cases

118.16   *R v Smith* 1999 2 Cr App R (S) 212. The defendant was convicted of murder and attempted murder. There was a history of bad feeling and violence between the victim and another, K. The defendant took a gun to a nightclub. He and K watched the two victims leave the club and the defendant gave the gun and ammunition to K saying 'Cap him, cap him'. K fired at one victim and missed. He fired again and the victim fell to the ground. The other victim ran to K and tried to kick him but slipped and fell. The defendant said to K 'Ain't you going to end him?' K then shot him on the floor. The bullet passed through his heart sac. The defendant and K left. The first victim through a miracle survived. The second victim died. The defendant was serving a sentence for rape and was sentenced to custody for life and 25 years. Held. A clear motive is absent. We conclude that there was a grievance, which ran so deep to cause these offences. That puts it at the upper end of the range of 14 to 20 years. Had it not been that he was serving the rape sentence and his age the sentence might be at the top namely 20. However, **18 years** substituted concurrent to custody for life. [The report does not state the defendant's age or any details of the rape or the sentence for the rape.]

See also EXPLOSIVE OFFENCES – *Kill the victim, intending to*

MUTINY

See PRISON MUTINY

NEWTON HEARING

See **GUILTY PLEA, DISCOUNT FOR** – *Newton hearing, defendant takes part in*

NOXIOUS THING

For administering etc a noxious thing see **OFFENCES AGAINST THE PERSON ACT 1861 s 23** and **OFFENCES AGAINST THE PERSON ACT 1861 s 24**

NUISANCE, PUBLIC

See **PUBLIC NUISANCE**

Where the offence is connected with obtaining money dishonestly see **THEFT ETC**

Where the offence is connected with harassment see **HARASSMENT (s 4 OR PUBLIC NUISANCE)**

See also **PUBLIC ORDER ACT 1986** and **STALKING**

OBSCENE PUBLICATIONS

See **PORNOGRAPHY**

119   OBSTRUCTING A POLICE OFFICER

119.1   Police Act 1996 s 89(2)

Summary only. Maximum 1 month and/or Level 3 (£1,000). When the Criminal Justice Act 2003 s 280(2) & Sch. 26 Para 47 is in force the maximum will increase to 51 weeks[1]. The Home Office do not expect this to occur before September 2006.

Magistrates' Court Sentencing Guidelines January 2004

119.2   For a first time offender pleading not guilty. Entry point. Is a discharge or a fine appropriate? Consider the impact on the victim. Examples of aggravating factors for the offence are attempt to impede arrest, group action, and premeditated. Examples of mitigating factors for the offence are genuine misjudgement, impulsive action and minor obstruction. Examples of mitigation are age, health (physical or mental), subsequent co-operation with the police, and genuine remorse. Starting point fine B. (100% of weekly take home pay/weekly benefit payment)

For details about the guidelines see **MAGISTRATES' COURT SENTENCING GUIDELINES** at page 483.

120   OBSTRUCTING THE CORONER/BURIAL, PREVENTING

120.1   Both offences are against the common law.

---

1   Criminal Justice Act 2003 s 280(2) & Sch. 26 Para 47

Indictable only. No maximum provided so the maximum is life.

Guideline remarks

120.2 *R v Godward* 1998 1 Cr App R (S) 385 *at 388.* LCJ. The defendant pleaded guilty to obstructing the Coroner. The most important factor is the intention of the accused. If it appears that the intention was to obstruct the course of justice by disposing of or concealing a body, and so making it difficult or impossible to bring home a charge against the defendant or another person, then the offence merits a sentence at the top end of the appropriate scale.

Obstructing the Coroner

120.3 *R v Godward* 1998 1 Cr App R (S) 385. LCJ. The defendant pleaded guilty to obstructing the Coroner. She complained to the police that her boyfriend who had recently been released from prison had broken into her flat. Officers visited the flat and noticed a strong smell and discovered a body in a cupboard. It had been there for over five months. Parts were severely decomposed and it was infested with maggots and flies. The hands of the deceased were tied behind his back with cords, which secured a bloodstained towel. He was wearing only a vest and socks and there were slash marks. In the cupboard was a pair of bloodstained trousers. Pathologists found no fractures or wounds to the body and there were no signs of a heart attack or stroke. It was impossible to certify a cause of death. The deceased was 51 and he had had a sexual relationship with the defendant. There was evidence that the defendant was violent and domineering towards him. The defendant said she left him in her house with a prostitute and another woman and returned to find the deceased slumped on the floor. She realised that he was dead and she and one of the women put him in a cupboard. She was in a state of blind shock and panic. Before the body was found police had twice called on her when they were trying to trace him after he was reported missing. The judge said he did not accept her explanation and that there had been some form of violence but she was not necessarily involved in it. Held. It was not possible to infer that her intention was to conceal from the authorities that violence had occurred. It is at least possible and perhaps more likely that the defendant's intention was shock and panic. There was persuasive evidence that the smell had preyed on her imagination and had been a form of torment. **3 years** not 4.

Disposing of/concealing body after drug overdose

120.4 *R v Peddler* 2000 2 Cr App R (S) 36. The defendant, a heroin addict, pleaded guilty to preventing the burial of a corpse. Residents complained of a foul odour at his flat and the police attended and found a badly decomposing body. It was estimated death had taken place six weeks before. The defendant said the deceased had wanted heroin and may have used his syringe, which contained heroin of great strength. He said he was frightened because the circumstances were similar to those when his wife died. He was 37 and had a long list of previous convictions. Held. 18 months was appropriate. However, because he had now rehabilitated himself from drugs and his partner had MS, **12 months** not 18.

R v Whiteley 2001 2 Cr App R (S) 119. The defendant, a heroin addict, pleaded guilty to conspiracy to prevent the burial of a corpse. He also failed to answer his bail for which he received 3 months consecutive. The deceased, D, a heroin addict, and recently released from prison arrived at a block of flats either drunk or under the influence of drugs. He was unsteady, muddled and drowsy. At 10.30 pm a neighbour heard an occupant of the flat of his girlfriend say, 'Take him out of the flats.' Later she heard an occupant say he was unable to move D. She next saw D being dragged to a green at the rear of the flats. His body was next taken wrapped in a carpet, curtain and newspapers to a ditch in a country lane. He was found three days later and death had been caused by opiate poisoning. The flat was described as a drugs den. The defendant was arrested and said they panicked and he had bought a car to dispose of the body. He had also helped with the wrapping of the body. He was 35 and had two drug convictions and a conviction for possession of a bladed article. Held. It was a serious offence capable of interfering with the administration of justice and causing real grief to the bereaved. As the defendant was not present at the time of the death, so didn't make the initial decision and because he had fewer convictions and played a lesser role than his co-defendant who received 30 months, **18 months** not 30.

R v Munday 2003 1 Cr App R (S) 623. The defendant made an early plea to preventing the burial of a body and to burglary. The victim J, met C who was a heroin addict and formed a relationship with him. The victim moved into accommodation with C and the defendant. The victim was last seen about a year later. Enquiries led the police to the defendant who, after initially denying it, admitted his involvement about a month later. He said that one night after a good deal of drink and drugs he had fallen asleep. He was told by C the next morning that the victim had died as a result of a heroin overdose. She was 21 and had taken heroin the night before for the first time in her life. C prevailed upon the defendant to obtain a car to transport the body to a place where it could be disposed of. The body was taken to a wooded area where C had dug a shallow grave and buried the body. The defendant's role was limited to sitting in the car shining the headlights at the scene. Police officers took the defendant to the scene and a subsequent postmortem confirmed that she had died of a heroin overdose. C later pleaded guilty to manslaughter on the basis that he knew that the victim was suffering and possibly on the point of dying; he recognised the need to call an ambulance but did nothing. He received 5 years. The burglary was of an unoccupied dwelling committed at night. £700 of goods was stolen. The defendant's fingerprints were found inside but in his interview he denied his involvement. He then changed his account and said that he had gone to the premises and waited in the car whilst his companion had committed the burglary. The sentencing judge read out part of the statement of the victim's mother. 'I cry every single day. These things will never leave us. Neither will the feeling of horror and sadness we all feel for the loss of [J], and the way she was treated with such disrespect by being left in that lay-by while the people responsible just got on with their lives as though nothing had happened, and we were going out of our minds with worry.' The defendant was 31 with convictions going back to 1995 predominantly for dishonesty. He was in breach of his licence for a 2 year sentence for two burglary charges and two theft charges. He was sentenced on the basis he acted to avoid being implicated in these events. Held. The proper sentence following a plea of guilty is $2^1/_2$ years. That sentence remains consecutive to the 2 years imposed (unaltered) for the burglary and consecutive to the 243 days' for the recall. **$4^1/_2$ years** (plus recall) not 6 years (plus recall).

R v Butterworth 2004 1 Cr App R (S) 255. The defendant pleaded guilty to obstructing the coroner. He and others were taking drugs at his address. One of them died and the defendant said he didn't want to call an ambulance. The deceased's girlfriend protested but she was overruled. After dark the body was taken to a nearby playing field. The clothing was removed and other clothing was put on the body. After the defendant had come back from work the girlfriend tried to change the defendant's mind. He threatened her. The next day the body was found and the girlfriend made a statement to the police about it. He was 39. Held. The offence was committed to avoid the detection of drug offences. It was aggravated by the attempt to remove forensic evidence. It was callous and offensive to the friends and family of the deceased. **3 years** not 3 years 10 months.

See **PERVERTING THE COURSE OF JUSTICE/CONTEMPT OF COURT/PERJURY ETC –** *Evidence, interfering with – Bodies*

OBSTRUCTIONS ON A RAILWAY LINE, PLACING

See **RAILWAY OFFENCES**

OBTAINING PROPERTY AND SERVICES BY DECEPTION

See **DECEPTION, OBTAINING PROPERTY AND SERVICES BY**. Where the offence is in essence theft the case is listed under **THEFT ETC**

121   OFFENCES AGAINST THE PERSON ACT 1861 S 18

121.1   Wounding or causing grievous bodily harm with intent to do some grievous bodily harm or with intent to resist or prevent the lawful apprehension or detainer of any person.

Indictable only. Maximum sentence life.

There is a new offence of committing an offence with intent to commit a sexual offence, see Sexual Offences Act 2003 s 62.

CHAPTERS in this book are in bold capitals. The ***paragraph titles*** are in bold italics. Where a chapter (e.g. arson) has subsections, the **subsections** are in lower case bold.

Anti-Social Behavioural orders Where the defendant has acted in a manner than caused or was likely to cause harassment, alarm or distress to one or more persons not in the same household as the defendant and it is necessary to protect persons from further anti-social acts by him/her the court may make this order[2].

Automatic life For offences committed before 4/4/05, section 18 is a specified offence for automatic life[3].

Dangerous Offender provisions For offences committed on or after 4/4/05 where there is a significant risk to members of the public of serious harm etc. there is a mandatory duty to pass a life sentence when it is justified and otherwise a sentence of imprisonment for public protection[4]. For offenders under 18 the duty is to pass detention for life, detention for public protection or an extended sentence[5].

Football Where the offence was committed relevant to a football match and where there are reasonable grounds to believe that making a banning order would help to prevent violence or disorder at or in connection with any regulated football match; the court must make a Football Banning Order, under the Football Spectators Act 1989 s 14A and Sch 1, para 1.

Licensed premises Where the offence is committed on licensed premises the court may prohibit the defendant from entering those premises or any other specified premises without the express consent of the licensee or his agent[6]. The order shall last from 3 months to 2 years[7].

Longer than commensurate sentences and extended sentences It is a violent offence[8] for the purposes of passing a longer than commensurate sentence [Powers of

---

2   Crime and Disorder Act 1998 s 1C
3   Powers of Criminal Courts (Sentencing) Act 2000 s 109(5)
4   Criminal Justice Act 2003 s 225
5   Criminal Justice Act 2003 s 226 and 228
6   Licensed Premises (Exclusion of Certain Persons) Act 1980 s 1(1)
7   Licensed Premises (Exclusion of Certain Persons) Act 1980 s 1(3)
8   Powers of Criminal Courts (Sentencing) Act 2000 s 161(3)

Criminal Courts (Sentencing) Act 2000 s 80(2)] and an extended sentence (extending the licence) [Powers of Criminal Courts (Sentencing) Act 2000 s 85(2)(b)]. The orders cannot be made for offences committed before 30/9/98 or after 3/4/05.

Sexual Offences Prevention Order There is a discretionary power to make this order when it is necessary to protect the public etc[9].

Working with children Where the offence is against a child (aged under 18), the defendant is aged 18 or over and s/he is sentenced to 12 months or more or a hospital order etc. the court <u>must</u> disqualify him/her from working with children unless satisfied s/he is unlikely to commit any further offences against a child when the court must state its reasons for not doing so[10]. For a defendant aged less than 18 at the time of the offence the court must order disqualification if s/he is sentenced to 12 months or more and the court is satisfied that the defendant will commit a further offence against a child[11]. The court must state its reasons for so doing.

The division of the cases into categories does not mean that each category has its own sentencing tariff. The number of categories only indicates how many cases have been reported recently.

Crown Court statistics – England and Wales – Males 21+ – "Wounding or other act endangering life"
121.2

Year	Plea	Total Numbers sentenced	Type of sentence %					Average length of custody (months)
			Discharge	Fine	Community sentence	Suspended sentence	Custody	
2002	Guilty	624	1	–	3	1	92	50.7
	Not guilty	405	–	–	2	0	96	60.5
2003	Guilty	585	0	0	4	2	90	46.9
	Not guilty	426	0	0	1	0	94	57.7

For details and explanations about the statistics in the book see page vii

121.3   *Guideline remarks*
Att-Gen's Ref. No 44 of 1994 1995 16 Cr App R (S) 865. LCJ. The general level of sentencing for an offence under s 18 is of the order of 4 years and upwards. It is frequently a misconception that unless some object is held in the hand, no weapon has been used. An attacker who uses shod feet, or who bites someone is just as much using a weapon as someone who wields an object in his hand.

Att-Gen's Ref. Nos. 59, 60 & 63 of 1998 1999 2 Cr App R (S) 128. LCJ All offences under s 18 are serious because they involve the deliberate or intentional causing of serious injury. Some instances are more serious than others: the use of a firearm, a razor, a knife, a broken bottle, a club, a baseball bat, or a pick helve, or something of that sort, has usually been held to aggravate the offence. The courts have also, however, been obliged to recognise that injuries of almost equal seriousness can be caused by kicking with a shod foot or biting. It is also of course possible to inflict serious injury with the bare fist, although this is usually regarded as less serious, partly because in that instance the offender may lack the premeditation usually shown by a defendant who has armed himself with a dangerous weapon. Perhaps the least inexcusable example of an offence

9 Sexual Offences Act 2003 s 104 & Sch. 5
10 Criminal Justice and Court Services Act 2000 s 28
11 Criminal Justice and Court Services Act 2000 s 29

under s 18 is where a defendant entitled to defend himself responds with unreasonable and excessive force directed against an aggressor. Even then a custodial sentence, probably of some length, will usually be appropriate. In any other case a custodial sentence will almost invariably follow.

Att-Gen's Ref. No 29 of 2001 2002 1 Cr App R (S) 253. A sentence of only 18 months, without the benefit of a plea will only be merited in the most exceptional circumstances. The essence of the offence which marks it out for a substantial custodial sentence is the specific intent to do serious bodily harm, which even in cases of provocation or stress simply cannot be excused. In s 18 cases the court is less flexible in its approach than in relation to lesser assaults and is much less inclined to leniency in the face of personal mitigation. Nonetheless in appropriate cases, the courts will be merciful and sentences towards the bottom end of a wide ranging band which is likely to range between **2¹/₂ years** when the injury is relatively minor, and the circumstances of the offence and the defendant deserving of leniency, **up to as much as 10 years** in the case of horrific or sadistic injuries where mitigating circumstances are absent.

Acid etc attack

121.4   *R v Newton* 1999 1 Cr App R (S) 438. The defendant was convicted of GBH with intent and robbery. The defendant was having extreme difficulty in coming to terms with the separation from his wife. He bought paint stripper and was warned it would burn. He discussed it with the safety officer at work. It contained phenol capable of causing serious burns to skin and eyes. He added hydrochloric acid to the mixture and put it in a Flash bathroom cleaner bottle. It was potentially cancer inducing. He went to the shop where his wife worked on a motor cycle wearing a motor cycle helmet, balaclava and gloves. He paid for a packet of cigarettes and when the wife opened the till he squirted the mixture into her face. She ran to the storeroom and he followed her. He sprayed more of the mixture on her front, head and back. He ran back into the shop and stole £65 and some cheques. The wife was in extreme pain. The burns covered about 10% of her body. She was in hospital for 5 days. Her burns healed remarkably well. After the police had released the defendant, an anonymous letter was received by the police saying he would be attacked. He staged a fake attack on himself. The judge described him as evil, vengeful and scheming. He had no previous convictions. **12 years** for the GBH not 15 and 8 not 10 concurrent for the robbery.

R v Jones 1999 1 Cr App R (S) 473. The defendant was convicted of GBH with intent and false imprisonment. In a gangland feud the defendant was seeking revenge. The defendant, the victim and others were involved in a substantial credit card fraud. He maintained that the victim owed him several thousand pounds and made an attempt to recover it. The victim stopped his car to make a telephone call. The defendant spayed him with acid from a squeezy bottle shouting abuse. The victim tried to run away and the defendant followed squirting the acid over his face and arms. The victim was put in his car and questioned about the money while the car was being driven. His requests to be taken to hospital were ignored. The defendant jumped out at some traffic lights. The acid had ³/₄ hour to wreak havoc on his face. He had extensive full thickness burns and the loss possibly permanently of an eye. The defendant was 30 and had nine court appearances for criminal damage, burglary, theft, drugs, two ABH and other matters. The defendant was sentenced for conspiracy to defraud for the credit card offences and possession of a loaded firearm and received 4 years imprisonment. Held. **16 years** for the GBH was in the proper range for such a determined, remorseless and vicious attack. The fact the victim was a former confederate does not necessarily entitle him to a discount. However, the sentence should have been concurrent not consecutive to the 4 years.

R v Carrington 1999 2 Cr App R (S) 206. The defendant was convicted of GBH with intent. The victim and the defendant lived together for almost 6 years. She asked him to leave her flat, which he did. He agreed to pay his contribution to the bills. The following day he visited her and she was unrelenting. She asked him to leave and he became rather upset. Some time later he approached her when she was on the way to work. He said he wanted to talk to her. She stepped back, saw a Lucozade bottle and liquid was thrown on her face. She ran into her work place and colleagues doused her face with water. She spent 1 week in hospital. Gradually her eyes improved and she no longer suffers from any disability. She was expected to have eye discomfort up to 8 to 11 months after the attack. For a period after that they would feel abnormal. The damage to her clothing was consistent with sulphuric acid. Had she not received prompt assistance there could have been very severe consequences for her sight. The defendant was 57 and showed no remorse. 9 years previously he had a conviction for ABH on his wife. Held. Despite his ill health **6 years** was appropriate.

R v Rai and Robinson 2000 2 Cr App R (S) 120. The defendants K and E were convicted of conspiracy to commit GBH with intent. E was also convicted of GBH. K's girlfriend broke off the relationship when he went to prison because she did not want to mix with criminals. He would not accept it was over and pestered her and her family over the telephone. The calls also contained threats, like, 'If I can't have you, then no-one can'. On his release he was warned by the police to stay away from her. He continued to call her and was twice more warned. To stop him calling she said she was going to marry someone else but he followed her and drove past her when she was in the street. She walked to work and E who had been in prison with K threw concentrated nitric acid over her from a bottle. Perhaps anticipating the attack she moved her head and the acid hit the side of her head. The side of her head and her neck dissolved. She suffered the most acute agony. She was taken to hospital and she lost her right ear with significant scarring to her face, neck, scalp and chest. Her facial appearance was altered. Seven months later K called her again. The judge passed longer than commensurate sentence of 15 years. He did not state that the reason was their propensity to violence. Held. The injuries were horrific. It was unnecessary to extend the sentence as **15 years** was not inappropriate. (The previous convictions were not listed.)

Baseball bat, bottle (unbroken), plank of wood etc

121.5   *Att-Gen's Ref. No 56 of 2000* 2001 1 Cr App R (S) 439. The defendant was convicted of wounding with intent. The victim after drinking went to stay in someone's house and among others there was the defendant aged 27 whose group had also been drinking. That group was watching an adults only channel on television which caused some embarrassment to the women in the victim's group. There was an atmosphere, which led to words being exchanged. The victim and one of the women went into the garden. After a while one of the women complained that the defendant had tried to kiss her. The victim told the defendant that he should leave the house. There was a baseball bat by the front door. At some stage, the victim picked up the baseball bat and took it outside. An argument developed about some property being taken to the garden where some people were going to sleep. The baseball bat was passed to the victim and then seized by the defendant. The defendant then struck the victim on the head with the bat three times, twice when he was on the ground. One of the women tried to get between the defendant and the victim, but the defendant side-stepped her and kicked the victim in the stomach. The victim had two wounds, one 10 cm long and the other 6 cm long, which required stitching. He had bruising on his arm. The judge accepted that the offender had struck the first blow in the mistaken belief that the victim had been intending to hit him with the bat. The offender was of good character and had expressed remorse. He was sentenced to 200 hours' community service and £1,500 compensation. He had carried out just over 160 hours' community service. Held. We would have expected a sentence within the bracket of **2 to 3 years**. Taking into account it was a reference and one where he will now loose his liberty for the first time and he had performed a substantial amount of the community service **9 months** substituted with the outstanding amount of the compensation quashed.

Att-Gen's Ref. No 31 etc. of 2004 Re DB 2005 1 Cr App Rep (S) 377 at 386. The defendant DLB was convicted of wounding with intent to do GBH. The victim and a friend were in the town centre when they passed a group of four to five young men including the defendant. One of the defendant's group said "Are you going to bottle him?" The defendant, who was holding a glass bottle, chased the victim into a chip shop. He pushed the victim against the counter and hit him a number of times on the head, shoulders and upper body with the bottle. The defendant then left without the bottle (which had remained intact). The victim was bleeding and was taken to A and E where he was treated with staples for a 2 cm and a 1.5 cm cut to his head. He also had pain in the right shoulder and hand. He recovered physically but remained wary of the defendant and his associates. Three months after the incident, the defendant approached the victim and said that he had got the wrong person. He gave his details to the victim and was later arrested. In interview he said that he had got the wrong person and that he did not realise that he had the bottle in his hand. He was 20 with previous convictions for driving offences including aggravated vehicle taking for which he received a CRO. Held. This was an unprovoked attack upon an innocent victim who suffered head injuries. He had chased and cornered the victim and had used a bottle to reign repeated blows. $3^1/_2$ **years** would have been the correct sentence. $2^1/_2$ **years** as this was a reference, not 2 years CRO.

Biting   See Fighting – *Biting*

Blackmail, and   See Blackmail – *Serious violence inflicted*

Burglary, and – See *Robbery/burglary/aggravated burglary, and*

Children against   See Cruelty to Children – *Offences Against the Person Act 1861 s 18*

Crime of passion   See *Passion, crime of/emotional attack and Relationship attacks*

Defendants aged under 21 – Guidelines

121.7   *Att-Gen's Ref. Nos. 59, 60 & 63 of 1998* 1999 2 Cr App R (S) 128. LCJ In sentencing young offenders the court will of course have regard to the welfare principle expressed in s 44 of the Children and Young Persons Act 1933: the younger the offender the less the justification in any ordinary case for treating the offender exactly as if he or she were an adult. It must be recognised that an effective means of protecting the public in the future is to reform a criminal whether young or old. Sentencers must, however, always bear in mind that the welfare of the young offender is never the only consideration to be taken into account. When an offender, however young, deliberately inflicts serious injury on another there is a legitimate public expectation that such offender will be severely punished to bring home to him the gravity of the offence and to warn others of the risk of behaving in the same way. If such punishment does not follow, public confidence in the administration of the criminal law is weakened and the temptation arises to give offenders extra-judicially the punishment, which the formal processes of law have not given. When we speak of the public we do not forget the victim, the party who has actually suffered the injury, and those close to him. If punishment of the offender does little to heal the victim's wounds, there can be little doubt that inadequate punishment adds insult to injury.

Defendant aged under 14

121.8   *R v Haley* 1998 2 Cr App R (S) 226. The defendant pleaded guilty to GBH with intent. Two girls persuaded the victim aged 13 to go to a flat. At the flat the defendant and another were there and the victim was accused of stealing a benefit book. The defendant aged 12 and one of the girls kicked and punched the victim. The victim was threatened with a ferret and was twice burnt with a cigarette. She was given the opportunity to confess and then the kicking would start again. It lasted for about $2^1/_2$ hours until the occupier returned. The victim had severe bruising and abrasions to her head, face, back and chest. She also had burns and remains severely disturbed by the experience. The defendant had no convictions. He had had a very disturbed childhood. He was in care and had many expulsions from school because of disruptive behaviour and fighting. Held. The offence could properly be described as torture. We have considered the extreme youth of the victim and the sustained nature of the detention and the attack. **3 years** detention was upheld.

Att-Gen's Ref. Nos. 60 and 61 of 1997 1998 2 Cr App R (S) 330. The defendants were convicted of wounding with intent. The defendant W aged 12 enquired of another girl whether she had been writing things about someone. She denied it. B also 12 handed W a razor blade and said "Go on, slash her." They approached another girl aged 14 and asked her the same question. She also denied it. W hit her across the face with the razor blade. She needed 26 stitches and is permanently scarred. B had convictions. Three days before the offence a supervision order had been made for theft, two assaults with intent to resist arrest, assault on police and obstruction. Less than 3 weeks before the wounding she committed ABH and robbery. Six weeks after the wounding she committed affray. In the same month and 3 months later she committed three criminal damage offences. W had no convictions. The judge imposed a supervision order on each. W had responded well to it. Held. If they had been adults a sentence of 5 years would have been imposed. Taking into account it was a reference, B sentence increased to **18 months** detention and W's to **12 months**.

R v W. 2003 1 Cr App R (S) 502. The defendant, now 12 was convicted when he was 10 of causing GBH with intent. A woman driving saw a group of three or four boys standing over a badly injured six year old child who was obviously in great pain and fear. The child had been hit by the defendant with a piece of concrete about the size of a brick causing nasty injuries to his face including serious cuts and bruises particularly around his right eye. In addition, there had been a fire at the scene and a stick which had been burned had been applied to the child's back. The defendant had bragged about committing the offence afterwards. The child was kept in hospital for three days. The child told police that he had gone to collect balls and tried to put out a grass fire when the defendant and others arrived. There was an argument over golf balls whereupon the defendant set upon him and pushed him into the fire. Others had assaulted him too. The defendant suffered from attention deficit hyperactivity disorder, learning difficulties, a short attention span and a poorly developed short-term memory. His reading age was about half that of his actual age. His mother had done her very best and he was on medication that possibly had some side effects that resulted in the loss of control that led to the offence in question. It appeared that the local authority did not put into affect the powers that they had to produce some positive steps that would have assisted him. However, up to date reports described him as a very pleasant young man, with signs of immaturity. Held: This was a most serious offence; however, four years represented a third of his life. **3 years** not 4 detention.

Defendant aged 14–15

121.9   *R v Islam* 2002 2 Cr App R (S) 118. The defendant pleaded guilty to robbery and GBH with intent. He was acquitted of racially-aggravated GBH with intent. The victim, a 75-year-old man was walking home with a bag, which contained a flask and his cap. The defendant who was in a group of three approached him, grabbed the plastic bag and punched him. The victim struggled and he either fell or was pushed to the ground. He was then kicked in the head on a number of occasions. The victim became disorientated and confused. He was taken to hospital and he had facial swelling, a virtually closed eye, cuts over and under that eye, a broken nose, fractures to his cheekbone and both orbital rims. He had a number of operations with plates and splints inserted. He was there for 10 days and was unable to go home so went to a rest home. He needed new teeth, had problems with his balance and nose. Seven months later he had not recovered. The defendant boasted about it to friends. He was 14 with findings of guilt for ABH, battery and burglary. The pre-sentence report said he showed remorse. Held. The injuries are truly horrific. Age has to be looked at in the greatest detail. This joint attack with shoes or boots compares with those where weapons are held in their hands. **4 years** detention was in no way manifestly excessive.

R v Tabu 2002 2 Cr App R (S) 500. The defendant pleaded guilty to Section 18. The prosecution accepted a plea of not guilty to attempted murder. On a Saturday, he watched the victim repairing his car. The victim asked what he wanted and he said he was just watching. A quarter of an hour later the victim was concerned and went to close his garage door. He felt a sudden pain from the back of the head. He saw the defendant standing by him holding something. He didn't remember how many times he was hit but saw the defendant was holding a machete. The defendant ran off. The victim had a fractured skull and a severe laceration penetrating to the bone in his fore-head. There were some defence injuries. The police contacted the boy's father and the boy admitted to him that he had attacked the victim. He said he had gone to look for anyone working on the Sabbath. He said he had concealed the machete down his trousers and repeatedly hit the victim. He said he had to be "cut off." The father, Dr. Tabor told the police that he had been concerned about his son's mental state for some time and he had misquoted a section of the Bible. The boy had a very disturbed mental state. He was 15 with no convictions. There was no Mental Health Act disposal available. After the sentence, the Judge was told the boy had served 1 year on remand, which would not count, to his sentence. The reports written after the sentence said he was doing extremely well. He was now 16. Held. It was a very difficult sentencing exercise. The Judge was right to refer to the requirement for the protection of the public. **5 years** with 2 years extended licence not 7 years detention.

R v M 2003 1 Cr App R (S) 245. The defendant was convicted of Section 18. He when aged 14 and 3 months, was walking in a street with five other youths in the evening. The victim aged 38, who suffered from a disability caused by a motorbike accident, was walking the other way. The group taunted him, abused him and jostled him. As the victim walked past they threw earth and stones at him and continued to abuse him. The victim called them idiots and walked back towards them as the defendant entered a church garden broke off a stake holding a sapling and ran up behind the victim. With a baseball type swing the defendant hit him on the back of the head with the stake. There was a distinct crack and the victim lay motionless on the ground. The youths ran off. The victim had fractures to the skull and had not the hospital been near he might well have died. He was in hospital for 4 months and there was limited progress to independent living. At trial the defendant admitted the blow but denied the intent. He had a troubled background with extreme behavioural difficulties at school and elsewhere. There was theft, truanting, damage to property and fighting. He was excluded from school after fights virtually on a weekly basis and he had thrown a chair and scissors at a teacher. There was a problem with drugs. A social worker said, "He was raised in an atmosphere of abuse and intimidation. He has a tendency to meet violence with violence. He finds it near impossible to walk away when he feels under physical threat". A psychiatrist said, "He had a socialised conduct disorder and the defendant had described how he had had many fights over the years. He says he uses weapons including knives, bats, pieces of wood and bottles and he would use anything he could pick up. He also said he will not stop unless the opponent is unconscious, bleeding profusely, run off, crying on the ground or he is dragged off by his mates. The worst injuries he had inflicted were a stab, biting a man's ear off and this case. After being challenged he experiences excitement and not fear. When asked about the brain damage to the victim he said he was not really bothered about it." Another psychiatrist said he had a Severe Conduct Disorder with a high risk of committing similar offences in the future. He had convictions for theft and driving and in 2000 an affray. In 2001 there was another Section 18 offence for which he received a 6 month Detention and Training Order. He had a dispute with a boy and insulted the boy's mother. She told her partner who confronted him and the defendant initiated a brawl. He bit part of an ear off causing significant injury. The offence was committed when he was on bail for this case. The Judge in this case said he posed a very serious risk to the public. She said her duty was to protect them. Held. Where a defendant is as young as this detention for life should only be imposed in exceptional circumstances and as a last resort where there was no alternative. The defendant remains a serious danger to the community for the foreseeable future. **Detention for life** was justified. The notional determinate sentence of 7 years was not manifestly excessive. The specified period of $3^1/_2$ years was reduced by 4 months to take into account the 4 months in custody before his sentence.

Att-Gen's Ref Nos. 54–56 of 2004 2005 1 Cr App R (S) 402. The defendants S (16), G (17) and W (16) pleaded guilty to GBH with intent. G pleaded guilty three months earlier than W and S. The three approached the 14 year old victim and W took his bike and rode it away. The others followed. The victim tried to retrieve his bike. W rammed the bike into his right leg, causing him to fall. All three defendant's then began punching and kicking him about the head and body whilst the victim pleaded with them to stop. S suggested that they kill him by popping his head on some nearby spikes. After repeatedly kicking and punching him in the face they dragged him to the spiked railings. On W's suggestion they dragged him to the canal, took off his jacket, swung him backwards and forwards and threw him in. When he surfaced they threatened to throw rocks at him but he swam to the other side. His left elbow was broken in three places and he had bruising and abrasions to his face and head. Each had mitigation: S had lost his grandfather, W had lost his baby and G had pleaded guilty at the first opportunity. None of them had any previous convictions for violence; W had a poor criminal record for dishonesty. Held. This was a terrible offence, in its persistence, in the variety of violence, in the numbers involved and in its culmination. The physical injuries were serious and included multiple fractures. The appropriate sentence was **3 years detention**, but as they had been at liberty, **2 years** Detention and Training Order as this was a reference for S and G (not a CPRO), 12 month DTO for W as he had spent 7 months on remand (not counting) (not a CRO).

Old case *R v Baldwin* 1997 2 Cr App R (S) 260. (For a summary of this case see the first edition of this book).

Defendant aged 16–17 – Baseball bat, plank of wood etc

121.10 *Att-Gen's Ref. Nos. 56 and 57 of 1996* 1997 2 Cr App R (S) 286. The defendants were convicted of wounding with intent and affray. M was also convicted of common assault. The defendants M then 16 and S then 21 who were brothers spent a New Year's Eve drinking and afterwards outside S's home an argument developed between S and his girlfriend. A group of loud boisterous people who had been drinking passed the house and approached the defendants. The defendants went inside to arm themselves with a golf club and mop handle. A fight developed. They kicked one of them after he had been knocked down and was lying curled up and defenceless. They also used their weapons on him. Someone from the group tried to intervene and was attacked with the weapons with such force the head came off the club and the mop handle broke. The first victim was taken to hospital and wounds to his head, the bridge of his nose and under his eye were stitched. He also had bruises to the head, neck and shoulders. The second victim did not go to hospital and had a swollen and cut head. M told the police the group had interfered with their argument. He said the group had tried to kick in the front door. There was no damage to the door. The judge said the truth lay somewhere between the two conflicting versions and there was an element of provocation and self defence. S was on bail for one offence at the time of the offence and M two offences. S had convictions for breach of the peace and causing harassment etc. That offence related to a fight. M had no convictions when the offence took place. Since then he had pleaded guilty to attacking a fish and chip shop owner after he had accused him of being gay. He had also been convicted of affray after he and others had entered a supermarket where a member of staff was beaten up and the defendant had produced an air pistol and threatened to kill a member of staff. He was given a community sentence order for both incidents. Both were sentenced to a Community Service Order and had completed their 180 and 200 hours and M had paid the compensation of £400 ordered. Held. Making the most generous assumptions in favour of the defendants the appropriate sentence would have been between **12 and 15 months**. Because of their behaviour since and the circumstances the Community Service Orders would not be altered.

Defendant aged 16–17 – Bricks etc

121.11   *Att-Gen's Ref. No 18 of 1998* 1999 1 Cr App R (S) 142. The defendant pleaded guilty on the day after his trial was due to start to wounding with intent. He was also committed for sentence for dangerous driving and disqualified driving. At 10.30 pm outside a supermarket, the defendant then 16 approached the victim aged 18 apparently looking for a fight. A fist fight developed. The defendant picked up a brick and threw it in the victim's face causing heavy bleeding. As the victim staggered away the defendant threw the brick again into his face with full force. A friend intervened. The victim required 30 stitches. He suffered severe headaches. He was permanently scarred. He lost 2% of his vision in one eye. He feels nervous when he goes out alone. The defendant had 24 convictions for burglary, theft, criminal damage, ABH and offences in relation to motor cars. He had been sentenced to detention three times. One of the two ABH convictions was with a baseball bat on a woman. She was hit on the head and required seven stitches. He was sentenced to 1 year and 6 months consecutive for the driving offences. Held. The appropriate total was 4 years detention. As it was a reference **3 years** detention substituted.

Defendant aged 16–17 – Glassing

121.12   *Att-Gen's Ref. Nos. 36 and 37 of 1998* 1999 2 Cr App R (S) 7. The defendants L and J pleaded guilty to false imprisonment and L pleaded guilty to wounding (the October incident). J also pleaded to wounding with intent and unlawful wounding and L also pleaded guilty to affray (the September incident). In September at about 9.25 pm the defendant J then 17 picked a fight with one of a group of students and punched one of them in the mouth and face several times. He then took a bottle of beer off the victim and smashed it over his head. The students made off. L then 15 and J pursued them throwing rubbish from a skip at them. A passer-by was walking her dog and J attacked her with a broken bottle. She had a 3″ wound to her cheek and 1″ wounds to her nose and chin. For a number of weeks she could not talk properly or eat solid foods and she was off work for 9 weeks. The defendants were released on bail and about 4 weeks later at about 9 pm J and L approached a group of teenagers. J jumped on one of them aged 16, and started to struggle with him. L threatened the group, and was restrained by a member of his group. J then said to L "Come on, let's go and get the filthy Paki". J and L then followed three of them to a path running along a lake. J and L forced the three to climb over the gate into the park and threatened to "batter" or kill them. Once in the park the three were forced to sit upon a bench. J punched one of them in the face and pushed a lighted cigarette into his face causing burn marks. L forced him against a tree, and J said he was going to kill him. The three were terrified and ran away, with L in pursuit. One climbed over some spiked railings, and suffered a 5 cm and 2 cm cut to his thigh. Both were deep. This was L's wounding charge. One of the three managed to run away and the third was forced by J and L to walk across the park until he too escaped. The three teenagers were so terrified that they were unable to estimate the period of time during which they had been detained. Both J and L were arrested and when interviewed disputed the victims' account of events. J had an ABH conviction involving an attack with two others on a man in the early hours. The man was knocked to the ground, kicked and punched. J had also been cautioned for affray and assaulting a police officer. J had a serious history of drug and alcohol abuse. J received $3^{1}/_{2}$ years for the wounding with intent and 6 months for the false imprisonment. Held. The intimidation of the teenagers was deliberate and sustained and the offence had a very unpleasant racist overtone, which demanded immediate custody. Had J pleaded not guilty a total of **7 years** detention would have been appropriate for the s 18 and false imprisonment offences. On a plea of guilty **5 years** would have been merited. Taking into account it was a reference and the false imprisonment **4 years** detention for the s 18 offence.

Att-Gen's Ref. Nos. 59, 60 & 63 of 1998 Re O'Brien 1999 2 Cr App R (S) 128. LCJ. The defendant, O was convicted of GBH with intent. The victim challenged O about some rumours O was said to have spread. O denied the matter and the victim became annoyed. The victim then punched O in the face and a fight began. After a few minutes the victim and O became tired and stopped. The victim had had the better of the fight. O, nursing a cut lip, entered a local shop in a "very excited mood" and asked to borrow a toy cricket bat so that he could hit someone with it. He left the shop empty-handed. O then approached the victim, holding an empty beer bottle, which he broke against a lamp-post and then ran at the victim, holding it. The victim ran but fell. O caught up with him and stabbed him more than once to the body using the broken bottle, causing immediate heavy bleeding. Someone pulled O back and O ran. Two builders ran to the victim's assistance and he was taken to hospital in their van. He had a $^{1}/_{2}$ cm cut to his arm, a 4 cm superficial laceration to his chest and a deep laceration to his left armpit. He had lost a substantial amount of blood. The main artery to the arm had two large wounds in it and the main vein to the arm was completely divided, as were several major nerves, which provided nerve supply to the left arm. His operation lasted some 5 hours. The armpit wound was life threatening. The prompt actions of the builders helped to prevent a fatal consequence. The victim remained in hospital for a week. On his discharge he was unable to use his left arm, which was devoid of any feeling. He continues to be disabled with regard to his arm. He has had to learn to write with his other hand and is permanently scarred. O admitted that he had been involved but contended that it was self-defence. O had one conviction when 14 for robbery. He had shown remorse and had a good employment record. O received a £1,000 compensation and combination order. Since the sentence favourable reports had been received. Held. Following a contested trial the appropriate sentence, even for someone of this age, would have been **5 years** detention. It was right to make a very substantial reduction to reflect the efforts, which the offender has undoubtedly made. **3 years** detention substituted. The compensation order was quashed.

Att-Gen's Ref. No 28 of 2004 2005 1 Cr App R (S) 163. The defendant pleaded guilty to wounding with intent to do GBH. The 23-year-old victim was standing outside a nightclub with his female cousin and a friend when the defendant, who was very drunk, and another youth approached them. There was an exchange of words, the cousin ran back to the nightclub for help, and the victim got between his friend and the defendant to try and calm things down. The defendant took hold of the victim's arm and held it while he pushed a broken bottle into the victim's face at least six times. The victim had cuts to face and arm. The wounds needed twenty stitches and gluing, and he suffered the following day from post concussion syndrome. There was a victim impact statement which said that he had visible scars on his head and face, his hair had not grown back over a wound to his eyebrow and he was very self conscious about his scarring. He had lost social confidence, was nervous about going out on his own and did not sleep properly. The defendant, 17 at the time of the offence, had a substantial criminal record of over thirty offences, including for common assault, arson being reckless as to whether or not life would be endangered, ABH, and offences contrary to section 4 and 6 of the Public Order Act. It was said some remorse was demonstrated and he had a difficult background. His father died when he was three and after that his mother had been in a psychiatric hospital. In custody he had completed a course and was taking an anger management course. Held. The judge was too influenced by the defendant's personal circumstances and paid too little regard to the gravity of defendant's conduct in repeatedly using a broken bottle to the face of an entirely innocent victim at night in the street. The appropriate sentence would have been **4 years** detention. Taking into account double jeopardy **3** years detention not 18 month DTO.

Defendant aged 16–17 – Kicking man on ground

121.13   *R v Robinson and McManus* 1998 1 Cr App R (S) 72. The defendant M pleaded guilty to GBH with intent. The defendant R pleaded guilty to just GBH. The white defendants who were drunk came across the victim who was black walking home from work. M aged 16 ran after him and knocked him out of the way. He was raving and shouting. R aged 18 started pushing him in the chest and grabbing his suit lapels. As he wouldn't let go the victim took a swing at him. R still would not go and a fight ensued. The victim was knocked out. A witness saw M punch him to the ground and kick him in the head. The witness moved in between them. Punches were thrown at him and the M continued to kick the victim. The witness ran and was chased by R. M then jumped on the victim's head. The victim required 22 stitches to his head and face. He had multiple lacerations round the eye. There was a danger his retina might become detached. His scarring to his right eye might be permanent. His headaches and vertigo would take several months to resolve. He was afraid to leave his home. R's plea was based on a late participation in the joint enterprise and preventing the witness from assisting the victim. Held. It wasn't racially motivated but it was horrific. Taking into account the mitigation particularly the remorse **4 years** detention not **3** for M and **2 years** not **3** for R.

R v Bevan 2003 2 Cr App R (S) 311. The defendant was convicted of causing grievous bodily harm with intent. At about 10 pm two 16-year-olds were on their way to meet a friend when they came across the defendant and another, R. All four were the same age and attended the same school. They chatted and the four walked on together. The defendant and R took it in turns to drink from bottle of vodka and coke. The four eventually reached some playing fields where the victim, aged 58, was walking towards them. R asked him for cigarette and the man replied that he did not smoke and continued walking. R walked with him and suddenly punched him hard to the side of his head and he fell. At that point the defendant ran over and kicked him four or five times as he tried to get up. R stood and watched. The other two called to the defendant to stop, which he did. The victim was lying on the ground trying to shield himself. R then began to kick the victim hard about the head and face and this continued for some time. The defendant stood by. R ignored the shouts of the other 2. R bent down to the unconscious victim, felt for a pulse and commented that he was still breathing. The victim was left lying on his back in the field seriously injured. About 3 hours later, a passer-by telephoned for an ambulance after finding the victim barely conscious. He was in a coma and had multiple injuries about the head and face, right wrist and right eye. It was suspected that he suffered brain damage. He had severe facial bruising, a fractured nose and was unable to open his right eye. He suffered post-traumatic amnesia. Following his eventual discharge his family noticed personality, behavioural and cognitive changes with memory and attentional problems. Acute anxiety prevented him from walking outside in the dark. He was diagnosed with left frontal brain damage that affected the right side of his body. There was significant deficit in his ability to move $6^1/_2$ months after the attack. Speech was still badly affected 2 years later. He was told that he would only ever be 80% of the person he had once been and that that would take at least 9 years from the attack. The injuries caused considerable distress to his family. He was receiving a raft of different therapies. The day after the attack the defendant handed himself in to the police. He said in interview that he went to help R and had kicked the victim a number of times. He was 16 and of effectively good character and the risk of re-offending was perceived to be low. Held. This was a terrible attack. Notwithstanding the good character and youth of the defendant, the sentence, following a trial was appropriate. **6 years** detention upheld.

Old case. *Att-Gen's Ref. No 51 of 1996* 1997 2 Cr App R (S) 248, for a summary of this case see the first edition of this book.

Defendant aged 16–17 – Knives

121.14 *Att-Gen's Ref. Nos. 30 and 31 of 1998* 1999 1 Cr App R (S) 200. The defendants pleaded to GBH with intent. At 10.30 pm, the defendant K then 16 who was with 15–20 other youths in the street, ran towards the victim. K challenged him about an earlier incident and held him in a headlock. K punched him several times on the head and held his hands while others struck him. G also hit him with a crutch. The victim fell to the ground and G hit him across the back of the head with a crutch. K kicked him on the head. K jumped in the air and landed with both feet on the victim's head. Others asked him to stop and he carried on. It only stopped when someone said he had been killed. An ambulance arrived and his pulse was found to be weak. There were no fractures or brain damage. He was confused. He had bruising, lacerations and grazing. He was in hospital for 2 weeks. He had unreliable memory problems. He required psychiatric counselling. He made a remarkable complete physical recovery. G admitted punching him five or six times and kicking him in the face. G had a conviction for damaging property. K had convictions for common assault, handling, burglary, damaging property and possession of an offensive weapon. He had had a short sentence of detention. Held. Taking into account the ages of the defendants, the mitigation, the plea and it was a reference K **21 months** detention and G **12 months** detention not 8 and 4 months.

Att-Gen's Ref. Nos. 59, 60 & 63 of 1998 Re Hussein 1999 2 Cr App R (S) 128. LCJ. The defendant Hussein, H pleaded guilty to wounding with intent. H aged 16 and the victim aged 17 attended the same school. They were both queuing up for lunch and H pushed in front of the victim and others in the queue. The victim objected and a teacher intervened H was told to leave. Both H and the victim swore at each other. Then H left threatening to hit the victim. A teacher spent 10 minutes trying to calm him down. After lunch H confronted the victim and challenged him to a fight. The victim was reassured by H and his friends that it would only be a fist fight involving the two of them. One of the H's friends assured the victim that H did not have a knife. H raised his open hands in the air to confirm that that was so. H and the victim then walked to a small car park followed by a large group of other pupils wanting to watch the fight. A fist fight started. The victim appeared to be getting the better of H, which involved punching and kicking. three of H's friends tried to join in by kicking out at the victim. They were, however, stopped by the others. The victim, fearing that the offender's friends would try and join in again, decided to stop the fight. He turned away from H to return to school. H produced a knife, which he had concealed in his clothing, and he stabbed the victim in the back with it. The victim immediately ran off, pursued initially by the offender and ran down onto a railway track in order to escape. He was found slumped at the side of the track in a semi-conscious state. The victim had a single stab wound to his back. The knife had penetrated the chest and cut the lung, causing severe internal bleeding. The victim was left with a permanent and disfiguring scar to his back. H's record contained some minor offences of theft. H had spent 5 months in a secure unit and had shown "a good deal of remorse". He had responded well to that. H was sentenced to a supervision order with attendance at a Youth Justice Centre. The Centre said H's attendance had been excellent, both for his time keeping and his level of participation. Held. The proper order on a plea of not guilty would have been of the order of **4¹/₂ years** detention. For a plea of guilty the appropriate sentence would have been **3¹/₂ years** detention. Because of H's progress **2¹/₂ years** substituted.

Att-Gen's Ref. No 75 of 1999 2000 2 Cr App R (S) 146. LCJ. The defendant was convicted of wounding with intent. The victim aged 40 left a shop with his young son and heard the defendant's friend swearing. He asked him to be quiet and the defendant aged 17 and his friend told him to "Fuck off." The victim asked again for them not to use such language in earshot of his son. The defendant ran up to the victim and a scuffle ensued. The victim tried to defend himself. The victim was held in a headlock and was punched three or four times to the head. They fell to the ground. They got up and the defendant crouched in front of the victim and began swaying as the friend shouted encouragement. The two youths then walked away. They were very drunk. The son was very upset. The victim was bleeding profusely. The defendant was then heard to boast he had laid into the man with a knife. The knife was thrown onto some waste ground. The victim had a 2 cm cut and there was haematoma. He was in hospital for 2 days and a month later he had to have an operation to remove a blood clot. The defendant had no previous convictions for violence and had not served a custodial sentence. The juvenile centre where he was detained spoke highly of him. Held. **4 years** would have been appropriate. Taking into account the mitigation and it was a reference **3 years** detention not 15 months.

R v Reed 2002 1 Cr App R (S) 219. The defendant pleaded guilty to wounding with intent. The victim with friends visited a number of pubs and in one saw the defendant aged 17 looking through a window at one of them. He had been to school with her and she tried to ignore him. The group left the pub and saw the defendant with his friends waiting outside. The defendant's group set about trying to provoke a fight. The victim's group made it clear they were not interested. With no provocation the victim was stabbed in the chest. He then sat on the ground and was kicked in the face. Fortunately there was an ambulance nearby and he was rushed to hospital. He had a stab wound to the lower chest and his chest wall was penetrated. He was in hospital for a week and then had to be re-admitted in a serious condition four days later in severe pain. He then remained in hospital for three weeks. The defendant was arrested and said he took the knife in case he met a group he disapproved of. He said he just swung and hit the victim. He did not suggest the victim was any threat to him. He was in breach of a conditional discharge for obstructing the police and threatening behaviour. The risk of re-offending was assessed as high. He had a favourable prison report although he had been involved in a fight. Held. We bear in mind his age. It was sheer good fortune the injury was not life threatening. He deliberately set out armed with a knife looking for a fight. Too many young men have knives all too ready to use them on innocent members of the public. Offences of this kind are far too prevalent. **4 years** was not excessive.

See also *R v B* 2005 Unreported 11/2/05 Early plea. Cut from the hairline to just above the top lip. Then striking out at the victim 3 or 4 times causing a 1″ laceration. 45 stitches. Because of plea and age **4 years'** detention not 5.

Defendant aged 16–17 – Punishing the victim, motive to

121.15   *Att-Gen's Ref. No 25 of 1998* 1999 1 Cr App R (S) 351. The defendant was

convicted of GBH with intent. The victim aged then 16 parked his caravanette in the street and it was damaged. The victim sought to discover the culprit and was told it was the defendant. He and two male friends approached the defendant and the situation escalated. The defendant went into his house and came back armed with a sword and struck the two friends. Neither was cut. The victim and the two friends left to play golf and returned with the victim's uncle and a golf club. Words were exchanged and the golf club was put on the ground. The victim asked the defendant to come round the corner to talk. The defendant then struck the victim in the face with the club. A large area of skin was gouged out and the jawbone was broken. He was in hospital for three days. Six metal plates were inserted in his face to repair the fractures. He will be permanently scarred and have shooting pains. The defendant maintained it was self-defence. He had two convictions for ABH, an assault on police and various offences of dishonesty. Before trial he was convicted of burglary and theft. He was sentenced on the basis he felt threatened. Held. Because of the defendant's age, the fact he felt threatened and other mitigation the sentence of **18 months** detention was not unduly lenient.

Defendant aged 16–17 – Robbery/Burglary/Aggravated burglary, and

121.16 *R v Mills* 1998 Re Holder 2 Cr App R (S) 128 at 143. LCJ. The defendant pleaded guilty at the earliest opportunity to wounding with intent. In the early hours he when 16 broke into the home of a couple in their mid 70s. He took a large knife from the kitchen went upstairs and confronted the man who had been disturbed. He demanded money and told the man not to look at him. The wife appeared and he pointed the knife at the man's temple. The man tried to persuade him there was no money. He ignored this and continued intimidating the couple. He started searching and became increasingly aggressive and threatening telling them he would kill them. It seems that he made as if to stab the woman and her husband pushed her backwards and tried to avoid the knife. The man managed to seize the defendant's wrist for a minute and shortly after the defendant left with money and jewellery. In fact the man had been stabbed and he collapsed. He had a punctured lung with injuries to his head and back. He was in hospital for eight days. The defendant claimed to be very drunk at the time and he had a problem with alcohol. He showed little remorse. The defendant was unemployed with nine findings of guilt mostly for theft and criminal damage. Held. He had menaced this couple and the man was fortunate to survive. **9 years** was entirely appropriate.

Att-Gen's Ref. Nos. 33 of 2000 2001 1 Cr App R (S) 355. The defendant pleaded guilty at a late stage to wounding with intent. He was also committed for sentence for burglary and handling. The defendant entered the flat of a vulnerable man who was something of a recluse through an unlocked door at 1.00 am. The man had an artificial leg, was of low intellect and suffered from depression. He was too frightened to sleep in the bedroom because it had been broken into before. The defendant entered the living room where the victim was and started to shout abuse. The victim went into the bedroom and the defendant followed. The defendant hit the victim with his walking stick until the stick broke. The victim retreated into the kitchen and the defendant followed repeatedly shouting, "Motherfucker." The victim was struck with a saucepan and a crutch. The victim escaped to the front garden and the defendant followed again and attacked him with fists and feet. The blows were aimed at his head and shoulders. The victim fell and the defendant aimed a kick at his head and a neighbour intervened. The neighbour went to call an ambulance and the defendant renewed the attack by running over his body and kicking him. He then left and told a friend a false story to explain his lack of shirt, which was not believed. He took the friend to the front garden and showed him the victims motionless body. He continued to call the victim "Motherfucker." The victim had extensive bruising to the head, face, trunk and arm with other bruising. He had a 2 cm laceration on his forehead, which required stitching. Four ribs were fractured. A psychiatrist said the offence had had a serious impact upon his social functioning. He had to be moved to hospital as a place of safety. The defendant was just 16 and on bail at the time. He had three convictions and since the offence he was given a conditional discharge for possession of a bladed weapon, criminal damage and failure to surrender. He showed some signs of remorse. Held. This was a very serious offence because the victim was vulnerable, he was attacked at home, a variety of weapons were used, the attack was sustained and in different areas, there were serious consequences for the victim's physical and mental health and he was on bail. We would have expected **5 years** detention. Taking into account it was a reference **4 years** not 3.

Defendant aged 16–17 – Transport company etc, victim working for

121.17   *Att-Gen's Ref. No 69 of 1999* 2000 2 Cr App R (S) 53. The defendant pleaded guilty when the case was listed for trial to GBH with intent. The defendant then 16 and a friend boarded a bus. The defendant recognised the driver as someone who had ordered him off a bus before and he told his friend if he tried it again he was going to hit him. The defendant produced a Saver ticket, which the driver thought had an altered date. The defendant became aggressive. The driver took the ticket and asked the defendant to leave. The defendant became irate and produced a knife with a 4 to 6″ blade. He then held the driver with his hand and thrust the knife towards the ribs. The driver raised his arm and was stabbed just below the elbow. The friend who had tried to stop it pulled the defendant off the bus. The friend took the knife and gave it to the police. The victim had a 9 cm wound and had an operation to repair the muscles, tendons and nerves. He suffers from weakness in the power of his grip and it was anticipated he would be able to return to work. The defendant admitted it in interview and showed remorse. The defendant had a caution for possession of an offensive weapon namely a knife but no convictions. He spent 6 months in custody awaiting trial. The psychological report described him as on the borderline of mental retardation and naïve and simplistic. He was given probation and had made excellent contact in the 16 weeks since then. It was said if the constructive work continued his risk for re-offending could be reduced from low to medium to very low. Held. Applying *Att-Gen's Ref. Nos. 59, 60 and 63 of 1998* 1999 2 Cr App R (S) 128 the sentence was unduly lenient. We would have expected $3^1/_2$ **years** detention. Taking into account his progress and that it was a reference $2^1/_2$ **years** detention not probation.

Drug offences, linked to

See SUPPLY OF DRUGS – *Drug gang using violence*

Extended sentences (i.e. licence extended)

121.18   Powers of Criminal Courts (Sentencing) Act 2000 s 85

R v Allen 2005 1 Cr App R (S) 7. The defendant pleaded guilty to causing GBH with intent. At 10.45 pm on a Saturday the defendant and the co-defendant went into a nightclub with two females. Inside there was a man, P with whom there was altercation. Staff prevented it from getting out of hand. At about 2am the defendant's group went to get some food from a take-away which they ate on a bench outside the nightclub. At 2.30am P and another left the nightclub and walked passed the defendant's group. P shouted abuse saying he wanted to "Fuck [the defendant] up the arse". P took off his jacket and punched the defendant in the mouth causing him to bleed. The defendant believed that P was going to strike him again so he struck him to the face, knocking him backwards. The defendant then kicked him to keep him down. He kicked P 4 or 5 times to the head and to the body and he stamped on his head with one foot, twice, before his girlfriend pulled him away. P was extremely seriously injured. He was found to have a traumatic brain injury, with a haematoma in the front left lobe, a fractured skull of the left orbit, the phenoid bone and the floor of the anterior cranial fossa. There was extensive skull swelling. He required 24-hour care; he suffered from epilepsy and had lost much of the sight of one eye. He was paralysed down one side and was unable to walk unaided. His speech was affected, he was unable to write and read properly, had memory loss and depression. When arrested the appellant admitted that he had stamped on P's head. He was 18 with two convictions for inflicting GBH, two for ABH and two for common assault. The defendant's previous record revealed a long-standing violent nature and there was a high-risk of re-offending. He was genuinely remorseful. Held. Referring to *R v Nelson* 2002 1 Cr App R (S) 565, a longer than commensurate sentence should be imposed only where there is a risk of further offences which may cause death of some physical or psychological injury. Also, there may be cases in which, because of the power to impose an extended licence period, a longer than commensurate sentence may not be necessary. Further, referring to *R v Briggs* 2003 2 Cr App R (S) 615. The purpose of the extended licence is to hold above the defendant's head the sword of recall from his licence in the event of further offending." **7 years** with an extended licence period of 3 years, not 10 years imprisonment.

See also EXTENDED SENTENCES

Fighting – Biting

121.19 *Att-Gen's Ref. No 44 of 1994* 1995 16 Cr App R (S) 865. LCJ. It is frequently a misconception that unless some object is held in the hand, no weapon has been used. An attacker who uses shod feet, or who bites someone is just as much using a weapon as someone who wields an object in his hand.

Att-Gen's Ref. No 29 of 2001 2002 1 Cr App R (S) 253. The defendant pleaded guilty to ABH. She was convicted of wounding with intent and common assault. She was in a pub with her sister and saw a group of workers from a bakery having a belated Christmas party. She used to work there. There had been a dispute between her husband and one of their husbands. Previously the wives had been friends for 15 years. There was an attempt to resolve the dispute and the sister ended up assaulting one of them and being ejected from the pub. The argument continued outside and the defendant struck the woman she had fallen out with. This was the ABH. At some stage the defendant suffered a blow to the head possibly by hitting the pavement. The situation calmed down and one of the victim's colleagues tried to take her back inside. The defendant grabbed the colleague's hair and pulled her to the ground. This was the common assault. A woman from the bakery, G intervened and there was a struggle with the defendant. G held the defendant's face while the defendant held her hair. G pushed her finger into the defendant's mouth and the defendant bit it. She gripped it for some time. She let go and then bit her nose so some of the flesh was bitten off. The defendant was scratched to the face. G lost the lowest part of her nostril which the police preserved. The graft was unsuccessful. Her injury was disfiguring. She had a small wound to her finger. The first victim had a badly swollen eye and other bruises and swellings to her arms, legs and head. The second victim had hair loss and bruising. The defendant was 41 and of positive good character. She had a stable family, two teenage children and she was suffering stress at the time. The judge said the usual sentence is 3 years and the least he could impose was 18 months. Held. The judge was at liberty to take a lenient view of the case. There was strain at work, the offence was in anger and after a struggle. It was wholly out of character. But it was a vicious attack with permanent disfigurement. The lowest sentence was **2¹/₂ years** but because it was a reference the sentence will remain.

Fighting when the major injuries are caused by the fall, not any blow – Guideline remarks

121.20 *R v Coleman* 1992 13 Cr App R (S) 508. LCJ. The defendant was sentenced for manslaughter. We are considering a person who receives a blow, probably one blow only, to the head or face, is knocked over by the blow and unfortunately cracks his head on the floor or the pavement, suffers a fractured skull and dies. It is to be distinguished sharply from the sort of case where a victim on the ground is kicked about the head. It is to be distinguished sharply from the sort of case where a weapon is used in order to inflict injury. It is to be further distinguished from where the actual blow itself causes the death. This is the case of a fall almost accidentally resulting in a fractured skull. The starting point for manslaughter for this type of offence is 12 months on a plea of guilty. Then one looks at the mitigation and aggravating features. No pre-meditation, a single blow of moderate force, remorse and immediate admissions are all mitigation. Indications that the defendant is susceptible to outbreaks of violence, the assault was gratuitous and unprovoked, more than one blow all tend to aggravate the offence.

R v Hickman 2001 2 Cr App R (S) 261. The defendant pleaded guilty to GBH (s 20). The principles in *R v Coleman* 1992 13 Cr App R (S) 508 were applied. (So they would also apply to s 18, but to a lesser extent than manslaughter and s 20 because in a s 18 case there is an intent to cause GBH unlike the other two offences.)

Fire, by

121.21 *R v Griffin* 1999 1 Cr App R (S) 213. The defendant pleaded guilty to arson with intent to endanger life and causing GBH with intent. The defendant was distressed with the break up of his relationship with the victim. He wrote to his family telling them what he was about to do. The victim came to the premises to pick up some clothing and he pointed a knife at her. She was told she would not get out alive and he stabbed her in the chest. He followed her to the bedroom where he locked the door. There was a struggle over the knife in which the defendant received severe injuries to his hands. After this he recovered the knife and stabbed her several times. By now she was having trouble breathing. Further stab wounds were inflicted and she was told to open her legs. The children then knocked on the front door and he told them to go away. He returned to the bedroom and stabbed her once again in the cheek. The victim became unconscious and awoke up to find a burning duvet on the bed. She got up to get away and the defendant pushed her to the floor and threw the burning duvet over her, which she managed to throw off. She lost consciousness but awoke and escaped. She had burns to her shoulders, arms, hands and feet. The defendant had a significant mental illness and some minor previous convictions. Held. Because of the plea and the authorities **9 years** not 11 concurrent for both offences.

R v Parker 2000 2 Cr App R (S) 60. The defendant was convicted of GBH with intent. He had earlier pleaded guilty to arson being reckless whether life would be endangered. The defendant and the victim lived in the same block of flats. They spent an evening together and the defendant in the early hours returned to his flat and decided someone had entered it. He with others went to the victim's other address and would not accept his denials. They took him back to the defendant's flat by car and the victim noticed that the defendant had a petrol can on his lap. After they arrived at the defendant's flat the defendant continued to assert that the victim had entered his flat. He was kept there in all 1 hour. At 10.30 pm he said he had until 11.00 pm or I'll burn you. As 11.00 pm drew closer the defendant counted off the minutes. At 11.00 pm he unscrewed the lid on the petrol can and the victim felt petrol splashing over his head and body. He then heard the click of a cigarette lighter and the petrol ignited. The victim ran from the flat in great pain. He heard the defendant shouting for him to get his coat off and felt water going over him. He had skin hanging off his chin and elbows and his hands looked as if his fingers had split open. The defendant who had burnt his own hands trying to help had followed him. A motorist took him to hospital. He had 19% burns to his entire head, chest and upper arms. 12% of the area was partial thickness and the remaining 7% was full thickness. He sustained burns to both hands. He had dreadful scarring. The defendant said the victim was his best friend and he would regret it for the rest of his life. He was 27 and had two convictions for possession of an offensive weapon, two public order offences drug possession and dishonesty. **10 years** was in no way manifestly excessive.

See also ARSON – *Arson – Intending Life would be Endangered – Violent attack, part of a*

Glassing – Guideline remarks

121.22   *Att-Gen's Ref. No 20 of 1993* 1994 15 Cr App R (S) 797. LCJ. We have been referred to a number of decisions indicating the level of sentence appropriate for "glassing cases" (in s 18 cases). In *R v Harwood* 1979 1 Cr App R (S) 354, Lord Widgery LCJ said that nothing less than **3 years** would be appropriate for deliberate glassing. We have been referred to *R v Ronaldson* 1990 12 Cr App R (S) 91, where in circumstances similar to those in the present case a sentence of **5 years** was upheld. Other authorities tend to suggest that the appropriate sentence for offences of this kind is of that order.

Att-Gen's Ref. No 14 of 2000 2001 1 Cr App R (S) 55. Glassing offences are extremely dangerous. Terrible and permanent injuries can be inflicted in a split second.

R v Pritchard 2003 1 Cr App R (S) 263. The defendant pleaded guilty to Section 18. Held. Using a glass to lacerate the face is a significantly aggravating factor because of the appalling long term consequences that may occur. Where an offence is committed in cold blood, with premeditation and the motive of revenge, the sentence would be significantly longer than the **4 years** here.

Glassing – Less than 3 years' imprisonment

121.23   Att-Gen's Ref. No 15 of 1998 1999 1 Cr App R (S) 209. The defendant pleaded guilty to wounding with intent. The victim who knew the defendant from schooldays saw what he thought was the defendant and others pestering a woman outside a public house. The woman came over and spoke to the victim about it. The victim asked the defendant, "Do you have a problem with that." The defendant said, "No." About $1^1/_2$ hours later the defendant, who appeared drunk, approached and threatened the victim. He said, "I have now got a problem with you." He was told to go away but he pushed the victim backwards. He was told to go away again but he continued putting his face very close to the victim. Eventually the victim thought he was about to throw a punch and he pushed him and he fell over. Shouts were exchanged. The defendant was told to desist by a friend of his but didn't. He attempted to get round the friend and reach the victim but didn't. He then went into the public house for 3–5 minutes and came out. There was the sound of breaking glass and the victim's face was cut open. He had multiple lacerations. There was a deep 2 cm cut and a deep 3 cm cut. The saliva duct was cut. He was in hospital for a couple of days and will have permanent scarring to the face. The defendant accepted he had a pint glass in his hand. The defendant was then 18. He pleaded not guilty to an offence under s 18 but guilty to s 20. It was set down for trial but there was no time to hear it. The trial was put back and he then failed to answer his bail and had to be arrested. Two months later he pleaded guilty to an offence under s 18. He had a conviction for common assault. He was sentenced on the basis the glass was not broken before the single blow. Held. *Att-Gen's Ref. No 20 of 1993* 1994 15 Cr App R (S) 797 makes it clear that 6 months was unduly lenient. If the defendant had not been released $2^1/_2$ years would be substituted. However, as the defendant had been at liberty for 4 months, was in work and now drinks in very small amounts **2 years** substituted.

Att-Gen's Ref. No 79 of 1999 2000 2 Cr App R (S) 124. The defendant pleaded guilty to wounding with intent. He had earlier pleaded guilty to an alternative s 20 offence. The defendant then 18 had been drinking and was standing outside an Indian restaurant. He had a beer glass from the restaurant in his pocket and the victim, a 20-year-old student, seems to have slightly bumped into him. There may have been a mumbling and the victim and his friend walked on. The defendant approached the victim from behind and there was a confrontation. After a very short fight he took the glass from his pocket and smashed it into the victim's face. Immediately the defendant said, "Oh no, what can I have done?" The victim needed 16 stitches to cuts on his eyebrow, cheek, chin and lip. His scars will be permanent. He suffered from nightmares and from a complex about his face. The defendant had references and an excellent character. He showed real remorse. He received 8 months and had been released from the sentence with a tag. Held. The judge was in error to say in chambers that in the region of 12 months was merited, that there was no great distinction between s 18 and 20 and to consider drink as a mitigating factor. Our approach must be tempered by the fact the judge said there was not much to distinguish s 18 and 20 before the plea. Giving maximum value to the factors in mitigation the least sentence that could properly be imposed was **18 months**. Taking into account his release and that it was a reference we substitute **12 months** detention.

Att-Gen's Ref. No 67 of 1999 2000 2 Cr App R (S) 380. The defendant pleaded guilty to GBH with intent. The defendant's partner of 3 years left her and started a relationship with the victim. She appeared to accept the situation. In the early hours of New Years Day 1999 she went into a club where the victim was drinking. Someone heard the defendant say while pointing at the victim, "She's getting it tonight. She is definitely getting it tonight." The defendant picked up a lager bottle and asked whether it was empty. She was asked what she wanted it for and was informed, "You'll see in a minute." She then walked over to the victim and struck the victim in the face with it. It broke quite easily and caused a dreadful wound, which required 17 stitches. The victim was disfigured for life. The defendant surrendered to the police. The defendant was 24 and had a daughter aged 8. Six weeks before the offence she had had a miscarriage and she was expecting another child. She suffered from depression. She had convictions for possession of an offensive weapon and prostitution. Held. Taking into account it was a reference **2 years** not probation.

Glassing – 3 years and less than 4 years' imprisonment appropriate

121.24   *Att-Gen's Ref. No 24 of 1998* 1999 1 Cr App R (S) 278. The defendant was convicted of wounding with intent. The victim was with his girlfriend at a public house. They went to the bar and the victim was next to the defendant who said something. The victim couldn't hear it and asked the defendant what he had said. The defendant smashed a beer glass into his face. The defendant aged 27 had convictions over 13 years principally for theft, motor vehicle and motoring offences. However, there were offences for two assaults on police, ABH and common assault. He had received for those 3 months detention, probation and a community service order. Held. We would have expected a sentence in the order of **5 years**. However, as it was a reference and the defendant had 7 weeks before his planned release **3 years 9 months** not 2 years.

Att-Gen's Ref. Nos. 59, 60 and 63 of 1998 1999 2 Cr App R (S) 128. LCJ. The defendant G pleaded guilty to wounding with intent. G then aged 18, and the victim, aged 15, attended a birthday party at a nightclub. G was observed behaving in an intimidating way towards some other youths, who did not include the victim. G accosted a guest who sought to avoid any further confrontation and walked away. However, he told the victim what had happened. The victim then approached G to calm down the situation. He asked the offender what was the problem, but the offender did not respond. The victim then said to the offender, "Just chill out, it's a party". About 5–10 minutes later G beckoned the victim to come over to him. An argument developed and G suddenly turned and threw a pint glass into the victim's face. The glass broke, causing immediate wounds to his face and heavy bleeding. The victim was found to have a deep 4 cm laceration to the cheek, which extended down to the bone, a 2 cm laceration across his nose, which also extended down to the bone, a laceration to his lip, and other small superficial lacerations. A fragment of glass was removed from his eye. The victim has received permanent facial scarring as a result of the assault. The attack had a profound effect on his schooling. He was very reluctant to return to school at all because of his embarrassment at his facial appearance and his loss of confidence and interests had been marked. In interview he admitted being drunk. He denied that he had assaulted the victim. He expressed remorse. The offender has some offences of dishonesty on his record, but no violence and no custodial sentences. He was expelled from school. Held. Had the offender pleaded not guilty the appropriate sentence would then have been **4 years** detention. As he pleaded guilty the appropriate sentence would have been **3¹/₂ years**. As it was a reference **2¹/₂ years** not 18 months.

Att-Gen's Ref. No 14 of 2000 2001 1 Cr App R (S) 55. The defendant was convicted of wounding with intent. The defendant who had drunk five to six pints of lager and the victim aged 17 who had drunk ¹/₂ pint of lager were in the same wine bar. The defendant who was tipsy was acting in a partly aggressive manner on the dance floor. He was staring at the victim and his friends. The defendant thought they were laughing at him and he spoke to one of the victim's friends and said, "Have you got a problem." The friend said there wasn't and said they didn't want any trouble. He waved a wine glass in the man's face. He then asked, "Have you got a problem now." He was told three times they didn't want any trouble. He then picked up a pint glass and waved it in the victim's direction. The victim stood up to attract the attention of a doorman and the defendant swung the glass into the victim's face and punched him. The victim bled heavily and became unconscious. He had a deep laceration to his face stretching from the bridge of his nose around the cheek to his lip. His wounds required 44 stitches. The scarring was likely to be permanent. He had problems with his right eye. The defendant said he feared he would be attacked. The defendant was 35 and had six court appearances. Five of which were for public order offences or ABH. He suffered from post-traumatic stress due to an attack on him in 1995. His nose was severed with a knife when he went to the assistance of a publican who was in trouble with some youths. He also had been good in preventing serious clashes between clients at a charity dealing with people with tempers. The risk of re-offending was assessed as high due to mental illness and alcohol. Held. Glassing offences are extremely dangerous. Terrible and permanent injuries can be inflicted in a split second. Taking into account he had been a victim, his charity work and it was a reference **3¹/₂ years** not 2.

Att-Gen's Ref. No. 25 of 2002 2003 1 Cr App R (S) 130. The defendant was convicted of Section 18 wounding. The victim was with her friends in a club and the defendant was with H. The defendant walked over to the victim and said, "You better tell your friend (meaning D) not to touch my fucking hair or I'll knock her the fuck out." The defendant and the victim then spoke amicably and the defendant walked away. H then grabbed D's hair, pulled her to the floor and punched her to the head on a number of occasions. The victim tried to assist D and asked H what was going on. The victim then felt something hit her face. It was a glass that the defendant had smashed in her face. The victim felt skin hanging down her nose and blood spurting into her eyes. The defendant then took hold of the victim's hair and using her arm, which was in plaster, delivered several "upper cut blows" to her face. The defendant was pulled away and taken out of the club where she shouted threats to the victim and told her what she would do to her. The victim had a 6 cm wound over the bridge of her nose extending down both of her cheeks. There were two smaller wounds one of which was above the left eye. Twenty stitches were required. In interview the defendant said she was unaware she had cut the victim. She was 21 and the sole carer of her two year old daughter. She was also on probation for affray but had been a model prisoner. The Crown said it was unprovoked and there was permanent scarring albeit feint. Held. We note the glass was not broken for use, it was a single blow, her record, it was a trial and the concerns about the defendant's behaviour when in drink. We adopt the **5 year** starting point in *Att-Gen's Ref. No. 20 of 1993* 1994 15 Cr App R (S) 797 and in normal circumstances **4 years** not 2 would be in line with the authorities. Bearing in mind her personal circumstances and it was a reference **3 years**.

Old case *Att-Gen's Ref. No 67 of 1997* 1998 2 Cr App R (S) 420, (for a summary of the case see the first edition of this book.)

Glassing – 4 years and less than 5 years imprisonment appropriate

121.25   *R v Dooley* 1999 2 Cr App R (S) 364. The defendant pleaded guilty to wounding with intent. The victim and the defendant were in a public house. The defendant walked passed the victim, stopped walked back, picked up a pint glass, raised it and smashed it into the back of the victim's head. The glass broke and the defendant punched him on the back of the head. The defendant then picked up a chair and raised that. The landlord approached and the defendant left. The victim had four lacerations of 5, 5, 4 and $1\frac{1}{2}$ cm long. He required 17 stitches. When arrested the defendant said the victim called his sister a slag. He was sentenced on the basis the attack had lasted 3 seconds and the victim had discharged himself from hospital on the same day. The defendant had been detained under s 38 of the Mental Heath Act from 10 months after the offence and it was continuing. It was for intermittent psychotic illness. He had an emotionally unstable personality disorder of the borderline type as well as features of a dyssocial personality disorder. He did not meet the treatment criteria for a mental health disposal. The defendant was 28 with numerous convictions for violence and dishonesty. The longest sentence he had received was 21 months for burglaries. **4 years** not 6.

R v Bishop 2000 2 Cr App R (S) 416. The defendant was convicted of GBH with intent. The victim and the defendant were in the ladies' lavatory in a nightclub together and there was a harmless exchange. An altercation developed involving hair pulling and both of them ended up on the ground. Things calmed down and the victim left the lavatory. Outside the defendant thrust a beer bottle into the victim's face. There was a 15 to 17 cm cut to the victim's cheek. The defendant was then 20 with a debilitating disease called Lupus, asthma and eczema. She also had a young son. **4 years** not 6.

R v Reader 2000 2 Cr App R (S) 442. The defendant was convicted of GBH with intent, ABH and criminal damage. Mr Bhangra, Mr Sheldrick and Mr Bhogal went to a public house, then went to buy some food and then Mr Bhangra went back to the public house. When he didn't return Mr Sheldrick went in. There was then an altercation between the three as to whether they should go home. The defendant with a half-full glass of beer approached Mr Bhangra and Mr Sheldrick who were at a van and asked, "Did you smash my glasses? I hope it was an accident. I'm the only one who smashes glasses." A girl who he was with told him to stop. He punched Mr Bhangra in the face and he fell down unconscious. This was the ABH. Other men joined the defendant and he asked, "What are you doing standing up for a Paki?" The defendant and three others started to kick the van. This was the criminal damage. Someone opened the rear doors of the van and Mr Sheldrick got out and as he stood up the defendant struck him with his glass of beer shattering the glass. The victim had a deep 3 cm laceration to his forehead with two superficial lacerations to each side. He was left with scarring and developed depression. When he went out he feared he would be attacked. Mr Bhangra had bruising and soreness to his eye and cheek. The van had dents to its side panels, wings and bonnet. The back door had been pulled off its hinges. Held. As there was a racist motive $4\frac{1}{2}$ **years** with other concurrent sentences was appropriate.

R v Pritchard 2003 1 Cr App R (S) 263. The defendant pleaded guilty to Section 18. He married the victim in 1980. They had two children now aged 17 and 12. After three years, she ceased to have any affection for him. She said five years ago he had seen her talking to another man on holiday and he had punched her, knocked her to the ground and kicked her. He claimed the marriage was good. Both received treatment for depression. In August 2001, she moved out of the matrimonial home taking one of her children. He then started to persistently call her both in person and on the telephone begging her to return. She refused to return. Three weeks after she left, contrary to his promises, he went to her house where she lived with her father,. He persuaded her to return to his home to talk through their problems. When there he offered her a cup of tea. As she went into the kitchen, he grabbed her by the hair and punched her repeatedly to the face. She was terrified and promised to return to stop him continuing. She heard breaking glass and felt a thumping sensation to her face. She was knocked to the floor and kicked. She had been glassed and had tried to protect herself. The defendant said nothing and drove off in the family car. Nearby he went straight across a roundabout at a motorway junction. He demolished signs and came to rest in the middle of a busy carriageway. He told doctors in hospital he had tried to commit suicide. She had eight lacerations to her head, forearm, finger, hand and elbow. In interview he said his relationship was excellent and at the house she had said she had found someone else and the room began to get smaller. Everything had gone dark and thereafter he had no memory of the events. He was 42 and had convictions for robbery and two for ABH. The most recent was in 1983. The pre-sentence report said there was deep remorse and the risk of re-offending was at the lower end of the scale. Further he accepted his marriage was over. He told the psychiatrist he took an overdose 2–3 days before the offence at a time when he discovered she was having an affair. Held. She had horrific bruising and swelling to her face and she was likely to be permanently scarred. Using a glass to lacerate the face is a significantly aggravating factor because of the appalling long term consequences that may occur. Where an offence is committed in cold blood, with premeditation and the motive of revenge, the sentence would be significantly longer than the **4 years** here. That was well within the permissible range.

Glassing – 5 or more years imprisonment appropriate

121.26 *R v Gould* 2000 2 Cr App R (S) 173. LCJ. The defendant changed his plea to guilty of GBH with intent. He and his friend went drinking together and had an argument about computer games. The defendant stood up and punched his friend to the head and body. The friend tried to defend himself and the defendant picked up a glass and drove it into the area round his ear causing the glass to break. The defendant ran off. The victim had a large flap laceration, which extended from the neck up over his chin as far as the ear and back. He needed 25 stitches. When interviewed the defendant could not explain his conduct. The defendant was now 21. In 1996 he was convicted of affray. When 19 he was convicted of a Public Order Act 1986 offence and a s 20 offence (6 months). The defendant after drinking and an argument threw a glass at another man causing severe facial injuries. As he ran off he threw a concrete boulder at him which hit the victim's chest. The pre-sentence report referred to a need to control his drinking and develop anger management techniques. The psychiatric report referred to a likelihood of further violent offending. There were references saying he was responsible when not in drink. Held. The **5 years** detention was not at the top of the bracket. It was entirely appropriate.

Att-Gen's Ref. No 43 of 2000 2001 2 Cr App R (S) 381. The defendant was convicted of wounding with intent. The defendant was separated from his wife and was living with another woman. The wife and the victim were in a relationship. She moved out of the matrimonial home and shortly before the offence she moved back in. In the evening the defendant was seen to be in a rage looking wild and very angry. He was angry because his wife would not leave the matrimonial home. He went to the public house where his wife and her friend were and picked up a wine glass and thrust it into the friend's face. The glass shattered. The victim had a large laceration in his left eye, and lacerations to his forehead and cheek. A piece of glass was protruding from his lower left eyelid. The surgeon said it was one of the most severe ocular injuries he had seen for some time. He had lost virtually all his sight in the left eye and the right eye was at risk of developing symptomatic inflammation. It was becoming very sensitive to light. He was unable to return to work. The defendant was 37 and had convictions for violence. In 1984 and 1996 he was convicted of criminal damage and in 1997 burglary. In 1997 he was convicted of ABH and threatening words with intent to cause fear or provocation of violence. These offences were committed against his wife. He had an excellent work record. Held. This was a very grave offence. Taking into account the mitigation and that it was a reference **5 years** not $3^1/_2$.

Hammer, bars and shovels etc, with

121.27   *Att-Gen's Ref. No 19 of 1998* 1999 1 Cr App R (S) 275. The defendant was convicted of two wounding with intent counts and affray. He was committed for sentence for ABH. The ABH matter related to an unprovoked attack on a white victim with a bottle. The victim had just left a restaurant with his girlfriend. The victim was with three to five Asians. He left sniggering. The victim's nose was cut and his spectacles were broken. He was convicted. Whilst on bail for that offence and three weeks after the offence he made an unprovoked attack on a young man who had just left a nightclub with his girlfriend. He used a lump hammer and the victim suffered a 3 and 2 cm cut. He also lost consciousness. The defendant was arrested nearby and lashed out at the police officer with a belt. He was released on bail. Less than a week later he committed the second GBH offence. A girl knocked on the victim's door saying there were two men she wanted to get rid of. The victim saw the defendant and another and walked the girl to a telephone box. The two men approached the victim and he was threatened. The other man tried to start a fight. The victim's friends managed to calm things down. The victim returned home and then decided to tell the father of the other man he was causing trouble. The victim and his friends left and the defendant and the other man appeared. They were shouting and trying to start a fight. Without any warning the defendant lunged forward and struck the victim on the top of the head with a claw hammer. The victim had a 7 and 10 cm long cut. Beneath was a skull fracture and the brain had been lacerated indicating a blow of extreme force. There was a risk of brain damage and epilepsy. There was a comparatively superficial 3 cm wound on the back of the head. The defendant was 19 and had no relevant previous convictions. Held. We would have expected a sentence of 6 years in total. Taking into account it was a reference and he was showing signs of maturity 6 months for the ABH, 3 years and 5 years for the GBH concurrent substituted for **$3^1/_2$ years** in total.

Att-Gen's Ref. No 81 of 2000 2001 2 Cr App R (S) 90. The defendant pleaded guilty to GBH with intent on the day his trial was listed. The defendant lived near the victim and at 1am repeatedly hit his head and body with a shovel. He said, "I'm going to fucking kill you." The victim's daughter saw the attack from her bedroom and ran out. He ignored her pleas to him to stop. The victim had a large skull fracture, a fracture to his forearm, a 5 cm laceration to his temple, a deep 5 cm laceration to his elbow and a superficial laceration to his forearm. He was in hospital for 5 days and made a good recovery. The defendant was 36 and had no convictions. The judge sentenced him on the basis that the victim had been aggressive, thrown stones at his house and made a noise early in the morning. The victim ran at him swinging his fist. The defendant used excessive self-defence. The prosecution did not accept that account. Held. Accepting the defence version, which was in stark contrast to the victim's without evidence, was wrong. It is difficult to see how the judge found severe provocation. Taking into account it was a reference **15 months** immediate imprisonment not 18 months suspended.

R v Laker 2002 1 Cr App R (S) 64. The defendant pleaded guilty to GBH with intent and affray. After drinking he was argumentative and aggressive to all and sundry and threatened the victim who he suggested had forced himself on his sister 16 years previously. This suggestion was quite untrue. Eventually he was arrested and the police took him home and de-arrested him because they thought he had calmed down. When they had left he took a hollow metal bar weighing 0.4 kilos to the victim's house and knocked on the door. When the victim's girlfriend answered it he pushed her out of the way and stormed into the lounge where he confronted the victim about his sister. The victim said he didn't know what he was talking about. With the victim defenceless in the chair he struck him about the head and face with multiple blows. He also struck him on the inside of his forearm which was extremely painful. Next he ripped his watch off cutting his arm and smashed it. Also smashed was his mobile phone. Then he struck the victim's knees causing him to fall to the ground where he struck him with the bar 23 times. The victim was told, "You're fucking dead." and was in agony. He was blinded by blood and spat his teeth out until he became unconscious. The victim was taken to hospital and three fractures to the jaw and eight lacerations were found. Seven teeth had been knocked out and 36 stitches were required. There were other injuries. The doctor said the injuries were significant but not life threatening. Police found him near a taxi office and he climbed onto the roof of some shops. When a police officer approached he said, "I've got a 9mm. I'm going to blow you away." He was eventually overpowered. This was the affray matter. The victim's life had permanently changed and he had to give up his job which he was proud of. He was permanent scarred. Parts of his teeth were embedded in his lips. The defendant was 29 and had an unattractive record but only one conviction for violence in very different circumstances. There was 141 days left of his licence to serve from an earlier sentence. Since his sentence he had performed well in prison and now displayed remorse. Held. This dreadful case called for a severe sentence. **8 years** was richly deserved.

Att-Gen's Ref. (No 68 of 2002) 2003 1 Cr App R (S) 498. The defendant was convicted of wounding with intent. The victim was 25. The defendant arrived at a public house at about 8.45 pm. During the course of the evening he said to the victim: "I pity anyone who starts with me tonight, they're all fucking wankers." At about 10:30 pm the defendant told the victim that he wanted to see him outside where there was a confrontation (but no violence), following which the victim prevented him from re-entering the public house. The defendant walked off; the victim went back in. Shortly after midnight, the victim left the public house and crossed the road. The defendant retrieved a claw hammer that he had hidden in a refuge bin earlier and without any provocation struck the victim on the head with the hammer. The victim fell to the ground where the defendant continued to strike him using the hammer. CCTV showed eight forceful blows at the victim's head, some of which connected. The defendant delivered about six further blows, striking the victim's left forearm as he tried to defend himself. The defendant's jacket came off his shoulders inhibiting his ability to strike further and enabling the victim to restrain the defendant. The police arrived and arrested him. In interview he said that he was pretty drunk. The victim had a 1 cm laceration to the side of the head, two 2 cm lacerations to the back of the head, a deep S-shaped laceration on the forearm, two lacerations near the elbow and bruising to the ribcage. Muscle to the wrist flexors was divided and nineteen stitches were needed to close the deep laceration. The defendant had previous convictions for ABH in 1990 and a more recent public order offence. A psychiatric report said he had a deep and intense hostility towards his real father. The risk of similar outbursts of irrational violence was already lower since his incarceration. That risk will fall to entirely acceptable levels once he rids himself entirely of these leftovers from a disturbed past. Held: The use of a claw hammer was certainly no less serious than when a glass is used in the face and sentences of the order of 5 years would be expected. Taking into account that this was a reference, **4 years** not **2½**.

R v Robertson 2003 1 Cr App R (S) 143. The defendant pleaded guilty to Section 18. He and the victim were alcoholics living in local authority housing for alcoholics. They went to hospital to visit the defendant's twin brother who was ill. On their return the defendant went straight to an off-licence while the victim went to his room where another resident joined him. An hour later, the defendant went to the victim's room and pushed the door open. The defendant asked the victim to come with him to show him something, which he did. Fifteen seconds later the defendant went back to the room and the other resident asked, "What's wrong?" The defendant showed him the broken handle of a hammer and went to his room. The other resident went out of the room and saw the victim lying on the floor with a dent in his head and blood running from it. He tried to stop the flow of blood and a specialist crew from the hospital arrived. His condition was critical. The victim had a depressed fracture of the skull, which left him with memory impairment, speech impediment, dysfunction of the arm and an increased risk of epilepsy. Police went to the defendant's room and he told police what had happened was not his concern. He admitted the offence in the custody suite and made a no comment interview. He was 39 with one conviction, namely possession of an offensive weapon for which he was fined £100. The probation officer was concerned at the risk of re-offending, which was described as significant although when he wasn't drinking there was minimal risk. However with drinking and stress there was a tendency for an explosive temper. In custody the defendant had been addressing his alcoholism. **Held.** It was a horrific attack with terrible effects. However the highest starting point should have been **9 or 10 years** so with the plea **7 years** not 9.

R v Hudson 2003 2 Cr App R (S) 327. The defendant pleaded guilty to wounding with intent. The victim had been involved in a long relationship with Miss F and had a daughter, aged 6. He was an alcoholic and suffered from epilepsy. Miss F began a relationship with the defendant and broke off her relationship with the victim. The victim's subsequent behaviour led Miss F to complain to the police on over 100 occasions. His behaviour ranged from phoning her 3 or 4 times a day, shouting at her in the street, visiting her house and making threats. Child contact arrangements were conducted through solicitors. On the day of the attack the victim phoned Miss F with a view to seeing their daughter. Miss F had reacted with hostility. The defendant had become aware of the extent of the unwanted approaches by the victim and went looking for him. He visited and left a message with the victim's sister: "Tell him I'll kill him." The sister noticed that he was carrying a hammer. The victim was later walking the street when the defendant pulled up in his lorry, got out and attacked him with a hammer. He hit him on the head a number of times and kicked and punched him whilst he was on the ground. He left him there bleeding. He was later found wandering in the street with blood on his face. A CT scan revealed a haematoma with a gross midline shift of the brain. He had a left-sided skull fracture which extended to the base of the skull. He was lucky to survive but remained very ill. His health had not been good prior to the attack. He had in fact since died. On arrest the defendant denied the attack but subsequently admitted it. The defendant was effectively of good character and had been in good employment. He had four children from his previous marriage. A psychiatrist reported that he was riddled with remorse and that the risk of re-offending was low. **Held.** This was a case where the defendant acted out of a sense of seeking to protect the woman with whom he was living. He conducted a very severe attack that caused the victim most serious, life-threatening injuries. **6 years** upheld.

Att- Gen's Ref. No 12 of 2004 2005 1 Cr App R (S) 147. The defendant pleaded guilty to causing GBH with intent. He had been married for eight years and there were three children of that relationship, but the marriage had been in difficulties for some years. He had become abusive and jealous towards his wife. Three years before the attack his wife told him she wanted to leave and after that he threatened violence towards her several times. She was in bed when he came in and he became irritated with her, taking her mobile phone from her and pulling out the landline from its socket. His wife followed him out of the bedroom and tried to run down the stairs but fell and hurt herself although not seriously. She asked him to call an ambulance because she was frightened of him and he refused. She lay on the floor for about twenty minutes and then tried to sit up. As she did so he hit her three times with a hammer, only stopping when their thirteen year old son heard the noise and intervened to protect his mother by threatening his father with a knife. The victim sustained multiple lacerations on her head and two depressed skull fractures, needing surgery and four or five days in hospital. It was argued that the aggravating features were that the attack was in the victim's home, that there were three children asleep in the house, the attack was unprovoked, it took place when the victim was lying defenceless on the floor, a hammer was used on the head, a thirteen year old boy witnessed it and it only ceased when the boy intervened. The defendant, 52, had no previous convictions and was hardworking. He had had three to four cans of beer that evening and the attack took place against a background of depression and morbid jealousy. Held. The appropriate sentence was in the order of **5^1/$_2$ to 6 years**. As it was a reference **4^1/$_2$** not 3.

Att-Gen's Ref No 30 of 2004 2005 1 Cr App R (S) 212. The defendant pleaded guilty on the first day of trial to one count of wounding with intent. The defendant and the victim were in a public house. The victim went to put some credits in the jukebox when the defendant said to him that he still had three credits left. The victim said if the credit were still there after his selection had been played the defendant could have them. The defendant left the public house but then returned to pick up his tools. He hit the victim three times with a hammer, twice on the head and once, because he moved, on the shoulder. He shouted 'That'll teach you to take my free credits and threw an ashtray at the victim, which missed. He was still abusing him as the victim left. The next day the victim was taken to hospital and was found to have a depressed skull fracture and damage to the membrane lining the brain. The blow had been of considerable force and had driven bone, hair and skin fragments into the skull surface. Fourteen clips were needed to close the site. He also had a cut to his right ear and a numb shoulder. He spent three days in hospital. After the assault the victim experienced daily headaches for a month, then pain around the scar area. He experienced a constant high pitched noise in his head which interfered with his sleep. There was a risk in the future of epilepsy. He was not allowed to drive or play football for six months. He became shy and quiet whereas before he had been sociable and confident. He found it harder to concentrate. He avoided two nearby towns in case he met the defendant and he lost his job. The defendant surrendered to the police and said he was too drunk to remember the incident. He said he had drunk fourteen pints of lager and bitter. His basis of plea was that he had been working all day without food or drink so that the drink had a more marked effect; that he did not recall the assault but admitted forming a drunken intent to cause the victim GBH. Further he bitterly regretted the incident and surrendered to the police as soon as he knew what had happened. He had previously contested the intent necessary for GBH because of his drunken state but when he learnt of the medical evidence that three blows were struck he accepted the necessary intent. The aggravating features were said to be the use of the hammer, the unprovoked attack on a stranger in a public place, the repeated blows only stopped by others intervening, the deliberate and forceful blows to the head and the serious and lasting consequences. The defendant, 29, had over forty previous convictions including robbery, ABH, burglary, criminal damage, handling and public order offences. The last offences of violence were over ten years ago. There was genuine remorse and he had not behaved violently for a number of years. He had a difficult personal history with a history of drug abuse and he had made a significant effort to improve his behaviour with some success. Held. This was a very savage attack on a wholly innocent person. The critically important feature was the extent of the injuries causing serious long-term consequences. The proper sentence would have been **5^1/$_2$–6 years** so as it was a reference **4^1/$_2$ years** not 3.

R v Horrocks 2005 1 Cr App R (S) 414. The defendant pleaded guilty to GBH with intent. The victim had been drinking in a public house and his behaviour had become irritating. The defendant had also been drinking but agreed to give the victim a lift in his van. During the journey the defendant said that the victim picked up a hammer, which the defendant tried to retrieve. A tug of war developed and the defendant lost his temper. He hit the victim on the head with the hammer and pushed him out of the van. Seeing the victim get up, the defendant turned the van around, got out and hit the victim two or three more times on the head with the hammer. The defendant's partner saw him covered in blood and went and found the victim lying unconscious. The defendant washed the hammer and dumped his clothing. The victim had a depressed skull fracture, multiple scalp lacerations and bruising to his head. His ear was hanging on by skin fragments and a finger was fractured. He had to attend a rehabilitation centre and his prognosis was uncertain. He had hearing loss, fits and memory loss. When the defendant was arrested he said "I take it the bloke is still alive". He was a binge drinker. He expressed remorse and suffered with depression. He was 29 with previous violence convictions including ABH, affray, wounding, possessing an offensive weapon and knife point robbery for which he had received community and custodial sentences. Held. The defendant had left the victim for dead and tried to cover his tracks. Despite knowing his own capacity for terrible violence when drunk, he has continued to abuse alcohol. **12 years** was severe but justifiably so.

Kicking – Guideline remarks

121.28   *Att-Gen's Ref. No 44 of 1994* 1995 16 Cr App R (S) 865. LCJ. It is frequently a misconception that unless some object is held in the hand, no weapon has been used. An attacker who uses shod feet, or who bites someone is just as much using a weapon as someone who wields an object in his hand.

R v Islam 2002 2 Cr App R (S) 118. Attacks by kicking with shoes or boots compares with those where weapons are used.

Kicking victim on ground after drinking

121.29   *Att-Gen's Ref. Nos. 33 of 1997* 1998 1 Cr App R (S) 352. The defendant pleaded guilty to GBH with intent and ABH. The two victims E and W were out celebrating the birthday of one of them and had had a considerable amount to drink. At about 1.45 am they walked along a road looking for a taxi. The defendant then 22 and H had also had a lot to drink and an argument developed between the two couples. As E walked passed he was hit on the back of his head and fell to the ground. The defendant struck E in the face knocking him backwards and his head hit the pavement and rendered him unconscious. As E lay on the ground the defendant repeatedly kicked him on the head and stamped on it with considerable force, causing bleeding. The defendant then joined H in assaulting W. Passers-by gave first aid to E and succeeded in preventing further attacks on W. The defendant then returned to E and as a police car arrived he jumped on his head, kicked it and stamped on it. The defendant and H walked off and were caught and than ran off again. They were eventually apprehended. E was bleeding profusely from the head and was unconscious. In hospital he showed no verbal or eye-opening responses. X-rays revealed no internal injury apart from soft tissue trauma to the neck. There was bruising to the eye, swelling to his cheek and grazes to the shoulder. He regained consciousness a day later. The defendant was of good character and showed remorse. Held. The appropriate sentence giving generous construction to the facts in favour of the defendant was **3 years**. The best for him on a guilty plea would have been **2 years**. As it was a reference **12–15 months** would have been appropriate. As he had completed the 240 hours' community service ordered, was now in full time employment and with hesitation it was not appropriate to order a short sentence.

Att-Gen's Ref. No 18 of 2001 2001 2 Cr App R (S) 521. The defendant was convicted of GBH with intent. He had pleaded to GBH without the intent. The defendant then 19 and the victim had been drinking. At about 1.15am the victim who owned a bicycle shop and two young women were sitting on a bench and the defendant joined them. The defendant's larger brother and two others came up to them and the victim said to the brother, "You're a fat bastard." The defendant punched him in the face and others crowded round punching him in the head. The brother kicked him in the head. The victim was pulled to the ground and as he lay motionless the defendant kicked him four or five times with considerable force. Witnesses said it was sickening. The victim had a large bruise on the back of the head and blood from the mouth. He had a serious brain injury. His responses were tested and were the lowest possible. He was still effected. His co-ordination was poor, he was unsteady on his feet, he had reduced mental faculties and he was unable to ride a bicycle. Two years after the incident he was expected to have recovered most of his lost functions. The defendant had no convictions for violence. He showed remorse. Held. We would have expected a sentence of **5 to 6 years**. Taking into account it was a reference **4 years** not 3.

R v Allen 2005 1 Cr App R (S) 7. The defendant pleaded guilty to causing GBH with intent. At 10:45 pm on a Saturday the defendant and the co-defendant went into a nightclub with two females. Inside there was a man, P, with whom there was altercation. Staff prevented it from getting out of hand. At about 2am the defendant's group went to get some food from a take-away which they ate on a bench outside the nightclub. At 2.30 am P and another left the nightclub and walked passed the defendant's group. P shouted abuse saying he wanted to "Fuck [the defendant] up the arse". P took off his jacket and punched the defendant in the mouth causing him to bleed. The defendant believed that P was going to strike him again so he struck him to the face, knocking him backwards. The defendant then kicked him to keep him down. He kicked P 4 or 5 times to the head and to the body and he stamped on his head with one foot, twice, before his girlfriend pulled him away. P was extremely seriously injured. He was found to have a traumatic brain injury, with a haematoma in the front left lobe, a fractured skull of the left orbit, the phenoid bone and the floor of the anterior cranial fossa. There was extensive skull swelling. He required 24-hour care; he suffered from epilepsy and had lost much of the sight of one eye. He was paralysed down one side and was unable to walk unaided. His speech was affected, he was unable to write and read properly, had memory loss and depression. When arrested the appellant admitted that he had stamped on P's head. He was 18 with two convictions for inflicting GBH, two for ABH and two for common assault. The defendant's previous record revealed a long-standing violent nature and there was a high-risk of re-offending assessment. He was genuinely remorseful. Held. Referring to Nelson 2002 1 Cr App R (S) 565, a longer than commensurate sentence should be imposed only where there is a risk of further offences which may cause death or some physical or psychological injury. Also, there may be cases in which, because of the power to impose an extended licence period, a longer than commensurate sentence may not be necessary. Further, referring to Briggs 2003 2 Cr App R (S) 615: The purpose of the extended licence is to hold above the defendant's head the sword of recall from his licence in the event of further offending." **7 years** with an extended licence period of 3 years, not 10 years imprisonment.

Old cases *R v Reynolds* 1997 2 Cr App R (S) 118, *R v Richards* 1998 1 Cr App R (S) 87. (for a summary of these cases see the first edition of this book.)

Kicking victim on ground after drinking – Group attack

121.30   *Att-Gen's Ref. Nos. 76 of 1998* 1999 2 Cr App R (S) 362. The defendant made an early guilty plea to GBH with intent. The victim and the defendant aged 28 had been drinking. The victim was chased into a car park by a group of youths. There was no escape and he was knocked to the ground and kicked. He got up. Someone punched him and they both fell to the ground and youths began kicking the victim. He was curled up in a defensive position. Someone called out that they had called the police and the youths moved away. There was nothing to say the defendant had played a part in any of this. The defendant then walked up and asked if he was alright. The victim believing the defendant was part of it said, "I'll get you back one day." The defendant replied, "I didn't hurt you, but if you want me to …" He then stamped on his head six times. A witness said it was vicious. He was said to be very drunk but able to boast as to what he had done afterwards. The victim was described as slipping into a coma and had blood coming from his nose and mouth. He had bleeding in the back and side of his brain. It was a traumatic brain injury from which it is unlikely he will make a full recovery. Three months later he was allowed home from hospital for weekends but needed constant care. Eight months later he could only walk with difficulty and his sight and speech were still impaired. The basis of plea was that the complainant abused him and struck the defendant. The defendant had four violent convictions one of which was punished with imprisonment. The defendant expressed remorse. His partner and child were facing difficulties. Held. Taking into account that it was a reference and the mitigation **5 years** not 3.

R v Jama and Oliver 2000 2 Cr App R (S) 98. The defendants J and O made a late plea to GBH with intent. A minor incident developed in a public house between O and the victim. Later O was evicted and waited outside. As the victim left J and O were together. O approached the victim and there was a scuffle. They were parted and the victim walked away. He next saw J, O and another coming towards him. O confronted the victim and J took an estate agent's board and hit the victim with its post. He made heavy determined blows to the head. A witness thought he was going to be killed and telephoned the police. A witness saw a second man punching out with both fists at the victim. He saw a third man watching. Another witness said he saw three men punching and kicking a man on the floor. That witness told them to leave him alone and two stopped and one carried on kicking and stamping on his face, head and body. The victim had fractured ribs and a ruptured spleen, which had to be removed. This has affected his immune system. He has permanent tinnitus in his ear and blurred vision. The injuries were life threatening. He wanted to be a sound engineer, which is now not practical. The defendants expressed shame and remorse. J was 30 and had a long list of convictions including wounding, ABH, two for cruelty to animals and possession of an offensive weapon. O was 23 and had less violent convictions but had one for robbery. J's basis of plea was that he struck one blow with the estate agent's board and delivered two or three kicks. Held. This was a truly brutal, sustained attack with consequences that the victim will have to endure long after the defendants are released. If there was a trial **7^1/$_2$ to 8 years** could not be criticised. **6 years** was not manifestly excessive.

Att-Gen's Ref. Nos. 44 and 45 of 2001 2002 1 Cr App R (S) 283. The defendant S was convicted of GBH with intent. G pleaded guilty to the same offence. No one saw the start of the attack near a kebab van. The victim who had spent the evening in pubs was slightly built and 5' 2" One witness saw S then 21 holding the victim against a wall punching him 8–12 times in the face and head. The victim fell to the ground and lay motionless on his back. A group then kicked him to the head and upper body. S delivered 10–15 hard kicks like a footballer kicking a ball. G then 19 kicked him 10 times and said, "That's how you fucking do it." A witness tried to stop it and lay across the prone body. He shouted for them to stop and he was kicked powerfully and frequently to the body, head and chest. A woman tried to use her mobile phone to call the police and another woman punched her. A witness who had been in the army and was trained in first aid saw the victim and found no pulse or signs of life. He found the victim had swallowed his tongue and cleared the victim's airway. He commenced resuscitation and the victim remained unconscious throughout. The victim was taken to hospital and on the Glasgow coma scale he was 3. He was in hospital for nearly 3 weeks. Six months afterwards he was still having nightmares and had only just returned to work. He was on anti-depressants and his concentration wasn't what it should have been. He was seeing a clinical psychologist. The man who lay prone on the body had bruising to his eye, jaw and ribs. When interviewed, S said he had been drinking and had taken an ecstasy pill. He made no comment about the attack. G said he had no memory of the attack. S had convictions mostly for dishonesty and motoring offences. There was a s 20 glassing. G's record was not as bad and included ABH. S showed no remorse. Held. This was a particularly bad case. The facts are too shocking to require any further elaboration. This was a sustained and vicious unprovoked assault, which could have resulted in the death of the victim. The appropriate sentence for S after his trial was **7 years** and for G on his plea **5 years**. As it was a reference **6 years** not 4 for S and ordinarily we would have imposed on G 4 years. However, because of the delay and 4 years would make him a long-term prisoner **3 years 9 months** not 3 years detention instead.

Old case *Att-Gen's Ref. Nos. 62 and 63 of 1997* 1998 2 Cr App R (S) 300, (for a summary of the case see the first edition of this book.)

Knives, with – 5 years or less appropriate

121.31   *Att-Gen's Ref. No 27 of 1999* 2000 1 Cr App R (S) 237. The defendant was convicted of wounding with intent. In July 1996, the victim who was black was with a group of mostly black friends. They visited a nightclub and a group of white youths started making insulting remarks to his group. A slanging match developed which the defendant then 21, was not part of. A missile hit the victim then he and others left and a fracas developed outside. A Mr Selby spat in the victim's face and the victim threw him to the ground and stood over him. He also stabbed the victim in the right leg. While the victim was dealing with Mr Selby the defendant stabbed the victim in the buttocks. The victim ran off. A Swiss army knife was found close by with the victim's blood and the defendant's fingerprints on it. The victim had 11 lacerations in the buttocks and a 2 cm cut to his thigh. The defendant said he had been drinking and could not recall much. The defendant was not tried until March 1999 through no fault of his. The defendant had a lengthy criminal record although he had never had a custodial sentence before. He was on probation at the time. Held. Taking into account the mitigation the sentence should have been **2¹/₂ years**. As it was a reference **22 months** not 15.

Att-Gen's Ref. No 26 of 2000 2001 1 Cr App R (S) 188. The defendant pleaded guilty to wounding with intent. It was not at the first opportunity. The victim who was 18 drunk about 7 or 8 pints of lager. The defendant aged 21 and the victim both ended up in a nightclub. The defendant was involved in two incidents with other young men there. The victim left the club and saw his friend being attacked by the defendant and another. Witnesses said it was unprovoked. The victim intervened and witnesses said the victim was getting the better of the defendant until they saw four or five jabs to the victim's face. The victim shouted he's got something in his hand. Blood was seen on the victim's face. The victim remembered the defendant squared up to him and the defendant's hand flashed in front of the victim three or four times really fast. The victim had four lacerations cause by a very sharp knife. Two were over the forehead penetrating down to the bone and required nerve and muscle repair. Another one caused cartilage damage. One was 14 cm and one 12 cm long. The scarring was extremely serious, as it was permanent and very disfiguring. The victim was changed from an ambitious outgoing man to a withdrawn one who finds profound difficulties with his work and social life. The defendant had convictions although he had never had custody before. He was of limited intelligence. Because of medical opinion he was sentenced on the basis he used a very sharp knife. Held. When a victim is seriously injured in an unprovoked attack the offender must be seriously punished. Were it not for the particular factors and that it was a reference the sentence would be substantially higher. $4^1/_2$ **years** not $3^1/_2$ years.

R v White 2003 2 Cr App R (S) 354. The defendant pleaded guilty to wounding with intent. He was involved in a fight with G, another drug user. Later that evening the defendant armed himself with a 10-inch knife and went and found G in a park. He stabbed him in the back once without warning. G suffered a 3 cm cut and significant blood loss. His left kidney had to be surgically removed. Other witnesses were sufficiently intimidated to say that they had seen nothing. The defendant threw the knife into a canal and gave a false account to the police. The defendant had had an horrific upbringing. He was 19 and had 5 convictions for violence (albeit none at this level). The PSR said he had a 6 year history of drug abuse. There was no formal mental illness. Held. There was nothing impulsive about this attack. He had threatened witnesses. Because of the plea **5 years detention** not 7.

Knives, with – More than 5 years appropriate

121.32 *Att-Gen's Ref. No 86 of 1998* 2000 1 Cr App R (S) 10. The defendant was convicted of wounding with intent, ABH and having an offensive weapon. In the early hours of New Year's Day the victim and his girlfriend paused to kiss outside a block of flats on their way home. Two girls told them to do that outside their own house. As they started to leave the defendant who had been drinking arrived. He said, "I'm telling you to leave." He ran after them stood in front of them and punched the victim several times. The victim punched back. A co-accused arrived and tried to separate them. He was punched by the victim and then joined in the attack. The defendant then produced a knife and the victim raised his arm to defend himself. The knife cut through his jacket and the muscle and tissue of his arm and caused a chip fracture to his left elbow and an 8×7 cm wound in his forearm. The co-accused called an ambulance. The ambulance arrived and the crew were confronted by about seven people. The crew did not think it safe to render any assistance and called the police. In a further attack on the victim he was knocked to the ground, punched and kicked. He was assaulted again by the defendant who then went into the block of flats where he lived and came out carrying a baseball bat. The victim fled. The victim's fracture required a metal plate and 25 stitches. He was in hospital for 4 days. He fell behind with his Master's Degree. When the defendant was sentenced the victim still had restricted movement of his arm. The defendant had no convictions for violence. Held. We would have expected a sentence of **6 years**. Because it was a reference $4^1/_2$ **years** not 2.

Att-Gen's Ref. No 52 of 2001 Unreported 30/7/01. 7 years would be the least sentence for this attack with a Stanley knife on the partner of girl who the defendant fancied.

Att-Gen's Ref. No. 18 of 2002 2003 1 Cr App R (S) 35. The defendant pleaded guilty to Section 18 at a late stage and Section 20. The 16 year old schoolboy victim was walking in the street and overtook the defendant and B who were together. The defendant shouted "Twat" at him. When the victim reached the Bus Terminus the defendant barged into him and stabbed him with a knife in the stomach with a 5" to 6" blade. The victim was in hospital for eight days. The wound was 2cms long and entered the peritoneal cavity and breached the bowel. The boy ran and sought help. Two days later there was bad feeling within B's family and B's girlfriend. There was a disturbance in the street. R ran to a car and broke the side window with A in it. The defendant armed with what A thought was a knife slashed all four tyres, R kicked the car and A tried to drive off. The defendant leant in through the broken window and tried to drag A out of the car. In doing so, he inflicted two small puncture wounds to A's arm. The defendant was arrested nearby and admitted involvement in the incident but denied wounding A. Six days later he was arrested for the first attack and made no comment in interview. The basis of plea for the car attack was that the weapon was a piece of metal and not a knife. Also the injury was caused by A moving around in the car. The defendant was 23 with convictions for assault on police more than once, robbery and more than one common assault all in 1995. There was a wounding and assault with intent to resist arrest in 1996, and two robberies in 1997. Thereafter there had been burglaries and dishonesty but no violence save two criminal damage offences in 2001. He was sentenced to 15 months on each consecutive. *Held.* The authorities demonstrate that the bracket where knives are used is **3 to 8 years**. We would have expected **6 years**. As it was a reference **5 years** substituted; with section 20 penalty the same, making **6 years 3 months**.

Att-Gen's Ref. No. 132 of 2001 2003 1 Cr App R (S) 190. The defendant pleaded guilty to Section 18. He was an alcoholic and lived with the victim in a home for the homeless. Each had a room. Another resident, M, refused the defendant's girlfriend entry into the home. A few days later, the defendant remonstrated to M, the victim and another about that. The victim tried to calm the defendant down and told him to leave. The defendant punched the victim and the other resident and left. The police were called but the victim did not want to pursue the matter. The three residents complained to the landlord about the defendant's behaviour and the defendant was given a week to leave the home. The defendant told an acquaintance that he was going to sort out those responsible. The day before he had to go and after he had been drinking, he went to the victim's room and ransacked it turning over the furniture and belongings. He then went to M's room and found M and the victim there. He accused the victim of getting him evicted and punched him on the face, causing him to fall to the floor. He then kicked him several times to the head and body causing the victim's nose to bleed heavily as he lay unconscious. The defendant then left to fetch a knife and returned. M tried to rouse the victim and the defendant kicked the victim twice more. He then stabbed the victim nine times in the lower back and buttocks while the victim lay motionless on the floor. The defendant shouted, "Die you bastard," and "Right you bastard you are going to die." A witness was also hit and the defendant left. Shortly after, another resident found the defendant crying and he told her, "I just could not control myself any longer. It has been boiling up for ages. I've done it". Police found him in a very agitated state and he handed the knife over and said, "He deserved it the bastard. He got me kicked out of my flat." The victim underwent major surgery in which his colon and upper rectum were removed. He came very close to death. After the operation he had major organ failure and he had further surgery and was in hospital for five months. He suffered lasting damage and continuing pain. He has a colostomy, walks with a limp and lacks sensation and muscle control in parts of his body. The defendant was 31 and of good character in employment as a gardener. The people he worked for were astonished at his behaviour and wrote letters of support. He expressed remorse. *Held.* The starting point should have been **9 years** and with a plea **at least 6 years**. Because it was a reference **5 years** substituted for 4.

R v Webster 2004 2 Cr App R (S) 413. The defendant pleaded guilty on re-arraignment to wounding with intent to cause GBH. He had been at a club with a woman, R, with whom he had had a relationship. She danced with the victim, V, at the club. She and the defendant became separated, he went home, and she went home with the victim. Shortly after she arrived home the defendant rang her bell and when she wouldn't let him in he kicked the door open, and ran upstairs to her flat. He stabbed the victim in the back of his head with a Stanley knife and then cut his face from below his ear to the corner of his mouth. He would have a scar for life with damage to the nerves on the victim's face. The victim was also afraid of going out and was worried he would have difficulties finding a girlfriend because of the scar. His eventual basis of plea was not acceptable to the prosecution and there was Newton hearing with the V and R giving evidence. The Judge said he found the defendant wholly unworthy of belief. The defendant, 28, had a short criminal record and no offences of violence. It was said on his behalf that there was a relatively low level of premeditation, it was not a sustained assault, and apart from the scarring the injuries had healed. The aggravating features were use of a bladed instrument which would inevitably cause serious injury, the assault was not entirely unpremeditated as he had the knife with him and entered the flat with the blade exposed, he barged his way in and committed an unprovoked attack on a stranger. Held. When a defendant pleads guilty three months after a plea and directions hearing and then advances an untruthful version of events which requires the victim and an eyewitness to relive the experience and have their truthfulness challenged, he is only entitled to limited credit for his plea. It was impossible to say that **9 years** was excessive.

R v Marsh 2004 2 Cr App R (S) 429. The defendant pleaded guilty to wounding with intent and theft. The victim was his ex-partner, P. They had lived together for 6 years and during that time he had been violent towards her although, she said, 'not excessively so'. The cause of his violence was his heavy drinking. He was also injecting heroin although there were periods when he was trying to stop this. They had 2 children. 12 weeks before the offence he had started using heroin again and she asked him to leave and sort himself out. He would visit the children from time to time and there were episodes of theft from her to finance his drug taking. On the day of the offence he saw her in town and said he was going to smash her house up and 'get her with this' – although she couldn't see what he had in his hand. He later went to her house and caused damage and stole items. At 7.30 pm he went to the house and slashed her face with a Stanley knife. She had three deep slashes to her face which required numerous stitches, two superficial wounds to her arm, and a deep wound to her arm which required stitches. She said she thought he was trying to kill her. She had changed her phone and asked to be re-housed. She suffered flashbacks and nightmares, had permanent scars and suffered loss of feeling to her forehead. The defendant, 29, had some 50 previous convictions for offences including theft, possession of an offensive weapon and robbery. A pre-sentence report said he had suffered frequent violence when a child from his alcoholic father, as had his mother and siblings. He had been using heroin for five years. Police had frequently attended the home he shared with the victim following assaults by the defendant on the victim. Sometimes these assaults were in front of the children. Once he had threatened her with an axe and a screwdriver. He was assessed as having a high risk of re-offending and posed a high risk especially to his victim. He had expressed remorse for the attack but tended to minimise the effect of his violence on his victim. The court had a statement from her saying that she found his sentence harsh, she had visited him in prison and he had apologised to her. Also he was a different person off drugs and that she would have been happy with a sentence of 4 or 5 years. Held. There was no mitigation other than the plea of guilty. Insufficient credit was given for that plea. The sentence was reduced from 10 to **8** years.

Att-Gen's Ref No 26 of 2004 2005 1 Cr App R (S) 118. The defendant was convicted of wounding with intent to cause GBH. The defendant and the victim had been good friends, but in recent times the defendant claimed that the victim owned him money. The defendant and an older man went to confront the victim in his home. After an argument they left but returned about 3 minutes later. The victim, in the face of demands, said that he had no money and was unemployed. The victim was fearful that the defendant had a weapon and picked up a walking stick to defend himself. The defendant's friend took the walking stick and the defendant took out a knife with a 7" blade and struck the victim's neck. The victim tried to run out of his house and was pursued by the defendant and struck him in the head. The defendant hit the victim over the head and body with the walking stick and broke it. The wounds bled profusely from a 3" wound to the neck requiring 18 stitches and a 4" wound to the back of the head requiring 15 stitches. He had physical scarring, nightmares and severe headaches. When interviewed he said that he acted in self-defence. He was 35 with good character. Held. This was a very serious case of wounding with intent that occurred in the victim's home. The degree of premeditation including fetching a weapon and disarming the victim. There was a repeated attack. Following a trial **7 years**, but as this was a reference, **6 years** not 3 years 9 months.

[The sentences have risen following the court's change in attitude to knives. A similar trend can be found in the cases listed under **MANSLAUGHTER**]

Old cases. Ignore them before *R v Pollin* 1997 2 Cr App R (S) 356; *R v McPhee* 1998 1 Cr App R (S) 201 (see **121.34**), and *Att-Gen's Ref. No 4 of 1998* 1998 2 Cr App R (S) 388, (for a summary of the first and last cases see the first edition of this book.)

Life was appropriate

121.33   *Att-Gen's Ref. No 88 of 1998* 1999 2 Cr App R (S) 346. The defendant, a serving prisoner was convicted of wounding with intent. Another prisoner was talking to a police officer in a therapy workshop. He approached from behind and plunged a screwdriver into the prisoner's back, saying, "That's for you, you fucker," and later, "The fucker deserved it." The screwdriver was used with considerable force and was buried up to its 10 cm hilt. The defendant had asked for the screwdriver 10 minutes before. The victim was taken to hospital and the screwdriver was seen on X ray to be 1 cm from the heart. He was lucky to be alive and lucky not to have suffered catastrophic injuries. The defendant said the victim had made repeated unwanted advances to him and he just flipped. The defendant had 26 previous court appearances including robbery, and burglary. In the robbery he threatened a pharmacist with a knife demanding drugs. While serving his sentence for that offence he attacked a fellow prisoner with a Stanley knife. He slashed the back of his neck and stabbed him in the side of the body. He received 2 years for an offence under s 20. Psychiatrists said he suffered from marked instability of mood and behaviour. He had a strong sense of being persecuted. Not particularly frequently he heard voices. He had a severe personality disorder. He presents a risk of further violent offences. Treatment was unlikely to be successful. The judge sentenced him to 7 years as a longer than commensurate sentence. Held. The instance offence was very serious. It required a very long sentence. He was unstable. He cannot be dealt with under the Mental Health Act. There is a substantial risk he will re-offend. He represents a grave danger to the public and will remain so for the indefinite future. The appropriate sentence was **life** with 5 years specified.

Life was not appropriate

121.34   *R v McPhee* 1998 1 Cr App R (S) 201. LCJ. The defendant pleaded guilty to wounding with intent. He was 27 and had been a serving soldier for 4 or 5 years. Two days before the incident the victim and the defendant were drinking and the defendant was taking ketamine, a drug with psychedelic properties. At one stage the victim was aggressive. The next day the victim again spent a substantial time drinking and went to bed before midnight. He was awoken by loud banging on his front door. The defendant was outside and when the door was opened the defendant punched the victim about the head and face. The victim said the defendant had a metal rod but the defendant denied this. The victim was knocked back into a chair and the defendant was shouting incoherently. He said, "I'm going to do you in," and he accused the victim of stitching up one of the defendant's friends and that he was going to kill him. Two others came in and assaulted the victim. One claimed the victim owed him money but the victim told him to 'piss off'. As the victim stood up to hand over some money the defendant stabbed him in the chest and lower back. The defendant told him not to go to the police but did assist in trying to stem the blood. He then said if he went to the police his brother would come down from Scotland and "finish him off". The defendant left and the victim went to a friend's room to recuperate. 45 minutes later the defendant returned under the influence of drugs with a machete. The threats were repeated and he left. The victim went to hospital and the wound was sutured. One wound was a 1″ laceration involving skin and fat. The other was 1″ and very shallow. The defendant was arrested and admitted the offence and said that he was under the influence of drugs and that he picked up the knife and was so worked up in his head. In 1988 he had convictions for breach of the peace, and two assault on police officers for which he was admonished. In 1994 he was fined for common assault. He had punched the manager of a restaurant during a fracas. In 1995 he was fined for vandalism. In 1996 he was given probation for ABH on his wife who was accused of infidelity. The psychiatric report said, 'he posed a high risk of further offending. His anger remains whether or not he is under the influence. He fails to see he has a choice or could have acted differently. The public need to be protected from his potential to commit violent offences.' Another report said, 'the defendant described feelings of intense anger and he thought about stabbing and beating up people. He has a personality disorder characterised by an incapacity to experience guilt and antisocial behaviour. There was also a pattern of escalating violence.' The judge described the attack as savage, mindless, and very dangerous. He also said the defendant posed a serious danger to the public for an indefinite time. Since then a report said he did not have a personality disorder but had severe difficulty with anger control. Held. It cannot be said that he is likely to represent a serious danger to the public for an indeterminate time. Accordingly life is inappropriate. The previous convictions are not of a type or number which by themselves would justify anything other than a commensurate sentence. A commensurate sentence is sufficient and it is not necessary to pass a longer than normal sentence. It was worth **9 years** and because of the guilty plea **7 years** not life.

Life Sentence/Automatic life sentence – Fixing specified term

121.35   *R v Lee* 2001 1 Cr App R (S) 1. The defendant pleaded guilty to GBH with intent. The defendant had convictions for GBH with intent, and wounding. He was sentenced to automatic life and the judge considered 12 years was appropriate if a determinate sentence was passed. He thought 8 years should be specified. This was reduced to 6 years 9 months to take into account the period on remand. Held. 6 years would have been appropriate for a determinate sentence. He was entitled to $^1/_2$ not a $^1/_2$ discount so 3 years specified making it **1 year 9 months**.

See also *Att-Gen's Ref. No 82 of 2000* 2001 2 Cr App R (S) 289

Longer than commensurate sentences (frequently wrongly called extended sentence)

121.36   Powers of Criminal Courts (Sentencing) Act 2000 s 80(2)(b). ... the custodial sentence shall be...where the offence is a violent or sexual offence, for such longer term (not exceeding the maximum) as in the opinion of the court is necessary to protect the public from serious harm from the offender. (previously the Criminal Justice Act 1991 s 2(2)(b).)

R v McPhee 1998 1 Cr App R (S) 201. LCJ. Not appropriate here. See **121.34**.

See also Longer than Commensurate Sentences

Motorists   See *Vehicles*

Passion, Crime of/Emotional attack

121.37   *Att-Gen's Ref No 99 of 2002* 2003 2 Cr App R (S) 290. The defendant pleaded guilty to causing grievous bodily harm with intent on the day fixed for his trial. He had been an amateur boxer and he and his fiancé went to a pub where they met two male friends, H and D. At closing time, the defendant and his fiancé invited H and D back to their home to have more to drink. At about 1.45am, the defendant was in the kitchen with D. He then went into the living room and saw H kissing his fiancé where he lost his temper and punched H repeatedly in the face and head. H was knocked to the floor where the defendant kicked him and possibly stamped on him. H suffered bruising and bleeding to his face, and his jaw was fractured in two places. There was some permanent disability. The defendant and D took the unconscious H into the street where the defendant put him into the recovery position. An ambulance and the police attended. The defendant made full admissions to the physical acts. He had no convictions for offences of violence. *Held*. The starting point was **4 years**. However, because this was a reference, **30 months** not a deferred sentence coupled with a compensation order.

R v Hudson 2003 2 Cr App R (S) 327. The defendant pleaded guilty to wounding with intent. The victim had been involved in a long relationship with Miss F and had a daughter, aged 6. He was an alcoholic and suffered from epilepsy. Miss F began a relationship with the defendant and broke off her relationship with the victim. The victim's subsequent behaviour led Miss F to complain to the police on over 100 occasions. His behaviour ranged from phoning her 3 or 4 times a day, shouting at her in the street, visiting her house and making threats. Child contact arrangements were conducted through solicitors. On the day of the attack the victim phoned Miss F with a view to seeing their daughter. Miss F had reacted with hostility. The defendant had become aware of the extent of the unwanted approaches by the victim and went looking for him. He visited and left a message with the victim's sister: "Tell him I'll kill him." The sister noticed that he was carrying a hammer. The victim was later walking the street when the defendant pulled up in his lorry, got out and attacked him with a hammer. He hit him on the head a number of times and kicked and punched him whilst he was on the ground. He left him there bleeding. He was later found wandering in the street with blood on his face. A CT scan revealed a haematoma with a gross midline shift of the brain. He had a left-sided skull fracture which extended to the base of the skull. He was lucky to survive but remained very ill. His health had not been good prior to the attack. He had in fact since died. On arrest the defendant denied the attack but subsequently admitted it. The defendant was effectively of good character and had been in good employment. He had four children from his previous marriage. A psychiatrist reported that he was riddled with remorse and that the risk of re-offending was low. *Held*. This was a case where the defendant acted out of a sense of seeking to protect the woman with whom he was living. He conducted a very severe attack that caused the victim most serious, life-threatening injuries. **6 years** upheld.

Att-Gen's Ref. No 87 of 2003 2005 1 Cr App R (S) 68. The defendant was convicted of wounding with intent, harassment (s. 4(1) of the Harassment Act 1997). The victim and the defendant lived in a relatively close-knit community and it is clear that the victim had made the acquaintance of the defendant's girlfriend. That relationship developed through text messages. The defendant became intensely jealous and suspected that there was more to the relationship. The victim was at work in a shop when the defendant approached him and without warning, took out a bag of two ice lollipops enclosed in plastic (Ice Pops) which were between 6–8″ long and struck the victim over the head with them 4 or 5 times with sufficient force to cause a 5 cm laceration over the left frontal region of the head (requiring 5 stitches) and a 5cm laceration on the right side (requiring 4 stitches). He left the shop threatening to kill the victim. Thereafter he phoned the victim and threatened him. 2½ months later they met by chance. The defendant approached the victim and pointing a Stanley Knife at him asked him whether he had anything to tell him. The defendant then threatened the victim who managed to run off. The defendant and his girlfriend had been together for 11 years and they had 2 children. He said that he had bought the lollipops for his children. It was accepted that the second meeting had occurred by chance. He was of good character, with severe learning difficulties and dyslexia. He was someone who had been unable to control his temper at the time. Held. The lowest sentence was **2 years** for the GBH with intent and **12 months consecutive** for the harassment. As he had completed 100 hours of CPO and as this was a reference, **18 months and 6 months consecutive** respectively.

See also *Relationship attacks*

Police officers on duty as victims

121.38   *Att-Gen's Ref. No 78 of 2000* 2002 1 Cr App R (S) 500. The defendant was convicted of four counts of GBH with intent and two counts of ABH. All the victims were police officers on duty in police cars. Two police offers decided to stop the defendant's Nissan four-wheel drive after they did a vehicle check. They flashed the lights of their car and the Nissan stopped. As the officers got out the Nissan drove across a grassy area and the officers were unable to follow. They caught up with it when it returned to the road and the Nissan stopped and reversed twice into their car at considerable speed. There was a further chase and the Nissan reversed into their car again at speed. These were the ABH counts. One officer received acute neck strain and back strain. The other sustained neck strain. Shortly after the Nissan rammed another police car, a Vectra, on the off-side front wing and then rammed it on the nearside pillar. The Nissan then drove at a third police car, a Fiesta, and the car was badly damaged. The Vectra then pursued the Nissan and the Nissan rammed the police car six times. The defendant was arrested shortly after he had left the vehicle with another man. He denied being the driver. The two occupants of the Fiesta received whiplash injuries and received cuts to the face and arm, the two occupants of the Vectra also received whiplash injuries and one had misaligned teeth. All the officers returned to work. The defendant was 30 and had convictions for perverting the course of justice, assaulting a constable (3 months), reckless driving (9 months), reckless driving (12 months) and threatening behaviour for which he was fined. Held. The gravity of using a vehicle as a weapon increases when it is used repeatedly and at police officers. In many authorities the vehicle is used at a body. Here it was used at a car in which officers were in. Happily the officers were not as injured as they might have been. We would expect **6 to 7 years**. As it was a reference **5 years** not 4.

R v Wight 2003 1 Cr App R (S) 228. The defendant was convicted of Section 18. He was acquitted of attempted murder. The defendant set out to steal cars and to burgle dwelling houses if the occasion arose. He had a long-bladed screwdriver and a knife. In a village he broke into a car and started to hot wire the engine. He was seen and the owner, a PC, was told. He went to the car, told the defendant he was a police officer and showed him his warrant card. The defendant got out of the car holding a knife and screwdriver, one in each hand. He was told to drop them and the defendant just walked towards him saying, "Piss off" or "Go away." The PC backed off and the defendant ran off down the street and jumped over a fence. The PC followed and found the defendant and the defendant said, "Right I'll hurt you." The PC held his ground and the defendant raised his hand, rushed forward and stabbed him in the chest to the depth of 2″. The PC reeled back and he was stabbed in the chest with the knife. The defendant kept trying to stab him and stabbed him in the arm and the leg. As the PC tried to stand up he was stabbed in the chest again. The defendant ran off. An artery had been ruptured. He would have died if the paramedics had not arrived very quickly. The defendant was then almost 24 with a bad record going back to when he was 15 including ABH when he bit a police officer, dishonesty, TDA, discharge of noxious gas, and in 2000 affray for which he received 15 months. For this he was still on licence. Held. The circumstances demonstrate his violent tendencies. The convictions and the circumstances were an adequate basis for a longer than commensurate sentence. **10 years** as a commensurate sentence was not manifestly excessive. The Judge did not err with **15 years** as a longer than commensurate sentence.

Att-Gen's Ref. No 99 of 2003 2005 1 Cr App R (S) 151. The defendant was convicted of GBH with intent to resist or prevent the lawful apprehension of himself. He was also convicted of affray. Two police officers were called to a Working Man's Club where there had been a disturbance involving members of the defendant's family. The victim police officer spoke to the defendant who told him to 'fuck off'. The victim then noticed that the club manager was being attacked by another man and went to help the manager. While he was struggling with the attacker, the defendant grabbed his neck, squeezed his throat, pushed him onto his knees, punched him in the head knocking him to the ground, stamped on his face, and kicked him repeatedly in the head and near his throat. The defendant then attacked the other police officer and only stopped when he was sprayed with CS gas. The victim was taken to hospital and discharged later that night. His head was painful to touch, he had two small cuts on his face and head, one side of his face and his jaw were swollen and he had a black eye. He had a wound to his upper lip that needed four stitches. A medical report said that eight months after the attack he suffered from persistent double vision for which he might have to have surgery, headaches and a persistent click in his jaw. He had just returned to light police duties. The defendant, 38, had previous convictions for drugs, dishonesty and violence. He had two previous convictions for ABH and one for assault on police. Since the offence he had sought to address his alcohol and anger management problems. At the time of the events his wife was mentally unwell. Before the appeal court there was a letter from the defendant expressing remorse and a letter from the prison showing he was an enhanced prisoner and was being trained by the Samaritans. Held. It was true that the victim's injuries were not of the utmost severity but although the consequences of violent conduct are important, the nature of the defendant's conduct is even more important. The appropriate sentence for the GBH was **5 years** imprisonment. As it was a reference and the due to the significant progress he was making in prison it was not necessary to make him a long term prisoner and **3 years 11 months** not 30 months.

R v Butler 2005 1 Cr App R (S) 712. The defendant was convicted of attempting to cause GBH with intent to resist arrest or prevent lawful detention. At a previous hearing he had pleaded guilty to two offences of handling stolen goods, making off without payment and giving a false name with the intention of perverting the course of justice. The defendant was stopped by PC Poyser on the M11 for driving with excessive speed. He had a woman passenger. The officer attempted to arrest him for driving whilst disqualified and the defendant provided a false name. He resisted arrest and punched the officer twice in the chest. He then got back into the car while PC Poyser tried to pull him out and another officer tried to pull the ignition keys out. The woman passenger punched PC Poyser in the face several times. An off duty officer stopped to help and tried to pull the defendant out of the car. The defendant started the engine and drove off, taking with him PC Poyser who had his foot in the driver's footwell. The vehicle gathered speed and the defendant steered towards the central barrier shouting 'You're going to die you bastard'. He then swerved away from the barrier and braked causing PC Poyser to release his grip and tumble across the motorway. PC Poyser suffered a broken nose, numerous cuts, grazes, bruises and severe body pains. PC Mann had been dragged 10 yards before he was thrown clear and had bruising to his arms and a cut to his finger. The car was later found abandoned and in it were a stolen briefcase and printer, which were the subject of one of the stolen goods charges. The career of PC Poyser who had served 24 years in the police force ended. Held. This was a very clear and deliberate attempt to cause really serious injury to a police officer. The sentence of **10 years** for the attempt to cause GBH was fully justified. The other sentences were ordered to run concurrently.

R v Huntroyd 2005 1 Cr App R (S) 442. The defendant was convicted of attempting to cause GBH with intent. The victim, a police officer, was on foot patrol, where via CCTV a car had been noticed in the service area of some shops. The passenger of the car was holding a can of lager. The officer approached the service area and the defendant drove towards the officer who moved into the middle of the road, and signalled the defendant to stop. He appeared to acknowledge the officer and started to pull the vehicle over as if to stop. He then put the car into gear and drove straight at the officer who tried to move out of the way but could only turn away whereby the car, travelling between 15 and 20mph, struck him on the back of his legs. The officer ended up on the roof of the car hanging onto the sunroof. The defendant accelerated down a busy high street, went the wrong way round a roundabout and continued to try to throw the officer off the car by swerving from side to side, and by accelerating and braking suddenly. He tried to close the sunroof on the officer's fingers. When he reached the end of the road, he turned left at such speed that the car lurched across to the wrong side of the road and the officer was thrown into the road. The defendant was using his partner's car without her permission and was a disqualified driver. The officer sustained a fracture of the scaphoid bone (which the jury had doubts was a really serious injury so the conviction was for an attempt instead). He was unable to return to work until 6 months after the incident and was having difficulty in sleeping. The defendant was 31 with an extensive drug and alcohol history and a bad record for dishonesty and violence. He had 3 convictions for disqualified driving. Held. The intent weighed heavily against the defendant. This was a police officer doing his duty. The defendant's manner of driving after the initial impact clearly demonstrated an intent to cause really serious harm. **9 years** was wholly appropriate.

Old cases. *R v Hall 1997 1 Cr App R (S) 62.*

Prison officers, against

121.39   *Att-Gen's Ref. No 88 of 1998* 1999 2 Cr App R (S) 346. The defendant, a serving prisoner was convicted of wounding with intent. Another prisoner was talking to a police officer in a therapy workshop. He approached from behind and plunged a screwdriver into the prisoner's back, saying, "That's for you, you fucker," and later, "The fucker deserved it." The screwdriver was used with considerable force and was buried up to its 10 cm hilt. The defendant had asked for the screwdriver 10 minutes before. The victim was taken to hospital and the screwdriver was seen on X ray to be 1 cm from the heart. He was lucky to be alive and lucky not to have suffered catastrophic injuries. The defendant said the victim had made repeated unwanted advances to him and he just flipped. The defendant had 26 previous court appearances including robbery and burglary. In the robbery he threatened a pharmacist with a knife demanding drugs. While serving his sentence for that offence he attacked a fellow prisoner with a Stanley knife. He slashed the back of his neck and stabbed him in the side of the body. He received 2 years for a s 20 offence. Psychiatrists said he suffered from marked instability of mood and behaviour. He had a strong sense of being persecuted. Not particularly frequently he heard voices. He had a severe personality disorder. He presents a risk of further violent offences. Treatment was unlikely to be successful. The judge sentenced him to 7 years as a longer than commensurate sentence under the longer than normal provisions. Held. The instance offence was very serious. It required a very long sentence. He was unstable. He cannot be dealt with under the Mental Health Act 1983. There is a substantial risk he will re-offend. He represents a grave danger to the public and will remain so for the indefinite future. The appropriate sentence was **life** with 5 years specified.

See also PRISONERS – *Total sentence when sentence consecutive to the sentence being served*

Punishing the victim, motive to

121.40   *R v Lee* 2001 1 Cr App R (S) 1. The defendant pleaded guilty to GBH with intent. The victim who worked in a store sold and delivered a bed to the defendant's girlfriend. The victim was attracted to her and sent her a letter expressing his feelings. The defendant and two other men went to the store. The defendant grabbed him, pushed him back and told him to leave his girlfriend alone. He then repeatedly punched him and the victim fell to the floor. He knelt on his neck and punched him in the face. He stood up and kicked the victim in the ribs. The two other men prevented a colleague of the victim from helping him. Later the defendant kicked the victim again on the back of the head two or three times and stamped on his head five times. The attack lasted about 2 minutes and the blows might well have killed him. The victim had a fractured skull but no brain damage. He had a small bruise above his eye, a swelling on the jaw and some scrapes over the temple. He was in hospital for 2 days twice. The defendant had convictions for GBH with intent, and wounding. He was sentenced to automatic life. Held. It was a very serious and vicious attack. It was premeditated. It was amazing no more serious damage was caused. **6 years** would have been appropriate for a determinate sentence.

R v Frost 2001 2 Cr App R (S) 124. The defendant pleaded guilty to GBH with intent. The victim who knew the defendant visited a friend in a block where the defendant lived. As he was leaving he saw the defendant and the co-accused and he was seized and bundled into the defendant's flat. He was put on a bed, the door was blocked and an iron was turned on. The victim said he had done nothing wrong. Both punched him in the face and head and then pulled him to the floor where he was kicked in the side and back. The defendant held his arms and neck tightly while the other put the hot iron on his naked back. While he screamed the others laughed. He was dragged into the hallway where the other man hit him in the face with the iron. The defendant held his hands and kicked him. His face was hit against a cupboard. The victim managed to struggle free and escape. [No medical report is referred to.] He was told the defendant wanted to give him £2,000 to keep his mouth shut. The defendant had a significant number of convictions for violent, driving and dishonesty offences. In 1991 when 15, he was found guilty of an offence under s 18 and received a supervision order. He had stabbed a police officer in the face with a screwdriver after a car chase. He told the probation officer that the victim had burgled his flat. His risk of re-offending was assessed as high but he had a good prison report. He was sentenced to automatic life, which was quashed because there were exceptional circumstances. Held. This was a very nasty attack. It was persistent, calculated and vicious and involved two people. **5 years** substituted.

Att-Gen's Ref. No 20 of 2004 2005 1 Cr App R 615. The defendant was convicted of Section 18 wounding. The victim went with three friends at 3.30am to buy food from a petrol station near his home. The defendant pulled up at the petrol station in a car with two others and tried to get petrol from a pump but it didn't operate at that hour without advance payment. He went to the cashier's window pushing in front of the victim and his friends. The victim protested. The defendant returned to his car, signalled the other passengers to get out and took a steering lock from the boot of his car. One of his passengers had a knife. The man with the knife stabbed the victim and the defendant hit him over the head with the steering lock. The victim tried to escape and the defendant chased him and hit him again. The victim got up and tried to escape and the defendant hit him again with the steering lock in a swinging motion with both hands above his shoulder. The defendant got into his car and drove away. The victim had three stab wounds and, as a consequence of blood loss, suffered severe brain injury. He was left blind, immobilised with no useful movement in any limb, confined to a wheelchair, doubly incontinent and totally dependant on 24-hour specialist nursing. No change was expected. The consequences for him and his family members were devastating. Following these events there was a search for the attackers although the other two involved were not found. The defendant was arrested at Stansted airport with a one-way ticket to Spain. His defence was alibi. Six aggravating features were said to be that he instigated the attack and enlisted others to take part; that the steering lock and knife were used as weapons; that the victim was unarmed; that the attack was planned; that the injuries were severe and permanent. The defendant, 29, was of previous good character. There was psychiatric evidence that he suffered from depression and claustrophobia. A letter from the chaplain of the prison said he was hard working and determined to contribute to society in a constructive manner on release and that he was a simple likeable character vulnerable to manipulation. A letter from the mother of one of his children spoke in graphic terms of the effects on the children of his imprisonment. Held. The least appropriate sentence following a trial for this very grave offence was **12** years. As it was a reference and to a limited extent, the personal mitigation, **9 years** not 5.

Old cases *Att-Gen's Ref. No 49 of 1996* 1997 2 Cr App R (S) 144; *Att-Gen's Ref. Nos. 8 and 9 of 1997* 1998 1 Cr App R (S) 98 and *R v McDonagh* 1998 2 Cr App R (S) 195, (for a summary of these cases see the first edition of this book.)

Racist attack

121.41   *Att-Gen's Ref. Nos. 29–31 of 1994* 1995 16 Cr App R (S) 698. LCJ. It cannot be too strongly emphasised that where there is a racial element in an offence of violence, that is a gravely aggravating feature.

R v Reader 2000 2 Cr App R (S) 442. The defendant was convicted of GBH with intent, ABH and criminal damage. Mr Bhangra, Mr Sheldrick and Mr Bhogal went to a public house, then to a buy some food and then Mr Bhangra went back to the public house. When he didn't return Mr Sheldrick went in. There was then an altercation between the three as to whether they should go home. The defendant with a half-full glass of beer approached Mr Bhangra and Mr Sheldrick who were at a van and asked, "Did you smash my glasses? I hope it was an accident. I'm the only one who smashes glasses." A girl who he was with told him to stop. He punched Mr Bhangra in the face and he fell down unconscious. This was the ABH. Other men joined the defendant and he asked, "What are you doing standing up for a Paki?" The defendant and three others started to kick the van. This was the criminal damage. Someone opened the rear doors of the van and Mr Sheldrick got out and as he stood up the defendant struck him with his glass of beer shattering the glass. The victim had a deep 3 cm laceration to his forehead with two superficial lacerations to each side. He was left with scarring and developed depression. When he went out he feared he would be attacked. Mr Bhangra had bruising and soreness to his eye and cheek. The van had dents to its side panels, wings and bonnet. The back door had been pulled off its hinges. As there was a racist motive **4½ years** with other concurrent sentences was appropriate.

See also **RACIALLY-AGGRAVATED OFFENCES**

Razor blades

121.42   *Att-Gen's Ref. Nos. 60 and 61 of 1997* 1998 2 Cr App R (S) 330. The defendants were convicted of wounding with intent. The defendant W aged 12 enquired of another girl whether she had been writing things about someone. She denied it. B also 12 handed W a razor blade and said "Go on, slash her." They approached another girl aged 14 and asked her the same question. She also denied it. W hit her across the face with the razor blade. She needed 26 stitches and is permanently scarred. B had convictions. Three days before the offence a supervision order had been made for theft, two assaults with intent to resist arrest, assault on police and obstruction. Less than 3 weeks before the wounding, she committed ABH and robbery. Six weeks after the wounding she committed affray. In the same month and 3 months later she committed three criminal damage offences. W had no convictions. The judge imposed a supervision order on each. W had responded well to it. Held. If they had been adults a sentence of **5 years** would have been imposed. **18 months** detention for B and **12 months** detention for W substituted.

Relationship attacks– *Men attacking wives and partners, or ex-wives or ex-partners* *– Less than 5 years appropriate*

121.43   *R v Mannion* 1999 2 Cr App R (S) 240. The defendant pleaded guilty to GBH with intent, ABH and common assault. After 17 years of married life the defendant's wife left the matrimonial home. About 2 weeks later they met to discuss the end of their marriage and the financial arrangements. The wife returned to where she was living. As she was sitting in her car outside the house the defendant appeared. He opened the car door, struck her in the face and pulled her hair, saying, "You're not having half. I'll kill you first." He was angry and walked off. The police arrested him and she suffered from two cuts and a graze. Nine days later his wife spent the evening with a male friend, the victim, and both went home to his house. The victim noticed a car was following their car home. They entered the house. There was a loud banging on the front door. Fearing that it might be the defendant because the victim had received abusive telephone calls from him he asked the defendant's wife to go upstairs. He did not answer the door and rang the police. The defendant smashed the front window and ran upstairs after the victim. The victim tried to barricade the defendant's wife and himself in the bedroom but the defendant burst in and hit him on the head with a small wrench. The wrench belonged to the victim. He beat the victim with the wrench until the victim seized it. He then struck the victim with a hammer. The wife tried to intervene and was repeatedly punched as she tried to intervene. The police arrived and arrested the defendant. The victim had multiple fractures to his arm and lacerations to his head and forehead. The wife had a cut to her eye and bruising to her legs. The defendant said he had employed a private detective to prove to his family that the victim was a confidence trickster. The basis for the plea was he went unarmed to the house to reason with his wife. The victim was armed with a hammer. He did not intend to assault or injure his wife. The defendant aged 56 was effectively of good character. He had many positive attributes. Held. Because the judge strayed from the agreed basis of plea and the mitigation **3 years** not 4. The other 1 month and 12 month concurrent sentences would remain.

Att-Gen's Ref. No 92 of 1998 2000 1 Cr App R (S) 13. The defendant pleaded guilty at the first opportunity to wounding with intent and assault with intent to resist arrest. In January 1998 after 12 years of marriage the defendant aged 40 separated from his wife, the victim. The wife left taking the three children with her. At 2am on 31 May 1998 the defendant after drinking went to where his wife was living with a hatchet and a kitchen knife. He broke into the house by breaking panes of glass. He climbed the stairs with the knife in one hand and the hatchet in the other and told his wife (who had woken and moved to the landing) that she was a dead woman. He raised the hatchet and hit her on her face with the blunt side. He raised it again and she pulled it from him and tried to take refuge between the children's bunk beds. He began a sustained attack with fists and booted feet and she became unconscious. Most of this took place in front of the children aged 13, 10 and 7 one of whom called the police. His 7-year-old son tried unsuccessfully to get the knife off his father. The defendant was present in the house for about 10 minutes. He then left. The victim was taken to hospital and stayed there for 9 days. She had extensive bruising on the back of her neck and shoulder, a huge haematoma on her head, swelling and bruising to both thighs and above the eye, and a huge swelling above the temple. She also had swellings to both ears, both cheeks, her lip, neck, chest and under her armpit. There were no fractures. When police arrested him he stripped to the waste and wielded a wooden walking stick at them and punched an officer a number of times. In interview he said he was devastated when his wife left him. The victim had continuing pain and has lost concentration and memory. The children had sustained distressing consequences also. The defendant at the time was profoundly disturbed following a mining accident, which caused a depressive illness resulting in a change of character. Since the offence he had improved. He had expressed deep and genuine remorse. He had been imprisoned for 3 months for assaulting a police officer during the miner's strike. There were no convictions for the best part of 20 years nor evidence of any prior violence to wife or children. The risk of re-offending was low. The prison report was "glowing." Held. Were it not for the exceptional circumstances a sentence very considerably in excess of 4 years would have been appropriate. 2 years was on the border between lenient and unduly lenient. The mitigation was very substantial. The **2 years** sentence was not altered.

Att-Gen's Ref. No 61 of 2000 2001 2 Cr App R (S) 66. The defendant pleaded guilty to two counts of GBH with intent and unlawfully wounding. The defendant had a relationship with the victim. Both sides claimed the other was violent. The defendant did not accept it was over. On the day of the offence he was at her flat mending her stereo and gave her and her daughter lifts. He said he wanted to see her and he loved her. That evening she went with her father to a public house. He remained nearby parked in a van. They communicated by text messages and she indicated she did not want to see him. He twice offered her a lift. The victim left the public house and as she was walking to a nightclub with a friend he approached her and he was persuaded to leave her alone. He was on CCTV in the town centre from 12–2 am. He then approached her in a club and grabbed her by the shoulder and stormed out. A taxi took her and a man to her flat and as they crossed some grass the defendant told the man to get away from her. He lunged at her in the neck, face and back. The man tried to assist her and he later discovered he had a number of cuts to his fingers. The defendant then called the police and said he had stabbed his girlfriend. When they arrived he said he did it and told the police who had arrested the other man that he didn't do anything. Two knives were found on the ground. Her neck wound was 2.5 cm long and was superficial but near to a major blood vessel. The other wounds were 1.5 and 2 cm's long. The defendant was 31 and had no convictions. He told police that he saw them snogging and she taunted him. Held. The appropriate sentence was in the order of **4½ years**. As it was a reference **3½ years** not 3.

R v Standing 2003 1 Cr App R (S) 253. The defendant pleaded guilty to Section 18. He and the victim had lived together for about 10 years. They had a daughter aged 8, who the defendant had looked after from when she was 6 months to 6 years old. He had a residence order in his favour. The victim also had an elder child. Since then there had been resumed co-habitation and a further estrangement when the daughter remained with her mother. On 5 December 2000, the victim's brother had died of an overdose. The victim asked the defendant's help with her loss and to help with the child care arrangements. On 23 December 2000, she asked him to her address and to look after the children while she went out with a male friend. She went out drinking and the defendant drank 16–18 bottles of Stella Artois. The elder daughter rang the victim to warn her about the amount the defendant had drunk. On her return, an argument ensued. She told him to sort out his drinking. On his account she said, "I am going to make sure you never have contact with (your daughter) again." The elder daughter phoned the police and a struggle developed which moved to the kitchen. He then picked up a knife and stabbed her in the chest, back and hand. He immediately phoned the emergency services. She needed major surgery. The main injury, which was to the chest was millimetres away from the main subclavian and carotid arteries and jugular vein. Had any of these been penetrated the wound would have been fatal. On her hand the digital nerve to her index finger was divided. A back calculation of his alcohol level was 200 mg in 100 ml of blood. Her reading was 190 mg. He was 42 and of good character, save for a theft in 1975 and a drugs offence in 1982. Held. We have paid particular attention to his evident remorse expressed in words, which is common, and his action in calling help at once. There was an evident lack of premeditation, a sudden loss of self-control, his effective good character and that he was acting against his consuming interest in having a residence or contact order with his daughter. **4 years** not 8.

R v Pritchard 2003 1 Cr App R (S) 263. The defendant pleaded guilty to Section 18. He married the victim in 1980. They had two children now aged 17 and 12. After three years, she ceased to have any affection for him. She said five years ago he had seen her talking to another man on holiday and he had punched her, knocked her to the ground and kicked her. He claimed the marriage was good. Both received treatment for depression. In August 2001, she moved out of the matrimonial home taking one of her children. He then started to persistently call her both in person and on the telephone begging her to return. She refused to return. Three weeks after she left, contrary to his promises, he went to her house where she lived with her father,. He persuaded her to return to his home to talk through their problems. When there he offered her a cup of tea. As she went into the kitchen, he grabbed her by the hair and punched her repeatedly to the face. She was terrified and promised to return to stop him continuing. She heard breaking glass and felt a thumping sensation to her face. She was knocked to the floor and kicked. She had been glassed and had tried to protect herself. The defendant said nothing and drove off in the family car. Nearby he went straight across a roundabout at a motorway junction. He demolished signs and came to rest in the middle of a busy carriageway. He told doctors in hospital he had tried to commit suicide. She had eight lacerations to her head, forearm, finger, hand and elbow. In interview he said his relationship was excellent and at the house she had said she had found someone else and the room began to get smaller. Everything had gone dark and thereafter he had no memory of the events. He was 42 and had convictions for robbery and two for ABH. The most recent was in 1983. The pre-sentence report said there was deep remorse and the risk of re-offending was at the lower end of the scale. Further he accepted his marriage was over. He told the psychiatrist he took an overdose 2–3 days before the offence at a time when he discovered she was having an affair. Held. She had horrific bruising and swelling to her face and she was likely to be permanently scarred. Using a glass to lacerate the face is a significantly aggravating factor because of the appalling long term consequences that may occur. Where an offence is committed in cold blood, with premeditation and the motive of revenge, the sentence would be significantly longer than the **4 years** here. That was well within the permissible range.

Att-Gen's Ref. No. 98 of 2002 2003 2 Cr App R (S) 563. The defendant pleaded guilty to attempting to cause GBH with intent. He, aged 45 and the victim, aged 52, had been married for about 5 years. However, after 2 years, the marriage started to deteriorate because of the defendant's heavy drinking. After 3 years they split up and the victim obtained a non-molestation order in the County Court. He breached that order and was committed to prison for 7 days (suspended). About 4 months later, in the early hours of New-Year's day, the victim heard a bang downstairs. She tried to put on a light but it seemed to her as if the electricity had been switched off. She went downstairs to turn it back on and noticed that the lower half of the front door was smashed and the door was open. Her husband approached her wearing a balaclava rolled up on his head. He had with him a crowbar which he was wielding. She tried to escape out of the front door and was struck on the back of her head. She managed to escape to the front garden but the defendant struck her on the front of her head. He struck her a third time. She screamed for help. The defendant throttled her. The victim's son came to her aide and punched the defendant who then left the scene. The defendant smelt of alcohol. Police later found that the electricity had been turned off at the fuse box. The victim had soft-tissue swelling to her forehead, a cut to her nose and multiple superficial scratches. The defendant was interviewed and following initial denials said that the victim had attacked him. He had a recent drink-related driving offence for which he received 2 year's probation but was otherwise he was of exemplary character. He was given full credit for his plea. There was evidence of a mental condition resulting from his service in the forces that led to his heavy drinking. Held. The attack was pre-meditated and unprovoked, in the middle of the night, using a weapon, in breach of a suspended Court order, whilst he was subject to a probation order and there was a history of him acting violently towards the victim. Where the Court is sentencing a man of good character with a very positive side to his character in the past, such mitigation cannot excuse offending of this kind. The sentence of 2 years was unduly lenient. However, the defendant had been released $3^1/_2$ months before the reference and had started to rebuild his life. Further, whilst he served his prison sentence, had to do so on a segregation wing because of the public service that he had given. **$3^1/_2$ years** would have been appropriate, but the sentence remained unchanged in the circumstances.

Relationship attacks – Men attacking wives and partners, or ex-wives or ex-partners – 5–9 years appropriate

121.44   *R v Carrington* 1999 2 Cr App R (S) 206. The defendant was convicted of GBH with intent. The victim and the defendant lived together for almost 6 years. She asked him to leave her flat, which he did. He agreed to pay his contribution to the bills. The following day he visited her and she was unrelenting. She asked him to leave and he became rather upset. Some time later he approached her when she was on the way to work. He said he wanted to talk to her. She stepped back, saw a Lucozade bottle and liquid was thrown on her face. She ran into her work place and colleagues doused her face with water. She spent 1 week in hospital. Gradually her eyes improved and she no longer suffers from any disability. She was expected to have eye discomfort up to 8 to 11 months after the attack. For a period after that they would feel abnormal. The damage to her clothing was consistent with sulphuric acid. Had she not received prompt assistance there could have been very severe consequences for her sight. The defendant was 57 and showed no remorse. 9 years before he had a conviction for ABH on his wife. Held. Despite his ill health **6 years** was appropriate.

Att-Gen's Ref. No 3 of 2000 2001 1 Cr App R (S) 92. The defendant was convicted of GBH with intent. The defendant had an intermittent relationship with the victim for about 5 years. The defendant returned home about 2 am under the influence of crack cocaine. He found the victim and two male friends there and demanded to know what had happened to his motor car. He believed the three had sold it to buy heroin. He was armed with a knife and his manner was threatening. He was also asking for £100 to buy crack. He left and returned carrying a full jug sized kettle of boiling water. He poured it over the victim's back and shoulders. He fetched a sheet soaked in cold water and she wrapped herself in it. She was terribly burnt and in agony. She suffered from 16% to 22% mixed depth burns. Some 80% of her back was scarred. She was in hospital for $3^1/_2$ weeks. The defendant claimed it was an accident. He had 16 court appearances as an adult. He had convictions for robbery, dishonesty and two for ABH. Held. We would have expected a sentence of **at least 6 years**. Taking into account it was a reference **5 years** substituted for 3.

Att-Gen's Ref. No 42 of 2000 2001 1 Cr App R (S) 393. The defendant pleaded guilty during the trial to four counts of false imprisonment, making a threats to kill, ABH and inflicting GBH. The defendant had a troubled relationship with a 23-year-old woman who from time to time returned to her mother. In June 1997, he slapped her and pulled her by the hair into the cellar. He pushed her into the coal cellar and shut her inside. He released her after two hours. He became angry again and told her to go back in. She did so because she feared an assault. This continued over 4 days although from time to time she was let out. This was the first count. In July 1997, she gave birth. A week later he punched her and pushed her down the cellar steps and locked her in the coalhouse. He let her out to feed the baby and picked up a crossbow and loaded it with a bolt. He told her he could kill her and get away with it. She believed she was going to be killed. This lasted for about a minute. He punched and kicked her and put a belt round her neck, which he pulled tight. This activity was the second false imprisonment count and the threats to kill. In November 1997 they moved to a flat. In December he punched and kicked her. He grabbed her between the legs and twisted them. He tore her right labia majora, causing her bleeding and immense pain. She said she wanted to end her life and he said, "go on then" and gave her some Tamazepam tablets, which she took. The offender became extremely violent and pushed her head through a plasterboard wall. He forced her to swallow shampoo to bring up the tablets, which she did. At 9–10 pm he tied her to a stool with flex and put a sock in her mouth. He slapped and punched her until the early hours. This activity was the third false imprisonment. He was then sentenced to 30 months imprisonment for wounding etc which involved fighting men unrelated to the victim. The last false imprisonment was when he punched her, made her undress and tied her to the bedposts. He whipped her back and legs. She had black eyes, cut lips, a swollen face, bruising to her body and wheal marks. The ABH related to when he punched her and pushed a burning cigarette against her chest. This was followed by more punching. The GBH involved an incident when they were out with friends and he slapped her. She refused to go home. He said he would break her jaw. He grabbed her hair and dragged her to the front door. The friends told him to stop. He kicked and punched her in the face. She was taken to the kitchen where it was repeated. She was pregnant again. He banged her head on the floor. She had to be taken to hospital. He was taking crack or heroin during all the false imprisonments and the occasion of the ABH. He was arrested and she gave evidence at the trial. Just before she was to be cross-examined he pleaded guilty. The defendant had helped police in an unrelated matter. **6 or 7 years** was appropriate. Because it was a reference **5 years** not 30 months, consecutive to 11 months for breach of his licence.

Att-Gen's Ref. No 89 of 2000 2001 2 Cr App R (S) 309. The defendant pleaded guilty on the day his trial was listed to GBH with intent, ABH and criminal damage. The defendant was married for 18 years and there were a number of examples of his violence to her. She moved out and he discovered where she was living. He went there and she would not let him in so he forced his way in. He punched and kicked her. Their younger son went to find help. The older son pleaded with him to stop. The defendant pulled her into the kitchen and armed himself with a wine bottle. A neighbour persuaded him to put it down and he picked up a knife and stabbed her in the abdomen and shoulder. The police arrived and he was arrested. The victim had two wounds one through her liver. The victim of the ABH was someone who the defendant thought was associating with his wife. The victim was driving his car and the defendant parked his car so as to block the victim's route. The defendant opened his car door and struck him a number of times. He pulled his shirt off and kicked the car causing a large indentation, (the criminal damage). The victim had swelling and bruising. The defendant was 37 and had no convictions. Held. The appropriate sentence was **5 years**. As it was a reference **4 years** not 30 months. The time on licence should be extended to 7 years under the Powers of the Criminal Courts (Sentencing) Act 2000, s 85.

R v Symeon 2002 1 Cr App R (S) 211. The defendant was convicted of GBH with intent. He pleaded guilty to an offence under s 20, which was not accepted and was acquitted of attempted murder. The victim moved in with him and she found him extremely possessive and jealous. He tried to control her. The relationship was extremely stormy and the police were called at least once. She broke it off twice but took him back at his request. After about 9 months she moved out and he made abusive and threatening telephone calls to her. He also sent her text messages. She made it plain that the relationship was over and she wanted no contact with him. She consulted the police who advised her to obtain an injunction and they warned him to stay away from her. The threatening messages continued and he said the children would have a dead mother and threatened to tell them she was a prostitute. At around midday she arrived home from work and received a text message saying he was going to get her for this. Then she received another threatening phone call and he said he had been following her and watched her with another man. A short time later he broke into the house with a loud crash and ran towards her shouting, "Prostitute. You're a dead mother. If I can't have you, no one can. I'd rather we both die." He then punched her several times and started to throttle her. She struggled and fell to the floor and he kicked her repeatedly to the face, nose, chest and body. Suddenly he stopped and he sat on the floor crying saying she did not deserve to live. Seeing he had a knife she ran to a neighbour's house and banged on the door. The neighbours were too frightened to open the door. He followed her shouting, "I'm going to kill you." He trapped her in the porch grabbed her hair, dragged her backwards and punched her to the face and chest. She fell to the floor and he kicked her in the head, chest and arms until she lost consciousness. The neighbour called the emergency services and she was taken to hospital. She had four cuts to her scalp the largest of which was 17 cm and exposed the scull bone, It needed 30 stitches. There were cuts and bruising elsewhere to her head, two black eyes, other bruising to her face, neck, hands and legs. She had two broken teeth and suffered from severe headaches for some time. The defendant was arrested and found to have a 9″ knife on him and another knife in his car. He was of good character. Held. This was not a sudden unpremeditated explosion of violence by a man at the end of his tether marked by immediate remorse. It was a campaign of intimidation of a particularly unpleasant nature despite a police warning. The attack could have proved fatal. **8 years** was not excessive.

R v Marsh 2004 2 Cr App R (S) 429. The defendant pleaded guilty to wounding with intent and theft. The victim was his ex-partner, P. They had lived together for 6 years and during that time he had been violent towards her although, she said, 'not excessively so'. The cause of his violence was his heavy drinking. He was also injecting heroin although there were periods when he was trying to stop this. They had 2 children. 12 weeks before the offence he had started using heroin again and she asked him to leave and sort himself out. He would visit the children from time to time and there were episodes of theft from her to finance his drug taking. On the day of the offence he saw her in town and said he was going to smash her house up and 'get her with this'– although she couldn't see what he had in his hand. He later went to her house and caused damage and stole items. At 7.30 pm he went to the house and slashed her face with a Stanley knife. She had three deep slashes to her face which required numerous stitches, two superficial wounds to her arm, and a deep wound to her arm which required stitches. She said she thought he was trying to kill her. She had changed her phone and asked to be re-housed. She suffered flashbacks and nightmares, had permanent scars and suffered loss of feeling to her forehead. The defendant, 29, had some 50 previous convictions for offences including theft, possession of an offensive weapon and robbery. A pre-sentence report said he had suffered frequent violence when a child from his alcoholic father, as had his mother and siblings. He had been using heroin for five years. Police had frequently attended the home he shared with the victim following assaults by the defendant on the victim. Sometimes these assaults were in front of the children. Once he had threatened her with an axe and a screwdriver. He was assessed as having a high risk of re-offending and posed a high risk especially to his victim. He had expressed remorse for the attack but tended to minimise the effect of his violence on his victim. The court had a statement from her saying that she found his sentence harsh, she had visited him in prison and he had apologised to her. Also he was a different person off drugs and that she would have been happy with a sentence of 4 or 5 years. Held. There was no mitigation other than the plea of guilty. Insufficient credit was given for that plea. The sentence was reduced from 10 to **8 years**.

Att- Gen's Ref. No 12 of 2004 2005 1 Cr App R (S) 147. The defendant pleaded guilty to causing GBH with intent. He had been married for eight years and there were three children of that relationship, but the marriage had been in difficulty for some years. He had become abusive and jealous towards his wife. Three years before the attack his wife told him she wanted to leave and after that he threatened violence towards her several times. She was in bed when he came in and he became irritated with her, taking her mobile phone from her and pulling out the landline from its socket. His wife followed him out of the bedroom and tried to run down the stairs but fell and hurt herself although not seriously. She asked him to call an ambulance because she was frightened of him and he refused. She lay on the floor for about twenty minutes and then tried to sit up. As she did so he hit her three times with a hammer, only stopping when their thirteen years old son heard the noise and intervened to protect his mother by threatening his father with a knife. The victim sustained multiple lacerations on her head and two depressed skull fractures, needing surgery and four or five days in hospital. It was argued that the aggravating features were that the attack was in the victim's home, that there were three children asleep in the house, the attack was unprovoked, it took place when the victim was lying defenceless on the floor, a hammer was used on the head, a thirteen year old boy witnessed it and it only ceased when the boy intervened. The defendant, 52, had no previous convictions and was hardworking. He had had three to four cans of beer this evening and the attack took place against a background of depression and morbid jealousy. Held. The appropriate sentence was in the order of **5¹/₂ to 6 years**. As it was a reference **4¹/₂** not 3.

Relationship attacks – Men attacking wives and partners, or ex-wives or ex-partners – 10 or more years appropriate

121.45   *R v Newton* 1999 1 Cr App R (S) 438. The defendant was convicted of GBH with intent and robbery. The defendant was having extreme difficulty in coming to terms with the separation from his wife. He bought paint stripper and was warned it would burn. He discussed it with the safety officer at work. It contained phenol capable of causing serious burns to skin and eyes. He added hydrochloric acid to the mixture and put it in a Flash bathroom cleaner bottle. It was potentially cancer inducing. He went to the shop where his wife worked on a motor cycle wearing a motor cycle helmet, balaclava and gloves. He paid for a packet of cigarettes and when the wife opened the till he squirted the mixture into her face. She ran to the storeroom and he followed her. He sprayed more of the mixture on her front, head and back. He ran back into the shop and stole £65 and some cheques. The wife was in extreme pain. The burns covered about 10% of her body. She was in hospital for 5 days. After the police had released the defendant, an anonymous letter was received by the police saying he would be attacked. He staged a fake attack on himself. The judge described him as evil, vengeful and scheming. He had no previous convictions. **12 years** for the GBH not 15 and 8 not 10 concurrent for the robbery.

R v Moseley 1999 1 Cr App R (S) 452. The defendant pleaded guilty to GBH with intent and wounding with intent. The defendant and the woman (the second victim) intended to get married. However, she became increasingly concerned, disillusioned and depressed about it. She needed medication. She confided in the licensee of a public house (the first victim). She became attracted to him and spent a night with him. She told the defendant who was upset, very angry and for the first time was violent to her. He punched her and the engagement was broken off. He was asked to leave her house where they were living. Later there was much discussion and she said she wanted to be with the first victim. He appeared to accept it and moved out. One night the two victims spent the evening at a nightclub and went back to her house. At about 4 or 5 am the defendant entered the house with a wheel brace. The first victim was struck several hard blows to his head and body. She was hit on the head as well. Her pleas to stop were ignored and the attack went on for a while. The defendant went straight to the police. He told them his mind had gone. The first victim had a large depressed fracture of the skull causing permanent disability. He had to be re-educated to read and write and to communicate. He suffered severe headaches. His skin was de-sensitised. His business came to an end. He was unable to go out alone. His stuttering and inability to pronounce many words was unlikely to improve. The second victim had lacerations to her head, which required 18 stitches. She had bruising to her arm and swelling to her hands. She found it extremely difficult to come to terms with what had happened and became something of a recluse. The defendant showed considerable remorse and had no convictions for violence. A psychiatrist did not consider he posed a risk to the public in general. Held. There was no provocation. We accept he was under emotional strain and the attack was out of his normal character. The sentence was severe and the crime merited it. **10 years** in total (6 +4) upheld.

Revenge

121.46 *Att-Gen's Ref. No. 132 of 2001* 2003 1 Cr App R (S) 190. The defendant pleaded guilty to Section 18 and driving without due care. He was an alcoholic and lived with the victim in a home for the homeless. Each had a room. Another resident, M, refused the defendant's girlfriend entry into the home. A few days later, the defendant remonstrated to M, the victim and another about that. The victim tried to calm the defendant down and told him to leave. The defendant punched the victim and the other resident and left. The police were called but the victim did not want to pursue the matter. The three residents complained to the landlord about the defendant's behaviour and the defendant was given a week to leave the home. The defendant told an acquaintance that he was going to sort out those responsible. The day before he had to go and after he had been drinking, he went to the victim's room and ransacked it turning over the furniture and belongings. He then went to M's room and found M and the victim there. He accused the victim of getting him evicted and punched him on the face, causing him to fall to the floor. He then kicked him several times to the head and body causing the victim's nose to bleed heavily as he lay unconscious. The defendant then left to fetch a knife and returned. M tried to rouse the victim and the defendant kicked the victim twice more. He then stabbed the victim nine times in the lower back and buttocks while the victim lay motionless on the floor. The defendant shouted, "Die you bastard," and "Right you bastard you are going to die." A witness was also hit and the defendant left. Shortly after, another resident found the defendant crying and he told her, "I just could not control myself any longer. It has been boiling up for ages. I've done it". Police found him in a very agitated state and he handed the knife over and said, "He deserved it the bastard. He got me kicked out of my flat." The victim underwent major surgery in which his colon and upper rectum were removed. He came very close to death. After the operation he had major organ failure and he had further surgery and was in hospital for five months. He suffered lasting damage and continuing pain. He has a colostomy, walks with a limp and lacks sensation and muscle control in parts of his body. The defendant was 31 and of good character in employment as a gardener. The people he worked for were astonished at his behaviour and wrote letters of support. He expressed remorse. Held. The starting point should have been **9 years** and with a plea **at least 6 years**. Because it was a reference **5 years** substituted for 4.

Robbery/Burglary/Aggravated burglary, and – Guideline remarks

121.47 *Att-Gen's Ref. No. 1 of 1995* 1996 1 Cr App R (S) 11. LCJ. We wish to stress that anyone who breaks into someone else's home, in the middle of the night, with the intention of inflicting grievous bodily harm, particularly if he takes others with him and has weapons, can expect to receive a substantial sentence. An offence of that kind is outrageous. Here **6–7 years** would have been appropriate.

Robbery/Burglary/Aggravated burglary, and

121.48   *R v Rogers* 1998 1 Cr App R (S) 402. The defendant pleaded guilty to causing GBH with intent and two burglaries. The victim was aged 87 and lived on her own in a large detached house. In January 1995 the defendant broke into her house and was sentenced to 9 months detention for it. After being released on 1 November 1996 he broke in again and stole milk and other items. On 25 November 1996 he broke in again after the victim had gone to bed. He entered her bedroom and repeatedly struck her in the face. He put his hands around her throat as if to throttle her. When she regained consciousness she had difficulty in breathing. He was under the influence of heroin. The victim went to hospital and numerous cuts and bruises were found. The doctor believed pressure would have to be applied for some time to leave the marks he found on her neck. The defendant's prints were found and he was arrested the next day. The defendant was 20 when sentenced. He had five drug-related cautions for burglary, theft, TDA etc. The judge described the photographs as, 'truly revolting.' He was sentenced to 2 years for the first burglary, 5 years' concurrent for the second burglary and 12 years' consecutive to the 2 years for the GBH. Held. If there had been a trial **12 years** would have been appropriate for the GBH. For a plea **9 years** was appropriate. The 5 years concurrent was right. The consecutive sentence of 2 years was right because he had preyed on the house. Therefore **9 years** and 2 consecutive not 12 and 2 years.

R v Dudeye 1998 2 Cr App R (S) 430. The defendant pleaded guilty to wounding with intent and robbery. The defendant then 18 and the victim were on a train. As the train pulled out of a station the defendant sat next to the victim and produced a knife. He tried to grab her briefcase and she wouldn't give it to him. A struggle developed. He wanted her shoulder bag and said, 'Give me the fucking bag or I'll kill you to death.' He stopped her getting off at the next station and repeated the threat to kill her. She managed to alight at the station after that and he followed. He was holding the strap of the bag and he stabbed her four times. He cut the handle of the bag and ran off leaving her bleeding profusely. She had a punctured lung, internal chest bleeding and a stab wound that required stitching. In interview he admitted it and said he was sorry. He said he was drunk at the time. He had convictions for robbery, threatening behaviour, common assault and several previous for burglary and dishonesty. He had previously been sent to detention. The longest period was 6 months. The robbery was on a woman travelling on a tube train. He told her he would punch her in the face. The defendant left Somalia when he was 9. His mother and her children were refugees. He was taken into care. He used alcohol as an escape. **8 years** not 10 YOI.

Att-Gen's Ref. Nos. 43 and 44 of 2002 2003 1 Cr App R (S) 364. The defendant G pleaded during his trial to aggravated burglary and Section 18. The defendant B was convicted of the same counts. G and his wife were separated and she was now co-habiting with B. G and B entered her ex husband's bedsit at night. While the victim was in bed G struck him about the head with a 14″–15″ bar, saying, "Now I am going to kill you. I have nothing to lose." The blows were to the legs body and head. G had previously told the victim that he was to be killed. B remained in the communal area of the bed-sit and at one stage B said in effect enough is enough. This caused a pause but the attack was resumed and B did nothing more to stop it. The victim lost consciousness and awoke with a large cut to his head. This injury was treated with 14 sutures. The scar remains. G was arrested and was aggressive and abusive to the police. In interview he said the victim was, "a short arsed, bald-headed stupid wanker. When I find the man who has done this job I will shake his hand. My only regret is whoever done it didn't do the job properly because the prick is still alive." G was 22 and with no convictions for serious violence. The pre-sentence report said there was a high risk of re-offending. B was then 31 and had served a short sentence for a motoring offence. Held. For an offence of this kind, where there is no guilty plea the least sentence that can be passed was of **the order of 8 years** and sentences higher than that would not be considered manifestly excessive. G's guilty plea and stated remorse can carry no significant weight. G's sentence should have been **8 years**. As it was a reference **7 years** not 3¹/₂. B had not involved himself in the actual attack, although he had facilitated it. His proper sentence would be **5 to 6 years**. As it was a reference **4 years** not 2.

R v Marcus 2004 1 Cr App R (S) 258. The defendant pleaded guilty to s 18, wounding and two counts of robbery. A murder charge was dropped because the prosecution couldn't prove the causal link. At about 5 pm, after smoking crack he went to a house to steal money for drugs. The 84 year old occupier saw him on his window ledge. The occupier challenged him and the defendant jumped on him and hit him. The defendant then knelt on him and continued to attack him using a key in his fist. He kept demanding £10. The victim's wife aged 86 pleaded with the defendant to stop. He pulled the victim to the top of the stairs and pushed him down them. He then punched and kicked the wife. This was the s 20 count. He ransacked their clothing which was in the hall and made off with about £80. They were both treated for multiple bruising and abrasions to their faces and bodies. The wife was put in a home for observation and a few days later fell off her commode, struck her head and died. In the first four interviews the defendant denied attacking them but in the fifth he confessed. He was 31 with eleven previous for robbery, two for attempted robbery, four for burglary and three for ABH. He showed remorse. Held. Those who select elderly or otherwise vulnerable people as victims and then invade their homes will receive very severe sentences. Such vulnerable people have to be protected, and this court will do everything it can to provide that protection. Lengthy prison sentences will normally be absolutely inevitable. The sentence had to reflect his appalling record. However 20 years would not have been appropriate after a trial so **12 years** not 14.

See also **ROBBERY** – *Domestic premises Victim over 65 Victim injured or attacked and Victim seriously injured*

Self defence, excessive

121.49 *Att-Gen's Ref. No 81 of 2000* 2001 2 Cr App R (S) 90. The defendant pleaded guilty to GBH with intent on the day his trial was listed. The defendant lived near the victim and at 1am repeatedly hit his head and body with a shovel. He said, 'I'm going to fucking kill you.' The victim's daughter saw the attack from her bedroom and ran out. He ignored her pleas to him to stop. The victim had a large skull fracture, a fracture to his forearm, a 5 cm laceration to his temple, a deep 5 cm laceration to his elbow and a superficial laceration to his forearm. He was in hospital for five days and made a good recovery. The defendant was 36 and had no convictions. The judge sentenced him on the basis that the victim had been aggressive, thrown stones at his house and made a noise early in the morning. The victim ran at him swinging his fist. The defendant used excessive self-defence. The prosecution did not accept that account. Held. Accepting the defence version, which was in stark contrast to the victim's without evidence, was wrong. It is difficult to see how the judge found severe provocation. Taking into account it was a reference **15 months** immediate imprisonment not 18 months suspended.

Series of offences

121.50 *Att-Gen's Ref. No 19 of 1998* 1999 1 Cr App R (S) 275. The defendant was convicted of two wounding with intent counts and affray. He was committed for sentence for ABH. The ABH matter related to an unprovoked attack on a white victim with a bottle. The victim had just left a restaurant with his girlfriend. The victim was with three to five Asians. He left sniggering. The victim's nose was cut and his spectacles were broken. The defendant was convicted. Whilst on bail for that offence and 3 weeks after the offence he made an unprovoked attack on a young man who had just left a nightclub with his girlfriend. He used a lump hammer and the victim suffered a 3 and 2 cm cut. He also lost consciousness. The defendant was arrested nearby and lashed out at the police officer with a belt. He was released on bail. Less than a week later he committed the second GBH offence. A girl knocked on the victim's door saying there were two men she wanted to get rid of. The victim saw the defendant and another and walked the girl to a telephone box. The two men approached the victim and he was threatened. The other man tried to start a fight. The victim's friends managed to calm things down. The victim returned home and then decided to tell the father of the other man he was causing trouble. The victim and his friends left and the defendant and the other man appeared. They were shouting and trying to start a fight. Without any warning the defendant lunged forward and struck the victim on the top of the head with a claw hammer. The victim had a 7 and 10 cm long cut. Beneath was a skull fracture and the brain had been lacerated indicating a blow of extreme force. There was a risk of brain damage and epilepsy. There was a 3 cm comparatively superficial wound on the back of the head. The defendant was 19 and had no relevant previous convictions. Held. We would have expected a sentence of **6 years** in total. Taking into account it was a reference and he was showing signs of maturity 6 months for the ABH, 3 years and **5 years** for the GBH concurrent substituted for $3^1/_2$ in total.

R v Moseley 1999 1 Cr App R (S) 452. The defendant pleaded guilty to GBH with intent and wounding with intent. The defendant and the woman (the second victim) intended to get married. However, she became increasingly concerned, disillusioned and depressed about it. She needed medication. She confided in the licensee of a public house (the first victim). She became attracted to him and spent a night with him. She told the defendant who was upset, very angry and for the first time was violent to her. He punched her and the engagement was broken off. He was asked to leave her house where they were living. Later there was much discussion and she said she wanted to be with the first victim. He appeared to accept it and moved out. One night the two victims spent the evening at a nightclub and went back to her house. At about 4 or 5 am the defendant entered the house with a wheel brace. The first victim was struck several hard blows to his head and body. The second victim was hit on the head as well. Her pleas to stop were ignored and the attack went on for a while. The defendant went straight to the police. He told them his mind had gone. The first victim had a large depressed fracture of the skull causing permanent disability. He had to be re-educated to read and write and to communicate. He suffered severe headaches. His skin was desensitised. His business came to an end. He was unable to go out alone. His stuttering and inability to pronounce many words was unlikely to improve. The second victim had lacerations to her head, which required 18 stitches. She had bruising to her arm and swelling to her hands. She found it extremely difficult to come to terms with what had happened and became something of a recluse. The defendant showed considerable remorse and had no convictions for violence. A psychiatrist did not consider he posed a risk to the public in general. Held. There was no provocation. We accept he was under emotional strain and the attack was out of his normal character. The sentence was severe and the crime merited it. **10 years** in total (6 +4) upheld.

R v Iyegbe 2001 Unreported 18/10/01. The defendant was convicted of two woundings with intent and pleaded guilty to five robberies on minicab drivers. **10 years** not 12 in all.

Strangling, choking etc.

121.51 *R v Enstone* 2003 1 Cr App R (S) 168. The defendant pleaded guilty to attempting to strangle with intent to cause GBH, (Offences against the Person Act 1861 Section 21). The defendant married in 1989 and had two children but by 1999 the marriage was in difficulties. During that year he had an affair and by mid 2000 he and his wife were sharing a home and a bed but barely talking. In late 2000 his wife started to see another man and during the last weekend of January 2001, the man spent the night. That night the defendant came home unexpectedly and the man ran from the house leaving his mobile phone and jacket behind. The affair was discovered but not the man's name. The defendant threatened suicide, woke his son and told him about it. He wrote some suicide notes, was depressed and had a morbid interest in his Samuri swords, which he gave to his brother for safekeeping. The marriage was over and each side consulted solicitors. Nearly two weeks after the discovery of the man with his wife, he told his wife he had discovered the man's name and suggested they have their last meal together. That evening he said he was going to work whereas he had given the job up in January. At 9 pm he sent an affectionate text message to his wife and at 11 pm he rang her but she didn't get to the phone in time. At 11.30 pm a neighbour saw someone matching the defendant's description acting suspiciously and entering the house. In the early hours the wife went downstairs for water and found the defendant. She went back to bed and he joined her. He was naked and asked for a cuddle and it was refused. He grabbed her and lay on top of her. He produced what appeared to be rope, which he wrapped around his wife's wrist and passed across her throat in an attempt to tie it around her other wrist. When she shouted and struggled he dropped the rope and put his hands around her neck and squeezed. She struggled and he let go. Then he put a pillow over her face so she could not breathe. She fought free but he grabbed her and strangled her again. She almost lost consciousness and she wet the bed. She managed to say, "I love you" to try to make him stop and he did. He said he was sorry and she ran for help. When she dialled 999 he pulled the telephone wires out but she managed to reconnect them. In hospital she had abrasions on the neck and multiple petechiae to her neck, face and eyes. They were consistent with up to $\frac{1}{2}$ minute of strangulation. He was arrested and said, "I didn't mean to kill her. I only meant to frighten her." He also said he was having a breakdown and that he had just snapped. His mobile rang and while the officers were distracted he stabbed himself in the stomach several times. He cried and said he wanted to die. He was taken to hospital and he had seven cuts to the abdomen requiring 20 stitches. He was 36, of good character and with testimonials. A psychiatrist said there was marked distress probably from an adjustment disorder. He told the writer of the pre-sentence report his wife was largely responsible for her near demise. The Judge said it was fortunate he had not caused worse injuries but he would receive credit for stopping when he did. He also said he posed no risk to the public. Held. The difficulty with strangulation is there is a fine line between success and failure. Had he persisted for only a little longer his wife would have died. **6 years** was tough but appropriate.

Unprovoked attack

121.52   *Att-Gen's Ref. No 19 of 1998* 1999 1 Cr App R (S) 275. The defendant was convicted of two wounding with intent counts and affray. He was committed for sentence for ABH. The ABH matter related to an unprovoked attack on a white victim with a bottle. The victim had just left a restaurant with his girlfriend. The victim was with three to five Asians. He left sniggering. The victim's nose was cut and his spectacles were broken. He was convicted. While on bail for that offence and 3 weeks after the offence he made an unprovoked attack on a young man who had just left a nightclub with his girlfriend. He used a lump hammer and the victim suffered a 3 and 2 cm cut. He also lost consciousness. The defendant was arrested nearby and lashed out at the police officer with a belt. He was released on bail. Less than a week later he committed the second GBH offence. A girl knocked on the victim's door saying there were two men she wanted to get rid of. The victim saw the defendant and another and walked the girl to a telephone box. The two men approached the victim and he was threatened. The other man tried to start a fight. The victim's friends managed to calm things down.

The victim returned home and then decided to tell the father of the other man he was causing trouble. The victim and his friends left and the defendant and the other man appeared. They were shouting and trying to start a fight. Without any warning the defendant lunged forward and struck the victim on the top of the head with a claw hammer. The victim had a 7 and 10 cm long cut. Beneath was a skull fracture and the brain had been lacerated indicating a blow of extreme force. There was a risk of brain damage and epilepsy. There was a 3 cm comparatively superficial wound on the back of the head. The defendant was 19 and had no relevant previous convictions. Held. We would have expected a sentence of **6 years** in total. Taking into account it was a reference and he was showing signs of maturity 6 months for the ABH, 3 years and 5 years for the GBH concurrent substituted for **3¹/₂** in total.

Att-Gen's Ref. No 24 of 1998 1999 1 Cr App R (S) 278. The defendant was convicted of wounding with intent. The victim was with his girlfriend at a public house. They went to the bar and the victim was next to the defendant who said something. The victim couldn't hear it and asked the defendant what he had said. The defendant smashed a beer glass into his face. The defendant aged 27 had convictions over 13 years principally for theft, motor vehicle and motoring offences. However there were offences for two assaults on police, ABH and common assault. He had received for those 3 months detention, probation and a community service order. Held. We would have expected a sentence in the order of **5 years**. However, as it was a reference and the defendant had 7 weeks before his planned release **3 years 9 months** not 2 years.

R v Richards 2002 1 Cr App R (S) 133. The defendant was convicted of wounding with intent. The defendant then 19 and a friend met a 44 to 45-year-old gay man, the victim, through a gay chat line. The man paid for their train fares from London to Swansea and took them to his house where they had sex. He provided them with food, accommodation, drink and money for three days. On the fourth day the man was asked to pick them and another up from a club and he did so. On the way home they bought food and cannabis. When they got home they drank beer and whisky and smoked the cannabis. The friend left the room and the defendant without warning or cause cut the victim across the throat using a serrated kitchen knife. He also stabbed him and as the victim tried to get away the defendant continued to attack him causing multiple wounds to the victim's head and body. Eight were serious and the attack only stopped when the friend re-entered the room. The three men left leaving the victim who managed to telephone for an ambulance. The friend returned to London and told his mother who told the police. The knife was left at the scene and was 19 cm long with a serrated double edge. It had a forked tip which had one fork broken off and the blade was bent at right angles to the handle. In hospital the victim was found to have a 6–7 cm laceration on his neck and a 5 cm stab wound. There were multiple complications and he was on an artificial ventilator for nearly a month. The defendant was arrested and said the victim wanted sex, he was resisting and the victim tried to stab him. The defendant had a conviction in 1995 for two robberies with an imitation firearm and an aggravated burglary. He was then 14¹/₂ and received 2 years detention. His risk of re-offending was described as high. The judge said the victim was only saved by the prompt and highly competent medical treatment. The judge did not pass an automatic life sentence because the defendant did not create an unacceptable danger to the public and because the other offence was when he was 14¹/₂ and there was no actual violence on his record. Held. **12 years** was not manifestly excessive.

Att-Gen's Ref. No 68 of 2002 2003 1 Cr App R (S) 498. The defendant was convicted of wounding with intent. The victim was 25. The defendant arrived at a public house at about 8.45 pm. During the course of the evening he said to the victim: "I pity anyone who starts with me tonight, they're all fucking wankers." At about 10.30 pm the defendant told the victim that he wanted to see him outside where there was a confrontation (but no violence), following which the victim prevented him from re-entering the public house. The defendant walked off; the victim went back in. Shortly after midnight, the victim left the public house and crossed the road. The defendant retrieved a claw hammer that he had hidden in a refuge bin earlier and without any provocation struck the victim on the head with the hammer. The victim fell to the ground where the defendant continued to strike him using the hammer. CCTV showed eight forceful blows at the victim's head, some of which connected. The defendant delivered about six further blows, striking the victim's left forearm as he tried to defend himself. The defendant's jacket came off his shoulders inhibiting his ability to strike further and enabling the victim to restrain the defendant. The police arrived and arrested him. In interview he said that he was pretty drunk. The victim had a 1 cm laceration to the side of the head, two 2 cm lacerations to the back of the head, a deep S-shaped laceration on the forearm, two lacerations near the elbow and bruising to the ribcage. Muscle to the wrist flexors was divided and nineteen stitches were needed to close the deep laceration. The defendant had previous convictions for ABH in 1990 and a more recent public order offence. A psychiatric report said he had a deep and intense hostility towards his real father. The risk of similar outbursts of irrational violence was already lower since his incarceration. That risk will fall to entirely acceptable levels once he rids himself entirely of these leftovers from a disturbed past. Held. The use of a claw hammer was certainly no less serious than when a glass is used in the face and sentences of the order of 5 years would be expected. Taking into account that this was a reference, **4 years** not **2¹/₂**.

Att-Gen's Ref No 30 of 2004 2005 1 Cr App R (S) 212. The defendant pleaded guilty on the first day of trial to one count of wounding with intent. The defendant and the victim were in a public house. The victim went to put some credits in the jukebox when the defendant said to him that he still had three credits left. The victim said if the credits were still there after his selection had been played the defendant could have them. The defendant left the public house but then returned to pick up his tools. He hit the victim three times with a hammer, twice on the head and once, because he moved, on the shoulder. He shouted 'That'll teach you to take my free credits and threw an ashtray at the victim, which missed. He was still abusing him as the victim left. The next day the victim was taken to hospital and was found to have a depressed skull fracture and damage to the membrane lining the brain. The blow had been of considerable force and had driven bone, hair and skin fragments into the skull surface. Fourteen clips were needed to close the site. He also had a cut to his right ear and a numb shoulder. He spent three days in hospital. After the assault the victim experienced daily headaches for a month, then pain around the scar area. He experienced a constant high pitched noise in his head which interfered with his sleep. There was a risk in the future of epilepsy. He was not allowed to drive or play football for six months. He became shy and quiet whereas before he had been sociable and confident. He found it harder to concentrate. He avoided two nearby towns in case he met the defendant and he lost his job. The defendant surrendered to the police and said he was too drunk to remember the incident. He said he had drunk fourteen pints of lager and bitter. His basis of plea was that he had been working all day without food or drink so that the drink had a more marked effect; that he did not recall the assault but admitted forming a drunken intent to cause the victim GBH. Further he bitterly regretted the incident and surrendered to the police as soon as he knew what had happened. He had previously contested the intent necessary for GBH because of his drunken state but when he learnt of the medical evidence that three blows were struck he accepted the necessary intent. The aggravating features were said to be the use of the hammer, the unprovoked attack on a stranger in a public place, the repeated blows only stopped by others intervening, the deliberate and forceful blows to the head and the serious and lasting consequences. The defendant, 29, had over forty previous convictions including robbery, ABH, burglary, criminal damage, handling and public order offences. The last offences of violence were over ten years ago. There was genuine remorse and he had not behaved violently for a number of years. He had a difficult personal history with a history of drug abuse and he had made a significant effort to improve his behaviour with some success. Held. This was a very savage attack on a wholly innocent person. The critically important feature was the extent of the injuries causing serious long-term consequences. The proper sentence would have been **5¹/₂–6 years** so as it was a reference **4¹/₂ years** not 3.

Att-Gen's Ref. No 31 etc. of 2004 Re DB 2005 1 Cr App Rep (S) 377 at 386. The defendant DLB was convicted of wounding with intent to do GBH. The victim and a friend were in the town centre when they passed a group of four to five young men including the defendant. One of the defendant's group said "Are you going to bottle him?" The defendant, who was holding a glass bottle, chased the victim into a chip shop. He pushed the victim against the counter and hit him a number of times on the head, shoulders and upper body with the bottle. The defendant then left without the bottle (which had remained intact). The victim was bleeding and was taken to A and E where he was treated with staples for a 2 cm and a 1.5 cm cut to his head. He also had pain in the right shoulder and hand. He recovered physically but remained wary of the defendant and his associates. Three months after the incident, the defendant approached the victim and said that he had got the wrong person. He gave his details to the victim and was later arrested. In interview he said that he had got the wrong person and that he did not realise that he had the bottle in his hand. He was 20 with previous convictions for driving offences including aggravated vehicle taking for which he received a CRO. Held. This was an unprovoked attack upon an innocent victim who suffered head injuries. He had chased and cornered the victim and had used a bottle to reign repeated blows. **3¹/₂ years** would have been the correct sentence. **2¹/₂ years** as this was a reference, not 2 years CRO.

Old cases *R v Thomas* 1997 2 Cr App R (S) 148, (for a summary of the case see the first edition of this book.)

Vehicles, after using – (including road rage)

121.53 *Att-Gen's Ref. No 60 of 1996* 1997 2 Cr App R (S) 198. The defendant was convicted of ABH and wounding with intent. The defendant after drinking heavily argued with his sister in the street. He threw a can of drink into the road and it struck a car. The driver got out to remonstrate with the defendant. The defendant threatened him and kicked him hard in the testicles, (the ABH). The sister and the driver tried to push the defendant away and the passenger, an off duty police officer got out of the car. He tried to restrain the defendant and told him to calm down. The defendant pushed him back and forced him against a wall. The defendant persistently bit his ear growling and roaring like a wild animal. The driver and the sister tried to pull the defendant away but failed. The driver went to the boot of the car to find a torch to hit him with. Unable to find one he returned with a wheelbrace and hit the defendant with it. The defendant then turned to face the driver, shouted abuse and moved towards him aggressively. The sister managed to push him away and he left. The driver followed him and he was threatened. Both the victims were detained overnight in hospital. The driver had swollen testicles. The passenger had 18 stitches for three bite marks in the ear of 2.5, 3.5, and 0.8 cm long. He was off work for 5 weeks and he and his family suffered great stress and upset. Four months later he was still in pain. The victim required five stitches to his head. The defendant had convictions for ABH and criminal damage. He had forced his way into his former girlfriend's flat and had punched and kicked her current boyfriend about the face and head. The probation officer thought he posed no significant risk. There was significant personal mitigation. Held. Giving weight to that the minimum sentence for the wounding was 3 years. Because of the delay and it was a reference **2 years** substituted for the wounding and 6 months concurrent for the ABH remaining.

Vehicles, using vehicle as a weapon (incl. driving off with victim clinging to car)

121.54   *Att-Gen's Ref. No 13 of 2001* 2001 2 Cr App R (S) 497. The defendant pleaded guilty on the day fixed for his trial to GBH with intent and dangerous driving. A month earlier he pleaded guilty to driving whilst disqualified and perverting the course of Justice. The defendant tailgated a number of vehicles including a van. He shouted to his passenger about the van driver, "Hurry up," and flashed his lights and made gestures. The driver pulled over and the defendant pulled up behind the van. The van driver got out and walked towards the defendant who drove his car straight at him at speed. The van driver was thrown onto the bonnet of the car and hit his face on the windscreen. He fell off and the defendant drove away. The victim had a badly broken wrist and cuts and bruises to his face. The defendant went to the police station with a bogus receipt for his car and made a statement saying he had sold his car. The defendant was 25 and had convictions for dangerous driving (twice) and disqualified driving (7 times) with 36 similar offences taken into account. He had had three probation orders, a 6 month detention order and a combination order. He had references. He was sentenced to a combination order with 100 hours' community service and 3 years' probation. He had performed 60 out of the 100 hours' community service and was within 6 weeks of completing the course he was required to undertake. Held. We would have expected the order of **5 years** made up of 4 years for the GBH and 1 for the perverting count. Taking into account it was a reference, the partial completion of the community service, $2\frac{1}{2}$ years for the GBH and 6 months consecutive for the perverting matter and 2 for ABH making **3 years**.

R v Evans 2002 2 Cr App R (S) 34. The defendant was convicted of GBH with intent, ABH and dangerous driving. He went to a pub and drank 'quite an amount of alcohol'. There was an incident with C but it all calmed down. When the pub closed he went outside and started some horseplay which developed into a fight. His ex-girlfriend intervened to try to calm the situation and he made a threatening gesture towards her as if to hit her. Two brothers who were both judo experts intervened and had no difficulty in inflicting one or two punches on him and putting him on the ground. The defendant in a rage about being humiliated, went home, got his pick up truck and went to the road where the brothers were walking home with C. He drove onto the pavement and deliberately straight at the three men. C was struck a glancing blow and was not seriously injured. One brother got out of the way. The other was hit and carried for about 20 metres before he fell to the ground. He sustained fractures to the spinal column and it was initially thought he would be totally paraplegic. He could have been killed, but made a remarkable recovery. He had recovered the use of his legs, although the use of his hands and arms had been gravely impaired and would not recover further. The defendant was 23 and effectively of good character with references, which said the offence, was out of character. Held. The aggravating factors were it was a relatively heavy truck used as a weapon of revenge. After the perceived insult there was ample time for the defendant to come to his senses. The injuries were severe and permanently disabling. **8 years** was on the high side but not manifestly excessive.

R v Fazal 2005 1 Cr App R (S) 591. The defendant pleaded guilty on re-arraignment, but in circumstances where he was entitled to full credit for his plea, to causing GBH with intent. He was working part time as a minibus driver and took on board a group of twelve people in the early hours. On arrival an argument developed about the fare to be paid. F made racist comments and tried to make his friends refrain from paying. Some of the group subjected him to sustained racial abuse and F was persistent in his racial insults. F got out of the minibus and effectively challenged the defendant to a fight. The defendant shouted back and as the group started to move away he reversed and then accelerated forwards aiming his taxi at F. F got out of the way but the victim, who was on a zebra crossing, was struck. The defendant did not realise he had hit him and dragged him under the minibus for a short distance. The victim's girlfriend who was still in the minibus alerted him to what had happened and he stopped. He then pushed her out of the minibus and drove some distance away but 10 minutes later phoned the police and returned to the scene where he was arrested. The victim, who had not made any provocative remark to the defendant, was seriously injured. He had fractures at the base of his skull, his left temple and his jaw. There was a major injury to the hip and grazing to his shoulders hands and knees. He suffered significant problems with his eyesight and there would be a permanent defect in his sight. The victim impact statement revealed that he was in intensive care for seven days and was unable to work for six and a half months. At the age of 14 he was the Midland Youth Boxing Champion but he was unable to follow this sport after his injuries. He had hoped to rejoin the army but could not now do that. The defendant, 23, had one wholly unrelated conviction for which he received an attendance centre order. He was working as a taxi driver to pay for his LLB law course at University. His first child was born shortly after these events. He was in employment with N Power and was considered a good employee in line for promotion. Two psychiatric reports indicated that he had suffered from depression after these events, with panic attacks and post-traumatic stress disorder. He was assessed as posing a risk of self-harm and at one point was thought to be unfit to stand trial. There were impressive testimonials and a helpful and favourable prison report. Held. The defendant did not try to hide and gave himself up to the police. We do not underestimate the significance of the racial taunting in this case. He was provoked by sustained racist remarks to behave in a way wholly out of character and has suffered significantly both professionally and personally as a result. His sense of remorse and regret is real and substantial. Given the exceptional mitigation and as an act of mercy on the particular facts of this case we are persuaded by a narrow margin that notwithstanding the appalling injuries **3 years** not 4.

R v Butler 2005 1 Cr App R (S) 712. The defendant was convicted of attempting to cause GBH with intent to resist arrest or prevent lawful detention. At a previous hearing he had pleaded guilty to two offences of handling stolen goods, making off without payment and giving a false name with the intention of perverting the course of justice. The defendant was stopped by PC Poyser on the M11 for driving with excessive speed. He had a woman passenger. The officer attempted to arrest him for driving whilst disqualified and the defendant provided a false name. He resisted arrest and punched the officer twice in the chest. He then got back into the car while PC Poyser tried to pull him out and another officer tried to pull the ignition keys out. The woman passenger punched PC Poyser in the face several times. An off duty officer stopped to help and tried to pull the defendant out of the car. The defendant started the engine and drove off, taking with him PC Poyser who had his foot in the driver's footwell. The vehicle gathered speed and the defendant steered towards the central barrier shouting 'You're going to die you bastard'. He then swerved away from the barrier and braked causing PC Poyser to release his grip and tumble across the motorway. PC Poyser suffered a broken nose, numerous cuts, grazes, bruises and severe body pains. PC Mann had been dragged 10 yards before he was thrown clear and had bruising to his arms and a cut to his finger. The car was later found abandoned and in it were a stolen briefcase and printer, which were the subject of one of the stolen goods charges. The career of PC Poyser who had served 24 years in the police force ended. Held. This was a very clear and deliberate attempt to cause really serious injury to a police officer. The sentence of **10 years** for the attempt to cause GBH was fully justified. The other sentences were ordered to run concurrently.

R v Huntroyd 2005 1 Cr App R (S) 442. The defendant was convicted of attempting to cause GBH with intent. The victim, a police officer, was on foot patrol, where via CCTV a car had been noticed in the service area of some shops. The passenger of the car was holding a can of lager. The officer approached the service area and the defendant drove towards the officer who moved into the middle of the road, and signalled the defendant to stop. He appeared to acknowledge the officer and started to pull the vehicle over as if to stop. He then put the car into gear and drove straight at the officer who tried to move out of the way but could only turn away whereby the car, travelling between 15 and 20mph, struck him on the back of his legs. The officer ended up on the roof of the car hanging onto the sunroof. The defendant accelerated down a busy high street, went the wrong way round a roundabout and continued to try to throw the officer off the car by swerving from side to side, and by accelerating and braking suddenly. He tried to close the sunroof on the officer's fingers. When he reached the end of the road, he turned left at such speed that the car lurched across to the wrong side of the road and the officer was thrown into the road. The defendant was using his partner's car without her permission and was a disqualified driver. The officer sustained a fracture of the scaphoid bone (which the jury had doubts was a really serious injury so the conviction was for an attempt instead). He was unable to return to work until 6 months after the incident and was having difficulty in sleeping. The defendant was 31 with an extensive drug and alcohol history and a bad record for dishonesty and violence. He had 3 convictions for disqualified driving. Held. The intent weighed heavily against the defendant. This was a police officer doing his duty. The defendant's manner of driving after the initial impact clearly demonstrated an intent to cause really serious harm. **9 years** was wholly appropriate.

See also *Att-Gen's Ref. No 78 of 2000* 2002 1 Cr App R (S) 500. See **Police officers on duty as victims**

Victim under 10

121.55   *R v Alston* 2004 2 Cr App R (S) 362. The defendant pleaded guilty on re-arraignment to causing GBH with intent. He had been drinking at his brother's flat with others and became aggressive. He was involved in a fight which spilled out onto the landing. A neighbour came out to investigate. The defendant's brother apologised for him and the defendant went back into the flat after looking at the neighbour in an aggressive way. 15 minutes later there was more shouting and the neighbour went out again and saw the defendant holding his brother by the throat trying to punch him. She had not closed her door and her three year old autistic son followed her out and ran towards the defendant, evading her grasp. She went to press the panic button in her flat. The defendant picked up the boy, who was chuckling at the game, held him at head height, and then threw him down with all his force. The boy had two skull fractures, injuries which were severe and life threatening. He was in hospital for some three weeks. He made a good recovery but there was a risk he might suffer from epilepsy and hearing problems. The defendant, aged 18, was of previous good character. A pre-sentence report said there was a high risk of him re-offending as he had behaved in a highly unpredictable manner and his motivation was unknown. He was now sickened and appalled by his behaviour. He had a troubled childhood and was involved in alcohol and cannabis abuse. It was possible he had an attention deficit disorder when younger. A psychiatric report concluded he was not suffering from any illness or learning disability. Post-sentence prison reports said he had made some progress in education and suffered from anxiety and depression. Held. The case was unique and notwithstanding the defendant's age and plea **10 years** YOI was not excessive.

Victim caused permanent disability/Very serious injuries

121.56   *R v Meredith and Craven* 2000 1 Cr App R (S) 508. The defendant C was convicted of GBH with intent. In October 1997 the victim and the defendant C's brother got in an argument in a public house. They then fought and the victim seemed to be getting the better of the brother. They were separated and the brother was bleeding. The victim got into a chair. Then C punched the victim and he fell to the floor and was motionless. A fracas developed between a bystander and C. M then punched the victim in the head three or four times and kicked him in the stomach. M also stamped and kicked him on his head and shoulders. C then picked up a chair and brought it down on the victim's head four or more times. The injuries were the worst the consultant had ever seen. An eye was knocked out of its socket and was on his cheek held by the optic nerve, which was damaged. He was blind in that eye and had reduced vision in the other. Every bone in his face was broken. His mid face area was mobile. He was on a ventilator for 4 days and they could not operate on him for 13 days because of his condition. There was no hint of remorse or regret. C was 40 and had a long record. Most were minor but in 1985 he received $2^{1}/_{2}$ years for robbery and in 1996 he received 6 months for unlawful wounding and violent disorder. In December 1996 he was arrested for supplying cannabis in a public house. In 1998 he was sentenced to 27 months for it. M was given automatic life because he had a conviction for manslaughter. Held. It was sadistic and sustained cruelty. **12 years** was towards the top of the sentencing bracket but was not outside it. However, the total sentence of 12 years and 27 months consecutive for the drugs was too long so the sentences were made concurrent.

R v Cloud 2001 2 Cr App R (S) 435. The defendant was convicted of GBH with intent. Around midnight there was an argument and then a fight outside a public house involving the defendant and his two younger brothers. The victim aged 35, told them to break it up and he was attacked. He went back into the pub and returned with a fire extinguisher which was wrestled from him and he was thrown or knocked to the ground. The fire extinguisher was discharged and the defendant swung it in a golf swing at the victim's head as he lay on the ground. He suffered two skull fractures and nearly lost his life. There was serious and irreversible brain damage. He will need full time care for the rest of his life and could regain limited speech and possibly some degree of continence. **10 years** not 13. [The age and character of the defendant is not revealed.]

R v Bevan 2003 2 Cr App R (S) 311. The defendant was convicted of causing grievous bodily harm with intent. At about 10 pm two 16-year-olds were on their way to meet a friend when they came across the defendant and another R. All four were the same age and attended the same school. They chatted and the four walked on together. The defendant and R took it in turns to drink from bottle of vodka and coke. The four eventually reached some playing fields where the victim, aged 58, was walking towards them. R asked him for cigarette and the man replied that he did not smoke and continued walking. R walked with him and suddenly punched him hard to the side of his head and he fell. At that point the defendant ran over and kicked him four or five times as he tried to get up. R stood and watched. The other two called to the defendant to stop, which he did. The victim was lying on the ground trying to shield himself. R then began to kick the victim hard about the head and face and this continued for some time. The defendant stood by. R ignored the shouts of the other 2. R bent down to the unconscious victim, felt for a pulse and commented that he was still breathing. The victim was left lying on his back in the field seriously injured. About 3 hours later, a passer-by telephoned for an ambulance after finding the victim barely conscious. He was in a coma and had multiple injuries about the head and face, right wrist and right eye. It was suspected that he suffered brain damage. He had severe facial bruising, a fractured nose and was unable to open his right eye. He suffered post-traumatic amnesia. Following his eventual discharge his family noticed personality, behavioural and cognitive changes with memory and attentional problems. Acute anxiety prevented him from walking outside in the dark. He was diagnosed with left frontal brain damage that affected the right side of his body. There was significant deficit in his ability to move $6^{1}/_{2}$ months after the attack. Speech was still badly affected for 2 years later. He was told that he would only ever be 80% of the person he had once been and that that would take at least 9 years from the attack. The injuries caused considerable distress to his family. He was receiving a raft of different therapies. The day after the attack the defendant handed himself in to the police. He said in interview that he went to help R and had kicked the victim a number of times. He was 16 and of effectively good character and the risk of re-offending was perceived to be low. Held. This was a terrible attack. Notwithstanding the good character and youth of the defendant, the sentence, following a trial was appropriate. **6 years** detention upheld.

R v Hudson 2003 2 Cr App R (S) 327. The defendant pleaded guilty to wounding with intent. The victim had been involved in a long relationship with Miss F and had a daughter, aged 6. He was an alcoholic and suffered from epilepsy. Miss F began a relationship with the defendant and broke off her relationship with the victim. The victim's subsequent behaviour led Miss F to complain to the police on over 100 occasions. His behaviour ranged from phoning her 3 or 4 times a day, shouting at her in the street, visiting her house and making threats. Child contact arrangements were conducted through solicitors. On the day of the attack the victim phoned Miss F with a view to seeing their daughter. Miss F had reacted with hostility. The defendant had become aware of the extent of the unwanted approaches by the victim and went looking for him. He visited and left a message with the victim's sister: "Tell him I'll kill him." The sister noticed that he was carrying a hammer. The victim was later walking the street when the defendant pulled up in his lorry, got out and attacked him with a hammer. He hit him on the head a number of times and kicked and punched him whilst he was on the ground. He left him there bleeding. He was later found wandering in the street with blood on his face. A CT scan revealed a haematoma with a gross midline shift of the brain. He had a left-sided skull fracture which extended to the base of the skull. He was lucky to survive but remained very ill. His health had not been good prior to the attack. He had in fact since died. On arrest the defendant denied the attack but subsequently admitted it. The defendant was effectively of good character and had been in good employment. He had four children from his previous marriage. A psychiatrist reported that he was riddled with remorse and that the risk of re-offending was low. Held. This was a case where the defendant acted out of a sense of seeking to protect the woman with whom he was living. He conducted a very severe attack that caused the victim most serious, life-threatening injuries. **6 years** upheld.

R v Moore and Feeney 2004 2 Cr App R (S) 153. The defendants M and F were both convicted of causing GBH with intent. Both defendants went at night to F's mother's address to eject the 35 year old victim who was a drug addict on methadone. F's mother, a chronic alcoholic, had allowed the victim to stay. Once inside the house F punched the victim while his mother tried to stop him and M joined in the assault. Both defendants kicked and stamped on the victim while he was lying on the floor bleeding from his injuries, and then carried him to a grass verge two doors away from F's mother. They made no attempt to call the emergency services. M wiped their fingerprints from the light switches and doorknobs inside the house. The victim had a fractured skull and jaw and was in a persistent vegetative state. If medical care was removed he would die. He was unlikely to improve. The Judge said that both defendants bore an equal responsibility for the injuries caused. Both defendants were aged 25. For F it was said his previous excellent character and his good work record should be taken into account. He had also made great efforts to help his mother. Held. The sentences were manifestly excessive. The Judge was right not to differentiate between the two defendants. **12 years**, not 15 years, for both.

R v Desourdy 2004 2 Cr App R (S) 188. The defendant pleaded guilty to causing GBH with intent. He did this on the second occasion the case was set for trial and then on a basis which required a Newton hearing, during the course of which he accepted the Crown's case. The defendant and two others attacked a man who was the worse for drink on the eighth floor of a block of flats. They had been searching for two men who the defendant said had attacked him earlier. The three men had between them a chair leg and a stick of some sort and launched an attack on the victim. The defendant hit and kicked the victim and when he fell on the floor the defendant stamped on his face several times and jumped on it landing with both feet. For a short time the men left the victim bleeding and severely injured. The defendant then returned and dragged him down the concrete steps allowing his head to bang on each step for about two storeys, when one of the others came and helped him carry the victim out of the premises. The victim suffered considerable bruising to his body, extensive bruising to his brain, multiple fractures to the floor of his cranium, his facial skeleton was partially detached, both his cheek bones were fractured, part of his spine was fractured and his brain was badly swollen. He underwent extensive surgery. At the time of sentence he could not walk unaided because of problems with balance and weakness in his lower limbs. This also prevented him from dressing, washing or attending to his toilet needs or cooking. Because of the deficit in his skull he had to wear a helmet at all times to protect himself from further brain injury in the case of a fall. In due course a plate was to be inserted. His speech was slurred, he had problems in swallowing, he suffered from blurred vision making reading and watching television difficult and from considerable mood swings and anxiety. He was unable to care for himself and needed help 24 hours a day. He suffered from severe headaches and needed to be accompanied when he left the house. The defendant, aged 22, had previous convictions including ABH (12 months imprisonment). He had shown no remorse at any stage. Held. This was a savage and brutal attack for which the defendant must bear the greater responsibility for the attack and the appalling consequences. The attack showed features of callousness and in the absence of disinhibiting factors such as drink or drugs was akin to sadistic cases. The only significant mitigation was the defendant's age. **11 years** was entirely appropriate in the circumstances.

R v Alston 2004 2 Cr App R (S) 362. The defendant pleaded guilty on re-arraignment to causing GBH with intent. He had been drinking at his brother's flat with others and became aggressive. He was involved in a fight which spilled out onto the landing. A neighbour came out to investigate. The defendant's brother apologised for him and the defendant went back into the flat after looking at the neighbour in an aggressive way. 15 minutes later there was more shouting and the neighbour went out again and saw the defendant holding his brother by the throat trying to punch him. She had not closed her door and her three year old autistic son followed her out and ran towards the defendant, evading her grasp. She went to press the panic button in her flat. The defendant picked up the boy, who was chuckling at the game, held him at head height, and then threw him down with all his force. The boy had two skull fractures, injuries which were severe and life threatening. He was in hospital for some three weeks. He made a good recovery but there was a risk he might suffer from epilepsy and hearing problems. The defendant, aged 18, was of previous good character. A pre-sentence report said there was a high risk of him re-offending as he had behaved in a highly unpredictable manner and his motivation was unknown. He was now sickened and appalled by his behaviour. He had a troubled childhood and was involved in alcohol and cannabis abuse. It was possible he had an attention deficit disorder when younger. A psychiatric report concluded he was not suffering from any illness or learning disability. Post-sentence prison reports said he had made some progress in education and suffered from anxiety and depression. Held. The case was unique and notwithstanding the defendant's age and plea **10** years YOI was not excessive.

Att-Gen's Ref. No 20 of 2004 2005 1 Cr App R 615. The defendant was convicted of Section 18 wounding. The victim went with three friends at 3.30am to buy food from a petrol station near his home. The defendant pulled up at the petrol station in a car with two others and tried to get petrol from a pump but it didn't operate at that hour without advance payment. He went to the cashier's window pushing in front of the victim and his friends. The victim protested. The defendant returned to his car, signalled the other passengers to get out and took a steering lock from the boot of his car. One of his passengers had a knife. The man with the knife stabbed the victim and the defendant hit him over the head with the steering lock. The victim tried to escape and the defendant chased him and hit him again. The victim got up and tried to escape and the defendant hit him again with the steering lock in a swinging motion with both hands above his shoulder. The defendant got into his car and drove away. The victim had three stab wounds and, as a consequence of blood loss, suffered severe brain injury. He was left blind, immobilised with no useful movement in any limb, confined to a wheelchair, doubly incontinent and totally dependant on 24-hour specialist nursing. No change was expected. The consequences for him and his family members were devastating. Following these events there was a search for the attackers although the other two involved were not found. The defendant was arrested at Stansted airport with a one-way ticket to Spain. His defence was alibi. Six aggravating features were said to be that he instigated the attack and enlisted others to take part; that the steering lock and knife were used as weapons; that the victim was unarmed; that the attack was planned; that the injuries were severe and permanent. The defendant, 29, was of previous good character. There was psychiatric evidence that he suffered from depression and claustrophobia. A letter from the chaplain of the prison said he was hard working and determined to contribute to society in a constructive manner on release and that he was a simple likeable character vulnerable to manipulation. A letter from the mother of one of his children spoke in graphic terms of the effects on the children of his imprisonment. Held. The least appropriate sentence following a trial for this very grave offence was **12** years. As it was a reference and to a limited extent, the personal mitigation, **9 years** not 5.

R v Horrocks 2005 1 Cr App R (S) 414. The defendant pleaded guilty to GBH with intent. The victim had been drinking in a public house and his behaviour had become irritating. The defendant had also been drinking but agreed to give the victim a lift in his van. During the journey the defendant said that the victim picked up a hammer, which the defendant tried to retrieve. A tug of war developed and the defendant lost his temper. He hit the victim on the head with the hammer and pushed him out of the van. Seeing the victim get up, the defendant turned the van around, got out and hit the victim two or three more times on the head with the hammer. The defendant's partner saw him covered in blood and went and found the victim lying unconscious. The defendant washed the hammer and dumped his clothing. The victim had a depressed skull fracture, multiple scalp lacerations and bruising to his head. His ear was hanging on by skin fragments and a finger was fractured. He had to attend a rehabilitation centre and his prognosis was uncertain. He had hearing loss, fits and memory loss. When the defendant was arrested he said "I take it the bloke is still alive". He was a binge drinker. He expressed remorse and suffered with depression. He was 29 with previous violence convictions including ABH, affray, wounding, possessing an offensive weapon and knife point robbery for which he had received community and custodial sentences. Held. The defendant had left the victim for dead and tried to cover his tracks. Despite knowing his own capacity for terrible violence when drunk, he has continued to abuse alcohol. **12 years** was severe but justifiably so.

Water, boiling

121.57   *Att-Gen's Ref. No 3 of 2000* 2001 1 Cr App R (S) 92. The defendant was convicted of GBH with intent. The defendant had an intermittent relationship with the victim for about 5 years. The defendant returned home at about 2am under the influence of crack cocaine. He found the victim and two male friends there and demanded to know what had happened to his motor car. He believed the three had sold it to buy heroin. He was armed with a knife and his manner was threatening. He was also asking for £100 to buy crack. He left and returned carrying a full jug sized kettle of boiling water. He poured it over the victim's back and shoulders. He fetched a sheet soaked in cold water and she wrapped herself in it. She was terribly burnt and in agony. She suffered from 16% to 22% mixed depth burns. Some 80% of her back was scarred. She was in hospital for $3^{1}/_{2}$ weeks. The defendant claimed it was an accident. He had 16 court appearances as an adult and he had convictions for robbery, dishonesty and two for ABH. Held. We would have expected a sentence of at least 6 years. Taking into account it was a reference **5 years** substituted for 3.

122   OFFENCES AGAINST THE PERSON ACT 1861 s 20

122.1   Malicious GBH or wounding

Triable either way. On indictment maximum 5 years. Summary maximum 6 months and/or £5,000.

The Criminal Justice Act 2003 creates a summary maximum sentence of 51 weeks, a minimum sentence of 28 weeks and Custody plus. The Home Office says they do not expect to introduce these provisions before September 2006.

There is a new offence of committing an offence with intent to commit a sexual offence, see Sexual Offences Act 2003 s 62. A section 20 offence would be an obvious offence to link with this new offence.

Anti-Social Behavioural orders Where the defendant has acted in a manner that caused or was likely to cause harassment, alarm or distress to one or more persons not in the same household as the defendant and it is necessary to protect persons from further anti-social acts by him/her the court may make this order[12].

Extended sentences under CJA 2003 For offences committed on or after 4/4/05 there is a mandatory duty to pass an extended sentence when there is a significant risk to members of the public of serious harm etc.[13]. See **EXTENDED SENTENCES**.

Football Where the offence was committed relevant to a football match and where there are reasonable grounds to believe that making a banning order would help to prevent violence or disorder at or in connection with any regulated football match; the court must make a Football Banning Order, Football Spectators Act 1989 s 14A and Sch 1, para 1.

Licensed premises Where the offence is committed on licensed premises the court may prohibit the defendant from entering those premises or any other specified premises without the express consent of the licensee or his agent[14]. The order shall last from 3 months to 2 years[15].

Longer than commensurate and extended sentences It is a violent offence for the purposes of passing a longer than commensurate sentence [Powers of Criminal Courts (Sentencing) Act 2000 s 80(2)] and an extended sentence (extending the licence) [Powers of Criminal Courts (Sentencing) Act 2000 s 85(2)(b)]. The orders cannot be made for offences committed before 30/9/98 or after 3/4/05.

Sexual Offences Prevention Order There is a discretionary power to make this order when it is necessary to protect the public etc[16].

Working with children Where the offence is against a child (aged under 18), the defendant is aged 18 or over and s/he is sentenced to 12 months or more the court must

---

12 Crime and Disorder Act 1998 s 1C
13 Criminal Justice Act 2003 s 227–228
14 Licensed Premises (Exclusion of Certain Persons) Act 1980 s 1(1)
15 Licensed Premises (Exclusion of Certain Persons) Act 1980 s 1(3)
16 Sexual Offences Act 2003 s 104 & Sch. 5

disqualify him/her from working with children unless satisfied s/he is unlikely to commit any further offences against a child when the court must state its reasons for not doing so[17]. For a defendant aged less than 18 at the time of the offence the court must order disqualification if s/he is sentenced to 12 months or more and the court is satisfied that the defendant will commit a further offence against a child[18]. The court must state its reasons for so doing.

Crown Court statistics – England and Wales – Males 21+ – "Other woundings etc."
122.2

Year	Plea	Total Numbers sentenced	Type of sentence %					Average length of custody (months)
			Discharge	Fine	Community sentence	Suspended sentence	Custody	
2002	Guilty	6,070	5	4	38	4	46	16.1
	Not guilty	1,171	3	5	29	2	54	18
2003	Guilty	5,631	5	3	36	4	49	15.8
	Not guilty	1,255	3	4	27	3	57	16.5

For details and explanations about the statistics in the book see page vii

Magistrates' Court Sentencing Guidelines January 2004 – Wounding

122.3   For a first time offender pleading not guilty. Entry point. Are Magistrates' sentencing powers sufficient? Consider the impact on the victim. Examples of aggravating factors for the offence are abuse of trust (domestic setting), deliberate kicking/biting, extensive injuries, group action, offender in position of authority, on hospital/medical or school premises, pre-meditated, prolonged assault, victim particularly vulnerable, victim serving the public and weapon. Examples of mitigating factors for the offence are minor wound and provocation. Examples of mitigation are age, health (physical or mental), co-operation with the police, genuine remorse and voluntary compensation. Consider committal for sentence. Give reasons if not awarding compensation.

For details about the guidelines see MAGISTRATES' COURT SENTENCING GUIDELINES at page 483.

Guideline remarks

122.4   *R v Clare* 2002 2 Cr App R (S) 445. Where there has been an attack involving a single blow the first consideration is the strength of the blow and the second is the consequences for the victim.

Children – See CRUELTY TO CHILDREN – **Offences Against the Person Act 1861 s 20**

Defendant 18–20

122.6   *R v Robinson and McManus* 1998 1 Cr App R (S) 72. The defendant M pleaded guilty to GBH with intent. The defendant R pleaded to just GBH. The white defendants who were drunk came across the victim who was black walking home from work. M aged 16 ran after him and knocked him out the way. He was raving and shouting. R aged 18 started pushing him in the chest and grabbing his suit lapels. As he wouldn't let go the victim took a swing at him. R still would not go and a fight ensued. The victim was knocked out. A witness saw M punch him to the ground and kick him in the head. The

17 Criminal Justice and Court Services Act 2000 s 28
18 Criminal Justice and Court Services Act 2000 s 29

witness moved in between them. Punches were thrown at him and the M continued to kick the victim. The witness ran and was chased by R. M then jumped on the victim's head. The victim required 22 stitches to his head and face. He had multiple lacerations round the eye. There was a danger his retina might become detached. His scarring to his right eye might be permanent. His headaches and vertigo would take several months to resolve. He was afraid to leave his home. R plea was based on a late participation in the joint enterprise and preventing the witness from assisting the victim. Held. It wasn't racially motivated but it was horrific. Taking into account the mitigation particularly the remorse **4 years** not 3 for M and **2 years** YOI not 3 for R.

R v Clarke 1999 2 Cr App R (S) 400. See **122.13**

Fighting where the injuries are caused by the fall not any blow – Guideline remarks

122.7 *R v Coleman* 1992 13 Cr App R (S) 508. LCJ. The defendant was sentenced for manslaughter. We are considering a person who receives a blow, probably one blow only, to the head or face, is knocked over by the blow and unfortunately cracks his head on the floor or the pavement, suffers a fractured skull and dies. It is to be distinguished sharply from the sort of case where a victim on the ground is kicked about the head. It is to be distinguished sharply from the sort of case where a weapon is used in order to inflict injury. It is to be further distinguished from where the actual blow itself causes the death. This is the case of a fall almost accidentally resulting in a fractured skull. The starting point for manslaughter for this type of offence is 12 months on a plea of guilty. Then one looks at the mitigation and aggravating features. No premeditation, a single blow of moderate force, remorse and immediate admissions are all mitigation. Indications that the defendant is susceptible to outbreaks of violence, the assault was gratuitous and unprovoked, more than one blow all tend to aggravate the offence.

Fighting where the injuries are caused by the fall not any blow – Cases

122.8 *R v Hickman* 2001 2 Cr App R (S) 261. The defendant pleaded guilty to a Section 20 GBH and ABH at the first opportunity. The defendant and his girlfriend went to a party and then a pub. When she said she was leaving he followed her down the street and shouted at her. Two people D and R told him to leave the girl alone. He punched R once to the back of the head and the D intervened to separate them. The defendant threw a punch at D which missed. The girlfriend and D tried to calm him down. Someone seized the defendant and D and the girlfriend again intervened to separate them. The defendant punched D to the face. D fell and his head hit a raised part of the pavement. The girlfriend walked him away and unsuccessfully attempted to phone an ambulance. D and R were taken to hospital. D's injuries were catastrophic. He was found to have a large blood clot over his brain with bruising and trauma to the brain. He suffered dense spastic weakness to an arm and leg, disordered eye movements, which produced double vision, and a significant loss of vision in both eyes. The defendant attended voluntarily at a police station after he had seen a newspaper report of the incident. He said he was in temper and struck D. D's recovery was slow. He had severe cognitive impairment, memory impairment, poor concentration and an impaired bladder and bowel function. He was unable to read and write. He also had depression and anxiety which at times were overwhelming. A year later he had not significantly improved. He remained unable to walk and was incontinent. R had tenderness around an eye and his jaw. The defendant was 19 in employment and an amateur boxer. He was of good character and showed genuine remorse. Held. It was a difficult sentencing exercise. It was a one-off loss of self-control. It was unprovoked and he didn't stop when people tried to make him. The principles in *R v Coleman* 1992 13 Cr App R (S) 508 were applied. **2 years** YOI not 3.

R v Gilbert 2001 2 Cr App R (S) 450. The defendant pleaded guilty to GBH on the first day of his trial for that and a section 18 count (not guilty verdict). There was an altercation between the defendant aged 21 and the victim aged 26 over something trivial. They were both affected by alcohol. Each felt increasingly provoked by the other. Anger escalated and each refused to heed the calls made to them to back off. The victim was as anxious to continue the confrontation and was as provocative. The defendant then punched the victim once very hard in the face. The victim fell back and struck his head on the ground causing bleeding in the brain. When the defendant heard that the police wanted to see him he surrendered himself saying he hadn't had any sleep and his conscience made him go to the police. The victim underwent two brain operations. Nine months later he was still suffering language difficulties both in comprehension and expression. It was doubted whether he would ever return to work. When 17, the defendant had a conviction for assault on the police and was given community service. When 18 he was conditionally discharged for damaging property. The CSO was ordered to continue. When 19 there was another conviction for damaging property. There were later convictions for threatening behaviour and drunk and disorderly. The basis of plea was that he acted initially in self-defence but his response was an over reaction. Held. Concentrating on the blow **21 months** was severe but not manifestly excessive. (The medical details are scant.)

Old cases *R v Ambrose* 1997 1 Cr App R (S) 404.

See also **Serious but unexpected injuries**

Glassings

122.9   *R v Robertson* 1998 1 Cr App R (S) 21. The defendant pleaded guilty to a s 20 wounding. The defendant was watching football in a public house with friends. The victim realised he was being spoken to by the defendant said, 'Pardon.' The defendant said do you want to be scarred. The victim said, 'No thanks.' The defendant grabbed him and showed him a glass and said, 'You would be if I pushed that in your face.' The victim did not take this as a threat as he thought he was drunk. The defendant then faced the victim and thrust a glass into his face, which broke. The defendant was arrested and said he did not recall the incident and was drunk at the time. He expressed remorse. The victim suffered a $2^1/_2''$ cut above the eye and two cuts below. The defendant was suffering anxiety about work and had difficulty controlling his drinking. He had only a drink/drive conviction. His medical notes referred to unexplained acts of violence when he had been drinking. The defendant has now accepted his alcohol problem. Held. The court should look with care at sentences over 2 years. It was a serious offence involving a glass. **2 years** not 30 months.

R v Singleton 1998 1 Cr App R (S) 199. The defendant was convicted of unlawful wounding. He was acquitted of an offence under s 18. The defendant was in a wine bar with his sister and his girlfriend. The victim spoke to his sister in an objectionable and sexual way. The victim went to order drinks and on his way back walked past the defendant who stood up on the foot rest of his stool and picked up a glass. He swung his arm and smashed the glass into the victim's face. The defendant was taken out of the bar and he told the owner the victim had started it. The victim had very serious injuries to his eye and face. At the trial over 6 months later he was still undergoing treatment. The left eye remains at significant risk of severe visual loss or blindness. It was a 'very severe injury.' There was a small life long risk of the healthy right eye being affected by sympathetic ophthalmia. The defendant was arrested and said it was an accident after the victim had punched him. He was of good character with references. Held. We have regard to the very serious injuries and the strong personal mitigation. **2 years** not 3.

Knives

122.10   *R v Farrar* 2002 2 Cr App R (S) 63. The defendant changed his plea to guilty to unlawful wounding and ABH. A section 18 count was dropped. The defendant held a house warming party and at about 12.20am one of the guests made an unfortunate but well meaning joke. There was then an argument between him and his partner who was one of the people present. The maker of the joke approached and said to the defendant, 'Sorry, cheer up' and patted him with a friendly gesture. The defendant headbutted him which cut his forehead. That victim was taken to hospital and the cut required six stitches. There was bruising to the bridge of the nose and discolouration to an eye. The party continued and at about 5am the defendant became involved in an argument with his partner's brother about a long standing family issue about the different ethnicity between the defendant and his partner. It culminated in a struggle but no one was injured. The brother left the house and a short while afterwards the defendant followed with a large carving knife. Outside a neighbour was being dropped off by a friend. The neighbour saw the defendant's demeanour and was concerned about walking past him. The friend decided to reverse into a side street and take a different route. The defendant approached the car and asked, 'What are you doing hanging around here?' The friend said, 'Nothing.' The defendant kept on asking him what he was doing and then asked him for a lift home. He did this in a threatening manner. The friend said, 'Get lost.' The defendant then smashed the car window and lunged at him with a knife. The friend who was a doorman opened the car door, forced the defendant backwards and punched out at him. He managed to restrain the defendant who kept on struggling violently. Police arrived and arrested the defendant. The victim was taken to hospital and found to have a deep wound to his index and ring finger. The radial digital nerve was divided and he would have permanent loss of normal sensation. The defendant was interviewed and admitted hitting the window but claimed he was set upon by the victim. Afterwards he was an in patient for 5 days at an acute psychiatric unit. He was 29 and had a conviction for ABH in 1996 for which he received CSO. He had been teased at school because of his gypsy origins. He had become an apprentice welder, which led to him graduating from University in computer studies. He worked for Rolls Royce and was buying his house with his partner. A psychiatrist said he suffered from anxiety in crowds and with strangers. In 1999 he had been badly assaulted in a nightclub. The risk of the defendant causing further harm to the public was assessed as high. Held. This was an extremely bad case of wounding. It was very nasty but **2¹/₂ years** not 3¹/₂. There was nothing wrong with the 6 months consecutive for the ABH.

Longer than commensurate sentences – (frequently wrongly called extended sentences)

122.11   Powers of Criminal Courts (Sentencing) Act 2000 Section 80(2)(b) … the custodial sentence shall be … where the offence is a violent or sexual offence, for such longer term (not exceeding the maximum) as in the opinion of the court is necessary to protect the public from serious harm from the offender. (previously Criminal Justice Act 1991 Section 2(2)(b))

R v Jowett-Hall 2003 1 Cr App R (S) 138. The defendant pleaded guilty to Section 20 on a Section 18 indictment on the first day of his trial when the victim had arrived at Court. In August 2000 he was sentenced to 12 months for ABH on his then girlfriend. During that sentence he started to correspond with the next victim. When he was released he immediately went to live with her and her baby. The relationship went reasonably well for the first few months but he started to drink heavily and there were arguments. Five weeks before the expiry of his prison licence and after attempts at reconciliation the victim decided she could take no more abuse and said she was going for a walk. While she was changing the baby nappies he took a 6″ knife from the kitchen drawer and put it in his pocket. She asked him to put it back in the cutlery drawer and he replied he would, "rip her eye out with it". She was becoming distressed and frightened. Wearing only pyjamas she took her baby and ran into the street. He followed shouting for her to return and that she wouldn't last long. As she ran he seized her hair and stuck the knife into her neck. Still with the baby in her arms she pulled it out and ran to a friend. He was 32 and had been taken into care aged 2. He had suffered physical and sexual abuse and rejection. There were fifty five previous offences on twenty occasions. There were many for dwelling burglaries, dishonesty and drugs. In 1986, when 17 for arson endangering the life of his then girlfriend and child he was sentenced to life which was reduced by the Court of Appeal to 7 years youth custody. In 1996 he received probation for ABH, common assault and burglary. The violent offences involved attacks on women with whom he was having a relationship. The pre-sentence report said, "His current behaviour followed a distinct pattern where feeling threatened or slighted he attacked her with such force the knife broke in her neck. I do not believe it was a momentary loss of control, but a calculated action on his part to bring her under his control. The combination of emotions represents a powder keg waiting to be ignited by the right spark. Two of his former supervising officers assess him as a highly dangerous man with woman with whom he has a relationship. I fully concur. I am concerned he will be released to repeat his pattern on a new set of victims." Held. The risk of re-offending is high. A heavy sentence was demanded. The Recorder was right to invoke Section 80(2)(b). The maximum is 5 years. **4½ years** was the right sentence because of the very grave circumstances and the continuing risk he poses. If the Recorder could have passed a longer sentence he would have had every justification.

R v Lovett 2003 1 Cr App R (S) 320. The defendant pleaded guilty to Section 20 on a Section 18 indictment. After drinking cider and vodka, taking cannabis and cocaine, he had an argument with the victim in the victim's girlfriend's kitchen. The defendant then took a knife from the kitchen drawer and slashed the victim's face. The victim slumped to the floor and the defendant said, "I'm fucking going to kill you." The girlfriend interposed her body between them and the defendant left. There was no real motive. The victim had a deep laceration over his eyelid and across the bridge of his nose. There was also a 1 cm cut over his upper eye lid and a 2 cm superficial laceration to the cheek. The plea of guilty was based the defendant being too drunk to form a specific intent. The defendant was 28. His violent and alcohol offences were: two ABH offences in 1992, assault on police and drunk and disorderly in 1995, excess alcohol in 1998, drunk and disorderly in 2000 and possession of a bladed instrument in 2001. The pre-sentence report said all his offences were drink related and that he presents a high risk of harm to the public. The psychiatrist said his violence appears to have an impulsive element and he is likely to cause injury in the future. Held. This was a very serious offence, committed by a man who presents a continuing danger to the public of serious harm. The description of the injuries does not describe their seriousness, nor how very close the victim came to sustaining very serious damage indeed. He could have lost an eye. His throat could have been cut. The Judge was right to make the offence longer than commensurate. The defendant had little option but to plead guilty. The credit for the plea is minimal. This is one of the exceptional cases where the Judge was right to take the view that the protection of the public must be paramount. **5 years** (the maximum) was the right sentence.

For general principles see LONGER THAN COMMENSURATE SENTENCES

Public houses/After drinking

122.12   *R v McNellis* 2000 1 Cr App R (S) 481. The defendant pleaded guilty to unlawful wounding on an indictment for wounding with intent. After a lengthy drinking session there was an argument between him and his friend, the victim, in a flat. The defendant waved a knife at the victim, which he had earlier used to open bottles. The victim obtained a meat cleaver from the kitchen and a fight developed in which the victim hit him with it on the shoulder causing a wound 4.5 cm long and 1.5 cm deep. The defendant then stabbed the victim four times in quick succession in the shoulder, upper arm and twice in the chest with the knife. In hospital the victim deteriorated rapidly due to the severity of the wounds. Holes were found in the left and right ventricles of his heart. He was 4 days in intensive care and was in hospital for 24 days. The defendant was 37 and had numerous convictions for a variety of offences with many for dishonesty. He had served prison sentences. The longest was 9 months. The judge accepted the he was not entirely to blame. On appeal it was argued there was insufficient discount for the plea. Held. The wounds were of the utmost severity and could have led to death. The plea should not have been accepted. **4¹/₂ years** was a severe sentence but it did not cross the threshold of being manifestly excessive.

Old case *R v Byrne* 1998 1 Cr App R (S) 105, (for a summary of the case see the first edition of this book.)

Road rage   See **ROAD RAGE** – *Offences against the Person Act 1861 s 20*

Serious injuries – Unexpected

122.13   *R v Jane* 1998 2 Cr App R (S) 363. The defendant pleaded guilty at the Magistrates' Court to GBH. The defendant bought some tins of lager from a shop and drank them. He returned and stole two more cans. A few minutes later he tried to steal some more but the shopkeeper locked the door. He tried to leave but the shopkeeper stood in his way and held his arm telling him to wait until the police arrived. A struggle developed and the shopkeeper fell to the floor. A friend of the defendant pushed the door open and the shopkeeper continued to try to stop him leaving. The defendant kicked him in the face and left. The shopkeeper's eye was seriously injured. There was no likelihood of the vision returning to normal. There was a small risk of sympathetic ophthalmia occurring in the uninjured eye causing reduced vision in that eye. The defendant was arrested and made full admissions. He said he kicked out in frustration and had not intended to cause any injury. He was 23 and had been in the army and the experience had affected him mentally. He had a conviction for threatening behaviour. He showed remorse and had a number of impressive character references. He had also attended an alcohol rehabilitation course. Held. He lashed out in a panic. There was no suggestion that he intended to do serious harm. **2¹/₂ years** not 3¹/₂.

R v Clarke 1999 2 Cr App R (S) 400. The defendant pleaded guilty at the first opportunity to GBH and threatening words and behaviour. After the defendant's Rugby team had won the League cup the defendant and players etc. went to celebrate and ended up in a nightclub. Shortly after 1am the doorman of the club said the defendant had bumped into him. The defendant said it was accidental but was asked to leave and did so. He began shouting at the doorman and kicked the door. This was the Public Order offence. At about the same time, the victim (a complete stranger to the defendant) left the club and walked down an alleyway. The defendant overtook him and punched him in the face with the back of his fist. The defendant thought he was the doorman. The force of the blow knocked the victim to the ground and he hit his neck and head against a building. The defendant walked off not realising the victim had been seriously injured. Members of the public flagged down a passing ambulance and he was taken to hospital. His neck was fractured at the base of the skull and he was placed in a halo jacket, which he had to wear for 6 months. Five months later it was hoped that the fracture would unite and the outlook was 'good.' The injury was potentially fatal and there was the possibility of severe and irreparable neurological damage. The defendant surrendered voluntarily to the police. He showed genuine remorse and apologised unreservedly to the victim. He was 19 and of good character and with an admirable record and fifteen testimonials about charity work etc. Held. For any unprovoked blow of this nature, which causes the serious, albeit fortunately not long term injury which this blow caused, the assailant must expect to go straight to custody. There was a great deal of mitigation and the attack was limited and unpremeditated. **6 months** YOI not 18 and 1 month not 6 for the Public Order Act offence remaining concurrent.

Serious injuries, very

122.14   *R v Brindle* 2003 1 Cr App R (S) 9. The defendant pleaded guilty to dangerous driving and Section 20. He had pleaded at the Magistrates' Court to failing to report or stop and no insurance. After borrowing a friend's Escort car, he drove three friends at excessive speed in a 30mph area without insurance. When driving on the wrong side of the road the car struck a pedestrian who was stepping off a traffic island. The victim, aged 16, was thrown into the air and landed on the car and then the road. The car's estimated speed was 50mph and it was abandoned round the corner where the occupants ran off. Eleven days later the defendant surrendered to the police. The victim spent three weeks in intensive care and eight weeks in hospital. As well as fractures and multiple abrasions he suffered extensive head injuries causing brain injury which it was hoped would improve over two years. The defendant was 20 with convictions but none involving vehicles. The Judge said short of killing the victim he could not have caused more harm. Held. This was an exceptional piece of bad driving. He did not deliberately drive the vehicle as a weapon. **21 months** detention on both concurrent not $4^1/_2$ years for the Section 20. 6 years not 15 years disqualification.

R v Bell 2003 1 Cr App R (S) 543. The defendant indicated his plea of guilty at the first opportunity to GBH (s.20). It was some time before his plea was accepted. The victim was walking near to his home when he heard the sound of breaking glass. He past a comment to the defendant that he believed that the defendant had been responsible. The defendant, who appeared to be agitated and smelt strongly of alcohol, became aggressive, removed his jacket, adopted a boxing stance and pushed the victim. The defendant struck the victim three times in the face. He fell to the ground. The defendant then kicked him with sufficient force to leave a shoe imprint on his face. One witness described the defendant stamping on the victim's head. There were appalling injuries. His cheekbone was fractured, the floor of his left eye-socket dropped so his eyesight had been permanently affected and his vision blurred, he needed dental treatment and treatment for damage to his sinuses and misalignment of his nose. His consequential disabilities are permanent. The defendant admitted kicking the victim in interview but said that he had been out drinking with a friend. He was sentenced on the basis that he had had so much to drink that he was unable to form an intent to cause grievous bodily harm (as originally indicted). The defendant was 22. He had a significant record of violence: six years earlier he had been convicted on four occasions of common assault and there were also convictions for assaulting a police officer and assault occasioning actual bodily harm. For the last two offences he was ordered to perform 180hours of community service. There had been no further offences in the previous five years. Two prison reports described the defendant as mature and disciplined. Held. The judge should have (and had) started from a point very close to the maximum (5 years). The defendant merited this sentence. **$3^1/_2$ years** unchanged.

Sporting

122.15   *R v Calton* 1999 2 Cr App R (S) 64. The defendant pleaded guilty to GBH. His plea of not guilty to GBH with intent was accepted. He was aged 19 and played in a schools' rugby match. The victim was on the ground after a ruck and was getting up. The defendant who was on the opposing side kicked him to the side of the head. There was a loud crack. He was sent off and when interviewed said he kicked him because the victim had tried to grab his ankles. The victim had a fracture to his mandible. Six months later he was still having problems with his jaw and was still in pain. The defendant was a student with no convictions and five testimonials. He didn't want to play rugby again. The risk of re-offending was assessed as low. The judge sentenced him on the basis it was a fit of temper. There was a good prison report. Held. Custody was necessary but **3 months** detention not 12.

R v Moss 2000 1 Cr App R (S) 307. The defendant was convicted of GBH. According to the victim he was at the bottom of a ruck in a rugby game and was getting up when the defendant who was on the opposing team punched him in the face knocking him to the ground. He was disorientated and his eye bled. A witness said he was 10′ from the ruck and both players were throwing punches. The defendant denied hitting the victim. The victim was found to have a blow out fractured eye socket with entrapment of both fat and muscle. This had to be reduced and a titanium mesh was inserted to reconstruct the orbital floor. He was in hospital for five weeks. Ten days after his release he was suffering from diplopia. There was 16 months delay before sentence. The defendant was 35 with a conviction for conspiracy to defraud. There were no convictions for violence. The risk for re-offending was assessed as extremely unlikely. He was married with children and his small business would suffer severe hardship or collapse if he remained in custody. There were eight character references. His prison conduct was commendable. Held. **8 months** was not too long.

R v Bowyer 2002 1 Cr App R (S) 448. The defendant was convicted of GBH. In the final of a Rugby Union competition there was a scrum and when it broke up the victim went to defend his team's line. The defendant struck him a very severe blow which knocked him off his feet. The blow broke his jaw in two places and split his gum. His lower incisors were pushed backwards. Two plates were inserted which would remain there permanently. The defendant faced three trials after the first jury could not agree and the second was struck by illness. The defendant was 36 and treated as of good character although he had old convictions for ABH and threatening behaviour. It was out of character and he was a hard working family man with children. Held. This kind of gratuitous violence on the field is not to be tolerated. Acts of physical violence off the ball in sporting events must receive custodial sentences. **8 months** was severe but not excessive let alone manifestly excessive.

R v Tasker 2002 1 Cr App R (S) 515. The defendant pleaded guilty to unlawful wounding at the Magistrates' Court. The defendant was playing in a local Sunday league football match. The score was 0–0 until the victim's team scored a disputed goal. His players protested but it was allowed. Thereafter things deteriorated rapidly. He was later cautioned by the referee after an incident with one of the opposing players and spoken to by the referee after that. Matters came to a head following a foul and there was a flare up between the players during which the victim was pulled to the ground. Before he could get up the defendant came across the field and kicked him in the face. The victim could hardly see and the game was abandoned. An X-ray of the victim showed a fracture of the lower eye socket and possibly another one under the cheek bone. When interviewed the defendant said it was, 'just a rush of blood, a silly moment'. He was 29 and of good character in full time employment. Held. There was no provocation. He had been cautioned and deliberately went over and kicked him. Very serious injuries were caused. Looking at the authorities **6 months** not 12.

R v Ahmed 2002 2 Cr App R (S) 535. The defendant pleaded guilty to Section 20 and common assault. He was acquitted of Section 18. During a soccer match the defendant was involved in a scuffle with the opposing goalkeeper in which he punched the goalkeeper in the face. His nose was broken and bled profusely. The referee intervened and sent the defendant off. As the red card was held up he punched the referee in the face. The referee said it was with a fist. The defendant said it was with an open hand. The blow caused bruising and soreness to the cheek. This was the common assault. The defendant left the pitch and within 30 seconds he had walked behind the goal where the goalkeeper was receiving treatment for his nose on the ground. He moved quickly towards him and kicked him in the face. This caused a broken jaw and broken eye socket. The victim spent three nights in hospital. His jaws were wired together and three metal plates and thirteen screws were inserted. The defendant was arrested three months later and admitted pushing the referee. He was 22 and had been convicted four times for violence and five times for Public Order Act offences. The FA had already banned him from playing soccer and fined him £500. He was a former crack addict. Held. What occurred was very much more serious than any of the reported cases. A great majority of them involve a single punch by a man of good character. They indicate some allowance is to be made for misconduct on a football or rugby pitch, having regard to the fact that there is an element of consent on the part of the victim to some degree of bodily contact and plainly acts upon a pitch which within a public house would constitute an assault, are not, by reason of the sport an assault. Here the referee did not consent to any physical contact and was particularly defenceless with his arm raised with the red card. The goalkeeper was lying on the ground defenceless. So if there is a lower tariff for those engaged in the sport it does not avail the defendant. He has shown himself to be violent and unruly on numerous occasions. He is a manifest danger on a football pitch. **30 months** and 4 months consecutive were neither individually or cumulatively a day too long.

See also *R v Ahmed* 2002 2 Cr App R (S) 535.

Stalking

See STALKING – **Offences Against the Person Act 1861, s 20**

Unprovoked/unwarranted attack in the street

122.16   *R v Clare* 2002 2 Cr App R (S) 445. The defendant pleaded guilty to Section 20 at the Magistrates' Court and was committed for sentence. Around midnight the victim, aged 26 was walking home after a night out. He passed the defendant who he knew slightly from his school days and who was with Nicola and Daniel. The defendant shouted, "Prick". Some minutes later the victim realised the defendant was walking besides him and was being sarcastic and annoying in his attitude. The victim told him to piss off. He was punched in the face and fell to the ground losing consciousness. When he came round Nicola was asking him if he was alright and the defendant was standing nearby saying, "I'm sorry. I didn't mean it." The victim had a broken jaw and a fractured cheekbone. In hospital he had a metal plate and four screws fixed to his jaw and was there for two days. He may have to have another operation. The defendant was 27 with no previous convictions. The defence relied on the fact he had run to get help for Nicola and had not run off and that he had resigned from his job because he was so worried about the court case. The Judge held a Newton hearing where the defendant gave evidence and was disbelieved. The pre-sentence report said he was remorseful and considered there was little chance of him committing a similar offence in the future. The Judge held it was gratuitous violence after he had been drinking. Held. The blow was obviously hard because the victim lost consciousness. The consequences were reasonably severe. However **18 months** not $2^1/_2$ years.

R v Bell 2003 1 Cr App R (S) 543. The defendant indicated his plea of guilty at the first opportunity to GBH (s.20). It was some time before his plea was accepted. The victim was walking near to his home when he heard the sound of breaking glass. He past a comment to the defendant that he believed that the defendant had been responsible. The defendant, who appeared to be agitated and smelt strongly of alcohol, became aggressive, removed his jacket, adopted a boxing stance and pushed the victim. The defendant struck the victim three times in the face. He fell to the ground. The defendant then kicked him with sufficient force to leave a shoe imprint on his face. One witness described the defendant stamping on the victim's head. There were appalling injuries. His cheekbone was fractured, the floor of his left eye-socket dropped so his eyesight had been permanently affected and his vision blurred, he needed dental treatment and treatment for damage to his sinuses and misalignment of his nose. His consequential disabilities are permanent. The defendant admitted kicking the victim in interview but said that he had been out drinking with a friend. He was sentenced on the basis that he had had so much to drink that he was unable to form an intent to cause grievous bodily harm (as originally indicted). The defendant was 22. He had a significant record of violence: six years earlier he had been convicted on four occasions of common assault and there were also convictions for assaulting a police officer and assault occasioning actual bodily harm. For the last two offences he was ordered to perform 180hours of community service. There had been no further offences in the previous five years. Two prison reports described the defendant as mature and disciplined. *Held.* The judge should have (and had) started from a point very close to the maximum (5 years). The defendant merited this sentence. **2¹/₂ years** unchanged.

R v Jeffrey 2004 1 Cr App R (S) 179. The defendant pleaded guilty to GBH (s.20). At 11.30 pm as the victim was walking to a nightclub he came across the defendant. The defendant punched the victim in the face and the victim's head hit the pavement fracturing his skull. As a result he suffered permanent hearing loss and the onset of tinnitus. Dental work was also required. It transpired the defendant held some ancient animosity against the victim. The defendant was 23 with convictions for burglary, theft, possession of drugs and criminal damage. He was convicted of common assault in 2000, in 2001 and four times in 2002, one of which was racially aggravated. Three of the common assault offences were committed 8 days before this offence. The racially aggravated offence was committed four weeks before. His risk assessment was "high". **2¹/₂ years** not 3¹/₂.

Old cases *R v Byrne* 1998 1 Cr App R (S) 105 and *R v Curry* 1998 2 Cr App R (S) 410 (For a summary of these cases see the first edition of this book.)

Vehicle, caused by a

122.17   *R v Wildman* 1998 1 Cr App R (S) 236. The defendant was convicted of unlawful wounding and dangerous driving. He was acquitted of section 18. The defendant had a somewhat stormy relationship with his girlfriend over three years and they had two children. In one of the many separations the girlfriend met the victim and she said they were never more than friends. The defendant became reconciled with his girlfriend but was jealous of the victim. On Boxing Day the victim had too much to drink and sat beside the girlfriend. The defendant stared at him and she stood up. As she did so the victim stroked her leg and the victim was ejected from the club. At 1am on New Years Day the defendant after drinking told some acquaintances that he was looking for the victim. The defendant then drove away and saw the victim after he had left a pub worse for drink. He turned his car round and drove it at the victim. There was an issue whether the victim was on the pavement or in the road at the time. The defendant told the girlfriend the victim had walked into the middle of the road and he had put his foot down. The victim was very seriously injured. He had a fracture to his face with multiple lacerations and contusions. He stopped breathing in the ambulance. He was paralysed and unconscious initially. By the trial he had improved considerably but was left with a personality change which was likely to be permanent. The defendant was 25 and had no convictions for violence but had one for criminal damage arising out of an argument with his girlfriend. *Held.* The courts treat very seriously any offence committed by means of misuse of a motorcar. It is indeed a lethal weapon. If a car is driven at speed at someone it is always likely that serious injury may result. **4 years** was correct. (The report does not refer to the estimated speed of the car.)

R v Brindle 2003 1 Cr App R (S) 9. The defendant pleaded guilty to dangerous driving and Section 20. He had pleaded at the Magistrates' Court to failing to report or stop and no insurance. After borrowing a friend's Escort car, he drove three friends at excessive speed in a 30mph area without insurance. When driving on the wrong side of the road the car struck a pedestrian who was stepping off a traffic island. The victim, aged 16, was thrown into the air and landed on the car and then the road. The car's estimated speed was 50mph and it was abandoned round the corner where the occupants ran off. Eleven days later he surrendered to the police. The victim spent three weeks in intensive care and eight weeks in hospital. As well as fractures and multiple abrasions he suffered extensive head injuries causing brain injury which it was hoped would improve over two years. The defendant was 20 with convictions but none involving vehicles. The Judge said short of killing the victim he could not have caused more harm. Held. This was an exceptional piece of bad driving. He did not deliberately drive the vehicle as a weapon. **21 months** detention on both concurrent not $4^1/_2$ years for the Section 20. 6 years not 15 years disqualification.

123 Offences Against the Person Act 1861 s 20 – Racially-Aggravated

123.1 Crime and Disorder Act 1998 s 29

Triable either way. On indictment maximum 7 years. Summary maximum 6 months and/or £5,000.

Anti-Social Behavioural orders Where the defendant has acted in a manner that caused or was likely to cause harassment, alarm or distress to one or more persons not in the same household as the defendant and it is necessary to protect persons from further anti-social acts by him/her the court may make this order[19].

Extended sentences under CJA 2003 For offences committed on or after 4/4/05 there is a mandatory duty to pass an extended sentence when there is a significant risk to members of the public of serious harm etc.[20] See **Extended Sentences**

Football Where the offence was committed relevant to a football match and where there are reasonable grounds to believe that making a banning order would help to prevent violence or disorder at or in connection with any regulated football match; the court must make a Football Banning Order under the Football Spectators Act 1989, s 14A and Sch 1, para 1.

Licensed premises Where the offence is committed on licensed premises the court may prohibit the defendant from entering those premises or any other specified premises without the express consent of the licensee or his agent[21]. The order shall last from 3 months to 2 years[22].

Sexual Offences Prevention Order There is a discretionary power to make this order when it is necessary to protect the public etc[23].

Working with children Where the offence is against a child (aged under 18), the defendant is aged 18 or over and s/he is sentenced to 12 months or more the court must disqualify him/her from working with children unless satisfied s/he is unlikely to commit any further offences against a child when the court must state its reasons for not doing so[24]. For a defendant aged less than 18 at the time of the offence the court must order disqualification if s/he is sentenced to 12 months or more and the court is

19 Crime and Disorder Act 1998 s 1C
20 Criminal Justice Act 2003 s 227–228
21 Licensed Premises (Exclusion of Certain Persons) Act 1980 s 1(1)
22 Licensed Premises (Exclusion of Certain Persons) Act 1980 s 1(3)
23 Sexual Offences Act 2003 s 104 & Sch. 5
24 Criminal Justice and Court Services Act 2000 s 28

satisfied that the defendant will commit a further offence against a child[25]. The court must state its reasons for so doing.

For basic principles about racially-aggravated offences see **RACIALLY-AGGRAVATED OFFENCES**

Magistrates' Court Sentencing Guidelines January 2004 – Wounding

123.2   For a first time offender pleading not guilty. Entry point. Are Magistrates' sentencing powers sufficient? Consider the impact on the victim. Examples of aggravating factors for the offence are abuse of trust, deliberate kicking/biting, extensive injuries, group action, offender in position of authority, on hospital/medical or school premises, pre-meditated, prolonged assault, victim particularly vulnerable, victim serving the public and weapon. Examples of mitigating factors for the offence are minor wound, provocation. Examples of mitigation are age, health (physical or mental), co-operation with the police, voluntary compensation and genuine remorse. Consider committal for sentence. Give reasons if not awarding compensation.

For details about the guidelines see **MAGISTRATES' COURT SENTENCING GUIDELINES** at page 483.

Knives, with

123.3   *Att-Gen's Ref. No 19 of 2004* 2005 1 Cr App R (S) 73. The defendant pleaded guilty to racially aggravated unlawful wounding. A 16-year-old black youth (K) was sitting with two black friends at a railway station when he said "Hello" to a girl with who he had been at school. She was with the defendant and told K to "Fuck off". The defendant went over to K and became aggressive and threatening and called him a "Fucking black monkey". The girlfriend sought to pull him off, but he produced a folding knife and slashed K across the left side of the neck causing a significant wound, which required 18 stitches. There was no interview. The defendant was 27 with a significant record. At the time of this offence he had been sentenced to a DTTO only 4 weeks earlier. Held. The sentence was unduly lenient. There was a substantial wound to a vulnerable part of the victim caused by a folding knife that the defendant was carrying with him. His girlfriend had tried to stop him. The wounding itself would have attracted $2^{1}/_{2}$ years and the racial element would have attracted $1^{1}/_{2}$ years, making **4 years**. As this was a reference, 2 years and 1 year making **3 years**, not 10 months.

124   OFFENCES AGAINST THE PERSON ACT 1861 SECTION 21

124.1   Attempting to choke, suffocate or strangle etc. with intent to commit etc. an indictable offence

Indictable only   Maximum sentence life imprisonment

Dangerous Offender provisions For offences committed on or after 4/4/05 where there is a significant risk to members of the public of serious harm etc. there is a mandatory duty to pass a life sentence when it is justified and otherwise a sentence of imprisonment for public protection[26]. For offenders under 18 the duty is to pass detention for life, detention for public protection or an extended sentence[27].

Longer than Commensurate sentences and Extended sentences Section 21 is a violent offence for the purposes of passing a longer than commensurate sentence

25 Criminal Justice and Court Services Act 2000 s 29
26 Criminal Justice Act 2003 s 225
27 Criminal Justice Act 2003 s 226 and 228

[Powers of Criminal Courts (Sentencing) Act 2000 s 80(2)] and an extended sentence (extending the licence) [Powers of Criminal Courts (Sentencing) Act 2000 s 85(2)(b)] where the offence leads, or is intended or likely to lead, to a person's death or to physical injury to a person[28]. The orders cannot be made for offences committed before 30/9/98 or after 3/4/05.

Sexual Offences Prevention Order There is a discretionary power to make this order when it is necessary to protect the public etc[29].

Where the intent is to bugger see **RAPE** – *Anal* or rape see **RAPE** and where the intent is to cause serious bodily harm see **OFFENCES AGAINST THE PERSON ACT 1861 SECTION 18** – *Strangling, choking etc.*

125   OFFENCES AGAINST THE PERSON ACT 1861 S 23

125.1   Administering etc poison or noxious thing etc so as to endanger life or inflict GBH.

Indictable only. Maximum sentence 10 years.

Imprisonment for public protection For offences committed on or after 4/4/05 when there is a significant risk to members of the public of serious harm etc. there is a mandatory duty to pass a sentence of imprisonment for public protection[30]. For offenders under 18 the duty is to pass detention for public protection or an extended sentence[31].

Sexual Offences Prevention Order There is a discretionary power to make this order when it is necessary to protect the public etc[32].

Drugs – Class A

125.2   *R v Dorosz* 2001 2 Cr App R (S) 476. The defendant pleaded guilty at the first opportunity to two counts of supplying heroin and administering heroin so as to endanger life. The victim visited his flat. At the request of the victim he injected her with heroin. Later she injected herself. One evening she brought heroin and cocaine to his flat. They both injected themselves with heroin and cocaine probably four or five times. He probably gave her two of them and she gave herself the rest. He asked her several times whether she was alright and she always said she was. She seemed to be enjoying it. Apart from one occasion he always put the heroin in the syringe to ensure she was taking less than he was. He left her to sleep on the sofa. In the morning he rang his workplace to say he was unwell and went back to bed. He woke again at 1 pm and could not wake her. He called for an ambulance and she could not be resuscitated. Police arrived and he gave them above account although in less detail. An expert said she possibly died from heroin and cocaine. He also said she had taken heroin up her nose, which the defendant said he had not seen. He was 28 and of good character. He gave a full account to the coroner although he was not obliged to. He was arrested two months later. He was a computer programmer, which rewarded well. He had developed a fascination with altered states of the mind and had abused drugs including heroin from time to time. He had impressive character witnesses. He was genuinely remorseful and the pre-sentence report said that the event had been devastating for him. Held. There were many factors in his favour. **2¹/₂ years** on each count concurrent not 3¹/₂.

---

28 Powers of Criminal Courts (Sentencing) Act 2000 s 161(3)
29 Sexual Offences Act 2003 s 104 & Sch. 5
30 Criminal Justice Act 2003 s 224–226
31 Criminal Justice Act 2003 s 226 and 228
32 Sexual Offences Act 2003 s 104 & Sch. 5

Neighbours

125.3 *R v Cronin-Simpson* 2000 1 Cr App R (S) 54. The defendant was convicted of three counts of causing a noxious thing to be administered so as to endanger life. The defendant's mother lived next door to the victims who detected a strong smell of fumes in their house. It appeared to be either petrol or ammonia. Liquid was seen to be pouring down the walls. The three occupants began to feel ill and suffer from nausea. One of them discovered a brick had been removed in the loft between the two houses. Police found a number of containers of petrol and other liquids in the mother's house. Local authority inspectors also found three pipes running in a cavity wall into the neighbours' house which were found to contain petrol. There were also holes in the plasterwork. The defendant was unfit to be interviewed and spent a short time in a psychiatric hospital. She gave no clue as to the reason for the offence. She gave detail of some disputes with the neighbours but said she had not had any problems with them. She was 62 with some minor convictions for criminal damage and abusive behaviour. She refused to co-operate with a psychiatric report. The judge said the ammonia and petrol mix was extremely dangerous. After sentence a report said she had a hysterical personality disorder and a paranoid personality. She was suspected of suffering paranoid delusions. There were no signs of a major mental illness. Her prison behaviour was above standard. Held. Because the neighbours did not suffer more than feeling ill and nausea and because of her medical condition **4 years** not 6.

126 OFFENCES AGAINST THE PERSON ACT 1861 s 24

126.1 Administering etc poison or noxious thing etc with intent to injure, aggrieve of annoy.

Indictable only. Maximum sentence 5 years.

General principles

126.2 *R v Jones* 1990 12 Cr App R (S) 233. The right approach is to equate the offence with either an Offences against the Person Act 1861, s 20 offence or a serious ABH.

Neighbours etc, unexplained administering to

126.3 *R v Nasar* 2000 1 Cr App R (S) 333. The defendant pleaded guilty to three counts of causing a noxious thing to be administered with intent. On three occasions she mixed a sleep inducing tablet with food or drink and gave it to friends or relations on the pretext it was beneficial for some supposed ailment. On the last occasion having drugged the woman she tied her up and bundled her unconscious into a suitcase and took her from her house into a car to move her to another house. She asked two friends who had come to visit her to give her a lift. As she was struggling with the suitcase the friends heard the victim calling from inside the suitcase. They opened the case and found the victim semi-conscious inside. On two of the occasions the victims were hospitalised and all three victims lost consciousness. The first drug was fluoxetine, which the defendant had been prescribed for her depression. The second drug was probably sleeping pills, which were also proscribed to her or her disabled daughter. The third drug was most probably Temazepan and an anti-depressant drug called Dothiepin. She was arrested and claimed the last victim asked for the tablets and she put her in the box because the victim was nearly unconscious and she could not find a pushchair. She couldn't speak English and showed a lot of concern for her mentally disabled daughter who required constant attention. The psychiatrist diagnosed a somatised anxiety state, which was a form of mental illness. She was sentenced on the basis the true explanation was unknown but she did not intend to cause any permanent harm. She received 1, 1 and 12 months concurrent. Held. Because of the defendant's age (not stated) and antecedents **12 months** was a severe sentence but it was fully merited for these deliberate acts which certainly in relation to the last matter could well have caused death. [The serious aspect seems to be the false imprisonment of the last victim, which was not something she was charged with.]

Prank etc

126.4 *R v Callaghan* 2001 2 Cr App R (S) 333. The defendant pleaded guilty to causing a noxious thing to be administered with intent to injure or annoy and common assault. He had known the young victim for some time and she had recently purchased a house from him. He agreed to do some carpentry work in the house for her before she moved in if she helped him. While she was out of the room he slipped a prescription only drug into her glass. Its effects were sedation, drowsiness and confusion. Combined with alcohol the effects could be more severe. She became unconscious. When she came round the next morning, on her skin just below the knicker line the defendant had written "In here" and an arrow pointing to her private parts. She was horrified and she became frightened. The next day he asked her if she remembered falling over in the garden and said he had written over her to show how inebriated she was. Traces of the drug were found in her glass and a half-consumed packet of the same drug was found at the defendant's home. He denied the offence when interviewed. The basis of plea was that there was no indecent motive and it was a joke. Also he had not needed to remove any of her clothing. He was 52 and of good character with character witnesses. Held. The dominant consideration is the victim. The drug was calculated to render her unconscious and the drawing on, her which was an invasion of her person, aggravated the offence. **6 months** was just as it should have been.

R v Gantz 2005 1 Cr App R (S) 582. The defendant was convicted of causing a noxious thing to be administered with intent. He and a friend flew from Israel to London. The previous night he had been to a party and taken an ecstasy tablet and smoked cannabis as well as drinking. He also had some cocaine although he claimed he did not knowingly take that. Also travelling to London was the victim, who was pregnant, and her grandmother. The victim was previously unknown to the defendant. The defendant got into conversation with her at the airport and on the plane he was sitting quite close to her. He drank from a bottle of Schnapps on the plane and the cabin crew asked him to stop. He refused and they confiscated the bottle. Next he got into conversation with the victim and handed her a cup of coffee that the flight attendant had made for her. She didn't like the taste and only drank a sip. He asked her to go to a party with him in London and she refused. She perceived him as persistent in his advances although she told him she was married. He later offered to get her an orange juice which she drank. After she had drunk the juice she noticed bits at the bottom of the glass. After that she felt a little unwell and had a rapid pulse with affected vision. She was thought to be suffering from a panic attack. When the plane landed she was taken to hospital and her blood and urine were found to contain traces of ecstasy. Near to where the defendant had been sitting there was an empty Diazepam packet and three ecstasy tablets. It was the Crown case that he had been trying to make her susceptible to his advances by means of the drug. The defendant was 31 and of good character. He never showed any remorse. Held. The fact that the noxious substance was a Class A drug was a seriously aggravating factor. Other aggravating factors were that the victim was a wholly innocent woman, she had not encouraged the defendant's attentions and she was pregnant. When she discovered she had had something administered to her she panicked and was very distressed. The incident was on an aeroplane with limited medical facilities, which would have increased her distress and fear. Although **3 years** was at the upper end of the range of sentence it was not manifestly excessive.

Security staff, directed at

126.5   *R v Sky* 2000 2 Cr App R (S) 260. The defendant pleaded guilty to causing a noxious thing to be taken with intent, common assault, theft and breach of bail. A security guard at Marks and Spencer was informed the defendant had stolen a bottle of vodka. Outside the store he tried to apprehend him and the defendant sprayed a substance in his face. The guard was temporarily blinded and had difficulty in breathing. He also had a burning sensation to his face. The defendant escaped. The guard's eyes were bloodshot and he was treated with antibiotics and eye drops. When interviewed the defendant said he acted out of panic. He had been given the substance by another and did not known what it was. He was 28 with numerous convictions for dishonesty including twenty two for theft. One was for failing to surrender. The majority were spent. Held. **21 months** for the spray offence was not manifestly excessive. The theft sentence, 1 month and breach of bail sentence, 2 months remained consecutive making **2 years** in all.

Victim under 10

126.6   *R v Liles* 2000 1 Cr App R (S) 31. The defendant pleaded guilty to causing a noxious thing to be administered. Two brothers aged 5 and 6 years visited the defendant who was 52. They knew the defendant and they lived in the same road. The defendant used isobutyle nitrate which was similar to amyl nitrate. During their visit he allowed them to inhale some. The boys felt dizzy and unwell. Some was spilt on the face and clothing of the youngest. His mother noticed that his eyes were full of tears and his face bright red. He was taken to hospital and allowed home. The defendant had been in trouble in the past for a number of different matters. He was sentenced on the basis that there was no sexual content. Held. Because of the plea and frankness **2 years** not 3.

127   OFFENSIVE WEAPON, POSSESSION OF AN

127.1   Prevention of Crime Act 1953 s 1

Triable either way. On indictment maximum sentence 4 years. Summary maximum 6 months and/or £5,000.

Football It is a relevant offence under the Football Spectators Act 1989 s 14A and Sch 1, para 1. Where (a) the accused was at or attempting to enter or leave the premises or journeying to and from the football premises or the offence related to a match, the offence was committed during a journey and the court makes a declaration that the offence related to football matches and (b) there are reasonable grounds to believe that making a banning order would help to prevent violence or disorder at or in connection with any regulated football match, the court must make a Football Banning Order (except where the defendant is given an absolute discharge).

Licensed premises Where the offence is committed on licensed premises and the defendant resorted to violence or offered or threatened to resort to violence the court may prohibit the defendant from entering those premises or any other specified premises without the express consent of the licensee or his agent[33]. The order shall last from 3 months to 2 years[34].

Magistrates' Court Sentencing Guidelines January 2004

127.2   For a first time offender pleading not guilty. Entry point. Is it so serious that only custody is appropriate? Consider the impact on the victim. Examples of aggravating factors for the offence are group action or joint possession, location of offence, offender

---

33 Licensed Premises (Exclusion of Certain Persons) Act 1980 s 1(1)
34 Licensed Premises (Exclusion of Certain Persons) Act 1980 s 1(3)

under influence of drink or drugs, people put in fear/weapon brandished, planned use and very dangerous weapon. Examples of mitigating factors for the offence are acting out of a genuine fear, weapon carried only on a temporary basis, no attempt to use the weapon and offence not premeditated. Examples of mitigation are age, health (physical or mental), co-operation with the police, genuine remorse and voluntary compensation.

For details about the guidelines see **Magistrates' Court Sentencing Guidelines** at page 483.

Guideline case

127.3   *R v Celaire* 2003 1 Cr App R (S) 610. We largely, although not entirely, adopt the proposals of the Sentencing Advisory Panel, dated May 2000. This judgement is guidance not a straightjacket to sentencers. The carrying of knives is extremely dangerous because the production of a knife to threaten people, in circumstances of potential violence, has the capacity to cause serious escalation of such violence. A balance has to be struck between the fact that the offence does not in itself involve physical injury and the public's legitimate concern that a culture of carrying weapons encourages violence and may lead to more serious criminal behaviour. It is necessary to consider the offender's intention, the circumstances of the offence and the nature of the weapon involved. It may often be helpful for a sentencer to ask the sort of questions posed in relation to firearms in *R v Avis* 1998 2 Cr App R (S) 178, that is to say to consider the nature of the weapon involved, the use to which it may be put and the defendant's intention in carrying it and the defendant's previous record. As to intention there are, in our judgment, three specific factors, which may aggravate the offence. First, there may be a specifically planned use of the weapon, to commit violence or threaten violence or intimidate others. Secondly, the offence may be motivated by hostility towards a minority individual or group, which may give rise to an aggravating feature, such as racial motivation within the Crime and Disorder Act 1998 s 28. Thirdly, we would regard it as an aggravating aspect if the defendant was acting under the influence of alcohol or drugs while carrying such a weapon.

Aggravating and Mitigating factors

As to the circumstances of the offence, these may be aggravated if its commission takes place at particularly vulnerable premises such as a school, (which may give rise to the possibility of a separate charge under the Criminal Justice Act 1988 s 139A), or a hospital or other place where vulnerable people may be present. Likewise, an offence may be aggravated if committed at a large public gathering, especially one where there may be a risk of disorder; or, if committed on public transport or on licensed premises or on premises where people are carrying out public services, such as in a doctor's surgery or at a social security office. Finally the offence will obviously be aggravated if it is committed while the defendant is on bail. That, of course, is a statutorily aggravating feature under the Criminal Justice Act 1991 s 29(2). As to the nature of the weapon, some weapons are inherently more dangerous than others. But the nature of the weapon will not be the primary determinant as to the seriousness of the offence, because a relatively less dangerous weapon, such as a billiard cue, or a knuckle-duster, may be used to create fear and such an offence may be at least as serious as one in which a more obviously dangerous weapon, such as a knife or an acid spray, is being carried for self-defence or no actual attempt has been made by the offender to use it. On the other hand, light may be shed on an offender's intention if he is carrying a weapon, such as a flick knife or a butterfly knife, which is offensive per se, or a weapon designed or adapted to cause serious injury. Mitigation will be found if the weapon was being carried only on a temporary basis. As in most other cases, there will be mitigation arising from personal factors, co-operation with the police and a timely plea of guilty. A defendant, with previous convictions for violence or carrying weapons, who is convicted of carrying a particularly dangerous weapon, in circumstances aggravated by any of the factors which we have identified and doing so with the clear intention of causing injury or fear, can expect to receive a sentence **at or near the statutory maximum**. In relation to an adult offender of previous good character, the custody threshold will almost invariably be passed where there is a combination of dangerous circumstances and actual use of the weapon to threaten or cause fear. The nature of the weapon and other aggravating or mitigating factors will bear on the length of the custodial term.

Custody may still be appropriate, depending on the circumstances, where no threatening use was made of the weapon. Alternatively, depending on the circumstances, there will be cases where, absent aggravating features of the kind which we have identified and where no threat has been made and where the weapon is not particularly dangerous, the custody threshold may not be passed and a community sentence towards the top end of the available range may be appropriate. Of course, if the defendant has previous convictions for violence or for other weapon offences, then the sentence imposed on him or her is likely to be longer.

Consecutive or concurrent to the other offence

Where the weapons offence was committed in conjunction with another offence, the usual considerations in relation to totality will apply. A concurrent sentence will usually be appropriate if the weapons offence is ancillary to another more serious offence. Where the weapons offence is distinct and independent of another offence, a consecutive sentence will usually be called for.

Other orders

The sentencing court will also wish to bear in mind its powers to order forfeiture which will almost inevitably follow, and its powers to make a compensation order.

Self protection, claim of

127.4 *R v Proctor* 2000 1 Cr App R (S) 295. The defendant was convicted of possessing an offensive weapon. Police spoke to him and he was taken to a police station and was searched. They found a plastic bottle containing ammonia. He said it was for his own protection and had been carrying it for 2–3 days. He also feared a particular individual was going to stab him. The ammonia strength was similar to household solutions and if sprayed into the eyes could cause extreme discomfort. He was 23 with convictions for dishonesty. He had served 12 months for burglary and theft but had been out of trouble for some time. Held. Offences of this nature are serious. **9 months** was severe but not manifestly excessive.

Young offenders Guideline remarks

127.5 *R v Celaire* 2003 1 Cr App R (S) 610. So far as young offenders are concerned, the courts will of course, in passing sentence, have regard to their statutory duty to prevent offending by children and young persons, under the Crime and Disorder Act 1998 s 37 and the need to have regard to the welfare of the child by virtue of the Children and Young Persons Act 1933 s 44. It will almost invariably be appropriate, in the case of young offenders, to obtain a pre-sentence report before proceeding to sentence.

See also BLADED ARTICLE, POSSESSION OF A

128 OFFICIAL SECRETS ACTS

128.1 Official Secrets Act 1911 s 1
Indictable only. Maximum sentence 14 years.

Official Secrets Act 1920 and 1989

Various penalties. Some offences are triable only on indictment, some are either way and some are summary only.

Journalists, handing material to

128.2   *R v Shayler* 2002 The Times 6 Nov. CCC High Court Judge. The defendant an ex-Security Service officer was convicted of three counts under "the Official Secrets Act". He handed documents to The Mail and twenty nine were returned. Most of them related to security and intelligence matters and were classified from "Classified" up to and including "Top Secret". They related to the interception of communications. He left the country and articles based on the papers were published. Attempts to extradite him from France failed. Sentencing remarks. Your blinkered arrogance has led you to the dock. I accept you motivation was to expose what you thought was wrong, not a desire for money or as a ploy to begin a new career as a journalist. You lack any real insight into what you were doing or any intelligent foresight into its consequences. I was minded to send you to prison for 18 months but I take into account the $3^1/_2$ months you spent in a French prison. (Where possible the facts are taken from *R v Shayler* 2001 1 WLR 2206, his House of Lords case on a preliminary matter. Treat news reports with care.)

Selling defence secrets, unsuccessful

128.3   *R v Bravo* 2002 Times and Daily Telegraph 2 Feb and Internet sites. CCC The Recorder of London. The defendant pleaded guilty to five counts under the Official Secrets Act (presumably including 1911 Act, s 1) and five theft counts. He asked for two secrets counts to be taken into consideration. He was a security guard for a private firm at British Aerospace and obtained documents from unlocked security cabinets while on night patrols. He tried to sell the documents, which contained British, and NATO secrets. The documents related to defence systems for Harrier jump jets to stop radar locking onto them, electronic decoy systems for warships and electronic warfare. The documents had a colour system indicating that the documents could threaten life and cause serious damage to operational effectiveness etc. He telephoned the Russian Embassy but only reached an answerphone. He therefore posted the documents with his pager number. When the documents were found to be missing he was suspected. His fingerprints were found at the scene. He was followed. Shortly after the theft, an MI5 agent contacted him and arranged a meeting. Bravo said he had more documents. He was asked what he wanted and he said, "Money, as much as I can get." He was arrested and 200 pages of defence secrets were found in the carriers of his motorbike. There was no evidence that national or allied secrets were prejudiced. Had he succeeded those interests would have been substantially prejudiced. He considered he was in a dead-end job and wanted money to go to Spain. He was 30 and a British National of Spanish descent with financial problems. He was described as a loner and typical opportunist spy. He claimed that he had not appreciated the seriousness of what he had done. Sentencing remarks. Although I accept you were motivated by financial gain a lengthy jail term was necessary to deter others. Anyone who has put at risk his country's security must receive long sentences. **11 years**. (Treat news reports with care.)

R v Parr 2003 The Times and Daily Telegraph 30 Nov 02, Daily Telegraph and Guardian 5 April 03 and Internet sites. CCC The Recorder of London. The defendant pleaded guilty to two counts under the Official Secrets Act 1911 s 1 and seven counts under the Theft Act. He handed over 56 floppy disks and 14 sets of documents relating to seven sensitive defence projects to someone who he thought was from the Russian Embassy. They included the stealth cruise missile system and the Storm Shadow system. In fact he had been dealing with an MI5 officer from the start. He thought he would receive £25,000 in the first stage of an espionage operation which would net him

£130,000. He was arrested. The defendant had worked at BAE Systems Avionics for 15 years where he was a test co-ordinator in charge of a department making circuit boards for key weapon systems. It was the same place Raphael Bravo (see above) worked. He was 46 and a former soldier. His sole motive was money. None of the systems were compromised. He was of good character and claimed he was worried about being made redundant. Sentencing remarks. A substantial sentence was needed to reflect public abhorrence and to deter others. **10 years**. (Treat news reports with care.)

OLD DEFENDANT

See **DEFENDANT** – *Elderly*

129   OPIUM

General characteristics

129.1   *R v Mashaollahi* 2001 1 Cr App R (S) 96. Opium is most often imported from traditional opium growing countries in small quantities for personal use. It is not commonly traded on the street and there is no evidence that its use is widespread or that it is likely to increase significantly. The current classification of opium as a class A drug is on the premise that it is to be regarded as being every bit as harmful as other class A drugs. Weight for weight, where street value is concerned, heroin is considered to be approximately eight times more valuable than opium. On this basis, a consignment of 40 kilos of opium at 100% purity would be equivalent in value to five kilos of heroin at 100% purity, importation of which, under the current sentencing guidelines, attracts a sentence of 14 years and upwards on a contested case. We understand that the ratio to apply to convert opium to morphine or heroin would be 10:1 i.e. 10 kilos of opium would be needed to produce 1 kg of morphine or heroin assuming average levels of purity. In practice, it is virtually impossible to buy heroin or cocaine of 100% purity on the street. They are invariably cut or otherwise adulterated by the admixture of some harmless substance. The extent of criminality depends on the extent of the drug itself and not of the harmless substance. But with opium the position is different. It is a crude mixture of many different chemicals contained in the juice of the seed capsule of the opium poppy, papaver somniferum. Incisions are made in the capsule from which the latex oozes out and when collected and allowed to dry in the air forms a dark sticky mass known as raw opium. For non-medical purposes, such as either smoking or eating the substance, the raw opium is boiled in water, strained to remove insoluble materials and then evaporated to form a sticky paste known as prepared opium. The significant feature is that it is still the natural derivative of the plant, and, save exceptionally, it is not adulterated by the addition of any further substances. It was pointed out to us that the morphine constituent of opium tended to show a considerable variation. However, since we are dealing with the composite product of the plant, we think that any enquiry as to the percentage of one particular constituent, even though it is by itself a class A drug, would introduce a needless complication to the sentencing process.

For details of the sentences imposed see **SUPPLY OF DRUGS (CLASS A, B AND C)** – *Opium*

See also **DRUG USERS; IMPORTATION OF DRUGS; POSSESSION OF DRUGS; PRODUCTION OF DRUGS** and **SUPPLY OF DRUGS (CLASS A, B AND C)**

OUTRAGING PUBLIC DECENCY

See **PUBLIC DECENCY, OUTRAGING**

PARKING   See **ROAD TRAFFIC**

130   PAROLE

See also **CURFEW SCHEME, HOME DETENTION** for an example of the basic principle.

131   PASSPORT OFFENCES

131.1   Various offences and penalties

Note with the increase in penalties in *R v Kolawole* 2005 2 Cr App R (S) 71. some recent cases are not listed as they are no longer a guide to the suitable penalties. All cases before R v Kolawole 2005 should be viewed with care.

See also **BIGAMY/MARRIAGE OFFENCES** – *Immigration controls, to evade* and **IMMIGRATION OFFENCES**

Guideline case – Using false passports

131.2   *R v Singh* 1999 1 Cr App R (S) 490. There have been a number of inconsistent cases in offences involving false passports. The use of false passports appears to be on the increase. A passport is an important document that confers rights upon the lawful holder. It is, in our judgment, necessary that the integrity of passports should be maintained. It follows that to use a false passport is a serious offence, whatever the precise nature of the offence. Good character and personal circumstances are of very limited value. Sentences should generally be on a deterrent basis, for the reasons given in *R v Osman* 1999 1 Cr App R (S) 230. Extensive or sophisticated alteration of a passport will always be an aggravating feature. Cases involving the use of false passports will almost always merit a significant period of custody. This will usually be within the range of **12–18 months** (previously 6 to 9 months), even on a guilty plea by a person of good character. (This extract has been updated by *R v Kolawole* 2005 2 Cr App R (S) 71 which increased the penalties.)

Guideline remarks

131.3   *R v Takyi* 1998 1 Cr App R (S) 372. The integrity of the passport system is of such public importance that other than in unusual circumstances custodial sentences will follow convictions for the improper use of a passport. The length of the sentence will vary infinitely with the facts of the case.

False passport, using or possessing

131.4   *R v Kolawole* 2005 2 Cr App R (S) 71. The defendant pleaded guilty at the Magistrates' Court to two charges of possessing a false instrument and two driving offences. Police stopped his car and asked him to produce identification. He produced a driving licence in the name of Johnson. Police found a forged Nigerian passport and a stolen British passport in the name Johnson. The Nigerian passport had his photograph in it. He was 28 with no known previous convictions. 8 months on each consecutive (**16 months**) was not manifestly excessive.

False passport, using or possessing – part of large organisation

131.5   *R v Cheema* 2002 2 Cr App R (S) 356. The defendant was convicted of having custody or control of false instruments namely 12 false passports. The defendant arrived at Birmingham airport from Amsterdam with 12 counterfeit Greek and German passports with Asian names and £2,500. He had been in Amsterdam 1 day and the passports were not of the best quality and were unlikely to deceive an immigration official. He was treated as a courier. He was 65 with two convictions in 1974 for conspiracy to assist illegal entry for which he received 42 months. In 1996 he received 7 years for importing 17 kilos of heroin. Held. A courier in the drugs trade is not treated less seriously than a person carrying drugs for his own use. The same approach is required in the illegal trade in false passports. Couriers are a necessary element in this unlawful trade. Sentences need to deter others. But **3 years** not 4.

R v Stanca 2004 1 Cr App R (S) 264. The defendant pleaded guilty at the Magistrates' Court to 9 offences of unlawfully having forged instruments. He was stopped as he was about to board a ferry to the Hook of Holland. He produced a Dutch passport and Customs found 2 Italian passports, 3 French ID cards, 3 Portuguese ID cards, a Portuguese ID document and French ID document. He said he had arrived in the UK two days before to pick up documents by arrangement. He also said he was a Romanian with now Dutch nationality who needed money for medical bills for his father in Romania. He said he received £3000 as advance payment. He was 27 with no convictions. He was sentenced as a courier with full knowledge of what he was doing. Held. The increased concern about these offences should be taken into account but **15 months** not 21.

Making false statements

131.6   *R v Walker* 1999 1 Cr App R (S) 43. The defendant pleaded guilty to making a false statement to obtain a passport. The defendant came to Britain from Zimbabwe and remained after the permitted period had expired. He applied for a passport in a different name with a false date and false place of birth. He was 31 and of good character. He had given evidence for the prosecution in a serious criminal matter. Held. Passport application offences are to be treated seriously. They have the potential to undermine the immigration control system. As the maximum is 2 years **9 months** not 18 was appropriate to take into account the plea and to leave room for more serious offences.

Producing passports, being involved in

131.7   *R v Munir and Khondu* 2003 1 Cr App R (S) 124. The defendants M and K were convicted of conspiracy to possess paper etc. for making false passports and making a document (a driving licence) with intent to deceive. Earlier M had pleaded to handling six stolen passports. Police and Immigration officers searched a workshop premises where some legitimate printing was done and M's flat above. In the workshop they found a printing press and printing equipment. In the flat were the stolen passports, a computer, a page from a passport and several blank driving licences and some plastic laminates. The computer was found to contain a large number of files indicating it had been used to create false passports and other false documents. False acetates were found to produce false stamps. Several blank driving licences were also found. The prosecution case was that K was in charge and M was a worker. They forged British passports by obtaining stolen passports, removing the personalised page and replacing it with a computer generated forged page and photograph. It was for profit. Further this was the largest quantity of forged documentary material seen by the Immigration Service forgery section. K was the proprietor of the printing company. Neither had any relevant criminal record. The Judge said that over the recent weekends interracial violent disorder had occurred and passport forgery tends to increase the tensions in society. He gave 2 years for the handling and 12 months for the driving licence, all concurrent. Held. It was right for the Judge to use the forgery cases for counterfeiting money to work out the sentence. The violent disorder was too remote from the defendants' conduct to have any effect on the sentence. We see why the defendants think that factor increased their sentences. In order to demonstrate justice has been done, **6¹/₂ years** for K not 7¹/₂ and **4¹/₂ years** not 5 for M.

Someone else's passport, using

131.8   *R v Osman* 1999 1 Cr App R (S) 230. The defendant pleaded guilty to using a false instrument at the Magistrates' Court. The defendant went to Gatwick Airport to board a flight to the US. He produced a passport in the name of Morgan and was arrested. When interviewed he said he wanted to start a new life in the US because he feared that his application for political asylum would fail in this country. He had left Sudan because he claimed he had been tortured. Held. The fact a defendant is under personal pressure e.g. a refugee does not excuse the conduct. The courts must discourage those attempting to abuse the system. **9 months** was right.

132   PATIENTS, ILL TREATING ETC

132.1   Ill treatment or neglect of mental patients

Mental Health Act 1983 s 127

Triable either way. On indictment maximum 2 years. Summary maximum 6 months and/or £5,000.

Extended sentences under CJA 2003 For offences committed on or after 4/4/05 there is a mandatory duty to pass an extended sentence when there is a significant risk to members of the public of serious harm etc[1]. See **EXTENDED SENTENCES**

Sexual Offences Prevention Order There is a discretionary power to make this order when it is necessary to protect the public etc[2].

Elderly patients

132.2   *R v Spedding* 2002 1 Cr App R (S) 509. The defendant was convicted of 11 counts of ill-treating patients. He was a registered mental nurse working in a home for elderly mental patients. The prosecution said he was a lazy, heavy-handed, cruel nurse whose ill treatment was systematic, prolonged and distressing. It ran from February 1997 to May 1999. None of the patients were fit to give evidence. The judge sentenced him to **12 months** on two counts and 9 months on the rest. The sentences were all concurrent and the defendant only appealed the 12 month sentences. One of the sentences was reduced because of the judge's approach and the other was confirmed. [The facts are not listed because the approach of the judge was criticised and the appeal did not centre on whether the sentences were manifestly excessive.]

See also **INDECENT ASSAULT ON A WOMAN** – *Breach of trust – Nurse*

133   PENSION OFFENCES

133.1   Various offences including many under the Pensions Act 1995.

1   Criminal Justice Act 2003 s 227–228
2   Sexual Offences Act 2003 s 104 & Sch. 5

Failing to pay money into employees' company fund

133.2   *R v Dixon* 2000 2 Cr App R (S) 7. The defendant pleaded guilty at the Magistrates' Court to nine offences contrary to the Pensions Act 1995, s 49(8) and 115(1). He was company secretary and finance director of a ceramic company and trustee of the occupational pension scheme involving payment of part of the 60 employees' pay to the managers of the scheme. Six of the charges related to payments of about £80,000 in total from the company to the scheme which were all made but were 10 to 53 days late. The last three charges related to payment of about £40,000 due but not made. This sum will be replaced from public funds with the possibility of lost interest to the fund as a result. A cheque was issued when there appeared sufficient overdrawing facilities but the bank did not honour it and soon after the company went into receivership at the instigation of the bank. During the period of the offences the bank was reducing the overdraft facilities month by month from £1.5m. The defendant was unaware the delay of payments was a criminal offence. A letter from the pension adviser said payments should be made to avoid late payment fees but said nothing about it being a criminal offence. When he discovered it was an offence he wrote to the regulatory authority and explained the position. When interviewed he candidly accepted his failure and explained the reasons for it. He delayed payment in an attempt to preserve the jobs when the company was beset with debts. He was of good character. A £2,500 penalty had already been paid. Held. The offences have only recently been introduced and were being replaced with one which requires fraudulent evasion of payment. The desire to keep the company going rather than a selfish motive and his frankness with the authority were significant mitigation. 3 and 6 months custody was wrong and it should have been a financial penalty. £250 fine for the first 6 charges and £500 for the others making **£3,000** fine in total.

See also COMPANY FRAUDS AND FINANCIAL OFFENCES

PERJURY

See PERVERTING THE COURSE OF JUSTICE/CONTEMPT OF COURT/PERJURY ETC

For Perjury Act 1911, s 3 see BIGAMY/MARRIAGE OFFENCES

PERMITTING

For permitting premises to be used for drug supply see the end of the SUPPLY OF DRUGS (CLASS A, B AND C) chapter at **183.74**.

For permitting premises to be used by a girl under 13 or under 16 for sexual intercourse see PROSTITUTION, CHILD PROSTITUTES (see chapter **144**)

134   PERVERTING THE COURSE OF JUSTICE/CONTEMPT OF COURT/PERJURY ETC

134.1   Perverting the course of Justice. Common law offence.

Indictable only. No maximum provided so the maximum is life.

Contempt of Court Act 1981 s 12 (Magistrates' Courts), s 14 (and all other courts which have power to commit to prison for contempt)

Triable at the court the offence was committed. Maximum 2 years except for Magistrates' Court where 1 month and/or £2,500.

The Criminal Justice Act 2003 creates a summary maximum sentence of 51 weeks, a minimum sentence of 28 weeks and Custody plus. The Home Office says they do not expect to introduce these provisions before September 2006.

Detention Contemnors aged 18–20 may be sentenced to detention[3]. There is no power to sentence a contemnor under 18 to custody[4].

Perjury Act 1911 s 1

Perjury in judicial proceedings.

Indictable only. Maximum 7 years[5].

Criminal Justice and Public Order Act 1994 s 51

Intimidation of witnesses, jurors etc.

Triable either way. On indictment maximum 5 years. Summary maximum 6 months and/or £5,000.

Crown Court statistics – England and Wales – Males 21+
134.2

Year	Plea	Total Numbers sentenced	Type of sentence %					Average length of custody (months)
			Discharge	Fine	Community sentence	Suspended sentence	Custody	
Perverting the course of Justice								
2002	Guilty	992	2	2	38	3	55	7.1
	Not guilty	106	3	2	18	5	72	16.8
2003	Guilty	916	3	4	38	3	51	7.9
	Not guilty	103	2	–	18	5	72	21.5
Perjury								
2002	Guilty	19	–	11	32	–	58	8
	Not guilty	4	–	–	–	75	25	12
2003	Guilty	39	5	5	38	10	41	12.9
	Not guilty	3	–	–	–	33	67	18

For details and explanations about the statistics in the book see page vii.

Guideline remarks – Perjury

134.3   *R v Archer* 2003 1 Cr App R (S) 446. There are many factors to be considered when determining the appropriate level of sentence for perjury and related offences. There is not any distinction to be drawn whether the proceedings contaminated were civil or criminal. Perjury may be comparatively trivial in relation to criminal proceedings or very serious in relation to civil proceedings. No doubt whether the proceedings were civil or criminal is one of the factors proper to be considered. There are many others. We do not purport to give an exhaustive list. They include the number of offences committed; the timescale over which they are committed; whether they are planned or spontaneous; whether they are persisted in; whether the lies which are told or the fabrications which are embarked upon have any actual impact on the proceedings

---

3 Powers of Criminal Courts (Sentencing) Act 2000 s 108.
4 *R v Byas* 1995 16 Cr App R (S) 869
5 Criminal Justice Act 1948 s 1(1) and (2).

in question; whether the activities of the defendant draw in others; what the relationship is between others who are drawn in and the defendant.

Guideline remarks – Perverting the course of justice etc

134.4   *R v Williams* 1995 16 Cr App R (S) 191. The defendant was convicted of an attempt to intimidate a witness in civil proceedings. Held. People who are tempted to involve themselves in seeking to deter witnesses from giving evidence, or true evidence, must realise that a prison sentence is inevitable, whatever their own personal mitigation and good character might be.

R v Khan 2001 2 Cr App R (S) 553. Such offences undermine the whole process of justice and they are to be treated seriously and will in most cases merit a custodial sentence to run consecutively to any other sentence.

Assisting defendants/Tipping defendants off etc

134.5   *R v Rayworth* 2004 1 Cr App R (S) 440. The defendant pleaded guilty to perverting the course of justice. A series of robberies took place where a car was used as a getaway vehicle. The car had been purchased from the defendant. Police officers attended the defendant's premises and sought to identify the purchaser. The defendant told the police that he had sold the vehicle to three males but did not have the sales invoice with him and did not know the identity of the purchasers. He said he would provide them with the details later. Another robbery was committed. 2 days later, other officers visited the defendant. They were handed a sales invoice book with a fictitious name and address for the purchasers of the vehicle. The defendant gave the officers vague descriptions of three men and said he would not recognise them again. He signed a statement to this effect. However, telephone billing showed the defendant had telephoned one of the three men three minutes after the police had been to visit him and there were a further 9 calls. He also contacted the other 2 men. He left an incriminating message almost immediately after the first police visit. He initially denied the offences but subsequently admitted his role. He had no previous convictions. Held. The significant matters were the nature of the principal offences (serious robberies), the fact that there was a further robbery after the first visit to the defendant by the police. Further, the defendant immediately contacted the robbers after the police had visited. **2$^{1}/_{2}$ years** upheld.

Att-Gen's Ref. No 31 etc. of 2004 Re SL 2005 1 Cr App R (S) 377 at 392. SL and BL pleaded guilty to perverting the course of public justice. The defendants were married. The wife, BL became friends with a man, K, at work. The relationship was volatile and K bullied her to get her into his car where he assaulted her and refused to let her out. He then told her that he loved her and wanted to marry her. She was released but the following morning K arrived at her house when she was alone and banged and kicked the door repeatedly before leaving. She called the police. The next day he telephoned her three times and said that he was coming to get her and that no one could save her. She phoned her cousin who phoned her brother. The cousin and brother stabbed K to death later that evening. These two men ran into the basement of the defendants' home, which was unlocked. They were covered in blood and sweating. They changed into clean clothes which they took from the washing line and asked the wife to call them a taxi. She refused but the men left anyway when the husband told them to go. The police arrived at the scene but could find no relevant clothing or blood. The defendants denied that they had seen the men. The defendants were initially arrested for murder and conspiracy to murder and remanded in custody. The wife admitted what had happened and said that she was told that her cousin and brother had had a fight with the deceased. The husband also admitted that he had seen the men. They were both of good character. Held. **12 months** immediate custody was not unduly lenient and there were exceptional circumstances in this case justifying suspension. Specifically, the defendants had already spent time in custody in relation to even more serious offences for which they would not be entitled to credit of the sentence were either not suspended or suspended and activated.

Evidence, interfering with – General

134.6 *R v Foley* 2003 1 Cr App R (S) 261. The defendant pleaded guilty to doing an act intending to pervert the course of Justice, based on impeding the coroner's enquiry. She allowed a cousin of hers to live at her home for a short time. One morning she found him dead on her living room floor. She picked up a piece of coiled silver foil, which was next to the body and threw it out of the window. Death was a result of alcohol and diamorphine. She admitted the offence to the police and told them where to find the article. The Judge found that the discovery of the body was a very traumatic event, with young children in the house and she was in shock. He also accepted she acted out of panic and impetuously and she was deeply depressed and remorseful at what she had done. Held. The penal purpose here was to mark the gravity of the offence and yet, give due weight to the unusual mitigating circumstances. **6 months conditional discharge** not 4 months imprisonment.

Att-Gen's Ref. No 31 etc. of 2004 Re SL 2005 1 Cr App R (S) 377 at 392. SL and BL pleaded guilty to perverting the course of public justice. The defendants were married. The wife, BL became friends with a man, K, at work. The relationship was volatile and K bullied her to get her into his car where he assaulted her and refused to let her out. He then told her that he loved her and wanted to marry her. She was released but the following morning K arrived at her house when she was alone and banged and kicked the door repeatedly before leaving. She called the police. The next day he telephoned her three times and said that he was coming to get her and that no one could save her. She phoned her cousin who phoned her brother. The cousin and brother stabbed K to death later that evening. These two men ran into the basement of the defendants' home, which was unlocked. They were covered in blood and sweating. They changed into clean clothes which they took from the washing line and asked the wife to call them a taxi. She refused but the men left anyway when the husband told them to go. The police arrived at the scene but could find no relevant clothing or blood. The defendants denied that they had seen the men. The defendants were initially arrested for murder and conspiracy to murder and remanded in custody. The wife admitted what had happened and said that she was told that her cousin and brother had had a fight with the deceased. The husband also admitted that he had seen the men. They were both of good character. Held. **12 months** immediate custody was not unduly lenient and there were exceptional circumstances in this case justifying suspension. Specifically, the defendants had already spent time in custody in relation to even more serious offences for which they would not be entitled to credit of the sentence were either not suspended or suspended and activated.

Evidence, interfering with – Bodies

134.7 *R v Lang* 2002 2 Cr App R (S) 44. The defendant changed his plea to guilty of perverting the course of justice in concealing a body knowing he had been killed and two counts of supplying cocaine. The defendant's uncle shot and killed a fellow criminal at close range with a shotgun probably over a dispute over drugs. The defendant dug a grave in his uncle's garden and helped his uncle bury the body. The grave was covered by a patio. Later he spent time with his brother in a hotel at his uncle's expense. He was nearby when his uncle was arrested and firearms attributed to the uncle were found in a vehicle not far away. His fingerprints were found on wrappings associated with two overalls found by police in the uncle's garden. The uncle was convicted of the murder of the fellow criminal. The defendant told police that while he was digging the grave the uncle was mopping up blood inside the house. He said he was called unexpectedly to assist and couldn't say no because he was scared of the uncle who had been violent to him before and threatened him on the day. The uncle was drunk and had a shotgun in his hand. On two occasions he bought cocaine for another when he bought his own cocaine. He owed that person money. He was 33 and had a number of dishonesty convictions. In 1995 he received $4^1/_2$ years for possession of firearms and a CS canister, possession of drugs with intent to supply and possession of counterfeit currency. He was released 11 months before the pervert offence. The judge said the facts which lie behind the offences bear all the hallmarks of professional organised crime. It was professional crime to conceal a professional execution by a professional criminal. Held. It was possible to infer that the judge was associating the defendant with the killing. **6 years** not 8 consecutive to the 1 year for the drugs' convictions.

See also **Obstructing the Coroner/Burial, Preventing**

Incriminating innocent people

134.8   *R v Sadiq* 1999 2 Cr App R (S) 325. The defendant pleaded guilty to perverting the course of justice. In June 1996 the defendant started to live with his girlfriend, the victim. On 28 April 1997 the relationship ended and 3 days later he visited her and there was an argument and he was excluded from the flat. She borrowed his car and returned it on 12 May 1997. They met in the street near her home and he took her house keys and said he was going to her flat to collect his passport. She said she would call the police and he said if she did she would be in one hell of a lot of trouble. She did contact the police who took her home and it was clear he had been in the flat. He gave the keys to a neighbour. Later the same day he called the police claiming to be her previous boyfriend. He tried to disguise his voice and said the victim was about to receive a delivery of drugs. Police thought the call was a hoax in response to the keys. The next day he made another call pretending to be the ex-boyfriend and said he was aware they had been to the flat and told them they had missed the drugs. He suggested they look under the washing machine. Later he made another call giving his true name and said he understood they wanted to talk to him about the keys. The flat was searched and 11 grams of amphetamine and 20 grams of cannabis were found under the washing machine. The drugs were made up in several bags to make it look like she was dealing in drugs. The judge said it was a 'deliberate, calculated attempt' to get the young woman of good character into serious trouble with the police. The defendant had 'serious convictions.' **2 years** not 3.

Att-Gen's Ref. No 85 of 2001 2002 2 Cr App R (S) 13. The defendant was convicted of doing acts tending to pervert the course of justice. In November and December 1998 the defendant had sex with the victim unbeknown to her boyfriend. She falsely told the victim that her relationship with her boyfriend was over. She arranged to go out with the victim and some of his friends on 24 December but never arrived. In the early hours of Christmas Day she was with her boyfriend at his home. The victim went to her home saw the gas fire on and assumed she was in. The defendant was worried as she was often drunk and he had often climbed in through her window as she was too inebriated to let him in. He climbed in through a window and telephoned the boyfriend using her telephone assuming she was there, pretending to be a friend of the boyfriend. Two calls were received and the telephone display showed they were being made from the defendant's home. She called the police. When the police went to her home they found the victim with a knife and a tape which he had used to break the window and saw where entry had been gained. He was arrested for burglary and kept in custody. The defendant that day made two witness statements saying the defendant had developed an obsession with her and had sent her flowers, love songs etc at work. He had arrived uninvited at her home although she had not told him where she lived. She said she was frightened of him and had had to improve her security. She had not given him permission to enter her home and as a result of the break in she was terrified. The victim was charged with burglary and harassment and was remanded into custody. Police found photographs of the defendant at the victim's home and she claimed in another witness statement she had not given them to him saying they must have been removed from her house without authority. She gave the police letters, a tape and a card which he had given her. The victim remained in custody till 12 January 1999 when the proceedings were discontinued. She continued with her account and said she wanted the proceedings against the victim to continue. The effect on the victim was severe and he needed psychiatric help. Because of the allegations he had problem in obtaining access to see his son and found difficulty in forming relationships because of his distrust of others. She wasn't interviewed until November 1999 when she maintained her story. Her second trial started 2 years and 4 months after the offence. She was 41 with no convictions except some for drink/drive. The relationship with the boyfriend ended and she had since married someone else. They had taken over a pub and had invested a lot of energy and money into it. She was sentenced to 180 hours CSO, £1,000 costs and £700 compensation to the victim. 69.5 hours were performed and the penalties had been paid. The court heard the appeal nearly 3 years after the offence. Held. False complaints of a serious offence sexual or otherwise leading to the arrest of an innocent man/woman call for sentences of immediate imprisonment even on a plea of guilty. It is even more serious when the alleged offence is very grave. Burglary and harassment are grave offences. If the conviction had been obtained in 1999 the sentence would have been counted in months if not years. In light of the delay, her marriage, the way she had established herself, the CSO performed and the payment of penalties the judge was entitled to ask whether custody was necessary. Although we do not say we would have reached the same decision the sentences were not disturbed.

Att-Gen's Ref. Nos. 6–8 of 2000 2002 2 Cr App R (S) 341. LCJ. [The defendants J and R were convicted of conspiracy to commit acts tending to pervert the course of justice. The defendant a police officer pleaded guilty to the same offence. They were involved in planting Class A drugs in the car of the policeman's estranged wife. The starting point was **10–12 years**.]

R v Pearson 2002 Unreported 30/8/02. The defendant pleaded guilty to perverting the course of justice and theft. She bought a stereo music system on HP. Her husband was violent to her and her marriage split up. Her husband failed to pay maintenance and she became in dire financial straits. She and others devised a scheme to fake a burglary so she wouldn't have to pay the HP premiums. A man, X was selected to be set up. She gave her flat keys to someone and he entered the flat, broke a window and took the stereo. She reported the burglary and the stereo was found at X's address. Eventually she admitted what had happened. She was of good character and her pre-sentence report was very good and positive. Held. This was a very serious offence. It was carefully planned. The aggravating feature was X's arrest. Perverting will almost inevitably attack a sentence of imprisonment. **8 months** cannot be criticised.

R v Milroy-Sloan 2003. Times and Daily Telegraph news reports 14 June CCC Judge (Simon) Smith The defendant was convicted of two counts of perverting the course of Justice. She accused Neil Hamilton, the ex-Tory MP and his wife of rape. An arthritic pensioner was also accused of being involved. She was a trainee teacher and mother of four. Held. It was a cynical attempt to make money. It's becoming all too easy for people to sell false allegations against well-known people. The courts have to deal firmly with it. **3 years**. (Treat news reports with care.)

R v Collins 2005 1 Cr App R (S) 103. The defendant pleaded guilty to perverting the course of public justice. During the course of theft of a transit van, the van's owner was run over and killed. The defendant's boyfriend was identified as possibly involved. When the defendant was seen by police she provided a preliminary statement in which she said that she had been aware of the incident, having heard about it on television.

She said that she had not talked to her boyfriend about it. Her boyfriend was arrested but denied any involvement. She made full statement (s.9 CJA 67) stating that the personality of her boyfriend had changed and he had been observed by her as unable to sleep and having been distressed. She stated that her boyfriend had told her that he had gone out with a friend to "do a little tickle" (steal a car) and that the friend had admitted running over the victim and that her boyfriend had been the person responsible thereafter for telephoning the ambulance in relation to what had occurred. She said that she had been very shocked by what she ad been told and she detailed a conversation that she had overheard between her boyfriend and his friend talking about their involvement in the matter. Both boyfriend and his friend were arrested and changed with murder, then remanded in custody. 2 months later the defendant told the police that the conversation that she had recounted had in fact never happened and that she had lied. The police interviewed her and she admitted her witness statement contained lies. She was 19 and had no previous convictions. She had two small children ($2^1/_2$ and $5^1/_2$), had suffered depression and had attempted suicide on two occasions. She was heavily pregnant when she made her witness statement. Held. There was nothing wrong in principle in custody. The making of a witness statement implicating people in an offence of murder, falsely, strikes at the very heart of the administration of justice. A custodial sentence on a young mother kept away from her young children means the impact of such a sentence is worse than it would be for someone else not in that situation committing the same offence. **9 month's detention**, not 18.

Jury interference

134.9   *R v Boodhoo* 2002 1 Cr App R (S) 33. The defendant pleaded guilty to perverting the course of justice. He acted as a juror and on the second day of the trial he asked his fellow jurors, 'What if they offered us a bribe?' There was then a series of calls and meetings between him and the defendants in the trial. He was paid £1,000 in cash and told them the views of the jurors and was told to do what he could. In fact the jury was not corrupted. Another juror pleaded guilty and gave evidence for the prosecution. Some of the defendants in the first trial were convicted and others acquitted in the pervert trial. The judge said he was the central figure. He was 37 and had co-operated with the police. Held. Any event which threatens the integrity of the jury system will inevitably attract a custodial sentence. **4 years** was entirely appropriate.

R v Baxter 2003 1 Cr App R (S) 241. The defendant pleaded guilty to intimidation contrary to the Criminal Justice and Public Order Act 1994 Section 51. Although he had earlier pleaded not guilty the Judge gave him full credit for his plea. His brother was standing trial for aggravated burglary and after the first day the defendant followed one of the jurors in his car. Although the juror tried to shake him off by speeding and other manoeuvres the defendant kept following him. Eventually the juror went to his place of work and the defendant parked nearby. The police were summonsed and the defendant gave a false name. The juror was discharged from the jury and the rest of the jury convicted the brother. The defendant was 25 with a poor record essentially for dishonesty. His last custodial sentence was in 1997 for ABH for which he received 28 days. He was in a stable relationship and in good employment. Held. Intimidation of jurors is an increasing problem. Although this case was serious it was not the most serious. The defendant might have a sense of grievance because of the Judge's remarks that this was one of the most serious cases. Considering the 5 year maximum, **2 years** not 3.

Old case *R v Mitchell-Crinkley* 1998 1 Cr App R (S) 368, (for a summary of this case see the first edition of this book.)

Newspaper reporting

134.10   *R v MGM* 2002 Daily Telegraph news 20/4/02. High Court. The defendant, a publishing company accepted they were in contempt of court. There was a trial of Leeds United footballers at Hull Crown Court about an attack on an Asian student. The judge had stressed to the jury that any issue of racism was not part of the prosecution's case. While the jury was considering their verdict the Sunday Mirror printed an interview with the victim's father. The report said the father said it was a racist attack. The father had agreed to the interview on condition it would not be published till after the verdicts. It caused the trial to be 'derailed' which would be 'lengthy, expensive and traumatic for the complainant, his family, witnesses and defendants alike.' The total cost for the aborted trial was £1.113 m and the retrial was £1.25 m. The company said it was the result of wrong legal advice and they apologised unreservedly. Two lawyers had been dismissed and the Editor had resigned on the basis that he was ultimately responsible. Held. In the absence of mitigating information we find it difficult to escape the conclusion that the assurances given to the father were simply overridden. The defendant's good record and their attitude since this matter came to light make it possible to reduce the fine to £75,000. The costs to be paid were £54,160. [News reports should be treated with care.]

R v Express Newspapers 2004 The Times news 26/11/04. High Court. The defendant, a publishing company were found in contempt of court. A 17 year old girl made allegations that she was gang raped in the Grosvenor House Hotel by Premiership footballers. Suspects were arrested who denied the allegations. The Star newspaper named two footballers. Guidelines from the Attorney-general and advice from the police not to name suspects were given including one the day before. The advice was not to protect footballers' reputations but because identity was in issue and evidence could be compromised if certain material had appeared before all the ID procedures had been completed. No-one was ever charged because of lack of evidence. The defendants claimed to have overlooked the guidelines. Held. The aggravating feature was that the press had been repeatedly told not to name or carry photographs of the players. **Fine £60,000**. [News reports should be treated with care.]

Outbursts in court

134.11   *R v Lewis* 1999 Unreported 22/10/99. The six defendants were judged to be in contempt of court. They went to court to see a friend being sentenced. The friend was given 6 months. The Assistant Recorder heard a disturbance and cries of 'terrible' and 'disgusting' with people pointing at the bench. The defendants said they were upset because the court had been misled by the victim's impact statement. The defendants were all of good character and apologised unreservedly. Each was in gainful employment or had home responsibilities. Held. In a situation like this it is often tactically wise for a judge merely to rise and leave the courtroom, and for those who wish to behave badly to do so in his absence. It was not suitable for the contempt to be dealt with by another court because that would have blown the whole thing out of proportion. The defendants should be dealt with quickly and they should know their fate as soon as possible. This contempt was at the low end of the scale. The custody threshold was not crossed. The situation could have been dealt with by a strong judicial reprimand coupled if necessary with a fine or discharge. 7 days was wholly wrong in principle and quashed. **No order** substituted.

Perjury – To assist your own case

134.12   *R v Dunlop* 2001 1 Cr App R (S) 133. The defendant pleaded guilty to two counts of perjury. In 1991, the defendant was tried for murder and gave evidence that he had not gone to the victim's house shortly before her death. The jury failed to agree and he gave the same evidence again at the retrial. That jury couldn't agree and he was discharged. In fact shortly before her death he had been in a fight at a stag do and beaten a man and gouged his eyes such that he was in hospital for 4 days. Afterwards he went round to see the victim of the murder and on his account she made fun of him and his injuries and he lost his temper and strangled her. After the trials he formed a relationship with another woman and they had a child. The relationship didn't last and she found another boyfriend. He then stabbed her several times and smashed the facial bones of the boyfriend with a baseball bat. He received 7 years for those offences. In prison he confessed to the murder to a prison officer. He said he was sick of violence and wanted help. He also wrote a letter to an ex-girlfriend confessing to the murder. He was sincere in accepting the distress he had caused to the family of the deceased. He was about 37 when sentenced with convictions for a firearm offence, an offensive weapon offence, eight offences against the person and 18 offences for dishonesty. A psychiatric report said he suffered from a number of abnormal personality traits. Held. The offences were very serious. The case was aggravated by the perjury being at a very grave trial and it was repeated. No criticism could be made if the judge had given 3 years on each consecutive so there was no fault with **6 years** concurrent on each but consecutive to the 7 years.

R v Archer 2003 1 Cr App R (S) 446. The defendant, Lord Archer, was convicted of procuring a false alibi, two counts of perverting the course of public justice, swearing a false affidavit and perjury. In 1986 he was a successful writer, ambitious politician and deputy chairman of the Conservative Party. The News of the World published articles saying he had sex with a prostitute and that money was handed to her at Victoria Station to silence her. The Star newspaper effectively repeated the News of the World's allegation with added details. The co-accused who was a casual friend created a false alibi for the appellant. He received £12,000 in cash and was told the defendant would help him with his film script. At the libel trial against The Star newspaper the prostitute gave her account and the defendant gave false evidence. A diary with false entries written by his secretary was relied on. In 1999 the co-accused approached Max Clifford, a public relations man. Held. The secretary was an employee and therefore vulnerable to suggestions made by her employer. The co-accused was corrupted by money. Considering the length of time over which these offences were committed, the perceived involvement of others, and the persistence in dishonest conduct **4 years** was not manifestly excessive.

Photographs taken of courtrooms – Guideline remarks

134.13   *R v D* 2004 The Times 13/5/04. LCJ. Photographs taken by mobile phones have become a major problem in the Crown Court, the Magistrates' Court and the civil courts. Photographs can easily be passed on electronically. Intimidation of juries and witnesses is a growing problem in criminal cases. Recently there have been physical attacks on prosecution counsel. Illegal photography has the potential to gravely prejudice the administration of justice. Factors to consider are the nature of the trial; the potential disruption of the trial and the potential for misuse. Mitigation factors are plea, youth, a genuine apology and ignorance or naivety of the person involved. Where security is less than this case a sentence of less than the 12 months here may well be appropriate. In some case "the clang of prison gates" will be enough. In other cases e.g. a foreign tourist in ignorance of the law it may be imprisonment is inappropriate and a fine would be correct.

Photographs taken of courtrooms – Cases

134.14   *R v D* 2004 The Times 13/5/04. LCJ. The defendant pleaded guilty to contempt of court. His brother was at the top of Class A drugs gang and his trial which was both lengthy and complex was underway. He was a double A prisoner and the security was very significant. There was a protected witness who had received 7 years imprisonment. The Judge had indicated that he would have imposed a 28 year sentence without the assistance. The witness was attended by a great deal of security. Those in the public gallery were searched but allowed to keep their mobiles. Just before the day's hearing ended the defendant leant towards the secure dock and took a photograph of his brother with his mobile. He was arrested and the mobile examined. There were three photographs of interest. One was of the court canteen, another of witness box and the judge's bench which was of poor quality and the third was of his brother with a prison officer visible. The police were very concerned the identity of the officer was revealed. The Judge considered this was a chilling development. He was worried that the jury could have been frightened and the trial abandoned. The defendant had a number of convictions some of which were for drugs. He made an unreserved apology. Held. The aggravating factor was the fact it was a long and serious trial of a double A prisoner. We bear in mind the protected witness in the trial and **12 months** sentence was severe but cannot be interfered with.

Police officer as defendants

134.15 *R v Hesse* 2004 2 Cr App R (S) 215. The defendant pleaded guilty on rear-raignment to perverting the course of public justice. He was a serving police officer and had investigated an allegation of racially aggravated harassment by youths against an Asian family running a newsagents. The family decided not to pursue the matter. Instead of taking a statement from them to that effect, he created a false statement purporting to come from one of the family indicating he did not wish to pursue the case. He also created a false interview record with one of the youths, a juvenile, showing that the juvenile had confessed to the offence. He created false pocket book entries claim-ing to have visited the victim and interviewed them. He submitted a false crime record claiming that he had interviewed the youth who had committed the offence and that the victim had declined to prosecute. The documentation did not bear scrutiny and if any enquiries had been made it would have become immediately apparent that all the documentation was false. The mitigation claimed that he was in the wrong job. He found even the training for the job stressful. During his service it was apparent he was a worrier, panicker, incompetent and unwell. A medical report showed that 3 years before there were concerns about his mental health which raised the question of whether or not he could stay in the police force. By the time of the offence he had become moderately depressed. After sentence his mental condition had deteriorated and he had attempted suicide, he was then transferred to an open prison where his mental state improved. Held. There was no justification for interfering with **15 months**.

Prosecution/conviction, to avoid

134.16 *R v Saxena* 1999 1 Cr App R (S) 170. The defendant, a doctor, pleaded guilty to two counts of perverting the course of justice. The pleas were not entered at the first opportunity. The defendant was in a minor traffic accident and was charged with failing to stop, failing to report and due care. He was interviewed and denied being the driver. He approached a colleague who worked as a doctor in prison and asked her if she would like to earn £200. He asked her to write a note saying he was on duty in the prison at the time of the accident. She contacted the police. After he was convicted of the offences he repeatedly contacted her and she told the police about it. The police arranged for her to meet him with a tape recorder on her. He again asked her to give evidence for him at his appeal despite the fact she repeatedly said she could not recall whether he was working that day. He encouraged her to make false entries in her diary and offered her money and a trip to India. The defendant was arrested and denied the offences. He had a conviction for obtaining property by a deception for which he received a suspended sentence. He was about 47 and would be struck off as a doctor. He had health difficulties and was the sole carer of his 6-year-old son. Held. The case was serious. The offence was repeated. **3 months and 6 months consecutive** were not manifestly excessive.

R v Wake 1999 2 Cr App R (S) 403. The defendant pleaded guilty to perverting the course of justice. The defendant after celebrating in a pub drove his car into two elderly men who had just got off a bus. Both died very shortly afterwards. His car was very seriously damaged. He did not stop but drove the car to a wood where he abandoned it. He wrenched off the cowling around the ignition to make it look like it had been hot-wired. He went back to the pub and asked a friend to drive him home. On the way he threw some clothing out of the window because it was impregnated with glass. He told his wife if the police called he should say the car had been stolen. He went back to the pub and when he arrived home the police were there and he was told the two victims had died. He denied any knowledge of the accident and lied during several interviews but admitted it in a later interview. He had convictions but had not served a custodial sentence. He was only prosecuted for due care. The judge said the sentence had to be more than the charges he avoided namely two death by dangerous driving. Held. That approach was wrong. The offences were separate. Within 24 hours the defendant had given his account of what had happened and the prosecution could have charged whatever offence they liked. He had drawn his wife into the offence. **2 years** not $4^1/_2$.

R v Dowd and Huskins 2000 1 Cr App R (S) 349. The defendants D and H changed their plea to guilty of perverting the course of justice. H also pleaded to driving without due care and attention when originally charged with dangerous driving. H drove D in his father's car on a bendy unlit road with no pavement just less than an hour after lighting up time. The victims were walking in the same direction on the right hand side of the road. The car was on the wrong side of the road and hit the victims. One died instantly and the other was very seriously injured. H drove on and told a witness he thought he had knocked someone over. The car's front indicator surround was broken. H and D returned to the scene to retrieve the missing pieces. H met C who he knew and told him that he thought he had hit someone and was told, 'he looks all right he's sat' and was advised to leave. That person when he learnt of the fatality told the police of the conversation. H was insistent that D and others agreed to dispose of the car. H and D drove to a field and set the car on fire. H then reported the car as stolen and with D and others agreed a false version of events. C then told H of the fatality and that he had told the police that H was the driver. H went to the police and told then he had been involved in an accident and that subsequently the car had been stolen. In interview he gave the agreed version but later admitted he had lied about the car being stolen and admitted burning the car. D was then arrested and told the truth. H was 27 and had convictions for a public order offence, theft and in 1996 perverting the course of justice. In that case he had an accident causing damage, fled and reported the car stolen. D was 25 and had convictions for theft and attempted theft for which he ultimately received probation. Held. **18 months** not 3 years for H and **9 months** not 18 for D.

R v Charlton and Mealing 2000 2 Cr App R (S) 102. The defendants C and M pleaded guilty to conspiracy to pervert the course of justice. C also pleaded to perverting the course of justice. M was a director of a car repair company, which employed C. A customer was lent a car while his Nissan was being prepared. His wife was killed in it in an accident and the tyres were found to be faulty and that might have contributed to the accident. The car was also found to be uninsured. The defendants said the Nissan was received as payment and the other car was sold by M to C. This was to avoid blame for the lack of insurance. When C was interviewed he produced false receipts as proof of the transfer. Later they admitted the truth. Three days later C was stopped for speeding and he gave his brother's name and an incorrect address. He was found to be almost twice over the alcohol limit. C was 29 and M was 43 and neither had any relevant convictions. M's pre-sentence report referred to panic attacks and stress as a result of the offence and said it was an ill-judged attempt to protect his business. C's report referred to stress. Held. Because M was older and the employer he should receive more for the conspiracy. **18 months** not 3 years for him. C **15 months and 3 months consecutive** not 2 and 1 years consecutive.

R v Francis-McGann 2003 1 Cr App R (S) 57. The defendant was convicted of perverting the course of Justice. He was a serving army Captain having had nine years of service. When driving, a speed camera photographed his car and when he received the notice he contacted the Criminal Justice Unit saying it could not be him as his car had been exported. He was advised to send in evidence of the exportation. He sent in a letter headed with the army insignia giving details of the "exportation" by him, which was not true. The letter said the car had then been replated. He was interviewed and said he could not be sure whether it was his vehicle and challenged the telephone conversation. He had a clean licence and an army officer spoke of his abilities. The army said a community penalty or a custodial sentence would lead to a discharge. The Judge said he would be failing in his duty if he passed any other sentence than custody and gave him **three months** and £1,030 prosecution costs order. Held. We agree with the Judge's comments. On a number of occasions the Court has emphasised that where people persist in perverting the course of Justice to avoid persecution custody is inevitable. The gravamen was the interference with the administration of Justice and the persistence. It was wholly out of character and will have a disastrous impact on him. It is important for the Court to have serious regard to the effects of any sentence on an individual. We hope a future employer or the Army will bear in mind his good service and the Army should consider whether it is really inevitable that he should lose his commission.

R v Mitchell 2003 1 Cr App R (S) 508. The defendant pleaded guilty to perverting the course of justice. An accident occurred between a cyclist and a vehicle driven by the defendant. The cyclist suffered a serious head injury. Although not the defendant's fault, he drove on after the accident without stopping. The defendant and the co-owner of the vehicle took a series of steps to avoid the police detecting the fact that the Peugeot car had been involved in an accident. Two days later, the co-owner offered the Peugeot to his niece and a week later the car was sold to her. Two days later the police were shown the defendant's and the co-owner's garage premises but they failed to mention their ownership of the Peugeot or the work that they had done on it. The following day the co-owner repaired damage to the body of the vehicle and they both re-sprayed it. They were arrested and the defendant initially denied the offence; before eventually making full and frank admissions. The defendant was 24 and of previous good character. Held. Perverting the course of justice is invariably a serious matter because it strikes at the root of the of the criminal justice system. Important factors are the length of time during which the deception continues, the nature of the deception as well as its success in producing a false result. In this case the aggravating features were the length of time over which the offence was committed and the varied ways in which the police were misled. Further, in this case the co-owner received a sentence of 8 months which contributed to the reduction from **1 year** from 2.

R v Manning 2004 2 Cr App R (S) 405. The defendant pleaded guilty to two counts of possession of cannabis with intent to supply and was convicted of perverting the course of justice. The defendant and W, a co-defendant in the perverting the course of justice count were in a flat with V, the victim and a woman, drinking. There was an argument between W and the defendant and the woman saw that W had a gun. W and the defendant went into the kitchen. Shortly afterwards V followed. V then came out of the kitchen having been shot. The defendant called the emergency services saying someone had been shot after someone was messing around with a gun they didn't know was loaded. He could be overheard telling W to leave the flat with the gun. The woman was asked to leave, which she did with W who had the gun in a bag. Police officers arrived and found the defendant in the flat. He told them V had left the flat to get some cigarettes, come back and collapsed and he didn't know where V was shot. Three kilos of cannabis were found in the flat or nearby. In a subsequent police interview he said he had shot V accidentally in the kitchen, summoned the emergency services and told W to get rid of the gun. W was acquitted of murder. The pervert count was based on one day's events. The defendant, 28, had six previous convictions three of which were for violence. He received six months imprisonment in 2001 for ABH. The defendant's case was he acted in panic and the accidental death of his friend and flatmate had made a real impact on him and caused him to re-appraise his life. He had suffered depression and needed treatment in hospital for this. Held. **2 years** not 3 years for the pervert count consecutive to 2 years for the drugs matter.

R v Adams 2004 2 Cr App R (S) 410. The defendant pleaded guilty at the first opportunity to perjury. She gave evidence on behalf of an old friend of hers who was being tried for possession of Class A drugs with intent to supply. She said she had been in the premises the night before the police had raided the house and had not seen any drugs. She said twice in cross-examination she had never been in trouble with the law and also that she had never had anything to do with drugs. In fact she had spent convictions for theft, handling stolen goods, forging a document and using a false instrument in respect of drugs. She had been addicted to heroin. The trial was stopped because her lies were discovered and in a subsequent trial her friend was convicted and sentenced to six and a half years imprisonment. The defendant had made efforts to put her past life behind her and had moved away from where she had taken drugs. She had got herself off heroin and found employment. She did not realise at the time the gravity of her offence. A pre-sentence report demonstrated the remarkable progress she had made recently. Held. Anyone who deliberately tells lies on a court of law can expect severe punishment. If the perjury is aimed at avoiding conviction for a grave offence, as in this case, punishment must be commensurate with the gravity of that offence. **18 months** not 2 years.

Prosecution/conviction, to avoid – Frustrating the Breath Test procedure

134.17   *R v Melender* 2003 2 Cr App R (S) 370. The defendant was convicted of driving without due care and attention and doing an act intended to pervert the course of justice. He was acquitted of causing death by careless driving. He had pleaded to driving whilst disqualified, without insurance and failing to stop. The victim was dropped by car near his home after a party in a residential street subject to a 30 mph limit. He got his rucksack from the boot ad as he stepped into the road he was hit by the defendant's black Mercedes travelling at about 40 mph and died. The defendant parked his Mercedes and left the area. Later he approached a police station and confessed that he had been involved. He said that he had been out for 2 pints; that he was travelling at about 40 miles an hour; he had not had time to brake; he had panicked and hence parked and ran to a friend's house where he opening a bottle of wine and drank. (The verdicts indicated that the jury were sure that he had drunk to frustrate any breath test procedures). He was 43 with 22 previous convictions including numerous road traffic offences: no insurance, excess alcohol, three offences of failing to provide a specimen and nine offences of driving whilst disqualified. He had received sentences of up to 18 months imprisonment. Held. **2½ years** not 5 for the pervert. The other (non-custodial) sentences were not subject to appeal.

Prosecution/conviction, to avoid – Giving false name on arrest etc.

134.18   *R v Saxon* 1999 1 Cr App R (S) 385. The defendant pleaded guilty to perverting the course of justice. Police stopped him when he was driving a car. He gave his brother's name because he was disqualified from driving. He was asked to produce documents at a police station. When they were not produced his brother was summonsed for failing to produce. The brother spoke to the defendant and the defendant went to the police and said he had lied. He was 22 with a conviction for drink/drive.

The pre-sentence report recommended community service, said he had expressed remorse and said the chance of re-offending was low. Held. Custody was right but applying *R v Howells* 1999 1 Cr App R 335 **2 months** not 4 months.

Att-Gen's Ref. Nos. 62–65 of 1996 1998 1 Cr App R (S) 9. The defendants S, J, M and B pleaded guilty to perverting the course of justice at the earliest opportunity. S also pleaded guilty to dangerous driving, failing to stop and failing to report. S drove his car with M at between 38 and 47 and the car was swerving. There was a 30 mph speed limit and he hit a pedestrian who was thrown into the air. He didn't stop. He abandoned the car and the two went to the home of J and B. The four agreed to report that the car had been stolen. The car was set on fire and it was effectively destroyed. The victim was taken to hospital. She had a massive head injury and fractures to her cheek bone, eye socket, jawbone and knee. She had a large wound on her forehead and blood in her ear. She was in hospital for 16 days. The police were told it had been stolen. Next day the four confessed to the police and were arrested. The victim made a full recovery but has permanent scarring. The prosecution suggested the driving was borderline between careless and dangerous driving. S and J were 22, M 28 and B 27. S had a speeding conviction in 1990. The rest were of good character. M was a mother of four children one of whom was 11 and blind. B was a mother of two children and was expecting a third. She suffered from cerebral palsy and has since married J. The four showed remorse. There was almost a year's delay before sentence. The judge gave S 6 months suspended and conditionally discharged the rest. Held. Remorse and delay were not reasons to suspend the sentence. For S a total sentence of **12 months** would have been appropriate. As it was a reference 8 months would have been appropriate. As the prosecution said **6 months** was the appropriate sentence we substitute 3 months on each consecutive making 6 months. J's sentence is **2 months**. M's sentence is **1 month** and because of the child that would be **suspended**. B sentence is **1 month** and as an act of mercy with the sentence passed on M that would also be **suspended**.

R v Sookoo 2002 Unreported 20/3/02. The defendant gave a false name on arrest. Held. In many cases the addition of a perverting count was unnecessary and only served to complicate the sentencing process. Where as in this case, the defendant had attempted to hide his identity and failed, a specific separate count should not be laid. Where there were serious aggravating features like a great deal of police time and resources were involved or innocent members of the public had been arrested as a consequence, a specific count could be justified. The attempt here was unsophisticated and it was inevitably going to fail. **3 months** not 9 concurrent to 6 months for the other matter.

R v Gosling 2003 1 Cr App R (S) 295. The defendant pleaded guilty to perverting the course of Justice, aggravated vehicle taking and driving whilst disqualified. He was also committed for sentence for no insurance and excess alcohol. In December 2001, after drinking to excess he took his brother's car without his consent. On a by-pass he lost control of the car hit the central crash barrier, rebounded across three carriageways and hit the nearside crash barrier. The car and the crash barriers were extensively damaged. When the police arrived, he gave his brother's name and the address they shared. At the police station he persisted with the false name. Three days later the police discovered his true identity and when questioned again the defendant admitted he had given a false name. He was 28, with a bad record for dishonesty with 14 convictions for various kinds of theft. In February 2001, he was disqualified for 2 years for dangerous driving. After that he had been convicted of driving whilst disqualified and was given a 180 hours community punishment order and further disqualified The Judge gave him 18 months for the pervert and no penalty on the other offences. There were concurrent disqualification orders with 2 years or until he had passes the extended test on the excess alcohol charge. Held. The pervert was at the very bottom of the range of seriousness for that kind of offence. The aggravated vehicle taking, aggravated by the alcohol and the driving whilst disqualified for the third time in a year was significantly the most serious matter. **3 months** not 18 for the pervert. 9 months for the vehicle taking and 3 months concurrent for the disqualified driving concurrent. So total 12 months not 18. The disqualification will remain.

Old case *R v Johnson* 1998 1 Cr App R (S) 168, (for a summary of this case see the first edition of this book).

Statement, making a false witness

134.19   *R v Evans* 1998 2 Cr App R (S) 72. The defendant pleaded guilty at the first opportunity to perverting the course of justice. The defendant was in a pub with his friend Y. There was bad feeling between Y and M. M assaulted Y and they were both ejected from the pub. The defendant remained inside and when he went out he found Y outside injured. Y told him he had been assaulted by M and another. The defendant made a witness statement describing events he said he had seen outside implicating M and another. He attended an ID parade and picked out H as the other man. He confirmed that with another witness statement. A few days before the trial of M and H at the Crown Court he withdrew his statement. He was interviewed and admitted he hadn't seen anything outside and made the statement out of misguided loyalty. He was 25 with minor unrelated convictions and a good work record. The employer wrote a testimonial. Held. The offence struck at the heart of the administration of justice. It created the risk of an innocent man being convicted. The judge was entitled to be influenced by the prevalence the making of false statements in his area. As the maximum sentence for giving a false statement (under the Criminal Justice Act 1967, s 89) is 2 years the sentence was reduced from 2 to **1 year**.

Witness interference – Guideline remarks

134.20   *R v Khan* 2001 2 Cr App R (S) 553. Cases where threats are used against potential witnesses are generally more serious than those where the offender merely tries to persuade (with or without a bribe) a witness to retract or change his or her evidence. Where threats are used the sentence may well be in the range of **12 months to 2 years** depending on the circumstances, including the seriousness of the threats.

R v Chinery 2002 2 Cr App R (S) 244. The defendant was convicted of two counts of witness intimidation. Held. The offences are very serious. Witnesses are indispensable. They must not be pressurised. Sentences invariably contain an element of deterrence.

Witness interference – Arson

134.21   *R v Gerrard* 2004 2 Cr App R (S) 47. The defendant, pleaded guilty to arson being reckless as to whether life would be endangered and four counts of taking revenge against witnesses. The defendant had previously been tried and acquitted on a charge of causing grievous bodily harm. Two of the witnesses in that trial were the victim's mother and girlfriend. The defendant went to the mother's mid terraced house at 3.30 am and threw a homemade petrol bomb at the front door. The mother was in the house and four others were asleep in it at the time. The mother heard an explosion and saw flames round the front door. She roused the others and phoned the fire brigade. At that time the fire fighters were on strike. People in the house extinguished the fire. The next day the defendant wrote to a friend saying that he had blown this front door and that there was 'loads more to come'. A week later the mother received an anonymous letter saying 'time is here for you to suffer grass' and the word 'die'. The next day the girlfriend received an anonymous letter saying 'we are coming for you grass.' Three days later the mother received an anonymous letter saying 'obsession to die grass bang'. On the same day the girlfriend received an anonymous letter saying 'agony is not over grass'. In a victim impact statement the mother referred to suffering loss of sleep, having time off work, and being reluctant to leave the house unoccupied. The defendant was 34 and had 8 findings of guilt and 15 previous convictions mainly for dishonesty and driving offences, but including criminal damage and a number of ABHs. In a report the defendant described his continuing anger and resentment towards the victims. He did not accept that this anger had caused enduring problems for the victims. The report concluded that the risk of re-offending was high and there was a risk of him committing the same offences again. Since the report was written he had attended a Calm Course to address his anger. **Held.** This was a very serious case of its kind as it was a revenge attack against witnesses. The house was mid terraced and there was a risk not just to the 5 people in the house he fire bombed but to the occupants of adjoining houses. Real fear and alarm was caused. There was no warning and the defendant did not raise any alarm. However he pleaded guilty, he had no previous convictions for arson, there was no personal injury to anyone and the petrol bomb was not thrown at a person or through or at a window. It was thrown at the door and the design was to frighten. The case was towards the top end because of the motivation. **6 years** not 7 for the arson. **1** year's imprisonment on the 3 witness revenge counts consecutively to the sentence for arson upheld, making **7 years** not 8.

Witness interference – Threats, no

134.22   *R v Khan* 2001 2 Cr App R (S) 553. The defendant was convicted of interfering with the peace or comfort of an occupier, unlawful eviction, theft and doing an act intending to pervert the course of justice. The victim a single mother aged 33, her boyfriend and her three children including her baby rented a flat owned by the defendant. He harassed her and unlawfully evicted. He broke much of her property and stole some of her property. After a couple of hours after they discovered the damage, the boyfriend went to the flat to pick up some of her baby's clothes. He was met by the defendant and four others and he said they had no right to be there. One of them replied it was 'fuck all to do with him' and the defendant wanted his house back. That man was aggressive and threatening and the boyfriend found him intimidating. The boyfriend was told to leave immediately and if the victim returned to the flat her face would be rearranged. The lock on the flat door was changed. Police attended and found the defendant and four other men inside and the defendant said he was repossessing the flat for non-payment of rent. The defendant was released on bail with a condition not to contact directly or indirectly any prosecution witness. Two months later, a car in which the defendant was a passenger approached the boyfriend. The man who had intimidated him got out of the car and asked to see the victim. They both went to where the victim was living and the man asked her how much she wanted to drop the case. When she told him to deal with the solicitors the man became aggressive and told her if the defendant went to prison she would get nothing. He also said the most she would get would be £1,500, with half paid now and the rest when the case was dropped. The defendant was 26 and of good character. His wife was ill and spoke no English. **Held.** There was no basis for interfering with the 16 months for the three flat offences. Perverting offences are treated seriously because they undermine justice. **8 months** for it was not excessive. Neither was 2 years in total in any way excessive.

R v Underwood Re A 2005 1 Cr App R (S) 478 at 490. The defendant pleaded guilty to fifteen counts of harassment contrary to s. 4 and one count of intimidating a witness. The offences took place over about $3^1/_2$ years and were similar. The victims were aged between 14 and 17. The defendant would begin by approaching and sometimes appearing to befriend the victims. He made them flex their biceps and felt their arms, chests and legs. He would ask them to lean over and perform squatting exercises while he rested his weight against their backs or buttocks. He often required them to perform these exercises in his car or in some lonely area. In some cases they were harassed in this way for periods exceeding three years. Some saw him daily, others less frequently.

He undoubtedly intimidated the victims. The separate witness intimidation concerned a victim of harassment who came across the defendant by accident. The defendant said to him "I want you out of this … better for you if you were not involved". They talked for about 20 minutes. The basis of plea included a denial of a threat made but an acceptance that the victim would have felt intimidated. He was 43 with a very long record including 30 months for threats to kill that occurred after these offences. Most of his previous convictions were for violence on police officers and offences of dishonesty. Held. He represented a danger to young men. An overall sentence of 5 years for harassment was not arguably manifestly excessive nor was a consecutive **12-months** for witness intimidation.

(For more details see **Harassment and Unlawful Eviction of Tenants**)

Witness interference – Bribing police officers

134.23   *R v Hurrell* 2004 2 Cr App R (S) 23. The defendant pleaded guilty to perverting the course of justice, and driving with excess alcohol. He was seen driving badly in the early hours on a country road and stopped by police. One of the officers asked him to take breath test. The defendant got into the police car but procrastinated when asked to provide a sample and eventually offered the police officer money so that he would not have to take the test. He refused to provide a sample of breath and was arrested. After he had been cautioned he offered the officer £2,000 to forget about the test. On the way to the police station he continued to try to bribe the officers. On arrival at the police station he provided a sample. He was aged 43 and of previous good character. A pre-sentence report said that he was deeply remorseful and that there was little risk of him re-offending. There were 3 impressive character references before the sentencing judge. Held. Those who offer bribes to a police officer must expect a custodial sentence, especially when the offer is made on a number of occasions, as was the case here. Any attempt to bribe a police officer in the course of his duty is serious as it seeks to deter public officials from performing important public duties. The sentence was manifestly excessive. It was an impulsive offence by a man of previously good character who was a highly respected businessman. **3 months** imprisonment not **12 months.**

Witness interference – Threats, with

134.24   *R v Smith* 2001 1 Cr App R (S) 229. The defendant pleaded guilty to nine charges of intimidating a witness at the Magistrates' Court. A complaint was made that the defendant had indecently assaulted a young lady. In February 1999 the defendant drove his car at one of the witnesses and another young lady saw it. The defendant was arrested and released on bail on condition he did not contact that lady. In June 1999 he made a number of threatening and abusive telephone calls to her home. A recorder was installed on the telephone. The first was abusive and threatening. Three threatened death. Another asked to speak to her saying he was going to kill her. The rest were similar. She was terrified. The defendant was arrested and he denied making the calls. His plea was only forthcoming after an expert had identified his voice. He was convicted of the indecent assault and had served the 6 months detention. He was 20 and was of previous good character. Held. The judge said it was an ongoing campaign of harassment and intimidation with the aim of striking fear and to persuade her not to give evidence. He gave limited credit for the plea because it was extremely late. **2 years** YOI not 2¹/₂.

R v Rogers 2002 1 Cr App R (S) 272. The defendant pleaded guilty to witness intimidation. A 12-year-old boy gave a statement to the police, which concerned his grandmother and the defendant's two younger brothers. The victim was walking to a park and the defendant started to abuse and threaten him saying if he got his brothers into trouble he would kill him and his family and attack him with a bottle. Further he was not to tell anyone or he would be killed and if his mother contacted the police she would be killed as well. The defendant's speech was slurred and he smelt of alcohol. The boy was very frightened but the grandmother who had heard what was going on came out and told him to stop. The victim ran home and told his mother who told the police. The defendant was interviewed and denied the offence. The boy said the defendant head-butted him but he was sentenced on the basis their heads came close together. He was 18 and on probation for criminal damage. Held. The offence was not premeditated and was an isolated occasion. The defendant did not seek out the witness nor did he pursue a campaign of threats or violence against him. But there was actual and direct physical confrontation accompanied by intimidating threats of violence. We take into account his youth but he was on probation. A significant custodial sentence was justified but **18 months YOI** not 2 years.

R v Chinery 2002 2 Cr App R (S) 244. The defendant was convicted of two counts of witness intimidation. He was a DJ in a nightclub where there was a fight in the ladies' lavatory between his former wife and a barmaid, his wife to be. There were three witnesses. The wife to be was charged with common assault and appeared at the Magistrates' Court. The next day the three witnesses were in the nightclub and the defendant pulled one of them that had made a statement to the police to one side and said, 'Why did you give a statement? Bad things happen to people who grass. You want to watch your back.' She said, 'Don't threaten me.' He replied, 'I am just warning you. Watch your back.' She was upset, shocked and in fear for her safety. The victim told her friends and one of them spoke to the defendant and said he should not threaten her friend. He said, 'You're all grasses and you best watch your backs.' She was infuriated and very intimidated. The next morning the first victim called the police and asked to withdraw her statement. Five days later the second victim gave a statement about both incidents. The defendant was arrested and denied the incidents. He was 43 and of good character with references. He supported his four children and his now wife's two children. Held. The offences are very serious. Witnesses are indispensable. They must not be pressurised. Sentences invariably contain an element of deterrence. It was not wrong to pass consecutive sentences. The judge was entitled to pass 3 and 3 months making **6 months** in all.

R v Lawrence 2005 1 Cr App R (S) 432. The defendant pleaded guilty to threatening to take revenge on a witness. He was living with his father and the relationship was fraught. They returned home after bingo and drinking and at about 4.30am they argued about money and the defendant punched his father. The father left the flat and telephoned the police. When he returned with the police, the defendant refused to let them in. Officers forced entry, and it appeared that the defendant had left the flat. The father remained in the flat, only to find the defendant behind him. The father left and again called the police who returned to the flat and found the defendant hiding inside a cupboard. As he was led to police custody he shouted the words: "You paedophile. I'm gonna tell all the mums you're a paedophile. I'll get bail and kill you" and "I'm gonna write to all the mums and tell them you're a paedophile". He was 35 and had twenty years of offending of every type including threatening behaviour, ABH and wounding and every sentence available. There was a high risk of re-offending. Held. The threats were made when he was drunk and the latter part of the threats were made from police custody at a time when they clearly could not be fulfilled. **8 months** (with full credit for the plea) not 16.

Old case *R v Bryan* 1998 2 Cr App R (S) 109, (for a summary of this case see the first edition of this book).

Witness interference – Cases – Violence to the witness or damage to his/her property, with

134.25 *R v Edmunds* 1999 1 Cr App R (S) 475. The defendant was convicted of an offence under the Criminal Justice and Public Order Act 1994, s 51. The defendant had a relationship with the victim who was 16. He assaulted her twice and the police were told. She did not support a prosecution. They were further assaults and she started a relationship with someone else. He stayed at her address, as she was afraid to make him leave. She realised he was stealing cars and property from cars. He assaulted her again and was given a lift by him in a car which she realised was stolen. She then informed the police about his stolen cars and made a statement about it. That evening she received a telephone call from him after he had been released on police bail saying he was, 'going to carve her up and stab her. It won't be worth her walking the streets because I've got so many people after her. If they don't get her I will'. A quarter of an hour later he rang again saying he was going to smash her place up. When she returned home she found, 'Grass. Remember this.' in nail polish on a mirror with an arrow pointing to a decapitated teddy bear. A table lamp was smashed, her belongings were strewn across her room and all the photographs were taken from their frames. The judge said that his violence had led to her withdrawing three complaints. He was now 22 with a substantial record for dishonesty. He had lost his liberty more than once but had no convictions for violence or threatening violence. **3 years** not 4.

Att-Gen's Ref. Nos. 110 and 111 of 2001 2002 2 Cr App R (S) 546. The defendants, D made a very late plea to conspiracy to handle cars. D also pleaded to obtaining a money order by deception (4 months concurrent), witness intimidation and common assault, (1 month concurrent). D was 38 with a 10 year gap in his record till a similar car ringing conspiracy conviction in 1997 for which he received 12 months. While in prison for that his wife left him taking most of the furniture with her. He claimed on his insurance for a non-existent burglary. This was the deception count. The witness intimidation against D was arranging to have his former partner, J, (not his wife), who was a prosecution witness in the conspiracy and the deception matter to be attacked in order to fabricate a case of assault against her. Two women were recruited and one punched her and the other was to be a witness. The women were to report that his co-defendant in the conspiracy was the assailant. When D was arrested for this he "shoved aside" the officer, (the common assault). He was also in breach of a conditional discharge for making phone calls to J threatening violence. D had been released on a tag. Held. It was an elaborate car-ringing fraud. D's part shortly after his release from prison for a similar offence was a particularly aggravating factor. The witness intimidation was very serious in its planning, execution and purpose with a particularly unpleasant assault. Taking into account it was a reference for the conspiracy 3 years not 18 months Bearing in mind the totality **12 months consecutive** not 6 for the intimidation. The other sentences remaining making 4 years in total. (Because it was a reference and the other longer sentences this case is of little assistance.)

R v Atkin 2003 2 Cr App R (S) 263. The defendant pleaded guilty at the Magistrates' Court to assaulting a witness, contrary to Criminal Justice and Public Order Act 1994 s 51. The victim was raped by the defendant's brother. She was working at a restaurant when one lunchtime she served the defendant who asked her what time the restaurant closed. At about 3 pm the victim set off to walk home. As she reached the car park the defendant grabbed her arm from behind and swung her round. There was a struggle and the victim fell backwards onto a car where she hit her forehead on the boot. The defendant then dragged the victim into a garden area and said, "I hope you're going to move far away, otherwise I'm going to make your life hell". The victim was terrified. The defendant said, "He gave you oral sex and you enjoyed it and you knew it". The victim denied that she had had oral sex, at which the defendant started to punch her in the face a number of times. The victim fell to the floor, protecting her head. Passers-by told the defendant to stop but she did not do so. She told them, "You don't know what she's done". The defendant then kicked the victim in the lower back and she pulled her hair before punching her in the face again then walking off. The victim was treated for bruising to her head, her nose, right cheek and lower back. She had a cut and swollen upper lip. Some of her hair had been pulled out. She became too frightened to go to work. When interviewed the defendant admitted the assault. She said that she had lost her temper but denied that it was premeditated; claiming all she wanted to do was to talk to the victim. She was 36 and of good character. A pre-sentence report stated there was a relatively low risk of further offending and a lengthy custodial sentence would have serious implications for her and for her children who would be put into care. She had been treated for depression. There were 13 character witnesses. Held. Any attack on a witness was a very serious offence as the courts rely on such people. An aggravating factor was that the attack was such a vicious one. In ordinary circumstances a deterrent sentence was appropriate. A custodial sentence was required to mark the gravity of this offence and to deter others, even taking into account the mitigating factors. Bearing in mind that the defendant was a single mother with four children aged between 5 and 7 and that the children would have to be placed into care, **15 months** not 2 years.

Old case R v Watmore 1998 2 Cr App R (S) 47, (for a summary of this case see the first edition of this book).

See also ASSISTING OFFENDERS

PHOTOGRAPHS

For indecent photographs see PORNOGRAPHY

For photographing courtrooms see PERVERTING THE COURSE OF JUSTICE/CONTEMPT OF COURT/PERJURY – *Photographs taken of courtrooms*

135   PLANNING OFFENCES

135.1   Town and Country Planning Act 1990 s 179, 187, 189 194 and 210 etc

Offences concerning enforcement notices, orders requiring discontinuance, making false statements in an application and tree order offences respectively.

All triable either way. On indictment maximum fine only (except for s 194 where the maximum is 2 years). Summary maximum £20,000 for s 179, 187 and 210, and £5,000 for s 189 and 194.

Crown Court statistics – England and Wales – Males 21+
135.2

Year	Plea	Total Numbers sentenced	Type of sentence %					Average length of custody (months)
			Discharge	Fine	Community sentence	Suspended sentence	Custody	
2002	Guilty	10	10	90	–	–	–	–
	Not guilty	6	–	100	–	–	–	–
2003	Guilty	10	50	50	–	–	–	–
	Not guilty	2	–	100	–	–	–	–

For details and explanations about the statistics in the book see page vii.

Enforcement notices

135.3   Old case. *R v Ayling* 1996 2 Cr App R (S) 266.

PLEA

See **GUILTY PLEA, DISCOUNT FOR**

POISON

For administering etc poison see **OFFENCES AGAINST THE PERSON ACT 1861, S 23** and **OFFENCES AGAINST THE PERSON ACT 1861, S 24**

136   POLICE OFFICERS

Defendants, as

136.1   *R v Keyte* 1998 2 Cr App R (S) 165. Held. Police officers are given considerable powers and privileges. If they dishonestly abuse their position and do so for profit, then not only must a prison sentence follow but it must of necessity be a severe sentence.

R v Nazir 2003 2 Cr App R 671. The Judge said that the public should have absolute faith and trust in their police officers who by the nature of their job, have extensive powers and responsibilities. Those who do exploit that trust must inevitably serve a prison sentence. Held. We agree.

See also **OBSTRUCTING A POLICE OFFICER**; **CORRUPTION** – *Police officers as defendants*; **MISCONDUCT IN PUBLIC OFFICE** – *Police officers as defendants* and **THEFT ETC** – *Police officers as defendants*.

POLLUTION

See **ENVIRONMENTAL OFFENCES**

137   PORNOGRAPHY

137.1   Sexual Offences Act 2003 s 48–50

Causing etc. a person to be involved in pornography, controlling a child involved in pornography or arranging child pornography. These offences commenced on 1/5/04.

Triable either way. On indictment maximum 14 years. Summary maximum 6 months and/or £5,000.

The Criminal Justice Act 2003 creates a summary maximum sentence of 51 weeks, a minimum sentence of 28 weeks and Custody plus. The Home Office says they do not expect to introduce these provisions before September 2006.

For offences committed before 1/5/04 the two offences which follow would be charged.

Protection of Children Act 1978 s 1

Taking, distributing, publishing etc indecent photographs etc.

Triable either way. On indictment maximum 10 years[6]. Summary maximum 6 months and/or £5,000.

Criminal Justice Act 1988 s 160

Possession of indecent photographs etc.

Triable either way. On indictment maximum 5[7] years. Summary maximum 6 months and/or level 5 fine (£5,000).

Imprisonment for public protection For all three offences committed on or after 4/4/05 when there is a significant risk to members of the public of serious harm etc. there is a mandatory duty to pass a sentence of imprisonment for public protection[8]. For offenders under 18 the duty is to pass detention for public protection or an extended sentence[9].

Longer than commensurate sentences and extended sentences All offences under Protection of Children Act 1978 are sexual offences[10] for the purposes of passing a longer than commensurate sentence [Powers of Criminal Courts (Sentencing) Act 2000 s 80(2)] and an extended sentence (extending the licence) [Powers of Criminal Courts (Sentencing) Act 2000 s 85(2)(b)]. The orders cannot be made for offences committed before 30/9/98 or after 3/4/05. See EXTENDED SENTENCE, EXTENDED SENTENCES and LONGER THAN COMMENSURATE SENTENCES.

Notification For both the older offences (a) where the photograph showed a person under 16 and (b)(i) the defendant is 18 or over or (ii) the defendant is sentenced to at least 12 months imprisonment; the defendant must notify the police within 3 days (or 3 days from his/her release from imprisonment, hospital etc.) with his/her name, home address, national insurance number etc. and any change and addresses where s/he resides for 7 days[11] (in one or more periods) or more in any 12 month period[12]. See SEX OFFENDERS' REGISTER

Working with children For all the offences where the defendant is aged 18 or over and s/he is sentenced to 12 months or more the court must disqualify him/her from working with children unless satisfied s/he is unlikely to commit any further offences against a child when the court must state its reasons for not doing so[13]. For a defendant aged less than 18 at the time of the offence the court must order disqualification if s/he is sentenced to 12 months or more and the court is satisfied that the defendant will commit a further offence against a child[14]. The court must state its reasons for so doing.

Sexual Offences Prevention Order For all offences there is a discretionary power to make this order, when the notification (q.v.) criteria are present and when it is necessary to protect the public etc[15].

---

6 This maximum sentence was increased from 3 years to 10 years on 11 January 2001, Criminal Justice and Court Services Act 2000 s 41(1).
7 This offence was until 11 January 2001 a summary only offence, Criminal Justice and Court Services Act 2000 s 41(3).
8 Criminal Justice Act 2003 s 224–226
9 Criminal Justice Act 2003 s 226 and 228
10 Powers of the Criminal courts (Sentencing) Act 2000 s 161(2)(a)
11 Sexual Offences Act 2003 s 84(1)(c) & (6)
12 Sexual Offences Act 2003 s 83 & Sch. 3 Para 13 & 15
13 Criminal Justice and Court Services Act 2000 s 28
14 Criminal Justice and Court Services Act 2000 s 29
15 Sexual Offences Act 2003 s 104 & Sch. 3 Para 13 & Sch 5 Para 63

As the maximum has been increased by Parliament significantly for both offences those cases before 2001 should not be considered a true guide to the likely sentence for offences committed after that date.

Obscene Publications Act 1959 s 2

Publishing an obscene article or having an obscene article for publication for gain.

Triable either way. On indictment maximum 3 years. Summary maximum 6 months and/or £5,000.

Prosecutors tend to avoid this Act perhaps because it does not trigger notification, working with children etc. orders.

Crown Court statistics – England and Wales – Males 21+ Possession of obscene material

137.2

Year	Plea	Total Numbers sentenced	Type of sentence %					Average length of custody (months)
			Discharge	Fine	Community sentence	Suspended sentence	Custody	
2002	Guilty	174	5	6	41	3	45	16.3
	Not guilty	29	7	10	17	3	62	12.8
2003	Guilty	484	2	4	36	2	56	13.1
	Not guilty	34	3	15	12	3	68	18.2

For details and explanations about the statistics in the book see page vii.

Guidelines case – Indecent photographs etc.

137.3 *R v Oliver* 2003 1 Cr App R 28. Subject to two matters, we adopt the Sentencing Panel's advice dated August 2002. The two primary factors determining the seriousness of a particular offence are the nature of the indecent material and the extent of the offender's involvement with it. As to the nature of the material, it will usually be advisable for sentencers to view for themselves the images involved, unless there is an agreed description of what those images depict. We take five different levels of activity, derived from the COPINE Project's description of images, namely: (1) images depicting erotic posing with no sexual activity; (2) sexual activity between children, or solo masturbation by a child; (3) non-penetrative sexual activity between adults and children; (4) penetrative sexual activity between children and adults; (5) sadism or bestiality.

As to the nature of the offender's activity, the seriousness of an individual offence increases with the offender's proximity to, and responsibility for, the original abuse. Any element of commercial gain will place an offence at a high level of seriousness. In our judgement, swapping of images can properly be regarded as a commercial activity, albeit without financial gain, because it fuels demand for such material. Wide-scale distribution, even without financial profit, is intrinsically more harmful than a transaction limited to two or three individuals, both by reference to the potential use of the images by active paedophiles, and by reference to the shame and degradation to the original victims.

The sentence

The choice between a custodial and non-custodial sentence is particularly difficult. On the one hand, there is considerable pressure, demonstrated by Parliament increasing the maximum permissible sentence, to mark society's abhorrence of child sexual abuse and child pornography by the use of custody. On the other hand, there is evidence that sex offender treatment programmes can be effective in controlling offenders' behaviour and thus preventing the commission of further offences. In any case which is close to the custody threshold, the offender's suitability for treatment should be assessed with a view to imposing a community rehabilitation order with a requirement to attend a sex offender treatment programme. The appropriate sentence should not be determined by the availability of additional orders, or by the availability of treatment programmes for offenders in custody. We stress that the proposals we make are guidelines intended to help sentencers. They are not to be construed as providing sentencers with a straightjacket from which they cannot escape. We bear in mind the current state of over-crowding in our prisons, and that a custodial sentence should only be imposed when necessary. We also bear in mind the public concern in this area to which we have already referred. In our judgement, **a fine** will normally be appropriate in a case where the offender was merely in possession of material solely for his own use, including cases where material was downloaded from the Internet but was not further distributed, and either the material consisted entirely of pseudo-photographs, the making of which had involved no abuse or exploitation of children, or there was no more than a small quantity of material at Level 1. A **conditional discharge** may be appropriate in such a case if the defendant pleads guilty and has no previous convictions. But a discharge should not be granted, as we have earlier indicated, for the purpose of avoiding the requirement of registration under the Sex Offenders Act 1997. Possession, including downloading, of artificially created pseudo-photographs and the making of such images, should generally be treated as being at a lower level of seriousness than pos-sessing or making photographic images of real children. But there may be exceptional cases in which the possession of a pseudo-photograph is as serious as the possession of a photograph of a real child: for example, where the pseudo-photograph provides a particularly grotesque image generally beyond the scope of a photograph. It is also to be borne in mind that, although pseudo-photographs lack the historical element of likely corruption of real children depicted in photographs, pseudo-photographs may be as likely as real photographs to fall into the hands of, or to be shown to, the vulnerable, and there to have equally corrupting effect. It will usually be desirable that a charge or count in an indictment specifies whether photographs or pseudo-photographs are involved. A **community sentence** may be appropriate in a case where the offender was in possession of a large amount of material at Level 1 and/or no more than a small number of images at Level 2, provided the material had not been distributed or shown to others. For an offender with the necessary level of motivation and co-operation, the appropriate sentence would be **a community rehabilitation order with a sex offender programme**. The custody threshold will usually be passed where any of the material has been shown or distributed to others, or, in cases of possession, where there is a large amount of material at Level 2, or a small amount at Level 3 or above. A custodial sentence of up to **six months** will generally be appropriate in a case where (a) the offender was in possession of a large amount of material at Level 2 or a small amount at Level 3; or (b) the offender has shown, distributed, or exchanged indecent material at Level 1 or 2 on a limited scale, without financial gain. A custodial sentence of between **6–12 months** will generally be appropriate for (a) showing or distributing a large number of images at Level 2 or three; or (b) possessing a small number of images at Levels 4 or 5.

A custodial sentence between **12 months and 3 years** will generally be appropriate for (a) possessing a large quantity of material at Levels 4 or 5, even if there was no showing or distribution of it to others; or (b) showing or distributing a large number of images at Level 3; or (c) producing or trading in material at Levels 1 to 3. Sentences **longer than 3 years** should be reserved for cases where (a) images at Levels 4 or 5 have been shown or distributed; or (b) the offender was actively involved in the production of images at Levels 4 or 5, especially where that involvement included a breach of trust, and whether or not there was an element of commercial gain; or (c) the offender had commissioned or encouraged the production of such images. An offender whose conduct merits more than three years will merit a higher sentence if his conduct is within more than one of categories (a), (b) and (c) than one where conduct is within only one such category. Sentences approaching **the 10-year maximum** will be appropriate in very serious cases where the defendant has a previous conviction either for dealing in child pornography, or for abusing children sexually or with violence. Previous such convictions in less serious cases may result in the custody threshold being passed and will be likely to give rise to a higher sentence where the custody threshold has been passed. An extended sentence may be appropriate in some cases, even where the custodial term is quite short: see *R v Nelson* 2002 1 Cr App R (S) 565.

The levels of sentence which we have indicated are appropriate for adult offenders after a contested trial and without (save to the extent that we have referred to them) previous convictions.

Aggravating factors

They are

(i)   if the images have been shown or distributed to a child;

(ii) if there are a large number of images. It is impossible to specify precision as to numbers. Sentencers must make their own assessment of whether the numbers are small or large. Regard must be had to the principles presently applying by virtue of *R v Canavan, Kidd and Shaw* 1998 1 Cr App R 79;

(iii) the way in which a collection of images is organised on a computer may indicate a more or less sophisticated approach on the part of the offender to trading, or a higher level of personal interest in the material. An offence will be less serious if images have been viewed but not stored;

(iv) posting images on a public area of the Internet, or distributing them in a way that makes it more likely they will be found accidentally by computer users not looking for pornographic material, will aggravate the seriousness of the offence;

(v)   the offence will be aggravated if the offender was responsible for the original production of the images, particularly if the child or children involved were members of the offender's own family, or were drawn from particularly vulnerable groups, such as those who have left or have been taken from their home or normal environment, whether for the purposes of exploitation or otherwise, or if the offender has abused a position of trust, as in the case of a teacher, friend of the family, social worker, or youth group leader;

(vi) the age of the children involved may be an aggravating feature. In many cases it will be difficult to quantity the effect of age by reference to the impact on the child. But in some cases that impact may be apparent. For example, assaults on babies or very young children attract particular repugnance and may, by the conduct depicted in the image, indicate the likelihood of physical injury to the private parts of the victim. Some conduct may manifestly (that is to say, apparently from the image) have induced fear or distress in the victim, and some conduct which might not cause fear or distress to an adolescent child, might cause fear or distress to a child of, say, six or seven.

Mitigating factors

Some, but not much, weight should be attached to good character. A plea of guilty, by virtue of the Powers of Criminal Courts (Sentencing) Act 2000 s 152 is a statutory mitigating factor. The extent of the sentencing discount to be allowed for a plea of guilty will vary according to the timing and circumstances of the plea. The sooner it is tendered, the greater is likely to be the discount: see, for example, *R v Barber* 2002 1 Cr App R (S) 548.

Magistrates' Court Sentencing Guidelines January 2004– Indecent photographs

137.4   For a first time offender pleading not guilty. Entry point. Are Magistrates' sentencing powers sufficient? Consider the impact on the victim. Examples of aggravating factors for the offence are abuse of trust, commercial gain, involvement in production, large number of images and particularly young or vulnerable children. Examples of mitigating factors for the offence images at the lowest categories of COPINE (seek advice from the clerk) (The COPINE (Combating Paedophile Information Networks in Europe) Project was founded in 1997 and is based in the Department of Applied Psychology, University College Cork, Ireland), one photograph only, possession for own use and pseudo images. Examples of mitigation are age, health (physical or mental), co-operation with the police, genuine remorse and voluntary compensation. Consider committal for sentence. Give reasons if not awarding compensation.

For details about the guidelines see **MAGISTRATES' COURT SENTENCING GUIDELINES** at page 483.

Guidelines for the procedure to be followed – Indecent photographs

137.5   *R v Thompson* 2005 1 Cr App R (S) 1. The following practices should be adopted in the drafting of indictments. The same practices might also be adopted in the selection of images for presentation in summary proceedings.

1)   In cases where there are significant numbers of photographs, in addition to the specific counts, the inclusion of a comprehensive count covering the remainder is a practice that should be followed.

2)   The photographs used in the specific counts should, if it is practicable, be selected so as to be broadly representative of the images in the comprehensive count. If agreement can then be reached between the parties that (say) 5 images at level 2, 10 at level 3, and 2 at level 4 represent 500 level 2, 100 level 3 and 200 level 4 images in the comprehensive count of 800 images, the need for the judge to view the entirety of the offending material may be avoided.

3)   Where it is impractical to present the court with specific counts that are agreed to be representative of the comprehensive count there must be available to the court an approximate breakdown of the number of images at each of the levels. This may best be achieved by the prosecution providing the defence with a schedule setting out the information and ensuring that the defence have an opportunity, well in advance of the sentencing hearing, of viewing the images and checking the accuracy of the schedule.

4)   Each of the specific counts should in accordance with what was stated by this court in Oliver make it clear whether the image in question is a real image or a pseudo-image. The same count should not charge both. As this Court pointed out in Oliver, there may be a significant difference between the two and where there is a dispute, then there should be alternative counts. In the majority of cases there will be no doubt as to whether the image in question should be dealt with either as a real image or a pseudo-image.

5)   Each image charged in a specific count should be identified by reference to its "jpg" or other reference so that it is clear with which image the specific count is dealing.

6)   The estimated age range of the child shown in each of the images should where possible be provided to the Court.

Guideline remarks – Pornography

137.6   *R v Holloway* 1982 4 Cr App R (S) 128 at 131. Fining pornographers does not discourage them. The only way of stamping out this filthy trade is by imprisonment for first offenders and all connected with the commercial exploitation of pornography: otherwise front men will be put up and the real villains will hide behind them.

R v Pace 1998 1 Cr App R (S) 121. The sale of pornographic books, films and tapes on a commercial sale justify sentences of imprisonment for first offenders. The sentences will be comparatively short when appropriate. Salesmen, projectionists, owners and suppliers behind the owners should be at risk of losing their liberty.

R v Tunnicliffe and Greenwood 1999 2 Cr App R (S) 88. There may be cases where prison was not necessary.

Articles

137.7   Sentences for Child Pornography 2003 Crim L R 81

Basis of plea, – No proper basis of plea

137.8   *R v Thompson* 2005 1 Cr App R (S) 1. The defendant pleaded guilty to 12 counts of possessing indecent photographs or pseudo-photographs of children. The defendant's computer was seized after a search warrant was executed and was found to have contained over 3,700 indecent images of children downloaded from commercial sites on the internet which had subsequently been deleted. He initially denied knowledge before admitting downloading and then deleting them. He was 52, married with three children and of good character. Two of the photographs in two of the counts contained 5 or 6 year-old girls engaged in intercourse with adults. The other 9 counts were representative of the other photographs seized. Because the photographs were notcategorised into the quantities at the different levels, it was impossible to say how many of the remaining photographs fell into category 4 (see R v Oliver 2003 2 Cr App R (S) 15). It would not be right to make an assumption against the defendant as to thenumber of images at the different levels which were encompassed within the remaining images. Held. On the information before him, the judge could not properly conclude that the appellant was in possession of that large quantity of material at level **4.9 months** not 2 years.

Importation   See IMPORTATION OF A PROHIBITED/RESTRICTED ARTICLE – *Pornography*

Internet, The – Guideline case

137.9   *R v Oliver* 2003 1 Cr App R 28. The increased access to the Internet has greatly exacerbated the problem in this area by making pornographic images more easily accessible and increasing the likelihood of such material being found accidentally by others who may subsequently become corrupted by it. This additional risk adds to the culpability of offenders who distribute material of this kind, especially if they post it on publicly accessible areas of the Internet. Merely locating an image on the Internet will generally be less serious than downloading it. Downloading will generally be less serious than taking an original film or photograph of indecent posing or activity.

Internet, downloading from – Custody not appropriate

137.10   *R v Bowden* 2000 2 Cr App R (S) 26. The defendant pleaded guilty to 12 counts of taking indecent photographs and nine counts of possessing indecent photographs of children. The defendant had taken his computer hard drive for repair where the repairer found indecent material on it. Police in a different operation police seized his computer hard drive and floppy discs. That material contained indecent images of boys under the age of 16. The defendant had downloaded the images from the Internet and either printed them out or stored them on disk. All images were downloaded for the defendant's own use. The defendant who was a schoolteacher had no previous convictions. Held. The defendant was not a risk to the public therefore a **conditional discharge for 12 months** was appropriate, not 4 months' imprisonment.

R v S 2000 2 Cr App R (S) 388. The defendant pleaded guilty to one count of taking indecent photographs of children. His estranged wife found pornographic images of children on his computer. They were of a sexual nature. Police then searched his home and seized the equipment. In interview he admitted downloading the material from the Internet. It was accepted the material was for his own use. He was a 33-year-old architect and of positive good character. There were six references. He had undertaken private psychiatric counselling. The psychiatric report said, "the defendant was not a paedophile and was unlikely to become one. He was responding to therapy and was unlikely to re-offend." Held. Taking into account the sentence in *R v Bowden* 2000 2 Cr App R (S) 26, 4 months was a manifestly excessive sentence. A **conditional discharge for 12 months** was appropriate.

R v Malone 2001 2 Cr App R (S) 203. The defendant pleaded guilty at the Magistrates' Court to taking indecent photographs of a child. The defendant's employer became aware that the defendant was using the Internet at work to visit pornographic websites and informed the police. The police seized his computer and found no indecent images. But they found indecent images of children on a back-up cartridge, mostly of girls between 13 and 14 naked or performing sex acts on adults. The defendant had no convictions and had lost his job. The pre-sentence report emphasised his insight into the seriousness of what he had done. The sentencing judge noted that the defendant had downloaded the images for personal use but could not conceive that anyone would download such photographs unless they had paedophile tendencies. Held. Taking into account *R v Toomer* 2001 2 Cr App R (S) 30 custody was not required. As the defendant was not distributing the images and had lost his job and spent 4 weeks in custody a **conditional discharge** was appropriate not 6 months. [The court reduced the period of Registration to 5 years which appears illegal because there can be no registration when the defendant is conditionally discharged.]

R v Wild 2002 1 Cr App R (S) 156. The defendant pleaded guilty to 15 counts of taking indecent photographs. Police executed a search warrant at his home. He was asked about indecent images and he told them he had deleted the images from his computer. Experts were able to recover the images from the hard drive of the computer. The images involved children of both sexes from about 2 to 3 months to 13 years. Many showed children engaged in sexual activity including apparent intercourse and oral sex. He said he had been sent the pictures unsolicited. They had been stored. Held. This was grave conduct because of the ages and numbers of children. However it did not cross the custody threshold and could have been dealt with by a **substantial fine**. As he had served a custodial sentence **conditional discharge** substituted for 4 months. [His age and character are not revealed. The judgment was considered a nullity because there is no appeal for a committal for sentence case when less than 6 months is imposed, *R v Wild* 2002 1 Cr App R (S) 162.]

R v Turpin 2002 1 Cr App R (S) 323. LCJ. The defendant pleaded guilty to 19 counts of taking indecent photographs. He asked for 21 other offences to be taken into consideration. Police executed a search warrant at his home and seized his computer which had indecent images on it. The images involved children from about 5 to 12 years who were in a variety of indecent situations. Some children were alone, some with other children and some indulging in explicit sexual acts with children and adults. The defendant said he had downloaded them from the Internet over a 4 month period. He was 29, married, in work and of good character. A psychiatrist said there was no evidence of psychosexual abnormality by way of deviant interest with sexual arousal. Although the defendant denied it, the pre-sentence report concluded he derived sexual pleasure from the images, but presented a low risk of re-offending. He had suffered high level of anxiety before sentence. Held. The degree of obscenity was high. However, there was no distinction between this case and *R v Wild* 2002 1 Cr App R (S) 156, so the case did not cross the custody threshold. Therefore 1 year **community rehabilitation order** not 8 months.

R v Owens 2002 1 Cr App R (S) 216. The defendant pleaded guilty to five counts of taking indecent photographs. They were not specimen counts. Trading Standards Officers searched his home during a trade mark investigation and took some floppy disks. Four contained images of young girls displaying their vaginas and the fifth showed a naked boy touching a naked girl's vagina. He admitted that he had downloaded the material from the Internet. There was no suggestion he had links with others or that he had distributed the material. He was now 40 and of good character with very positive references. He was dishonourably discharged from the RAF after 21 years service and had lost his family home. He received 6 months' imprisonment which he had almost served. Held. The pictures were very nearly at the bottom of the scale of indecency. However upsetting this material may be there is an element of the pathetic as well. He looked at five indecent pictures, briefly obtaining some lonely sexual gratification and now faced a very bleak future. The conviction had had a devastating effect on his unfortunate wife and their family. An immediate custodial sentence was not appropriate. We would have imposed a **probation order with treatment** so his interest could be addressed. Alternative a **substantial fine** would be sufficient punishment. As he had nearly served his sentence **conditional discharge** substituted. [The court reduced the period of Registration to 5 years which appears illegal because there then could be no registration when the defendant is conditionally discharged[16]. This anomaly was later removed by Sexual Offences Act 2003 s 134.]

Internet, downloading from – Custody appropriate

137.11 *R v Makeham* 2001 2 Cr App R (S) 41. The defendant pleaded guilty to three offences of taking an indecent photograph of a child. The defendant asked for 61 other such offences to be taken into consideration. The defendant's girlfriend became concerned about file names found on the defendant's computer and contacted the police. The police found images on a power box of young children engaging in mutual masturbation and oral sex and a video clip of a young girl being abused by an older man. The defendant, who was 41 years of age, had no previous convictions. The sentencing judge noted that the defendant did not have the pictures in his possession for profit or gain. Held. By downloading images of children from the Internet the defendant was perpetuating child abuse therefore a custodial sentence was necessary. **6 months** not 9 months was appropriate.

R v Evans 2004 The Times 22 March. LCJ. The defendant pleaded guilty at the first opportunity. The report does not reveal what the counts were. He had a habitual and compulsive habit to make or obtain indecent photographs of children. Some were downloaded. Some he created himself. Police found 140,000 images. The overwhelming majority were level 1. Some were level 2 and 3. Twelve were level 4. He had never had any inappropriate contact with any child nor had he ever circulated the material. He was 48, with no convictions and had positive references. He was socially and emotionally isolated. A probation officer said she did not think a custodial sentence would be likely to deal with potential future risks. The pre-sentence report recommended an extended supervision order. The Judge bore in mind the vast number of pictures, the fact some were of very young children and the way the pictures were organised. Held. There had to be a custodial sentence. The three year extended sentence was entirely sensible. But **18 months** not 27.

16 *R v Wild* [2002] 1 Cr App R (S) 162.

R v Pardue 2004 1 Cr App R (S) 105. The defendant pleaded guilty at the first opportunity to 17 charges of making 28 indecent photographs of children at the Magistrates' Court. Police seized over 100 printed images of children from a cupboard and over 1,000 images from his computer. The images featured children between 6–13. They were engaged in masturbation of themselves and each other. There was oral sex with adult males and adult penetration of the vagina and anus. The images were level 1–4. He said he had paid for access on the internet and they were for his own use. He was 41 with no convictions living with his parents. Held. He had only admitted the 17 charges so he fell to be sentenced for 6–12 months not 15. He had little choice but to plead so 10 months instead.

Internet, downloading from – Worst type of material

137.12   *R v Tatam* 2005 1 Cr App R 256. The defendant pleaded guilty at an early stage to 18 counts of making indecent photographs of a child, one count of possession of indecent photographs and one count of attempted buggery. The defendant, aged 35, had used his credit card to access child pornography on a website based in Texas. As a result of the enquiry Operation Ore his home and work address were searched and officers seized computer equipment, video tapes and compact and optical discs. They recovered a folder next to his bed containing 350 pornographic pictures of children. The counts of making indecent photographs were samples of individual images, and the one count of possession of indecent photographs represented the totality of the material seized. In all the defendant had 495,524 indecent photographs of children and this was the largest seizure of child pornography during Operation Ore in the UK. 472,000 were at level 1: (nudity and no sexual activity), over 9,000 at level 2: (sexual activity between children and solo masturbation), about 11,000 at level 3: (non penetrative sexual activity between children and adults), over 3000 at level 4: (penetrative sexual activity between children and adults), and 336 at level 5: (images of sadism involving children adults and bestiality). He had downloaded the images and stored most of them on computer hard drives under specific category headings such as scatology, bondage, extreme, rape, burning, vomiting and torture. One of the images was of a 3–6 year old girl, fully naked, hanging upside down. She was bound by a rope and gagged. An object was being inserted into her vagina. A video was seized from his home showing him encouraging a dog to commit buggery with his girlfriend, although it was accepted by the prosecution that there had been no penetration. This was the attempted buggery count. There was no evidence that he had distributed the images to anyone else. He was of good character. Held. This was a case of exceptional gravity with aggravating features namely the vast number of images; the organisation of the images showing a high level of interest in the material; the significant number of particularly young children who had been abused for the purposes of making the images. The sentences of **5 years** imprisonment with an **extension period of 1 year** for 15 counts of making an indecent photograph from February 2001 onwards; **2** years concurrent for 3 counts of making indecent photographs of a child during 1997 and 1999; **4** years concurrent for 1 count of possession of indecent photographs of a child and **3 months** concurrent for attempted buggery were not excessive individually or in their totality.

Internet, downloading from – Relevant previous convictions

137.13   *R v James* 2000 2 Cr App R (S) 258. The defendant pleaded guilty to six counts of taking indecent photographs. Police search the address of his co-defendant where the defendant also lived. Items connected with the co-defendant were seized. They also searched the defendant's computer and discs and found 18,500 indecent photographs depicting the images of 'young' children and animals. The defendant said he had downloaded the images from the Internet and they were for his personal use. The defendant, who was 37, had a previous conviction for possessing indecent photographs of children (he received 4 months). He said he wanted help. The sentencing judge noted that to download such images perpetuated the abuse of children. Held. We agree with the judge. This is a disgusting trade. He had plenty of opportunity to obtain help after his last conviction. But **18 months** not 2 years.

R v Hopkinson 2001 2 Cr App R (S) 270. The defendant pleaded guilty at the Magistrates' Court to six offences of taking indecent photographs of a child. They were sample counts. The police executed a search warrant at the defendant's home and seized his computer. About 550 images of males under the age of 16 were found. There were also duplicates. The images depicted children in nude poses or engaging in sexual activity with other children or adults. They had been down loaded from the Internet or sent by email. The defendant had co-operated with the police and claimed the material had been sent unsolicited. The judge rejected that. The defendant was 66 and had previous convictions for taking indecent photographs of children, two offences of buggery and one of gross indecency. He showed no remorse. The pre-sentence report said until he changed his attitudes the risk of re-offending could not be discounted. The judge gave credit for the images not being used to corrupt children or anyone else and that the defendant was not using the pictures for commercial gain. Held. The matters to be borne in mind are the number of images and the convictions for similar offences. The offence was not an isolated case and it appeared to some degree to be systematic. It was more serious because of his history and his involvement with a group who he had corresponded with called 'Gay Teen boys'. Therefore **12 months** was not a manifestly excessive sentence.

R v Grosvenor 1994 1 Cr App R (S) 122. The defendant pleaded guilty at a very early stage to 18 counts of possession of pseudo photographs of children and one count of making such a photograph. He was a single man who lived alone and spent a large amount of time on the internet using chat rooms and downloading. Police examined his computer and found 8,785 images of which a large number were illegal. The illegal images were level 1, 3 and 4 ranging from nude adolescent girls to rape and buggery of very young children by adults. His basis of plea was he did not know the precise detail of the images when down loading, he was not searching for images of assaults on children and the images in 12 of the counts had been deleted. He was 31 and in employment. The offences were all committed in breach of a 3 year probation order for 3 offences of unlawful sex with a 15 year old. Except for these offences he had made an excellent response to the order, but concern was expressed about the risk of re-offending. He was sentenced to **2 years with a 3 year extension**. Held. The children's young ages, the large number of images and his previous convictions meant the sentence could well have been longer.

Internet, posting images on

137.14   *R v Bolingbroke* 2001 1 Cr App R (S) 277. LCJ. The defendant pleaded guilty at the Magistrates' Court to six offences of distributing indecent photographs of a child and ten offences of processing indecent photographs of a child for distribution. After an investigation the defendant was identified as the person responsible for posting indecent images of children on a bulletin board on the Internet. Over 3 months he had posted numerous articles all with indecent photographs of children. On the last day he posted 61 articles attaching 145 images. Police seized his computer equipment and found 6,000 similar images. The images were of children who were between the ages of 5 and 8 some of whom appeared to be distressed. He made immediate admissions and said he started using chatrooms and it had snowballed and he'd been involved for 18 months. There were records of chatroom conversations in which he had boasted of his part in obtaining the images. It was not suggested the offences were committed for gain. The defendant was of good character and was a cleaner. The judge made the sentences for distribution consecutive to those for possession. Held. These images are available to a very, very large audience. They can have a corrupting effect. Even if persons of good character were committing these offences without any desire for profit a very firm stance had to be taken. As the distribution could not have taken place without possession the offences should be concurrent so **3 years** not 4.

Internet, sending images to others

137.15   *R v Toomer* 2001 2 Cr App R (S) 30. The defendant pleaded guilty to 30 offences of taking indecent photographs or pseudo photographs of children and to two offences of distributing the same photographs. He approached a friend and gave him a computer disc to do some printing work. The disk contained (in a part not for printing) pornographic pictures of children. Police were informed and his premises were searched. The pornographic images were of children between the ages of 3 and 13 engaging in sexual intercourse with other children and adults (both vaginal and anal) and oral sex were found. He explained that he had gained access to the material through chat rooms and logging on to the ICQ system. He said he had been doing it for 2 years and he was hooked. Not only had he downloaded the material he had traded in the images but not commercially. He was of good character. He showed remorse and recognised the seriousness of the offences. The sentencing judge noted that he was not involved in the abuse or incitement of children. Held. Having regard to the personal use of the images, the maximum was (then) 3 years the appropriate sentence for the distributing offences was **18 months** not 24 months.

R v Toomer Re Powell 2001 2 Cr App R (S) 30 at 35. The defendant pleaded guilty to an offence of taking an indecent photograph of a child, two offences of possessing an indecent photograph of a child and one offence of distributing an indecent photograph of a child. He asked for 50 offences including distribution to be taken into consideration. Police executed a search warrant at his home address and he immediately admitted being in possession of obscene material on his computer and disks. When interviewed he admitted he had possessed pictures of children and distributed them to others on the Internet. He had downloaded 16000 images from the Internet and created 229 pseudo photographs. A large number were of children and many showed them in sexual positions. There was no obvious commercial element. This defendant was of positive good character and had been Mayor of his town. The images were not produced for commercial gain. Held. The sentences should have been concurrent. Having regard to the personal use of the images the appropriate sentence was **18 months** not 3 years.

R v Wild 2002 1 Cr App R (S) 156. Distribution or further dissemination of obscene material is almost inevitably likely to be an aggravating factor. Whether it causes the custody threshold to be passed depends on the extent of the distribution.

R v Ashman 2003 1 Cr App R 308. The defendant pleaded at the Magistrates' Court to 12 counts of making indecent photographs and 3 counts of distributing them. They were specimen counts for 200 indecent images. Police searched his home under a warrant and found numerous images of indecent boys between about 9 and 14. Typically they were in a state of sexual arousal, with masturbation, oral sex and buggery by adults and in one case by another boy. They appeared to have been printed from the computer. He initially denied showing them to anyone but later admitted to sending them three times to America by E-mail. That was not for commercial gain but in exchange for others photographs. In interview he said his fantasy was being a child and having sex with other children. He was 54 and had been a priest for most of his life, firstly as an Anglican and then as a Roman Catholic. He was of good character with a large number of letters. He was deeply remorseful and had sought assistance. Held. The effect of these convictions will continue to be profound. There is no suggestion he ever directly sought out to abuse children. However **2 years** was not manifestly excessive.

Internet, sending images to others – There must be a count in the indictment

137.16   *R v Wild* 2002 1 Cr App R (S) 156. The defendant pleaded guilty to 15 counts of taking indecent photographs. The judge took into account that the defendant had sent the images to others. This was admitted. Held. Before that can be taken into account it should be reflected in a specific count.

Magazines etc, producing etc

137.17   *R v Caley* 1999 2 Cr App R (S) 154. The defendant was convicted of distributing indecent photographs of a child and possessing indecent photographs of children for distribution. He wanted to produce a magazine and approached a friend and asked for his help. He gave the friend a CD-ROM containing sexually explicit photographs of children. He told the friend he wanted to sell copies at £50 each. The friend looked at the file and found photographs of young children in various sexual poses and states of undress. The friend was so shocked he phoned the police. The police searched the defendant's home and found computer equipment and 26 floppy disks containing 670 images of children, aged between 3 and 16. The images were of children with each other and with adults. The defendant said he had obtained the pictures from the Internet and claimed he wanted to infiltrate a paedophile ring. He had no relevant convictions. The sentencing judge noted 'there must be an element of deterrence in this sentence'. Held. We agree. The material was foul. The (then) penalties may be thought to be somewhat inadequate. **30 months** was not manifestly excessive.

Mail order

137.18   *R v Lamb* 1998 1 Cr App R (S) 77. The defendant pleaded guilty to five counts of having obscene articles for gain. Each count concerned a different video. Four involved sadomasochism and one involved animals. Police raided his premises and they found five obscene videos, some video recorders and postage bags and stamps. The defendant said he made his living by running a mail order business. His address book and sales showed the sales were not trivial. He said he had obtained the animal video unintentionally. He was 38 with three similar previous convictions. They involved the sale of pornography on a larger scale than the present offence. He received consecutive offences totalling 5 years. Held. The judge may have been too greatly influenced by the previous convictions. The total exceeded the maximum and was too long. **30 months** on each concurrent substituted.

Sadomasochism and animals

137.19   *R v Lamb* 1998 1 Cr App R (S) 77. The defendant pleaded guilty to five counts of having obscene articles for gain. Each count concerned a different video. Four involved sadomasochism and one involved animals. Police raided his premises and they found five obscene videos, some video recorders and postage bags and stamps. The defendant said he made his living by running a mail order business. His address book and sales showed the sales were not trivial. He said he had obtained the animal video unintentionally. He was 38 with three similar previous convictions. They involved the sale of pornography on a larger scale than the present offence. He received consecutive offences totalling 5 years. Held. The judge may have been too greatly influenced by the previous convictions. The total exceeded the maximum and was too long. **30 months** on each concurrent substituted.

R v Tatam 2005 1 Cr App R 256. The defendant pleaded guilty at an early stage to 18 counts of making indecent photographs of a child, one count of possession of indecent photographs and one count of attempted buggery. The defendant, aged 35, had used his credit card to access child pornography on a website based in Texas. As a result of the enquiry Operation Ore his home and work address were searched and officers seized computer equipment, video tapes and compact and optical discs. They recovered a folder next to his bed containing 350 pornographic pictures of children. The counts of making indecent photographs were samples of individual images, and the one count of possession of indecent photographs represented the totality of the material seized. In all the defendant had 495,524 indecent photographs of children and this was the largest seizure of child pornography during Operation Ore in the UK. 472,000 were at level 1: (nudity and no sexual activity), over 9000 at level 2: (sexual activity between children and solo masturbation), about 11,000 at level 3: (non penetrative sexual activity between children and adults), over 3000 at level 4: (penetrative sexual activity between children and adults), and 336 at level 5: (images of sadism involving children adults and bestiality). He had downloaded the images and stored most of them on computer hard drives under specific category headings such as scatology, bondage, extreme, rape, burning, vomiting and torture. One of the images was of a 3–6 year old girl, fully naked, hanging upside down. She was bound by a rope and gagged. An object was being inserted into her vagina. A video was seized from his home showing him encouraging a dog to commit buggery with his girlfriend, although it was accepted by the prosecution that there had been no penetration. This was the attempted buggery count. There was no evidence that he had distributed the images to anyone else. He was of good character. Held. This was a case of exceptional gravity with aggravating features namely the vast number of images; the organisation of the images showing a high level of interest in the material; the significant number of particularly young children who had been abused for the purposes of making the images. The sentences of **5 years** imprisonment with an **extension period of 1 year** for 15 counts of making an indecent photograph from February 2001 onwards; **2** years concurrent for 3 counts of making indecent photographs of a child during 1997 and 1999; **4** years concurrent for 1 count of possession of indecent photographs of a child and **3 months** concurrent for attempted buggery were not excessive individually or in their totality.

Shop assistants

137.20   *R v Pace* 1998 1 Cr App R (S) 121. The defendant was convicted of possessing an obscene article for gain. He worked for about 4 months in an unlicensed sex shop in Soho. Much of the stock was hard pornography. He was there on both days 3 months apart when police raided the shop. He was tried in respect of three videos and acquitted of two. The video he was convicted of showed digital penetration of female anuses and vaginas by the female or other females and scenes of urination, buggery and anal and vaginal "fisting." The sentencing judge said he was a "front man" who was either unable or unwilling to identify the operators of the shop. The defendant was 50 with no relevant convictions. He suffered from a history of depressive illnesses. Held. The sale of pornographic books, films and tapes on a commercial sale justify sentences of imprisonment on first offenders. The sentences will be comparatively short when appropriate. Salesmen, projectionists, owners and suppliers behind the owners should be at risk of losing their liberty. **3 months** was not manifestly excessive.

R v Ibrahim 1998 1 Cr App R (S) 157. LCJ. The defendant pleaded guilty to 13 counts of possessing obscene articles for gain. They were videos and magazines depicting bondage, flagellation and cruelty to women. There was violence and torture to women which glorify their degradation. No children or animals were depicted. Six articles related to the first police visit. Two to the second police visit and five related to a third police visit. In October 1994 police found the defendant behind a counter in Soho talking to people and pointing to a screen where bound and gagged women were being whipped by a man. He said he was in charge of the premises but refused to answer questions how the business worked. In January 1995 there was another police visit and the defendant was again behind the counter. He said he had been employed for 3 months and his job was to sell the videos and magazines. Six days later he was seen arriving at the shop with another. Two laundry bags of videos were taken into the shop and the defendant said he was in charge of the shop. The defendant had convictions but of a different character. He was sentenced on the basis he was a salesman but not the owner. He received **18 months** on each while the other man received 150 hours' community service at the Magistrates' Court. Held. It is difficult to imagine material more degrading to women. The October matter was a low level offence. He was minding the shop and not taking the profits. **6 months** was appropriate. His later persistent conduct was a serious aggravating factor. The other two groups of offences were worth **12 months** concurrent but **consecutive** to the 6 months. So the original sentence was rearranged but the length was the same.

R v Tunnicliffe and Greenwood 1999 2 Cr App R (S) 88. The defendants T and G pleaded guilty on the day of their trial to having an obscene article for gain. Police officers went to a partitioned-off area of a shop in Manchester which was not licensed and found T behind a till, magazines and videos. The police officer requested videos and T went to the rear of the shop and returned with five videos. The officer asked to look at them. He did so and left. They showed three people having sex and oral sex. Ten days later a search warrant was executed. T was again behind the counter and G arrived saying the shop had nothing to do with him. T admitted selling the videos and receiving 10% of the money paid. The videos were not of the worst kind. None showed children or animals. G's basis of plea was he was allowed to use the flat above in exchange for performing a supervisory role in the shop. He paid the bills and was paid £50 on occasions. T involvement was for 2 months and G's for 4 months. T was 27 and treated as of good character. G was 47 with some irrelevant convictions. Held. We are surprised the Crown asked the Magistrates to decline jurisdiction. There was no evidence that the problem in Manchester was the same as the problem in West End of London at the time of *R v Holloway* 1982 4 Cr App R (S) 128. There may be cases where prison was not necessary. Applying *R v Ollerenshaw* 1999 1 Cr App R (S) 65, **6 weeks** not 3 months for G and **1 month** not 2 for T.

Shop owners

137.21   *R v Singh* 1999 2 Cr App R (S) 160. The defendant pleaded to nine counts of having obscene articles for sale and was committed for sentence. The police visited the defendant's shop and seized magazines. Most were returned and some were destroyed. The defendant continued to sell pornography. A police offer visited the shop and was shown some videos by an assistant (not the defendant). He then asked for "more unusual stuff." The assistant went to a back room and came back with two videos depicting acts of torture and "anal fisting." A week later a search warrant was executed and videos and magazines were seized. [The report does not indicate what seven of the counts related to.] He was 52 with no convictions and a wife and five children. Held. The police visit should have warned the defendant. **6 months** was fully merited.

Taking etc photographs – Victims aged under 16 – Guideline remarks

137.22   *R v Bayliss* 2000 1 Cr App R (S) 412. Where there is a commercial aspect to the taking of indecent photographs of children the courts will take a strong line intending to discourage that kind of activity.

R v Saunders 2004 2 Cr App R (S) 459. The defendant pleaded guilty to taking photographs children. Held. *R v Oliver 2003* is not a straight jacket. Its momentum is downloading. The taking of photographs gives rise to serious aspects with this offending. Generally there will evidence of manipulation, devious conduct and the like leading to children being groomed.

Taking etc photographs – Victims aged under 13

137.23   *R v Saunders* 2004 2 Cr App R (S) 459. The defendant pleaded guilty to taking photographs children. There were 22 TICs involving photographs. He was arrested on suspicion of indecent assault. His home was searched and a cassette was found. It showed images of three different daughters of friends of his. He admitted he filmed it. There was a 5 year old girl sitting naked. He concentrated on her genital area. A naked 9 year old girl was in the shower and doing gymnastics. He chased her. He persuaded her to fully expose her genital area and took every opportunity to zoom in on that area. A naked girl asleep and watching TV and a 9 year old girl asleep were also filmed. He admitted downloading similar images from the internet onto his computer. One girl became angry that the "good times" had come to an end. This led her to becoming alienated from her family. She was expected to have serious personality problems and have great difficulty in forming lasting relations with men. The 5 year old withdrew into herself. She will not talk and has become very isolated. The defendant had 5 court appearances for 14 offences. All involved indecent assaults and indecent photographs of young girls. He showed no remorse. Held. His record was appalling. The risk required the most earnest and firm attention. **4** years with **3 years extension** was thoroughly merited.

Taking etc photographs – Victims aged 13–15

137.24   *R v Bayliss* 2000 1 Cr App R (S) 412. The defendant pleaded guilty to three counts of taking indecent photographs of a child and one count of unlawful sexual intercourse with a girl under 16. The defendant, who was 52 at the time of conviction, picked up a 15-year-old girl who was working as a prostitute. The defendant had sexual intercourse with the girl and then took a series of indecent photographs of her. This was the basis of two of the photograph counts. On that and other occasions he videoed his sexual intercourse with the girl. He met the second victim, through an escort agency when she was 13 years of age. Her mother organised her availability to men. 34 photographs were taken of the second victim. The photographs showed the girls with provocative expressions and standing in sexually suggestive positions. The police searched his home and found pictures of women of various ages in varying degrees of indecency. There was also video and computer equipment. He was sentenced on the basis he thought the girls were 16 or over but was reckless about their ages. The defendant had no convictions and was a retired school inspector. He had had a 'life time of honourable service to the community'. The judge noted that this was an extraordinarily difficult and unusual case as the girls had consented to the photographs as part of their sordid trade. He gave 6 months for the unlawful sex and concurrent sentences for the taking of photographs on that girl and 3 months consecutive for the photograph of the other girl. Held. The purpose behind the offences is the protection of children and that includes protection from themselves. Neither girl was corrupted by him. We might well have made up the sentences in a different way. However, **9 months** in total was not an excessive sentence.

R v Grigg 1999 1 Cr App R (S) 443. The defendant pleaded guilty to two counts of taking indecent photographs of children. He was a friend of the father of the victims who were girls aged 14 and 10 at the time. He had friends who ran a model agency and he asked the girls if they would like to be models. Primitive contracts were drawn up. Legitimate videos were made of the children wearing sundresses ostensibly to help them obtain contracts for modelling children's clothes. Others were in their underwear and he paid them small sums. As a school governor he became involved in converting an air-raid shelter into a museum. The victims came along to help. He then asked the girls to pose without their clothes on in the air-raid shelter. The girls reluctantly agreed and there were indications that he put pressure on the victims to consent. He withdrew while they undressed and wasn't present while they filmed each other naked. There was no sexual activity involved in the filming, nor were there any close-up shots. The girls told their parents who told the police. He was 52, in poor health and of good character. Held. Maybe the videos were not obscene but he had prevailed upon the girls one of whom was only 10 to pose naked for a camera. We accept that the film was not for his own sexual gratification. The breach of trust not only to the victims' parents but also as a school governor meant it had to be a custodial sentence. **9 months** was not manifestly excessive.

Young offenders Guideline case – Indecent photographs etc.

137.25 *R v Oliver* 2003 1 Cr App R 28. These kind of offences very rarely result in the prosecution or cautioning of offenders under the age of 18. When such a person has to be sentenced, the appropriate sentence is likely to be a **supervision order with a relevant treatment programme**. We draw attention, however, as did the Panel, to the apparent present shortage of adequate treatment programmes for young sex offenders.

138 POSSESSION OF DRUGS

138.1 Misuse of Drugs Act 1971 s 5(2)

Triable either way. On indictment maximum 7 years for Class A drugs, 5 years for Class B drugs and 2 years for Class C drugs. Summary maximum 6 months and/or £5,000 for Class A drugs, 3 months and/or £2,500 for Class B drugs and 3 months and/or £1,000 for Class C drugs.

The Criminal Justice Act 2003 creates a summary maximum sentence of 51 weeks, a minimum sentence of 28 weeks and Custody plus. The Home Office says they do not expect to introduce these provisions before September 2006.

Drug Abstinence Order This was repealed on 4 April 2005.

Crown Court statistics – England and Wales – Males 21+
138.2

Year	Plea	Total Numbers sentenced	Type of sentence %					Average length of custody (months)
			Discharge	Fine	Community sentence	Suspended sentence	Custody	
Class A								
2002	Guilty	519	10	16	40	1	31	13.9
	Not guilty	44	5	16	32	2	39	10.5
2003	Guilty	472	12	14	38	1	34	13
	Not guilty	51	6	16	31	–	47	26.5
Class B								
2002	Guilty	287	24	28	33	1	11	8.9
	Not guilty	21	19	43	24	–	14	18.7
2003	Guilty	307	23	31	30	0	13	12.4
	Not guilty	17	24	29	–	–	35	11.3
Class C								
2002	Guilty	10	40	–	20	–	30	2.3
2003	Guilty	5	20	40	20	–	20	0.9

There were 12 and 8 possession offences in 2002 and 2003 respectively where the class of the drug was not recorded. There were no not guilty Class C offences in either year. For details and explanations about the statistics in the book see page vii.

Guideline case – Class A

138.3 *R v Aramah* 1982 76 Cr App R 190. LCJ. It is at this level that the circumstances of the individual offender become of much greater importance. Indeed the possible variety of considerations is so wide, including often those of a medical nature, that we feel it is impossible to lay down any practical guidelines. On the other hand the maximum penalty for simple possession of Class A drugs is 7 years and there will be very many cases where deprivation of liberty is both proper and expedient.

Guideline case – Cannabis

138.4 *R v Aramah* 1982 76 Cr App R 190. LCJ. When only small amounts are involved being for personal use, the offence can very often be met with a fine. If history shows, however, a persistent flouting of the law, imprisonment may become necessary.

See also **Cannabis – Class C (previously B) Does Reclassification Affect the Guidelines for Cannabis Supply?** (At **138.9**)

Magistrates' Court Sentencing Guidelines January 2004 – Class A

138.5 For a first time offender pleading not guilty. Entry point. Is it serious enough for a community penalty? An example of an aggravating factor for the offence is an amount other than a very small quantity. An example of a mitigating factor for the offence is very small amount. Examples of mitigation are age, health (physical or mental), co-operation with the police, and genuine remorse. Consider forfeiture and destruction.

Magistrates' Court Sentencing Guidelines January 2004 – Class B and C

138.6 For a first time offender pleading not guilty. Entry point. Is a discharge or a fine appropriate? An example of an aggravating factor for the offence is large amount. An example of a mitigating factor for the offence is small amount. Examples of mitigation are age, health (physical or mental), co-operation with the police, and genuine remorse. Consider forfeiture and destruction. Starting point fine B. (100% of weekly take home pay/weekly benefit payment)

For details about the guidelines see **Magistrates' Court Sentencing Guidelines** at page 483.

Causing dangerous driving, taking while

138.7 *R v O'Prey* 1999 2 Cr App R (S) 83. The defendant pleaded guilty to perverting the course of justice, driving whilst disqualified and possession of cannabis. He was committed for sentence for driving whist unfit through drugs. Police stopped his car because it was being driven "terribly" on the M3. He gave a false name (presumably the perverting matter). He admitted he had smoked cannabis and spat some out. He was then 24 with dishonesty convictions and had received custody for robbery. He was disqualified for 2 years for drink/drive. Held. The judge was in a difficult position because he had not been charged with dangerous driving. He could not be sentenced for it by using the cannabis count. The proper sentence for the driving whilst disqualified was 3 months, for the perverting count 3 months, for the unfit charge 6 months and 1 month (not 3 years) concurrent for the cannabis. The rest were consecutive making **12 months** not 3½ years.

Prisoners

138.8 *R v Donovan* 2003 2 Cr App R (S) (Unpaginated – at the front of 2003 2 Cr App R (S) Part 2). The defendant pleaded guilty to possessing crack cocaine and possessing heroin. The defendant was visited by his wife in prison where they were observed kissing open-mouthed. The defendant was seen to put his hand down the front of his trousers and to try to get his hand towards his backside. He was searched and found to have 13 wraps (total 1.63 grams) of crack and 24 wraps (total 3.99 grams) of heroin concealed in the cheeks of his backside. He made no comment in interview. He was 36 and serving life for murder. Prior to that he had one drug-related conviction for simple possession (£50 fine). His wife received 6 months for supplying the drugs. Held. With regard to the seriousness of and prevalence of drugs in prison, **30 months** upheld.

See also SUPPLY OF DRUGS (CLASS A, B AND C) – *Prisoners*

Individual drugs

Cannabis – Class C (previously B) – Does reclassification affect the guidelines for cannabis possession?

138.9   *R v Herridge* 2005 Unreported 26/5/05. For supply Parliament clearly intended no change. However there was a reduction in the maximum for possession. A reduction should be made.

Cannabis – Class C (previously B) Cases

138.10   *R v Djahit* 1999 2 Cr App R (S) 142. The defendant pleaded guilty to possession of heroin with intent to supply and possession of cannabis. The cannabis was found at his home. Held. The proper sentence for this low level retailing of heroin was 4 years. 12 months concurrent for the cannabis was manifestly excessive. **2 weeks** concurrent substituted.

R v Hughes 1999 2 Cr App R (S) 329. The defendant was convicted of possession of 1.35 kilos cannabis. Police stopped a car and searched the defendant for drugs. The cannabis was found in his pocket. He was arrested and denied the drugs were found in his pocket. He was 22 and of good character and unemployed. The pre-sentence report said he was continuing to deny it and recommended CSO. Held. *R v Aramah* 1982 76 Cr App R 190 does not imply the only appropriate penalty is a financial one. The offence will usually cross the CSO threshold. However, **40 hours' CSO** not 80.

Cocaine – Class A

138.11   *R v Nawaz* 1999 1 Cr App R (S) 142. The defendant pleaded guilty to possessing crack cocaine. A count of supplying was left on the file. Police watched the defendant and the co-defendant, H leave H's house. They separated and H picked up something on the ground near a fence. He rejoined the defendant and they both walked back to the H's house. They were arrested and the police found three wraps of crack cocaine on the defendant. He was a widower aged 31 with two children. He was in receipt of benefits. He had a number of previous convictions but none for drugs. He had been to prison before for perjury (12 months) and assault on police (3 months concurrent). H was convicted of supply. **8 months** not 12 months.

Old cases *R v Scarlett* 1995 16 Cr App R (S) 745.

Heroin – Class A

138.12   *R v Campbell* 2001 2 Cr App R (S) 369. The defendant was convicted of possession of heroin and crack cocaine. It was treated as a plea of guilty. He was acquitted of possessing the same amounts with intent to supply. Police saw him behaving suspiciously in an area known for the sale of drugs. He appeared to be buying drugs. They moved in and he ran off. He was caught and tried to swallow something. He eventually spat out four wraps. Three contained 383 mgs of heroin and the fourth contained 193 mgs of crack cocaine. The total value was £20. He was a drug addict and in 1996 he had been convicted of three offences of supplying cocaine and received 4 years. Afterwards he was deported. **10 months** not 18.

See also AMPHETAMINE; CANNABIS; DRUG USERS; ECSTASY; LSD; OPIUM, and SUPPLY OF DRUGS (CLASS A, B AND C)

PREMISES

For permitting premises to be used for drug supply see the end of the SUPPLY OF DRUGS (CLASS A, B AND C) chapter at **183.72**.

For permitting premises to be used by a girl under 13 or under 16 for sexual intercourse see PROSTITUTION, CHILD PROSTITUTES (see chapter **144**)

PRISON

For the need to consider prison overcrowding see BASIC PRINCIPLES – *Prison overcrowding*

See also ESCAPE FROM CUSTODY and PRISONERS

139 PRISON CONDITIONS, HARSH

139.1 Occasionally Judges do take into account the effect of prison on the defendant. Reductions have been made because the defendant speaks little English, has no family in this country, or is blind or disabled. However where reductions are made they are not necessarily particularly great.

A reduction in sentence can be made

139.2 *R v Soares* 2003 Unreported 5/9/03. The defendant was arrested on 12 February 1999 and was made a Category A exceptional risk prisoner. He was detained in the Special Security Unit at Belmarsh prison. The cell was small. There was little natural light. Metal grids and mesh covered the exercise yard and limited the light. There was no proper view of the sky. For most of the time the defendant was alone in his cell with only three prison officers to associate with. Contact with the outside world was limited. After he had been in the unit for a year he was allowed three open visits. His wife and son came from France twice. His mother came from Brazil once. After convictions there were no open visits. The only free telephone contact was once a month through an interpreter. Otherwise he would have to pay £200 a time. His trial lasted from May 2000 to June 2000 when a new jury was sworn and then to 25 July 2001(sic). During the trial he was continually stripped searched sometimes eleven times a day. The High Court sentencing Judge reduced the sentence from 27 to 24 years (11%) because the defendant had no family in this country. A critical report from Amnesty International on the Special Security Unit was relied on by the defence. The defence said the defendant had suffered serious depressive illnesses as a result of the conditions and the conditions amounted to inhuman and degrading treatment under Article 3 of the European Convention on Human Rights. Held. This Court cannot decide whether the conditions amounted to inhuman and degrading treatment because we have heard no argument. The Judge was right not to reduce the sentence because the detention was unlawful. We are inclined to the view that a Judge would be entitled to take pre-sentence conditions into account. If he thought they aggravated the effect of the detention he might adjust the sentence. The appeal was dismissed.

140   PRISON MUTINY

140.1   Prison Security Act 1992 s 1

Indictable only. Maximum sentence 10 years.

Longer than Commensurate sentences and Extended sentences Prison Mutiny is a violent offence for the purposes of passing a longer than commensurate sentence [Powers of Criminal Courts (Sentencing) Act 2000 s 80(2)] and an extended sentence (extending the licence) [Powers of Criminal Courts (Sentencing) Act 2000 s 85(2)(b)] where the offence leads, or is intended or likely to lead, to a person's death or to physical injury to a person[17]. The orders cannot be made for offences committed before 30/9/98 or after 3/4/05.

140.2   *Cases*

R v Mitchell and Pipes 1995 16 Cr App R (S) 924. LCJ. The defendants M and P were the ringleaders of a prison riot in which £117,000 worth of damage was caused and a prison van was 'hot wired' and used to ram the hospital gate. The van then drove round the perimeter wall and it was then used as a launch pad in an attempt to scale a wall. It was also driven at speed at prison and police officers. M attacked an officer while keys were snatched and stopped others going to his aid. P was armed and masked and tried to stop people surrendering. Held. The Prison Security Act 1992 was passed because Parliament was concerned about unrest and riots in prison. **5 years** and 5 years YOI respectively concurrent to sentences being served were entirely appropriate.

R v Whiteman and Others. 2004. 2 Cr App R (S) 312. The defendants W, B, Bt, S and D were charged with participating in a prison mutiny at Rochester YOI. W pleaded guilty and B and Bt changed their pleas to guilty some 6 months later. S changed his plea to guilty 3 days after B and Bt. D was convicted of this count and a further count of false imprisonment. The mutiny lasted from 7.30 pm to 4.30 am the following day. The violence began when D threw a flask towards prison officers. Items were smashed and B threw a chair towards officers, although it did not hit them. W threw items at officers, one of whom took refuge in a cell and became trapped there when other officers were forced out of the wing. D and W demanded his keys, W threatened the officer with a chair leg and struck him on the hand. The officer could hear threats such as 'torture the screw'. At one point he was produced with a letter opener held to him as a threat. He was handcuffed painfully, taped around the chest to a chair, and a pillow case was put over his head. Another prisoner hit him over the head with a broom handle or pool cue producing a lot of blood and possibly he passed out. B and Bt were not involved in any violence towards this officer and B said he tried to help him. S, Bt and B helped to build barricades. Offices were ransacked and beds and sheets were set on fire. When the control and restraint teams came they had furniture and hot water thrown at them. Held. The judge was right to work from the basis that anyone who joined in was committing a serious offence, that any involvement required a substantial sentence and that it was not necessary to take into account the precise degree of involvement. Although W received credit for an early plea his conduct was sufficiently serious that it was inevitable that his starting point would have been higher than others. This was a serious offence of its kind. W, B, Bt and S were properly sentenced to **4 years** imprisonment and D to **6 years**.

PRISON OVERCROWDING

For need to consider prison overcrowding see **BASIC PRINCIPLES** – *Prison overcrowding*
See also **ESCAPE FROM CUSTODY** and **PRISONERS**

17 Powers of Criminal Courts (Sentencing) Act 2000 s 161(3)

141   PRISON OFFICERS AS DEFENDANTS

Breaching their trust to prisoners

141.1   *R v Fryer* 2002 2 Cr App R (S) 122. [The report does not make it clear what the offences were but it was probably ABH.] Three Wormwood Scrubs officers punched and kicked a prisoner in the segregation unit for $1^1/_2$ to 2 minutes. The assault was followed by bogus charges and disciplinary proceedings against the prisoner. Held. Breach of trust does not simply mean protection of the prisoner. A prisoner is entitled to receive protection that the law provides him with from prison officers. It is a breach of trust so far as the responsibilities of the prison officers are concerned, to society generally. The damage does not stop with the damage such as it may be to the prisoner. The damage is to the fabric of the prison system, to the proper administration of the prisons, to the need for those who are in prison, and for those who regard the prison system as playing a significant social role, to have confidence in it. Those who are in prison are not to be abused in a way which is likely to undermine yet more their alienation from society. Prisoners are entitled to the protection of the law, from assaults on them by prison officers. Society is entitled to the proper discharge of the onerous responsibilities which prison officers undertake. They are heavy responsibilities.

See also **ABH** – *Prison officers assaulting prisoners* and *Supply of Drugs (Class A, B and C) – prisoners, supply to Class A – Prison Officers*

142   PRISONERS

Defendant badly treated by other prisoners

142.1   *R v Nall-Cain* 1998 2 Cr App R (S) 145. The defendant, Lord Brocket was sentenced to 5 years for a false £4.5m insurance claim. While in prison his diary was stolen by a gang of prisoners for sale to the press. Other prisoners blackmailed him and threats were made to him and his family. A prisoner went to his aid and was assaulted and wounded. The leader of the gang was arrested and charged with theft, GBH, and blackmail but none of the other prisoners who could give evidence were prepared to give evidence. He was moved from one prison to another on a number of occasions. When prison officers were absent he was accused of being a grass. He was stabbed in the hand and repeatedly kicked and punched. His shoulder was dislocated and he received a black eye. Since he moved to an open prison 12 months ago there were no further incidents but he said he was fearful. Held. The different wording of the Criminal Appeal Act 1907, s 4(3) and the Criminal Appeal Act 1968, s 11(3) means there is now a wider power to alter sentences. The authorities do not speak with one voice. *R v Kirby* 1979 1 Cr App R (S) 215; *R v Kay* 1980 2 Cr App R (S) 284 and *R v Parker* 1996 2 Cr App R (S) 275 show that a defendant's treatment by other inmates is not generally a factor the Court of Appeal can have regard to. A prisoner maltreated has a number of avenues of redress open to him. The difficulties of adjudicating upon the disputes preclude us from taking them into account. The appeal is dismissed.

Total sentence when sentence consecutive to the sentence being served

142.2   *R v Ali* 1998 2 Cr App R (S) 123. The defendant was convicted of prison mutiny, and two counts of GBH with intent. A prisoner P hit two prison officers with a metal part of a bed causing serious injuries to their heads. The short- and long-term damage to them was great. Neither had been able to return to work. P said he had been threatened to do this by the defendant and it was the signal for a riot. P gave evidence for the prosecution. The defendant was 32 with 20 previous including manslaughter and wounding with intent. He was sentenced to 6 years for the mutiny and 12 years for each GBH. The sentences were concurrent to each other and consecutive to the 9 year sentence for the wounding which he was serving making **21 years** in all. The judge said, the regard the principle of totality should be minimal. The defence did not appeal the individual sentences but appealed the total sentence. Held. The total is very long indeed. The judge is to be commended for the stern attitude he took which the court supports. We hope the message will be conveyed to anyone contemplating acts of this sort. It is inevitable the sentences should be consecutive. The judge was right not to be persuaded by the arguments of totality.

R v Singh 1999 1 Cr App R (S) 445. The defendant was convicted of possession of 4.9 grams of heroin with intent to supply. He was a serving prisoner with about 9 months to serve of a 12 year sentence. The judge thought he should serve his sentence and then 2 years extra and passed originally a 4 year sentence consecutive. When informed that this would make him a long-term prisoner he reduced the sentence to 3 years 10 months. Held. He was still a long-term prisoner because of the 12 year sentence and both sentences were treated as one term. So **3 years** substituted to achieve the Judge's intention of 2 extra years.

R v Parker 2000 Crim LR 494. The Judge considered that a sentence which kept him a short-term prisoner was too short. Held. The authorities established that the effect of converting a short-term prisoner to a long-term prisoner was a relevant consideration. If the effect of that was disproportionate then make an appropriate discount. However, here the sentence was appropriate.

See also **ABH** – *Prison officers, against*; OFFENCES AGAINST THE PERSON ACT **1861, S 18** – *Prison officers, against* and *Prison Mutiny*

PROCURING

For procuring the execution of a valuable security in which the defendant intended to steal see THEFT ETC

143   PRODUCTION OF DRUGS

143.1   Misuse of Drugs Act 1971 s 4(2)(a) and (b)

Triable either way, unless the defendant could receive the minimum sentence of 7 years for a third drug trafficking offence when the offence is triable only on indictment.

On indictment the maximum is life for Class A drugs, 14 years for Class B and C[18] drugs (for offences committed before 29/1/04 the maximum for Class C drugs is 5 years). Summary maximum 6 months and/or £5,000 for Class A and B drugs and 3 months and/or £2,500 for Class C drugs.

Drug Abstinence Order This was repealed on 4 April 2005.

Confiscation For production offences[19] the court <u>must</u> follow the Proceeds of Crime Act 2002 procedure for offences committed on or after 24 March 2003[20] and Drug Trafficking Act 1994 procedure for offences committed before that date.

---

18 Criminal Justice Act 2003 s 284 & Sch. 28 Para 1
19 Proceeds of Crime Act 2002 s 75 and Sch 2 para 1(1)(a) or Drug Trafficking Act 1994 s 1(1)(a) (depending on the date of the offence).
20 Proceeds of Crime Act 2002 (Commencement No 5, Transitional Provisions, Savings and Amendment) Order 2003

Minimum sentences For offences committed on or after 30 September 1997, production carries a minimum 7 years for a third Class A drug trafficking offence[21]. See SUPPLY OF DRUGS (CLASS A, B AND C) – *Persistent Class A offenders*

Travel Restrictions For offences committed on or after 1/4/02 where 4 or more years imprisonment is appropriate the Court is under a duty to consider whether it is appropriate to make a travel restriction order[22]. Where there is a direction in the order the Secretary of State may retain the defendant's passport[23].

Magistrates' Court Sentencing Guidelines January 2004 – Class A Production and supply

143.2 For a first time offender pleading not guilty. Entry point. Are Magistrates' sentencing powers sufficient? Consider the impact on the victim. Example of aggravating factors for the offence are commercial production, large amount, deliberate adulteration, quantity, sophisticated operation supply to children and venue, e.g. prison or educational establishment. An example of a mitigating factor for the offence is small amount. Examples of mitigation are age, health (physical or mental), co-operation with the police, and genuine remorse. Consider forfeiture and destruction.

For details about the guidelines see MAGISTRATES' COURT SENTENCING GUIDELINES at page 483.

For production of cannabis see CANNABIS – *Cultivation of Etc*

See also IMPORTATION OF DRUGS, POSSESSION OF DRUGS, and SUPPLY OF DRUGS (A, B AND C)

PROSECUTION, GIVING EVIDENCE FOR THE

See INFORMANTS/GIVING EVIDENCE FOR THE PROSECUTION

144   PROSTITUTION, CHILD PROSTITUTES

144.1   Sexual Offences Act 2003 s 47–50

Paying for sexual services of a child, causing or inciting child prostitution, controlling a child prostitute and facilitating child prostitution etc. respectively.

These sections came into force on 1/5/04. Offences committed before this date are charged under Sexual Offences Act 1956. As the definition of a child is for these sections someone under 18 some of the now unlawful activity was lawful before 1/5/04.

All the offences are triable either way (except for s 47 [paying for sexual services of a child] when the child is under 16. Then the offence is indictable only).

On indictment maximum 14 years. Summary maximum 6 months and/or £5,000.

Confiscation For all Sexual Offences Act 2003 s 48, 49 and 50 offences the court must follow the Proceeds of Crime Act 2002 procedure[24].

Imprisonment for public protection For all offences committed on or after 4/4/05 when there is a significant risk to members of the public of serious harm etc. there

---

21 Powers of Criminal Courts (Sentencing) Act 2000 s 110
22 Criminal Justice and Police Act 2001 s 33
23 Criminal Justice and Police Act 2001 s 33(5)
24 Proceeds of Crime Act 2002 s 6 and s 75 and Sch 2 para 4(2) as inserted by Sexual Offences Act 2003 s 139 and Sch 6 para 46(2).

is a mandatory duty to pass a sentence of imprisonment for public protection[25]. For offenders under 18 the duty is to pass detention for public protection or an extended sentence[26].

Notification For an offence of for s 47 [paying for sexual services of a child] where (a) the victim was under 16 and (b)(i) the defendant is 18 or over or (ii) is sentenced to 12 months imprisonment or more, the defendant must notify the police within 3 days (or 3 days from his/her release from imprisonment, hospital etc.) with his/her name, home address, national insurance number etc. and any change and addresses where s/he resides for 7 days[27] (in one or more periods) or more in any 12 month period[28]. See SEX OFFENDERS' REGISTER

Working with children Where (a) the prostitute is a child [for these provisions a child is someone under 18], (b) the defendant is aged 18 or over and (c) s/he is sentenced to 12 months or more etc. hospital order etc. the court must disqualify him/her from working with children unless satisfied s/he is unlikely to commit any further offences against a child when the court <u>must</u> state its reasons for not doing so[29]. For a defendant aged less than 18 at the time of the offence the court must order disqualification if s/he is sentenced to 12 months or more and the court is satisfied that the defendant will commit a further offence against a child[30]. The court must state its reasons for so doing.

Sexual Offences Prevention Order For section 47 offences there is a discretionary power to make this order when it is necessary to protect the public etc[31].

Guideline remarks

144.2   *Att-Gen's Ref. Nos. 91, 119 and 120 of 2002,* 2003 2 Cr App R (S) 338. In *R v Millberry* 2003 2 Cr App R (S) 142 at par 8, the Lord Chief Justice said, 'There are, broadly three dimensions to consider in assessing the gravity of an individual offence of rape. The first is the degree of harm to the victim; the second is the level of culpability of the offender; and the third is the level of risk proposed by the offender to society. The gravity of each case will depend very much upon the circumstances and it will always be necessary to consider an individual case as a whole taking into account the three dimensions.'

It will be necessary to take account of similar considerations in all cases of sexual interference, whether amounting to rape or not. However, that is not all. In all classes of sexual offences, there will also be the need to deter others from acting in a similar fashion.

Coercion, violence or threats, with

144.3   *R v Lassman* 2003 1 Cr App R (S) 505. The defendant pleaded guilty to living on the earnings of prostitution. The victim first met the defendant when she was 15 in 1997. He moved into her house and they had sexual intercourse for the first time on her 16th birthday. She experimented with heroin and quickly became addicted to that drug. Initially the defendant's earnings support his and her habits; however, she quickly started to steal to supplement their income. Shortly before the victim's 17th birthday, the defendant was sentenced to custody for an offence of unlawful sexual intercourse (with another young woman). After his release, the defendant and the victim moved into an unfurnished flat together and both resorted to stealing to fund their habits. When she was

25 Criminal Justice Act 2003 s 224–226
26 Criminal Justice Act 2003 s 226 and 228
27 Sexual Offences Act 2003 s 84(1)(c) & (6)
28 Sexual Offences Act 2003 s 83 & Sch. 3 para 29
29 Criminal Justice and Court Services Act 2000 s 28 & Sch 4 as amended by Sexual Offences Act 2003 s 139 & Sch 6 Para 44(5)(a)
30 Criminal Justice and Court Services Act 2000 s 29
31 Sexual Offences Act 2003 s 104 & Sch. 3 Para 29 & Sch. 5 Para 62

17 the defendant said that he had been supporting their habits for long enough and introduced her to working as a street prostitute charging £20 a client. She would service between five and eight clients a night, closely observed by the defendant. The proceeds were spent on drugs, which now included crack cocaine. In July 1999 he was imprisoned and the victim returned to live with relatives; however, following his release she returned to live with him and to prostitution. Later the same month, he was returned to prison for outstanding warrants and the victim found that she was pregnant. Her parents arranged for her undergo detoxification. Following his release approximately 2 months later, the defendant went to live with the victim and her parents. A baby was born months later. He was again arrested and imprisoned for robbery, before being released about 10 months later and returned to live with the victim's parents. He again told her to resume prostitution and was required by the defendant to meet as many clients as she could each night. When she asked not to work, some six months later, the defendant became violent and assaulted her. She continued to solicit clients. Her child died a little over a year later. The same day the defendant required the victim to continue soliciting and he dragged her into a motorcar. The two of them were arrested at the squat where they lived weeks later. The period in the indictment was 19 months, 14 of which he had been in custody. The defendant was 33 with 15 previous convictions mainly for dishonest. Two were for unlawful sexual intercourse, one in 1989 and one in 1998. He showed a lack of remorse and presented a high risk of re-offending. During the 19-month period to which the indictment referred the defendant had been in custody for fourteen months. He had demonstrated an unwillingness to undertake a sex offenders' programme. We have regard to the youth of the victim, to the fact that the defendant coerced her initially and that he then continued to coerce her. However **4 years** not 5.

Girl aged 13–15

144.4 *R v Sisson* 2002 1 Cr App R (S) 353. The defendant pleaded guilty to permitting premises to be used by a girl under 16 for sexual intercourse. The defendant who lived in Newcastle upon Tyne was a female friend of the mother of a girl T. T then aged 15 was a regular and welcome visitor to the defendant's home. The defendant accessed Internet chat rooms and a met a man from Hastings. She introduced T to the chat room and T met a man, M. T gave her age on the Internet as 17. The defendant told M that T was only 15. The man from Hastings travelled to Newcastle to meet T and M decided to join him. The defendant took them to her home where T was babysitting. M had sex with T. The next day T and the two men spent the afternoon together and then went to the defendant's home. T telephoned her parents to say she had been asked to baby-sit and she would be staying overnight. M again had sex with T. The girl had been given a quarter bottle of schnapps and some vodka and was encouraged to have sexual discussions with M. After a Newton hearing in which T gave evidence the judge found that T had been put under pressure to go into the bedroom. The defendant was 32 and had a child aged 11 who was severely disabled with autism and two younger children who were being looked after her husband while the defendant was in prison. The judge found the defendant obtained a degree of pleasure of a perverted nature from what had occurred and it was a very gross breach of trust. Also she had set it up and put her under pressure to take part. Held. It was obvious why the men were travelling to Newcastle. **14 months** was a severe sentence but it was justified.

145 PROSTITUTION, CONTROLLING PROSTITUTES ETC.

145.1 There are four main offences

1 & 2 Sexual Offences Act 2003 s 52 and 53

Causing or inciting another person to become a prostitute for gain etc. and controlling prostitutes

These sections came into force on 1/5/04. Offences committed before this date are charged under Sexual Offences Act 1956 s 30 (Living on immoral earnings) (now repealed), Sexual Offences Act 1956 s 33–4 (Brothel offences) (not repealed) etc.

3 Sexual Offences Act 1956 s 33A (not repealed)

Keeping a brothel

The two new offences and the old Sexual Offences Act 1956, s 30 and s 33A are triable either way.

On indictment maximum 7 years. Summary maximum 6 months and/or £5,000.

The Criminal Justice Act 2003 creates a summary maximum sentence of 51 weeks, a minimum sentence of 28 weeks and Custody plus. The Home Office says they do not expect to introduce these provisions before September 2006.

4 Sexual Offences Act 2003 s 57–9 replaced on 1/5/04 Nationality, Immigration and Asylum Act 2002 s 145

Trafficking in prostitution

All offences both old and new are triable either way. On indictment maximum 14 years. Summary maximum 6 months and/or £5,000.

Confiscation For all Sexual Offences Act 1956 s 2, 3, 9, 22, 24, 28–31, 33 and 34 offences[32] committed on or after 24 March 2003[33] the court must follow the Proceeds of Crime Act 2002 procedure. For all Sexual Offences Act 2003 s 52, 53, 57–9 offences the court must follow the Proceeds of Crime Act 2002 procedure[34].

Extended sentences under CJA 2003 For offences under s 52–3, committed on or after 4/4/05 there is a mandatory duty to pass an extended sentence when there is a significant risk to members of the public of serious harm etc.[35]. See EXTENDED SENTENCES

Working with children Where (a) the prostitute is a child, (b) the defendant is aged 18 or over and (c) s/he is sentenced to 12 months or more etc. hospital order etc. the court must disqualify him/her from working with children unless satisfied s/he is unlikely to commit any further offences against a child when the court must state its reasons for not doing so[36]. For a defendant aged less than 18 at the time of the offence the court must order disqualification if s/he is sentenced to 12 months or more and the court is satisfied that the defendant will commit a further offence against a child[37]. The court must state its reasons for so doing.

Sentencing trends. For adults the sentences where there is no coercion are likely to remain stable or fall but there will be a much more concerted effort to strip the defendant of his/her profits using where possible the pathetically limited new powers. For offences against children the sentences will remain high.

Guideline case

145.2   *R v Farrugia* 1979 69 Cr App R 108 at 113. In the absence of any evidence of coercion, whether physical or mental, or of corruption **2 years** is probably adequate. Anything exceeding 2 years should be reserved for a case where there is an element of coercion or there is some strong evidence of corruption.

---

32 Proceeds of Crime Act 2002 s 6 and s 75 and Sch 2 para 8
33 Proceeds of Crime Act 2002 (Commencement No 5, Transitional Provisions, Savings and Amendment) Order 2003
34 Proceeds of Crime Act 2002 s 6 and s 75 and Sch 2 para 4(2) as inserted by Sexual Offences Act 2003 s 139 and Sch 6 para 46(2).
35 Criminal Justice Act 2003 s 227–228
36 Criminal Justice and Court Services Act 2000 s 28
37 Criminal Justice and Court Services Act 2000 s 29

Coercion, violence or threats, with

145.3 *R v Powell* 2001 1 Cr App R (S) 261. The defendant was convicted of living on prostitution. He was acquitted of ABH. The defendant met the victim socially and moved into a flat he owned. He offered her work in a sauna and she agreed. When she went there and saw girls in skimpy underwear she realised what she was being asked to do and left. When she got back to the flat he demanded she work as a prostitute. She agreed because she was frightened of him. She started working as a prostitute between 10am and 4 and he demanded all the money she earned. She said she was unable to leave because he threatened her. She took drugs to take her mind off what she was doing and her weight dropped from 10 to 8 stone. After 6 weeks she was allowed to go home. She estimated she had earned £7,000. A month later she suffered a breakdown and tried to harm herself. It was considered she had suffered personality damage as a result of her experiences. He was 38 and had convictions for theft, handling, offensive weapon and criminal damage. In 1997 he had received 18 months concurrent for two domestic burglaries. Held. **5 years** was severe having regard to the maximum but not too long.

R v Lassman 2003 1 Cr App R (S) 505. The defendant pleaded guilty to living on the earnings of prostitution. The victim first met the defendant when she was 15 in 1997. He moved into her house and they had sexual intercourse for the first time on her 16th birthday. She experimented with heroin and quickly became addicted to that drug. Initially the defendant's earnings support his and her habits; however, she quickly started to steal to supplement their income. Shortly before the victim's 17th birthday, the defendant was sentenced to custody for an offence of unlawful sexual intercourse (with another young woman). After his release, the defendant and the victim moved into an unfurnished flat together and both resorted to stealing to fund their habits. When she was 17 the defendant said that he had been supporting their habits for long enough and introduced her to working as a street prostitute charging £20 a client. She would service between five and eight clients a night, closely observed by the defendant. The proceeds were spent on drugs, which now included crack cocaine. In July 1999 he was imprisoned and the victim returned to live with relatives; however, following his release she returned to live with him and to prostitution. Later the same month, he was returned to prison for outstanding warrants and the victim found that she was pregnant. Her parents arranged for her undergo detoxification. Following his release approximately 2 months later, the defendant went to live with the victim and her parents. A baby was born months later. He was again arrested and imprisoned for robbery, before being released about 10 months later and returned to live with the victim's parents. He again told her to resume prostitution and was required by the defendant to meet as many clients as she could each night. When she asked not to work, some six months later, the defendant became violent and assaulted her. She continued to solicit clients. Her child died a little over a year later. The same day the defendant required the victim to continue soliciting and he dragged her into a motorcar. The two of them were arrested at the squat where they lived weeks later. The period in the indictment was 19 months, 14 of which he had been in custody. The defendant was 33 with 15 previous convictions mainly for dishonest. Two were for unlawful sexual intercourse, one in 1989 and one in 1998. He showed a lack of remorse and presented a high risk of re-offending. During the 19-month period to which the indictment referred the defendant had been in custody for fourteen months. He had demonstrated an unwillingness to undertake a sex offenders' programme. We have regard to the youth of the victim, to the fact that the defendant coerced her initially and that he then continued to coerce her. However **4 years** not 5.

Owner etc of premises used for prostitution

145.4 *R v Elul* 2001 2 Cr App R (S) 321. The defendant pleaded guilty to four counts of living off prostitutes. The defendant came to this country in 1997 and from 1999 he and his wife were in the business of providing sexual services. He advertised for prostitutes in South Africa and 20 came over to the UK. The business started at one flat and then police kept observations on two other flats and typically there were two girls at each of the flats. There was no coercion or corruption and the business was run hygienically. The defendant took 50% of the earnings less a fee for the receptionist. His benefit was £105,600 and there was a confiscation order for £12,340 made. He was 30 and of good character. His wife was cautioned. Held. It was a carefully organised and professional criminal enterprise but **12 months** not 18.

R v Rousseau 2003 1 Cr App R (S) 60. The defendant pleaded guilty to living on the earnings of prostitution. His premises were divided between where he lived and a brothel. He was deeply involved taking on substantial debt to pay for setting it up. He was paid £30 per client, which covered the room and the advertising. He was 29 and treated as of good character. He told police he was looking after it for a friend. He absconded and was given 2 months consecutive for the bail offence. Held. **6 months** not 9 with other sentence remaining which will enable him to be released. (This is one of the shortest judgements ever and does not reveal time period, overall profits or the standards of hygiene etc.)

R v Middleton 2005 1 Cr App R 195. The defendant pleaded guilty to two counts of living on the earnings of prostitution. The second count was committed while he was on bail for the first. He owned a shop selling sex toys and lingerie and upstairs he ran a massage parlour. When undercover police officers visited the premises they were offered sexual services as well as massage and the women there indicated they sometimes earned as much as £1,000 per week. They told the officers the defendant recruited them by advertising. An undercover police officer spoke to the defendant and he explained the range of services on offer. The defendant, 61, had no relevant previous convictions. It was accepted that there were no aggravating features such as threats or the use of force, coercion or corruption. The women were of age and acted voluntarily. There was no evidence of disruption to neighbouring trades. Held. These were well-organised offences involving up to twenty women. **6 months** not 9 for the first count remaining **consecutive to 3 months** on count two. (Regretfully there is no reference to the amount of benefit the defendant might have received.)

Old case. *R v Malik* 1998 1 Cr App R (S) 115, (for a summary of this case see the first edition of this book).

Trafficking – Guideline remarks

145.5   *Att-Gen's Ref No 6 of 2004* 2005 1 Cr App R (S) 83. Human trafficking is a problem which confronts not only this country but many other countries. It is degrading and produces untold misery to girls all over the world. The message has to be sent out that this type of activity is despicable, cannot be tolerated by a civilised society and that those involved will be sentenced to lengthy terms of imprisonment.

Trafficking – Cases

145.6   *Att-Gen's Ref No 6 of 2004* 2005 1 Cr App R (S) 83. The defendant was convicted of three counts of kidnapping, incitement to rape, three counts of living off immoral earnings and procuring a girl for sexual intercourse. He pleaded guilty to 7 counts of assisting illegal immigration. Girls from Romania were promised work in Britain and assisted with false passports to come. When they arrived they were held against their will, corrupted and coerced to work as prostitutes. One aged 17 was assaulted and threatened that food and water would be withheld. She still refused and was locked in a room and then forcibly undressed. She was terrified. Luckily she managed to escape and alerted the police. The defendant's address was searched and the paraphernalia of prostitution was found. Police were then able to make enquires. Another girl aged 16 was assisted to enter the country and told she had to repay the money spent by working as a prostitute. She said she was also coerced into marriage. Another girl aged 16 was sold to a pimp for £7,000. She later returned to the defendant and earned between £600 and £1,000 a day all of which was taken. 7 girls were the subject of charges. Two were rescued before being mistreated. £204,396 was traced as having been in his bank deposits. He lived extravagantly and owned a Ferrari. The defendant was an Albanian with a British passport. He was 26 with effectively no convictions. The Judge gave him 10 years. Held. This case has echoes of the days of slavery and the characteristics of a campaign of rape. The illegal entry counts **5 years**. The kidnap counts **10 years**. The incitement to rape **8 years**. For one of the girl's counts 5 + 10 + 8 consecutive making **23 years** in all.

146   PUBLIC DECENCY, OUTRAGING

146.1   Common law

Triable either way[38]. On indictment maximum 7 years. Summary maximum 6 months and/or £5,000. (For offences committed before 20/1/04 the offence is indictable only. There is no maximum fine or term of imprisonment provided the sentence is not inordinate *R v Morris* 1951 34 Cr App R (S) 210.)

Anti-Social Behavioural orders Where the defendant has acted in a manner that caused or was likely to cause harassment, alarm or distress to one or more persons not in the same household as the defendant and it is necessary to protect persons from further anti-social acts by him/her the court may make this order[39].

Guideline remarks

146.2   *Att-Gen's Ref. Nos. 91, 119 and 120 of 2002*, 2003 2 Cr App R (S) 338. In *R v Millberry* 2003 2 Cr App R (S) 142 at par 8, the Lord Chief Justice said, 'There are, broadly three dimensions to consider in assessing the gravity of an individual offence of rape. The first is the degree of harm to the victim; the second is the level of culpability of the offender; and the third is the level of risk proposed by the offender to society. The gravity of each case will depend very much upon the circumstances and it will always be necessary to consider an individual case as a whole taking into account the three dimensions.'

It will be necessary to take account of similar considerations in all cases of sexual interference, whether amounting to rape or not. However, that is not all. In all classes of sexual offences, there will also be the need to deter others from acting in a similar fashion.

Children, involving

146.3   *R v Gaynor* 2000 2 Cr App R (S) 163. The defendant was convicted of outraging public decency. He had been sentenced to 4$\frac{1}{2}$ years for indecent assault on a male. Three weeks after his release on licence police who had mounted a surveillance operation on him and saw him looking at children in a playground 30 to 40 yards away. He took out his penis and masturbated. He was not calling out or gesticulating to any child. No child came near. When arrested he denied it. He was 63. He had an appalling record. In 1976, 1979, 1980, 1985, 1992, and in 1996 he was sentenced to 6 months, 2, 3, 5 years, 4 years 9 months and 4$\frac{1}{2}$ years respectively for various indecent assault offences on children under 14. The total convictions for indecent assault was 11. Held.

38 Criminal Justice Act 2003 s 320
39 Crime and Disorder Act 1998 s 1C

He has to be kept out of the way of children for a long time. **3 years** not 5 years consecutive to the 1 year, 22 weeks and 4 days passed for breach of the licence.

Longer than commensurate/Extended, can the sentence be?

146.4   *R v Gaynor* 2000 2 Cr App R (S) 163. As the offence is not listed in the definition under the Criminal Justice Act 1991, s 31 [now the Powers of Criminal Courts (Sentencing) Act 2000 s 161(2)] extended sentences cannot be passed.

See also **PORNOGRAPHY**

PUBLIC HEALTH

See **ENVIRONMENTAL OFFENCES** and **HEALTH AND SAFETY OFFENCES**

147   PUBLIC NUISANCE

Common law so indictable only. No maximum provided so the maximum is life.

Where the offence is connected with obtaining money dishonestly see **THEFT ETC**

Where the offence is connected with harassment see **HARASSMENT S 4 OR / PUBLIC NUISANCE**

See also **PUBLIC ORDER ACT 1986** and **STALKING**

PUBLIC ORDER ACT 1986 S 2

See **VIOLENT DISORDER**

148   PUBLIC ORDER ACT S 4

148.1   Public Order Act 1986 s 4

Using threatening, abusive or insulting words or behaviour.

Summary only. Maximum sentence 6 months[40] and/or Level 5 fine (£5,000).

Football Where the offence (a) is under Public Order Act 1986 s 4(1)(a); and (b) was committed relevant to a football match and (c) where there are reasonable grounds to believe that making a banning order would help to prevent violence or disorder at or in connection with any regulated football match; the court must make a Football Banning Order, under the Football Spectators Act 1989 s 14A and Sch 1, para 1[41]. The Court of Appeal has considered that it didn't think there was any reason why the position should be any different for an offence under Public Order Act 1986 s 4(1)(b) but left the point open as the court hadn't heard any argument on the point[42].

---

40 Where the jury convict the defendant of an offence under s 4 as an alternative to a racially-aggravated offence the maximum sentence at the Crown Court is the Magistrates' Courts maximum, Public Order Act 1986 s 7(4), R v Alden 2002 2 Cr App R (S) 326
41 R v O'Keefe 2004 1 Cr App R (S) 402
42 R v O'Keefe 2004 1 Cr App R (S) 402

Licensed premises Where the offence is committed on licensed premises and the defendant resorted to violence or offered or threatened to resort to violence, the court may prohibit the defendant from entering those premises or any other specified premises without the express consent of the licensee or his agent[43]. The order shall last from 3 months to 2 years[44].

Magistrates' Court Sentencing Guidelines January 2004

148.2 For a first time offender pleading not guilty. Entry point. Is it serious enough for a community penalty? Consider the impact on the victim. Examples of aggravating factors for the offence are football related, group action, on hospital/medical or school premises, people put in fear, victim serving the public and vulnerable victim. Example of mitigating factors for the offence are minor matter and short duration. Examples of mitigation are age, health (physical or mental), co-operation with the police, genuine remorse and voluntary compensation. Give reasons if not awarding compensation.

For details about the guidelines see **MAGISTRATES' COURT SENTENCING GUIDELINES** at page 483.

Defendant aged 15–16

148.3 *R v Howells Re Marston* 1999 1 Cr App R (S) 335 at 344. LCJ. The defendant pleaded guilty to ABH. While serving the 9 months detention he pleaded guilty to the Public Order Act 1986, s 4 count for an offence which was committed before the first one and received 3 months consecutive. Both pleas were at the Crown Court. In the first offence (second plea) the victim was returning home in his car with his 14-year-old son and sounded his horn to encourage two youths who were fighting to move off the road. One of them shouted abuse and his car was hit. He stopped and he was sworn at so he left the car. A youth ran at him and fearing for his safety the victim struck him. A group of youths surrounded him shouting, "You're going to die" and other threats. The victim got back in his car and his car door was struck by a baseball bat. The bat was swung at the victim who ducked and it missed him. He drove home, called the police and went outside where about 20 youths were approaching the house. Wooden fencing was ripped up and wood and bricks were thrown at him and his family. A brick struck his father on the leg and a piece of wood struck his girlfriend. The police arrived and the group dispersed and when they left the group returned. More abuse was shouted. None of the witnesses identified the defendant then 15 in taking part in any of the violence and the case against him was based on an admission that he had been shouting abuse. The second incident was about 4 weeks later, (for details see **ABH**). He had a relatively minor dishonesty conviction and two dishonesty cautions. He was said to be remorseful and ashamed. He had been taken away from his family by the local authority. Held. The first incident was an utterly disgraceful and inexcusable episode, but abusive language by a 15 year old, however deplorable, **did not merit custody**. 4 months detention for the ABH and no separate penalty for the s 4 offence not 12 months in all.

149 PUBLIC ORDER ACT 1986 s 4A

149.1 Using threatening, abusive or insulting words or behaviour etc causing harassment etc with intent to cause harassment etc.

Public Order Act 1986, s 4A

43 Licensed Premises (Exclusion of Certain Persons) Act 1980 s 1(1)
44 Licensed Premises (Exclusion of Certain Persons) Act 1980 s 1(3)

Summary only. Maximum sentence 6 months[45] and/or Level 5 fine (£5,000).

Anti-Social Behavioural orders Where the defendant has acted in a manner that caused or was likely to cause harassment, alarm or distress to one or more persons not in the same household as the defendant and it is necessary to protect persons from further anti-social acts by him/her the court may make this order[46].

Licensed premises Where the offence is committed on licensed premises and the defendant resorted to violence or offered or threatened to resort to violence, the court may prohibit the defendant from entering those premises or any other specified premises without the express consent of the licensee or his agent[47]. The order shall last from 3 months to 2 years[48].

Magistrates' Court Sentencing Guidelines January 2004

149.2   For a first time offender pleading not guilty. Entry point. Is it serious enough for a community penalty? Consider the impact on the victim. Examples of aggravating factors for the offence are football related, group action, high degree of planning, night time offence, victim specifically targeted and weapon. An example of a mitigating factor for the offence is short duration. Examples of mitigation are age, health (physical or mental), co-operation with the police, genuine remorse and voluntary compensation. Give reasons if not awarding compensation.

For details about the guidelines see **MAGISTRATES' COURT SENTENCING GUIDELINES** at page 483.

150   PUBLIC ORDER ACT 1986 S 4 AND 4A – RACIALLY-AGGRAVATED

150.1   Fear or provocation of violence and intentional harassment, alarm or distress when the activity is racially aggravated.

Crime and Disorder Act 1998 s 31 and the Public Order Act 1986 s 4 and 4A

Triable either way. On indictment maximum 2 years. Summary maximum 6 months and/or £5,000.

Anti-Social Behavioural orders Where the defendant has acted in a manner that caused or was likely to cause harassment, alarm or distress to one or more persons not in the same household as the defendant and it is necessary to protect persons from further anti-social acts by him/her the court may make this order[49].

Licensed premises Where the offence is committed on licensed premises and the defendant resorted to violence or offered or threatened to resort to violence, the court may prohibit the defendant from entering those premises or any other specified premises without the express consent of the licensee or his agent[50]. The order shall last from 3 months to 2 years[51].

Sexual Offences Prevention Order For both offences there is a discretionary power to make this order when it is necessary to protect the public etc[52].

45 Where the jury convict the defendant of an offence under s 4 as an alternative to a racially-aggravated offence the maximum sentence at the Crown Court is the Magistrates' Courts maximum, Public Order Act 1986 s 7(4) and R v Alden 2002 2 Cr App R (S) 326
46 Crime and Disorder Act 1998 s 1C
47 Licensed Premises (Exclusion of Certain Persons) Act 1980 s 1(1)
48 Licensed Premises (Exclusion of Certain Persons) Act 1980 s 1(3)
49 Crime and Disorder Act 1998 s 1C
50 Licensed Premises (Exclusion of Certain Persons) Act 1980 s 1(1)
51 Licensed Premises (Exclusion of Certain Persons) Act 1980 s 1(3)
52 Sexual Offences Act 2003 s 104 & Sch. 5

Magistrates' Court Sentencing Guidelines January 2004 – Section 4

150.2   For a first time offender pleading not guilty. Entry point. Is it so serious that only custody is sufficient? Consider the impact on the victim. Examples of aggravating factors for the offence are group action, motivation for the offence was racial or religious, on hospital/medical or school premises, people put in fear, setting out to humiliate the victim, victim serving the public and vulnerable victim. Example of mitigating factors for the offence are minor matter and short duration. Examples of mitigation are age, health (physical or mental), co-operation with the police, genuine remorse and voluntary compensation. Give reasons if not awarding compensation.

For details about the guidelines see MAGISTRATES' COURT SENTENCING GUIDELINES at page 483.

Magistrates' Court Sentencing Guidelines January 2004 – Section 4A

150.3   For a first time offender pleading not guilty. Entry point. Is it so serious that only custody is appropriate? Consider the level of racial aggravation and the impact on the victim. Examples of aggravating factors for the offence are football related, group action, high degree of planning, motivation for the offence was racial or religious, night time offence, setting out to humiliate the victim, victim specifically targeted and weapon. An example of a mitigating factor for the offence is single incident. Examples of mitigation are age, health (physical or mental), co-operation with the police, evidence of genuine remorse and voluntary compensation. Give reasons if not awarding compensation.

For details about the guidelines see MAGISTRATES' COURT SENTENCING GUIDELINES at page 483.

General approach

See RACIALLY AGGRAVATED OFFENCES – *General approach*

Police officers, against

150.4   *R v Jesson* 2000 2 Cr App R (S) 200. The defendant pleaded guilty at the Magistrates' Court to racially aggravated threatening, abusive or insulting wordsor behaviour with intent to cause harassment etc. Police officers tried to arrest the defendant's cousin and the defendant intervened. He was abusive to an Asian police officer and brought his face close to the officer repeatedly. Each time the officer stepped back and told him to calm down. The defendant shouted, 'You Paki' and repeatedly shouted, 'Fuck off Paki.' He was arrested and in the interview said he was drunk. He had several previous convictions including a number for threatening behaviour andone for ABH for which he was sent to prison for 12 months. **6 months** substituted for 9 months.

R v Jacobs 2001 2 Cr App R (S) 174. The defendant was sentenced for racially-aggravated harassment and common assault. [Her plea is not revealed.] She was arrested and taken to a police station. While she was being searched a police officers asked her to remove her rings. She replied, 'I don't want you Paki filthy hands on me, I don't want that Paki touching me.' She spoke to the custody sergeant and continued to shout racial abuse and began to struggle. Later she shouted racial abuse in the cell. She admitted the offence in interview. She was 20 and had one public order previous conviction in 1997. **3 months** substituted for 9 months.

R v Fitzgerald 2004 1 Cr App R (S) 436. The defendant pleaded guilty to racially aggravated harassment. It was offered at the earliest opportunity. Police had been summoned to a shop where the defendant was being restrained by two members of the public. He was shouting obscenities at them and his nose was bleeding. He was handcuffed and struggled violently. He called one officer a "Fucking Nigger", "a whore" and "a cunt" and threatened her and her family. When police transport arrived he said "I want a white boy to do it, you fucking wog" and "Wog go back to where you came from, up a fuck-ing tree, wog, cunt." He was drunk. He was 40 and had seven previous convictions for harassment and many offences of violence (including wounding with intent). A signif-icant number were aimed at the police. Further threats were made at the police station. There was a negative pre-sentence report. The risk of further offending was assessed as high. Held. This was a case in which the racial aggravation of the offence was inherent and integral to the offence itself. It was not possible or sensible to assess the overall criminality involved in such a discrete way. In such cases, the Court must assess the seriousness of the conduct involved and its criminality as a whole. **10 months**, not 21.

Public officials, ticket collectors etc, against

150.5   *R v Miller* 1999 2 Cr App R (S) 392. The defendant pleaded guilty at the Magistrates' Court to racially aggravated threatening words and behaviour and travel-ling on a railway without a ticket. He was committed for sentence. Mr Shafi, a railway conductor approached the defendant on a train and asked to see his ticket. He hadn't got one and pretended he had lost it. The conductor pressed him and the defendant became abusive calling him a Paki. He was ordered to leave the train. The defendant refused and said, 'What's your problem? You're all the same you Pakis, why don't you fucking go back to India.' He was left on the platform and he continued to swear at Mr Shafi. He said, 'I feel like head-butting you. You fucking Paki, why don't you fuck off?' and 'You cunts are all the same, you Pakis.' The victim thought he was going to be hit and he found the incident so upsetting he went off work sick. The defendant was arrested and was abusive to the police. He was 35 with an appalling record. It included three robberies, three public order offences, two possessions of an offensive weapon, an affray, an ABH and a wounding. Held. The facts were weighted so heavily against him the discount for the plea was marginal. **18 months** was severe but fully justified.

151   PUBLIC ORDER ACT 1986 S 5

151.1   Using threatening, abusive or insulting words or behaviour etc likely to cause harassment etc.

Public Order Act 1986 s 5

Summary only. Maximum sentence Level 3 fine (£1,000).

Anti-Social Behavioural orders Where the defendant has acted in a manner that caused or was likely to cause harassment, alarm or distress to one or more persons not in the same household as the defendant and it is necessary to protect persons from further anti-social acts by him/her the court may make this order[53].

Fixed penalty £80 (£40 if under 16)[54]

Football The offence is a relevant offence under the Football Spectators Act 1989 s 14A and Sch 1, para 1. Where (a) the offence was committed during a period relevant to a football match and (b) the accused was at or attempting to enter or leave the prem-ises or journeying to and from the premises or the offence related to a match the court must make a Football Banning Order, where there are reasonable grounds to believe that making a banning order would help to prevent violence or disorder at or in con-nection with any regulated football match (except where the defendant is given an absolute discharge).

---

53 Crime and Disorder Act 1998 s 1C
54 The Penalties for Disorderly Behaviour (Amount of Penalty) Order 2002 Para 2 and Sch. Part II as amended.

Licensed premises Where the offence is committed on licensed premises and the defendant resorted to violence or offered or threatened to resort to violence, the court may prohibit the defendant from entering those premises or any other specified premises without the express consent of the licensee or his agent[55]. The order shall last from 3 months to 2 years[56].

Magistrates' Court Sentencing Guidelines January 2004

151.2   For a first time offender pleading not guilty. Entry point. Is a discharge or a fine appropriate? Consider the impact on the victim. Examples of aggravating factors for the offence are football related, group action and vulnerable victim. Examples of mitigating factors for the offence are stopped as soon as police arrived and trivial incident. Examples of mitigation are age, health (physical or mental), co-operation with the police, genuine remorse and voluntary compensation. Give reasons if not awarding compensation. Starting point fine B. (100% of weekly take home pay/weekly benefit payment)

For details about the guidelines see **MAGISTRATES' COURT SENTENCING GUIDELINES** at page 483.

152   PUBLIC ORDER ACT 1986 S 5 – RACIALLY OR RELIGIOUSLY AGGRAVATED

152.1   Crime and Disorder Act 1998 s 31 and the Public Order Act 1986 s 5

Summary only. Maximum fine Level 4, (£2,500).

Football The offence is a relevant offence under the Football Spectators Act 1989 s 14A and Sch 1, para 1. Where (a) the offence was committed during a period relevant to a football match and (b) the accused was at or attempting to enter or leave the premises or journeying to and from the premises or the offence related to a match the court must make a Football Banning Order, where there are reasonable grounds to believe that making a banning order would help to prevent violence or disorder at or in connection with any regulated football match (except where the defendant is given an absolute discharge).

Licensed premises Where the offence is committed on licensed premises and the defendant resorted to violence or offered or threatened to resort to violence, the court may prohibit the defendant from entering those premises or any other specified premises without the express consent of the licensee or his agent[57]. The order shall last from 3 months to 2 years[58].

General approach

See **RACIALLY AGGRAVATED OFFENCES** – *General approach*

Magistrates' Court Guidelines January 2004

152.2   For a first time offender pleading not guilty. Entry point. Is it serious enough for a community penalty? Consider the impact on the victim. Examples of aggravating factors for the offence are group action, motivation for the offence was racial or religious, setting out to humiliate the victim and vulnerable victim. Examples of mitigating factors for the offence are stopped as soon as police arrived and trivial incident. Examples of mitigation are age, health (physical or mental), co-operation with the police, genuine remorse and voluntary compensation. Give reasons if not awarding compensation.

For details about the guidelines see **MAGISTRATES' COURT SENTENCING GUIDELINES** at page 483.

---

55 Licensed Premises (Exclusion of Certain Persons) Act 1980 s 1(1)
56 Licensed Premises (Exclusion of Certain Persons) Act 1980 s 1(3)
57 Licensed Premises (Exclusion of Certain Persons) Act 1980 s 1(1)
58 Licensed Premises (Exclusion of Certain Persons) Act 1980 s 1(3)

QUEEN'S EVIDENCE, GIVING

See INFORMANTS/GIVING EVIDENCE FOR THE PROSECUTION

153 RACIAL REMARKS, JUDICIAL

Race of defendant, Judge referring to it

153.1 *R v George* 1994 Unreported 3/11/94. In sentencing the Judge referred to the colour of the defendants' skin. Held. In the normal case the colour, race and religion of the victims and defendants are wholly irrelevant. There may be exceptional cases such as public order offences inspired by racial or colour prejudice or religious beliefs, where reference to those motives and to the race, religion or colour of those involved as victims, or as offenders, will be necessary for a proper explanation to be made of the circumstances of the offence. This was not such a case. For a Judge to refer to the fact that the defendants were black can only leave in the minds of the defendants and their relatives and friends the suspicion that the defendants' colour was a factor in the judge's mind when he passed sentence. We make a specific reduction so there is no lingering sense of injustice.

R v Odewale and Others 2004 2 Cr App R (S) 240. The defendants were convicted of conspiracy to defraud financial institutions by means of identity theft. The judge said, 'a disproportionate number of participants in these sorts of crimes, are either Nigerians or people who have connections to other Nigerians, the court has a responsibility ... to seek to deter others'. Held. The judge should not have made those remarks and it is regrettable that he did so. The language used may well have given the impression that their Nigerian background added to the defendants' sentences. We take this specific failing into account when adjusting the sentences.

154 RACIALLY-AGGRAVATED OFFENCES

154.1 Crime and Disorder Act 1998 s 29–32

On indictment Offences Against the Person Act 1861 s 20, ABH, and Protection from Harassment Act 1997, s 4–7 years. Common assault, Public Order Act 1986 s 4 and 4A and Protection from Harassment Act 1997 s 2–2 years. Summary maximum 6 months and/or £5,000.

Public Order Act 1986 s 5 Summary only Maximum Level 4 fine (£2,500).

Magistrates' Court Sentencing Guidelines January 2004 Racially or religiously aggravated offences

154.2 There are special provisions on racial and religious aggravation, under the Crime and Disorder Act 1998 as amended. There are two forms of aggravation: an offence is racially or religiously aggravated EITHER if it is racially or religiouslymotivated, OR if in committing the offence the offender demonstrates racial or religious hostility (e.g. by making a racist remark). The guideline case for sentencingfor these offences is Kelly and Donnelly 2001, and three situations should be treated separately:

i) there are a few specific racially or religiously aggravated offences in the Crime and Disorder Act, which have higher maximum penalties than the non-aggravated versions of those offences (e.g. common assault, ABH, criminal damage, etc). Where a defendant is convicted of one of these special offences, the court should determine its sentence for the basic offence (such as criminal damage or assault), and then decide how much to add for the racial or religious aggravation. When the sentence is announced, the court should state how much it added to the basic offence in order to reflect the racial or religious aggravation.

ii) most offences do not have a specific racially or religiously aggravated version, however. Here, the general principle applies, which is that racial or religious aggravation is a factor that should increase the severity of the sentence.

iii) where an offender is convicted of an offence which has a racially or religiously aggravated version, but is convicted only of the basic offence, it is wrong in principle to pass a higher sentence on racial or religious grounds. If the racially or religiously aggravated version of the offence is not charged or not proved, that is the end of the matter.

General approach

154.3   *R v Saunders* 2000 2 Cr App R (S) 71. Racism must not be allowed to flourish. The message must be received and understood in every corner of our society. Racism is evil. Those who indulge in racially aggravated violence must expect to be punished severely. Generally speaking following a trial a period of up to 2 years should be added to the term of imprisonment otherwise appropriate. Consider the sentence in two stages. Relevant factors will include the nature of the hostile demonstration, its length, whether isolated, repeated, or persistent; its location, whether public or private; and the number both of those demonstrating and those demonstrated against.

R v Morrison 2001 1 Cr App R (S) 12. *R v Saunders* 2000 2 Cr App R (S) 71 does not mean that the maximum that can be added is 2 years. The amount will depend on all the circumstances.

R v Kelly and Donnelly 2001 2 Cr App R (S) 341. First determine what the appropriate sentence was for the offence without the racial element and then determine the appropriate sentence for the racial element. Each part should be publicly identified. The factors seriously aggravating the racial element in relation to the offender's intention are planning, the offence being part of a pattern of racist offending, membership of a group promoting racist activity, and the deliberate setting up of the victim for the purposes of humiliating him or being offensive towards him. The factors seriously aggravating the racial element in relation to the impact on the victim are if the offence took place in the victim's home, or the victim was particularly vulnerable, or providing a service to the public, or if the timing or location of the offence was such to maximise the harm or distressed caused, or the expressions of racial hostility were repeated or prolonged, or if fear and distress throughout a particular community resulted from the offence or if particular distress was caused to the victim or the victim's family. These factors should be added to the factors in *R v Saunders* 2000 2 Cr App R (S) 71.

R v Beglin 2003 1 Cr App R (S) 88. The defendant pleaded guilty to racially aggravated common assault. Held. Any offence that is racially aggravated is serious because of its impact not only on the victim but on the public who should rightly be outraged at such behaviour. The Court in *R v Kelly and Donnelly* 2001 2 Cr App R (S) 341 was astute not to provide any automatic mechanism in respect of the amount that should be added for racial aggravation, since there are so many factors which have to be taken into account which distinguish one racially aggravated assault from another. Counsel are obliged to draw the Court's attention to R v Kelly and Donnelly 2001 2 Cr App R (S) 341 and the Judge should announce what the two parts are.

R v O'Brien 2003 2 Cr App R (S) 390. The defendant pleaded to racially aggravated criminal damage. He was given 2 months with an uplift of 12 months making a 14 month sentence. The defence said the uplift was too great. Held. We note the Sentencing Advisory Panel recommended the two stage approach and an enhancement within the range of 40–70%, but the sentencer should not be constrained by those figure. There may be cases where the two stage approach is not appropriate. Take the case of a burning book, with slight monetary value but important racial or religious associations. There could be circumstances in which a mechanical or even the flexible application of the 40–70% will not be appropriate. It may fail to regard the overall view. There may be cases where the entire nature of the offence is changed by reason of the racial or religious aggravation. (For further details of the case see page **42.3**.)

R v Fitzgerald 2004 1 Cr App R (S) 436. The R v Kelly and Donnelly approach is not applicable in all cases. Here the racial aggravation is so inherent and integral to the offence it is not possible sensibly to assess the overall criminality in such a discrete way. In such cases the Court must assess the seriousness of the conduct and its criminality as a whole.

Joint enterprises

154.4   *R v Davies and Ely* 2004 2 Cr App R (S) 148. The defendants pleaded guilty to wounding with intent. A group attacked a mixed race victim. A witness heard a member of the group say, "You black bastard. I am going to cut you." The Judge found that as the group set off there was no element of racial motivation. He sentenced them to 5 years for the wounding with 1 years added to reflect the racial aggravation. Held. The Judge made no finding as to who said the offending words and it would have been impossible for him to do so. It is open to all members of the group to be convicted of the s 18 offence on a joint enterprise basis but that same basis is not apt to make all members of the group liable for the added aggravating feature. 5 years substituted.

Offences other than under the Crime and Disorder Act 1998 s 29–32

154.5   Powers of Criminal Courts (Sentencing) Act 2000 s 153. If an offence other than one under sections 29–32, was racially aggravated, the court shall treat that fact as an aggravating factor (i.e. increase the sentence) and shall state in open court that the offence was so aggravated. [Summarised.]

The following have racially or religiously aggravated chapters: **ABH**, **Burglary Common Assault**, **Criminal Damage**, **Harassment**, **s 2**, **Harassment**, **s 4**, **Offences Against the Person Act 1861**, **s 20**, **Public Order Act 1986** **s 4** and **4A**, **Public Order Act 1986** **s 5**,

See also **Threats to Kill** – *Racist defendants*

155   Racist Offences

Guideline remarks

155.1   *Att-Gen's Ref. Nos. 29–31 of 1994* 1995 16 Cr App R (S) 698. LCJ. It cannot be too strongly emphasised that where there is a racial element in an offence of violence, that is a gravely aggravating feature.

Possession of racially inflammatory material

155.2   Public Order Act 1986 s 23

Triable either way. On indictment maximum 2 years. Summary maximum 6 months and/or £5,000.

R v Gray 1999 1 Cr App R (S) 50. The defendant pleaded guilty to possession of racially inflammatory material with a view to distribute it. Three months after serving a three year sentence for assaulting a police officer police raided his address where he was living as a lodger. The prime occupier was his landlord. The house was used for the production of a right-wing magazine designed to appeal to the British National Party and football fans. The magazines contained violent intolerance of groups because of their race, religion and political views. The landlord was also the prime mover in the magazine. Five hundred copies were found and Eighty eight were in the defendant's bedroom. Held. Old cases are no longer an adequate guide to sentencing practice. **12 months** was not in any way excessive. As the offence was committed to soon after his release it was entirely appropriate for him so serve the outstanding period of the first sentence which the sentencing judge had made concurrent.

The following chapters have racially or religiously aggravated sections: ABH, BURGLARY, COMMON ASSAULT, CRIMINAL DAMAGE, HARASSMENT, S 2, HARASSMENT, S 4, OFFENCES AGAINST THE PERSON ACT 1861 S 20, PUBLIC ORDER ACT 1986 S 4 and 4A, PUBLIC ORDER ACT 1986 S 5,

See also THREATS TO KILL – *Racist defendants*

156 RAILWAY OFFENCES

156.1 Various offences and penalties including

Malicious Damage Act 1861 s 35

Placing wood etc on a railway etc with intent to obstruct or overthrow any engine etc.

Indictable only. Maximum Life.

Malicious Damage Act 1861 s 36

Obstructing engines or carriages on railways etc.

Triable either way. On indictment maximum 2 years. Summary maximum 6 months and/or £5,000.

Offences Against the Person Act 1861 s 32

Placing wood etc on railway etc with intent to endanger passengers.

Triable either way. On indictment maximum Life. Summary maximum 6 months and/or £5,000.

Dangerous Offender provisions For offences committed on or after 4/4/05 where there is a significant risk to members of the public of serious harm etc. there is a mandatory duty to pass a life sentence when it is justified and otherwise a sentence of imprisonment for public protection[1]. For offenders under 18 the duty is to pass detention for life, detention for public protection or an extended sentence[2].

Sexual Offences Prevention Order For Offences Against the Person Act 1861 s 32 there is a discretionary power to make this order when it is necessary to protect the public etc[3].

Offences Against the Person Act 1861 s 33

Casting stones etc on railway etc with intent to endanger passengers.

Indictable only. Maximum Life.

Offences Against the Person Act 1861 s 34

Doing or omitting anything so as to endanger passengers etc.

Triable either way. On indictment maximum 2 years. Summary maximum 6 months and/or £5,000.

1 Criminal Justice Act 2003 s 226 and 228
2 Sexual Offences Act 2003 s 104 & Sch. 5
3 Powers of Criminal Courts (Sentencing) Act 2000 s 109(5)

Crown Court statistics – England and Wales – Males 21+
156.2

| Year | Plea | Total Numbers sentenced | Type of sentence % | | | | | Average length of custody (months) |
			Discharge	Fine	Community sentence	Suspended sentence	Custody	
2002	Guilty	–	–	–	–	–	–	
	Not guilty	1	–	–	100	–	–	–
2003	Guilty	1	–	–	100	–	–	–
	Not guilty	1	–	–	–	–	100	12

For details and explanations about the statistics in the book see page vii

Defendant under 16

156.3   *R v H* 2000 2 Cr App R (S) 280. The defendant pleaded guilty to three counts of placing obstructions on a railway. (Because of the sentence imposed it is assumed it was under s 35.) He, when 14 placed a concrete troughing lid on a railway line which was struck by a train. He did the same again four days later and the lid was also hit by a train. Three days later a train hit another obstruction. In no case was there any injury or serious accident. The defendant and his co-defendant aged 22 were arrested and made full admissions. However, they both blamed each other. They had envisaged themselves as some sort of private army and gave themselves a quasi-military status. They wore military style clothing. The defendant was given 5 years and since his sentence had made excellent progress. A report said he had learnt a salutary lesson and developed a heightened awareness of the reason he had offended. Held. The danger was plain for all to see. Obstructions can cause the most horrendous accidents. The age differential was so great the primary responsibility must be borne by the older defendant. Because of his age, the reports and mercy **3 years** detention substituted.

R v S and P 2004 1 Cr App R (S) 94. The defendant P pleaded guilty and S was convicted of placing matter on a railway line with intent to obstruct an engine. They placed a concrete troughing lid across the tracks on the Birmingham to Wolverhampton railway line. It was on an embankment just before a bridge. The lid was 2′–3′ long and normally rested by the side of the track. An office worker saw the boys and ran to remove the lid. A train hit the lid and dust and bits of concrete showered the office worker. The train continued undamaged, but there was potential damage and derailment. The track speed limit was 60 mph. P's basis of plea was he intended to disintegrate the lid but not derail the train. P was aged 14 and S 12. Both were of good character. P gave evidence for the prosecution. S was described as less mature and naïve. Held. Given the self-evident danger of a serious accident which might have led to loss of life it must be custody. But because of *R v H* 2000 2 Cr App R (S) 280 **2 years detention** not 3. (This case won't encourage many people to plead and give evidence for the prosecution. Ed.)

Defendant aged 16–17

156.4   *R v Leech* 2001 Unreported 8/11/01. A 16 year old pleaded guilty to three counts of endangering passengers (s 34). He dropped a 32 lb boulder onto the track which was hit by a train. The other offences were a piece of wood and a stone on other days. He was of good character. **18 months** detention and training upheld.

Endangering passengers

156.5   *R v Keane* 2002 1 Cr App R (S) 383. The defendant pleaded guilty to endangering the safety of rail passengers (Offences Against the Person Act 1861, s 34) and failing to surrender to his bail. The defendant dragged a bench along the platform of South Croydon Station and threw it onto the track. Moments later a train travelling at 55 mph struck the bench which caught under its front and it became entangled with the train's front axle. After the train had stopped the driver spoke to the defendant. The defendant said he had worked on the railways for 30 years. In fact he was sacked from his job on the railway in 1995 because of alcohol problems. After the conductor had left the train the defendant entered the conductor's van with a key he already had. He stole the conductor's jacket and £20 cash which was in a pocket. No-one was injured but an expert said if the bench had wrapped round one of the wheels the train would probably have derailed. Police stopped the defendant and he was heavily intoxicated. He said he had little recollection of what had happened but was angry about being sacked. He failed to answer to his bail and was arrested nearly four months later. The defendant was 58 and had no convictions but had a long-standing problem with drink. There was a letter saying he was a hard working and conscientious member of the local community. The judge said he must have caused the driver very considerable alarm and a great deal of inconvenience to passengers. Held. **15 months** cannot be faulted, but 1 month not 3 months consecutive for the bail offence.

See also **HEALTH AND SAFETY OFFENCES** – *Railway accidents*

157   RAPE

157.1   Sexual Offences Act 2003 s 1

Sexual Offences Act 2003 s 5 (when the victim is a child under 13)

For offences committed before 1/5/04 the offence is contrary to Sexual Offences Act 1956 s 1. The new section widens the offence to include oral penetration by a penis. It also restricts the defence of lack of consent.

All three offences are indictable only with a maximum sentence of life.

CHAPTERS in this book are in bold capitals. The *paragraph titles* are in bold italics. Where a chapter (e.g. arson) has subsections, the **subsections** are in lower case bold.

Automatic life All three offences (incl. attempts) committed before 4/4/05 are specified offences for automatic life[4].

Dangerous Offender provisions For both offences committed on or after 4/4/05 where there is a significant risk to members of the public of serious harm etc. there is a mandatory duty to pass a life sentence when it is justified and otherwise a sentence of imprisonment for public protection[5]. For offenders under 18 the duty is to pass detention for life, detention for public protection or an extended sentence[6].

Longer than Commensurate sentences and Extended sentences All three offences are sexual offences[7] for the purposes of passing a longer than commensurate sentence [Powers of Criminal Courts (Sentencing) Act 2000 s 80(2)] and an extended sentence (extending the licence) [Powers of Criminal Courts (Sentencing) Act 2000 s 85(2)(b)]. These provisions will continue to apply to offences committed after 29/9/98 and before 4/4/05. See **LONGER THAN COMMENSURATE SENTENCES** and **LONGER THAN COMMENSURATE SENTENCES**.

Notification For all three offences the defendant must notify the police within 3 days (or 3 days from his release from imprisonment, hospital etc.) with his name, home

---

4   Criminal Justice Act 2003 s 226 and 228
5   Sexual Offences Act 2003 s 104 & Sch. 5
6   Powers of Criminal Courts (Sentencing) Act 2000 s 109(5)
7   Criminal Justice Act 2003 s 225

address, national insurance number etc. and any change and addresses where he resides for 7 days[8] (in one or more periods) or more in any 12 month period[9]. See SEX OFFENDERS' REGISTER

Working with children Where (a) the offence is against a child (aged under 18), (b) the defendant is aged 18 or over and (c) he is sentenced to 12 months or more or a hospital order etc. the court *must* disqualify him from working with children unless satisfied he is unlikely to commit any further offences against a child when the court must state its reasons for not doing so[10]. For a defendant aged less than 18 at the time of the offence the court must order disqualification if he is sentenced to 12 months or more and the court is satisfied that the defendant is likely to commit a further offence against a child[11]. The court must state its reasons for so doing.

Sexual Offences Prevention Order For all three offences, there is a discretionary power to make this order when it is necessary to protect the public etc[12].

Sentencing trends. Most of the recent sentences passed have been loyal to *R v Billam* 1986 82 Cr App R 347 and *R v Millberry* 2003 2 Cr App R (S) 142. The Attorney-General has made widespread use of his power to appeal sentences in sex cases which will no doubt mean that judges who pass lenient sentences will be less likely to do so. There is a consistency and predictability absent in the sentencing of many other offences. Life sentences are going to be even more common.

Crown Court statistics – England and Wales – Males 21+
157.2

Year	Plea	Total Numbers sentenced	Type of sentence %					Average length of custody (months)
			Discharge	Fine	Community sentence	Suspended sentence	Custody	
Rape of a female								
2002	Guilty	212	–	–	2	0	96	80.6
	Not guilty	334	0	0	0	–	99	90.2
2003	Guilty	216	–	–	0	0	98	81.8
	Not guilty	346	–	–	–	–	99	92Class B
Rape of a male								
2002	Guilty	14	–	–	–	–	100	77
	Not guilty	21	–	–	–	–	100	97.4
2003	Guilty	12	–	–	–	–	92	80.7
	Not guilty	21	–	–	–	–	100	97.9

For details and explanations about the statistics in the book see page vii.

Guideline case

157.3 *R v Millberry* 2003 2 Cr App R (S) 142. (R v Millberry 2003 confirms the guidance *in R v Billam* 1986 8 Cr App R (S) 48 with expansions. Ed)

We act on the advice of the Sentencing Advisory Panel. The courts should consider; (1) the degree of harm to the victim; (2) the level of culpability of the offender; and (3) the level of risk proposed by the offender to society. While rape will always be a

8   Criminal Justice Act 2003 s 226 and 228
9   Powers of Criminal Courts (Sentencing) Act 2000 s 161(2)(a)
10 Sexual Offences Act 2003 s 84(1)(c) & (6)
11 Criminal Justice and Court Services Act 2000 s 29
12 Sexual Offences Act 2003 s 104 & Sch. 3

most serious offence, its gravity will depend very much upon the circumstances of the particular case.

Length of the custodial sentence

What should be the starting points for sentences after a contested trial? In R v Billam 1986 **5 years** was the figure in a contested case where there was no aggravating feature, **8 years** the figure where there were certain aggravating features and **15 years plus** for a defendant who has carried out a campaign of rape. **Life imprisonment** was 'not inappropriate' if the offenders behaviour, 'has manifested perverted or psychopathic tendencies or gross personality disorder where the offender is likely, if at large, to remain a danger to women for an indefinite time'.

The **5 year** starting point

5 years should continue to be appropriate for a single offence of rape on an adult victim by a single offender manifesting none of the features after a contested trial.

Aggravating factors

The Panel identified nine aggravating factors. (The panel at para 32 of their report said, "These factors would indicate a sentence of above the 5 year starting point. The presence of one or more such factors could, depending on the degree of their seriousness, raise the sentence about the starting point of 8 years." It is to be assumed the Court of Appeal is inviting a similar approach.) The nine factors are:

i.   The use of violence over and above the force necessary to commit the rape

ii.   The use of a weapon to frighten or injure the victim

iii. The offence was planned

iv.   An especially serious physical or mental effect on the victim; this would include, for example, a rape resulting in pregnancy, or in transmission of a life-threatening or serious disease

v.   Further degradation of the victim, e.g. by forced oral sex or urination on the victim (referred to in Billam as 'further sexual indignities or perversions')

vi.   The offender has broken into or otherwise gained access to the place where the victim is living (mentioned in Billam as a factor attracting the eight-year starting point)

vii. The presence of children when the offence is committed (c.f. *R v Collier* 1992 13 Cr App R (S) 33)

viii. The covert use of a drug to overcome the victim's resistance and/or obliterate his or her memory of the offence

ix.   A history of sexual assaults or violence by the offender against the victim.

Extended and longer than commensurate sentences

In all cases of rape, Sentencers should consider whether it would be appropriate to impose a longer than commensurate sentence or an extended sentence or both under PCC(S)A 2000, s 80 and 85.

The 8 year starting point

After a contested trial where there is present any of the following features:

i)   the rape is committed by two or more offenders acting together;

ii)   the offender is in a position of responsibility towards the victim (e.g. in the relationship of medical practitioner and patient, teacher and pupil); or the offender is a person in whom the victim has placed his or her trust by virtue of his office or employment (e.g. a clergyman, an emergency services patrolman, a taxi driver, or a police officer);

iii) the offender abducts the victim and holds him or her captive;

iv) the rape of a child, or a victim who is especially vulnerable because of physical frailty, mental impairment or disorder, or learning disability;

v) racially aggravated rape, and other cases where the victim has been targeted because of his or her membership of a vulnerable minority (e.g. homophobic rape);

vi) repeated rape in the course of one attack (including cases where the same victim has been both vaginally and anally raped);

vii) the rape by a man who is knowingly suffering from a life-threatening sexually transmissible disease, whether or not he has told the victim of his condition and whether or not the disease was actually transmitted.

The **8 year** starting point is recommended either because of the impact of the offence upon the victim or the level of the offender's culpability, or both. The Panel adds that factors reflecting a high level of risk to society, in particular evidence of repeat offending, will indicate a substantially longer sentence. The seven grounds for raising the starting point to eight years each can, depending on the circumstances, vary in gravity. In a really bad case it can mean a higher figure is appropriate.

15-year starting point

15 years and upwards is the starting point for a campaign of rape. This is recommended where the offender has repeatedly raped the same victim over a course of time as well as for those cases involving multiple victims.

Life sentence

A **life sentence** will not be 'inappropriate' where the offender 'has manifested perverted or psychopathic tendencies or gross personality disorder, and where he is likely, if at large, to remain a danger to women for an indefinite time'. Unless there are exceptional circumstances (as now defined in *R v Offen* 2001 2 Cr App R (S) 44) if a defendant has a previous conviction for rape or a conviction for another serious offence he will be subject to an automatic sentence of life imprisonment under the Powers of Criminal Courts (Sentencing) Act 2000 s 109.

Mitigating factors and guilty pleas

The reason why the courts are prepared to and should reduce sentences substantially for a guilty plea is because it is well known that victims of rape can find it an extremely distressing experience to give evidence in open court about what has happened to them, even where their identity is protected. Having to give evidence, and especially being cross-examined, can make a victim relive the offence. We have seen many victim impact statements that make this clear. Obviously the distress which is avoided is greater the earlier the victim is informed so the discount should be reduced if there is not an early plea. There is also the fact that the plea demonstrates that the offender appreciates how wrong his conduct was and regrets it. While it is desirable to avoid taking up the time of the court and incurring expense unnecessarily, this is less important in mitigation than the other two factors we have just mentioned. We stress that the maximum credit should only be given for a timely guilty plea.

The defendant's good character

While the fact that an offender has previous convictions for sexual or violent offences can be a significant aggravating factor, the defendant's good character, although it should not be ignored, does not justify a substantial reduction of what would otherwise be the appropriate sentence.

The role of guidelines

We would emphasise that guidelines can produce sentences which are inappropriately high or inappropriately low if sentencers merely adopt a mechanistic approach to the guidelines. It is essential that having taken the guidelines into account, sentencers stand back and look at the circumstances as a whole and impose the sentence which is appropriate having regard to all the circumstances. Double accounting must be avoided and can be a result of guidelines if they are applied indiscriminately.

Guideline remarks

157.4 *Att-Gen's Ref. No. 6 of 2002* 2003 1 Cr App R (S) 357. Held. Where aggravating features have to be taken into account, there is no artificial limit beyond which the court cannot go in reflecting those aggravating features.

Att-Gen's Ref. No. 91 119 and 120 of 2002 2003 2 Cr App R (S) 338. Courts should consider 1, the degree of harm to the victim, 2, the culpability of the offender and 3, the risk posed by the offender. In all classes of sexual offences there will also be the need to deter others.

Abduction/false imprisonment etc, and – Guideline cases

157.5   On 1/5/04[13] the offences of abduction was repealed[14].

R v Millberry 2003 2 Cr App R (S) 142. LCJ. Guideline case The **8 year** starting point is appropriate after a contested trial where the offender abducts the victim and holds him or her captive. The **8 year** starting point is recommended either because of the impact of the offence upon the victim or the level of the offender's culpability, or both. The Panel adds that factors reflecting a high level of risk to society, in particular evidence of repeat offending, will indicate a substantially longer sentence. The seven grounds for raising the starting point to eight years each can vary in gravity. In a really bad case it can mean a higher figure is appropriate.

Abduction/false imprisonment etc., and – Cases

157.6 *Att-Gen's Ref. No 27 of 1998* 1999 1 Cr App R (S) 259. The defendant was convicted of false imprisonment, ABH, rape, attempted rape and indecent assault. In 1995 there was an arranged marriage in Pakistan between the defendant and the victim. She came to England and lived with the defendant and his brother, mother and sister. She was prevented from leaving and when they moved from Preston she was humiliated, abused and mocked. She was prevented from speaking to her family in Pakistan and having contact with the outside world. She did not share her husband's bedroom. She was not permitted to do anything without the permission of her mother in law. When she passed a note to a neighbour he told her not to speak to neighbours without his permission. He hit her, threw her against the floor and raped her. He tried to anally rape her. The police arrived and the victim was seen by a doctor. She had a healing laceration to her neck, two small lacerations and tenderness to her face and three anal fissures, which were sufficiently tender that an internal examination was not possible. She had lacerations and/or abrasions on her hand, back, legs and breast. The false imprisonment lasted 8–10 weeks. He was 28 and was of good character with testimonials. He was under the influence of his mother. The victim had discussed with him the possibility of reconciliation. His mother, brother and sister were also convicted of false imprisonment. Held. The sentences of **4½ years** for the rape and **1 year consecutive** for the false imprisonment **were lenient**. The judge was particularly well placed to impose appropriate sentences. Neither sentence nor the total were unduly lenient.

---

13 Sexual Offences Act 2003 (Commencement Order) 2004
14 Sexual Offences Act 2003 s 140 & Sch 7

R v E 2000 1 Cr App R (S) 78. The defendant pleaded guilty to two rapes and false imprisonment. Five months after his release from prison he lay in wait in the evening for a 58-year-old widow who lived in the same block of flats as he did to return. When she did he forced her into his flat and brutally raped her. Threatening her with a knife he forced her upstairs to her flat and raped her again. The victim was then kept in her flat against her will until the next afternoon. The first rape was violently painful. In 1992 he had been convicted of two counts of rape on his stepdaughter when she was between the ages of 12 and 16. He repeatedly raped her over 4 years. He had received 10 years. After 8 years he was released on licence. The judge passed an automatic life sentence considering 18 years would have been appropriate otherwise. Held. The rapes were extremely bad. The appropriate determinate sentence would have been **15 years** not 18.

R v McStay 2003 1 Cr App R (S) 176. The defendant was convicted of rape, indecent assault, false imprisonment and theft. The victim an, 18 year old virgin, worked in a restaurant as a waitress where the defendant aged 35 worked in a more responsible position. The two stayed behind at the end of an evening for a cup of coffee after the restaurant had closed. He started kissing her and would not stop when she tried to push him away. He put her under his arm and carried her to the locker room despite her screams. He put her to the floor and pushed some industrial waste paper tissue in her mouth. He took a roll of sellotape and wrapped it round her head many times. She was forced to breathe through her nose. He then forced himself on top of her and attempted rape. She continued to protest and struggle. He told her it would not take long and his anger increased. She wanted to go to the lavatory and he stood over her while she relieved herself. He next removed the tape and made her kneel and pushed his penis into her mouth. Then he gagged her and pushed her to the floor. Next she was dragged to a booth where he raped her and ejaculated. She was allowed to leave in abject distress. The incident lasted about two hours. He then took money from the restaurant and fled. Physical injury to her was relatively modest. In 1993 he was convicted of rape The Judge gave him automatic life. Held. It was a protracted ordeal, late at night with imprisonment, gagging and repeated sexual indignities. There was not a scrap of remorse. In this sort of case the bracket goes **up to 15 years**. The notional term of 15 years was at the top end but not manifestly excessive.

Old cases. *R v Dooley* 1994 15 Cr App R (S) 703; *Att-Gen's Ref. No 16 of 1993* 1994 15 Cr App R (S) 811 and *R v Masood* 1997 2 Cr App R (S) 137 (for a summary of the case see **157.39**).

Acquaintance rape

157.7 *R v Millberry* 2003 2 Cr App R (S) 142. LCJ. The starting point is that cases of 'relationship rape' and 'acquaintance rape' are to be treated as being of equal seriousness to cases of 'stranger rape', with the sentence increased or reduced, in each case, by the presence of specific aggravating or mitigating factors. Rape is rape, and cannot be divided in this way into more and less serious offences. It can be just as traumatic to be raped by someone you know and trust who has chosen you as his victim, as by a stranger who sexually assaults the first man or woman who passes by. It is up to the courts to take all particular circumstances of a case into account before determining the appropriate penalty.

R v Devitt 2001 2 Cr App R (S) 354. The defendant was convicted of rape. Previously he had had sex with the victim about six times. She said they were dating rather than in a serious relationship. He said he was in love. He arrived at her house and asked for sex but she told him to leave, which he did. The next day she decided he was to be told that she did not want to see him again. Three days later he went to her house with a friend and was told she did not want to see him again and to leave. He did but he tapped on the window and eventually she let him back in to talk. They talked for about 2¹/₂ hours with her children upstairs. He began to touch her thigh and she made it clear she wasn't interested in sex. He put his leg over hers and pulled down his tracksuit bottoms. He pulled her head towards his groin. She pushed him away and moved to another sofa. She made it clear she wanted him to go and he locked the front door and put the key in his pocket. He called her a bitch and threatened her. She was extremely frightened and he pushed her head aggressively. She was worried about the children and that he had the key. She went upstairs because she didn't think he would do anything with her daughter in the bedroom. He grabbed the daughter and lashed out at the victim. He apologised to the daughter and took her to her room. He returned, ordered the victim about and kicked her several times in the chest. He told her how he had battered a friend and she was going to be taught a lesson and that she made him sick. She was told how he was going to hurt her, and he forced her to perform oral sex and he performed oral sex on her. He raped her after he had put his fingers in her vagina. After 5 minutes he ejaculated. The victim suffered bruising. When interviewed he said she consented. He was 27 years old, and had served 15 months in custody before but had no sex convictions. Held. **8 years** not altered, but it was wrong to extend the licence by 4 years.

Old case. *R v Diggle* 1995 16 Cr App R (S) 163.

Aiding and abetting etc

157.8 *Att-Gen's Ref. No 12 of 2001* 2002 2 Cr App R (S) 382. [The defendant aided and abetted the rape of a baby of some friends by her partner. 4 years was lenient but not disturbed.]

Old case *R v Reid* 1998 2 Cr App R (S) 10, (for a summary of this case see the first edition of this book.)

AIDS

157.9 See *Sexually transmitted disease – Defendant has*, DEFENDANT – *AIDS, Defendant has* and VICTIMS – *Victim fears she will contract AIDS from sex attack*

Anal rape – (female victim)

157.10 *R v Millberry* 2003 2 Cr App R (S) 142. Guideline case LCJ. There is no inherent distinction between anal and vaginal rape. Where a victim is raped both vaginally and anally by the offender, this should be treated (for the purposes of the higher starting point) as repeated rape.

R v Bowley 1999 1 Cr App R (S) 232. The defendant was convicted of anal rape of a woman. The defendant had been drinking with the victim, who was a 34-year-old married woman and other patrons in a pub. The group drunk a lot and engaged in a game of strip poker. The defendant had made it clear to the victim that he wanted sex with her and during the evening had kissed her. In the early hours of the morning the victim drove herself home and was followed by the defendant. The victim's car suffered two burst tyres and she was persuaded by the defendant to accept his offer of a lift home. The defendant did not stop at the woman's house but drove to a nearby car park. The victim feared for her safety and jumped from the car, however as a consequence she lost consciousness. When the victim awoke she was on the backseat of the car and the defendant was having anal intercourse with her. She received bruises and abrasions. The defendant was 37 and had no convictions. The judge described it as dreadful, humiliating, degrading and painful. Held. The fact that this was anal rape was a powerful aggravating feature. The fact that the victim was unconscious or semi-conscious, D had taken advantage of her drunken state and he drove past her house to a car park were all also aggravating factors. **7 years** was not so severe we should quash it.

R v H 1999 1 Cr App R (S) 470. The defendant pleaded guilty to two counts of rape on his estranged wife and one count of possessing a firearm with intent to cause fear. The defendant had been married for 13 years although the marriage had deteriorated. Following incidents of violence and sexual abuse the wife moved out of their home. The victim went to the defendant's house during her lunch break after a request by the defendant and was detained for 4–4½ hours. During this time she was sexually assaulted, anally raped twice and terrified by the defendant brandishing a handgun. She was also assaulted and threatened and in constant fear of being shot. She received bruises and abrasions and was in considerable pain. The defendant was a fireman who had been traumatised by the misery and violence he had seen. He had lapsed into drink, drugs and violence. Since his conviction the defendant realised the full extent of his actions He had sought and obtained help. His wife had considerably forgiven him his conduct. He received 10 years for the anal rape and lesser concurrent sentences for the other counts. Held. Due to the defendant's improvement of attitude **7 years** was more appropriate than 10 years.

R v Triggs 2000 2 Cr App R (S) 179. The defendant was convicted of attempted rape and anal rape. The victim aged 13 had an argument with her mother, packed her bags and left home. She went to some grassland and was reading a book when the defendant approached her from behind. He dragged her into some bushes and held a knife to her throat. He undressed her and unsuccessfully tried to rape her. Then he anally raped her. The victim had three small tears in her anus. The defendant was 28 with 14 previous convictions including a firearm offence but no sex offences. He had a very rudimentary knowledge of sexuality and relationships. He had little education and a number of other problems from his childhood. The judge said there was a very real risk of further offending and causing serious harm. Later an expert said the risk was low. **12 years** not 14 years.

R v Persico 2004 1 Cr App R (S) 262. The Judge sentenced the defendant saying anal rape was more serious. Sentence reduced.

See also *R v Ishizawa* 1998 Unreported 10/12/98.

See also *Male rape* and BUGGERY

Attempted rape – Is it a violent offence?

157.11   *R v Robinson* 1993 96 Cr App R 418. Attempted rape was a violent offence for the purposes of the Powers of Criminal Courts (Sentencing) Act 2000 s 80(2)(b) previously the Criminal Justice Act 1991, s 2(2)(b). (The court is able to pass longer than normal sentences and extend the sentences, for offences committed before 4/4/05.)

Attempted rape – Guideline case

157.12   *R v Billam* 1986 82 Cr App R 347. LCJ. The starting point for attempted rape should normally be less than for the completed offence, especially if it is desisted at a comparatively early stage. But, attempted rape may be made by aggravating features into an offence even more serious than some examples of the full offence. (*R v Millberry* 2003 2 Cr App R (S) 142 did not refer to attempted rape)

Attempted rape – Cases

157.13   *R v Mills* 1998 2 Cr App R (S) 252. The defendant pleaded guilty to attempted rape, having called the victim as a witness at the committal hearing. Two weeks after being told his relationship with the victim was over he waited for her to return to her house. He had been drinking. When she returned at about 2am he dragged her down the road and pushed her to a grassy area. He took out his penis but had no erection. He made threats to kill her and ripped away at her tights. She struggled and after a verbal exchange he desisted. He pulled her to her feet and punched her. He started to take her to a nearby garage but she managed to escape. He told police he had drunk 10 pints of beer. He had a conviction for manslaughter when after drinking he had fought with another man. Both he and the victim had weapons. The rape victim attended the Court of Appeal saying they 'were back together'. Held. The fact the offence was not completed was not without its importance. **3 years** not 6.

R v Kamil 2004 1 Cr App R (S) 460. The defendant was convicted of attempted rape. A party was held by some students including the defendant, the victim and her boyfriend. Late in the evening the victim and her boyfriend were shown to their bedroom for the night. They had sex in that room and then returned to the party. They went upstairs again at about midnight when they were intimate again after which the boyfriend went downstairs to the party and the victim went to sleep. The next thing she remembered was being awoken in the early hours by a movement on top of her. She realised that it was not her boyfriend. The defendant was pushing into her body but was too high to enter her vagina. She was scared and shouted. She pulled herself up. The defendant stepped back off the bed holding his trousers and tried to do up his flies. He opened the door which hit a bedside table that had been placed close to the door and left the room. The victim went downstairs to find her boyfriend, crying hysterically. Police were called and later found the defendant. He declined to answer any questions in interview. The attack had a very serious effect on her and her family as well as a devastating effect on the defendant's family. He was of good character. Held. The defendant desisted as soon as the victim awoke. Bearing in mind his age and his good character, **3 years** not 4.

See also *Att-Gen's Ref. No 6 of 1998* 2 Cr App R (S) 423. **8 years** imprisonment for a series of attempted rapes on a social worker over the period of about one hour.

Old cases. *Att-Gen's Ref. No 11 of 1993* 1994 15 Cr App R (S) 490; *R v Diggle* 1995 16 Cr App R (S) 163.

Breach of trust/in a position of responsibility to victim

157.14   *R v Millberry* 2003 2 Cr App R (S) 142. Guideline case LCJ. The **8 year** starting point is appropriate after a contested trial the offender is in a position of responsibility towards the victim (e.g. in the relationship of medical practitioner and patient, teacher and pupil); or the offender is a person in whom the victim has placed his or her trust by virtue of his office or employment (e.g. a clergyman, an emergency services patrolman, a taxi driver, or a police officer). The **8 year** starting point is recommended either because of the impact of the offence upon the victim or the level of the offender's culpability, or both. The Panel adds that factors reflecting a high level of risk to society, in particular evidence of repeat offending, will indicate a substantially longer sentence. The seven grounds for raising the starting point to eight years each can vary in gravity. In a really bad case it can mean a higher figure is appropriate.

Att-Gen's Ref. No 51 of 2001 2002 1 Cr App R (S) 80. 8 years' imprisonment for a man who raped an 18 year old girl who was the daughter of his friend, and whom she called 'uncle'.

Att-Gen's Ref. Nos. 35 etc. of 2003 Re Coles 2004 1 Cr App R (S) 499 at 515. The defendant was convicted of rape, attempted rape and 3 indecent assaults. He ran a modelling agency promoting aspiring models. The first victim was 18 and was persuaded to have nude photographs taken by the defendant. He raped her without a condom, to ejaculation, ignoring her pleas to stop. She sought treatment for rashes and bumps as a result of the activity. The second victim (aged 25) posed nude and was jumped on by the defendant; he touched her breasts and vaginal area and then tried to force her legs apart. He digitally penetrated her (indecent assault). The third victim (aged 21) was lying naked on a bed during a photographic shoot when the offender pinned her down and attempted to kiss her. He tried to take his trousers down. She shouted "Fuck off" and the defendant got off her. He was convicted of attempted rape. The fourth victim (aged 29) was also was persuaded to have nude photographs taken. The defendant jumped on her and tried to pin her down; she managed to get away. The fifth victim (aged 18) posed nude and had explicit photographs taken. The defendant digitally penetrated her before she was able to get away without further harm. The defendant was 41 with convictions for violence that were between 22 and 8 years old. He had no convictions for sexual offences. Held. He deliberately placed himself in a position on five separate occasions where he knew that such an opportunity might present itself to him with total disregard for the wishes of the women involved. The offences were a breach of trust and there was a continuing risk. A total sentence of **10 years** should have been passed (**7 years** for rape, 3 years consecutive for attempted rape and 18 months for each indecent assault). As this was a reference, **8 years** (7 years for the rape and 12 months consecutive for each other offences, but concurrent to each other) not 7.

Att-Gen's Ref. No 3 of 2002 2004 1 Cr App R (S) 357. The defendant was convicted of two counts of rape and ten counts of indecent assault. The defendant was a psychiatrist. Twenty years ago MR had been referred to him by her GP. She was vulnerable and had disabilities. After several months of counselling the defendant suggested that they should have a sexual relationship. He touched her breast but she pushed him away (indecent assault). Twenty one years ago, SMF, a student nurse, was having difficulties in her marriage and had suffered a breakdown. She fell under the defendant's spell and in the end she was persuaded against her will to submit to sexual intercourse. This happened twice. The experience had damaged her relationships with men (rape × 2). Another patient, AS, was a nurse who was initially treated for anorexia. The defendant kissed her passionately and put a hand between her legs in the area of her crotch (indecent assault x 2). Eighteen years ago, PAH was referred to him for an eating disorder. She complained of a bad back. He positioned himself behind her, placed his hands just over her hips, slid his left hand down, took hold of her crotch and kissed the back of her head (indecent assault). After a complaint from another patient, the defendant was suspended (sixteen years ago). Six years later he took up private practice where HSM started to see him and became dependant on the counselling sessions. She was persuaded to start a sexual relationship with him and masturbated him. He also penetrated her digitally and other similar offences occurred. After five years he ended the relationship (indecent assault × 3). After that relationship a 16/17 year old, NAH, started treatment at the defendant's house. He groomed her over a period of time before massaging her breasts under her bra, her front and her buttocks (indecent assault). Held. The two rapes were a serious breach of trust between a medical practitioner and a patient. The proper sentence ought to have been **above 8 years**. It had been right to sentence the defendant for consecutive sentences for the offences that occurred after he had been suspended. The breach of trust element was a serious aggravating feature and occurred over a period of time (see *R v Propkop* 1995 16 Cr App R (S) 598 and *R v Pike* 1996 1 Cr App R (S) 4). These most recent indecent assaults should have attracted sentences of the **very least 4 years**. The total sentence should have been **12 years**. Hence, because this was a reference, for the rapes **7 years**; for the recent indecent assaults, **3 years** consecutive, making a total of **10 years** not 8.

Old cases. *Att-Gen's Ref. No 11 of 1993* 15 Cr App R (S) 490; *R v Angol 1994* 15 Cr App R (S) 727; *R v Mason 1995* 16 Cr App R 860 and *R v Sellars 1998* 1 Cr App R 117. (For a summary of the last case see the first edition of this book.)

See also *Fathers, by and, Stepfathers/step grandfathers, Victim aged less than 10, Victim aged 13–15*

Brother, by and INCEST

Burglars/robbers, by

157.15 *R v Millberry* 2003 2 Cr App R (S) 142. A sentence above **5 years** as the starting point is appropriate when one of the nine aggravating factors is present. The presence of one or more such factors could, depending on the degree of their seriousness, raise the sentence above the starting point of 8 years. Factor vi is "the offender has broken into or otherwise gained access to the place where the victim is living (mentioned in Billam as a factor attracting the eight-year starting point). (Note An intent to burgle is not quite the same as an intent to break in. It could be assumed that where there is a predetermined intent to rape, rob or steal the starting point would be higher. Much will depend on the facts.)

Att-Gen's Ref. No 47 of 1999 2000 1 Cr App R (S) 446. The defendant was convicted of having a firearm with intent to commit robbery, indecent assault and rape. After midnight, a 15-year-old boy answered a knock at the front door and the defendant and another chased the boy in. There were five or six children in the flat asleep. A loaded gun was held to a 15 year old's head. They ordered all four people in the room to get on the floor and not look at them. Money, jewellery and drugs were demanded. Personal items were seized from them. Two were hit with the gun for no obvious reason and one was tied up with a sheet. Oral sex was demanded at gunpoint. The other man attempted to rape a 19-year-old girl, then ordered her into kitchen and raped her. He hit her with the gun. Then the defendant made her perform oral sex at gunpoint and raped her. The house was searched and they left. The gun was thought to have been loaded. The victim was very seriously traumatised. The defendant was arrested and denied involvement. He was then 20 and had no convictions. He was an illegal overstayer from Jamaica in the process of being deported. There was no underlying psychiatric condition. Held. The sentence should have been **14 years**. But because it was a reference, his good character and youth **11¹/₂ years** not 9.

Old cases. *Att-Gen's Ref. No 16 of 1993* 1994 15 Cr App R (S) 811; *R v Thomas* 1995 16 Cr App R (S) 686, *R v Akram* 1997 Unreported 13/3/97 and *R v Shafiq* 1998 2 Cr App R (S) 12. (For a summary of the last case see the first edition of this book.)

Concurrent or consecutive sentences for two or more sex offences

157.16 *R v Khan* 2001 2 Cr App R (S) 285. Consecutive sentences for these two rapes was not wrong.

R v Price 2003 2 Cr App R (S) 440. The defendant was convicted of rape and indecent assault. The victim lived with her two children when she met the defendant. A relationship developed and they lived together for four months. She experienced his violent temper and mood swings and as a result the eldest daughter aged 16 moved out. One night, the victim went to bed and the defendant wanted sex. She refused and he put his hand around her neck, kissed her forcibly and got on top of her. He held her hands above her head, and ignored her protests and crying. There was sex to ejaculation then he got off and apologised. Within a fortnight she moved out of her own home (with her remaining daughter). She was persuaded a week later to return but following further violence, the defendant was persuaded to leave her home. A few days later, in the early hours he phoned her and said he wanted to talk. She firmly told him that the relationship was over whereby he became abusive. He arrived uninvited at her home shortly afterwards and let himself in. He was initially calm but threatened to rape her, humiliate her and make her feel as bad as he felt. When she made it clear that she wanted him to leave, he pushed her onto a sofa and removed her trousers as she kicked out. He ripped her knickers and tried to kiss her. He later calmed down but he demanded her knickers to prevent her from showing them to anyone. He remained in the house for a considerable time. Police were eventually called to the house and arrested the defendant. He was interviewed but denied the offences. He was 35 with no previous convictions of any significance. A pre-sentence report suggested that he was a "higher risk of re-offending". Held. Relationship or acquaintance rape should be treated as equally serious as cases of stranger rape. In cases of this kind, the starting point should be **5 years** in a contested case. Further, in this case, there was nothing wrong in principle or inappropriate with consecutive sentences as these were two quite distinct incidents some time apart. **5 years and 3 years consecutive** upheld.

R v Hinds 2003 2 Cr App R (S) 455. The defendant was convicted of thirty two serious offences against eight girls aged 11–16 including rape, buggery and indecent assault. Held. For these offences, there was no reason why the judge should not impose consecutive sentences. (For more detail see page **157.46**)

Date rape   see *Acquaintance rape*

Defendant under 18 – Guideline case

157.17   *R v Millberry* 2003 2 Cr App R (S) 142. LCJ. Guideline case Even in the case of young offenders, because of the serious nature of the offence custody will normally be the appropriate disposal. Nonetheless the sentence should be 'significantly shorter for young offenders'.

Defendant aged 10–13

157.18   *Att-Gen's Ref. No 18* of 1999 1 Cr App R (S) 246. The defendant was convicted of a number of counts of rape, incest, indecent assault, buggery and attempted buggery against his sisters and brother over a seven year period beginning when the defendant was 12 or 13. The abuse started when the defendant was 10 or 11. The defendant raped his older sister when she was 14 or 15 and the defendant was 12 or 13. The defendant raped his younger sister, O when she was 11, and the defendant was 15. His abuse of her had started when she was 9. He would attack her in her bed and in the shower. It is estimated that she was abused over fifty times. The abuse continued until she was 15. She put up with the activity because her father had also raped her. The defendant began to abuse his brother when he was 13 and the defendant was 15 or 16. The defendant made his brother, S, masturbate him and perform oral sex on him and eventually buggered him. Force and inducements were used. O now lives as a lesbian saying she cannot bear a penis near her after what the defendant and her father did to her. All the victims were gravely damaged. S eventually ran from home and went to live with his aunt never to return. The defendant, who was 31 at the time of conviction, had committed no sexual offences since his adolescence. The defendant did not pose a danger to the community now. Held. The sentencing task was immensely difficult. **3 years 8 months** was a lenient sentence, but not unduly lenient.

R v B 2001 1 Cr App R (S) 431. The defendant aged 12 pleaded guilty to four rapes on a boy aged 11. **2 years** not 4 detention but the 11 months on remand remaining consecutive.

R v JC 2005 1 Cr App R 37. The defendants JC and A were convicted of rape having pleaded guilty to indecent assault and indecency with a child. JC was 13 and 14 and A was 17 at the time of the offences; 15 and 18 respectively at sentence. V was the victim of the rape. With a friend, she had some alcohol and went socialising. They were approached by the defendants who separated V from her friend. Together they pushed V up the road (JC took the lead). She tried to run away but she was pushed and fell onto the road with her head against the pavement. She screamed, but then she was raped by each defendant in turn. A raped her anally and JC raped her vaginally. She was literally in the gutter and screaming in pain. In interview they said that it was consensual. JC indecently assaulted RM. He was attracted to her; she was not interested. On one occasion he chased her into an alleyway, put her into a headlock forced his hands down her trousers, touched her bottom and tried to go round the front. Later she was physically sick (6 months). The indecency with a child concerned both defendants and the victim, SC. They got to know her and started to treat her like a sex object. She was met by the defendants and told by JC that she was going to lose her virginity that day. She was taken to a male public lavatory and forced to perform oral sex on JC and A (who masturbated and ejaculated over her jacket) (12 months each). Some weeks later, JC phoned SC and told her to meet him. In an alleyway JC forced SC to perform oral sex on him. He then masturbated and wiped his penis on her jacket (2 years consecutive). JC then took her to his home and was joined by A who forced SC to perform oral sex on him (2 years consecutive). Each victim was badly affected. Both JC and A were of good character. The sentences imposed gross indecency were unlawful. Held. As far as the rape was concerned, looking at the dimensions to consider in assessing gravity, (*R v Millberry* 2003 2 Cr App R (S) 142) there were 3 features: the degree of harm to the victim, the culpability of the defendant and the risk posed to society by the defendant. If the defendants had been adults their offences of rape would have attracted **10 years** or more after a trial. **7 years** was imposed for the rape but the overall sentences were **9 years**. The additional 2 years for the indecency offences were quashed but the sentence for rape was increased to 9 years; no separate penalty was imposed for the other offences (see *R v Mills* 1998 2 Cr App R (S) 128. The Court of Appeal had the power to increase individual sentences to reflect the over all criminality "Taking the case as a whole" (see *R v Sandwell* 1985 80 Cr App R 78) as long as the total sentence was not increased. So **9 years** detention each.

Defendant aged 14–15

157.19 *R v M* 2000 1 Cr App R (S) 188. The defendant pleaded guilty to two attempted rapes of an 18 year old woman. The defendant, who was 14 at the time of the offences, followed the woman and a girlfriend after they left a party. He led the woman into an estate on the pretext that she could find a telephone box pretending to help her. He began to touch her and she pushed him away. He persisted and pinned her against a car and grabbed her breasts and put his hand between her legs and squeezed her vagina. She screamed and he put his hand over her face and then bit her cheek. She screamed again. He touched her breasts and kissed them and then pulled down her trousers. Her pleas for him to stop were ignored and he turned her round and attempted to penetrate her anus. He then pushed her to the ground and then let her get up and dragged her to a dustbin area. She cried uncontrollably and she was pushed to the ground again. He attempted to penetrate her vagina but police who had been summonsed by neighbours arrived. She was crying hysterically. When interviewed he pretended she was consenting. The defendant had breached a conditional discharge for indecency. Held. It was a terrifying attack carried out with grim persistence. The defendant was of a young age. A good secure unit report contributed to a reduction from 5 to **3¹/₂ years** detention.

Old cases. *R v McIntosh* 1994 15 Cr App R (S) 163; *R v Suleman* 1994 15 Cr App R (S) 569; *R v Powell* 1994 15 Cr App R (S) 611; *R v Stone 1995 16 Cr App R 407; R v Brumwell* 1996 1 Cr App R (S) 213; *R v Bennett* 1997 Unreported 11/3/97; *R v Tack* 1997 Unreported 7/7/97; *R v Stepton* 1998 2 Cr App R (S) 319.

Defendant aged 16–17

157.20 *R v S* 2001 2 Cr App R (S) 491. The defendant was convicted after a trial of rape. The defendant then aged 16 raped a 17 year old virgin from the school he had attended. He called out to her while she was waiting for a friend and invited her to his house. She refused. He pulled her in. After she resisted, she was pushed onto a sofa and he inserted his fingers into her vagina. He then forced her onto the floor and put his fingers in again. She was struggling. He then raped her while she struggled. There were no injuries. He had been excluded from school with a bad school report. When on bail he also earned an unfavourable assessment from a NACRO programme, which he had to leave. At the trial he alleged consent. He was treated as of good character. Held. Because of his age **4 years** not 5 detention.

R v S 2001 Unreported 14/9/01. The defendant pleaded guilty to rape. He was aged 16 at conviction. The victim was 15 years old. He thought she consented to start with and during the act she tried to push him off. He was sentenced on the basis he was reckless and had carried on regardless. Held. Because of *R v Greaves* 1999 1 Cr App R (S) 319, the court had to pass a sentence that was less than *Greaves*. Therefore **12 month's** detention and training not 30 months.

R v Millberry 2003 2 Cr App R (S) Re Mi at p 158. The defendant pleaded guilty on re-arraignment to rape. He met the victim who was 15 two weeks before the offence. The defendant invited him back to his house and after some initial horseplay pulled him to the floor, pulled down his trousers and engaged in oral sex. He then pinned the victim down, by kneeling on his arms, pulled down his trousers and had anal sex. He threatened the victim that if he told anyone he would make it worse for him. The following day he was arrested and made full admissions. The defendant was 17 at the time of the offence and 18 at his sentence. He had one caution for a minor indecent assault on an 11 year old boy about a year before the rape. There was a perceived high risk of re-offending. A psychiatric report said that the defendant was having difficulty adjusting to the fact that he was a homosexual. His emotional and social development had a number of deficits. Held. The starting point should be 5 years. However, there were aggravating features: the age of the victim and force used, albeit it was within the range that can be inherent in the case of forcible rape. **4 years detention** not 5.

R v M 2005 1 Cr App R (S) 218. The defendant pleaded guilty on re-arraignment to one count of kidnapping and one count of rape. He approached a woman in an alleyway and talked to her; when she tried to move away he pulled her arm and produced a knife. He then forced her at knife-point to walk along with him to a park. In the course of this walk she cried and pleaded with him to release her. At the park he forced her to perform oral sex on him by holding the knife under her chin, threatening to kill her, and grab-bing hold of her head. When he stopped she got up and bent down to get her bag; he told her to remain in that position and take her trousers down and she refused. After a brief struggle he pulled her trousers and underwear down and raped her as she was lean-ing over the bench. He then dragged her across to the play area, told her to lie on her back and raped her again. He also took some money from her handbag. She ran out of the park and told a couple what had happened. He was traced through his DNA. The defendant was 16 at the time of the offence. He had sixteen previous convictions including possessing a bladed article, ABH and possession of an offensive weapon. The defendant had shown remorse and had made substantial efforts to improve himself in custody. Held. The defendant had a bad record. He had the chance of responding to community punishments but chose not to. This offence attracted the starting point of eight years owing to the aggravating features: abduction, two rapes, forced oral sex and the use of a knife. Progress in custody did not mean the sentence should be reduced. For this appalling case there was nothing whatever wrong with **6 years detention** for the rape and 3 years concurrent for the kidnapping.

R v JC 2005 1 Cr App R 37. The defendants JC and A were convicted of rape having pleaded guilty to indecent assault and indecency with a child. JC was 13 and 14 and A was 17 at the time of the offences; 15 and 18 respectively at the time of the sentence. V was the victim of the rape. With a friend, she had some alcohol and went socialising. They were approached by the defendants who separated V from her friend. Together they pushed V up the road (JC took the lead). She tried to run away but she was pushed and fell onto the road with her head against the pavement. She screamed, but then she was raped by each defendant in turn. A raped her anally and JC raped her vaginally. She was literally in the gutter and screaming in pain. In interview they said that it was consensual. JC indecently assaulted RM. He was attracted to her; she was not interested. On one occasion he chased her into an alleyway, put her into a headlock forced his hands down her trousers, touched her bottom and tried to go round the front. Later she was physically sick (6 months). The indecency with a child concerned both defendants and the victim, SC. They got to know her and started to treat her like a sex object. She was met by the defendants and told by JC that she was going to lose her virginity that day. She was taken to a male public lavatory and forced to perform oral sex on JC and A (who masturbated and ejaculated over her jacket) (12 months each). Some weeks later, JC phoned SC and told her to meet him. In an alleyway JC forced SC to perform oral sex on him. He then masturbated and wiped his penis on her jacket (2 years consecutive). JC then took her to his home and was joined by A who forced SC to perform oral sex on him (2 years consecutive). Each victim was badly affected. Both JC and A were of good character. The sentences imposed gross indecency were unlawful. Held. As far as the rape was concerned, looking at the dimensions to consider in assessing gravity, (Millberry 2003 Cr App Rep (S) 31) there were 3 features: the degree of harm to the victim, the culpability of the defendant and the risk posed to society by the defendant. If the defendants had been adults their offences of rape would have attracted **10 years** or more after a trial. **7 years** was imposed for the rape but the overall sentences were **9 years**. The additional 2 years for the indecency offences were quashed but the sentence for rape was increased to 9 years; no separate penalty was imposed for the other offences (see *R v Mills* 1998 2 Cr App R (S) 128. The Court of Appeal had the power to increase individual sentences to reflect the over all criminality "Taking the case as a whole" (see *R v Sandwell* 1985 80 Cr App R 78) as long as the total sentence was not increased. So **9 years** detention each.

Defendant aged 18–20

157.21   *R v Broadhead* 2000 1 Cr App R (S) 3. The defendant pleaded guilty to the rape of his stepbrother's wife. The defendant, who was 19, was a frequent visitor to the house. One day the defendant entered the house, where the victim and her two young children were. He was holding a knife and refused to put it down. He grabbed the woman and held the knife to her face. The defendant made threats towards the children and made the woman go into a bedroom and remove her clothing. He raped her, performed oral sex on her and made her reciprocate. The sentencing judge recognised that the defendant posed a significant risk within the community. The defendant had previous convictions, which were not relevant. A guilty plea did not hold as much credit as for others as the defendant was caught in the act. Held. Taking into account that a weapon was used to frighten the victim and her children and that the offence included sexual indignities over and above rape **9 years detention** was not a manifestly excessive sentence.

Att-Gen's Ref. No 54 of 1998 2000 1 Cr App R (S) 219. The defendant was convicted of two counts of rape, both anally and vaginally, on a 17-year-old student. The defendant, who was 19 at the time of conviction was drinking in the pub where the victim worked. He offered to walk her home but she declined. At 4.30 pm she left the pub and the defendant followed her. He called the victim offensive names and eventually picked her up in bear hug and dragged her along 100 yards to a thorny thicket. He threatened to kill her if she did not do what she wanted. The defendant tore off the victim's clothes and anally raped her briefly. He then placed his penis in her mouth and then penetrated her vagina. He pulled her hair, sucked her breasts and then took £15 from the victim. He returned £10. During the incident he slapped her causing red marks. She suffered stress and trauma. The defendant was treated as of previous good character.

Held. We would have expected **7 or 8 years** YOI. As it was a reference, the sentence of **6 years** was upheld.

Old cases. *R v Barrie* 1998 Unreported 18/7/97, *R v Matthews* 1998 1 Cr App R (S) 220, *R v Reid* 1998 2 Cr App R (S) 10 and *R v Shafiq* 1998 2 Cr App R (S) 12. (For a summary of the last three cases see the first edition of this book.)

Defendant aged over 65   See *Historic cases*

Defendant, inadequate

157.22   *Att-General's Ref. No. 69 of 2001* 2002 2 Cr App R (S) 593. The defendant was convicted of rape and indecent assault, for which he received no penalty. The victim was 58 and suffered from Huntington's chorea, an appalling progressive disease of the brain. This caused her to suffer from dementia and impairment of the intellectual function, memory and understanding, together with associated psychotic symptoms. She had an IQ of 52 and was a "defective within the meaning of the Sexual Offences Act 1956 s 45. Her condition meant she lost her inhibitions and had a tendency to invent or fill gaps in her memory. She was discharged from the psychiatric department of a hospital and went to a residential care home. Shortly after that the defendant and his brother, M went to visit another resident, P at the home. The defendant was 29 with an IQ of 52. He had a reading and perceptual age of a 9 years old. In some respects he performed like a 6 year old. All four of them were in P's room and there was some horseplay and P encouraged the defendant to ask the victim for sex, which took place. The prosecution case was she repeatedly said words like, "No" and "Stop it". M participated and attempted oral sex and touched her breasts. A care worker heard shouting and discovered the victim with her pants down. The defence was consent. He received 3 years with a 3 years extension. Both sides appealed. Held. It was a very difficult sentencing decision. The defence suggestion that there should have been a guardianship order was wrong because the case was not wholly exceptional such as to warrant a non-custodial. She was very vulnerable with child-like tendencies. The aggravating features were that vulnerability, her age and that it took place in a nursing home. The vulnerability was seriously aggravating. Without his impairment the correct sentence would have been 8 years. The correct sentence would have been **5 years**. Because of the need for a substantial discount as it was a reference and the extended period the sentence was not increased.

See also **DEFENDANT** – *Inadequate*

Delay

See *Historic abuse* and **INDECENT ASSAULT ON A MAN** –*Historic abuse* and **INDECENT ASSAULT ON A WOMAN** – *Historic abuse*

False claim of rape, making

See **PERVERTING THE COURSE OF JUSTICE/CONTEMPT OF COURT/PERJURY ETC.** *Incriminating innocent people*

False Imprisonment, and

See *Abduction/false imprisonment etc., and*

Fathers, by

157.23   *Att-Gen's Ref. No 29 of 1998* 1999 1 Cr App R (S) 311. The defendant pleaded guilty to three rapes and five indecent assaults on his daughter over a period of 6 years when she was between the ages of 11 and 17. When the victim's mother was away from the house the defendant would return home to his daughter and abuse her. The abuse began by touching her genitals over and under her clothing. When the girl was 13 or 14 the abuse progressed to digital penetration of her vagina. He abused her weekly over six years. The rapes took place when the victim was 15. The defendant was 49 years of age and of good character. At the time of conviction he continued to have a close relationship with his daughter, the girl was extremely fond of her father. The sentencing judge had passed sentence as though this offence was one of incest. Held. Substantial allowance should be given for the fact that these offences of rape were akin to incest. The appropriate sentence was if not **5 years** very close to 5. As this was a reference **3¹/₂ years** not 2 years.

Att-Gen's Ref. No 8 of 1999 2000 1 Cr App R (S) 56. The defendant was convicted of five counts of rape and one count of indecent assault. Four counts of rape were on his daughter and one on his daughter's friend. He and his wife were divorced and his daughter lived with her mother. He looked after her daughter, who was 8, when her mother was in hospital. First he indecently assaulted her and thereafter raped the child on a number of occasions. The defendant made the child smell amyl nitrate and would perform oral sex upon her. The defendant took his daughter and another child, who was 13, to a caravan site. During the stay he anally raped the second child and again raped his daughter. The rapes were over three years. He was 37 and a warrant officer in the army and of good character. He would be dismissed from the army and lose considerable pension rights. Held. The defendant was in a position of responsibility to both victims. The lowest sentence that could be imposed was **12 years**. Taking into account that this is a reference **10 years**.

Att-Gen's Ref. No 75 of 1998 2000 1 Cr App R (S) 102. The defendant pleaded guilty to four rapes, three buggeries and six indecent assaults against his two daughters over a period eleven years in one case and four years in the other. Some were specimen counts. The pleas were very late. He placed his penis against the girls' genital areas and digitally penetrated their anuses and vaginas. The defendant also used sex aids on the children. The defendant raped and buggered the victims. He would place a pillow over the face of the older child to prevent her sounds being heard. The defendant administered entinox from a gas cylinder to the younger child. The older child was abused from the age of 6 to 17 and the younger child from 6 to 10. The defendant was 45 at the time of conviction and lacked remorse. Held. These were grave offences against victims of a tender age. Taking into account the late guilty plea and the lack of remorse the appropriate sentence was **12–14 years**. As it was a reference **10 years** not 7 years.

R v R 2000 2 Cr App R (S) 239. The defendant pleaded guilty to three rapes and other sex offences on his daughter over 9 years. The first offence was rape when she was 13. **14 years** not 16 years.

Old cases *Att-Gen's Ref. No 23 of 1997* 1998 1 Cr App R (S) 378 (for summary of case see 1ˢᵗ edition of this book) and *R v C* 1998 2 Cr App R (S) 303. [**10 years** for a father who was convicted of two counts of rape, one of buggery and one of indecent assault on his daughter when she was 15 upheld.]

See also INCEST

Fathers/mothers by – with torture

157.24 *R v W & W* 1999 1 Cr App R (S) 268. The defendant F, the victim's father, pleaded guilty to eleven counts of rape, four counts of GBH with intent, four counts of indecent assault and five counts of cruelty to a child. The defendant M, the victim's mother, pleaded guilty to four counts of GBH with intent, four counts of indecent assault and two counts of cruelty to a child. The defendants were a married couple who had five children who were aged between 17 and 3 when the case came before the court. They lived with their children in squalor with rubbish being collected inside the house and the only lavatory facilities being a bucket. He disconnected the water and there was an overpowering smell in the house. They denied access to health visitors. W had had sexual intercourse with his eldest child since her 12th birthday. The child was also forced to perform oral sex and masturbate her father; she was paid £1 a time. She was also paid £25 for her mother to beat her. M tied her daughter to a bed, used a vibrator on her vagina and urinated in her mouth whilst the male defendant videoed the act. Videos were found depicting the eldest child being beaten and tortured by her mother with the father watching. The girl was tied to a metal bar on the ceiling and penetrated by a vibrator vaginally and anally. The victim was also made to tie her baby brother to his playpen and suck his penis. The 15-year-old daughter also described how she had been repeatedly raped since her 12th birthday. She was tied up and hit by the father with a cane. She was found to have knife and cigarette burns on her. The children were withdrawn and one aped the sexual behaviour she had seen. The sentencing judge said that the defendants had descended deep into a pit of human degradation. Held. No parallel could be drawn between the facts of this case and any other case. The judge did not err. **Life imprisonment**, with 21 years as the notional determinate sentence and 14 years as the specified period for the male defendant not wrong. **15 years** for the female defendant not altered.

R v M and M 2000 1 Cr App R (S) 296. The defendant, F, and his wife, M were convicted of repeatedly raping, buggering and indecent assaulting their seven children and grandchildren over a period of 34 years. F was sentenced for eleven rapes and four buggery on his children and nine rapes and buggery on his grandchildren. M was sentenced for three rapes and two buggeries. Their children suffered abuse for 13 years between 1961 and 1974 and their grandchildren were abused from 1982 to 1995. The defendants engaged in vaginal and anal intercourse with the victims, and inserted such items as screwdrivers, part pickaxe handles, razor blades, pins and knitting needles into the victims. One had his foreskin pinned over his penis and another razor blades inserted into her vagina. One had both ends of a pitchfork inserted into their bodies. A daughter and granddaughter had knitting needles inserted into their vaginas in an attempt to procure abortions. The children were forced to abuse each other and the defendants invited family members, neighbours and friends to use the victims for sexual gratification. Some were taken away for the weekend by strangers in exchange for money. Degradation and humiliation was used as a tool to subjugate them. M held their heads and watched. She humiliated them and when they wet their beds she made them stand for hours in soiled sheets. The children were still disturbed and one continues to mutilate herself. F was now 68 with a heart condition. He was of good character and had been in the RAF. M was 67 and not in good health. The sentencing judge considered that it would not be appropriate to pass an indeterminate sentence because at the end of a substantial sentence it would be unlikely that the defendants would represent a serious danger to the public. He considered F was the prime mover. Held. It was beyond belief. They were abused and tortured for pleasure. The offences were of unique gravity and sentences of very substantial length had to passed. **25 years** for F and **14 years** for M were neither excessive nor wrong in principle.

Firearm, with

157.25 *R v H* 1999 1 Cr App R (S) 470. The defendant pleaded guilty to two counts of rape on his estranged wife and one count of possessing a firearm with intent to cause fear. The defendant had been married for 13 years although the marriage had deteriorated. Following incidents of violence and sexual abuse the wife moved out of their home. The victim went to the defendant's house during her lunch break after a request by the defendant and was detained for 4–4$\frac{1}{2}$ hours. During this time she was sexually assaulted, anally raped twice and terrified by the defendant who was brandishing a handgun. She was also assaulted and threatened and in constant fear of being shot. She received bruises and abrasions and was in considerable pain. The defendant was a fireman who had been traumatised by the misery and violence he had seen. He had lapsed into drink, drugs and violence. Since his conviction the defendant realised the full extent of his actions. He had sought and obtained help. His wife had considerably forgiven him his conduct. He received 10 years for the anal rape and lesser concurrent sentences for the other counts. Held. Due to the defendant's improvement of attitude **7 years** was more appropriate than 10 years.

Att-Gen's Ref. No 47 of 1999 2000 1 Cr App R (S) 446. The defendant was convicted of having a firearm with intent to commit robbery, indecent assault and rape. After midnight, a 15-year-old boy answered a knock at the front door and the defendant and another chased the boy in. There were five or six children in the flat asleep. A loaded gun was held to a 15 year old's head. They ordered all four people in the room to get on the floor and not look at them. Money, jewellery and drugs were demanded. Personal items were seized from them. Two were hit with the gun for no obvious reason and one was tied up with a sheet. Oral sex was demanded at gunpoint. The other man attempted to rape a 19-year-old girl, then ordered her into kitchen and raped her. He hit her with the gun. Then the defendant made her perform oral sex at gunpoint and raped her. The house was searched and they left. The gun was thought to have been loaded. The victim was very seriously traumatised. The defendant was arrested and denied involvement. He was then 20 and had no convictions. He was an illegal overstayer from Jamaica in the process of being deported. There was no underlying psychiatric condition. Held. The sentence should have been **14 years**. But because it was a reference, his good character and youth **11¹/₂ years** not 9.

Old cases. *R v C* 1993 14 Cr App R (S) 642, *R v Suleman* 1994 15 Cr App R (S) 569 and *R v Shafiq* 1998 2 Cr App R (S) 12. (For a summary of the last case see the first edition of this book.)

General (i.e. No aggravating feature)

157.26 *R v Millberry* 2003 2 Cr App R (S) 142. Guideline case LCJ. **5 years** should continue to be appropriate for a single offence of rape on an adult victim by a single offender manifesting none of the features (listed under **Guideline Case**) after a contested trial.

R v Bamforth 1999 1 Cr App R 123. The defendant pleaded guilty to rape. He when 23, wandered round the streets looking for and fantasising about sexual intercourse. The victim aged 19 was walking at night with her boyfriend and the defendant took a fancy to her. He followed them for some while until the victim about two streets from her home persuaded the boyfriend he should leave her to make her way the last few yards. Once she was alone he stole up behind her and seized her from behind. He put his hands over her breasts and held her by the neck. He squeezed the neck tightly and when she screamed he pushed her fingers down her throat. He dragged her to a playing field and notwithstanding her desperate struggles and her screams pushed her to the ground. He stripped her and raped her and left her naked to make her way to the nearest house. Nearly a year later his DNA was matched and when told of the match he admitted the offence. The victim became withdrawn, depressed and left her university without completing the first year. She continued to experience nightmares. Held. Had he fought the case 8 years would have been appropriate. Because of his plea at the first opportunity, **6 years** not 8.

Att-Gen's Ref. No 23 of 2000 2001 1 Cr App R (S) 155. The defendant pleaded guilty to rape. The victim and the defendant had helped each other in past as they lived in adjacent flats. They had been friendly for about two years. She had occasionally cooked meals for him. She had not responded to his interest in her. At 11 pm she knocked on his door and asked his help to move a box into her children's bedroom. He got out of bed, agreed to help and got dressed. After helping her they smoked and had tea. She told him about her debts and he said he would pay them off if she had sex with him. She declined. He asked her to masturbate him and she again declined. He pulled down his trousers and pants and started to masturbate in front of her. She avoided looking at him. After a few minutes, he pulled down her shorts and raped her. Eventually she pushed him off and he continued to masturbate and ejaculated over her carpet. He then left. The rape was very brief. During the night he left a number of telephone messages apologised for his behaviour. The next morning he put £10 note through the door. When arrested he made immediate admissions. The victim found it difficult to remain in her flat and often had nightmares about the rape. The defendant was 37 and a farm labourer. He had no previous offending of any gravity and was of very limited intelligence. He had very few close friends and his family was somewhat over protective of him. He showed remorse. Held. It is axiomatic that in a rape case a non-custodial sentence cannot be justified save in wholly exceptional circumstances. **3¹/₂ years** was appropriate. Because it was a reference, **2¹/₂ years** not probation with treatment.

Att-Gen's Ref. No 44 of 1999 2000 1 Cr App R (S) 317. LCJ. The defendant pleaded guilty to two counts of rape on women with whom he was previously acquainted. Both were committed when he was drunk. The defendant met the first victim at a fun fair and sometimes visited her house, staying the night. After a period of time the victim sought to avoid the defendant. The defendant came to her door one evening and was let in by the victim's young daughter. The defendant made advances towards the victim, which she rebuffed. The defendant then became angry and ordered that the child be put to bed. He said they were going to have some fun tonight and she indicated it was time he left. The child became distressed but the defendant made threats to the victim if she did not put the child to bed. When the woman returned from putting the child to bed she was frightened and in tears. He ordered her to remove her clothing and he removed his trousers and underwear. Fearful of what might happen she complied with the request. The victim realised that she was about to be raped and asked the defendant to wear a condom, which she provided; he refused to do this. He raped her then attempted to penetrate her anus and then raped her vaginally again. The victim felt physically sick. He stayed the night on her sofa and told her nothing was going to stop him doing the rape. They had sex in the morning because she wanted to get rid of him. The defendant knew the second victim and would often arrive at her house drunk. The defendant was found banging on her window and she let him in so that he did not wake her 18-week-old baby. The defendant produced a knife and claimed he had stabbed six people with it. She asked him to leave and he told her he was having her tonight. She began to cry and he waved the knife about. The defendant forced the woman to perform oral sex on him. He then pushed her onto the sofa and raped her. She managed to flee and ran to another house and by chance the first victim came to help her. The police were called and the defendant was arrested on the second victim's sofa. The defendant, who was 24, was of good character. Held. The fact that a knife was used in the second attack and that in both cases young children were present made this a very serious case. As the prosecution suggested he had initially been a welcome guest in both rapes the appropriate sentence was **5 years**. As it was a reference **4 years** not altered.

See also *Att-Gen's Ref. No 43 of 2001* 2002 1 Cr App R (S) 30 and *Att-Gen's Ref. No 69 of 2001* 2002 2 Cr App R (S) 593 [Woman with mental disabilities].

Old cases. *R v Shields* 1994 15 Cr App R (S) 775, *Att-Gen's Ref. No 28 of 1993* 16 Cr App R (S) 103, *R v Doe* 1995 16 Cr App R (S) 718 and *R v Ford* 1998 2 Cr App R (S) 74. (For summary of last case see the first edition of this book.)

See also INCEST

Guilty plea – Guideline case

157.27 *R v Millberry* 2003 2 Cr App R (S) 142. Guideline case LCJ. The reason why the courts are prepared to and should reduce sentences substantially for a guilty plea is because it is well known that victims of rape can find it an extremely distressing experience to give evidence in open court about what has happened to them, even where their identity is protected. Having to give evidence, and especially being cross-examined, can make a victim relive the offence. We have seen many victim impact statements that make this clear. Obviously the distress which is avoided is greater the earlier the victim is informed so the discount should be reduced if there is not an early plea. There is also the fact that the plea demonstrates that the offender appreciates how wrong his conduct was and regrets it. While it is desirable to avoid taking up the time of the court and incurring expense unnecessarily, this is less important in mitigation than the other two factors we have just mentioned. We stress that the maximum credit should only be given for a timely guilty plea.

Historic cases – Guideline case

157.28 *R v Millberry* 2003 2 Cr App R (S) 142. LCJ. Where the offence is reported many years after it occurred and where the offender at the time of sentencing is old, even in their eighties, the same starting points should apply. The fact that the offences are stale can be taken into account but only to a limited extent. It is after all always open to an offender to admit the offences and the fact that they are not reported earlier is often explained because of the relationship between the offender and the victim which is an aggravating factor of the offence. A different factor that could cause the court to take a more lenient view than it would otherwise is the consequence, which results from the age of the offender. In these cases the experience is that the offender may be only a danger to members of the family with whom he has a relationship. So this is a dimension that can be taken into account if there is a reduced risk of re-offending. In addition, the court is always entitled to show a limited degree of mercy to an offender who is of advanced years, because the impact that a sentence of imprisonment can have on an offender of that age.

Historic cases – Examples

157.29 *R v Anderson* 1999 1 Cr App R (S) 273. The defendant was convicted of three attempted rapes, seven indecent assaults, and three indecency with children counts. The offences occurred between 1972 and 1982 on three girls. The defendant was a lodger of the first victim's grandmother. The victim and her family stayed there for seven months when the girl was 11. She recalled that she was assaulted on more than one occasion. The first time the defendant touched her vagina under her knickers. The second victim, A, was the granddaughter of the defendant's partner, and cousin of the first victim. When A was 7 or 8 the defendant would baby-sit for her. He would walk around the house naked and invite A to touch his penis. D would masturbate in front of A and digitally penetrate her vagina. On one occasion the defendant masturbated over her arm. When the victim was 10 the defendant attempted to have intercourse with her. Between the ages of 10–14, A was indecently assaulted about twice a week by the defendant. When A was 15 the defendant attempted to rape her again, however, A held a knife to his throat and he never touched her again. The third victim was a friend of A's. She was indecently assaulted many times over a 3 year period and when she was aged 10 the defendant attempted to rape her. The defendant who was about 56 when the offences began and 77 at the time of conviction had no previous convictions. The sentencing judge said that the victims and their families were entitled to trust the defendant but his conduct had caused them irreparable damage. Held. **8 years** accurately reflected the scale and criminality of the defendant's behaviour. However, due to the defendant's age and as an act of mercy, **6 years** not 8 years.

R v Matthews 1999 1 Cr App R (S) 309. The defendant pleaded guilty to two counts of attempted rape and two counts of indecent assault on a girl of 10. The defendant who was then 18 was the brother of the victim's stepfather. The defendant admitted that on two occasions his penis had touched the outside of the victim's vagina, but that he had stopped when he realised what he was doing was wrong. The defendant also admitted that he had had oral sex with the child on more that one occasion. The victim, a mother of five, stated how the defendant's conduct has stifled her ability to communicate with others over the past 30 years and how she had received counselling. He admitted the matters when interviewed and expressed remorse. The defendant, who was 49 at the time of conviction, was of exemplary character. He had been in the same job for 29 years and was buying his house on mortgage. Held. Had he been dealt with at the time he would have received Borstal. Taking into account the delay of 30 years before the case came before the court and that the defendant was a man of limited intellect with learning difficulties 30 months was excessive. Therefore **12 months**.

R v King 1999 2 Cr App R (S) 376. The defendant was convicted of one count of rape, two counts of buggery and sixteen counts of indecent assault. The defendant targeted seven children who came from vulnerable and deprived backgrounds. He would buy them presents and show an interest in them while belittling their families. He introduced them to alcohol and cannabis. The offences took place over a period of nineteen years and involved touching the genital areas of the children, forcing the children to masturbate him and then engaging in sexual intercourse. The first victim was 7 when the abuse began and it lasted four years. Her sister was abused from when she was 4 and when she was 11 or 12 he raped her. He continued raping her regularly after that and she took an overdose at 19 and had psychiatric treatment. The abuse on her then stopped. Her brother was abused from 11 and he was given cannabis as a reward. The boy was forced to masturbate him regularly. On one occasion he tried to bugger him. Another boy was abused from 10 leading to masturbation, oral sex and then buggery. The defendant had three-way sex with him and his 19-year-old girlfriend. The abuse ended when the boy was 13. Three other girls were abused through oral sex etc from when they were aged 15, 12 and sometime after she was 8. His control was mostly emotional. The abuse seriously affected the children. The defendant, who was 52 at the time of conviction, had no previous convictions. He was blind in one eye and had severe arthritis. One blow could cause him to lose the sight in his other eye. He was not considered a serious threat to children now. The judge said that the defendant had sexually corrupted young children chosen by him for their vulnerability. Held. For this prolonged insatiable depravity involving children of both sexes a long sentence was called for. It was to punish and deter. **18 years** was not manifestly excessive.

Att-Gen's Ref. No 64 of 1998 1999 2 Cr App R (S) 395. The defendant pleaded guilty at an early stage to eleven charges of rapes and indecent assault against his two nieces. There were three rapes and an attempted rape. They took place over 9 years. The offences came to light twelve years after the offending against the two girls stopped. The victim's mother died when the nieces were 5 and 6 so they had to live with their grandmother. After her death the girls had to live with the defendant and his wife. The defendant had already begun to indecently assault the younger of the two girls before she lived with him. It started when she was 5. When she was 9 the abuse turned into rape. This became a regular event. The defendant then began to indecently assault the older girl. The assaults were of a particular unpleasant character. The offences came to light 10 to 12 years after they had been committed. The effect on the girls was very serious. From time to time they would run away from home and the elder girl tried to commit suicide. The defendant had a conviction for attempted rape of the third sister when she was 15 years old (he received an 18 month suspended sentence). There were no offences since then. He was 46. The girls, now women, asked that the defendant be allowed home. Held. **10 years** would have been appropriate. Taking into account the time that had elapsed since the offences and the fact that this was a reference, **7 years** not 3 years.

Att-Gen's Ref. No 18 of 1999 2000 1 Cr App R (S) 246. The defendant was convicted of a number of counts of rape, incest, indecent assault, buggery and attempted buggery against his sisters and brother over a seven year period beginning when the defendant was 12 or 13. The abuse started when the defendant was 10 or 11. The defendant raped his older sister when she was 14 or 15 and the defendant was 12 or 13. The defendant raped his younger sister, O when she was 11, and the defendant was 15. His abuse of her had started when she was 9. He would attack her in her bed and in the shower. It is estimated that she was abused over fifty times. The abuse continued until she was 15. She put up with the activity because her father had also raped her. The defendant began to abuse his brother when he was 13 and the defendant was 15 or 16. The defendant made his brother, S, masturbate him and perform oral sex on him and eventually buggered him. Force and inducements were used. O now lives as a lesbian saying she cannot bear a penis near her after what the defendant and her father did to her. All the victims were gravely damaged. S eventually ran from home and went to live with his aunt never to return. The defendant, who was 31 at the time of conviction, had committed no sexual offences since his adolescence. The defendant did not pose a danger to the community now. Held. The sentencing task was immensely difficult. **3 years 8 months** was a lenient sentence, but not unduly lenient.

Att-Gen's Ref. No 13 of 2000 2001 Cr App R (S) 89. At least **8 years** was expected for a father, now 70 and in bad health, who committed a series of rapes on his daughters twenty seven years earlier.

R v Fowler 2002 2 Cr App R (S) 463. The defendant pleaded guilty to eight counts of rape, eight counts of indecent assault, eight counts of gross indecency and arson. He received 6 years, 18 months, 12 months and 3 $^1/_2$ years respectively all concurrent. The sex counts were specimen counts. In 2000, he lived alone with his four-year-old son. There was an allegation he had indecently assaulted two small children and his son was taken into care. Shortly after he attempted to kill himself by setting light to clothing and bedding in his house. He was drunk and fell asleep. The fire brigade arrived and he was taken to hospital. After his release he was seen by chance by a man who complained to the police about the defendant's abuse between 1972 and 1975 when he was between 8 and 11 and the defendant was 14–17. He looked after the victim while their mothers went shopping. The victim had craved affection and enjoyed the closeness and affection of the defendant. The activity was licking his anus, masturbation, oral sex (both ways) and buggery. The victim said he enjoyed the foreplay but not the buggery. That made him scream and cry. The defendant denied the allegations when questioned. He was now 44 with various convictions for dishonesty but only one sex offence in 1977 involving under age sex. The pre-sentence report said he did not give the impression of regret and he sought to minimise the effects on the victim. The psychiatric report said there was no mental disorder and he had been sexually abused as a child. His upbringing was miserable with no parental direction. The offences were now twenty eight to thirty years old. The Judge found breach of trust and profound emotional effect on the victim. Held. First you have to consider what is the likely sentence he would have been given at the time. Secondly, that will be a powerful factor in deciding the proper sentence. Thirdly fix the sentence considering all the circumstances as they are now. We assume he would have been sent to Borstal. The factors are the considerable effect on the victim, the substantial risk of further offences and his personal mitigation. **2 years** substituted.

Att-Gen's Ref. Nos. 91, 119 and 120 of 2002 re TAG 2003 2 Cr App R (S) 338 at 341. The defendant was convicted of two rapes, two indecent assaults and two counts of cruelty to children. In late 1980 or early 1981, his daughter told her friend aged 13 to wait in her bedroom. The defendant came in, pinned her against a wall, forced her to the floor and raped her. He threatened to kill her if she told anyone. Previously he had shown her pornographic and violent films. While doing this he had frequently felt her breasts. She was a virgin and since then had suffered repeated nightmares. As an adult she had matrimonial problems which needed counselling that may refer back to the rape. Between August 1980 and August 1982 he took another of her daughter's friends aged 12 or 13 on a motorbike to a field where he forced her to the ground, put his arm round her throat, slapped her and raped her. Her lip bled and he blamed her for struggling. In about 1973, when his son was 7 he severely smacked him. When he was 8 he made the boy stand on a chair in front of his sister before pulling down his trousers and whipping him with the buckle end of a belt. He used extreme violence on his daughter for her most minor transgressions. He would strike her with a knife and throw her round the room. He abused her verbally and carved "I hate you" on her bed head. He put her in the lavatory and banged her head on the door. When she was 8 or 9 and lying between her parents in bed she woke up to find him pressing her vagina. He was 54 and when 20 or 21 he was given a suspended sentence for rape. The PSR said there was a high risk of further offending. Held. Each rape on its own called for **8 years at least** because of the age of the victim. If concurrent the total sentence should have been **12 years** for each of the rapes and 3 years for each of the cruelty counts consecutive making 15 years. 15 months was the least sentence for the assaults because of the girls' age, their vulnerability and the breach of trust. Those sentences should be concurrent to the others. Because it was a reference **11 years** for the rapes and 2 years consecutive for the cruelty making **13 years** not 8 years for the rapes, 3 for the cruelty and 9 months for the assaults all concurrent.

Att-Gen's Ref. No 3 of 2002 2004 1 Cr App R (S) 357. The defendant was convicted of two counts of rape and ten counts of indecent assault. The defendant was a psychiatrist. Twenty years ago MR had been referred to him by her GP. She was vulnerable and had disabilities. After several months of counselling the defendant suggested that they should have a sexual relationship. He touched her breast but she pushed him away (indecent assault). Twenty one years ago, SMF, a student nurse, was having difficulties in her marriage and had suffered a breakdown. She fell under the defendant's spell and in the end she was persuaded against her will to submit to sexual intercourse. This happened twice. The experience had damaged her relationships with men (rape x 2). Another patient, AS, was a nurse who was initially treated for anorexia. The defendant kissed her passionately and put a hand between her legs in the area of her crotch (indecent assault x 2). Eighteen years ago, PAH was referred to him for an eating disorder. She complained of a bad back. He positioned himself behind her, placed his hands just over her hips, slid his left hand down, took hold of her crotch and kissed the back of her head (indecent assault). After a complaint from another patient, the defendant was suspended (sixteen years ago). Six years later he took up private practice where HSM started to see him and became dependant on the counselling sessions. She was persuaded to start a sexual relationship with him and masturbated him. He also penetrated her digitally and other similar offences occurred. After 5 years he ended the relationship (indecent assault x 3). After that relationship a 16/17 year old, NAH, started treatment at the defendant's house. He groomed her over a period of time before massaging her breasts under her bra, her front and her buttocks (indecent assault). Held. The two rapes were a serious breach of trust between a medical practitioner and a patient. The proper sentence ought to have been **above 8 years**. It had been right to sentence the defendant for consecutive sentences for the offences that occurred after he had been suspended. The breach of trust element was a serious aggravating feature and occurred over a period of time (see *R v Propkop* 1995 16 Cr App R (S) 598 and *R v Pike* 1996 1 Cr App R (S) 4). These most recent indecent assaults should have attracted sentences of the **very least 4 years**. The total sentence should have been **12 years**. Hence, because this was a reference, for the rapes **7 years**; for the recent indecent assaults, **3 years** consecutive, making a total of **10 years** not 8.

See also *R v Fowler* 2002 2 Cr App R (S) 463.

Homophobic rape

157.30 *R v Millberry* 2003 2 Cr App R (S) 142. LCJ. Guideline case The **8 year** starting point is appropriate after a contested trial where the victim has been targeted because of his or her membership of a vulnerable minority (e.g. homophobic rape). The **8 year** starting point is recommended either because of the impact of the offence upon the victim or the level of the offender's culpability, or both. The Panel adds that factors reflecting a high level of risk to society, in particular evidence of repeat offending, will indicate a substantially longer sentence. The seven grounds for raising the starting point to eight years each can vary in gravity. In a really bad case it can mean a higher figure is appropriate.

See also *Anal rape*

Husbands, by

see *Relationship rape*

Intruders – Breaking into premises etc as a trespasser

157.31 *R v Millberry* 2003 2 Cr App R (S) 142. A sentence **above the 5 years** is the starting point when one of the nine aggravating factors is present. The presence of one or more such factors could, depending on the degree of their seriousness, raise the sentence about the starting point of 8 years. Factor vi is "the offender has broken into or otherwise gained access to the place where the victim is living."

Att-Gen's Ref. No 51 of 1999 2000 1 Cr App R (S) 407. The defendant pleaded guilty to the rape of a woman while she was asleep. He broke into the house of the victim, who was an ex-neighbour. On previous occasions he had made inappropriate comments towards the victim. On the night of the offence the victim had consumed a great deal of alcohol and had gone to bed. She awoke in the night when she realised that someone was having sexual intercourse with her. At first she thought it was her boyfriend, when she realised it was not she shouted and the defendant left. The victim rang a friend and was sobbing violently and was very upset. When interviewed the defendant denied he had been at the house. When intimate samples were analysed he then said she had consented. The defendant, who was 46, had no relevant convictions. Held. The claim of consent was a very unattractive feature of the case. The appropriate sentence taking into account it was a reference, his character and other matters was **6 years** not 4 years.

Old cases. *Att-Gen's Ref. No 10 of 1995* 2 Cr App R (S) 122.

Life sentence is appropriate

157.32 *R v Millberry* 2003 2 Cr App R (S) 142. Guideline case LCJ. Life imprisonment was 'not inappropriate' if the offenders behaviour, 'has manifested perverted or psychopathic tendencies or gross personality disorder where the offender is likely, if at large, to remain a danger to women for an indefinite time'.

Att-Gen's Ref. No 14 of 1998 1999 1 Cr App R (S) 205. The defendant pleaded guilty to rape and GBH (s 18). At about 2am he attacked the victim aged 42 from behind as she was walking home. He struck her on the head with a house brick, causing her to lose consciousness more than once and dragged her along a road. For over 2 hours he used repeated violence including kicks to the head and striking her with her belt, which had a metal buckle. The victim managed to break free and ran to her home. He chased her and started attacking her again. There she managed again to break free but was recaptured again. He said she had done it now and told her to take her clothes off. She was raped while her throat was squeezed and her head hit. She had difficulty in breathing. Suddenly he stopped, apologised and tried to comfort her. She asked him to knock on her door to wake her son and he did so. He was arrested nearby and later expressed remorse. She was bleeding extensively and was in hospital for 3 days. She had extensive bruising to her face, her throat and upper body. There were multiple lacerations to her face which required stitching. Her facial scars would be permanent. Six months later she was still suffering pain with permanent tinnitus. She had to move home with her children aged 16 and 13. It appeared he was only aroused when violence was used. He had been released from an 18 month sentence for indecent assault and ABH one month earlier. At 1am he had forced entry into the victim's house where she lived with her two young children. He woke her and pulled lumps of hair from her head. He tore her clothes and demanded money. He struck her with his fists knocking her to the floor. He was 29. Held. He did represent a serious danger to the public for an indeterminate time. Therefore **life** not 11 years. 7 years specified.

R v W & W 1999 1 Cr App R (S) 268. The defendant F, the victim's father, pleaded guilty to eleven counts of rape, four counts of GBH with intent, four counts of indecent assault and five counts of cruelty to a child. The defendant M, the victim's mother pleaded guilty to four counts of GBH with intent, four counts of indecent assault and two counts of cruelty to a child. The defendants were a married couple who had five children who were aged between 17 and 3 when the case came before the court. They lived with their children in squalor with rubbish being collected inside the house and the only lavatory facilities being a bucket. He disconnected the water and there was an overpowering smell in the house. They denied access to health visitors. W had had sexual intercourse with his eldest child since her 12th birthday. The child was also forced to perform oral sex and masturbate her father; she was paid £1 a time. She was also paid £25 for her mother to beat her. M tied her daughter to a bed, used a vibrator on her vagina and urinated in her mouth whilst the male defendant videoed the act. Videos were found depicting the eldest child being beaten and tortured by her mother with the father watching. The girl was tied to a metal bar on the ceiling and penetrated by a vibrator vaginally and anally. The victim was also made to tie her baby brother to his playpen and suck his penis. The 15 year old daughter also described how she had been repeatedly raped since her 12th birthday. She was tied up and hit by the father with a cane. She was found to have knife and cigarette burns on her. The children were withdrawn and one aped the sexual behaviour she had seen. The sentencing judge said that the defendants had descended deep into a pit of human degradation. Held. No parallel could be drawn between the facts of this case and any other case. The judge did not err. **Life imprisonment**, with 21 years as the notional determinate sentence and 14 years as the specified period for the male defendant not wrong. **15 years** for the female defendant not altered.

Old cases. *Att-Gen's Ref. No 5 of 1998* 1998 2 Cr App R (S) 442; *R v Jabble* 1999 1 Cr App R (S) 298; *R v Pullen* 2000 2 Cr App R (S) 114; *Att-Gen's Ref. No 5 of 1998* 1998 2 Cr App R (S) 442; *R v Low* 1998 1 Cr App R (S) 68 and *R v Rodwell* 1998 2 Cr App R (S) 1 (for summary of the last three cases see the first edition of this book).

Life Sentence/Automatic life sentence – Fixing specified term

157.33   *R v E* 2000 1 Cr App R (S) 78. The defendant pleaded guilty to two rapes and one false imprisonment. He had many previous convictions including two rapes (10 years' concurrent). Held. If it hadn't been automatic life, 15 years would be appropriate, taking into account the guilty plea. The trial judge fixed the specified period too high at 12 years. The practice is to fix it at $\frac{1}{2}$ the appropriate determinate sentence, unless there was good reason not to. As the defendant had spent 145 days in custody before sentence, **8 years** for the specified period substituted.

R v Stokes 2000 2 Cr App R (S) 187. The defendant pleaded guilty to seven counts of indecent assault, one attempted rape and seven counts of rape. He had previously been convicted of attempted rape and had been sentenced to 4 years. The judge had indicated that without the life sentence provisions 9 years would be appropriate. Held. The Judge was wrong to just deduct a third. He should have deducted a half and the time on remand.

R v McStay 2003 1 Cr App R (S) 176 at 180–1. The Judge passed an automatic life sentence. Held. Judges should deduct the period in custody after they have divided the notional determinate sentence in half. The amount of time in custody should be an exact figure and not rounded up or down. If the figure is not known it is not wrong for the Judge to fix the term and add, "less the number of days spent in custody for this offence, with liberty to apply within 28 days in default of agreement as to that number of days." We recommend that Judges imposing automatic life should after stating the period, the method of calculation, and the effect of the specified period he should add words to the effect that the defendant will remain in custody unless and until the Parole Board is satisfied that it is no longer necessary for the protection of the public he should be detained. That will stop any misunderstanding as to the period.

See also *R v Rodwell* 1998 2 Cr App R (S) 1; *R v Jabble* 1999 1 Cr App R (S) 298; *R v Pullen* 2000 2 Cr App R (S) 114 and Manslaughter *– Life Sentence/Automatic life sentence – Fixing specified term*

Longer than commensurate sentences

157.34   Powers of Criminal Courts (Sentencing) Act 2000 s 80(2)(b)… the custodial sentence shall be … where the offence is a violent or sexual offence, for such longer term (not exceeding the maximum) as in the opinion of the court is necessary to protect the public from serious harm from the offender. (Previously the Criminal Justice Act 1991, s 2(2)(b).)

R v Robinson 1993 96 Cr App R 418. Attempted rape was a violent offence under the Act.

R v Howatt 1996 Unreported 8/7/96. The defendant was convicted of rape. He forced his way into the victim's flat, threats with a knife then raped her. He had four previous convictions for indecent assault. The use of the section must not result in a sentence out of all proportion to the sentence that would otherwise be imposed. **15 years** not 18.

R v L 2000 2 Cr App R (S) 177. The defendant pleaded guilty to two counts of rape and one of indecent assault on his 12-year-old stepson. He touched the boy and was told to stop. The defendant got him to the floor and the boy screamed and was buggered. His mother walked in and the defendant stopped. On a caravan holiday the defendant buggered him again. The defendant was 53 and had twenty one convictions including attempted rape (receiving 18 months) and two indecent assaults (receiving CD and CSO). The last offence was 15 years ago. The judge passed a longer than commensurate sentence of 9 years. Held. As his last offence was 15 years ago it was taking things too far to say there was current dangerousness. Therefore it was wrong to pass a longer than commensurate sentence so **9 years** substituted.

See also Longer than Commensurate Sentences and *Persistent offender*

Male rape

157.35   *R v Millberry* 2003 2 Cr App R (S) 142. Guideline case LCJ. The same guidelines should apply in principle to male and female rape, with factors relevant to only one gender (such as pregnancy resulting from the rape of a woman) taken into account on a case-by-case basis.

*See also **Anal rape (female victim)**, Buggery and **Homophobic rape***

Mothers See ***Fathers/mothers, by – With Torture***

Newspapers, and

157.36 For an article about rape sentences and newspaper reporting 1998 Crim LR 455.

Oral rape

157.37 (For offences committed on or after 1/5/04)

R v Millberry 2003 2 Cr App R (S) 142. The fact it is oral rape does not mean that the rape is any less serious than vaginal or anal rape. It is true there is no risk of pregnancy. However there are dangers in oral rape of sexually transmitted diseases particularly where no protective action is taken.

Oral rape – Cases

157.38 *R v Ismail* 2005 Unreported 15/2/05. The defendant pleaded guilty at the PDH to rape and sexual assault on a female. In the early hours he approached the victim aged 16 and walked with her. He repeatedly asked her for sex and she refused saying she was a virgin. He asked her to go back to look for his phone. She refused. Next he grabbed her from behind and dragged her onto a grass verge. She struggled and he held her hair. She managed to ring 999. He put his hands inside her underwear and touched her vaginal area. She asked him to stop which he did. He then pulled down his trousers to his thighs and forced her to suck his penis. He threatened to stab her if she did comply with his demands. She was slapped and punched about the head and face. He ejaculated in her mouth. Because of the 999 call the incident could be timed to 12 minutes. She sustained no physical injuries but was exceedingly upset and distressed. He was 18 with no convictions. Held. Her age was a substantial aggravating factor. **6 years detention** upheld.

Previous conviction for rape or attempted rape/serious offence

See *Life sentence/automatic life* and Extended Sentences

Prostitutes, on

157.39 *R v Cole* 1993 14 Cr App R (S) 764. The law will uphold the prostitute's right to say "no". But by the very nature of her trade she is prepared to have sex with any man who pays for it and the hurt she may suffer is to some extent different from another woman and that is a factor the court can take into account.

R v Masood 1997 2 Cr App R (S) 137. The defendant, aged 20, pleaded guilty to rape and false imprisonment. He picked up a 16-year-old prostitute in his car punched her 3–4 times and she lost consciousness. The attack involved various sexual activities which lasted over 4 hours. He had no convictions. Held. We do not disagree with *R v Cole* 1993 14 Cr App R (S) 764, but the remarks are not germane here. The very act of intercourse to someone who has never experienced it before, if she is unwilling and is taken by surprise, can be in itself an inexpressibly appalling event. Intercourse by itself with a prostitute might be to some extent less appalling, but the catalogue of other indecencies, of gratuitous violence, of false imprisonment, of gratuitous additional insults and threats is something which is as painful to a prostitute as it would be to anyone else. It was for the courts to give the protection to prostitutes they sadly too often need. We take no account of the fact she was a prostitute. **9 years** concurrent was severe but not manifestly excessive.

Att-Gen's Ref. No 28 of 1997 2 Cr App R (S) 206. LCJ. The defendant was convicted of five rapes over 6 years. Each was on a different prostitute. He always refused to wear condom just before sex. Held. Prostitutes were entitled to the protection of the law as much as anyone else. They were in particular need of protection. **8 years** was the least sentence appropriate. Because it was a reference **6 years**.

R v Khan 2001 2 Cr App R (S) 285. The defendants N, T, and K were convicted of two rapes, three false imprisonment and a robbery. The defendant J was convicted of one rape, two false imprisonments and a robbery. There were three attacks on prostitutes. J was only involved in two and the others in all three. The first and third victims were the same. The first victim was persuaded by N to get in a car. The car was driven off to a nearby car park. T and K got in and a hand was placed over her mouth. She was forced by the threat of a knife to have sex with the three in turn. She supplied them with a condom. The second victim was picked up by J, driven to a secluded spot and the other three defendants got in. She struggled, punched and kicked them. They took £25 from her and ejected her from the car. The first victim was attacked again shortly after. She went through the same ordeal as she had on the first occasion. The defendants were now aged 20, 19, 21 and 20 respectively. All had no previous convictions. N had received cautions. T, K, and J were assessed as a risk for re-offending. The judge gave N and J an extra $^{1}/_{2}$ year because they had been the ones who had picked up the girls in question. Held. The attacks were planned. The robbery was very unpleasant. Consecutive sentences for the two rapes was not wrong. The picking up of the girls did not add to N and J's responsibility so **10 years** not $10^{1}/_{2}$ years detention for N. **10 years** detention for T upheld. **8 years** detention for K upheld. **6$^{1}/_{2}$ years** detention not 7 for J.

Racially aggravated rape

157.40 *R v Millberry* 2003 2 Cr App R (S) 142. LCJ. Guideline case The **8 year** starting point is appropriate after a contested trial for racially aggravated rape. The **8 year** starting point is recommended either because of the impact of the offence upon the victim or the level of the offender's culpability, or both. The Panel adds that factors reflecting a high level of risk to society, in particular evidence of repeat offending, will indicate a substantially longer sentence. The seven grounds for raising the starting point to eight years each can vary in gravity. In a really bad case it can mean a higher figure is appropriate.

Relationship rape – Guideline case

157.41 *R v Millberry* 2003 2 Cr App R (S) 142. LCJ. The starting point for sentence is that cases of 'relationship rape' and 'acquaintance rape' are to be treated as being of equal seriousness to cases of 'stranger rape', with the sentence increased or reduced, in each case, by the presence of specific aggravating or mitigating factors. Rape is rape, and cannot be divided in this way into more and less serious offences. It can be just as traumatic to be raped by someone you know and trust who has chosen you as his victim, as by a stranger who sexually assaults the first man or woman who passes by. It is up to the courts to take all particular circumstances of a case into account before determining the appropriate penalty. Where, for example, the offender is the husband of the victim there can be, but not necessarily will be, mitigating features that clearly cannot apply to a rape by a stranger. On the other hand, as is confirmed by the research commissioned by the Panel, because of the existence of a relationship the victim can feel particularly bitter about an offence of rape, regarding it as a breach of trust. This may, in a particular case, mean that looking at the offence from the victim's point of view, the offence is as bad as a 'stranger rape'.

Where there is a relationship, the impact on a particular victim can still be particularly serious. In other cases this may not be the situation because of the ongoing nature of the relationship between the offender and the victim. In such a situation the impact on the victim may be less. It may also be the case where, while the offender's conduct cannot be excused, the continuing close nature of the relationship can explain how a particular offender came to commit what is always a serious offence that is out of character. There can be situations where the offender and victim are sharing the same bed on a regular basis and, prior to retiring to bed, both had been out drinking and, because of the drink that the offender consumed, he failed to show the restraint he should have. It would be contrary to common sense to treat such a category of rape as equivalent to stranger rape.

In *R v M* 1995 16 Cr App R (S) 770 a man had been sentenced to 3 years' imprisonment for rape committed on his wife. He appealed to this Court, presided over by Taylor CJ, who reduced the sentence to 18 months. It was a case where the victim had told the appellant that the marriage was finished. The appellant had then gone out drinking. When he returned home, he went to bed with his wife and asked her for intercourse. She broke away from him but intercourse took place against her wishes. No violence was used towards her. The appellant expressed remorse about what he had done and immediately admitted the matter when it was raised by the police. The Court emphasised that a custodial sentence was inevitable and Lord Taylor CJ said:

'There is a distinction between a husband who is estranged from his wife and has parted from her and returns to the house as an intruder either by forcing his way in or by worming his way in through some device and then rapes her, and a case where, as here the husband is still living in the same house and indeed, with consent occupying the same bed as his wife. We do not consider this class of case is the same as the former class.' (at p 772)

We agree but we emphasise that today we would not have allowed that appeal. We would not regard three years as an excessive sentence on the facts set out in the judgement, which may not reveal the full picture. We do, however, in relation to the 18 months' sentence, emphasise that today a sentence of 18 months' imprisonment would only be appropriate in a minority of cases where the impact upon the victim has not been great.

Relationship rape – Guideline remarks

157.42 *R v Berry* 1988 10 Cr App R (S) 13. In some instances the violation of the person and defilement and inevitable features where a stranger rapes a woman are not always present to the same degree when the defendant and victim previously had a long-standing sexual relationship.

R v W 1993 14 Cr App R (S) 256 at 260. LCJ. It should not be thought that a different and lower scale of sentencing attaches automatically to rape by a husband as against that set out in Billam (the then guideline case). All will depend on the circumstances of the individual case. Where the parties were cohabitant normally at the time and the husband insisted on intercourse against his wife's will, but without violence or threats, the considerations identified in *R v Berry* 1988 10 Cr App R (S) 13 and approved in *R v Thornton* 1990 12 Cr App R (S) 1 will no doubt be an important factor in reducing the level of sentencing. Where, however, the conduct is gross and does involve threats or violence, the facts of the marriage, of long cohabitation and that the defendant is no stranger will be of little significance. Between these two extremes there will be many intermediate degrees of gravity which judges will have to consider case by case.

Relationship rape – living together

157.43 *R v M* 1995 16 Cr App R (S) 770. LCJ. Principles considered. There must be a distinction between those who are estranged and return as an intruder and those who share the same house or bed. Here, where the victim consented to sharing the same bed, no violence was used, the defendant showed remorse and pleaded guilty.

Att-Gen's Ref. No 24 of 1999 2000 1 Cr App R (S) 275. The defendant pleaded guilty to raping his estranged wife. He and his wife were no longer in a relationship but they continued living in same house. The victim went to bed and the defendant jumped on her and pinned her down. He placed tape over her mouth and nose so she had difficulty breathing. She was dragged downstairs and struck three or four times across the face. He tied her legs to the bed with rope and told her he was going to kill himself. He added he had not decided whether she was also going to die. She was told she was not going to see the children again. He held the Stanley knife against her wrist and had oral sex with her while saying he had been planning it for days. She begged him not to have oral sex but he continued for about 10 minutes. She cried and he raped her. She believed she was going to be killed. He attempted to commit suicide with pills. The defendant, who was now 26 years of age, had no previous convictions and had a good work record. He suffered from acute depression. Held. The appropriate sentence was **6 years** but as the defendant was in state of acute depression **5 years** was appropriate. As this was a reference and he had not been given custody before, **3½ years** not probation with treatment.

R v G 2000 1 Cr App R (S) 70. The defendant was convicted of three counts of rape, one ABH and one common assault on his wife. He was 34 and she 44. The defendant had been married to his wife for thirteen years when the offences took place. He became violent towards her and put pillows over her face until she almost passed out. On two occasions she did pass out. He forced his wife to have sex with him every night for three months until she left. He would put his wife in a headlock and then force her to have sex with him. She repeatedly told him she did not want sex. It hurt her every time they had sex and that was the basis of the ABHs and common assault. Once when she was scared after being raped he wrapped a tie around her neck and tightened it until she could not breathe. Her head was pulsating and she lost her voice for 4–5 days. Her lower lip was blue. One of the rapes was anal while she cried. When interviewed he made a complete denial of the offences. He was mentally retarded with some long spent convictions. The judge concluded he was dangerous and he enjoyed the violence on his wife. Held. This was a particularly distasteful and persistent episode of serious sexual misconduct and violence over a considerable time. **10 years** was severe not a manifestly excessive.

R v H 2001 1 Cr App R (S) 181. The defendant was convicted of rape on his wife and two specimen counts of indecent assaults on his daughter (from 13 years onwards). They had lived together since 1983. His wife was pinned down on the bed and raped despite the fact she was unwilling. They had consensual sex after the rape and before sentence. The daughter said from when she was 13 she was regularly assaulted by her father who touched her breasts and vagina area despite her objections. It happened weekly for over a year. The investigation into the daughter's assault caused the rape to come to light and there was a considerable delay between the rape in September/October 1998 and the sentence a year later. He was aged 36 with no previous convictions and a good work character. He was not thought a danger to young g irls in the future. He had lost his family, his job and his home. **3 and 2 years consecutive** not 4 and 2 years consecutive.

Att-Gen's Ref. No. 26 of 2002 2003 1 Cr App R (S) 134. The defendant was convicted of attempted rape, indecent assault and ABH. For three years the defendant and the victim had a happy relationship. In 1999 he moved in with her but started to drink excessively and became possessive. In 2001 he issued an ultimatum. Unless she married him he would leave. He claimed he felt like a lodger, providing the money and getting nothing in return. In the same month, he demanded sex and seized her hair from behind and pulled her upstairs. She reminded him the children would soon be returning from school. He pushed her into the bedroom and removed his clothes. Next he tore off her jeans and knickers and said, "I'm going to get 10 years for rape. He forced her to perform oral sex and told her he was going to stick it up her arse. He tried to do this but didn't have an erection. Then he told her to spread her legs apart and that he was going to put his fist inside her and rip her insides out. He did put his fist inside her causing extreme pain but no injuries. When she pushed him he slapped her. When she reached for the phone he pulled it from the wall. He hit her and she seized his testicles. She managed to break a window with the telephone receiver and call for help. He continued to punch her and neighbours forced the front door. They found her with a swollen face and bleeding mouth. Doctors found bruising near an eye and the nose, tender jaw, ribs and loin, a suspected injury to her ear drum and blood in her urine. For some time afterwards she continued to have ringing sounds in her ear and psychological difficulties. He was 52 with no sex convictions nor had he served a prison sentence. His release date was four months away. Held. We would have expected a total sentence of **at least 4 years**. Taking into account all the factors and that it was a reference **3 years**.

R v Price 2003 2 Cr App R (S) 440. The defendant was convicted of rape and indecent assault. The victim lived with her two children when she met the defendant. A relationship developed and they lived together for four months. She experienced his violent temper and mood swings and as a result the eldest daughter aged 16 moved out. One night, the victim went to bed and the defendant wanted sex. She refused and he put his hand around her neck, kissed her forcibly and got on top of her. He held her hands above her head, and ignored her protests and crying. There was sex to ejaculation then he got off and apologised. Within a fortnight she moved out of her own home (with her remaining daughter). She was persuaded a week later to return but following further violence, the defendant was persuaded to leave her home. A few days later, in the early hours he phoned her and said he wanted to talk. She firmly told him that the relationship was over whereby he became abusive. He arrived uninvited at her home shortly afterwards and let himself in. He was initially calm but threatened to rape her, humiliate her and make her feel as bad as he felt. When she made it clear that she wanted him to leave, he pushed her onto a sofa and removed her trousers as she kicked out. He ripped her knickers and tried to kiss her. He later calmed down but he demanded her knickers to prevent her from showing them to anyone. He remained in the house for a considerable time. Police were eventually called to the house and arrested the defendant. He was interviewed but denied the offences. He was 35 with no previous convictions of any significance. A pre-sentence report suggested that he was a "higher risk of re-offending". Held. Relationship or acquaintance rape should be treated as equally serious as cases of stranger rape. In cases of this kind, the starting point should be **5 years** in a contested case. Further, in this case, there was nothing wrong in principle or inappropriate with consecutive sentences as these were two quite distinct incidents some time apart. **5 years and 3 years consecutive** upheld.

Att-Gen's Ref. Nos. 35 etc. of 2003 Re TG 2004 1 Cr App R (S) 499 at 512. The defendant was convicted of rape and causing GBH to his partner. The victim was 57. She formed a relationship with the defendant, who moved in with her. She suffered with heart problems and asthma. She suffered violence at his hands and made complaints on twenty two occasions. The two had not had sexual relations for many months and she wanted him to leave. One afternoon the defendant had been drinking and began to physically torment the victim, punching her about the body and flicking her in the head with his fingers. The police were called and put him out of the house. He returned that night. The next day he spent drinking at her flat and was drunk by the evening. The victim went to bed in her own room and closed the door. The defendant barged his way in, she asked him to leave. "I want to fuck you" he replied. He wet herself. He climbed on top of her, removed her underwear and held her whilst she was on all fours and raped her forcefully, causing her pain. He attempted to force a cider bottle into her anus. It was degrading. The next day the defendant returned to the victim's home, very drunk. He immediately began to abuse the victim, by punching her several times to the face and biting her arm. He took her mobile phone. Fortunately she was able to run to a neighbour's kitchen. She was taken to hospital with 39 bruises, a broken nose, a bite mark and a closed eye. There was redness and tenderness of the vulva and perianum showed laxity and redness of the anal verge. When interviewed the defendant made no reply. The defendant denied rape at trial and asserted he acted in self-defence in relation to the section 18. The victim was hospitalised during the course of her evidence. He was 51. Held. The offences called for consecutive sentences. This was a brutal rape that merited **7 years** (more if it stood alone) and not 5 years. The violence warranted an additional **12 months** (not 3 years concurrent). **8 years** in total, not 5.

Att-Gen's Ref. No 44 of 2004 2005 1 Cr App R (S) 263. The defendant was convicted of rape. The victim and the defendant lived in the defendant's house and had developed a consensual sexual relationship in the three months before the rape. The victim accepted that in that time if she indicated she did not want sex the defendant respected her decision. They were both abusing alcohol. One evening when they were both drunk he wanted to have sexual intercourse and she refused. He tried to prise her legs open, she refused and ran downstairs. She then returned to the bedroom and told him she did not want sexual intercourse. He accepted that. The next day he refused to give her money and the two of them spent the evening in the house eating and drinking. He became drunk. She said she was not so drunk. When they were in the bedroom he tried to kiss him and she resisted and told him she did not want that to happen. He became violent, pulling her by the arms, but she broke free. He went towards her with raised fists and said 'I could fucking do you'. He pulled her to the bed by her hair, forced her pyjama bottoms off, pinned her arms down, used his knees to prise her legs opened and raped her. Afterwards he apologised for raping her. She reported the rape to her supervisor at work the next day and then saw a nurse at the local doctor's surgery. Both gave evidence of her distress. She had fingertip bruising to her upper arms, shoulders and some bruising to her inner thighs. In an impact statement eight months later she said she had been through five jobs in six months; she had been on anti-depressants and she was having difficulty in her then relationship because she could not trust her boyfriend. She had become subdued and was unable to socialise. She was afraid of the dark. It was suggested to her in cross- examination that she was exaggerating the effect of the rape. It was submitted that aggravating features were that the force and threats went beyond what was necessary for the commission of the offence and the victim had to re-live her ordeal and subject herself to searching cross-examination. The defendant was treated as having no relevant convictions. Held. The defendant has a right to contest guilt. It is not the place of the prosecution in a reference to be critical of the fact that the case was contested. It may be there was some degree of exaggeration in the impact statement. This was a dreadful incident but there was not the sort of violence which is normally an aggravating feature. It did not lead to significant bruising. Drink had affected both parties. The fact that there had been a pre-existing relationship could not of itself be regarded as a mitigating factor but any case of this kind does have to be approached with a degree of common sense. **3 years** was lenient and the appropriate sentence would have been **4 years**, but it was not unduly lenient.

Old cases. *R v Henshall* 1995 16 Cr App R (S) 388; *R v Pearson* 1996 1 Cr App R (S) 309; *R v Thorpe* 1996 2 Cr App R (S) 246; *R v Dredge* 1998 1 Cr App R (S) 285, *R v W* 1998 1 Cr App R (S) 375 and *R v Mountaine* 1998 2 Cr App R (S) 66 (for a summary the last three cases see the 1st edition of this book).

Relationship rape – Living apart

157.44   *R v H* 1999 1 Cr App R (S) 470. The defendant pleaded guilty to two counts of rape on his estranged wife and one count of possessing a firearm with intent to cause fear. The defendant had been married for thirteen years although the marriage had deteriorated. Following incidents of violence and sexual abuse the wife moved out of their home. The victim went to the defendant's house during her lunch break after a request by the defendant and was detained for 4–4½hours. During this time she was sexually assaulted, anally raped twice and terrified by the defendant who was brandishing a handgun. She was also assaulted and threatened and in constant fear of being shot. She received bruises and abrasions and was in considerable pain. The defendant was a fireman who had been traumatised by the misery and violence he had seen. He had lapsed into drink, drugs and violence. Since his conviction the defendant realised the full extent of his actions. He had sought and obtained help. His wife had considerably forgiven him his conduct. He received 10 years for the anal rape and lesser concurrent sentences for the other counts. Held. Due to the defendant's improvement of attitude **7 years** was more appropriate than 10 years.

R v Millberry 2003 Re M 2 Cr App R (S) at p 154. The defendant pleaded guilty, days before trial, to rape. From about mid–1996 the defendant and the victim had a relationship. In January 2000 they had a child and thereafter lived together until November 2000 when the defendant moved out. In December the defendant stayed in the flat with the victim whilst he visited his daughter. However, he became involved in a fight with the victim's new boyfriend and refused to accept that his relationship with the victim was over. Reluctantly, the victim let him visit again at Easter 2001. He arrived at the flat. That evening, after the victim had retired to bed, the defendant appeared in her bedroom and held a knife to her cheek. She suggested that they went downstairs to avoid waking the child. When she entered the lounge she noticed some rope and handcuffs. She was handcuffed and tied to a bar that had been attached to a skirting board. Her underwear was removed by the defendant and a video camera was placed opposite her legs which had been tied in an open position. The defendant briefly performed oral sex on her and rubbed his penis against her mouth before penetrating her. The victim was then released from the handcuffs and he made her select a vegetable and place it in her vagina. After masturbating himself, the defendant removed the vegetable and penetrated her again. He subsequently ejaculated over her face and urinated over her chest, belly and legs. The incident lasted 5 hours. Police searched the flat and found a notebook in which the defendant had detailed an attack called 'The rape and humiliation of the package ending in her death'. Initially in interview he said that the sexual activity had taken place with the victim's consent and that the similarity between what was written and what had happened had been coincidental. He was 32. A probation report assessed the risk of similar offending to be relatively high. Held. The offence was planned and there was considerable humiliation and degradation of the victim. The effect on the victim was substantial. **9 years upheld with an extended licence of 5 years** unchanged because of concerns of the probation officers.

R v Millberry 2003 Re L 2 Cr App R (S) at p 156. The defendant pleaded guilty to two offences of rape and one of attempted rape. For about a year the defendant was involved in a relationship with the victim. After it ended she made it clear that she did not want reconciliation. About a month later the defendant came to the victim's home and made a threat of rape but left. About a month after this, the victim returned home to find that the defendant had broken in. He said to her "I'm your worst fucking nightmare" and placed both of his hands around her neck and said that he was going to "do this, then I'm going to kill myself". She undressed to order and not withstanding her resistance he raped her and attempted anal rape. The victim was crying throughout. Later he raped her again in her own bed, before masturbating and rubbing his ejaculate into her chest. During the night there were another three rapes and again the matter concluded as it had done before. There was an attempt to have sex with her the following morning. She was forced to remain in the flat until noon the next day when they both left. She managed to enter a shop alone and broke down. The defendant was then arrested. During inter-view he said that she had consented. Subsequently the victim was unable to enter her own home, was receiving counselling and may not be able to form another relationship with a man. He was 48 and of positive good character. Held. His plea only entitled him to a modest reduction, particularly in view of the attitude he adopted in interview. The course of conduct which continued over 7 hours was horrendous, humiliating and frightening for the victim. She thought that her life was in danger. **10 years** unchanged, however, the **extended sentence was reduced to 4 years** from 7.

Att-Gen's Ref. Nos. 35 etc. of 2003 Re HN 2004 1 Cr App R (S) 499 at 508. The defendant was convicted of three offences against his wife: vaginal rape, wounding with intent and intimidating a witness. After nine years of marriage (and four children) the victim said that she no longer wanted a sexual relationship with the defendant. They subsequently went on a family holiday where, one night, he held her down, ignored her protestations and raped her to ejaculation. Although the defendant was drinking heavily he had never been violent towards her. About nine months after the rape, the victim made contact with an old flame over the internet and soon began an affair. She told the defendant that she wanted to end the marriage. He wanted it to continue. On one occasion the victim and the defendant were talking about their problems and he stabbed her in the stomach with a kitchen knife. She ran to her mother's house where an ambulance was summoned. There was a 3 cm stab wound, the stomach wall had been perforated and there were small tears in the mesentery. She remained in hospital for about four weeks. He said that it had been an accident, but accepted that his wife's affair had upset him, although not greatly. He was released on bail with a condition not to contact her. He telephoned her and put emotional pressure upon her. Her daughter also started to receive text messages from the defendant. The victim received further communications from the defendant and an answerphone message which purported to come from the wife of the man with whom she was having a relationship stat-ing that the victim should leave this man alone. In fact the message had been left by a friend of the defendant's sister at the instigation of the defendant. There were other letters and calls from the defendant and his sister. When re-interviewed he denied that he had put pressure on her. He was 43, a serving police officer and of good character. Held. The rape was no less serious because it was committed within marriage. **5 years** was appropriate (not 4). The wounding demanded a substantial consecutive custodial sentence. Allowing for totality, **2 ¹/₂ years consecutive** (not 4 concurrent). The witness intimidation warrant-ed 12 months consecutive (not concurrent). As this was a reference, **7 ¹/₂ years**, reduced from 8 ¹/₂ not 4

See also *Att-Gen's Ref. No 64 of 1999* 2000 1 Cr App R (S) 529, [for this rape and kidnap at least **4** would be imposed]

Old cases. *R v Cox* 1995 16 Cr App R (S) 72; *R v Malcolm* 1995 16 Cr App R 151; *R v D* 1996 2 Cr App R (S) 342; *R v Mills* 1998 2 Cr App R (S) 252 (for summary see page **157.13**).

Repeated rape in one attack

157.45   *R v Millberry* 2003 2 Cr App R (S) 142. LCJ. Guideline case The **8 year** start-ing point is appropriate after a contested trial for repeated rape in the course of one attack (including cases where the same victim has been both vaginally and anally raped). The **8 year** starting point is recommended either because of the impact of the offence upon the victim or the level of the offender's culpability, or both. The Panel adds that factors reflecting a high level of risk to society, in particular evidence of repeat offending, will indicate a substantially longer sentence. The seven grounds for raising the starting point to eight years each can vary in gravity. In a really bad case it can mean a higher figure is appropriate.

R v Steward 2005 1 Cr App R (S) 19. The defendant was convicted on four counts of rape. At about 4am a 24-year-old woman was staying in a bedroom in a hotel in Brighton. She was awakened by a noise by the door of her room. She opened the door a little to find the defendant lying on the floor of the corridor. He put his foot in the door and prevented her from shutting it. He said he needed to get into his friend's room to get some money. When the victim tried to close the door the defendant jumped to his feet and forced his way in. She screamed. He put his hand over her mouth and his other arm round her body. He said she must not scream or he would break her jaw. He threatened to smash her head against the wall and to kill her. He pinned her to the bed. He threatened to kill her with a gun. He locked the door and told her to get under the bed covers. She made to a run out of the door. The defendant caught her and dragged her back to the bed. She tried to reach the phone. He pulled it out of its socket. He said that if she tried that again that he would kill her. He told her to remove her pyjamas and put on her day clothes. She did so. He then told her to undress as he was going to rape her. She undressed; he raped her twice anally and twice vaginally. In addition, he forced her to perform oral sex upon him. He ejaculated in her vagina. She went to reception with him and bought him some cigarettes and he left. Police were called and the defendant was arrested near the hotel. He claimed consent and that she had given him her room number when he had seen her in the street. At the time of the attack he was three times the drink-drive limit and had taken Ecstasy and other drugs. He was 19 and had previous convictions for false imprisonment and robbery (5 years earlier) and GBH (1 year earlier). Held. Of the aggravating features identified in Millberry 2003 2 Cr App Rep (S) 31, 5 or 6 were present here. There was an especially serious mental element on the victim whose job required her to stay frequently in hotel bedrooms and she further feared that she might have been infected with HIV. There was also the degradation of the forced oral sex. It was entirely appropriate to impose a sentence significantly above the 8-year starting point. **12 years** was severe but not manifestly excessive.

Robbers

See *Burglars/robbers, by*

Series of rapes/campaign of rape

157.46   *R v Millberry* 2003 2 Cr App R (S) 142. LCJ. Guideline case. **15 years and upwards** is the starting point for a campaign of rape. This is recommended where the offender has repeatedly raped the same victim over a course of time as well as for those cases involving multiple victims. (Note. In fact those who conduct a campaign of rape usually satisfy the criteria for a life sentence)

R v W & W 1999 1 Cr App R (S) 268. The defendant, F, the victim's father, pleaded guilty to eleven counts of rape, four counts of GBH with intent, four counts of indecent assault and five counts of cruelty to a child. The defendant M, the victim's mother, pleaded guilty to four counts of GBH with intent, four counts of indecent assault and two counts of cruelty to a child. The defendants were a married couple who had five children who were aged between 17 and 3 when the case came before the court. They lived with their children in squalor with rubbish being collected inside the house and the only lavatory facilities being a bucket. He disconnected the water and there was an overpowering smell in the house. They denied access to health visitors. W had had sexual intercourse with his eldest child since her 12th birthday. The child was also forced to perform oral sex and masturbate her father; she was paid £1 a time. She was also paid £25 for her mother to beat her. M tied her daughter to a bed, used a vibrator on her vagina and urinated in her mouth whilst the male defendant videoed the act. Videos were found depicting the eldest child being beaten and tortured by her mother with the father watching. The girl was tied to a metal bar on the ceiling and penetrated by a vibrator vaginally and anally. The victim was also made to tie her baby brother to his playpen and suck his penis. The 15-year-old daughter also described how she had been repeatedly raped since her 12th birthday. She was tied up and hit by the father with a cane. She was found to have knife and cigarette burns on her. The children were withdrawn and one aped the sexual behaviour she had seen. The sentencing judge said that the defendants had descended deep into a pit of human degradation. Held. No parallel could be drawn between the facts of this case and any other case. The judge did not err. **Life imprisonment**, with 21 years as the notional determinate sentence and 14 years as the specified period for the male defendant not wrong. **15 years** for the female defendant not altered.

Att-Gen's Ref. No 45 of 1998 1999 1 Cr App R (S) 461. The defendant was convicted of two counts of rape on two separate women. The defendant, who was now 26 years of age, began a consensual sexual relationship with the first victim, but the relationship ended. The defendant continued to pester the girl, who was then 18 years old. One evening after he had been drinking the defendant called at the victim's flat and persuaded her to let him in. The defendant pushed her onto the sofa, tore her nightdress, called her a bitch and raped her. The victim repeatedly pleaded with the defendant to stop. After the victim was allowed to use the toilet she was raped again. The defendant was arrested but released on bail. During this time the defendant raped a second woman who was the fiancé of a relative of his. The defendant called at her flat and was admitted. The defendant made advances towards the woman and would not leave. He picked her up in a fireman's lift and carried her upstairs, then raped her. The defendant ejaculated over the right side of her face and hair. The defendant left saying that he would return the following night. The defendant had a history of violence predominately on men. However, two convictions were for offences of violence on his then partner. The court took into account that the defendant committed an offence whilst on bail and that he attacked the victims when he knew they would be alone. Held. Taking into account it was a reference **9 years** not 6 years.

Att-Gen's Ref. No 8 of 1999 2000 1 Cr App R (S) 56. The defendant was convicted of five counts of rape and one count of indecent assault. Four counts of rape were on his daughter and one on his daughter's friend. He and his wife were divorced and his daughter lived with her mother. He looked after her daughter, who was 8, when her mother was in hospital. First he indecently assaulted her and thereafter raped the child on a number of occasions. The defendant made the child smell amyl nitrate and would perform oral sex upon her. The defendant took his daughter and another child, who was 13, to a caravan site. During the stay he anally raped the second child and again raped his daughter. The rapes were over 3 years. He was 37 and a warrant officer in the army and of good character. He would be dismissed from the army and lose considerable pension rights. Held. The defendant was in a position of responsibility to both victims. The lowest sentence that could be imposed was **12 years**. Taking into account that this is a reference **10 years**.

Att-Gen's Ref. No 44 of 1999 2000 1 Cr App R (S) 317. See **157.26**

Att-Gen's Ref. No 47 of 1999 2000 1 Cr App R (S) 446. The defendant was convicted of having a firearm with intent to commit robbery, indecent assault and rape. After midnight, a 15 year old boy answered a knock at the front door and the defendant and another chased the boy in. There were five or six children in the flat asleep. A loaded gun was held to a 15 year old's head. They ordered all four people in the room to get on the floor and not look at them. Money, jewellery and drugs were demanded. Personal items were seized from them. Two were hit with the gun for no obvious reason and one was tied up with a sheet. Oral sex was demanded at gunpoint. The other man attempted to rape a 19 year old girl, then ordered her into kitchen and raped her. He hit her with the gun. Then the defendant made her perform oral sex at gunpoint and raped her. The house was searched and they left. The gun was thought to have been loaded. The victim was very seriously traumatised. The defendant was arrested and denied involvement. He was then 20 and had no convictions. He was an illegal overstayer from Jamaica in the process of being deported. There was no underlying psychiatric condition. Held. The sentence should have been **14 years**. But because it was a reference, his good character and youth **11¹/₂ years** not 9.

R v Khan 2001 2 Cr App R (S) 285. See **157.39**

R v Hinds 2003 2 Cr App R (S) 455. The defendant was convicted of thirty two serious offences against 8 girls M, E, H, D, W, N, G and R aged 11–16 including rape, buggery and indecent assault. Three girls were raped. The defendant was about 27 when the offences started about 11 years before conviction. His mother was the commandant of an organisation for children with an interest in horses. The defendant was the farm manager. M was 12 when 2 years of abuse began. She was repeatedly raped and buggered. Once she was raped with such gratuitous violence that she bled. M was also forced to give the defendant oral sex. There was for her eight rapes, two buggeries and one indecent assault charged. E, the younger sister of M, was 11 when about 3 years of abuse began. She was raped on five occasions. The defendant forced her to have oral sex to ejaculation and once forced her to swallow his semen. He sent other rangers on the farm off site so that he could bugger her. The defendant kissed H, aged 14 and ran his hands over her body as she lay on a sofa. He also kissed D aged 14 and digitally penetrated her. W was 13 when she was pulled onto the defendant's lap. He then forced his hand down inside her clothing. When N was 14 the defendant took her for a walk off the site. He tried to kiss her then forced her to the ground and forcibly raped her. On another occasion she was made to give him oral sex then he raped her. He assaulted G when she was babysitting for him. R was nearly 14 when he kissed and assaulted her in the stables. He was arrested about 10 years after the abuse had started and denied it all. He had one irrelevant previous conviction. Whilst in custody he had successfully completed a sex offenders' programme. Held. N had written about the dreadful effect the offences had on her. No doubt others could have written similar accounts. For these offences, there was no reason why the judge should not impose consecutive sentences. This was a case that attracted a sentence of more than 15 years. There was violence, repeated rapes, careful planning, the victims had been subjected to further indignities and the victims were young. A sentence of substantially more than 15 years was appropriate. **18 years** upheld for each of the rapes and buggeries against M. **20 years** for the rapes against E and N upheld.

See also CONCURRENT OR CONSECUTIVE SENTENCES FOR TWO OR MORE RAPES

Old cases. *R v Henshall* 1995 16 Cr App R (S) 388, *R v M* 1996 2 Cr App R (S) 286, *Att-Gen's Ref. No 28 of* 1997 2 Cr App R (S) 206 (for short summary see **157.39**), *R v Rodwell* 1998 2 Cr App R (S) 1 and *R v Mountaine* 1998 2 Cr App R (S) 66. (For a summary of the last two cases see the first edition of this book.)

Sexually transmitted disease, defendant has

157.47 *R v Millberry* 2003 2 Cr App R (S) 142. LCJ. Guideline case. The **8 year** starting point is appropriate after a contested trial for rape by a man who is knowingly suffering from a life-threatening sexually transmissible disease, whether or not he has told the victim of his condition and whether or not the disease was actually transmitted. The **8 year** starting point is recommended either because of the impact of the offence upon the victim or the level of the offender's culpability, or both. The Panel adds that factors reflecting a high level of risk to society, in particular evidence of repeat offending, will indicate a substantially longer sentence. The seven grounds for raising the starting point to eight years each can vary in gravity. In a really bad case it can mean a higher figure is appropriate.

Stepfathers/step grandfathers

157.48   *R v Millberry* 2003 2 Cr App R (S) 142. LCJ. Guideline case The **8 year** start-ing point is appropriate after a contested trial for where the offender is in a position of responsibility towards the victim. The **8 year** starting point is recommended either because of the impact of the offence upon the victim or the level of the offender's cul-pability, or both. The Panel adds that factors reflecting a high level of risk to society, in particular evidence of repeat offending, will indicate a substantially longer sentence. The seven grounds for raising the starting point to eight years each can vary in gravity. In a really bad case it can mean a higher figure is appropriate.

Att-Gen's Ref. No 12 of 1998 1999 1 Cr App R (S) 44. The defendant pleaded guilty to two rapes and three indecent assaults. The prosecution was told of the guilty pleas a day before his trial. The offences were on his stepdaughter aged then between 11 and 13 over an 18 month period. The mother left her children in his care while she worked long hours in the evening. The defendant due to his epilepsy was unable to work. The offences started when he was 23 with touching her breasts and vagina over her clothing. Later there was digital penetration, oral sex and then full sex. He gave her cig-arettes. He was 23 when the offences started and of good character. Held. The discount for the plea should be reduced because the girl had been left in suspense for so long. The appropriate sentence was **at least 7 years**. Because it was a reference and the other circumstances **6 years** not 4.

Att-Gen's Ref. No 23 of 1999 2000 1 Cr App R (S) 258. The defendant was convicted of two counts of indecent assault and one count of rape against his stepdaughter when she was between the ages of 11 and 13. The defendant was convicted 20 years after the offences took place. When the victim was 11 the defendant married her mother. The abuse began almost immediately. The defendant touched the girl's vagina over her underwear. She told him to stop. When the victim was 12 she had to go to hospital for an injection. She became drowsy and fell asleep. When she woke, she was in a car in a country lay-by. She found the defendant on top of her trying to force her legs open. She screamed and cried and he slapped her across her face and called her a frigid bitch. He drove her home and sent her to bed. Just before her 13th birthday the defendant came into her bedroom, put his hand over her mouth and raped her. Her vagina was bleeding. He bullied her and told her if she told anyone her mother would die. The victim suffered considerably as a result of the abuse. She had very low self-esteem and could not relate to her husband. She was forced to seek counselling. The defendant, who was 57 at the time of conviction, suffered ill health. He had a conviction for unlawful sexual intercourse with a girl under 13 and was released from prison only months before this abuse began. The victims of those offences were his stepdaughters from a previous relationship. Held. Taking into account the short period of time from the defendant's release from prison and when this new abuse started and the effect on the victim 4 years was unduly lenient. The appropriate sentence was **9 years**. As this was a reference **7 years**.

Att-Gen's Ref. No 71 of 1999 2000 2 Cr App R (S) 83. The defendant was convicted of three rapes, one indecent assault and one gross indecency. The offences were over a 9 month period against his stepdaughter when she was 7 or 8 years old. While his wife was out he raped her and tried to make her suck his penis. It went close to her face. He also performed oral sex on her. The medical evidence referred to the injury to the girl as being slight. The defendant was 38 and had convictions (no details given). The pre-sentence report said he was holding the girl responsible for the offences. There was a significant risk of re-offending. Held. There was no mitigation. The sentence should have been **10 or 11 years**. Because it was a reference **9 years** substituted for 6. 2 years for the indecent assaults increased to 3 but remaining concurrent.

See also **BUGGERY** – *Stepfathers*

Old cases. *R v M* 1996 2 Cr App R (S) 286 and *Att-Gen's Ref. No 5 of 1996* 2 Cr App R (S) 434.

Stranger rape – Guideline case

157.49   *R v Millberry* 2003 2 Cr App R (S) 142. LCJ. In drawing the balance it is not to be overlooked, when considering 'stranger rape', the victim's fear can be increased because her assailant is an unknown quantity. Is he a murderer as well as a rapist? In addition, when a rape is committed by a stranger in a public place, not only is the offence horrific to the victim, it can also frighten other members of the public.

Street attack on victim

157.50   *R v Chowdury* 1999 2 Cr App R (S) 269. The defendant was convicted of rape on a stranger. The victim, who was partially deaf in both ears, was walking home at about 2am. She had drunk about thirteen bottles of beer. The defendant began to follow her and then caught up with her and said, 'I want you to come home with me.' He tugged at her sleeve and she managed to pull free. He continued to walk behind her and then dragged her off the road to a secluded spot. He pushed her to the ground and raped her. The victim went back to the road and screamed hysterically. The victim said she felt humiliated, violated and ashamed. She found her dealings with the police extremely traumatic. The defendant, who was 30 years old, was of extremely limited intellect and was a continuing danger to women. Held. The serious impact the offence had on the victim was the strongest aggravating factor making the starting point 8 years. The other factors including the dragging her to a quiet spot and him being a continuing danger to women means **10 years** was entirely justified.

R v Maidment 2000 1 Cr App R 457. The defendant pleaded guilty, to rape. The plea was indicated four days before trial. At about 2.30am the 17 year old victim was walking home. He attempted to engage her in conversation and she ignored him. As she continued walking he followed her and she became increasingly uneasy. As she quickened her pace he caught up with her and placed his hand on her buttocks. She removed his hand and he moved in front of her to block her path. He seized her and pinned her against a wall. Her struggling was in vain. He slapped or punched her on her head several times and ended up on the ground. He got on top of her and put his fingers in her vagina. He produced a bottle of amyl nitrate and told her to sniff it and she refused to do it. He then raped her. He told her to get up and she continued with her journey shaking with fear. When she reached her home he followed her in. She went to her brother's room and when she and her brother went to the hall he had left. She had bruising, a cut lip and scratches. When arrested he continued to deny the offence until confronted with the evidence of a DNA match. He was 32 with no relevant convictions. Held. His conduct was very serious indeed. Because of the gratuitous violence and her being waylaid at night after a trial it would have warranted a sentence of the dimension of **8 years**. Taking into account his late plea that would be discounted to **6 years**.

Att-Gen's Ref. No. 6 of 2002 2003 1 Cr App R (S) 357. The defendant was convicted of rape and indecent assault. He and two friends went to a nightclub and saw the victim aged 17 and her female friend. He made a nuisance of himself, dancing close to her and making passes at her. She made it clear she was not interested in him and said she had a current boyfriend. This didn't stop him following her about the club. At 2am the club was empty except for the five of them. They left and talked outside for a time and the two girls fell over. The two girls then decided to walk to a taxi rank and the three men followed. The defendant said he would stay with the two girls and his two friends left. The victim went to a phone box and the defendant followed. She called her boyfriend and as she left the phone box he pushed her back in and banged her head on the wall of the kiosk. He seized her by the back of the neck and forced her to the ground. As he kissed her face he said, "Do as I say or I'll kill you." To emphasise this he hit her across the face a number of times and took off her jacket and unzipped her trousers. He forced more than one of his fingers into her vagina and after a struggle she ran off. She was crying and screaming for help and he pursued her, grabbed her and pulled her to the ground. Next he pulled off her top and while she was lying in a puddle in the pouring rain he licked her vagina. Then he put his fingers inside and raped her. She repeatedly asked why and he said, "You shouldn't be so fucking pretty. It's your fault." She managed to spray him with a can of deodorant and run away. She was completely naked and he ran after her shouting he hadn't finished and he was going to kill her. She banged on the windows of a house and was let in. By now she was hysterical. He was picked out on an ID parade and the DNA from the can matched. Since the attack she was extremely reluctant to go out at night, found it difficult to sleep, was on medication and her sex life with her boyfriend was almost non-existent. He was 18 and in his last year at school and working at a fast food outlet. There were no previous convictions. He was sentenced to 6 and 2 years concurrent. The pre-sentence report said he remained a continuing threat to young girls but the Judge said there was nothing more than normal to be found in such cases. Held. The Judge's approach to the risk factor was perfectly proper. For an adult **8 years and upwards** would be the proper range and **10 years** could not be characterised as manifestly excessive. Taking into account the age of the defendant **7 years and upwards** would be proper. Therefore 6 years was unduly lenient. However as it was a reference it would not be appropriate to alter it.

R v JC 2005 1 Cr App R 37. The defendants JC and A were convicted of rape having pleaded guilty to indecent assault and indecency with a child. JC was 13 and 14 and A was 17 at the time of the offences; 15 and 18 respectively at sentence. V was the victim of the rape. With a friend, she had some alcohol and went socialising. They were approached by the defendants who separated V from her friend. Together they pushed V up the road (JC took the lead). She tried to run away but she was pushed and fell onto the road with her head against the pavement. She screamed, but then she was raped by each defendant in turn. A raped her anally and JC raped her vaginally. She was literally in the gutter and screaming in pain. In interview they said that it was consensual. JC indecently assaulted RM. He was attracted to her; she was not interested. On one occasion he chased her into an alleyway, put her into a headlock forced his hands down her trousers, touched her bottom and tried to go round the front. Later she was physically sick (6 months). The indecency with a child concerned both defendants and the victim, SC. They got to know her and started to treat her like a sex object. She was met by the defendants and told by JC that she was going to lose her virginity that day. She was taken to a male public lavatory and forced to perform oral sex on JC and A (who masturbated and ejaculated over her jacket) (12 months each). Some weeks later, JC phoned SC and told her to meet him. In an alleyway JC forced SC to perform oral sex on him. He then masturbated and wiped his penis on her jacket (2 years consecutive). JC then took her to his home and was joined by A who forced SC to perform oral sex on him (2 years consecutive). Each victim was badly affected. Both JC and A were of good character. The sentences imposed for gross indecency were unlawful. Held. As far as the rape was concerned, looking at the dimensions to consider in assessing gravity, (Millberry 2003 Cr App Rep (S) 31) there were 3 features: the degree of harm to the victim, the culpability of the defendant and the risk posed to society by the defendant. If the defendants had been adults their offences of rape would have attracted **10 years** or more after a trial. **7 years** was imposed for the rape but the overall sentences were **9 years**. The additional 2 years for the indecency offences were quashed but the sentence for rape was increased to 9 years; no separate penalty was imposed for the other offences (see *R v Mills* 1998 2 Cr App R (S) 128. The Court of Appeal had the power to increase individual sentences to reflect the over all criminality "Taking the case as a whole" (see *R v Sandwell 1985 80 Cr App R 78*) as long as the total sentence was not increased. So **9 years** detention each.

Two or more men acting together

157.51 *R v Millberry* 2003 2 Cr App R (S) 142. LCJ. Guideline case The **8 year** starting point is appropriate after a contested trial where the rape is committed by two or more offenders acting together. The **8 year** starting point is recommended either because of the impact of the offence upon the victim or the level of the offender's culpability, or both. The Panel adds that factors reflecting a high level of risk to society, in particular evidence of repeat offending, will indicate a substantially longer sentence. The seven grounds for raising the starting point to eight years each can vary in gravity. In a really bad case it can mean a higher figure is appropriate.

R v Khan 2001 2 Cr App R (S) 285. See **157.39**

Victim aged under 13 – Guideline cases/remarks

157.52 *R v Millberry* 2003 2 Cr App R (S) 142. LCJ. Guideline case. The **8 year** starting point is appropriate after a contested trial where the offender rapes a child. The **8 year** starting point is recommended either because of the impact of the offence upon the victim or the level of the offender's culpability, or both. The Panel adds that factors reflecting a high level of risk to society, in particular evidence of repeat offending, will indicate a substantially longer sentence. The seven grounds for raising the starting point to eight years each can vary in gravity. In a really bad case it can mean a higher figure is appropriate.

R v Corran 2005 Unreported 2/2/05. The Court considered the wider definition of rape and offences against children under 13. No precise guidance can be given. The appropriate sentence is likely to lie within a very wide bracket. There will be very few cases in which immediate custody is not called for even for young offenders. There will be some offences where there is no question of consent and where significant aggravating features are present where long determinate or life sentences will be called for. The presence of consent is material particularly for young defendants. The age of the defendant, of itself and when compared with the age of the victim is also an important factor. A **very short period of custody** is likely to suffice for a teenager where the other party consents. In exceptional cases like this one a **non-custodial sentence** may be appropriate for a young defendant. If the offender is much older than the victim a substantial term of imprisonment is called for. Other factors include the nature of the relationship between the two and their respective characters and maturity, the number of occasions when penetration occurred, the circumstances of the penetration, including whether contraception was used, the consequences for the victim, emotional and physically, the degree of remorse and the likelihood of repetition. A reasonable belief that the victim was 16 will also be a mitigating factor. Pre Act authorities such as *R v Bulmer 1989 11 Cr App R (S) 586, R v Oakley* 1990 12 Cr App R (S) 215 and *R v Bough* 1997 1 Cr App R (S) 55 which indicate a sentence in the order of **15 months** for a defendant in his 20s will continue to provide assistance.

Victim aged under 13

157.53 *R v Anderson* 1999 1 Cr App R (S) 273. See **157.29**

R v King 1999 2 Cr App R (S) 376. See **157.29**

Att-Gen's Ref. No 64 of 1998 1999 2 Cr App R (S) 395. The defendant pleaded guilty at an early stage to eleven charges of rapes and indecent assault against his two nieces. There were three rapes and an attempted rape. They took place over 9 years. The offences came to light 12 years after the offending against the two girls stopped. The victim's mother died when the nieces were 5 and 6 so they had to live with their grandmother. After her death the girls had to live with the defendant and his wife. The defendant had already begun to indecently assault the younger of the two girls before she lived with him. It started when she was 5. When she was 9 the abuse turned into rape. This became a regular event. The defendant then began to indecently assault the older girl. The assaults were of a particular unpleasant character. The offences came to light 10 to 12 years after they had been committed. The effect on the girls was very serious. From time to time they would run away from home and the elder girl tried to commit suicide. The defendant had a conviction for attempted rape of the third sister when she was 15 years old (he received an 18 month suspended sentence). There were no offences since then. He was 46. The girls, now women, asked that the defendant be allowed home. Held. **10 years** would have been appropriate. Taking into account the time that had elapsed since the offences and the fact that this was a reference, **7 years** not 3 years.

Att-Gen's Ref. No 18 of 1999 2000 1 Cr App R (S) 246. See **Para 157.29**

Att-Gen's Ref. No 28 of 1999 2000 1 Cr App R (S) 314. LCJ. The defendant pleaded guilty to two counts of attempted rape, four counts of indecent assault and one count of indecency with a child at the first opportunity. The victim was the 6 year old daughter of the woman with whom he was living with. The defendant asked the victim to put his penis in her mouth and to masturbate him, which she refused to do. The defendant then masturbated in front of her. The defendant lay with his penis exposed and made the girl lie on top of him. The defendant also digitally penetrated the girl at least three times and placed his penis between her legs and pushed his penis between the cheeks of her bottom. On a later occasion he penetrated her anally. She said it hurt and he stopped. The victim told her mother and he left the house that evening. The child's anus was not damaged but her character had been affected by the events. Previously she was affectionate and cheerful but now she was quiet, withdrawn, tearful and afraid of men. Her sleep was disturbed. The defendant admitted the matters in interview. He was 24 and of good character. He was assessed as having a high risk of re-offending. He expressed regret and disgust towards himself. Held. After a trial the appropriate sentence would have been in the order of **6 years**. Taking into account the early plea, which saved the victim the trauma of the fear of giving evidence, and that he had spent time in a bail hostel **4 years** would be appropriate. However, as it was a reference **3 years** was suitable. **30 months** was unduly lenient, but it would not be appropriate to increase the sentence by 6 months.

R v Maishman 2000 1 Cr App R (S) 419. The defendant pleaded guilty to two rapes and ABH of a 7-year-old girl. He rented a room in the girl's stepfather's public house where she lived. The defendant on Christmas evening had a few drinks with her family and played with the children. After the girl had had a happy day she went to bed. At night he entered her bedroom and carried her to his room. Once in his room she called for her mother and he punched her in the eye and told her to be quiet. He undressed her and then had vaginal and anal sex with her. He tried to make her perform oral sex on him. He also punched her on the nose causing it to bleed. At one stage he covered her face with a pillow. Next morning when the mother asked the girl about the injuries the defendant seemed overprotective towards her. The girl said she had fallen over. At hospital she was treated for a black eye and a bruised nose and forehead. Later the girl was able to say what had happened. The defendant was arrested and said he could recall little of what had happened on Christmas Day because he was drunk. Four days after the rapes a paediatrician found bruising to the inside of her mouth and a tear on the inside of her lip. There was a deep cut at the base of her hymen and an acute fissure in her anus. The child's personality changed. She now wakes up crying, wets her bed and has nightmares. She plays by herself and is clingy and frightened. He was now 45 and had no relevant convictions. The judge said the offence was cruel and vicious and would have long lasting effects on her. Held. The effect on her was devastating and disastrous. The attack was depraved. The aggravating features were the age of the child; the age gap between them; the two rapes; the violence before and after the rapes; the attempt to perform oral sex; the effects on the victim and the breach of trust. If there had been a trial **14–16 years** would be appropriate. Because the case was o verwhelming **14 years** was at the top of the bracket but not manifestly excessive.

Att-Gen's Ref. No 12 of 2001 2002 2 Cr App R (S) 382. [The defendant aided and abetted the rape of a baby of some friends by her partner. 4 years was lenient but not disturbed.]

R v Corran 2005 Unreported 2/2/05. The defendant aged 20 pleaded guilty to rape. The victim was 12 and looked 16. Every feature of mitigation that could be present was present. Held. A **non custodial** would have been appropriate. As he had spent 5¹/₂months in custody **CD** instead.

Old case R v Stepton 1998 2 Cr App R (S) 319. **9 years** not 7 for buggery of this 9 year old boy by a 44 year old who pleaded guilty.

See also *Stepfathers/step grandfathers*

Victim aged 13–15

157.54 *R v Millberry* 2003 2 Cr App R (S) 142. LCJ. Guideline case The **8 year** starting point is appropriate after a contested trial where the offender rapes a child. The **8 year** starting point is recommended either because of the impact of the offence upon the victim or the level of the offender's culpability, or both. The Panel adds that factors reflecting a high level of risk to society, in particular evidence of repeat offending, will indicate a substantially longer sentence. The seven grounds for raising the starting point to eight years each can vary in gravity. In a really bad case it can mean a higher figure is appropriate.

R v Triggs 2000 2 Cr App R (S) 179. The defendant was convicted of attempted rape and anal rape. The victim aged 13 had an argument with her mother packed her bags and left home. She went to some grassland and was reading a book when the defendant approached her from behind. He dragged her into some bushes and held a knife to her throat. He undressed her and unsuccessful tried to rape her. Then he anally raped her. The victim had three small tears in her anus. The defendant was 28 with 14 previous convictions including a firearm offence but no sex offences. He had a very rudimentary knowledge of sexuality and relationships. He had little education and a number of other problems from his childhood. The judge said there was a very real risk of further offending and causing serious harm. Later an expert said the risk was low. **12 years** not 14 years.

R v S 2001 Unreported 14/9/01. The defendant pleaded guilty to rape. He was aged 16 at conviction. The victim was 15 years old. He thought she consented to start with and during the act she tried to push him off. He was sentenced on the basis he was reckless and had carried on regardless. Held. Because of *R v Greaves* 1999 1 Cr App Rep (S) 319, the court had to pass a sentence that was less than *Greaves*. Therefore **12 month's** detention and training not 30 months.

R v Millberry 2003 2 Cr App R (S) Re Mi at p 158. The defendant pleaded guilty on re-arraignment to rape. He met the victim who was 15 two weeks before the offence. The defendant invited him back to his house and after some initial horseplay pulled him to the floor, pulled down his trousers and engaged in oral sex. He then pinned the victim down, by kneeling on his arms, pulled down his trousers and had anal sex. He threatened the victim that if he told anyone he would make it worse for him. The following day he was arrested and made full admissions. The defendant was 17 at the time of the offence and 18 at his sentence. He had one caution for a minor indecent assault on an 11 year old boy about a year before the rape. There was a perceived high risk of re-offending. A psychiatric report said that the defendant was having difficulty adjusting to the fact that he was a homosexual. His emotional and social development had a number of deficits. Held. The starting point should be 5 years. However, there were aggravating features: the age of the victim and force used, albeit it was within the range that can be inherent in the case of forcible rape. **4 years detention** not 5.

Att-Gen's Ref. Nos. 91, 119 and 120 of 2002 re TAG 2003 2 Cr App R (S) 338 at 341. The defendant was convicted of two rapes, two indecent assaults and two counts of cruelty to children. In late 1980 or early 1981, his daughter told her friend aged 13 to wait in her bedroom. The defendant came in, pinned her against a wall, forced her to the floor and raped her. He threatened to kill her if she told anyone. Previously he had shown her pornographic and violent films. While doing this he had frequently felt her breasts. She was a virgin and since then had suffered repeated nightmares. As an adult she had matrimonial problems which needed counselling that may refer back to the rape. Between August 1980 and August 1982 he took another of her daughter's friends aged 12 or 13 on a motorbike to a field where he forced her to the ground, put his arm round her throat, slapped her and raped her. Her lip bled and he blamed her for struggling. In about 1973, when his son was 7 he severely smacked him. When he was 8 he made the boy stand on a chair in front of his sister before pulling down his trousers and whipping him with the buckle end of a belt. He used extreme violence on his daughter for her most minor transgressions. He would strike her with a knife and throw her round the room. He abused her verbally and carved "I hate you" on her bed head. He put her in the lavatory and banged her head on the door. When she was 8 or 9 and lying between her parents in bed she woke up to find him pressing her vagina. He was 54 and when 20 or 21 he was given a suspended sentence for rape. The PSR said there was a high risk of further offending. Held. Each rape on its own called for **8 years at least** because of the age of the victim. If concurrent the total sentence should have been **12 years** for each of the rapes and 3 years for each of the cruelty counts consecutive making 15 years. 15 months was the least sentence for the assaults because of the girls' age, their vulnerability and the breach of trust. Those sentences should be concurrent to the others. Because it was a reference **11 years** for the rapes and 2 years consecutive for the cruelty making 13 years not 8 years for the rapes, 3 for the cruelty and 9 months for the assaults all concurrent.

See also **Stepfathers/step grandfathers** and *R v Tack* 1997 Unreported 7/7/97.

Old cases. *R v Stone* 1995 16 Cr App R 407, *R v Brumwell* 1996 1 Cr App R (S) 213, *Att-Gen's Ref. No 36 of 1995* 1996 2 Cr App R (S) 50, *R v M* 1996 2 Cr App R (S) 286, *R v Matthews* 1998 1 Cr App R (S) 220, *R v Canavan Re S* 1998 1 Cr App R (S) 243 *at 251* and *R v Geary* 1998 2 Cr App R (S) 434.

Victim aged 16–17

157.55   *R v Maidment* 2000 1 Cr App R 457. The defendant pleaded guilty, to rape. The plea was indicated four days before trial. At about 2.30am the 17-year-old victim was walking home. He attempted to engage her in conversation and she ignored him. As she continued walking he followed and she became increasingly uneasy. As she quickened her pace he caught up with her and placed his hand on her buttocks. She removed his hand and he moved in front of her to block her path. He seized her and pinned against a wall. Her struggling was in vain. He slapped or punched her on head several times and she ended up on the ground. He got on top of her and put his fingers in her vagina. He produced a bottle of amyl nitrate and told her to sniff it and she refused to do it. He then raped her. He told her to get up and she continued with her journey shaking with fear. When she reached her home he followed her in. She went to her brother's room and when she and her brother went to the hall he had left. She had bruising, a cut lip and scratches. When arrested he continued to deny the offence until confronted with the evidence of a DNA match. He was 32 with no relevant convictions. Held. His conduct was very serious indeed. Because of the gratuitous violence and her being waylaid at night after a trial it would have warranted a sentence of the dimension of **8 years**. Taking into account his late guilty plea that would be discounted to **6 years**.

Victim aged over 65

157.56 *R v Millberry* 2003 2 Cr App R (S) 142. LCJ. Guideline case The **8 year** starting point is appropriate after a contested trial where the offender rapes a victim who is especially vulnerable because of physical frailty, mental impairment or disorder. The **8 year** starting point is recommended either because of the impact of the offence upon the victim or the level of the offender's culpability, or both. The Panel adds that factors reflecting a high level of risk to society, in particular evidence of repeat offending, will indicate a substantially longer sentence. The seven grounds for raising the starting point to eight years each can vary in gravity. In a really bad case it can mean a higher figure is appropriate.

Old cases. *R v Thomas* 1995 16 Cr App R (S) 686; *R v Mason* 1995 16 Cr App R (S) 860.

Victim, bad effect on

157.57 *R v Millberry* 2003 2 Cr App R (S) 142. A sentence above the **5 years** as the starting point is appropriate when one of the nine aggravating factors is present. The presence of one or more such factors could, depending on the degree of their seriousness, raise the sentence about the starting point of 8 years. Factor iv is an especially serious physical or mental effect on the victim; this would include, for example, a rape resulting in pregnancy, or in transmission of a life-threatening or serious disease

R v Chowdury 1999 2 Cr App R (S) 269. The defendant was convicted of rape on a stranger. The victim, who was partially deaf in both ears, was walking home at about 2am. She had drunk about 13 bottles of beer. The defendant began to follow her and then caught up with her said, 'I want you to come home with me.' He tugged at her sleeve and she managed to pull free. He continued to walk behind her and then dragged her off the road to a secluded spot. He pushed her to the ground and raped her. The victim went back to the road and screamed hysterically. The victim said she felt humiliated, violated and ashamed. She found her dealings with the police extremely traumatic. The defendant, who was 30 years old, was of extremely limited intellect and was a continuing danger to women. Held. The serious impact the offence had on the victim was the strongest aggravating factor making the starting point 8 years. The other factors including the dragging her to a quiet spot and him being a continuing danger to women means **10 years** was entirely justified.

Victim initially consents to sexual familiarity – Guideline case

157.58 *R v Millberry* 2003 2 Cr App R (S) 142. LCJ. Where, for example, the victim has consented to sexual familiarity with the defendant on the occasion in question, but has said 'no' to sexual intercourse at the last moment, the offender's culpability for rape is somewhat less than it would have been if he had intended to rape the victim from the outset. This is not to say that any responsibility for the rape attaches to the victim. It is simply to say that the offender's culpability is somewhat less than it otherwise would have been. The degree of the offender's culpability should be reflected in the sentence, but, given the inherent gravity of the offence of rape, the sentence adjustment in such a case should, we think, be relatively small.

Victim initially consents to sexual familiarity

157.59 *R v Greaves* 1999 1 Cr App R (S) 319. The defendant pleaded guilty to the rape of a 17 year old woman after she initially consented but then withdrew her consent. The victim was friendly with the defendant and asked him to come to the flat where she was staying. Shortly after his arrival sexual intimacy took place and the couple began to have sexual intercourse. However the victim at this late stage said, 'No Steve. This isn't what I want. Stop.'. The defendant did not stop until the act of sexual intercourse was completed. The defendant, who was aged 34, had no previous convictions of a sexual nature. The trial judge attached a great deal of significance to the disparity in ages between the defendant and the victim; this was not appropriate, the girl was over the age of consent. Held. **18 months** not $3\frac{1}{2}$ years.

R v S 2001 Unreported 14/9/01. The defendant pleaded guilty to rape. He was aged 16 at conviction. The victim was 15 years old. He thought she consented to start with and during the act she tried to push him off. He was sentenced on basis he was reckless and had carried on regardless. Held. Because of *R v Greaves* 1999 1 Cr App R (S) 319, the court had to pass a sentence that was less than *Greaves*. Therefore **12 month's** detention and training not 30 months.

Victim does not want the defendant sent to prison/Victim has forgiven him

157.60 *R v Dredge* 1998 1 Cr App R (S) 285. The victim suffered an extremely painful and degrading rape. However, she said she wanted the relationship to continue and to marry him. The victim was not prepared to give evidence. Held. The views of the victim are always a factor to be taken into account. That also has to be balanced, however, against the public interest that a sentence which is appropriate is passed. For further details see the first edition of this book.

R v Mills 1998 2 Cr App R (S) 252. The defendant pleaded guilty to attempted rape, having called the victim as a witness at committal hearing. Two weeks after being told his relationship with the victim was over he waited for her to return to her house. He had been drinking. He dragged her down the road and pushed her to a grassy area. He took out his penis but had no erection. He made threats to kill her and ripped away at her tights. She struggled and after a verbal exchange he desisted. He pulled her to her feet and punched her. He started to take her to a nearby garage but she managed to escape. He told police he had had 10 pints of beer. He had previous for manslaughter when he fought with another man. Both had weapons. The victim attended the Court of Appeal saying they 'were back together'. Held. The victim of a crime cannot tell the court that because she has forgiven the defendant they should treat the crime as not having happened. But we can take it into account. **3 years** not 6.

R v S 1998 Unreported 3/12/98. Insufficient account taken of the view of the victim so sentence reduced.

R v Perks 2000 Crim LR 606. The opinions of the victim and the victim's close relatives on the appropriate level of sentence should not be taken into account except (a) where the sentence passed on the offender was aggravating the victim's distress and (b) where the victim's forgiveness or unwillingness to press charges provided evidence that his or her psychological or mental suffering must be very much less than would normally be the case.

See also VICTIMS and DEATH BY DANGEROUS DRIVING, CAUSING – *Victims, the views of the relatives of* and *R v N* 2000 Unreported 5/5/99.

Old cases. *R v Henshall* 1995 16 Cr App R (S) 388.

Victim exposing herself to danger

157.61 *R v Billam* 1986 82 Cr App R 347. LCJ. Victim exposing herself, e.g. accepting a lift, is not a mitigating factor.

Victim mentally defective

157.62 *R v Millberry* 2003 2 Cr App R (S) 142. LCJ. Guideline case The **8 year**

starting point is appropriate after a contested trial where the victim is especially vulnerable; has a mental impairment or disorder, or learning disability. The **8 year** starting point is recommended either because of the impact of the offence upon the victim or the level of the offender's culpability, or both. The Panel adds that factors reflecting a high level of risk to society, in particular evidence of repeat offending, will indicate a substantially longer sentence. The seven grounds for raising the starting point to eight years each can vary in gravity. In a really bad case it can mean a higher figure is appropriate.

Att-Gen's Ref. No. 69 of 2001 2002 2 Cr App R (S) 593. The defendant was convicted of rape and indecent assault, for which he received no penalty. The victim was 58 and suffered from Huntington's chorea, an appalling progressive disease of the brain. This caused her to suffer from dementia and impairment of the intellectual function, memory and understanding, together with associated psychotic symptoms. She had an IQ of 52 and was a "defective" within the meaning of the Sexual Offences Act 1956 s 45. Her condition meant she lost her inhibitions and had a tendency to invent or fill gaps in her memory. She was discharged from the psychiatric department of a hospital and went to a residential care home. Shortly after that the defendant and his brother, M, went to visit another resident, P at the home. The defendant was 29 with an IQ of 52. He had a reading and perceptual age of a 9 year old. In some respects he performed like a 6 year old. All four of them were in P's room and there was some horseplay and P encouraged the defendant to ask the victim for sex, which took place. The prosecution case was she repeatedly said words like, "No" and "Stop it". M participated and attempted oral sex and touched her breasts. A care worker heard shouting and discovered the victim with her pants down. The defence was consent. He received 3 years with a 3 years extension. Both sides appealed. Held. It was a very difficult sentencing decision. The defence suggestion that there should have been a guardianship order was wrong because the case was not wholly exceptional such as to warrant a non-custodial. She was very vulnerable with child-like tendencies. The aggravating features were that vulnerability, her age and that it took place in a nursing home. The vulnerability was seriously aggravating. Without his impairment the correct sentence would have been **8 years**. The correct sentence would have been **5 years**. Because of the need for a substantial discount as it was a reference and the extended period the sentence was not increased.

Victim's previous sexual experience

157.63   *R v Billam* 1986 82 Cr App R 347. LCJ. Old guideline case. It is irrelevant.

Violence, with (including offences of GBH etc)

157.64   *R v Millberry* 2003 2 Cr App R (S) 142. A sentence **above the 5 years** as the starting point is appropriate when one of the nine aggravating factors is present. The presence of one or more such factors could, depending on the degree of their seriousness, raise the sentence about the starting point of 8 years. Factor vi is "the offender has broken into or otherwise gained access to the place where the victim is living. (Note An intent to burgle is not quite the same as an intent to break in. It could be assumed that where there is a predetermined intent to rape, rob or steal the starting point could be higher. Much will depend on the facts.)

R v W & W 1999 1 Cr App R (S) 268. See **157.46**

R v Maishman 2000 1 Cr App R (S) 419. See page **157.53**.

Att-Gen's Ref. Nos. 35 etc. of 2003 Re TG 2004 1 Cr App R (S) 499 at 512. The defendant was convicted of rape and causing GBH to his partner. The victim was 57. She formed a relationship with the defendant, who moved in with her. She suffered with heart problems and asthma. She suffered violence at his hands and made complaints on twenty two occasions. The two had not had sexual relations for many months and she wanted him to leave. One afternoon the defendant had been drinking and began to physically torment the victim, punching her about the body and flicking her in the head with his fingers. The police were called and put him out of the house. He returned that night. The next day he spent drinking at her flat and was drunk by the evening. The victim went to bed in her own room and closed the door. The defendant barged his way in, she asked him to leave. "I want to fuck you" he replied. She wet herself. He climbed on top of her, removed her underwear and held her whilst she was on all fours and raped her forcefully, causing her pain. He attempted to force a cider bottle into her anus. It was degrading. The next day the defendant returned to the victim's home, very drunk. He immediately began to abuse the victim, by punching her several times to the face and biting her arm. He took her mobile phone. Fortunately she was able to run to a neighbour's kitchen. She was taken to hospital with 39 bruises, a broken nose, a bite mark and a closed eye. There was redness and tenderness of the vulva and perianum showed laxity and redness of the anal verge. When interviewed the defendant made no reply. The defendant denied rape at trial and asserted he acted in self-defence in relation to the section 18. The victim was hospitalised during the course of her evidence. He was 51. Held. The offences called for consecutive sentences. This was a brutal rape that merited **7 years** (more if it stood alone) and not 5 years. The violence warranted an additional **12 months** (not 3 years concurrent). **8 years** in total, not 5.

Old cases. *R v Thomas* 1995 16 Cr App R (S) 686, *R v Thorpe* 1996 2 Cr App R (S) 246, *R v Masood* 1997 2 Cr App R (S) 137, (for summary see page **157.39**), *R v Matthews* 1998 1 Cr App R (S) 220, *R v Reid* 1998 2 Cr App R (S) 10, *Att-Gen's Ref. No 14 of 1998* 1999 1 Cr App R (S) 205, (for summary of last three cases see the first edition of this book.).

158   RELIGIOUSLY AGGRAVATED OFFENCES

158.1   Criminal Justice Act 2003 Section 145(2)

Where "the offence is ... religiously aggravated, the court must treat that fact as an aggravating factor and must state in open court that the offence was so aggravated."

Powers of Criminal Courts (Sentencing) Act 2000 Section 153(2)

"If the offence was ... religiously aggravated, the court shall treat that fact as an aggravating factor (that is to say, a factor that increases the seriousness of the offence); and shall state in open court that the offence was so aggravated."

Magistrates' Court Sentencing Guidelines January 2004

Racially or religiously aggravated offences

158.2   There are special provisions on racial and religious aggravation, under the Crime and Disorder Act 1998 as amended. There are two forms of aggravation; an offence is racially or religiously aggravated EITHER if it is racially or religiously motivated, OR if in committing the offence the offender demonstrates racial or religious hostility (e.g. by making a racist remark). The guideline case for sentencing for these offences is Kelly and Donnelly 2001, and three situations should be treated separately:

i)   there are a few specific racially or religiously aggravated offences in the Crime and Disorder Act, which have higher maximum penalties than the non-aggravated versions of those offences (e.g. common assault, ABH, criminal damage, etc). Where a defendant is convicted of one of these special offences, the court should determine its sentence for the basic offence (such as criminal damage or assault), and then decide how much to add for the racial or religious aggravation. When the sentence is announced, the court should state how much it added to the basic offence in order to reflect the racial or religious aggravation.

ii) most offences do not have a specific racially or religiously aggravated version, however. Here, the general principle applies, which is that racial or religious aggravation is a factor that should increase the severity of the sentence.

iii) where an offender is convicted of an offence which has a racially or religiously aggravated version, but is convicted only of the basic offence, it is wrong in principle to pass a higher sentence on racial or religious grounds. If the racially or religiously aggravated version of the offence is not charged or not proved, that is the end of the matter.

REMAND

See CUSTODY, DISCOUNT FOR TIME SPENT IN

REPORT

See FAILING TO STOP/FAILING TO REPORT

RESENTENCED, THE DEFENDANT IS

See DEFENDANT – *Resentenced, discount for being*

159   RESTRAINING ORDER, BREACH OF

159.1   Protection from Harassment Act 1997 s 5

Triable either way. On indictment maximum sentence 5 years. Summary maximum 6 months and/or £5,000.

The Criminal Justice Act 2003 creates a summary maximum sentence of 51 weeks, a minimum custodial sentence of 28 weeks and Custody plus. The Home Office says they do not expect to introduce these provisions before September 2006.

Anti-Social Behavioural orders Where the defendant has acted in a manner that caused or was likely to cause harassment, alarm or distress to one or more persons not in the same household as the defendant and it is necessary to protect persons from further anti-social acts by him/her the court may make this order[15].

Guideline remarks

159.2   *R v Pace* 2005 1 Cr App R (S) 370. The defendant was convicted of breaching a restraining order Held. The relevant factors are the nature of the act giving rise to the breach, the effect on the victim, whether the breach was the first of that order, the defendant's record and in particular how he had previously responded to community penalties.

Breach after some compliance

159.3   *R v Kasoar* 2002 2 Cr App R (S) 260. The defendant pleaded guilty to breaching

15 Crime and Disorder Act 1998 s 1C

a restraining order. He had a relationship with the victim for about a year and a half from 1995. After the break up he used to park his car outside her place of work. She ignored that. After she got married in 1996 he constantly followed her from her work to her home. That disrupted her relationship and she separated from her husband. In January 2000 there was harassment and assault and he was convicted and sentenced to CSO. The day after the sentence he started telephoning her. It lasted for 'months.' In July 2000 he was arrested for it and sent to prison. A restraining order was made. After nearly a year he went to her home where she was with her boyfriend and shouted, 'You fucking bitch.' She went inside and he continued to shout. She was upset and angry about his interference in her life again. All his convictions were for pestering the victim. The pre-sentence report referred to the defendant being unable to recognise that his behaviour constituted harassment and that he did not wish to address this continuing domestic violence. His risk assessment for re-offending was high. **12 months** was severe but wholly justified.

R v Pace 2005 1 Cr App R (S) 370. The defendant was convicted by the Magistrates' Court of breaching a restraining order. In April 2003 he was required not to contact or harass M. In October 2003 he met her by chance when he was drunk. He accosted her by holding out his hands and saying he wanted to hug her. She told him to go away but he wouldn't. He grabbed her under the chin, she pushed him away and walked off and he followed her. He said 'I've got a blade. Come here' while putting his hand in his pocket. She ran to a phone box and called the police. The incident lasted 10 minutes. The defendant, 39, had 75 previous convictions and as a young man had served custodial sentences for offences of dishonesty and violence. Since 2001 he had a number of convictions including damage to property, assault on a police officer and possession of an offensive weapon. This conviction put him in breach of a community rehabilitation order imposed in April 2003. He had not complied with that order. There was 38$^3/_4$ hours completed of a community punishment order imposed in August 2003 for shoplifting and handling. He was about to be the subject of breach proceedings in that matter for failing to work on two occasions. The pre-sentence report said the root of his problems was drink and drug misuse. The likelihood of re-offending was assessed as high. Held. This was the first breach, it was not premeditated, his conduct was influenced by drink. The persistence of his behaviour and the threat of serious violence, together with his disregard of community penalties in the past, were aggravating features. The judge gave insufficient weight to the fact this offence was spontaneous, it was the first breach and he had managed to go without breaching the order for 6 months. **18 months** not 2 years.

Early breach

159.4 *R v Burke* 2001 Unreported 26/7/01. The defendant pleaded guilty to breach of a restraining order and criminal damage and later he made a belated plea to threats to kill. He had a 6 year stormy relationship with the one of the victims. He harassed her and in 1994 stabbed her. For that he was convicted of wounding with intent and received 4 years. On his release he resumed the relationship and it remained extremely stormy. Many incidents were reported to the police and she feared for her life. In May 2000 the relationship ended and in August 2000 he was sentenced to 3 months for harassment and a restraining order was made. Because of time served on remand he was released immediately. The victim was so scared she stayed overnight with friends and visited her disabled elderly mother during the day. Five days after the order was made he entered the mother's flat from the garden. He pushed the arthritic lady to the ground, used foul and abusive language and threatened to shoot both victims. The flat was ransacked and he damaged a window, a table, china ornaments, a clock, a gas fire, a kettle and electrical equipment. The mother went outside to get help and he told her he was going to shoot her daughter and her current boyfriend. He also said, 'I've got a gun.

Do you want to see it?' He then sat on a wall until the police arrived. When he was charged he threatened to repeat his behaviour. He was 37 with 23 convictions and had had 10 periods of custody. As well as the offences already mentioned he had convictions for GBH with intent, assault on police, two affrays and two threatening words or behaviours. Held. The offences were in breach of the court order. It was permissible to make the 2 years for the breach of the order consecutive to the threats to kill, because the threats to kill were outside the flat after the breach offence was committed. The total of **5 years** was appropriate but the criminal damage sentence should be made concurrent not consecutive.

Persistent breaches

159.5   *R v Lumley* 2001 2 Cr App R (S) 110. The defendant pleaded guilty to breaching a restraining order. The offence took place three weeks after his release from prison for a similar offence. In August 1998, he was sentenced to 8 months for two counts of harassment and a threats to kill matter. A restraining order was made. It contained a prohibition from contacting either directly or indirectly his former partner, the victim. There were persistent breaches of the order, although the victim did write to him when he was in prison. In April 1999 he was put on probation for common assault, threatening behaviour and harassment. In October 1999, he was sentenced to 6 months for breaching the restraint order and the probation order. The probation order continued. Two weeks later, at 9.15 pm he and another went to the victim's home and rang the bell twice. The police were called but when they arrived he had gone. The victim and her new partner were distressed, angry and extremely afraid. The defendant was arrested and gave a false alibi. In March 2000, he was sentenced for breaching the probation order on a date after the current offence. He received 6 months and the probation order was revoked. He was 28 with a long history of offending. His pre-sentence report said his heroin use had depleted what self- control he had left. Held. The harassment (not revealed) was at the lower end of the scale. The persistent nature of the breaches did call for a more substantial sentence. The fact he had served a 6 month sentence since the offence was important. **18 months** not $2^1/_2$ years. [Factually the judgment is far from clear.]

R v Dadley 2005 1 Cr App R (S) 455. The defendant pleaded guilty to (1) breaching a restraining order, (2) assault with intent to resist arrest and (3) driving whilst disqualified. Two years earlier the defendant was convicted of harassing his former partner; a Community Punishment Order and a restraining order were imposed. Fourteen months later he breached the restraining order and received a Community Rehabilitation Order. He was made subject of a second restraining order. A month later he breached that restraining order and was given 4 month's custody. A further restraining order was made. Six months later he breached the restraining order and received another 4 month sentence. Another restraining order was made. Seventeen days later he made calls to her mobile phone the last of which she answered at 11.30 pm. The call lasted for 15 minutes and she was put in fear of the defendant (Offence 1). Some three months later the defendant was seen driving (Offence 3). When he was stopped and arrested for breach of the restraining order he resisted arrest (Offence 2). When interviewed he denied having contacted the victim but later pleaded guilty to having made the call three months earlier. He had an alcohol dependency but was ashamed of his behaviour. He represented a high risk of reoffending. He was 42 with (other than the harassment and breach of restraining order offences) previous for criminal damage which was associated to the victim. Held. The *R v Liddle and Hayes* 2001 1 Cr App R (S) 131 series of considerations were relevant. There was an extremely serious history of breaches whereby the victim had been frightened by the conduct and requires protection. However, there was only one breach that was to be sentenced and this was not a s. 4 offence. A sentence in excess of the 15 month guideline was appropriate. However **20 months** not 30.

Serious breach, one

159.6 *R v Goble* 2004 2 Cr App R (S) 12. The defendant pleaded guilty to breach of a restraining order. He claimed title to some unregistered land at the side of his house and in November 1995 he was declared a vexatious litigant. A neighbour G built a house on his land and sold it to Mr L and Miss G. The only access to this house was a path on the unregistered land claimed by the defendant. The defendant objected to the access and began a campaign against G, Mr L and Miss G. This resulted in the defendant's conviction for harassment in September 2001. The magistrates made a 12month community rehabilitation order and a restraining order under which he was prohibited from approaching etc G, Mr L and Miss G. He breached the order in 2002 by making a series of unfounded allegations against them to the police; he alleged that they had made racial taunts; that they had threatened him with a handgun and a shotgun; that they had assaulted him and that they had committed criminal damage. The police interviewed Mr L and Miss G and searched their house. The defendant, aged 64, had an extensive record for offences of dishonesty and had served terms of imprisonment, the longest $4^1/_2$ years including a consecutive 6 month sentence for contempt of court. He had convictions for doing an act intended to pervert the course of justice, and for intimidating a witness or juror, and for using threatening etc words. The pre-sentence report assessed the risk of re-offending as high, and it said that the defendant intended to continue the dispute with his neighbours. A psychiatric report concluded that he had minimal insight into his behaviour and remained fixated with t he dispute, and that he suffered from a delusional disorder. The Judge said 'that to say he made his neighbours' life a misery was a gross understatement'. Held. His actions caused great anxiety and because of them the victims had put their house up for sale. There was a pattern of behaviour. He wilfully flouted the law and its processes in relentless pursuit of his objectives. The Judge was right to have the factors of punishment and deterrence predominantly in mind. Given the defendant's background, obsessive behaviour, offences committed and the effect on the victims **2 years** was not a day too long.

See also PUBLIC ORDER ACT 1986 and STALKING

REVENUE, CHEATING THE PUBLIC

See TAX FRAUD

RICH DEFENDANT

See DEFENDANT – *Rich*

160   RIOT

160.1   Public Order Act 1986 s 1

Indictable only. Maximum sentence 10 years.

Imprisonment for public protection For offences committed on or after 4/4/05 when there is a significant risk to members of the public of serious harm etc. there is a mandatory duty to pass a sentence of imprisonment for public protection[16]. For offenders under 18 the duty is to pass detention for public protection or an extended sentence[17].

Longer than Commensurate sentences and Extended sentences Riot is a violent offence for the purposes of passing a longer than commensurate sentence [Powers of Criminal Courts (Sentencing) Act 2000 s 80(2)] and an extended sentence (extending the licence) [Powers of Criminal Courts (Sentencing) Act 2000 s 85(2)(b)] where the offence leads, or is intended or likely to lead, to a person's death or to physical injury to a person[18]. These provisions will continue to apply to offences committed after 29/9/98 and before 4/4/05. See LONGER THAN COMMENSURATE SENTENCES and EXTENDED SENTENCES

Sexual Offences Prevention Order There is a discretionary power to make this order when it is necessary to protect the public etc[19].

Crown Court statistics – England and Wales – Males 21+

160.2

Year	Plea	Total Numbers sentenced	Type of sentence %					Average length of custody (months)
			Discharge	Fine	Community sentence	Suspended sentence	Custody	
2002	Guilty	58	–	–	–	2	98	49.9
	Not guilty	3	–	–	–	–	100	76
2003	Guilty	28	=	–	7	–	93	40.2
	Not guilty	7	–	–	–	–	100	54.4

For details and explanations about the statistics in the book see page vii.

Guideline remarks

160.3 *R v Tyler* 1993 96 Cr App R (S) 332. Two defendants were convicted of riot and two offences of violent disorder. After a poll tax demonstration buildings were damaged and police attacked. Held. It is not the individual act that is the essence of the offence here. It is the use of violence in circumstances where so many people are present as to cause or inspire fear in the general public. One must look at the individual act in the context of that fear. When it occurs in a busy street the dangers are obvious.

R v Najeeb 2003 2 Cr App R (S) 408. The defendants pleaded guilty to riot. Held. The authorities stress the importance of the distinction between riots which are premeditated and pre-planned and those which are spontaneous.

Cases

160.4 *R v Najeeb* 2003 2 Cr App R (S) 408. The defendant N, Q, M, R, Al, P, L, Az, H, Ha, Qu, K, Kh and Ra pleaded guilty to riot at the first opportunity. There was a disturbance at Oldham. One and a half months later there was another at Burnley which was held to be a racist attack on Asians. Two weeks later, the Leader of the BNP made a speech at Bradford. The City Council cancelled a Festival planned for the next day. The Anti Nazi League assembled in Bradford in response to an assembly by the National Front party which the police had banned. The Asian community was concerned about the need to defend themselves. By 2 pm serious disorder broke out

16 Criminal Justice Act 2003 s 224–226
17 Criminal Justice Act 2003 s 226 and 228
18 Powers of Criminal Courts (Sentencing) Act 2000 s 161(3)
19 Sexual Offences Act 2003 s 104 & Sch. 5

between rival Asian and white males. Arrests were made and Asian youths threw missiles smashing windows. Then the police were targeted. A white man seriously stabbed an Asian male. Asian males were running amok carrying sticks and baseball bats which were used against pubs and shops. Police decided to drive the youths out of the city centre to prevent destruction. As they were pushed back premises were attacked with stones, petrol bombs etc. Two police horses were stabbed and the police who were heavily outnumbered were attacked with metal fencing and a cross bow. Two garages were completely gutted. Stolen cars were set alight and driven at the police. Four hundred police attended from different forces. Three hundred police were injured. Businesses were ruined and £27 m worth of damaged caused. The prosecution relied on video evidence. Held. The origin of this riot began in fear. This riot was of the utmost gravity. It lasted about 12 hours. As the hours passed there were clear signs of organisation among the rioters. They covered their faces and changed their clothes because of what they intended to do. The rioters defied the senior members of the Asian community who tried to calm matters. Deterrent sentences were called for so good character and personal mitigation were of comparatively little weight. If any ringleader had been convicted we would have expected a sentence at or near the statutory maximum of **10 years**. A persistent participant who threw petrol bombs or used a cross bow or drove a car at police if convicted would receive between **8 and 9 years**. Those who participated over a number of hours and threw missiles more dangerous than stones like gas cylinders, knives, fences or poles or who set fire to cars would receive after a trial **6–7 years**. For those present for a significant period repeatedly throwing missiles like bricks and stones would expect after a trial **5 years**. All defendants expressed remorse. All except P gave themselves up to police. N was seen at 4 pm and at 6.48 pm when he was in a hostile crowd. He threw one missile. He was 28 with references. **3 years** not 4. Q was in the front line of the riot early in the evening. He threw a missile at the police and armed himself with a broken lamp pole. In a group he struck a police van three times. He threw a gas cylinder towards the police knocking an officer over. He left for $2^{1}/_{2}$ hours and returned with a change of clothing. His face was covered and he threw a burning object at a stolen car. He hurled a gas cylinder at police from a short distance and knocked another officer over. He suffered from a mental illness namely mania which creates an elation in mood, overactivity, grandiose ideas and over confidence. A psychiatrist said at the time his thought processes and reasoning were affected. Held. The Judge gave insufficient reduction for this so **2 years** not 4. M was present for 5 hours and he threw an object at the police lines. He was in the vicinity of two cars which were being damaged and nearby when a petrol bomb was thrown. He had convictions including a common assault some time ago. His wife spoke no English and they had a child with a congenital heart defect. **4 years** was not excessive. R was present between 6 and 7 hours and he covered his face. He threw a missile at police lines four times. His child died in deeply distressing circumstances. He looked after his disabled sister. There was no distinction between him and M so **4 years** upheld. Al was seen throwing missiles on several occasions over a 20 minute period. At one stage he was masked. Al was aged 21 of good character and was described as a highly motivated student with a University place available. Held. Because of the mitigation **3 years** not 4. P was first involved at 6.30 pm and he remained in the crowd till the early hours. About 9 pm he threw missiles at police three times and was wearing a mask. P threw two more missiles at about 11 and shortly after midnight. On a number of occasions he was at or near the front of those confronting the police. There was nothing wrong with **4 years**. L was present for a three hour period and was seen with a metal bar and on a number of occasions throwing stones at police. When arrested he put forward false alibis. He had no relevant convictions. **4 years 9 months** was not manifestly excessive. Az was seen throwing stones and missiles at the police. He was also seen near a burning barricade and an overturned car. On occasions he was hooded. He was

25 and of good character. **4 years 9 months** upheld. H was repeatedly throwing missiles at the police. He was present for about 8 hours. H pulled his hood up on his jacket. He was 26 with no relevant convictions. **4$^1/_2$ years** upheld. Ha participated for over 2 hours and on 6 separate occasions threw stones and other missiles at the police. He also attacked a police van and picked up a metal fence and threw it at a police van. Ha was hooded for most of the time and encouraged others with victory signs. He was 21 with perhaps obstructing the police as his only relevant conviction. **4 years 9 months** was not manifestly excessive. Q participated for 4 hours and threw 9 missiles at the police. He brandished a large light tube to encourage others. Q was 21, of good character and with references. **4 years 9 months** was not manifestly excessive. K was present for about 3 hours. He threw two missiles at police, carried burning debris and tried to ignite something in his hand. Q rolled a beer barrel towards the police and threw a petrol bomb directly at police. He was 28 with no relevant conviction except obstructing police. **6$^1/_2$ years** was not manifestly excessive. Kh started by behaving peacefully and then he changed his clothes. He then was with a group which damaged a car, helped to erect a barricade and threw missiles at police. When arrested he lied. Kh was 20 with no relevant convictions and had references. **5 years** was not manifestly excessive. Ra was present for 5 hours. He threw missiles several times, instructed others how to damage a car which was set alight and pushed towards the police. He was repeatedly in the front line. He was 20, of good character and had 6 references. **5 years** was not manifestly excessive.

(One defendant pleaded to Violent Disorder. See VIOLENT DISORDER – *Riot, part of*)

161 ROAD RAGE

Guideline remarks

161.1 *R v Hassan and Schuller* 1989 RTR 129. LCJ. The habit of drivers getting out of their cars, loosing their tempers and striking other road users seems to be increasing. If it occurred a prison sentence will follow.

R v Normanton 2003 The Times 21/7/03. The defendant pleaded guilty to road rage ABH. Held. Custody is almost inevitable even where the defendant is of good character. Road rage must be firmly dealt with because of the prevalence and its unacceptable nature.

ABH

161.2 Offences Against the Person Act 1861 s 47

Triable either way. On indictment maximum 5 years. Summary maximum 6 months and/or £5,000.

R v Doyle 1999 1 Cr App R (S) 383. The defendant was convicted of ABH. The defendant, driving a lorry sounded his horn at a woman in a car. At the give way lines at a roundabout he got out and went to the car. Another motorist, the victim fearing he was going to assault or abuse the women went over to the car. The defendant without saying a word punched him five or six times in the face causing him to fall to the ground. He then kicked him five times in the legs. The victim was in his 60s and had bruising to an eyebrow a 5mm cut to an eye and a bleeding nose. The defendant was 36 with a number of previous for dishonesty and two for violence (GBH and common assault). The court was entitled to take a more serious view that in earlier cases as the offence has become more prevalent. Use the more recent cases. **12 months** was not excessive.

R v Sharpe 2000 1 Cr App R (S) 1. The defendant was convicted of ABH. The defendant started to reverse into a parking space the victim had found. The victim then left his car to stand in the space. The defendant's car continued to reverse. The victim went over to the defendant's car and opened the driver's door. The defendant then got out of the car and head butted the victim causing a broken nose. The defendant was treated as being of good character. These attacks are on the increase and the courts must indicate that they will not be tolerated. Custody is almost inevitable. Where there is any significant injury the period will be months rather than weeks even if the defendant is of good character. A substantial sentence was justified, but **8 months** substituted for 12 months.

R v Normanton 2003 The Times 21/7/03. The defendant pleaded guilty on re-arraignment to ABH. The victim was driving in an area he didn't know and the defendant was very close behind him. The victim stopped without indicating to ask for directions. The defendant sounded his horn, pulled up sharply alighted and asked the victim why he hadn't indicated. The victim said he shouldn't have been so close behind. The exchange continued and then the defendant hit the victim in the face knocking him to the ground. Bystanders tried to stop the defendant leaving but he got away in his car. The victim suffered a black eye, numbness to his face and a graze to his elbow. The defendant was interviewed and relied on self defence. He was 23 and of positive good character. He was in employment. Held. Because of the personal mitigation, 6 weeks not 3 months. £350 not £500 compensation. £350 prosecution costs order quashed.

Old case. *R v Maben* 1997 2 Cr App R (S) 341, (For summary of this case see the first edition of this book.)

Affray

161.3   *R v Heightley* 2003 2 Cr App R (S) 95. The defendant pleaded guilty to affray. He and a friend and the friend's daughter crossed a road at about 6 pm. O who was 75 drove by. The defendant thought that his car had driven too close to him and he banged violently on the bonnet several times. O drove round a corner and got out of his car. The defendant went over to him. There was an argument and a fight started between them. Blows were exchanged. O suffered cuts in the area of his ear and left temple. The defendant punched O and forced him back into his car and he drove away. Sadly, very shortly after driving off, he suffered a heart attack from which he never recovered. The defendant was arrested the next day and interviewed. He made no comment and later submitted a statement admitting involvement in fight but asserted that O had been the first to use violence. No basis of plea was agreed. The defendant had a record that included affray in 1992, several offences against property and many for dishonesty. He had served substantial periods of imprisonment, the longest was 30 months. Moses J when sentencing said 'It does not matter precisely what happened at the car, how many blows were struck or precisely where they landed, but it is plain that you lost control of yourself at the time, that you were hopelessly out of control, angry and aggressive, to an extent and for a period way that Mr O was unable to defend himself'. Held. First, it was more serious as it concerned a motoring offence; secondly it involved an assault by a younger man on, obviously, a much less fit and much older man; and thirdly, the defendant's record is no mitigation. **15 months** not 2 years.

See also **AFFRAY**

Wounding (Section 20)

161.4   *R v Khan* 2003 2 Cr App R (S) 100. The defendant, aged 19, pleaded guilty to unlawful wounding. The victim drove her car with a friend and her three-year-old daughter. She passed a car containing the defendant and three other young men. She sounded her horn as she thought that they had driven discourteously or dangerously. Insults were exchanged. The other car was in front of her and she tried to pass but the other car blocked her way. The men shouted aggressively at her. She got out of her car and walked towards the car. The defendant got out and both sides shouted. Then the defendant headbutted her in the face causing her to stagger and bleed. She suffered a large wound to her upper lip and had to have 14 stitches. One of her front teeth was chipped, requiring dental treatment. She became nervous when driving. The defendant had no previous convictions and some excellent references. Held. Motorists are not in a different position from any other member of the public. In many ways they owe more of an obligation of self-control than does the ordinary pedestrian because they have particular obligations towards other road users. This was a serious incident and involving gratuitous violence which is exactly the sort of conduct that the Courts are obliged to take a serious view of. However **12 months detention** not 18.

See also OFFENCES AGAINST THE PERSON ACT 1861 S 20

Old cases. Ignore them. The tariff has gone up.

162   ROAD TRAFFIC

162.1   The following offences are listed separately: CARELESS DRIVING; DANGEROUS DRIVING; DEATH BY CARELESS DRIVING; DEATH BY DANGEROUS DRIVING; DISQUALIFIED DRIVING; DRINK DRIVING; EXCISE LICENCE, FRAUDULENT USE ETC.; FAILING TO PROVIDE A SPECIMEN; FAILING TO STOP; INSURANCE, NO; ROAD RAGE; SPEEDING; TACHOGRAPH AND OTHER DRIVERS' HOURS OFFENCES; TAKING MOTOR VEHICLES and VEHICLE INTERFERENCE.

Magistrates' Court Sentencing Guidelines January 2004

162.2   In all cases, consider the safety factor, damage to the roads, commercial gain and if the driver is not the owner, with whom prime responsibility should lie. The penalties are for a first time offender pleading not guilty.

Offence	Penalty points	Maximum penalty	Suggested penalty
Driver offences Not supplying details	3[2]	Level 3 E	B
Licence offences No driving licence, where could be covered[3]	–	Level 3	A
Licence offences Driving not in accordance with provisional licence[4]	3–6	Level 3 E	A
♦ No excise licence	–	Level 3 or 5 times annual duty (whichever greater)	Actual duty lost and penalty of Guideline fine[5]
Lights Driving without lights	–	Level 3	A
Ownership Not notifying DVLA of change etc	–	Level 3	A
Parking In a dangerous position	3	Level 3 E	A
Parking I In a Pelican/Zebra crossing area	3	Level 3 E	A
Test Certificate Not held	–	Level 3	A
Traffic Offences			
Failing to comply with height restrictions	3	Level 3 E	A
Failure to comply with red traffic light	3	Level 3 E	A
Failure to comply with stop sign	3	Level 3 E	A
Failure to comply with double white lines	3	Level 3 E	A

Failure to give precedence at Pelican or Zebra crossing	3	Level 3 E	A
Driving			
♦ Driving in reverse on motorway	3	Level 4 E	B
♦ Driving in reverse on slip road.	3	Level 4 E	A
♦ Driving in wrong direction on motorway.	3	Level 4 E	B[6]
♦ Driving off carriageway – central reservation	3	Level 4 E	A
♦ Driving off carriageway – hard shoulder	3	Level 4 E	A
♦ Driving on slip road against no entry sign	3	Level 4 E	A
♦ Doing U turn	3	Level 4 E	A6
Fast lane			
♦ Vehicle over 7.5 tonnes or drawing trailer in fast lane	3	Level 4 E	A
Learners			
♦ Learner or excluded vehicle	3	Level 4 E	A
Stopping			
♦ Stopping on hard shoulder of motorway	–	Level 4	A
♦ Stopping on slip road of motorway	–	Level 4	A
Walking			
♦ Walking on motorway or slip road	–	Level 4	A
♦ Walking on hard shoulder or verge	–	Level 4	A
Defects			
♦ Brakes	3	Level 4 E	A
♦ Steering	3	Level 4 E	A
♦ Tyres (per tyre)	3	Level 4 E	A
♦ Loss of wheel	3	Level 4 E	A
♦ Exhaust emission	–	Level 3	A
♦ Other offences	–	Level 3	A
Loads, danger of injury by			
♦ Condition of vehicle, accessories and equipment	3	Level 4 E	A
♦ Purpose of use/number of passengers/ how carried	3	Level 4 E	A
♦ Weight position or distribution of load	3	Level 4 E	A
♦ Insecure load	3	Level 4 E	A
♦ Overloading or exceeding maximum axle weight	–	Level 5	A[7]
Brakes	3	Level 5 E	C
Steering	3	Level 5 E	C
Tyres (per tyre)	3	Level 5 E	C
Loss of wheel	3	Level 5 E	C
Exhaust emission	–	Level 4	C
Other offences	–	Level 4	C

Loads			
Condition of vehicle, accessories and equipment	3	Level 5 E	C
Purpose of use/number of passengers/ how carried	3	Level 5 E	C
Weight position or distribution of load	3	Level 5 E	C
Insecure load	3	Level 5 E	C
Overloading or exceeding maximum axle weight	–	Level 5	C[9]
Operator's licence			
Not held	–	Level 4	C
Speed limiters-When applicable			
Not being used or incorrectly calibrated	–	Level 4	C

For details about the guidelines see MAGISTRATES' COURT SENTENCING GUIDELINES at page 483.

1   Fixed Penalty Order 2000. It only applies when the fixed penalty procedure is used.

2   If Company owned, use higher fine when unable to apply endorsement as a minimum.

3   E.g. If licence not renewed, but would have covered class of vehicle driven, or holder of full licence has lost or misplaced it.

4   Includes where no licence ever held.

5   Guideline fine is Starting point A (1–4 months unpaid duty), Ax2 (4–6 months), Ax3 (6–12 months) subject to a maximum of twice the duty.

6   Consider disqualification.

7   Plus increase in proportion to % overloading. Examine carefully evidence of responsibility for overload and if for commercial gain relating to the owner increase the fine.

8   For an owner/driver take net turnover into account as appropriate.

9   Plus increase in proportion to % overloading.

163   ROBBERY

163.1   Theft Act 1968 s 8

Indictable only. Maximum sentence life imprisonment.

CHAPTERS in this book are in bold capitals. The *paragraph titles* are in bold italics. Where a chapter (e.g. arson) has subsections, the **subsections** are in lower case bold.

Anti-Social Behavioural orders Where the defendant has acted in a manner that caused or was likely to cause harassment, alarm or distress to one or more persons not in the same household as the defendant and it is necessary to protect persons from further anti-social acts by him/her the court may make this order[20].

Automatic life For offences committed before 4/4/05, robbery is a specified offence for automatic life if the offender had in his possession a firearm or imitation firearm[21]. See *Automatic life*

20 Crime and Disorder Act 1998 s 1C
21 Powers of Criminal Courts (Sentencing) Act 2000 s 109(5)

Drug Abstinence Order This was repealed on 4 April 2005.

Dangerous Offender provisions For offences committed on or after 4/4/05 where there is a significant risk to members of the public of serious harm etc. there is a mandatory duty to pass a life sentence when it is justified and otherwise a sentence of imprisonment for public protection[22]. For offenders under 18 the duty is to pass detention for life, detention for public protection or an extended sentence[23].

Longer than Commensurate sentences and Extended sentences Robbery is a violent offence for the purposes of passing a longer than commensurate sentence [Powers of Criminal Courts (Sentencing) Act 2000 s 80(2)] and an extended sentence (extending the licence) [Powers of Criminal Courts (Sentencing) Act 2000 s 85(2)(b)] where the offence leads, or is intended or likely to lead, to a person's death or to physical injury to a person[24]. These provisions will continue to apply to offences committed after 29/9/98 and before 4/4/05. See *Longer than commensurate sentences*

Restitution Orders There is power to make a restitution order under Powers of Criminal Courts (Sentencing) Act 2000 s 148.

Sexual Offences Prevention Order There is a discretionary power to make this order when it is necessary to protect the public etc[25].

Sentencing predictions. Sentences for robbery will remain high as they continue to cause so much fear among the public.

Sentencing Advisory Panel The Panel have produced a report which can be found at www.sentencing-guidelines.gov.uk

Crown Court statistics – England and Wales – Males 21+

163.2

Year	Plea	Total Numbers sentenced	Type of sentence %					Average length of custody (months)
			Discharge	Fine	Community sentence	Suspended sentence	Custody	
2002	Guilty	2,486	0	0	5	1	93	48
	Not guilty	614	0	–	3	1	95	61.5
2003	Guilty	2,375	0	0	7	1	91	46.7
	Not guilty	628	0	0	6	0	92	61.8

For details and explanations about the statistics in the book see page vii.

Guideline remarks

163.3   *Att-Gen's Ref. Nos. 20 and 21 of 1992* 1994 15 Cr App R (S) 152. Those who seek to prey upon the vulnerable carriers of money will be treated severely by the courts.

Armed robbery   See *Firearm, with*

Attempted robbery – Automatic life

163.4   *R v Buckland* 2000 2 Cr App R (S) 217. LCJ. Attempted robbery is not a 'serious offence' for the purposes of Crime (Sentences) Act 1997, s 2 (now Powers of Criminal Courts (Sentencing) Act 2000 s 109 (automatic life). For more detail see **163.6**.

22 Criminal Justice Act 2003 s 225
23 Criminal Justice Act 2003 s 226 and 228
24 Powers of Criminal Courts (Sentencing) Act 2000 s 161(3)
25 Sexual Offences Act 2003 s 104 & Sch. 5

Automatic life

163.5   Powers of Criminal Courts (Sentencing) Act 2000 s 109(2) and (5)(h). The court shall impose a life sentence (for his second) serious offence. Section 109(5)(h) defines robbery as, "Robbery where, at some time during the commission of the offence, the offender had in his possession a firearm or imitation firearm is a serious offence within the meaning of that Act". (available only for offences committed before 4/4/05)

Att-Gen's Ref. No 71 of 1998 1999 2 Cr App R (S) 369. (Note. The Cr App R has the wrong year for the reference.) Section 2(5)(h) includes joint enterprise. Whether the offence falls within para (h) depends on the basis of the offender's participation. If he was party to a robbery which to his knowledge involved the possession of a firearm it qualifies. If a firearm was produced or used contrary to his own understanding and belief about the robbery we doubt it would qualify. Here he didn't carry the firearm but he knew of it so he qualified.

Automatic life – Exceptional circumstances

163.6   *R v Buckland* 2000 2 Cr App R (S) 217. LCJ. The defendant was convicted of attempted robbery and possessing a firearm on arrest [Firearms Act 1968, s 17(2)]. The defendant entered a branch of Barclays Bank and joined a queue for Customer Service. When his turn came, he passed an envelope with a note which read 'This is a robbery, give us the money, I have a gun.' The note was signed by him in his correct name and on the back of the envelope was typed his name and address. He made no attempt to disguise himself and produced no gun. The clerk who took it seriously told him he needed to go to the counter. The defendant said 'You better go and get it. I want £100,000.' The clerk activated the alarm and the defendant sat and waited quietly. At one point he went to the cashier's window and said he hadn't got all day. He was told to sit down and obediently did so. He was arrested without a struggle and an imitation handgun costing £1.50 was found in his tracksuit pocket. He gave his occupation as 'Saving the planet.' The defendant was 31 and was a persistent but relatively minor offender with a conviction for having a firearm with intent to resist arrest. He had picked up a starting pistol, which fired caps and he was stopped by police for firing it and his boisterous and drunken behaviour. He ran off and fired the pistol once. He was sentenced to 4 years' imprisonment. He suffered from drug-induced psychosis. He had a glowing prison report. He was sentenced to automatic life after the judge found no exceptional circumstances. Held. The incompetence, lack of aggression, the fact no physical injury could have been caused and the imitation gun was not produced, no gain was made, and any distress caused to the staff was far from extreme were exceptional circumstances. He did not present a serious danger to the public. The judge's starting point of 7 years was too high. Sentence varied to **4¹/₂ years**.

For cases where there is no firearm count see *Firearms, with – No Firearm Count*

Banks, Building Societies, security guards etc

163.7   *Att-Gen's Ref. Nos. 65–6 of 2001* Unreported 26/10/01. The defendant S was convicted of robbery. Before trial the defendant H changed his plea to guilty. Four men were involved in the robbery of a security van. The guard was attacked by two of them who were not S or H. The two were wearing balaclava helmets and were armed with an axe and a machete. The guard was struck on the head with the axe. Fortunately, because of his protective headgear, he suffered no injury. He was also hit on the arm causing no more than a graze. A security box with £3,268 in cash was stolen. S then 20 was the getaway driver and H then 19, sat beside him wearing a balaclava helmet throughout the robbery. H's basis of plea was that when the two assailants got out of the car he was unaware that weapons were to be used. When he saw the weapons he decided not to go with the other two and he remained in the car. H had convictions for criminal damage, having an air rifle, theft of a bicycle and three offences of possession of cannabis with intent to supply and a similar offence involving amphetamine. He had served 6 months' detention for breach of probation. S had convictions, mainly for burglary and theft but included interfering with a motor vehicle and going equipped for theft, affray and ABH. He had served three custodial sentences. The longest one was 2 years 3 months. Held. It has to be recognised that since *Att-Gen's Ref. Nos. 72 and 73 of 1995* 1996 2 Cr App R (S) 438 sentences have increased for these sorts of serious offences where weapons are used. Where young men choose to arm themselves with weapons capable of causing really serious injury they must expect very long sentences. The more so if they make use of them. The proper sentence for S who received 6 years was **8 years** detention. Because it was a reference 7 years instead. The basis of plea for H was supported by the fact he just remained in the car. Courts ought to encourage people who at the last minute decide not to go through with a criminal enterprise and who withdraw their own involvement even if they remain a party to what is going on. Having regard to that factor, his plea and his bad criminal record, his sentence of **4 years** cannot be unduly lenient.

Banks, Building Societies, high value targets, security guards etc (no firearms)

163.8   *R v Exley and Day* 2000 2 Cr App R (S) 189. The defendant D pleaded guilty to robbery on re-arraignment. Police kept a cash delivery under observation where a guard and a police officer disguised as a guard pretended to deliver cash to a bank. Two men ran up and the officer was sprayed with corrosive liquid from a bottle. Both men ran to a waiting car which was driven off by D. A police car blocked the exit and the three men ran off. D had convictions. Held. The getaway driver is an important feature in the offence of robbery. His role was pivotal to the success of it. **7 years** consecutive to 1 year for an unrelated wounding count was not excessive.

Att-Gen's Ref. Nos. 20 of 2000 2001 1 Cr App R (S) 178. The defendant pleaded guilty to robbery at a late stage, and to being carried in a taken conveyance, going equipped, TDA, theft, driving whilst disqualified and other lesser charges. A witness outside a store saw four men in a car pulling scarves over their faces while a guard was delivering cash to the store. As the guard removed the cash bags from the van the rear door of the van was pushed against his back trapping his legs. He pushed the door open and saw three men including the defendant. They had hold of his trolley. He grabbed one of the bags and was hit on the hand by what he thought was a screwdriver. The men carried another screwdriver. The three went to the front of the van and one called out, 'Go and get some more.' The guard managed to lock the door and the men escaped in the car. The guard's finger and back were sore. £2,250 in coins was stolen. Only the defendant was arrested. The car was taken the night before. A nearby house had been used as a safe house. The defendant was 23 and most if not all the offences were committed whilst he was on bail. He had convictions but they were not for serious offences. For some of the other offences he received in total 12 months consecutive to the robbery sentence. Held. Men collecting or delivering cash are particularly vulnerable. Offences committed against them are prevalent. Courts should impose substantial custodial sentences. Bearing in mind it was a reference and the principles of totality **4¹/₂ years** not 3 for the robbery consecutive to the 12 months.

R v Betson and Others 2004 2 Cr App R (S) 270. The defendants B, C and H were convicted with others of conspiracy to rob the De Beers Diamond Exhibition at the Millennium Dome. The jewellery bound to be worth £5m and could have been worth between £30–£40m. The issue for the Jury was whether their intention was to rob or steal. B drove a JCB adapted to carry three extra people and crashed it through a perimeter fence and a shuttered door in the Dome to the diamond exhibition. C wearing a gas mask threw smoke grenades, which posed a risk to people in an enclosed environment, being irritant and potentially toxic. C used a Hilti gun to attack the glass cabinet holding the jewels. Each of these defendants had a plastic bottle of ammonia. The gang had been under police surveillance for some time and waiting officers arrested them. There had been two earlier aborted attempts at the robbery. Some witnesses said they were shocked and that the experience was nerve wracking. B had a considerable record for dishonesty but nothing for violence or robbery. Held. This was not a run of the mill bank robbery, it was meticulously planned with months of preparation including aborted attempts. The target was unique and the rewards would have been immense. Although abnormal it was not a case where ruthless violence was contemplated. Ammonia was carried but firearms were not and we pay particular regard to that. For B and C **15** years not 18. For C **12 years** not 15 years.

Burglary, during   See *Domestic premises*

Car Jacking

163.9   *R v Thompson* 2003 1 Cr App R (S) 54. The defendant pleaded guilty to robbery. Car jacking offences are particularly prevalent at the moment. The offences are committed quickly. The detection rates are not high. Those who commit these offences must expect substantial sentences. (For further details see **163.41**)

Att-Gen's Ref. No 31 etc. of 2004 Re AM 2005 1 Cr App R (S) 377 at 384. The defendant AM pleaded guilty to robbery. She approached the victim who was sitting in a car making a phone call. The defendant opened the drivers' door and asked the victim to call the police because her boyfriend had taken her child. The victim offered to drive the defendant to wherever the child was. The defendant then tried to grab the car keys and following a struggle slapped the victim across the face. Part of the bunch of keys broke off and the defendant ran off with the broken off part and the victim's mobile phone. The victim drove away but returned a few minutes later and the defendant tried to open the car door. The same thing happened again soon afterwards. The defendant was arrested and the phone was restored to the victim. The offence was motivated by the defendant's need to finance her heroin addiction. She was drug-free at sentence. She was remorseful and maintained her plea despite the victim being unwilling to give evidence. An additional report indicated that she was undertaking drug tests to try and secure full parental responsibility and she continued to take necessary steps to address her drug use. She was 20 with no previous convictions for robbery. Held. Although the sentence was low it was not in the public interest to return her to prison. **8 months'** detention unchanged.

Car Jacking – Firearm, with   See *Firearm, with – Car Jacking*

Commercial/industrial premises

163.10   *R v Ginley* 2002 2 Cr App R (S) 277. The defendant was convicted of manslaughter and attempted robbery. The 57-year-old victim and his disabled wife were helping out at their frozen food warehouse. Because of ill health they were semi retired and their sons had taken the business over. In 1987 the victim had had a triple bypass and his wife was paralysed down one side and in a wheelchair. In the late morning the defendant and another entered the warehouse. One pulled a balaclava down over his face and demanded to know where the safe was. He put a knife with a 10″ blade to the victim's throat and put him in a headlock. There was a scuffle in which the victim was prodded in the ribs a number of times with the knife. The wife pointed to the safe in the office and picked up a walking stick to go to her husband's aid. The second man who was masked grabbed her stick and pushed her in her wheelchair to the other side of the office away from the panic button. The victim shouted the police were on their way and the robbers left believing the panic button had been pressed. The victim then pressed the panic button and the police attended quickly. The victim gave the number of the car to an officer, collapsed and died of a heart attack. The pathologist said, 'death could have occurred at any time but trauma and excitement could precipitate a heart attack. More likely than not the victim would have been alive had it not been for the struggle.' The defendant was 21 when sentenced and had convictions but none for violence. Held. The judge quite rightly took the view that this was a robbery of an extreme kind. It was a prepared robbery. There was nothing wrong with **9 years** for the robbery without considering the death. The 3 years extra for the death was wholly appropriate. **12 years** upheld.

Custody not necessary

163.10a   *Att-Gen's Ref. No 37 of 2004* 2005 1 Cr App R (S) 295. The defendant pleaded guilty to attempted robbery and possessing a firearm at the time of committing an indictable offence. He had an argument with his mother who had told him not to return to her house. He went to a sub post office close to his mother's home with an air pistol with him. When the sub postmaster was alone the defendant pulled a gun from the waistband of his trousers and told the postmaster to fill a plastic bag with money and not push any alarms. The postmaster fearing that he would be shot, dived below the counter and pushed alarms. The defendant fled without any money. He was arrested about two hours later. When he was told there was CCTV in the shop he accepted he was responsible and took the police officers to the gun. The gun was an air pistol in working order which was capable of casing a fatal wound and fulfilled the criteria for a lethal barrelled weapon. The defendant, 20, had two cautions but no convictions. The pre-sentence report set out that his upbringing had been unhappy and he had left home when he was 16. He began drinking heavily and discovered matters about his family history which caused him distress. The risks of future offending were described as low. There was a report from a consultant psychiatrist which said that at the time of the offence he was suffering from a depressive illness, which clouded his judgement, complicated by his alcohol dependency. He concluded the defendant was in state of crisis and wanted to be caught. The judge imposed a **3 year community rehabilitation order** with a condition that the offender works with a psychiatric counsellor. The probation report for the Court of Appeal was positive. Held. Sentencing is not a mechanical exercise. The sentencer has to do justice not only to the offender but has to exercise his judgement in seeking to provide ultimately more protection for the public. The course taken was an exceptional and justified.

Death is caused See MANSLAUGHTER – *Burglars/Robbers/Thieves, by*

Defendant aged 10–13 – Domestic robberies

163.11   *R v Lindsay* 1999 2 Cr App R (S) 230. The defendant pleaded guilty to robbery and two counts of burglary. He was 13 when the offences were committed and when he was sentenced. The offences took place within five weeks. The burglaries were daytime domestic burglaries. The occupiers returned home to find drawers etc had been rifled. In the first burglary a video and cash were stolen. In the second jewellery and cash worth about £2,000 was taken. He was arrested and released. A week later he and another robbed a 14 year old schoolboy on his paper round. The boy was pushed and one of the robbers produced a knife and demanded his Walkman. The earphones were pulled from his neck. The defendant had been cautioned for robbery and ABH. He had had a disruptive home life and had been permanently excluded from school. The judge sentenced him on the basis that the other had the knife. The report from where he was detained was in part positive but also said he was abusive and aggressive. Considering *R v Fairhurst* 1986 8 Cr App R (S) 346 and *R v Wainfur* 1997 1 Cr App R (S) 43, **2 years** detention in all not 3.

Defendant aged 10–13 – Street robbery

163.12   *R v McKay* 2000 1 Cr App R (S) 17. The defendants M, A, and T pleaded guilty to robbery and ABH as an alternative to s 18 GBH. L was convicted of false imprisonment and ABH. A 15 year old boy was approached on a railway station platform by two girls and a boy, M, A and T aged then 13, 14 and 13 respectively. They demanded money and cigarettes and threatened to beat him up. The boy handed over 42p and two cigarettes. T said, 'Let's punch and kick him.' M and T kicked him about the face. A joined in and scratched him. L then 16 got off a train and asked what was going on and the four then attacked him. The victim was hit with a padlock and chain. M got a piece of wood and hit him on the legs with it. The boy ran away and they caught him and carried on beating him. As trains came in they crowded round him and pretended he was drunk. L took the padlock and chain off the others and also stopped one of then using a broken bottle on the boy. A lighter was put to the boy's hair and it was singed. A bicycle was thrown at him. His coat was taken from him. The whole incident lasted 35–40 minutes and the four left. The victim was in hospital for 5 days. He was unable to leave his home for a month. He had extensive bruising to the face, eyes, nose, mouth, back, shoulder and hands. One eye was swollen shut. The pictures were alarming and it was possible to see chain marks and probable footprints. M and L had no findings of guilt. A and T had cautions. When sentenced they were 14, 14, 16, and 17. The defence suggested that the serious feature was the assault and not the robbery. No custodial sentences were available for the assault for those who were 14. Held. It was a merciless attack on a defenceless harmless youth. It was one single incident. The removal of the coat underlines that. It was appropriate to rely on Children and Young Persons Act 1933, s 53(3), (now Powers of Criminal Courts (Sentencing) Act 2000 s 91). The sentences of **2 years** detention (one being a YOI order) for M, T, and A were within the appropriate range. As L made serious efforts to prevent the attack becoming absolutely disastrous his sentence was reduced from 21 months to **15 months**.

R v T and F 2001 1 Cr App R (S) 294. The defendant F pleaded guilty to robbery. The defendant T pleaded guilty to handling. The victim was walking home when F grabbed her from behind and pressed a closed penknife into her neck. F demanded her handbag and dragged and pushed her over a small fence. The victim fell and F grabbed her bag off her shoulder and ran off. The defendants both then 13 were arrested and T pointed out a bin where the bag was found. £15 cash was missing. T admitted being given £5. A month later the victim still had a fear of being out alone. F's mother died in childbirth. Her father's whereabouts was unknown. F came to the UK to live with her step-grandmother and grandfather several years before. Because of her behaviour they were unable to look after her. She had placements with foster parents and in local authority residential units. She was difficult, absconded and took part in petty offending and anti-social behaviour. While on remand in a secure unit she made good progress. A psychologist said she was in dire need of therapeutic help. Her social worker said that a detention and training order would mean she would leave the secure unit where she was doing well. Held. Taking into account her age and the mitigation **18 months** not 2¹/₂ years' detention.

R v T 2004 Unreported 9/11/04. The defendant aged 10 pleaded guilty to three false imprisonment counts, GBH, two ABHs and two robberies. He and two others dragged a 12 year old boy to a shed outside a derelict bungalow. The boy was put in a dustbin and punched and kicked to the head and body. He was taken into the bungalow where two more boys joined the assailants. The boy was struck with chair legs about the head and body. He was next taken to the bathroom where he was taunted and told to wash or else he would be killed. Then the boy was taken to the living room where he was tied to a bench with electrical flex. When the boy managed to stand up he was kicked in the stomach which caused him to fall after which one of them stamped on his face.

In hospital he was treated for extensive bruising. Shortly after on the same day, the defendant and two others approached J and K aged 12 and 11. They asked for money and dragged them to the bungalow. They were put in the same shed and their bags were taken. The defendant picked up a metal bar. J was taken to the bungalow, searched and some biscuits taken from him. The defendant hit him with the bar. L was taken from the shed, searched and also had biscuits taken from him. Both boys were pushed into chairs. The defendant jumped on K and another jumped on and kicked J. The boys were told to suck one of the boy's "dicks", to kiss each other, spit in each others mouths and put their tongues in each others mouths. The boys refused. J's trousers and boxer shorts were taken off. K started screaming and he was told if he didn't stop he would be killed. A passer-by heard what was going on and the assailants ran away. All the victims were seriously traumatised. The defendant had a chaotic and traumatic childhood. His father was killed. He was permanently excluded from school at 8. He was disruptive and aggressive at placements. He was heavily involved in anti-social behaviour. An anti-social behaviour order was made a few weeks before the offences. The pre-sentence report recommended s 91 detention. Held. It is very rare for someone of the defendant's age to be detained. But a s 91 detention order was essential for the boy and the public. **3 years** did take into account the guilty plea.

Defendant aged 14–15 – Domestic premises

163.13   *R v Pinkney* 1998 1 Cr App R (S) 57. The defendant pleaded guilty at the first opportunity to attempted robbery. The defendant then 15 and two others went to the home of an elderly lady who lived in a flat in an old peoples' complex intending to commit burglary. He carried a knife which he held close to her face when she answered the door. She called for help and the three ran away. She was greatly upset and was taken to hospital for a check up. Four months later he voluntary attended the police station and eventually admitted his role and took police to where the knife was recovered. He showed genuine remorse and increasing signs of maturity. Held. It is inappropriate to impose detention under s 53(2) (now the Powers of the Criminal Courts (Sentencing) Act 2000, s 91) on a person of this age unless no other course is suitable. So 30 months under s 53(2) reduced to **2 years** YOI.

Defendant aged 14–15 – Firearm, with – Shops, public houses, petrol stations etc

163.14   *R v W* 2002 2 Cr App R (S) 528. The defendant pleaded guilty to conspiracy to rob and having a firearm with intent to commit an indictable offence. There were 3 co-accused R aged 17, D aged 18 and J aged 15. At 9.15 pm the four defendants approached a small relatively isolated shop. W had his father's air pistol and some balaclavas taken from his home. R who was armed with a baseball bat and J who had the gun entered the shop and confronted the owner. W was a lookout some distance away. D, who was to have entered the shop, changed his mind and didn't take part. R and J had balaclavas on and J pointed the gun at the shopkeeper and demanded money. The shopkeeper shouted at them and they fled hitting a display of sweets with the baseball bat. Nothing was taken. The Judge found they had spent the day discussing and planning the robbery and D had played a significant part in the planning. W lived at home with his parents and had no findings of guilt against him. His family was supportive and he assisted his disabled father. He was bright and capable at school although he had begun to truant and associated with a "negative peer group." He had written to the victim apologising for the offence. The pre-sentence report said it was a fantasy which got out of control and the risk of further offending was low. There were six letters from neighbours, teachers etc. who bore witness to his normally good character. R and J received 3 years and D received 30 months consecutive to a breach of a combination order (3 months). D had 10 findings of guilt including burglary and robbery. R had theft and an attempted theft. J had a TDA. The defence argued the sentence was manifestly excessive and showed no distinction between the older co-defendants who had previous convictions. Held. It is clear that he is a "normally decent young man" who has acted out of character and committed a very serious crime. There is no reason to doubt the risk assessment. He is genuinely remorseful. However this very serious offence will normally attract a severe sentence containing a deterrent element. The Judge had explained his reasons which could not be faulted. **3 years** detention was well within the range and certainly not manifestly excessive.

Defendant aged 14–15 – Firearm, with – Shops, public houses, petrol stations etc – Imitation

163.15   *R v Brown and Roberts* 2002 1 Cr App R (S) 274. The defendants B and R were convicted of robbery, possession of an offensive weapon and common assault. R demanded a cigarette from a man who was walking across a supermarket car park. The man refused their request and shouted abuse. R produced a knife and lunged at him. The man seized his wrist and twice got the better of him while R was swinging a knife and the incident ended. Within minutes they entered the supermarket's petrol station having changed into dark clothes and put on balaclava helmets. R was holding a knife at least 9' long and B had an imitation gun which was quite realistic. They shouted, 'Give us your fucking money.' Some £10 notes were handed over to R while B banged his gun on the till. When interviewed they denied involvement. They were now 17 but then they were 15. At trial they relied on alibis. B had a long record starting when he was 10. Regularly he had committed a large number of offences including burglary, handling, ABH, threatening words, common assault, criminal damage, theft and vehicle interference etc. While on bail for the robbery he was convicted with R of ABH in which he struck the victim with a leather belt and both received 10 months detention and training order. R's record started at 11 and paralleled Bs. Both abused alcohol and drugs. B's offending was said to be impulsive with no thought of the consequences to him or others. His risk assessment was high with a real possibility of harm to others being caused. B and R had family difficulties and B was living with R's family. Held. The court must carefully consider the principles in *R v Storey* 1984 6 Cr App R (S) 104 but will apply them in light of the sentencing practice developed since then. The court has to be prepared in appropriate cases to make examples of juveniles who commit these types of offences. **6 years** detention was severe but fully merited.

Defendant aged 14–15 – Series of robberies

163.16   R v Barker 2001 2 Cr App R (S) 75. The defendant pleaded guilty to three sets of offences. The first in time was robbery and theft. The second was robbery and the third was robbery, false imprisonment and threatening to damage property. The first started when a taxi with a passenger slowed down to make a turn. Four youths started to kick the taxi and the driver stopped. The defendant then 14 attempted to drag the passenger from the cab while another attacked him. The defendant took his luggage and ran off with it. His watch was taken and the driver who was trying to help the passenger lost a bag with £45 in it. The luggage was recovered. Ten days later a taxi called at a pub to pick up a fare called Barker. Three got in and when the taxi reached the destination the defendant walked round to the driver's side and leant though the window. He refused to pay the fare and was brandishing a knife. The driver was searched and between £70 to £80 was taken. Three days later the defendant was arrested and he denied the offence. He was bailed. Thirteen days later he rushed into a discount store where a 21 year old was working on her own. A 12 year old was in the store. He ran straight to the assistant carrying a knife and demanded money. She refused to give him any money and he became angry. She moved to the back of the shop and he threatened to slash her. He lashed out at her demanding the till be opened. The panic alarm was pressed and the police arrived quickly. He jumped over the counter and threw milk bottles at the front door. The young girl ran out and the assistant was prevented from leaving. Police used CS gas but were prevented from entering because the defendant threatened to slash the assistant. She was forced to write a note saying please leave and a threat to burn the shop down. He sprayed lighter fuel at the victim. He lit the can turning it into a small blow-torch. He closed the front door, locked the shutters and a siege began. He blamed the assistant for him being locked up for 3 months. He took £65 in cash and started a num-ber of fires. He pointed two small imitation handguns which were owned by the victim's father at the police. Two hours 10 minutes after he arrived he surrendered. The 12 year old was very distressed. The father of the assistant suffered emotionally, and the victim suffered from shock, bruising and swellings. The defendant had four convictions for assaulting a police officer, three for threatening behaviour, and one of affray, ABH, com-mon assault, attempted robbery, assault with intent to rob, damaging property being reckless whether life was endangered and having an offensive weapon. When 13 he threw a concrete slab at a bus injuring a passenger. Also when 13 he threatened a man with a knife. The attempted robbery was on someone sitting in a motor vehicle when he wore a stocking mask and brandished a knife. His past offences were frequently violent and involved weapons. He was in breach of a supervision order and he was excluded from school. He was almost illiterate and innumerate, but since his sentence he had made huge efforts to catch up. **Held.** The discount for the store offences has to be limited. Because of his age and the authorities **6 years** detention not 10.

R v P 2004 2 Cr App R (S) 343. The defendant pleaded to assault with intent to rob, robbery, four attempted robberies linked to four false imprisonment counts and two thefts. They were all committed within five days when the boy was 15. He hit a 12 year old boy with a stick whilst demanding money and his mobile. He tricked another boy to produce his mobile and stole it. This was repeated on another boy. He threatened to hit a 15 year old boy with a bat unless he handed over his phone. The boy did and the defendant snatched it. He detained four 14 year old boys in a park for a "considerable time". He threatened to knife them if they tried to leave. He demanded money and forced one to dance and reduced another to tears. He had a good relationship with his bail support worker. A doctor recommended psychological intervention for chronic depression. **Held.** He was not a lost cause. **3 years detention** not 4. (There is no reference to his previous convictions and many other details.)

Defendant aged 14–15 – Street robbery

163.17 *R v Manghan and Manghan* 2000 1 Cr App R (S) 6. The defendants P and B who were brothers pleaded guilty to robbery and five counts of theft. They targeted old ladies, jostled them and stole their purses or handbags. The first offence was on a 77 year old woman on a bus and she lost her purse. The next day they distracted the bus driver and pushed the victim up the front of the bus. Her purse was stolen. On the same day they operated in precisely the same way on a woman aged 70. The next day two other women were attacked. One was 69 and the other 77. They both lost their purses and one was very upset. On same day they jostled an elderly lady and stole her purse. This was the robbery. P was interviewed and said, 'Fuck the old ladies. I don't give a fuck about them.' He was 16 and had four findings of guilt and a conviction mostly for dishonesty. He had received 15 months for burglary. B was then 14 had two findings of guilt and two convictions of a relatively minor nature. The defendants said they needed the money for drugs. **Held.** Even with young defendants it was proper to include a deterrent element. Because of their age and the plea **4 years** detention for P and **3¹/₂ years** for B not 5 for both.

R v McKay 2000 1 Cr App R (S) 17. The ages of the defendants were 13–15. See **163.12**

R v J-R and G 2001 1 Cr App R (S) 377. The defendant J-R pleaded guilty to robbery and G was convicted of robbery. They were both 14. The victim aged 14 was walking

home and saw J-R, G and another youth S. He increased his speed. S shouted out for
him to stop and G grabbed him by the collar and punched him in the face. The victim
was led into an alleyway. He was surrounded and they demanded money. G produced
a knife and held it to the victim's throat. The contents of his bag were tipped onto the
ground. A pen, pencil and pencil sharpener were taken. The three walked off. The victim suffered from nightmares, became withdrawn and was frightened to go out alone.
His school results suffered. Previously he had been happy go lucky and successful. J-R
was of excellent character. He bitterly regretted his actions. His risk of re-offending was
low. G was the ringleader. In recent years he had aggressive and problematic behaviour.
He did not attend school. Held. The judge was right to bear in mind the increase in
street robbery. The effects on the victims can be disastrous as in this case. J-R's sentence was reduced from 20 months to **15 months** detention. G's sentence was reduced
from 3 years to **30 months**.

R v Joseph 2001 2 Cr App R (S) 398. The defendant was convicted of attempted
robbery. At 11.40 pm the victim was walking home carrying his lap top computer. The
defendant then 14 and two others approached him. He was asked for 10p and one of
them flicked off his glasses. One of the three jumped on them and they broke. The
defendant asked him if he wanted a fight and punched him in the face and headbutted
him six or seven times. He told the others to take the victim's wallet and computer. He
also produced a knife and the victim ran off. The victim was chased, tackled and fell to
the ground. He held onto his computer as the group tried to take it off him. Eventually
the victim managed to run away. The incident had lasted between 5 and 10 minutes. The
victim had swelling to his jaw, bruising to his eye and scratches to his face. He needed
5 stitches for a cut above his eye. A tooth was chipped and his ribs were sore. The
laptop was damaged and he had to replace his glasses. The defendant had no convictions and was a hard working student. The probation officer said the offence was out of
character. The judge said he was a big lad and bigger than the victim. Held. A balance
is required between the youth of the defendant and deterrence and the effect of a long
sentence upon the perception of the defendant. The sentence of **3 years** detention was
not manifestly excessive.

R v Sahadeo 2002 2 Cr App R (S) 564. The defendant pleaded guilty to three robberies,
one attempt and possessing a firearm whilst committing one of the offences. When 14,
he and his co-accused and another approached two 17 year old students. They separated the students and demanded money. The co-accused produced a gun and held it to the
face of one of the students. His mobile phone, cash cards and cash were stolen. The
defendant punched the other student twice in the face and stole similar property from
him. The two students were terrified. One believed he might have been shot. On the
same day, shortly afterwards the defendant and his co-accused approached two brothers aged 15 and 17. They told them they had a knife and one of the brothers was
punched in the face. They were told to empty their pockets and a small amount of cash
was stolen from them. The other had nothing worth stealing. The defendant was arrested later that day and denied the offences. He was 15 when sentenced and had a bad
record with a robbery conviction and 290 days left from a 3year sentence for a different offence. The Judge described the gun, which belonged to one of the others as,
"lethal looking." He also regarded prevalence of this sort of crime in the area. Held.
He was entitled to take that into account having obtained evidence about it. Applying
Att-Gen's Ref. Nos. 4, and 7 of 2002 2002 2 Cr App R (S) 345, there was undoubtedly
some aggravating features, namely more than one offence, more than one offender,
the poor record and above all the gun. Had the defendant been an adult or close to it
7 years with the 290 days consecutive would have been stern but unappealable. Solely
because of his age **4 years detention** for the robbery, **1 year** consecutive for the firearm
consecutive to the 290 days.

Att-Gen's Ref No. 31 etc of 2004 Re TM 2005 1 Cr App R (S) 377 at 381. The defendant TM was convicted of robbery and intimidation contrary to s. 51(1) of the CJPOA 1994. He approached an acquaintance and asked for money and cigarettes. Following a refusal they play-fought and the defendant's jacket was ripped. He became abusive and violent, beating the victim about the body until he had parted with a mobile phone worth £280. Subsequently the defendant made a call threatening violence to the victim and his parents if they called the police. There was a high risk of re-offending. However, the victim did not want the defendant to receive a custodial sentence. The defendant had 'real problems' with his schooling and lacked social skills. He was 15 and had recent previous convictions for indent assault, TDA and criminal damage and had received supervision and attendance centre orders. Held. The defendant had real problems. Unless his offending behaviour was tackled he would commit more serious crime. Custodial sentences would be the only option available to the courts where these offences were committed, unless there were exceptional circumstances. There were here and he had responded positively to the original sentence. If could not be said that the original order was inappropriate. If he goes off the rails again the courts have ample power. **24 month Supervision Order** with a 90-day ISSP coupled with a 6-month curfew unchanged. This type of order can achieve better long term protection for the public than a short custodial sentence.

Old cases *R v Fenemore* 1998 1 Cr App R (S) 167 and *R v Deegan* 1998 1 Cr App R (S) 291, (for a summary of these cases see the first edition of the book.)

Defendant aged 14–15 – Taxi drivers etc

163.18 *R v Hilden* 1999 1 Cr App R (S) 388. The defendant pleaded guilty to robbery, three burglaries, a theft and making off without payment. He asked for three matters including a burglary to be taken into consideration. When he was 15 he directed a taxi to a quiet place and demanded money from the driver. He held a razor at the driver's neck. The driver said he hadn't any until he saw he had been cut and handed over £35. The defendant ran off. The driver was bleeding heavily and was taken to hospital. He had a 1″ cut to his hand and a 5″ cut on his cheek and a 4½″ cut to his neck. When arrested the defendant made a full admission. He said he had not meant to cut the driver. His offending began when he was 12. The offences included burglary, intimidating witnesses and offences involving motor vehicles. He had eight appearances at the Youth Court usually for a plurality of offences sometimes as many as 10 or 12. He had a depressing family history. His father was in prison for his second rape offence. His mother and stepfather were alcoholics. There was a history of abuse. Held. The injuries were dreadful. Because of his age **4 years** not 5

Defendant aged 16–17 – Domestic

163.19 *R v Roberts* 1999 2 Cr App R (S) 194. The defendant pleaded guilty to robbery. When 17 he and another knocked on the door of a 52 year old man who was disabled with arthritis of the spine and neck. The victim was pushed the length of the hallway and pinned against the wall. The victim protested and was punched. He was dragged into the living room by his wrist causing bruising to his wrist and forearm. The other youth began to dismantle electrical equipment and the victim protested. He was pushed violently against the wall. His head was banged and his face pushed backwards. Because of his arthritis he was in considerable pain. He was told that if he did anything he would be slashed to pieces and would be killed. They claimed he owed someone some money. He was also slapped and told if he informed the police he'd be cut up and killed. They demanded money. £60 was handed over. They stole property worth about £1,500 and left. The victim had trouble sleeping and felt unable to return to his flat. The defendant had previous convictions for theft but none for violence. There was a Newton hearing and in all material respects he was disbelieved. Held. Because of his age and the discount for the plea, albeit reduced, **4 years** not 6.

Old case *Att-Gen's Ref. No 30 of 1997* 1998 1 Cr App R (S) 349, (for a summary of this case see the first edition of the book.)

Defendant aged 16–17 – Firearm, with – Banks – Imitation

163.20   *R v Jephson* 2001 1 Cr App R (S) 18. The defendant pleaded guilty to attempted robbery. A hoax call was made to the police to set the robbery up. [The content and purpose is not revealed.] The defendant then 17 with two others entered a bank. She did not attempt to conceal her face. Her co-defendant pointed an imitation gun, which fired small pellets at the bank clerk. Money was demanded and she held out a bag. No money was handed over and the three left. One of the victims had received counselling. She became depressed and was on medication. She was unable to return to work. Another victim suffered from anxiety. The defendant had no convictions and lived in a stable home. The risk of re-offending was described as low. She expressed her remorse and wrote to the victim saying she appreciated the misery she had caused. The co-defendants who were older received 5 years' detention and imprisonment. Held. 5 years for the co-defendants could not be criticised. As she stood further away from the planning and to some extent had been caught up rather than joined up in their enterprise **4 years** detention not 5.

Defendant aged 16–17 – Firearm, with – Imitation – Post Offices etc

163.21   *Att-Gen's Ref. No 52 to 55 of 1999* 2000 1 Cr App R (S) 450. The defendants T, L, B and J pleaded guilty to robbery. L also pleaded to attempted robbery. After $1\frac{1}{2}$ hours reconnaissance and careful planning the four defendants entered a sub-Post Office and news agency. They were dressed in camouflage clothing and wore masks. T had a hammer, which he used to smash the security video. Two imitation firearms were carried. There were four customers and four members of staff. They shouted, 'Get to the floor.' A firearm was waved and those inside were terrified. Two of the staff were working in the Post Office part and they were told to 'Open the fucking door.' The guns were pointed at them and they opened the door. It was opened and the staff left leaving the keys inside. The door closed and they demanded the door to be opened again. The staff tried to explain that couldn't be done as the keys were inside. The guns were discharged and one of the staff thought her colleague had been shot. The demands and the explanations continued until they left. One had demanded the till be opened and £200 was taken. They ran to a hostel because there was no getaway transport. The defendants were arrested and the guns recovered. They were both blank firing pistols and one had a live round in it. They were granted bail. Eight months later L confronted a boy who went to the same school as him. L and his friends bullied him. L asked to use his mobile phone and tried to grab it. He tried to run from L but was followed. L produced a Stanley knife and held it to his stomach. The boy thinking he was to be stabbed broke free and escaped. T and B were 17, J 16 and L 15 years old. T had no previous convictions, B had been cautioned, J had a conviction and a caution. L had been dealt with for violence. L received an indication that on a plea to the attempted robbery he would receive a concurrent sentence. Held. Had they been adults the sentences would be in the region of **10 years**. Bearing in mind their youth and the mitigation **7 years** would be appropriate. Because it was a reference **5 years** detention not 2.

For sentencing principles about Post Offices, see **Post offices**

Defendant aged 16–17 – Firearm, with – Imitation – Street etc robbery

163.22   Old case. *Att-Gen's Ref. No 47 of 1996* 1997 2 Cr App R (S) 194.

Defendant aged 16–17 – Firearm, with – Imitation – Trains

163.23   *Att-Gen's Ref. Nos. 7–10 of 2000* 2001 1 Cr App R (S) 166. The defendants K and W pleaded guilty to two robberies and were convicted of an attempted robbery. The defendant W also pleaded guilty to possessing an imitation firearm with intent. The defendants S and P were convicted of attempted robbery and two robberies. The boys then all aged 16 travelled on the Amersham part of the London Underground. K threw a bottle at the victim N aged 17. W had a gun which was waved in the N's face. N pushed it away and moved to the next carriage. He told two other boys C aged 18 and S aged 16 who had seen what had happened who also became victims that it was an imitation gun. The defendants moved as well and swore and abused the victims. N was asked if he had any money. N showed them his wallet was empty. C's rucksack was searched and W asked him to produce his wallet. £8 was taken from it. W searched S's rucksack and £35 was taken from his wallet. The victims were told they would be shot if they reported what had happened. W told them that he knew they attended Amersham College which he had discovered from their belongings. K had convictions and was in breach of a supervision order. He had been given 2 months' custody for an offence committed after the robbery. S was of good character. P at the time of the robbery had a conviction for which he was conditionally discharged and since then he had been convicted of theft. W had convictions and was in breach of a supervision order. He had been cautioned for ABH and the possession of an air weapon. K received 4 months' detention. S and P were given 80 and 90 hours' CSO. W was given a combination order with 100 hours' CSO. S had failed to comply with his CSO. Breach proceedings were instituted and he was given another 20 hours. No hours had been completed. P performed no hours of his CSO and breach proceedings were instituted against him. W had completed his CSO. Held. *Att-Gen's Ref. No 6 of 1994* 1995 16 Cr App R (S) 343 applies to offences committed on trains and other forms of public transport. Save in wholly exceptional circumstances robberies committed against young people on public transport must be met by custodial sentences. **18 months** for W and **12 months** for the rest would have been appropriate. Taking into account it was a reference, the mitigation and that W had completed his CSO **12 months** in a YOI for W and K and **6 months** detention for S and P.

Defendant aged 16–17 – Post offices

163.24 *Att-Gen's Ref. No 79 of 2001* 2002 1 Cr App R (S) 460. The defendant pleaded guilty to robbery. He and his co-defendant were under police observations. The co-defendant, W, entered a Post Office and grocer's shop pretending to make an enquiry about a savings account. The shop was staffed by a 62, 67 and 79 year old. He re-entered wearing a mask with the defendant who had zipped up his jacket up to conceal the lower part of his face and wore a baseball cap. They rushed in and W seized the manageress of the grocer's department's coat and put a knife with an 8″ blade to her back. She was pushed towards the sub-Post Office and her face was pushed against the wall. He said, 'Give me the money or I'll stab her'. She was petrified, screaming, crying and shouting. The defendant took the money that was passed through the security hatch while the woman was held with the knife now at her throat. Police officers entered the shop and the defendant tried to escape by running into the street. They were arrested. £1,000 was found in their possession. The manageress had to give up her job. The defendant had previous convictions for dishonesty and possession of drugs. He was on bail for a comparatively minor robbery, offences of burglary and possession of heroin. After receiving 12 months YOI, a Youth Court sentenced him to 4 months consecutive for those offences. Since his sentence he had taken a grip on his life and cleared himself of his drug problem. He was due to be released in the not too distance future. Held. Despite the mitigating features we would have expected **3 to 3¹/₂ years** detention. Taking into account it was a reference and the sentence imposed by the magistrates **2¹/₂ years** substituted.

For sentencing principles about Post Offices, see *Post Offices*

Defendant aged 16–17 – Shops

163.25 *R v B* 2001 1 Cr App R (S) 303. The defendant pleaded guilty to robbery. He, when 16, went into the shop part of a service station in the evening with a mask on. The cashier saw him holding a bag which was later discovered to contain a plastic imitation gun. He asked for cash and she told him not to be stupid. She thought it was a joke and went though the door behind the counter. When she came back he had gone. He had no convictions and was depressed with suicidal thoughts. Reports indicated the offence was a cry for help. Held. It was a serious offence but **12 months** detention and training not 18 would be sufficient.

Defendant aged 16–17 – Street etc robberies

163.26 *R v Manghan and Manghan* 2000 1 Cr App R (S) 6. The defendants P and B who were brothers pleaded guilty to robbery and five counts of theft. They targeted old ladies, jostled them and stole their purses or handbags. The first was on a 77 year old woman on a bus and she lost her purse. The next day they distracted the bus driver and pushed the victim up the front of the bus. Her purse was stolen. On the same day they operated in precisely the same way on a woman aged 70. The next day two other women were attacked. One was 69 and the other 77. They both lost their purses and one was very upset. On the same day they jostled an elderly lady and stole her purse. This was the robbery. P was interviewed and said, 'Fuck the old ladies. I don't give a fuck about them.' He was 16 and had four findings of guilt and a conviction mostly for dishonesty. He had received 15 months for burglary. B was then 14 had two findings of guilt and two convictions of a relatively minor nature. They said they needed the money for drugs. Held. Even with young defendants it was proper to include a deterrent element. Because of their age and the plea **4 years** detention for P and **3½ years** detention for B not 5 for both.

Att-Gen's Ref. No 21 of 1999 2000 1 Cr App R (S) 197. The defendant pleaded guilty at the first opportunity to attempted robbery. The victim aged 69 was walking along the pavement when the defendant then 17 ran up behind him and pushed him to the ground. The defendant stood over him and demanded his wallet. The victim shouted for help and the defendant placed his hand over the victim's mouth. He continued to demand the wallet. Two members of the public in a car stopped and shouted out and the defendant ran off. In a long chase he was caught. The victim had an orbital fracture to his eye socket, a cut above the eye requiring three stitches, swelling and bruising. There was some permanent disfigurement. He felt unable to use public transport and felt uncomfortable in the presence of strangers. He lost confidence and had difficulty in sleeping. The defendant was of good character with references. He had spent 4 months in custody before sentence. Held. The appropriate sentence for an adult of good character would be **3 years**. Taking into account his age and that it was a reference **18 months** YOI not probation.

Att-Gen's Ref. No 57 and 58 of 1999 2000 1 Cr App R (S) 502. LCJ. The defendant L was convicted at the Youth Court of robbery, burglary (both offences involving the defendant G) and shoplifting. She pleaded guilty to attempted robbery. G was convicted of another robbery on the same victim, possession of cannabis and theft. They were committed for sentence. L when 16 and G when 15 followed the victim aged 12 and demanded her jacket. They grabbed her arm and L pulled the jacket off. There had been long term intimidation of her by the two defendants. Three months later they went to the victim's home and demanded money. They entered uninvited and stole shopping vouchers worth £30 and left. Two days later G confronted the victim in a park, searched her and removed £30. Police arrested the two and cannabis was found on G. L's shoplifting was of goods worth £95 and G's theft was bedding from her children's home. The attempted robbery was on a 43-year-old woman who was walking home.

Someone grabbed her handbag and tried to snatch it. A struggle ensued and the victim was dragged to the ground. At that point L joined in and both tried to wrench the handbag from her grasp. The victim was kicked. A motorist disturbed them and the two made off. L had been convicted of damage to property, common assault, disorderly behaviour and a drugs offence. She was conditionally discharged. She had had limited contact with her family. She had been on remand for 6 weeks. The probation officer said she had made positive steps to make a fresh start and a custodial sentence might have a serious and detrimental effect on her ability to protect herself from more sophisticated offenders. She said she was a damaged individual who had attempted suicide. She had been affected by media interest because the victim had committed suicide although the prosecution did not suggest the two defendants were responsible for it. G had convictions for affray, two shopliftings, disorderly behaviour, two ABHs and other assaults. Her upbringing was turbulent and her response to supervision was poor. She was pregnant. However there were signs of improvement. Since sentence she had demonstrated a high level of commitment and was showing signs of responsibility. Held. We don't view these offences just through the eyes of the defendants. Supervision orders were unduly lenient. Parents are incensed when their children are victimised by others. Custody of some months was required. Taking into account the time passed, their co-operation with the authorities and the pregnancy it would be destructive and cruel to impose custody now.

Att-Gen's Ref. Nos. 11 and 12 of 2000 2001 1 Cr App R (S) 30. The defendants F and T pleaded guilty at the first opportunity to five counts of robbery. They when 16 with three others of similar ages robbed five 15 year old school boys who were sitting by a river. They went up to them and asked the boys about three other boys and left. Five minutes later they approached the victims from behind and F who was the largest held a kitchen knife with an 8″ blade to a boy's throat. The knife poked into the boy's Adam's apple. He told the others not to move or, 'He's going to get it.' The others joined in the attack. T took £10 from one boy. T wore no disguise unlike the others. F demanded a boy's wallet and took £16 and his watch worth £25. His hands and neck were checked for jewellery. The second victim was struck in the stomach and his mobile and wallet were taken. His shirt was pulled to check for jewellery. He was straddled and punched five or six times to the head causing bruising. The third victim had his wallet snatched which contained £20 and a door key. He was punched near his eyebrow and his wrists, socks and neck were checked. He was threatened again. The fourth victim was forced to hand over his watch. The fifth was robbed at knifepoint. A different knife with a 3″ blade was poked into his neck and he thought he was going to be stabbed. £9 was taken and he was told to jump in the river. The robberies were interrupted by the stolen mobile phone being called and the attackers ran away. The second and the third victims received bruises. T was not personally involved with the violence. T had no convictions and made full admissions to the police. His risk assessment for re-offending was described as very low. F was treated as of good character. Both showed remorse and had references etc. T was due to be released in 9 days time and had employment to go to. Held. Attacks of this kind are very frightening indeed. The offence is rife. The effect on them of being sentenced twice is likely to be very much greater than in the case of older and more experienced offenders. The sentences substituted were very substantially reduced. The effective sentences substituted were F **18 months** YOI not 8 and T **12 months** YOI not 6. Because of the change in the sentences for young offenders, lesser sentences starting dated from the date of the Court of Appeal ruling were imposed.

Att-Gen's Ref. Nos. 53–57 of 2001 Unreported Judgment 31/7/01. H and T pleaded guilty to two robberies. The two victims of the first robbery were walking home when by threats the defendants and others forced them into two different cars, threatened them and beat them up. They were told they were going to be raped and killed. One victim was hit with a hockey stick. H held a metal bar. They said an acquaintance of his had been stripped and tied up. He was going to have his teeth smashed out and his ears cut off. A gold chain was taken. At different times both victims managed to leave the cars when they were travelling at about 40 mph. Both had to taken to hospital but had surprisingly minor injuries. The next day, the third victim was also walking home and he was knocked over by a car driven by H. He was punched and kicked by a group of men while they demanded money. When he managed to run away he was jumped on, punched and kicked again. His visa card, bank credit card and mobile phone was taken. He suffered a cut, grazes and a very sore jaw. H played the major role in both incidents. He was 23 with previous convictions including robbery. T was 17 but he played a significant role. Held. The appropriate sentences for H would have been **6 years at the very least**. 18 months was absurdly low. Because it was a reference 18 months deducted so **4¹/₂ years**. T sentence should have been **4 years detention** only because of his age not 18 months. As it was a reference **2¹/₂ years** substituted.

R v Lang 2001 2 Cr App R (S) 175. The defendant pleaded guilty to two robberies, handling and theft. He then 17 approached an 18-year-old boy and asked to see his ring and bracelet. A man with the defendant started to shout and swear at the victim threatening to cut off his finger if he didn't remove the ring. The bracelet was taken and the victim was forced to remove his ring. The other man said, 'If you tell anyone I'm going to put a gun to your head and blow your head off.' This was the handling count. Six days later the defendant and another ran up to two 14-year-old boys and the defendant demanded one of the boy's rings. When the boy refused he threatened to stab him. The victim pretended he couldn't remove it and the defendant pulled it off. He also took a bracelet. Next he pulled down his collar and saw a gold chain which he also took. The victim said it was a Christmas present and the defendant said, 'I don't care. It's my Christmas present now.' The total value of the items was £300. This was one of the robbery counts. The other attacker pointed a screwdriver at the other boy and asked him for jewellery. He threatened to stab that boy and searched him. A £325 bracelet was taken. This was the theft count. The next day the defendant and two others followed two brothers aged 13 and 15 and another. They asked for money and jewellery and the boys said they didn't have any. One of the attackers put a screwdriver into a boy's cuff and threatened to stab him if he was lying. After pushing and shoving a hat was taken. The older brother feared he would be stabbed and was very frightened. When arrested he made limited admissions. He had 22 previous convictions predominately for dishonesty. There was one robbery and one common assault. He had received comparatively short custodial sentences. He abused ecstasy and alcohol. Held. The number and nature of the offences called for a strong deterrent sentence. The appeal over the **3¹/₂ years** detention sentence had no merit.

Att-Gen's Ref. Nos. 19–21 of 2001 2002 1 Cr App R (S) 136. There was an attempted robbery and a robbery. A 16 year old was not involved in the death of one of the victims. Following a plea the equivalent of **4 years** was not unduly lenient.

Att-Gen's Ref. No 98 of 2004 2005 1 Cr App R (S) 716. The defendant pleaded guilty at the PDH hearing to robbery and ABH. The events were captured on CCTV. The victim had phoned for a taxi from a phone box at about 2.00am and was keeping warm by staying in the phone box while he waited. The defendant was seen on the CCTV trying to break into a parked car nearby. He and three others walked towards the phone box. The victim stepped outside thinking they wanted to use the phone. The defendant and one other attacked him, punching his face and knocking off his glasses. He was knocked to the ground and kicked in the shoulder, head and back. He did not offer any resistance. The defendant and others searched his pockets as he lay on the ground and took £64 cash, a mobile telephone and some disposable cigarette lighters. The defendant and one of the others returned and the defendant stamped on him. They walked off and again the defendant came back and kicked and stamped on the victim. This was the subject of the ABH count. The victim had deep bruising of the head, back and shoulders. The defendant was 17 at the time, 18 at the time of sentence. He had a conviction for possession of a bladed article some four years previously and had been cautioned for offences of theft and ABH when he was 12 and criminal damage when he was 13. Aggravating features were that the robbery was committed by a group of four on a single person; that it took place at night; that shod feet were used as weapons; that the use of violence went beyond that required for the robbery and that there was subsequent and gratuitous violence after the robbery had been committed. Held. The appropriate sentence was at least **5 years** detention in a young offenders institution. As it was a reference **4 years** detention not 30 months.

Old cases. *R v Mills Re King* 1998 2 Cr App R (S) 128 at 136, *R v Mills Re Maloney* 1998 2 Cr App R (S) at 138 and *R v Mills Re Howe* 1998 2 Cr App R (S) at 142, (for a summary of these cases see the first edition of the book.)

Defendant aged 16–17 – Street etc robberies – Mobile phones

163.27   *Att-Gen's Ref. Nos. 4 and 7 of 2002 and R v Q* 2002 2 Cr App R (S) 345. LCJ. A reference and an application for leave to appeal were listed together. The defendant Q was convicted of robbery. The victim aged 14 was on his paper round. The defendant aged 17 approached him wearing surgical gloves and holding a claw hammer above his head. He said, 'Give me your fucking phone now.' The victim handed it over and it was worth about £80. He was a persistent offender, (no details given) and was on bail. The judge said the message needs to go out that to those that do this that they will serve a custodial sentence of a substantial length. A deterrent sentence is demanded. Held. The judge was absolutely right. Punishment will be severe. Custodial sentences will be the only option unless there are exceptional circumstances irrespective of age and lack of previous convictions. **3 years** detention substituted for 4 years. That would not have happened if there had been violence used, or there was more than one offence or if the defendant had been older.

Defendant aged 16–17 – Taxi drivers

163.28   *Att-Gen's Ref. Nos. 7–10 of 2000* 2001 1 Cr App R (S) 166. The defendants K and W pleaded guilty to two robberies and were convicted of an attempted robbery. The defendant W also pleaded guilty to possessing an imitation firearm with intent. The defendants S and P were convicted of attempted robbery and two robberies. The boys then all aged 16 travelled on the Amersham part of the London Underground. K threw a bottle at the victim N aged 17 and W waved a gun in the N's face. N pushed it away and moved to the next carriage. He told two other boys – C aged 18 and S aged 16 – who had seen what had happened and became victims, that it was an imitation gun. The defendants moved as well and swore and abused the victims. N was asked if he had any money. N showed them his wallet was empty. C's rucksack was searched and W asked him to produce his wallet. £8 was taken from it. W searched S's rucksack and £35 was taken from his wallet. The victims were told they would be shot if they reported what had happened. W told them that he knew they attended Amersham College which he had discovered from their belongings. K had convictions and was in breach of a supervision order. He had been given 2 months custody for an offence committed after the robbery. S was of good character. P at the time of the robbery had a conviction for which he was conditionally discharged and since then he had been convicted of theft. W had convictions and was in breach of a supervision order. He had been cautioned for ABH and the possession of an air weapon.

K received 4 months' detention. S and P were given 80 and 90 hours' CSO. W was given a combination order with 100 hours' CSO. S had failed to comply with his CSO.

Breach proceedings were instituted and he was given another 20 hours. No hours had been completed. P performed no hours of his CSO and breach proceedings were instituted against him. W had completed his CSO. Held. *Att-Gen's Ref. No 6 of 1994* 1995 16 Cr App R (S) 343 applies to offences committed on trains and other forms of public transport. Save in wholly exceptional circumstances robberies committed against young people on public transport must be met by custodial sentences. **18 months** for W and **12 months** for the rest would have been appropriate. Taking into account it was a reference, the mitigation and that W had completed his CSO **12 months** in a YOI for W and K and **6 months** detention for S and P.

Old case. *Att-Gen's Ref. Nos. 35 and 37 of 1997* 1998 1 Cr App R (S) 344, (for a summary of this case see the first edition of this book.)

Defendant aged 18–20

163.29 Where age is not treated as significant e.g. where the defendant has convictions the cases for defendants who are 18–20 are listed in the general categories.

See also *Att-Gen's Ref. Nos. 35 and 37 of 1997* 1998 1 Cr App R (S) 344. For a summary of this case see the first edition of this book.

Defendant aged 18—20 – Firearm, with

163.30 *R v Brownbill and Dorrian* 1999 2 Cr App R 331. The defendants B and D both then 18 pleaded guilty to robbery and possession of a firearm on arrest. D had also pleaded guilty at the Magistrates' Court to aggravated vehicle taking. In the incident he was a passenger. At about 21.45, the defendants burst in to a convenience store wearing balaclava helmets. D pointed a gun at the owner and demanded the till be open and B was armed with a knife. D seized £220 cash from the till and some cigarettes. B seized some bottles of spirits. The total value of goods stolen was £500. An off duty police officer pursued them and they were caught. The property was recovered and the gun found. It was unloaded damaged air pistol. They both admitted the offence. B had convictions including non-domestic burglary and wounding with intent for which he received 18 months detention. He was in breach of his licence. D had convictions for burglary and motor vehicle offences but had not had a custodial sentence. B's risk assessment was high. The judge sentenced B to automatic life with 4¹/₂ years specified based on? of 7 years. D was sentenced to 7 years detention. Held. It was a very serious robbery. If they had been adults 7 years would have been fully justified. Because of their age the sentence for D was reduced to **6 years** detention. B's specified period was reduced to 3 years (being half 6 years).

Defendant aged 18–20 – Street etc robberies – Mobile phones

163.31 *Att-Gen's Ref. Nos. 4 and 7 of 2002 and R v Q* 2002 2 Cr App R (S) 345. LCJ. The defendant was convicted of robbery and assault with intent to commit robbery. The defendant then aged 18 with two others confronted two 16-year-old victims as they were walking in a town centre. The defendant grabbed one and demanded his mobile. He threatened to stab him and produced a knife which he pointed at his chest. His mobile and bus pass was stolen. The second victim was asked for jewellery and his mobile. A threat to stab him was made and his hand was jabbed causing a small cut. The defendant and another each headbutted him. A member of the public intervened and the robbery was abandoned. The defendant was the ringleader and was of good character. Held. The appropriate detention was **4 years** not 6 months. Because it was a reference **3¹/₂ years** substituted.

Domestic premises

163.32 *R v Gabbidon and Bramble* 1997 2 Cr App R (S) 19. The defendant G pleaded guilty to robbery. He was convicted of wounding with intent to resist apprehension. B was convicted of three robberies and assault with intent to resist apprehension. B was comfortably over 6 foot tall. He was 37 and a professional burglar. He had 12 burglary convictions and two aggravated burglary convictions since he was 14. For the last three offences he had received 6 years. On his release from a period in custody when he was acquitted he was the subject of surveillance. The defendant entered the home of a mother who was at home with her two young children and a woman friend. He had a mask on and carried a crowbar. He demanded jewellery and the adults handed over their rings. They were pulled upstairs. Following the robbery both women had slept badly and had been very scared in the home. Three nights later, B entered another home where another mother lived with her husband, her children aged 2 years and 7 months and their nanny. He demanded property. The nanny managed to lock herself into the library and call the police. This did not seem to affect the defendant. The defendant threatened to hurt the baby. He pushed the husband who was holding the baby but the husband saved the baby from injury. The defendant left 20 seconds before the police arrived with cash, credit cards and a handbag. All three adults suffered from trauma. Five days later B and G entered the home of a couple aged 66 and 69 who were entertaining an 82 year old. B had a handkerchief across his face and carried a crowbar. The husband tried to hit B but was pushed to the floor where B held a screwdriver to his eye. B attacked the 82 year old and held him down. B threatened to shoot them and G demanded the safe be opened. The wife opened the safe because she was so frightened about the older man. Her ring and watch were taken as well as the jewellery in the safe. The couple's main worry was that the older man would be killed. The husband had bruises and was in a great deal of pain. G was chased by police who caught him when he leapt onto a fence. They seized his legs and he kicked out. He raised a metal jemmy and brought it down on the head of a policeman with some force. There was a lot of blood and the officer required three stitches. All three incidents terrified the occupants and had the potential for long term trauma. G was 32 and had 16 burglary convictions. The judge said B gloried in the effect he could produce terror. G received 16 years for the robbery and 1 year consecutive for the wounding. B received 21, 22, and 27 years concurrent for the robberies with 6 months concurrent for the assault. B's sentences was made longer than commensurate under the then Criminal Justice Act 1991, s 2(2)(b). The judge had considered 18 years suitable for the B's overall figure and added 50% under the then s 2(2)(b). G's sentence was not made longer than commensurate. **Held.** We have conducted a full review of the authorities. The case falls to the top of the range although not the very worst of their kind. The very worst are those involving firearms and where gratuitous violence to the extent of torture is used. Top of the range sentences must correlate sensibly and fairly with the indeterminate sentences of life for comparable murders, i.e. in 'robberies that went wrong.' Here the burglars wished the houses to be occupied to increase their haul by causing fear to open safes etc. The trauma of the victims can cause lasting psychological damage. The judge was under a duty to extend B's sentences. There was a clear need to protect the public. The 18 years and 9 years consecutive sentence for B was out of scale. Without extending the sentence **15 years** would have been appropriate. To reflect the need to protect the public, 5 additional years was right making 20 years in all. The correct sentence for G would have been **12 years** with **9 years** on a plea and 12 months consecutive for the GBH. Therefore G's sentence was reduced from 17 to **10 years**.

Att-Gen's Ref. Nos. 108–9 of 2002 2003 2 Cr App R (S) 608. The defendants were convicted of manslaughter, conspiracy to rob and threatening to kill. The defendant, together with a third man, went to the victim's 12th floor flat to rob him. They recruited another to trick the victim into opening his front door. After the door was opened all three burst in. The victim ran to his bedroom where his 3 year old daughter was asleep. The men demanded the keys to his sports car and the victim refused. One of the men had a folding knife; the other had a claw hammer. One of them threatened to shoot him. One of them grabbed his daughter and threatened to kill her. The victim, in panic, threatened to climb out of the window unless they released the child. Then a man held onto the child and the victim climbed out of the window. The three defendants left. As the victim was clinging to the ledge the police arrived at the foot of the block and as they went in the defendants were leaving. The police were told a different floor from the one on which the events were taking place. Inside the flat, a friend tried to pull the victim back in but the victim lost his friend's grasp and fell to his death. One defendant denied presence, the other admitted presence but denied playing any part in the robbery. Both defendants were 22, one was of good character, the other had one conviction for possessing a bladed article 3 years earlier. Held. There were 3 male invaders who were armed with at least one and probably two weapons. The threats that they made to the child were despicable and understandably induced intense fear. The defendants left without rendering him any assistance and they sought to mislead the police about where he might be found. The manslaughter would normally attract a sentence of between **10 and 12 years**; the conspiracy to rob, a sentence of at least 7 years. For the manslaughter, 6 years was unduly lenient; **9 years** substituted. For the conspiracy to rob, 4 years was unduly lenient; 6 years substituted. All concurrently.

R v Underwood and others Re C 2005 1 Cr App R (S) 478 at 497. The defendant pleaded guilty to conspiracy to burgle and rob. The group targeted elderly people in their home by tricking them or forcing their way in. The average age of the victims was 80. They would steal a car and change the number plate. The defendant was always the driver whilst his co-defendant, H would pose as the official in order to gain entry. The first robbery concerned an 84 year old who was home alone when she heard a knock at the door. She was told that he was installing a washing machine at a neighbouring property. She gradually became aware that there was someone else in the property. After an untidy search upstairs, the two men left. During that day, seven further burglaries and an attempted burglary took place involving elderly victims. A total of £3,000 of cash was stolen. One victim had her wedding ring and some jewellery stolen. Eleven days later a 76 year old gentleman who suffered from acute angina was robbed. As he tried to stand up he was threatened with a fist and forced to sit down again. His life savings were stolen. When the police arrived he had a severe attack of angina. He died two months later. On the same day a couple aged 76 and 75 were threatened with knives. The defendant had been pressured into acting as the driver by his elder and more experienced co-defendants. He was 20 and was effectively of good character. H had received 9 years. Held. This team had deliberately targeted elderly and vulnerable people. However, given the defendant's youth, his lack of criminal sophistication, the limited role that he played, **6 years** detention not 8.

See also **Burglary – Aggravated**

Domestic premises – Victim over 65 – Guideline remarks

163.33   *R v O'Driscoll* 1986 8 Cr App R (S) 121. LCJ There is a tendency for burglars to select as victims elderly or old people living on their own. It is plain why. First of all they are not likely to offer much resistance, and the chances are that they have got not inconsiderable sums of money concealed about the house. Where thugs, because that is what they are, select as their victims old folk and attack them in their own homes and then torture them – that is what happened here – in order to try to make them hand over their valuables in this most savage fashion, then this sort of sentence (**15 years**) will be the sort of sentence they can expect. One hopes this court may have some effect in protecting these old folk from this sort of savage, sadistic, cruel and greedy attack.

Att-Gen's Ref. Nos. 32 and 33 of 1995 1996 1 Cr App R (S) 376. LCJ Both defendants pleaded to aggravated burglary. One also pleaded guilty to attempted robbery. The general effect of the cases is that where an elderly victim, living alone, is attacked by intruders and is injured the likely sentence will be in **double figures**. We wish to stress that attacks on elderly people in their homes are particularly despicable and will be regarded by the court as deserving severe punishment. Elderly victims living alone are vulnerable, not only because of their lack of assistance but also because of their own weakness and isolation. Any attack on such a person is cowardly and can only be expected attract a very severe punishment indeed.

R v Dunn 2002 1 Cr App R (S) 95. We bear in mind the principles in *R v O'Driscoll* 1986 8 Cr App R (S) 121.

R v Marcus 2004 1 Cr App R (S) 258. Those who select elderly or otherwise vulnerable people as victims and then invade their homes will receive very severe sentences. Such vulnerable people have to be protected, and this court will do everything it can to provide that protection. Lengthy prison sentences will normally be absolutely inevitable.

Domestic premises – Victim over 65 or vulnerable

163.34   *R v Hearne* 1999 1 Cr App R (S) 333. The defendant pleaded guilty to robbery. The defendant got to know a 90 year old lady when cleaning her windows. He offered to help her when she moved home. It was agreed he would get £10 and any furniture she didn't want. After some discussions about tea-chests he inexplicably pushed her on her bed. He told her to be quiet and pulled one of her jumpers over her face and knotted it. He said, 'Keep quiet I want your money.' He took £30 and ran off. She went after him. Eight hours later he went to the police station and confessed to the crime and said he spent the money on crack. He had character witnesses. Held. Generally 5 years is not a day too long. However, here **3 years** instead.

R v Collins 2001 2 Cr App R (S) 433. The defendant was convicted of robbery. The defendant called at the victim's flat pretending to be from the Water Board. He was let in and 4–5 minutes later the defendant's brother who was also pretending to be a workman was let in. The victim, aged 86 became suspicious and they asked for £25 for work done. The victim went upstairs to get money from his safe. The brother went to the safe and the defendant pushed the victim onto the bed and tried to put a gag into his mouth. That failed but he was held down for about 5 minutes while the brother rifled the safe. They took five watches, a ring, some commemorative coins and £60. The defendant was 29 with convictions for 13 burglaries and attempted burglaries, three for robbery and had received four custodial sentences one of which was 6 years. Held. **12 years** was at the top end but not manifestly excessive. There was a significant element of deterrent.

Att-Gen's Ref. No 113 of 2001 2002 2 Cr App R (S) 269. The defendant pleaded guilty to five counts of robbery on the date his case was listed for trial. The victims were all elderly and attacked in their own homes after dark. He had been released from prison for 5 months. He was masked and they were terrified. He demanded money and he put his hand over two of their mouths. He brushed passed one and caused her to fall. Another victim was tied up. Money and small items were taken. The offences were on two separate nights just 2 weeks apart. The defendant had seventeen court appearances for thirty five offences. They included robbery, rape, burglary, assault, theft, possession of offensive weapons, motor vehicle offences and unlawful sexual intercourse. In 1988 he gained entry to an 85 year old lady's house by pretending to be a police officer. He bound gagged and raped her. In 1989 he broke into an 81 year old lady's flat at 1am. He tied her up, gagged her and searched for money. She was raped at gunpoint. In 1989 he received 18 years for offences of robbery and rape. He was 47 with a long history of drink and drug abuse. The risk of re-offending was assessed as exceptionally high. He believed he had caused his victims little harm and refused to take part in programmes for offence focused work. The judge was not satisfied the offences were violent and sentenced him in total to $9^1/_2$ years. Held. Bearing in mind the ages of the victims and what was done to each of them, the real possibility of fractures, asphyxia and cardiac arrest each was a violent offence. **Life** substituted.

R v McDonnell 2003 2 Cr App R (S) 117. The defendant pleaded guilty to three robberies, six burglaries, two thefts and one attempted burglary. The burglaries targeted elderly victims. In January 2000, he entered a pensioner's house and went to the bathroom and turned on the taps, saying that he was checking the water. He took £80 and a ring. The same day the defendant arrived at the home of another pensioner saying he was from the water board. He took a wallet with £200 from a bedroom. Ten days later the defendant visited an 82 year old and said that he was from the electricity board and that he wanted to check the premises. Nothing was taken. On the same day he told an 88 year old he was from the electricity board. He looked around but took nothing. 5 days later, a 76 year old lady opened her door. He pushed it so hard that the security chain broke, knocking her backwards into a chair. He took a pension book and purse. Later, he told an elderly lady he was from the Council. He and another went upstairs and stole about £450 in cash. He told a lady in her 80s he was from the police before pushing her backwards causing her to fall. He rushed inside and stole her handbag containing £900 in cash. When she tried to stop him she was knocked to the floor. The robberies again targeted elderly victims. In October 2001, he forced a frail 81 year old man into his rear room where he and another searched and threatened him. A wallet containing £90 was taken. The man was shocked, shaken and upset and had to have medical assistance. Two weeks later, an 85 year old man was forced back into his home by the defendant and another man. His arm was held behind his back. When neighbours intervened, the pair ran off with £400 in cash. The defendant was later arrested and interviewed where he admitted the robberies and volunteered various information concerning offences that he asked to be taken into consideration (driving offences, handling stolen goods, six burglaries, three attempted burglaries and one theft). The thefts were opportunistic. In February 2000 an 85 year old lady arrived at home and put her shopping down at her front door. He stole it. The other theft was an unlocked car with the keys in it. The defendant was 23 with a number of convictions, mostly for driving matters. He had four convictions for burglary; one resulting in a 12 month sentence. Held. There were aggravating circumstances. He had targeted elderly people. Secondly, he told the victims he was from one of the utilities or from the police. Thirdly, on occasions the appellant used force knocking elderly occupiers backwards. The robbery offences were particularly vicious as the defendant having knocked at the door of elderly people, forced them back into their homes before stealing their possessions. Fourthly many of these offences were committed whilst he was on bail. Fifthly the frequency of these offences clearly denote that he is a professional and regular burglar who has been undeterred by the previous sentences. **12 years** severe but upheld.

Domestic premises – Victim over 65 or vulnerable – Victim injured or attacked

163.35   *Att-Gen's Ref. No 1 of 1999* 1999 2 Cr App R (S) 398. The defendant pleaded guilty to five robberies. In all of them the defendant had forced his way into the homes of elderly people. The first robbery was on a 71 year old who was pushed to the floor when he opened his door. He was then pushed into his sitting room where the defendant demanded money. The defendant shouted and said he was on drugs. He obtained £230 and pulled out the telephone wires. Eight months later he returned and pushed the same victim to the floor. He took cash from his pockets and £130 in all. The victim was threatened with a radio. The telephone wires were cut and the victim was very distressed. The second robbery was on an 88-year-old man. The defendant was wearing a balaclava and pushed the victim over. The victim had £215 taken from his pockets and his wrist was hurt. $3^1/_2$ weeks later he returned and climbed through a window and seized the same victim's arms and stole £110. The other robbery was on an 84-year-old woman who suffered from a heart condition. She lived with her lodger aged 79. He entered their home wearing a balaclava and demanded money. The lodger tried to push him out and a struggle ensued. The lodger fell to the floor and the woman was pushed in the chest and stumbled. He took £40 from her purse and she suffered an anginal attack. She said she was in total fear.

The defendant was arrested and said the money was for drugs. He expressed remorse. Held. He had targeted the homes of the elderly. Attacks on the elderly in their homes were despicable and deserved severe punishment. They are vulnerable not only because they lack assistance and support but because of their weakness and feeling of isolation. Fear and anxiety are ever present and that blights the future. The first visit to the victims was worth **6 years** and the second visit **8 years**. The total should have been 8. Because it was a reference **6 years** not 4. [The defendant's age and character is not revealed.].

Att-Gen's Ref. No 89 of 1999 2000 2 Cr App R (S) 382. The defendant was convicted of robbery. The victim, D lived alone and was 69 years old and frail. The defendant had robbed him previously. The defendant knocked on his door and forced his way in. He demanded money and produced a knife. The victim was pushed to the floor and sat upon. The defendant pushed his Adam's apple with a lot of pressure. The telephone cable was ripped from the wall and wrapped around his neck. The victim was in pain and passed out. The incident had lasted about 15 minutes. When he came to he found £120 and a £20 souvenir coin was stolen. The victim was taken to hospital and found to have redness to the front of his neck. The defendant was 32 and had 29 convictions. In 1979 there were two burglaries and other offences for which he received 9 months youth custody. In 1987 there were three robberies, a residential burglary, three thefts and a blackmail for which he received 5 years. Except for the burglary the victim was D. In 1991 the defendant received 3 years for robbery and a non-residential burglary. In 1993 he received 7 years for a robbery and two burglaries. The 1993 convictions all involved the same 64-year-old victim and each involved a knife. He was on licence. Held. The sentence should have been in **double figures** even though the injuries were not the gravest. Applying *Att-Gen's Ref. No 1 of 1999* 1999 2 Cr App R (S) 398 the starting point was 10 years. Because it was a reference **8 years** not 6. The powers should have been exercised about the breach of the licence. 443 days were ordered to run consecutive.

Att-Gen's Ref. No 48 of 2000 2001 1 Cr App R (S) 423. The defendant pleaded guilty to robbery. Police watched the defendant paying attention to elderly pedestrians near sheltered accommodation. He was seen trying to open a door and a window. He approached the victim aged 79 in the street and was told he couldn't come into the block because of incidents in the past. The defendant pushed past the victim and went in. He was seen by a witness inside to be agitated and he claimed to be delivering pizzas. He went to the victim's flat and when the door was opened he forced his way in. The victim was pushed and fell on the floor face down. The defendant went through his pockets and took £24. The victim was then punched on the mouth and nose. The sideboard was searched and the defendant left. The victim suffered from pains in his ribs and tenderness. The defendant was 36 and had been convicted of 49 offences. They started when he was 13 and were mostly for burglary or theft. In 1993 he had received 5 years for robbery, residential burglary, burglary and theft. In 1996 he received 3 extra years for three robberies committed about the time of the 1993 offences. They were on elderly victims who had been assaulted in their own homes. 13 months after the defendant had been released from that sentence he committed this offence. Held. The sentences for a single offence when a defendant had pleaded guilty range between **4 and 7 years. 4 years** was lenient but not unduly lenient. It fell at the bottom of the range which are permissible. One factor in the decision is as it was 4 years he would have to serve a greater proportion of the sentence and be subject to more stringent conditions on his release.

R v Dunn 2002 1 Cr App R (S) 95. The defendant pleaded guilty to robbery, an attempted robbery and two counts of theft. The robbery was on a husband aged 86 and wife aged 78. The husband suffered from cancer and had heart problems. They lived in housing for the elderly. At about 10.30 pm while the wife went to check the front door the defendant entered the living room where the husband was. The defendant started to open drawers and cupboards. When the wife returned she told him to leave and he said, 'I want some money or I'll kill you.' He continued searching. She told him to leave her husband alone and he repeated his threats and demand. She told him to kill her and he grabbed her by the throat, squeezed and dug his fingers into her neck causing marks to her neck. She had breathing difficulties and eventually he let go and left. Both the victims found the incident frightening and she felt unable to leave the house at all for 2 weeks. About $2^1/_2$ hours later he entered the bedroom of his next victims by climbing in through a window. One of them, the wife, jumped out of bed and as she screamed for her husband tried unsuccessfully to push the defendant out. He knocked her to the floor, raised his fist and said, 'Where's the money? I want money.' The husband got out of bed and seized a walking stick. He repeatedly struck the defendant who kicked out at him. The defendant tried to leave by the front door but it was locked. The husband continued to hit him and the defendant jumped out of the window. The wife suffered scratches and her hand was sore. She feared the defendant would return. Nothing was taken but some ornaments of great sentimental value were damaged. The thefts were from supermarkets. The defendant had a substantial record but no convictions for violence. Held. The **10 year** sentence was severe but in all the circumstances justifiably so.

Att-Gen's Ref. Nos. 38 and 39 of 2004 2005 1 Cr App R (S) 267. The defendants D and R pleaded guilty to robbery at preliminary hearings, D some three months before R, because R breached his bail. The two men and another went at about 1.00 am to the home of the victim, a frail 57 year old man who they knew had learning difficulties. The victim needed help in carrying out basic activities such as washing and shaving. He had been the target of local children pestering him for money and he had sometimes complied with the requests. One of the children he had given money to was R's stepson, aged 10, to whom he had given £10 the day before this offence. The three men called at the house. The victim woke up and opened the door. They pushed him back into the doorway and D restrained him and punched him in the face. They asked him for money and he told them about £100 he had, the totality of his savings from benefits. R at least went upstairs and took the money. A neighbour called the police and the three men were discovered hiding in a hedge. The victim suffered fractures to his right cheek bone and eye socket. R suggested in interview that he was concerned in case the victim was abusing his stepson. This suggestion was later withdrawn. Both men claimed to have been heavily drunk. It was submitted that aggravating features were that the offence was committed at night time, serious injury was caused and both offenders at the time attributed unsavoury motives to the victim's behaviour towards children. R, 21, had a number of previous convictions mainly for burglary, theft and motoring offences. D, 39, had a substantial criminal record with over 100 previous convictions mostly for burglary, theft and minor offences. A pre-sentence report said that both sought to minimise their blameworthiness and revealed no sense of remorse. Held. The aggravating features were that a vulnerable and frail man was targeted; the offence involved an invasion of his house a night; gratuitous violence was used; significant injury resulted and a group of men were involved. The real test is vulnerability not age. Deterrent sentences are required. 3 years for both men was unduly lenient. The appropriate sentence would have been in the range of **$6^1/_2$ to 7** years. As it was a reference $5^1/_2$ years was substituted for both men.

Old cases. *R v Lee* 1995 16 Cr App R (S) 60 and *R v Owen* 1998 1 Cr App R (S) 52, (for a summary of this case see the first edition of this book.)

For when there is a s 18 count see OFFENCES AGAINST THE PERSON ACT 1861 s 18 – *Robbery/Burglary/Aggravated burglary*

Extended sentences (Old law)

163.36 *Att-Gen's Ref. No. 92 of 2002* 2003 2 Cr App R (S) 80. The defendant, M, pleaded guilty to two counts of robbery. In the first robbery M with another, H, who acted as lookout, went into a general store. M was wearing a mask. He shouted at Mrs S, who was working in the shop, "Give me the money you Paki bastard". The defendant held a 9" knife in his right hand and pushed Mrs S to the floor as she reached for the phone. He shouted at her to open the till and pushed her head onto the till and pushed the knife into her face causing a small cut above her lip. Next he placed the knife between her thumb and forefinger and threatened: "If you don't open the till I'll cut your finger off". She still resisted so he held the knife to her neck. She then opened the till and £250 and some cigarettes were taken. The two men made off. The second robbery occurred on the same day at about 9.30 pm. H asked R for a word in the gents; once there M entered. H punched R in the face and M joined in, punching him several more times in the face. R was searched by the defendant who said "Make it easy for yourself, give him your wallet or I'll kill you". A doorman entered and dragged the defendant, who was holding R's wallet, off. Both escaped. R suffered numerous bruises and a black eye. M was arrested later and claimed not to have been involved in the first robbery but had been present in the public house at the time of the second. He was re-interviewed and admitted to his involvement in the first. He was 35 and had been sentenced to 6½ years for 3 knife point robberies. Shortly following his release he had stolen the handbag of an 87 year old who had just arrived home in her disabled carriage. He received 3 years. He committed the current offences with 463 days of his licence remaining. Held. The aggravating features were the use of a knife, the violence inflicted on Mrs S, the degree of premeditation, the fact that it was a vulnerable small shop and M's high risk of re-offending, as assessed by the probation officer. **6 or 7 years** would have been appropriate. **5 years 9 months** was lenient and upheld but the sentence should be extended so with the licence 10 years in all.

See also EXTENDED SENTENCES

Firearm, with – Guidelines

163.37 *R v Turner* 1975 61 Cr App R 67 at 90. It is not in the public interest that even for grave crimes, sentences should be passed which do not correlate sensibly and fairly with the time in prison which is likely to be served by someone who has committed murder in circumstances in which there were no mitigating circumstances. The courts must have a range of penalties to deal with abnormal crime like bad cases of espionage, horrid violence like the *Richardson* torture case and bomb outrages. Bank robberies, which are common occurrences, should not be treated as abnormal crimes but as crimes of gravity. The normal sentence for anyone taking part in a bank robbery or the hold-up of a security or Post Office van should be **15 years** if firearms are carried and no serious injury done. The fact that a man has not much of a criminal record is not a powerful factor in cases of this gravity. The total sentence for those that commit two or more should not normally be more than **18 years**. This is about the maximum for the category of offences we describe as, 'wholly abnormal.' The judge was right to make a distinction between the look out and those who went into the bank and held up the staff with guns.

R v Adams and Harding 2000 2 Cr App R (S) 274 at 277. The starting point must be *R v Turner* 1975 61 Cr App R 67 which suggests that the maximum sentence for more than one armed robbery should be 18 years. However, R v Turner 1975 was decided when the sentencing climate was very different from today. For one thing remission was one third. Recent examples of sentencing is *R v Schultz* 1996 1 Cr App R 451 in which sentences of 25 years were upheld for more than one offence of armed robbery. Here but for the fact that life sentences were imposed we would not consider 25 years as manifestly excessive.

Firearms, with – Consecutive or concurrent sentences

163.38   *R v Greaves and Jaffier* 2004 2 Cr App R (S) 41. LCJ. The policy which should be adopted is to make the firearm sentence consecutive. That gives a clear message to those who commit crimes of this nature that if they carry a weapon when committing a robbery they will receive an additional sentence.

Firearm, with – No firearm count

163.39   *R v Eubank* 2002 1 Cr App R (S) 11. LCJ. The defendant pleaded guilty to a single count, robbery. There was an issue whether the defendant had a firearm. The judge held a Newton hearing and concluded that the defendant at least had an imitation weapon. Held. Before the defendant is convicted of such a grave offence he is entitled to have a verdict of the jury. The appropriate course was to include a count in the indictment to make their position clear. As there was no count it was wrong to sentence him on the basis he had a firearm.

R v Flamson 2002 2 Cr App R 208. The prosecution tells the Judge there is no dispute about the firearm. Automatic life upheld.

R v Murphy 2003 1 Cr App R (S) 181. In 1997 the defendant pleaded guilty to robbery. There was no firearm count. The prosecution did not agree the basis of plea and the Judge held a Newton hearing and concluded the defendant had something with him, which looked like a gun. He was sentenced and released. He robbed a petrol station and his accomplice had a gun. He was convicted of robbery and again there was no firearm count. The second Judge read the transcript from the Newton hearing from the first robbery and passed an automatic life sentence. Held. *R v Eubank* 2002 1 Cr App R (S) 11 applied. In both cases there should have been separate firearm counts. It was inappropriate to hold a Newton hearing. The proceedings were flawed so the life sentence was quashed.

R v Corps 2003 1 Cr App R (S) 418. The defendant pleaded guilty to attempted robbery. The plea was indicated at his first appearance at the Crown Court. A count of possessing an imitation firearm was left on the file. A community rehabilitation order was revoked. When 20, he consumed a large quantity of alcohol and possibly some drugs. He borrowed a gun and about 4 pm. entered a fast food restaurant and showed a member of staff the gun and left without buying any food. At about 9.15 he returned and asked for a portion of chips. He told the staff a man was coming to the restaurant with a gun and since he also had a gun he could protect the restaurant owners. The manager refused to give him any free food and the defendant pulled out the gun and aimed it at the manager, the rest of the staff numbering four and the manager's 15 year old son. Throughout this he was swearing and uttering threats to kill the staff. He referred to the gun as a BB gun indicating a ball bearing gun and ultimately laughed and left tucking the gun into his trousers. He ran away and was apprehended after a struggle in which he shouted abuse. When in the police van he kicked out causing it to rock. The manager had appreciated the gun was not real. In the police station he didn't deny the allegations and said he felt sorry for what he had done. The basis of plea was the gun was a plastic gun capable of firing soft pellets. He had a poor record including common assault and a public order offence, for which he had received the rehabilitation order. The pre-sentence report said he had had a troubled and difficult upbringing with problems with alcohol and drugs. Further he was a vulnerable and chaotic young man lacking motivation or aim in life with an IQ of 77. The Judge said he gave him $^1/_2$ off. Held. **3 years** detention not 4.

R v Benfield 2004 1 Cr App R (S) 307. LCJ. The defendant pleaded guilty to robbery. The prosecution case was he was armed with a firearm. There was no issue about the firearm raised at the hearing. He received automatic life. Held. It is appears his counsel did not direct their minds to the issue (of the automatic life provisions). The fact there was no (dispute) about the possession of the firearm must be established. There should be no doubt about the position for the subsequent and the prior offence. If it isn't (dealt with) the matter must be resolved in favour of the defendant. The life sentence is set aside.

R v Townsend 2004 1 Cr App R (S) 281. The defendant pleaded to robbery and the prosecution counsel said leading counsel for the defence tells me his robbery previous conviction involved an imitation firearm. He was sentenced to automatic life. Held. We do not seek to undervalue authority *R v Eubank* 2002 1 Cr App R (S) 11. We are faced with different views in *R v Flamson* 2002 2 Cr App R 208 and *R v Murphy* 2003 1 Cr App R (S) 181. It is not proper to gloss the statute to require there be a separate firearms count. We should follow *R v Flamson* 2002 2 Cr App R 208. *R v Murphy* 2003 1 Cr App R (S) 181 was decided per incuriam.

R v Hylands 2004 Crim L R 154. The defendant was convicted of robbery. The defence did not expressly admit the defendant had a firearm. The Judge held the defendant was in joint possession of a firearm. Held. We accept that had the jury been asked they would have found the defendant in possession of the firearm. *R v Murphy* 2003 1 Cr App R (S) 181 and *R v Eubank* 2002 1 Cr App R (S) 11 are binding on us. The provisions only apply where the defendant admits the firearm or the jury return a special verdict. Life sentence quashed.

See also *Automatic life*

Firearm, with – Banks, Building Societies, security guards etc – Imitation

163.40   *R v Law* 1998 2 Cr App R (S) 365. The defendant pleaded guilty to robbery. He and another wearing masks attacked a security guard as he was delivering cash to a bank. They threatened the guard with a machete and what turned out to be an imitation gun. £6,000 was stolen. They escaped in a waiting van, which was found abandoned nearby. There a passer-by was threatened and the three men left in a car that had been parked there the day before. The car was followed and all but £1,200 was recovered. The judge said it was carefully planned and executed. The defendant was now 22. Held. The authorities indicate sentences a little lower than the 10 year sentence had been passed for similar offences and age of the defendant. The LCJ has said age and personal mitigation can play but a limited part. Severe sentences must be passed. Sentences will vary according to how prevalent the offence is. **10 years** was entirely appropriate.

R v Buckland 2000 2 Cr App R (S) 217. See **163.6**.

Firearm, with – Car Jacking

163.41   *R v Thompson* 2003 1 Cr App R (S) 54. The defendant T, pleaded guilty to robbery and possessing a firearm. The victim was driving to work and pulled into a petrol station. T and his co-defendant, S who had a knife approached the victim one on each side of the car. T lifted his jumper and showed the victim a gun. T demanded the car keys and the victim's wallet. They were produced and T drove away in the car with S. The police chased the car and it crashed into some railings. S was trapped in the car. A Bruni unloaded firearm was found in the car. T ran off but was caught. In interview T denied the offence. T was 18 with one conviction for an offence of possession of a bladed article (a knife with an 8″ blade) one month before for which he was on bail. S received 8 years and 2 years consecutive. Held: Such offences are particularly prevalent at the moment. The offences are committed quickly. The detection rates are not high. Those who commit these offences must expect substantial sentences. It was aggravated by two people being involved, because that increases the level of intimidation. The consecutive sentences were right. At that age **6 years** and **2 years** detention for the robbery **consecutive** could be described as crushing. It was severe but not manifestly excessive.

Firearm, with – Domestic – Imitation

163.42   *R v Delaney* 1998 1 Cr App R (S) 325. The defendant D made a late plea to robbery and making use of a firearm with intent. The defendants M and H were convicted of the same counts. At about 4.20am four men wearing balaclava masks broke into the first floor of a pub where the publican and his family lived. One carried an imitation but realistic firearm. They entered the bedroom of the publican's 12-year-old daughter. The publican came in and the man with the gun seized him. The publican believed he would be killed if he did not co-operate. At gunpoint he handed over the keys to the safe and deactivated the alarm. They threatened to tape his mouth and he begged them not to, as he was asthmatic. He showed them the cash tills and deactivated a further alarm. £1,893 and some jewellery were taken. The police arrived as the gang was leaving and the gun was pointed at an officer. 'Firearm' was shouted out and police had to stand back and the gang escaped. D was 34 with a substantial number of previous convictions including robbery and manslaughter. M was 42 with 15 convictions including burglary, robbery and rape. H was 27 and had four convictions including GBH and burglary. The judge said the family was terrorised and he gave $2^{1}/_{2}$ years' discount for D's late plea. D received **11$^{1}/_{2}$ years** and the other two received **14 years**. Held. This was a very grave offence. It is imperative courts impose exemplary sentences. Applying *R v Brewster* 1998 1 Cr App R (S) 181, **14 years** was tough but not manifestly excessive. The discount for the late plea was within the judge's discretion.

Firearm, with – Imitation General

163.43   *Att-Gen's Ref. No 84 of 2003* 2004 2 Cr App R (S) 510. The defendant pleaded guilty at PDH hearing to assault with intent to rob and possession of an imitation firearm with intent to commit an indictable offence. He had arranged to meet the victim, who had advertised some jewellery for sale, at a public house. When the victim showed him the jewellery, the defendant hit him on the head with an air pistol a number of times. The victim and others detained the defendant at the scene. The air pistol was not capable of being fired. The victim was taken to hospital and treated for minor cuts and bruising. He later experienced bouts of tiredness and giddy spells. The defendant, 22, had no previous convictions. It was submitted that aggravating features were that the offences were premeditated and that the defendant carried a weapon and used it to cause injury. There were a number of references and the defendant expressed remorse. He owed money and did not plan this offence alone. Held. This offence occurred in a public place and there was actual violence. 18 months imprisonment was unduly lenient. The appropriate sentence would have been **3$^{1}/_{2}$–4 years**. Because it was a reference **3 years** not 18 months.

Firearm, with – Persistent offenders

163.44   *R v Avis* 1998 Re Goldsmith 2 Cr App R (S) 178 at 192. LCJ Goldsmith pleaded guilty to attempted robbery and having a firearm with intent to commit an indictable offence. In June 1997, he entered a jeweller's shop and asked to see a ring. He left returning an hour later and again asked to see the ring. He produced a starting pistol threatening to shoot the jeweller if he did not open the till. The jeweller tried to 'bluff him'. The gun was fired into the ceiling and Goldsmith left the shop. He was arrested nearby. The gun was a .22 pistol capable of firing .22 pellets. The jeweller and his wife were terrified. The defendant later wrote to the jeweller expressed the hope that he had not been too upset. He suggested that if the jeweller had been on his own he might have shot him but that he wouldn't do that in front of a lady. He advised that the next time someone came to rob him with a gun, he should let them take what was there. The defendant was 49 and was a persistent armed robber. In 1968 he had two convictions for assault with intent to rob involving firearms. In 1971, he was sentenced to 2 years for offences that included using a firearm with intent to resist arrest. In 1979, he went to prison for 6 years for offences that included possession of a firearm and ammunition. In 1985 he was sentenced to 15 years for six armed robberies or attempted robberies and in 1994 he was sentenced to 8 years concurrent for armed robbery. He was released in August 1996. The judge said that viewed in isolation 10 years' imprisonment was the correct sentence but when he considered the need to protect the public, a longer sentence of **15 years** was appropriate. Held. The long sentences he had served had done nothing to deter him. Even without resorting to s 2(2)(b) of the 1991 Act (longer than commensurate sentences now governed by the Powers of Criminal Courts (Sentencing) Act 2000 s 80(2)(b)), **10 years** was justified for this armed robbery. The judge was right that the s 2(2)(b) power should be exercised. It is clear from his record the letter to the jeweller, he is likely to commit further offences of this very serious kind. The sub-section requires that the court 'shall' pass such sentence 'as is in the opinion of the court necessary to protect the public from serious harm from the offender'. Since a previous 15 year sentence did not deter him from re-offending, it is difficult to see how the necessary period of protection required should be any shorter. The sentence was an entirely proper one.

R v Adams and Harding 2000 2 Cr App R (S) 274. The defendant H was convicted of two counts of robbery, GBH with intent, attempted robbery and making use of a firearm to avoid arrest. On the three robbery matters he was also convicted of possessing a firearm with intent to commit robbery. On the last robbery there were two counts of firearms with intent. The defendant A was convicted of the last robbery and with the two firearm counts. The first robbery was on a Securicor guard who was delivering money to a Building Society. The guard was shot in the lower leg and foot and £20,000 was stolen. The second was an attempted robbery of another Securicor guard who was delivering money to the Midland Bank. A handgun was used and the guard was forced to hand over an empty cash box. In the third robbery another Securicor guard was delivering £25,000 cash to Lloyds Bank. A Webley revolver which was adapted to fire shotgun cartridges was produced by H and the cash box taken. Police officers intervened and H pointed a revolver at an officer. A was standing nearby with a stun gun in his pocket. A and H were arrested. They both had been involved in an earlier armed robbery. H received 12 years and A 8 years. As a result both received automatic life. Held. If it hadn't been life **25 years** could not be considered manifestly excessive for H. Because of the previous for armed robbery **16 years** notional determinate sentence was not wrong for A.

Old cases *R v Woodruff and Hickson* 1998 1 Cr App R (S) 424, See **163.45**.

Firearm, with – Post Offices

163.45 *R v Woodruff and Hickson* 1998 1 Cr App R (S) 424. The defendants W and H were convicted of conspiracy to rob, robbery, having a firearm with intent and having an imitation firearm with intent. The conspiracy to rob was based on 4 months of observations when the two were seen visiting Post Offices and watching deliveries of cash take place. Vans carrying money were also followed. For the robbery W and H posed as customers in a Post Office. They were armed with a loaded handgun, an imitation handgun and a bottle of ammonia. They waited till the security guard had finished delivering the cash and then entered the secure area. An assistant tried to intervene and W produced a loaded gun and H banged his head against the window. £33,500 was taken. Their defence was it was a theft not a robbery. The judge said they were professionals who carried out the robbery meticulously. W was 61 and H was 54. In 1969 W had received 14 years for armed robbery. In 1979 he received 15 and 18 years for armed robberies. In 1976 H had received 12 years for robbery. In 1985 he had received 6 years for handling. W was mentally ill. Held. No distinction should be drawn between a robbery that takes place in a bank, a security van, a Post Office van or a sub-Post Office. Post Offices are soft targets staffed by defenceless men and women. It is a reasonable inference that they would have used the gun if need arose. As the conspiracy was not carried out it should be treated as one robbery. **15 years** not 17.

Att-Gen's Ref. No 37 of 2004 2005 1 Cr App R (S) 295. The defendant pleaded guilty to attempted robbery and possessing a firearm at the time of committing an indictable offence. He had an argument with his mother who had told him not to return to her house. He went to a sub post office close to his mother's home with an air pistol with him. When the sub postmaster was alone the defendant pulled a gun from the waistband of his trousers and told the postmaster to fill a plastic bag with money and not push any alarms. The postmaster fearing that he would be shot, dived below the counter and pushed alarms. The defendant fled without any money. He was arrested about two hours later. When he was told there was CCTV in the shop he accepted he was responsible and took the police officers to the gun. The gun was an air pistol in working order which was capable of casing a fatal wound and fulfilled the criteria for a lethal barrelled weapon. The defendant, 20, had two cautions but no convictions. The pre-sentence report set out that his upbringing had been unhappy and he had left home when he was 16. He began drinking heavily and discovered matters about his family history which caused him distress. The risks of future offending were described as low. There was a report from a consultant psychiatrist which said that at the time of the offence he was suffering from a depressive illness, which clouded his judgement, complicated by his alcohol dependency. He concluded the defendant was in state of crisis and wanted to be caught. The judge imposed a **3 year community rehabilitation order** with a condition that the offender works with a psychiatric counsellor. The probation report for the Court of Appeal was positive. Held. Sentencing is not a mechanical exercise. The sentencer has to do justice not only to the offender but has to exercise his judgement in seeking to provide ultimately more protection for the public. The course taken was an exceptional and justified.

For sentencing principles about Post Offices, see *Post offices*

Firearm, with – Post Offices etc – Imitation

163.46 *Att-Gen's Ref. Nos. 52 to 55 of 1999* 2000 1 Cr App R (S) 450. The defendants T, L, B and J pleaded guilty to robbery. L also pleaded to attempted robbery. After 1¹/₂ hours reconnaissance and careful planning the four defendants entered a sub-Post Office and news agency. They were dressed in camouflage clothing and wore masks. T had a hammer, which he used to smash the security video. Two imitation firearms were carried. There were four customers and four members of staff. The defendants shouted, 'Get to the floor.' A firearm was waved and those inside were terrified. Two of the staff were working in the Post Office part and they were told to 'Open the fucking door.' The guns were pointed at them and they opened the door. The staff left leaving the keys inside. The door closed and the robbers demanded the door be opened again. The staff tried to explain that couldn't be done as the keys were inside. The guns were discharged and one of the staff thought her colleague had been shot. The demands and the explanations continued till they left. A robber demanded the till be opened and £200 was taken. They ran to a hostel because there was no getaway transport. The defendants were arrested and the guns recovered. They were both blank firing pistols and one had a live round in it. They were granted bail. Eight months later L confronted a boy who went to the same school as him. L and his friends bullied him. L asked to use his mobile and tried to grab it. The boy tried to run from L but was followed. L produced a Stanley knife and held it to his stomach. The boy thinking he was to be stabbed broke free and escaped. T and B were 17, J 16 and L 15 years old. T had no previous convictions, B had been cautioned, and J had a conviction and a caution. L had been dealt with for violence. L received an indication that on a guilty plea to the attempted robbery he would receive a concurrent sentence. Held. Had they been adults the sentence would be in the region of **10 years**. Bearing in mind their youth and the mitigation **7 years** would be appropriate. Because it was a reference **5 years** detention not 2.

Att-Gen's Ref. No 74 of 1999 2000 2 Cr App R (S) 150. LCJ. The defendant was convicted of theft, attempted robbery and having a firearm with intent. The defendant and another entered a village shop and post office wearing masks and gloves. One had what appeared to be a handgun and the other a knife. The gunman shouted, 'It's a hold up,' and 'Give us your money.' The gunman shouted at the two customers, one of whom was retired and the other 79 years old to lie on the floor. The door to the Post Office section was kicked open. The men attempted to open the safe but the assistant did not have a key. The alarm went off and the two men fled. The defendants were arrested driving away in a stolen car. The assistant had experience of another robbery and did not want to return to work. One customer feared for his life and the other couldn't stop crying. The weapon was found and it was low powered unloaded air pistol which was not in working order. The defendant was 22 and had a bad criminal record although he had not served a prison sentence. He was released on bail and committed further offences. Held. The vulnerability of Post Offices has not decreased. **6 years** would be the minimum. Because it was a reference **5 years** substituted.

R v McCarthy 2003 1 Cr App R (S) 626. LCJ. The defendant pleaded guilty to a robbery at a sub-post office in Liverpool. At around 08:35 the owner opened the front door and shutters. He was confronted by the defendant, wearing a balaclava, who demanded money. The defendant forced the shopkeeper to the floor and tied his hands behind his back with duct tape. He asked questions about the safe in the post office before placing a silver duct tape over the shopkeeper's mouth, kneeling on his back and pressing a metallic object to the back of his head. A short while later the sub-postmistress arrived with her assistant. The assistant was tied with duct tape and struck twice to the back of the head with a gun that the defendant was holding. He kept shouting orders and waving the gun. He threatened to shoot anyone who moved. The postmistress was prodded with the gun and dragged towards the post office door. She opened the safe and the defendant grabbed a quantity of cash. He made his escape with £12,020 in cash. He hid in bushes close by for some time before giving himself up when the police arrived. He told the police where he had left the blank cartridge firing pistol. It and the money were recovered. In interview the defendant made full admissions. Since the robbery, the postmistress had slept badly and felt stressed. She had nightmares and had felt depressed. The other post officer worker also felt stressed and was unable to sleep. The defendant was 28 and had previous convictions for mostly driving-related offences and offences of burglary which resulted in non-custodial sentences. He had been under some pressure to commit this offence in that he had borrowed money from money lenders. They had confiscated his car and the tools of his trade and then put him under some pressure to commit the robbery. Held. Had this defendant not pleaded guilty at the first opportunity the sentence could not have exceeded 10 to 12 years. So **8 years** not ten years.

R v Greaves and Jaffier 2004 2 Cr App R (S) 41. LCJ. The defendant J aged 22 pleaded guilty to 2 robberies, an attempted robbery and 2 possessions of an imitation firearm whilst committing a Sch. 1 offence and possession of an imitation firearm on arrest. 2 robberies and a burglary were TICed. The defendant G aged 34 pleaded late to the same attempted robbery and possession of a prohibited weapon (a CS gas canister.) J was the organiser and recruiter. The premises were visited previously. In the first offence the manager of a sub post office was robbed of £5,000. A co-accused pointed a gun at him and told him not to touch any alarms. The manager put the money in a bag and pushed it under the security screen. J picked it up. Both men were wearing masks. More money was demanded but the manager said he couldn't open the safe. A month later J went into a travel agents with another man, both wearing masks. One had a gun. A man and his 14 year old son were customers in the premises. J herded them and two members of staff behind the counter, money was demanded and a cashier had a gun held to her head. £2,346.00 and the cashier's mobile phone were stolen. Eight days later J and G went to a sub post office ran by Mr O who was being assisted by a 67 year old woman. The two defendants, wearing masks, burst into the premises. J and G kicked at the door but Mr O managed to keep the door closed for some time. Eventually it was partially opened. Mr O sounded the alarm. Money was demanded. G sprayed Mr O in the eyes and face with CS gas, he was overcome with gas and coughing, and he suffered gashes and bruising. J and G ran out without taking any money. G had previous convictions for robbery and one drugs offence for which he was sentenced to 4½ years. J had 3 previous convictions for robbery. J had given assistance to the police. The judge said that the terror caused could only be imagined and that these were professional crimes. Held. The proper course is to impose a separate and consecutive sentence if arms are used in the course of a robbery. For G for the robbery **6 years** not 7 and for the CS canister **2 years** not 3, making a total of 8 years not 10. For J: the total of the sentence was too high bearing in mind that he pleaded guilty at the first opportunity, his record, his age, his help to the police and that the weapon was an imitation. **9 years** not 14 for the robberies and **3 years consecutive** not no separate penalty for the firearms, making a total of **12 years** not 14.

Old cases see *R v Lea* 1997 2 Cr App R (S) 215. (For a summary of this case see the first edition of this book.)

For sentencing principles about Post Offices, see **Post offices**

Firearm, with – Security guards carrying money

163.47   *R v Adams and Harding* 2000 2 Cr App R (S) 274. The defendant H was convicted of two counts of robbery, GBH with intent, attempted robbery and making use of a firearm to avoid arrest. On the three robbery matters he was also convicted of possessing a firearm with intent to commit robbery. On the last robbery there were two counts of firearms with intent. The defendant A was convicted of the last robbery and with the two firearm counts. The first robbery was on a Securicor guard who was delivering money to a Building Society. The guard was shot in the lower leg and foot and £20,000 was stolen. The second was an attempted robbery of another Securicor guard who was delivering money to the Midland Bank. A handgun was used and the guard was forced to hand over an empty cash box. In the third robbery another Securicor guard was delivering £25,000 cash to Lloyds Bank. A Webley revolver which was adapted to fire shotgun cartridges was produced by H and the cash box taken. Police officers intervened and H pointed a revolver at an officer. A was standing nearby with a stun gun in his pocket. A and H were arrested. They both had been involved in an earlier armed robbery. H received 12 years and A 8 years. As a result both received automatic life. Held. If it hadn't been life **25 years** could not be considered manifestly excessive for H. Because of the previous for armed robbery **16 years** notional determinate sentence was not wrong for A.

Att-Gen's Ref. No 84 of 2001 2002 2 Cr App R (S) 226. The defendant pleaded guilty at the first opportunity to attempted robbery and having a firearm with intent to resist arrest. In the evening, Securicor guards were supplying cash machines in Regent Street in London. The defendant approached and was disguised with a cap with ear flaps and a scarf. He held out a firearm in front of him at arms length from a guard. It was a few inches from the guard's chest and he said, 'Give me the money.' The guard was scared and dropped the cartridge with £22,000 in it and then tried to apprehend the defendant in a headlock. The gun was pressed to his chest and a violent struggle ensued. With the help of his colleague they wrestled the defendant to the ground and with the help of some American students and other helpers the gun and money were put out of reach. The police arrived and the defendant continued to struggle. The defendant tried to bite a hand of a student. The firearm was a double action revolver with four bullets in the chamber. The ejector rod was bent and the cylinder axis pin missing so it could not be operated in the normal way. However, it could be fired by holding the cylinder manually. He said another had supplied him with the firearm and the man drove him to the cash dispenser. The prosecution agreed there must have been a second man. He was now 23 with no convictions and favourable references. A psychologist said he was clinically anxious and depressed and was assessed as someone who was very compliant. A prison report said he was, 'very timid, nervy and very vulnerable.' Held. Personal factors in relation to offences of this gravity can have only a very small effect in determining what the appropriate sentence is. We would have expected a sentence for these two offences of **at least 8 years**. Because it was a reference, the progress he is making in prison **5 years** for the attempt and 1 consecutive for the firearm making **6 years** not 2 and 1 consecutive.

R v Murdoch 2004 2 Cr App R (S) 207. The defendant pleaded guilty to robbery, attempted robbery and two counts of possession of an imitation firearm while committing an offence. In the first incident he robbed a Securicor employee who was holding a cash box containing £25,000 at gun point. He pointed a Browning type handgun at him and told him to give him the box or he would shoot. The victim stepped back in shock and the defendant tried to take the box. A second robber appeared with a handgun. There was a struggle and the victim was gripped round the neck by the other robber and was hit on the head by both robbers. His helmet prevented any injuries. One of the robbers ripped the box from the victim and ran off. A dye was activated on the notes inside the box, which was found damaged but not opened nearby. In the second incident two weeks later the defendant went by appointment to the home of a man who had advertised a watch for sale in Loot for £5,700. Someone calling herself 'Jeanette' had made the appointment by phone. The defendant told the victim he had come to see the watch on behalf of his sister. The victim noticed that the defendant's hands were shaking, became uneasy and took the watch back. The defendant punched him in the face and reached towards his waist where the victim saw a gun in his waistband. The victim pushed him out of the house. Police found an imitation pistol adapted to discharge steel ball bearings in the defendant's girlfriend's bedroom. They found a double-barrelled imitation Derringer pistol adapted to discharge .22 bulleted cartridges at his home address. The defendant, aged 23, had some 24 previous convictions including one for possessing a firearm without a certificate for which he was sentenced to two years imprisonment. Held. The starting point of 18 years was too high. At no stage was the firearm discharged. There were physical tussles but no apparent injuries in both cases. Neither robbery was of the criminally sophisticated type. This defendant is not in the major league of armed robbers. The correct starting point was 14 years. **12** years not 15 years for the Securicor robbery, **8 years** concurrent on the other three counts, not 15 years concurrent.

Old case. *R v Devlin and Cotter* 1997 1 Cr App R (S) 68, (For summary of this case see the first edition of this book.)

Firearm, with – Series of robberies

163.48   *R v Turner* 1975 61 Cr App R 67. The court is alive to the problems arising when men are kept in prison for very long periods of time. On the other hand it is only just that those who are making a career out of crime should receive more serious punishment than those who have committed only one grave crime. Something must be added to the sentence for those who have committed more than one robbery but the maximum total sentence should not be more than **18 years**. The maximum refers to crimes that are not 'wholly abnormal.'

R v Adams and Harding 2000 2 Cr App R (S) 274. The defendant H was convicted of two counts of robbery, GBH with intent, attempted robbery and making use of a firearm to avoid arrest. On the three robbery matters he was also convicted of possessing a firearm with intent to commit robbery. On the last robbery there were two counts of firearms with intent. The defendant A was convicted of the last robbery and with the two firearm counts. The first robbery was on a Securicor guard who was delivering money to a Building Society. The guard was shot in the lower leg and foot and £20,000 was stolen. The second was an attempted robbery of another Securicor guard who was delivering money to the Midland Bank. A handgun was used and the guard was forced to hand over an empty cash box. In the third robbery another Securicor guard was delivering £25,000 cash to Lloyds Bank. A Webley revolver which was adapted to fire shotgun cartridges was produced by H and the cash box taken. Police officers intervened and H pointed a revolver at an officer. A was standing nearby with a stun gun in his pocket. A and H were arrested. They both had been involved in an earlier armed robbery. H received 12 years and A 8 years. As a result both received automatic life. Held. If it hadn't been life **25 years** could not be considered manifestly excessive for H. Because of the previous for armed robbery **16 years** notional determinate sentence was not wrong for A.

R v Parkinson 2003 2 Cr App R (S) 160. The defendant pleaded guilty to one count of robbery and one of attempted robbery. He indicated pleas of guilty at the preliminary hearing. Two associated offences of possessing an imitation firearm whilst committing a specified offence were ordered to lie on file, despite the defendant admitting that one of these offences involved the use of an imitation firearm. At about 10.40 am, with another man, the defendant entered a building society and went up to the counter. One of the two men produced a gun, pointed it at the cashier and demanded money repeatedly. The cashier started to count some money and tried to press the alarm button but was so shaken she could not press it. She did manage to kick a bar which caused the screens to come up closing off the serving area from the side where the customer and the robbers were. As a result both men left. On their way out they demanded money from a customer but she refused. They were caught on CCTV camera. At about 11.30 the same morning the defendant with another man went into another building society. One of them demanded money from a cashier. He had a gun in his hand and walked around the counter. After that cashier had opened her till he grabbed some money and went to other cashiers and demanded that they did the same. Money was obtained from them too. The two men ran out with £12,700. He was arrested about 3 months later and in interview made full admissions to both offences saying that he had produced a plastic pistol on the first occasion and had demanded money. He said that he had needed the money for drugs. He was 37 and had been before the courts on 15 occasions, mainly for offences of dishonesty and violence. In January 1989, for robbery of a building society and possessing a firearm he received sentences totalling eight years. In 1994, whilst unlawfully at large he robbed a security guard using a firearm. The security guard had been shot in the leg. He received a total sentence of 14 years. With the exception of periods when he was unlawfully at large he was in custody from the time of his arrest on the 1989 matters until his release on parole in December 1999. Although the defendant was liable to automatic life the judge found that there were exceptional circumstances. Held. These were horrid offences. However, they were not sophisticated.

There was more than one robber but not a gang. There were no physical injuries. The defendant's record was an aggravating feature. There were personal matters which led the judge to find that there were exceptional circumstances (although these are not specified in the report). **14 years** not 16.

R v Greaves and Jaffier 2004 2 Cr App R (S) 41. LCJ J. pleaded guilty at the first opportunity to two counts of robbery and two counts of possession of an imitation firearm whilst committing a Sch. 1 offence and an attempted robbery and possession of an imitation firearm on arrest. G. pleaded on the day of his trial to the last robbery, the firearm count and possession of a CS gas canister. The first robbery was on a sub-post office by J. and another wearing ice hockey masks. A gun was pointed at the manager, money demanded and £5,000 stolen. A month later, J and another entered a travel agent stole £2,300 with the same features as listed above. Two members of staff were herded behind a counter and all the time the staff and customers were menaced by a gun. Eight days later, G. and J. burst into a sub-post office and J. kicked at the panel at the post office section. The man in charge managed to hold the door closed. The door was partially open and G. spayed CS gas into the man's eyes and face. He was overcome and suffered gashes and bruising. J. was the organiser and recruiter for the robberies. All the premises were visited prior to the robbery. On each a stolen car was used as a getaway vehicle. J. asked for two robberies and a burglary to be taken into consideration. J. was 22 with three previous convictions for robbery and he gave information to the police. G. was 33 and had a previous conviction for robbery and a drugs offence for which he received 4½ years. **12 years** not 14 for J. **8 years** not 10 for G.

Firearm, with – Shops, public houses etc

163.49 *Att-Gen's Ref. No 56 of 1999* 2000 1 Cr App R (S) 401. The defendant pleaded guilty to robbery, having a firearm with intent, burglary and making off without payment. He stayed at a guesthouse and left without paying. The owners discovered a wallet containing £50 had been stolen from the private quarters. A week later he went to a public house, drank 2 pints and left. A few minutes later he returned and ordered a drink. He approached the barmaid from behind and said, 'Open the fucking till.' He took money and told the barmaid to go upstairs. Once upstairs he bound her hands and ankles with tape and flex. Referring to the gun he said, 'You don't think this is fucking real?' and fired it against the wall. He taped her mouth and threatened to come back with friends if she gave the police his description or said anything about him. When arrested he threatened to kill the officers but later admitted the offences. The defendant was 39. In 1984 he was made the subject of a hospital order with a restriction order for robbery, aggravated burglary, burglary and ABH. He had tied up a man, inflicted multiple cuts and poured hot water into the wounds. The robbery was with a large spanner when the victim was threatened, bound and gagged. The medical report said there was no formal medical illness but he had an obsessional aspect to his personality with compulsive thoughts. He ruminated about revenge and had considerable difficulty in controlling anger. The writer thought, 'the threats to the officers were important. The offences were a mixture of a desire for money and a need to assert himself aggressively. He had longstanding personality difficulties. He was a very inadequate man who finds it impossible to live a settled life and was untreatable. He is a significant and ongoing risk to the public. The risk is unpredictable and ever present.' The report was based on a great deal of material about him. Held. An appropriate determinate sentence was **9 years**. He presents a serious danger to the public for an indeterminate time. A **life sentence with 4½ years specified** substituted for 6 years.

Firearm, with – Shops, public houses, petrol stations etc – Imitation

163.50 *Att-Gen's Ref. No 17 of 1998* 2000 1 Cr App R (S) 174. The defendant pleaded guilty to robbery, supplying cannabis, supplying amphetamine sulphate, being concerned in the supply of cannabis, two counts of handling stolen goods and affray. A month after his release from prison and when on licence he supplied a small quantity of cannabis to undercover police officers. Just over a month later he supplied the same officers in the same place amphetamine sulphate. He introduced the officers to someone who supplied cannabis. He was arrested. He handed seven stolen T-shirts to the manager of an amusement arcade and was connected with three others worth in total £190. He was again arrested. He next walked over some parked cars when drunk and seized a man who told him to get off. He pushed him against a wall and threatened him. The victim went home to telephone the police and the defendant banged on his front door loudly. He barged his way in and seized the victim by the throat. The victim was pinned against the wall and threatened with a beating if he reported the matter to the police.

Five days later when on bail for two sets of charges he entered a petrol station wearing a balaclava, and gloves. He was carrying a handgun. He told the attendant to hand him the money in the till. The attendant handed over £100. The defendant made off and discarded the gun, balaclava and outer clothing in a stream. They were recovered and the gun was a plastic pistol but resembled a firearm and was able to discharge a pellet. He was arrested. Next someone who worked in a hostel where the defendant was living found a cassette player and stereo system in a communal room. They had been stolen from a daytime burglary of an 84-year-old man. He was arrested again. He had recently served an 18 month sentence for burglary. He was a chronic alcoholic and had deeply sad personal circumstances. He pleaded guilty to robbery at the earliest opportunity. He was given 4 years for the robbery with the other sentences concurrent with no order for the breach of licence. Held. We would expect **at least 7 years** for the robbery even with a plea. We would also expect the 8 months unexpired period of his licence to be activated and consecutive sentences for the offences on bail. We would expect a total of **at least 8 years**. As it was a reference **6 years** substituted.

R v Murphy 2003 1 Cr App R (S) 181. The defendant was convicted of robbery. He pleaded guilty to dangerous driving. There was no firearm count. He and another entered a petrol station and the co-defendant produced a gun and demanded money. £150 was handed over and the two men fled in a car. They went to a public house but they were refused a drink because they were drunk. They went back to car and it was stopped by police because of the car was being driven erratically. The gun was found and £145. The gun was an inert replica of a Colt revolver. It had a blocked barrel and was incapable of discharging any projectile. He was 36 with the main relevant previous being a robbery in 1997 for which he received 3 years. In that case the defendant had something which looked like a gun. There was six months left on his licence from the earlier robbery. The Judge passed an automatic life sentence consecutive to the six month breach. Held. There should have been a firearm count. The proceedings were flawed so the life sentence was quashed. The appropriate determinate sentence was $8^1/_2$ **years. 8 years** substituted remaining consecutive.

R v Corps 2003 1 Cr App R (S) 418. The defendant pleaded guilty to attempted robbery. The plea was indicated at his first appearance at the Crown Court. A count of possessing an imitation firearm was left on the file. A community rehabilitation order was revoked. When 20, he consumed a large quantity of alcohol and possibly some drugs. He borrowed a gun and about 4 pm. entered a fast food restaurant and showed a member of staff the gun and left without buying any food. At about 9.15 he returned and asked for a portion of chips. He told the staff a man was coming to the restaurant with a gun and since he also had a gun he could protect the restaurant owners. The manager refused to give him any free food and the defendant pulled out the gun and aimed it at the manager, the rest of the staff numbering four and the manager's 15 year old son. Throughout this he was swearing and uttering threats to kill the staff. He referred to the gun as a BB gun indicating a ball bearing gun and ultimately laughed and left tucking the gun into his trousers. He ran away and was apprehended after a struggle in which he shouted abuse. When in the police van he kicked out causing it to rock. The manager had appreciated the gun was not real. In the police station he didn't deny the allegations and said he felt sorry for what he had done. The basis of plea was the gun was a plastic gun capable of firing soft pellets. He had a poor record including common assault and a public order offence, for which he had received the rehabilitation order. The pre-sentence report said he had had a troubled and difficult upbringing with problems with alcohol and drugs. Further he was a vulnerable and chaotic young man lacking motivation or aim in life with an IQ of 77. The Judge said he gave him ¹/₃ off. Held. **3 years** detention not 4.

R v Davies. 2003 2 Cr App R (S) 621. The defendant pleaded guilty to robbery and to possession of a firearm with intent to cause fear of violence. Shortly before 9.30 pm the female victim was at work in an off-licence. The defendant entered the shop and grabbed her by the back of the neck and put a gun to the side of her face. He made go to the storeroom and then made her lock the door of the shop. He took her to the storeroom again where he blindfolded her and made her sit in a chair. He then took cash and cigarettes and made her walk in front of him to unlock the door. Police had been called already and the defendant arrested soon after leaving the off-licence hiding in a wheelie bin. He admitted the offence in interview. The gun was a replica. He had a drug habit and debts. He was 30 and had a record of 121 offences of almost every type except robbery. The longest sentence he had received was 2 years but he had been in prison for 7 of the last 10 years. He indicated remorse. Held: For an offence of this kind a period of **6–8 years** on a plea of guilty is the normal range of sentence for a crime in which a firearm or other weapon is used. **7 years** concurrent, not 10 years.

Firearm, with – Street robbery – Imitation

163.51   *Att-Gen's Ref. No 13 of 1998* 1999 1 Cr App R (S) 140. The defendant pleaded guilty at the first opportunity to robbery and having an imitation firearm with intent. The victim aged 69 was confronted by the defendant as he walked along road. The defendant aged 18 held up an air gun and said, 'Give me your money or I'll blow your head off.' The victim gave him his wallet with some small change in it. He assured him that all he had and the defendant walked away. The area was searched and the defendant was found with an airgun in his waistband with two pellets in the breech. The defendant said he had been drinking and expressed remorse. He was of good character. He was given a deferred sentence. Since them he had spent £3,000 to go on a course. The money was said not to be recoverable. Held. We would have expected a **4 years** sentence. Because it was a reference and the other features **2¹/₂ years** detention.

R v McDonald 2001 2 Cr App R (S) 546. The defendant pleaded guilty to two counts of robbery and possessing a firearm at the time of committing the offence. Two students were walking home and they were followed. They were eventually surrounded and someone, not the defendant produced an imitation pistol. They were told to put their cash etc on the ground. A wallet, credit cards and cash was taken. The pistol was found at the defendant's address. The defendant was arrested and he said he received £5 from the robbery. He was sentenced on the basis the pistol was produced without his complicity or consent. In 1986 he was sentenced to 5 years for two robberies, a s 18 wounding and 'two other similar offences', an aggravated burglary and offences of criminal damage. He cared for his ill mother. His automatic life sentence was quashed and **4¹/₂ years** substituted.

Att-Gen's Ref. N s 21 and 22 of 2003. 2004 2 Cr App R (S) 63. H pleaded guilty toTDA, 2 counts of robbery and 2 counts of possession of a firearm while committing robbery. W pleaded guilty to allowing himself to be carried and was convicted of the same robbery and firearm counts as H. In the first robbery the victim was walking along a road shortly after 6.00 pm when the car pulled up with its wheels on the pathway. Two men got out. H had a hand gun and said 'Give me the bag'. Fearing for her life the victim gave him her bag. Later the same evening the second victim was sitting in his stationary car when he heard men shouting at him to get out of the car. Three men came to the car door. He heard one of them say 'Get him with the gun'. He heard H say 'Shoot him' two or three times. He saw one of the men holding a gun and was in fear and got out of the car. The three men got into the car but could not start it. The victim tried to take the ignition keys away and again someone shouted for him to be shot. The victim helped them to start the car and they drove off. The firearm used was never recovered but it was accepted that it was an imitation. H, aged 23 had numerous previous convictions starting from when he was 15 and including burglary, theft and possession of an offensive weapon. He had no convictions for robbery or firearms offences. He had a cocaine habit costing him £50.00 per day. W was aged 23, had not carried a weapon or uttered threats and he had played a lesser role than H. He had a shorter but similar criminal record and was also addicted to drugs. Held. There was no substantial violence. In sentencing the distinction between a real and an imitation firearm is relevant, as it indicates the level of violence to which the defendant may be prepared to go. **8 years** for H and **9 years** for W upheld.

Firearm, with – Taxi drivers, delivery staff etc – Imitation

163.52   *R v Wright* 2000 2 Cr App R (S) 459. The defendants H and S pleaded guilty to two robberies. The defendant W pleaded to a robbery and aiding and assisting an offender. A taxi driver went to pick up a fare and H got in the cab and pointed a replica pistol at the driver's chest. The driver handed over the cab keys, about £10 in coins and £34 from the driver's wallet. H ripped the radio hand set out and ran to a waiting car throwing the keys in a nearby alleyway. W was the driver of the car and S was a passenger. They drove off. The pistol was capable of firing blanks. 27 hours later another taxi driver went to pick up a fare. H approached him, asked for the keys and produced a gun. H opened the cab door, demanded money and was given £316 and a cheque for £95. As H walked away he pointed the gun at the taxi and the gun went off. H again ran to a car where W drove them off with S as a passenger. Both taxi drivers were in fear of their lives. H was sentenced on the basis the gun went off accidentally and W on the basis on the second occasion he only knew afterwards there had been a robbery. S's role was as a lookout. H was 18 with eight convictions including burglary, assault and theft. He had not been sentenced to a custodial term before. H was treated as the dominant personality. S and W were treated as of good character. S was 20 and W 21. W bitterly regretted his involvement. H received **8 years**, S **7 years** and W **6 years**. Held. The use of the gun and the discharge of it even accidentally were major aggravating factors. Taxi drivers are vulnerable and attacks on them are increasing. Taxi drivers, milkmen and postmen go about the streets carrying money and are entitled to look to the courts for protection. If taxi drivers are not protected members of the public, including women will be forced to make their own way home. The offences were planned. The judge could have passed consecutive sentences. The sentences were rightly severe and not excessive let alone manifestly excessive.

R v Harvey 2002 1 Cr App R (S) 127. The defendant pleaded guilty to robbery. A take-away meal was delivered to the defendant's address and as he paid for it he noticed a considerable sum in the employee's wallet. Two hours later he ordered another meal to another address and when the employee arrived he and another robbed him of £700 with a gun. There were no substantial physical injuries caused. Later the victim saw the defendant in a car and told the police. He was 37. Six weeks earlier he had been released from a 7 year sentence for robbery with 3 years concurrent for indecent assault. It was a Post Office robbery in which £15,000 had been stolen by a violent assault by him and others. He also had convictions for s 20 wounding, ABH, indecent assault and assault with intent to resist arrest. He had served the unexpired period of his licence. Held. It was deliberately planned. There were a number of aggravating features including the firearm, the trick to lure the victim, the vulnerability of those running the service and his record, but **8 years** not 12.

Old cases. *R v Jackson* 1998 1 Cr App R (S) 259, *R v Shaw* 1998 2 Cr App R (S) 233, (For summary of these cases see the first edition of this book.)

See also *Taxi drivers etc*

Firearm, with – Victim injured

163.53   *R v Adams and Harding* 2000 2 Cr App R (S) 274. The defendant H was convicted of two counts of robbery, GBH with intent, attempted robbery and making use of a firearm to avoid arrest. On the three robbery matters he was also convicted of possessing a firearm with intent to commit robbery. On the last robbery there were two counts of firearms with intent. The defendant A was convicted of the last robbery and with the two firearm counts. The first robbery was on a Securicor guard who was delivering money to a Building Society. The guard was shot in the lower leg and foot and £20,000 was stolen. The second was an attempted robbery of another Securicor guard who was delivering money to the Midland Bank. A handgun was used and the guard was forced to hand over an empty cash box. In the third robbery another Securicor guard was delivering £25,000 cash to Lloyds Bank. A Webley revolver which was adapted to fire shotgun cartridges was produced by H and the cash box taken. Police officers intervened and H pointed a revolver at an officer. A was standing nearby with a stun gun in his pocket. A and H were arrested. They both had been involved in an earlier armed robbery. H received 12 years and A 8 years. As a result both received automatic life. Held. If it hadn't been life **25 years** could not be considered manifestly excessive for H. Because of the previous for armed robbery **16 years** notional determinate sentence was not wrong for A.

Att-Gen's Ref. No 84 of 2003 2004 2 Cr App R (S) 510. The defendant pleaded guilty at PDH hearing to assault with intent to rob and possession of an imitation firearm with intent to commit an indictable offence. He had arranged to meet the victim, who had advertised some jewellery for sale, at a public house. When the victim showed him the jewellery, the defendant hit him on the head with an air pistol a number of times. The victim and others detained the defendant at the scene. The air pistol was not capable of being fired. The victim was taken to hospital and treated for minor cuts and bruising. He later experienced bouts of tiredness and giddy spells. The defendant, 22, had no previous convictions. It was submitted that aggravating features were that the offences were premeditated and that the defendant carried a weapon and used it to cause injury. There were a number of references and the defendant expressed remorse. He owed money and did not plan this offence alone. Held. This offence occurred in a public place and there was actual violence. 18 months imprisonment was unduly lenient. The appropriate sentence would have been **3¹⁄₂–4 years**. Because it was a reference **3 years** not 18 months.

Life sentence – General principles

163.54   *R v Baker* 2001 2 Cr App R (S) 191. Held. *R v Chapman* 2000 1 Cr App R (S) 377 held that a discretionary life sentence imposed for the purposes of public protection and not for the purposes of pure retribution or deterrence had to be passed under the longer than commensurate sentence provisions for violent or sexual offences.

See also *Automatic life* and *Attempted robbery – Automatic life*

For cases to determine whether the offence carries automatic life see *Firearm, with – No firearm count*

Life sentence was appropriate, a

163.55 *Att-Gen's Ref. No 56 of 1999* 2000 1 Cr App R (S) 401. The defendant pleaded guilty to robbery, having a firearm with intent, burglary and making off without payment. He stayed at a guesthouse and left without paying. The owners discovered a wallet containing £50 had been stolen from the private quarters. A week later he went to a public house drank 2 pints and left. A few minutes later he returned and ordered a drink. He approached the barmaid from behind and said, 'Open the fucking till.' He took the money and told the barmaid to go upstairs. Once upstairs he bound her hands and ankles with tape and flex. Referring to the gun he said, 'You don't think this is fucking real?' and fired it against the wall. He taped her mouth and threatened to come back with friends if she gave the police his description or anything about him. When arrested he threatened to kill the officers and later admitted the offences. The defendant was 39. In 1984 he was made the subject of a hospital order with a restriction order for robbery, aggravated burglary, burglary and ABH. He had tied up a man, inflicted multiple cuts and poured hot water into the wounds. The robbery was with a large spanner when the victim was threatened, bound and gagged. The medical report said there was no formal medical illness but he had an obsessional aspect to his personality with compulsive thoughts. He ruminated about revenge and had considerable difficulty in controlling anger. The writer thought the threats to the officers were important. The offences were a mixture of a desire for money and a need to assert himself aggressively. He had longstanding personality difficulties. He is a very inadequate man who finds it impossible to live a settled life and is untreatable. He is a significant and ongoing risk to the public. The risk is unpredictable and ever present. The report was based on a great deal of material about him. Held. An appropriate determinate sentence was **9 years**. He presents a serious danger to the public for an indeterminate time. A **life sentence** with $4^1/_2$ years specified substituted for 6 years.

Att-Gen's Ref. No 113 of 2001 2002 2 Cr App R (S) 269. The defendant pleaded guilty to five counts of robbery on the date his case was listed for trial. The victims were all elderly and attacked in their own homes after dark. He had been released from prison for 5 months. He was masked and they were terrified. He demanded money and he put his hand over two of their mouths. He brushed passed one and caused her to fall. Another victim was tied up. Money and small items were taken. The offences were on two separate nights just 2 weeks apart. The defendant had 17 court appearances for 35 offences. They included robbery, rape, burglary, assault, theft, possession of offensive weapons, motor vehicle offences and unlawful sexual intercourse. In 1988 he gained entry to an 85-year-old lady's house by pretending to be a police officer. He bound gagged and raped her. In 1989 he broke into an 81-year-old lady's flat at 1am. He tied her up, gagged her and searched for money. She was raped at gunpoint. In 1989 he received 18 years for offences of robbery and rape. He was 47 with a long history of drink and drug abuse. The risk of re-offending was assessed as exceptionally high. He believed he had caused his victims little harm and refused to take part in programmes for offence focused work. The judge was not satisfied the offences were violent and sentenced him in total to $9^1/2$ years. Held. Bearing in mind the ages of the victims and what was done to each of them, the real possibility of fractures, asphyxia and cardiac arrest each was a violent offence. **Life** substituted.

Life sentence wasn't appropriate

163.56 *R v Barker* 2003 1 Cr App R (S) 172. The defendant pleaded guilty to robbery and common assault. At about 5.10 pm he entered a fancy Dress shop and the proprietor thought he looked gormless. He put his hand in his pocket and said, "Give me the money in the till. I've got a gun." She waited to see if a gun was produced and when it wasn't, he repeated his demand. She said, "Show me the gun and I'll show you my Rottweiler." She was confident he didn't have a gun and was not particularly frightened of him. She tried to usher him out of the shop. He suddenly turned round and punched her in the mouth. He tried to hit her again, but she blocked his arm and hit him back in self defence. She managed to restrain him by putting her weight on him. The proprietor managed to ring the police and he struggled free. She hit him in the face and then sat on him till the police arrived. She suffered a deep cut to her lower lip and some cuts inside the lower lip. The Judge passed a discretionary life sentence with a 21 month recommendation. Held. A discretionary life sentence can only be imposed if the relevant offence was one that called for a very severe sentence. The offence was not of sufficient severity so the sentence quashed. (For further details see **163.68**.)

Longer than commensurate sentences (frequently wrongly called extended sentences) – Is it a violent offence?

163.57   Powers of Criminal Courts (Sentencing) Act 2000 s 80(2)(b). ... the custodial sentence shall be ... where the offence is a violent or sexual offence, for such longer term (not exceeding the maximum) as in the opinion of the court is necessary to protect the public from serious harm from the offender. [Previously the Criminal Justice Act 1991, s 2(2)(b).]

Powers of Criminal Courts (Sentencing) Act 2000 s 161(3). a violent offence is an 'offence which leads, or is intended or likely to lead, to a person's death or physical injury to a person.'

R v Cochrane 1994 15 Cr App R (S) 708. The defendant pleaded guilty to robbery. Held. The definition of a violent offence does not require that the physical injury be serious. It does not include psychological harm. Here no injury was actually done. Sometimes shock may amount to ABH. This was not that case. The defendant denied he intended to cause physical injury. The judge accepted that. It was not necessary to show that injury was a necessary or probable consequence. The only issue was whether the acts were likely to lead to physical injury. Here it could have done if the shopkeeper had resisted or the defendant had lost control. 6 years was arguably too high if the sentence was commensurate with the facts of the offence. However, it was a perfectly proper sentence for a man foreseeably likely to cause serious harm to the public.

R v Palin 1995 16 Cr App R (S) 888. LCJ. A robbery was committed with an imitation weapon. Held. Considering *R v Cochrane* 1994 15 Cr App R (S) 407 and the statutory definition of 'violent offence' the Act did not apply.

R v Johnson 1998 1 Cr App R (S) 126. The defendant pleaded guilty to three robberies and a s 20 wounding which were concerning four separate attacks on minicab drivers. He had three previous convictions for robbery. The defence contended that in the three robberies there was no evidence that he intended injury to the victims. The judge passed a longer than commensurate sentence. Held. Applying *R v Cochrane* 1994 15 Cr App R (S) 407 the judge was entitled to come to that view. In little more than a week four drivers were subjected to attacks with a knife. In three of the attacks the defendant produced a knife to reinforce demands for money and/or jewellery. In one case a driver was stabbed in the chest. One driver was told he would be killed.

R v Blades 2000 1 Cr App R (S) 463. The defendant pushed a 74-year-old woman in the middle of the back causing her to fall to the ground. She sustained cuts and bleeding to her knees. The judge was mindful of the psychological harm caused to old victims by attacks of this kind. Held. Injuries of this kind should be regarded as serious. The section did apply. For more details see **163.76**.

R v Grady 2000 2 Cr App R (S) 468. The defendant entered an off-licence and threatened an assistant with two knives. She was uninjured but was in a considerable state of shock. The judge said the offence was worth **7 years** but made it 11 years as a longer than commensurate sentence. Held. It was entirely a question of fact for the judge to decide whether the offence was a 'violent offence.' To establish that physical injury was intended where none ensued will be difficult in most cases, but to find it was likely is a very different matter. Applying *R v Cochrane* 1994 15 Cr App R (S) 708 the judge was entirely justified in saying it was a violent offence. **11 years** was not too high. For further details see **163.67**.

R v Baker 2001 2 Cr App R (S) 191. Held. *R v Palin* 1995 16 Cr App R (S) 888 held that robbery carried out by a man with an imitation firearm was not a 'violent offence.' That decision is binding. The life sentence must be quashed.

Att-Gen's Ref. No 113 of 2001 2002 2 Cr App R (S) 269. The defendant pleaded guilty to five counts of robbery. The victims were all elderly and attacked in their own homes after dark. He was masked and they were terrified. He demanded money and he put his hand over two of their mouths. He brushed passed one and caused her to fall. Another victim was tied up. The judge was not satisfied the offences were violent. Held. Bearing in mind the ages of the victims and what was done to each of them, the real possibility of fractures, asphyxia and cardiac arrest each was a violent offence. The defendant was lucky not to have caused physical injury and this demonstrates its likelihood.

R v Bowmer 2001 Unreported 11/12/01. [It was not a violent offence here.]

Longer than commensurate sentences, how much extra?

163.58   *R v Avis* 1998 Re Goldsmith 2 Cr App R (S) 178 at 192. LCJ The defendant pleaded guilty to attempted robbery and having a firearm with intent to commit an indictable offence. In June 1997, he entered a jeweller's shop and asked to see a ring. He left returning an hour later and again asked to see the ring. He produced a starting pistol threatening to shoot the jeweller if he did not open the till. The jeweller tried to 'bluff him'. The gun was fired into the ceiling and Goldsmith left the shop. He was arrested nearby. The gun was a .22 pistol capable of firing .22 pellets. The jeweller and his wife were terrified. The defendant later wrote to the jeweller expressed the hope that he had not been too upset. He suggested that if the jeweller had been on his own he might have shot him but that he wouldn't do that in front of a lady. He advised that the next time someone came to rob him with a gun, he should let them take what was there. The defendant was 49 and was a persistent armed robber. In 1968 he had two convictions for assault with intent to rob involving arms. In 1971, he was sentenced to 2 years for offences that included using a firearm with intent to resist arrest. In 1979, he went to prison for 6 years for offences that included possession of a firearm and ammunition. In 1985 he was sentenced to 15 years for six armed robberies or attempted robberies and in 1994 he was sentenced to 8 years concurrent for armed robbery. He was released in August 1996. The judge said that viewed in isolation 10 years' imprisonment was the correct sentence but when he considered the need to protect the public, a longer sentence of 15 years was appropriate. Held. The long sentences he had served had done nothing to deter him. Even without resorting to s 2(2)(b) of the 1991 Act (extending sentences), 10 years was justified for this armed robbery. The judge was right that the s 2(2)(b) power should be exercised. It is clear from his record and the letter to the jeweller, he is likely to commit further offences of this very serious kind. The sub-section requires that the Court 'shall' pass such sentence 'as is in the opinion of the court necessary to protect the public from serious harm from the offender'. Since a previous 15 year sentence did not deter him from re-offending, it is difficult to see how the necessary period of protection required should be any shorter. The sentence was an entirely proper one.

R v Winfield 1999 2 Cr App R (S) 116. The defendant was convicted of robbery. He and two others were in a public house. One followed the victim, who had drunk about 5 pints, into the lavatory. The victim's gold chain was seized and there was a struggle. The victim received a bite on the finger. The defendant and the other man joined them and all three kicked and punched the victim. The door was closed to stop those who had heard the commotion from entering. The victim became unconscious and lost his gold chain, his bracelet, a gold watch, a ring and £30. Police found him covered in blood with a boot mark on his forehead. At hospital he was found to have a 2" cut to his head and bruising to his temple, nose, cheek and near his eye. He stayed there for a few days. The defendant had a bad record (details not given). The judge found the defendant was not the instigator but the No 2. He was given an extended sentence of 8 years. Held. There is substance in the criticism that he was no more involved than the third man and should have been sentenced on that basis. Ordinarily the offence would warrant 5 years. The court had to balance the need to protect the public and ensure the sentence is not out of all proportion to the nature of the offending. It must also ensure there is no double counting. Double counting is when a sentence has a deterrent factor built in and is extended without taking into account that existing deterrent factor. That deterrent factor caters for the necessity to protect the public. **6 years** not 8.

R v Blades 2000 1 Cr App R (S) 463. The defendant made a late guilty plea to robbery. An elderly victim was pushed over in the street and her handbag was stolen. He had very many previous convictions and was on licence for similar offences. Held. The offence was worth 4–5 years. A 2 year extension was appropriate so **7 years** plus 1 year consecutive for the breach of licence. For more details see **163.76**.

See also LONGER THAN COMMENSURATE SENTENCES

Mobile phones

See *Street robbery – Mobile Phones*

Persistent offenders

163.59   *R v Taylor* 2002 1 Cr App R (S) 490. The defendant pleaded guilty to robbery. Three months after his release from custody he and another entered a small village Post Office and general store. They had stocking masks and were carrying knives and a hammer. They pushed the terrified victim to the back and held the knives to his throat. One was a large thick knife for cutting meat. They threatened to chop off the defendant's head and asked for the safe keys. They were given the keys to the front door to delay them. When they realised they demanded the correct keys and threatened him again. He said there was a time lock on the safe and handed them £10 from his pocket. They asked if he had any jewellery or watches and armed police entered the shop. There was £18,000 in the safe and the victim was terrified. The defendant said he had a serious crack and heroin habit. He had an appalling record with 25 offences for theft and kindred matters. In 1991 he had two convictions for robbing a taxi driver. He received $2^1/_2$ years. In 1996 he robbed a post office with an imitation firearm. The firearm was a toy gun in a bag and his accomplice had a cucumber in a bag to look like a firearm. He received 7 years. The co-defendant had 39 offences of theft and kindred matters but no convictions for robbery. He received 6 years and the judge said he hadn't drawn any real distinction between the culpability of the two defendants. There were 684 days unexpired on his licence. The judge said severe deterrent sentences were necessary. Held. We agree with the judge about deterrent sentences. He was entirely correct to treat this offence as an extremely serious offence. Courts will protect these vulnerable premises. The offence was aggravated by the very substantial knife. The disparity between his sentence, (twice as much) and the co-defendant was a little too great so **10 years** substituted. The 684 days were not reduced and were to remain consecutive.

Att-Gen's Ref. No. 92 of 2002 2003 2 Cr App R (S) 80. The defendant, M, pleaded guilty to two counts of robbery. In the first robbery M with another, H, who acted as lookout, went into a general store. M was wearing a mask. He shouted at Mrs S, who was working in the shop, "Give me the money you Paki bastard". The defendant held a 9" knife in his right hand and pushed Mrs S to the floor as she reached for the phone. He shouted at her to open the till and pushed her head onto the till and pushed the knife into her face causing a small cut above her lip. Next he placed the knife between her thumb and forefinger and threatened: "If you don't open the till I'll cut your finger off". She still resisted so he held the knife to her neck. She then opened the till and £250 and some cigarettes were taken. The two men made off. The second robbery occurred on the same day at about 9.30 pm. H asked R for a word in the gents; once there M entered. H punched R in the face and M joined in, punching him several more times in the face. R was searched by the defendant who said "Make it easy for yourself, give him your wallet or I'll kill you". A doorman entered and dragged the defendant, who was holding R's wallet, off. Both escaped. R suffered numerous bruises and a black eye. M was arrested later and claimed not to have been involved in the first robbery but had been present in the public house at the time of the second. He was re-interviewed and admitted to his involvement in the first. He was 35 and had been sentenced to $6^1/_2$ years for 3 knife point robberies. Shortly following his release he had stolen the handbag of an 87 year old who had just arrived home in her disabled carriage. He received 3 years. He committed the current offences with 463 days of his licence remaining. **Held.** The aggravating features were the use of a knife, the violence inflicted on Mrs S, the degree of premeditation, the fact that it was a vulnerable small shop and M's high risk of re-offending, as assessed by the probation officer. **6 or 7 years** would have been appropriate. **5 years 9 months** was lenient and upheld but the sentence should be extended so with the licence 10 years in all.

R v McDonnell 2003 2 Cr App R (S) 117. The defendant pleaded guilty to three robberies, six burglaries, two thefts and one attempted burglary. The burglaries targeted elderly victims. In January 2000, he entered a pensioner house and went to the bathroom and turned on the taps, saying that he was checking the water. He took £80 and a ring. The same day the defendant arrived at the home of another pensioner saying he was from the water board. He took a wallet with £200 from a bedroom. 10 days later the defendant visited an 82-year-old and said that he was from the electricity board and that he wanted to check the premises. Nothing was taken. On the same day he told an 88-year-old he was from the electricity board. He looked around but took nothing. 5 days later, a 76-year-old lady opened her door. He pushed it so hard that the security chain broke, knocking her backwards into a chair. He took a pension book and purse. Later, he told an elderly lady he was from the Council. He and another went upstairs and stole about £450 in cash. He told a lady in her 80s he was from the police before pushing her backwards causing her to fall. He rushed inside and stole her handbag containing £900 in cash. When she tried to stop him she was knocked to the floor. The robberies again targeted elderly victims. In October 2001, he forced a frail 81-year-old man into his rear room where he and another searched and threatened him. A wallet containing £90 was taken. The man was shocked, shaken and upset and had to have medical assistance. Two weeks later, an 85-year-old man was forced back into his home by the defendant and another man. His arm was held behind his back. When neighbours intervened, the pair ran off with £400 in cash. The defendant was later arrested and interviewed where he admitted the robberies and volunteered various information concerning offences that he asked to be taken into consideration (driving offences, handling stolen goods, six burglaries, three attempted burglaries and one theft). The thefts were opportunistic. In February 2000 an 85-year-old lady arrived at home and put her shopping down at her front door. He stole it. The other theft was an unlocked car with the keys in it. The defendant was 23 with a number of convictions, mostly for driving matters. He had four convictions for burglary; one resulting in a 12-month sentence. **Held.** There were aggravating circumstances. He had targeted elderly people. Secondly, he told the victims he was from one of the utilities or from the police. Thirdly, on occasions the appellant used force knocking elderly occupiers backwards. The robbery offences were particularly vicious as the defendant having knocked at the door of elderly people, forced them back into their homes before stealing their possessions. Fourthly many of these offences were committed whilst he was on bail. The fifthly the frequency of these offences clearly denote that he is a professional and regular burglary who has been undeterred by the previous sentences. **12 years** severe but upheld.

Post Offices

163.60 *Att-Gen's Ref. No 9 of 1989* 1990 12 Cr App R (S) 7. LCJ. Businesses such as small Post Offices coupled with sweet-shops are particularly susceptible to attack. They are easy targets. The courts must provide such protection as they can for those who carry out the public service of operating those Post Offices and sweet-shops, which fulfil a very important public function. The only way in which the court can do that is to make it clear that if people do commit this sort of offence, then, inevitably a severe sentence containing a deterrent element will be imposed to persuade others it is not worth a candle.

Att-Gen's Ref. No 7 of 1992 1993 14 Cr App R (S) 122. LCJ It has to be realised that corner shops, sub-Post Offices etc are very often staffed by only one person, who may be unable to defend himself or herself. It is unlikely there will be any sophisticated security there, and it is a prime target for someone who wants to enrich himself quickly and successfully. It is therefore very important that the courts should indicate by the sentences passed that that type of offence will be punished severely.

R v Woodruff and Hickson 1998 1 Cr App R (S) 424. No distinction should be drawn between a robbery that takes place in a bank, a security van a post office van, or a sub Post Office. Post Offices are soft targets staffed by defenceless men and women.

R v Taylor 2002 1 Cr App R (S) 490. See **163.59**.

When with firearms see **paras 163.24 and 163.45–163.53**

Public servants (Doctors etc) when with firearms

163.61 *Att-Gen's Ref. No 45 of 2000* 2001 1 Cr App R (S) 413. The defendant pleaded guilty to false imprisonment and robbery. A doctor visited a female patient who was a heroin addict and the also defendant's girlfriend. He explained to the defendant and the patient that he was not going to prescribe any medication. They explained their displeasure and then the doctor tried to leave. The defendant's activity caused the doctor to ask, 'Are you barring my exit.' The defendant replied, 'I've done 7 years and I'll do it again.' The defendant then armed himself with a large knife and held the knife at the doctor's chest. He demanded the doctor's bag. The doctor who was frightened gave the defendant two tablets. The defendant demanded a sleeping pill, which he was given. The doctor was allowed to leave but was in a highly distressed condition. Fortunately the doctor had a driver who became suspicious and called the police who arrived. The defendant appeared to be under the influence of drink or drugs or both and the police found him incoherent. The defendant had an appalling record including offences of violence and dishonesty. He was on licence at the time. Held. A sentence of **4 or 5 years** would be appropriate. However as it was a reference the **30 month** sentence was not altered.

Security vehicles

See **Banks, building societies, security guards etc**

Series of robberies

163.62 *R v Brown* 1998 2 Cr App R (S) 257. The defendant pleaded guilty to unlawful wounding and robbery; two counts of offering to supply drugs; six counts of robbery; and an attempted robbery. The defendant approached a man in the street and took £10. He used a knife and caused a wound to the man's cheek. He was arrested and bailed. He offered two plain clothes officers ecstasy and cannabis. He was arrested and found to have neither. He was released on bail. The other robberies were on minicab drivers who were threatened with a knife and had money and other items taken. The last was where after he had threatened a driver with a knife a struggle took place and the defendant fled empty handed. He was picked out at ID parades. He had only recently been released from prison. For all but two of the robberies he was on bail twice. In 1982 he received 3 years for robbery, in 1993 he received 2 years for robbery, in 1993 he was convicted of 13 offences of which 4 were robbery and received 2 years and also in 1993 he was convicted of 6 offences 4 of which were robbery and received 4 years. Those robberies were very similar to the latest offences. He received 4 years for the street robbery, 6 years for the robberies and 3 years for the attempt consecutive making 13 years in all. The judge made it an extended sentence. The defence did not suggest the making of the extended sentences was wrong. Held. Without considering the powers to extend the worrying features of this case meant a sentence of between 6 or 7 years would be justified even after a guilty plea. None of the sentences could be faulted but the total should be **10 years** not 13.

R v Ebanks 1998 2 Cr App R (S) 359. The defendant pleaded guilty to five robberies and asked for 15 robberies and three attempted robberies to be taken into consideration. The robberies followed a similar pattern and were committed between January and April 1997. He entered small shops and demanded money. There was no actual violence but he was extremely aggressive. He always threatened the staff with a knife and told them they would be cut. One example was on Tie Rack. It was not an impulsive robbery. He waited till there was one assistant. He entered the shop and moved about aggressively causing a display cabinet to fall to the ground. He passed the assistant a note saying, 'Put the money in the bag or I will cut you.' He was holding a Stanley knife. The assistant was very frightened and he made sure he got all the money there was. He was caught red handed in another shop and identified on ID parades. He co-operated with the police. In all about £6,000 was taken. He was 33 and had dishonesty and drug convictions going back to 1981. In 1994 he received 6 years for two robberies and possession of an imitation firearm with intent with seven robbery TICs. There was 13 months left on his licence to run. Held. The number of offences was a very relevant factor. **15 years** was severe but not manifestly excessive.

Att-Gen's Ref No 105 of 2002 2003 2 Cr App R (S) 319. The defendant pleaded guilty to 2 robberies, one burglary and perverting the course of justice. He asked for other offences to be taken into consideration. Hence, in total there were 7 robberies, 4 burglaries (2 commercial and 2 domestic), 3 thefts and one perverting the course of justice, all committed over a 2-month period. At 7.15 am the defendant stopped the car he was driving and asked the victim for directions. He got out and said "Number one, I need to rob you". He rammed his hands into the victim's pockets, searched them and took his wallet (containing £13, a credit card and a debit card). He got back into his car and drove off. A week later at 5.40am the second victim was walking to work when he saw the defendant sitting at a bus stop. They knew each other and walked together. After saying their good-byes and separating the defendant approached the victim from behind, seized him with an arm round the neck, choked him and took his wallet from his back pocket. He forced him against a wall, took his house keys, cigarettes and a lighter. The defendant ran off. The burglary count concerned a laundrette where entry was gained and cash-operated machines were forced with a screwdriver. Police were called by a neighbour and arrived to find the defendant on the roof. He gave a false name. He was found to have a torch and screwdriver. In interview he admitted the burglary and said that he had a £300 per day crack habit. He was interviewed in relation to the indicted robberies and made full admissions. The other robberies were firstly, calling a taxi, punching the driver twice in the face and stealing his waist bag containing £30. Secondly, trapping the owner of a take-away behind the till before smashing the till and taking cash, his jacket and phone. Thirdly, with another man attacking a taxi driver and taking £75. Fourthly, threatening another victim with a pair of scissors and taking a 2o inch gold chain and a mobile phone. Fifthly a taxi driver driving the defendant and another was restrained whilst £10 and his mobile phone was taken. When the driver went to give chase his legs were closed in the car door. The defendant was 26 with 75 previous convictions but none for robbery. There were 23 offences of dishonesty (including 12 burglaries), 6 offences of violence and he had experience every type of disposal. He had been given community service for his most. recent (burglary) offence. It was accepted (and demonstrated by his post-sentencing behaviour) that he was not prepared to properly address his drugs problem. Held. Of course it is in the interests of the public that those who commit criminal offences in order to feed their drug habit should, if possible, be weaned from that habit; because, if they are, the public may, in the future, suffer less from the depredations than they have in the past. On the other hand, the imposition of a community penalty for offences of robbery, taking into account many other offences including offences of robbery, even if the offence at the time of sentence was a promising candidate for a DTTO, would usually be wholly inappropriate, having regard to the public interest and the interests of the victims. Because it was a reference, **4 years** not a community rehabilitation order.

See also *R v Gabbidon and Bramble* 1997 2 Cr App R (S) 19 See **163.32**.

Series of robberies – Returning to rob the same person again

163.63   *Att-Gen's Ref. No 1 of 1999* 1999 2 Cr App R (S) 398. The defendant pleaded guilty to 5 robberies. In all of them the defendant had forced his way into the homes of elderly people. The first robbery was on a 71–year-old man who was pushed to the floor when he opened his door. He was then pushed into his sitting room where the defendant demanded money. The defendant shouted and said he was on drugs. He obtained £230 and pulled out the telephone wires. Eight months later he returned and pushed the same victim to the floor. He took cash from his pockets and £130 in all. The victim was threatened with a radio. The telephone wires were cut and the victim was very distressed. The second robbery was on an 88 year old. The defendant was wearing a balaclava and pushed the victim over. The victim had £215 taken from his pockets and his wrist was hurt. $3^{1}/_{2}$ weeks later he returned and climbed through a window and seized the same victim's arms and stole £110. The other robbery was on an 84-year-old woman who suffered from a heart condition. She lived with her lodger aged 79. He entered their home wearing a balaclava and demanded money. The lodger tried to push him out and a struggle ensued. The lodger fell to the floor and the woman was pushed in the chest and stumbled. He took £40 from her purse and she suffered an anginal attack. She said she was in total fear. The defendant was arrested and said the money was for drugs. He expressed remorse. Held. He had targeted the homes of the elderly. Attacks on the elderly in their homes were despicable and deserved severe punishment. They are vulnerable not only because they lack assistance and support but because of their weakness and feeling of isolation. Fear and anxiety are ever present and that blights the future. The first visit to the victims was worth **6 years** and the second visit **8 years**. The total should have been 8. Because it was a reference **6 years** not 4.

Sexual

163.64   *R v Christian* 2003 1 Cr App R (S) 1. The defendant was convicted of attempted robbery and indecent assault. The victim was walking on a footpath, which opened onto an isolated small garage area. The defendant who was drunk grabbed her from behind and tried to pull her over and tried to put his hands over her mouth. Next he put his mouth on her breast and squeezed it. He tried to take her rings off and lunged at her shoulder bag but was unable to dislodge it. Then he moved his hands down to the woman's crotch and tried to lift up her skirt. She managed to elbow him in the stomach and punch him in the groin. He eventually released his grip and she escaped. Nothing was stolen and she suffered no physical injuries. Three days later she saw him again and he said, "I ain't fucking finished with you yet, bitch". She ran away. Two days later he was arrested and denied the offences. Less than a month earlier, he had assaulted a 13 year old and had grabbed her jacket. She managed to get free. When on bail for this he committed the attempted robbery. He was convicted by the Magistrates for the assault for an unknown offence and received a community rehabilitation order. There were no other convictions. He told the psychiatrists he had been an alcoholic for 20 years and usually drank himself into oblivion. The psychiatrist's report for the Magistrates' Court considered he was a chronic alcoholic and had a disorganised personality who posed a risk, as he does not appear to appreciate personal boundaries. The psychiatrist for the Crown Court said he posed a risk when under the influence of alcohol. Further his alcohol abuse had lead to personality changes in terms of poor social behaviour and loss of impulse control. He said he was likely to reoffend when he resumes his heavy alcohol intake. The pre-sentence report said he poses a high risk to the public and indications suggest that violence would be characteristic of the high likelihood of sexual offending. The Judge made the sentences concurrent and made an extended sentence with the licence part 5 years. Held. The two offences showed a pattern. **4½ years** in total was lenient. He was unlikely to co-operate with rehabilitation. For a chronic alcoholic with anti-social and anti-women tendencies a long period of supervision is necessary for the protection of the public. The extension was not wrong.

R v Huczek 2003 1 Cr App R (S) 97. The defendant was convicted of robbery and indecent assault. The victim saw him on her train as she was returning home around midnight. When he alighted at her stop she was concerned and walked quickly. He seized her from behind and put a sharp implement to her throat. Her ponytail was grabbed and he pushed her towards an alcove. He demanded her purse and then money. £15 was handed over. Next he placed his hand down her top and began to touch her breast. As she cried, he told her that he was going to put fingers up her and that she was going to be raped or killed. She refused to take down her trousers and he pulled her ponytail down hurting her. She was terrified and loosened the zip to her trousers. He forced his finger into her vagina, which hurt. Next he demanded a blow job, telling her to get to her knees. Saying suck it or I'll kill you, he forced her to have oral sex. He ejaculated into her mouth as she was choking and could not breathe. While she still cried with her eyes shut and while frozen to the spot, he told her that he was going to rape her. When she opened her eyes he had gone. She ran home and was crying so much she could not speak. There was bruising to her knees but an anogenital examination revealed no external or internal injury. As a result of the attack she was looking for somewhere else to live. The defendant was 31 with 16 previous court appearances for burglary, robbery (1991 probation), ABH, arson, threatening words, common assault and dishonesty. His only custodial sentence was 12 months YOI in 1989. The pre-sentence report said he continued to deny the offence and there was a high risk of re-offending. He was sentenced to 3 years for the robbery and 5 years consecutive for the indecent assault with a 2 year licence extension. The defence said the consecutive sentences were wrong, as it was all part of the same incident. Held. There was some force in this. She was in great fear and distress. It was two phases of one single incident. 8 years was not manifestly excessive so 5 years and **8 years** for the indecent assault concurrent.

Shops, off-licences, take away restaurants, estate agencies etc – Guideline remarks

163.65   *Att-Gen's Ref. No 7 of 1992* 1993 14 Cr App R (S) 122. LCJ It has to be realised that corner shops, sub-post offices etc. are very often staffed by only one person, who may be unable to defend him or herself. It is unlikely there will be any sophisticated security there, and it is a prime target for someone who wants to enrich himself quickly and successfully. It is therefore very important that the courts should indicate by the sentences passed that that type of offence will be punished severely.

Shops, off-licences, take away restaurants, estate agencies etc – 5 years or less appropriate

163.66 *Att-Gen's Ref. No 67 of 1998* 1999 2 Cr App R (S) 152. The defendant pleaded guilty to robbery. He entered a Co-Op without any disguise. He went to the till and said, 'Give me the notes.' The assistant thought he was joking and he showed her a note, which said, 'Give me the notes because I have a gun pointing right at you.' His hand was in his pocket and seemed to be pointing something. She was very frightened and handed over £250. He was arrested and found with £130. He was of good character and had financial and marital problems. He had always been in work until a few years before when he lost his job. A business he set up failed. He was depressed and had turned to alcohol. He received 6 months and was due to be released in about 2 weeks. Held. The bracket is **4 to 5 years**. Taking into account it was a reference and his anticipated release **3^1/$_2$ years** instead.

R v Bishop 2000 1 Cr App R (S) 899. The defendant pleaded guilty to two counts of attempted robbery. He changed his plea a month before the trial. He entered an estate agent, which acted as a building society wearing a false beard and hat, which covered most of his face. He went to the cashier and said, 'CS gas, give me all your money.' He was pointing a small aerosol at her. The cashier said she didn't have any money. He repeated the demand and she repeated the reply. He then left. 1^1/$_4$ hours later he entered a village general store wearing the same disguise. He tried the same ploy with the can again. When the proprietor went for the panic button he fled. He was driven away by the co-defendant. He had no convictions. He was under severe personal stress. The driver of the getaway car received 2 years. The defence said there was disparity and the sentence was excessive. Held. We need to protect the staff in small premises, who tend to be vulnerable women. He was carrying a purported weapon. It appears wholly out of character. There is some force in the disparity point but not much. **3 years** not 5. (The case is listed under *Shops* because the amount of money on the premises makes it more similar to a shop than a building society.)

Att-Gen's Ref. No 68 of 1999 2000 2 Cr App R (S) 50. The defendant was convicted of attempted robbery. He was unexpectedly made redundant and he spent the day drinking. He set off to walk home and was shouting loudly in the street. He entered an estate agency smelling strongly of drink and asked to shelter from the rain. He was told he could. A couple of minutes later he suddenly approached an assistant and said, 'You've been fucking stupid.' His hand was in his pocket and the victims thought it was a gun. He told her and her colleague to get in the back and demanded cash. He swore and seized the woman assistant round the neck and again pushed his fingers in his pocket so it appeared to be a weapon. He pointed it to the side of her head. They thought he was deranged and he said, 'Get the cash or she's dead.' She was told to get on the floor. The male assistant found the petty cash tin but there was no key so the defendant threw it to the ground. That assistant was also ordered to get on the floor. He tried to find a cupboard to put the female assistant in but there wasn't one. She was pushed into a hallway and she managed to escape. The defendant then fled leaving his rucksack. The defendant said he had no recollection of the incident and said he was sorry. No injury was caused. He was 33 with no violent convictions and no convictions in the 1990s. A report said at the time he was severely depressed and his mother extremely ill. At the trial only the male assistant was required to give evidence and his account was not challenged. He was sentenced to 6 months and there was a hearing to consider whether the sentence should be increased. He had been released on a tag which was removed about a month ago. Held. The normal sentence would have been **3 years**. Taking into account the 'triple jeopardy' **2 years** substituted.

Old cases *Att-Gen's Ref. No 18 of 1997* 1998 1 Cr App R (S) 151 (for summary see the first edition of this book.)

Shops, off-licences, take away restaurants, estate agencies etc – More than 5 years appropriate

163.67   *R v Grady* 2000 2 Cr App R (S) 468. The defendant was convicted of robbery. He entered an off licence and pulled a balaclava or mask over his face. He went to the counter and said, 'Open the door I've got a knife.' The assistant saw a small knife in his hand and opened the counter door. She was forced to open a wall safe and a bag was taken which did not contain much. The defendant demanded that the main safe be opened. The assistant deliberately took the wrong key and she was unable to open the safe. He continued to demand the safe be opened and said, 'I'll give you 5.' She also saw a larger knife with a 14" blade. He was handed two cash bags from the till float. The defendant lost the knifes and said, 'Where's my fucking knives you bitch.' The defendant then left and £559 was found to have been taken. The victim was left in a considerable state of shock. He had an appalling record including offences of robbery with knives and one on the same premises. He had received 12 years for robberies and 5 years shortly after his release. The judge said the offence was worth **7 years** but made it 11 years as an extended sentence. Held. It was entirely a question of fact for the judge to decide whether the offence was a 'violent offence. Applying *R v Cochrane* 1994 15 Cr App R (S) 708 the judge was entirely justified in saying it was a violent offence. **11 years** was not too high.

Att-Gen's Ref. No 16 of 2000 2001 1 Cr App R (S) 144. The defendant pleaded guilty to robbery and possession of $2\frac{1}{2}$ ecstasy tablets. He went to a cashier in a video hire shop wearing a balaclava and gloves and carrying an 8" knife and a bag. He demanded money and banged on the counter. The knife was pointed at the victim in a threatening way. She had difficulty in opening the till and the defendant became impatient and shouted for her to hurry. Eventually the till was opened and over £300 was taken. He left the shop and caused the glass panel in the door to shatter cutting the finger of woman from another shop who was trying to lock the door. After the robbery he was in a stressed state. He expressed remorse. He was in breach of a combination order for two ABHs and two common assaults. That was a fight in a pub. He had been released from prison and was now said to be free of drink and drugs. Held. We would have expected the sentence to be **5 or 6 years**. Taking into account it was a reference and that he had been released **4 years** not 9 months consecutive to the 1 month for the breach.

Att-Gen's Ref. No. 149 of 2002 2003 2 Cr App R (S) 559. The defendant pleaded guilty to 3 counts of robbery of off-licences on the day of trial. In the first robbery the cashier was working alone. The defendant entered with a female. He had a hood on and his accomplice wore a scarf round her face. The defendant pulled a kitchen knife with a 10-inch blade, pointed it at the cashier and demanded the "fucking money". The defendant started taking money and the cashier ran into an office and the activated alarm. The couple left. They had taken £200. Fingerprints left on the till were the defendant's. 2 weeks later, the same cashier was working (with another) at the same off-licence. The defendant and a female entered the shop dressed in a similar fashion as before. He produced the same knife and made similar demands. While the till was being emptied the defendant demanded that the safe was opened. Bags of money were taken from the safe as well as a large quantity of cigarettes. The defendant was much more aggressive and threatening on this occasion than before. About 2 weeks later again the defendant and a male entered a different off-licence where the manageress was working alone. They both had hoods up. Both had their faces covered. The defendant started waiving a chisel about and demanding that the safe was opened. He put his arm round her neck and held the chisel to it. He ordered that the CCTV tape was removed. The till and the safe were emptied of about £300 and cigarettes were taken. The phone lead was ripped but the manageress managed to activate the alarm. Police officers arrived and caught the defendant hiding nearby. In interview he made no comment. He was 28, addicted to drugs and had a bad record for offences including robbery. Held: There were three separate robberies committed by two people. Weapons were brandished and there were acts of overt violence. Vulnerable premises were targeted and the same premises was targeted on two occasions. Elements of disguise and planning were present

Old case *R v Ebanks* 1998 2 Cr App R (S) 359, (for a summary of this case see the first edition of this book.)

Shops, off-licences, take away restaurants, estate agencies etc – Injuries caused

163.68 *Att-Gen's Ref. No 17 of 2000* 2001 1 Cr App R (S) 96. The defendant pleaded guilty to ABH. He was convicted of two assaults with intent to rob. He and another entered a take away restaurant and enquired about the menu. Suddenly the defendant sprayed ammonia from a plastic bottle into the owner's face. She screamed in shock, suffered pains in the eye and had difficulty in breathing. Both men went to the staff side of the counter and looked for cash. The co-owner arrived and was also sprayed with ammonia. He partly protected his face with his arm. It caused him considerable pain to one eye. The men ran off with nothing. The victims went to hospital for treatment. The bottle was left behind and contained ammonia with strength at the top range for household solutions. His defence was he complained about food, which had been eaten by his brother and had been threatened and chased by the owners. He had been sentenced on 14 occasions before for theft, burglary, robbery, handling and possession of a firearm. He had received 30 months' youth custody and 8 years' imprisonment. At the time of his arrest he had failed to attend for a handling matter. Held. There was no mitigation. Taking into account his record we would have expected a sentence in the order of **6 years**. As it was a reference **4¹/₂ years** substituted for 30 months.

Att-Gen's Ref. No 22 of 2001 2002 1 Cr App R (S) 46. The defendant pleaded guilty to robbery and going equipped for theft. At 11am he went into a newsagent and waited for the customers to leave. Then he went behind the counter where the assistant was and held a knife to her throat. Her blouse was pulled up and she was pushed to the floor. He twisted her wrist and put his foot on her elbow. He took a money bag and left. Outside the shop people detained him. £205 was found in the money bag. The victim said she had injuries but there was no evidence as to their nature. The knife had been bought for the robbery the day before. He was now 20 with no convictions. Two weeks before he had left home after an argument with his parents. He had no where to stay and no money. Remorse and shame was expressed. He was sentenced to a combination order and had done what was required by the order. 22 hours' CSO had been performed. Employment had been obtained. Held. Allowing for his age, no record, remorse and there were no serious injuries caused the proper sentence was **3 years**. Because it was a reference and the efforts he had made during his combination order **18 months** YOI instead.

R v Barker 2003 1 Cr App R (S) 172. The defendant pleaded guilty to robbery and common assault. At about 5.10 pm he entered a fancy Dress shop and the proprietor thought he looked gormless. He put his hand in his pocket and said, "Give me the money in the till. I've got a gun." She waited to see if a gun was produced and when it wasn't, he repeated his demand. She said, "Show me the gun and I'll show you my Rottweiler." She was confident he didn't have a gun and was not particularly frightened of him. She tried to usher him out of the shop. She thought he either had a mental problems and he was in a daze. He suddenly turned round and punched her in the mouth.

He tried to hit her again, but she blocked his arm and hit him back in self defence. She managed to restrain him by putting her weight on him. She asked the cleaning lady to ring the police but she was too flustered to do it. The proprietor managed to ring the police and he struggled free. She hit him in the face and then sat on him till the police arrived. She suffered a deep cut to her lower lip and some cuts inside the lower lip. At hospital she was advised to have stitches but declined. The incident had an unsettling effect on her. The defendant had a number of convictions for violence including a section 20 offence. The first psychiatrist said he was suffering from a mental illness and was dangerous. The second one said there was a high risk of further violent offences. The third one said he found no evidence of mental illness and that the defendant said he intends to kill a man on his release and does not appear to be willing to cooperate with any source of help. The third one said he poses a threat of serious harm and should be subject to hospital order with a restriction order and he poses a threat of serious harm. A report before the Court of Appeal said he suffers from a significant disorder of personality. No bed was available when he sentenced and on his appeal. The Judge passed a discretionary life sentence with a 21 month recommendation based on a notional determinate period of 42 months. Held. We are firmly of the view that he poses a serious risk and a **hospital order with a restriction order** is the best disposal. The life sentence was wrong because it wasn't an offence of sufficient severity. We have warned counsel that we would if the life sentence was quashed impose a longer than commensurate sentence and invited him to withdraw his appeal. He declined to do so. The commensurate sentence should be 4 years. The public requires a longer than commensurate sentence of 6 years making a total sentence in custody of **10 years**. His licence will be extended to the full amount permissible namely to the end of the 10 year period. (The judgement is incomprehensible because Courts do not add commensurate and longer than commensurate sentences together, 10 years seems out of line for a shop robbery with a punch, 10 years seems an unjust result for a man who needs treatment and was only facing a 21 month recommendation and because an extended licence means the licence is extended beyond the period it would otherwise end which is 10 years. Many would feel the original sentence was fairer to the defendant and gave a better production to the public on the defendant's release.)

Att-Gen's Ref. No. 92 of 2002 2003 2 Cr App R (S) 80. The defendant, M, pleaded guilty to two counts of robbery. In the first robbery M with another, H, who acted as lookout, went into a general store. M was wearing a mask. He shouted at Mrs S, who was working in the shop, "Give me the money you Paki bastard". The defendant held a 9" knife in his right hand and pushed Mrs S to the floor as she reached for the phone. He shouted at her to open the till and pushed her head onto the till and pushed the knife into her face causing a small cut above her lip. Next he placed the knife between her thumb and forefinger and threatened: "If you don't open the till I'll cut your finger off". She still resisted so he held the knife to her neck. She then opened the till and £250 and some cigarettes were taken. The two men made off. The second robbery occurred on the same day at about 9.30 pm. H asked R for a word in the gents; once there M entered. H punched R in the face and M joined in, punching him several more times in the face. R was searched by the defendant who said "Make it easy for yourself, give him your wallet or I'll kill you". A doorman entered and dragged the defendant, who was holding R's wallet, off. Both escaped. R suffered numerous bruises and a black eye. M was arrested later and claimed not to have been involved in the first robbery but had been present in the public house at the time of the second. He was re-interviewed and admitted to his involvement in the first. He was 35 and had been sentenced to $6^1/_2$ years for 3 knife point robberies. Shortly following his release he had stolen the handbag of an 87 year old who had just arrived home in her disabled carriage. He received 3 years. He committed the current offences with 463 days of his licence remaining. Held. The aggravating features were the use of a knife, the violence inflicted on Mrs S, the degree of premeditation, the fact that it was a vulnerable small shop and M's high risk of re-offending, as assessed by the probation officer. **6 or 7 years** would have been appropriate. **5 years 9 months** was lenient and upheld but the sentence should be extended so with the licence 10 years in all.

Att-Gen's Ref No. 135 of 2002 2003 2 Cr App R (S) 649. The defendant was convicted of robbery. At 1.30pm, a 17-year old cashier was working alone in a convenience store. He noticed two men wearing hoods hanging around outside. They entered the shop wearing balaclavas and holding large kitchen knives. The cashier was told to open the till and had his face slashed (8–9 cms cut). The robbers stole £715 in cash and left having told the cashier to lie on the floor. Police recovered a balaclava and 2 kitchen knives that were linked by DNA to the defendant. He made no comment when interviewed and then denied the offence in a further interview. He was 32 and had a bad criminal record although he had not previously committed any violent offences. Held. These stores are all too vulnerable to attack. There was a serious wound inflicted; there was more than one robber, each of whom had a knife; the victim was young and on his own. There had been a degree of premeditation as they had armed themselves and wore balaclavas. At the time of the offence he was on licence for an offence of burglary. **7 years** not 4 reduced to **6 years** because this was a reference.

Old case. *Att-Gen's Ref. No 58 of 1996* 1997 2 Cr App R (S) 233, (for a summary of this case see the first edition of this book.)

Street etc robbery (including premises open to the public) – Guideline remarks

163.69   *Att-Gen's Ref. No 6 of 1994* 1995 16 Cr App R (S) 343 at 345. LCJ. Street robberies make the public afraid to walk out alone. The public require protection. There must be an element of deterrence to protect the public. Even a first offender must expect a period of custody.

R v Edward and Larter 1987 Times 3/2/87. LCJ. The defendants were convicted of robbery and received 5 years. Held. Judges should impose long sentences on muggers who attack others particularly women at night in urban areas. The amount of money was beside the point. [This case has been recently relied on by the Court of Appeal.]

Att-Gen's Ref. Nos. 19–21 of 2001 2002 1 Cr App R (S) 136. There can be little doubt that the two forms of criminal conduct which causes the public most concern are domestic burglary and street robberies. The effect of such offences goes way beyond the dreadful trauma suffered by the immediate victim and causes large sections of the public to alter their lifestyle to seek to avoid the danger. People are afraid to go out of their homes.

Street etc robbery (including premises open to the public) – Cases

163.70   *R v Luck and Woollard* 1999 1 Cr App R (S) 248. The defendant L pleaded guilty to four robberies and an attempted robbery and W pleaded guilty to five robberies and an attempted robbery. W was then 17 years old and L 16. In the first incident L pleaded to one robbery and W to two robberies. A 14-year-old schoolboy was intimidated by three youths with what looked like a knuckle-duster. Threats were made by one of them that another boy had ripped someone's tongue out and stabbed someone. The victim handed over £10 and the group left. The returned and extracted another £10. The victim's friend was threatened that he would be pushed through the wall. He handed over £1 and was told if he didn't hand over more the shit would be kicked out of him. Nothing was handed over and he was not attacked.

A week later W and six other youths surrounded a 17-year-old boy near the scene of the earlier robbery. They took his packet of cigarettes and searched him taking £13. They tried to rob his younger brother of his jacket but he resisted and they gave up. W pleaded guilty to robbery of them both. The same day seven youths surrounded a

16 year old and others. The boy's wallet was taken. He didn't resist as he had an injured hand. Another boy was told that if he didn't hand over money he would be knifed. No knife was produced and nothing taken. L pleaded guilty to the attempt and W to the robbery. They were arraigned and W pleaded guilty to all his matters and L only one but changed the pleas later. They were bailed. Five months later L and W attacked C a 16 year old and a 14 year old in a shopping centre. C's neck was seized and he was told they had a knife. The boys handed over their bags. L had convictions for two offences of criminal damage, assault, three burglaries, theft, handling and vehicle taking. Several were committed when he was on bail and he was subject to a supervision order. W had convictions for shoplifting, vehicle taking, theft and threatening words. Held. They had been given every opportunity. Their **3¹/₂ years** detention (under different provisions) was not manifestly excessive.

Att-Gen's Ref. No 34 of 1999 2000 1 Cr App R (S) 322. LCJ. The defendant pleaded guilty to robbery 4 months after the PDH hearing. The defendant who had partly covered his face with a shirt came up to the victim in a park and grabbed him by his jacket. He also grabbed hold of a valuable gold chain, which was round his neck. The defendant produced a hypodermic syringe, which appeared to contain a brown liquid and accused the boy of selling drugs to his brother. He held the syringe about a foot away from his neck and threatened to give him AIDS if he didn't get the chain off. The boy was terrified and the syringe was moved close to the boy's legs in a stabbing motion. Eventually the chain was undone. The defendant ran off with it. The next day he went to the shop where the boy worked and asked if he was accusing him of being the robber. He warned the boy not to make trouble for himself. He was arrested and gave an alibi. He was 25 and had convictions for burglary, common assault, drink/drive and failing to provide a specimen. They were all drug related. He didn't co-operate with a probation order and was given CSO for the breach, which he breached again and he then served a short period of custody. There were reports from drug rehabilitation units, which said 'He was committed to overcoming his addiction and was doing his utmost to sort out his life. He arranged his own interviews and all tests were negative. To interfere with the programme would jeopardise the recovery. He was now in a residential unit. The progress was very good. The stay would be for up to 9 months funded by the council.' The risk to the public was now described as being very low. He was given **18 months' suspended** and a suspended sentence supervision order. Held. What distinguishes this from the normal case of a defendant saying they will cure themselves is that here he has taken vigorous, persistent, constructive and determined action. That made it exceptional so the sentence could be suspended. The sentence did not fall outside the options open to the judge.

Att-Gen's Ref. No 30 of 2001 2002 1 Cr App R (S) 164. The defendant pleaded guilty to two counts of robbery on the day his trial was listed. At about 2.10am he when 25 and another spoke to the victim. They then lurked in an alleyway and tripped him up. He was pushed into the alleyway and pinned down. The other man held a knife to his neck. They demanded his wallet and he was rolled over so his pockets could be searched. They found nothing and took his watch. He was made to stand so they could check for his wallet and then they walked off laughing. The victim was very shaken and had a small nick in his neck from the knife. About 10 minutes later the next victim was dragged into an alleyway by the same two. The other man raised a knife to the victim's face and demanded his wallet. They searched his pockets and took his mobile and his wallet containing £5–10 and some bank cards. The other man asked for his PIN number and moved the knife closer to his throat. The number was given and they ran off. The attack had lasted about 30 seconds. Shortly after £110 was drawn from the victim's bank account. The defendant then surrendered himself to the police and identified his accomplice. When interviewed he said he was no more than a look out, although he did search the men's pockets. He said the money was for drugs but he didn't receive any. The defendant was said to be in fear of the other man. He was injured and said that they were caused by the other man and that was why he gave himself up. He had convictions for minor offences of dishonesty, four common assaults and driving offences. The risk of re-offending was described as significant. Held. 12 months was unduly lenient. A proper sentence could not be less than **3 years**. As it was a reference **2¹/₂ years** substituted.

See also *R v Ezair* 2001 Unreported 14/11/01. 3 years and 1 year consecutive upheld for defendant who robbed students in a city were there were over 700 robberies of students in that area.

R v Martin 2003 1 Cr App R (S) 172. The defendant changed his plea to guilty to assault with intent to rob. The victim was walking along a residential street at dusk and the defendant grabbed her from behind around her neck. He shouted, "Give me your purse." A struggle ensued and he held her in a headlock. Eventually he forced her to the ground in the middle of the road. The victim screamed, curled herself into a ball and kicked out at him. A witness thought he tried to hang onto him and he eventually struggled free and ran off when two cars approached. Her boyfriend joined her and together they managed to find him and he ran away again. She was terrified and thought she did not have any definite injuries but most of her body was aching. He was 31 with 22 appearances for sentence for 42 offences. They included burglaries and supplying Class A drugs. He was a heroin addict and in breach of a two year probation order for dangerous driving. His risk of re-offending was assessed as high. Held. An offence will not be mitigated if the vulnerable victim happens to be someone who, albeit chosen by the defendant, turns out to be more robust than might be expected. A severe sentence was called for but **3 years** not 3 years 10 months.

R v Underwood and others Re K 2005 1 Cr App R (S) 478 at 494. The defendant pleaded guilty to robbery. At around 1.30 am H was working as a prostitute and was picked up by the victim, V. V drove to what he thought was her home (but was in fact the defendant's). V locked his car, went inside and removed his clothing. V felt insecure and changed his mind. As V went to re-clothe, the defendant burst in holding a broomstick. V refused to lie down on the side of the bed and was struck on the left side of his face. H stole his car keys and his briefcase and possessions (including his clothing, watch, wallet and necklace.) He was forced to give up his PIN number. He was tied-up naked and left in the flat. He managed to untie himself and tried to escape. He was locked in. After hanging from the 3ʳᵈ storey window he managed to get back into the room and finally prised open the front door. V found his clothes by his car and alerted the police. V lost a number of very valuable papers including his birth certificate and passport. The defendant's basis of plea was that the offence was not pre-meditated and that he was angry when H returned with a client. The defendant had previous convictions for kidnapping and blackmail for which he was on licence, having received 4 years. Held. As this was not pre-meditated **4 years** not 6.

Street etc robbery (including premises open to the public) – Injuries caused

163.71 *R v Winfield* 1999 2 Cr App R (S) 116. The defendant was convicted of robbery. He and two others were in a public house. One followed the victim who had drunk about 5 pints into the lavatory. The victim's gold chain was seized and there was a struggle. The victim received a bite on the finger. The defendant and the other man joined them and all three kicked and punched the victim. The door was closed to stop those who had heard the commotion from entering. The victim became unconscious and lost his gold chain, his bracelet, a gold watch, a ring and £30. Police found him covered in blood with a boot mark on his forehead. At hospital he was found to have a 2″ cut to his head and bruising to his temple, nose, cheek and near his eye. He stayed there for a few days. The defendant had a bad record (details not given). The judge found the defendant was not the instigator but the No 2. He was given an longer than commensurate sentence of 8 years. Held. There is substance in the criticism that he was not more involved than the third man. Ordinarily the offence would warrant **5 years**. We must ensure the sentence is not out of all proportion to the nature of the offending and there is no double counting. Double counting is when a sentence has a deterrent factor built in and is extended without taking into account that existing deterrent factor. That deterrent factor caters for the necessity to protect the public. **6 years** not 8.

Att-Gen's Ref. Nos. 24 and 25 of 2000 2001 1 Cr App R (S) 237. The defendants E and M were convicted of robbery. They stopped an 18 year old who was running for a bus. They pretended to be police officers and dragged him to a dark alley. One held him while the other punched him. He was forced to the ground. They took £14 cash from his wallet. Police on the roof of a nearby building saw it and arrested the defendants. The victim suffered bruising and his spectacles were bent. The lenses were scratched. At the trial they claimed the victim made a racist remark and he was chased and had fallen over. E was now 30 and had nine court appearances for offences including ABH and robbery. M was now 31 and had 9 court appearances when he was aged 10 to 20. They were all for minor dishonesty. He was brought up in care. Both were sentenced to 6 months and had been released. Held. The differences between the defendants did not require different sentences. We would have expected **4 years** imprisonment. Because it was a reference and they had been released **3 years** substituted.

Att-Gen's Ref. Nos. 150–1 of 2002 2003 2 Cr App R (S) 658. The defendants pleaded guilty to robbery and attempted robbery. At about 9.20 pm the first victim was sitting on a bench at a railway station when the defendants came and sat alongside him. One of them moved very close and said "Listen, I don't want to hit you" and demanded his phone and a ring. The victim handed over his ring and phone. Money was further demanded and he handed over £5.70. The defendants then boarded a train. The second victim was on the train when one of the defendants (KW) sat near him and asked to see his phone. He refused. KW threatened to kick him in the mouth. Again the victim refused. KW called for the other defendant (AW) and told him to give the victim a kick-ing. AW threatened him with a kicking. KW grabbed hold of his jumper and saw a gold chain beneath and pulled it hard. He demanded the chain but the victim declined to hand it over. Both defendants demanded the phone and the chain. KW then kicked the victim, punched him twice and spat in his face. The police were called and both defendants were arrested. They were both picked out at identification parades but denied any involvement in interview. AW was 18 and KW was 20. Held. The offences involved the use of actual violence including kicking of one of the victims; mobile phones were targeted; and there were two robbers working together. **4 years** would have been appropriate. The combination orders imposed were unduly lenient, and **30 months detention** was substituted.

Att-Gen's Ref. Nos. 19–21 of 2001 2002 1 Cr App R (S) 136. There was an attempted robbery and a robbery. For those adults not involved in the death of one of the victims the appropriate sentence was **6 years**.

Old case. Att-Gen's Ref. No 44 of 1997 1998 2 Cr App R (S) 349, (for a summary of this case see the first edition of the book.)

Street etc robbery – Mobile phones – Guideline remarks

163.72   *Att-Gen's Ref. Nos. 4 and 7 of 2002 and R v Q 2002* 2 Cr App R (S) 345. LCJ. A Home Office Study shows a marked increase in mobile thefts and robberies. In 2000 there were 470,000 thefts and robberies including attempts from those 16 or over. There were 15,000 from those aged 11–15. The risk of theft for those aged between 11 to 16 is five times higher. Offences have at least doubled in 2 years. We have to adopt a robust sentencing policy. Punishment will be severe. Custodial sentences will be the only option unless there are exceptional circumstances irrespective of age and lack of previous convictions. The authorities indicate the sentencing bracket is **18 months to 5 years**. Without a weapon the upper limit is **3 years**. If there the defendant has a number of convictions or there is a substantial violence the upper limit may be **more than the 3 and 5 years**.

R v Dallison 2005 Unreported 21/2/05 The defendant pleaded guilty to robbery. The 3 year upper limit in the Att-Gen's Ref. No 4 and 7 of 2002 does not apply to this frightening robbery on a train.

Street etc robbery – Mobile phones

163.73   *Att-Gen's Ref. Nos. 4 and 7 of 2002* 2002 2 Cr App R (S) 345. LCJ. The defendant S pleaded guilty to three robberies and two thefts. The defendant who was on bail, approached a 14-year-old boy who was with five friends and grabbed him by the collar. The victim was dragged to the nearby shopping centre, pushed against a wall and searched. The defendant threatened to beat him up if he did not hand over his mobile phone. The victim was then pushed to the floor. The robbery ended. About a month later he stole a mobile phone and jewellery. About another month later the defendant was with another who approached the victim. He asked to borrow his mobile phone because 'he had been mugged.' The victim said he didn't have one. The defendant pulled up his top to cover his nose and mouth and joined them. He told the victim not to be stupid and not to look at them. They took his phone and unclipped his watch. The other youth took his gold chain. The items were worth £175. The victim was frightened. The next day he blocked the path of an 18 year old in the street. The defendant accused him of stealing his mobile and was asked to prove his was a different type and then when it was shown the defendant tried to seize it. The defendant's accomplice ran off with it. The defendant then threatened to beat the victim up if he did not give him some money. He was given some money and then ran off. He was 19 and had three convictions including stealing a bicycle when he scuffled with the owner. He spent 93 days in custody and the judge gave him a community rehabilitation order with 60 hours of community punishment. Held. **4 years' detention** was the starting point. The plea reduced it to 3 years and because it was a reference **$2^1/_2$ years** substituted.

Att-Gen's Ref. Nos. 150–1 of 2002 2003 2 Cr App R (S) 658. The defendants pleaded guilty to robbery and attempted robbery. At about 9.20 pm the first victim was sitting on a bench at a railway station when the defendants came and sat alongside him. One of them moved very close and said "Listen, I don't want to hit you" and demanded his phone and a ring. The victim handed over his ring and phone. Money was further demanded and he handed over £5.70. The defendants then boarded a train. The second victim was on the train when one of the defendants (KW) sat near him and asked to see his phone. He refused. KW threatened to kick him in the mouth. Again the victim refused. KW called for the other defendant (AW) and told him to give the victim a kicking. AW threatened him with a kicking. KW grabbed hold of his jumper and saw a gold chain beneath and pulled it hard. He demanded the chain but the victim declined to hand it over. Both defendants demanded the phone and the chain. KW then kicked the victim, punched him twice and spat in his face. The police were called and both defendants were arrested. They were both picked out at identification parades but denied any involvement in interview. AW was 18 and KW was 20. Held. The offences involved the use of actual violence including kicking of one of the victims; mobile phones were targeted; and there were two robbers working together. **4 years** would have been appropriate. The combination orders imposed were unduly lenient, and **30 months detention** was substituted.

The sentences have gone up. Ignore all cases before the *Att-Gen's Ref. Nos. 4 and 7 of 2002*.

Street etc. robbery – Previous convictions for robberies

163.74 *R v Greenland* 2003 1 Cr App R (S) 375. The defendant pleaded to robbery. As the victim walked home from a tube station, he attacked her from behind and tried to pull her handbag away. She resisted and he repeatedly punched her to the face. Ultimately she let go of the bag and he ran off with it and was chased by two doormen who caught him. The bag was recovered in tact and he was arrested. She had a cut and bruise to her eye, was badly upset and frightened. In interview he admitted the offence and said he had waited at the tube for a victim. He was a crack addict and had numerous convictions including 3 robberies. One in 1985, (detention centre) one in 1990, (hospital order) and one in 1992 (2 months). He had other convictions for possession weapons in public places. Held. He was caught virtually red handed. Although he was entitled to some credit for his plea he was not entitled to full credit. This kind of robbery is prevalent and becoming increasingly so. Such robberies are serious and this is a particularly serious example. People are entitled to be safe and feel safe on the streets and to know the courts will do their best to ensure their safety. This kind of conduct merits condign punishment. **6 years** is not manifestly excessive.

R v Riahi 2003 2 Cr App R (S) 29. LCJ. The defendant pleaded guilty to 10 robberies which were committed over a two-month period. All the victims were aged 16 to 19. The defendant, sometimes accompanied by others, engaged the victims in conversation and, using a combination of trickery and intimidation, stole their mobile telephones, cash and bankcards. In some cases the victims was searched and threatened, which included threats to stab. He used accomplices to back up his threats. In one attack he enticed three students from a shopping centre to a stairway where the students were set upon by six robbers. After he had seized a phone from a victim he said, "If you block this phone I'll come and find you and get you." To another he said, "Don't make me slash you." The other offences were similar. He was 19 years old and had a very bad record including two robberies, ABH and dishonesty. The pre-sentence report indicated that he represented a risk to the public. Held. The starting point was between **5 and 6 years**. The defendant did not indicate any true sense of remorse. He did not take any steps to admit his offending until he had been identified. The number of offences which were involved took it outside the less than four-year starting bracket. **4 years detention** not 6.

Street etc robbery – Vehicles, luring victims into their cars and attacking them

163.75 *Att-Gen's Ref. Nos. 53–57 of 2001* Unreported Judgment 31/7/01. H and T pleaded guilty to two robberies. The two victims of the first robbery were walking home when by threats the defendants and others forced them into two different cars, threatened them and beat them up. They were told they were going to be raped and killed. One victim was hit with a hockey stick. H held a metal bar. They said an acquaintance of his had been stripped and tied up. He was going to have his teeth smashed out and his ears cut off. A gold chain was taken. At different times both victim managed to leave the cars when they were travelling at about 40 mph. Both had to taken to hospital but had surprisingly minor injuries. The next day, the third victim was also walking home and he was knocked over by a car driven by H. He was punched and kicked by a group of men while they demanded money. When he managed to run away he was jumped on, punched and kicked again. His visa card, bank credit card and mobile phone was taken. He suffered a cut, grazes and a very sore jaw. H played the major role in both incidents. He was 23 with previous convictions including robbery. T was 17 but he played a significant role. Held. The appropriate sentences for H would have been **6 years at the very least**. 18 months was absurdly low. Because it was a reference 18 months deducted so **4¹/₂ years**. T sentence should have been **4 years detention** only because of his age not 18 months. As it was a reference **2¹/₂ years** substituted.

Street etc robbery – Victim over 65

163.76 *Att-Gen's Ref. No 48 of 1998* 1999 2 Cr App R (S) 48. The defendant pleaded guilty at the first opportunity to attempted robbery and handling. The victims of the attempted robbery were a married couple aged 82 and 78. They walked to their car after collecting their pensions. As they reached the car the defendant who was then 19 demanded the wife's purse. He was armed with two walking sticks. She got in the car and locked it. He then demanded money from the husband. The defendant raised his hand and the husband saw a black metal barrel. The husband said he was sure it was a gun from his years in the RAF. He told the defendant not to waste his time and the defendant ran away. The couple said they were shaken by the incident. The defendant was arrested and the officer found a weight bar. He also had a number of cigarette lighters, which had been stolen, in a burglary. In interview he admitted the attempted robbery and having the weight bar at the time. He also said he had been drinking and taking pills and was absolutely desperate for money. He was released on bail and committed further offences, which were dealt with in the Magistrates' Court. He had convictions for theft and a non-domestic burglary. He was sentenced to a combination order with a 100 hours' CSO. He attended twice and then for $3^{1}/_{2}$ months failed to attend. Held. A sentence in the region of **3 years** was appropriate. Because of his age and that it was a reference **2 years** detention substituted.

R v Buck 2000 1 Cr App R (S) 42. The defendant pleaded guilty to two robberies after the judge had ruled the ID evidence admissible. Both victims had to attend the court expecting to give evidence. The defendant watched the first victim aged 77, collect her pension and he followed her. He grabbed her round the neck from behind and threw her to the ground. He dragged her down a path to some bushes. She banged her head and became dazed. He took the pension book with the money still in it. She had a cut to her elbow and a bruise to her leg and forehead. An hour and a half later the next victim aged 79 collected her pension. As she was walking along the street the defendant grabbed her handbag and the strap broke. He ran off with it. The defendant was 29 with 52 offences of burglary, theft, handling and six drug-related offences. He had served 5 custodial sentences. The judge gave him 6 years on each concurrent. Held. The appropriate individual sentences are **5 years and 4**. The individual sentences would be **3 years each but consecutive**.

R v Blades 2000 1 Cr App R (S) 463. The defendant made a late guilty plea to robbery. The defendant pushed a 74 year old woman in the middle of the back causing her to fall to the ground. She sustained cuts and bleeding to her knees. He grabbed her handbag which contained £11. The defendant was arrested and the bag returned. In 1991 he brandished a gun in a burger restaurant and demanded the takings. He received 5 years. In 1994 he snatched cash and banking documents from a victim in a wheelchair (9 months). One year after his release and within 33 days, he committed two street robberies and two street thefts and another street offence. The victims were a care worker, a mother with a 2-month-old baby, a disabled woman and a 82 and 72-year-old woman respectively He received 4 years and was on licence for it at the time of the new offence. There was 1 year to run. He was 33. The pre-sentence report said he was addicted to crack and the offence was committed when his drug use was out of control. The judge was mindful of the psychological harm caused to old victims by attacks of this kind. He was sentenced to a longer than commensurate sentence of 10 years but there was no order about the breach of licence. Held. The offence was worth **5 years**. A 2 year extension was appropriate so 7 years plus 1 year consecutive for the breach of licence making **8 years**.

R v Howe and Graham 2001 2 Cr App R (S) 479. LCJ. The defendants H and G pleaded guilty to robbery. Their cases were unrelated but heard together because they were simi-lar. H and another approached the victim aged 73 as she was walking. She was pushed which caused her to stagger back. She didn't fall but her handbag with personal items and £14 was taken. The two ran off. Two passers-by followed them and asked them for the bag. H used insulting words and one of them was hit on her face. The 73 year old was very shocked and upset. H was 24 with 107 convictions and 28 TICs since he was 14. They included 26 burglaries, 15 thefts and a robbery. He had eight custodial sentences one of which was for 5 years. He was in breach of probation and a conditional discharge. The judge sentenced him to 5 years on the basis he struck the passer-by. This was denied and there was no Newton hearing. G approached his victim aged 76 as she was walking alone from behind. He pushed her and she turned and screamed. She tried to hang onto her bag but G eventually got it off her and ran away. It contained cash and personal items. He was 26 and had eight previous court appearances. His convictions included two for robbery which was one incident. The defence said he was in dire financial straits and had not eaten for several days. He received 4 years. Held. In each case the handbag was snatched with no more force than necessary. No threats or weapons were used. The striking of the passer-by should have been ignored. Both sentences should be **4 years**.

R v Simpson 2002 2 Cr App R (S) 234. LCJ. The defendant made an early guilty plea to manslaughter and two robberies. The first victim, an 89-year-old lady was returning to her flat after picking up her pension and doing some shopping. As she was walking up the stairs to the flat the defendant pulled her shopping bag firmly backwards. It contained her purse with £6 in it. She tried to resist and he gave it a heavier pull. She fell backwards and slid down the concrete stairs. He ran off with the bag. She was found to have a fracture to her neck and femur. A plate and screws were inserted. The operation appeared straight forward but she suffered two consequential chest infections and died about a month after the robbery. Almost immediately after the first robbery, the defendant 'thumped' a 76-year-old lady in the back and then pulled at her bag. It contained her pension book, documents and purse. The victim had just returned from collecting her pension. He pulled at it until she let go and drove away. The defendant was now 40 with convictions going back to the early 70s. Over the years he had been in and out of prison for dishonesty and driving offences. In 1995 he received 4 years for two robberies and one of the victims was an 83 year old lady who was followed from picking up her pension and knocked to the ground. The second robbery was similar. After the manslaughter offence he was sentenced to 3 years for burglary and serious driving offences. He needed £200 a day for heroin. Held. These offences are mean beyond words, easy to commit, highly prevalent and dangerous both to life and limb of the elderly victims. When they are committed by dangerous acts and death occurs severe sentences are called for. There can be no fault with the sentence of **7 years** for the robberies because of his record and the circumstances. The 10 years for the manslaughter as an overall sentence could not be faulted. The sentences remained consecutive to the sentence he was serving.

Att-Gen's Ref. Nos. 108 of 2001 2002 2 Cr App R (S) 294. The defendant made an early guilty plea to robbery. When 19 she approached an 88-year-old lady from behind and pulled her shopping bag. The victim held on and there was a struggle in which the victim swung round and fell to the ground. The defendant seized the bag and ran off but was detained by the public. While they waited for police to arrive she made two attempts to run off. The purse contained £17. The victim had a wound to her head and her shoulder was broken in four places. She needed a major operation, which effectively provided a new shoulder. There was also a hairline fracture to the pelvis. She was eventually released from hospital but would have to live in a home rather than independently. The defendant was interviewed and said it was easy money and she was desperate for drugs. There were no relevant convictions and she was 6 months pregnant. She showed remorse. Held. We would have expected **3$\frac{1}{2}$ years** YOI taking into account the injuries, the victim was targeted and the defendant's pregnancy. As it was a reference **2$\frac{1}{2}$ years** YOI not 18 months.

Street etc robbery – Victim taken to a cash machine

163.77   *R v Targett and Watkins* 1999 2 Cr App R (S) 282. The defendants T and W pleaded guilty to robbery and false imprisonment. They followed a man into a public lavatory. The man went into a cubicle, which had no lock. They pushed the door open despite effort by the victim to stop them and T threatened him with a Swiss Army knife. The victim was sitting on the lavatory with his trousers down. T demanded his wallet saying he was a crack head and he'd use the knife. The wallet was examined and the man was allowed to dress. They took £5. They saw his credit cards and asked him how much he could obtain from a cash machine. He said £30. They told him he was to be taken to a cash machine and T said he had a gun and he wasn't afraid to use it. W told the victim to remove his jewellery and two rings and a watch worth about £40. They were stolen. The victim was taken to a cash machine and told again that T was not afraid to use the gun. He was unable to obtain any money either inside or outside the bank. On his way to another machine the victim was able to escape into a shop. The incident had lasted about 20 minutes. They were arrested soon afterwards. T was 33 and W 41 with records (details not given). They were both addicted to various substances. The judge said that without a guilty plea 9 years would have been appropriate. Held. The judge was right to consider the offence was more serious than a straightforward street robbery. **6 years** was at the top of the bracket but was not manifestly excessive.

R v Gordon and Foster 2001 1 Cr App R (S) 200. The defendants G and F pleaded guilty at the first opportunity to robbery and ABH. A 17-year-old student in the street at night asked the defendants what the time was. G grabbed him by the throat and pinned him against the wall. He was asked if he had anything on him. The victim said, 'Nothing,' and he was told that wasn't good enough and was made to empty his pockets. G punched him and repeated the demand. F stood close by as if to hide what was going on. The victim handed over some keys and loose change. His wallet was taken and F looked through it. The victim was so frightened he handed over his bank card. F grabbed his arm and together they took him to the nearest cash point. On the way he was further threatened. They discovered he only had £1.70 in the account. He was taken round the side of the bank and was punched and headbutted. The victim managed to escape. He had a swollen and cut lip and swelling to his head. He also suffered from dizzy spells. G was 26 with 6 convictions including ABH. F was 28 and had been sentenced 13 times largely for dishonesty. The offences included ABH and possession of a bladed article. Held. **5 years** was not manifestly excessive.

Att-Gen's Ref. No. 127 of 2001 2003 1 Cr App R (S) 83. The defendant was convicted with his brother of robbery. At about 6 p.m. the brother approached the victim, a 21 year old student and offered to sell him a shirt. The offer was declined and the defendant came within a few inches of the victim's face and was aggressive. The brothers were taller and broader than the victim. The victim's Walkman was taken. The shirt offer was made again and the victim declined the offer and the brother persisted. The victim showed his wallet was empty of cash and the brother saw his bankcard. The brother put his arm around the victim's shoulder escorted him up the road asking about his bank account. As the victim protested, the defendant approached holding a Stanley knife, which was held to the defendant's face. The defendant repeatedly threatened to use it and on occasions said, "Well maybe we should just kill him anyway". The victim was terrified. The offender was also aggressive to passers-by. The victim was obliged to walk 1^1/$_2$ miles to a cash point. The victim revealed his PIN number and £300 was taken from the machine. Eight further attempts were made to obtain money but they were all unsuccessful. The victim was then made to walk ^{3}/$_4$ of a mile while the threats continued. Then he was released with no physical injury. At trial the defence run was that the £300 was for drugs. The defendant was now 24 with a deprived background. His father had assaulted him and he had attempted suicide. He had been before the Courts on 18 occasions for 63 offences including 12 for violence. His last sentence was for affray, 2 offences of assaulting the police and common assault. He was described as immature with a drink problem. The Judge sentenced him to 3 years consecutive to 3 months for the breach of his licence, which had 186 days outstanding. The brother who was younger received 3 years detention. Held. This was a serious robbery. We take into account his background and his progress in prison. We would have expected at least **6 years**. As it was a reference **5 years** substituted remaining consecutive to the breach sentence.

Taxi drivers etc – Guideline remarks

163.78 Att-Gen's Ref. No 38 of 1995 1996 2 Cr App R (S) 103. LCJ Taxi drivers are particularly vulnerable; they operate alone and they are at the whim of the passenger to be taken where the passenger asks. It is this court's job to see they are properly protected and anyone who is minded to attack a taxi driver must receive a substantial sentence of imprisonment.

Taxi drivers etc – Cases

163.79 *R v Johnson* 1998 1 Cr App R (S) 126. The defendant pleaded guilty to three robberies, a s 20 wounding and two TDA counts. The first minicab driver drove the defendant and felt something sharp near his ribs. It was a knife. The defendant demanded money and took over £50 in notes and £15 in loose change. He also demanded his gold chains and took them as well. He ran off taking the car keys. Six days later the defendant produced a knife on the second minicab driver. He stabbed him in the chest and ran off. He was in hospital for 5 days. The same evening he grabbed another minicab driver by the hand and produced a knife. He pushed it into his stomach and demanded money and jewellery. He took £86. The driver kicked him to stop him driving off and the defendant lunged at him with a knife. The defendant drove off in the car. The next evening the defendant and another were in another minicab and the driver was directed to a dead-end street. The defendant grabbed the driver from behind and forced his neck against the headrest. The other man produced a knife, which was held against his chest. They demanded money and said if he resisted he would be killed. His wallet containing about £50 and has mobile was taken. He was forced out of the car and they drove off in it. The defendant was 29 with three previous convictions for robbery. One was in 1993 and the other two were in 1994. He received 5 years concurrent on each and was released 3 months before the fist minicab robbery. The judge sentenced him to 10 years. Held. He had deliberately targeted minicab drivers because they were vulnerable. He either used a knife or was a party to the use of a knife. He was prepared to use violence on the one who was wounded. 7 years for the robberies cannot be faulted. The sentence as an overall sentence cannot be faulted.

R v Okee and West 1998 2 Cr App R (S) 199. The defendants O and W pleaded guilty at the last minute to robbery. W used a minicab a number of times to move his belongings from his hostel to his new address. O helped him. At the end of the last journey W seized the ignition key and the driver struggled and seized it back. The driver got out and the two manhandled him and tried to hit him. The victim dodged the blows. Then O hit him causing injury to the driver's forehead and kept hold of him while W went to the car and stole money from the ashtray. In interviewed they concocted contradictory lies. O was 20 and had two convictions for robbery. For the last one he received 3 years. W was 21 and had an attempted robbery conviction for which he received 3 years. The judge passed a $4^1/_2$ year sentence saying with no plea it would have been 5 years. The defence said there was insufficient credit given. Held. Those who run their not guilty pleas to the wire should know that the discount will be substantially and visibly reduced. The 10% discount here was ample. However the starting point is too high. **3 years 9 months** detention and imprisonment substituted.

R v Brown 1998 2 Cr App R (S) 257. The defendant pleaded guilty to unlawful wounding and robbery; two counts of offering to supply drugs; six counts of robbery; and an attempted robbery. The defendant approached a man in the street and took £10. He used a knife and caused a wound to the man's cheek. He was arrested and bailed. He offered two plain clothes officers ecstasy and cannabis. He was arrested and found to have neither. He was released on bail. The other robberies were on minicab drivers who were threatened with a knife and had money and other items taken. The last was where after he had threatened a driver with a knife, a struggle took place and the defendant fled empty handed. He was picked out at ID parades. He had only recently been released from prison. For all but 2 of the robberies he was on bail twice. In 1982 he received 3 years for robbery, in 1993 he received 2 years for robbery, in 1993 he was convicted of 13 offences of which 4 were robbery and received 2 years and also in 1993 he was convicted of six offences four of which were robbery and received 4 years. Those robberies were very similar to the latest offences. He received 4 years for the street robbery, 6 years for the robberies and 3 years for the attempt consecutive making 13 years in all. The judge passed a longer than commensurate sentence. The defence did not suggest the making of the longer than commensurate sentences was wrong. Held. Without considering the powers to extend the worrying features of this case mean a sentence of between 6 or 7 years would be justified even after a guilty plea. None of the sentences could be faulted but the total should be **10 years** not 13.

See also *Firearm, with – Taxi Drivers etc – Imitation*

Trains, buses etc

163.80 *Att-Gen's Ref. Nos. 35 and 36 of 2000* 2001 1 Cr App R (S) 327. LCJ. The defendant H aged 27 pleaded guilty to two robberies. The defendant D was convicted of robbery. The defendants approached the victims G aged 15 and F aged 16 and another at a railway station. They called out to them in a hostile manner. H got G in a loose headlock and asked him if he had a mobile. G said 'No.' H took £2 in change which had been proffered. A train arrived and the defendants and the victims entered different carriages. After the train left the station the defendants moved to the victims' carriage. There was another intimidating verbal exchange and D tried to persuade H to leave them alone. One boy got away but the defendants blocked the other two from leaving. The victims ran to the other end of the carriage and were chased. H pushed G into a seat and demanded his fucking money. G handed over his wallet containing £20. H searched F and took his mobile phone and camera. These were returned. The train arrived at a station and defendants told the victims they would have to travel back to London with them but F was able to tell staff at the a station what had happened. D gave a false name, failed to attend an ID parade and failed to answer to his bail. H expressed remorse. H had convictions mainly for dishonesty and was on probation. He had drug and alcohol problems. D's record was similar and he was on probation for assaulting a police officer. Held. Applying *Att-Gen's Ref. Nos. 7–10 of 2000* 2001 1 Cr App R (S) 166 the starting point for H is **3 years** and for D is **30 months**. Taking into account it was a plea and a reference **2 years** not 4 months for H. Taking into account D was involved in one offence 2 years for him.

R v Dikko 2002 2 Cr App R (S) 380. The defendant pleaded guilty to robbery. The victim was near the terminus of a London Underground journey and was alone in a carriage when the defendant came through the connecting door. The defendant sat next to her and said in an authoritative manner that she was going to give him everything she had. Frightened she took out her purse and he took her keys, bankcards and cash and demanded to know her PIN number which she gave him. He said he would not hurt her. She asked for her keys and he gave them back. He demanded details of her car and she was very frightened because he showed her what appeared to be a handle of a knife in his waist band. The train arrived at its destination and he left and withdrew £400 from her account. He was arrested and denied the offence in interview. He was 19 with 5 non-relevant convictions, (details not given). Held. The public is entitled to travel unaccompanied in safety. The victim was in terror. **3 years** YOI was unimpeachable.

R v Dallison 2005 Unreported 21/2/05 5 years upheld after a plea for this particularly frightening robbery in the confined space of a train

Att-Gen's Ref. Nos. 21 and 22 of 2004 Unreported 11/11/04. Those in gangs who prey on innocent travellers on the Underground can expect to receive deterrent sentences and save in the most exceptional cases e.g. extreme youth can expect custody. Even young offenders should expect a significant period of DTO and in some cases long term detention.

Victims, elderly

See **Domestic premises – Victim Over 65** and **Street etc. robbery – Victim over 65**

Victim seriously injured

163.81   *R v Evans* 2000 1 Cr App R (S) 454. The defendant pleaded guilty to robbery. He entered an antiques shop and took out a bottle or gas container which he used as a cosh. He struck the 59-year-old lady that ran the shop with it on the side of her face. She was propelled back against a wall and fell unconscious. He then stole jewellery from the cabinets worth about £1,200 and left her bleeding and unconscious on the floor. The incident was recorded on CCTV. She was found by another shopkeeper. She was taken to hospital and found to have blood over the surface of the brain. There was bruising to the brain. Her scalp was injured. She was in hospital for 11 days. She had loss of hearing, problems with her balance and she would never be able to return to work. Her hearing in her right ear and her sense of taste and smell would never recover. She had difficulty with strangers and her quality of life had been very seriously and permanently impaired. He was 30 with convictions in South Africa but was treated as of good character. He had no mental illness. His behaviour had changed after a motor accident. Held. The injuries were horrific, but **8 years** not 10.

R v Hooley 2001 2 Cr App R (S) 105. The defendants H, R and F pleaded guilty to robbery. The R and F had changed their pleas. The defendants had all used the village store which the victim aged 62 managed. Shortly after 10 pm F entered the store with some tape and a balaclava. The victim took the cash drawers to the back of the shop where F was waiting wearing a mask and hat and holding an iron bar in a threatening way. He had picked up the bar in the shop. He asked for money and the victim turned to go to the office. F struck him with the bar on the shoulder and the victim fell to his knees. He was made to open the safe and hand over the money. The next thing he remembered after being unconscious for $1/_2$ hour was crawling to a take away. The defendants had done nothing to assist him. He was in intensive care for 3 weeks. He had broken ribs on both sides of his chest. His lung was punctured. He had bruising on his shoulder and arms. His jaw and cheekbones were fractured and plates had to be inserted. There was a cut to his eye and his eye socket had been knocked slightly backwards. He required a tracheotomy. An expert said, 'He had subjected to kicking and/or stamping with substantial force. He had been punched and hit with a weapon like an iron bar.' H said F was in the shop for about $1/_2$ hour and then H and R stole £1,600 in cash, a large quantity of cigarettes. Previously he had lied about his involvement. The property was divided and items were burnt. H was sentenced on the basis that he did not believe any violence was to be used and his role was that of a lookout. H was 21 with ten convictions including offences of violence and dishonesty. R was 29 with three convictions including affray and ABH. F was 30 with eight convictions including four for violence. He had not served a prison sentence. The judge said it was well planned and ruthlessly executed. Held. **10 years** not 13 for H and **8 years** not 11 for H and R.

Att-Gen's Ref. Nos. 108 of 2001 2002 2 Cr App R (S) 294. The defendant made an early guilty plea to robbery. When 19 she approached an 88-year-old lady from behind and pulled her shopping bag. The victim held on and there was a struggle in which the victim swung round and fell to the ground. The defendant seized the bag and ran off but was detained by the public. While they waited for police to arrive she made two attempts to run off. The purse contained £17. The victim had a wound to her head and her shoulder was broken in four places. She needed a major operation, which effectively provided a new shoulder. There was also a hairline fracture to the pelvis. She was eventually released from hospital but would have to live in a home rather than independently. The defendant was interviewed and said it was easy money and she was desperate for drugs. There were no relevant convictions and she was 6 months pregnant. She showed remorse. Held. We would have expected **3¹/₂ years** YOI taking into account the injuries, the victim was targeted and the defendant's pregnancy. As it was a reference **2¹/₂ years** YOI not 18 months.

See also **OFFENCES AGAINST THE PERSON ACT 1861, S 18** – *Robbery, and*

Withdrawing from robbery plan

163.82   *Att-Gen's Ref. Nos. 65–6 of 2001* 2001 Unreported 26/10/01. H pleaded guilty to robbery of a guard of a security van. H then 19 sat beside the getaway driver wearing a balaclava helmet throughout the robbery. H's basis of plea was that when the two assailants who attacked the guard got out of the car he was unaware that weapons were to be used. When he saw the weapons he decided not to go with the other two and he remained in the car. Held. The basis of plea for H was supported by the fact he just remained in the car. Courts ought to encourage people who at the last minute decide not to go through with a criminal enterprise and who withdraw their own involvement even if they remain a party to what is going on.

164   SCHOOL, FAILURE TO SECURE REGULAR ATTENDANCE

164.1   Education Act 1996 s 444(1)

Parent with child who fails to attend regularly.

Summary only. Maximum Level 3 £1,000.

Education Act 1996 s 444 (1A)

Parent who knows child is failing to attend regularly, and fails to cause him to attend.

Summary only. Maximum 3 month and/or Level 4 (£2,500). When the Criminal Justice Act 2003 s 280(2) & Sch. 26 Para 47 is in force the maximum will increase to 51 weeks. The Home Office do not expect this to occur before September 2006.

Fixed penalties The Anti-Social Behaviour Act 2003 s 23[1] and Education Act 1996 444A(1) introduce a new power to authorised local education authority, school staff and the police to issue Fixed Penalty Notices.

Parenting order For both offences there is power to make a parenting order under the Crime and Disorder Act 1998 s 8.

Magistrates' Court Sentencing Guidelines January 2004 – Section 444A

164.2   For a first time offender pleading not guilty. Entry point. Is it serious enough for a community penalty? Examples of aggravating factors for the offence are harmful effect on other children in the family, lack of parental effort to ensure attendance, parental

---

1   In force 27/2/04, Anti-Social Behaviour Act 2003 (Commencement No 1 and Transitional Provisions Order 2003

collusion and threats to teachers, pupils and/or officials. Examples of mitigating factors for the offence are physical or mental health of child and substantial history of bullying, drugs etc. Examples of mitigation are age, health (physical or mental), subsequent co-operation with the Education Authority and genuine remorse. Consider a parenting order where appropriate.

For details about the guidelines see MAGISTRATES' COURT SENTENCING GUIDELINES at page 483.

165   SENTENCES SERVED FOR WHICH THE CONVICTION WAS LATER QUASHED

165.1   R v Exley and Day 2000 2 Cr App R (S) 189. The defendant is not entitled to any discount when sentenced for another offence.

166   SEXUAL OFFENCES PREVENTION ORDER, BREACH OF

(previously breach of a Sex Offender Order)

166.1   On 1/5/04 the Sexual Offences Act 2003 replaced the Sex Offenders Order with the Sexual Offences Prevention Order. Sex Offenders Orders made before 1/5/04 continue.

Breaches of both orders are offences contrary to Sexual Offences Act 2003 s 1(1) and (2)

Triable either way. On indictment maximum 5 years. Summary maximum 6 months and/or £5,000.

Guideline remarks

166.2   *R v Brown* 2002 1 Cr App R (S) 1. The police obtained a Sex Offender Order for the defendant. Held. It would be wholly illogical if, against that background (an order for the protection of children) a judge did not have the protection of children foremost in his mind. The remarks in *R v Chief Constable of Avon and Somerset, ex p B Judgement 5/4/00* were obiter. The actual quality of the acts which considered the breach are by no means the only consideration in determining its seriousness.

Children, order made to protect

166.3   *R v Brown* 2002 1 Cr App R (S) 1. The defendant was convicted of three breaches of a Sex Offender Order. Shortly before his release the police obtained a Sex Offender Order for him which prohibited him from contact, communication, association or befriending children under the age of 16. On the evening of his release he spoke to a 14 year old and was with him for over an hour. He occasionally put his arm around the boy's shoulder. Next morning he waved a £5 note towards a 13 year old and later approached and made a sexual remark to a 14-year-old boy. He was 35 with some 'run of the mill' offences and six sex convictions. They were two indecent assaults on a female under 16, gross indecency with a child and outraging public decency for which he received 18 months. He had apparently an irresistible attraction to children. The judge said he posed a very serious risk to children. Held. The breaches were serious because of the speed they took place and the number. **3 years** was not manifestly excessive.

R v Clark 2003 1 Cr App R (S) 6. The defendant pleaded guilty to two breaches of his order. He had indicated his plea at the Magistrates' Court. The defendant had a perverted interest in girls aged about 9 or 10. In 1996, he was convicted of attempted abduction of a girl in that age-range and impersonating a police officer. He received 3 years and was ordered to serve the unserved part of a sentence for indecent assault on a girl. Soon after his release, he was seen by police seeking the company of young girls. The Magistrates' Court made a Sex Offender Order restricting his freedom of activity and in particular saying he was not to reside where people under 16 resided and he must not remain where people of under 16 were present. He complied with the order for about a year and then moved to a house where there were boys aged 3 and 18 months. He also failed to notify the police of his change of address. He was given 3 years and 3 months consecutive for the notification breach. Held. There was no suggestion of targeting of girls. The sentence was too close to the maximum so **18 months** instead. 3 months was correct but as the facts were the same it should be concurrent.

R v Wilcox 2003 1 Cr App R (S) 199. The defendant pleaded guilty to doing five acts prohibited by his Sex Offending Order. The day before he was acquitted of a number of indecent assaults on females. In 1998, he was convicted of indecent assault on a girl under 14. He had touched her private parts at a fete. He was put on probation for 3 years and in 2001 he was made the subject of a Crime and Disorder Act Section 2 order. It was recognised it would make his business difficult to conduct as it provided equipment for children's parties. There was a proviso that he could arrange such events and manage the business side. A month later on 2 June, he arranged a four year old's party and remained throughout. On 22 June at a hearing when he was present the order was varied to permit him to attend the functions to set up and dismantle the equipment but not to be present within an hour before the start or within an hour after the end of the functions. On 8, 15, 20, 27 and 29 July he remained at parties for children where his equipment was used and on two occasions he assisted children to use his inflatable aeroplane. The Judge said that he treated the order with contempt. Held. The real offence was the continual breach of the order. Custody was inevitable. Bearing in mind his background **1 year** not 2.

R v Munday 2003 2 Cr App R (S) 112. The defendant pleaded guilty to a breach of a sex offender's order. His earlier plea was changed but he later pleaded again. There were various incidents between 1991 and 2001 when he had loitered near schools or befriended children. The sex offender order was made on the basis of eleven findings of fact including an attempted abduction of a young girl from a jumble sale, possession of children's underwear, photographs, toys and so-called love letters and other items connected with children. After the order was made police explained it to him. Two months later, they specifically said he was not to visit F's family home where there were four children. Six and a half weeks later police saw him there. The defendant admitted he was a regular visitor and had stayed overnight. The parents of the children had invited him but did not allow him to be with the children unsupervised. He was 58 with twelve convictions. There were sexual offences in 1977, 1979 and 1990 when he had received 30 months. The pre-sentence report asked for a significant custodial sentence so that he could have treatment. The risk of committing sex offences against children was assessed as high. He was of low intelligence. The Judge said it was a serious breach but nothing had happened. No treatment was offered in prison but it was offered on his release. Held. Bearing in mind his plea and that it was by invitation and *R v Wilcox* 2003 1 Cr App R (S) 199 2 years was too long. **12 months** and **immediate release** substituted.

R v Adams 2004 2 Cr App R (S) 78. The defendant pleaded guilty before magistrates to three charges: that being a sex offender he had failed to notify a change of address and name and obtaining a pecuniary advantage, an employment, by deception. The defendant had been convicted in 1995 of offences of indecent assault and possessing indecent photographs of young boys and sentenced to 6 years. On release he registered his address as required and registered a change of address three years later in 2001. A routine check later that year showed he had moved without notifying the police. He went to the Netherlands and stayed there until late 2002, when he went to live in Brighton. Documents from his address in Brighton showed that he had changed his name by deed poll in 2002. He had been working as a fairground attendant, a job which brought him into contact with children. He had got that job by not disclosing his previous convictions and this was the basis of the third charge. A pre-sentence report said that although while previously in custody he underwent a number of treatment programmes he retained his own views on child sexuality but kept these to himself to get parole. He felt hemmed in by the rules of registering after his release and by not being able to mix with children. He felt that by lifting children on and off rides, chatting to them and seeing them in the toilet he could satisfy his basic sexual needs and could avoid re-offending. Held. The defendant had made a determined effort to avoid the registration requirements. Consecutive sentences on the first two charges were appropriate. **1 year** not **2** for the failure to notify the change of address consecutive to **2 years** for the failure to notify a change of name and **6 months** for the obtaining, making a total of **3¹/₂ years** not **4¹/₂**.

R v Moore 2005 1 Cr App R (S) 575. The defendant pleaded guilty, not at the first opportunity but well before trial to four counts of breaching a sex offender order. In April 2001 he was made the subject of a sex offender order prohibiting him (i) from unsupervised access to or control of any child under 16, and (ii) from inviting in any child under 16 or allowing any such child access to his home unless accompanied by his or her parent. He was a frequent visitor at his brother's home where his 11-year-old nephew lived. Count one related to October 2003 when a young boy came to this house to visit the nephew. The defendant allowed the boy to enter the house and helped him with decorating work. There was no suggestion of impropriety. The second count related to an occasion when there was a family scheme to go ice skating, and the defendant manipulated the situation so that he was left alone in a car with two teenage boys of the family both under 16. The third and fourth counts related to the next day when the defendant was seen walking the family dog and was in the company of a 9 year old boy and another young boy, a friend of the 9 year old. He was then seen in the company of the friend alone. The defendant, 36, had a bad record of serious sexual abuse against young boys. Between 1995 and 2001 sexual offences were committed which led to prison sentences. He also had convictions for burglary offences. Held. The judge was entitled to take the view that he was a danger to young boys and deliberately and flagrantly breached the order four times. **3 years** not **6 years**.

R v Cox 2005 1 Cr App R (S) 588. The defendant pleaded guilty at the Magistrates' Court to breaching a sex offender order. On December 4th 2003 a sex offender order was made prohibiting him from having any contact with a child under 16 or from having any child under 16 in any accommodation occupied by him. This order was to last for ten years. On the 31st of December 2003 he was seen speaking to five children all under 16, four were boys and one a girl. They were traced and said that he had done a little dance and winked at them. He had invited one of them to feel his muscles and opened his shirt to show them his chest. He had asked one boy to come back at 2.00 pm when he would have something for him. The defendant, 66, had a history of sex offending going back to 1961. His victims were often young boys and he had convictions for six offences of indecent assault on a male, six of gross indecency, three of indecent exposure, one of buggery and one of attempted buggery. A psychiatric assessment in 1999 found he had strong paedophile tendencies. A pre-sentence report referred to a very high risk of re-offending and expressed grave concerns regarding the risk he posed to children and young people. Held. It is necessary to look carefully at the circumstances of the specific breach. The circumstances give rise for real concern especially as it took place only a few weeks after the order was imposed. But what happened was limited to one occasion and it took place outside his flat so that the actual conduct did not place this breach at the very highest level of seriousness. Taking into account that the maximum sentence is 5 years, that he pleaded guilty at the first opportunity, and his age and failing health **2¹/₂ years** not 4.

Name, – failing to notify new name

166.4   *R v Pike* 2004 Unreported 9/12/04 (sub nom R v Spencer 2004). The defendant pleaded guilty to failing to notify the use of a new name and perverting the course of justice. He was arrested in Worthing and gave the name Gibson and a false date of birth. There was no record of that name so the police cautioned him. Two months later he was arrested in Cambridge very drunk with two stolen bottles of Brandy with him. He gave the name Spencer and a false date of birth. This was the pervert count. He was 44 with over two hundred offences mostly for drunkenness and indecency. There was minor dishonesty, violence and indecent assault (for which in 1998 he received 2¹/₂ years). He had eight appearances for failing to notify a change of name or address (for one he received 18 months). Held. The message was not getting through. **18 months** upheld but because of totality **3 months** not **9 consecutive** for the perjury.

Police officers, conduct directed towards

166.5   *R v Beech* 2002 1 Cr App R (S) 7. LCJ. The defendant made a late guilty plea to breaching his Sex Offender Order. The order prohibited him from being drunk in any place other than a dwelling and using threatening, abusive or insulting words etc towards any female. The day after it was made he was released. He stayed at police accommodation as he was prepared to co-operate with them and because of the local media publishing inaccurate details about him. He and police officers visited a number of pubs and had a considerable amount to drink. His behaviour deteriorated and he was taken into custody. While there he was abusive and threatening in particular to a woman police sergeant. It was a torrent of abuse and threats including, 'Bitch, I'm going to shag you and bury you, you whore.' She found it frightening and unnerving. He apologised. He was 37 and had one court appearance for sex offences namely rape and indecent assault for which he received 9 years. There were also 13 appearances for drugs, assault, affray, harassment and threatening behaviour etc. A dyssocial personality disorder which was exacerbated by alcohol and illicit substances was diagnosed. His risk of re-offending was assessed as extremely high and he presented a serious risk of harm to the public particularly women. The judge identified a history of failing to comply with court orders. He was due to be released in a few days. Held. There is no doubt the defendant finds it very difficult to behave in a manner which is other than extremely antisocial. It was precisely this sort of behaviour the order was designed to avoid. In normal circumstances even for someone with the defendant's background 12 months would not be proportionate for these remarks, however distressing they were to the sergeant. However, we can take into account the risk he poses himself and the public. It is important the arrangements for his release are in place so **12 months** is not manifestly excessive. The public are entitled to be protected.

See also SEX OFFENDERS' REGISTER

167   SEX OFFENDERS' REGISTER

167.1   Sexual Offences Act 2003 s 80–92

The requirements are not listed as they concern the operation of a sentencing provision which for reasons of space are not included in the book.

Can the need to register contribute to a reduction in sentence

167.2   *Att-Gen's Ref. No 50 of 1997* 1998 2 Cr App R (S) 155. The sentencing judge thought 9 months was appropriate for two counts of indecent assault. He said, 'That would require registration for 10 years which would be an absurd additional burden. I have no discretion.' He passed a 6 month sentence which required 7 years of notification. Held. The judge was wrong to reduce the sentence. It is the duty of judges to implement the sentencing powers that have been given to them by Parliament.

See also SEX OFFENDERS' ORDER, BREACH OF

168   SEXUAL ACTIVITY – BREACH OF TRUST

168.1   Sexual Offences Act 2003 s 16–19

Sexual activity with a child, in the presence of a child etc. when abusing a position of trust. In force from 1/5/04.

For offences committed before 1/5/04 the offence is Sexual Offences (Amendment) Act 2000 s 3 (now repealed).

Having sexual intercourse or engaging in other sexual activity with a person under 18 years when in a position of trust to that person.

Both old and new offences are triable either way. On indictment maximum 5 years. Summary maximum 6 months and/or £5,000.

Extended sentences under CJA 2003 For offences under s 16–19, committed on or after 4/4/05 there is a mandatory duty to pass an extended sentence when there is a significant risk to members of the public of serious harm etc.[2]. See EXTENDED SENTENCES

Longer than commensurate sentences and extended sentences Sexual Offences (Amendment) Act 2000 s 3 is a sexual offence[3] for the purposes of passing a longer than commensurate sentence [Powers of Criminal Courts (Sentencing) Act 2000, s 80(2)] and an extended sentence (extending the licence) [Powers of Criminal Courts (Sentencing) Act 2000, s 85(2)(b)]. These provisions will continue to apply to offences committed after 29/9/98 and before 4/4/05. See EXTENDED SENTENCES and LONGER THAN COMMENSURATE SENTENCES

Notification For offences under (a) Sexual Offences Act 2003 s 16–19 and the defendant is at least 20 and (b) offences under Sexual Offences (Amendment) Act 2000 s 3 where the defendant was sentenced to imprisonment or detained in a hospital or given community service for at least 12 months, the defendant must notify the police within 3 days (or 3 days from his/her release from imprisonment, hospital etc.) with his/her name, home address, national insurance number etc. and any change and addresses where s/he resides for 7 days[4] (in one or more periods) or more in any 12 month period[5]. See SEX OFFENDERS' REGISTER

Working with children Where the defendant is aged 18 or over and s/he is sentenced to 12 months or more the court must disqualify him/her from working with children unless satisfied s/he is unlikely to commit any further offences against a child when the court must state its reasons for not doing so[6]. For a defendant aged less than 18 at the time of the offence the court must order disqualification if s/he is sentenced to 12

2   Criminal Justice Act 2003 s 227–228
3   Powers of Criminal Courts (Sentencing) Act 2000 s 161(2)(a)
4   Sexual Offences Act 2003 s 84(1)(c) & (6)
5   Sexual Offences Act 2003 s 83 & Sch 3 Para 16 & 25
6   Criminal Justice and Court Services Act 2000 s 28

months or more and the court is satisfied that the defendant will commit a further offence against a child[7]. The court must state its reasons for so doing.

Sexual Offences Prevention Order There is a discretionary power to make this order, when the notification (q.v.) criteria are present and when it is necessary to protect the public etc[8].

Crown Court statistics – England and Wales – Males 21+ – Abuse of Trust (including Sex Offender notification offence)
168.2

| Year | Plea | Total Numbers sentenced | Type of sentence % | | | | | Average length of custody (months) |
			Discharge	Fine	Community sentence	Suspended sentence	Custody	
2002	Guilty	5	–	–	–	–	100	7.7
	Not guilty	1	–	–	–	–	100	18
2003	Guilty	12	8	-	42	8	42	3.8
	Not guilty	3	-	33	–	–	67	37.5

For details and explanations about the statistics in the book see page vii.

Guideline remarks

168.3   *Att-Gen's Ref. Nos. 91, 119 and 120 of 2002,* 2003 2 Cr App R (S) 338. In *R v Millberry* 2003 2 Cr App R (S) 142 at para 8, the Lord Chief Justice said, 'There are, broadly three dimensions to consider in assessing the gravity of an individual offence of rape. The first is the degree of harm to the victim; the second is the level of culpability of the offender; and the third is the level of risk proposed by the offender to society. The gravity of each case will depend very much upon the circumstances and it will always be necessary to consider an individual case as a whole taking into account the three dimensions.'

It will be necessary to take account of similar considerations in all cases of sexual interference, whether amounting to rape or not. However, that is not all. In all classes of sexual offences, there will also be the need to deter others from acting in a similar fashion.

Exposing himself to children

168.4   *R v Eyre* 2005 1 Cr App R (S) 15. The defendant was convicted of abusing a position of trust contrary to s. 3(1)(b) of the Sexual Offences (Amendment) Act 2000. He was a teacher at a primary school. One lunchtime the 9 year old victim went to the classroom in a small mobile unit where the defendant was in order to see her sister and friend. When she arrived, the defendant asked her sister and the friend to leave whilst the victim was asked to stay. He took her into a cloakroom, removed his penis from his clothing and exposed it to her before putting it back in his clothing. The victim became upset, burst into tears and went to the headmistress. The defendant declined to comment in interview. He was 29, of good character and had a daughter of 5. He lived separately in the same property as his partner. There would likely be an investigation by the Social Services to consider whether his 5 year old daughter could live in the same household as him. He had been a teacher for seven years. His career was at an end. He had been abused and had had to leave the area. Held. An immediate custodial sentence was inevitable and **15 months** was (if anything) on the low side.

---

7   Criminal Justice and Court Services Act 2000 s 29
8   Sexual Offences Act 2003 s 104 & Sch. 3

Sexual intercourse

168.5   *R v Hubbard* 2002 2 Cr App R (S) 473. The defendant pleaded guilty to three counts of abuse of trust on a 15 year old pupil of his. He was head of department at a secondary school. She was vulnerable but sexually experienced and found him easy to talk to about her personal problems. Consensual sexual intercourse took place on three occasions. It was revealed because she told her friends. The defendant was 43 and was full of remorse. His marriage ended in divorce. Held. This Act is to protect girls like this. **2 years** was not manifestly excessive. The judge was entitled to extend his licence by 2 years.

R v MacNicol 2004 2 Cr App R (S) 6. The defendant pleaded guilty to two counts of sexual activity with girls both aged 16 to whom he was in a position of trust, being their school teacher. With one girl he had sexual relations, which fell short of intercourse, with her full consent. After his arrest he made full and frank admissions to this matter and he also admitted having fully consensual intercourse on one occasion with the other girl. That relationship had begun when they exchanged text messages. He had a good employment record. The Judge also passed a 33 month extended licence period (no appeal made). Held. It was an important factor that two girls not one were involved. He was entitled to substantial credit for his co-operation with the police, particularly in respect of the second matter, and for his early pleas. Total concurrent sentences of **15 months** were not excessive.

Sexual intercourse, without

168.6   For cases under the old law see also INDECENT ASSAULT ON A MAN – *Breach of trust* and INDECENT ASSAULT ON A WOMAN – *Breach of trust*

169   SEXUAL ACTIVITY WITH A CHILD FAMILY MEMBER

169.1   Sexual Offences Act 2003 s 25–26

Sexual activity with a child family member and inciting a child family member to engage in sexual activity.

These sections came into force on 1/5/04. Offences committed before this date are charged as INCEST etc. The definition of child family member is much wider than those with close blood connections.

For a defendant aged 18 or more and where there is penetration[9] the offences are indictable only. Maximum sentence 14 years. Otherwise the offences are triable either way. Maximum sentences 14 years and 5 years if the defendant is under 18. Summary maximum is 6 months and/or £5,000.

The Criminal Justice Act 2003 creates a summary maximum sentence of 51 weeks, a minimum sentence of 28 weeks and Custody plus. The Home Office says they do not expect to introduce these provisions before September 2006.

Detention Both offences are specified offences enabling defendants aged 14–17 to be detained[10].

Imprisonment for public protection For offences committed on or after 4/4/05 when there is a significant risk to members of the public of serious harm etc. there is a mandatory duty to pass a sentence of imprisonment for public protection[11]. For offenders under 18 the duty is to pass detention for public protection or an extended sentence[12].

9 Penetration means "penetration of a vagina or anus or a mouth with a penis", Sexual Offences Act 2003 s 25(6) and 26(6).
10 Powers of Criminal Courts (Sentencing) Act 2000, s 91(2)(a) as amended by Sexual Offences Act 2003 s 139 & Sch 6 Para 43(2)
11 Criminal Justice Act 2003 s 224–226
12 Criminal Justice Act 2003 s 226 and 228

Notification Where the defendant (a) is at least 18 or (b) s/he has been sentenced to imprisonment, detention in hospital s/he must notify the police within 3 days (or 3 days from his/her release from imprisonment, hospital etc.) with his/her name, home address, national insurance number etc. and any change and addresses where s/he resides for 7 days[13] (in one or more periods) or more in any 12 month period[14]. See **SEX OFFENDERS' REGISTER**

Working with children Where (a) the defendant is aged 18 or over and (b) s/he is sentenced to 12 months or more or a hospital order etc. the court <u>must</u> disqualify him/her from working with children unless satisfied s/he is unlikely to commit any further offences against a child when the court must state its reasons for not doing so[15]. For a defendant aged less than 18 at the time of the offence the court must order disqualification if s/he is sentenced to 12 months or more and the court is satisfied that the defendant is likely to commit a further offence against a child[16]. The court must state its reasons for so doing.

Sexual Offences Prevention Order There is a discretionary power to make this order, when the notification (q.v.) criteria are present and when it is necessary to protect the public etc[17].

The chapter is divided into three sections, (A) General, (B) Penetrative sex and (C) Sexual activity without penetration.

A General

Guideline case – Old guideline case for incest

169.2   *Att-Gen's Ref. No 1 of 1989* 1989 90 Cr App R 141. LCJ The gravity of the offence of incest varies greatly according, primarily, to the age of the victim and the related matter, namely the degree of coercion or corruption. Aggravating factors, whatever the age of the girl may be, are:

(1) If there is evidence that the girl has suffered physically or psychologically from the incest;

(2) If the incest has continued at frequent intervals over a long period of time;

(3) If the girl has been threatened or treated violently by or was terrified of the father;

(4) If the incest has been accompanied by perversions abhorrent to the girl, e.g. buggery or fellatio;

(5) If the girl has become pregnant by reason of the father failing to take contraceptive measures;

(6) If the defendant has committed similar offences against more than one girl.

Possible mitigating features are:

(1) A plea of guilty. It should be met by an appropriate discount, depending on the usual considerations, that is to say how promptly the defendant confessed and his degree of contrition and so on;

(2) If it seems that there was a genuine affection on the part of the defendant rather than the intention to use the girl simply as an outlet for his sexual inclinations;

(3) Where the girl has had previous sexual experience;

---

13 Sexual Offences Act 2003 s 84(1)(c) & (6)
14 Sexual Offences Act 2003 s 83 & Sch. 3 Para 26
15 Criminal Justice and Court Services Act 2000 s 28
16 Criminal Justice and Court Services Act 2000 s 29
17 Sexual Offences Act 2003 s 104 & Sch. 3

(4) Where the girl has made deliberate attempts at seduction;

(5) Where, as very occasionally is the case, a shorter term of imprisonment for the father may be of benefit to the victim and the family.

(The rest of the guidelines are split up into the various sections in this chapter for the different ages for the victim.)

Guideline remarks

169.3   *Att.-Gen's Ref. Nos. 91, 119 and 120 of 2002,* 2003 2 Cr App R (S) 338. In *R v Millberry* 2003 2 Cr App R (S) 142 at para 8, the Lord Chief Justice said, 'There are, broadly three dimensions to consider in assessing the gravity of an individual offence of rape. The first is the degree of harm to the victim; the second is the level of culpability of the offender; and the third is the level of risk proposed by the offender to society. The gravity of each case will depend very much upon the circumstances and it will always be necessary to consider an individual case as a whole taking into account the three dimensions.'

It will be necessary to take account of similar considerations in all cases of sexual interference, whether amounting to rape or not. However, that is not all. In all classes of sexual offences, there will also be the need to deter others from acting in a similar fashion.

B Penetrative sex

Girl aged 13–15 years – Old Guideline case for incest

169.4   *Att-Gen's Ref. No 1 of 1989* 1989 90 Cr App R 141. LCJ. Where the girl has achieved the age of 13 it will in most cases mean she has achieved puberty. This of course is the demarcation line chosen in the 1956 Act. Sentences in this area seem to vary between about **2 years to 4 or 5 years** on a plea of guilty, depending on the mitigating or aggravating factors. A broad guide to the level of sentence where the girl is 13 to 16 and where there has been no plea of guilty is that a sentence between about **5 years and 3 years** seems on the authorities to be appropriate. Much the same principles will apply as in the case of a girl over 16, though the likelihood of corruption increases in inverse proportion to the age of the girl. [Note. The imprisonment figures in this guideline case were issued before the charges to the release dates brought about by the Criminal Justice Act 1991, s 32–40. The figures should be considered in line with the Practice Statement (Crime Sentencing) 1992 95 Cr App R 948. However since then the actual release dates are not greatly different and in recent years the courts have been slow to make reductions because of the 1991 changes.]

Girl 13–15 years – Fathers

169.5   *R v MH* 2001 2 Cr App R (S) 454. The defendant pleaded guilty to seven counts of incest with his daughter over a period of six years when the girl was 15 to 21. When the girl started a sexual relationship with a boyfriend he resented it and after an incident between him and the boyfriend that relationship broke up. He decided he was going to teach her about sex. He engaged in sexual activity with her when she was aged 14 without active protest on her part. She simply suffered what was going on. On her 15th birthday he first had sexual intercourse her. He would sleep in her bedroom and have intercourse with her 2–3 times a week often with his wife's (the girl's mother) knowledge. He moved out of the family home with his daughter and the two effectively lived as husband and wife. She permitted that to keep the peace and because she was financially dependant on him. He was 47 and had no relevant convictions. The sentencing judge said that the defendant had destroyed the young womanhood of his natural daughter and destroyed the trust that should exist between a father and daughter. Held. The sentencing judge was correct in his remarks, therefore **4¹/₂ years** was high but we will not disturb it.

Girl/Woman aged 16 or more – Guideline case

169.6 *Att-Gen's Ref. No 1 of 1989* 1989 90 Cr App R 141. LCJ. At one end of the scale is incest committed by a father with a daughter in her late teens or older who is a willing participant and indeed may be the instigator of the offences. In such a case the court usually need do little more than mark the fact that there has been a breach of the law and little, if anything, is required in the way of punishment. A broad guide to the level of sentence where there has been no plea of guilty is: where the girl is over 16, generally speaking a range from **3 years down to a nominal penalty** will be appropriate depending, in particular, on whether force was used, on the degree of harm, if any, to the girl, and the desirability, where it exists, of keeping family disruption to a minimum. The older the girl the greater the possibility that she may have been willing or even the instigating party to the liaison, a factor which will be reflected in the sentence. In other words, the lower the degree of corruption, the lower the penalty.

Girl/woman aged 16–20 years – Fathers

169.7 *R v B* 1999 1 Cr App R (S) 174. The defendant pleaded guilty to incest with his daughter and supplying cannabis to her. The defendant, who was 42 years of age, had spent the evening with his daughter, who was aged 20. Both of them had been drinking heavily and shared a cannabis cigarette. The defendant and his daughter were sleeping in the same room, though in separate beds. During the night the defendant asked his daughter to join him in his bed and engaged in sexual intercourse with her. The woman did not move nor communicate with her father during the act. She pretended to be asleep. When he pleaded guilty she said she wanted to withdraw the complaint and that she loved him. The defendant had no relevant convictions. The sentencing judge noted that the defendant had abused his position of trust and had taken advantage of his daughter's vulnerability as she was under the influence of alcohol and cannabis. Held. The hitherto good relationship between the father and daughter should not be disrupted longer than was necessary therefore **6 months** not 18 months.

Girl/Woman aged 16 or more – With pregnancy/baby born

169.8 *R v M* 2003 1 Cr App R (S) 283. The defendant pleaded guilty to eight counts of incest. He lost contact with his daughter very early in her life. They met again when she was 23 and shortly after he moved in with her and her four children. They were both alcoholics. About two to three weeks later, when she was 24 and they were both drunk sex took place. Sexual intercourse continued with consent and without force from November 1997 to December 2000 when she went to the police. In 1999 she gave birth to his child, which was proved by scientific evidence. There was no genuine affection between the two and he just used her as a sexual outlet. He accepted that what he had done had had a serious impact on his daughter. He was 45 with no convictions of any real significance and a depressive disorder. The pre-sentence report said the risk of committing a similar offence was slim and there was no longer any contact between them. The psychiatrist said he showed genuine remorse and he had become suicidal. Held. The duration of the relationship, the birth of the child, the serious impact on the daughter and his age and maturity were serious aggravating features. **2¹/₂ years** might be regarded as high but it was not manifestly excessive. However the circumstances were not present to warrant an extended licence period so that was quashed.

R v GM 2002 1 Cr App R (S) 112. The defendant was convicted of three counts of incest. They were representative counts for a 21 month period of regular incest with his daughter. He was acquitted of rape and other counts of incest for a different period. A fortnight after his 15ᵗʰ birthday his then girlfriend of a similar age gave birth to a daughter, the victim. That relationship continued on a tenuous basis for two years or so. They then lost touch. Twelve years later he met her again. There was perfectly proper contact for two years or more. The defendant's marriage then broke up. He continued to see his daughter and just short of her 17th birthday the relationship became sexual. She had had no other sexual experience before. When she became pregnant, he encouraged her to have a late termination for his own protection. In a state of some depression she made a suicide attempt. He was 38 with no other convictions. The trial judge came to the clear conclusion that his relationship always had selfish and manipulative elements. He also considered the relationship contributed to her depression. Held. The fact that the two had not grown up in the same household was a relevant consideration and provides some differentiation from a case when a man exploits a girl who has been dependant upon him as a parent. Neither the termination nor her mother's suspicions made to him deterred him from continuing. There was a proper basis for saying some emotional damage had been done to her. **$3^{1}/_{2}$ years not 5**.

R v B 2003 1 Cr App R (S) 91. The defendant pleaded guilty to five counts of incest. At the time the defendant was on licence for murdering his wife in 1973. Having been released in 1990 he re-established contact with his daughter. She had left her husband and had with her her three children. In 1996 he began a sexual relationship with her (then aged 24), with intercourse taking place on 10 occasions. No contraception was used and the daughter became pregnant; however the child died when she was a few months old. By 1997 the relationship was over, although was not reported until 2000. On arrest the defendant made a full confession. The daughter had consented fully and letters written by her reflected the love that she felt for him. He was 63. There was no element of corruption or seduction and the defendant had provided her with emotional and financial support during the relationship. **9 months not 18**.

C Sexual activity without penetration

Father/stepfather, by – Victim under 10 – Less than 3 years appropriate

169.9   *R v Lennon* 1999 1 Cr App R (S) 19. The defendant, who was 52, was convicted of indecent assault on the 9 year old daughter of his co-habitee. The defendant had masturbated and subsequently jumped onto the victim, pulled off her trousers and underwear and attempted to penetrate her with his penis. It was treated as a single act. Held. Each sentence must be tailored to the particular facts. **2 years** was not manifestly excessive. [Facts are in short supply in this case.]

Att-Gen's Ref. No 35 of 1998 1999 1 Cr App R (S) 400. The defendant, who was 61, pleaded guilty to four counts of indecent assault on two girls aged between 7 and 11. The victims were the daughters of the defendant's girlfriend with whom he was staying. The defendant invited the victim into his bed when he was naked and subsequently placed his penis between their legs. The defendant was arrested but without any evidence except for the girls there was no prosecution for a year. This conduct occurred on a second occasion after the defendant had shown the victims a pornographic video. The defendant was treated as being of good character. The judge noted the defendant remained a high risk unless his behaviour was fully addressed. Held. The appropriate sentence was **12–18 months** considering his age and the plea. As it was a reference **9 months** was appropriate not a probation order.

Att-Gen's Ref. No 72 of 1999 2000 2 Cr App R (S) 79. The defendant was convicted of six counts of indecent assault, one of indecency and taking an indecent picture. The first girl, H, his stepdaughter, was abused when she was 4 or 5, 5 or 6 and 7 twice. The second girl, G had been fostered and then adopted when she was 12. She was abused when she was 13 or in one count possible younger. His early abuse was touching the girl's vagina in the bath. When H was 7 she made her touch his penis. G was asked to play strip poker and when she lost they both had all their clothes off and the defendant became all excited and asked her to touch him. She refused. Later he made G unroll a condom on his erect penis. G was also asked twice to lie on a scanner once with her bra and once without. He also made her masturbate him to ejaculation. Both girls had to give evidence. The defendant was of good character and had given up his job to be a Minister and was highly regarded by the church. He lost his home, his job and his vocation. He showed no remorse. **2¹/₂ years** in total not 12 months.

Att-Gen's Ref. No 15 of 2001 2001 2 Cr App R (S) 532. LCJ. The defendant was convicted of gross indecency on his 4 year old stepdaughter and perverting the course of justice. The defendant had consumed a considerable amount of alcohol when his wife found him astride the girl. The defendant had pulled down the child's underwear and was masturbating over her. His wife came in and found him astride the girl and there was semen on the crotch of her knickers and her T-shirt. The defendant tried to destroy the evidence by putting the sheet in the washing machine while she attempted to prevent it. She also tried to call the police and he ripped the phone out of the socket. When she tried to use her mobile to call the police he snatched it. He was arrested and denied the incident. The defendant, who was 23 years of age, had no relevant convictions. He was in the Navy with promotion prospects. He was dismissed from the services, lost £8,000 in pension rights and lost Navy quarters. He also lost being with his two daughters and his stepdaughter. He received 6 months for the indecency and 2 months consecutive for the perverting. Held. The 2 months was adequate and rightly consecutive. A sentence must be imposed as a deterrent. The appropriate sentence was **2¹/₂ years**. As it was a reference **18 months** not 6 months.

Father/stepfather, by – Victim under 10 – 3 to 4 years appropriate

169.10   *Att-Gen's Ref. No 32 of 1998* 1999 1 Cr App R (S) 316. The defendant pleaded guilty to five offences of indecent assault and one of indecency, with the daughter of his co-habitee, who was between the ages of 6 and 8. The defendant, who was aged 44, admitted to behaving indecently with the child on between 15 and 20 occasions, which included simulating sexual intercourse, digital penetration of the victim's vagina and anus, and mutual oral sex. The child was extremely traumatised and had to receive treatment for her mental condition. The defendant had no previous convictions and had demonstrated genuine remorse. The psychiatrist's report stated that the defendant had distorted the boundaries between affection and sexuality with his stepdaughter. The judge noted that the defendant was not a 'true paedophile' and presented a low risk of re-offending. Held. **3 years** was lenient but not an unduly lenient.

Att-Gen's Ref. No 61 of 1998 1999 2 Cr App R (S) 226. LCJ. The defendant pleaded guilty to eight counts of indecent assault on the handicapped daughter of the woman with whom he cohabited. The victim suffered from quadriplegia, cerebral palsy and dystonia, which affected her limb movements and voice. The defendant was the father figure of the house. Over a 2 year period when the victim was between the ages of 9 and 11 the defendant forced the victim to masturbate him, digitally penetrated her, performed oral sex on her and forced her to reciprocate. The acts were not reported and it wasn't until 3 years later that her school nurse was told about it. The defendant, who was 40, had no previous convictions for similar behaviour. The judge noted that the child's trust had been abused and the child's innocence betrayed. Held. The appropriate sentence on a trial was 4 years or more. On a plea it should have been **3 years**. As it was a reference **2 years** not probation.

Father/stepfather, by – Victim under 10 – More than 4 years appropriate

169.11   *Att-Gen's Ref. No 66 of 1999* 2000 1 Cr App R (S) 558. The defendant was convicted of seven counts of indecent assault on his three daughters, who were aged between 7 and 13 over a period of 4 or 5 years. The defendant's wife had died and he had been left to look after the victims and a fourth child, a boy aged 10. The conduct included digital penetration touching the victim's breasts, simulating sexual intercourse and forcing the victims to masturbate him. Two of the victims left home at the age of 13 because of the defendant's conduct. The defendant, who was 51, had previous convictions though none had a sexual element and these were not taken into account by the sentencing judge, though the serious breach of trust was noted. Held. Taking into account the case of *R v Lennon* 1999 1 Cr App R (S) 19 and *R v L* 1999 1 Cr App R (S) 347 the appropriate sentence for these offences was **4¹/₂–5 years**. As this was a reference, **3¹/₂ years** not 2¹/₂ years.

Att-Gen's Ref. No 77 of 2000 2001 2 Cr App R (S) 94. The defendant was convicted of six counts of indecent assault against his two daughters who were between the ages of 9 and 14. The defendant was a strong disciplinarian and as such his daughters feared him. The defendant began to abuse his eldest daughter when she was 10. The defendant touched the girl's breasts and vagina, digitally penetrated her and simulated sexual intercourse with her. When the defendant's younger daughter was between the ages of 9 and 13 he subjected her to abuse such as digital penetration, sucking her breasts and simulating sexual intercourse with her. The abuse was over a 4 year period. The defendant, who was 52 years of age at the time of conviction, had no previous convictions. Held. The appropriate sentence was **4 years**. As it was a reference **3 years** was appropriate not 12 months.

Att-Gen's Ref. No 2 of 2001 2001 2 Cr App R (S) 524. The defendant pleaded guilty to seven counts of indecent assault against his stepdaughter when she was between the ages of 8 and 15. The defendant, who was 100% disabled and wheelchair-bound, forced the victim to masturbate him and take his penis in her mouth. The defendant was 49 years of age. Held. The appropriate sentence was **5 years**. Having regard that this was a reference and the serious disability faced by the defendant which would render imprisonment more difficult to bear **2 years** was appropriate not a probation order.

Father/stepfather, by – Victim aged 10–12

169.12   *R v L* 1999 1 Cr App R (S) 347. The defendant pleaded guilty to six counts of indecent assault on his daughter aged 12. The offences took place over a period of three months when the victim was in the sole care of her father and consisted of, touching the victim's breasts and vagina, placing her hand on his erect penis when it was exposed and through his clothing and pinning her down whilst kissing her. The defendant, who was 46 years of age, had no previous convictions. The pre-sentence report said unless he addressed his offending there was a high risk of re-offending. The trial judge had regard to the fact that there was no force, no threats and no penetration but that children were entitled to protection from the courts. Held. These offences were a gross breach of trust and as the defendant was unwilling to accept the seriousness of what had happened **2 years** was not manifestly excessive.

Att-Gen's Ref. No 43 of 1999 2000 1 Cr App R (S) 398. LCJ. The defendant was convicted of two counts of indecent assault on his daughter, who was aged between 10 and 11, and one count of gross indecency. The offences took place when the victim's mother was either asleep or out of the house. The defendant rubbed his penis on the victim's vaginal area, stroked her breasts and forced the victim to hold his penis. The defendant, who was 45, had no previous convictions. The probation officer said he was unlikely to offend again. The judge noted that these were not the worst assaults imaginable as there had been no violence or threat of violence and no penetration. The defendant was sentenced to 6 months. Held. The sentence was unduly lenient. The appropriate sentence for these offences was **15–18 months**; having regard that this was a reference **9 months**. As the defendant had already served his 6 months it would be destructive and advanced no relevant public interest for him to be returned to prison.

170   SEXUAL ACTIVITY WITH MENTALLY DISORDERED PERSONS

170.1   Sexual Offences Act 2003 s 34–35

Section 34 Inducement etc to procure sexual activity with a person with a mental disorder.

Section 35 Causing a person with a mental disorder to engage in sexual activity by inducement etc.

Both sections in force from 1/5/04. Where there is penetration both offences are triable only on indictment. Maximum Life. Otherwise triable either way. On indictment maximum 14 years. Summary maximum 6 months and/or £5,000.

For offences committed before 1/5/04 the offence is Sexual Offences Act 1956 s 7 and 9 (now repealed).

Section 7 Unlawful sexual activity with a woman who is a defective.

Section 9 Procurement of a defective.

Both are triable only on indictment maximum 2 years.

Imprisonment for public protection For offences committed on or after 4/4/05 when there is a significant risk to members of the public of serious harm etc. there is a mandatory duty to pass a sentence of imprisonment for public protection[18]. For offenders under 18 the duty is to pass detention for public protection or an extended sentence[19].

Longer than commensurate sentences and extended sentences All four offences are sexual offence[20] for the purposes of passing a longer than commensurate sentence [Powers of Criminal Courts (Sentencing) Act 2000, s 80(2)] and an extended sentence (extending the licence) [Powers of Criminal Courts (Sentencing) Act 2000, s 85(2)(b)]. These provisions will continue to apply to offences committed after 29/9/98 and before 4/4/05. See EXTENDED SENTENCES and LONGER THAN COMMENSURATE SENTENCES

Notification For offences under Sexual Offences Act 2003 s 30–7 (but not the 1956 s 7 and 9 offences) where the defendant was sentenced to imprisonment or detained in a hospital or given community service for at least 12 months, the defendant must notify the police within 3 days (or 3 days from his/her release from imprisonment, hospital etc.) with his/her name, home address, national insurance number etc. and any change and addresses where s/he resides for 7 days[21] (in one or more periods) or more in any 12 month period[22]. See SEX OFFENDERS' REGISTER

Working with children Where the defendant commits a Sexual Offences Act 2003 s 30–5 against a child or a Sexual Offences Act 1956 Act s 7 or 9 and is aged 18 or over and s/he is sentenced to 12 months or more the court must disqualify him/her from working with children unless satisfied s/he is unlikely to commit any further offences against a child when the court must state its reasons for not doing so[23]. For a defendant aged less than 18 at the time of the offence the court must order disqualification if s/he is sentenced to 12 months or more and the court is satisfied that the defendant will commit a further offence against a child[24]. The court must state its reasons for so doing.

Sexual Offences Prevention Order For offences under Sexual Offences Act 2003 s 30–5 (but not the 1956 s 7 and 9 offences) there is a discretionary power to make this order when it is necessary to protect the public etc[25].

18 Criminal Justice Act 2003 s 224–226
19 Criminal Justice Act 2003 s 226 and 228
20 Powers of Criminal Courts (Sentencing) Act 2000 s 161(2)(a)
21 Sexual Offences Act 2003 s 84(1)(c) & (6)
22 Sexual Offences Act 2003 s 83 & Sch 3
23 Criminal Justice and Court Services Act 2000 s 28
24 Criminal Justice and Court Services Act 2000 s 29
25 Sexual Offences Act 2003 s 104 & Sch. 3

Sexual intercourse

170.2   *R v Young* 2005 1 Cr App R (S) 45. The defendant pleaded guilty at the first opportunity to having sexual intercourse with a defective (s. 7(1)) The victim was a woman aged 27 who had severe learning difficulties (mental age of 6 or 7). In the early hours the defendant with another knocked on her door. She knew the defendant. As she opened the door they pushed their way in and demanded sexual favours. The defendant then had sex with her. The other man assisted the defendant and inserted his finger into her vagina a couple of times. The defendant was of previous good character, showing remorse and shame. Held. There was no real difference between this case and *R v Adcock* 2000 1 Cr App R (S) 563 and the maximum sentence was 2 years. **9 months** instead of 15.

171   SEXUAL ASSAULT BY PENETRATION

171.1   Sexual Offences Act 2003 s 2

Penetrating the vagina or anus of another person who does not consent. (The penetration can be by part of the defendant's body or anything else[26].) This section came into force on 1/5/04.

Indictable only. Maximum sentence Life.

Automatic life Offences committed before 4/4/05 are specified offences (including attempted offences) for automatic life[27].

Dangerous Offender provisions For offences committed on or after 4/4/05 where there is a significant risk to members of the public of serious harm etc. there is a mandatory duty to pass a life sentence when it is justified and otherwise a sentence of imprisonment for public protection[28]. For offenders under 18 the duty is to pass detention for life, detention for public protection or an extended sentence[29].

Notification The defendant must notify the police within 3 days (or 3 days from his release from imprisonment, hospital etc.) with his name, home address, national insurance number etc. and any change and addresses where he resides for 7 days[30] (in one or more periods) or more in any 12 month period[31]. See SEX OFFENDERS' REGISTER

Working with children Where (a) the offence is against a child (aged under 18), (b) the defendant is aged 18 or over and (c) he is sentenced to 12 months or more or a hospital order etc. the court must disqualify him from working with children unless satisfied he is unlikely to commit any further offences against a child when the court must state its reasons for not doing so[32]. For a defendant aged less than 18 at the time of the offence the court must order disqualification if he is sentenced to 12 months or more and the court is satisfied that the defendant is likely to commit a further offence against a child[33]. The court must state its reasons for so doing.

Sexual Offences Prevention Order There is a discretionary power to make this order when it is necessary to protect the public etc[34].

26 Sexual Offences Act 2003 s 2(1)
27 Powers of Criminal Courts (Sentencing) Act 2000 s 109(5)as amended by Sexual Offences Act 2003 s 139 & Sch 6 Para 43(3)
28 Criminal Justice Act 2003 s 225
29 Criminal Justice Act 2003 s 226 and 228
30 Sexual Offences Act 2003 s 84(1)(c) & (6)
31 Sexual Offences Act 2003 s 83 & Sch. 3 Para 17
32 Criminal Justice and Court Services Act 2000 s 28
33 Criminal Justice and Court Services Act 2000 s 29
34 Sexual Offences Act 2003 s 104 & Sch. 3

Although before the change in the law these offences would have to be charged as
INDECENT ASSAULT ON A MAN (q.v.) and INDECENT ASSAULT ON A WOMAN (q.v.) the
insertion of fists, bottles etc into a woman who does not consent is best equated with
RAPE (q.v.) with an aggravating element.

Guideline remarks

171.2   *Att-Gen's Ref. Nos. 91, 119 and 120 of 2002* 2003 2 Cr App R (S) 338. In
R v Millberry 2003 2 Cr App R (S) 142 at para 8, the Lord Chief Justice said, 'There
are, broadly three dimensions to consider in assessing the gravity of an individual
offence of rape. The first is the degree of harm to the victim; the second is the level of
culpability of the offender; and the third is the level of risk proposed by the offender to
society. The gravity of each case will depend very much upon the circumstances and it
will always be necessary to consider an individual case as a whole taking into account
the three dimensions.'

It will be necessary to take account of similar considerations in all cases of sexual
interference, whether amounting to rape or not. However, that is not all. In all classes of
sexual offences, there will also be the need to deter others from acting in a similar fashion.

Att-Gen's Ref. No 104 of 2004 2005 1 Cr App R (S) 666. The new offence with life as
a maximum must mean that sentences for digital penetration must be a higher level than
what would have been appropriate for indecent assault.

171.3   *Cases*

Att-Gen's Ref. No 104 of 2004 2005 1 Cr App R (S) 666. The defendant pleaded
guilty at a preliminary hearing to assault by penetration. The victim was a 23-year-old
married woman who had gone to neighbour's house with her husband for a drink. The
defendant was also there. The victim was very much the worse for drink when she
announced she was going home and as her husband was staying at the neighbour's
house for a time she would leave the door open for him. She went to bed and woke at
5.45 am with the defendants arm round her. She was frightened and jumped out of bed.
The defendant was naked from the waist down. He put his trousers on and she told him
to leave. When the defendant left she locked the door and called her husband. He came
home and found her in a state of shock and called the police. The victim felt sore in the
vagina. She noticed two buttons on her pyjama top had been undone. The defendant
was arrested not long afterwards and eventually admitted that he had digitally penetrated her for five to ten minutes and that he had touched one of her breasts. He said he
had taken alcohol cannabis and amphetamine. The defendant, 31, had nine previous
convictions for violence or dishonesty. There were no offences of a sexual nature. He
had not previously been sentenced to custody. A psychiatrists report said that after the
offence he developed a major depressive disorder. He was assessed as having the potential to pose a serious harm to women if his cognitive skills and awareness did not
improve, and there was a moderate risk he would re-offend. Aggravating features were
said to be that the offence was committed in the defendant's home; that the victim was
very vulnerable; that she was asleep in bed and that she had consumed a large quantity
of alcohol. Held. Having regard to the aggravating features of intrusion into the victim's
home when she was asleep and vulnerable the appropriate sentence after a trial would
have been **6 years**. With the guilty plea the appropriate sentence was **4 years**. Because
it was a reference **3 years 3 months** substituted not 18 months.

172   SEXUAL ASSAULT ETC. CHILDREN

172.1   Sexual Offences Act 2003 s 6–15

Assault of a child by penetration[35] (s 6), Sexual assault of a child (s 7), Causing etc. a child to engage in sexual activity (s 8 & 10), Sexual activity with a child (s 9), Engaging in sexual activity in the presence of a child (s 11), Causing a child to watch a sex act (s 12), Section 9–12 offences committed by persons under 18 (s 13), Arranging or facilitating a child sex offence (s 14) and Grooming (s 15).

These sections came into force on 1/5/04. Offences committed before this date are charged with indecent assault etc.

Sections 6 is indictable only. Section 8, 9 and 10 are indictable only where there is penetration. Otherwise the offences are triable either way. Sections 7, 12–15 are triable either way. Maximum sentences are:- Section 6 and 8 (where there is penetration), life. Sections 7, 8 (no penetration), 9, 10 and 14, 14 years. Sections 11, 12 and 15, 10 years. Section 13, 5 years. Summary maximum is 6 months and/or £5,000.

Automatic life Sections 6 and 8 (where there is penetration) committed before 4/4/05 are specified offences (including an attempted offence) for automatic life[36].

Confiscation For all Sexual Offences Act 2003 s 14 offences the court must follow the Proceeds of Crime Act 2002 procedure[37].

Dangerous Offender provisions For offences when 1) under s 6 and 8, 2) when there is penetration, 3) when committed on or after 4/4/05 and 4) where there is a significant risk to members of the public of serious harm etc. there is a mandatory duty to pass a life sentence when it is justified and otherwise a sentence of imprisonment for public protection[38]. For offenders under 18 the duty is to pass detention for life, detention for public protection or an extended sentence[39].

Detention Sexual Offences Act 2003 s 13 is a specified offence enabling defendants aged 14–17 to be detained[40].

Extended sentences under CJA 2003 For offences under s 13 and committed on or after 4/4/05 there is a mandatory duty to pass an extended sentence when there is a significant risk to members of the public of serious harm etc.[41]. See EXTENDED SENTENCES

Imprisonment for public protection For offences 1) where the maximum sentence is 14 or 10 years (see above), 2) committed on or after 4/4/05 and 3) when there is a significant risk to members of the public of serious harm etc. there is a mandatory duty to pass a sentence of imprisonment for public protection[42]. For offenders under 18 the duty is to pass detention for public protection or an extended sentence[43].

Notification For offences under (a) Sections 6, 8–12 and 15, (b) Sections 7 and 14 where the defendant was (i) 18 or over or (ii) s/he was sentenced to at least 12 months imprisonment, (c) Section 13 where the defendant has been sentenced to at least 12 months imprisonment; the defendant must notify the police within 3 days (or 3 days from his release from imprisonment, hospital etc.) with his name, home address,

---

35 Penetration means "penetration of a vagina or anus or a mouth with a penis", Sexual Offences Act 2003 s 6(1), 8(2), 9(2) and 10(2).
36 Powers of Criminal Courts (Sentencing) Act 2000 s 109(5) as amended by Sexual Offences Act 2003 s 139 & Sch 6 Para 43(3)
37 Proceeds of Crime Act 2002 s 6 and s 75 and Sch 2 para 4(2) as inserted by Sexual Offences Act 2003 s 139 and Sch 6 para 46(2).
38 Criminal Justice Act 2003 s 225
39 Criminal Justice Act 2003 s 226 and 228
40 Powers of Criminal Courts (Sentencing) Act 2000 s 91(1)(c) as amended
41 Criminal Justice Act 2003 s 227–228
42 Criminal Justice Act 2003 s 224–226
43 Criminal Justice Act 2003 s 226 and 228

national insurance number etc. and any change and addresses where he resides for 7 days[44] (in one or more periods) or more in any 12 month period[45]. See SEX OFFENDERS' REGISTER

Sexual Offences Prevention Order There is a discretionary power to make this order, when the notification (q.v.) criteria are present and when it is necessary to protect the public etc[48].

Working with children Where (a) the offence is against a child (aged under 18), (b) the defendant is aged 18 or over and (c) he is sentenced to 12 months or more or a hospital order etc. the court <u>must</u> disqualify him from working with children unless satisfied he is unlikely to commit any further offences against a child when the court must state its reasons for not doing so[46]. For a defendant aged less than 18 at the time of the offence the court must order disqualification if he is sentenced to 12 months or more and the court is satisfied that the defendant is likely to commit a further offence against a child[47]. The court must state its reasons for so doing.

The chapter is divided into three sections, (A) General, (B) Penetrative sex, (C) Sexual activity without penetration and D Sexual activity in the presence of a child and causing a child to watch a sex act.

Crown Court statistics – England and Wales – Males 21+
172.2

Year	Plea	Total Numbers sentenced	Type of sentence %					Average length of custody (months)
			Discharge	Fine	Community sentence	Suspended sentence	Custody	
Unlawful sexual intercourse with girl under 13								
2002	Guilty	27	–	–	15	4	81	41.4
	Not guilty	2	–	–	–	–	100	75
2003	Guilty	19	–	–	5	5	89	44.4
	Not guilty	4	–	–	–	–	100	61.5
Unlawful sexual intercourse with girl under 16								
2002	Guilty	101	2	2	24	1	71	10.9
	Not guilty	5	–	–	–	–	100	11.2
2003	Guilty	107	1	2	21	2	74	11.7
	Not guilty	9	11	11	–	–	78	10.6

For details and explanations about the statistics in the book see page vii.

A General

Guideline remarks

172.3 *Att-Gen's Ref. Nos. 91, 119 and 120 of 2002*, 2003 2 Cr App R (S) 338. In *R v Millberry* 2003 2 Cr App R (S) 142 at para 8, the Lord Chief Justice said, 'There are, broadly three dimensions to consider in assessing the gravity of an individual offence of rape. The first is the degree of harm to the victim; the second is the level of culpability of the offender; and the third is the level of risk proposed by the offender to

44 Sexual Offences Act 2003 s 84(1)(c) & (6)
45 Sexual Offences Act 2003 s 83
46 Criminal Justice and Court Services Act 2000 s 28
47 Criminal Justice and Court Services Act 2000 s 29
48 Sexual Offences Act 2003 s 104 & Sch. 3

society. The gravity of each case will depend very much upon the circumstances and it will always be necessary to consider an individual case as a whole taking into account the three dimensions.'

It will be necessary to take account of similar considerations in all cases of sexual interference, whether amounting to rape or not. However, that is not all. In all classes of sexual offences, there will also be the need to deter others from acting in a similar fashion.

R v Watkins 1998 1 Cr App R (S) 410. The significance of an 11-year-old girl consenting is limited.

R v Corran 2005 Unreported 2/2/05. The Court considered CJA 2003 s 7 and 8. The presence of consent is material particularly for young defendants. The age of the defendant, of itself and when compared with the age of the victim is also an important factor. Factors will include the nature of the assault or penetrative activity and the period it lasted. Other factors include the nature of the relationship between the two and their respective characters and maturity, the number of occasions the assault occurred, the circumstances of the assault, the consequences for the victim, emotional and phys-ically, the degree of remorse and the likelihood of repetition. Pre-Act authorities will continue to be of assistance, subject to them being viewed through the prism of the increased sentence for sexual assault from 10 to 14 years. In relation to s 7 offences, the custody threshold will not always be passed. Generally speaking, despite the similar maximum penalties s 7 offences will be less serious than s 8, 9 and 10 offences. Section 11 and 12 offences will usually attract a lesser sentence than that appropriate for sexual activity with a child contrary to s 5, 7, 8, 9 or 10. Factors relevant to sentence will include the age and c

Internet – Guideline remarks

172.4   *Att-Gen's Ref. No. 39 of 2003 2004 1 Cr App R (S) 468.* Where a man consid-erably older than a teenager makes contact with young girls using the internet and this leads to sexual offences against the girls, it needs to be clearly understood that sentences will be towards the top of the range.

B Penetrative sex

Guideline remarks

172.5   *R v Corran* 2005 Unreported 2/2/05. The Court considered penetrative sex under the CJA 2003 s 9 and 10. The presence of consent is material particularly for young defendants. The age of the defendant, of itself and when compared with the age of the victim is also an important factor. Other factors include the nature of the relationship between the two and their respective characters and maturity, the number of occasions when penetration occurred, the circumstances of the penetration, includ-ing whether contraception was used, the consequences for the victim, emotional and physically, the degree of remorse and the likelihood of repetition. Offences contrary to CJA 2003 s 5 will generally attract a heavier penalty than those contrary to s 9 or 10.

Att-Gen's Ref. No 104 of 2004 2005 1 Cr App R (S) 666. The starting point for assault by penetration should generally be somewhat lower than rape, that is in the region of **4 years**. If non-penile penetration is by an object of such size and character that, whether by reference to the age of the victim or otherwise, there is a significant risk of physical injury, the starting point should be **5 years**. The R v Millberry aggravating and mitigating features and higher starting points should also apply to assault by penetra-tion. If the degree of penetration or the time which penetration lasts is minimal, a lower starting than 4 or 5 years is likely to be appropriate. For young offenders the sentence should be significantly shorter than that for an adult.

Digital penetration – Guideline remarks

172.6 *Att-Gen's Ref. No 104 of 2004* 2005 1 Cr App R (S) 666. The new offence of penetration in s 2 with life imprisonment as the maximum must mean that the sentences to be passed for digital penetration are at a higher level than would be appropriate for indecent assault. We note that digital penetration was always regarded by the courts as a particular serious type of indecent assault.

Digital penetration – Cases

172.7 *Att-Gen's Ref. No 104 of 2004* 2005 1 Cr App R (S) 666. The defendant pleaded guilty at a preliminary hearing to assault by penetration. The victim was a 23 year old married woman who had gone to neighbour's house with her husband for a drink. The defendant was also there. The victim was very much the worse for drink when she announced she was going home and as her husband was staying at the neigh-bour's house for a time she would leave the door open for him. She went to bed and woke at 5.45am with the defendant's arm round her. She was frightened and jumped out of bed. The defendant was naked from the waist down. He put his trousers on and she told him to leave. When the defendant left she locked the door and called her husband. He came home and found her in a state of shock and called the police. The victim felt sore in the vagina. She noticed two buttons on her pyjama top had been undone. The defendant was arrested not long afterwards and eventually admitted that he had digitally penetrated her for five to ten minutes and that he had touched one of her breasts. He said he had taken alcohol, cannabis and amphetamine. The defendant, 31, had nine previous convictions for violence or dishonesty. There were no offences of a sexual nature. He had not previously been sentenced to custody. A psychiatrists report said that after the offence he had developed a major depressive disorder. He was assessed as having the potential to pose serious harm to women if his cognitive skills and awareness did not improve, and there was a moderate risk he would re-offend. Aggravating features were said to be that the offence was committed in the defendant's home, that the victim was very vulnerable, that she was asleep in bed and that she had consumed a large quantity of alcohol. Held. Having regard to the aggravating features of intrusion into the victim's home when she was asleep and vulnerable the appropriate sentence after a trial would have been **6 years**. With the guilty plea the appropriate sentence was **4 years**. Because it was a reference **3 years 3 months** substituted not 18 months.

Girl aged 10–12

172.8 *R v Murray* 1998 1 Cr App R (S) 395. The defendant pleaded guilty to unlaw-ful sexual intercourse with a girl under the age of 13. He met the victim, who was 12, near his home as she took a short cut. She approached the defendant and asked him for a cigarette. A conversation took place between the two and the victim consented to have sexual intercourse with the defendant. The girl had had sex before. The defendant was 40 and had a conviction for indecent assault on a woman in 1996. In 1985 he was convicted of indecent assault on his 9 year old stepdaughter. The sentencing judge noted that the defendant was unable to contain his sexual appetite and took advantage of a solitary girl. Held. She was vulnerable and the age difference is appalling. **4 years** was a reasonable sentence.

Att-Gen's Ref. No 106 of 2002 2003 2 Cr App R (S) 423. The defendant pleaded guilty to two counts of unlawful sexual intercourse with a girl under 13. The victim, V, was 12 at the time of the offences and was a friend of the defendant's stepson. She met the defendant at a party at his house. The defendant started sending her text messages and in one suggested that they should meet. They met in a park and he drove her to a lay-by where they had sex on the back seat of his car. She had been a virgin. They had

sex in similar circumstances on a separate occasion. When the victim's brother challenged the defendant about matters, the defendant pleaded with him not to involve the
police or the rest of the family. The brother did. The defendant was arrested but made
no comment in interview. By the time of sentence V had become upset and withdrawn
and initially could not cope with being at school where she had been the subject of
ridicule. Events had turned the family upside down. A report opined that future risk to
the public might be reduced (to low) if a sex offender programme was undertaken. He
was 32 and had no previous convictions for sexual offences. Held. There were two
offences. **2¹/₂ years** not 12 months concurrent.

Victim aged 10–12 – Breach of trust

172.9   *R v Watkins* 1998 1 Cr App R (S) 410. The defendant pleaded guilty to three
counts of unlawful sexual intercourse with a girl under the age of 13 and one count of
incitement to unlawful sexual intercourse with a girl under 13. The defendant was
friendly with the 11 year old daughter of his neighbour. He asked her whether she
would like to label some items for a car boot sale. He bought her cigarettes, cake and
chips. Later she went with a youth, Hill, to the defendant's home. The defendant
showed the victim a pornographic video and then told the victim to remove her trousers.
The defendant had sexual intercourse with the girl and next actively encouraged Hill to
also engage in sexual intercourse with her. He then told her if she told anyone he
would get his brother to kill her. He had sex with the girl on two other occasions. The
defendant was 55 and had convictions, but none of a sexual nature. He was of limited
intelligence. The sentencing judge noted that an offence of this type was the most serious type of unlawful sexual intercourse. Held. Unlawful sexual intercourse with a girl
under 13 carries a maximum sentence of life, as would rape on a girl under 13. The
sentence must reflect that the significance of an 11 year old girl consenting is limited.
This was not the very worse case of its kind and there was no extreme degradation,
therefore **7 years** not 10 years was appropriate. Had it been a fight 10 years would have
been appropriate. **6 years** concurrent for the incitement count remained.

R v Ssejjuko 1998 2 Cr App R (S) 262. The defendant pleaded guilty to sexual intercourse and indecent assault on a girl aged 11. He was acquitted of rape on the same girl.
In late 1996 he touched her breasts over her clothing. He said that was with her consent
and that she was flirtatious with him. In January 1997, he went in the early hours to the
mother's house when the mother was out and insisted he be let in. He woke the victim
up. Sexual intercourse took place. He said she was flirtatious, encouraging and consenting. He was 26 and of good character and expressed remorse. The judge said he
knew she was a virgin and it must have been painful for her as he caused her internal
injuries. He also said there was a degree of breach of trust because the mother had on
numerous occasions let him and his girlfriend look after her children. Held. The judge
was right in his observations but his view about the defendant's perception of her age
was wrong. Considering the authorities **2 years and 3 months concurrent** not 3 years
and 3 months consecutive.

R v M 2002 2 Cr App R (S) 99. The defendant was convicted of sexual intercourse of
a girl aged 12 and was found not guilty of rape. The parents of three children went out
for the evening leaving them with the victim who was 12 years 8 months, the defendant's 19 year old brother and another. During the evening the defendant and a friend
arrived and beer and cider were drunk. The defendant took the victim upstairs put his
hand inside her trousers, touched her vagina and had intercourse with her which lasted
two minutes. The victim told the parents. When interviewed the defendant denied
the offence. He was sentenced on the basis he knew she was 12, he knew she had had
a very great deal to drink and was greatly affected by it, that he was sexually experienced and persuaded her to agree, she was a virgin and he was in breach of trust. The

defendant was 20 and immature. The risk of re-offending was assessed as high with a high risk of harm to young females. Since sentence he was considered a suicide risk. The defence said there was no breach of trust. Held. In the broad view there was a breach of trust to enter their home and interfere with the victim. **3½ years** detention was not manifestly excessive.

R v Fidler 2001 1 Cr App R (S) 349. The defendant was convicted of unlawful sexual intercourse with an 11 year old girl. He was acquitted of rape. He was the boyfriend of the victim's mother and stayed intermittently at the home. He was a father figure to the girl. The defendant had intercourse with the girl in December 1998 and made her pregnant. The girl's child was born only 10 days after her mother had given birth to the defendant's child also. The child's birth was very traumatic, as she was not expecting it until it happened. When interviewed he said he was aware she had started having periods. The defendant was 24 and had an IQ of only 66 which is in the bottom 1%. He had three previous convictions for theft from graves and had served a prison sentence. The sentencing judge said that this was a grave offence and was not substantially less serious than rape. Held. The defendant knew that the girl had started her periods and was therefore at risk of becoming pregnant. He had a duty to treat the girl with paternal care rather than to seduce her. It was a grave case and he was in a position of trust. However, taking into account his IQ **3½ years** not 7 years.

Old cases. *R v Polly* 1997 1 Cr App R (S) 144.

Girl aged 13–15 – General

172.10   *R v Offord* 1999 1 Cr App R (S) 327. The defendant pleaded guilty to two counts of unlawful sexual intercourse with a 15 year old girl. Over 3 months there was consensual sex eight times. They were discovered when the girl's mother found a love letter he had written to her. He was 36, married with three children and four step children. The judge said he took the initiative and in a sense had corrupted her. He was treated as of good character. A psychiatrist said he was an inadequate, vulnerable man with a very disadvantaged childhood. Held. This was a serious offence by a man of mature years. **15 months** was not manifestly excessive.

R v Hancocks 2000 1 Cr App R (S) 82. The defendant pleaded guilty to unlawful sexual intercourse with a 13 year old girl, indecent assault and indecency with a child. The victim, who was almost 14, met the defendant as she was going to meet a friend. The victim did not have any money for the bus so asked the defendant for 37 pence. He asked the victim how old she was and was told 13. He offered her money if she would return to his flat with him. The defendant ordered a taxi and they went to a supermarket where he bought the victim some lager and cigarettes. After the two went back to the defendant's flat he began to undress her and performed oral sex on her. The victim then engaged in sexual intercourse with the defendant. He then performed oral sex on her again and she masturbated him. He tried to make her stay by holding her arm saying he wanted to have sex again. She managed to get free and run out. The defendant, who was 52 years of age, had previous convictions, though none for sexual offences. He expressed remorse but his risk of re-offending was assessed as high. Held. The maximum is 2 years. Taking account of the defendant's guilty plea and that he was not in a position of trust **9 months** not 18 months was appropriate.

Att-Gen's Ref. No. 39 of 2003 2004 1 Cr App R (S) 468. The defendant pleaded guilty to five offences of unlawful sexual intercourse with a girl under the age of 16 and six offences of indecent assault. The first victim, K, was 11 when the defendant first communicated with her via an internet chat room. She said that she was 16, the defendant said that he was 19 (in fact he was 32). They met a number of times. After about 6 months, just after her 13th birthday, the defendant initiated sexual contact and then consensual intercourse on at least 6 occasions as well as fellatio and masturbation;

sometimes in the presence of her friends. The defendant met C through K. After C's 13th birthday the defendant asked her to masturbate him and this soon led onto partial and then full intercourse. She also performed fellatio upon him after some coercion. Both girls experienced emotional problems after these experiences. He was 34, of good character and remorseful. He was sentenced under the Sexual Offences Act 1956. Held. Where a man considerably older than a teenager makes contact with young girls using the internet and this leads to sexual offences against the girls, it needs to be clearly understood that sentences will be to the top of the range. For unlawful sexual intercourse: **18 months** not 15 to run consecutively for each girl; for the indecent assaults (except count 19) 12 months rather than 3; for count 19 (the fellatio in respect of C) 18 months rather than 3 again to be consecutive for each girl. The total sentence of **5$^1/_2$ years** would be reduced to 4$^1/_2$ as this was a reference and an extended licence period of 2$^1/_2$ years was added.

For the rule about indecent assault with consent sentences should not exceed the 2 year maximum available for Sexual Offences Act 1956 s 6 see **INDECENT ASSAULT ON A WOMAN** – *Should the sentence exceed the 2 year max under SOA 1956 s 6?*

Girl aged 13–15 – Breach of trust

172.11   *R v Lane* 1999 1 Cr App R (S) 415. The defendant pleaded guilty at the Magistrates' Court to unlawful sexual intercourse with a girl who was aged 15 and two counts of indecent assault. He was doing building work for the mother of a friend of the victim. He met the friend, the victim and another girl and showed them his penis. The victim telephoned the defendant and initiated a sexually explicit conversation. He met her and one of her friends and took them to a secluded lane where they consented to masturbate him. On a separate occasion the defendant took the two girls to his house and the victim consented to sexual intercourse with him on two occasions during the same day. Later in the month he drove two other girls aged 14 and 15 to a canal where they masturbated him of their own volition. He touched one girl's breasts and kissed the other girl's breasts over her clothing. These were the indecent assault matters. The defendant was 31 and had two previous convictions though neither were of a sexual nature. Held. Important consideration should have been given to the extent to which the victim agreed to and encouraged the behaviour of the defendant. It may be said he was in a position of trust but that did not seriously aggravate the offence here. The indecent assaults were at the bottom of the scale. **9 months** not 15 months was appropriate.

R v Goy 2001 1 Cr App R (S) 43. The defendant pleaded guilty to unlawful sexual intercourse with a 15 year old. She was a baby-sitter for the defendant's daughter and stepdaughter. After she had put the children to bed he knelt between her legs and they kissed. Intercourse lasted about 3–4 minutes and he withdrew without ejaculating. It did not appear that she resisted him. The defendant, who was 24, had one previous conviction for burglary of a non-dwelling. Held. The aim of the legislation is to ensure that girls are protected. The victim was 15$^1/_2$ so there was not a vast discrepancy in age between them so **3 months** not 9 months.

Att-Gen's Ref. No 80 of 2000 2001 2 Cr App R (S) 72. The defendant pleaded guilty to indecent assault and four counts of unlawful sexual intercourse with a 13 year old girl. She was a virgin and met the defendant, as he was the stepbrother of a friend of her sister. She suggested sex and he was initially reluctant, as he didn't want to hurt her. The two began a sexual relationship. There was pressure on the girl not to see him but they ran away using a milk delivery van he used for work. Within hours police discovered them. The defendant, who was more than twice the victim's age, contacted the victim after he had been charged, which was a breach of his bail conditions. As a consequence the defendant served 22 days' imprisonment. He was sentenced to 100 hours' CSO which he had almost completed. Held. A custodial sentence should have been made at the first instance, however the defendant had served a period of imprisonment, and as it was a reference the **community service order** was undisturbed.

R v Reeves 2002 1 Cr App R (S) 15. The defendant pleaded guilty to attempted unlawful sexual intercourse with a 15 year old girl. There were two short attempts. He was 30 and of good character.**18 months** was not manifestly excessive.

R v Garrity 2002 1 Cr App R (S) 38. **12 months** not 18 for a 30 year old man who pleaded guilty to unlawful sexual intercourse with a 13 year old girl. He was 60 and of good character. The girl was vulnerable and damaged and had a mental age of 7–8. Had there been a trial and no remorse 2 years would not have been inappropriate.

Girl aged 13–15 – Girl becomes pregnant

172.12   *R v Clement* 2000 2 Cr App R (S) 153. The defendant pleaded guilty to three counts of unlawful sexual intercourse with girls under the age of 16. The defendant, who was 26 years of age, had sexual intercourse with a 14 year old girl at her home during her parents' absence. A few days later he had sex with her in his van. The victim told him her true age and he said it did not matter. The girl became pregnant. He took two other girls out in his van and had sexual intercourse with one of them off the road in an overgrown area. She was 13 years old and said it was painful. It lasted a few minutes and she said she wasn't ready for it. He stopped and went back to the van and told the other girl who was also 13 that he wanted to talk to her. The same thing happened to that girl. During the sex she twice asked him to leave her alone. He continued and then took the girls back and told them not to tell anyone. He had a borderline personality disorder. The judge gave him $1^1/_2$, $1^1/_2$ and 1 year consecutive. He gave him maximum credit for his early plea. Held. This was a campaign of sexual intercourse against underage girls, one of whom became pregnant. Nevertheless **3 years** not 4.

C Sexual Activity without penetration

Guideline remarks – Child victims

172.13   *R v Lennon* 1999 1 Cr App R (S) 19. The court reviewed forty three authorities on indecent assault on a child. Held. It is never easy to sentence in these cases. The circumstances of each case will vary greatly. The judge must tailor the sentence to the particular facts. In most cases the personal circumstances of the defendant will have to take second place behind the plain duty of the court to protect victims and to reflect the clear intention of Parliament that offences of this kind are to be met with greater severity than in former years when the position of the victim may not have been so clearly focused in the public eye.

R v Stapley 2001 1 Cr App R (S) 302. LCJ. The defendant, aged 67 and of good character, fondled the breasts of a 13 year old. He showed her indecent photographs. Held. The courts have to have regard to the public perception of the way offences of this sort are treated and have to make it plain, in order to discourage and to deter others, that custodial sentences will invariably be passed.

R v Corran 2005 Unreported 2/2/05. The Court considered CJA 2003 s 7 and 8. The presence of consent is material particularly for young defendants. The age of the defendant, of itself and when compared with the age of the victim is also an important factor. Factors will include the nature of the assault or penetrative activity and the period it lasted. Other factors include the nature of the relationship between the two and their respective characters and maturity, the number of occasions the assault occurred, the circumstances of the assault, the consequences for the victim, emotional and physically, the degree of remorse and the likelihood of repetition. Pre-Act authorities will continue to be of assistance, subject to them being viewed through the prism of the increased sentence for sexual assault from 10 to 14 years. In relation to s 7 offences, the custody threshold will not always be passed. Generally speaking, despite the similar maximum penalties s 7 offences will be less serious than s 8, 9 and 10 offences.

For cases under the old law see INDECENT ASSAULT – *Victim under 10, Victim aged 10–12* **and** *Victim 13–15*

D Sexual activity in the presence of a child, causing a child to watch sex act

Guideline remarks

172.14   *R v Corran* 2005 Unreported 2/2/05. *CJA 2003* s 11 and 12 offences will usually attract a lesser sentence than that appropriate for sexual activity with a child contrary to s 5, 7, 8, 9 or 10. Factors relevant to sentence will include the age and character of the defendant, the age of the child, the nature and duration of the sexual activity engaged or, in the case of s 12, depicted in the image, the number of occasions when the activity is observed, the impact on the child, the degree of remorse shown and the likelihood of repetition.

173   SEXUAL ASSAULT TOUCHING

173.1   Sexual Offences Act 2003 s 3

Touching another person who does not consent.

This section came into force on 1/5/04.

Triable either way. On indictment maximum 10 years. Summary maximum 6 months and/or £5,000.

Detention The offence is a specified offence enabling defendants aged 14–17 to be detained[49].

Imprisonment for public protection For offences committed on or after 4/4/05 when there is a significant risk to members of the public of serious harm etc. there is a mandatory duty to pass a sentence of imprisonment for public protection[50]. For offenders under 18 the duty is to pass detention for public protection or an extended sentence[51].

Notification For offences where the defendant was (a) under 18 and sentenced to imprisonment of at least 12 months or (b) the defendant was 18 or over and (i) the victim was under 18 or (ii) the defendant was sentenced to imprisonment or detained in a hospital or given community service for at least 12 months; the defendant must notify the police within 3 days (or 3 days from his/her release from imprisonment, hospital etc.) with his/her name, home address, national insurance number etc. and any change and addresses where s/he resides for 7 days[52] (in one or more periods) or more in any 12 month period[53]. See SEX OFFENDERS' REGISTER

Sexual Offences Prevention Order There is a discretionary power to make this order, when the notification (q.v.) criteria are present and when it is necessary to protect the public etc[54].

Working with children Where (a) the offence is against a child (aged under 18), (b) the defendant is aged 18 or over and (c) he is sentenced to 12 months or more or a

---

49 Powers of Criminal Courts (Sentencing) Act 2000 s 91(2)(a) as amended by Sexual Offences Act 2003 s 139 & Sch 6 Para 43(2)
50 Criminal Justice Act 2003 s 224–226
51 Criminal Justice Act 2003 s 226 and 228
52 Sexual Offences Act 2003 s 84(1)(c) & (6)
53 Sexual Offences Act 2003 s 83 & Sch 3 Para 18
54 Sexual Offences Act 2003 s 104 & Sch. 3

hospital order etc. the court must disqualify him from working with children unless satisfied he is unlikely to commit any further offences against a child when the court must state its reasons for not doing so[55]. For a defendant aged less than 18 at the time of the offence the court must order disqualification if he is sentenced to 12 months or more and the court is satisfied that the defendant is likely to commit a further offence against a child[56]. The court must state its reasons for so doing.

For sentencing for this behaviour before the change in the law see INDECENT ASSAULT ON A MAN and INDECENT ASSAULT ON A WOMAN

Guideline remarks

173.2 *Att-Gen's Ref. Nos. 91, 119 and 120 of 2002* 2003 2 Cr App R (S) 338. In *R v Millberry* 2003 2 Cr App R (S) 142 at para 8, the Lord Chief Justice said, 'There are, broadly three dimensions to consider in assessing the gravity of an individual offence of rape. The first is the degree of harm to the victim; the second is the level of culpability of the offender; and the third is the level of risk proposed by the offender to society. The gravity of each case will depend very much upon the circumstances and it will always be necessary to consider an individual case as a whole taking into account the three dimensions.'

It will be necessary to take account of similar considerations in all cases of sexual interference, whether amounting to rape or not. However, that is not all. In all classes of sexual offences, there will also be the need to deter others from acting in a similar fashion.

174   SEXUAL CAUSING A PERSON TO ENGAGE IN SEXUAL ACTIVITY WITHOUT CONSENT

174.1   Sexual Offences Act 2003 s 4

This section came into force on 1/5/04.

Where the activity involves the penetration of victim's anus or vagina, mouth with a penis or penetration of another person's anus or vagina with the victim's penis or something else by the victim or the other person's mouth with the victim's penis the offence is indictable only. Maximum sentence Life.

Offences with other activity are triable either way. On indictment maximum 10 years. Summary maximum 6 months and/or £5,000.

Automatic life Offences (including attempted offences) committed before 4/4/05 are specified offences for automatic life[57].

Dangerous Offender provisions For offences committed on or after 4/4/05 where there is a significant risk to members of the public of serious harm etc. there is a mandatory duty to pass a life sentence when it is justified and otherwise a sentence of imprisonment for public protection[58]. For offenders under 18 the duty is to pass detention for life, detention for public protection or an extended sentence[59].

Notification The defendant must notify the police within 3 days (or 3 days from his release from imprisonment, hospital etc.) with his name, home address, national

---

55 Criminal Justice and Court Services Act 2000 s 28
56 Criminal Justice and Court Services Act 2000 s 29
57 Powers of Criminal Courts (Sentencing) Act 2000 s 109(5)as amended by Sexual Offences Act 2003 s 139 & Sch 6 Para 43(3)
58 Criminal Justice Act 2003 s 225
59 Criminal Justice Act 2003 s 226 and 228

insurance number etc. and any change and addresses where he resides for 7 days[60] (in one or more periods) or more in any 12 month period[61]. See **Sex Offenders' Register**

Sexual Offences Prevention Order There is a discretionary power to make this order when it is necessary to protect the public etc[64].

Working with children Where (a) the offence is against a child (aged under 18), (b) the defendant is aged 18 or over and (c) he is sentenced to 12 months or more or a hospital order etc. the court must disqualify him from working with children unless satisfied he is unlikely to commit any further offences against a child when the court must state its reasons for not doing so[62]. For a defendant aged less than 18 at the time of the offence the court must order disqualification if he is sentenced to 12 months or more and the court is satisfied that the defendant is likely to commit a further offence against a child[63]. The court must state its reasons for so doing.

For sentencing for this behaviour before the change in the law see **Indecent Assault on a Man, Indecent Assault on a Woman** and where there is penetration see **Rape**.

Guideline remarks

174.2   *Att-Gen's Ref. Nos. 91, 119 and 120 of 2002* 2003 2 Cr App R (S) 338. In *R v Millberry* 2003 2 Cr App R (S) 142 at para 8, the Lord Chief Justice said, 'There are, broadly three dimensions to consider in assessing the gravity of an individual offence of rape. The first is the degree of harm to the victim; the second is the level of culpability of the offender; and the third is the level of risk proposed by the offender to society. The gravity of each case will depend very much upon the circumstances and it will always be necessary to consider an individual case as a whole taking into account the three dimensions.'

It will be necessary to take account of similar considerations in all cases of sexual interference, whether amounting to rape or not. However, that is not all. In all classes of sexual offences, there will also be the need to deter others from acting in a similar fashion.

Sexual Intercourse

For sexual intercourse without consent see **Rape**

For sexual intercourse with a girl under 13, see **Rape** and **Sexual Assaults etc. Children**

175   Sexual Offences Act 1956 s 5

175.1   Having unlawful sexual intercourse with a girl under 13.

Indictable only. Maximum sentence for full offence 10 years, and for an attempt 7 years.

This offence was abolished on 1/5/04. Offences since that date are charged under Sexual Offences Act 2003 s 9. See **Sexual Assault etc. Children**

---

60 Sexual Offences Act 2003 s 84(1)(c) & (6)
61 Sexual Offences Act 2003 s 83 & Sch. 3 Para 19
62 Criminal Justice and Court Services Act 2000 s 28
63 Criminal Justice and Court Services Act 2000 s 29
64 Sexual Offences Act 2003 s 104 & Sch. 3

Automatic life Offences committed before 4/4/05 are specified offences for automatic life[65].

Longer than Commensurate sentences and Extended sentences Sexual Offences Act 1956, s 5 is a sexual offence[66] for the purposes of passing a longer than commensurate sentence [Powers of Criminal Courts (Sentencing) Act 2000, s 80(2)] and an extended sentence (extending the licence) [Powers of Criminal Courts (Sentencing) Act 2000, s 85(2)(b)]. The orders cannot be made for offences committed before 30/9/98 or after 3/4/05. See EXTENDED SENTENCES and LONGER THAN COMMENSURATE SENTENCES

Notification The defendant must notify the police within 3 days[67] (or 3 days from his release from imprisonment, hospital etc.) with his name, home address, national insurance number etc. and any change and addresses where he resides for 7 days[68] (in one or more periods) or more in any 12 month period[69]. See SEX OFFENDERS' REGISTER

Sexual Offences Prevention Order There is a discretionary power to make this order when it is necessary to protect the public etc[72].

Working with children Where the defendant is aged 18 or over and he is sentenced to 12 months or more or a hospital order etc. the court must disqualify him from working with children unless satisfied he is unlikely to commit any further offences against a child when the court must state its reasons for not doing so[70]. For a defendant aged less than 18 at the time of the offence the court must order disqualification if he is sentenced to 12 months or more and the court is satisfied that the defendant will commit a further offence against a child[71]. The court must state its reasons for so doing.

For cases under the old and the new law see SEXUAL ASSAULTS ETC. CHILDREN – *Girl Aged Less than 13*

176   SEXUAL OFFENCES ACT 1956 s 6

176.1   Sexual intercourse with a girl aged under 16.

Triable either way. On indictment maximum 2 years. Summary maximum 6 months and/or £5,000.

This offence was abolished on 1/5/04. Offences from that date are charged under Sexual Offences Act 2003 s 9. See SEXUAL ASSAULT ETC. CHILDREN

Longer than Commensurate sentences and Extended sentences The offence is a sexual offence for the purposes of passing a longer than commensurate sentence[73] [Powers of Criminal Courts (Sentencing) Act 2000, s 80(2)] and an extended sentence (extending the licence) [Powers of Criminal Courts (Sentencing) Act 2000, s 85(2)(b)]. The orders cannot be made for offences committed before 30/9/98 or after 3/4/05. See EXTENDED SENTENCES and LONGER THAN COMMENSURATE SENTENCES

Notification If the defendant is aged 20 or over, he must notify the police within 3 days[74] (or 3 days from his release from imprisonment, hospital etc.) with his name,

65 Powers of Criminal Courts (Sentencing) Act 2000 s 109(5)
66 Powers of Criminal Courts (Sentencing) Act 2000 s 161(2)(a)
67 Sexual Offences Act 2003 s 80–82
68 Sexual Offences Act 2003 s 84(1)(c) & (6)
69 Sexual Offences Act 2003 s 83
70 Criminal Justice and Court Services Act 2000 s 28
71 Criminal Justice and Court Services Act 2000 s 29
72 Sexual Offences Act 2003 s 104 & Sch. 3
73 Powers of Criminal Courts (Sentencing) Act 2000 s 161(2)(a)
74 Sexual Offences Act 2003 s 80–82

home address, national insurance number etc. and any change and addresses where he resides for 7 days[75] (in one or more periods) or more in any 12 month period[76]. See **SEX OFFENDERS' REGISTER**

Sexual Offences Prevention Order There is a discretionary power to make this order when it is necessary to protect the public etc[79].

Working with children Where the defendant is aged 18 or over and he is sentenced to 12 months or more the court must disqualify him from working with children unless satisfied he is unlikely to commit any further offences against a child when the court must state its reasons for not doing so[77]. For a defendant aged less than 18 at the time of the offence the court must order disqualification if s/he is sentenced to 12 months or more and the court is satisfied that the defendant will commit a further offence against a child[78]. The court must state its reasons for so doing.

For rule about indecent assault with consent sentences should not exceed the 2 year maximum available for Sexual Offences Act 1956 s 6 see **INDECENT ASSAULT ON A WOMAN –** *Should the sentence exceed the 2 year max under Sexual Offences Act 1956 s 6?*

For cases under the old and the new law see **SEXUAL ASSAULTS ETC. CHILDREN –** *Girl aged 13–15*

177   SEXUAL OFFENCES ACT 1956 S 25 AND 26

177.1 This offence was abolished on 1/5/04. Offences since that date are charged under Sexual Offences Act 2003 s 9. See **PROSTITUTION, CHILD PROSTITUTES**

Section 25: Permitting a girl under 13 to use premises for sexual intercourse

Indictable only. Maximum sentence life.

Section 26: Permitting a girl under 16 to use premises for sexual intercourse

Triable either way. On indictment maximum 2 years. Summary maximum 6 months and/or £5,000.

Longer than Commensurate sentences and Extended sentences Sexual Offences Act 1956, s 25 and 26 are both sexual offences[80] for the purposes of passing a longer than commensurate sentence [Powers of Criminal Courts (Sentencing) Act 2000, s 80(2)] and an extended sentence (extending the licence) [Powers of Criminal Courts (Sentencing) Act 2000, s 85(2)(b)]. The orders cannot be made for offences committed before 30/9/98 or after 3/4/05. See **EXTENDED SENTENCES** and **LONGER THAN COMMENSURATE SENTENCES**

Working with children Where the defendant is aged 18 or over and s/he is sentenced to 12 months or more etc. the court must disqualify him/her from working with children unless satisfied s/he is unlikely to commit any further offences against a child when the court must state its reasons for not doing so[81]. For a defendant aged less than 18 at the time of the offence the court must order disqualification if s/he is sentenced to 12 months or more and the court is satisfied that the defendant will commit a further offence against a child[82]. The court must state its reasons for so doing.

---

75 Sexual Offences Act 2003 s 84(1)(c) & (6)
76 Sexual Offences Act 2003 s 83
77 Criminal Justice and Court Services Act 2000 s 28
78 Criminal Justice and Court Services Act 2000 s 29
79 Sexual Offences Act 2003 s 104 & Sch. 3
80 Powers of Criminal Courts (Sentencing) Act 2000 s 161(2)(a)
81 Criminal Justice and Court Services Act 2000 s 28
82 Criminal Justice and Court Services Act 2000 s 29

Guideline remarks

177.2 *Att-Gen's Ref. Nos. 91, 119 and 120 of 2002*, 2003 2 Cr App R (S) 338. In *R v Millberry* 2003 2 Cr App R (S) 142 at para 8, the Lord Chief Justice said, 'There are, broadly three dimensions to consider in assessing the gravity of an individual offence of rape. The first is the degree of harm to the victim; the second is the level of culpability of the offender; and the third is the level of risk proposed by the offender to society. The gravity of each case will depend very much upon the circumstances and it will always be necessary to consider an individual case as a whole taking into account the three dimensions.'

It will be necessary to take account of similar considerations in all cases of sexual interference, whether amounting to rape or not. However, that is not all. In all classes of sexual offences, there will also be the need to deter others from acting in a similar fashion.

Girl aged 13–15

177.2 *R v Sisson* 2002 1 Cr App R (S) 353. The defendant pleaded guilty to permitting premises to be used by a girl under 16 for sexual intercourse. The defendant who lived in Newcastle upon Tyne was a female friend of the mother of a girl T. T then aged 15 was a regular and welcome visitor to the defendant's home. The defendant accessed Internet chat rooms and a met a man from Hastings. She introduced T to the chat room and T met a man, M. T gave her age on the Internet as 17. The defendant told M that T was only 15. The man from Hastings travelled to Newcastle to meet T and M decided to join him. The defendant took them to her home where T was babysitting. M had sex with T. The next day T and the two men spent the afternoon together and then went to the defendant's home. T telephoned her parents to say she had been asked to baby-sit and she would be staying overnight. M again had sex with T. The girl had been given a quarter bottle of schnapps and some vodka and was encouraged to have sexual discussions with M. After a Newton hearing in which T gave evidence the judge found that T had been put under pressure to go into the bedroom. The defendant was 32 and had a child aged 11 who was severely disabled with autism and two younger children who were being looked after by her husband while the defendant was in prison. The judge found the defendant obtained a degree of pleasure of a perverted nature from what had occurred and it was a very gross breach of trust. Also she had set it up and put her under pressure to take part. Held. It was obvious why the men were travelling to Newcastle. **14 months** was a severe sentence but it was justified.

178 SEXUAL OFFENCES ACT 2003 S 62

178.1 Committing any offence with the intention of committing a relevant sexual offence.

This offence starts from 1/5/04.

Triable either way. On indictment maximum 10 years. Summary maximum 6 months and/or £5,000.

Imprisonment for public protection For offences committed on or after 4/4/05 when there is a significant risk to members of the public of serious harm etc. there is a mandatory duty to pass a sentence of imprisonment for public protection[83]. For offenders under 18 the duty is to pass detention for public protection or an extended sentence[84].

83 Criminal Justice Act 2003 s 224–226
84 Criminal Justice Act 2003 s 226 and 228

Longer than Commensurate sentences and Extended sentences Sexual Offences Act 2003 s 62 is a sexual offence[85] for the purposes of passing a longer than commensurate sentence [Powers of Criminal Courts (Sentencing) Act 2000, s 80(2)] and an extended sentence (extending the licence) [Powers of Criminal Courts (Sentencing) Act 2000, s 85(2)(b)]. These provisions will continue to apply to offences committed after 29/9/98 and before 4/4/05. See EXTENDED SENTENCES and LONGER THAN COMMENSURATE SENTENCES

Notification The defendant must notify the police within 3 days[86] (or 3 days from his release from imprisonment, hospital etc.) with his name, home address, national insurance number etc. and any change and addresses where he resides for 7 days[87] (in one or more periods) or more in any 12 month period[88]. See SEX OFFENDERS' REGISTER

Sexual Offences Prevention Order There is a discretionary power to make this order when it is necessary to protect the public etc[91].

Working with children Where the defendant is aged 18 or over and he is sentenced to 12 months or more or a hospital order etc. the court <u>must</u> disqualify him from working with children unless satisfied he is unlikely to commit any further offences against a child when the court must state its reasons for not doing so[89]. For a defendant aged less than 18 at the time of the offence the court must order disqualification if he is sentenced to 12 months or more and the court is satisfied that the defendant will commit a further offence against a child[90]. The court must state its reasons for so doing.

Guideline remarks

178.2   *R v Wisniewski* 2004 The Times 20/12/04. The defendant pleaded guilty to two counts of battery with intent to commit a sexual offence (s 62). Held. The offence is new but the conduct is not new. Pre-Act authorities particularly *R v Millberry* 2003 2 Cr App R (S) 142 (see RAPE), *Att-Gen's Ref. Nos. 37 etc. of 2003* 2004 1 Cr App R (S) 499 (see RAPE) and *R v Nelson* 2002 1 Cr App R (S) 565 (see EXTENDED SENTENCES) should continue to guide sentencers. In relation to battery with intent, the factors of particular relevance include the method and degree of force used, the nature and extent of the indecency perpetrated and intended, the degree of vulnerability of and harm to the victim, the duration and general circumstances of the attack, including the time, day and place where it occurred and the level of risk posed by the offender to the public. The good character of the offender will afford only limited mitigation. In consequence of the maximum sentence of 10 years compared with life for rape, save where a great deal of violence is used, the level of sentence for battery with intent will generally be lower than the appropriate sentence for rape.

Cases

178.3   *R v Wisniewski* 2004 The Times 20/12/04. The defendant pleaded guilty at the Magistrates' Court to two counts of battery with intent to commit a sexual offence (s 62). In the early hours the first victim was walking on her own and the defendant asked her for a light. She was rude to him and kept on walking. He asked for a light again and took hold of her by the shoulder and then by her waist. He lifted her over a wall and she struggled and swore. He kept hold of her jacket and she managed to struggle free. She had bruising and scratching and some fingernail marks on her shoulder.

---

85 Powers of Criminal Courts (Sentencing) Act 2000 s 161(2)(a)
86 Sexual Offences Act 2003 s 80–82
87 Sexual Offences Act 2003 s 84(1)(c) & (6)
88 Sexual Offences Act 2003 s 83
89 Criminal Justice and Court Services Act 2000 s 28
90 Criminal Justice and Court Services Act 2000 s 29
91 Sexual Offences Act 2003 s 104 & Sch. 3

When she got home she was sick. About a week later another woman was walking home after a night out. He appeared to have her mobile in his hand and was trying to tempt her with it. She walked on. Further on he again held out the mobile and seized her saying, "You and me sex, sex, you and me." He dragged her into a church yard and forced her to the ground. She shouted and he lay on top of her. She was hysterical and a man heard her screams and came out. The defendant ran off. The victim was very upset and tearful. In interview the defendant denied the offence but he was picked out on an ID parade. He was of good character. The Judge sentenced him on the basis that in the second incident the intent was to rape and made a deportation order. Held. Both attacks were at night. No weapon was used or blows struck and the indecency that actually occurred was of a limited nature. The victim in the second incident was deeply upset. **18 months** not 2 years consecutive to **3¹/₂ years** not 5 making **5 years** not 7.

SHIPPING OFFENCES

Where the prosecution is connected with Health and Safety see **HEALTH AND SAFETY –** *Shipping*

SLAUGHTERHOUSES

See **ENVIRONMENTAL OFFENCES –** *Slaughterhouses and animal incinerators*

179   SOCIAL SECURITY FRAUD/HOUSING BENEFIT FRAUD ETC

179.1   Social Security Administration Act 1992, s 112

False representations for obtaining benefit etc.

Summary only. Maximum 1 month and/or Level 5 fine (£5,000). When the Criminal Justice Act 2003 s 280(2) & Sch. 26 Para 47 is in force the maximum will increase to 51 weeks. The Home Office do not expect this to occur before September 2006.

Social Security Administration Act 1992, s 111A & 114

Dishonest representation to obtain benefit/fraudulent evasions

Triable either way. On indictment maximum 7 years. Summary maximum 6 months and/or £5,000.

The Criminal Justice Act 2003 creates a summary maximum sentence of 51 weeks, a minimum sentence of 28 weeks and Custody plus. The Home Office says they do not expect to introduce these provisions before September 2006.

Statistics The Court in *R v Graham* 2005 1 Cr App R (S) 640 at para 26 was told that in 2002 benefit fraud was estimated at £2 billion. There were between 12,000 and 14,000 prosecutions with 80% dealt with at the Magistrates' Court. Less than 150 defendants were sent to prison. The average sentence was between 6 and 9 months.

Many offences can also be charged under the Theft Act 1968, false instruments, forgery etc. See also **THEFT ETC**

Guideline case

179.2   *R v Stewart* 1987 85 Cr App R 66. LCJ. Welfare benefit offences are easy to commit and difficult and expensive to track down. However, it must be remembered that they are non-violent, non-sexual and non-frightening crimes. In some cases immediate unsuspended imprisonment (or youth custody) is unavoidable. The sentence will depend on an almost infinite variety of factors, only some of which it is possible to forecast. The factors are (i) a guilty plea; (ii) the amount involved and the length of time over which the defalcations were persisted in (bearing in mind that a large total may in fact represent a very small amount weekly); (iii) the circumstances in which the offence began (e.g. there is a plain difference between a legitimate claim which becomes false owing to a change of situation and on the other hand a claim which is false from the very beginning); (iv) the use to which the money is put (the provision of household necessities is more venial than spending the money on unnecessary luxury); (v) previous character; (vi) matters special to the offender, such as illness, disability, family difficulties, etc; (vii) any voluntary repayment of the amounts overpaid. Before sentencing the offender the court should consider (i) whether a custodial sentence is really necessary? The fraud cases dealt with in the Crown Court are likely to be relatively serious and a non-custodial sentence may often be inappropriate; (ii) if a custodial sentence is necessary, can the court make a community service order as an equivalent to imprisonment, or can it suspend the whole sentence? (The law for suspending sentences has changed since these guidelines were issued.) It seems to us that a suspended sentence or (especially) a community service order may be an ideal form of punishment in many of these cases; (iii) if not, what is the shortest sentence the court can properly impose? We do not think that the element of deterrence should play a large part in the sentencing of this sort of case in the Crown Court.

R v Graham 2005 1 Cr App R (S) 640. The Stewart guidelines do not need revision save to take account of inflation. There will be cases in which the court will be justified in passing sentences with a deterrent element.

Magistrates' Court Sentencing Guidelines January 2004 – S 112

179.3   For a first time offender pleading not guilty. Entry point. Is it serious enough for a community penalty? Examples of aggravating factors for the offence are claim fraudulent from the start, fraudulent claims over a long period, large amount, organised group offence and planned deceptions. Examples of mitigating factors for the offence misunderstanding the regulations, pressured by others and small amount. Examples of mitigation are age, health (physical or mental), co-operation with the police, genuine remorse and voluntary compensation. Give reasons if not awarding compensation.

For details about the guidelines see **MAGISTRATES' COURT SENTENCING GUIDELINES** at page 483.

Compensation – Guideline case

179.4   *R v Stewart* 1987 85 Cr App R 66. LCJ. So far as compensation is concerned, where no immediate custodial sentence is imposed, and the amount of overpayment is below, say, £1,000 or thereabouts, a compensation order is often of value. This will usually only be the case when the defendant is in work. Counsel for the Crown must be equipped with the relevant information to enable the court to come to a proper conclusion on this matter. [Since 1987 the value of money has fallen considerably.]

Compensation – Will the department attempt to recover the sum? Duty to ascertain

179.5   *R v Stewart* 1987 85 Cr App R 66. LCJ. It may well be advisable as a first pre-caution for the court to inquire what steps the department proposes to take to recover their loss from the offender. Counsel for the Crown should be equipped to assist the court on this aspect of the matter.

Over £1,000 under £20,000 – Guideline Case

179.6 *R v Stewart* 1987 85 Cr App R 66. LCJ. A short term of up to about **9 or 12 months** will usually be sufficient in a contested case where the overpayment is less than, say, £20,000. (As amended by *R v Graham* 2005 1 Cr App R (S) 640.

Over £1,000 under £10,000 – Cases

179.7 *R v Rosenburg* 1999 1 Cr App R (S) 365. The defendant was convicted of nine counts of obtaining property by a deception. The defendant claimed income support on the basis of an alleged degenerate arthritic condition and that he wasn't working or receiving income. In fact he was running an agency for dancers. The paperwork for the business was found at his house and £22,000 was paid into a bank account and £21,000 into her wife's bank account during the period. He received rent from two properties let to tenants and during the period sold a Porsche car and a villa in Spain. The loss in the counts was £2,500, which were treated by the judge as specimens for a total loss of about £30,000 over a $2^1/_2$ year period. Held. *R v Clark* 1996 2 Cr App R (S) 351 meant he had to sentenced for the £2,500 loss only. **2 years** not $2^1/_2$ years.

R v Evans 2000 1 Cr App R (S) 144. The defendant was convicted of twenty counts of furnishing false information and procuring the execution of securities by deception. She had earlier pleaded guilty to four further similar counts. Over $4^1/_2$ years she was involved in a housing benefit fraud involving eleven different claims, which were repeated over and over again. The prosecution said they were sample counts for a £25,000 fraud. The total loss in the twenty four counts was £2,807. She gave a slightly wrong National Insurance number, an address that did not exist, false details of employers, a variety of false names and submitted false tenancy agreements. She was 32 and had two dishonesty convictions. The judge described it as a highly sophisticated, professional fraud and that she was the major player. Held. Because of earlier authorities the court was not able to sentence on the basis of sample counts. Therefore **2 years** not 3.

R v Graham Re W 2005 1 Cr App R (S) 640 at 652. The defendant was convicted of thirteen counts of benefit fraud. He claimed sickness benefit to which he was not entitled from May 1997 to July 2001. In that time he worked as a street trader and there was evidence that he had made sixteen trips to France and that on three of those trips he came back with alcohol and cigarettes in his car. He also made payments on a mortgage from September 1998 totalling £21,600. The first count was a charge of false accounting relating to a Form A2 completed by the defendant in 1997. Counts 2–11 related to falsification of a document required for an accounting purpose, namely a paid order in his name, covering the period August 2000 to July 2001. Count 12 was obtaining £1,048.74 on or about April 28 1997 by representing that he was entitled to claim income support and was therefore entitled to mortgage interest benefit. Count 13 was an identical offence committed on June 14 2001. The total period in issue was in excess of £90,000 but the sums involved in the counts in the indictment totalled £3,100. The judge approached sentencing on the basis that the sum in excess of £90,000 could all be traced back to the fraudulent A2 form. The defendant, 64, was a family man with daughters and grandchildren. His father was dying from cancer at the time of sentencing and had since died. The defendant suffered from chronic degenerative osteoarthritis. He was not able to sit or stand for long periods or walk unaided for further than 50metres. He had undergone numerous operations to his knee and shoulder. As a result he suffered from depression. Since being sentenced he had undergone surgery twice and needed crutches. Held. The judge erred in imposing a sentence on count 1 intended to reflect the receipt of over £90,000. The defendant only stood to be sentenced for offences of fraud totalling approximately £3,100. **12 months** not 30 months.

£10,000 and up to £20,000

179.8   *R v Smethurst* 1998 Unreported 23/11/98. The defendant pleaded guilty to three offences of obtaining property by deception and two offences of false accounting. He asked for eighty four similar offences to be taken into consideration. Between 1991 and 1996 the defendant defrauded the DSS of £12,258.60. He had started legitimately to claim benefit for himself and his partner in February 1990, but when his partner started to work in April 1991 he failed to disclose that. She continued in work until October 1996. He was interviewed on three occasions. He admitted that his wife had been working, but initially claimed that he did not think that she was earning sufficient to affect their entitlement to benefit. Later he admitted that he knew he should have reported that she was working and he realised that, if he had done so, it would have reduced the benefits they were receiving. He was 44 and had a number of minor convictions for dishonesty as a young man, but he fell to be treated as if he was of good character. There were two character references. **9 months** not 21.

R v Bendris 2000 2 Cr App R (S) 183. The defendant pleaded guilty to conspiracy to obtain property by a deception. Over $4^1/_2$ years he claimed Income Support for a fictitious male using a document that stated that the person had entered the UK in 1994 and a false passport with the defendant's photograph on it. After just over three years his brother continued the scheme with the defendant signing a new claim form to give substance to the conspiracy. The amount claimed was in excess of £10,000. He was 35 and had one conviction in 1998 for obtaining by a deception for which he received a non-custodial sentence. Held. Applying *R v Ellison* 1998 2 Cr App R (S) 382 **10 months** not 15.

Old case. *R v Ellison* 1998 2 Cr App R (S) 382, (for a summary of this case see the first edition of the book.)

Top of the range offences – Guideline case

179.9   *R v Stewart* 1987 85 Cr App R 66. LCJ. At the top of the range, requiring substantial sentences, perhaps of $2^1/_2$ **years and upwards**, are the carefully organised frauds on a large scale in which considerable sums of money are obtained, often by means of frequent changes of name or address or of forged or stolen documents. These offenders are in effect professional fraudsmen, as is often apparent from their previous records. They have selected the welfare departments as an easy target for their depredations and have made a profitable business out of defrauding the public in this way. The length of the custodial sentence will depend in the first instance on the scope of the fraud. Of course, as in all fraud cases, there may be a variety of mitigating circumstances and in particular a proper discount for a plea of guilty should always be given.

R v Graham 2005 1 Cr App R (S) 640. The defendant pleaded guilty at the Magistrates Court and at the first opportunity to ten offences of benefit fraud. She asked the court to take four hundred and seventy one offences into consideration. She received benefits from December 1992 to 2002. Investigations revealed that she had been in employment since June 1992. During the period in question she had received income support totalling £34,500 and housing benefit of £16,000. Five of the charges related to housing benefit and five to income support. The four hundred and seventy one offences she asked to be taken into consideration related to income support paid on a weekly basis from September 1993 to February 2003. When arrested and interviewed she made full admissions. The defendant, 36, lived with her dependant son who was 17 at the time of sentence. She was of good character and showed genuine remorse for her actions. She was deeply distressed by her contact with the police and courts. The offences were committed against a background of very modest earnings and she had been unable to cope. She had suffered from abusive relationships in the past which had had a bad effect on the defendant and on her son who had been repeatedly excluded from school. Medical records showed she suffered from severe depression and had attempted suicide on two occasions. Held. There were serious aggravating features; she persisted in her fraud over a period of 10 years and her claims to benefit were fraudulent from the outset. **18 months** not 2 years 6 months.

See also **TAX FRAUD**

SOLDIERS

See **ARMED FORCES, MEMBERS OF**

180   SOLICITORS

180.1   There is no tariff for defendants who are solicitors. The fact a defendant is a solicitor may or may not be relevant to the sentence. Where the offence is committed as part of the defendant's work as a solicitor it is likely to be a relevant factor. In a case of careless driving it is likely to be irrelevant.

Theft etc.

180.2   *R v Neary* 1999 1 Cr App R (S) 431. The defendant pleaded guilty at the first opportunity to twelve counts of theft. Since 1971 he had been a solicitor who became a senior partner in a distinguished firm. In the early 1990s his property interests, business and consultancy work gave him a 'very great income'. However, he was badly affected by the property crash. He managed a family trust fund, which had property which was let to Glasgow District Council. The defendant kept the rents and failed to pay the lessor and the lease was forfeited. The fund lost between £800,000 and £1.1 m. He spent the money on a business venture, repaying a bank loan, reducing his overdraft etc. The amount stolen was £135,230. In the property company he was entrusted to manage he stole £153,500 using 2/3 of the money to pay off a loan. The total loss was £288,730, which was stolen between November 1991 and November 1992. When interviewed he denied the offences and about 9 months later in 1994, he left the country. In 1997 he returned voluntarily and the proceedings against him started. From then he co-operated with the authorities. He was of previous unblemished character with an impressive array of testimonials including references to his charity work. In 1995 he was made bankrupt. The defendant had been an international rugby player. He had played for England forty three times and had been captain for two years. Held. *R v Clark* 1998 2 Cr App R (S) 95 only provides guidelines. Each case has its own special features. It was a very serious continuing breach of trust by a man in a very senior position. **5 years** was not manifestly excessive.

R v Torkonaik 2005 1 Cr App R (S) 126. The defendant was convicted of fifteen counts of theft, two of obtaining a money transfer by deception, one of false accounting, two of obtaining property by deception, one of forgery and one of perjury. He was a 36 year old solicitor who stole £300,000 from his clients, the Legal Services Commission and the DSS. The most serious offence was committed against B, who fell off a girder and sustained serious multiple injuries and fractures. From the resulting £100,000 settlement, B was told it was £18,000 from which the defendant kept £3,000. The defendant put £75,000 into a bond in his own name and failed to repay £10,000 to the LSC in costs. Another offence involved the theft of £1,100 from a dead man's estate. The defendant stole large sums from other personal injury clients and failed to repay sums to the LSC. In another case, he failed to repay the LSC costs (£113,000) for a civil claim against a local authority. He also continued to claim a client's pension from the DSS after that client had died. Proceedings were brought by the Law Society in respect of B's claim. The defendant lied about his possession of certain crucial papers (which were in fact in the boot of his car). Held. Considering *R v Clarke* 1998 2 Cr App R 137, the **8 years** was not manifestly excessive. There was considerable damage to the public confidence in the legal system and there was the greater public interest that the court should take a severe and stern view of such offences. This was a bad breach of trust where the victims were vulnerable and weak who had a particular need to be able to repose absolute confidence and trust in the defendant as their solicitor. The offences of theft deserved 7 years; in addition the offences of perjury and forgery were particularly serious as they were committed by an officer of the Court. Consecutive sentences were appropriate as a matter of principle. The fact that funds were available to pay compensation were not a feature of mitigation.

See also **Money Laundering** – *Solicitors*

Specimen

See **Failing to Provide a Specimen**

181 Speeding

181.1   Road Traffic Regulation Act 1984 s 89 (1)

Summary only. Maximum Level 3 fine, £1,000. Level 4 (£2,500) if on motorway. Discretionary disqualification. Obligatory endorsement. 3–6 points.

Magistrates' Court Sentencing Guidelines January 2004

181.2   For a first time offender pleading not guilty. Entry point. Is a discharge or a fine appropriate? Examples of aggravating factors for the offence are LGV, HGV, PCV, PSV, or minicabs, location/time of day/visibility, serious risk and towing caravan or trailer. Examples of mitigation for the offence are emergency established. Examples of mitigation are co-operation with police and fixed penalty not taken up for a valid reason. Consider disqualification until test is passed where appropriate. New drivers 6 points means automatic revocation of the licence.

Legal speed limit	Excessive speed mph	Fine	Guideline penalty points
20–30 mph	Up to 10 mph	A	3
40–50 mph	Up to 15 mph		
60–70 mph	Up to 20 mph		
20–30 mph	From 11–20 mph	A	4 or 5
40–50 mph	From 16–25 mph		or
60–70 mph	From 21–30 mph		Disqualify for up to 42 days
20–30 mph	From 21–30 mph	B	6
40–50 mph	From 26–35 mph		or
60–70 mph	From 31–40 mph		Disqualify for up to 56 days

Starting point fine A (50% of weekly take home pay/weekly benefit payment)
Starting point fine B (100% of weekly take home pay/weekly benefit payment)

For details about the guidelines see MAGISTRATES' COURT SENTENCING GUIDELINES at page 483.

182   STALKING

182.1   Offences Against the Person Act 1861, s 18, 20 and 47

For penalties see **ABH** and OFFENCES AGAINST THE PERSON ACT **1861** s **18** and OFFENCES AGAINST THE PERSON ACT **1861** s **20**

182.2   Research Lorraine Sheridan, a lecturer in psychology at Leicester University who has written extensively about stalking has identified four types of stalker. 1. Angry or bitter former partners account for half of the incidents. They often threaten violence against their ex-partners and his or her property. The threats should be taken seriously. 2. Infatuated harassers account for 20% and see their target as a fantasy "beloved". They generally seek out their victims by non-malicious means. These include leaving notes, quizzing their friends or loitering near their address or place of work, hoping for an accidental meeting. The threat is not considered high risk and such behaviour can often be discouraged through discussion. 3. Delusional fixation stalkers are more sinister. They genuinely believe they are having a relationship with their victim. Making up 15% of stalkers, they talk about their sexual intentions, rather than romantic love, and often suffer from mental illness or borderline personality disorders. They might bombard their victims, who are often professionals of elevated status, with telephone calls, letters or visits. Victims are advised to take legal advice. 4. The most dangerous type is sadistic stalkers who make up 13% of cases. They consider their target to be their prey and want to make their target feel powerless. They target those who seem stable and content, leaving subtle, nasty clues to show they have been in their victims' homes. They should be taken very seriously. Victims should consider moving to a secret address. www.le.ac.uk/pc/lph1/lph1.html

ABH

182.3   *R v Smith* 1998 1 Cr App R (S) 138. The defendant was convicted of ABH. The defendant developed an obsession with a woman with whom he had had a relationship. She made it clear the relationship was completely over. Over 4 years he telephoned her, sent her offensive letters, watched her, loitered outside her place of work, followed her, and confronted her even after she told him how distressed she was. He was warned by her employers, the police and was bound over by the Magistrates' Court on several occasions. He brought County Court proceedings against her, which were dismissed and the judge warned him. The psychiatrist said the victim suffered clinical depression, which would require a year's treatment. He also said she would remain mentally scarred for life. The defendant was not mentally ill but had suffered depression at one stage. The judge, unlike the reports, was satisfied he still presented a risk to the victim. Held. Here the judge was entitled to disagree with the writers of the reports. The defendant had no previous convictions. **21 months** substituted for $2^1/_2$ years.

R v Haywood 1998 1 Cr App R (S) 358. The defendant pleaded guilty to two counts of ABH and then later pleaded to another ABH. The defendant developed an obsession with a nurse with whom he had had a relationship. After their relationship broke down he shouted at her, he telephoned her, appeared outside her house, hammered on the door, sent a frightening note to her, wrote to her employers saying she was stealing drugs from the hospital and threw a rock through her window. She obtained an injunction and he put her obituary in the local paper. Notices were put up at her place of work, windows broken, her windscreen shattered, and many taxis ordered for her. She became mentally and physically ill. He was arrested and pleaded guilty. It had been over a 2 month period. When in custody he ordered another taxi and arranged for a firm of undertakers to send her a letter treating her as a client. He was convicted of two counts (one before and one after his arrest) of ABH and sentenced to **3 years and 1 year consecutive**. On the day he was sentenced the victim received another letter containing a picture of a gravestone with her details on it saying she died in pain. She continued to receive threatening and frightening letters. He instructed solicitors to falsely claim property from her and telephone messages were left at her place of work. She believed she was going to be killed. He had no other convictions. For these later matters he was sentenced to 3 years consecutive. The first 3 year sentence was reduced to 2 so making the sentence **6 years** not 7 years.

R v Notice 2000 1 Cr App R (S) 75. The defendant was convicted of ABH. The victim aged 48 worked as a manager at a building society. He looked into her office most weekdays, mouthed obscenities at her, watched her leave work and left a note under her windscreen. The company then installed cameras and a security guard. She started to keep a log. The defendant continued to stare and make lewd remarks. He banged on her car roof in stationary traffic and approached her in the street saying he loved her. She was moved to another branch. The defendant was arrested but 7 months later he spoke to her in a street in an aggressive tone. She was counselled for distress and a psychiatrist said she suffered from a generalised anxiety state. The defendant claimed she was harassing him. He had convictions for minor matters including three cases of indecent exposure. He was not mentally ill. There was 19 months between the first and last incident with 16 specified incidents. **15 months** not 2 years.

Offences Against the Person Act 1861, s 20

182.4   Old case. *R v Bustow* 1997 1 Cr App R (S) 144.

STATEMENTS, GIVING FALSE

For the making of false witness statements see PERVERTING THE COURSE OF JUSTICE/CONTEMPT OF COURT/PERJURY ETC – *Statement, making a false witness*

STOP

See FAILING TO STOP/FAILING TO REPORT

183   SUPPLY OF DRUGS (CLASS A, B AND C)

183.1   Misuse of Drugs Act 1971, s 4(3)(a)–(c) and 5(3)

Triable either way unless the defendant could be sentenced to a 7 year minimum sentence under the Powers of Criminal Courts (Sentencing) Act 2000, s 110(2) when the offence is triable only on indictment. On indictment maximum Life for Class A drugs, 14 years for Class B and C[92] drugs (for offences committed before 29/1/04 the maximum for Class C drugs is 5 years). Summary maximum 6 months and/or £5,000 for Class A and B drugs and 3 months and/or £2,500 for Class C drugs.

92 Criminal Justice Act 2003 s 284 & Sch. 28 para 1

The Criminal Justice Act 2003 creates a summary maximum sentence of 51 weeks, a minimum sentence of 28 weeks and Custody plus. The Home Office says they do not expect to introduce these provisions before September 2006.

CHAPTERS in this book are in bold capitals. The *paragraph titles* are in bold italics. Where a chapter like this one has subsections, the **subsections** are in lower case bold.

Approach What matters is the scale of the dealing, which is not solely determined by the amount of drugs found[93]. As the Court of Appeal has determined courts are not to distinguish between drugs in the same class[94]. All the Court of Appeal cases about drugs in the same class can be used to estimate the likely sentence. So if the drug you are considering is heroin, cases for cocaine and ecstasy will provide assistance.

Confiscation For all supply offences[95] the court <u>must</u> follow the Proceeds of Crime Act 2002 procedure for offences committed on or after 24 March 2003[96] and Drug Trafficking Act 1994 procedure for offences committed before that date.

Drug Abstinence Order This was repealed on 4 April 2005.

Minimum sentences For offences committed on or after 30 September 1997, supply carries a minimum 7 years for third Class A drug trafficking offence[97]. See *Persistent Class A offenders*

Travel Restrictions For offences committed on or after 1/4/02 where 4 or more years' imprisonment is appropriate the Court is under a duty to consider whether it is appropriate to make a travel restriction order[98]. Where there is a direction in the order the Secretary of State may retain the defendant's passport[99].

Working with children Where the offence is supplying, offering to supply or being concerned in the supply Class A drugs to a child (aged less than 18), the defendant is aged 18 or over and s/he is sentenced to 12 months or more etc. hospital order etc. the court must disqualify him/her from working with children unless satisfied s/he is unlikely to commit any further offences against a child when the court must state its reasons for not doing so[100]. For a defendant aged less than 18 at the time of the offence the court <u>must</u> order disqualification if s/he is sentenced to 12 months or more and the court is satisfied that the defendant will commit a further offence against a child[101]. The court must state its reasons for so doing.

This chapter is divided up into (A) General, (B) Amphetamine, (C) Cannabis, (D) Cocaine, (E) Ecstasy, (F) Heroin. (G) LSD, (H) Magic Mushrooms, (I) Opium, (J) Steroids and (K) Permitting premises to be used for the supply of drugs.

---

93 *R v Singh* 1988 10 Cr App R (S) 402 at 406
94 *R v Thompson* 1997 2 Cr App R (S) 223
95 Proceeds of Crime Act 2002 s 75 and Sch 2 para 1(1)(a) (b) and (c) or Drug Trafficking Act 1994 s 1(1)(a) (depending on the date of the offence).
96 Proceeds of Crime Act 2002 (Commencement No 5, Transitional Provisions, Savings and Amendment) Order 2003
97 Powers of Criminal Courts (Sentencing) Act 2000, s 110
98 Criminal Justice and Police Act 2001 s 33
99 Criminal Justice and Police Act 2001 s 33(5)
100 Criminal Justice and Court Services Act 2000 s 28
101 Criminal Justice and Court Services Act 2000 s 29

A General

Crown Court statistics – England and Wales – Males 21+

Production, supply and possession with intent to supply a controlled drug
183.2

Year	Plea	Total Numbers sentenced	Type of sentence %					Average length of custody (months)
			Discharge	Fine	Community sentence	Suspended sentence	Custody	
Class A								
2002	Guilty	2,398	1	1	11	1	86	40.9
	Not guilty	581	1	1	2	0	96	64.7
2003	Guilty	2,731	1	0	13	2	84	41.1
	Not guilty	598	0	1	3	1	94	66
Class B								
2002	Guilty	892	3	4	33	4	56	19.5
	Not guilty	184	1	2	11	3	82	28.5
2003	Guilty	1,016	3	4	40	5	48	19.6
	Not guilty	167	3	4	18	2	71	26.8
Class C								
2002	Guilty	17	12	–	47	–	41	9.4
	Not guilty	4	–	–	–	–	100	35.3
2003	Guilty	23	13	9	30	4	39	24.7
	Not guilty	3	33	–	33	–	33	30

There were 61 and 107 offences of supply etc. offences in 2002 and 2003 respectively where the class of the drug was not recorded. For details and explanations about the statistics in the book see page vii.

Class A – Guideline cases

183.3   *R v Aramah* 1982 76 Cr App R 190. LCJ. The sentence will largely depend on the degree of involvement, the amount of trafficking and the value of the drugs being handled. It is seldom that a sentence of less than 3 years [now increased, see *R v Singh* 1998 below will be justified and the nearer the source of supply the defendant is shown to be, the heavier will be the sentence. There may well be cases where sentences similar to those appropriate to large scale importers may be necessary. It is unhappily all too seldom that those big fish amongst the suppliers get caught.

R v Singh 1988 10 Cr App R (S) 402 at 406. LCJ. The starting point for possession with intent to supply Class A drugs 'is in general **5 years at least**.' following a conviction. It should be noted … that the assistance which can be derived from the amount of the drug actually found in the possession of the defendant is limited. It is the scale and nature of the dealing which are the material factors.

Class A – Guideline remarks

183.4   *R v Beevor* 2001 2 Cr App R (S) 362. The sentence largely depended on the degree of involvement, the amount of trafficking and the value of the drugs. The purity of the drugs needed consideration. Personal mitigation however strong does not necessarily reduce the sentence below a certain level.

Att-Gen's Ref. Nos. 99–102 of 2004 2005 Unreported 7/2/05. Generally speaking those responsible for organising the importation of Class A drugs will attract somewhat higher sentences than for those organising distribution in this country. The difference is not likely to be great.

Class B and cannabis – Guideline case

183.5   *R v Aramah* 1982 76 Cr App R 190. LCJ. Class B particularly cannabis. The supply of massive quantities will justify sentences in the region of **10 years** for those playing anything more than a subordinate role. Otherwise the bracket should be between **1 to 4 years** imprisonment, depending on the scale of the operation. Supplying a number of smaller sellers – wholesale if you like – comes at the top of the bracket. At the lower end will be the retailer of a small amount to a customer. Where there is no commercial motive (for example, where cannabis is supplied at a party), the offence may well be serious enough to justify a custodial sentence.

See also **Cannabis, Does reclassification affect the guidelines for cannabis supply?**

Magistrates' Court Sentencing Guidelines January 2004 – Class A, B and C

183.6   For a first time offender pleading not guilty. Entry point. Are Magistrates' sentencing powers sufficient? Consider the impact on the victim. Example of aggravating factors for the offence are commercial supply, deliberate adulteration, large amount, sophisticated operation, supply to children and venue, e.g. prisons, educational establishments. An example of a mitigating factor for the offence is no commercial motive and small amount. Examples of mitigation are age, health (physical or mental), co-operation with the police, and genuine remorse. Consider forfeiture and destruction.

For details about the guidelines see MAGISTRATES' COURT SENTENCING GUIDELINES at page 483.

Assisting the authorities

183.7   *R v Aramah* 1982 76 Cr App R 190 at 192. It is particularly important that offenders should be encouraged to give information to the police, and a confession of guilt coupled with considerable assistance to the police can properly be marked by a substantial reduction.

Believing the drugs to be a different drug

183.8   *R v Bilinski* 1987 9 Cr App R (S) 360. The amount of mitigation for this will obviously depend upon all the circumstances amongst them the degree of care exercised by the defendant.

R v Young 2000 2 Cr App R (S) 248. The defendant pleaded guilty to possession with intent to supply heroin and cannabis. She went to visit her boyfriend who was a prisoner serving life. She was told she was to be searched and she produced two balloons from her underwear containing the drugs. The heroin was 10.7 grams of unknown purity (worth at street value £900 and £1,000) and the cannabis was 25.9 grams. She was told it was a one off and she would be paid £75. She was shocked to learn one contained heroin. She was 45 with no convictions. She had a number of problems. Two sons lived with her and one of them had considerable difficulties. An older son suffered from muscular dystrophy and she had four other sons. She was described as vulnerable, lonely and suffered from low esteem. She was not in good health. She was sentenced on the basis she may not have known it was heroin and she thought it was cannabis. Held. Smuggling drugs into prison is an offence of extreme gravity. It is becoming more prevalent. Had she known it was heroin she could have expected a sentence of 5 years. **2$^{1}/_{2}$ years** was entirely correct.

R v Ngiam 2002 1 Cr App R (S) 150. The defendant pleaded guilty to possessing 50 kilos of heroin (at 47%) with intent to supply. She was sentenced on the basis she thought it was cannabis and she was a courier. Held. The fact she believed it was cannabis was a mitigating factor but it did not mean the judge was obliged to sentence her as if it was cannabis.

Att-Gen's Ref. No. 146 of 2002 2003 2 Cr App R (S) 640. The defendant pleaded guilty to possessing 982 grams of heroin (363 grams at 100%) at the first opportunity. Police boarded a train believing a gun was on board and inspected a holdall. The defendant denied it was his. Police found a plastic gun and the defendant then admitted it was his holdall. He took the heroin from his carrier bag and tried to conceal it on his body. When challenged he said it was cannabis. The basis of plea was that he was a courier who believed it was cannabis and acted because he had a drug debt. There were differences about the debt in his account to the police and the pre-sentence report writer. He was 35 with a conviction for supplying cannabis for which he received 6 months. Held. We consider the opportunity the offender might have had to satisfy himself of the true nature of the drugs. The drugs were wrapped. The false account was to water down the degree of his admission in that regard. The degree of discount needs not be particularly high. 7–7$^1/_2$ years as a starting point is not excessive. Because he believed it was cannabis **5 years** is proper. Because it was a reference **4 years**.

See also IMPORTATION – *Believing the goods to be a different drug*

Children etc. Supplying to/using as couriers

183.8a   Misuse of Drugs Act 1971 s 4A[1] Where the offender has reached 18 and the offence under s 4(3) was committed on or in the vicinity of school premises at a relevant time or the offender uses a courier under 18 the court must treat that factor as an aggravating factor.

Class A – Large scale conspiracy

183.9   *Att-Gen's Ref. Nos. 90 and 91 of 1998* 2000 1 Cr App R (S) 32. The defendants S and F pleaded guilty to a conspiracy to supply Class A and Class B drugs. The prosecution case was that the conspiracy from February to September 1997 was to supply large quantities of drugs to wholesalers. They were organisers and brokers. Police put a bug in F's car and police heard reference to amphetamine, ecstasy and cocaine. There was also reference to 50,000 pills, 100 kilos, a ton of cannabis, 200 kilos of cannabis and sums of money up to £250,000. There was evidence of F taking large quantities of money to Ireland and Holland. There was mass of observation material and links with those connected with drugs. The defendant S after an extended period of legal argument pleaded on a limited basis, which was not accepted by the prosecution. There was a Newton hearing and the defence accepted the prosecution evidence. F had pleaded earlier. S was 42 and of good character. F was 54 and had a conviction for importing 600 kilos of cannabis for which he received 10 years. Held. Had the offence been contested **14 years** would have been appropriate. With an early plea **12 years** would have been appropriate. Because it was a reference **10 years** each not 6 for S and 5 for F.

Att-Gen's Ref. Nos. 99–102 of 2004 2005 Unreported 7/2/05. W changed his plea to guilty to three conspiracies to supply (cocaine, cannabis resin and cannabis) three months after the PDH. He was the principle conspirator, buying directly from the importers. He rented three storage units. In one was found 14.8 kilos of cocaine (11 kilos at 100%), a hydraulic press, electronic scales etc. In another 5.7 kilos of cannabis and £200,000 in cash. Analysis of incomplete computer records show 142 kilos of cocaine (not including the 14.8 kilos), 566 kilos of cannabis resin and 434 kilos of cannabis were handled. The conspiracy lasted at least 18 months. W had a share in a light aircraft. Held. The Judge's starting point of **20 years** was at the bottom of the appropriate bracket. The discount to 12 years was too generous. For an early plea we would have

---

1   Inserted by Drugs Act 2005 s 1 (commencement date awaited)

expected **13–14 years**. For his plea we would expect **15–16 years**. Because it was a reference we will not interfere.

Death is caused

183.10   *R v Lucas* 1999 1 Cr App R (S) 78. The defendant pleaded guilty to supplying heroin. He bought three £10 bags of heroin and then joined his girlfriend at home. They drank and he injected himself with heroin. He passed the syringe to his girlfriend. He then went to the local shop to buy beer and left her apparently asleep. On his return he couldn't rouse her and called an ambulance. The paramedics arrived and she was already dead. She was found to have $3^{1}/_{2}$ times the legal limit of alcohol for drivers and a high level of unmetabolised heroin which suggested she died shortly after injecting herself. Death was thought to have been caused by a combination of drugs and alcohol. The defendant was interviewed and made a frank confession. He said she had only used heroin twice before. There was genuine remorse. Following the death he made a number of suicide attempts. He was now drug free. He was 36 with no relevant convictions. He had abused drugs and alcohol for many years. He had been treated from time to time for depression and had not always been very well. **3 years** not 5.

R v Ashford 2000 1 Cr App R (S) 389. The defendant pleaded guilty to supplying heroin at the Magistrates' Court. The defendant was living at a bail hostel and another resident who was very drunk asked for some heroin. The defendant said no, but later after being pestered gave him some. The other resident took it and died during the night. He was sentenced on the basis heroin was not the cause of death. Death was caused by asphyxia after vomit had been swallowed. The defendant had served five custodial sentences for dishonesty. He expressed remorse. The prison report said he was traumatised by the death and he was displaying a very high motivation to address his drug problem. **2 years** not 3.

R v Bull 2000 2 Cr App R (S) 81. The defendant pleaded guilty at the first opportunity to supplying ecstasy. He gave two ecstasy tablets to his sister's boyfriend without charge. The boyfriend and the sister went to a nightclub where they stayed several hours. He drank a number of double whiskeys as well as a lot of water. He was seen to be sweating a lot. The two came home at 2.30pm. He was found dead the next morning. He died of heart failure. It was discovered he had an abnormality of the heart and ecstasy contributed to the heart failure. If he hadn't taken the ecstasy it is unlikely he would have died. When questioned by the police the defendant admitted he had given him the tablets. The defendant was 21 and lived with his parents. He was in regular employment and working hard. He had no convictions and had a deep sense of remorse, which led to a depressive illness and a suicide attempt. Held. He must not receive a disproportionate sentence because of the tragic and appalling consequences of the supply. **9 months** not 18.

R v Dorosz 2001 2 Cr App R (S) 476. The defendant pleaded guilty at the first opportunity to two counts of supplying heroin and administering heroin so as to endanger life (Offences Against the Person Act 1861, s 23). The victim visited his flat. At the request of the victim he injected her with heroin. Later she injected herself. One evening she brought heroin and cocaine to his flat. They both injected themselves with heroin and cocaine probably four or five times. He probably gave her two of them and she gave herself the rest. He asked her several times whether she was alright and she always said she was. She seemed to be enjoying it. Apart from one occasion he always put the heroin in the syringe to ensure she was taking less than he was. He left her to sleep on the sofa. In the morning he rang his workplace to say he was unwell and went back to bed. He woke again at 1 pm and could not wake her. He called for an ambulance and she could not be resuscitated. Police arrived and he gave them the above account although in less detail. An expert said she possibly died from heroin and cocaine. He also said she had taken heroin up her nose, which the defendant said he had not seen. He was 28 and of good character. He gave a full account to the coroner although he was not obliged to. He was arrested 2 months later. He was a computer programmer, which rewarded well. He had developed a fascination with altered states of the mind and had abused drugs including heroin from time to time. He had impressive character witnesses. He was genuinely remorseful and the pre-sentence report said that the event had been devastating for him. Held. There were many factors in his favour. **2¹/₂ years** on each count concurrent not 3¹/₂.

R v Anderson 2001 Unreported 9/11/01. On a guilty plea the range is 2¹/₂ to 3¹/₂ years.

See also MANSLAUGHTER – *Drug abuse*

Defendant under 18 – Class A

183.11   *R v M* 2001 1 Cr App R (S) 101. The defendant pleaded guilty to two counts of possession of heroin with intent to supply. The defendant then aged 16 was stopped on his bicycle. He was searched and police found two bags containing 55 grams of heroin at 28–29% purity in his pocket. He was heard to shout out to some youths to contact his mother about a leak, which was interpreted as a coded message indicating there were drugs at his home. Police found 13 grams of heroin of 30% purity there. The total was the equivalent of 19 grams at 100% purity. They also seized £9,170 in cash. He had no convictions. The pre-sentence report indicated that he was naïve and had fallen in with bad company. He was keen to demonstrate that he had changed his attitude and keen to pursue his education. On remand he was described as a model resident. Held. This was a serious offence. It was trafficking for a substantial profit. Even taking into account the substantial mitigation **3 years** detention was not manifestly excessive.

R v Hussain 2001 2 Cr App R (S) 273. The defendant pleaded guilty to possession of heroin with intent to supply and supplying heroin. An undercover police officer contacted the defendant then aged 15 on his mobile phone and arranged to meet him so he could be supplied with three wraps. The defendant went to the meet on his bicycle and was arrested when he arrived. Six wraps of heroin containing 1.04 grams were found on him. Their value was £100. £57.96 was found at his home. When interviewed he said he had sold 8–10 wraps for £10 before. He said he had found the drugs. He agreed the money at his home was drug profits. He was treated as being of good character. He came from a good home. Held. The judge was right to include an element of deterrent in the sentence. **2 years detention and training** not 3 years detention.

R v Coudjoe 2002 2 Cr App R (S) 205. The defendant pleaded guilty on the day of his intended trial to possession of heroin and cocaine with intent to supply. Then 15, the defendant was seen by police acting suspiciously and he was searched. In his second and under pair of tracksuit bottoms police found nine wraps of heroin containing 913 mgs at 44% purity and seven wraps of crack cocaine at 56% purity. In his coat pocket was 118 mgs of heroin at 46% purity. He was on bail at the time. The pre-sentence report indicated he did not take hard drugs and had a blasé attitude to the dangers of supplying them. His risk of re-offending was assessed as significant. He had two non-drug relatively minor convictions. His account was rejected in a Newton trial. He was sentenced on the basis that he was going to supply friends. He was not sentenced on the basis he was going to trade on the street. Held. A severe sentence was called for but because of his youth **18 months** detention not 30.

Determining the scale of the supply

183.12   *R v Singh* 1988 10 Cr App R (S) 402 at 406. LCJ. It should be noted ... that the assistance which can be derived from the amount of the drug actually found in the possession of the defendant is limited. It is the scale and nature of the dealing which are the material factors.

R v Djahit 1999 2 Cr App R (S) 142. The defendant pleaded guilty to possession of heroin with intent to supply and possession of cannabis. The police arrived to execute a search warrant at his shop and adjoining flat. Two bags of heroin were found in a door panel near his kitchen. Two further bags were found in a kitchen cupboard. A small amount of heroin was found in one of his socks. The total weight was 21.5 grams with a street value of £2,150. The purity was not ascertained. £6,005, a list of names and addresses, a set of scales and bags were found. The defendant accepted the paraphernalia belonged to him but the list did not. Held. One count of possession with intent to supply does not prevent the judge from taking into account the admitted level of dealing as reflected by the sums of money and drugs paraphernalia found. If, however, there is a dispute about the level of dealing and no conviction on a count which reflects dealing over a period of time, then the sentencing judge must exercise care, see for example *R v Canavan* 1998 1 Cr App R (S) 243; *R v Thompson and Smith* 1997 1 Cr App R (S) 289 and *R v Johnson* 1984 6 Cr App R (S) 227.

R v Brown 2000 1 Cr App R (S) 300. The defendant was convicted of being concerned in the supply of controlled drugs and possession with intent to supply. The counts were based on one occasion. The defendant's car was stopped and he was searched. Police found five small bags of cannabis and nearly £700. At his home in his sister's room there were scales, 100 self sealing bags, £7,520 in cash and two Building Society account books in her name. £43,000 was in the accounts. There was no scientific link between any of the money and the defendant. The judge sentenced him on the basis of 'the wider picture.' He was sentenced on the basis of a period of 33 months with profits of £33,000. Held. The judge was bound to sentence for the single offence. The prosecution could have avoided the difficulties if they had drafted six substantive counts against him which the sister faced (assisting another to retain the proceeds of drug trafficking). The sentence was reduced from $3\frac{1}{2}$ years to 9 months consecutive on each making **18 months**.

R v Morris 2001 2 Cr App R (S) 297 at para 18. The amount of Class A or B drug with which a defendant is involved is a very important but not solely the determinative factor in sentencing. Evidence as to the scale of dealing can come from many sources other than the amount with which a defendant is directly connected.

R v Lee 2005 Unreported 22/2/05. The defendant pleaded guilty to two supply counts. She claimed she was holding the drugs for another as a custodian. A Newton hearing was held. After hearing the defendant the Judge asked the prosecution counsel if there was any PII material. Counsel elected not to adduce any. The Judge then saw him in chambers. Afterwards counsel gave the defendant information that the defendant had been dealing drugs on a different day. Held. The Judge erred. There was no evidence to support the claim about the other day.

Distinction, don't draw a distinction between drugs in the same class

183.13 *R v Thompson* 1997 2 Cr App R (S) 223. The defendant pleaded guilty to two counts of supplying ecstasy. The judge sentenced him on the basis that ecstasy was more serious than other Class A drugs so passed a higher sentence than the guidelines. Held. The court has said on a number of occasions that there should be no distinction between the various drugs in a class. The sentence was reduced.

Drug addicts

See – **Retailing low level class A – Drug addicts**

183.14   Save for this group (and possibly those who supply Class B drugs) drug addicts should not expect a discount for being an addict. For more detail see **Drug Users**.

Drug gang using violence

183.15   *R v Brocklesby* 1999 1 Cr App R (S) 80. The defendants D and P were brothers and were convicted of conspiracy to supply heroin and crack cocaine, wounding Andrew Mournian (s 18), falsely imprisoning Andrew Mournian, ABH on Philip Parker, falsely imprisoning Philip Parker, kidnap and falsely imprisoning Natham Burton and kidnapping and falsely imprisoning Anthony Newton. D was also convicted of wounding Philip Parker (s 18) and having a sawn-off shotgun with intent to cause fear to Philip Parker. The two defendants were the organisers and principles of a highly successful and lucrative heroin and crack cocaine business. They only supplied individual users but engaged others to do the selling. [The judgment may be missing a 'not' before 'only in the preceding sentence.] They had hundreds of customers and made an estimated minimum of £8,000 a week. The blatant drug dealing was only possible because of the fear they and their henchmen generated. The fear was generated by extreme violence, nothing short of a reign of terror involving guns and knives in order to protect the empire and discourage or punish those perceived to be informers. P was more prominent. Andrew Mournian was thought possibly to have been an informer. He was held prisoner and D slashed his arm with a knife and threatened to stab him in the eye. P tried to break his leg with the back of an axe. He was punched and kicked with D saying, 'Let's fucking kill him.' D sewed up each arm with ordinary thread because of the loss of blood. This caused great pain and distress. D also bit his nose making threats. Later D and another attacked Philip Parker a drug addict by throwing knives at and into his leg. The blade came out of the other side. The knife was held to his eye and threats to kill him were made. A knife was thrown which fractured his ankle. A sawn-off shotgun was held at his head moved a few inches and discharged. After returning from hospital he was accused of stealing money. He was punched and kicked. His face was burnt with a soldering iron. His tooth was damaged with a knife. He smashed a glass window trying to escape and cut himself badly. Natham Burton aged 17, was a customer and owed them money. He was kidnapped off the street and taken to a house. He was threatened with knives and knives were thrown at his feet. The defendants set others on to him to punch and kick him. He managed to escape through a window. Anthony Newton was taken by force to a house. He was punched and told he was a police informer. He was hit with knives and head butted. He fell backwards into a bath, which contained water. P told D to electrocute him. A radio with mains leads was held over the bath. Newton managed to run to a nearby house but was caught and attacked again. He was imprisoned overnight. A police officer found him next day. The defendants were arrested. D was 31 with an extensive criminal past. He had convictions for robbery, violence, firearms and drugs. P had a similar record and some of the offences had been committed jointly. Their longest sentences were 5 and $4^{1}/_{2}$ for robbery respectively. D received 7 years for the drug conspiracy and 7 years for one of the kidnapping offences and 7 years for the firearm offence all consecutive making **21 years** in all. P was sentenced to 9 years for the drug conspiracy and 6, 3 and 4 years consecutive for the other incidents making **22 years** in all. Held. The only question was whether the totals were manifestly excessive for this campaign of terror, designed to protect the lucrative drug operation. These were two gangsters who cared nothing for those they hurt. They used fear, violence and brutality to a quite dreadful extent. They showed no mercy. We are quite satisfied the sentences were not excessive.

R v Smith Re S 2002 1 Cr App R (S) 386 at 394. The defendants C and S pleaded guilty to kidnapping. A drugs deal went wrong and one of those involved, J and his family fled fearing J would take the blame for the money and drugs which disappeared. J was arrested and bailed. S, C and another kidnapped J and drove him along a motorway demanding the return of the drugs and the money. They 'thumped' him and threatened to kill him and throw him out of the moving car. C made a number of calls on his mobile suggesting someone who might enjoy torturing J for fun. J was handcuffed and taken to a building where he was assaulted. After the three left he remained a prisoner for 24 hours until a ransom was paid. J made a statement to the police, which contained false details about the culprits and said he didn't want any action taken. Later he gave a full and true statement. There was considerable delay before sentence. **3 years** not 4.

R v Bediako and Martin 2001 The Times 16/10/01. Manslaughter, two counts of kidnapping and two counts of false imprisonment. Held. **7 years** reduced from 14.

Att-Gen's Ref. Nos. 58–66 of 2002 147 SJ 296. P, the founder member of a drug gang habitually using firearms and violence was sentenced for murder and three counts of attempted murder. The rest were each sentenced for possessing firearms with intent to endanger life and conspiracy to supply Class A and B drugs. The gang supplied drugs including heroin, crack cocaine and cocaine, 7 days a week 24 hours a day. Guns were used for the members own protection and to enforce territorial claims. Safe houses were used to cut and prepare drugs. They would wear dark clothing, balaclavas and bullet proof vests. Discipline was maintained by terror. Held. The drugs conspiracy count merits without guns **up to 10 years**. For someone of full age and at the centre of activity the total sentence when aggravated by firearms should have been close to **20 years**. All the sentences were reduced because it was a reference. The ages of the defendants relate to their age during the conspiracy.

Individual sentences. G, T, B and S were the senior members of the gang. B pleaded on the first day of his trial on the basis he had not discharged a firearm nor had been present when one was discharged. The others were convicted. G was a very significant player. He savagely beat another youth with a butt of a gun. He bundle a rival gang member into a car and then subjected him to Russian Roulette. G was seen bagging up guns G was 18–19 and was convicted. He had no convictions. Held for G. **12 years detention** reduced from 14 not 9. T was immediately below the leader of the gang. He confronted members of rival gangs during which guns were discharged. T was 22–3 and had a previous conviction for possessing a CS gas canister, supplying cocaine and supply of heroin and cocaine. Held for T. **12 years** reduced from 14 not 8. B was very senior member of the gang. B was 19–20 with no relevant previous. Held for B. **10 years** reduced from 12 not 8. S exchanged weapons and bought drugs and was "up to his neck in it". He was 20–1 with a conviction for possessing ammunition. Held for S. **12 years** reduced from 14 not $7^1/_2$. For the junior members they were much less involved with the firearms. D aged 22 held a gun at someone. C, aged 19 made crack cocaine at a flat. He was arrested with wraps of crack and heroin. M, aged 15 was linked to 18 snap bags. O, aged 23 sold drugs and couriered a revolver to P. Pr aged 20 was linked by DNA to a sworn off shotgun and was caught running from a house were a revolver was found. Their sentences of **7 years, 6 years, $4^1/_2$ years detention, $5^1/_2$ years detention** and **6 years** were lenient but not unduly lenient.

R v Burgess 2004 2 Cr App R (S) 85. The defendant was convicted of kidnapping. The victim owed him money for drugs. The defendant saw the victim's car parked outside a flat where crack could be bought. When the victim came out he was dragged into a car by D and taken to a flat. The victim was aged 56 and in poor health. He was kept in a damp and unheated room in a flat for about 10 hours. The defendant threatened, punched, and gave him electric shocks with a stun gun. He contacted the victim's daughters and demanded £3,500. She went to the flat and saw her father. She was present when a threat was made to use the stun gun again. When she left, the defendant told her that if she contacted the police he would have no hesitation in 'taking her father out'. She did contact the police and arrangements were made for the victim to be released on payment of the money. The daughter handed over marked money and he was released. The defendant aged 35 had been before the courts on sixteen previous occasions including aggravated burglary, burglary and section 18 wounding. Held. There was violence of a particularly unpleasant kind although the victim only suffered minor injuries. The victim's family were involved. The sentence was more severe than was appropriate to the circumstances. $7^1/_2$ **years** not 9. (There was no conviction for supply but the facts are analogous.)

Entrapment (and similar situations)

183.16   *R v Tonnessen* 1998 2 Cr App R (S) 328. The defendant pleaded guilty to supplying heroin. The defendant was approached by a man who claimed to know her. He was accompanied by two others who turned out to be from the *News of the World*. They said they worked for a Sheikh and they were instructed to buy drugs. She was a heroin addict and a cannabis user and said they were widely available. They said they wanted to buy heroin and asked her whether she was prepared to get it for them. They gave her £50 and she bought four wraps of heroin. She and a friend spent the rest of the evening with them. Immediately after her name and photograph appeared in the paper. The police felt obliged to arrest her and she admitted the offence. After the publicity she was assaulted and received a threat to her life. She was 31 and had already served a prison sentence for an unrelated offence. She had no supply convictions. She suffered from a serious pre-cancerous condition. The judge did not refer to the involvement of agent provocateurs and appeared not to have taken it into account. The defence said there could be considerable mitigation where it can be shown that the offence would not otherwise have been committed. It is legitimate for policemen to entrap criminals. When the entrapment is by a journalist even more consideration and more weight should be given. Held. We consider there is substance in those submissions. However it merited immediate custody. We cannot ignore she was set up. If these men had been police officers that would provide mitigation. Different considerations must apply to investigatory journalists. Their purpose was perfectly honourable. But we feel the public would be left with a sense of unease by the identification in the paper. The consequences were most unfortunate. It is appropriate to reflect the entrapment in the sentence. It should have been expressly mentioned in the remarks. In the exceptional circumstances we reduce the sentence from **12 months** to 6.

R v Springer 1999 1 Cr App R (S) 217. The defendant pleaded guilty at the Magistrates' Court to three charges of supplying heroin and was committed to the Crown Court. The defendant was a suspected drug dealer. The police tested their suspicions by making three telephone calls. He was asked, 'Have you got anything.' He replied, 'Yeah,' and arrangements were made to meet him. In response to each call a meeting was arranged and about 1.5 grams of heroin was supplied. The calls were recorded and the meetings were videoed. The defence argued that he was entitled to a discount because of entrapment. Held. There was a need for the police to adopt this method of detection. There was need for there to be more than one supply to provide evidence he was a dealer. This was not a case of entrapping a suspect into supplying drugs who would otherwise never have engaged in that activity. *R v Underhill* 1979 1 Cr App R (S) 270 at 272 applied. Here there was legitimate police activity and not activity that could provide mitigation or a reduction at all. (For further details see later in this section *Heroin – Class A – Street dealer*)

R v Mayeri 1999 1 Cr App R (S) 304. The defendant pleaded guilty at the earliest opportunity to four counts of supplying ecstasy. One tablet was involved in each case. Four undercover police officers approached him in a nightclub and he agreed to sell them a tablet for £10. He claimed there was an element of entrapment. The defendant relied on *R v Tonnessen* 1998 2 Cr App R (S) 328. Held. The entrapment argument is not a good one. Where undercover officers discover a man is prepared to sell drugs by approaching him it is not a matter the courts need normally take into account as amounting to entrapment. It might be said 'Seller beware.' These premises are frequently used to sell drugs.

R v Davidson 2003 1 Cr App R (S) 12. Held. Although the police behaved impeccably, the escalating progress of the supply was to a degree fuelled by their suggestions, (which contributed to the reduced sentence). (For further details see *Ecstasy – 10,000 tablets or more*) For more information about entrapment see **para 63.1.**

Indictment/Charge, must restrict yourself to what is alleged in

183.17   *R v Twisse* 2001 2 Cr App R (S) 37. We recognise the importance of only sentencing for the criminality proved or admitted. This established principle of law is now reinforced by the European Convention of Human Rights, art 6. If the prosecution can prove the defendant has been acting as a supplier over a substantial time it can put the court in a position to sentence properly by one of three ways. (1) charging a number of offences of supply or possession supply at different dates; (2) charging a conspiracy over a prescribed period; (3) charging him with being concerned in the supply over a specified period contrary to the Misuse of Drugs Act 1971, s 4(3)(b). If the indictment is not drawn as we have suggested and the defendant does not ask for offences to be taken into consideration judges should refrain from drawing inferences to the extent of the defendant's criminal activities, even if those inferences are inescapable having regard to admissions made or equipment found. In other words a defendant charged with one offence of supply cannot receive a more substantial sentence because it is clear he has been dealing for 9 months: but the court is not required to blind itself to the obvious. If he claims that the occasion in question was an isolated transaction, that submission can be rejected. He can be given the appropriate sentence for that one offence without the credit he would receive if he really were an isolated offender.

Informing on the defendant, his/her family

183.18   *R v Catterall* 1993 14 Cr App R (S) 724. The defendant's father called the police because he and his wife were concerned the defendant was under the influence of drink or drugs. They did it entirely in the interests of their son. Held. His father and mother care so much about his future they were prepared to disclose the offences to the police. They are likely to support his efforts to give up his habit. The court should take those facts into account and give him a further discount. The sentence will be reduced from 4 years to **2 years**, a reduction entirely due to his father's action.

R v Ferrett 1998 2 Cr App R (S) 384. The defendant pleaded guilty to four counts of supplying ecstasy, a count of supplying amphetamine and two counts of supplying cannabis. A teenage girl died after taking ecstasy and amphetamine. The defendant's mother and others told the police he might have been the supplier of the drugs. The defendant was interviewed and denied supplying the deceased but admitted supplying another. He was 18 when sentenced and of good character. Held. A total of **5 years** would have been appropriate. However applying *R v Catterall* 1993 14 Cr App R (S) 724 he is entitled to a further discount because of the credit due to his family for taking the course they did. So 4$^{1}/_{2}$ **years** YOI not 7. (For further details see **Ecstasy –** *Class A – Retail supply*)

Innocuous substances, material turns out to be

183.19   *R v Porter* 1999 2 Cr App R (S) 205. The defendant pleaded guilty at the Magistrates' Court to attempting to possess amphetamine with intent to supply. Police watched someone walk from a car to the defendant at a railway station. They shook hands and walked to the car. The defendant got in and left shortly after carrying a plastic bag. The police stopped him and he struggled. In the bag were 4,063 tablets and he said they were speed (i.e. amphetamines). In fact the tablets were not a controlled drug. If they had been amphetamine they would have been worth between £8,000 and £12,000. When interviewed he said his job was to travel from Wales and collect the drugs. He was 27. **12 months** not 30.

Medicines – Where the drugs are not Class A, B or C see **Medicine Offences**

Persistent Class A supplier etc – Minimum 7 years

183.20   Powers of Criminal Courts (Sentencing) Act 2000, s 110. Where a person is convicted of a class A drug trafficking offence committed after 30 November 1999 and was 18 or over and he has been convicted of two other class A drug trafficking offences one of which was committed after he had been convicted of the other the court shall impose a sentence of imprisonment of at least 7 years except where the court is of the opinion that there are particular circumstances which relate to any of the offences or to the offender which would make it unjust. [This section is summarised and is slightly amended by Criminal Justice and Court Services Act 2000.]

Persistent Class A supplier etc – Minimum 7 years – Plea of guilty

183.21   Powers of Criminal Courts (Sentencing) Act 2000, s 152(3) Where a sentence is to be imposed under the Powers of Criminal Courts (Sentencing) Act 2000, s 110 after a plea of guilty nothing in that section shall prevent the court from imposing a sentence of 80% or more of the minimum period. [Section summarised. The section means if s/he pleads guilty the court can impose a sentence, which is 80% or more of the minimum term.]

R v Brown 2000 2 Cr App R (S) 435. The defendant pleaded guilty at the first opportunity to supplying crack cocaine, supplying heroin and possession of cocaine. Police were conducting a drugs operation in the Kings Cross area of London and the defendant gave an officer a piece of paper with a telephone number on it and told them to call it if they wanted drugs. An officer rang the number and the defendant told them where they should meet. Two officers went to flat as directed and one purchased 164 mgs of crack for £20 and another officer asked for heroin and crack but was told there was no crack left and was given 105 mgs of heroin for £20. When the defendant was arrested nearly 3 months later he had 1.6 mgs of crack on him. He was 45 and had three convictions for supplying drugs, two of which were for Class A drugs. He also had two convictions for possession of an offensive weapon and one for possession of a bladed article. He was sentenced to $6\frac{1}{2}$ years for the supply counts with 6 months consecutive for a breach of a CSO. There was a concurrent sentence for the possession offence. The defence said either the Judge started too high or failed to give the full 20% discount for the guilty plea. Held. We agree and as he didn't indicate which we adjust the supply sentence to **5 years 8 months** and because of totality the 6 months should run concurrently.

R v Willoughby 2003 2 Cr App R (S) 357. The defendant pleaded guilty to five counts of supplying heroin. He had two relevant previous convictions. The Court examined Powers of the Criminal Courts (Sentencing) Act 2000 s 110 and152. Held. The wording was tortuous. The Judge did not have to start at 7 years here. (Little of significance to the sections was said.)

Persistent Class A supplier etc – Minimum 7 years – Unjust, meaning

183.22   *R v Hickson* 2002 1 Cr App R (S) 298. One is not looking for exceptional circumstances; one is looking at the particular circumstances of the offence and the offender.

Persistent Class A supplier etc – Minimum 7 years – Cases

183.23   *R v Harvey* 2000 1 Cr App R (S) 368. The defendant was convicted of supplying two small wraps of heroin. Each was worth £20. He had been arrested in a police drugs operation in the Kings Cross area of London. He was on bail for drug offences at the time. He was 57 with convictions going back to 1962. The first sixteen appearances were for dishonesty. From March 1997 they included drug offences. Those included possessing cannabis with intent to supply, conspiracy to supply drugs, possession of heroin with intent to supply (for which he received 6 years) and supplying heroin (for which he received 4 years). The judge imposed the 7 year minimum sentence saying that would not be unjust. Held. Applying *R v Munson* 1998 Unreported 23/11/98 (where a defendant in very similar circumstances save that that defendant made a late guilty plea had his 7 year sentence described as a 'tough sentence, but ... a deliberately tough sentence.' and one that was not manifestly excessive.) The sentence is not manifestly excessive. Parliament has chosen 7 years as the standard penalty on a third conviction, which meets the conditions in the section. The object is plainly to require courts to impose a sentence of at least 7 years where but for the section they would not or might not do so. The judge was entitled to pass the **7 years** minimum sentence.

[Since this case was decided the rules about the imposition of mandatory sentences have been considered under the Human Rights legislation by *R v Offen (No 2)* 2001 1 Cr App R 372. Those changes are not dealt with here.]

R v Stenhouse 2000 2 Cr App R (S) 386. The defendant pleaded guilty to supplying heroin on four separate occasions. A police officer called a number and was told to ring back in 15 minutes. He did so and spoke to the defendant. They agreed to meet. The defendant was given £10 and the undercover officer was given a wrap, which contained 52 mgs of heroin. The other offences were similar. He had convictions for possession of drugs and two for supplying Class A drugs. The last conviction was in 1997 for supplying one methadone tablet for which he was given probation at the Magistrates' Court. He had been in custody from December 1998 to July 1999 when he was released because of the Custody Time Limit provisions. He was sentenced in December 1999 to the 7 year minimum term. Since his arrest he had made valiant attempts to conquer his drug addiction. Held. His efforts to break his drug habit were rare and he should be encouraged to continue with his efforts. The sentence because of the combination of circumstances was unjust so **3 years** substituted.

R v Willoughby 2003 2 Cr App R (S) 357. The defendant pleaded guilty to five counts of supplying heroin. Over three weeks he sold wraps of heroin to undercover officers five times. The amounts were five wraps for £40 (212 mg.), a wrap for £20 (26 mg.), 5 wraps for £50 (389 mg.), a number of wraps for £40 (253 mg.) and 4 wraps (199gms) when he was arrested. The amounts were at 100%. He was 46 with numerous convictions primarily for theft and related matters. In 1986 for supply he received 30 months and in 1992, again for supply, he received 42 months. He qualified for a minimum 7 year sentence. He was in breach of a conditional discharge for possession of heroin. The Judge said he started at 9 years and gave him $6^1/_2$ years. Held. The Judge did not have to start at 7 years here. No complaint could have been made if the Judge had started at 8 years. $6^1/_2$ **years** meets the Justice of the case.

Pretending goods were prohibited drugs

183.24   *R v Chambers and Barnett* 1999 1 Cr App R (S) 262. The defendants C and B pleaded guilty to offering to supply ecstasy and going equipped to cheat. The defendants went to a rave with some innocuous tablets. They tried to sell them as ecstasy. B tried to sell one to an undercover police officer. C was 26 with no convictions. B was 19 with a conviction for deception. It was contended it was a deception case not tainted by any stain of the Drug Trafficking Act offences. Held. We don't entirely agree with that submission as it still contributed to the 'raves plus drug' scene which the police and courts are trying to stamp out. However, no damage and possibly some good would have been done to the purchasers. **12 months** imprisonment and YOI not 18 months.

R v Prince 1999 2 Cr App R (S) 419. The defendant pleaded guilty to offering to supply cocaine. Police mounted a surveillance operation in Moss Side. There were thirteen days of video evidence and he appeared in only one of them. Because there was no link with others being sentenced the Court of Appeal decided to look at the facts of his case in isolation. An undercover officer approached someone and asked for 'a stone.' He said he had none and the defendant approached and sold her a wrap for £20. It was 208 grams of paracetamol. The defendant later accepted a stone meant crack cocaine. He was 38 and had been addicted to drugs particularly cocaine for some time.

He had a long list of convictions mainly for dishonesty to finance his addiction. He was in breach of his licence following his release from a $2\frac{1}{2}$ year sentence for robbery. There were 224 days left to serve. He had no drug convictions. Held. It was important the sentence reflected that what was sold was not a controlled drug. 18 months was too long. **12 months** substituted.

R v Tugwell 2001 2 Cr App R (S) 501. The defendant pleaded guilty to possession of cannabis and ecstasy and two counts of offering to supply fake ecstasy. Held. Supplying fake drugs is not simply a case of obtaining money by fraud but it involves a lesser degree of criminality than supplying real drugs.

R v McNab 2002 1 Cr App R (S) 304. The defendants Mc, L, B and M were convicted of conspiracy to offer to supply ecstasy. The conspiracy was to offer people in night-clubs large amounts of fake ecstasy, which in fact contained various mixtures of ketamine, ephedrine and caffeine. They were non-controlled but did have dangerous side effects. Tablet presses were imported from Thailand and the pills were given dove and other motifs to make them look like ecstasy. M was the main player. L operated the laboratory company and was the financial backer and controller of the conspiracy. There were four tablet factories. B played a main part liaising between L's company and the various makers of the tablets. He also organised deliveries and the provision of minders. Mc was involved in the Scottish end and played a slightly smaller part. The judge said the lowest figure for the value of the tablets ran into six figures and the potential into seven figures. It was a fraud on a massive scale. Held. The judge was right to start by looking at the sentences for drug trafficking rather than fraud. It is not just a fraud. These drugs were not harmless. There is a danger that people who buy fake pills may not find the effect they want and then when they buy the real thing they take increased quantities and put themselves in serious danger even death. To suggest the purchasers are not innocent victims because they are buying illegal drugs is misguided. They are the real victims of the drugs trade even if they are not innocent. The 2 year maximum for ketamine is not a material factor. It couldn't relate to a conspiracy of this size. There can be no criticism of M's **11 years** and L and B's **9 years**. (Mc received **3 years and 11 months** and only appealed his conviction.)

Att-Gen's Ref No 90 of 2001 2003 2 Cr App R (S) 164. The defendant was convicted of conspiracy to offer to supply ecstasy to another. L pleaded guilty. The defendant had an interest in pharmaceuticals and sought to manufacture, using ketamine, ephedrine and caffeine, a drug giving similar affects to MDMA. None of the proposed constituents were controlled drugs, but their combined effects would enhance and stimulate the car-diovascular and central nervous systems. He purchased 300,000 calcium lactate tablets and 25 kilos of calcium lactate powder to use as a binding agent. He acquired 230 kilos of ketamine from Germany and ephedrine from Pakistan. He rented an industrial unit, purchased a cement mixer to mix the drug and a tablet press, again from Germany which was able to produce tablets with a suitable logo. Covert surveillance heard him describe his plans for manufacture and his intention to 'take the piss out of the system'. After production, there was a discussion between L and the defendant about customers becoming sick and re-orders stopped as the pills gave people headaches. Another chemical, scopolamine was added to the next batch of tablets. These pills were discov-ered throughout the country. When he was arrested, six weeks later a search discovered enough powder to manufacture another 850,000 tablets. When interviewed he admitted manufacturing stimulant tablets but said he had not made any tablets for months and months. It was submitted that the aggravating features were that this was a sophisti-cated operation involving an investment of at least £140,000; that the defendant had ignored the potential adverse side effects of which he was aware; and that the defendant targeted the young and vulnerable who might feel that they were immune to the effects of ecstasy and take more of the fake or real drug. The defendant was 40 with one

relevant conviction for trafficking cannabis 15 years previously. Held. He was unques-
tionably the principal conspirator and spent a considerable amount of time, research and
money on his venture. The appropriate starting point in relation to fake ecstasy tablets
was in the order of **10 years**. Because the defendant was sentenced for a second time,
7 years not 5.

See also *Cocaine – Class A – Offering to supply/Deceiving the buyer* and *Ecstasy –
Class A – Offering to supply/Deceiving the buyer*

Prisoners, supply to – Class A – Cocaine or heroin – Guideline remarks

183.25 *R v Bower* 2002 1 Cr App R (S) 483. The message has to go out to those who
succumb to threat or persuasion to take drugs into prison that if they do so they will
lose their liberty for a very long time indeed. Good character and absence of previous
convictions notwithstanding.

Prisoners, supply to – Class A – Cocaine or heroin – Cases

183.26 *R v Batt* 1999 2 Cr App R (S) 224. The defendant was convicted of possessing heroin with intent to supply. She went to prison to smuggle 4.9 grams of heroin
to her son. She was 60. She fought her case on the basis she had been threatened. She
was suffering from depression and was at serious risk of having a nervous breakdown
and possible suicide attempts. She had an unfortunate background. She has been traumatised by a series of events, which have occurred in her family. Two of her sons were
imprisoned for robbery. Another son had a serious accident in Germany such that they
considered turning off his life support machine. He has severe brain damage and will
require 24 hour nursing for the rest of his life. She is playing a major part in that. That
has left her in a vulnerable and exhausted state. Another son suffered a brain haemorrhage and died leaving a wife and two children. She was unable to come to terms with
that. Her daughter suffers from epilepsy. Her brother aged 69 who lives next door to her
is disabled. She had served the equivalent of a year in prison. The defence did not con-
tend the 3 year sentence was wrong but asked for the sentence to be suspended as an
act of mercy. Held. The rejection of the defence of duress does not mean there was
no element of pressure. We have well in mind the case of *R v Prince* 1996 1 Cr App R
(S) 335. This is an exceptional case. We do not want to undermine the seriousness of
the offence as set out in *R v Prince* 1996, but the factors here enable us to take an
exceptional course. We don't criticise the judge but she has now served a significant
period in custody. 3 years was in no way inappropriate. However, **2 years suspended**
substituted.

R v Ellingham 1999 2 Cr App R (S) 243. The defendant pleaded guilty at the Magistrates'
Court to possessing heroin with intent to supply. She went to visit her boyfriend in prison.
When she was searched the drugs were found in her mouth. It was 0.1 grams with a street
value of £10. She admitted it in interview. She said her boyfriend had said he would kill
himself in a call two days earlier. She was 20 and of good character. Held. Her good
character was of comparatively little mitigating significance. The sentence of **3 years** YOI
was not excessive applying *R v Prince* 1996 1 Cr App R (S) 335.

R v Appleton 1999 2 Cr App R (S) 290. The defendant pleaded guilty to possessing
heroin with intent to supply and three counts of possessing Class B drugs. He was a
serving prisoner who had his cell searched. Officers found two plastic wraps, each containing ten foil wraps of heroin (total of 0.74 grams at 32%), two foil wraps of heroin
(0.15 grams at 31%) and a cling film wrap of 0.56 grams of amphetamine sulphate. He
was arrested and admitted the offences. He was sentenced on the basis that he was
looking after the drugs for someone else. He was 29 and was nearing the end of a 7 year
sentence for robbery, ABH, using a firearm to resist arrest and possessing a firearm.
He had four court appearances before that mainly for dishonesty. There were no

convictions for drugs. Held. The court supports a policy of giving long additional sentences to those involved with drugs in prison. They will be dealt with severely as shown in *R v Prince* 1996 1 Cr App R (S) 335. The fact he was minding them rather than dealing does not necessarily mean a shorter sentence. Those who mind the drugs prevent the real dealers being caught. Those that do the minding and then protect the dealer cannot receive any mercy. It would be different if the person was prepared to name the dealer and assist the police. Otherwise we see little reason to reduce the sentence. The **5 years** sentence was entirely appropriate and we do not wish to alter the message we wish to send out by saying the total sentence of 12 years is too long.

R v Hamilton 2000 1 Cr App R (S) 91. The defendant pleaded guilty to possession with intent to supply 6.02 grams of heroin. On Christmas Eve she visited an associate of her husband in prison. The associate was serving 6 years for drugs' offences. A sniffer dog gave a positive indication and later she handed over a knotted condom with the heroin from her mouth. She was arrested and admitted the offence in interview. She was 32 and of good character. She was the sole carer of her three children aged 15, 10 and 9. The youngest had both physical and learning difficulties, which had led to behavioural problems. Her husband had indicated that if she helped him with the associate he would spend Christmas with her. That time was a particularly difficult time of year as it was the anniversary of the death of her 2 year old son who died in a cot death tragedy. She was on anti-depressant medication and receiving bereavement counselling. Held. Mitigation features happen in almost every case. It is often the wife, the ex-wife or the mother of children who is selected. Applying *R v Prince* 1996 1 Cr App R (S) 335 there were not here exceptional circumstances for the sentence to be suspended. **2 years** upheld.

R v Cowap 2000 1 Cr App R (S) 284. The defendant pleaded guilty to possession with intent to supply $^1/_2$ gram of cocaine. Previously she had pleaded not guilty and the case had been listed for trial. She went to visit her ex-boyfriend in prison. An officer noticed something in her mouth. She struggled but the drugs were retrieved. The cocaine was 96% pure and worth between £40 and £50. She was 31 and unemployed. She had quite an appalling record for unrelated offences mainly for dishonesty and prostitution. She was addicted to heroin and/or cocaine. The judge said considering her background she was well aware of the risks she was taking. Held. Even taking into account her late plea and the pressure from her former boyfriend **4 years** could not be criticised.

R v Young 2000 2 Cr App R (S) 248. The defendant pleaded guilty to possession with intent to supply heroin and cannabis. She went to visit her boyfriend who was a prisoner serving life. She was told she was to be searched and she produced two balloons from her underwear containing the drugs. The heroin was 10.7 grams of unknown purity (worth at street value £900 and £1,000) and the cannabis was 25.9 grams. She was told it was a one off and she would be paid £75. She was shocked to learn one contained heroin. She was 45 with no convictions. She had a number of problems. Two sons lived with her and one of them had considerable difficulties. An older son suffered from muscular dystrophy and she had four other sons. She was described as vulnerable, lonely and suffered from low esteem. She was not in good health. She was sentenced on the basis she may not have known it was heroin and she thought it was cannabis. Held. Smuggling drugs into prison is an offence of extreme gravity. It is becoming more prevalent. Had she known it was heroin she could have expected a sentence of 5 years. **$2^1/_2$ years** was entirely correct.

R v Bower 2002 1 Cr App R (S) 483. The defendant pleaded guilty to supplying 340 mgs of heroin to her boyfriend in prison. She was observed passing it to him on CCTV. Its' street value was £28. In interview she said her boyfriend had threatened her with violence. She was 18 and of good character. The pre-sentence report and the psychiatrist's report said she was quiet, shy and vulnerable and that the boyfriend was older and of a violent disposition. In prison she was doing extremely well, obtaining qualifications and rebuilding her relationship with her mother. Held. **2 years** YOI was severe but not manifestly excessive.

Att-Gen's Ref. No 75 of 2002 2003 1 Cr App R (S) 557. (5 months consecutive to another sentence was far too low but because of circumstances the sentence was not altered.)

R v Wilkinson 2003 1 Cr App R (S) 148. The defendant was convicted of supplying 0.36 grams of heroin. He visited an inmate in prison and was caught on CCTV passing something to him. It was a knotted plastic package with the heroin inside. The inmate was called by the defence to give evidence. After his conviction he admitted the supply and claimed duress. He was 19 and had twenty three convictions on nine occasions including dishonesty, violence criminal damage and public order. His only detention was in 2001 for an affray for which he received 6 months YOI consecutive to dangerous driving and other offences making 12 months in all. It was about retaliation over a damaged car. Held. Because of his comparative youth, family commitments and the cautious optimism in the pre-sentence report **3 years** YOI not 4.

R v Witten 2003 2 Cr App R (S) 33. The defendant pleaded guilty to possessing heroin with intent. She arrived at Whitemoor Prison with her three young children (aged 6, 5, and 3) to see her partner who was serving an 11 year sentence for conspiracy to supply heroin. The prison dog gave a positive indication and she was strip-searched. One gram of heroin had been concealed between her buttocks. She subsequently admitted the offence and indicated that this was a pre-arranged attempt as a result of a telephone discussion with her partner. The defendant was 26. She said her partner had placed pressure on her to commit the offence and subjected her to emotional blackmail. Held. The problem of drugs within prisons is too well known to need any emphasis. This Court has a responsibility to ensure that those who try to smuggle drugs into a prison, even in the circumstances which have been described and even though they have dependent children receive significant punishment. Mitigating features do not excuse the offence and do not avoid the need for a deterrent sentence. The Court has to take into account the effect of the sentence on the family, particularly with female defendants. **2 years** not $3^1/_2$.

R v Waheed 2004 1 Cr App R (S) 183. The defendant pleaded guilty to possession with intent to supply heroin and cannabis. He was stopped and searched when he went to visit a prisoner. He was wearing two pairs of underpants and two wraps of drugs were found. They were 3.1 grams of heroin (at 59%) and 3.58 grams of cannabis. He gave no comment at the interview. After pleading guilty he absconded. At the Crown Court he claimed duress and his account was rejected at a Newton hearing. He was 24. Held. 3 grams of heroin goes a long way in prison and the holder has considerable power to corrupt and disturb good discipline. But insufficient credit was given for plea before venue so **5 years** not 7.

Old cases *R v Slater* 1998 2 Cr App R (S) 415, and *R v Prince* 1996 1 Cr App R (S) 335, (for a summary of these cases see the first edition of this book)

See also **POSSESSION OF DRUGS** *– Prisoners*

Prisoners, supply to – Class A – Prison officers

183.27   *R v Whenman* 2001 2 Cr App R (S) 395. The defendant pleaded guilty to three counts of supplying heroin and possession with intent to supply heroin. They were specimen counts representing 15–20 transactions. They all related to the same prisoner. The defendant was arrested and said the prisoner had some information on him and he was pressurised first to supply cannabis and then heroin. He said threats were made which included violence to younger members of his family. A package was sent to an address and the defendant was called and told where to go. He collected it and took it to the prison kitchen and passed the package over in the whites' room. He received no payment. Police found one of the packages and it contained 4 grams of heroin. The defendant was 45 and of good character. The risk of re-offending was assessed as significant. He had three character witnesses and a certificate for nomination for a prison award. Held. The supply of Class A drugs to a serving prisoner is a most serious offence, *R v Prince* 1996 1 Cr App R (S) 335. We have considered the mitigating and aggravating features and **7 years** was not excessive.

R v Walker 2003 2 Cr App R (S) 351. The defendant was convicted of possessing heroin (34 grams at 69% purity) with intent, possessing ecstasy (12 tablets) with intent and possessing cannabis (124 grams) with intent. He had worked as a prison officer for 9 years. He left his prison and was under observation throughout. He drove to the local village and picked up a crisp packet from behind a telephone box. He then returned to the prison. He was arrested and searched and the drugs were found in his jacket and in his car. He was interviewed and said that a good informant had told him about the drugs. Before the prison service he had been in the armed forces and had had a flawless career in both. Held. The seriousness and gravity of this offence was aggravated by his position of trust. Further, he had in the past recovered drugs (although this is not clear when from the report). **9 years** upheld.

R v Mills 2005 1 Cr App R (S) 180. The defendant pleaded guilty to possessing heroin with intent to supply. He was a prison officer who was stopped and searched as he went into prison and was found to have two bags of heroin in his underwear containing in total 9.35 g of heroin at 20% purity. He immediately admitted he was carrying heroin into the prison for an inmate, and gave the inmate's name. He said the package had been give to him on the previous evening by a woman at a railway station, and he also named her. She was his co-defendant. He said he was to be paid £400 for delivering the drugs. He told police he had smuggled a package two weeks earlier into the prison for the same man There was a significant delay before he was sentenced which was not his responsibility, and he offered to give evidence for the prosecution against his co-defendant. He had no previous convictions. The pre-sentence report set out the background to the offending of financial and considerable emotional stress for the defendant. His family was suffering hardship because of his wife's lengthy illness and an industrial accident to his son. One of the prisoners had acquired information about his financial position and used it to apply pressure on him. His wife left him. Held. It was rightly said by the judge that the fact that the defendant was a prison officer increased the seriousness of the offence as he knew the problems caused by drugs in prisons. The only reason for reducing his sentence was he that he had offered to give evidence against his co-defendant. It was difficult to imagine anyone co-operating more with the authorities than he had. So **6 years** not 7.

Prisoners, supply to – Cannabis

183.28   *R v Doyle* 1998 1 Cr App R (S) 79. The defendant pleaded guilty to possessing cannabis resin with intent to supply. She went to visit her boyfriend in prison and she was strip searched after a sniffer dog made a detection. 8.7 and 10.4 grams of cannabis resin was found in her underclothes. It was worth about £70. She was under a fair amount of emotional pressure because she had found her boyfriend very depressed and possibly suicidal when she had visited him before. She was 28 and had lost both her jobs, which had caused her and her elderly parents difficulty and distress. She is now unable to pay the mortgage on the parents' house and the parents were in poor health. She had no convictions. Held. The need to deter is of very great importance. Taking into account the extenuating circumstances **12 months** not 18.

R v Farooqi 1999 1 Cr App R (S) 379. The defendant pleaded guilty at the Magistrates' Court to possessing cannabis with intent to supply. He went to visit a friend in prison.

A sniffer dog alerted the staff and a £15 wrap of cannabis was found. It contained 1.91 grams. He admitted the offence. He said the previous night he had been given the package by three men who threatened to harm his family if he didn't carry out their instructions. He was 22 and single. He lived with his parents and was unemployed. As a juvenile he had a conviction for robbery for which he was fined. In 1996 he was convicted of possessing cannabis and obstructing the police. In 1997 he was convicted of blackmail and he was given a combination order. He had been the victim of a violent assault and suffered from depression and headaches. The risk of re-offending was described as minimal. Held. Even where the quantity is small the offence should be treated seriously. A sentence of **12 months** is likely to be passed even on a plea. 6 months is not the tariff in these cases. The appeal must be dismissed.

R v Alger 2005 1 Cr App R (S) 347. The defendant pleaded guilty on re-arraignment to possession of cannabis resin with intent to supply. He tried to pass 12.3 gm of cannabis resin to a prison inmate while visiting him. The defendant, 36, had a number of previous convictions including burglary and dishonesty. In 2001 he was sentenced to a two year community rehabilitation order and 12 month DTTO for possession of amphetamine and supply of heroin. In July 2002 he breached the orders and was re-sentenced to 8 months imprisonment. In September he was given a conditional discharge for possession of cannabis. Held. The previous conviction for supply was an aggravating feature. Those caught passing or attempting to pass drugs to prisoners must expect a sentence designed to deter others. The sentence of **21 months** imprisonment was severe but not manifestly excessive.

Old case. *R v Freeman* 1997 2 Cr App R (S) 234, (for a summary of this case see the first edition of the book.)

Purity – What is required?

183.29   *R v Morris* 2001 2 Cr App R (S) 297. We have considered a large number of authorities. The relevant principles are the amount of Class A or B drug with which a defendant is involved is a very important but not solely the determinative factor in sentencing. Evidence as to the scale of dealing can come from many sources other than the amount with which a defendant is directly connected. Amounts should generally be based on the weight of drug involved at 100% purity, not its street value: see *R v Aramah* 1982 4 Cr App R (S) 407 at 409 and *R v Ronchetti* 1998 2 Cr App R (S) 100 at 104 as to cannabis; *R v Aranguren* 1994 99 Cr App R 347 at 351 as to cocaine; *R v Warren & Beeley* 1996 1 Cr App R 120 at 123A as to ecstasy and *R v Wijs* 1999 1 Cr App R (S) 181 at 183 as to amphetamine. But, in some circumstances, reference to the street value of the same weight of different drugs may be pertinent, simply by way of cross check. E.g. 1 kilo of LSD is worth very much more than 1 kilo of heroin, and 1 kilo of amphetamine is worth very much more than 1 kilo of cannabis. Weight depends on purity. The purity of drugs such as cocaine and heroin, and amphetamine powder, can be appropriately determined only by analysis. The weight of drugs such as ecstasy, in tablet, or LSD, in dosage, form, can generally be assessed by reference to the number of tablets or doses and, currently, an assumed average purity of 100 mgs of ecstasy (*R v Warren & Beeley* 1996 1 Cr App R (S) 233 at 236) and 50 micrograms of LSD (*R v Hurley* 1998 1 Cr App R (S) 299 at 304) unless the prosecution or defence, by expert evidence, show the contrary (*R v Warren & Beeley* 1996 1 Cr App R (S) 233 at 236, and *R v McPhail* 1997 1 Cr App R (S) 321 at 322) Purity analysis is essential for sentencing purposes for cases of importation, or in other circumstances, where 500 grams or more of cocaine, heroin or amphetamine are seized. It may be desirable in cases where quantities less than 500 grams of those substances are seized. But, bearing in mind the cost of purity analysis and that analysis may cause delay, purity analysis will not generally be required where a defendant is in possession of only small amounts consistent with either personal use or only limited supply to others. In such a case the court can be expected to sentence only on the basis of a low level of retail dealing, but taking into account all the other circumstances of the particular case. But, as purity can indicate proximity to the primary source of supply, if there is reason for the prosecution to believe that a defendant in possession of a small quantity of drugs is close to the source of supply and is wholesaling rather than retailing, it will be necessary for purity analysis to be undertaken before a court can be invited to sentence on this more serious basis. In the absence of purity analysis or expert evidence, it is not open to a court to find or assume levels of purity, except in the case of ecstasy and LSD in the circumstances to which we have referred.

Retailing, low level – Class A

183.30   *R v Djahit* 1999 2 Cr App R (S) 142. The appropriate sentence following a trial for low level retailing of a Class A drug, with no relevant previous convictions, i.e. selling to other addicts in order to be able to buy drugs for his own consumption and to earn enough to live very modestly is **about 6 years**. A plea at the earliest opportunity will reduce the sentence by about $1/_4$ to $1/_3$. Personal circumstances may reduce it further. If the defendant is able to show that he is no longer addicted to Class A drugs then a reduction may also be appropriate. [*R v Afonso* 2004 (see below) changes this so the 6 year tariff does not apply to drug addicts but to commercial supplies, those with stock and those who repeatedly supply.]

R v Twisse 2001 2 Cr App R (S) 37. It has been said that the *R v Djahit* 1999 (see above) decision does not lie entirely comfortably alongside what has been said in a number of other cases which suggest a longer sentence. We have looked at a wide range of reported cases, which suggest a longer sentence. All indicate a sentence of between **5 and 7 years**: in other words the offender may expect about 6 years which can be increased or mitigated. We are persuaded it is not necessary to review the existing tariff. As has been pointed out in *R v Djahit* the present level of sentencing does seem to bear a sensible relationship with those importing quantities of drugs.

Retailing low level Class A – Drug addicts – Guideline remarks

183.31   *R v Afonso* 2004 The Times 14/9/04. We review the tariff. Where the offender is an out of work drug addict whose motive is solely to finance his addiction, who holds no stock of drugs and made few retail sales 6 years is too high. Addict's culpability is likely to be less than many other suppliers. For some adults and young offenders a **DTTO** will be appropriate. For a first drug supply following a trial the defendant should be a short-term prisoner. For a plea at the first reasonable opportunity the sentence should be **2–2$1/_2$ years**. The sentence for young offenders is likely to be less.

Retailing low level Class A – Drug addicts – Cases

183.32   *R v Afonso* 2004 The Times 14/9/04. The defendant pleaded guilty at the earliest moment to four counts of supplying heroin, two counts of supplying crack cocaine and being concerned in the supply of heroin. An undercover officer entered a homeless centre and met the defendant. He asked if she was looking for heroin. Two phone calls were made and a third man was met. The officer was handed a wrap of heroin for £10. Three days later the officer was supplied with £20 worth of cocaine and he arranged another man to supply the officer with heroin. The next day the defendant supplied the officer with crack. Four and six days later he supplied the officer with £10 worth of heroin. The defendant was 37 and had a £150 a day crack addiction. He had no convictions for drugs but he had a substantial record over a four year period for particularly shoplifting. He had had a variety of sentences including a DTTO. The risk of reoffending was assessed as high he reverted to his old ways. **3$1/_2$ years** not 5.

Retailing to the vulnerable or young

183.33   *R v Djahit* 1999 2 Cr App R (S) 142. Selling to the vulnerable or the young will increase the sentence, see *R v Barnsby* 1998 2 Cr App R (S) 222 and *R v Doyle* 1988 10 Cr App R (S) 5. Introducing people to heroin will also increase the sentence, see *R v Singh* 1988 10 Cr App R (S) 402.

R v Kitching 2000 2 Cr App R (S) 194. The defendant was convicted of five charges of supplying cannabis resin and herbal cannabis. He was a cleaner at Ampleforth School. Pupils approached him for cannabis and he supplied a 17 year old with £10's worth and £45's worth for which he charged £5 delivery. He supplied a 15 year old with £18.50's worth. Another 17 year old was sold £20's worth on two occasions. A 16 and 17 year old were each supplied with £20's worth. One of the pupils informed the school and the defendant was arrested. He was 28 and of good character. Held. The judge was in error to describe the offences as committed in breach of trust. The offences were very serious which merited immediate custody. This was less serious than *R v Nolan* 1992 13 Cr App R (S) 144 so **18 months** on each concurrent not 2 years.

Warehouseman – Class A

183.34   *R v Harvey* 1997 2 Cr App R (S) 306. The defendant pleaded guilty to possessing ecstasy with intent to supply. He and his co-defendant were working in a café and police searched the premises and found 900 ecstasy tablets. The defendant had started work there the night beforehand and was so short of cash he was living in his car. He was told the drugs belonged to a drug baron and understood he would be in danger if he didn't comply with the request to assist. Following a Newton hearing the judge indicated that the basis for sentence was that the café was a wholesale distribution point where the 900 tablets were split for onward dispatch. The defendant was neither an organiser nor a chief. He was a warehouseman with a duty to repackage the goods for later collection. There was nothing to suggest this wasn't the first occasion he was involved, but there was clearly substantial trust placed in him. He did it for an undisclosed benefit, which might have been to keep his job. He was desperately short of money. The judge found he had made no benefit. The previous convictions were disregarded. He had spent his youth in children's homes. Held. Because of the plea, his personal circumstances and the sentence on the co-defendant **3¹/₂ years** not 5.

For basic principles about the different drugs see **CANNABIS, ECSTASY, HEROIN, LSD** and **OPIUM**

B Amphetamine – Class B

183.35   *R v Wijs Re Rae* 1999 1 Cr App R (S) 181 at 185. The defendant pleaded guilty to two counts of possessing cannabis and a count of possessing temazepan. He was convicted of possessing amphetamine with intent to supply. Police officers stopped a vehicle in which he was a passenger. He gave false answers. Inside a carrier bag under the seat in front of him was found a large block of amphetamine. It had a dry weight of 606 grams (95% pure), the equivalent at 100% purity of 575 grams and a street value of £75,600. He was 32 and had a long criminal record stretching back to 1979, which included drug convictions in 1980 and 1984. In 1989 he was sentenced to 7 years for robbery. The judge said he was a medium wholesaler, right at the start of the chain. Held. We are in full agreement with the observations of the judge but **3 years** not 5.

R v Horrigan 2001 Crim LR 1957. The defendant D pleaded guilty to two counts of being concerned in the supply of cannabis and a similar count for supplying amphetamine. P pleaded guilty to five counts of supplying amphetamine. The pleas were entered at the first opportunity. They and other co-defendants were members of a family, which sold drugs. The police decided to make test purchases. D was at his father's home. The house had a padlocked gate through which cannabis was passed. Police made two £10 test purchases on different days. P sold the drug from his home. Those who wanted heroin were directed to two other family members. P sold them £10 deals of amphetamine on 4 different days. He appeared to get it from a box with 3–4 oz of drugs in it. Police found scales and small bags at P's house. D was 22 and P 41. D was said to be assisting in his father's 'shop.' P accepted dealing for 3 weeks. D had many convictions before 1997 for petty offences but only two for driving whilst disqualified since. P had a long list of convictions, which had always been dealt with at the Magistrates' Court. Neither had any drug convictions. Held. D's sentence reduced from 15 to 9 months on each concurrent and P's from 4 to **3 years** on each concurrent.

See also AMPHETAMINE

C Cannabis – Class C (previously B)

Cannabis – Class C (previously B) – Does reclassification affect the guidelines for cannabis supply?

183.36   *R v Mitchell 2004* Unreported 9/11/04. The defendant pleaded guilty to importing cannabis. Held. R v Donovan *2005 1 Cr App R (S) 65* makes clear that in light of the raised maximum penalty for cannabis the reclassification of cannabis should not result in any reduction in sentence.

R v Herridge 2005 Unreported 26/5/05. For supply Parliament clearly intended no change. Where the cannabis is for own use a reduction should be made.

Cannabis – Class C (previously B) – less than 1 kilo (at 100%)

183.37   *R v Donovan* 2005 1 Cr App R (S) 65. The defendant was convicted of possessing 409.9g of cannabis with intent to supply and two counts of simply possessing cannabis (218.2 g and 5.61 g). Police stopped a vehicle being driven by the defendant and noticed a strong smell of cannabis. The defendant admitted being in possession of cannabis and was arrested. He was searched at the police station where police found 5.61 g. His home was searched and in the living room, the freezer and the fridge the police found the 218.2 grams in three large amounts. In the bedroom they found a number of large packages containing 409.9 g of cannabis. They also found a cannabis grinder and a roll of clingfilm that had been used to wrap some of the cannabis. He declined to answer questions in interview; at trial he said the cannabis was for his own (extensive) use. The Judge indicated that he would view the defendant as someone who subsidised his own consumption by dealing in a comparatively small way. The defendant worked in the music industry where consumption was commonplace. He was 25 with convictions for simple possession of class B. Held. Possession with intent to supply cannabis would almost inevitably attract a custodial sentence; even though cannabis has been re-classified. Having regard to the fact that judge treated this matter as though the defendant had pleaded guilty to all three counts and the very limited extent to which the defendant was involved in supply and his previous effectively good character, supported by impressive character references, **6 months**, not 12.

Cannabis – Class C (previously B) – Large scale dealing – Couriers

183.38   *R v Freeder* 2000 1 Cr App R (S) 25. The defendant was convicted of possessing cannabis resin with intent to supply. Police saw the defendant speeding and followed him. He was stopped and they noticed he was nervous. He could not supply an address so he was arrested. At the police station officers became suspicious of the back seat and when it was removed they found 48 kilos of cannabis resin. It was discovered the car had arrived from Spain seven days earlier with another driver. At Portsmouth a drug detector had not indicated a presence of drugs. The defendant had arrived at Gatwick eight days before his arrest. He denied all knowledge of the drugs. In 1988 he received 15 months for possession with intent to supply cannabis. In 1996 in Morocco he received 2 years for possession of cannabis with intent to export it. His arrest was shortly after his release from that offence. The judge said he was passing a draconian sentence because of the size of the operation. **5 years** not 7.

R v Odey 2001 2 Cr App R (S) 388. The defendant pleaded guilty to possession of cannabis with intent to supply and dangerous driving. Police tried to stop the defendant in a van because a door was not secure and he was not wearing a seat belt. He accelerated away and drove at speed and dangerously until he lost control of the van and skidded into a lamppost. He then ran off and fell. He said it was because the van was stolen but in fact there were 143 kilos of cannabis worth about £400,000 in the back. Police found £2,000 in cash at his home. He was interviewed and refused to comment. He had received no benefit. The basis of plea was that he was a courier on a single occasion. He was 35 and had no drug convictions. He had not served a custodial sentence. Held. We anticipate he was expecting some significant financial benefit. 5 years would have been appropriate if he had contested the case, but because of the plea **3 years 9 months** substituted for 5.

R v Baldwin 2002 The Times 22/11/02. LCJ. The defendant pleaded guilty to conspiracy to supply cannabis and being concerned in the supply of amphetamine. He was a courier for a large scale drugs enterprise. At the beginning of the police investigation he was sent to prison for $2^1/_2$ years for possession of cannabis with intent to supply. He served his sentence. Later he was charged with couriering a heat dealing device for amphetamine packing. (There are no details about the cannabis matter.) Until 1993 he was regularly appearing before the courts mostly for dishonesty. There was some violence but no drug offences. There was then a gap till 1998 when there was a section 20 wounding matter. There was employment for him. He had served the equivalent of 12 months imprisonment. Held. He does not represent a high risk of direct harm to the public. He has shown he can hold down responsible employment. Bearing in mind the prison overcrowding and the good prospects he is not going to prey on the public again there are advantages to a fine. A further 12 month sentence is not going to protect the public. So **immediate release** and a **£5,000 fine**. (The problem with this report is there are no details of the cannabis matter and no reference to the impact of the fact that he had already been sentenced for other offences connected with the drug enterprise.)

Old cases. *R v Netts* 1997 2 Cr App R (S) 117 and *R v Fairburn and McCarthy* 1998 2 Cr App R (S) 4. (For summaries of these cases see the first edition of this book.)

Cannabis – Class C (previously B) – Large scale dealing – Organisers and others

183.39   *R v Cunningham* 1999 2 Cr App R (S) 261. The defendant pleaded to possessing cannabis with intent to supply. The police watched him drop off what they believed were drugs at his parents' address. Two days later they arrested him as he was driving to that address. Two holdalls were found in his vehicle, which together contained fifteen 1 kilo blocks of cannabis. Five further blocks were found at his parents' address, which were identical to the others. The street value was over £100,000. £900 was found in the defendant's home. The defendant was 45 and traded in oriental crafts and wood carvings. He had convictions dating from 1973 to 1984. His last four convictions were drug related and included supplying Class A drugs for which he received 6 months suspended. He had never been to prison before. He was not the ringleader. **4 years** not 5.

R v Chisholm 1999 2 Cr App R (S) 443. The defendants C, F, Wa, K, Wr and T pleaded guilty to conspiracy to supply cannabis and to a lesser extent amphetamine. The Crown dropped a count referring to supplying Class A drugs after difficulties including witness problems became apparent. Pleas were entered after a 5–6 week pre-trial hearing. C ran a major supply organisation for Class B drugs in the North-East under the cover of his business in sale and repair of vehicles. His right-hand man and chief of staff was K, Wa and Wr were helpers and took part in the day to day running of the yard. They cut the amphetamine, couriered the drugs and money and looked after them. T supplied the drugs to Teesside and F purchased the drugs from C and sold them to South Tyneside. F was described as a sort of area manager. The offence lasted for 15 months. Police mounted a surveillance operation. with observation posts and covert listening devices. Police picked up conversations referring to 60 kilos in Spain, £250,000 in the boot of a car and 45 drums, 50, 100, 300, 200 kilos of either cannabis or amphetamine. The sentencing judge referred to the conspiracy as being on a massive scale and one never seen before in that part of the world. C was 39 and had a bad record with 14 appearances in court. He had received 5 years in 1989 but had no drug related convictions. F was 42 with a dismal record including two crimes of violence. He had no drug convictions. Wa was 35 with a number of previous convictions including one for drugs. K was 41 with 40 previous convictions, but none for drugs. Wr was 36 with a better record than the first four. T was 49 with virtually no convictions. C relied on the limited confiscation order of £40,000, indicating limited assets, the judge's remark that the defendant's were entitled to explore the legality of the covert operation, the fact that the Crown would not have accepted a plea to Class B until then and 11 years on a plea did not leave enough room for more serious cases. Held. 11 years gave a discount of less than 25% from the maximum. The judge must have pitched it too high. C's sentence was reduced to **10 years**. That wasn't regarded as tinkering. Because F's involvement was over only 2¹/₂ months and the reduction made for C his sentence was reduced from 7 to **5¹/₂ years**. Wa's sentence was reduced from 7 to **6 years**. Because of the reduction for C. K's sentence was reduced from 8 to **7 years** and Wr's and T's sentence was reduced from 7 to **6 years**.

R v Milton 2002 Unreported 28/10/02. The defendant was convicted of conspiracy to supply cannabis. 400 kilos of cannabis (10% of which was skunk) was imported from Holland. It was worth £1.7m. He was in regular contact with his co-conspirator for 4 weeks and this was considered to be planning. He travelled to Holland for what was a purchase enquiry making contact with a convicted Dutch drug importer. Although another paid for the drugs the defendant arranged the transport. The Judge considered he was a major participant in the importation. Two months before the offence he was released from prison for a cannabis supply offence for which he received 30 moths. Held. The Judge's approach could not be faulted. **10 years** was severe but not wrong. (It is not clear why he wasn't indicted with importation.)

R v Turvey 2003 1 Cr App R (S) 75. The defendant changed his plea to guilty of possessing 1,981 kilos of cannabis with intent. He hired a van in his own name and purchased a mobile phone in a false name. In a surveillance operation he was seen to drive the van into a yard where the drugs were loaded into his van. He signed for the goods in the same false name. He drove the van to near his home and the van was seen to drive there in a circle. He was arrested. The drugs were worth £6.9m–£8.3m. He was 35 with convictions for assaulting a police officer (fined) and possession of a controlled drug. Held. The proper starting point was **9 years**. Taking into account his plea with a full discount and character the proper sentence would be **6 years**.

Old cases *Att-Gen's Ref. Nos. 19 to 22 of 1997* 1998 1 Cr App R (S) 164 (For a summary of the case see the 1ˢᵗ edition of this book.)

Cannabis – Class C (previously B) – Small retail dealer

183.40   *R v Fantom* 1999 2 Cr App R (S) 275. The defendant pleaded guilty to possessing cannabis with intent to supply, supplying cannabis resin and possession of cannabis and amphetamines. For 3 months the defendant had supplied a boy aged 17 with cannabis. The police searched his flat and found £1,000 in cash and three pieces of cannabis, a smoking pipe, a set of scales, some glucose powder, a roll of cling film and some amphetamine. They searched him and found two pieces of cannabis. £145 in cash was found in a wallet. He was interviewed and said he used cannabis everyday and admitted selling it to whoever came to the flat. The cannabis weighed 137.6 grams. He was 29 with 17 unrelated previous convictions. Held. The *R v Aramah* 1982 76 Cr App R 190 guidelines suggest 1 to 4 years. Here **2 years** not 3.

R v Kitching 2000 2 Cr App R (S) 194. The defendant was convicted of five charges of supplying cannabis resin and herbal cannabis. He was a cleaner at Ampleforth School. Pupils approached him for cannabis and he supplied a 17 year old with £10's worth and £45's worth for which he charged £5 delivery. He supplied a 15 year old with £18.50's worth. Another 17 year old was sold £20's worth on two occasions. A 16 and 17 year old were each supplied with £20's worth. One of the pupils informed the school and the defendant was arrested. He was 28 and of good character. Held. The judge was in error to describe the offences as committed in breach of trust. The offences were very serious which merited immediate custody. This was less serious than *R v Nolan* 1992 13 Cr App R (S) 144 so **18 months** on each concurrent not 2 years.

R v Horrigan 2001 Crim LR 1957. The defendant D pleaded guilty to two counts of being concerned in the supply of cannabis and a similar count for supplying amphetamine, P pleaded guilty to five counts of supplying amphetamine. The pleas were entered at the first opportunity. They and other co-defendants were members of a family, which sold drugs. The police decided to make test purchases. D was at his father's home. The house had a padlocked gate through which cannabis was passed. Police made two £10 test purchases on different days. P sold the drug from his home. Those who wanted heroin were directed to two other family members. P sold them £10 deals of amphetamine on four different days. He appeared to get it from a box with 3–4 oz of it in it. Police found scales and small bags at P's house. D was 22 and P 41. D was said to be assisting in his father's 'shop.' P accepted dealing for 3 weeks. D had many convictions before 1997 for petty offences but only two driving whilst disqualified since. P had a long list of convictions, which had always been dealt with at the Magistrates' Court. Neither had any drug convictions. Held. D's sentence reduced from 15 to **9 months** on each concurrent and P's from 4 to **3 years** on each concurrent.

R v Barber 2002 1 Cr App R (S) 548. The defendant pleaded guilty before venue to possessing cannabis with intent to supply, possession of cannabis and possession of cannabis with intent to supply. Police officers executed a search warrant at a Golf Club intending to search the defendant's locker. The defendant arrived and his car was searched and police found twelve 9 oz bars of cannabis resin. He had £167 on him and he said it was 3 kilos worth and it was fractionally under 3 kilos. At the police station he said there was a lump of cannabis at his home and police found 37.4 grams of cannabis resin there. At his mothers house they found 144 grams and £26,000 in a holdall. In the kitchen they found 46.5 grams and a set of scales. When interviewed he said he had bought the cannabis resin in the car that morning for £3,650. He admitted dealing and to making £550 profit per kilo. In 1998 he had two convictions for possessing cannabis and in 1999 a conviction for possessing cocaine. He received fines. The pre-sentence report said he was displaying a high level of motivation in favour of not offending again. Held. He deserved more than a? discount because his plea was before venue. **2¹/₂ years** not 3¹/₂.

Cannabis – Class C (previously B) – Social supply

183.41   *R v Roberts* 1998 1 Cr App R (S) 155. The defendant pleaded guilty to possessing cannabis with intent to supply, producing cannabis and possession of cannabis.

On 26 September 1996 the defendant was stopped by police and found to have a tin containing about 3 grams of cannabis bush. In his accommodation was found a set of scales, three packets of hemp seeds, £245 in cash, four cannabis plants, a sachet containing 1 gram of cannabis bush and two dolls containing four wraps with 10.74 grams of cannabis in them. He said he had been selling to mainly friends making £20 per oz so he did not have to pay for his cannabis. He had sold about 1 to 1½ oz a week that summer. He was sentenced on the basis he sold only to friends. He was 20 and was a student at Leeds University with no convictions. The sentencing judge granted him a certificate to appeal and he obtained bail. Held. The case passed the custody threshold. It was commercial supply albeit at the bottom end. It is important for people to know that if they are University students or others if they dabble even in small scale supply they are likely to loose their liberty. For deterrent reasons it was necessary to impose a custodial sentence. Applying *R v Black* 1992 13 Cr App R (S) 262, **2 months** YOI on each concurrent not 6 months.

R v Luke 1999 1 Cr App R (S) 390. The defendant pleaded guilty to supplying 6.8 grams of cannabis and possessing with intent to supply 84 grams. The defendant was a university student and was of good character. He had references. There was a written basis of plea, which said the first matter, was to a friend who had asked for it and he had initially refused to supply it. This was the first time he had sold it. The second amount was to be used by his flat mates. They had put the money together and some money was outstanding. He was holding the drugs till he was paid for. It was purchased in that amount as it was cheaper and it would mean others could concentrate on their revising. He was visiting a drug project to cure himself of his drug habit. **4 months** not 9 months.

See also CANNABIS

D Cocaine – Class A

Cocaine – Class A less than 1 kilo (at 100%)

183.42   *Att-Gen's Ref. No. 83 of 2003* 2004 2 Cr App R (S) 388. The defendant pleaded guilty at the Magistrates' Court to two counts of possession of drugs with intent to supply. The amounts were 29.4 grams of heroin and 120.2 grams of crack cocaine with a combined street value of between £6,500 and £7,500. The drugs were found during a police search of the defendant's house and on his person. He was minding the drugs for others in return for a loan for gambling. He said he knew what the crack cocaine was but he thought the heroin was amphetamine. The defendant, 44, had a number of previous convictions mostly for minor dishonesty, but none for drugs. Since he was sentenced he had completed 34 hours of a community punishment. He had given the names of the three people who he said had left the drugs with him. A pre-sentence report said he was at low risk of re-offending. Held. There was no evidence that the names supplied had been of any value to the police. The defendant acted for financial advantage. Involvement as a minder for others of a substantial quantity of Class A drugs required a sentence measured in years. The appropriate sentence would have been at least **4** years. Because it was a reference and the hours worked **2½ years** imprisonment not 240 hour community punishment.

R v Smitheringale 2005 1 Cr App R (S) 260. The defendant pleaded guilty on re-arraignment to possession of cocaine with intent to supply. A co-accused, P had been found not guilty. P had been seen to enter the defendant's shop carrying a package. The defendant left the shop with the same bag within a minute, put it in the boot of his car and drove off. Police officers stopped him and found a package containing 618 grams of cocaine (at 100%). He said he had agreed to act as a courier for the package for between £500 and £1,000. The defendant had two previous convictions for dishonesty between 1981 and 1987. In 1991 he was convicted of possessing drugs with intent to supply and fined, so those drugs were presumed to be Class B. He had no convictions since 1991. He was sentenced on the basis that he was a courier but still a key player. He remained in work while awaiting sentence. Held. **7 years** was a stern sentence but not outside the legitimate range or manifestly excessive.

Cocaine – Class A – Flat, dealing from (including telephone sales from flat)

183.43   *R v Day* 2000 2 Cr App R (S) 312. The defendant pleaded guilty to two counts of supplying cocaine and possessing cannabis resin. He was convicted of possessing ecstasy. There was a police operation and undercover officers telephoned the defendant and arranged meetings. On two separate occasions £50's worth of cocaine was sold. A search was made of the defendant's flat and 37.7 grams of cannabis and eight ecstasy tablets were found. Held. There was no material difference between this case and *R v Howard* 1996 2 Cr App R (S) 273 where the sentence was reduced to 4 years. **4 years** for the supply counts not 5$^{1}/_{2}$. [The other sentences remained shorter and concurrent.]

R v Underwood and others 2005 1 Cr App R (S) 478 at 484. The defendant pleaded guilty to offering to supply cocaine and heroin (separate counts). An undercover officer phoned the defendant and arranged a £50 heroin deal. The officer went to a co-defendant's (H's) address with another officer and was met by the defendant who took the money for the drugs that were handed over by another defendant. Two weeks later another officer phoned the defendant about crack cocaine and was told to phone him back in 10 minutes. The officer was then invited back to H's house. H invited the officer in and he was taken to the defendant's room where the defendant was found chipping rocks from a bigger ball of crack. There was no principal offender. The defendant was 55 with 30 years of offending including possessing class A. Held. The defendant made no profit or commercial gain from his activities and reflecting broad justice of the sentences imposed on H (3 $^{1}/_{2}$ years), the sentence should be **3$^{1}/_{2}$ years** concurrent not 5 years.

R v Alfonso 2005 1 Cr App R (S) 560. The defendant A pleaded guilty to four counts of supplying heroin, two of supplying cocaine and one of being concerned in supplying heroin. Undercover officers targeting a centre for the homeless met the defendant who offered him heroin. After making a phone call and meeting with someone else, the defendant sold £10 of heroin to the officer. Three days later he supplied the officers with £20 of cocaine and he arranged for another man to supply the officer with heroin. The next day he supplied the officer with crack obtained from another man, 4 days and 6 days later he supplied further £10s of heroin. He had a £150 per day addiction. He was a high risk of reoffending. He was 37 with previous for dishonestly but not for drug offences. He had received a DTTO in the past and more recently custodial sentences. Held. He was simply dealing to fund his own addiction and there were no aggravating features. **3$^{1}/_{2}$ years** not 5.

R v Alfonso Re S 2005 1 Cr App R (S) 560 at 566. The defendant S pleaded guilty to four offences of supplying heroin and three of supplying cocaine. Undercover officers made a phone call and spoke with the defendant who offered to supply heroin to them. The officers met with the defendant and his friend, J, who supplied them, over the course of 2 weeks, £10 and £20 amounts of heroin and crack totalling £80 over four occasions. On two occasions J was observed to have about 6 or 7 further wraps on him. The defendant, when interviewed, admitted handing packages to the officers but claimed not to have known what was in them. Both the defendant and J had travelled about 30 miles to target this particular area. The defendant had become addicted to drugs at a low point in his life but was drug free at the time of sentence. He represented a medium risk of reoffending. J had played the greater role and it was accepted that the defendant was not dealing for commercial gain. The defendant was 24 with one previous conviction for which he was conditionally discharged. J had a poor record including drug offences and was in breach of his licence. J was sentenced to 4 years. Held. A greater distinction should have been made between the defendant and J (although J's sentence may well have been a lenient one) hence **2¹/₂ years** and not 3 years 3 months.

R v Alfonso Re An 2005 1 Cr App R (S) 560 at 567. The defendant An pleaded guilty to five counts of supplying cocaine. He sold a total of 2.8 grams of cocaine to under-cover officers for a total of £240 over 5 different occasions. On the first occasion he retrieved a bag containing several wraps from some weeds and supplied £40 of crack. Following repeated requests he supplied other officers. It was not accepted that he only supplied the undercover officers and he was sentenced as a commercial trader with access to considerable stock. The risk of reoffending was assessed as low. He was drug free but HIV positive at the time of his sentence. He was 26 and of previous good character. Held. The original sentence did not reflect his previous good character, his plea and the aspect of his addiction. **4 years** not 5.

Cocaine – Class A – Offering to supply/Deceiving the buyer

183.44   *R v Prince* 1999 2 Cr App R (S) 419. The defendant pleaded guilty to offering to supply cocaine. Police mounted a surveillance operation in Moss Side. There were thirteen days of video evidence and he appeared in only one of them. Because there was no link with others being sentenced the Court of Appeal decided to look at the facts of his case in isolation. An undercover officer approached someone and asked for 'a stone.' He said he had none and the defendant approached her and sold her a wrap for £20. It was 208 grams of paracetamol. The defendant later accepted a stone meant crack cocaine. He was 38 and had been addicted to drugs particularly cocaine for some time. He had a long list of convictions mainly for dishonesty to finance his addiction. He was in breach of his licence following his release from a 2¹/₂ year sentence for robbery. There were 224 days left to serve. He had no drug convictions. Held. It was important the sentence reflected that what was sold was not a controlled drug. 18 months was too long. **12 months** substituted. Although the judge when he activated the 224 days left to serve didn't say whether they were consecutive or concurrent they should be served consecutively. The amount should be 6 months consecutive not 224 days.

See also **Pretending goods were prohibited drugs**

Cocaine – Class A – Social supply

183.45   *R v Williams* 2004 1 Cr App R (S) 119. The defendant pleaded guilty to perverting the course of justice and possession of cocaine. Later she pleaded to possession with intent to supply cocaine. Police executed a search warrant at her flat and found 12 rocks of crack in her underwear and £211. The drugs weighed 5.2 grams and were worth £500. She gave a false name and made no reply to the police questions. A month later she was re-interviewed and admitted the false name and said she was afraid of being deported. This was the perverting matter for which she received 3 months concurrent. She also said she was a prostitute and a substantial user of crack. The basis of plea was she lived with two other women and they had each paid £160 towards a block of crack. She cut it up so they could share it. She was of effective good character. Held. Cases where drugs are purchased on behalf of others who are not present are more serious than when they are all present. Because of the basis of plea **18 months** not 3 years.

Cocaine – Class A – Street dealing etc – Guideline remarks

183.46   *Att-Gen's Ref. No 84 of 2000* 2001 2 Cr App R (S) 336. The defendant pleaded guilty to two charges of supplying crack cocaine. Held. For those of good character who plead guilty to supplying more than once to an undercover officer the sentencing bracket is **4–5 years**. Personal qualities play a comparatively small part in determining the appropriate sentence.

Cocaine – Class A – Street dealing etc – *non commercial*

183.47   *R v Anderson* 2003 1 Cr App R (S) 421. The defendant pleaded guilty to supplying cocaine. An undercover police officer used audio equipment when making purchases of drugs. She asked the defendant for a couple of rocks of crack. The defendant said that he could arrange it and they agreed a price of £40. The defendant walked off and returned with some cellophane wraps, which were given to the officer in exchange for £40. He gave the officer a piece of paper with "Derek" and a phone number written on it. He told her that she could call him at any time to arrange another purchase. In interview he said that he was not a drug dealer, this was a one-off transaction and he had made no profit. He said that he had supplied the cocaine and given her his telephone number in order to impress her. The defendant was 36 at the time with ten convictions, including two for possessing cocaine. He had no previous convictions for supplying controlled drugs. His previous longest custodial sentence was 12 months' imprisonment. His version was accepted. Held **18 months** not 30 months. (Note. The prosecution's acceptance of the defendant's version seems absurd)

Cocaine – Class A – Street dealing etc – *Commercial*

183.48   *R v Cargill* 1999 2 Cr App R (S) 72. The defendant pleaded guilty at the Magistrates' Court to four counts of supplying crack cocaine, possessing crack cocaine with intent to supply and simple possession. A police operation was mounted to combat drugs. An undercover officer sought to purchase drugs and called the defendant's mobile number. A meeting was arranged and 1.4 grams of crack cocaine was bought for £100. This occurred three further times. The defendant struggled violently on arrest and said, 'I'm only trying to make a living.' Eleven rocks of crack cocaine were found in his car. He was of good character. The sentencing judge referred to the defendant's activities being sufficient to trigger the police operation. Held. We do not think that that is a permissible inference, as it is far more likely that his name cropped up when they were looking into far more serious dealers. That fact and *R v Howard* 1996 2 Cr App R (S) 273 persuades us to reduce the sentence from 6 to **5 years**.

R v Iqbal 2000 2 Cr App R (S) 119. The defendant pleaded guilty at the earliest opportunity to possessing crack cocaine, possessing crack cocaine with intent to supply and a bail offence. Police were in plain clothes trying to reduce drug supply. The defendant asked an officer, 'What do you want?' The officer replied, 'Rocks.' The defendant spat out two rocks of crack cocaine into his hand and was arrested. The cocaine was 0.694 grams at 80% purity. He produced 15 clingfilm wrapped packages of crack cocaine from his sock. Their weight was 2.9 grams at 83% purity. He was of good character. Held. The cases indicate that notwithstanding the mitigation in this case the level of sentencing for first offenders for this offence is of the order of **4½ years** which is what he received. Albeit at the upper end of the tariff it was not manifestly excessive.

Att-Gen's Ref. No 84 of 2000 2001 2 Cr App R (S) 336. The defendant pleaded guilty at the Magistrates' Court to two charges of supplying crack cocaine. A police operation was set up to combat drugs in Peckham. Audio and video tape was used The defendant asked an undercover officer if he wanted 'weed.' The officer said he wanted a rock. He gave the defendant £20. The defendant then disappeared and returned with 247 mgs of crack at 60% purity. Two weeks later he sold another rock which was again 247 mgs and 58% purity. He was arrested and declined to answer questions. He had arrived in this country two weeks before the first sale. He had quickly become addicted to cocaine. He was 29 with no convictions. Held. For those of good character who plead guilty to supplying more than once to an undercover officer the sentencing bracket is **4–5 years**. Personal qualities play a comparatively small part in determining the appropriate sentence. Taking into account that it was a reference and he had already been released **3 years** not 9 months.

R v Beevor 2001 2 Cr App R (S) 362. The defendant pleaded guilty to two counts of possession of cocaine, two counts of possession of heroin, supplying heroin, supplying cocaine, possessing heroin with intent to supply and possessing cocaine with intent to supply. Police stopped his car and 68 mgs of crack cocaine was found in his pocket. He had £279 in cash and a mobile telephone. He admitted he had been out that night selling heroin and cocaine. His home was searched and 81 wraps were found containing a total of 7.67 grams of heroin and 25 grams of cocaine (3.48 grams at 100%). The purity was 27%. There was also $\frac{1}{2}$ gram of heroin and 185 mgs of cocaine. He said he was a runner. He said he used the mobile for dealing and had been dealing for about two weeks because he couldn't pay his mortgage. For the last 2 years he had had a drug habit. He was spending £40 a day. He was 32 with no convictions. His family had paid £2,500 for a clinic for him. He was remorseful and the risk of him re-offending was described as low. The judge said he had been totally honest with the police. Held. The level of sentence for supplying and possession with intent to supply is in general on a conviction 5 years at least, *R v Singh* 1988 10 Cr App R 402 at 406. The sentence largely depended on the degree of involvement, the amount of trafficking and the value of the drugs. The purity of the drugs needed consideration. Personal mitigation however strong does not necessarily reduce the sentence below a certain level. **4 years** not 5.

Att-Gen's Ref. No 27 of 2002 2003 1 Cr App R (S) 102. The defendant pleaded guilty to two offences of supplying cocaine. An undercover police officer called a phone number and she asked for a 20 and a meeting was arranged. She then went there and made another call and minutes later the defendant arrived. The defendant spoke to an Asian man who passed the defendant a package who then asked the police officer what she wanted. £20 was exchanged for 0.29 grams of cocaine at 70%. The activity was recorded on tape. Later that day the events were repeated and 0.270 grams of 53% cocaine was exchanged for £20. Foil, cling film and £675 were found at his home address. In interview he said he was dealing in drugs under pressure from others. It was not suggested he was a principle. He was 23. Seventeen days before the offence he was released from a 4 year sentence for importing cocaine. He had flown from Jamaica with 223 grams of cocaine at 40% and had pleaded guilty. The defence contended in both cases he was under pressure with debts to pay off. He received 12 months on each count with 12 months consecutive for the breach of his licence. Held. On a conviction the sentence would be **at least 5 years** excluding the breach of licence. As there was no prospect of avoiding the conviction there should be one year off for the plea. As it was a reference **3 years** consecutive substituted.

Att-Gen's Ref. No. 60 of 2003 2004 2 Cr App R (S) 376. The defendant pleaded guilty to two counts of supplying heroin and one count of supplying cocaine. H, a co-defendant offered to supply undercover police officers. He then arrived at premises, and asked the defendant for the heroin. The defendant then passed him a package which was given to the officers. This contained 409mg of heroin at 44% purity. Five days later the defendant again handed H 4.01g of cocaine at 17 % purity to sell to officers. A month later H telephoned the defendant from the premises and asked him to bring 6g of heroin. He arrived and handed the bag to the officers; it contained 5.27 g of 33% heroin. He was sentenced on the basis that he was less involved than H; that he had carried the drugs for H and produced them on demand; that he was H's assistant and played no part in the organisation or planning of the offences; that his involvement was limited to the three occasion charged and that the drugs belonged to H. The defendant, 45, had two minor convictions of an unrelated nature. He had 'psychological problems'.

He assisted in the dealing over of five weeks. Held. The minimum starting point should have been **4 years** reduced to **3 years** for the plea. Because it was a reference **30 months**, not 12 months.

Old cases *R v Walker* 1998 2 Cr App R (S) 245 (For a summary of this case see the first edition of this book.)

E Ecstasy – Class A

Ecstasy Class A 10,000 tablets or more

183.49   *R v Davidson* 2003 1 Cr App R (S) 12. The defendant changed his plea on three counts of supplying ecstasy. He was a doorman at a club and became the subject of an undercover operation. One officer developed a relationship with him and the defendant made offers to supply him with significant quantities of drugs including ecstasy. In January he supplied 475 tablets of ecstasy for £1,065. In March two tablets were supplied as a sample. Five days later he supplied 10,200 tablets at £1.40 each making £14,280. The street value was between £70,000 and £100,000. £630 was found at his home. He was nearly 50 with no convictions. He said he was under financial difficulties following a business collapse. The pre-sentence report said the risk of re-offending was limited. Held. The Judge either didn't give him full credit for the plea or started too high. There was no reason to doubt as the Judge did he was a wholesaler's agent. Although the police behaved impeccably, the escalating progress of the supply was to a degree fuelled by their suggestions and the suggestion for the large supply originated with the officer. Together with the good character and the personal mitigation **7 years** not 9.

Ecstasy – Class A – Minder etc of the drugs

183.50   *R v Harris* 1998 1 Cr App R (S) 38. The defendant pleaded guilty to possessing ecstasy with intent to supply. Police searched his home address and found seven plastic bags containing 705 ecstasy tablets with a street value of between £5,600 and £10,500. He said he had minded the drugs for 10 days and thought he would be paid £50. He would not identify the person who asked him to mind them. The sentencing judge said that a minder performs an essential service to the dealer and is often close to the dealer. Held. The position of a minder will depend upon the amount of drugs involved and what inferences can be drawn from the surrounding circumstances. There may well be circumstances when the minder is more seriously involved than the courier. Bearing in mind the authorities **4 years** not 5.

Old case. *R v Spalding* 1995 16 Cr App R (S) 803.

Ecstasy – Class A – Offering to supply/Deceiving the buyer

183.51   *R v Chambers and Barnett* 1999 1 Cr App R (S) 262. The defendants C and B pleaded guilty to offering to supply ecstasy and going equipped to cheat. The defendants went to a rave with some innocuous tablets. They tried to sell them as ecstasy. B tried to sell one to an undercover police officer. C was 26 with no convictions. B was 19 with a conviction for deception. It was contended it was a deception case not tainted by any stain of the Drug Trafficking Act offences. Held. We don't entirely agree with that submission as it still contributed to the raves plus drug scene which the police and courts are trying to stamp out. However, no damage and possibly some good would have been done to the purchases. **12 months** imprisonment and detention not 18 months.

R v Tugwell 2001 2 Cr App R (S) 501. The defendant pleaded guilty to possession of cannabis and ecstasy and two counts of offering to supply ecstasy. At the Glastonbury pop festival two undercover officers wanting to buy ecstasy approached him. He sold four tablets to one officer at £30 and eight to another for £40. They were innocuous zinc tablets. He told the police this in interview. The other drugs were found on him. He was 35 with 12 court appearances. The convictions were for dishonesty including robbery and burglary. Held. He was not duped. Supplying fake drugs is not simply a case of obtaining money by fraud but it involves a lesser degree of criminality than supplying real drugs. This distinction was not reflected in the sentence. **15 months** not 2 years for the supply counts.

R v McNab 2002 1 Cr App R (S) 304. [The defendants were convicted of offering to supply large quantities of ecstasy. **9 years** and **3 years 11 months** upheld.]

See also *Pretending goods were prohibited drugs*

Ecstasy – Class A – Retail supply

183.52   *R v Ferrett* 1998 2 Cr App R (S) 384. The defendant pleaded guilty to four counts of supplying ecstasy, one count of supplying amphetamine and two counts of supplying cannabis. A teenage girl died after taking ecstasy and amphetamine. The defendant's mother and others told the police he might have been the supplier of the drugs. The defendant was interviewed and denied supplying the deceased but admitted supplying another. The police interviewed several of his friends and they admitted receiving drugs from the defendant. Some of the drugs were supplied near a school to pupils aged 15. The defendant denied it but admitted to the probation officer that he had supplied drugs for about a year and made about £80 a week. The judge did not attribute the girl's death to him. He was 18 when sentenced and of good character. There were eight character references. Following his detention his risk of re-offending was assessed as very low. Held. A total of 5 years would have been appropriate. However, he is entitled to a further discount because of the credit due to his family taking the course they did. So **4¹/₂ years** YOI not 7.

Att-Gen's Ref. No. 20 of 2002 2003 1 Cr App R (S) 279. The defendant pleaded guilty to possessing 786 ecstasy tablets with intent to supply. Traffic police stopped him for speeding and 24 ecstasy tablets were found in the car and 2 in his pocket. At his home there were 760 tablets and £202 in cash. The street value was £6,000–£12,000. He admitted selling drugs for about a year. He was 21, had no convictions but had a cocaine and ecstasy habit costing £300 a week with drugs debts. There was a good work record with written references. The Judge, Moses J, accepted the recommendation in the pre-sentence report and gave him a community rehabilitation order with 100 hours community punishment with a condition of attendance at a Think First programme and £200 costs. He said it afforded the most effective way of keeping the defendant away from drugs. The defendant had served the 100 hours and demonstrated a positive attitude to the order. Held. The Judge was right to say the range was **3–4 years**. Only in the most exceptional circumstances was a non custodial sentence right for commercial supply of Class A drugs. Unless this was adhered to the courts will be sending out the wrong message. This was not such an exceptional case. Taking into account it was a reference, the 100 hours served and other factors **2 years** substituted.

Att-Gen's Ref. No. 136 of 2002 2003 2 Cr App R (S) 545. The defendant pleaded guilty to two counts of possessing ecstasy with intent at the PDH. He pleaded guilty on the day of trial to three remaining counts of supplying ecstasy on the basis of commercial supply to 21 people. He had been arrested driving his car in which 12 tablets of ecstasy were found. He said that they were for his heroin-addict sons. At his home self-seal bags, £375 in cash and a notebook containing names and numbers were found. In interview he said he and a friend bought 60 ecstasy tablets the previous day (30 each). The tablets were for his sons. He said that his ex-partner was dealing and that the notebook and writing was hers. Expert analysis did not support this contention. He said that the £375 in cash was for household bills; although he was on unemployment benefit.

On the day of trial his ex-partner was to give evidence and the defendant changed his pleas to the remaining counts. The sentencing judge afforded him little, if any, credit. He had no previous convictions for drug offences and had gone for a relatively long period without committing any offences. He was 42 and genuinely remorseful. Held. This was commercial supply of a class A drug to a number of people over a number of weeks. The original sentence (100 hours CPO and a 12-month CRO) was simply wrong. A sentence of **3^1/$_2$ years upwards** would have been appropriate. Allowing for the near-completion of the original sentence and that he was to be sentenced again, **2 years**.

Old case. *R v Wright* 1998 2 Cr App R (S) 333, for summary of this case see the first edition of this book.

Ecstasy – Class A – Retail supply –Sales in nightclubs – Guideline remarks

183.53 *R v Rumble* 2003 1 Cr App R (S) 618. The defendant pleaded guilty to supplying ecstasy. Held. A sentence for social supply of ecstasy to friends involving no real profit is one which may in some circumstances be properly met with a non-custodial sentence. For commercial supply in nightclubs involving this sort of quantity of tablets sentences of about 4 years' imprisonment following a plea of guilty has been consistently upheld by this Court. But this was extensive social supply.

Ecstasy – Class A – Retail supply – Sales in nightclubs – Non commercial

183.54 *R v Rumble* 2003 1 Cr App R (S) 618. The defendant pleaded guilty to supplying ecstasy, possessing ecstasy with intent to supply and possession of amphetamine with intent to supply. The defendant was seen by the manager of a nightclub to approach a number of different people. The manager saw him pass a package to one of those people before being apprehended. 73 ecstasy tablets, 28.3 grams of amphetamine and £132 in cash were recovered from him. He was arrested and interviewed. He said he was one of a group of friends who habitually bought ecstasy and amphetamine, pooling their money to obtain the drugs cheaper. He said that he had bought 100 tablets the day before for distribution to friends and acquaintances that evening. He had been paid in advance and had made no profit. He became the wholesale supplier to that extended group of friends in order to maintain and enhance his reputation amongst them and to obtain their approval and appreciation of him. That evening he had distributed 20 and had taken the rest himself. The amphetamine was for him and his girlfriend. He was sentenced on that basis. The defendant was 36 with no previous convictions. He had been cautioned 4 months earlier for possessing amphetamine. Held. The defendant fell to be sentenced for acting as the supplier to a large number of friends and acquaintances of a class A drug inside a nightclub not for profit. A sentence for social supply of ecstasy to friends involving no real profit is one which may in some circumstances be properly met with a non-custodial sentence. For commercial supply in nightclubs involving this sort of quantity of tablets sentences of about four years' imprisonment following a plea of guilty has been consistently upheld by this Court. But this was extensive social supply. This was a serious example of social supply involving a very substantial number of tablets and a very large circle of those to whom they were to be supplied. **Two years** not three.

Ecstasy – Class A – Retail supply – Sales in nightclubs – Commercial motive

183.55 *R v Mayeri* 1999 1 Cr App R (S) 304. The defendant pleaded guilty at the earliest opportunity to four counts of supplying ecstasy. One tablet was involved in each case. Four undercover police officers approached him in a nightclub and he agreed to sell them a tablet for £10. He named his supplier. He was 22 and of good character. There was a 9 month wait before he was sentenced. He claimed there was an element of entrapment. The defendant relied on *R v Tonnessen* 1998 2 Cr App R (S) 328 Held.

The entrapment argument is not a good one. Where undercover officers discover a man is prepared to sell drugs by approaching him it is not a matter the courts need normally take into account as amounting to entrapment. It might be said 'Seller beware.' These premises are frequently used to sell drugs. There has to be a considerable element of deterrence. **2 years** was entirely justified.

R v Robotham 2001 2 Cr App R (S) 323. The defendant pleaded guilty to two counts of supplying ecstasy and possession of amphetamine. He was seen acting suspiciously by staff in a nightclub. He was taken to be searched and he produced 0.45 grams of amphetamine. He was told police would be called and he said he had 40–50 ecstasy tablets on him. When the police came he tried to run. A bag with 56 ecstasy tablets and fragments of about 5 more was found on the floor. He had £285 cash on him. His home was searched and 32 more tablets, glucose and plastic bags similar to the one found in the club were found. He was 32 with many previous including ones for possession of drugs. Held. **4¹/₂ years** was entirely correct.

R v Kesler 2001 2 Cr App R (S) 542. The defendant pleaded guilty at the Magistrates' Court to supplying ecstasy and possessing ecstasy with intent to supply. Police officers kept observation on the defendant outside a public house where members of the public approached him. Over an hour he was watched having short conversations with people and then he would put his hands in his pocket. He gave one female something which she put in her mouth. This was the first charge. Shortly after he was searched and police found 40 ecstasy tablets. He admitted he supplied the female with ecstasy. He was 22 and had no drug supply convictions. His convictions included robbery, dishonesty and possession of cannabis. He said he was under pressure because of debts. The judge gave a modest discount for the plea because he was caught red-handed. Held. **4 years** was not manifestly excessive.

R v Hendry 2002 1 Cr App R (S) 534. The defendant pleaded guilty to three counts of supplying ecstasy, possessing ecstasy with intent to supply and possession of an offensive weapon. The defendant worked unpaid as a doorman at a pub. Three police officers asked for ecstasy and he supplied them with 3 pills for £10. Six days later he supplied them with 3 more and two weeks later he supplied them with another 2. His car was searched and police found 63 pills and a rubber handled extendable baton. The basis of plea was he had bought tablets for a friend who declined to accept them. He said he was selling them off cheaply to get rid of them. He was then 24 with convictions but none for drugs. Reports spoke well of him. Held. These were persistent supplies with a drug store available but **4 years** not 5.

Att-Gen's Ref (No 71 of 2002) 2003 1 Cr App R (S) 515. The defendant indicated a guilty plea in the Magistrates Court on his first appearance and was committed for sentence for several counts of supplying ecstasy to undercover police officers in a nightclub. Six officers purchased between them a total of 17 pills from this defendant at a total price of £70. The first officer approached the defendant and asked "Are you able to sort me out?" The defendant agreed to sell him pills "£3 or £4 each or three for a tenner." Further similar purchases followed. On one occasion the defendant approached two officers and said "Are you boys looking for pills?" When arrested and searched, a further 32 tablets wrapped in five separate packages were seized from his jeans. He admitted in interview that he had bought 35 ecstasy tablets from a man called Tony at the club and that he had not intended to sell any further tablets that night. The basis of his plea was that this was a single night's transaction. The defendant was 21 and of good character. He had unsought testimonials from his employer and had the offer of continued full time employment. He had been released by the time of the reference. Held. The aggravating features are that this was a species of commercial supply and involved repeated offences. The conversations between the defendant and the undercover police officers and the number of transactions as well as the number of tablets found on him on his arrest, demonstrate that that night, at any rate, the offender was in business and holding himself out as a supplier of ecstasy tablets to willing customers, selling them in a place where he anticipated a ready market. The appropriate level of sentence was in the **region of 18 months**, however, having examined the impact of the prison sentence and the very impressive report from the employer, there was no public advantage in returning the defendant to prison so 5 months not varied although unduly lenient.

Old cases *R v Skidmore* 1997 1 Cr App R (S) 15, *R v Thompson* 1997 2 Cr App R (S) 223, and *R v Patel* 1998 1 Cr App R (S) 170. (For summaries of these cases see the first edition of this book.)

Ecstasy – Class A – Sales to friends/Joint purchases

183.56 *R v Wakeman* 1999 1 Cr App R (S) 222. The defendant pleaded guilty to offering to supply ecstasy, possession of ecstasy, two counts of possession of cocaine and two counts of possession of cannabis. Police kept watch outside a nightclub. They approached the defendant and he took something from his pocket and put it in his mouth. He began to walk away and the police held him. He was chewing something and was told to spit it out. Eventually he spat out what turned out to be six tablets of ecstasy. He was arrested and was found to have $^1/_2$ gram of cocaine and nearly 2 grams of cannabis resin. At his house a list was found, which he said were lists of pills which he was to get for friends. There were 14 names on it. In another list there were 18 names and 19 amounts in figures. He said it was money he owed friends so they might buy pills from him. The prosecution accepted that there had been no supply of drugs against the list and the money he had lent was to supply drugs in the future. Also the customers were friends who were existing users of ecstasy. The defendant was then just 21. Held. The basis of plea was wholly artificial. There was evidence that he was a drug dealer. All too often pleas are tendered on an artificial basis. It puts the judge in difficulty. We have to accept that basis now. Where there is supplying to friends and here where there is just an offer to supply the sentence will be less than usual sentences for commercial supply. **18 months** not 2 years.

R v Busby 2000 1 Cr App R (S) 279. The defendant pleaded guilty to possession of ecstasy and amphetamines with intent to supply. He entered a nightclub and was found to have 14 ecstasy tablets and 4 amphetamine tablets. He said he and his two friends had bought the drugs between them. He was going to give them their share. They were expecting to be in clubs for the best part of 24 hours. The defendant was then 27 and a self employed electrician. He had two Public Order Act convictions. The court considered *R v Denslow* 1998 unreported 6/2/98 where two heroin users bought together £300 worth of heroin. The dealer gave it to the defendant who gave half to his friend. He had been absolutely discharged for the supply count. The Court of Appeal said a count of supply would hardly ever be justified. Held. We don't doubt that observation. Possession of Class A drugs carries a maximum sentence of 7 years. This was not a trivial or technical offence. Possession on behalf of others to enable them to commit offences is more serious than possession simply for oneself. Trying to take the drugs into a nightclub through the security check is more serious. Custody was appropriate. 9 months was too long for someone who pleaded guilty at the first opportunity and had a lot to lose by way of home, standing and employment. The fact of imprisonment was a very large part of the punishment. Taking into account *R v Ollerenshaw* 1999 1 Cr App R (S) 65, **6 months** substituted.

R v Robertson 2000 1 Cr App R (S) 514. The defendant pleaded guilty at the earliest opportunity to possession of ecstasy with intent to supply and possession of cannabis. The defendant was driving his car when police stopped him. Drugs were found in the car. The police searched his home and found 28 ecstasy tablets. Some were divided into wraps of 6, 5 and 3 tablets. Quantities and names were found on notepaper. 14.33 grams of cannabis and drug paraphernalia were found. The basis of plea was that he was going to supply 20 of the tablets to the five persons on the list on a non profit making basis. He was of good character and was in extremely good and profitable employment which was now lost. He had purchased property on a mortgage. Held. Because of *R v Byrne* 1996 2 Cr App R (S) 34 and *R v Wakeman* 1999 1 Cr App R (S) 222, **12 months** instead of 18.

R v Bull 2000 2 Cr App R (S) 81. The defendant pleaded guilty at the first opportunity to supplying ecstasy. He gave 2 ecstasy tablets to his sister's boyfriend without charge. The boyfriend and the sister went to a nightclub where they stayed several hours. He drank a number of double whiskeys as well as a lot of water. He was seen to be sweating a lot. The two came home at 2.30 pm. He was found dead the next morning. He died of heart failure. It was discovered he had an abnormality of the heart and ecstasy contributed to the heart failure. If he hadn't taken the ecstasy it is unlikely he would have died. When questioned by the police the defendant admitted he had given him the tablets. The defendant was 21 and lived with his parents. He was in regular employment and working hard. He had no convictions and had a deep sense of remorse, which led to a depressive illness and a suicide attempt. Held. He must not receive a disproportionate sentence because of the tragic and appalling consequences of the supply. **9 months** not 18.

R v Dassu 2004 2 Cr App R (S) 402. The defendant pleaded guilty to one count of possession of ecstasy with intent to supply, six counts of possession of drugs (heroin × 2, cannabis × 2, cocaine and crack cocaine). The intent plea and two other pleas were entered as the trial was about to begin. Police followed a car in which he was the passenger and 214 ecstasy tablets were thrown out while a further one was found in the car, these tablets having a total value of £645. Police also found 4.28 g of heroin on the road and 0.14 g in the car. They found a 250 g bar of cannabis in the defendant's house, some further small amounts of cannabis, a small amount of cocaine and a small amount of crack cocaine. The total value of the drugs was about £1,800. The defendant pleaded guilty to the small amounts at a much earlier stage than he did to the 214 tablets, the 4.28 g of heroin and the 250 g bar of cannabis. His plea was on the basis that he was a heavy user of drugs and that his drug taking friends had financed the ecstasy tablets so they could be shared out amongst them all including the defendant. He had bought the 250 g of cannabis in bulk to minimise cost and in order to share half and half with a friend, so there was no commercial element in the supply. The defendant, 24, had a number of convictions for drugs although none for supply. A pre-sentence report said that he was making some attempts to control his addiction. Held. **3** years not 4.

R v Bennett 2001 Unreported 2/8/01. **1 year** not 3 on a plea for 21 pills.

R v Edwards 2001 Unreported 19/10/01. Social supply. The defendant was convicted of possession 29½ pills and he pleaded to supplying cocaine. **2 years** not 3.

Att-Gen's Ref No 71 of 2002 2003 1 Cr App R (S) 515. The defendant indicated a guilty plea in the Magistrates Court on his first appearance and was committed for sentence for several counts of supplying ecstasy to undercover police officers in a nightclub. Six officers purchased between them a total of 17 pills from this defendant at a total price of £70. The first officer approached the defendant and asked "Are you able to sort me out?" The defendant agreed to sell him pills "£3 or £4 each or three for a tenner." Further similar purchases followed. On one occasion the defendant approached two officers and said "Are you boys looking for pills?" When arrested and searched, a further 32 tablets wrapped in five separate packages were seized from his jeans. He admitted in interview that he had bought 35 ecstasy tablets from a man called Tony at the club and that he had not intended to sell any further tablets that night. The basis of his plea was that this was a single night's transaction. The defendant was 21 and of good

character. He had unsought testimonials from his employer and had the offer of continued full time employment. He had been released by the time of the reference. Held. The
aggravating features are that this was a species of commercial supply and involved
repeated offences. The conversations between the defendant and the undercover police
officers and the number of transactions as well as the number of tablets found on him
on his arrest, demonstrate that that night, at any rate, the offender was in business and
holding himself out as a supplier of ecstasy tablets to willing customers, selling them
in a place where he anticipated a ready market. The appropriate level of sentence was
in the **region of 18 months**, however, having examined the impact of the prison sentence and the very impressive report from the employer, there was no public advantage
in returning the defendant to prison so 5 months not varied although unduly lenient.

R v Mapp 2003 2 Cr App R (S) 293. The defendant pleaded guilty in the Magistrates'
Court to supplying two ecstasy tablets to a friend. He was seen on CCTV in an alley
passing small objects to another from a bag. He was seen to put the bag down his sock
and receive some money. A search of his sock revealed 20 further ecstasy tablets and
there were two others in his pocket. He was sentenced on a (surprisingly!) accepted
basis that he had only sold those two tablets to a friend who had requested them and
that the other tablets were for his own consumption. He had no previous convictions.
There was a "most excellent" prison report. Held. **8 months** not 21 months.

Old cases *R v Kramer* 1997 2 Cr App R (S) 81 and *R v Pettet* 1998 1 Cr App R (S) 399
(both of which are summarised in the first edition of this book.)

See also Ecstasy

F Heroin – Class A

Heroin – Class A less than 1 kilo (at 100%)

183.57 *Att-Gen's Ref. No. 146 of 2002* 2003 2 Cr App R (S) 640. The defendant
pleaded guilty to possessing 982 grams of heroin (363 grams at 100%) at the first
opportunity. Police boarded a train believing a gun was on board and inspected a
holdall. The defendant denied it was his. Police found a plastic gun and the defendant
then admitted it was his holdall. He took the heroin from his carrier bag and tried to
conceal it on his body. When challenged he said it was cannabis. The basis of plea was
that he was a courier who believed it was cannabis and acted because he had a drug
debt. There were differences about the debt in his account to the police and the pre-
sentence report writer. He was 35 with a conviction for supplying cannabis for which
he received 6 months. Held. We consider the opportunity the offender might have had
to satisfy himself of its true nature. The drugs were wrapped. The false account was to
water down the degree of his admission in that regard. The degree of discount needs not
be particularly high. 7–7½ years as a starting point is not excessive. Because he
believed it was cannabis **5 years** is proper. Because it was a reference **4 years**.

Att-Gen's Ref. No. 83 of 2003 2004 2 Cr App R (S) 388. The defendant pleaded guilty
at the Magistrates' Court to two counts of possession of drugs with intent to supply. The
amounts were 29.4 grams of heroin and 120.2 grams of crack cocaine with a combined
street value of between £6,500 and £7,500. The drugs were found during a police search
of the defendant's house and on his person. He was minding the drugs for others in
return for a loan for gambling. He said he knew what the crack cocaine was but he
thought the heroin was amphetamine. The defendant, 44, had a number of previous convictions mostly for minor dishonesty, but none for drugs. Since he was sentenced he had
completed 34 hours of a community punishment order. He had given the names of
the three people who he said had left the drugs with him. A pre-sentence report said he
was at low risk of re-offending. Held. There was no evidence that the names supplied
had been of any value to the police. The defendant acted for financial advantage.

Involvement as a minder for others of a substantial quantity of Class A drugs required a sentence measured in years. The appropriate sentence would have been at least **4 years**. Because it was a reference and the hours worked **2^1/$_2$ years** imprisonment not a 240 hour community punishment order.

Att-Gen's Ref. No. 81 of 2003 2005 1 Cr App R (S) 11. The defendant was convicted of possessing 4.1 kilos of heroin (959grams at 100% purity) with intent to supply. He was the driver and sole occupant of a taxi cab which was stopped by police who were acting on information received. Officers found a bag in the passenger footwell which contained heroin. The defendant denied knowledge of the drug and said that a passenger had left the bag in the taxi. He was 31 with a good character and references. Held. In the case of offences involving distribution, quantity was not the whole story. It is also important to consider how high up the chain of distribution the defendant was. He was clearly a well-trusted courier. The appropriate sentence would have been **9 years** not 5 so 8 because it was a reference.

Heroin – Class A – 1 to 10 kilos (at 100%)

183.58   *Att-Gen's Ref. Nos. 64 and 65 of 1997* 1999 1 Cr App R (S) 237. The defendants O and H pleaded guilty at the earliest opportunity to a conspiracy to supply heroin. Police officers saw the two walking along the street. O was carrying a large green holdall which was searched and was found to contain large amount of drugs. H had £310 cash at his home and a relatively small amount of drugs. O had £520 in cash and packaging bags used to distribute heroin at his home. The total drugs seized from the bag and his home was over 3^1/$_2$ kilos of heroin. At 100% it was 1^1/$_2$ kilos of heroin. H said he didn't know what was in the bag and had been asked to look after it by another for about a week or two. He knew it was drugs. O said he knew it was heroin and that he was going to dump it. They were said to be fairly high up the ladder of distribution. The prosecution accepted they were couriers. O was 28 and H was 40. O was of good character and H had no drug's convictions. Both had references. H had had some depressive illnesses in prison. Held. People who deal in Class A drugs must be dealt with severely to punish and deter. Taking into account the mitigation and that it was a reference **6 years** not 30 months.

Heroin – Class A – 10 to 50 kilos (at 100%)

183.59   *R v Sehitoglu and Ozakan* 1998 1 Cr App R (S) 89. The defendants S and O made early pleas to conspiracy to supply heroin. The defendants were subject to a surveillance operation. S and O were seen carrying holdalls After arrests police found in a flat 44 kilos of heroin (24 kilos at 100% purity), three semi-automatic pistols, two silencers which fitted two of the guns and some live ammunition. The drugs were worth £7–8 m. At another flat police found hydraulic presses and moulds for the compression of heroin into blocks. They were arrested and S had about £1,100 on him. £28,290, £3,500 and £1,680 in cash were found elsewhere. A card was found which was consistent with large scale drug dealing. Neither had convictions. S was 27 and O was 28. S gave information and evidence in a linked murder case, which his part had been crucial. He had also given information and assistance in a significant drugs conspiracy. He was due to give evidence in that case and he was described as the lynch pin in both cases. He and his family were very seriously at risk. The police were satisfied his account was true and accurate. The judge started at 25 for S and reduced it to 15 because of the assistance he had given. Held. The case falls into the highest category of drug trafficking. O was not right at the top of the conspiracy. On a trial the sentence for O and S would be in the region of **24 years**. Because of his plea **18 years** for O not 25 years. The information, assistance, evidence, given and the risks to S and his family mark this as a case where the maximum possible reduction should be made. Applying *R v King* 1985 7 Cr App R (S) 227 the reduction for S should be 2/3 off the starting figure before one considers the plea. The sentence should then be reduced to **8 years**.

R v Altun 1998 2 Cr App R (S) 171. The defendant was convicted of possessing 12.3 kilos of heroin with intent to supply. It was 5.8 kilos at 100%. Its wholesale value was £300,000. Police discovered the heroin in a clothing factory in London. As the police arrived the defendant made off. He was arrested in a hotel and found to have £2,000 cash on him. His fingerprints were found on some of the packages of heroin. The lease of the factory was in his name but he sublet it to another. He was 36 with no convictions and came to this country in 1988. The judge said he didn't know the part the defendant played and there was no evidence to show his role was other than a custodian. However, the value of the drugs showed he must have been a trusted member of the organisation having sophisticated involvement indicated by the cash found and that he registered at the hotel in a false name. The defence said he should be sentenced as a custodian. Held. The defendant was closer to the source of the supply than a mere minder of the drugs. However, **14 years** not 16.

R v Ngiam 2002 1 Cr App R (S) 150. The defendant pleaded guilty to possessing 50 kilos of heroin (at 47%) with intent to supply. Police stopped the car she was driving and found a large suitcase in the boot. It was padlocked and she said it wasn't hers. She was sentenced on the basis she thought it was cannabis and she was a courier. She had a conviction for importing 24 ecstasy tablets and some cannabis cigarettes. For that she received probation. Held. The fact she believed it was cannabis was a mitigating factor but it did not mean the judge was obliged to sentence her as if it was cannabis. If she thought it was heroin the appropriate sentence would be in the region of **15–20 years**. **6 years** was not manifestly excessive.

Heroin – Class A Over 50 kilos (at 100%)

183.60   *R v K* 2003 1 Cr App R (S) 12. The defendant pleaded guilty on the eighth day of his trial to conspiracy to supply heroin. The plea followed the production of documents, which established his guilt without doubt. The conspiracy had the same factual background as *R v Sehitoglu and Ozakan* 1998 1 Cr App R (S) 89 (see above). 44 kilos worth £7 m were seized. One defendant said that 15–22 kilos, then 80 kilos and then 100–150 kilos a time were being imported. The heroin was worth well in excess of £100 m. (The report does not make clear the involvement of the defendant.) The defence argued that the Judge was wrong to take 30 years as the starting point as there were others more involved abroad in the conspiracy. Held. The Judge was entitled to take **30 years** as his starting point and place the defendant for the head of the conspiracy in this country. He was entitled to put the defendant at that head. 4 years deduction properly reflects the plea on the eighth day, so **26 years** upheld.

Heroin – Class A – Couriers

183.61   *Att-Gen's Ref. Nos. 64 and 65 of 1997* 1999 1 Cr App R (S) 237. The defendants O and H pleaded at the earliest opportunity to a conspiracy to supply heroin. Police officers saw the two walking along the street. O was carrying a large green holdall. It was searched and was found to contain large amount of drugs. H had £310 cash at his home and a relatively small amount of drugs. O had £520 in cash and packaging bags used to distribute heroin at his home. The total drugs seized from the bag and his home was over 3½ kilos of heroin. At 100% it was 1½ kilos of heroin. H said he didn't know what was in the bag and had been asked to look after it by another for about a week or two. He knew it was drugs. O said he knew it was heroin and that he was going to dump it. They were said to be high up the ladder of distribution. The prosecution accepted they were couriers. O was 28 and H was 40. O was of good character and H had no drug's convictions. Both had references. H had had some depressive illnesses in prison. Held. People who deal in Class A drugs must be dealt with severely to punish and deter. Taking into account the mitigation and that it was a reference **6 years** not 30 months.

Heroin – Class A – Flat or shop, dealing from

183.62   *R v Weeks* 1999 2 Cr App R (S) 16. The defendant pleaded guilty to nine counts of supplying heroin. Police kept his flat under observation for nine days. They saw between 20 and 25 callers a day. He was arrested and the police found £245 and a wrap of heroin. Items consistent with handling drugs were found. He immediately admitted his involvement and said he had a drug habit, which cost him £100 a day. He said he was selling for someone else and was paid in drugs. He kept three bags for every ten he sold. He said he had been dealing for between 2 and 2½ months and selling to up to 30 callers a day. He was 24 and had convictions for burglary and aggravated vehicle taking. He had no convictions for drugs. In light of the authorities and the mitigation **5 years** not 7.

R v Djahit 1999 2 Cr App R (S) 142. The defendant pleaded guilty to possession of heroin with intent to supply and possession of cannabis. He had indicated his plea shortly after his PDH when he had pleaded not guilty. The police arrived to execute a search warrant at his shop and adjoining flat. The defendant was arrested. Two bags of heroin were found in a door panel near his kitchen. Two further bags were found in a kitchen cupboard. A small amount of heroin was found in one of his socks. The total weight was 21.5 grams with a street value of £2,150. The purity was not ascertained. £6,005, a list of names and addresses, a set of scales and bags were found. The defendant accepted the paraphernalia belonged to him but the list did not. Cannabis was found at his home address. The defendant had no convictions. The pre-sentence report indicated that he had been to a Dependency Unit and had become 'clean.' Held. He should have been given a full discount for his plea of guilty. The correct sentence for low level retailing is about 6 years. He appears to have solved his problems with heroin. The proper sentence was **4 years** not 6.

R v Williams 2000 2 Cr App R (S) 308. The defendant D pleaded guilty to a conspiracy to supply cocaine and another conspiracy to supply heroin. The defendants W and J pleaded not guilty to the same counts. Three months later they changed their pleas to guilty. Police targeted W and his and B's address in Oxford. They saw a large number of visitors to W's address who stayed for a very short period of time. Sometimes they would not enter the premises. On a few occasions small packages were seen to be exchanged for money. An undercover officer made a number of test purchases and was supplied with cocaine and heroin from the three defendants. W's address was searched. W was in the attic throwing drug deals out of the window. Heroin worth £6,000 with a purity between 32% and 57% was found. A set of electric scales was found at J's address. W was the principle figure. Each defendant had a bad record. W's assessment of re-offending was described as high. W's basis for plea was that he started to sell drugs to pay off a debt. He had let a supplier use his address until about four weeks before he was arrested when he supplied the drugs. He had six regular customers who were friends. J's basis was that he had not made any money out of the dealing. J's role was described as not marginal. D's risk assessment for re-offending was described as high until she overcame her drug dependency. The judge said he wanted to send a clear message to dealers who were agents of death and destruction. He expressed the gravest concerns about Class A drugs in Oxford. He said it was a medium sized operation. He rejected W's assertion there were only six regular customers. Held. Because the judge decided not to hear evidence about the factual disputes between the Crown and the defence he was bound to sentence on the basis of plea submitted by the defendants. Applying *R v Djahit* 1999 2 Cr App R (S) 142 the sentences were too long. The judge was in the best situation to judge the relative culpability of the defendants. W's sentence reduced from 8 to **6¹/₂ years**. J's reduced from 6 to **5 years** and D's from 5 to **3¹/₂ years**.

R v Twisse 2001 2 Cr App R (S) 37. The defendant pleaded guilty at the first opportunity to three counts of supplying heroin and offering to supply cocaine. Undercover officers rang the defendant's telephone number and as a result another man supplied the officer with a wrap of heroin. This was not represented in any count in the indictment. The next day another call was made and the officers were asked to come to an address and were supplied by the defendant with 0.342 grams of heroin at 36% purity. It cost £30 and the officers paid £15 and a video in part exchange. The next day there was another telephone call and visit and they were supplied again by the defendant with 0.273 grams of heroin at 35% purity. The value was £25 and they paid £15 and gave him two T-shirts. The next day they rang again and asked for heroin and cocaine. They were invited to the house and the defendant offered to sell them cocaine. The officer asked for heroin and was supplied with two wraps at £20 each. They contained 0.204 and 0.207 grams of heroin at 23% and 28% purity. A search warrant was executed and the defendant and his associate were arrested. He was frank in interview and said he had been dealing for 9 months. He said he bought drugs and used some himself and sold the rest. He had three previous convictions. They were a supply conviction and two possession convictions including one a month before the first sale. On that occasion the defendant had been conditionally discharged for possessing heroin. He said he was now drug free. The defence said it was on a small scale, he made no real profit and following *R v Djahit* 1999 2 Cr App R (S) 142 the starting point was 6 years. Held. You have to bear in mind the horrific picture of what it is like to live near someone trafficking in drugs. Supply is likely to cause offence and very often a good deal of fear. It did seem he made little profit. This was a team effort. **5 years** not 6.

R v Morris 2001 2 Cr App R (S) 297. The defendant was convicted of possessing heroin with intent to supply and possessing cocaine with intent to supply. He had pleaded guilty to simple possession of ecstasy. Police officers stopped the defendant, as he was about to get into a car. They searched him, and his flat. They found 23 ecstasy tablets, 23.37 grams of cocaine, the street value was up to £2,200, 42.5 grams of heroin the street value was up to £3,400. The appellant was arrested and interviewed and claimed the drugs were for his own use. He was 35 years of age and had nine previous court appearances mostly for robbery, sometimes including firearms. In 1993, he was sentenced to 11 years for attempted robbery and carrying a firearm with intent to commit an indictable offence. He was released on licence in 1998. He was ordered to serve the whole 1,670 days of the unexpired term of the 11 year sentence. (That was illegal, as the maximum is the time from the breach to the end of the sentence.[102]) The defence said the total was too long and the sentence was too high for one without a purity analysis. Held. Had the purity been known the defendant could not have been treated more favourably than he was and a sentence of less than 5 years would not have been appropriate. We agree with the observations in *R v Djahit* 1999 2 Cr App R (S) 142, and **5 years** for possession of two different Class A drugs, with intent to supply, cannot be excessive following a trial. The judge when considering the unexpired term of the licence did not pay sufficient regard either to the defendant's history following his release or to the principle of totality. 2¹/₂ years consecutive substituted for an order to serve the whole term.

R v Taylor 2005 Unreported 25/1/05. The defendant pleaded guilty early to possessing heroin with intent to supply. Police executed a search warrant at his home address. They found clingfilm wraps, weights with traces of heroin, dealers lists and £1,220. The defendant arrived during the search and police found on him a set of scales (with traces

102 Criminal Justice Act 1991, s 40A (4)(b) and (5)

of heroin and cocaine on them), £1,365, five wraps of heroin (86.31 grams worth £4,385 street value) and 2.19 grams of cocaine (£219 street value). At the station police found a further 1.39 grams of heroin on him. He was 19 and of good character. **5 years** not 7 detention.

R v Underwood and others 2005 1 Cr App R (S) 478 at 484. The defendant pleaded guilty to offering to supply cocaine and heroin (separate counts). An undercover officer phoned the defendant and arranged a £50 heroin deal. The officer went to a co-defendant's (H's) address with another officer and was met by the defendant who took the money for the drugs that were handed over by another defendant. Two weeks later another officer phoned the defendant about crack cocaine and was told to phone him back in 10 minutes. The officer was then invited back to H's house. H invited the officer in who was taken to the defendant's room where he was found chipping rocks from a bigger ball of crack. There was no principal offender. The defendant was 55 with 30 years of offending including possessing class A. Held. The defendant made no profit or commercial gain from his activities and reflecting broad justice of the sentences imposed on H (3 $^1/_2$ years), the sentence should be **3$^1/_2$ years** concurrent not 5 years.

R v Alfonso 2005 1 Cr App R (S) 560. The defendant A pleaded guilty to four counts of supplying heroin, two of supplying cocaine and one of being concerned in supplying heroin. Undercover officers targeting a centre for the homeless met the defendant who offered him heroin. After making a phone call and meeting with someone else, the defendant sold £10 of heroin to the officer. Three days later he supplied the officers with £20 of cocaine and he arranged for another man to supply the officer with heroin. The next day he supplied the officer with crack obtained from another man, four days and six days later he supplied further £10s of heroin. He had a £150 per day addiction. He was a high risk of reoffending. He was 37 with previous for dishonestly but not for drug offences. He had received a DTTO in the past and more recently custodial sentences. Held. He was simply dealing to fund his own addiction and there were no aggravating features. **3$^1/_2$ years** not 5.

R v Alfonso Re S 2005 1 Cr App R (S) 560 at 566. The defendant S pleaded guilty to four offences of supplying heroin and three of supplying cocaine. Undercover officers made a phone call and spoke with the defendant who offered to supply them heroin. The officers met with the defendant and his friend, J, who supplied them, over the course of two weeks £10 and £20 amounts of heroin and crack totalling £80 over 4 occasions. On two occasions J was observed to have about 6 or 7 further wraps on him. The defendant, when interviewed, admitted handling packages to the officers but claimed not to have known what was in them. Both the defendant and J had travelled about 30 miles to target this particular area. The defendant had become addicted to drugs at a low point in his life but was drug free at the time of sentence. He represented a medium risk of reoffending. J had played the greater role and it was accepted that the defendant was not dealing for commercial gain. The defendant was 24 with one previous conviction for which he was conditionally discharged. J had a poor record including drug offences and was in breach of his licence. J was sentenced to 4 years. Held. A greater distinction should have been made between the defendant and J (although J's sentence may well have been a lenient one) hence **2$^1/_2$ years** and not 3 years 3 months.

Heroin – Class A – Friends etc. supplying to

183.63   *R v Lucas* 1999 1 Cr App R (S) 78. The defendant pleaded guilty to supplying heroin. He bought three £10 bags of heroin and then joined his girlfriend at home. They drank and he injected himself with heroin. He passed the syringe to his girlfriend. He then went to the local shop to buy beer and left her apparently asleep. On his return he couldn't rouse her and called an ambulance. The paramedics arrived and she was already dead. She was found to have $3^1/_2$ times the legal limit of alcohol for drivers and a high level of unmetabolised heroin which suggested she died shortly after injecting herself. Death was thought to have been caused by a combination of drugs and alcohol. The defendant was interviewed and made a frank confession. He said she had only used heroin twice before. There was genuine remorse. Following the death he made a number of suicide attempts. He was now drug free. He was 36 with no relevant convictions. He had abused drugs and alcohol for many years. He had been treated from time to time for depression and had not always been very well. **3 years** not 5.

R v Giunta 2000 1 Cr App R (S) 365. The defendant pleaded guilty to possession of heroin with intent to supply, various possession of drug counts and production of cannabis. Police searched his home and found 120.9 grams of heroin of various purity worth £4,300, small amounts of cannabis, methadone, 50 temazepan tablets and an ecstasy tablet. There was also a cannabis plant, £765 in cash, some scales and a card with figures on it. He was interviewed and said all the drugs were his for his personal use but he had supplied and would supply fellow drug addicts. He had a long standing habit, which he had to finance. He had just a drink drive conviction. He was assessed as being of high risk for re-offending. He had a good reference from his employer and from the prison. He received 5 years for the supply count and short concurrent sentences for the other counts. **5 years** was not manifestly excessive.

R v Ashford 2000 1 Cr App R (S) 389. The defendant pleaded guilty at the Magistrates' Court to supplying heroin. The defendant was living at a bail hostel and another resident who was very drunk asked for some heroin. The defendant said no, but later after being pestered gave him some. The other resident took it and died during the night. He was sentenced on the basis heroin was not the cause of death. Death was caused by asphyxia after vomit had been swallowed. The defendant had served five custodial sentences for dishonesty. He expressed remorse. The prison report said he was traumatised by the death and he was displaying a very high motivation to address his drug problem. **2 years** not 3.

R v Smythe 2000 1 Cr App R (S) 547. The defendant pleaded guilty to possession of heroin with intent to supply. Police officers saw the defendant approach a woman on a bicycle. They spoke and there was an exchange of articles. The police approached and the defendant cycled off. He then discarded the bicycle and ran off. He threw away a wrap which was found to contain 1.82 grams of heroin of unknown purity worth £182. 0.21 grams of heroin was found at his house with £700, a pager and a mobile. He was 22 with 12 court appearances mainly for dishonesty. There were two drug possession appearances and three custodial sentences. The basis of plea was that he and two friends had clubbed together to buy the heroin and he was the one to approach the dealer. Held. It was regrettable that there was no written basis of plea. Also that matters like the money and the mobile etc. were opened which run contrary to the basis of plea. $4^1/_2$ years was a tariff sentence for a relatively low level dealer with a similar record to the defendant and allowing credit for the plea. This was a case when a purchase was not made in the presence of the others. **2 years** substituted.

R v Underdown 2002 1 Cr App R (S) 50. The defendant pleaded guilty to four counts of supplying heroin and possession of heroin with intent to supply on the first day of his trial. They were specimen counts covering two months activity. The purchasers were heroin users and lived in Aberaman in South Wales. They asked for heroin and after initially refusing to help them he regularly sold them heroin bought in Bristol. He then moved in with them. When the premises were searched heroin worth between £400 and £560 was found. He had no relevant convictions and had character witnesses. He had not had a custodial sentence before. **5 years** not 6.

Heroin – Class A – Intermediary etc

183.64   *R v Tonnessen* 1998 2 Cr App R (S) 328. The defendant pleaded guilty to supplying heroin. The defendant was approached by a man who claimed to know her He was accompanied by two others who turned out to be from the *News of the World*. They said they worked for a Sheikh and they were instructed to buy drugs. She was a heroin addict and a cannabis user and said they were widely available. They said they wanted to buy heroin and asked her whether she was prepared to get it for them. They gave her £50 and she bought four wraps of heroin. She and a friend spent the rest of the evening with them. Immediately after her name and photograph appeared in the paper. The police felt obliged to arrest her and she admitted the offence. After the publicity she was assaulted and received a threat to her life. She was 31 and had already served a prison sentence for an unrelated offence. She had no supply convictions. She suffered from a serious pre-cancerous condition. The judge did not refer to the involvement of agent provocateurs and appeared not to have taken it into account. The defence said there could be considerable mitigation where it can be shown that the offence would not otherwise have been committed. It is legitimate for policemen to entrap criminals. When the entrapment is by journalist even more consideration and more weight should be given. Held. We consider there is substance in those submissions. However, it merited immediate custody. We cannot ignore she was set up. If these men had been police officers that would provide mitigation. Different considerations must apply to investigatory journalists. Their purpose was perfectly honourable. But we feel the public would be left with a sense of unease by the identification in the paper. The consequences were most unfortunate. It is appropriate to reflect the entrapment in the sentence. It should have been expressly mentioned in the remarks. In the exceptional circumstances we reduce the sentence from **12 months** to 6.

Heroin – Class A – Large organisations

183.65   *Att-Gen's Ref. No 13–18 of 2004* 2005 1 Cr App R (S) 300. The six defendants were sentenced for a conspiracy to supply heroin between August and November. SM and her partner B, P and J were convicted after a trial. NM and JM (brothers of SM) pleaded guilty on the first day of trial. It was a significant and organised retail enterprise in Birmingham where the evidence came mainly from police observations and tapes. The drugs were sold for either cash or stolen goods. The conspiracy initially operated out of SM and B's flat where they lived with their five children. After an eviction hearing when it was suggested in court the premises were being used for drug dealing the operation moved to NM's flat, where he lived with his partner (not a defendant) and their two children. Throughout the conspiracy heroin of 50% purity was sold in £10 deals. Purchasers phoned the conspirators and the heroin was then delivered to them in a convenient location which included near a school and in a local recreation ground. Some of the street dealers involved seemed to be as young as 14 and 15, and some customers seemed to be of a similar age. Sometimes specific goods were stolen to order and traded at one third their retail value. It was estimated that 30–40 transactions were conducted each day. All the defendants had one or more convictions treated as not aggravating their sentences. SM and B were both 35. They were at the forefront of the conspiracy and dealt with the stolen goods. NM, 23, was an addict. His involvement began after the conspiracy moved to his home, and thereafter he was a significant contributor. JM, 36, was the most prolific street dealer, involved at both addresses. P, 19, was treated as the 'duty dealer' for street supply and was less involved than some of the others. He was not involved for the last five weeks of the conspiracy. J, 24, had an involvement which was limited in time to the first month of the conspiracy. He was present at the first address on occasions when dealing had taken place and on two specific occasions in the first month was concerned in the supply of drugs directly to purchasers. A pre-sentence report said that the educational system had failed him and he left school early but that he was well motivated to study and acquire qualifications which would enable him to secure employment. Held. The aggravating features were:

a significant scale of heroin dealing; a well organised conspiracy; a large number of people were involved in the distribution; some of the dealers and purchasers were young and drugs were sold close to a school and on a recreation ground; sometimes transactions were conducted relatively openly; children lived at the premises concerned; the receipt of stolen goods as payment encouraged criminal activity; the presence of young and very young children while heroin was being supplied. SM and B: in the light of the aggravating features a sentence at the top end was justified, noting particularly the impact this had on the community. An appropriate sentence for both after the trial would have been **10 years**, 5 years quashed and **8 years** substituted. NM: After a trial the appropriate sentence would have been **8 years**, taking into account his late plea and double jeopardy **5 years** not 3. JM: After a trial an appropriate sentence would have been **8 years**, taking into account his late plea and it was a reference **5¹/₂ years** substituted. P: The appropriate sentence was **7 years, 5 years** was substituted for the original sentence. J: The appropriate sentence was **6 years, 5 years** detention was substituted for the original sentence.

Heroin – Class A – Minder etc of the drugs

183.66   *R v Appleton* 1999 2 Cr App R (S) 290. The defendant pleaded guilty to possessing heroin with intent to supply and three counts of possessing Class B drugs. He was a serving prisoner who had his cell searched. Officers found two plastic wraps, each containing ten foil wraps of heroin (total of 0.74 grams at 32%), two foil wraps of heroin (0.15 grams at 31%) and a cling film wrap of 0.56 grams of amphetamine sulphate. He was arrested and admitted the offences. He was sentenced on the basis that he was looking after the drugs for someone else. Held. The fact he was minding them rather than dealing does not necessarily mean a shorter sentence. Those who mind the drugs prevent the real dealers being caught. Those that do the minding and then protect the dealer cannot receive any mercy. It would be different if the person was prepared to name the dealer and assist the police. [For further details see *Prisoners, supply to.*]

Old cases. *R v Arif* 1994 15 Cr App R (S) 895.

Heroin – Class A – Street dealer

183.67   *R v Barnsby* 1998 2 Cr App R (S) 222. The defendant pleaded guilty to four counts of supplying heroin. Outside a Drug Rehabilitation Centre, officers conducting an undercover drugs operation approached the defendant. He supplied two wraps of heroin to one officer and two further wraps to another officer. The next day he offered to supply an officer with a wrap and he fetched it from inside the centre. Later the same officer was supplied with another wrap. All the wraps had cost £10. The total weight was 484 mgs at about 50% purity and 238 mgs at 100% purity. He was arrested and after being shown the video he accepted his guilt. He was 36 and had been a heroin addict for the last 10 years. He had several previous convictions including possession of amphetamine in 1987 and possession of methadone in 1997. He was placed on probation each time. The judge said that the need to deter other drug dealers for the protection of all those vulnerable people using the centre took priority over the defendant's personal circumstances Held. The judge was right. There was nothing wrong with **5¹/₂ years**.

R v Stenhouse 2000 2 Cr App R (S) 386. The defendant pleaded guilty to supplying heroin on four separate occasions. A police officer called a number and was told to ring back in 15 minutes. He did so and spoke to the defendant. They agreed to meet. The defendant was given £10 and the undercover officer was given a wrap, which contained 52 mgs of heroin. The other offences were similar. He had convictions for possession of drugs and two for supplying Class A drugs. The last conviction was in 1997 for supplying one methadone tablet for which he was given probation at the Magistrates'

Court. He had been in custody from December 1998 to July 1999 when he was released because of the Custody Time Limit provisions. He was sentenced in December 1999 to the 7 year minimum term. Since his arrest he had made valiant attempts to conquer his drug addiction. Held. His efforts to break his drug habit were rare and he should be encouraged to continue with his efforts. The sentence because of the combination of circumstances was unjust so **3 years** substituted.

Att-Gen's Ref. No. 60 of 2003 2004 2 Cr App R (S) 376. The defendant pleaded guilty to two counts of supplying heroin and one count of supplying cocaine. H, a co-defendant offered to supply undercover police officers. He then arrived at premises, and asked the defendant for the heroin. The defendant then passed him a package which was given to the officers. This contained 409mg of heroin at 44% purity. Five days later the defendant again handed H 4.01g of cocaine at 17 % purity to sell to officers. A month later H telephoned the defendant from the premises and asked him to bring 6g of heroin. He arrived and handed the bag to the officers; it contained 5.27 g of 33% heroin. He was sentenced on the basis that he was less involved than H; that he had carried the drugs for H and produced them on demand; that he was H's assistant and played no part in the organisation or planning of the offences; that his involvement was limited to the three occasion charged and that the drugs belonged to H. The defendant, 45, had two minor convictions of an unrelated nature. He had 'psychological problems'. He assisted in the dealing over five weeks. Held. The minimum starting point should have been **4 years** reduced to **3 years** for the plea. Because it was a reference **30 months**, not 12 months.

Att-Gen's Ref. Nos. 58–9 of 2001 Unreported 27/7/01. We would have expected **6 years** if it had been fought.

R v Springer 1997 1 Cr App R (S) 217, (for a summary of this case see the first edition of this book.)

G LSD

Guidelines

183.68   *R v Hurley* 1998 1 Cr App R (S) 299. LCJ. It is wrong to consider some Class A drugs merit lesser sentences than others. Assuming the unit (the square containing the drug) is approximately 50 micrograms of pure LSD, the sentence for 25,000 units should in the ordinary case be **10 years** plus. For 250,000 or more units the sentence should ordinarily be **14 years plus**. Adjustment may be needed where it is shown the amount in the square varies significantly from the 50 micrograms figure. Where the seizure is of tablets or crystal in a form which permits a precise amount to be ascertained easily, then work out the number of 50 micrograms units which could be produced from that quantity and then implement the guidelines.

Cases

183.69   *R v Hurley* 1998 1 Cr App R (S) 299. LCJ. The defendant pleaded guilty to possessing LSD with intent to supply. He travelled from America and arranged for sheets of paper to be sent from California to a house, which he had access to. He received them and collected materials so he could impregnate the paper in a flat, which he had rented. The materials were trays, a perforating board, and measuring jugs, He successfully impregnated at least 319 sheets with each sheet having about 900 such impregnated squares which would give a total of 287,000 units of LSD. He was arrested. His home address in California was also searched and items were found which indicated he had a comparable operation in that country. His passport showed seven short trips to the United Kingdom and Peru in the last few years. A Newton hearing was held about the number units he intended to produce and the retail value of the units. The judge concluded that the 319 sheets were to be divided into 287,000 units, but rounded it down to 280,000 units. He decided the retail price was £3.75 per square and thus estimated the projected sale receipts to be over £1m. He described this operation as 'a very highly organised and professional enterprise' and as a 'massive drugs operation'. He said the credit for his plea must take into account that the evidence was overwhelming. The defendant had a number of 'very impressive written references.' and had various medical afflictions Held. The defendant was very heavily involved. The average LSD content of the squares was 31 micrograms, which fell substantially below the 50 micrograms average content, which we have treated as the standard unit. The number of squares should be notionally reduced to reflect that. The judge perhaps gave inadequate credit for the plea. Had this case been contested the appropriate sentence would have been **12 or 13 years**. With the plea of guilty the appropriate sentence was **10 years**.

See also **LSD**

H Magic Mushrooms – Class A

Retailing, small scale

183.70   *R v Thomas* 2005 2 Cr App R (S) 48. The defendant was convicted of possession of magic mushrooms with intent to supply. He was stopped at the Glastonbury Festival and searched. 73 individual self sealing bags containing magic mushrooms (140 grams) were found. He made an attempt to escape. When recaptured he said the bags were going for £10 and he had picked the mushrooms in Wales the year before. He also said there were 70–80 mushrooms in each bag and about 5,000 in all. He was 43 without previous convictions. He had struggled financially for many years. A psychiatric report said he had had 10 years of psychiatric problems and had been treated with antidepressants. It also said he found life difficult to deal with and only survived with the assistance of props. The risk of reoffending was described as low. Further he would have given some mushrooms to friends and sold some to cover the £100 ticket for the festival. Held. This may be equated with small scale retailing. If he had the same number of wraps of heroin he would have received after a trial a sentence of 4–6 years. Account was taken of his long standing problem with depression and the sales to friend and the financing of the ticket. We reject the submission that the drug should be treated differently from other Class A drugs. **2 years** was proper.

I Opium – Class A

Opium – Class A – Guidelines

183.71   *R v Mashaollahi* 2001 1 Cr App R (S) 96. The current classification of opium as a Class A drug is on the premise that it was to be regarded as being every bit as harmful as other Class A drugs. Weight for weight, where street value is concerned, heroin is considered to be approximately eight times more valuable than opium. On this basis, a consignment of 40 kilos of opium at 100% purity would be equivalent in value to five kilos of heroin at 100% purity, importation of which, under the current sentencing guidelines, attracts a sentence of 14 years and upwards on a contested case. There is at least the remote possibility that opium might be imported to convert it into morphine or heroin. In those cases base the sentence on the amount of heroin or morphine that could be produced from the opium seized. We understand that the ratio to apply in these circumstances would be 10:1 i.e. ten kilos of opium would be needed to produce one kilo of morphine or heroin assuming average levels of purity. The guideline for the possession of opium with intent to supply should be based on weight, cross-checked with street value to ensure that at least an approximate equivalence with heroin and cocaine is maintained. Because opium is the natural extract from the poppy and not a drug adulterated with other material the court should assume that it is unadulterated and of 100%

purity. Should the defence wish, by way of mitigation, to persuade a judge that the active ingredient was of a lesser percentage it is open to them to call the appropriate evidence. If the judge is presented with evidence which persuades him that a calculation based on the equivalent street value of heroin or cocaine would produce an unacceptably high sentence for opium offences, he would be entitled to disregard any cross-check based on the street value of heroin or cocaine. For importing 40 kilos or more of opium the sentence should be 14 years and upwards, and for 4 kilos or more the sentence should be ten years and upwards. There is one exception and that is where the importation of opium was carried out for the purpose of conversion into morphine or heroin the appropriate sentence should be based on the equivalent value of those drugs. [As this was a supply case it is a pity the court did not give guidelines about supply other than figures for importation from which a discount could be made.]

Opium – Class A – Cases

183.72   *R v Mashaollahi* 2001 1 Cr App R (S) 96. The defendant pleaded guilty to possessing opium with intent to supply. The opium was 28 kilos of raw opium and 2 kilos in sticks, probably representing some degree of adulteration. The street value of the consignment lay somewhere between £295,000 and £342,000. He was of good character. Held. Applying our guidelines it will be seen that the total importation fell into the ten years and upwards bracket. Having regard to the plea, the good character, and of somewhat less impact, the fact that he was acting as a warehouseman, we reduce the sentence from 14 years to **9 years**. [These are the only facts about the individual case recorded in the judgment.]

See also OPIUM

J   Steroids Class C

183.73   For an old case before steroids were made a Class C drug see *R v Wilson* 1998 1 Cr App R (S) 364 (best ignored).

K   Permitting premises to be used for the supply etc of drugs

183.74   Misuse of Drugs Act 1971, s 8.

Class A drugs – Supply

183.75   Triable either way unless the offence could qualify for a minimum 7 year sentence when the offence is triable only on indictment.

On indictment maximum sentence 14 years for Class A and B drugs and 5 years for Class C drugs. Summary maximum 6 months or £5,000 for Class A and B drugs and 3 months and £2,500 for Class C drugs.

Confiscation For supply offences[103] the court must follow the Proceeds of Crime Act 2002 procedure for offences committed on or after 24 March 2003[104] and Drug Trafficking Act 1994 procedure for offences committed before that date.

Inevitably the offence will qualify for a minimum sentence of 7 years for the third Class A drug trafficking offence[105].

---

103 Proceeds of Crime Act 2002 s 75 and Sch 2 para 1(1)(c) or Drug Trafficking Act 1994 s 1(1)(a) (depending on the date of the offence).
104 Proceeds of Crime Act 2002 (Commencement No 5, Transitional Provisions, Savings and Amendment) Order 2003
105 Applying Drug Trafficking Act 1994, s 1(1)(a) which defines a drug trafficking offence as doing or being concerned in … supplying a controlled drug where the … supply contravenes section 4(1) of the Misuse of Drugs 1971. (Section 4(1) does not create an offence.)

Addicts permitting dealing – Class A

183.76   *R v Kilby* 2002 2 Cr App R (S) 20. The defendant pleaded guilty to permitting premises to be used for the supply of heroin and attempted possession of heroin. Over 4 days he allowed his home to be used for the supply of heroin to four heroin addicts. There was no corruption or profit. He was frank with the police. He was 30 and for 11 years had been a heroin addict with convictions for supply and possession with intent to supply cannabis. There were a large number of other offences including theft. A drug treatment and testing order failed. **2 years** not 3.

R v Sykes 2002 2 Cr App R (S) 83. The defendant pleaded guilty to permitting premises to be used for the supply of heroin, possession of heroin and obstructing a constable. The prosecution dropped a supply count. Police went to his room at a hostel for the homeless to search it. He blocked the door and became quite aggressive. There was a struggle which no doubt gave the five other people in the room time to discard drugs they had onto the floor. They were small amounts consistent with personal use. The defendant had a single wrap of heroin on him. It was conceded the people all used heroin and were used to supplying each other by way of exchange or gift. He was 39 and a long-standing heroin addict and had a number of convictions mostly for dishonesty but including possession with intent to supply a kilo of cannabis. In 1998 he received 6 years for various burglaries including one where an 80-year-old lady was struck a number of times with a metal bar. He was in breach of his licence for that and 12 months consecutive for it was imposed. Held. The offence was to facilitate the use and exchange of heroin and was not to be equated with supply. Different considerations would apply if it was effectively a retail outlet. Taking into account his obstruction it was still too much so **3 years** not 4.

R v Phillips 2003 2 Cr App R (S) 61. The defendant pleaded guilty to allowing his premises to be used for supplying crack cocaine. Police raided the defendant's council house. A co-accused, B, was leaving as the officers arrived. B was searched and £2,000 and 32 wraps of cocaine were found. In the living room, near to where the defendant was sitting was a piece of silver foil, which contained 40 deals totalling 9.65 grams of crack cocaine. The defendant was interviewed and he admitted that for a month he had let two people use his premises to sell cocaine to other purchasers. He was paid in kind with drugs. He had offences of dishonesty and minor violence and six for drug offences. He was sentenced on the basis that he had not intended to deal himself. Held. The clear aggravating feature was that there was an element of profit; as against that, the period of use was relatively short, just about 1 month. **3¹/₂ years** not 4¹/₂.

Failing to take steps to stop dealing – Class A

183.77   *R v Coulson* 2001 1 Cr App R (S) 418. The defendant pleaded guilty to permitting premises to be used for the supply of heroin. A drug dealer and his accomplice dealt with drugs at the defendant's flat with his full knowledge. Police raided the flat and found a large amount of cash, drug paraphernalia and 16.7 grams of heroin at 30% purity. The defendant was arrested and said he knew what was going on and was scared. He had a long list of convictions. Thirty three were for dishonesty. He had served five custodial sentences. Held. *R v Bradley* 1997 1 Cr App R (S) 59 was substantially different. In that case the supply was very limited and this defendant's record is much worse. It is no precedent for reducing the **30 months** sentence. Without people like the defendant it would be difficult for people like this dealer to carry on their business. The appeal was dismissed.

R v Brock and Wyner 2001 2 Cr App R (S) 249. The defendants B and W were convicted of permitting premises to be used for supplying Class A drugs. W was the director and B the project manager of a charity drop-in centre for the homeless. It provided shelter, food, clothing, washing, advice and medical care. Police recorded videos of obvious dealing on and off the premises. The prosecution was that anyone working there would have seen the activity and they were unwilling to take steps to stop it. W said she did have policies to stop it and she was there only there 30% of the time. There was a policy of no non-prescribed drugs being allowed on the premises. A document said that it was not an offence to fail to pass on information to the police except for terrorism etc. The police were members of an Advisory Group at the centre and they complained about the problem. A policy of bans for those involved in drugs was formulated. A centre logbook showed the presence of people on the banned list. Police said the centre was unhelpful with information after someone died of drugs there. Also they said there was a lack of supervision. Three dealers gave evidence. One said it was a 'smack dealers' paradise.' They had a system of signals to warn each other about the staff. Another said staff saw it going on. When the police were called the staff told them in advance. The third said he had never been warned off and there were ten other dealers at one time. It wasn't necessary to be worried about the staff and deals were done openly. When he arrived 40–50 people rushed up to him. After the defendant's arrest fundamental changes were made. They were both 49 and with impeccable characters. They had character evidence in the highest terms. There was a 2^1/$_2$ year wait for trial and they had been in custody after sentence for 7 months before being granted bail. Held. This was serious because the drugs were Class A, there were several suppliers and the dealing may make their funding difficult when these refuges are vital for the homeless. They were also aware of the police concerns. However, there was no commercial gain and there was no evil motive. They were caring. The appropriate sentence would have been **18 months** not 4 and 5 years. In future longer may be appropriate. As they had served the equivalent of **14 months** it was not necessary to return them to custody for the 2 months.

R v Setchall 2002 1 Cr App R (S) 320. The defendant pleaded to permitting premises to be used for supplying heroin at the earliest opportunity. She was a single mother with three children aged 11, 4 and 1 years old. Police executed a search warrant at her home and found small quantities of heroin and cannabis. When interviewed she admitted that a long-standing friend of hers had become a heroin addict. She unsuccessfully tried to stop him and found that he was supplying heroin from her house to feed his and his girlfriend's addiction. She did not take steps to prevent it and it lasted 3 months. She co-operated with the police. In December 1998 she was given 12 months probation for permitting premises to be used for smoking cannabis and possession of a prohibited weapon. The judge said the offence was misguided loyalty and he appreciated it would have been difficult to stop it. He started at 18 to 24 months and reduced it to 12 months. Held. There was no evidence of profit. She was vulnerable and was used by those she tried to help. 18 months before she committed a similar offence and it should have served as a warning. There was no option but to send her to prison. There were no exceptional circumstances to suspend the sentence. The judge started too high. Because of her personal mitigation, early plea and frankness **4 months** substituted.

R v Williams 2002 1 Cr App R (S) 532. The defendant pleaded guilty to permitting premises to be used for supplying cocaine and possession of cocaine with intent to supply. She shared her house with her partner who was a Class A drug supplier. Police exercised a search warrant and she was searched. Police found a small amount of crack on her. She said she was carrying it for her partner because she was less likely to be searched than he was. It was said it was very difficult for her to do anything to arrest his activity. She was a mother of two young children. Held. She had little opportunity to exercise any will in the matter. The more serious offence was the possession with intent. **8 months** on each concurrent not 18 months and 3 months concurrent.

Premises used specifically for dealing – Class A
183.78   *R v Fitzpatrick* 2001 1 Cr App R (S) 15. The defendant pleaded guilty to

permitting premises to be used for supplying heroin. Undercover officers were escorted by guides to the defendant's flat to buy heroin on four occasions. On most of the occasions the purchase money was given to a guide. The money would be pushed through the letter box and a hand would then pass the drugs back through a letter box. There were a number of people in the flat besides the defendant. Officers entered the flat and found the defendant there and he was arrested. The defendant was the tenant of the flat and a heroin user. He was a diabetic and suffered from epilepsy. Held. Where a person is a regular dealer or provides facilities for others to carry on an established course of dealing over a substantial period sentences ought to reflect that. There was a significant difference between this case and *R v Bradley* 1997 1 Cr App R (S) 59 as in that case the supply might be called social. This was a retail outlet for all and sundry. It was used for an established business of supplying heroin. It is important that he was not himself actively involved in the supply of heroin. He took a passive role. He did not make a profit. Taking these matters into account and that his co-accused received 2 years, **3 years** substituted for 4¹/₂.

Premises used specifically for dealing – Cannabis

183.79 *R v Dowman and Dowman* 2003 1 Cr App R (S) 150. The defendant P pleaded to two counts of permitting premises to be used for the supply of cannabis and one count of supplying cannabis. Her husband, S pleaded guilty to four counts of permitting premises to be used for the supply of cannabis and two counts of supplying. Police conducted test purchases at their house where they had a joint tenancy. Neither lived there but S visited about twice a day. Both they and their son supplied cannabis. Her involvement was said to be two days. P's plea covered 6 weeks and S's plea covered 3 months. P was 41 and of good character. She was the sole carer of one of her daughter's children. S had one drugs previous. The son received 6 years imprisonment. Held. Despite the proposed changes we apply the law as it stands today. S must have known that his house had become a sort of retail shop where cannabis was regularly sold. **18 months** for her and **3 years** for him was at the upper end of the bracket but not manifestly excessive.

Prostitution, and – Class A

183.80 *R v Bradley* 1997 1 Cr App R (S) 59. The defendant pleaded guilty to permitting premises to be used for supplying cocaine, possessing cocaine and permitting premises to be used for habitual prostitution. The defendant was a tenant of a flat in the 'red light' district of Walsall. Over 6 or 7 years he had allowed his premises to be used as a brothel. As a by-product the premises had been used for smoking crack cocaine for 'a number of years.' Drug dealers had come to use the premises for the supply of drugs. The case against him was based on admissions he made. No drugs were found on the premises when the police raided them. In 1988 he had a conviction for supplying drugs for which he received 3 months at the Magistrates' Court. There were no previous convictions after that. The defence contended that the supply of drugs was very limited and *R v Gregory* 1993 14 Cr App R 403 meant 4 years was too long. Held. We should interfere on the basis of the submission. **2 years** substituted. [The other sentences remained lesser and concurrent.]

184 TACHOGRAPH AND OTHER DRIVERS' HOURS OFFENCES

184.1 Transport Act 1968 s 96(11), 97(1), 97A, 97AA, 98 and 99(5)

Contravening permitted driving time; using vehicle without proper recording equipment; driver failing to return proper recording sheet; forging etc the seals on recording equipment, contravening records regulations and making etc false record etc.

Sections 97AA and 99(5) are triable either way. On indictment maximum 2 years. Summary maximum £5,000.

Sections 96(11), 97(1), 97A and 98 are summary only. The maximum fines are Level 4 (£2,500), Level 5 (£5,000), Level 4 and Level 4 respectively.

Crown Court statistics – England and Wales – Males 21+ – Fraud, Forgery etc. associated with vehicle or driver records

184.2

Year	Plea	Total Numbers sentenced	Type of sentence %					Average length of custody (months)
			Discharge	Fine	Community sentence	Suspended sentence	Custody	
2002	Guilty	16	19	50	25	–	6	4
	Not guilty	13	–	38	38	–	23	4
2003	Guilty	50	10	32	40	2	16	6.6
	Not guilty	10	20	30	40	–	10	12

For details and explanations about the statistics in the book see page vii.

Magistrates' Court Sentencing Guidelines January 2004

184.3

Tachograph	Penalty points	Maximum penalty	Owner/operator	Driver or owner/driver
Not properly used	–	Level 5	C	B
Falsification or fraudulent use	–	Level 5	C	B
For an owner/driver, take net turnover into account as appropriate.				

Starting point fine B is 100% of weekly take home pay/weekly benefit payment and **starting point fine C is** 150% of weekly take home pay/weekly benefit payment.

For details about the guidelines see MAGISTRATES' COURT SENTENCING GUIDELINES at page 483.

Guideline remarks

184.4   *R v McCabe* 1989 11 Cr App R (S) 154. These offences were serious and caused danger to the public. The very fact that employees or drivers may regard them as bureaucratic interference with their livelihood was a reason for imposing a significant sentence.

Falsifying or failing to keep proper records

184.5   *R v Saunders* 2001 2 Cr App R (S) 301. The defendants S, H and W pleaded guilty at the Magistrates' Court to eleven, ten and six charges of making a false entries respectively. They were over 5, 5 and 6 months respectively. They were all drivers from the same company. Following a fatal accident which had nothing to do with the defendants police made enquires at their haulage company which revealed the offences. On two occasions H drove 380km on top of the mileage he had recorded. When interviewed the defendants made no comment. They were 39, 38 and 45 respectively. S and H were of good character and W had convictions but during the 1990s there was an improvement. He had no convictions of this kind. Each had family responsibilities. Six other drivers who faced fewer charges were prosecuted for the same offence and were given financial penalties. Held. Each had a financial motive for the offences, the extra wages. Members of the public were put in danger. The sentences need to be significant. **8 months** on each was not manifestly excessive.

Interfering with equipment to stop true recordings

184.6 *R v Potter* 1999 2 Cr App R (S) 448. The defendant pleaded guilty to five offences of making a false record [Transport Act 1968 s 99(5)], two offences of failing to use recording equipment [Transport Act 1968 s 97(1)(a)(iii)] and two offences of failing to have a daily rest period [Transport Act 1968 s 96(11)(a)] at the Magistrates' Court. He had an accident for which he wasn't to blame and his lorry was examined. The policeman was suspicious about the tachograph and arranged for it to be examined by an expert who discovered that a switch had been fitted which enabled the clock to run while there was no recording of speed and distance travelled. Earlier tachographs were found at his home address and in interview he admitted he had switched off the device. He said the device was installed 4 years previously and he had used it sparingly. The tachograph records were compared with his driver's journal. He was a 51-year-old owner-driver of good character with a substantial record of charitable works. Held. His positive good character militates very much in his favour. **3 months** not 9.

Persons in authority – Guideline remarks

184.7 *R v Raven* 1988 10 Cr App R (S) 354. The defendant was concerned in the management of a haulage company. He pleaded guilty to six charges of making false entries on a driver's sheet. The judge said, 'The deliberate alteration of tachographs with a view to profit is a shocking state of affairs. One only needs to have regard to the news on an almost daily basis to realise how important it is that safety regulations with regard to the use of heavy vehicles on the road are complied with and it must be obvious that those who come before the courts charged with effectively fraud but which give rise to matters of public danger, as these offences have done, must understand there will be serious consequences when and if they come to light. Where it is done for profit it dangerous and unfair competition for other traders.' Held. We agree with those comments.

R v McCabe 1989 11 Cr App R (S) 154. Where someone in authority was corrupting employees the offence was more serious than when committed by the employees and demanded a severe sentence to discourage others.

R v Saunders 2001 2 Cr App R (S) 301. We agree with the comments in *R v Raven* 1988 10 Cr App R (S) 354.

See also **ROAD TRAFFIC**

TAGGING

See **HOME DETENTION CURFEW SCHEME**

TAKING THE LAW INTO YOUR OWN HANDS

See **FALSE IMPRISONMENT** – *Taking the law into your own hands* and **BURGLARY** – *Aggravated – Revenge attack on a burglar*

185 TAKING MOTOR VEHICLES

185.1 Theft Act 1968 s 12

Summary only. Triable on indictment as an alternative to theft. Maximum sentence 6 months and/or Level 5 (£5,000) fine. There is power to commit for sentence with an either way offence[1].

Anti-Social Behavioural orders Where the defendant has acted in a manner that caused or was likely to cause harassment, alarm or distress to one or more persons not in the same household as the defendant and it is necessary to protect persons from further anti-social acts by him/her the court may make this order[2].

Disqualification from driving The offence carries discretionary disqualification[3]. No mandatory points[3].

Drug Abstinence Order This was repealed on 4 April 2005.

Endorsement The offence does not enable the recording of an endorsement[3].

Magistrates' Court Sentencing Guidelines January 2004

185.2   For a first time offender pleading not guilty. Entry point. Is it serious enough for a community penalty? Consider the impact on the victim. Examples of aggravating factors for the offence are group action, pre-meditated, related damage, professional hallmarks and vulnerable victim. Examples of mitigating factors for the offence are misunderstanding with the owner, soon returned and vehicle belonged to family or friend. Examples of mitigation are health (physical or mental), co-operation with police, genuine remorse and voluntary compensation. Give reasons for not awarding compensation.

For details about the guidelines see MAGISTRATES' COURT SENTENCING GUIDELINES at page 483.

See also AGGRAVATED VEHICLE-TAKING

186   TARIFF, CHANGE IN TARIFF YEARS LATER

Can you appeal?

186.1   *R v Graham* 1999 2 Cr App R (S) 312. The defendant was convicted of importing 665 kilos of cannabis in 1994. He received 12 years. In 1996 his appeal against conviction and sentence was dismissed. The Court of Appeal issued new guidelines for sentencing in cannabis cases in *R v Ronchetti* 1998 2 Cr App R (S) 100. The defendant's case was referred to the Court of Appeal by the Criminal Cases Review Commission and it was argued that the sentence should be 10 years. Held. The Commission was set up to refer possible miscarriages of justice to the Court of Appeal. It has an unfettered power to refer sentencing cases to the Court of Appeal. A defendant sentenced on the prevailing tariff cannot be described as a victim of a miscarriage of justice. An alteration in the statutory maxima or minima penalty cannot give rise to a legitimate grievance. Changes do not have retrospective effect.

187   TAX FRAUD

187.1   Many different offences and penalties but in particular:

Cheating the Public Revenue

1   Criminal Justice Act 1988 s 41
2   Crime and Disorder Act 1998 s 1C
3   Road Traffic Offenders Act 1988 s 9, 34, 97 and Sch. 2 Part II

Contrary to common law so penalty at large (maximum life) and triable only on indictment.

Value Added Tax Act 1994 s 72

Knowingly concerned in or taking steps with a view to the fraudulent evasion of VAT.

Triable either way. On indictment maximum 7 years. Summary maximum 6 months and/or £5,000 or three times the VAT whichever is greater.

Disqualification from driving This order may be appropriate for defendant whether or not s/he is the actual driver[4].

Crown Court statistics – England and Wales – Males 21+ – Revenue Law offence
187.2

Year	Plea	Total Numbers sentenced	Type of sentence %					Average length of custody (months)
			Discharge	Fine	Community sentence	Suspended sentence	Custody	
2002	Guilty	24	4	–	13	4	79	23
	Not guilty	20	–	–	5	–	95	41
2003	Guilty	12	8	–	–	8	83	23.4
	Not guilty	5	–	40	–	–	60	44

For details and explanations about the statistics in the book see page vii.

Guideline remarks

187.3   *R v Thornhill* 1980 2 Cr App R (S) 320. LCJ The defendant pleaded guilty to failing to deduct tax from employees' wages. The loss was £3,278. Held. Defrauding the Inland Revenue is a serious offence because it means defrauding the vast body of honest taxpayers. Those that plead guilty may well receive immediate imprisonment. **3 months** not 6 partly because his business might fail.

Att-Gen's Ref. Nos. 86–7 of 1999 2001 1 Cr App R (S) 505. The length of sentence will depend on a number of factors, the amount of tax evaded, the period of time the evasion took place, the efforts made to conceal the fraud, whether others were drawn in and corrupted, the character of the defendant, his personal gain, his plea and the amount recovered.

Value £1,000–£100,000

187.4   *R v Wells* 1999 1 Cr App R (S) 371. The defendant pleaded guilty to being knowingly concerned in the fraudulent evasion of VAT at the Magistrates' Court. His demolition company, which was registered for VAT, failed and he was left substantially in debt. Soon afterwards he borrowed £12,000 and opened a wine bar. Shortly after that his wife who looked after the administration and the accounts left him. Those duties fell to him and his experience of that was limited. He worked hard and the bar prospered although he was being pressed for payment of the debts. He was made bankrupt but because of the success of the wine bar the Receiver allowed the business to continue and it prospered. He was told by his accountant to register the company for VAT and sent him the forms. He didn't register although he was obliged to. Over 17 months the tax evaded was £28,000. Until he lost the tenancy the Customs didn't charge him. Then seeing no opportunity to recover the money they did charge him. He was 36 and of good character. Held. Sentences of 12 months or

---

4   R v Skitt 2005 2 Cr App R (S) 122. The defendants were sentenced for importing large quantities of cigarettes when duty had not been paid. Held. Disqualification is designed to deal with just these sorts of offences.

more are appropriate for this kind of fraud even on a plea. **8 months** fully took into account the delay.

Old cases. *R v Rogers* 1995 16 Cr App R (S) 720; *R v Aziz* 1996 1 Cr App R (S) 265.

Value over £1m

187.5 *Att-Gen's Ref. Nos. 86–7 of 1999* 2001 1 Cr App R (S) 505 [for facts see Unreported case Re conviction Judgment 23 Oct]. The defendants W and S were convicted of two offences of cheating the Inland Revenue, conspiracy to cheat and two offences of false accounting. The offences were over a 3 year period. W was convicted of another false accounting count. The defendants were involved in the sale of a distance learning course. They claimed copyright so it would be tax free. Payments were sent to an off shore company which they had set up after receiving legitimate tax advice. Some payments were diverted to another company. Documents were concealed during audits. The investigators raided their premises in 1996 and during the investigation W and another agreed to repay £200,000. The prosecution claimed it was window dressing and the defendants' knew it couldn't be treated as copyright payments. The total loss with interest was £1,979,808. W received not less than £500,000 and S not less than £200,000. The money was spent on property including a house for W bought for £423,428 and for S a flat costing £120,000 and another for S costing £49,000, cars including a Bentley for W costing £77,000 and credit card purchases for W of £17,872 and for S of £26,074. W was 53 and had earlier problems with the Inland Revenue [not it appears convictions]. S was 46 and of good character. She also had health problems. The trial lasted 4 months in which the judge said he would not be imposing imprisonment. He fined W £694,000 [following the quashing of one conviction £534,00] and S £106,000 [now £86,000]. There was a £16m compensation order. The financial penalties had been paid. Held. W's sentence should have been in the region of $4^{1}/_{2}$ years. As S was less involved and not involved in one of the counts which was a separate venture, the appropriate sentence was 18 months to 2 years. Taking into account the delay, that it was a reference and all the factors **18 months** for W and **6 months** for S.

R v Rogers 2002 1 Cr App R (S) 337. The defendant was convicted of two offences of cheating the Inland Revenue. He was an unqualified accountant and provided accounting services for contractors and sub-contractors in the building trade. Sub-contractors holding 715 vouchers were able to receive their money gross. Contractors under the SC60 scheme deducted tax at source and remunerated the sub-contractor net. The defendant on behalf of his clients submitted false SC60 forms indicating tax had been paid which had not been and then applied for the tax allowances. The profits were split equally between the contractor, the sub-contractor and the defendant. The extent of the fraud was in the region of £1 m. The judge said, 'the fraud was your idea, you masterminded it and led it throughout. You recruited vulnerable people and there was the possibility of corrupting young people. You were motivated by greed and had shown no remorse. In the witness box you were scheming, manipulative and dishonest. The only mitigation was you would be left with nothing and have to start again.' The defendant was 41 with no relevant convictions. Held. This was not mere evasion but positive cheating on a grand scale and over several years, all masterminded by the defendant. There was no benefit from a guilty plea and there were several aggravating features. The sentence of **7 years** was severe but not manifestly excessive. [The judgment does not accurately record the defence submissions.]

Old case. *R v Alibhai* 1992 13 Cr App R (S) 682.

Confiscation orders

187.6 Criminal Justice Act 1988 s 72(5). The court shall leave the (confiscation) order out of account in determining the appropriate sentence.

R v Andrews 1997 1 Cr App R (S) 279. The defendant who was sentenced for a £300,000 tax fraud was ordered to pay a £¼ m confiscation order. The Court of Appeal reduced the sentence because of the large order.

R v Rogers 2002 1 Cr App R (S) 337. *R v Andrews* 1997 1 Cr App R (S) 279 was decided without reference to s 72(5) and the court cannot reduce a sentence because of the confiscation order.

See also DUTY EVASION, SOCIAL SECURITY FRAUD/HOUSING BENEFIT FRAUD ETC

TDA

See TAKING MOTOR VEHICLES

188   TELEPHONE OFFENCES

188.1   Various offences including dishonesty offences and the Communications Act 2003 s 125 and 126, which on 18/9/03 replaced Telecommunications Act 1984 s 42 and 42A

New offences. (s 125) Dishonestly obtaining electronic communications services and (s 126) possession or supply of apparatus for contravening section 125.

Old offences Fraudulent use of a telecommunications system and possession or supply of anything for fraudulent purposes in connection with a telecommunication system.

All four offences are triable either way. On indictment maximum 5 years. Summary maximum 6 months and/or £5,000.

Harassment

See HARASSMENT S 2 – *Telephone calls* (**see para 86.6**) and HARASSMENT S 4 (OR PUBLIC NUISANCE) – *Telephone calls* (**see para 88.6**).

Landline phones, obtaining cheaper or free calls from

188.2   Old case. *R v Aslam* 1996 2 Cr App R (S) 377

Mobile phones, chipping

188.3   *R v Stephens* 2002 2 Cr App R (S) 291. The defendant pleaded guilty at the Magistrates' Court to having items in his custody and control (s 42A). A search warrant was executed at his address and in his workshop were found 75 mobiles which could be encoded and chips some of which could be used for encoding and computer equipment. These chips could modify mobiles to obtain free calls. He was frank and co-operative from his arrest and he said he had copied a system from the Internet. He sold the chips for about £10 and had made about £500. He was in employment earning a reasonable sum but had debts. There were two spent dishonesty convictions. It was very difficult to arrive at a figure for the loss but £11,000 was suggested. The potential was enormous. There was a delay of about a year. Held. Taking into account *R v Barber* 2002 1 Cr App R (S) 548 (about more than a 1/3 off for a plea before venue) **12 months** not 18.

For offences connected with mobiles see DANGEROUS DRIVING – *Magistrates' Court Sentencing Guidelines January 2004;* DEATH BY DANGEROUS DRIVING, CAUSING – *Mobile phone, defendant using;* ROBBERY – *Street robbery – Mobile phones*

TENANTS

See HARASSMENT AND UNLAWFUL EVICTION OF TENANTS

189   TERRORISM

189.1   Defendants are frequently indicted under the Explosive Substances Act 1883 s 2 and 3.

Indictable only. Maximum life.

Longer than Commensurate sentences and Extended sentences Terrorism will be a violent offence for the purposes of passing a longer than commensurate sentence [Powers of Criminal Courts (Sentencing) Act 2000 s 80(2)] and an extended sentence (extending the licence) [Powers of Criminal Courts (Sentencing) Act 2000 s 85(2)(b)] where the offence leads, or is intended or likely to lead, to a person's death or to physical injury to a person[5]. These provisions will continue to apply to offences committed after 29/9/98 and before 4/4/05.

Guideline case

189.2   *R v Martin* 1999 1 Cr App R (S) 477. LCJ. The defendants were convicted of conspiracy to cause explosions likely to endanger life or cause serious injury to property. They planned to attack electricity sub-stations with 37 bombs. Held. This crime was clearly abnormal within Lawton LJ's description in *R v Turner* 1975 61 Cr App R 67 at 90. We fully agree with the extract from *R v Byrne* 1976 62 Cr App R (S) 159 at 163. The reported cases show that the most severe sentences have been passed in cases involving a deliberate threat to human life. For example: *R v Hindawi* 1988 10 Cr App R (S) 104: **45 years**; *R v Basra* 1989 11 Cr App R (S) 527: **35 years**; *R v Kinsella* 1995 16 Cr App R (S) 1035: **35, 25, 16 years**; *R v Al-Banna* 1984 6 Cr App R (S) 426: **30, 35 years**; *R v Mullen* 1991 12 Cr App R (S) 754: **30 years**; *R v Taylor and Hayes* 1995 16 Cr App R (S) 873: **30 years**; *R v McGonagle and Heffernan* 1996 1 Cr App R (S) 90: **25, 23 years**; and *R v Al-Mograbi and Cull* 1980 70 Cr App R (S) 24: **12 years** (but the defendant pleaded guilty, was aged 19 and 'had she been of full adult age, the sentence might well have been 20 years or more.') The current level of sentencing in cases concerning terrorist explosions appeared to be in the range of **20 to 35 years**. But there are some cases, which fall outside the bracket, either above or below. The appropriate sentence will plainly depend on a large number of factors, including the likely result of any explosion, the target, the role, the nature, size and likely effect of any explosive device, the motivation and, where death, injury, or damage has been caused, the nature and extent of the death, injury and damage. When imposing sentences for conspiracies of this sort, the courts should remind themselves of the term actually served for murder, particularly murder in its more aggravated forms. But there can be no precise equivalence and conduct threatening the democratic government and the security of the state, and the daily life and livelihood of millions of people, has a seriousness all of its own. For conspiracies directed purely to the destruction of property the starting point should be somewhat wider than 'below 20 years'. In some cases below 15 will be appropriate. In a case such as this it would be unrealistic to ignore the threat to life and limb, since had the conspirators' plan been implemented it seems probable that some injury and loss of life would have resulted, whether intended or not. It is not appropriate to recast English sentencing practice to bring it into line with that in Northern Ireland, even assuming the level of sentences there are lower.

5   Powers of Criminal Courts (Sentencing) Act 2000 s 161(3)

Guideline remarks

189.3 *R v Byrne* 1976 62 Cr App R (S) 159 at 163. The defendants appealed their sentences under s 3 of the Explosives Act 1923. Held. Clearly conduct which is likely to endanger life is more grave than conduct which is likely to cause serious injury to property. In a particular case it may well be that the conduct is likely to do both; in other cases, conduct, although it is likely to do both, is more likely to endanger life than cause serious injury to property or vice versa. The maximum sentence should be reserved for the case with the type of explosive device which has, as its primary purpose (and I stress primary) to endanger life. It is unnecessary for us to specify what kind of explosive device we have in mind. Explosive devices differ considerably. A device which is primarily designed to endanger life may well attract the maximum sentence (then 20 years). On the other hand, if the primary purpose of the device is not to endanger life but to cause serious injury to property then a sentence less than the maximum may be appropriate. The deterrent aspect of sentences for using or conspiring to use explosive devices designed primarily to endanger life should be made clear.

Arson

189.4 *R v Cruickshank and O'Donnell* 1995 16 Cr App R (S) 728. LCJ. The two defendants pleaded guilty to conspiracy to commit arson with intent to cause, or being reckless as to, damage. They planted and set off a series of incendiary devices in shops in Leeds in order to advance the interests of Irish Republicanism. They did not aim to inflict physical injury but to damage property to a very considerable extent. Held. If all the devices in the five shops had ignited, the damage would have been enormous and the City would have looked like a City in the blitz. The emergency services would have been stretched to, and possibly beyond, their limits. £45,000 worth of damage was caused in one store. There would have been a high risk of injury to watchmen, firemen, bomb-disposal men, shop staff and the public generally. The gravamen of what was done was not an attack on an individual, but on the community as a whole. It had a political motivation. It must be clearly understood by activists for whatever cause, that to seek to de-stabilise the community or exert pressure must be met with severe deterrent sentences. Applying *R v Byrne* 1976 62 Cr App R (S) 159, **11 years** not 15 and **16 years** not 20.

Bombs – Lives at risk

189.5 *R v McCardle* 1999 1 Cr App R (S) note at 482. High Court Judge at Crown Court. The defendant was convicted of conspiracy to cause an explosion. He was a member of PIRA and the explosion was at Canary Wharf. Held. You did not intend to kill anyone, or cause really serious injury to anyone, nor did you personally appreciate the risks of those consequences. However, objectively there was a substantial risk of both death and injury and this conspiracy did, in fact, result in two deaths and many injuries, some of such a severity that the victims' lives will be permanently marred if not ruined. In addition, the conspiracy resulted in damage in excess of £150m and engendered terror and misery for many people. I accept that others did the planning and I make some allowance for that. The fact that there were deaths and serious injuries, whether or not you intended them, whether or not you appreciated the risk, is a serious aggravating feature of this offence. The law does and always should recognise, as one factor in sentencing, the consequences for others and I reject the submission that the deaths should be disregarded in determining the sentence for this offence. **25 years**.

R v Martin 1999 1 Cr App R (S) 477. LCJ. The defendants were convicted of conspiracy to cause explosions likely to endanger life or cause serious injury to property. They planned to attack electricity sub-stations with 37 bombs. The court reviewed past cases at the Court of Appeal and the Crown Court. Held. The judge was fully entitled to take the view that it called for a sentence of the utmost severity. The political, economic and social threat presented by this conspiracy was, perhaps, as great as in any of the cases we have considered. However, some weight must be given to the fact that death and injury, although likely, was not its primary object. Some reduction should be made in the sentence of 35 years. That sentence means, in real years, a minimum of $17^1/_2$ years and a maximum of 23 years and 4 months: that is the sort of term served by the perpetrator of a murder with severely aggravating features. **28 years** substituted.

R v Abedin 2002 The Times news report 28/2/02. High Court Judge at Crown Court. The defendant was convicted of conspiracy to cause an explosion. As a result of a long surveillance operation, MI5 nipped in the bud a plot that would have caused immense risk to life. The defendant who had extreme Islamic views had used a house and an industrial unit to stockpile bomb-making material. The defendant was born in Bangladesh and was 27. **20 years**. [Treat news reports with care.]

Proscribed organisations, belonging to

189.6   Terrorism Act 2000 s 11

Triable either way. On indictment maximum sentence 10 years. Summary maximum 6 months and/or £5,000.

R v Hundal and Dhaliwal 2004 2 Cr App R (S) 355. The defendants were convicted of belonging to a proscribed organisation, the International Sikh Youth Federation (ISYF). They were arrested on the 13th of January 2002 in a car which had arrived on a ferry from Calais. The car belonged to and was driven by D. Both had documents relating to the ISYF and both said they had been to a meeting of the ISYF in Cologne on the day of their arrest. Both said they were no longer members. It was accepted that neither man knew that the ISYF was proscribed in the UK and had been since March the 29th 2001. Held. As neither of the defendants knew that they were contravening UK legislation **12 months** not 30 months.

190   THEFT ETC

190.1   Theft Act 1968 s 1

Triable either way. On indictment maximum sentence 7 years. On summary maximum 6 months and/or £5,000.

The Criminal Justice Act 2003 creates a summary maximum sentence of 51 weeks, a minimum sentence of 28 weeks and Custody plus. The Home Office says they do not expect to introduce these provisions before September 2006.

Disqualification from driving If the offence is theft or attempted theft of a motor vehicle the offence carries discretionary disqualification[6]. The Crown Court may disqualify where a motor vehicle was used (by the defendant or another) to commit etc. the offence[7].

Drug Abstinence Order This was repealed on 4 April 2005.

Endorsement The relevant entries were removed from the Road Traffic Offenders Act 1988 so endorsement is no longer applicable for stealing a motor vehicle[8].

Fixed penalty £80 (£40 if under 16)[9]

Restitution Order There is power to make an order that the stolen goods etc. in the possession of the defendant or a third party be restored to the owner etc.[10].

---

6 Road Traffic Offenders Act 1988 s 9, 34, 97 and Sch. 2 Part II
7 Powers of Criminal Courts (Sentencing) Act 2000 s 147 (1)(a) & (3).
8 Road Traffic Act 1991 s 26 and Sch 2, para 32.
9 The Penalties for Disorderly Behaviour (Amount of Penalty) Order 2002 Para 2 and Sch. Part II as amended.
10 Powers of Criminal Courts (Sentencing) Act 2000 s 148(2)

The cases listed here include cases of obtaining money etc by deception, forgery, false accounting, making or using a false instrument and public nuisance where the essence of those offences is theft.

Crown Court statistics – England and Wales – Males 21+
190.2

Year	Plea	Total Numbers sentenced	Type of sentence %					Average length of custody (months)
			Discharge	Fine	Community sentence	Suspended sentence	Custody	
Theft from person								
2002	Guilty	908	5	4	33	2	55	13.7
	Not guilty	129	5	5	27	2	58	16.7
2003	Guilty	978	6	2	38	2	51	14.8
	Not guilty	115	6	10	30	1	52	21
Theft by an employee								
2002	Guilty	178	2	1	58	6	33	16
	Not guilty	30	–	3	33	–	63	17.3
2003	Guilty	131	2	7	41	5	44	13.9
	Not guilty	26	4	–	35	4	58	19.2
Theft or unauthorised taking from mail								
2002	Guilty	15	–	–	20	–	80	28.8
	Not guilty	3	–	–	–	–	100	28
2003	Guilty	19	–	–	32	–	68	17.2
	Not guilty	3	–	–	–	33	67	4.5
Theft from vehicle								
2002	Guilty	26	4	–	19	4	73	22.6
	Not guilty	2	–	–	–	–	100	9
2003	Guilty	25	–	–	32	4	64	14.8
	Not guilty	2	–	–	50	–	50	48
Theft from shops								
2002	Guilty	507	10	6	35	3	47	8.9
	Not guilty	86	8	23	31	2	34	8.1
2003	Guilty	522	15	6	35	1	43	9.6
	Not guilty	92	23	22	33	1	22	13.1
Theft of motor vehicle								
2002	Guilty	86	3	1	16	5	73	17.5
	Not guilty	39	8	10	21	–	59	22.2
2003	Guilty	90	4	2	26	2	66	18.2
	Not guilty	13	8	–	23	–	62	19.9

For details and explanations about the statistics in the book see page vii.

Magistrates' Court Sentencing Guidelines January 2004
190.3 For a first time offender pleading not guilty. Entry point. Is it serious enough

for a community penalty? Consider the impact on the victim. Examples of aggravating factors for the offence are high value, planned, sophisticated, adult involving children, organised team, related damage and vulnerable victim. Examples of mitigating factors for the offence are impulsive action and low value. Examples of mitigation are age, health (physical or mental), co-operation with police, genuine remorse and voluntary compensation. Give reasons for not awarding compensation.

For details about the guidelines see MAGISTRATES' COURT SENTENCING GUIDELINES at page 483.

Guideline remarks

190.4 *R (Sogbesan) v Inner London Crown Court* 2003 1 Cr App R (S) 408. The Court of Appeal is urging courts not to impose custody for economic crimes committed by persons of good character unless no other course is properly available. (For further details see *Breach of trust value less than £1,000.*)

R v Kefford 2002 2 Cr App R (S) 495. LCJ. In the case of economic crimes, e.g. obtaining undue credit by fraud, prison is not necessarily the only appropriate form of punishment. Particularly in the case of those who have no record of previous offending, the very fact of having to appear before a court can be a significant punishment. Certainly, having to perform a type of community punishment can be a very salutary way of making it clear that crime does not pay, particularly if a community punishment order is combined with a curfew order.

Advance fee fraud

See FRAUD – *Advance fee fraud*

Airport baggage handlers

190.5 *R v Dhunay* 1986 8 Cr App R (S) 107. For persistent pilfering from luggage at airports the starting point is **3 years**.

Betting, connected with/Sporting

190.6 *R v Ong* 2000 1 Cr App R (S) 404. The defendant pleaded on the first day of his trial to conspiracy to cause a public nuisance. The plan was to interfere with the lighting in a Premier Division football match so those placing bets in the Far East could make large sums of money. If the lights go out the match is abandoned and the bookmakers pay out on the then score. The defendant and another were prime movers in this country. They recruited a security guard at the ground who for £20,000 gave the defendant who was an electrical engineer access to the control room. Before the match started the defendants were arrested. The defendants were expected to gain substantial money. The Club would have incurred substantial financial loss estimated to be a six figure sum. He was of good character. Held. The practice of interfering with an important sporting fixture should be discouraged by severe sentences. **4 years** was not manifestly excessive.

Breach of trust – Guideline case

190.7 *R v Barrick* 1985 7 Cr App R (S) 142. LCJ Where a person in a position of trust, for example, an accountant, solicitor, bank employee or postman, has used that privileged and trusted position to defraud his partners or clients or employers or the general public of sizeable sums of money. He will usually, as in this case, be a person of hitherto impeccable character. It is practically certain, again as in this case, that he will never offend again and, in the nature of things, he will never again in his life be able to secure similar employment with all that that means in the shape of disgrace for himself and hardship for himself and also his family. It was not long ago that this type of offender might expect to receive a term of imprisonment of 3–4 years, and indeed a great deal more if the sums involved were substantial. More recently, however, the sentencing climate in this area has changed, and certainly so far as solicitors are concerned, has changed radically. Professional men should expect to be punished as severely as the others; in some cases more severely. We make the following suggestions. In general a term of immediate imprisonment is inevitable, save in very exceptional circumstances or where the amount of money obtained is small. Despite the great punishment that offenders of this sort bring upon themselves, the court should nevertheless pass a sufficiently substantial term of imprisonment to mark publicly the gravity of the offence. The sum involved is obviously not the only factor to be considered, but it may in many cases provide a useful guide. Where the amounts involved cannot be described as small but are less than £17,500, terms of imprisonment ranging from the very short up to about **21 months** are appropriate. Cases involving sums of between about £ 17,500 and £100,000 will merit a term of about **2–3 years**. Cases involving between £100,000 and £250,000 will merit **3–4 years**. Cases involving £250,000 and £1 m will merit **5–9 years** and cases over £1 m will merit **10 years or more**. The terms suggested are appropriate where the case is contested. In any case where a plea of guilty is entered, however, the court should give the appropriate discount. Where sums are exceptionally large, and not stolen on a single occasion, or the dishonesty is directed at more than one victim or groups of victims, consecutive sentences may be called for. As already indicated, the circumstances of cases will vary almost infinitely. The court will no doubt wish pay regard to: (i) the quality and degree of trust reposed in the offender including his rank; (ii) the period over which the fraud or the thefts have been perpetrated; (iii) the use to which the money or property dishonestly taken was put; (iv) the effect upon the victim; (v) the impact of the offences on the public and public confidence; (vi) the effect on fellow-employees or partners; (vii) the effect on the offender himself; (viii) his own history; (ix) those matters of mitigation special to himself such as illness; being placed under great strain by excessive responsibility or the like; where, as sometimes happens, there has been a long delay, say over two years, between his being confronted with his dishonesty by his professional body or the police and the start of his trial; finally, any help given by him to the police. [As adapted by *R v Clark* 1998 2 Cr App R (S) 95) which is itself now over 7 years old.]

R v Roach 2002 1 Cr App R (S) 44. The defendant stole money from a housebound 80 year old who she was employed to look after. Held. The guidelines in *Clark* and *Barrick* involved theft in breach of trust from employees, charitable bodies or other organisations of that kind. They are not directly in point at all in this case.

R v Hale 2002 1 Cr App R (S) 205. Because of a number of aggravating factors the judge passed a longer sentence (2 years instead of 21 months) than in *R v Clark* 1998 2 Cr App R (S) 137. Held. The judge was entirely justified in what he did. Sentencing is not a matter of mathematical calculation and guideline cases are intended simply as guidelines.

Breach of trust – Magistrates' Court Sentencing Guidelines January 2004

190.8   For a first time offender pleading not guilty. Entry point. Is it so serious that only custody is appropriate? Consider the impact on the victim. Examples of aggravating factors for the offence are casting suspicion on others, committed over a period, high value, organised team, planned, senior employee, sophisticated and vulnerable victim. Examples of mitigating factors for the offence are impulsive action low value, previous inconsistent attitude by employer, single item and unsupported junior. Examples of mitigation are age, health (physical or mental), co-operation with police, genuine remorse and voluntary compensation. Give reasons for not awarding compensation.

For details about the guidelines see **MAGISTRATES' COURT SENTENCING GUIDELINES** at page 483.

Breach of Trust – Value less than £1,000

190.9 *R v Randhawa* 1999 2 Cr App R (S) 209. LCJ. The defendant pleaded guilty to four counts of theft and one attempt (two at the Magistrates' Court and three at the Crown Court). The defendant then 18 was a checkout girl at Tesco and conducted a £50 cash back transaction without a customer being there. There was a random till check and she admitted a colleague had shown her how to obtain cash by retaining a receipt and typing the customer's details into the till and signing the freshly created receipt for cash back. She admitted doing that for a £50.70 transaction. A check was made and two similar transactions came to light. The four transactions were for about £50 and the total was some £200. There was one unsuccessful attempt. All the transactions were within a month. She was of good character and was soon to take her first year exams of a business degree course at Luton University. Held. Immediate custody was necessary but **2 months** YOI not 6.

R (Sogbesan) v Inner London Crown Court 2003 1 Cr App R (S) 408. The defendant (must have although this is not stated) pleaded guilty at the Magistrates' Court to two charges of theft and one charge of false accounting. He worked at the till at Safeways. He obtained credit card details of a customer and using those details a friend managed to buy a CD and have £50 cash back. This was repeated on the same day for a £18 phone voucher and another £50 cash back. The false accounting was based on the credit card documentation. The total loss was £216.99. The friends were given £20 and £10. In interview he made full admissions. He was 18 and of good character destined to start University. He had financial problems having bought a mobile and a car, which he could not afford. The pre-sentence report suggested a community rehabilitation order on the basis he needed guidance and support after which the chance of re-offending would be reduced to an absolute minimum. He received 1 months detention. Held. The Halliday Review has questioned the value of sentences of less than 12 months. The Court of Appeal is urging courts not to impose custody for economic crimes committed by persons of good character unless no other course is properly available. The custody threshold was not passed. The sentence was far outside the courts sentencing discretion. The Justices should have given a rehabilitation order. As he had served 1 week a conditional discharge substituted. (This case shows the unfairness of the Criminal Appeal Act 1968 Section 10(3), which prohibits the appeal of sentences of less than 6 months after a committal except by an appeal to the Divisional Court. Here the Justices could have committed the case so all the *defendants* could be sentenced together rather than *because* they thought more than 6 months imprisonment was appropriate. Ed.)

Breach of trust – Value £1,001–£5,000

190.10 *R v Mangham* 1998 2 Cr App R (S) 344. The defendant pleaded guilty to using a false instrument with intent and obtaining a money transfer by deception. The defendant was employed by an agency and one of her charges was a 95-year-old lady. She obtained the lady's National Savings passbook and forged her signature on a form enabling a cheque for £2,500 to be obtained. Four months later she did the same again obtaining another £2,500. She admitted it and pleaded at the first opportunity. She said the money went on domestic bills and presents for her family. She had two children aged 13 and 15. She had a previous conviction for theft, again as an employee and again in breach of trust. It was a cruel deception requiring a substantial sentence. Because of the plea **18 months** not 2 years.

R v Whitehouse and Morrison 1999 2 Cr App R (S) 259. The defendants W and M pleaded guilty to theft at the Magistrates' Court. W was employed by a haulage company and two lorries were left overnight at a locked depot full of clothing. The two defendants and two others entered the compound and took 35 boxes of clothing worth £17,700 and loaded them into a van they had hired earlier. The property was rapidly distributed. Police found some of the clothing hidden under a rug on the back seat of the car. As a result of what was said by one of the occupants of the car, police went to W's home and recovered 13 of the stolen boxes. W said he had sold some of the clothing for £700 in order to pay off debts. He also indicated that part of the motive was revenge against his employers who were not continuing his employment after a trial period. M was arrested and said he had loaded the van with 25 boxes and he had not had his cut from the proceeds. W was sentenced as the prime mover who had used his knowledge of the security procedures to effect the offence. He had recruited the others and used a stolen key. M was sentenced on the basis he had played a major part. W was 24 with three previous spent convictions for theft. M was also 24 and had a variety of dishonest convictions in the early 1990s. Held. The element of revenge was an aggravating factor which took W outside the guidelines in *Barrick* and *Clark*. **2 years** for W and **18 months** for M were severe but not manifestly excessive.

Breach of trust – Value £5,001–£10,000

190.11   *R v Barrick* 1985 7 Cr App R (S) 142. LCJ. Where the amounts involved cannot be described as small but are less than £17,500, terms of imprisonment ranging from the very short up to about **21 months** are appropriate when the case is contested. [As adapted by *R v Clark* 1998 2 Cr App R (S) 95.]

R v Griffiths 2000 1 Cr App R (S) 240. The defendant pleaded guilty to theft, false accounting, making a false instrument and using a false instrument at the Magistrates' Court. The defendant was treasurer of a football club. He provided falsified accounts, (the false accounting count). He forged an insurance certificate so he could pretend the premises were insured, (the using a false instrument count). To satisfy members he produced a bank statement indicating there was a balance in the club account of over £9,000. It was faxed to the bank and the bank reply said no such account existed, (the making a false instrument count). When bills weren't paid the police were called. When interviewed about the matter he agreed that between £7,300 and £7,500 had been stolen, (the theft count). It was over an 8 year period. He was 44 and a man with a good character with various references. It was said he tried to live up to the lifestyle of some of his friends. He owed £40,000 in loans and on credit card bills. He was humiliated in the community and was likely to lose his job and be divorced. He was depressed but had an exemplary prison report. The amount of money is only the starting point. It is not the sole consideration. It was over a long period and he had fobbed off the committee with a series of lies reinforced by the falsification of the accounts and other documents. Applying *R v Clark* it would be difficult to justify more than 18 months for the theft after a trial. The total sentence should have been 12 not 21 months. So **12 months** for the theft and 9 months concurrent for the other counts.

R v James 2000 1 Cr App R (S) 285. The defendant pleaded guilty to two counts of theft. She was a Post Office counter clerk. She stole twice. The total appears to be £7,318, (although the judgment is contradictory). She hid the theft by inflating the computerised records. She was a single parent with daughters aged 15 and 7. She was in debt. She denied it till the day of her trial. She had one spent dishonesty conviction. Applying *R v Clark* 1998 2 Cr App R 95, **9 months** substituted for 14 months.

R v Donaldson 2002 2 Cr App R (S) 140. The defendant pleaded guilty to theft, attempting to obtain property by deception and two counts of obtaining property by a deception. She asked for six offences to be taken into consideration. She was employed by a carer to a 90 year old who was at home after being released from hospital. The old lady needed 24-hour care. The defendant stole £3,300 in cash from a drawer and blank cheques. She forged the lady's signature on the cheques and tried to pay them into her bank account. She left her employment without notice. The banks were suspicious and the deception failed. She next started work caring for an 88-year-old lady who was immobile. Her employer allowed her to withdraw £250 in cash for her wages and housekeeping expenses. However, on six occasions she exceeded the limit and withdrew between £400 and £600 totalling £3,300. She then left that employment without notice the next day. She was questioned by the police and denied the offences and then failed to return to the police station when on bail. When she was next arrested she admitted the offences. She was 36 of good character with an unsettled background. In 1996 she suffered from postnatal depression. Her son went into care and her mother died. Held. These offences are serious and despicable but **18 months** not 2¹/₂ years.

Old cases. *R v Ross-Goulding* 1997 2 Cr App R (S) 348 and *R v Feakes* 1998 2 Cr App R (S) 295, (for a summary of these cases see the first edition of this book.)

Breach of trust – Value £10,001–£100,000

190.12 *R v Barrick* 1985 7 Cr App R (S) 142. LCJ. Where the amounts involved cannot be described as small but are less than £17,500, terms of imprisonment ranging from the very short up to about **21 months** are appropriate. Cases involving sums of between about £17,500 and £100,000 will merit a term of about **2–3 years**, when the case is contested. [As adapted by *R v Clark* 1998 2 Cr App R (S) 95.]

R v Kefford 2002 2 Cr App R (S) 495. LCJ. The defendant pleaded guilty to 12 thefts and asked for nine offences of false accounting to be taken into consideration. When 23 he made withdrawals from customer's accounts at the Building Society he worked at. He took windfall payments and signed a slip in their name. £11,120 was obtained. After he stopped it there were 5 months before he was detected. When interviewed he made an immediate confession. He had no convictions. He sold his home and paid the money back. He was under financial strain because of buying the house. He stopped when his finances improved. Held. **12 months** not 18 would have been the appropriate starting point. Because of the mitigation **4 months** not 12.

Old case *R v Husbands* 1998 2 Cr App R (S) 428 and *R v Kerr* 1998 2 Cr App R (S) 316, (for a summary of these cases see the first edition of this book.)

Breach of trust – Value £100,000–£1m

190.13 *R v Barrick* 1985 7 Cr App R (S) 142. LCJ. Cases involving between £100,000 and £250,000 will merit **3 to 4 years** would be justified. Cases involving £250,000 and £1m will merit **5–9 years**, when the case is contested. (As adapted by *R v Clark* 1998 2 Cr App R (S) 95.)

R v Neary 1999 1 Cr App R (S) 431. The defendant pleaded guilty at the first opportunity to 12 counts of theft. Since 1971 he had been a solicitor who became a senior partner in a distinguished firm. In the early 1990s his property interests, business and consultancy work gave him a 'very great income'. However, he was badly affected by the property crash. He managed a family trust fund, which had property which was let to Glasgow District Council. The defendant kept the rents and failed to pay the lessor and the lease was forfeited. The fund lost between £800,000 and £1.1m. He spent the money on a business venture, repaying a bank loan, reducing his overdraft etc. The amount stolen was £135,230. In a property company he was entrusted to manage he stole £153,500 using 2/3 of the money to pay off a loan. The total loss was £288,730, which was stolen between November 1991 and November 1992. When interviewed he denied the offences and about 9 months later in 1994, he left the country. In 1997 he returned voluntarily and the proceedings against him started. From then he co-operated with the authorities. He was of previous unblemished character with an impressive array of testimonials including references to his charity work. In 1995 he was made bankrupt. The defendant had been an international rugby player. He had played for England 43 times and had been captain for 2 years. Held. *R v Clark* 1998 2 Cr App R (S) 95 only provides guidelines. Each case has its own special features. It was a very serious continuing breach of trust by a man in a very senior position. **5 years** was not manifestly excessive.

R v Cook 2003 2 Cr App R (S) 315. The defendant pleaded guilty to 9 counts of theft. He had been employed as assistant bursar at a private school earning about £17,000 a year. He had a serious gambling addiction. Over a five-year period he stole about £225,000 from petty cash and from a safe. He made false entries in the school's accounting records both on the computer and in the manual records and destroyed slips showing that he had received the money. The offences came to light when colleagues found discrepancies. He was arrested after a thorough investigation. When interviewed he denied stealing any money and covering his tracks. He was a man of previous good character, a loyal friend and devoted father. He had rendered excellent service to the school. Whilst accepting that the sentence was in line with *R v Clark* 1998 2 Cr App R (S) 95, the appeal was made as a result of the decision *R v Kefford* 2002 2 Cr App R (S) 495. Held. The offences committed by the defendant were serious. They involved a breach of trust. They continued over a substantial period of time and they stopped only when the discrepancies in the school's accounts came to light. The judgement in Kefford did not modify sentencing practices when it came to breaches of trust involving substantial sums of money. **3 years** upheld.

R v Torkonaik 2005 1 Cr App R (S) 126. The defendant was convicted of 15 counts of theft, 2 of obtaining a money transfer by deception, 1 of false accounting, 2 of obtaining property by deception, 1 of forgery and 1 of perjury. He was a 36 year-old solicitor who stole £300,000 from his clients, the Legal Services Commission and the DSS. The most serious offence was committed against B, who fell of a girder and sustained serious multiple injuries and fractures. From the resulting £100,000 settlement, B was told it was £18,000 from which the defendant kept £3,000. The defendant put £75,000 into a bond in his own name and failed to Ray £10,000 to the LSC in costs. Another offence involved the theft of £1,100 from a dead man's estate. The defendant stole large sums from other personal injury clients and failed to Ray sums to the LSC. In another case, he failed to Ray the LSC costs (£113,000) for a civil claim against a local authority. He also continued to claim a client's pension from the DSS after he had died. Proceedings were brought by the Law Society in respect of B's claim. The defendant lied about his possession of certain crucial papers (which were in fact in the boot of his car). Held. Considering *R v Clarke* 1998 2 Cr App R 137, the **8 years** was not manifestly excessive. There was considerable damage to the public confidence in the legal system and there was the greatest public interest that the court should take a severe and stern view of such offences. This was a bad breach of trust where the victims were vulnerable and weak who had a particular need to be able to Rose absolute confidence and trust in the defendant as their solicitor. The offences of theft deserved 7 years; in addition the offences of perjury and forgery were particularly serious as they were committed by an officer of the Court. Consecutive sentences were appropriate as a matter of principle. The fact that funds were available to pay compensation were not a feature of mitigation.

Old case *R v Clark* 1998 2 Cr App R (S) 95, (for a summary of this case see the first edition of this book).

Breach of trust – Value more than £1m

190.14   *R v Barrick* 1985 7 Cr App R (S) 142. LCJ. Cases over £1m will merit **10 years or more**, when the case is contested. [As adapted by *R v Clark* 1998 2 Cr App R (S) 95.]

Car ringing

See *Vehicles – Car ringing*

Charging for work that is not necessary or not done

190.15 *R v Hafeez and Gibbs* 1998 1 Cr App R (S) 276. The defendant G changed his plea to guilty to conspiracy to obtain property by deception. G expressed a willingness to give evidence for the prosecution against H and another and the other two then changed their pleas to guilty. Over 7 months H, G and others agreed to defraud customers about work done and goods supplied in the garage trade. There were 10 loser witnesses who lost about £10,000. The prosecution case was that there were very substantially more vehicles involved than those belonging to the 10. Vehicles were deliberately damaged e.g. a car was put in fourth or fifth gear to burn out the clutch. This was called 'hitting.' All members of staff were instructed in 'hitting' cars. Bills were inflated. H was the prime mover who had invented the scheme and he owed and operated a number of businesses in the garage trade. G was an account clerk who had been involved for a comparatively short period of time. However he was a manager who did instruct employees to defraud customers. H was of good character and a family man. He had borrowed money so a compensation order of £10,000 could be paid. G was also of good character and had a supportive letter from the Council about his valuable work as a foster parent. Held. It was complex and audacious. It was more serious than the framework in *R v Barrick* 1985 7 Cr App R (S) 142. H involved a large number of other people and conducted a substantial business on a deeply dishonest basis. **3 years** was not excessive. The offer to give evidence weighs heavily in G's favour. His sentence reduced from 18 to **12 months**.

Charging for work that is not necessary or not done or overcharging – House repairs

190.16 *R v Ball and Ball* 2001 1 Cr App R (S) 171. The defendants A and N were father and son and jointly indicted. N pleaded guilty to two counts of obtaining money transfers by deception, one count of obtaining property by deception and one attempt. A was convicted of the three counts and the attempt count was left on the file. They told an 80-year-old widow that they had done work for her before and urgent work was needed on her roof. They said the side of the roof needed stripping out and the tiles needed mastic coating etc. The cost was £4,095. She paid £3,000 in cash and £1,095 in a cheque after they drove her to her bank. She was next told two beams in the roof needed replacing and that would cost £800. To pay for it she had to obtain a bank loan. Next they said the chimney stacks needed lowering because they were dangerous. The cost would be £1,200. Her stepson was present and informed the police. A was 42 and had spent convictions. N was 23 with convictions for dishonesty but it wasn't a bad record. Held. The victim was elderly, vulnerable and targeted. The offences were cowardly and courts will take a very serious view of them and impose substantial sentences. **4 years** for A and **3 years** for N were severe but not excessive.

R v Seymour 2002 2 Cr App R (S) 442. The defendant was convicted of obtaining property by deception. In summer 1999, a 50-year-old woman noticed her roof was leaking and contacted a company from Yellow Pages. A date was arranged and the defendant inspected the property and gave a quote of £3,000 for repairing the roof and painting five wall panels. Ten days later he arrived at the house with another. Over three days he and the other went up the roof and the defendant was paid the £3,000. The roof continued to leak and the householder and a surveyor found that no work had been done to the roof. The wall panels had been painted. Police discovered the business contact details were false. In August 2000, the defendant was questioned and claimed he had sub contracted the work. The defendant was 43 and of good character. He had character witnesses. His report suggested the risk of reoffending was relatively low. In September 2001, he received **15 months**. He appealed and relied on his character, the delay before sentence when he was in work and didn't reoffend and his family. Held. Householders are entitled to assume that if they employ people to work on their house the work will be done. No one should suffer from cowboy roofers. The sentence was wholly appropriate and entirely merited.

Old cases *R v Stewart* 1997 1 Cr App R (S) 71 and *R v Flynn* 1998 2 Cr App R (S) 413. (For summaries of these two cases see the first edition of this book.)

See also *R v Seymour* 2002 2 Cr App R (S) 442.

Charity offences

190.17 *R v Pippard and Harris* 2002 2 Cr App R (S) 166. The defendants were convicted of conspiracy to obtain money by deception. They set up a bogus charity, Helping Kids and kept the money collected. A genuine charity's name was usurped and one of the signatures of a local secretary was transferred to give the charity authenticity. That charity's number was misused on literature and put on the badges of those who collected the money. The defendants recruited collectors who were often the wives of serving officers to collect from pubs, ensuring the collectors made the contact and not the defendants. Small amounts were obtained and it was impossible to say how much. Both defendants had clean records and had good army service. Imprisonment would have serious consequences for their families. The judge said it was vital that public confidence in charities should be maintained so people continue to give to charities and that deterrent sentences were necessary. Held. It was a thoroughly dishonest scheme exploiting the public's goodwill. We agree with the judge's comments. **2 years** was consistent with the court's duty to stamp out dishonesty of this kind.

See also **FRAUD** – *Charity fraud*

Cheques

190.18 *R v Osinowo* 2001 Unreported 23/10/01. The defendant pleaded guilty on re-arraignment to handling. He also pleaded guilty to a bail offence for which he was fined. He allowed another, Q to use his bank account to pay in cheques. The victim discovered her chequebook had been taken and a cheque for £4,700 was paid into his bank account. He was charged and a verdict of not guilty was entered for that. Police searched his home and discovered a blank cheque. He said Q gave it to him. No attempt had been made to use the cheque. The defendant was a 23-year-old student of good character when the offence was committed. Since then he had been given a community service order and had not performed any work. His pre-sentence report said that that another order would not be appropriate. Held. The offence of handling is always serious and that certainly applies to cheques. A short custodial sentence was right and the judge was justified in suspending it. However, **4 months suspended** not 12.

Credit card offences – Guideline remarks

190.19 *R v Aroride* 1999 2 Cr App R (S) 406. Fraudulent use of credit cards or information about credit cards is a serious offence, since it undermines and exploits the modern system of telephone transactions using credit cards. Immediate and substantial terms of imprisonment will generally be called for. [This remark appears to relate to telephone ordering.]

Credit card offences

190.20 *R v Aroride* 1999 2 Cr App R (S) 406. The defendant pleaded guilty to attempting to obtain property by a deception at the Magistrates' Court. He acquired a copy of someone else's credit card statement. He then ordered some Porsche wheels and tyres worth £3,000 on the telephone and to pay for them gave the other person's name and card number. It was arranged the wheels should be delivered to the other person's house. The seller was suspicious and the wheels were in fact delivered by two plain clothes policemen who met the defendant outside the property. The defendant said he was the other person and signed a receipt. He denied he had made the telephone call. After pleading guilty he failed to attend the next hearing. The defendant was about 23 and a student who was short of money. Held. There was nothing wrong with an 8 month sentence. However, as the judge had not mentioned the credit for the plea the sentence was reduced to **7 months** consecutive to the bail sentence.

Credit facilities, obtaining

190.21 *R v Mills* 2002 2 Cr App R (S) 229. LCJ. The defendant pleaded guilty to two offences of obtaining services by deception. She completed an application for credit at a store and claimed that the Merseyside Fire Service had employed her for 3 years. This was untrue. Credit facilities were granted. For 12 months she had made the minimum payments. She made no more payments. With interest and charges, the account was £5,682.66 in debt. She also purchased goods to the value of £714 from another store. A 10% deposit was paid. She applied for credit to finance the balance. In her application she claimed to have been employed by Allwood Joinery for 6 years. This was quite untrue. Some months after a finance company issued a credit card to the appellant, which she then used. She said she had not knowingly applied for, or expected to receive, the card. By the time that account was closed, it was approximately £5,438 in debit, and only £43.76 had been paid. She was arrested and when interviewed she admitted that she had made the false representations on each application. She had borrowed £4,000 from her mother to pay off part of the debt. She was 33 years of age and the sole carer of two children aged 11 and 4. She had no previous convictions or cautions and had references. They said that she did voluntary work at a local charity shop and gave her time to a voluntary agency assisting parents with young children. A pre-sentence report recommended a community sentence. The judge said, 'Those who commit offences of this kind, knowing perfectly well that there is really no chance of them ever being able to pay for the goods concerned, go to prison.' Held. The appellant was deeply sorry for the way she had behaved and the offences had been committed to provide for her children. The first factor that has to be take into account is that apart from 'the clang of the prison door' type of sentence, which gives a prisoner the opportunity of knowing what is involved in imprisonment, the ability of the prison service to achieve anything positive in a short prison sentence is very limited. Secondly, with a mother who is the sole supporter of two young children, you must consider them if the sole carer is sent to prison. Finally, take into account the current situation with the female prison population. Since 1993 there has been a remarkable increase. Short prison sentences are always difficult for the prison service to accommodate. The ability to imprison mothers close to their homes in the community is difficult. The difficulties in the prison population to which we have referred does not mean that if an offence is such that it is necessary to send an offender to prison, they should not be sent to prison. But in a borderline case, where the offence does not in particular involve violence but is one with financial consequences to a commercial concern, it is very important to take into account the facts to which we have referred. The courts should strive to avoid sending people like her to prison and instead use punishments in the community. It is true that obtaining credit is easy. Commercial concerns are entitled to the protection of the courts. It was wrong in principle to send her to prison. The minimum period should be passed for this category of offending. If it was necessary to send her to prison, all that would be required was the clang of the prison door. One month not 8 months should have been imposed. It would have been right to impose a **community punishment** order in this case then but now we will make a community rehabilitation order for 6 months.

Company frauds

See COMPANY FRAUDS AND FINANCIAL SERVICES OFFENCES

Confidence tricks

190.22   *R v Salathiel* 1998 1 Cr App R (S) 338. The defendant Sa was convicted of six offences of obtaining by deception. The defendant Sm pleaded guilty to six theft and deception counts and the third defendant M pleaded guilty to three. Over nearly 3 years, the main victim who was in his 50s and lived with his parents was systematically swindled by the three defendants using false names. Sa befriended him and told him she needed a kidney operation and that gypsies were not covered by the Health Service. He gave her £1,000 and said he would Ray him from a legacy, which was expected shortly. This was followed by another request and payment of £1,000. £850 was then given for a poll tax bill. £4,000 was obtained to make up the £10,000 needed for the operation. The victim then became fond of Sa and believed she would marry him. Sa introduced Sm to the victim and Sm said she needed money for a divorce. The victim obtained a bank loan for £2,000 and paid the money over. Sa said she needed a further operation and the victim sold £1,300 of shares to pay the £1,700 requested. The victim borrowed £6,910 from his aunt to pay the various sums. Sa said the money would be paid back. The victim then discussed marrying M and he obtained a legacy of £28,000 and paid the aunt back. The money was paid to her estate as she had died. £26,500 was handed over for a caravan and site for them to live together. Sm also obtained £2,000 so she could buy a caravan to live near them. Finally Sm and M visited him. M had a black eye and they claimed all their inheritance had been taken in a mugging. They asked to take some ornaments, which he agreed to. While he cuddled with M, S took ornaments, which he hadn't agreed to give them. He called the police who discovered Sm and M had obtained £1,500 from a woman on the promise of an inheritance. The judge described Sa as scheming, greedy and heartless and the instigator. The judge said the case ranks among the gravest because of the number of people involved, the length of time it operated and the amount of money obtained from very vulnerable people. The judge sentenced Sa to **5 years**, M to **4 years** and Sm to **3 years**. Held. We endorse his tariff.

R v Mokoena 2004 2 Cr App R (S) 447. The defendant pleaded guilty, 'albeit late' to conspiracy to defraud. He had performed 'the classic confidence trick' on his victim. He approached his victim, giving a false name, exchanged phone numbers and phoned him the next day and arranged to meet him. The defendant was with another man at that meeting. They told the victim they were middle men acting for a man who ran a mine and sold raw gems, and that the victim could make 15% of the sale price if he acted as the buyer. They told him they were cutting out the real buyer. The next day the victim met the same two men and two more men at a hotel. One of the men, B, was posing as the man who ran the mine and the victim was introduced to him as the buyer. B produced two gems. The victim asked if they were real. The defendant produced another man who pretended to value the gems at £95,000. The victim agreed a price of £55,000 with B, but B said he needed a deposit. The defendant said he and his companion didn't have any money for the deposit, but they would pay the victim 50% of the profit if he paid it. The victim borrowed £8,500 from his father, £400 from someone else and put £100 of his own money in and gave the £9,000 to B in exchange for the gems. The gems were false. The defendant, 31, had no previous convictions. The victim had a number of convictions including convictions for dishonesty. Held. The victim was entitled to the protection of the law. It was a carefully planned and executed fraud. Because of the good character and the lack of aggravating features **18 months** not 2$\frac{1}{2}$ years.

Electricity or gas (including abstracting electricity)

190.23   *R v Hughes* 2000 2 Cr App R (S) 399. The defendant pleaded guilty to criminal damage, and two counts of theft of gas. A gas engineer went to the defendant's home and found that the gas meter had been removed so the gas supply by-passed the meter. The engineer capped the internal supply. About five months later another engineer found the cap had been removed and a home-made connection had been fitted. Gas was leaking from that connection. The defendant admitted that he had by-passed the system and said that he intended to pay for the gas when he could. He also claimed there was also a problem with his benefits, which had been suspended. The defendant was 36. He had been in the army and had been a lorry driver. Currently he was unable to work due to clinical depression. The previous year he had been sentenced to 2 months imprisonment for three fraudulent benefit offences. He was on probation for possession of a Class B drug. The pre-sentence report referred to the break up of his marriage and recommended probation. A custodial sentence was inevitable. However, the theft sentences were reduced from 6 months each to 3 months each. The 2 months criminal damage sentence was unchallenged and the all the sentences remained concurrent.

Financial services

See COMPANY FRAUDS AND FINANCIAL SERVICES OFFENCES

Handbag thefts

See *Pickpocket/theft from persons in public places*

Making off without payment

See MAKING OFF WITHOUT PAYMENT

Persistent offenders

190.24   *R v Dolphy* 1999 1 Cr App R (S) 73. The defendant was convicted of stealing £287. An elderly lady picked up her pension at the Post Office. He distracted her attention and stole £287. The defendant had convictions for dishonesty over 25 years. He had shortly been released from a three year sentence for three counts of theft totalling £1,500. They were all thefts from persons. **4 years** was severe but not excessive.

R v Richardson 2000 2 Cr App R (S) 373. The defendant pleaded guilty to theft and false imprisonment. The defendant at night visited the victim, a lady of 89 whom he knew. He asked to use the lavatory. She followed him. She said he should leave. He refused and appeared to be on drugs. He was aggressive and threatened to hurt her. He pushed her into her sitting room and forced her into an armchair. He tied a jumper over her face. He asked for £20. On a number of occasions she attempted to get out of the chair but he pushed her back. She was repeatedly threatened that she would be hurt if she told anyone about him. She allowed him to make a call for a taxi. When the taxi arrived he snatched her bag and stole £20. He tore the telephone wire from the wall. Because the telephone did not work and she could not manage the steps in the dark she had to stay in all night unable to contact anyone. Before the police started to look for him he went to a police station and confessed to a robbery. His account was very similar to the victim, although he claimed to have told her he wasn't going to hurt her. The defendant was very anxious she should not have to go to court and therefore did not contest her account. He had a bad record with 12 appearances in the last 10 years seven of which were for robbery. He had three convictions for burglary, three convictions for theft in a dwelling house and three convictions for theft from a person. He expressed remorse. The reason for his offending was crack cocaine. It was so serious a DTT order was inappropriate. In light of the mitigation **4 years** not 5 years substituted.

R v Vittles 2005 1 Cr App R (S) 31. The defendant pleaded guilty at the Magistrates' Court to theft, driving whilst disqualified and using a vehicle with no insurance. Twelve offences of theft and three of attempted theft were Tic'd. During the night he broke into a car parked the driveway of a home and stole a tool which was worth £20. The 15 Tics all related to similar offences in which he had stolen over £3500 worth of goods from parked cars. He admitted the offences in interview. He had a terrible criminal record for similar offences and a £900 a week drug addiction need. He also drove whilst on bail and disqualified. Held. The Judge rightly said community sentences had not worked. **3 years and 10 months** unchanged. An indefinite ASBO was reduced to a period of 5 years (the ASBO excluded the defendant from a significant area, where his crimes had predominated).

R v Clugston 2005 1 Cr App R (S) 139. The defendant pleaded guilty to 3 charges of obtaining property by deception at the Magistrates' Court. There were 11 TICs. He was released on bail and then pleaded to 5 similar offences with 8 TICs. He would find commercial premises close to a local restaurant. He would then visit the commercial premise and pretend to be connected in some way with the restaurant, either as an employee or as a supplier of wine. He would say that he had surplus champagne in stock and offer it at a favourable price. He would then disappear with the cash. In total there was £26,725 of deception over about 11 months. He admitted all of the offences and blamed a gambling addiction. He was 57 and had 16 court appearances for previous convictions, mainly for theft and obtaining by deception. He had received some substantial custodial sentences in the past. He was on licence at the time of these offences. The risk of reoffending was high. Held. There were a number of aggravating features: he was subject to licence, he committed one set of offences whilst he was on bail for the others; and he had previous convictions for offences of dishonesty. However because of the plea, **4 years** not 6.

Old cases. *R v Mullins* 1998 2 Cr App R (S) 372, (for a summary of this case see the first edition of this book.)

Pickpocket/Theft from persons in public places – Guideline remarks

190.25   *R v Gwillim-Jones* 2002 1 Cr App R (S) 19. A handbag may contain within it credit cards, diaries, telephone numbers, and personal items. The theft of a handbag may cause both inconvenience and distress to the victim, quite out of proportion to the intrinsic value of the handbag itself or any cash within it.

Pickpocket/Theft from persons in public places – Persistent offenders – Guideline remarks

190.26   *R v Spencer and Carby* 1995 16 Cr App R (S) 482. Where the offender has a long history of pick pocketing and can properly be considered a professional pickpocket, the sentences may well be in terms of years. Professional pick pocketing must be deterred. Both of these men fall into that category. They have not been deterred by short sentences. These offences can properly be viewed as more serious by reason of the appallingly long records of each for pick pocketing.

Pickpocket/Theft from persons in public places – Persistent offenders – Cases

190.27   *R v Dolphy* 1999 1 Cr App R (S) 73. The defendant was convicted of stealing £287. An elderly lady picked up her pension at the Post Office. He distracted her attention and stole £287. The defendant had convictions for dishonesty over 25 years. He had shortly been released from a three year sentence for three counts of theft totalling £1,500. They were all thefts from persons. **4 years** was severe but not excessive.

R v Bolt 1999 2 Cr App R (S) 202. The defendant pleaded guilty to theft. His accomplice stole a handbag from the floor of a pub near a customer and the two drove off together. He was 28 and had an appalling record. There were 30 convictions since he was 11. He had been sentenced to 3 and 5 years. This offence was committed 3 months after his release from the 5 years. The judge ignored the defence version that it was an impulse theft. Held. The judge should have indicated his view to counsel. An impulse theft is worth **12 months** not 2 years. There was no reason he should not serve the remainder of the earlier sentence.

R v Jarrett 2000 2 Cr App R (S) 166. The defendant changed his plea to guilty of theft. He and another took a hotel guest's purse from her bag while she was waiting at reception. They were so close she felt uncomfortable. Security staff saw them and they were arrested The purse was recovered. The defendant was 37 with numerous convictions including burglary, theft and attempted theft. He had nine convictions for stealing handbags or their contents and had been out of trouble for 2 years. Held. These offences are prevalent. People need to be protected especially from people like the defendant who can be described as a professional pickpocket. **18 months** was well within the appropriate range.

R v Gwillim-Jones 2002 1 Cr App R (S) 19. The defendant was convicted of attempted theft. The defendant sat on a barstool and dragged a woman's handbag towards him using his foot. Another customer who saw it grabbed him. The police arrested him. Seven weeks before he was placed on probation for two thefts of handbags or purses from women in pubs. He was placed on probation. He had 100 convictions for theft and seemed to target ladies handbags in pubs and shopping areas. Every type of penalty had been tried. None seemed to have any effect. He was 47 Held. He was plainly a professional. It is necessary for professional handbag thieves to know if they are caught they will receive severe sentences. **3 years** was appropriate.

R v McGee 2004 1 Cr App R (S) 399. The defendants M and H pleaded guilty to two counts of theft. A 77-year-old victim and his wife went into a lift and were followed by M. When the lift doors opened, the victim and his wife got out and M started arguing with a female associate. Whilst the victim was distracted, H stole the victim's wallet containing £100 from his back pocket. 3 days later, a 74-year-old was walking back to his hotel when he saw four people in front. A fight broke out involving two of them. M and H took the opportunity to take the victim's wallet (containing £20) from his back pocket. M pleaded guilty at the Magistrates' Court and was committed but sought to withdraw his guilty plea. H pleaded guilty at the Crown Court on the day of trial. Both men were professional criminals with long records with many offences of dishonesty. Held. Both were entitled to some credit but it was diluted. **4 years** not 5.

Old case *R v Mullins* 1998 2 Cr App R (S) 372, (for a summary of this case see the first edition of this book.)

Police officers as defendants

190.28   *R v Roberts* 1999 1 Cr App R (S) 381. The defendant was convicted of stealing a watch. He was a police constable with 19 years' service attached to CID with the temporary rank of detective constable. After a search, property including two watches was taken to a police station. It was lodged in a property store. Sometime later another officer noticed the defendant wearing one of the watches. He found the watch was missing from the store and reported it. When questioned the defendant said he was going to replace it and had mislaid his watch. No owner could be traced as all those questioned denied any knowledge of the watch. The watch was worth about £90. He was sentenced on the basis it was a moment of madness. He was 41 with a family and had lost his job. Held. There can be no compromise on the standard of integrity the public requires of serving policemen in relationship to the performance of their duties. Applying *R v Ollerenshaw* 1999 1 Cr App R (S) 65 **2 months** not 4.

See also **Police Officers**

Shoplifting – Guideline case

190.29   *R v Page* 2005 2 Cr App R (S) 221. Nothing we say is intended to affect the level of sentence appropriate for shoplifting by organised gangs. When this occurs repeatedly or on a large scale, sentences of the order of **4 years** may well be appropriate, even on a plea of guilty. If violence is used to a shopkeeper, after theft, so a charge